Surf Psychology on the Web!

The Internet and World Wide Web can be great sources for finding out what's new in psychology.

While new sites are cropping up all the time, and occasionally site names change, we will list a few areas that you can launch from. If you take the time to surf and look around, you will find things that will help you in the introductory psychology course (such as tips on how to study), or get information on majoring in psychology, finding a job, or going to graduate school.

The Web is also useful for doing research. Professional journals and organizations are going online—you can search for articles on any topic, or find APA guidelines for citing sources in a research paper or doing a lab.

We suggest these starting places:

http://www.gasou.edu/psychweb/psychweb.html
This site is chock-full of links to just about anything related to the field of psychology, and taking psychology courses. A must!

http://www.unipissing.ca/psyc/psycsite.htm
This site has a big list of servers and psychology news groups, with links to shareware, areas of research, and random fun home pages.

http://www.gamma.org
This site will link you to the sites of professional associations and journals. It is helpful if you are doing research and looking for sources.

http://www.med.harvard.edu:80/AANLIB/home.html
This is the site for the Whole Brain Atlas, if you're interested in the structure of the brain.

In addition, here are two home sites of psychology organizations. These are particularly useful if you are planning to major in psychology or pursue graduate studies.

http://www.apa.org (American Psychological Association)
http://www.hanover.edu/psych/APS/aps.html (American Psychological Society)

And these two additional psychology launchers carry links to other psychology indices and directories.

http://www.indiana.edu:80/~iuepsyc/psycjump.html (Psychology Jumping Stand)
http://ecuvax.cis.ecu.edu/academics/schdept/psyc/link.htm#G (Psych-Link Directory)

FIFTH EDITION

Psychology
AN INTRODUCTION

Josh R. Gerow

Indiana University – Purdue University at Fort Wayne

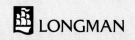
LONGMAN

An imprint of Addison Wesley Longman, Inc.

New York • Reading, Massachusetts • Menlo Park, California • Harlow, England
Don Mills, Ontario • Sydney • Mexico City • Madrid • Amsterdam

Acquisitions Editor: Catherine Woods
Developmental Editor: Phil Herbst
Supplements Editor: Diane Wansing
Project Coordination and Text Design: Ruttle, Shaw & Wetherill, Inc.
Cover Designer: Kay Petronio
Cover Photograph: Westlight/B. Ross
Photo Researcher: Carol Parden
Electronic Production Manager: Christine Pearson
Manufacturing Manager: Helene G. Landers
Electronic Page Makeup: Ruttle, Shaw & Wetherill, Inc.
Printer and Binder: R. R. Donnelley & Sons Company
Cover Printer: Phoenix Color Corp.

For permission to use copyrighted material, grateful acknowledgment is made to the copyright holders on pp. 631–632, which are hereby made part of this copyright page.

Library of Congress Cataloging-in-Publication Data
Gerow, Joshua R.
    Psychology : an introduction / Josh R. Gerow. —5th ed.
      p.   cm.
    Includes bibliographical references and indexes.
    ISBN 0-673-98095-2
    1. Psychology.   I. Title.
  BF121.G44   1997
  150–dc20

96-10424
CIP

ISBN 0–673–98095–2

1 2 3 4 5 6 7 8 9 10 – DOW – 99 98 97 96

To
Nancy S. Gerow
and
Christopher Steidle
Without them, there would be no book.

Brief Contents

Detailed Contents

6

Memory 186

7

Intelligence, Language, and Problem Solving 226

Preface

Psychology: An Introduction, now in its fifth edition, moves us ever closer to the vision I originally had for this text. The fifth edition offers fresh features and valuable new content that advance the goals that I've had from the start. Those goals include:

- **Making psychology come alive for the beginning student who will take few, if any, additional psychology classes.** *Psychology: An Introduction,* Fifth Edition, encourages the student to understand the basic methods, concepts, and principles of the whole field of psychology and their relevance to the real world. Acknowledging that we have many important questions in psychology for which answers are still being sought, it treats the wide array of points of view that make psychology an exciting field of study. This text's presentation of psychology as a vibrant, ongoing enterprise can be seen, for example, in the introduction to human memory in Chapter 6, in the treatment of theories of personality in Chapter 9, and in the discussion of motivation in Chapter 10.

- **Applying what we know about the psychology of human learning and memory to ensure that the student gets the most out of the text.** A major strength of this text from its inception has been its judicious drawing upon psychological and educational research and principles to help the student learn and remember what is learned. From the study guide on the endpapers to the topical organization of each chapter to the many other student-oriented features of this text, which are described later in the preface, *Psychology: An Introduction,* Fifth Edition, has been systematically designed to make learning easy.

- **Showing that psychology has emerged from a historical context.** Much of what we know in psychology comes from the past. A historical approach can be found, for example, in the coverage of sensory thresholds and adaptation in Chapter 3 and the history of treatments for the psychologically disordered in Chapter 13.

- **Meeting the challenge of human diversity.** *Psychology: An Introduction,* Fifth Edition, shows how culture, gender, age, and sexual orientation affect our lives. See, for example, coverage of gender and the brain in Chapter 2, or the role of culture in moral development in Chapter 8.

Highlights of the Fifth Edition

Granting that all the above goals and features are still important and still in this text, for a text in its fifth edition, a reasonable question is "What's new?" This edition of *Psychology: An Introduction* includes a number of significant new features to enhance learning as well as to update text material. Substantial changes that have been made in pedagogy, organization, and content are highlighted here.

New Pedagogical Features

This text has a history of incorporating useful features that make the content of psychology accessible and meaningful. A list of the established features is found later in this preface, under "Aids to Enhance Learning." With this fifth edition, the tradition continues with the addition of five new student-oriented learning aids.

- **Thinking Critically** boxes are paired with *Before You Go On* question items and are found four to six times per chapter. These small, marginal boxes pose questions designed to encourage students to think critically about what they are reading. These items were provided by the author and Dr. Shari Tishman of Harvard University, who defines critical thinking as thinking that involves interpreting, questioning, evaluating, and challenging the information presented in the text. I am confident that this new focus on critical thinking will foster the active use of information and make learning more effective and interesting.

- **Experiencing Psychology** is a feature now included with each chapter. Presented here are suggestions for projects or activities that students can do on their own. Each is designed to reinforce what they are reading about and make it more meaningful. The idea, of course, is to get the student *involved* in some aspect of psychology. This feature underscores one of the emphases of this text: real-world psychology.

- **Practicing Psychology** is paired with each *Chapter Summary*. The student is given a set of questions to answer, or problems to solve, that are designed to help the student understand material in the chapter that experience tells us is often difficult to grasp. Answers to the *Practicing Psychology* items are found at the back of the text, after the *Appendix.*

- **Using Psychology to Study Psychology** is a brief guide of study-skill advice derived from research in psychology and education. For each piece of advice at least one page reference to the text is given in which students can find more information. This feature is found on the endpapers.

- **Psychology on the Internet**, as its name implies, provides suggestions on how to find information about psychology on the Internet. In addition to general advice about using the net, specific psychology home-page locations are recommended. This feature can be found on the endpapers.

Organizational Changes

Psychology: An Introduction, Fifth Edition, still contains 15 chapters, a *Statistical Appendix,* and a *Topic* format that divides chapters into manageable chunks. In this edition, each chapter is divided into two comprehensible *Topics.* Coverage of intelligence (tests, theories, individual and group differences) is now incorporated with information on memory and a *Topic* on other cognitive processes (language and problem solving) in Chapter 7. This reorganization allows for an expanded treatment of the psychology of personality in Chapter 9. A number of other chapters and sections have been restructured to streamline the text or to make material more accessible.

Content Changes

- **New research and theory**. Over 220 new reference citations were added for this edition, most of them (more than 190) published in the 1990s. See, for example, expanded coverage of repressed memories in Chapter 6, the discussion of contemporary approaches to intelligence in Chapter 7, or the research on positive and negative symptoms in schizophrenia in Chapter 12.

- **Enhancement of cross-cultural psychology**. With the assistance of a consultant, Dr. Will Counts of Gateway College in Phoenix, Arizona, we have significantly expanded the coverage of gender, cultural, and ethnic issues in psychology that were found in earlier editions as well. This new material has been woven into extant material in the text. See, for example, the sections on ethnic differences in measured IQ in Chapter 7, moral reasoning in Chapter 8, and defining abnormality in Chapter 12.

- **Expanded psychobiological coverage**. With the assistance of a consultant, Dr. W. Jeffrey Wilson at Indiana-Purdue at Fort Wayne, we have added to the discussion of psychobiological issues. These additions are found, for example, in the section on early research on the brain in Chapter 1, in coverage of the endocrine system in Chapter 2, in the treatment of memory and the brain in Chapter 6, or in the sections on causes of major depression and schizophrenia in Chapter 12.

Following is a concise list of the key content changes by chapter.

Chapter 1, *Psychology: What Psychologists Do,* is a much streamlined chapter containing a new section on early research on the brain.

Chapter 2, *The Nervous Systems and Behavior,* includes new material on neurotransmitters, the endocrine system, and research on differences between male and female brains.

Chapter 3, *Sensation and Perception,* is a totally reorganized chapter, discussing sensory processes first, then perceptual issues, and including a refocused discussion of pain.

Chapter 4, *Varieties of Consciousness,* includes expanded coverage of sleep and dreaming.

Chapter 6, *Memory,* includes expanded and updated sections on repressed memories and memory and the brain.

Chapter 7, *Intelligence, Language, and Problem Solving,* is a virtually new chapter including new and updated coverage of theories of intelligence, and race and IQ.

Chapter 8, *Human Development,* includes new material on adolescence and adulthood.

Chapter 9, *Personality,* is a new chapter that expands coverage of Freud's psychosexual stages of development and gender and personality.

Chapter 10, *Motivation and Emotion,* is a reorganized chapter now discussing sexuality with other drives and adding an interim summary of motivational approaches.

Chapter 11, *Psychology, Stress, and Physical Health,* includes updated and new material on reacting to stressors and sexually transmitted diseases.

Chapter 12, *The Psychological Disorders,* is a heavily revised chapter containing new material on cultural differences in defining abnormality, comorbidity, personality disorders, antisocial personality disorder, schizophrenia, and positive and negative symptoms.

Chapter 13, *Treatment and Therapy,* contains new and revised material on the history of treatment, psychosurgery, antipsychotic drugs, deinstitutionalization, and evaluation of psychotherapies.

Chapter 14, *Social Psychology,* is a partially reorganized chapter containing an extended discussion of attributions.

Chapter 15, *Industrial/Organizational, Environmental, and Sport Psychology,* includes new material on personnel testing and training.

The Statistical Appendix, which has been streamlined, contains a new example used to present statistics.

Aids to Enhance Learning

Especially distinctive to *Psychology: An Introduction,* Fifth Edition, is its focus on making learning an effective, interesting, and meaningful experience. Discussed under "Highlights of the Fifth Edition" above were the pedagogic features new to this text: *Thinking Critically, Experiencing Psychology, Practicing Psychology,* and the endpaper features, *Using Psychology to Study Psychology* and *Psychology on the Internet.* Following are the features that have been an integral part of the text all along.

- **Chapter Outline and Vignette.** We know that before beginning to study textual material one should form something of an overview of what is to come. This process is aided by a complete *Chapter Outline* at the beginning of each chapter. Each outline is followed by a brief vignette, designed to arouse interest in the forthcoming subject matter and to raise questions addressed within the chapter.

- **Chapter Organization by Topic.** Dividing each of the book's 15 chapters into two short, but coherent *Topics* encourages spaced or distributed practice, long known to be superior to massed practice. A topical approach also fosters flexibility in making reading assignments. Instructors have had much success with this topical organization.

- **Examples and Applications.** We know that the more meaningful the material, the more efficient the learning and the better the retention of material. My rule of thumb has been to provide examples and applications at every opportunity. The more we can demonstrate psychology's relevance to the everyday lives of the student, the more effective we will be.

- **Boldface Key Words, Marginal Glossary, Alphabetized Glossary.** In large measure, learning about psychology is a matter of developing the proper vocabulary. Hence, key words and concepts are printed in the text in **boldface** type and immediately defined. Then each term is defined again in a marginal glossary. They are repeated in an alphabetized glossary at the end of the book.

- **Before You Go On Questions.** To promote *active learning,* sets of questions labeled *Before You Go On* appear at the ends of major sections of each chapter. This feature remains one of the most popular from the students' point of view. *Before You Go On* questions also further promote distributed practice by marking transitions from one content area to another.

- **Chapter Summaries.** The organizing of large amounts of information is prompted by *Chapter Summaries.* Each summary repeats all the *Before You Go On* questions in the chapter and presents brief answers, which are page referenced to the text.

Supplements for the Student

In addition to the features designed to enhance learning that have been built into the text, we have also provided a special student package called *MasterMind WorKit.* Here students will find all the tools necessary to gain a successful understanding of introductory psychology. This file includes the following booklets:

- *New:* **How to Succeed in This Course** (ISBN: 0–673–97908–3) is a concise, practical primer on study skills and includes suggestions on time management, listening and critical thinking, and exam preparation. In addition, this supplement contains learning objectives and outlines for each of the 15 textbook chapters. Materials were prepared by Josh Gerow and Judi M. Misale of Truman State University.

- *New:* **Making and Using Flash Cards** (ISBN: 0–673–97910–5) is a learning aid suggested by students in introductory psychology classes. This unit provides guidance about the construction of flash cards and how to use them for maximum benefit. Several flash cards of various types are also provided as models. This piece has been prepared by Josh Gerow.

- *New:* **Critical Thinking in Psychology** (ISBN: 0–673–97911–3) extends the commitment to critical thinking issues introduced in the text itself. This unit was created under the supervision of Dr. Shari Tishman of Project Zero at Harvard University. It contains exercises that promote critical thinking skills and can serve to stimulate discussion in the classroom.

- *New:* **Psychology and Anatomy: A Workbook for Students** (ISBN: 0–673–97909–1) provides both labeled and unlabeled anatomical drawings that facilitate classroom note-taking and supply essential visual support.

- **Practice Tests** (ISBN: 0–673–97872–9) include 25 multiple-choice and 10 true-false items for each chapter of the text. Two things make this supplement uniquely valuable. First, every item was written by Josh Gerow himself. Second, answers are provided in annotated form, informing the student about which alternatives are correct, and *why.*

- **SuperShell Student Tutorial Software** for Macintosh (ISBN: 0–673–97871–0) and IBM-PCs or compatibles (ISBN: 0–673–97870–2) will be available once again. Prepared by John Campbell of Methodist College, this popular interactive program provides students with self-paced instruction, including chapter review material, practice exercises, self-tests with immediate correct responses, and diagnostic feedback.

Supplements for the Instructor

Just as we have tried to do all we could to make learning as easy as possible for the student, so have we strived to make teaching as effortless as possible for the instructor. To that end, several supplements are available.

- **Instructor's Resource Kit** (ISBN: 0–673–97907–5) has been revised by Dr. Judi M. Misale of Truman State University. This resource offers a wealth of information for both beginning and experienced instructors. Features include chapter learning objectives and detailed outlines, suggested lecture topics, discussion ideas, classroom projects and demonstrations, expanded biographical profiles inclusive of contributions made to the field by women and minorities, updated timelines, plus critical thinking exercise suggestions. Also provided are media references, recent publication information including American Psychological Association titles, and suggested readings.

- *Two* **Test Banks** (ISBN: 0–673–97873–7 and ISBN: 0–673–97874–5) are also available to adopters. The first—fully edited, revised, and written by Josh Gerow—includes more than 2,000 multiple-choice and essay items. The second Test Bank, by Dr. Gary Piggrem of DeVry Institute of Technology, contains more than 1,500 test questions. Referenced to textbook page number, topic, and skill level, these items are designed to challenge student knowledge and comprehension at a range of levels.

- **TestMaster Computerized Test Bank** is a powerful test-generation system. It allows the instructor to construct test files using multiple-choice and essay items from both the Gerow test banks. The instructor can add new items or revise existing items. This software is available for both IBM (ISBN: 0–673–97876–1) and Macintosh (ISBN: 0–673–97875–3) computers.

- **Introductory Transparency Resource Package** (ISBN: 0–673–55811–8) includes nearly 200 four-color overhead transparencies accompanied by an annotated table of contents.

- **The CD-ROM for Psychology** has been designed exclusively as presentation software, using state-of-the-art technology. The disk links the electronic text to interactive exercises, animations, and video clips. It covers the core concepts in the discipline by applying a game approach to the learning of psychology. Dr. James Hilton of the University of Michigan and Dr. Charles Perdue of West Virginia State College served as consultants on this project.

- **The Psychology Encyclopedia Laser Disk** is also available for adopters in the latest version. This disk contains many still images, animation, and video segments, some of archival value. In addition, there is an array of media items available to qualified adopters, including electronic transparencies and full-length videos. Please see your local sales representative for details.

Acknowledgments

Preparing a package of materials such as this one is clearly a team effort. As has been the case with previous editions, I have had the support of a wonderful group of friends and colleagues. A simple mention here in the Preface seems woefully inadequate. I can only hope that each and all can see their good work reflected on the pages that follow.

As always, the first to acknowledge is my wife, Nancy, my best colleague and collaborator. Phil Herbst was the developmental editor for the fourth edition of *Psychology: An Introduction.* I was very pleased that he was able to serve in that role again. That the prose that follows is at all literate and sensible is fully to his credit. Catherine Woods is the psychology editor at Longman who has always supported all that I have wanted to do with this text—from adding features to bringing on consultants to enhance the content. I believe she shares my vision and goals for what this text should be. A special mention also for the three colleagues who contributed to this edition as consultants: Shari Tishman, Will Counts, and Jeff Wilson. Diane Wansing is the Longman Supplements Editor who managed to pull together so many pieces—and on schedule at that. Erica Smith served as Assistant Editor, Mark Paluch as Marketing Manager, and Gloria Klaiman, of Ruttle, Shaw & Wetherill, as Project Editor. To each of them, my heartfelt thanks as well.

Colleagues who served as reviewers are many. I appreciate their good work, as will the reader. Those who helped on this edition include: June Madsen Clausen, University of San Francisco; William Dwyer, University of Memphis; D. Brett King, University of Colorado at Boulder; Patsy Lawson, Volunteer State Community College; and Shawn Ward, LeMoyne College.

I would also like to acknowledge the reviewers whose input contributed to the fifth edition: Lynn Augsbach, Morehead State University; William M. Beneke, Lincoln University; Joyce Bishop, Golden West College; Shirley Cole-Harding, Minor State University; Marla J. Colvin, Cuyahoga Community College; James Dooley, Mercy College; John Flannagan, Eastern Kentucky University; Sue Gordon, Hudson Valley Community College; Martha B. Haslam, Laredo Community College; Barbara Honhart, Baker College; Robert Johnson, Arkansas State University; Neil J. Lavender, Ocean County College; Kit Lowder, Illinois Central College; William McVough, Weber State University; John Nichols, Tulsa Junior College; David Pick, Purdue University—Calumet; Gerald Rubin, Central Virginia Community College; Michael Shaughnessy, Eastern New Mexico University; Donald M. Stanley, North Harris College; Janice C. Stapley, Monmouth College; and Patrick S. Williams, University of Houston.

Josh R. Gerow

About the Author

Josh Gerow began his college training at Rensselaer Polytechnic Institute, where he majored in chemistry, and earned his B.S. in psychology at the University of Buffalo. At the University of Tennessee, Knoxville, he was awarded a doctorate in experimental psychology. His graduate area of specialization was developmental psycholinguistics. After teaching for two years at the University of Colorado at Denver, he joined the faculty at Indiana University–Purdue University at Fort Wayne (IPFW), an undergraduate institution, where he still teaches. Dr. Gerow has conducted research and published articles in the field of instructional psychology, focusing on factors that affect performance in introductory psychology. His teaching background is extensive: During his more than twenty-seven years as a college professor, he has taught courses on the psychology of learning, memory, the history of psychology, and his favorite course, introduction to psychology; he has brought college-level introductory psychology to high school students; and he has made frequent presentations at regional and national conferences on the teaching of psychology.

Psychology

OUTLINE

A very common question in our culture is " . . . and what do you do?" As soon as someone learns your name, they want to know "what you do." When I first left graduate school, and someone asked me what I did, my reply, spoken with pride and a smile, was "I'm a psychologist." The response was immediate and very predictable: "Oh, you're going to analyze my mind and tell me all about my problems." "No, no, I'm not that kind of psychologist," and off I'd go on a lecture on the different types of psychologists, as if I were in my introductory psychology class. I tried, "I teach at the university" for a while, but that always led to "What do you teach?" I'd say "psychology," and we were off again with the lecture on the variety of ways in which one can be a psychologist.

Perhaps one way to share my dilemma with you and to illustrate how wide is the range of interests of psychologists is to take you on a quick tour of a few of the offices and laboratories in the psychology department on my campus. If you were to ask what it is that psychologists do, I might answer, "Well, it's

Ken Bordens studying factors other than guilt or innocence that influence a jury in a criminal trial;

David Young researching the psychological adjustments of adolescents whose parents are undergoing a divorce;

Psychology: What Psychologists Do

Leni DeFonso studying ways in which skilled musicians and amateurs process music;

Carol Lawton examining how people acquire a 'sense of direction';

Bruce Abbott studying the question, 'If a rat is going to get shocked, would the rat rather know the shock is coming, or be surprised?';

Elaine Blakemore conducting research on how a child's understanding of gender impacts on his or her behaviors;

. . . and so much more—including what I do, studying how to help students learn psychology as efficiently as possible." Actually, the colleagues I've listed here constitute only about half of our psychology department. Their interests and activities go well beyond the one area of research I've mentioned here for each.

How do we get this variety, this range of subject matter, condensed into one, simple definition? This is exactly the goal of this first chapter.

TOPIC 1A What Is Psychology?

psychology *the science of behavior and mental processes*

Psychology is the science of behavior and mental processes. This is a fairly standard definition—one that millions of students before you have committed to memory. If there is a problem with this definition, it's that it is a bit sterile; it doesn't tell us very much about what psychologists actually study or how they go about it. It will take the rest of this book to fill in the details and make this definition truly meaningful. First, let's see what it means to say that psychology is a science; then we'll consider the subject matter of psychology.

The Goals of Psychology: Science and Practice

There are many ways to find out about ourselves and the world in which we live. Some of our beliefs are a matter of faith (There is a God—or there isn't). Some come through tradition, passed on from one generation to the next, accepted simply because "they said it is so." Some are credited to common sense ("Beat a dog often enough and sooner or later it will get mean"). Some of the insights we have about the human condition are taken from art, literature, poetry, and drama. Psychologists, however, claim that there is a better way to understand ourselves: by applying the values and methods of science.

One goal of psychology is to use scientific methods to discover and understand relationships that exist among the behaviors and mental processes of organisms. Put another way, one goal of psychology is to understand the *scientific laws* that govern our subject matter. In this context, a scientific law is a statement about one's subject matter that one believes to be true—not on the basis of faith, tradition, or common sense, but on the basis of evidence.

science *an organized body of knowledge gained through application of scientific methods*

What qualifies psychology to be a **science**? Simply put, a science is an organized body of knowledge gained through application of scientific methods. So to qualify as a science, a discipline has to demonstrate two things: (1) an organized body of knowledge and (2) the use of scientific methods.

Over the years, psychologists have accumulated a great deal of information about the behaviors and mental processes of organisms, both human and nonhuman. To be sure, we can still ask interesting and important questions for which psychologists do not yet have adequate answers. Not having all of the answers can be frustrating, but that is part of the excitement of psychology—there are still so many things to discover. The truth is, however, that psychologists *have* learned a lot, and what is known is reasonably well organized. You have in your hands one version of the organized collection of knowledge that is psychology. In terms of our first requirement, then, psychology is a science.

scientific methods *a series of systematic procedures involving observation, description, control, and replication*

Psychology meets the second requirement of a science because what is known in psychology has been learned (mostly) through the application of **scientific methods**—a series of procedures that involve observation, description, control, and replication.

Scientific methods reflect an attitude or an approach to problem solving. It is "a process of inquiry, a particular way of thinking," rather than a special set of procedures that must be followed rigorously (Graziano & Raulin, 1993, p. 2). There are guidelines, however. The basic process goes like this: The scientist (psychologist) makes observations about his or her subject matter. For example, you notice that some students get better grades on psychology tests than do others and there seems to be a relationship between where they sit in the room and their grades. On the basis of these observations, a **hypothesis** is developed. A hypothesis is a tenta-

hypothesis *a tentative explanation of some phenomenon that can be tested and either supported or rejected*

tive explanation of some phenomenon that can be tested and then either supported or rejected, an educated guess about one's subject matter. In our example you might hypothesize that bright, well-motivated students tend to sit as close to the front of a classroom as they can.

When studying behavior and mental processes, psychologists often find it convenient, if not necessary, to use nonhuman animals in their research. On the other hand, some psychologists are interested in nonhuman animals (such as armadillos) for their own sake.

The scientist now observes relevant events again. These observations are then analyzed to see if the hypothesis is well founded. Alternative hypotheses are also examined. Following this procedure, you may try to locate IQ test scores, GPAs, or SAT scores for the students in the class and then keep a careful record of where students sit. Is there any other way to explain why students at the front of the class do well on classroom tests? Perhaps they cheat more often. The results of an investigation are shared with others, who may test them further. Do bright, well-motivated students tend to sit toward the front of the room in other classes, or on other campuses?

A scientific hypothesis may be rejected or supported, but it cannot be "proven" as true. No matter how much support one finds for a hypothesis, there still may be other hypotheses (perhaps as yet unthought of) that will do a better job of explaining what has been observed.

The goal of many psychologists is to use scientific methods to learn more about their subject matter. But while all psychologists are scientists, most are *scientist-practitioners*. This means that they are not so much involved in discovering new scientific laws about behavior and mental processes as they are in applying what we already know. Of those psychologists who are practitioners, most are clinical or counseling psychologists. Their goal is to apply what we know to help people deal with problems that affect their ability to adjust to the demands of their environments, including other people.

Psychological practitioners can be found in many settings, dealing with a variety of issues. Some scientist-practitioners apply psychological principles to issues that arise in the workplace; these are industrial/organizational (or I/O) psychologists. Some use psychology to improve the performance of athletes. Others advise attorneys on how best to present arguments in the courtroom. Some intervene to reduce ethnic prejudice and to teach others how differing cultural values affect behaviors. Some establish programs to increase the use of automobile safety belts, while others help people train their pets.

Thus we say that psychology has two interrelated goals: (1) the understanding of relationships that exist among the behaviors and mental processes of organisms, and (2) the application of this understanding in the real world. The science of psychology and the practice of psychology are not mutually exclusive endeavors. Many psychologists who are practicing clinical, counseling, or industrial psychologists are also active scientific researchers. And much of the scientific research in psychology gets its initial spark or impetus from problems that arise in real-world applications of psychology (Hoshmand & Polkinghorne, 1992).

Before You Go On

What makes psychology a science?

What are the two major goals of psychology?

⊚⊚⊚ **Thinking Critically** ⊚⊚⊚

Can you think of any questions for which science would be an inappropriate technique to use?

The Subject Matter of Psychology

Trying to list everything that psychologists study would not be very instructive. The list would be much too long to be of any use. However, as our definition says,

Many sports psychologists can be considered "practitioners" of psychology. Using their knowledge of the scientific principles of psychology, they help athletes to attain their best performances.

the subject matter of psychology is behavior and mental processes. Let's explore more fully just what that means.

Psychologists study behavior. **Behavior** is what organisms do—their actions and responses. The behaviors of organisms are observable and—at least potentially—can be measured. If I am concerned with whether a rat will press a lever in some situation, I can observe its behavior directly. If I wonder about Susan's ability to draw a circle, I can ask her to do so and observe her efforts. Observable, measurable behaviors offer an advantage as subject matters of a science—they are *publicly verifiable*. That is, several observers (public) can agree on (verify) the behavior or the event being studied. We can agree that the rat did or did not press the lever or that Susan drew a circle raher than a triangle.

Psychologists study mental processes. As we shall soon see, when psychology emerged as a separate discipline in the late nineteenth century it was defined as the science of mental processes, or the science of consciousness. There are two types of mental processes: cognitions and affects. **Cognitions** are mental events such as perceptions, beliefs, thoughts, ideas, and memories. *Cognitive processes,* then, include activities such as perceiving, thinking, knowing, understanding, problem solving, and remembering. **Affect** refers to mental processes that involve one's feelings, mood, or emotional state.

Here we have a scheme we will encounter repeatedly: the *ABCs* that make up the subject matter of psychology. Psychology is the science of *a*ffect, *b*ehavior, and *c*ognition. To understand a person at any given time, or to predict what he or she will do next, we must understand what he or she is feeling (A), doing (B), and thinking (C).

Psychologists find it useful, and occasionally imperative, to define the subject matter of a given study using operational definitions. **Operational definitions** define concepts in terms of the procedures used to measure or create them. Let's look at a few examples.

Imagine that we wanted to look at the relationship, if any, between exposure to television and violence. Before we got very far, we would have to define what we meant by "exposure to television," and we'd have to specify exactly how we would go about measuring "violence." We would have to generate operational definitions for the behaviors we were to study. What if we wanted to compare the behaviors of hungry and nonhungry rats in a maze? What do we mean when we talk about a "hungry rat"? What we can do is offer an operational definition, specifying that—at least for our study—a "hungry" rat is one that has been deprived of food for 24 hours. We could also operationally define a hungry rat as one that has lost 20 percent of its normal body weight, thus defining the concept in terms of the procedures used to create the hunger.

Operational definitions are particularly useful when we are dealing with mental processes. How shall we define *anxiety* in a study comparing the exam performance of students who experience either high or low anxiety levels during test taking? How shall we define *intelligence* if we want to compare the intelligence of students who have had access to a preschool program with students who have not? Terms such as *anxiety* and *intelligence* are difficult to define precisely or in ways with which all psychologists would agree. Sometimes our only recourse is to use operational definitions and specify how we intend to measure these concepts. We might operationally define anxiety in terms of measurable changes in physiological processes such as heart rate, blood pressure, and sweat gland activity. We might operationally define intelligence as the score on a certain psychological test.

Operational definitions have their limitations. They may oversimplify truly complex concepts (surely there is more to intelligence than a few numbers from a test). On the other hand, they do allow us to specify exactly how to measure the behavior or mental process we are studying, so they help us communicate accu-

behavior *what organisms do; their actions and reactions*

cognitions *mental events such as perceptions, beliefs, thoughts, ideas, and memories*

affect *one's feelings, mood, or emotional state*

operational definition *a definition of a concept given in terms of the procedures used to measure or create that concept*

Is this student anxious? How would you operationally define "anxiety"?

Defining Right- and Left-Handedness

Approximately 90 percent of the population are right-handed, the remaining 10 percent are left handed. One fact revealed in research on handedness is that most people are not as strongly right-handed or left-handed as they may think. Try this. Ask friends and relatives whether they use their right hand or left hand to complete each of the following tasks. They are to indicate frequency on a 5-point scale: (1) Always Left, (2) Usually Left, (3) Equally Left and Right, (4) Usually Right, and (5) Always Right. Then find their average score (the sum of the six ratings, divided by six) to get an indication of handedness.

1. Write a letter legibly.
2. Throw a ball at a target.
3. Hold scissors to cut paper.
4. Deal playing cards.
5. Hold a toothbrush while cleaning teeth.
6. Unscrew the lid of a jar.

Now have your participants actually try the following task, using first one hand, then the other. You'll need a standard $8^{1}/_{2} \times 11$ inch sheet of paper on which you have drawn two sets of 100 little quarter-inch boxes or circles. (Something like:

▢▢▢▢▢▢▢ or ○○○○○○○○.)

When you say "go," your subject, using his or her right hand, is to tap each box or circle once, leaving a mark inside. They are to work as rapidly and accurately as possible. Allow 30 seconds, then call "stop." After a 30-second rest, have them do the same thing with the second set of targets, but now using the left hand. Add up the number of "hits" for each hand, i.e., marks *in* the target (on the line does not count). The hand that earned the higher score may be operationally defined as the dominant hand. Did the results match the participants' self report? Which measure (self report or this "test") provides the most accurate assessment of handedness?

rately with others. We will see many examples of operational definitions throughout this text.

Before You Go On

What do psychologists study?

What are operational definitions?

@@@@ **Thinking Critically** @@@@

What sorts of affects or cognitions might be particularly challenging for psychologists to define operationally? Why?

Psychological Approaches Past and Present

No two psychologists approach their subject matter exactly the same way. Each brings his or her own experiences, expertise, values, and prejudices to the study of behavior and mental processes. This is true today, and it always has been the case. In this section, we add to our definition of psychology by considering some of the major perspectives, or approaches, that have been developed throughout psychology's history.

Psychology's Roots in Philosophy and Science

Psychology did not suddenly appear full-blown as the productive scientific enterprise we know today. The roots of psychology are found in philosophy and science.

We credit the philosophers for first suggesting that it is reasonable and potentially profitable to seek explanations of human behaviors at a human level. Most of the earliest explanations tended to be at the level of God—or the gods. If someone suffered from fits of terrible depression, for example, it was because that someone had offended the gods. A few philosophers successfully argued that we might be able to explain why people do what they do and feel and think as they do without constant reference to God's intentions in the matter.

The French philosopher René Descartes (1596–1650) is a good example of such a philosopher. Descartes liked to think about thinking. As he "lay abed of a morning thinking" (which his schoolmaster allowed, since Descartes was so good at it), he pondered how the human body and mind produced the very process he was then engaged in–thinking. Descartes envisioned the human body as a piece of machinery–intricate and complicated, to be sure, but machinery nonetheless. If the body consisted essentially of tubes, gears, valves, and fluids, its operation must be subject to natural physical laws, and those laws could therefore be discovered.

Descartes went further. Humans possess more than just a body; they have minds. It is likely that the mind similarly functions through the actions of knowable laws, but getting at these laws would surely be more difficult. Here's where Descartes had a truly important insight. We can learn about the mind because the mind and the body interact with each other. That interaction takes place in the brain. We call Descartes' position in these matters *interactive dualism*–dualism because the mind and the body are separate entities, and interactive because they influence each other. Thus we have with René Descartes the real possibility of understanding the human mind and how it works.

Nearly a hundred years later a group of British thinkers moved that part of philosophy concerned with the workings of the human mind very close to what was soon to become psychology. This group got its start from the writings of John Locke (1632–1704). Locke was sitting with friends after dinner one evening discussing philosophical issues when it became clear that no one in the group really understood how the human mind comes to understand anything, much less complex philosophical issues. Locke announced that within a week he could provide the group with a short explanation of the nature of human understanding. What was to have been a simple exercise took Locke many years to finish, but it gave philosophers a new set of ideas to ponder.

One of Locke's major concerns was how we come to represent the world "out there" in the internal world of the mind. Others (including Descartes) had asked this question, and many assumed that we are born with certain basic ideas about the world, ourselves, and, of course, God. Locke thought otherwise. He believed we are born into this world with our minds quite empty, like blank slates (the mind as a blank slate, or *tabula rasa,* was not new with Locke–it had been introduced by Aristotle in the third century B.C.). So how *does* the mind come to be filled with all its ideas, and memories? Locke answered, "In one word, from *experience."* Locke and his followers came to be known as British **empiricists**, those who credit experience and observation as the source of mental life.

empiricists *those who credit experience and observation as the source of mental life*

Philosophers had gone nearly to the brink. They had raised intriguing questions about the mind, how it worked, where its contents (ideas) came from, how ideas could be manipulated, and how the mind and body influence each other. Could the methods of science provide answers to any of the philosophers' questions?

During the nineteenth century, natural science was making progress on every front. In 1859 Charles Darwin (1809–1882), back from a lengthy sea voyage on the *H.M.S. Beagle,* published his revolutionary *The Origin of Species,* which spelled out the details of evolution. Few nonpsychologists were ever to have as much influence on psychology. What Darwin did for psychology was to confirm that the human species was part of the natural world of animal life. The methods of science could be turned to try to understand this creature of nature called the human being. Darwin made it clear that all species of this planet are, in a nearly infinite number of ways, related to one another. The impact of this observation, of course, is that what we discover about the sloth, the ground squirrel, or the rhesus monkey may enlighten us about ourselves. Another concept that Darwin emphasized was

René Descartes was born in this small home in 1596. It is now a museum in a town near the center of France, which has been renamed "Descartes" in honor of the French philosopher.

Few nonpsychologists have influenced the science of behavior and mental processes to the extent that Charles Darwin has. Darwin emphasized the adaptation of species to their environment.

adaptation. Species will survive and thrive only to the extent that they can, over the years, adapt to their environments. Psychologists were quick to realize that adaptation to one's environment was often a mental as well as a physical process.

A year after the publication of *The Origin of Species* a German physicist, Gustav Fechner (1801–1887), published a volume that was unique as a physics text. Fechner applied his training in the methods of physics to the psychological process of sensation. How do we make psychological judgments about events in the environment? What, Fechner wondered, was the relationship between the physical characteristics of a stimulus and the psychological experience of sensing that stimulus? For example, if the intensity of a light is doubled, will an observer see that light as twice as bright? Fechner found that the answer was no. Using the precise scientific procedures of a physicist, Fechner went on to determine the mathematical relationship between physical aspects of stimuli and a person's psychological experience of those stimuli (Link, 1995). Fechner succeeded in applying the methods of science to a psychological question about the mind and experience.

The mid-1800s also found physiologists coming to a better understanding of how the human body functions. By then it was known that nerves carried electrical messages to and from various parts of the body, and that nerves serving vision are different from those that serve hearing and the other senses and are also different from those that activate muscles and glands. Of all the biologists and physiologists of the nineteenth century, the one whose work is most relevant to psychology is Hermann von Helmholtz (1821–1894). In the physiology laboratory, Helmholtz performed experiments and developed theories on how long it takes the nervous system to react to stimuli, how we process information through our senses, and how we experience color. These are psychological issues, but in the mid-1800s there was no recognized science of psychology as we know it today.

By the late nineteenth century, psychology's time had come. Philosophy had become intrigued with mental processes, the origin of ideas, and the contents of the mind. Physiology and physics had begun to look at the nervous system, at sensation and perception, and were doing so using scientific methods. Biologists were raising questions about relationships between humans and other species. What was needed was someone with a clear vision to unite these interests and methods and to establish a separate discipline. That person was Wilhelm Wundt.

Before You Go On

How did the philosophies of Descartes and Locke prepare the way for psychology?

How did the science of Darwin, Fechner, and Helmholtz influence the emergence of psychology?

The Early Years

It is often claimed that psychology began in 1879, when Wilhelm Wundt (1832–1920) opened his laboratory at the University of Leipzig. Wundt had been trained to practice medicine, had studied physiology, and had served as a laboratory assistant to the great Helmholtz. He also held an academic position in philosophy. Wundt was a scientist-philosopher with an interest in such psychological processes as sensation, perception, attention, word associations, and emotions.

For Wundt, psychology was the scientific study of the mind, of consciousness. His hypotheses were tested and retested in his laboratory under carefully controlled conditions. The focus of most of the work in Wundt's laboratory was to discover the basic elements of thought. Beyond that, Wundt wanted to see how they were related to one another and to events in the physical environment—the latter notion picked up from the work of Fechner. Wundt wanted no less than to systematically describe the basic elements of mental life. Because the psychologists in Wundt's laboratory were mostly interested in describing the structure of the mind and its operations, we refer to Wundt's approach to psychology as **structuralism**.

As Wundt's new laboratory was flourishing, an American philosopher at Harvard University, William James (1842–1910), took issue with the sort of psychology that was being practiced in Leipzig. James agreed that psychology should study consciousness, and should use scientific methods to do so. He defined psychology as "the science of mental life," a definition very similar to Wundt's. Still, he thought the German-trained psychologists were off-base trying to discover the contents and structure of the human mind. James argued that consciousness could not be broken down into elements. Consciousness is dynamic, a stream of events—personal, changing, and continuous. Psychology should be concerned not with the structure of the mind but with its function. The focus of psychology should be on the practi-

structuralism *associated with Wilhelm Wundt, the approach to psychology that seeks to understand the structure and operation of consciousness, or the human mind*

Late in the nineteenth century, Wilhelm Wundt (center) and his students gathered in his laboratory at the University of Leipzig to use scientific methods to study human consciousness.

functionalism *the approach to psychology that emphasized the utilitarian, adaptive functions of the human mind, or consciousness*

cal uses of mental life. In this regard, James was responding to Darwin's lead. To survive requires that a species adapt to its environment. How does the mind function to help organisms adapt and survive in the world?

James's practical approach to psychology found favor in North America, and a new type of psychology emerged, largely at the University of Chicago. Psychologists there continued to focus on the mind, but emphasized its adaptive functions. We refer to this approach as **functionalism**. Functionalists still relied on experimental methods, and introduced the study of animals to psychology, again reflecting Darwin's influence. One of the most popular textbooks of this era was *The Animal Mind* (1908). This book by Margaret Floy Washburn (1871–1939), the first woman to be awarded a PhD in psychology, addressed questions of animal consciousness and intelligence. One of the characteristics of functionalism was its willingness to be open to a wide range of topics—as long as they were in some way related to mental life, adaptation, and practical application. We can trace the origins of child, abnormal, educational, social, and industrial psychology to this approach.

In the early days of American psychology, societal pressure was such that earning a graduate-level education, or any academic appointment, was exceedingly difficult for women, no matter how capable they may have been (Furumoto & Scarborough, 1986; Scarborough & Furumoto, 1987). Still, one woman, Mary Calkins (1863–1930), so impressed William James that he allowed her into his classes although Harvard would not allow her to enroll formally (nor would Harvard award her a PhD, for which she met all academic requirements). Mary Calkins went on to do significant experimental work on human learning and memory and, in 1905, was the first woman elected president of the American Psychological Association (Madigan & O'Hara, 1992). Christine Ladd-Franklin (1847–1930) did receive a PhD, but not until 40 years after it was earned and Johns Hopkins University had lifted its ban on awarding advanced degrees to women. In the interim she authored an influential theory on how humans perceive color.

As bright young students were drawn to the science of psychology, new academic departments and laboratories began to prosper throughout the United States and Canada. Scientific psychology was well underway—as the scientific study of the mind, its structures, or its functions. Such was the case until early in the twentieth century, when John Watson turned psychology's attention to the study of behavior.

Before You Go On

When and where did psychology begin?
Compare and contrast structuralism with functionalism.

Behaviorism

While John B. Watson (1878–1958) was a student at Furman University his mother died, thus relieving one of the pressures he felt to enter the ministry. He enrolled instead as a graduate student in psychology at the University of Chicago. He had read about the new science of psychology as an undergraduate and thought Chicago—where many leading functionalists were—would be the best place to study. He was soon disappointed. It turned out that he had little sympathy or talent for attempts to study mental processes with scientific methods. Even so, he stayed on at the University as a psychology major, studying the behavior of animals.

With his new PhD in hand, Watson went to Johns Hopkins University, where, almost single-handedly, he changed both the focus and the definition of psychology. Watson argued that if psychology was to become a mature, productive science, it had to give up its preoccupation with consciousness and mental life, concentrating instead on events that can be observed and measured. That is, psychology should give up the study of the mind and study behavior; hence the name of a new approach: **behaviorism**.

Neither Watson nor the behaviorists who followed him claimed that people do not think or have ideas. What Watson did say was that such processes were not the proper subjects of scientific investigation. After all, no one else can share your thoughts or feelings. Watson argued that we should leave private, mental events to the philosophers and theologians and make psychology as rigorously scientific as possible. Watson once referred to behaviorism as "common sense grown articulate. Behaviorism is a study of what people do" (Watson, 1926, p. 724).

No one has epitomized the behaviorist approach to psychology more than B. F. Skinner (1904–1990). Skinner took Watson at his word and spent a long and productive career in psychology trying to demonstrate that we can predict and control the behaviors of organisms by studying relationships between their observable responses and the circumstances under which those responses occur (Lattal, 1992). What mattered for Skinner is how behaviors are modified by events in the environment. Behaviorists would not address the question of why a rat turns left in a maze by talking about what the rat wanted or what the rat was thinking at the time. Rather, they would try to specify the environmental conditions (the presence of food, perhaps) under which a rat is likely to make left turns. For more than fifty years, Skinner consistently held to the argument that psychology should be defined as "the science of behavior" (Skinner, 1987, 1990).

behaviorism associated with John Watson, the approach to psychology that argues for the scientific study of observable behavior alone, not mental processes

Before You Go On

Briefly summarize behaviorism.

Wundt's structuralism, the functionalism of the early American psychologists, and the behaviorism of Watson were mainstream academic approaches to psychology. In its day, each dominated the way that psychologists thought about their discipline. Since the late 1800s there have been other approaches to the science of behavior and mental processes that were influential in the past and that continue to influence the way we think about psychology. We'll briefly consider three.

Psychoanalytic Psychology

Early in the twentieth century Sigmund Freud (1856–1939), a practicing physician in Vienna, became intrigued with what were then called "nervous disorders." He was struck by how little was known about these disorders and, as a result, chose to specialize in psychiatry.

Freud was not a laboratory scientist. Most of his insights about the mind came from his careful observations of his patients and himself. Freud's works were particularly perplexing to the behaviorists. Just as they were arguing against a psychology that concerned itself with consciousness, here came Freud declaring that we are often subject to forces of which we are not aware. Our feelings, actions, and thoughts (A, B, and C) are often under the influence of the *unconscious mind,* wrote Freud, many of our behaviors are expressions of instinctive strivings. Freud's views were clearly at odds with Watson's. We call the approach that traces its origin to Sigmund Freud and that emphasizes innate strivings and the unconscious mind **psychoanalytic psychology**.

Humanistic Psychology

In many respects, the approach we call humanistic psychology arose as a reaction against behaviorism and psychoanalysis. The leaders of this approach were Carl

psychoanalytic psychology associated with Sigmund Freud, the approach to psychology that emphasizes the role of innate strivings and the unconscious mind

Sigmund Freud brought the psychoanalytic approach to psychology. Among other things, this approach emphasized the importance of instinctive strivings and the reality of an unconscious mind.

humanistic psychology *the approach to psychology that emphasizes the person, or the self, and personal growth and development*

Rogers (1902–1987) and Abraham Maslow (1908–1970). **Humanistic psychologists** take the position that the individual, or the self, should be the central concern of psychology. If we only concern ourselves with stimuli in the environment and observable responses to those stimuli, we are leaving the *person* out of the middle—and that's dehumanizing. Such matters as caring, intention, concern, will, love, and hate are real phenomena and worthy of scientific investigation whether they can be directly observed or not. Attempts to understand people without considering such processes are doomed. To the humanistic psychologists, the Freudian reliance on instincts was too controlling. Our biology notwithstanding, we are—or can be—in control of our destinies. Rogers, Maslow, and their intellectual heirs emphasized the possibility of personal growth and achievement. This approach led Rogers to develop a system of psychotherapy (see Topic 13B), and Maslow to develop a theory of human motivation (see Topic 10A).

Gestalt Psychology

Gestalt psychology *the approach to psychology that emphasizes perception; in particular, the selection and organization of information*

In the first quarter of the twentieth century, a group of German scientists was taking an approach to psychology decidedly different from that of Wundt, James, Watson, or Maslow. Under the leadership of Max Wertheimer (1880–1943), this approach became known as Gestalt psychology. **Gestalt psychology** focuses on perception, concerned in particular with how we select and organize information from the outside world. *Gestalt* is a German word difficult to translate literally into English. It means roughly "configuration," "whole," or "totality." In general terms, if you can see the big picture, if you can focus on the forest rather than the trees, you have formed a gestalt. Gestalt psychologists argued against trying to analyze perception or consciousness into discrete, separate entities. To do so would destroy the essence of what was being studied. "The whole is more than the sum of its parts," they said. When we look at a drawing of a cube, we do not see the individual lines, angles, and surfaces, but naturally combine these elements to form a whole, a gestalt, which we experience as a cube.

Early Research on the Brain and Behavior

Even before Wundt opened his laboratory, scientists were looking for relationships between structures of the brain and the behavior of organisms. One of the first to achieve success was Franz Joseph Gall (1758–1828). Gall stated that mental processes have their origins in the brain; to understand mental activity meant that one must understand the brain. He went further, suggesting that specific areas of the brain house specific psychological characteristics or faculties. Moreover, different people demonstrated different degrees of these psychological characteristics, which were innately determined.

So far, so good. But then Gall suggested that one could measure a person's psychological faculties by attending to the size and location of bumps on the skull. Speech, for example, was located at the very front of the brain, where orators seemed to have large protrusions; self-esteem was housed at the top, toward the rear. An associate, Johann Spurzheim, popularized Gall's ideas (to Gall's embarrassment). Spurzheim coined the term **phrenology** to mean the science of determining personal characteristics by the careful interpretation of bumps on the head! The new "science" became extremely popular, particularly in the United States, but gained little status among the scientific community.

phrenology *the now discredited notion that one could relate personal traits to the location of bumps on the skull*

One reason for the demise of phrenology—and Gall's view of the brain—was the work of Pierre Flourens (1794–1867). Flourens used the technique of **ablation**, or the systematic removal of small parts of the brain from living animals, to study each part's function. Flourens believed that human brains were not significantly different from those of other animals, so he used mostly dogs and pigeons in his work. He found that some lower brain structures (e.g., the cerebellum) did have rather specific functions, but he was unable to locate any specific functions in the largest structure of the brain, the cerebral cortex. He discovered, for example, that if some behavior was lost following the removal of an area of the cerebral cortex, that behavior often could be reacquired by some other area of the brain.

ablation *the process of surgically removing tissue from living organisms to study the effects of that removal*

A different means of studying relationships between the brain and behavior was discovered by Gustav Fritsch (1838–1927) and Eduard Hitzig (1838–1907) in 1870. They found that a mild electric current delivered to one side of a surgically

Johann Spurzheim made Joseph Gall's ideas about the brain popular. Spurzheim coined the term "phrenology" to describe what he referred to as the science of determining the personality of an individual by analyzing the bumps on his or her head.

exposed cerebral cortex elicited the movement of muscles in the *opposite* side of the body. Using dogs, they were soon able to map out areas on each side of the brain that corresponded to different muscle groups on the opposite side of the dog's body. Soon other scientists were using fine wire electrodes to search for other functions of brain areas. In 1929, Hans Berger, a German psychiatrist who had been experimenting with the technique for twenty years, reported that recording electrodes attached to a person's scalp could pick up and make a record of the general electrical activity of the brain; thus we have the first report of an **electroencephalogram (EEG)** in use.

electroencephalogram (EEG) *an instrument that measures and records the electrical activity of the brain, indicative of arousal*

Our discussion of the philosophical and scientific roots of psychology will not end in this chapter. We will return to matters of mind and brain, to the advantages and disadvantages of behaviorism and humanistic psychology. We will see Gestalt psychology again in our coverage of perception. We will certainly return to Freud and controversies about innate drives and levels of consciousness. We will return to history when we explore methods used to treat psychological disorders.

Before You Go On

Describe psychoanalysis, humanistic psychology, and Gestalt psychology.

Describe some of the early research that sought to relate the brain to behavior.

⊚⊚⊚ **Thinking Critically** ⊚⊚⊚

Suppose John Watson and Sigmund Freud met by chance on a train. What do you think they might have talked about? On what issues would they agree and disagree?

Contemporary Approaches to Psychology

Psychology has come a long way from those few students gathered around Wilhelm Wundt in his laboratory at Leipzig. Today there are well over 500,000 psychologists in the world, with about half working in the United States (Rosenzweig, 1992). The oldest organization of psychologists, the American Psychological Association (APA), claims nearly 120,000 members, and lists over 40 divisions to which its members belong (Fowler, 1992).

A recent survey from the APA lists 236 "psychological specialty areas" in which psychologists are employed. We'll encounter many of these specialty areas in the chapters that follow. Some areas of specialization are defined in terms of the behaviors studied (aviation psychology, social psychology, instructional psychology, health psychology, personality psychology, military psychology, cognitive psychology, psychology of religion, and so on). Others are defined in terms of the population (the individuals) being studied (animal psychology, industrial psychology, child psychology, cultural psychology, and so on). Still others include the practitioners of psychology (clinical psychologists, counseling psychologists, consumer psychologists, sports psychologists, and so on).

Indeed, as we approach the twenty-first century, the variety of tasks and careers available to those who call themselves "psychologist" is expansive. What unites them all, however, is the search to better understand the behavior and mental processes of organisms.

Key Principles in Psychology

Psychologists have learned a great deal about the behaviors and mental processes of organisms. Some of the conclusions that psychologists have reached are so important that they deserve special mention. The principles listed here can be considered part of our definition of psychology. You will see these principles reflected in the content of every chapter that follows.

1. *Our biological nature and our psychological nurture interact to make us who we are.* How much of who we are—our affect, behavior, and cognition—is the result

Recognizing that people live in a variety of cultures and ethnic environments, one of the aims of cultural psychology is to examine cultural sources of psychological diversity.

of our inheritance, our biological *nature*? How much of who we are reflects the influences of our environment and experiences, our *nurture*? Is intelligence inherited (nature) or due to experience (nurture)? Is aggressiveness inborn (part of our nature), or learned (reflecting our nurture)? Does alcoholism reflect one's innate nature, or is it a learned reaction to events in the environment?

In fact, nearly all behaviors and mental processes result from the interaction of inherited and environmental influences. In other words, a psychological characteristic is not going to be the result of either heredity or experience, but will reflect the interaction of both. "For all psychological characteristics, inheritance sets limits on, or creates a range of potentials for, development. Environment determines how near the individual comes to developing these potentials" (Kimble, 1989).

2. *No two persons are exactly alike.* This observation is psychology's most common and well documented. Given the diversity of genetic make-ups and environments, including social and cultural pressures, it is not surprising that people can be so different from one another. Not only is each organism unique and different from all others, but no one is the same from one point in time to another. Depending on your experiences, your mental processes and behaviors are different today from what they were yesterday. Most likely, you have not changed in any major way, but some observations that were true of you yesterday may not be true of you today.

Identical twins share the same genetic constitution. Similarities within pairs of identical twins may reflect their inheritance or their experiences. Their differences should reflect only their experiences.

Imagine that a psychologist wants to study your behavior and mental activity and draw some conclusions she can apply to people in general. Do you see the problem she is going to have? Indeed, because of the variability that exists among people, we find that psychologists seldom study just one person, hoping to draw conclusions about others. Because no two people are exactly alike, virtually all psychological laws are statements made "in general, in the long run, by and large." For example, we know that high school grades are reasonable predictors of success in college. But because people differ, the best we can do is generalize that students who do well in high school will *probably* do well in college.

3. *Our experience of the world may reflect something other than what is actually "out there."* This classic notion has a name: phenomenology. **Phenomenology** has to do with the study of events as they are experienced by the individual, not as they occur. We could get involved in some fairly deep philosophical discussions here, but we need not. What we need to appreciate and keep in mind is that, as active agents in the world, we each select, attend to, interpret, and remember different aspects of the same world.

Here's a simple, classic example attributed to the philosopher John Locke. Imagine that you have before you three pails of water. The water in the pail on your left is quite hot, the water in the pail on your right is nearly ice cold, and the water in the center pail is at about body temperature. You put your left hand into the hot water and your right hand into the cold. Then, after a minute, you place both hands in the center pail. What is its temperature? How does the water feel? To your left hand, the water seems cool, but to your right hand the very same water feels warm. Is the temperature of the water in the center pail cool or warm? A physicist may measure the temperature of the water in that center pail with astonishing accuracy. But we're not interested in the physics of the water. We're interested in the psychology of your experience of the water, and we may—with a smug smile—report that the water in the center pail is both warm and cool.

phenomenology *the study of events, not they occur, but as they are experienced by the individual*

The world is not always as it first appears. What is foreground and what is background in this drawing?

Here's another example (from Bruner & Goodman, 1947). Children are given the opportunity to manipulate the size of a small circle. They are asked to make the circle exactly the same size as a quarter. Most children overestimate the size of the coin. What is more interesting is that poor children overestimate the size of the coin to a significantly greater degree. To the poor children, quarters seem much larger than they actually are.

4. *For many questions in psychology, there are no simple answers.* There are many good questions in psychology for which there are, as yet, no good answers. For some questions we do have answers with which almost all psychologists agree. On the other hand, for other questions we don't even have reasonably acceptable hypotheses. What you will encounter in your study of psychology is that complex phenomena often have complex explanations.

As an example, let's briefly anticipate a subject we'll examine later when we cover psychological disorders. What causes schizophrenia? For now, we simply acknowledge that schizophrenia is one of the most debilitating of all psychological disorders, afflicting approximately 2.5 million people in the United States today. What causes the distortions in the way a person feels, thinks, and acts that define schizophrenia? The truth is that we don't know. We have several hypotheses, and each holds promise, but the issue is complex. Part of the answer is genetic: schizophrenia tends to run in families. Part of the answer is biochemical: the brains of persons with schizophrenia do not function the same as the brains of those who do not have schizophrenia. Part of the answer is environmental, or situational: stress and experience can bring on symptoms, or at least make symptoms worse than they would otherwise be. So what causes schizophrenia? Answer: a number of interacting factors, some genetic, some physiological, some environmental, perhaps all operating at the same time. And so it goes for virtually all our behaviors and mental processes.

If you're looking for simple answers to explain your behavior or the behavior of others, you are bound to be disappointed, but please don't be discouraged. Behaviors and mental processes are complex, and explaining them will not always be easy. Complexity in and of itself should not be worrisome. Behaviors and mental processes generally have multiple causes. Our challenge is to discover them.

5. *Psychology is relevant to our daily lives.* We might get an argument from biologists, chemists, physicists, geologists, and even some astronomers, but I'm willing to make the claim that no other science has more practical, useful application in the real world than psychology. In everyday life people can get by without thinking about physics or geology, but they cannot get by without thinking psychologically. They must take into consideration a multitude of sensations, perceptions, memories, feelings, and consequences of their actions if they are going to survive, and certainly if they are going to prosper. As you read about psychology on the following pages, you should be on the lookout for how the material you're reading can be put to use in your own life.

Here's an example you can put to use right now. When we get to the chapters on learning and memory, we'll see that information is easier to learn and remember if it is made meaningful. One of your jobs as a learner—as a student in a psychology class—is to make the material you are learning as meaningful as possible. What that means, among other things, is that you need to find ways in which you personally relate to the issues you are reading about. In psychology, finding such relevance is fairly easy. After all, the subject matter of psychology is the behavior and mental processes of organisms—and that includes you and me.

Before You Go On

Describe five key principles in psychology that will appear repeatedly throughout our study.

TOPIC 1A SUMMARY

In Topic 1A we have defined psychology as the scientific study of behavior and mental processes. That is, psychologists use scientific methods to study affect, behavior, and cognition. The goals of psychology are to discover and understand scientific laws that deal with its subject matter, and to apply these laws in the real world. We have also taken a look at psychology's history, noting that although it emerged as a separate scientific discipline only a hundred years ago, its roots in philosophy and science are much older. We've seen that the discipline of psychology includes many areas, approaches, and perspectives from which psychologists view their subject matter. This is true today, as it always has been. Now we need to consider in more detail just how psychologists go about doing what they do. These are the issues covered in Topic 1B.

TOPIC 1B The Research Methods of Psychology

In Topic 1A we saw that psychology is a science because it has an organized body of knowledge and because it uses scientific methods to discover and understand the laws of its subject matter. Scientific methods were defined in general terms as systematic procedures of observation, description, control, and replication. Now it is time to see what this definition means as it applies to the methods psychologists use. To understand psychology, it is imperative that we understand its research methods.

Observational Methods

Our discussion of research in psychology begins with comments about observational methods. Before we can explain what people do, we must first make valid observations of what people do. As it happens, there are several ways psychologists make observations, and there are steps they can take to ensure that their observations are valid.

Naturalistic Observation

Naturalistic observation involves carefully and systematically watching behaviors as they occur naturally, with no involvement from the observer. There is a logical appeal to the argument that if you are trying to understand what organisms do you should simply watch them in action, noting their behaviors and the conditions under which those behaviors occur.

As straightforward and appealing as naturalistic observation may sound, it does present a few difficulties. For one thing, if we want to observe people (or any other organism) acting naturally, we must make sure they do not realize we are watching them. As you know from your own experience, people may act very differently if they think they are being watched. You may do all sorts of things in the privacy of your home that you would never do if you thought someone was watching you.

A second potential problem is observer bias. **Observer bias** occurs when one's own motives, expectations, and previous experiences interfere with the objectivity

naturalistic observation *the careful, systematic observation of behaviors as they occur, without any involvement by the observer*

observer bias *a situation in which one's motives, expectations, and previous experiences interfere with the objectivity of observations*

Naturalistic observation requires skill and great patience. The observer here is using a night-vision lens to look for frogs as tape recorders play the frogs' mating call.

The data from surveys can tell us what a large sample of people think about a limited number of issues.

of the observations being made. It might be difficult for a researcher to be truly objective in her observations of children in a preschool setting if she is aware of the hypothesis under investigation, say, that boys are more verbally aggressive than girls. Observer bias may also result from gender and cultural bias. For example, men often have different visions of what constitutes "sexual harassment" than do women (see Fitzgerald, 1993). People from different cultural backgrounds, or ethnic groups, might have different views of what constitutes an "aggressive behavior." One remedy is to have observers note behaviors without knowledge of the hypotheses under investigation. Another protection against observer bias is to use several observers and rely only on those observations that are verified by a number of observers.

A third potential problem with naturalistic observation is more difficult to deal with. The behaviors you want to observe may not be there when you are. For example, if you are interested in conformity and want to observe people conforming naturally, in the real world, just where would you go? Where are you likely to observe conformity happening naturally? True, conformity behaviors are more likely to occur in some environments than in others. But there is no guarantee that during any particular day, week, or month the people you are watching will provide any evidence of conformity. If you manipulate a situation so that people are more likely to conform, you are no longer doing *naturalistic* observation. To use this method you often have to be lucky, and you almost certainly will have to be patient.

Although it has its problems, naturalistic observation is sometimes the most suitable method psychologists have available. For example, studying chimpanzees in zoos and laboratories will tell us little about how chimpanzees behave in their natural habitat. Examples also come from psychologists who have been frustrated in their attempts to study the language development of young children. By the time they are 3 or 4 years old, children demonstrate all sorts of interesting language behaviors. However, these children may be too young to understand and properly follow the instructions that many experiments require. They are almost certainly unable to respond sensibly to questions about their own language use. Perhaps all we can do is watch and listen carefully to young children as they use their language and try to determine what is going on by observing them as they interact naturally with their environments.

Before You Go On

What is naturalistic observation?

What steps need to be taken for the method to be successful?

Surveys

survey *the process of asking a large sample of persons a small set of questions*

When we want to make systematic observations about a large number of people, we may use a survey method. Doing a **survey** amounts to asking many people the same question or set of questions. The questions may be asked in person, in a telephone interview, or in a written questionnaire. Survey studies yield data that otherwise would be difficult to gather.

If we wanted to know, for example, whether there was a relationship between income level and the type of automobile one drives or television programs one watches regularly, we could ask about these issues in a survey of a large number of people. A survey can tell us what given segments of the population think or feel and can provide insights about preferences for products, services, or political candidates. If the cafeteria staff on your campus really wanted to know what students preferred to eat, they could survey a sample of the student population.

sample *a subset, or portion, of a larger population that has been chosen for study*

For survey data to be useful, the sample surveyed must be sufficiently large and representative of the population from which it was drawn. A **sample** is a subset, or portion, of a larger population that has been chosen for study. We would like to be able to generalize, or extend, observations beyond those persons in our sample. Cafeteria managers who survey only students attending morning classes may make observations that do not generalize to the larger population from which the sample was drawn.

Case Histories

The case history method provides another type of observational information. In the **case history method**, one person—or a small sample of people—is studied in depth, often over a long period. Use of this method usually involves a detailed examination of a wide range of behaviors. The method is retrospective, which means that we start with a given state of affairs (a situation that currently exists) and go back in time to see if there is any relationship between this state of affairs and previous experiences and events. We may use interviews or psychological tests as a means of collecting our data.

As an example, let's say that we are interested in Mr. X, a known child abuser. Our suspicion (hypothesis) is that Mr. X's own childhood experiences are related to his abuse of children. We talk to Mr. X at length and interview his family and friends—those who knew him as a child—to try to form a retrospective picture of Mr. X's childhood. If we find some clues—for example, Mr. X was often punished with severe spankings, or he missed class at school significantly more often than other children—we may then explore the early childhood experiences of other known child abusers, looking for common experiences that might be related to their abuse of children.

I have always been intrigued by the choices college students make when they decide on a major course of study. (Perhaps this is because when I started college, I was a chemistry major.) Why do some students major in psychology, whereas others choose mathematics or art as a major? Perhaps the case history method could provide some insights about issues related to one's choice of a major. How would we proceed? We would choose a sample of students, perhaps seniors, from each major, and ask them a series of penetrating (it is hoped) questions about their experiences, looking for things that students of one major had in common with each other, but not with students who chose other majors.

As we shall see, Freud based most of his theory of personality on his intensive examination of the case histories of his patients (and himself). An advantage of the case history method is that it can provide a wealth of information about a few individual cases. The disadvantage is that we have to be particularly careful when we try to generalize our findings beyond those individuals we have studied.

Before You Go On

How can surveys and case histories be used to help us understand behavior and mental processes?

Correlational Methods

As you know from your own experience, observations are often very useful in their own right. Observations about people's behaviors, thoughts, or feelings can provide us with interesting insights. How many people in North America *do* smoke cigarettes? What *do* the majority of Americans really think about abortions performed during the first trimester of pregnancy? How *do* most people feel about the making of a sequel to the movie *Forrest Gump*? However useful or insightful they may be in themselves, observations take the form of scientific laws only when they are consistently related to other observations. **Correlation** is a statistical procedure used to assess the degree to which sets of observations are lawfully related. To say that observations are correlated is to say that they are related to each other, or co-related.

case history method *the technique of studying (observing) one person (or a few persons) in depth, using interviews, tests, and the like*

@◎@◎ **Thinking Critically** @◎@◎

You have a hypothesis: people who like sports have more friends than those who do not like sports. How would you conduct three different studies, one using naturalistic observation, one using surveys, and one using case histories to investigate your hypothesis? What would be the strengths and weaknesses of each method?

correlation *a statistical procedure used to assess the degree to which sets of observed responses are associated (co-related) with each other*

We'll work through an example to see how this method works. Imagine that we are interested in learning whether there is a relationship—a correlation—between reading ability and performance in introductory psychology. The first thing to do is to generate acceptable operational definitions for the responses in which we're interested. How will we measure reading ability and performance in introductory psychology? Performance in introductory psychology is easy. We'll take that to be the total number of points earned by a student on classroom exams over the course of a semester. Reading ability is a little more of a challenge. We could design a test to measure behaviors we think reflect reading ability, but we're in luck. There are several tests of reading ability already available, and we decide to use the Nelson Denny Reading Test, the NDRT (Brown, 1973).

Now we're ready to collect some data (make our observations). We give a large group of students our reading test (the NDRT). Once the tests are scored, we have one large set of numbers. At the end of the semester, we add up the points earned by each of our students, and we have a second set of numbers. For each student we have a pair of numbers—one indicating reading ability, one indicating performance in the introductory psychology course. We want to know if these observations are correlated.

From here on, our method is more statistical than psychological. We enter our pairs of numbers into a calculator or a computer. A series of arithmetic procedures is applied, following prescribed formulas. The result is the **correlation coefficient**—a number between −1.00 and +1.00 that tells us about the nature and the extent of the relationship between the responses we have measured. What does this number

correlation coefficient *a number that indicates the nature (+ or −) and the degree (0.00 to +1.00 or −1.00) of the relationship between measured responses*

Although I've never done the study to confirm my suspicions, I suspect that there is a negative correlation between gymnastic ability and body size. How could we test this hypothesis?

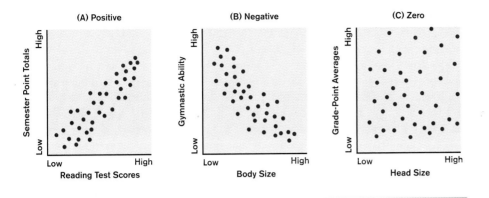

Figure 1.1

Positive, negative, and zero correlations. (A) A graph depicting the reading test scores and semester point totals earned by 40 students. These data indicate a positive (+) correlation between the two measured responses. As reading test scores increase, so do semester point totals. (B) A graph depicting the body size and gymnastic abilities of 40 students. These data indicate a negative (–) correlation between the two measured responses. As body size increases, gymnastic ability decreases. (C) A graph depicting the head sizes and grade-point averages of 40 students. These data indicate a zero (0) correlation between the two measured responses. There is no relationship between head size and grade-point average.

mean? How can one number be the basis for a scientific law? It takes experience to be truly comfortable with the interpretation of correlation coefficients, but we can make some general observations.

First let's deal with the sign of the correlation coefficient, which will be positive (+) or negative (–). A positive coefficient tells us that our two responses are related to each other, and that high scores on one of our responses are associated with high scores on the other. It also tells us that low scores on one measure are associated with low scores on the other. In our example, a positive correlation means that a student who does well on the reading test will probably do well in an introductory psychology course. Students who do poorly on the reading test are likely to earn lower grades in the course. As it happens, there is evidence that such is the case (e.g., Gerow & Murphy, 1980). Figure 1.1(A) shows what a graph of the scores in our example might look like and depicts a positive correlation. Here we see a major use of correlations: if we determine that two responses are correlated, we can use our observation of one to make predictions about the other.

What if our calculations yield a correlation coefficient that is a negative number? Here, too, we have a useful psychological law. We can still use scores on one response to predict scores on the other. But when our correlation coefficient is negative, we know that the relationship between the two responses is inverse. With negative correlation coefficients, high scores on one response predict low scores on the other. If we were to measure body size to see if it were related to gymnastic ability, we might find a negative correlation: large body sizes associated with poor gymnastic ability (low scores), and small body sizes associated with good gymnastic ability (high scores). Even if these two sets of observations are negatively correlated, we can still use body size to predict gymnastic ability. Figure 1.1(B) shows data depicting a possible relationship between gymnastic ability and body size, a negative correlation.

What if our correlation coefficient turns out to be zero, or nearly so (say, .003)? In this case, we would conclude that the two sets of observations we have made are simply not related to each other in any consistent, lawful way. Let's say that I worked from the faulty notion that intelligence is a function of brain size, and that head size tells us how big a person's brain is. If I were to measure both the head sizes of many students and their grade point averages, I would find that the correlation coefficient would be very close to zero. As correlations approach zero, predictability decreases. Figure 1.1(C) shows what a graph of data from two sets of unrelated measures would look like.

So much for the sign of the correlation coefficient. What about its numerical value? Again, it takes a little practice to get used to working with numbers such as −.46, +.55, and +.002. For now, let us just say that the closer we get to the extreme of +1.00 or −1.00, the stronger the relationship between the responses we have measured. That is, as our correlation coefficient approaches +1.00 or −1.00 (say, +.84 or −.93), we'll have increased confidence in our ability to predict one response knowing the other. The closer it gets to zero (say, −.12 or +.004), the weaker the relationship, or the less useful it is in making predictions. In general, the larger the sample (the more observations we make) the greater the confidence we can put in our correlation coefficient, whatever its value.

As you read this text, you'll encounter many studies that use a correlational analysis of measured observations. As you do, you'll need to keep in mind two important points. (1) *Cause-and-effect conclusions are inappropriate for correlational studies.* Even if two responses are well correlated with each other, we cannot claim that one causes the other. This can be a difficult point to remember. Sometimes logic overwhelms us. It does make sense that an inability to read will cause some students to do poorly in an introductory psychology class where reading is so important. Yes, it does make sense, but if all we know is that reading ability and grades are correlated, we can make no statement at all about cause and effect; we can say only that the two responses are related to each other. (2) *Even when two responses are well correlated, we cannot make predictions for individual cases.* As I said, reading ability and introductory psychology grades are positively correlated. By and large, students who read well do well in the course, and, by and large, students who do not read well do poorly. So, in general, we can use reading test scores to predict grades, but we have to allow for exceptions. A few poor readers may do very well, and a few excellent readers may still fail the course. Exceptions are to be expected. The farther from +1.00 or −1.00 our correlation coefficient is, the more exceptions we can expect. Like most of the scientific laws in psychology, statements of correlation hold true only "by and large," "generally," "in the long run," or "more often than not."

Before You Go On

What data are needed to calculate a correlation coefficient?

What does a correlation coefficient tell us about the relationship between two measured responses?

Experimental Methods

experiment *a series of operations used to examine possible cause-and-effect relations between manipulated events and measured events*

Most of what is known today in psychology has been learned by doing experiments. An **experiment** is a series of operations used to investigate relationships between manipulated events and measured events, while other extraneous events are controlled or eliminated. In the abstract that's quite a mouthful, but the actual procedures are not that difficult to understand.

The Basic Process

Experiments are designed to discover cause-and-effect relationships among variables. When we perform an experiment, we are no longer content to discover that two measured observations are simply related; now we want to be able to claim that, at least to some degree, one is caused by the other. To see if such a claim can be made, one manipulates one variable to see if that manipulation causes any measurable changes in another variable. A variable is simply something that can vary—

a measurable event that can take on different values. Experimental methods are described in terms of variables.

The events or conditions an experimenter manipulates are called **independent variables**. Those the experimenter measures are **dependent variables**—their value should *depend* on the experimenter's manipulation of independent variables. The hope is that the manipulation of the independent variable will cause predictable changes in the dependent variable—changes predicted by one's hypothesis. If there are changes in the dependent variable, the experimenter would like to claim that these changes are due solely to the influence of the manipulated independent variable. In order to make such a claim, the experimenter must show that all other variables that could have influenced what is being measured have been controlled or eliminated. Those factors that need to be eliminated from consideration are **extraneous variables** (extraneous means "not essential"). So, to do an experiment, a researcher manipulates independent variables, measures dependent variables, and eliminates or controls the effects of extraneous variables. If you haven't encountered this before, please don't be discouraged. Going over a couple of examples will help.

After a few quizzes in your biology class you notice that the student sitting in front of you is consistently scoring higher than you are—not by much, but by enough to be disturbing to you. You ask this student how she does it, and she tells you she has a system she learned in high school. To better remember a series of unrelated concepts, she weaves the terms together to form a story. Remembering the story is fairly easy and can be used to help recall terms for quizzes. This system sounds sensible to you, and you decide to test whether there is a cause-and-effect relation here (a decision that was also made by Gordon Bower and M. C. Clark, who performed such an experiment in 1969).

You get some volunteers from your introductory psychology class and divide them into two groups. One group (A) is asked to memorize a list of ten unrelated nouns. They are left to their own resources to learn the list however they choose. The other group (B) is asked to memorize the very same list of nouns, but they are told about the scheme of tying the words together to form a meaningful story and asked to use this strategy in learning the list.

Now for some terminology. Your hypothesis is that how people go about memorizing has an effect on how much one remembers. You have manipulated this process, so using or not using a strategy in memorizing is your *independent variable*. You believe this variable will have an effect on memory. How will you measure this to see if it is so—that is, what will be your dependent variable? You ask all of the students to return three weeks later. At that time you ask them to "write down as many of the words as you can recall from the list you learned three weeks ago." Thus, you operationally define your *dependent variable* to be the average number of words from the list recalled three weeks later. When you look at your data, you discover that on average, students in group A recall 3.5 words of the original 10, and those in group B (who made up stories) recall 8.2 words correctly. It seems that a story-generating strategy is useful in memorizing words. That strategy seems to cause significantly better recall.

Before we get too carried away, we had better consider the *extraneous variables* that might have been operating in this experiment. These are factors that might have affected the average recall of our two groups of students over and above what was manipulated (memorization strategy). Such factors should have been considered before you actually carried out the experiment, of course. What extraneous variables might be involved in this experiment? For one thing, we need to be certain that the students in each of our groups are of essentially the same academic ability to begin with. We'd have a problem if most of the students in group A were struggling students and those in group B were honor students. Furthermore, both groups of learners need to be presented with identical materials to be learned, and the words need to be presented in the same way to both groups.

independent variable *the event or situation manipulated by an experimenter to see if it will have a predicted effect on some other event or situation*

dependent variable *the event or situation measured by an experimenter to see if it has changed upon manipulation of an independent variable*

extraneous variables *those events or situations in an experiment that must be controlled or eliminated so as not to affect one's dependent variable*

When we are done with our experiment and find differences in the dependent variable, we want to be able to claim that these differences are due to our manipulation of the independent variable and to nothing else. This is a very important point. It is the extent to which extraneous variables are anticipated and eliminated that determines the quality of an experiment. Figure 1.2 reviews the steps in our example experiment.

Let's take a quick look at another potential experimental question. Suppose you hypothesize that a stimulating environment in early childhood will improve intellectual functioning at adolescence. You propose to do an experiment to seek support for your hypothesis. There are several ways of doing this kind of experiment, but this problem provides a good example of an experiment that could be done with rats. Manipulating the level of stimulation in the environments of young children would be unethical. Rats could be raised in cages that provide differing amounts of stimulation. When the rats approach maturity, you could test their ability to negotiate mazes or learn a variety of responses. Early exposure to stimulation

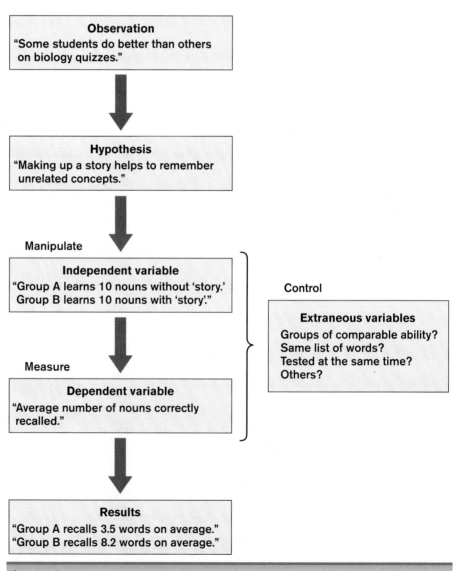

Figure 1.2

The steps, or stages, involved in doing an experiment. Note how the various types of variables are related to each other.

would be your independent variable, and scores on your tests of learning ability would be your dependent variable.

One advantage of using rats is that extraneous variables are usually easy to deal with. You seldom have to worry about past experience, inherited differences, parental influences, and the like (all of your rats have a known and very similar genetic history, and all have been reared in similar conditions). The problem with using rats is also obvious. Even if you do demonstrate your point with rats, you may then have to argue that the data you have collected for rats are, in some way, applicable to humans. In fact, several experiments of this sort have been done by Marion Diamond and his colleagues (Diamond et al., 1975).

Now that we have covered the essential procedures of doing experiments, we can examine some considerations that often determine the quality of an experiment.

Before You Go On

Describe the experimental process.

Exercising Control

The value of an experimental finding is related to the researcher's ability to eliminate or control the influence of extraneous variables. The most difficult extraneous variables to control are those that involve individual differences among the participants in the experiment. Such was the case in our example involving a memory strategy. In a typical experiment the independent variable is manipulated by presenting one group of participants with some treatment (e.g., a hint about how to memorize words) and withholding that treatment from another group (e.g., no hint). Participants in both groups are then measured to see if the treatment produced any effect. Participants who receive a treatment or manipulation are the **experimental group**. An experiment may have more than one experimental group, although our example experiment used just one. If an additional group of students had been available, we might have given them a different hint to aid their recall. Participants who do not receive the experimental treatment are the control group. An experiment usually has just one control group.

experimental group *participants in an experiment who receive a treatment or manipulation*

To make sure your control and experimental groups begin the experiment on equal footing you could do one of a number of things. You could try to match the groups on the characteristic of interest. In our example, you might have given all participants a different test of their recall skills before the experiment began and then assigned them to either group A or B so that the average scores on this test were equal, or nearly so.

A more common technique is to use **random assignment,** which means that each participant in the research has an equal chance of being assigned to any one of the groups used in your experiment. If assignment is truly random, then honor students would be equally likely to be in either of these two groups–the one that does or the one that doesn't get a hint about weaving the words into a story. Decisions to match or randomly assign participants to groups must be made before the experiment is begun.

random assignment *the selection of members of a population such that each participant has an equal chance of being in any of the study groups*

Another method of controlling for the differing past experiences of participants is called a **baseline design**. Although there are several such designs, each amounts to arranging things so that each participant serves in both experimental and control group conditions. Imagine, for example, that you wished to see if a particular drug caused an increase in the running speed of white rats. Using a baseline design, you'd first measure the running speed of rats without giving them the drug (a control, or baseline measure). Then you would check the running speed of the same rats after they were given some of the drug. Changes in their behavior (your

baseline design *a method in which a participant's performance with an experimental treatment is compared with performance without that treatment (the baseline)* dependent variable) could then be attributed to the drug (your independent variable). You would then check the running speed of the rats again, after the effects of the drug wore off, to see if their running behavior returned to its baseline rate.

Meta-analyses

Before we leave our discussion of research methods in psychology, there is a popular technique that deserves a brief note. Some experiments or correlational studies are impossible (or too expensive) to do on a large scale, with many participants.

For example, ethics prevent us from rearing children in isolation, deprived of environmental stimulation, but we might be able to identify a few adolescents who had relatively isolated, deprived childhoods. We might compare their learning abilities with those of adolescents whose childhood experiences were apparently normal and with adolescents who seem to have had stimulating childhood experiences. Our findings, based on only a few adolescents and with many variables not under careful control, would be tentative at best, no matter what those findings happened to be. But what if, over the years, many similar studies were conducted by different researchers in different places? Although each such study in and of itself would not be convincing, what if there were some way to combine the results of these studies? Such is precisely the intent of a procedure called **meta-analysis,** a statistical procedure of combining the results of many studies to more clearly see the relationship, if any, between independent and dependent variables. A meta-analysis minimizes the errors that can plague single, smaller studies (Schmidt, 1992).

meta-analysis *the statistical procedure of combining the results of many studies or experiments to determine if any commonalities exist*

Meta-analysis research sometimes uncovers relationships that are not clear in individual studies, and sometimes produces results that even contradict some of the studies being included. A meta-analysis by psychologist Janet Hyde and her associates (Hyde et al., 1990) examined gender differences in mathematics performance. These researchers analyzed 100 studies that involved the testing of a combined total of 3,175,188 participants (it's difficult to imagine one research project that could involve over 3 million people). These researchers found that there are

A meta-analysis by Janet Hyde and her colleagues combined data from over 100 separate research studies and found that differences between the mathematical skills of men and women were more similar than different.

not many differences between males and females in mathematical performance *on average*. Females do have a slight edge in computational skills in elementary and middle school, while males do a little better in mathematical problem solving in high school and college, particularly in tests of advanced mathematics. But any differences were found to be very small, and in most comparisons there were no real differences at all. This is the sort of finding that any one study, no matter how well conceived, is unlikely to give us.

Before You Go On

How do random assignment, baseline designs, and meta-analyses help to minimize error in psychological experiments?

Ethics in Psychological Research

Ethical and moral concerns can be found in all of the sciences; for most of them, ethical issues center on the application of knowledge. We know how to split the atom; should we build a bomb? We can manufacture effective insecticides; should we use them? We have the means to render people sterile; should we? We can use machines to keep people alive indefinitely; should we?

Psychology has something of a unique problem with regard to ethics. To be sure, ethical matters are important in the application of psychological knowledge, be it in diagnosis, therapy, counseling, or training. But in psychology, concerns about ethics are crucial in the *gathering* of information. After all, the objects of psychological research are living organisms. Their physical and psychological welfare need to be protected as their behaviors and mental processes are being investigated. Psychologists have long been concerned with the ethical implications of their work. Since 1953, the American Psychological Association has regularly revised *Ethical Principles of Psychologists* for practitioners and researchers (APA, 1992).

In planning research, psychologists assess the degree to which participants will be put at risk. What are the potential dangers, physical or psychological, that might accompany participation? Even if potential risks are deemed slight, they need to be considered and balanced in light of the potential good that might come from the research. Researcher Gregory Kimble put it this way: "Is it worth it? Do the potential benefits to science and eventually to animal and human lives justify the costs to be extracted here and now?" (Kimble, 1989, p. 499). Seldom will any

Even though the welfare of animals is carefully monitored in most laboratories, many animal rights activists would prefer that animals not be used in research under any circumstances. Such is the point of this demonstration.

one psychologist have to make the ultimate decisions about the potential benefits or risks of research. Advisory committees of researchers, familiar with the techniques and the problems of the proposed research, will have to approve the project before it begins.

What are some other ethical issues related to research in psychology?

1. The participant's confidentiality must be guaranteed. Often the person's name is not even used; instead, it is replaced with an identification number. No matter what participants are asked to do or say, they should be confident that no one will have access to their responses but the researchers.

2. Participation in research should be voluntary. No one should feel coerced or compelled to participate in psychological research. For example, college students cannot be offered extra credit for participating in psychological research unless other options are available for earning the same amount of extra credit. Volunteers should be allowed the option of dropping out of any research project, even after it has begun.

3. Persons should be included in experiments only after they have given their consent. Participants must know the risks of participation, why a project is being done, and what is expected of them. For example, no one can have access to your college records (your GPA, your entrance exam scores, and so on) without your specific knowledge and approval. Obviously, some small amount of deception may be required when doing experiments. Even so, the amount of deception needs to be balanced against the potential benefits of the research.

4. Particularly if participants have been deceived about the true nature of an experiment, and even if they haven't been, all participants should be **debriefed** after the experiment has been completed. That means that the project and its basic intent should be fully explained to all those who participated in it. Participants should also be provided with a copy of the results of the project when they are available.

debrief *the process of informing participants of the true and complete nature of an experiment after the experiment is over*

Published ethical guidelines for the use of animals in research are also quite stringent. Only experts trained and experienced in the proper and humane care and housing of animals should have responsibility for laboratory animals. Those experts must then provide training to all others working with the animals. Every effort must be made to avoid or minimize discomfort, illness, and pain. Putting animals in a situation in which they might experience injury, pain, or stress is acceptable only if no other procedure is available and the goal is justified by its prospective scientific, applied, or educational value. As with human subjects, there are usually review committees that approve the design of any research using non-human animals, where the major concern is the ethical, humane protection of the animals.

Before You Go On

What are some ethical issues that must be considered when doing psychological research?

TOPIC 1B SUMMARY

The major aim of this Topic was to describe in general terms the research methods used in psychology. We have learned that psychologists use scientific methods that can be classified as methods of observation, correlation, and experimentation. Most research begins with careful, reliable observation. In psychology this process may use naturalistic observation, surveys, or case history studies. Once observations have been made, we can discover the extent to which they are related to each other by using the statistical procedure of correlation. If two responses are correlated, we can use one to predict the other.

Experiments allow us to infer cause-and-effect relationships. Performing experiments involves manipulating independent variables and measuring dependent variables while controlling or eliminating the influence of extraneous variables. We've also learned that psychologists have concerns about the ethical implications of their work, be it with humans or nonhumans.

CHAPTER SUMMARY

Topic 1A

What makes psychology a science? What are the two major goals of psychology?

We may claim scientific status for psychology because it meets two criteria: it has an organized body of knowledge and it uses scientific methods. Psychology has two major interrelated goals: (1) to use scientific methods to discover and understand the laws that govern its subject matter, and (2) to apply what is already known about behavior and mental processes in the real world. /pp. 4–6

What do psychologists study? What are operational definitions?

The subject matter of psychology comprises the affects, behaviors, and cognitions of organisms. Operational definitions define concepts by specifying the procedures, or operations, used to measure or create those concepts. They help foster precise communication, but they can give the appearance of oversimplifying complex issues. /pp. 6–8

How did the philosophies of Descartes and Locke prepare the way for psychology? How did the science of Darwin, Fechner, and von Helmholtz influence the emergence of psychology?

Both Descartes and Locke directed the attention of philosophers to the study of the mind—how it interacts with the body and how it acquires understanding—and did so in the belief that the mind was part of the natural world. Darwin (biology), Fechner (physics), and Helmholtz (physiology) brought scientific methodology to bear on questions that were largely psychological. /pp. 9–10

When and where did psychology begin? Compare and contrast structuralism with functionalism.

We credit Wilhelm Wundt with having founded psychology when he opened his laboratory at the University of Leipzig in 1879. Wundt wanted to use scientific methods to discover both the contents and structure of the mind and how the mind operates. We call his approach structuralism. Following the lead of Charles Darwin and William James, the functionalist psychologists were also concerned with the mind and mental activity, but focused on the adaptive value (or function) of consciousness. The functionalists, including Washburn, added the study of animals to mainstream psychology. /pp. 11–12

Briefly summarize behaviorism.

Behaviorism (associated first with Watson and then Skinner) holds that the subject matter of psychology should be measurable and observable—thus, behavior. /pp. 12–13

Describe psychoanalysis, humanistic psychology, and Gestalt psychology. Describe some of the early research that sought to relate the brain to behavior.

Psychoanalytic psychology (associated with Freud) emphasizes instincts and the unconscious mind as influences on our behaviors. Humanistic psychology (associated with Rogers and Maslow) focuses on the person, emphasizing internal processes and the potential for growth and development. Gestalt psychologists were interested in how people select and organize their perceptions of the world, emphasizing the whole as more than the sum of its parts. Even in the eighteenth century, scientists understood that there was a relation between the brain and an organism's behaviors. Phrenology was an overly simple attempt to relate psychological traits to bumps on the skull. Flourens and Fritsch and Hitzig used ablation and electrical stimulation to study the brain's impact. /*pp. 13–16*

Describe five key principles in psychology that will appear repeatedly throughout our study.

(1) Who we are—our psychological functioning—is a result of the interaction of our biological nature and our psychological nurture. (2) In virtually any way imaginable, no two persons are alike. (3) Our experience of the world is influenced by psychological processes, such as expectation and motivation, as well as by what is "really" there to be experienced. (4) Most psychological phenomena are complex, and few questions in psychology have simple answers. (5) Psychology is a relevant science, with application to our daily lives. /*pp. 16–20*

Topic 1B

What is naturalistic observation? What steps need to be taken for the method to be successful?

Naturalistic observation is the careful, reliable observation of behaviors as they occur naturally. This method requires that (1) those being observed not be aware that they are being studied, (2) the observers' biases not influence observations, and (3) patience be exercised for those behaviors that occur infrequently. /*pp. 21–22*

How can surveys and case histories be used to help us understand behavior and mental processes?

Surveys provide a few responses (observations) from large samples of respondents, whereas case histories tend to provide detailed and specific information about just a few persons. In either case, one may discover relationships among the observations made. /*pp. 22–23*

What data are needed to calculate a correlation coefficient? What does a correlation coefficient tell us about the relationship between two measured responses?

To calculate a correlation coefficient, one needs to measure two responses made by the same group of persons, yielding a set of paired observations. Positive correlation coefficients tell us that high scores on one response are associated with (predict) high scores on the other, and that low scores on one response are associated with low scores on the other. Negative correlations tell us that the

two responses are inversely related, with high scores on one predicting low scores on the other, and vice versa. Correlation coefficients of zero (or nearly zero) tell us that our measured responses are not related to each other in any lawful way. The closer the coefficient is to its possible extreme of +1.00 or −1.00, the stronger the relationship between the responses, but in no case can one infer a cause-and-effect relationship from correlational data. /*pp. 23–26*

Describe the experimental process.

An experiment involves manipulating independent variables and measuring dependent variables while minimizing the influence of extraneous variables. Independent variables are those hypothesized to have a measurable effect on some behavior or mental process. To see if such is the case, one looks for changes in some measured dependent variable that are consistent with changes in the manipulated independent variable. In order to claim a cause-and-effect relationship between the independent and dependent variables, all other (extraneous) events that could have influenced the dependent variable must have been controlled or eliminated. /*pp. 26–29*

How do random assignment, baseline designs, and meta-analyses help to minimize error in psychological experiments?

The random assignment of participants to experimental (those who receive a treatment) or control (those who do not receive a treatment) conditions of an experiment ensures that each participant has an equal opportunity to be in any of the treatment groups of the experiment. Any existing differences among the participants should thus balance out over groups. With baseline designs, the same participants serve in both control and experimental group conditions, thus acting as their own control. A meta-analysis is a statistical procedure of control that combines the results of numerous smaller studies in one large analysis. /*pp. 29–31*

What are some ethical issues that must be considered when doing psychological research?

Participants in psychological research must have their confidentiality maintained. They should provide advised consent before voluntarily participating in the research and should be debriefed about the project when it is over. Above all else, with both humans and animals, one should always consider whether any potential risks in the research are offset by the present or future value of the results of the research. /*pp. 31–33*

PRACTICING PSYCHOLOGY

Understanding Correlations

Correlational studies show relationships between variables. If high scores on one variable predict high scores on another variable, the correlation is *positive*. If high scores on one variable predict low scores on another variable, the correlation is *negative*. As you know, demonstrating that two variables are related *does not* mean that a causal relationship exists. There may be a cause-and-effect relationship, but other explanations may exist as well. For example, two variables may be related because both have a causal relationship with a third variable. For each of the correlational studies described below, first decide whether the correlation is positive or negative, and then give *two* different explanations for each finding. [Suggested answers can be found on p. 571.]

1. A study of married couples found that the longer they had been married, the more similar were their opinions on social and political issues. [+ or -]

    Explanation #1:

    Explanation #2:

2. An intelligence test was given to all the children in an orphanage. The results showed that the longer children lived in the orphanage, the lower their IQ scores. [+ or -]

    Explanation #1:

    Explanation #2:

3. In a study of American cities, a relationship was found between the number of violent crimes and the number of stores selling pornography that depicted violence. [+ or -]

    Explanation #1:

    Explanation #2:

4. A college professor found that the more class absences students have, the lower their grade in the course tends to be. [+ or -]

    Explanation #1:

    Explanation #2:

5. A politician running against a candidate who had been in office for two terms pointed out that violent crime had increased steadily during those eight years during which the administration appropriated more and more money to fight crime. [+ or -]

    Explanation #1:

    Explanation #2:

6. It was found that elementary-school children who made high scores on a vocabulary test also tended to make high scores on a test of physical strength and muscular coordination. [+ or -]

    Explanation #1:

    Explanation #2:

7. Many studies have shown that there is an increased risk of lung cancer for those individuals who smoke, and that the more one smokes, the greater the risk. [+ or -]

    Explanation #1:

    Explanation #2:

OUTLINE

*A*ll of your behaviors, from simple to complex; every emotion you've ever experienced, from mild to extreme; all your thoughts, from the trivial to the profound—all of these can ultimately be reduced to molecules of chemicals racing in and out of the microscopically tiny cells that comprise your nervous systems.

So that we'll have an example to work with throughout this chapter, consider the simple matter of walking down a hallway late at night in your bare feet when all of a sudden—Ouch!—you've stepped on a tack. Roughly, here's what happened, with some intriguing questions you might ask yourself in parentheses.

The point of the tack punctures the sole of your foot and stimulates a nerve cell. (What's a nerve cell, and how does it "get stimulated"?) The cell stimulated by the tack sends a message to other, nearby nerve cells. (What do you mean, "message"? How do these messages get from one cell to another?) Messages race up your leg to your spinal cord. (What does the spinal cord look like? What does it do?)

Once in the spinal cord, messages go in two directions: up to the brain, and back down to muscles in your leg. (How do these messages get to my brain? Do they get to my brain first, or to those muscles in my leg?) The messages from your spinal cord get you to quickly lift your foot off the floor.

2

The Nervous Systems and Behavior

(Do you mean that my leg lifts off the floor without my brain even thinking about it?)

You realize that the source of your pain is a tack that someone left on the floor. Still hopping on one foot, you wonder who left the tack there, and start to get angry. (Where does "realization" take place? Isn't my memory involved in identifying a tack? Are there separate areas of the brain involved in emotions like anger?)

Even in a chain of events as simple as stepping on a tack, a remarkable series of biochemical and physiological reactions takes place. These reactions are the focus of this chapter.

T O P I C   2 A   Nerve Cells, and How They Communicate

Many physiological functions are necessary just to keep us alive. Among them are such processes as respiration, circulation, metabolism, and digestion. The focus of our discussion, however, will be on the major structures and functions of the human nervous systems. These are the aspects of our biology most intimately involved in our behaviors and mental processes.

The Neuron

neuron *a nerve cell that transmits information, in the form of neural impulses, from one part of the body to another*

Our exploration of the nervous system begins at the level of the nerve cell, or **neuron**, the microscopically small cell that transmits information, in the form of neural impulses, from one part of the body to another. Neurons were not even recognized as separate structures until about the turn of the century. To give you an idea of the sizes and numbers we're talking about, there are approximately 125 million specialized neurons that line the back, inside surface of each human eye, and an estimated 100 billion neurons in the human brain (Hubel, 1979; Kolb, 1989).

The Structure of Neurons

We may not be sure about snowflakes, but we can say with confidence that no two neurons are identical. Even so, most do have a few structures in common. Figure 2.1 illustrates these common features, and Figure 2.2 is a photograph that shows what a neuron actually looks like.

cell body *the largest concentration of mass of a neuron; contains the cell's nucleus*

One structure that all neurons are certain to have is a **cell body**, the largest concentration of mass of the neuron. It contains the nucleus of the cell, which, in turn, contains the genetic information that keeps the cell functioning. Extending away from the cell body are several tentaclelike structures called dendrites, and one particularly long structure called the axon. Typically, **dendrites** reach out to receive messages, or neural impulses, from nearby neurons. These impulses are sent to the cell body and then down the **axon** to other neurons, or to muscles or glands. Some axons are quite long—as much as 2 to 3 feet long in the spinal cord. Within a neuron, then, impulses go from dendrite to cell body to axon, and most of the trip will be made along the axon.

dendrites *extensions from a neuron's cell body that receive impulses*

axon *a long, tail-like extension of a neuron that carries impulses away from the cell body and to other cells*

myelin *a white, fatty covering found on some axons that insulates and protects them and speeds impulses along*

The neuron illustrated in Figure 2.1 has a feature not found on all neurons. The axon of this neuron has a cover, or sheath, of myelin. **Myelin** is a white substance made up of fat and protein found on about half the axons in an adult's nervous system. It is the presence of myelin that allows us to tell the difference between the gray matter (dendrites, cell bodies, and unmyelinated axons) and white matter (myelinated axons) we see when we look at sections of nervous system tissue. We tend to find myelin on axons that carry impulses relatively long distances. Neurons that carry messages up and down the spinal cord, for instance, have myelinated axons, whereas those that carry impulses back and forth across the spinal cord do not.

Myelin serves several useful functions. It protects the long, delicate axon. It acts as an insulator, keeping the activity of one neuron separate from those that happen to be nearby. Myelin speeds impulses along the length of the axon. Myelinated fibers carry impulses nearly 10 times faster than unmyelinated ones (up to 120 meters per second). Interestingly, myelin can be found only in vertebrate animals. Invertebrates have neurons and axons, but no myelin. In order to speed along neural impulses, invertebrates have developed some very fat (i.e., large diameter) axons. These axons are much easier to study than the relatively skinnier vertebrate axons. Because they don't have myelin, the speed of impulse conduction in invertebrates

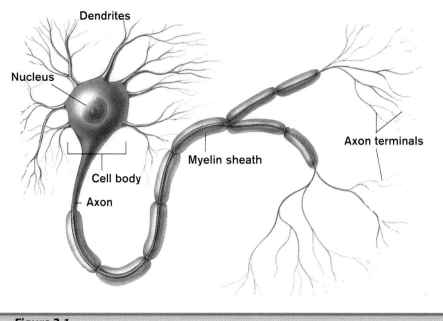

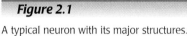

Figure 2.1

A typical neuron with its major structures.

is quite slow, which limits the size of these organisms—if they become too large, co-ordinated behaviors become impossible without rapid impulse transmission.

Whether they are myelinated or not, axons end in a branching series of bare end points called **axon terminals**. At the axon terminal, each neuron communicates with other neurons. To review: within a neuron, impulses travel from the dendrites to the cell body, to the axon (which may be myelinated), and then to axon terminals.

axon terminals the set of branching end points of an axon; where neurons begin to communicate with adjacent neurons

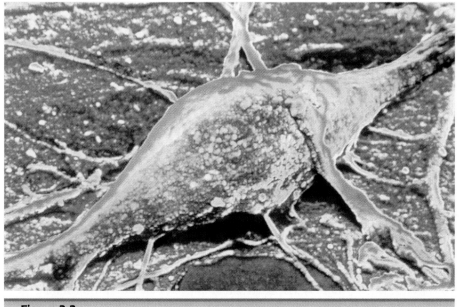

Figure 2.2

A photograph of a neuron taken through a powerful electron microscope.

Virtually no neurons are generated after birth. We are born with more neurons than we will ever have again. In fact, we are born with about twice as many neurons as we'll ever use. What happens to the rest? They just die off. Bryan Kolb (1989) of the University of Lethbridge in Canada gives us this analogy: In normal development, the brain is "constructed" in a manner rather like that in which a statue is chipped away from a block of granite. Rather than building up the finished product one small piece at a time, more material than one needs is available. What is needed or used is retained, and the rest dies away. Here is a related observation: In order to have billions of neurons in our brains at the time of birth, brain cells must be generated at a rate of about 250,000 per minute while the brain is being formed (Cowan, 1979). There are implications here about prenatal care, which we'll explore in Chapter 8.

The fact that dead neurons are not replaced with new ones makes them unique among cells. We constantly make new blood cells to replace lost ones. If we didn't, we could never donate a pint of blood. Lost skin cells are rapidly replaced by new ones. You rinse away skin cells by the hundreds each time you wash your hands. Neurons are different; once they're gone, they're gone forever. We're often in luck, however, because the *functions* of lost neurons can be taken over by other, surviving neurons. Also, recent evidence from research on tissue removed from the brains of adult mice suggests that when exposed to a substance called epidemal growth factor, new neurons, and cells that support them, *can* be generated (Reynolds & Weiss, 1992). Whether this research can be generalized to other species, or has any practical application, remains to be seen.

Have you noticed that discussing the structure of the neuron is nearly impossible without reference to the function of the neuron: the transmission of neural impulses? We have seen that impulses are typically received by dendrites, passed on to cell bodies, then to axons, and ultimately to axon terminals. We know that myelin insulates some axons and speeds neural impulses along, but we haven't yet considered exactly what a neural impulse is. Let's do so now.

Before You Go On

What are the major structures of a neuron?

The Function of Neurons

neural impulse *a rapid and reversible change in the electrical charges inside and outside a neuron; it travels from dendrite to axon terminal of a neuron*

The function of a neuron is to transmit neural impulses from one place in the nervous system to another. Let's start with a definition: A **neural impulse** is a rapid, reversible change in the electrical charges within and outside a neuron. This change in electrical charge travels from the dendrites to the axon terminal when the neuron fires. Now let's see what all that means.

Neurons exist in a complex biological environment. As living cells, they are filled with and surrounded by fluids. Only a very thin membrane (like a skin) separates the fluids inside a neuron from fluids outside. These fluids contain chemical particles called ions. **Chemical ions** are particles that carry a small, measurable electrical charge that is either positive (+) or negative (–). Electrically charged ions float around in all the fluids of the body, but are heavily concentrated in and around the nervous system. They come from the foods and liquids we eat and drink that are dissolved by our digestive system.

chemical ions *electrically charged (+ or –) chemical particles in solution*

Neurons that are just lying around not doing anything are said to be *at rest,* but "at rest" may not be a very accurate description. A tension develops between the electrical charge of ions that have been trapped *inside* the neuron and the electrical charge of ions that have been trapped *outside* the neuron. So, when it is at rest, the inside of the neuron has a negative (–) charge compared to the positive (+) charge on the outside. Positive and negative ions (having opposite charges) are attracted to each other. However, they cannot become balanced because the neuron's membrane keeps them separate.

The tension that results from the positive and negative ions' attraction to each other is called a **resting potential**. The resting potential of a neuron is about −70 millivolts (mV), which makes each neuron rather like a small battery. A D-cell battery of the sort used in a flashlight has two aspects (called poles), one positive and the other negative. The electrical charge possible with one of these batteries—its resting potential – is 1500 mV, much greater, of course, than that of a tiny neuron. The resting potential of a neuron is *negative* 70 millivolts (−70 mV) because we measure the inside of a neuron relative to the outside, and the inside is where the negative ions are concentrated.

When a neuron is stimulated to fire, or to produce an impulse, the electrical tension of the resting potential is released. Very quickly, the polarity of the nerve cell changes. For a brief instant (about one one-thousandth of a second) at one point along the length of the neuron, the electrical charge within the cell becomes more *positive* than the area outside the cell. The entire "charge" of the cell changes instantaneously. This new charge is called the **action potential**, or neural impulse. The electric potential is now about +40 mV, the positive sign indicating that the inside of the neuron is now more positive than the outside. There are more positive ions inside than outside. Now, for just a few thousandths of a second, there is a period, called the *refractory period,* during which the neuron cannot fire because there is no tension there to release as an action potential. In another fraction of a second, the neuron returns to its original state, with the tension redeveloped. It is ready to fire again.

To repeat, what happens is something like this. When a neuron is at rest, there is a difference between the electrical charges inside and outside the neuron (the inside being more negative). When the neuron is stimulated, the difference suddenly reverses, so that the inside becomes slightly positive. The tension of the resting potential then returns (see Figure 2.3).

Note: when an impulse "travels down a neuron," *nothing physically moves from one end of the neuron to the other.* The only movement of physical particles that occurs is the movement of the electrically charged ions into and out of the neuron through its membrane. What travels down the neuron is where this action potential takes place—where the release of tension of the resting potential occurs.

When a neuron is stimulated, it either transmits an impulse or it doesn't. It either fires or it doesn't, a fact called the **all-or-none principle**. This raises a psychological question: How does the nervous system react to differences in stimulus intensity? How do neurons react to the differences between a bright light and a dim

resting potential *the electrical tension resulting from the difference in electrical charge of a neuron where the inside is negatively charged and the outside is positively charged (about −70 mV)*

action potential *the short-lived electrical burst caused by the sudden reversal of electric charges inside and outside a neuron, such that the inside becomes positive (about +40 mV)*

all-or-none principle *the fact that a neuron will either produce a full impulse, or action potential, or will not fire at all*

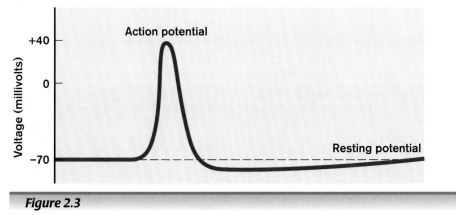

Figure 2.3

Changes in electrical potential that occur during the firing of a neuron. Note that the voltage is negative (−70 millivolts) when the neuron is "at rest," and positive (+40 millivolts) during the firing of the impulse. Note, too, that the entire process lasts but a few milliseconds.

one, a soft sound and a loud one, a tap on the shoulder and a slap on the back? The electrical charge of the resting potential is either released or it isn't. There is no in-between. We cannot say that for a dim light a neuron fires partially, releasing only some of the tension of its resting potential, while for brighter lights, more ions are exchanged. Part of the answer has to do with neural thresholds.

Neurons do not necessarily generate impulses every time they are stimulated. Each neuron has a level of stimulation that must be surpassed in order to get it to begin an impulse. The minimum level of stimulation required to get a neuron to fire is called the **neural threshold**. When this concept is coupled with the all-or-none principle, we have some insight about how we process stimulus intensities. High-intensity stimuli (bright lights, loud sounds, and so on) do not get neurons to fire more vigorously; they stimulate more neurons to fire or to fire more frequently. High-intensity stimuli are above the threshold of a greater number of neurons than are low-intensity stimuli. The difference in your experience of a flashbulb going off in your face and a candle viewed at a distance reflects the *number* of neurons in-volved and the *rate* at which they fire, not the degree or extent to which they fire.

Now that we've examined the individual nerve cell in some detail, we had better see how neurons communicate with each other—how impulses are transmitted from one cell to another. The story of how impulses travel between neurons is just as remarkable, but quite different from, the story of how impulses travel within neurons.

neural threshold *the minimum amount of stimulation necessary to get a neuron to fire*

⊚⊚⊚ **Thinking Critically** ⊚⊚⊚

As you probably realize by now, much of the information in this chapter is fairly technical. How will you manage your thinking to make sure that you are un-derstanding and retaining what you are reading?

Before You Go On

What is the basic process involved when a neuron fires?

EXPERIENCING PSYCHOLOGY

How Fast *Do* Neural Impulses Travel?

As neural impulses speed from one part of your body to another, they travel at incredibly high rates of speed. You step on a tack and it seems that the pain of that action is in your brain immediately. Can you measure neural impulse speeds without sophisticated equipment? Yes, you can with the help of a few friends and if you don't mind being just a little imprecise.

Ask 10 people to stand next to each other with their eyes closed, holding hands. At your signal, the first person is to squeeze the hand of the person next to him or her who will, in turn, squeeze the hand of the next person, and so on, until the last person has his or her hand squeezed and signals so by raising his or her free hand. At your signal, you start a stopwatch, and stop it at the signal that the last person has re-ceived a squeeze. Repeat the procedure until the time involved becomes reasonably stable. Divide that time by 10. Now have the same folks put their left hand on the right shoulder of the person standing next to them. At your signal, the first person is to squeeze the shoulder of whoever is standing to the left. This sec-ond person then squeezes the shoulder of the person to his or her left, and so on down the line, until the last person signals being squeezed. Again, repeat the procedure until the time interval stabilizes. Divide that time by 10.

Although it is a crude measure, the difference be-tween the two time intervals, after each has been di-vided by 10, represents the (average) time it takes for neural impulses to travel between the hand and the shoulder.

From: Rozin, P. & Jonides, J. (1977). Mass reaction time: Mea-surement of the speed of the nerve impulse and the duration of mental processes in class. *Teaching of Psychology, 4,* 91–94.

From One Cell to Another: The Synapse

The general location at which an impulse is relayed from one neuron to another is called the **synapse**. In the cerebral cortex of the human brain alone there are as many as one million billion synaptic interconnections among neurons (Edelman, 1992). Here's what happens at the synapse.

synapse the location where one neuron communicates with other cells via neurotransmitters

Synaptic Transmission

As we've noted, at the very end of an axon there are many branches, or axon terminals (see Fig. 2.1). Throughout any neuron, but concentrated in its axon terminals, are incredibly small containers called **vesicles**, which hold complex chemicals called neurotransmitters. **Neurotransmitters** are chemical molecules that will either excite or inhibit the transmission of a neural impulse at the synapse. When an impulse reaches the axon terminal, the vesicles near the neural membrane burst open and release the neurotransmitter they have been holding. The released neurotransmitter floods out into the **synaptic cleft**, the tiny space between two neurons. Note that neurons actually do not touch; they are separated by the synaptic cleft. Once in the synaptic cleft, some neurotransmitter molecules move to the membrane of the next neuron, where they may fit into "receptor sites" and enter the membrane. (See Figure 2.4.)

vesicles small containers concentrated in a neuron's axon terminals that hold neurotransmitter molecules

neurotransmitters chemical molecules released at the synapse that, in general, will either excite or inhibit a reaction in the cell on the other side of the synapse

synaptic cleft the actual space between a neuron and the next cell at a synapse

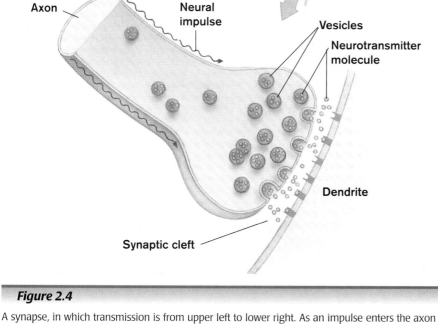

Figure 2.4

A synapse, in which transmission is from upper left to lower right. As an impulse enters the axon terminal, vesicles release neurotransmitter chemicals into the synaptic space or cleft. The neurotransmitter then either excites or inhibits an impulse in the next neuron.

Then what happens? Actually, any number of things. Let's look at a few. The most reasonable scenario for synaptic activity is that in which neurotransmitters float across the synaptic cleft, enter into receptor sites in the next neuron in a chain of nerve cells, and by so doing excite that neuron to release the tension of its resting potential and fire a new impulse down to its axon terminals. There, new neurotransmitter chemicals are released from vesicles, cross the synaptic cleft, and stimulate the next neuron in the sequence. This is the case when the neurotransmitter excites and stimulates the next neuron in a sequence to fire. These neurotransmitters are referred to as *excitatory*.

As it happens, there are many neurons throughout our nervous systems that hold neurotransmitters that have the opposite effect. When they are released, they flood across the synaptic cleft and work to prevent the next neuron from firing. We refer to these synapses as *inhibitory*.

If you think back to the last section, where we talked about neural thresholds, you may now better appreciate how that concept works. Imagine a neuron's dendrite, sitting at rest, with many axon terminals (of many neurons) just across the synaptic cleft. For this neuron to begin a new impulse, it may require more excitatory chemical than just one axon terminal can provide, particularly if nearby terminals are releasing inhibitory neurotransmitters about the same time.

The basic process I've just described also occurs at the synapse of neurons and nonneural cells. When a neuron forms a synapse with a muscle cell, for instance, the release of neurotransmitter from the neuron's axon terminals may excite that muscle to contract momentarily. Similarly, neurons that form synapses with a gland may cause that gland to secrete a hormone when stimulated by the appropriate neurotransmitter.

Neurotransmitters

Not long ago, it was believed that neurons produced and released one of just two neurotransmitters: those that excite further action, and those that inhibit neural impulse transmission. Now we realize that this view is much too simplistic. Today we know of nearly 60 neurotransmitters, and it is virtually certain that there are many others yet to be discovered. We'll run into neurotransmitters again when we discuss the actions of many drugs, when we consider what happens when memories are formed, and when we explore theories of what causes some psychological disorders. But for now, we ought to at least briefly note four of the better-known neurotransmitters.

Acetylcholine (pronounced "uh-see'-til-kōh'-leen"), or ACh, is found throughout the nervous system, where it acts as either an excitatory or inhibitory neurotransmitter, depending on where it is found. It is the most common neurotransmitter, and the first to have been discovered (in the 1920s). Not only is ACh found in the brain, but it commonly works in synapses between neurons and muscle tissue cells. One form of food poisoning, botulism, blocks the release of acetylcholine at neuron/muscle cell synapses, which can cause paralysis. The poisonous drug curare works in much the same fashion. Some other poisons (for example, the venom of the black widow spider) have just the opposite effect, causing excess amounts of ACh to be released, resulting in muscle contractions or spasms so severe as to be deadly. Nicotine is a chemical that in small amounts tends to increase the normal functioning of ACh, but in large doses acts to override the normal action of acetylcholine—a reaction that can lead to muscle paralysis and even death. Smoking or chewing tobacco seldom causes such a dramatic effect because large amounts of nicotine first stimulate a brain center that causes vomiting before too much nicotine has been absorbed into one's system (Palfai & Jankiewicz, 1991, p. 141). Acetylcholine is also implicated in normal memory function and is thus a prime candidate for research on memory problems, such as those found in Alzheimer's disease.

Norepinephrine is a common and important neurotransmitter that is involved in mood regulation. Norepinephrine is involved in the physiological reactions associated with high levels of emotional arousal—such as increased heart rate, perspiration, and blood pressure (Groves & Rebec, 1992). When there is an abundance of norepinephrine in a person's brain or spinal cord, the result can be a feeling of arousal, agitation, or anxiety. (One thing that cocaine does is increase the release of norepinephrine, leading to a state of agitation and a "high" mood state.) Too little norepinephrine in the brain and spinal cord has been associated with feelings of depression.

Dopamine, a common neurotransmitter also involved in mood regulation, is one that most intrigues psychologists. It is involved in a wide range of reactions. Either too much or too little dopamine within the nervous system seems to produce a number of effects, depending primarily on which system of nerve fibers in the brain is involved. Dopamine has been associated with the thought and mood disturbances of some psychological disorders. It is also associated with the impairment of movement: when there is not enough dopamine, we find difficulty in voluntary movement; too much and we find involuntary tremors.

Endorphins (there are several of them) are natural pain suppressors. By and large, what we call the pain threshold—the ability to tolerate different levels of pain—is a function of the production of endorphins (Watkins & Mayer, 1982). With excess levels of endorphins, we feel little pain; a deficit results in an increased experience of pain. When we are under extreme physical stress, endorphin levels rise. Many long-distance runners, for instance, often report a near-euphoric "high" after they have run great distances, as if their endorphins have kicked in to protect them against the pain of physical exhaustion.

We could easily continue this list, but for now it is the basic idea of what neurotransmitters do that matters: they are the agents that either excite or inhibit the transmission of neural impulses throughout the nervous system. That excitation or inhibition can have a considerable effect on our thoughts, feelings, and behavior.

Finally, so that our simplified description does not leave a false impression, let me make one point clear: neural impulse transmission is seldom a matter of just one neuron stimulating one other neuron that in turn stimulates yet one more. Remember that any neuron can have hundreds or thousands of axon terminals and synapses. Any neuron, then, has the potential for exciting or inhibiting (or being excited by or inhibited by) many other neurons.

Before You Go On

Summarize neural impulse transmission at the synapse.

Name and briefly describe the actions of four neurotransmitters.

Human Nervous Systems: The Big Picture

Now that we have a sense of how neurons work, both individually and in combination, let's step back for a moment to consider the context in which they function. Behaviors and mental activities require large numbers of integrated neurons working together in complex, organized systems. Figure 2.5 depicts these systems. I have also depicted the endocrine system in Figure 2.5. Although it is not composed

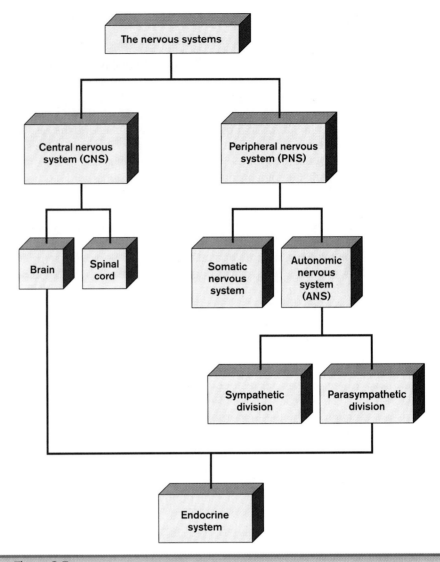

Figure 2.5
The various human nervous systems and how they are interrelated.

of neurons, the endocrine system interacts with the nervous systems in controlling behaviors and mental processes.

Organized Systems of Neurons

The major division of the nervous systems is determined wholly on the basis of anatomy. The **central nervous system (CNS)** includes all neurons and supporting cells found in the spinal cord and brain. This system of nerves is the most complex and intimately involved in the control of behavior and mental processes. The **peripheral nervous system (PNS)** consists of all neurons in our body that are *not* in the CNS—the nerve fibers in our arms, face, fingers, intestines, and so on. Neurons in the peripheral nervous system carry impulses either from the central nervous system to the muscles and glands (on *motor neurons*) or to the CNS from receptor cells (on *sensory neurons*).

The peripheral nervous system is divided into two parts, based largely on the part of the body being served. The **somatic nervous system** includes those neurons that are outside the CNS that serve the skeletal muscles and that pick up impulses from our sense receptors—the eyes and ears, for example. The other compo-

central nervous system (CNS) *neurons and supporting cells in the spinal cord and the brain*

peripheral nervous system (PNS) *neurons not found in the brain and spinal cord, but in the periphery of the body*

somatic nervous system *sensory and motor neurons outside the CNS that serve the sense receptors and the skeletal muscles* nent of the PNS is the **autonomic nervous system (ANS)**, where "autonomic" means about the same thing as "automatic." This implies that the activity of the ANS is largely (but not totally) independent of central nervous system control. The nerve fibers of the ANS are involved in activating the smooth muscles, such as those of the stomach and intestines, and the glands. The ANS does provide feedback to the CNS about all this internal activity.

Because the autonomic nervous system is so intimately involved in our emotional responding, we'll return to it again in that context. For now, we simply note that the ANS consists of two parts, the sympathetic division and the parasympathetic division. These two divisions commonly work in opposition to each other. The sympathetic division is active when we are in states of emotional excitement or under stress—like riding up that first huge incline of a roller coaster at an amusement park. The parasympathetic division becomes active when we are relaxed and quiet—as we might be late at night, after a long day at that amusement park, half asleep in the back seat on the drive home. The two divisions of the ANS each act on the same organs, but they do so in opposite ways.

There is good reason to categorize the various organizations of neurons. It helps make a very complex system easier to deal with, and it reminds us that not all neurons in our body are doing the same thing, for the same purpose, at the same time. Please keep in mind that the outline of Figure 2.5 is very simplified to this extent: the nerve fibers in each of the systems have profound influences on one another. They are not at all as independent as our diagram might imply.

The Endocrine System

As you can see, there is one other system depicted in the overview of Figure 2.5: the **endocrine system**, a network of glands that has its effects on behaviors through the secretion of chemicals, called *hormones*. All hormones travel through the bloodstream and have the effects on organs at some distance from where they were produced. The endocrine system is influenced by the central nervous system and, in turn, influences nervous system activity, but it is not a system of nerves. Many of the hormones produced by the glands of the endocrine system are chemically very similar to neurotransmitters and have many of the same effects. The endocrine system's glands and hormones are controlled by both the brain of the central nervous system and the autonomic nervous system. I have included the endocrine system in this discussion because its function is similar to that of the nervous systems: to transmit information from one part of the body to another.

There are several different endocrine glands scattered throughout our bodies. We'll discuss three of them to give you an idea of how this system works: the pituitary gland, the thyroid gland, and the adrenal gland. The sex glands are part of this system, but we'll have several opportunities to discuss their operation later. (There are glands in our bodies that are not part of the endocrine system because their secretions do not enter the bloodstream. They are called *exocrine* glands—tear glands and sweat glands are two examples.)

Perhaps the most important of the endocrine glands is the **pituitary gland**. It is often referred to as the *master gland,* reflecting its direct control over the activity of many other glands in the system. The pituitary is nestled just under the brain and secretes many different hormones.

One hormone released by the pituitary is the growth hormone. It regulates the overall growth of the body during its fastest physical development. Extremes of over- or underproduction cause the development of giants or dwarfs. The so-called growth spurt associated with early adolescence is due to the activity of the pituitary gland. It is the pituitary gland that stimulates the release of a hormone (that is actually produced elsewhere) that acts on the kidneys to regulate the amount of water held within the body. It is the pituitary that directs the mammary glands in

autonomic nervous system (ANS) *neurons in the PNS that activate smooth muscles and glands*

endocrine system *a network of glands that secrete hormones directly into the bloodstream*

pituitary gland *the "master gland" of the endocrine system that influences many others, controls such processes as body growth rate, water retention, and the release of milk from the mammary glands* the breasts to release milk after childbirth. In its role as master over other glands, the pituitary regulates the output of the thyroid and the adrenal glands, as well as the sex glands.

thyroid gland *endocrine gland that releases thyroxine, the hormone that regulates the pace of the body's functioning*

The **thyroid gland** is located in the neck. It produces a hormone called *thyroxine*. Thyroxine regulates the pace of the body's functioning—the rate at which oxygen is used and the rate of body function and growth. When a person is easily excitable, edgy, having trouble sleeping, and losing weight, he or she may have too much thyroxine in the system, a condition called *hyperthyroidism*. Too little thyroxine leads to complaints of lack of energy, fatigue, and a general inability to do much of anything, a condition called *hypothyroidism*.

adrenal glands *endocrine glands that release adrenaline, or epinephrine, into the bloodstream to activate the body in times of stress or danger*

The **adrenal glands**, located on the kidneys, secrete a variety of hormones into the bloodstream. The hormone adrenaline (more often referred to as *epinephrine*) is very useful in times of stress, danger, or threat. Adrenaline quickens breathing, causes the heart to beat faster, directs the flow of blood away from the stomach and intestines out toward the limbs, dilates the pupils of the eyes, and increases perspiration. When our adrenal glands flood epinephrine into our system during a perceived emergency, we can usually feel the resulting reactions. But, typical of endocrine system activity, these reactions may be delayed.

For example, as you drive down a busy street, a child suddenly darts out in front of you from behind a parked car and races to the other side of the street. You immediately slam on the brakes and twist the steering wheel, swerving to avoid hitting the child. As the child scampers away, oblivious to the danger just past, you proceed down the street. Then, about half a block later, your hormone-induced reaction strikes. You feel your heart pound, a lump forms in your throat, and you sense your mouth going dry as your palms turn sweaty. Why now? The incident is past. The child is safely across the street. You are no longer in any danger. The reason is that your reaction is largely hormonal, involving the adrenal glands, and it takes that long for the epinephrine from those glands to get through the bloodstream to have their effects.

When an emotion-arousing event takes place, we react first with our central and peripheral nervous systems. The endocrine system, working through the bloodstream, takes longer to have its effects. It may be some time after this accident before the driver will experience any emotional reactions.

Name the human nervous systems and indicate how they are related to one another.

What is the endocrine system and how does it operate?

In what ways are each of the nervous systems discussed in this section involved in an action like stepping on a tack as described at the beginning of this chapter?

TOPIC 2A SUMMARY

We cannot divorce who we are in this world from the biological bases of our behaviors and mental processes. Whatever else we may be, we are biological organisms, and it behooves us as students of psychology to appreciate the structures and functions of the nervous system. That living cells as tiny as neurons can provide the basis for all of our actions, mental or behavioral, is a notion that takes some time to get used to. Neurons do not act alone. The complexity of the individual nerve cell multiplies geometrically with the activity of neurotransmitters at synapses.

Neurons are microscopically tiny living cells, consisting of a cell body, dendrites, and axons. The axons of some neurons are covered with a myelin sheath that insulates these axons and speeds impulses along them. Neurons communicate with one another at synapses, where neurotransmitter chemicals are released from the vesicles stored in the axons' terminals. These neurotransmitters, of which there are many, work either to excite an impulse in a subsequent neuron or to inhibit the generation of a new impulse. Neural impulses involve the release of electrical tension caused by the imbalance of chemical ions concentrated inside and outside the walls, or membranes, of the neuron. Neurons are organized into interrelated systems, the most basic of which are the central nervous system and the peripheral nervous system. The endocrine system is a network of glands that interacts with the nervous systems and releases into the bloodstream hormones that affect our behaviors and mental processes.

TOPIC 2B The Central Nervous System

When we consider the central nervous system, the spinal cord and the brain, we can see most clearly how physiological structures and functions impact regularly on behavior and mental processes. When we examine the functions of the spinal cord we discover how certain stimuli from the environment can produce simple, reflexive responses.

Then there's the brain. The human brain. What is it like? A vast computer? The seat of understanding? The processor of information? A storehouse of memories of experiences past? A reservoir of emotion? The source of motivation? It is all of these, and more. It is in the brain that our conscious, voluntary actions begin. It is in the brain that our emotions are experienced and our cognitions are manipulated and stored.

Breaking down the central nervous system into small, manageable structures and discussing them one at a time is about the only choice we have. Still, when we fragment our discussion of the spinal cord and brain this way, we can lose sight of the reality that they make up a unified system in which all parts work together and interact with other complex systems. Some functions can be localized in specific areas or structures of the central nervous system, but the adaptability and integration of its many functions force us to consider the CNS as a whole, as more than the sum of its parts.

The Spinal Cord

As we have noted, the central nervous system consists of the brain and the spinal cord. In this section, we'll consider the structure and the function of the spinal cord, reserving our discussion of the brain for later.

The Structure of the Spinal Cord

spinal cord *a mass of interconnected neurons within the spinal column that transmits impulses to and from the brain and is involved in spinal reflex behaviors*

sensory neurons *neurons that carry impulses from the sense receptors to the CNS*

motor neurons *neurons that carry impulses away from the CNS to muscles and glands*

interneurons *neurons within the spinal cord or brain*

The **spinal cord** is a mass of interconnected neurons, within the spinal column, that looks rather like a section of rope or thick twine. It is surrounded and protected by the hard bone and cartilage of the vertebrae.

A cross-sectional view of the spinal column and the spinal cord is illustrated in Figure 2.6. Only a few structural details need to be mentioned. Note that the spinal cord itself is located in the middle of the spinal column, which reaches from your lower back to high in your neck, just below your brain. Then note that nerve fibers enter and leave the spinal cord from the side. Neurons or nerve fibers that carry impulses toward the brain or spinal cord are called **sensory neurons** or sensory fibers. Sensory neurons, and the impulses they transmit, enter the spinal cord on dorsal roots (dorsal means "toward the back"). Neurons and nerve fibers that carry impulses away from the spinal cord and brain to muscles and glands are called **motor neurons** or motor fibers. Impulses that leave the spinal cord on motor neurons do so on ventral roots (ventral means "toward the front"). Neurons within the central nervous system are called **interneurons**.

Also notice that the center area of the spinal cord itself consists of gray matter, rather in the shape of a butterfly, while the outside area is light, white matter. Remember, this means that the center portion is filled with cell bodies, dendrites, and unmyelinated axons, while the outer section is filled with myelinated axons. Both

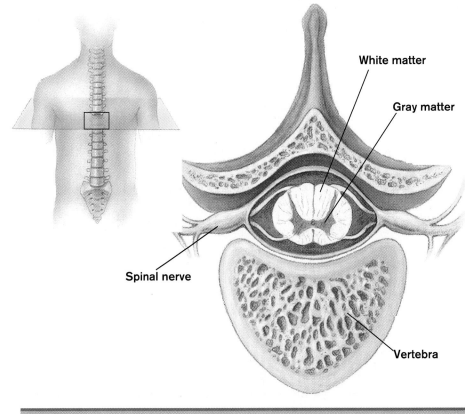

White matter

Gray matter

Spinal nerve

Vertebra

Figure 2.6

A cross-sectional view of the spinal column. Only the white matter and gray matter in the center represent actual spinal cord tissue.

of these observations about the structure of the spinal cord are keys to understanding its functions.

The Functions of the Spinal Cord

The spinal cord has two major functions, one of which is to transmit impulses rapidly to and from the brain. When sensory impulses originate in sense receptors below the neck and make their way to the brain, they do so through the spinal cord. When the brain transmits motor impulses to move or activate parts of the body below the neck, those impulses first travel down the spinal cord.

Impulses to and from various parts of the body leave and enter the spinal cord at different levels (impulses to and from the legs, for example, enter and leave at the very base of the spinal cord). If the spinal cord is damaged, the consequences can be disastrous, resulting in a loss of feeling from the part of the body served and a loss of voluntary movement (paralysis) of the muscles in the region. The higher in the spinal cord that damage takes place, the greater will be the resulting losses.

The second major function of the spinal cord is its role in **spinal reflexes**—simple automatic behaviors that occur without conscious, voluntary action of the brain. To understand how these reflexes work, follow along with the drawing in Figure 2.7. Here we have yet another drawing of the spinal cord, but we have added receptor cells in the skin, sensory neurons, motor neurons to muscles in the hand, and have labeled the neurons within the spinal cord as interneurons.

Let's trace your reaction to having your fingertip placed over the flame of a candle (assuming you're blindfolded at the time). Receptor cells in your fingertip respond to the flame, sending neural impulses racing along sensory neurons, through a dorsal root, and into the spinal cord. Then two things happen at almost the same time. Impulses rush up the ascending pathways of the spinal cord's white matter to your brain. Impulses also travel on interneurons and go right back out of the spinal cord through a ventral root on motor neurons to your arm and hand, where muscles are stimulated to contract, and your hand jerks back from the flame.

spinal reflexes *involuntary responses to a stimulus that involve sensory neurons, the spinal cord, and motor neurons*

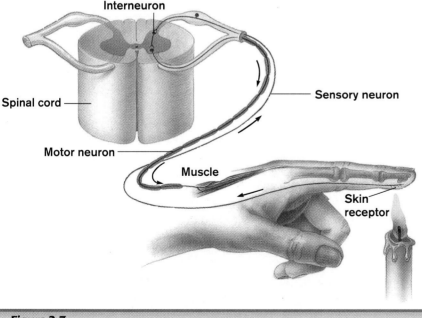

Figure 2.7

A spinal reflex. Stimulation of receptor cells in the skin, in turn, stimulates sensory neurons, interneurons, and motor neurons. Although a response is made without the involvement of the brain, impulses also travel up fibers in the spinal cord's white matter to the brain.

Here we have a simple spinal reflex. Impulses travel *in* on sensory neurons, *within* on interneurons, and *out* on motor neurons. We are involved with behavior. We have an environmental stimulus (a flame), activity in the central nervous system (neurons in the spinal cord), and an observable response (withdrawal of the hand).

There are a couple of observations I must make about the reflex of the type shown in Figure 2.7. First, the fact that impulses enter the spinal cord and immediately race to the brain is not indicated in the drawing. As you know, in a situation such as the candle flame example, you may jerk your hand back "without thinking about it," but very soon thereafter you *are* aware of what has happened. Awareness occurs in the brain, not in the spinal cord. It is also true that some reflexes are more simple than the one in Figure 2.7 in that no interneurons are involved. That is, it is possible for sensory neurons to form synapses directly with motor neurons inside the spinal cord. This is what happens in the familiar knee-jerk reflex. On the other hand, the complex pattern of behaviors involved in having one's finger burned in a flame actually involves many more than just three or four neurons.

Before You Go On

Why does damage to the spinal cord sometimes cause paralysis?

Describe the major features of the spinal reflex.

⊙⊙⊙ **Thinking Critically** ⊙⊙⊙

How would you explain a spinal reflex to a ten-year-old child?

The "Lower" Brain Centers

There are several ways in which we could organize our discussion of the brain. I'll use a simple scheme and divide the brain into two parts: the cerebral cortex and everything else—which I'm referring to as lower brain centers. Because the cerebral cortex plays so many important roles, this division is a reasonable one.

The lower brain centers are "lower" in two ways. First, they are physically located beneath the cerebral cortex. Second, they are the brain structures to develop first, both in an evolutionary sense and within the developing human brain. They are the structures we most clearly share with other animals. In no way should you think of these centers as being less important. As you will soon see, our very survival depends on them. You can use Figure 2.8 as a guide to locate the various structures as we discuss them.

The Brain Stem

As you look at the spinal cord and brain, you really cannot tell where one ends and the other begins. There is no abrupt dividing line separating these two aspects of the central nervous system. Just above the spinal cord there is a slight widening of the cord that suggests we are into brain tissue. Here, two important structures together form what we call the **brain stem**: the medulla and the pons.

The lowest structure in the brain is the **medulla**. In many ways, the medulla acts like the spinal cord in that its major functions involve involuntary reflexes. There are several small structures called *nuclei* (collections of neural cell bodies) in the medulla that control such functions as coughing, sneezing, tongue movements, and reflexive eye movements. You don't have to think about blinking your eye as something rushes toward it, for example; your medulla will produce that eye blink reflexively.

The medulla also contains nuclei that control breathing reflexes and that monitor the muscles of the heart to see that it keeps beating rhythmically. We *can* exercise some voluntary control over the nuclei of the medulla but only within limits. For example, the medulla controls our respiration (breathing), but we can override the medulla and hold our breath. We cannot, however, hold our breath until we die. We can hold our breath until we lose consciousness, which is to say until we

brain stem *the lowest part of the brain, just above the spinal cord, consisting of the medulla and the pons*

medulla *the structure in the brain stem where cross laterality begins; it contains centers that monitor reflex functions such as heart rate and respiration*

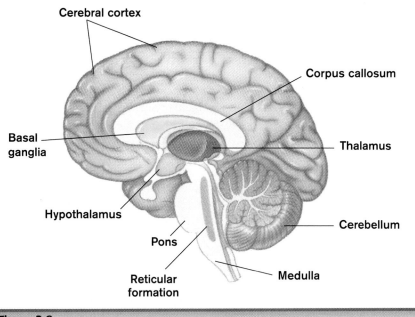

Figure 2.8

Some of the major structures of the human brain, of which the cerebral cortex is clearly the largest.

give up voluntary control; but the medulla then picks up where it left off, and breathing continues.

At the level of the medulla, nerve fibers to and from the brain cross over from right to left, and vice versa. Centers in the left side of the brain receive impulses from and send impulses to, the right side of the body. Similarly, the left side of the body sends impulses to, and receives messages from, the right side of the brain (which explains why electrically stimulating the correct area in the *left* side of the brain produces a movement in the *right* arm). This arrangement of fibers crossing from one side of the body to the opposite side of the brain is called **cross laterality**, and it takes place in the brain stem.

Just above the medulla is a structure called the pons. (The pons is one structure; there is no such thing as a "pon.") The **pons** serves as a relay station, a bridge (which is what *pons* means), sorting out and relaying sensory messages from the spinal cord and the face up to higher brain centers and reversing the relay for motor impulses coming down from higher centers. The cross laterality that begins in the medulla continues in the pons. Nuclei in the pons are also responsible, at least in part, for the rapid movement of our eyes that occurs when we dream (e.g., Sakai, 1985). Other centers in the pons are involved in determining our cycles of being awake and being asleep (Vertes, 1984).

cross laterality *the arrangement of nerve fibers crossing from the left side of the body to the right side of the brain, and from the right side of the body to the left side of the brain*

pons *a brain stem structure that forms a bridge, organizing fibers from the spinal cord to the brain and vice versa*

Before You Go On

Name the two brain stem structures, indicate their locations, and describe what they do.

⊚⊚⊚ **Thinking Critically** ⊚⊚⊚

Can you give an example not mentioned in the text of a bodily function that might be controlled by the medulla?

The Cerebellum

The **cerebellum** sits right behind your pons, tucked up under the base of your skull. Your cerebellum (literally, "small brain") is about the size of your closed fist. Its outer region (its cortex) is convoluted, meaning that the tissue there is folded in upon itself, creating many deep crevices and lumps.

cerebellum *a spherical structure at the rear base of the brain that coordinates fine and rapid muscular movements*

The major role of the cerebellum is in smoothing and coordinating rapid body movements. Most intentional, voluntary movements originate in higher brain centers (usually the motor area of the cerebral cortex) and are only coordinated by the cerebellum. Because of the close relationship between body movement and vision, many eye movements originate in the cerebellum.

Our ability to casually stoop, pick a dime off the floor, and slip it into our pocket involves a complex series of movements made smooth and regular by our cerebellum. When athletes train a movement, such as a golf swing or a gymnastic routine, we may say that they are trying to "get into a groove," so that their trained movements can be made simply and smoothly. In a way, such athletes are training their cerebellums. In fact, the cerebellum plays an important role in making movements that are "ballistic," which is to say that they occur without any sensory feedback. Examples would be catching a fast line drive hit right to you, playing a well-practiced piano piece, or quickly reaching out to save a priceless vase you just knocked off a table with your elbow. The cerebellum *learns* to make such movements, and thus is the focus of research by psychobiologists interested in how learning experiences are represented in the brain (Glickstein & Yeo, 1990; Kornhuber, 1974).

Few of our behaviors are as well coordinated or as well learned as the rapid movements we need to speak. The next time you're talking to someone, try to focus on just how quickly and effortlessly your lips, mouth, and tongue are moving—thanks to the cerebellum. Damage to the cerebellum disrupts speech, making it slurred. In fact, damage to the cerebellum disrupts all coordinated movements. One may shake and stagger when walking. Someone with cerebellum damage may appear to be drunk. (On what region of the brain do you suppose alcohol has a direct effect? The cerebellum.)

tremors *involuntary trembling movements*

Damage to the cerebellum can disrupt motor activity in other ways. If the outer region of the cerebellum is damaged, the result will be **tremors**, involuntary trembling movements, that occur when the person tries to move (called intention tremors). Damage to inner, deeper areas of the cerebellum leads to "tremors at rest,"

The ability of an athlete, such as this gymnast, to perform a complex, coordinated sequence of movements over and over again requires the involvement of the cerebellum.

and the limbs or head may shake or twitch rhythmically even when the person tries to remain still.

Before You Go On

Where is the cerebellum located, and what is its major function?

The Reticular Formation

The **reticular formation** is a different sort of brain structure. In fact, it is hardly a brain structure at all. It is a complex network of nerve fibers that begins in the brain stem and works its way up through and around other structures all the way to the top portions of the brain (Carlson, 1991).

Exactly what the reticular formation does, and how it does so, remains something of a mystery. It is involved in determining our level of activation or arousal. It influences whether we are awake, alert and attentive, drowsy, asleep, or at some level in between. Electrical stimulation of the reticular formation can produce EEG patterns of brain activity associated with being awake and alert. Classic research has shown us that lesions of the reticular formation cause a state of constant sleep in laboratory animals (Lindsley et al., 1949; Moruzzi & Magoun, 1949). In a way, the reticular formation acts like a valve that either allows sensory messages to pass from lower centers up to the cerebral cortex or shuts them off, partially or totally. What we don't know yet is what stimulates the reticular formation to produce its effects.

reticular formation *a network of nerve fibers extending from the base of the brain to the cerebrum that controls one's level of arousal*

The Limbic System

The **limbic system** is actually a collection of structures rather than a single unified one. It is of utmost importance in controlling the behaviors of nonhuman animals, which do not have as large or well-developed cerebral cortexes as humans. The limbic system controls many of the complex behavioral patterns we think of as instinctive. The limbic system is in the very middle of the brain. Its constituent parts are presented in Figure 2.9.

Within the human brain, parts of the limbic system are intimately involved in the display of emotional reactions. One center in the limbic system, the *amygdala,*

limbic system *a collection of structures near the middle of the brain involved in emotionality (amygdala and septum) and long-term memory storage (hippocampus)*

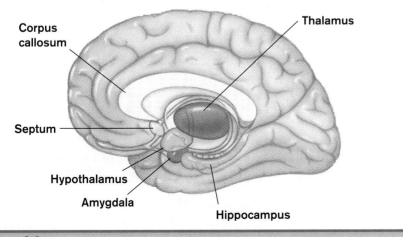

Corpus callosum

Thalamus

Septum

Hypothalamus

Amygdala

Hippocampus

Figure 2.9

A view of the brain showing structures deep within it. Among these, the septum, amygdala, and hippocampus constitute the limbic system. Given its proximity, it is easy to see why many scientists include the hypothalamus as part of the limbic system as well.

produces reactions of rage or aggression when stimulated, while another area, the *septum,* has the opposite effect, reducing the intensity of emotional responses when it is stimulated. The influence of the amygdala and the septum on emotional responding is immediate and direct in nonhumans. In humans, it is more subtle, reflecting the influence of other brain centers. The amygdala also plays an important role in helping to decide whether a stimulus is dangerous or not (Ekman, 1992; LeDoux, 1995).

Another structure in the limbic system, called the *hippocampus,* is less involved in emotion and more involved with the formation of memories. People with a damaged hippocampus are often unable to "transfer" experiences into permanent memory storage. They may remember events for short periods, and may be able to remember events from the distant past, but only if these events occurred before the hippocampus was damaged.

The Hypothalamus

hypothalamus *a small structure in the middle of the brain involved in feeding, drinking, temperature regulation, sex, and aggression*

The **hypothalamus** is often considered to be a part of the limbic system. It is located near the limbic system, and it, too, is involved in motivational and emotional reactions. Among other things, it influences many of the functions of the endocrine system, which, as we have seen, is involved in emotional responding.

The major responsibility of the hypothalamus is to monitor critical internal bodily functions. It has centers (nuclei again) that control feeding behaviors. It is sensitive to the amount of fluid in our bodies and indirectly gives rise to the feeling of being thirsty. The hypothalamus also acts something like a thermostat, triggering a number of automatic reactions should we become too warm or too cold. This small structure is also involved in aggressive and sexual behaviors. It acts as a regulator for many hormones. The hypothalamus has been implicated in the development of homosexual orientations (LaVay, 1991)—an implication we'll return to later. We'll also discuss the hypothalamus again when we study needs, motives, and emotions in later chapters.

The Basal Ganglia

basal ganglia *a collection of structures in front of the limbic system involved in the control of large, slow movements; a source of much of the brain's dopamine*

A curious set of tissues is the **basal ganglia**. The basal ganglia are a collection of small, loosely connected structures just in front of the limbic system. Like the cerebellum, the basal ganglia work primarily to control motor responding. Unlike the cerebellum, the role of the basal ganglia is more tied to large, slow movements—their initiation and their coordination. Although the basal ganglia are clearly related to the movements of some of our body's larger muscles, there are no pathways that lead directly from the ganglia down the spinal cord and off to those muscles.

Some of the functions of the basal ganglia have become clearer as we have come to understand Parkinson's disease—a disorder involving the basal ganglia in which the most noticeable symptoms are impairment of movement and involuntary tremors. At first there may be a tightness or stiffness in the fingers or limbs. As the disease progresses, it becomes difficult, if not impossible, to initiate bodily movements. Walking, once begun, involves a set of stiff, shuffling movements. In advanced cases, voluntary movement of the arms is nearly impossible. Parkinson's disease is more common with increasing age, afflicting approximately 1 percent of the population.

The neurotransmitter dopamine is usually found in great quantity in the basal ganglia. Indeed, the basal ganglia are the source of much of the brain's dopamine. In Parkinson's disease, the cells that produce dopamine die off, and as a result, levels of the neurotransmitter in the basal ganglia (and elsewhere) decline. As dopamine levels in the basal ganglia become insufficient, behavioral consequences are noted as symptoms of the disease. Treatment, you might think, would be to inject a lot of dopamine back into the basal ganglia. As it happens, that isn't possible:

simply put, there's no way to get the chemical in there so that it will stay. But another drug, L-dopa (in pill form), has the same effect: L-dopa increases dopamine availability in the basal ganglia, and as a result, the course of the disease can be slowed.

One treatment for Parkinson's disease has gotten considerable attention in the 1990s: the transplantation of brain cells from fetuses directly into the brain of someone suffering from the disease. After many studies with rats demonstrated that cells from the fetuses of rats could grow in the brains of adult rats—and increase the amount of dopamine there (e.g., Bjorklund et al., 1980)—the procedure was tried with humans. The results so far have been promising. Some studies have shown that transplanting brain cells from aborted human fetuses into the brains of persons with Parkinson's disease can actually reverse the course of the disease (e.g., Fahn, 1992; Freed et al., 1992; Spencer et al., 1992; Widner et al., 1992). As you can imagine, using brain cells from aborted fetuses—even to treat a devastating disease—is a procedure with profound ethical, legal, and political ramifications.

The Thalamus

The last structure to discuss as a lower brain center is the **thalamus**. It sits right below the cerebral cortex and is involved with its functioning. Like the pons, it is a relay station for impulses traveling to and from the cerebral cortex. Many impulses traveling from the cerebral cortex to lower brain structures, the spinal cord, and on to the peripheral nervous system pass through the thalamus. Overcoming the normal function of the medulla (e.g., by voluntarily holding our breath) involves messages that pass through the thalamus. The major role of the thalamus, however, involves the processing of information from the senses.

In handling incoming sensory impulses, the thalamus collects, organizes, and then directs sensory messages to the appropriate areas of the cerebral cortex. Sensory messages from the lower body, eyes, ears, and other sensory organs pass through the thalamus. For example, it is at the thalamus that nerve fibers from an eye are spread out and projected onto the back of the cerebral cortex.

Because of its role in monitoring impulses to and from the cerebral cortex, the thalamus has long been suspected to be involved in the control of our sleep-wake cycle (Moruzzi, 1975). Although the issue is not settled, some evidence (Lugaresi et al., 1986) suggests that nuclei in the thalamus (as well as the pons) do have a role in establishing a person's normal pattern of sleep and wakefulness.

thalamus *just below the cerebral cortex, the last sensory relay station; projects sensory impulses to the appropriate areas of the cerebral cortex*

Before You Go On

Indicate the locations and briefly describe the major functions of the reticular formation, limbic system, hypothalamus, basal ganglia, and thalamus.

The Cerebral Cortex

The human brain is a homely organ. There's just nothing very pretty about it. When we look at a human brain, the first thing we are likely to notice is the large, soft, lumpy, creviced outer covering of the cerebral cortex (cortex means "outer bark," or covering). The **cerebral cortex** (occasionally referred to as the cerebrum) of the human brain is significantly larger than any other brain structure. It is the complex and delicate cerebral cortex that makes us uniquely human.

cerebral cortex *the large convoluted outer covering of the brain that is the seat of voluntary action and cognitive functioning*

Lobes and Localization

Figure 2.10 presents two views of the cerebral cortex, one a top view, the other a side view. You can see from these drawings that the deep folds of tissue of the human cerebral cortex provide us with markers for dividing the cerebrum into major

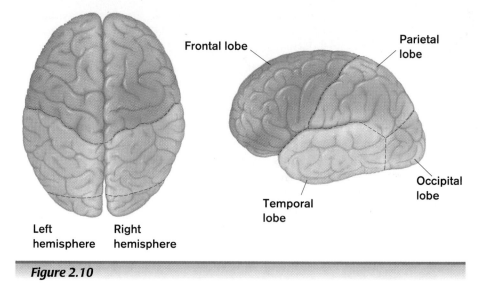

Figure 2.10

The human cerebral cortex is divided into left and right hemispheres, which, in turn, are divided into frontal, temporal, occipital, and parietal lobes.

areas. The most noticeable division of the cortex can be seen in the top view. Here, we can clearly see the deep crevice that runs down the middle of the cerebral cortex from front to back, dividing it into the left and right *cerebral hemispheres.*

A side view of a hemisphere (Figure 2.10 shows us the left one) allows us to see the four major divisions of each hemisphere, called "lobes." *The frontal lobes* (plural because there is a left and a right) are the largest and are defined by two large crevices called the central fissure and the lateral fissure. The *temporal lobes* are located at the temples, below the lateral fissure, with one on each side of the brain. The *occipital lobes,* at the back of the brain, are defined somewhat arbitrarily, with no large fissures setting them off, and the *parietal lobes* are wedged in behind the frontal lobes and above the occipital and temporal lobes.

Researchers have learned much about what normally happens in the various regions of the cerebral cortex, but many of the details of cerebral function are yet to be understood. There are three major areas that have been mapped: *sensory areas,* where impulses from sense receptors are sent; *motor areas,* where most voluntary movements originate; and *association areas,* where sensory and motor functions are integrated, and where higher mental processes are thought to occur. We'll now review each of these in turn, referring to Figure 2.11 as we go along.

Sensory Areas. Let's review for just a minute. Receptor cells (specialized neurons) in our sense organs respond to stimulus energy from the environment. These cells then pass neural impulses along sensory nerve fibers, eventually to the cerebral cortex. Senses in our body below our neck first send impulses to the spinal cord. Then, it's up the spinal cord, through the brain stem, where they cross from left to right and from right to left, on up to the thalamus, and beyond to the cerebrum. After impulses from our senses leave the thalamus, they go to a **sensory area**—an area of the cerebral cortex that receives impulses from our senses. Which sensory area is involved depends on the sense that was activated.

Reflecting their relative importance to us, large areas of the cerebral cortex are involved with vision and hearing. Virtually the entire occipital lobe processes visual information (labeled "visual area" in Figure 2.11). Auditory (hearing) impulses end up in large centers ("auditory areas") in the temporal lobes.

Our bodily senses (touch, pressure, pain, and so on) send impulses to a strip at the very front of the parietal lobe (labeled "body sense area" in Figure 2.11). In this

sensory areas *those areas of the cerebral cortex that ultimately receive neural impulses from sense receptors*

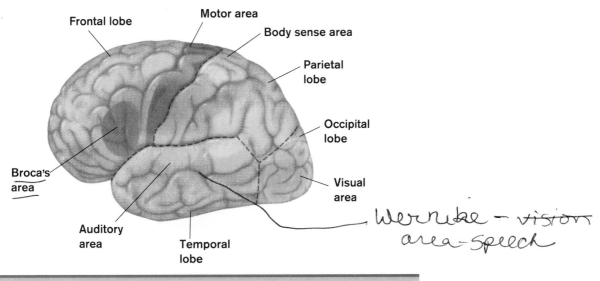

Handwritten note: Wernicke – vision area – speech

Figure 2.11

A side view of the left cerebral hemisphere, showing the four lobes of the cerebral cortex and areas of localization of function.

area of the parietal lobe we can map out specific regions that correspond to various parts of the body. When we do so, we find that some body parts—the face, lips, and fingertips, for example—are overrepresented in the body sense area of the cerebral cortex, reflecting their high sensitivity. In other words, some parts of the body,

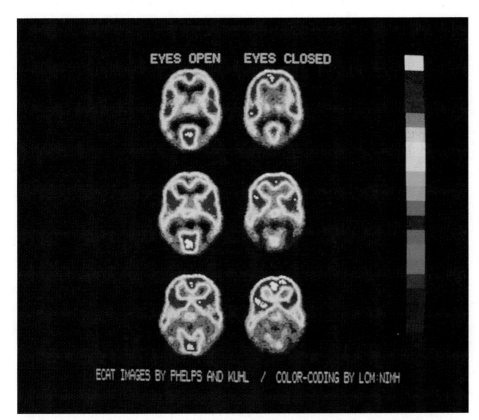

Using modern imaging equipment, we can actually see the occipital lobe's involvement in processing visual information—the occipital lobe is much more active when the subject's eyes are open than when they are closed.

even some very small ones, are processed in larger areas of the cortex than are other parts.

Finally, let's remind ourselves of cross laterality (page 53), the crossing over of information from senses on the left side of the body to the right side of the brain, and vice versa, that occurs in the brain stem. When someone touches your *right* arm, that information ends up in your left parietal lobe. A tickle to your left foot is processed by the right side of your cerebral cortex.

Motor Areas. We have seen that some of our actions, at least very simple and reflexive ones, originate below the cerebral cortex. Although lower brain centers, such as the basal ganglia, may be involved, most *voluntary* activity originates in the **motor areas** of the cerebral cortex—in strips at the very back of our frontal lobes. These areas (remember, there are two of them, left and right) are directly across the central fissure from the body sense areas in the parietal lobe (see Figure 2.11). I need to make the disclaimer that the actual, thoughtful decision-making process of whether one *should* move probably occurs elsewhere, almost certainly farther forward in the frontal lobes.

motor areas *those areas at the rear of the frontal lobes that control voluntary muscular movement*

Electrical stimulation techniques have allowed us to map locations in the motor areas that correspond to, or control, specific muscles or muscle groups. As is the case for sensory processing, we find that some muscle groups (such as those that control movements of the hands and mouth) are represented by disproportionally larger areas of cerebral cortex.

As you know, we also find cross laterality at work with the motor area. It is your right hemisphere's motor area that controls movements of the left side of your body, and the left hemisphere's motor area that controls the right side. Someone who has suffered a cerebral stroke (a disruption of blood flow in the brain that results in the loss of neural tissue) in the left side of the brain will have impaired movement in the right side of his or her body.

Association Areas. Once we have located the areas of the cerebral cortex that process sensory information and originate motor responses, we find that we still have a lot of cortex left over. The remaining areas of the cerebral cortex are called **association areas**—areas of the cerebrum where sensory input is integrated with motor responses; and where cognitive functions such as problem solving, memory, and thinking occur. There are three association areas in each hemisphere: frontal, parietal, and temporal. The occipital lobe is so "filled" with visual processing, there is no room left over for an occipital association area.

association areas *those areas of the frontal, temporal, and parietal lobes in which mental processes (planning, thinking, problem solving, memory) occur; where incoming sensory information is integrated with outgoing motor responses*

There is considerable support for the idea that so-called higher mental processes occur in the association areas. Frontal association areas are involved in many such processes. For instance, more than a century ago Pierre-Paul Broca (1824–1880) discovered that speech production and some other language behaviors are localized in the left frontal association area. Broca's conclusions were based on observations he made of human brains during autopsy. Persons with similar speech disorders commonly had noticeable damage in the very same region of the left hemisphere of the cerebral cortex. Logic led Broca to suspect that normal speech functions are controlled by this portion of the brain, which we now call *Broca's area* (see Fig. 2.11).

Damage to the very front of the right frontal lobe or to an area where the parietal and temporal lobes come together often interrupts or destroys the ability to plan ahead, to think quickly, or to think things through. Interestingly, these association areas of the brain involved in forethought and planning nearly cease to function when we are feeling particularly happy (e.g., George et al., 1995).

We should not get carried away with cerebral localization of function. Let's not fall into the trap of believing that separate parts of the cerebral cortex operate independently and have the sole responsibility for any one function. This will be particularly important to keep in mind as we look at the division of the cerebral cortex into right and left hemispheres.

Before You Go On

Given a side view of the brain, locate the four lobes of the cerebral cortex. What happens in the sensory, motor, and association areas?

The Two Cerebral Hemispheres—Splitting the Brain

The ancient Greeks knew that the cerebral cortex was divided into two major sections, or hemispheres. That there should be a division of the cerebral cortex into halves seems quite natural. After all, we have two eyes, arms, legs, lungs, and so forth. Why not two divisions of the brain? In the last 30 years, interest in this division into hemispheres has heightened as scientists have accumulated evidence that suggests that each half of the cerebral cortex may have primary responsibility for its own set of mental functions.

In most humans, the left hemisphere is the larger of the two halves, contains a higher proportion of gray matter, and is thought to be the dominant hemisphere (active to a greater degree in more tasks). We have already noted that a major language center (Broca's area) is housed in the left cerebral hemisphere. At least this is true for virtually all right-handed people. For some left-handers, language may be processed primarily by the right hemisphere. Because humans are so language oriented, not much attention was given to the "lowly" right hemisphere until a remarkable surgical procedure, first performed in the 1960s, gave us new insights about the cerebral hemispheres (Sperry, 1968, 1982; Springer & Deutsch, 1981).

Normally, the two hemispheres of the cerebral cortex are interconnected by a network of hundreds of thousands of fibers, collectively called the **corpus callosum** (see Figures 2.8 and 2.9). Through the corpus callosum, one side of our cortex remains in constant and immediate contact with the other. Separating the functions of the two hemispheres is possible, however, through a surgical technique called a **split-brain procedure**, which is neither as complicated nor as dangerous as it may sound. The procedure destroys the corpus callosum's connections between the two hemispheres and was first performed on a human in 1961 by Joseph Brogan in an attempt to lessen the severity of the symptoms of epilepsy. As an irreversible treatment of last resort, the split-brain procedure has been very successful.

Most of what we know about the activities of the cerebral hemispheres has been learned from split-brain subjects, both human and animal. One of the things that makes this procedure remarkable is that under normal circumstances split-brain patients behave normally. Only in the laboratory, with specially designed tasks, can we see the results of having made the hemispheres of the cerebral cortex function independently (e.g., Gazzaniga & LeDoux, 1978; Hellige, 1983; Metcalfe et al., 1995).

Experiments with split-brain patients confirm that speech production is a left-hemisphere function in a great majority of people. Suppose you have your hands behind your back. I place a house key in your left hand, and ask you to tell me what it is. Your left hand feels the key. Impulses travel up your left arm, up your spinal cord, and then cross over to your right cerebral hemisphere (remember cross laterality). You can tell me that the object in your hand is a key because your brain is intact. Your right hemisphere passes information about the key to your left hemisphere, and your left hemisphere directs you to say, "It's a key."

Now suppose that you are a split-brain subject. Now you cannot answer my question, even though you understand it perfectly. Why not? Your right brain knows that the object in your left hand is a key, but without your corpus callosum

corpus callosum *the network of nerve fibers that connects the two hemispheres of the cerebral cortex*

split-brain procedure *the surgical lesioning of the corpus callosum, which separates the functions of the left and right hemispheres of the cerebral cortex; a treatment of last resort for epilepsy* intact, it has no way to inform the left hemisphere, where speech production is located. You *would* be able to point out the key from among other objects placed before you, under the direction of the right cerebral hemisphere. Once your eyes saw you do so, they would communicate that information to your left hemisphere, and now it, too, would know, and tell us, what your right hemisphere knew all along.

A major task of the left hemisphere, then, is the production of speech and the use of language. But, I need to caution against overinterpretation. When results from split-brain studies were first made known, many people—psychologists and nonpsychologists—rushed to some premature conclusions. We now appreciate that virtually no behavior, virtually no mental process, is the simple and single product of just one hemisphere (Hellige, 1990). What is more reasonable to assert is that one hemisphere dominates the other in regard to, or may be the primary processing area for, certain actions and reactions. The left hemisphere *is* dominant in the perception and interpretation of speech. But some language processing seems to be more the responsibility of the right hemisphere. The right side of the cerebral cortex is more involved in processing common phrases and clichés, such as "How do you do?" or "Have a nice day!" (e.g., Kempler & Van Lanker, 1987).

Granted that we shouldn't overinterpret, what are some of the activities that are processed *primarily* in one hemisphere or the other? The left hemisphere can be given credit for processing most of our language skills, and given our heavy reliance on language, that's no small matter. Simple arithmetic tasks of calculation also seem to be primarily a left-brain function. Indeed, the left hemisphere has often been credited with the processing of information in an analytical, one-piece-at-a-time sort of way, although the data here are a bit tenuous (Hellige, 1990, p. 59).

What, then, of the right hemisphere? The clearest evidence is that the right hemisphere dominates in the processing of visually presented information (Bradshaw & Nettleton, 1983; Kosslyn, 1987). Putting together a jigsaw puzzle, for instance, uses the right hemisphere more than the left. Skill in the visual arts (i.e., painting, drawing, and sculpting) is associated with the right hemisphere. The right

We should be careful about overgeneralizing, but we can say that the left hemisphere of the cerebral cortex is involved in processing language, as when working a crossword puzzle. (As interested as my dog may appear, he has insufficient cerebral brain mass to work a crossword puzzle.) A major task of the right hemisphere is processing information about spatial relations, as when working a jigsaw puzzle. (Here we see the final piece of "the world's largest jigsaw puzzle.")

hemisphere is credited with being more involved in interpreting emotional stimuli and in expressing emotions. Consistent with the hypothesis that the left hemisphere tends to be analytical and sequential, the right hemisphere is thought to be better able to grasp the big picture—to see the overall view of things—and tends to be somewhat more creative.

Even these few possibilities are intriguing. It does seem that there are differences in the way the two sides of the cerebral cortex normally process information. But these differences are slight, and many remain controversial. In fact, we find that the more we study hemispheric differences, the more we discover similarities.

Before You Go On

What is a split-brain procedure, why has it been done on humans, and what have we learned from it?

The Two Sexes—Male and Female Brains

That there are anatomical differences between women and men is obvious. Here we are talking about the function of the brain, however, and we may fairly ask if there are any differences between the brains of men and the brains of women. Remember, we are asking about general differences; no two human beings brains are precisely the same. If there are differences in the anatomy of male and female brains, we must then ask if these differences are in any way significant. Do they have any measurable impact on psychological functioning?

It turns out that what appears to be a loaded issue can be resolved fairly easily. Except for those differences in the brains of males and females that are directly related to reproductive function (which are significant), there are very few differences that are of any real consequence (e.g., Unger & Crawford, 1992).

Here's an example of how research in this area has gone. One possibility that seemed intriguing was that the hemispheres of the cerebral cortex are more separate and distinct (more *lateralized*) in males than they are in females. At least one part of the corpus callosum in the brains of females seems consistently larger than it is in the brains of males. There is also evidence that women are more likely to recover from strokes than are men, perhaps because functions lost as a result of damage in one hemisphere can be taken over more easily by the other, undamaged hemisphere (McGlone, 1977, 1978, 1980). Another implication—usually left unsaid—is that intellectual functioning in women is more "balanced" than in men, whereas men are more likely to excel in the functioning of one hemisphere or the other. But further research failed to find any differences in lateralization (Bleier et al., 1987). Nor is there evidence that differences in lateralization are associated with any differences in cognitive abilities between men and women (e.g., Unger & Crawford, 1992). There is a difference in the lateralization of the brains of left-handed persons compared to right-handed persons (brains of left-handed persons are less lateralized, or less separate), but there are no significant differences in the cognitive abilities of left- and right-handed persons (Kocel, 1977).

Then, just as some researchers were prepared to give up on this line of study, a husband-and-wife team at Yale University, Drs. Sally and Bennett Shaywitz (she's a psychologist, he's a neurologist) published results of their work (Shaywitz et al., 1995). They watched the functioning, intact brains of men and women as they read nonsense words and tried to determine whether they rhymed. The Shaywitzes used a new method of brain imaging (called functional magnetic resonance imaging) that shows glimpses of areas of the brain that are active during even a very brief task. What they found was that when men attempted this process of sounding out nonsense words, they used a small portion of their left cerebral cortex, an area near Broca's area. Women used the same area, but also involved a similar area on the right side of their brains. Interestingly, the men and women performed the task equally well. The differences were only in *how their brains approached the task.* This

ⓒⓒⓒⓒ **Thinking Critically** ⓒⓒⓒⓒ

What kinds of conclusions about hemispheric specialization may be unwarranted? Why? Can one train or educate just one hemisphere of the cerebral cortex at a time?

was the first research to find a significant difference in brain function, not just brain structure.

Before You Go On

Are there any significant differences between the brains of females and the brains of males?

TOPIC 2B SUMMARY

Although we have learned a great deal about the human nervous system, its structures, and how it affects our thoughts, feelings, and behaviors, many mysteries remain to be solved. If nothing else, we have learned not to look for simple answers. We have also learned that a true understanding of behavior and mental processes requires a working knowledge of the underlying anatomy and physiology of the organism being studied. This observation will be reinforced in virtually every Topic that follows.

CHAPTER SUMMARY

Topic 2A

What are the major structures of a neuron?

Neurons are microscopically tiny, living cells consisting of a cell body, which contains the cell's nucleus; dendrites, which protrude from the cell body and usually receive impulses; and an axon, which carries an impulse away from the cell. The axons of some neurons are covered with a white, fatty myelin sheath that serves to protect and insulate the axon while speeding impulses along it. All axons, including myelinated ones, end with a set of bare, branching axon terminals. */p. 38*

What is the basic process involved when a neuron fires?

When a neuron is not firing, or is "at rest," the inside of the neuron is more negatively charged than the outside (the resting potential). When a neuron fires, the tension created by that imbalance of electrically charged chemical ions is quickly reversed. Where the impulse occurs, polarity changes, and for a very brief moment, the inside of the neuron becomes positive compared to the outside (the action potential). The all-or-none principle tells us that a neuron's firing either takes place totally or not at all; that is, there is no such thing as the partial firing of a

neuron. A neuron's threshold is the minimum amount of stimulation required to get a neuron to fire in the first place. */pp. 40–42*

Summarize neural impulse transmission at the synapse. Name and briefly describe the actions of four neurotransmitters.

At the synapse, a neural impulse triggers the release of neurotransmitter chemicals from small vesicles in the axon terminals. These chemicals flood into the synaptic cleft, embed themselves in receptor sites in the membranes of adjacent neurons, and, when sufficient amounts of the neurotransmitter are present, either excite or inhibit impulse transmission. Acetylcholine (ACh) is the most common neurotransmitter, and acts to either inhibit or excite impulse transmission. It is found in the CNS and at synapses between neurons and muscle cells. It activates muscle cell activity and has been implicated in normal memory function. Norepinephrine and dopamine are inhibitory neurotransmitters, the former implicated in reactions of agitation, arousal, and depression; the latter implicated in cognitive and affective reactions and in movement responses. Endorphins are a class of neurotransmitter involved in the suppression of, or reaction to pain. */pp. 43–45*

Name the human nervous systems and indicate how they are related to one another. What is the endocrine system and how does it operate?

See Figure 2.5. The major division is into CNS and PNS, where the CNS consists of the spinal cord and brain, and the PNS is divided into the somatic and autonomic nervous systems (ANS). The ANS is divided into sympathetic and parasympathetic divisions. The endocrine system is a network of glands that, under the influence of the brain and the ANS, secretes chemical substances called hormones into the bloodstream. These hormones then regulate or stimulate reactions in organs located at a distance from where the hormone is produced. The action of the endocrine system is particularly noticeable in states of emotionality. */pp. 45–49*

Topic 2B

Why does damage to the spinal cord sometimes cause paralysis? Describe the major features of a spinal reflex.

When the spinal cord is damaged, impulses originating in the brain to move parts of the body may not get past the damaged area to activate muscles, resulting in paralysis. Similarly, impulses from the lower extremities may not get past the injury to the brain for interpretation. In a spinal reflex, impulses enter the spinal cord on sensory fibers, may (or may not) form a synapse with interneurons, and then exit the spinal cord on motor fibers to activate a muscle response. At the same time, impulses are sent to the brain on fibers in the spinal cord's white matter. */pp. 51–52*

Name the two brain stem structures, indicate their location, and describe what they do.

The brain stem consists of the medulla, at the very base of the brain, which controls important reflexes, monitors heart rate and breathing, and is where cross laterality begins; and the pons, just above the medulla, which acts like a bridge, passing impulses between the spinal cord and the brain, continuing the process of crosslaterality. */pp. 52–53*

Where is the cerebellum located, and what is its major function?

The cerebellum is at the rear and base of the brain and is involved in the smoothing and coordinating of rapid muscular responses. */pp. 53–54*

Indicate the locations and briefly describe the major function of the reticular formation, limbic system, hypothalamus, basal ganglia, and thalamus.

The reticular formation extends from the brain stem through the middle of the brain to the cerebral cortex and is involved in maintaining levels of arousal. The limbic system, just above the brain stem, is involved in emotional expression (especially the amygdala and septum) and the transfer of information into long-term memory (hippocampus). The hypothalamus, which is near the limbic system, is involved in such motivated behaviors as feeding, drinking, sex, aggression, and temperature regulation. The basal ganglia, just in front of and above the limbic system, control slow body movement and produce much of the brain's dopamine. The thalamus, just below the cerebral cortex, is a final relay station for sensory impulses, which it projects up to the appropriate area of the cerebrum. */pp. 55–57*

Given a side view of the brain, locate the four lobes of the cerebral cortex. What happens in the sensory, motor, and association areas?

See Figures 2.10 and 2.11 to review the locations of the frontal, temporal, occipital, and parietal lobes, and the primary sensory, motor, and association areas. The sensory areas of the cerebral cortex (visual, auditory, and body sense) receive impulses (through the thalamus) from our senses. Voluntary motor activity is initiated in the motor area. Cognitive processing, such as memory, thinking, speech, planning, and problem solving, is thought to take place in the so-called association areas. */pp. 57–61*

What is a split-brain procedure, why has it been done on humans, and what have we learned from it?

The split-brain procedure severs the fibers of the corpus callosum, the structure that sends impulses back and forth between the two cerebral hemispheres, allowing them to operate independently. It is used as a treatment of last resort for epilepsy. Although one hemisphere may dominate the other in some functions, seldom does one have complete control of any important brain function. It is safe to say that language and speech are processed in the left hemisphere, while visual, spatial information is usually processed in the right. Less certain are the left hemisphere's dominance in simple calculations and the sequential, analytical processing of information, and the right hemisphere's involvement with the "big picture," the visual arts, and emotionality. */pp. 61–63*

Are there any significant differences between the brains of females and the brains of males?

Other than those brain structures that are involved in reproductive functioning, there seem to be few structural differences between the brains of females and the brains of males. Those that do exist have little known consequences in terms of function. One exception is the recent finding that women use small areas in both their left *and* right hemispheres when pronouncing words, while men use only the left hemisphere. There are no differences in abilities to perform this task, so the significance of these brain differences remains questionable. */pp. 63–64*

Damage to the CNS: What Happens If?

One way to review, and make sure that you understand the function of the various structures of the human nervous system, is to ask what would happen if a particular structure were damaged or destroyed by accident or illness. So, for each of the following briefly describe the consequences. (Suggested answers can be found on p. 571.)

1. Severing the spinal cord below the waist. _____
   _____
   _____

2. Severing the spinal cord at the base of the neck.
   _____
   _____

3. Destroying the medulla._____
   _____
   _____

4. Lesioning the pons. _____
   _____
   _____

5. Removing the cerebellum._____
   _____
   _____

6. Removing the corpus callosum. _____
   _____
   _____

7. Destroying the thalamus. _____
   _____
   _____

8. Cutting through the reticular formation. _____
   _____

9. Removing the occipital lobe._____
   _____

10. Destroying the very front portion of the left parietal lobe. _____
    _____

O U T L I N E

I've never tried this classroom demonstration, but when I was a graduate student at the University of Tennessee, I got to see it done about as well as it can be performed.

It was a grand old lecture hall. Nearly 600 students had settled down to listen to the day's lecture on perception. Suddenly a student burst through the doors at the rear of the hall. I recognized this student as the lecturer's graduate student assistant, but no one else in the class knew who he was. The graduate student stomped down the center aisle of the lecture hall, screaming foul obscenities at the professor. "Dr. X, you failed me for the last time, you *&@#$ so-and-so! You're going to pay for this!" The class was stunned. No one moved as the student leaped over the lectern to grab the professor.

The two struggled briefly, then—in clear view of everyone—there was a chrome-plated revolver. Down behind the lectern they fell. BANG! The students sat frozen in their seats as the graduate student raced out the side door that their professor had entered just minutes earlier. The professor lay sprawled on the floor, moaning loudly.

Six hundred stunned students just sat there. At just the proper dramatic moment, the professor slowly drew himself up to the lectern and in a calm, soft voice said, "Now I want everyone to write down exactly what you just saw here."

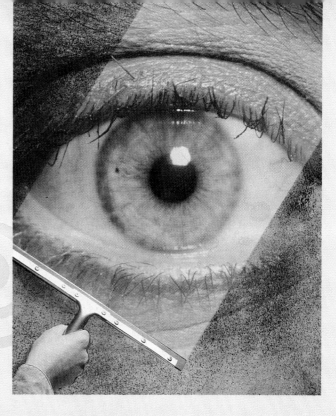

3

Sensation and Perception

You can guess what happened. The "enraged student" was described as being from 5'4" to 6'3" tall, weighing between 155 and 230 pounds, and wearing either a blue blazer or a gray sweatshirt. But the most remarkable misperception had to do with the gun. When the professor first reached the lectern, he reached into his suit coat pocket, removed the gun and placed it on top of his notes. When the student crashed into the room, the first thing that the professor did was to reach down, grab the pistol, and point it at the student. In fact, the student never had the gun. It was the professor who fired the shot that startled us all. *Fewer than 20 students of the 600 in class that day reported seeing these events as they actually occurred.* The overwhelming majority of witnesses claimed it was the crazy student who burst into the class with a gun in his hands.

Chapter 3 begins our discussion of information processing—how we find out about the world, make judgments about it, learn from it, and remember what we have learned. As this example demonstrates, our perception of the world often depends on factors that are not immediately apparent. This chapter addresses the question of how we find out about ourselves and the world in which we live. Answers begin with a consideration of how our senses work.

TOPIC 3A Sensory Processes

We do not experience any breaks in the way we process information. We hear someone say something in class and discover some time later that we remember what was said. If there were any subprocesses involved along the way, we were not aware of them. What we are going to do in this chapter, then, is somewhat artificial, at least in terms of our everyday experience. We're going to divide the initial stages of information processing into two subprocesses—sensation and perception.

We begin with a discussion of sensory processes, or what we often call sensation. **Sensation** is the process that yields our immediate experience of the stimuli in our environment. It is the process of receiving information and changing it into nervous system activity. The psychology of sensation deals with how our various senses do what they do. Sense receptors are the specialized neural cells in sense organs that change physical energy into neural impulses. In other words, each of our sense receptors is a **transducer**—a mechanism that converts energy from one form to another. A light bulb is a transducer. It converts electrical energy into light energy (and a little heat energy). Your eye is a sense organ that contains sense receptors that transduce light energy into neural energy. Your ear is a sense organ that contains sense receptors that transduce the mechanical energy of sound waves into neural energy.

Compared to sensation, perception is a more active, complex, even creative, process. It acts on stimulation received and recorded by the senses. **Perception** is a process that involves the selection, organization, and interpretation of stimuli. Perception is a more cognitive and central process than sensation. We say that our senses present us with information about the world in which we live, whereas perception represents (re-presents) that information, often flavored by our motivational states, our expectations, and our past experiences. In other words, ". . . we sense the presence of a stimulus, but we perceive what it is" (Levine and Shefner, 1991, p. 1).

Now, before we get into the story of how each of our sense organs goes about transducing physical energy from the environment into neural energy, we'll consider a few concepts that apply to all of our senses.

sensation *the process of receiving information from the environment and changing that input into nervous system activity*

transducer *a mechanism that converts energy from one form to another—a basic process common to all of our senses*

perception *the cognitive process of selecting, organizing, and interpreting stimuli*

Sensory Thresholds

psychophysics *the study of the relationship between the physical attributes of stimuli and the psychological experiences they produce*

Psychophysics is the study of relationships between the physical attributes of stimuli and the psychological experiences they produce. It is one of the oldest subfields in psychology. Many methods of psychophysics were developed before Wundt opened his psychology laboratory in Leipzig in 1879.

There are two ways to think about what psychophysics is all about. At a simple, applied level we can say that the techniques of psychophysics have been designed to assess the sensitivity of our senses, providing answers to such questions as, "Just how good *is* your hearing after all these years of playing in a rock band?" At a more theoretical level, we can think of psychophysics as providing a means of systematically relating the outside, physical world to the inner, psychological world. Now our question may be: "How much of a change in the physical intensity of this sound will it take for you to experience a difference in loudness?" Most psychophysical methods are designed to measure *sensory thresholds,* indicators of the sensitivity of our sense receptors. There are two types of sensory thresholds: absolute thresholds and difference thresholds.

Absolute Thresholds

Imagine the following experiment. You are seated in a dimly lighted room, staring at a small box. The side of the box facing you is covered by a sheet of plastic. Behind the plastic is a light bulb. I can decrease the physical intensity of the light bulb to the point where you cannot see it at all. I can also increase the light's intensity so that you can see it very clearly. I have many intensity settings available between these extremes. At what point of physical intensity will the light first become visible to you?

Common sense tells us that there should be some level of intensity below which you cannot see the light and above which you can. That level, that point, would be your absolute threshold. As you can see, sensory thresholds are related to sensitivity, but inversely. That is, as threshold values decrease, sensitivity increases. The lower the threshold of a sense receptor, the more sensitive it is.

Let's return to our imaginary experiment. I repeatedly vary the light's intensity and ask you to respond, "Yes, I see the light," or "No, I don't see the light," depending on your experience. In this experiment, I won't allow you the luxury of saying you don't know or aren't sure.

When this experiment is actually done, we discover something that at first seems strange. *I can* reduce the intensity of the light so low that you never report seeing it. And I *can* present light intensities so high that you always say you see them. However, there are intensities of the light to which you sometimes respond "yes" and sometimes respond "no," even though the actual, physical intensity of the light is unchanged.

In reality, there just isn't much that is absolute about absolute thresholds. They change from moment to moment, reflecting small, subtle changes in the sensitivity of our senses. They also reflect such factors as momentary shifts in our ability to pay attention to the task at hand—an issue we'll get back to soon. Because there are no set, absolute measures of sensory sensitivity, psychologists use the following operational definition of **absolute threshold**: the physical intensity of a stimulus that a person reports detecting 50 percent of the time. In other words, intensities below threshold are those detected less than 50 percent of the time, and

absolute threshold *the physical intensity of a stimulus that one can detect 50 percent of the time*

A consideration of absolute thresholds is not simply an academic exercise. Why put an expensive spice or herb in your cooking if no one can taste it? How much is needed so that it can be detected? These are questions of absolute threshold.

Professional wine tasters must be able to detect even the slightest j.n.d.'s between the varieties of wines they are tasting.

⊚⊚⊚⊚ **Thinking Critically** ⊚⊚⊚⊚

What examples could you provide to explain the differences between sensation and perception to those people who confuse these two processes?

difference threshold *differences in a stimulus attribute that can be detected 50 percent of the time*

just noticeable difference (j.n.d.) *the minimal change in a stimulus attribute, such as intensity, that can be detected*

intensities above threshold are those detected more than 50 percent of the time. This complication occurs for all of our senses, not just vision.

What good is the concept of absolute threshold? Determining absolute thresholds is not just an academic exercise. For one thing, as a measure of sensitivity, absolute threshold levels can be used to determine if one's senses are operating properly and are detecting low levels of stimulation (which is what happens when you have your hearing tested, for example). Engineers who design sound systems need to know about absolute thresholds; stereo speakers that do not reproduce sounds above threshold levels aren't of much use. Warning lights must be well above absolute threshold if they are to be of any use. How much perfume do you need to use for it to be noticed? How low must you whisper so as not to be overheard in a classroom? Do I really smell natural gas in the house, or is it my imagination? Can one basil leaf in the tomato sauce be detected, or will two be required? These are psychophysical questions about absolute thresholds as they pertain to everyday experiences outside the laboratory. As it happens, our sense receptors are remarkably sensitive, as the examples in Figure 3.1 attest.

Before You Go On

Define sensation and perception.

What is an absolute threshold, and how is it related to sensitivity?

Difference Thresholds

The truth is, we don't often encounter situations that test our abilities to detect very-low-intensity stimuli. We *are* often called upon to detect differences between or among stimuli that are above our absolute thresholds. The issue here is not whether the stimuli can be detected, but whether they are in some way different from each other. So, a **difference threshold** is the smallest difference between stimulus attributes that can be detected. As you may have anticipated, we do have the same complication here as we do when we try to measure absolute thresholds. To slight degrees, one's difference threshold for any stimulus attribute varies from moment to moment. So, again we say that to be above one's difference threshold, differences between stimuli need to be detected more than 50 percent of the time.

Here's an example. I present you with two tones. You hear them both (they are above your absolute threshold), and you report that they are equally loud. If I gradually increase the intensity of one of the tones, I will eventually reach a point at which you can just detect a difference in the loudness of the tones. This **just noticeable difference**, or **j.n.d.**, is the amount of change in a stimulus that makes it just noticeably different from what it was.

Figure 3.1
Examples of Absolute Threshold Values for Five Senses (i.e., These Stimuli Will Be Detected 50 Percent of the Time)

Vision	A candle flame seen from a distance of 30 miles on a clear, dark night
Hearing	The ticking of a watch under quiet conditions from a distance of 20 feet
Taste	1 teaspoon of sugar dissolved in 2 gallons of water
Smell	One drop of perfume in a three-room apartment
Touch	The wing of a bee dropped on your cheek from a height of 1 centimeter

From Galanter, 1962

The concept of just noticeable difference is relevant in many contexts. A parent tells a teenager to "turn down that stereo!" The teenager reduces the volume, but not by a j.n.d. from the parent's perspective, and trouble may be brewing. Does the color of the belt match the color of the dress closely enough? Can anyone notice the difference between the expensive ingredients in the stew and the cheaper ones?

Signal Detection

We've noted that sensory thresholds are not stable, fixed values. They vary from moment to moment and are defined in terms of probability—as a 50-percent point, above which attributes of stimuli, or their differences, can be detected.

To say that sensory thresholds change is the same thing as saying the sensitivity of our senses changes. It changes because of momentary shifts in attention and because of the random electrical activity of the nerve cells in our sensory systems.

When we are asked to determine if a stimulus has been presented, we are really being asked to judge if we can detect a signal against a background of other stimuli and randomly changing neural activity, called "noise." When we think of thresholds this way, we are using the basics of signal detection theory. **Signal detection theory** claims that stimulus detection is a decision-making process of determining if a signal exists against a background of noise (Green & Swets, 1966).

According to this theory, one's absolute threshold is influenced by many factors in addition to the actual sensitivity of one's senses. Random nervous system activity has to be accounted for. So do the person's attention, expectations, and biases. For example, in experiments to determine one's absolute threshold, people are more likely to say yes, they can detect a stimulus than they are to say no, they can't. Everything else being equal, there is a general tendency to say "yes" more often than "no" (Block, 1965).

Remember the absolute threshold study with which we began our discussion of psychophysics? I had a light in a box, changed the intensity of the light, and asked if you could see it. Your absolute threshold was the intensity of light to which you responded "yes" 50 percent of the time. Signal detection theory asks us

signal detection theory *the view that signal detection is a matter of decision making, of separating a signal from ground (background) noise*

EXPERIENCING PSYCHOLOGY

How Many Pennies Make a Difference?

Here's a simple demonstration of the nature of difference thresholds. All you need for this project are two identical small boxes (I use the boxes that Band-Aids come in) and two dollars worth of pennies. You can either make the called-for judgments yourself or use a volunteer to make the judgments for you. I'll assume that you have a volunteer to help you.

Begin with 10 pennies in each box. Have your volunteer compare the weights of the two boxes. (He or she should say they seem equally heavy, of course.) Now add a penny to one box (don't let your volunteer see what you are doing), and try again. Keep adding pennies (to the same box each time) until your volunteer detects a difference between the two. How many pennies did it take?

Now start with 50 pennies in each box, and repeat the same procedure. First judge the boxes as they are, then add one penny to one box and ask for another judgment. Add another penny, and then another until the volunteer detects a difference in the weight of the two boxes. How many pennies did it take?

Because you are starting with a heavier weight, it will take more pennies added to the box before you reach a *just noticeable difference* (or j.n.d.) for the 50 penny boxes than for the 10 penny boxes. You might actually weigh all the boxes involved and see if the difference (in weight—not pennies) is actually 5 times as great for the 50 penny boxes as for the 10 penny boxes.

to consider all of the factors that might have prompted you to say "yes" at any exposure to the light. What might some of these factors be? One might be the overall amount of light in the room. Wouldn't you be more likely to detect the signal of my light in a room that was totally dark as opposed to a room in which all of the standard lights were on? What if I had offered you a reward, say $5, each time you detected the light? Wouldn't you tend to say "yes" often, whether you were really sure of yourself or not? By the same token, if I were to fine you $1 for each time you said "yes" when the light was not really on, might you not become more conservative, saying "yes" only when you were very sure of yourself? Might we expect a difference in your pattern of saying "yes" or "no" depending on whether we tested you in mid-morning, or late in the day when you were tired?

Signal detection procedures take into account such factors as background noise (e.g., the amount of light in the room), levels of attention, and subject bias in determining sensory thresholds. The result is a better, clearer picture of sensory sensitivity.

Before You Go On

What is the difference between a difference threshold and a j.n.d.?
Briefly summarize signal detection theory.

Sensory Adaptation

sensory adaptation *the process in which our sensory experience tends to diminish with continued exposure to a stimulus*

Sensory adaptation occurs when our sensory experience decreases with continued exposure to a stimulus. There are many common examples of sensory adaptation. When we first jump into a pool or lake, the water feels very cold. But after only a few minutes we adapt and are reassuring our friends to "Come on in; the water's fine." When we first walk into a house in which cabbage is cooking, the odor is nearly overwhelming, but soon we adapt and do not notice it. When the compressor motor of the refrigerator first turns on, it seems to make a terribly loud noise—one we soon do not notice, until the motor stops and silence returns to the kitchen.

There is an important psychological point hidden in these common examples of sensory adaptation. It is that one's ability to detect the presence of a stimulus depends in large measure on the extent to which our sense receptors are being newly stimulated or have adapted. Our sense receptors respond best to *changes* in stimulation. The constant stimulation of a receptor leads to adaptation and less of a chance that that stimulation will be detected.

There is an exception to this use of the term *adaptation*. What happens when you move from a brightly lighted area to a dimly lighted area? Say you enter a darkened movie theater on a sunny afternoon. At first you can barely see, but in a few minutes, you are seeing reasonably well. What happened? We say that you've "adapted to the dark." Here we are using the term *adaptation* in a different way. **Dark adaptation** refers to the process in which the visual receptors become *more* sensitive with time spent in the dark.

dark adaptation *the process by which our eyes become more sensitive to light as we spend time in the dark*

Before You Go On

How does sensory adaptation relate to thresholds?

Vision

Discussing which of our senses is the most important is a silly exercise. Each sense is of value in helping us process information about the environment. (I enjoy eating and think highly of the sense of taste.) Nonetheless, vision is a very important sense for humans. Occasionally we equate our visual experience with truth, or reality, as in, "Seeing is believing." Remember, too, that the entire occipital lobe of the brain is devoted to the processing of visual information. In this section, we first consider both the stimulus for vision (light) and the receptor for vision (the eye).

The Stimulus for Vision: Light

Light is the stimulus for vision. Appreciating the nature of light can help us understand how it is related to our visual experiences. **Light** may be thought of as a wave form of radiant energy. What that means is that light radiates from its source in a manner we may represent as waves (which we call light waves).

Light waves have three important physical characteristics that are related to psychological experience: *wave amplitude, wavelength,* and *wave purity.* One of the ways in which light energy may vary is in its intensity. Differences in intensity correspond to differences in the wave amplitude of light. Refer to Figure 3.2 and assume that the two waves represent two different light waves. One of the physical differences between light A and light B is the wave amplitude of each. Our psychological experience of wave amplitude, or intensity, is **brightness**. The difference between a bright light and a dim light is due to the difference in wave amplitude. Dimmer-switches that control the brightness of light fixtures are controlling the amplitude of light waves.

Wavelength is the distance between any point in a wave and the corresponding point on the next cycle–from peak to peak, for example. In Figure 3.2, another difference between waves A and B is the wavelength of each, where A has the longer wavelength. It is difficult to imagine distances so small, but we can measure the length of a light wave. The unit of measurement is the **nanometer (nm)**, which is equal to one one-billionth of a meter, or one one-millionth of a millimeter.

The human eye responds only to radiant energy that has a wavelength between roughly 380 nm and 760 nm. This is the range of energy waves that constitute the *visible spectrum.* Wave forms of energy with wavelengths shorter than 380 nm (e.g., X rays and ultraviolet rays) are too short to stimulate the receptors in our eyes, and go unnoticed. Wave forms of energy with wavelengths longer than 760

light *a radiant form of energy that can be represented in wave form with wavelengths between 380 and 760 nanometers*

brightness *the psychological experience associated with a light's intensity, or wave amplitude*

wavelength *the distance between any point on a wave and the corresponding point on the next cycle of the wave*

nanometer (nm) *one millionth of a millimeter; the unit of measurement for the wavelength of light*

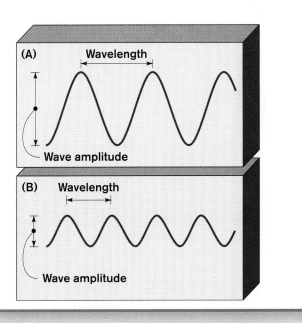

Figure 3.2

Representations of light waves differing in wavelength and wave amplitude. Wavelength gives rise to our experience of hue (or color) and wave amplitude determines our experience of brightness.

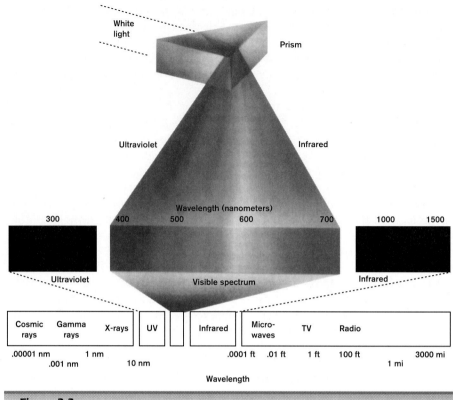

Figure 3.3

The spectrum of electromagnetic energy in wave form, of which light is but a small segment. Here we see that light is electromagnetic energy with a wavelength between 380 nm and 760 nm. As visible wavelengths change, our experience changes to produce a "rainbow."

nm (e.g., microwaves and radar) do not stimulate the receptor cells in our eyes either.

hue *the psychological experience of color associated with a light's wavelength*

Wavelength is the attribute of light energy that determines the **hue**, or color, we perceive. As light waves increase from the short 380-nm wavelengths to the long 760-nm lengths, our experience changes—from violet to blue to green to yellow-green to yellow to orange to red along the color spectrum (Figure 3.3). A source of radiant energy with a 700-nm wavelength will be seen as a red light. In fact, that's what a red light is. (A bright red light has a high amplitude, and a dim red light a low amplitude, but both have 700-nm wavelengths.) As we can see in Figure 3.3, if a light generated waves 550 nm long, it would be seen as a yellow-green light, and so on. Note that yellow-green is a single hue produced by wavelengths of light 550 nm long. It is not some combination of yellow and green. We simply have no other name for this hue, so we call it yellow-green.

Here's an apparently easy problem: I have two lights, one red (700 nm) and the other yellow-green (550 nm). I adjust the physical intensities of these lights so that they are equal. With both amplitudes equal, will the lights appear equally bright? Actually, they won't. The yellow-green light will appear much brighter than the red one. It will also appear brighter than a blue light of the same amplitude. We say that wavelength and wave amplitude interact to produce apparent brightness. Wavelengths in the middle of the spectrum (such as yellow-green) appear brighter than do wavelengths of light from either extreme, if their amplitudes are equal. I *can* get a red light to appear as bright as a yellow-green one, but to do so I'll have to increase its amplitude, which requires more energy, and is thus more expensive. Here is a fairly good argument that the lights on emergency vehicles should be yellow-green, not red. With everything else being equal, yellow-green lights appear brighter than red ones.

Now we need to consider a third characteristic of light waves: their degree of purity. Imagine a light of medium amplitude with all of its wavelengths exactly 700 nm long. The light would appear to be of medium brightness. Because the wavelengths are all 700 nm, it would appear red. More than that, it would appear as a pure, rich red. We call such a light **monochromatic** because it consists of light waves all of one (mono) length or hue (chroma). We seldom see such lights outside the laboratory because producing a pure, monochromatic light is expensive. The reddest of lights we see in our everyday experience have other wavelengths of light mixed in with the predominant 700-nm red. (If the 700-nm wave did not predominate, the light wouldn't look red.) Even the red light on top of a police car has some violet, green, and yellow light in it.

The physical purity of a light gives rise to the psychological experience called **saturation**. Pure, monochromatic lights are the most highly saturated; their hue is rich and obvious. As different wavelengths get mixed into a light, it becomes lower and lower in saturation, and starts to look pale and washed out.

What do we call a light that is of the lowest possible saturation, a light consisting of a random mixture of wavelengths of light? By definition, it is **white light**. It is something of a curiosity that white light is in fact as *impure* a light as possible. A pure light has but one wavelength; a white light contains many wavelengths. True white light is as difficult to produce as is a pure monochromatic light. Fluorescent bulbs produce a reasonable approximation, but their light contains too many wavelengths from the short, or blue-violet end of the spectrum to be truly white. Light from incandescent bulbs contains too many light waves from the orange and red end of the spectrum, even if we paint the inside of the bulb with white paint. A prism can break a beam of white light down into its various parts, giving us the experience of a rainbow of hues. Where did all those hues come from? They were there all along, mixed together to form the white light.

We have seen that three physical characteristics of light influence our visual experience. These relationships are summarized in Figure 3.4.

monochromatic *literally one-colored; a pure light consisting of light waves all of the same wavelength*

saturation *the psychological experience associated with the purity of a light wave; the most saturated lights are monochromatic, and the least saturated are white light*

white light *a light of the lowest possible saturation, containing a mixture of all visible wavelengths*

Before You Go On

In what ways do the major physical characteristics of light affect our psychological experience of vision?

The Receptor for Vision: The Eye

Vision involves changing (transducing, remember) light wave energy into the neural energy of the nervous system. This transduction of energy takes place in the eye, but most of the structures of the eye have little to do with transducing light energy into neural energy. Most structures are there to ensure that light waves that

Figure 3.4

The Relationships Between the Physical Characteristics of Light and Our Psychological Experience of That Light

Physical characteristic	Psychological experience
Wave amplitude (intensity)	Brightness
Wavelength	Hue
Wave purity	Saturation

These two interact

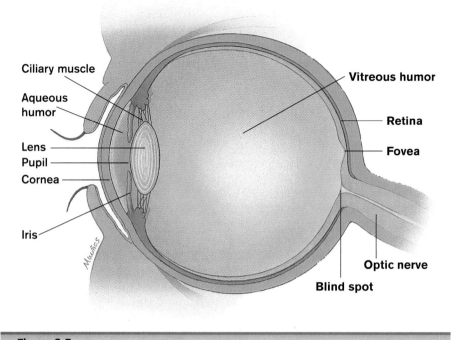

Figure 3.5

The major structures of the human eye.

cornea *the outermost structure of the eye that protects the eye and begins to focus light waves*

pupil *the opening of the iris, which changes size in relation to the amount of light available and to emotional factors*

iris *the colored structure of the eye that reflexively opens or closes the pupil*

lens *the structure behind the iris that changes shape to focus visual images in the eye*

ciliary muscles *small muscles attached to the lens that control its shape and focusing capability*

accommodation *in vision, the process in which the shape of the lens is changed by the ciliary muscles to focus an image on the retina*

enter the eye are well focused by the time they get back to the layer of cells that responds to them.

Using Figure 3.5 as a guide, let's trace the path of light as it passes through the eye, ultimately to produce a visual experience. Light enters the eye through the cornea. The **cornea** is the tough, round, virtually transparent outer shell of the eye. Those of you who wear contact lenses float them on your corneas. The cornea protects the delicate structures behind it and starts to bend the entering light waves in order to focus an image on the back surface of the eye.

Having passed through the cornea, light then travels through the **pupil**, which is an opening in the **iris**. The iris is pigmented, or colored. When we say that someone has blue, brown, or green eyes, we are referring to the color of the iris. The iris can expand or contract, changing the size of the pupil. This is a reflexive reaction, not something you can do by conscious effort. Changes in pupil size are usually made in response to the level of light present, opening wide when small amounts of light are present and getting smaller (protectively) in response to high-intensity lights. Increasing pupil size is also an automatic response that occurs with heightened levels of emotionality—an adaptive reaction to let in as much light as possible so that one can see clearly.

After the pupil, the next structure light encounters is the **lens**. As in a camera, the main function of the lens of the eye is to focus a visual image. Unlike a camera, the lens of the eye changes shape to bring an image into focus, becoming flatter when we try to focus on an object at a distance and becoming rounder when we try to view something up close. This, too, is a reflex. Obviously, lenses are not normally as hard as glass or they wouldn't be able to change their shape. Small, powerful muscles, **ciliary muscles**, push on the lens or relax in order to change the shape of the lens—a process called accommodation. Often an image does not focus as it should, because of the shape of the lens or a failure of **accommodation**. Sometimes even a healthy lens and functioning ciliary muscles can't get an image to focus because of the shape of the eyeball itself. The result is either nearsightedness or farsightedness. With age, lenses tend to harden, and ciliary muscles tend to weaken, making it difficult to focus and requiring us to use glasses to help out.

There is a space between the cornea and the lens filled with a clear fluid called **aqueous humor**. This humor (which means "fluid") provides nourishment to the cornea and the other structures at the front of the eye. The aqueous humor is constantly being produced and supplied to the space behind the cornea, filtering out blood to keep the fluid clear. If the fluid cannot easily pass out of this space, pressure builds within the eye, causing distortions in vision or, in extreme cases, blindness. This disorder is known as *glaucoma.* There is another, larger space behind the lens that is also filled with a fluid, or humor. This fluid is called **vitreous humor**. It is not nearly as watery as aqueous humor. It is thick and filled with tiny structures that give it substance. Its major function is to keep the eyeball spherical.

It is at the **retina** of the eye that vision begins to take place. Here, light energy is transduced into neural energy. The retina is really a series of layers of specialized cells at the back surface of the eye. These cells are nerve cells and can be thought of as part of the brain. The location of the retina and its major landmarks are shown in Figure 3.5. Figure 3.6 shows the retina in more detail.

To describe the retina, let's move from the back of the retina outward, toward the front. The layer of cells at the very back of the retina are the receptor cells for vision, the transducers, or photoreceptors, of the eye. It is here that light wave energy is changed into neural energy. There are two types of photoreceptor cells: **rods** and **cones**. They are aptly named because that's just what they look like: tiny rods and cones. Their tips respond to light wave energy and begin a neural impulse. The impulses travel down the rods and cones and pass on to (form a synapse with) other cells, also arranged in layers. Within these layers there is considerable combination and integration of neural impulses. No rod or cone has a single, direct pathway to the cerebral cortex of the brain. Impulses from many rods and cones are combined within the eye, by *bipolar cells* and *ganglion cells,* among others. Fibers from ganglion cells form the **optic nerve**, the collection of neurons that leaves the eye and starts back toward other parts of the brain.

The two main features of the retina depicted in Figure 3.5 are the fovea and the blind spot. The **fovea** is a small area of the retina where there are few layers of cells between the entering light and the cone cells that fill the area. There are no rods in the fovea, only cones, which are tightly packed together. Here at the fovea our *visual acuity,* or ability to discern detail, is best—at least in daylight or in reasonably high levels of illumination. If you were to try to thread a needle, you would want to focus the image of the needle and thread on the fovea.

aqueous humor *watery fluid found in the space between the cornea and the lens that nourishes the front of the eye*

vitreous humor *the thick fluid behind the lens of the eye that helps keep the eyeball spherical*

retina *layers of cells at the back of the eye that contain the photosensitive rod and cone cells*

rods *photosensitive cells of the retina that are most active in low levels of illumination and do not respond differentially to various wavelengths of light*

cones *photosensitive cells of the retina that operate best at high levels of illumination and that are responsible for color vision*

optic nerve *the fiber, consisting of many neurons, that leaves the eye and carries impulses to the occipital lobe of the brain*

fovea *the region at the center of the retina, consisting solely of cones, where acuity is best in daylight*

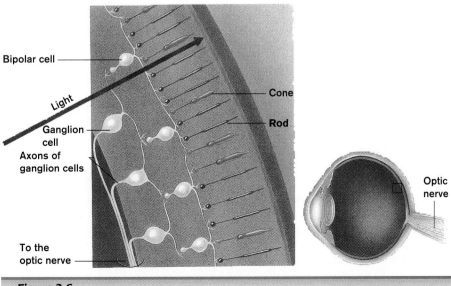

Figure 3.6

The major features of the human retina.

blind spot *the small region of the retina, containing no photoreceptors, where the optic nerve leaves the eye*

The **blind spot** is where the nerve impulses from the rods and cones, having passed through all those layers of cells, exit the eye. At the blind spot, there are no rods or cones—there's nothing there but the optic nerve threading its way back into the brain. Because there are no rods or cones, there is no vision here, which is why this area is called the blind spot. Figure 3.7 shows you how to locate your own blind spot.

Before You Go On

List the major structures of the eye, and describe the function of each.

More on Rods and Cones and What They Do

Let's now deal further with the two types of receptor cells in our retinas, rods and cones. Although they are both nerve cells, rods and cones do not look alike. There are other differences. In each eye, there are about 120 million rods, but only 6 million cones. They are not distributed evenly throughout the retina. Cones are concentrated in the center of the retina, in the fovea. Rods are concentrated in a band or ring around the fovea, out toward the periphery. These observations have led psychologists to wonder if rods and cones have different functions.

In fact, cones function best in medium to high levels of illumination (such as in daylight) and are primarily responsible for our experience of color. On the other hand, rods operate best under conditions of reduced illumination (as at twilight). They are more sensitive to low-intensity light. Our rods do not discriminate among wavelengths of light, which means that rods do not contribute to our appreciation of color.

Some of the evidence for these claims can be verified by our own experiences. Don't you find it difficult to distinguish among different colors at night or in the dark? The next time you are at the movies eating some pieces of candy that are of different colors, see if you can tell them apart without holding them up to the light of the projector. You probably won't be able to tell a green piece from a red one because they all appear black. You can't discriminate colors very well in a dark movie theater because you are seeing them primarily with your rods, which are very good at seeing in the reduced illumination of the theater but don't differentiate among wavelengths of light.

If you are looking for something small outside at night, you probably won't see it if you look directly at it. Imagine you are changing a tire along the road at night and you can't find one of the lug nuts you know is there someplace in the gravel. If

(A)

(B)

Figure 3.7

Two ways to locate your blind spot. (A) Close your right eye and stare at the cross (+). Hold the page about a foot from your left eye and slowly move the page around until the star falls on your blind spot and disappears. (B) Close your right eye and stare at the cross (+). Hold the page about a foot from your left eye and slowly move the page around until the break in the line falls on your blind spot. The line will then appear to be unbroken.

These two photos of lifeguard chairs approximate cone vision (daylight, clear, colorful) and rod vision (twilight, hazy, colorless).

you were to look directly at it, the image of the nut would fall on your fovea. Remember, your fovea consists almost entirely of cones. Cones do not operate well in relative darkness, and you won't see the nut. To have the best chance of finding it, you have to get the image of the nut to fall on the periphery of your eye, where your rods are concentrated.

One of the reasons nocturnal animals (such as many varieties of owls) function so well at night is that they can see well in the dark—because their retinas are packed with rods. Such animals usually have little or no fovea, or at least have

Animals who see well at night have a preponderance of rods in their retinas.

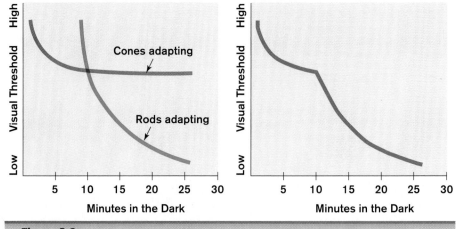

Figure 3.8

The dark adaptation curve. In the graph on the left we see that the cones begin adapting immediately, but then begin "dropping out" at about the 10-minute mark. Rods then begin adapting and continue until about 30 minutes have been spent in the dark. When these two curves are combined to give us a view of what happens in general with time spent in the dark, we have the curve at the right which shows the "rod-cone break."

fewer cones and are demonstrably color blind. (How you might test the color vision of an owl is discussed in Topic 5B, pages 176–177.)

Let's consider one other piece of evidence that supports the idea that our rods and cones provide us with two distinct types of visual experience. Let's take a closer look at what happens during dark adaptation. Dark adaptation is the process of our becoming more sensitive (our thresholds lowering) as we spend time in the dark. Figure 3.8 is a graphic representation of the dark-adaptation process. It shows us that with time spent in the dark, our sensitivity increases, or our threshold decreases. At first, we can see only very bright lights (say, the light reflected from a movie screen), then we can see dimmer lights (reflected from people in the theater), and then still dimmer ones (reflected from pieces of candy perhaps) are detected as our threshold drops. The entire process takes about 30 minutes.

But there is something strange going on. The dark-adaptation curve is not smooth and regular. At about the 8- to 10-minute mark, there is a change in the shape of the curve. This break in the smoothness of the curve is called the *rod-cone break*. At first, for 7 or 8 minutes, the cones increase their sensitivity (represented by the first part of the curve). But our cones are basically daylight receptors. They're not cut out for seeing in the dark, and after a few minutes, they have become as sensitive as they are going to get. They "drop out" of the curve. At about the same time, the rods begin lowering their threshold, becoming even more and more sensitive (represented by the part of the curve after the "break"). This explanation of rods and cones acting differently has remain unchallenged for over 60 years (Hecht, 1934).

Now that we've reviewed the nature of light and the basic structures of the eye, we'll examine how the neural impulses that leave our retinas make their way back to the occipital lobes of the cerebral cortex.

⊚⊚⊚ **Thinking Critically** ⊚⊚⊚

What evidence can you imagine that would be counter to this claim?

Before You Go On

Why can we claim that rods and cones provide us with two different kinds of visual experience?

The Visual Pathway After the Retina

To keep track of what happens to impulses once they have left the eyes at their respective blind spots, follow along with Figure 3.9. First recall that considerable visual processing takes place within the layers of the retina; there are, after all, many more rods and cones in the retina than there are ganglion cell fibers leaving it. Visual information continues to be altered as it races back to the visual area of the occipital lobe of the cerebral cortex.

One challenge in tracing the pathway of nerve fibers between the eyes and the cortex is simply a matter of sorting out left and right. To do so, I need to introduce the concept of left and right visual fields. When you look out at the world, everything off to your left is said to be in your left visual field, whereas everything you see off to your right is said to be in your right visual field. Figure 3.9 is drawn so that the left visual field is red and the right visual field is purple. What happens is that stimuli located in our left visual field end up in our right occipital lobe, and stimuli from our right visual field end up in our left occipital lobe.

The sorting out of which fibers in the optic nerve get directed where occurs largely in the **optic chiasma**. Look at Figure 3.9 again and notice that, in fact, each eye receives light energy from both visual fields. Light that enters our left eye from the left initiates neural impulses that cross at the optic chiasma and go over to the right side of the brain, whereas light that enters our left eye from the right visual field initiates neural impulses that go straight back to the left hemisphere. Now see if you can describe what happens to light that enters the right eye.

From the optic chiasma, nerve fibers pass through other centers in the brain. For example, there is, for each side of the brain, a cluster of cells, a *superior colliculus,* that controls the movement of our eyes over a patterned stimulus, perhaps fixing our gaze on some aspect of the pattern. Curiously, people who are totally blind

optic chiasma *the location in the brain where impulses from light in the left visual field cross to the right side of the brain, and impulses from light in the right visual field cross to the left side of the brain*

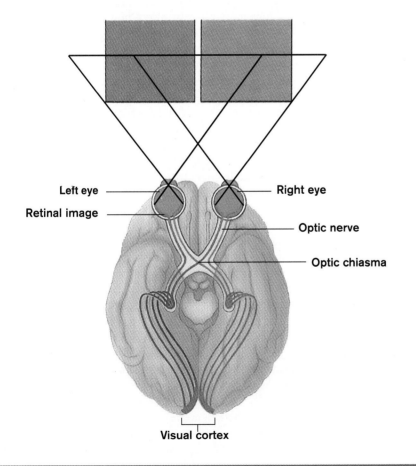

Left eye
Retinal image
Right eye
Optic nerve
Optic chiasma
Visual cortex

Figure 3.9

In keeping with the principle of cross laterality, stimuli from the left visual field are sent to the right occipital lobe for further processing, whereas stimuli from the right visual field are sent to the left occipital lobe.

because of damage to the occipital lobes of their cerebral cortex can still often locate visual stimuli in space. That is, they can point to a light they cannot "see"– probably an example of the superior colliculus at work (e.g.,Weiskrantz et al., 1974). Beyond the superior colliculus, nerve cells form synapses with neurons in the thalamus, which, as we saw in Chapter 2, project neural impulses to the layers of cells in the visual cortex of the occipital lobe.

An important point here is that vision doesn't really happen in our eyes. The eye *is* the structure that contains the transducers that convert light energy into neural impulses, but the actual experience of "seeing" a stimulus is something that happens in our brains. Our brains reassemble in our awareness one complete visual field that we experience as continuous, and not divided into right and left. The detection and interpretation of patterns of light, shade, color, and motion are functions of the cerebral cortex.

Before You Go On

Briefly trace the path of neural impulses from each eye to the cerebral cortex.

Color Vision and Color Blindness

Explaining how the eye codes or responds to various intensities of light is not difficult. High-intensity lights cause more rapid firings of neural impulses than do low-intensity lights, and high-intensity lights stimulate more cells to fire than do lights of low intensity. How the eye codes differing wavelengths of light to produce differing experiences of color, however, is another story. Here things are not simple at all. Two theories of color vision have received research support, even though both were proposed many years ago. As is often the case with competing theories that explain the same phenomenon, both are probably partially correct.

The older of the two theories of color vision is the *trichromatic theory*. It was first proposed by Thomas Young very early in the nineteenth century and was revised by Hermann von Helmholtz, the noted physiologist, about 50 years later.

As its name suggests, the trichromatic theory proposes that the eye contains *three* distinct receptors for color. Although there is some overlap, each receptor responds best to one of three **primary hues** of light: red, green, and blue. These hues are primary because by the careful combination of the three, all other colors can be produced. You see this in action every day on your TV screen, whose picture consists of a pattern of very small dots, each one being either red, green, or blue. From these three wavelengths alone, all other colors are constructed, or integrated. (Don't get confused here with the primary colors of pigment, which are red, blue, and yellow. These are the three colors of paint, dye, pastel, and so on that can be mixed together to form all other pigment colors. Our eyes respond to light, not to pigment, and the three primary hues of light are red, green, and blue.)

Because the sensitivity of the three types of receptors overlaps, when our eyes are stimulated by a nonprimary color, say, orange, the orange-hued light will stimulate each receptor to varying degrees to produce the experience of orange. What gives this theory credibility is that there really are such receptor cells in the human retina. Obviously, they are cones (which are responsible for color vision). The relative sensitivity of these three cone systems is shown in Figure 3.10.

Ewald Hering thought the Young-Helmholtz theory left a bit to be desired, and in 1870 he proposed a theory of his own, the *opponent-process theory*. Hering's position is that there are three pairs of visual mechanisms that respond to different wavelengths of light. One mechanism is a blue-yellow processor, one a red-green processor, and the third deals with black-white differences.

primary hues *red, green, and blue; those colors of light from which all others can be produced*

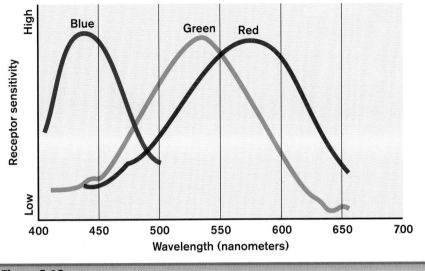

Figure 3.10

The relative sensitivities of three types of cones to lights of differing wavelengths. Although there is considerable overlap, each type is maximally sensitive to wavelengths corresponding to the primary hues of light: blue, green, and red.

Each mechanism is capable of responding to either of the two hues that give it its name, but not both. That is, the blue-yellow processor can respond to blue or to yellow, but cannot handle both at the same time. The second mechanism responds to red or to green, but not both. The third codes brightness. Thus, the members of each pair work to oppose each other, giving the theory its name. If blue is excited, yellow is inhibited. If red is excited, green is inhibited. A light may appear to be a mixture of red and yellow, but cannot be seen as a mixture of red and green because both red and green cannot be excited at the same time. (It *is* difficult to imagine what a "reddish green" or a "bluish yellow" would look like. Can you picture a light that is bright and dim at the same time?)

Although the opponent-process theory may at first appear overly complicated, there are some strong signs that Hering was on the right track. Excitatory-inhibitory mechanisms such as he proposed for red-green, blue-yellow, and black-white have been found. They are not at the level of rods and cones in the retina (as Hering had thought), but at the layer of the ganglion cells (see Figure 3.6) and also in a small area of the thalamus.

Support for Hering's theory also comes from our experiences with *negative afterimages.* If you stare at a bright green figure for a few minutes and then shift your gaze to a white surface, you will notice an image of a red figure. Where did that come from? The explanation for the appearance of this image is as follows: while you were staring at the green figure, the green component of the red-green process fatigued because of all the stimulation it was getting. When you stared at the white surface, both the red and green components of the process were equally stimulated, but because the green component was fatigued, the red predominated, producing the experience of seeing a red figure. Figure 3.11 gives an example for you to try.

Evidence supporting both theories of normal color vision has come from studies of persons with color vision defects. Defective color vision of some sort occurs in about 8 percent of males and slightly less than 0.5 percent of females. Most cases are genetic in origin. It makes sense that if cones are our receptor cells for the discrimination of color, people with some deficiency in color perception should have a problem with their cones. Such logic is consistent with the Young-Helmholtz theory. In fact, for the most common of the color vision deficiencies (dichromatism) there *is* a noticeable lack of one particular type of cone; which type

Figure 3.11

To illustrate the experience of color fatigue, or negative afterimages, stare at the blue circle for about 30 seconds; then quickly shift your gaze to a plain white surface. You should see the same figure, but it will appear yellow because the corresponding blue receptors are fatigued. Now try the same thing with the green triangle. What color did you see when you shifted your gaze?

depends on the color that is "lost." Those people who are red-green color blind, for instance, have trouble telling the difference between red and green. People with this type of color blindness also have trouble distinguishing yellow from either red or green. The deficiency is not in actually seeing reds or greens. It is in distinguishing reds and greens from other colors. Put another way, someone who is red-green color blind can clearly see a bright red apple; it just looks no different from a bright green apple.

Some color vision defects can be traced to cones in the retina, but damage to cells higher in the visual pathway are implicated in some rare cases of color vision problems. When such problems do occur, there are losses for both red and green, or losses for yellow and blue—color pairings predicted by the opponent-process theory (e.g., Schiffman, 1990).

Because cone cells that respond differentially to red, blue, and green light have been found in the retina, we cannot dismiss the trichromatic theory. Because there are cells that do operate the way the opponent-process theory predicts, we cannot dismiss that theory either. Well, which one is right? Probably both. Our experience of color likely depends on the interaction of cone cells and opponent-process cells within our visual pathway—a marvelous system indeed.

Before You Go On

Briefly summarize the trichromatic and the opponent-process theories of color vision.

Audition (Hearing)

There's no doubt that vision is an important sense. Try this little experiment on your own. Try to bypass your reliance on vision and spend the better part of a day doing without it. Try to go about your normal everyday activities blindfolded. One thing you will realize almost immediately is just how heavily you normally rely on vision. But consider for a moment the quantity and quality of information you do receive from your other senses. You soon may come to a new appreciation of your other senses as they inform you of the wonder of your environment: the aroma and taste of a well-prepared barbecue, the sounds of birds and music, the touch and feel of textures and surfaces, the sense of where your body is and what it's doing, the feedback from your muscles as you move. For the rest of Topic 3A, we'll briefly discuss several senses, noting, as we did for vision, the relevant stimulus for each and indicating in general how each sense receptor works. We'll start with hearing (more formally, *audition*) and then move to the chemical senses of taste and smell. We'll consider the skin senses of touch, pressure, and temperature. We'll cover those senses that help us maintain our balance and tell us where parts of our bodies are positioned. Finally, we'll take a look at pain—a sense as mysterious as it is important.

The Stimulus for Hearing: Sound

The stimulus for vision is light; for hearing, the stimulus is sound. Sound consists of a series of pressures of air (or some other medium, such as water) beating against our ear. We can represent these pressures as sound waves. As a source of sound vibrates, it pushes air against our ears in waves. As was the case for light waves, there are three major physical characteristics of sound waves: amplitude, frequency (the inverse of wavelength), and purity. Each is related to a different psychological experience. We'll briefly consider each in turn.

The *amplitude* of a sound wave depicts its intensity—the force with which air strikes the ear. The intensity of a sound determines the psychological experience we call **loudness**. That is, the higher its amplitude, the louder we perceive the sound. Quiet, soft sounds have low amplitudes.

Measurements of the physical intensity of sound are given in units of force per unit area (or pressure). Loudness is a psychological characteristic. It is measured by people, not by instruments. The **decibel scale** of sound intensity reflects perceived loudness. Its zero point is the lowest intensity of sound that can be detected, the absolute threshold. Our ears are very sensitive receptors and respond to very low levels of sound intensity. (In fact, if our ears were much more sensitive, we could hear molecules of air bouncing against our eardrums.) Sounds louder than those produced by jet aircraft engines or fast-moving subway trains (about 120 decibels) are experienced more as pain than as sound. Prolonged exposure to loud sounds causes varying degrees of deafness. The San (or the "Bushmen") of the Kalahari desert in Africa have significantly better hearing at older ages than do natives of the United States and Denmark. There may be several reasons for these differences, but the relative quiet of the desert environment certainly seems to be a significant factor (Berry et al., 1992). Figure 3.12 shows decibel levels for sounds we might find in our environment.

The second physical characteristic of sound to consider is *wave frequency,* the number of times a wave repeats itself within a given period. For sound, frequency

loudness *the psychological experience correlated with the intensity, or amplitude, of a sound wave*

decibel scale *a scale of our experience of loudness in which 0 represents the absolute threshold and 120 is sensed as pain*

Sound is a series of pressures of air that produce vibrations of the eardrum.

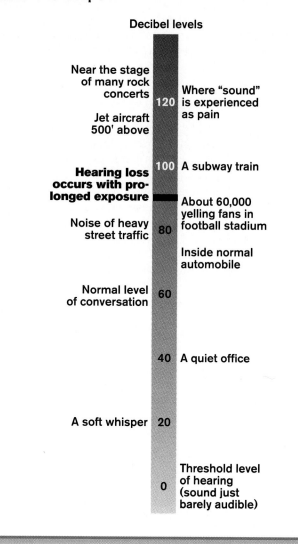

Decibel levels

Near the stage of many rock concerts

120   Where "sound" is experienced as pain

Jet aircraft 500' above

100   A subway train

Hearing loss occurs with prolonged exposure   About 60,000 yelling fans in football stadium

Noise of heavy street traffic   80

Inside normal automobile

Normal level of conversation   60

40   A quiet office

A soft whisper   20

0   Threshold level of hearing (sound just barely audible)

Figure 3.12

Loudness values in decibel units for various sounds.

hertz (Hz) *the standard measure of sound wave frequency that is the number of wave cycles per second*

pitch *the psychological experience that corresponds to sound wave frequency and gives rise to high (treble) or low (bass) sounds*

is measured in terms of how many waves of pressure are exerted every second. The unit of sound frequency is the **hertz**, abbreviated **Hz**. If a sound wave repeats itself 50 times in one second, it is a 50-Hz sound; 500 repetitions is a 500-Hz sound, and so on.

The psychological experience produced by sound wave frequency is pitch. **Pitch** is our experience of how high or low a tone is. The musical scale represents differences in pitch. Low frequencies correspond to bass tones, such as those made by foghorns or tubas. High-frequency vibrations give rise to the experience of high-pitched sounds, such as the musical tones produced by flutes or the squeals of smoke detectors.

Just as the human eye cannot respond to all possible wavelengths of radiant energy, so the human ear cannot respond to all possible sound wave frequencies. A healthy human ear responds to sound wave frequencies between 20 Hz and 20,000 Hz. If air strikes our ears at a rate less than 20 times per second, we will not hear a sound. Sound vibrations faster than 20,000 cycles per second cannot be heard, at least not by the human ear. Many animals *can* hear sounds with frequencies above 20,000 Hz, such as those produced by dog whistles.

A third characteristic of sound waves is *wave purity,* or *wave complexity.* You'll recall that we seldom experience pure, monochromatic lights. Pure sounds are also uncommon in our everyday experience. A pure sound would be one in which all waves from the sound source were vibrating at exactly the same frequency. Such sounds can be produced electronically, and tuning forks produce approximations, but most of the sounds we hear every day are complex sounds consisting of many different sound wave frequencies.

A tone of middle C on the piano is a tone of 256 Hz (again, this means that the source of the sound, here a piano wire, is vibrating 256 times per second). A pure 256-Hz tone consists of sound waves (vibrations) of only that frequency. As it happens, the middle C of the piano has many other wave frequencies mixed in with the predominant 256-Hz wave frequency. (If the 256-Hz wave did not predominate, the tone wouldn't sound like middle C.)

The psychological quality or character of a sound, reflecting its degree of purity, is called **timbre**. For example, each musical instrument produces a unique variety or mixture of overtones, so each type of musical instrument tends to sound a little different from all others. If a trumpet, a violin, and a piano were to play the same note, we could still tell the instruments apart because of our experience of timbre. In fact, any instrument can display different timbres, depending on how it is constructed and played.

With light, we found that the opposite of a pure light was white light—a light consisting of all wavelengths of the visible spectrum. Again, the parallel between vision and hearing holds up. If I have a sound source that can produce all the possible sound wave frequencies, what would it sound like? It would sound like a buzzing noise. The best example would be what one hears when a radio is tuned to a position between stations (FM works better than AM). This soft, buzzing sound, containing a range of many audible sound frequencies, is useful in masking or covering other unwanted sounds. We call a random mixture of sound frequencies **white noise**, just as we called a random mixture of wavelengths of light white light.

The analogy between light and sound, between vision and hearing, is striking. Both types of stimulus energy can be represented as waves. In both cases, each of the physical characteristics of the waves (amplitude, length or frequency, and purity or complexity) is correlated with a psychological experience. All of these relationships are summarized in Figure 3.13.

timbre *the psychological experience of wave purity by which we differentiate the qualities of tones*

white noise *a sound made up of a random mixture of audible sound wave frequencies*

Before You Go On

What are the three physical characteristics of sound, and which psychological experiences do they produce?

Figure 3.13
A Summary of the Ways in Which the Physical Characteristics of Light and Sound Waves Affect Our Psychological Experiences of Vision and Hearing

Physical characteristic	Psychological experience for vision	Psychological experience for hearing
Wave amplitude	Brightness	Loudness
Wavelength or frequency	Hue	Pitch
Wave purity or mixture	Saturation	Timbre

The Receptor for Hearing: The Ear

pinna *the outer ear, which collects and funnels sound waves into the auditory canal toward the eardrum*

eardrum *the outermost membrane of the ear; set in motion by the vibrations of a sound; transmits vibrations to the ossicles*

malleus, incus, and stapes *(collectively, ossicles) three small bones that intensify sound vibrations and transmit them from the eardrum to the oval window*

cochlea *part of the inner ear where sound waves become neural impulses*

basilar membrane *a structure within the cochlea that vibrates and thus stimulates the hair cells of the inner ear*

The energy of sound wave pressures is transduced into neural impulses deep inside the ear. As with the eye, most of the structures of the ear simply transfer energy from without to within. Figure 3.14 is a drawing of the major structures of the ear. We'll use it to follow the path of sound waves from the environment to the receptor cells.

The outer ear is called the **pinna**. Its function is to collect sound waves from the air around it and funnel them through the *auditory canal* toward the eardrum. Air waves push against the **eardrum** (technically called the *tympanic membrane*), setting it in motion so that it vibrates at the same rate as the sound source.

The eardrum then transmits vibrations to three very small bones (collectively called *ossicles*) in the middle ear. In order, they are the **malleus, incus, and stapes** (pronounced *stape-eez*). These bones pass vibrations on to the *oval window*, another membrane, like the eardrum, only smaller. As the ossicles pass sound vibrations to the oval window they amplify them, increasing their force.

When sound waves pass beyond the oval window, the vibrations are in the *inner ear*. The major structure of the inner ear is the snail-like **cochlea**, which contains the actual receptor cells–the transducers–for hearing. As the stapes vibrates against the oval window, fluid inside the cochlea is set in motion at the same rate. When the fluid within the cochlea moves, the **basilar membrane** is bent up and down. The basilar membrane is a small structure that runs about the full length of

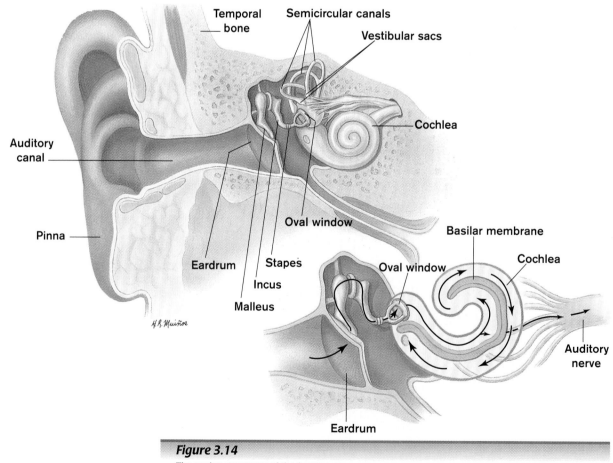

Figure 3.14
The major structures of the human ear.

the cochlea. Hearing takes place when very tiny **hair cells** are stimulated by the vibrations of the basilar membrane. Through a process not yet fully understood, the mechanical pressure of the basilar membrane on the hair cells starts neural impulses that leave the ear, traveling on the auditory nerve toward the temporal lobe. Thus, most of the structures of the ear are responsible for amplifying and directing waves of pressure to the hair cells in the cochlea, where the neural impulse begins.

hair cells *the receptor cells for hearing, located in the cochlea, stimulated by the vibrating basilar membrane; they send neural impulses to the temporal lobe of the brain*

Before You Go On

Summarize how sound wave pressures pass through the various structures of the ear.

The Chemical Senses

Taste and smell are referred to as chemical senses because the stimuli for both of them are molecules of chemical compounds. For taste, the chemicals are dissolved in liquid (usually the saliva in our mouths). For smell, they are dissolved in the air that reaches the smell receptors high inside our noses. The technical term for taste is *gustation;* for smell, it is *olfaction.*

If you have ever eaten while suffering from a head cold that has blocked your nasal passages, you appreciate the extent to which our experiences of taste and smell are interrelated. Most foods seem to lose their taste when we cannot smell them. This is why we differentiate between the *flavor* of foods (which includes such qualities as odor and texture) and the *taste* of foods. A simple test demonstrates this point nicely. While blindfolded, eat a small piece of peeled apple and a small piece of peeled potato, and see if you can tell the difference between the two. You shouldn't have any trouble with this discrimination. Now hold your nose very tightly and try again. Without your sense of smell to help you, such discrimination—on the basis of taste alone—is very difficult.

Taste (Gustation)

Our experience of the flavors of foods depends so heavily on our sense of smell, texture, and temperature that we sometimes have to wonder if there is any sense of taste alone. Well, there is. Even with odor and texture held constant, tastes can vary. Taste has four basic psychological qualities (and many combinations of these four): sweet, salt, sour, and bitter. Most foods derive their special taste from a unique combination of these four basic taste sensations. You should be able to generate a list of foods that produce each of these sensations. Have you noticed that it is more difficult to think of examples of sour- and bitter-tasting foods than of sweet or salty ones? This reflects the fact that we usually don't like bitter and sour tastes and have learned to avoid them. Beyond that, specific taste preferences are culturally conditioned—a reality you may have experienced the first time you visited a so-called "ethnic restaurant" that serves food from another culture (e.g., Berry et al., p. 135).

The receptor cells for taste are located in the tongue and are called **taste buds**. We have about ten thousand taste buds, and each one consists of several parts (Figure 3.15). When parts of taste buds die (or are killed by foods that are too hot, for example), new segments are regenerated. Fortunately, we are always growing new taste receptor cells. That observation in itself makes taste a unique sense: as recep-

taste buds *the receptors for taste located on the tongue*

Taste is a sense independent of smell, but the two usually combine to give us the experience of "flavor."

tor cells, taste buds are nerve cells, and we've already noted that nerve cells are usually not replaced when they die.

Different taste buds respond primarily to chemicals that produce one of the four basic taste qualities. Some receptor cells respond best to salts, whereas others respond primarily to sweet-producing chemicals, such as sugars. These receptors are not evenly distributed on the surface of the tongue; receptors for sweet tastes are concentrated at the tip of the tongue, for example. Nonetheless, all four qualities of taste can be detected at all locations of the tongue.

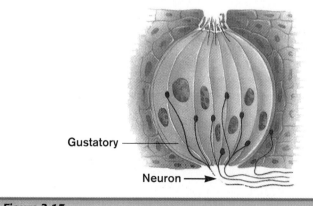

Gustatory ——

Neuron ——▶

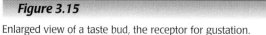

Figure 3.15

Enlarged view of a taste bud, the receptor for gustation.

Smell (Olfaction)

Smell is a poorly understood sense. It is a sense that often gives us great pleasure; think of the aroma of bacon frying over a wood fire or of freshly picked flowers. Smell can also produce considerable displeasure; consider the smell of a skunk, old garbage, or rotten eggs.

The sense of smell originates in hair cells located high in the nasal cavity, very close to the brain itself. We know that the pathway from these receptors to the brain is the most direct and shortest of all the senses (see Figure 3.16). What we don't understand well is how molecules suspended in air, gases, actually stimulate the small hair cells of the olfactory receptors to fire neural impulses.

The sense of smell is very important for many nonhumans. The dog's sense of smell is legendary. Many animals emit chemicals, called **pheromones**, that produce distinctive odors. Sometimes pheromones are released by cells in the skin, sometimes in the urine, and occasionally from special glands (in some deer, this gland is located near the rear hoof). One purpose of pheromones is to mark or delineate one's territory. If you take a dog for a walk around the block and discover that the pooch wants to stop and deposit small amounts of urine on just about every signpost, that dog is leaving behind a pheromone message that says, "I have been here; this is my odor—this is my turf."

It is likely that pheromone production is related to the sex hormones, even in humans. There is evidence that women who live in close quarters for very long, sharing the same air supply (and same pheromones, it is presumed), soon synchronize their menstrual cycles. The same thing occurs in rats when the only contact between them is that they share the same air supply and the same odors (McClintock, 1971, 1979). It is possible that humans use pheromones to attract members of

pheromones *chemicals that produce an odor used as a method of communication between organisms*

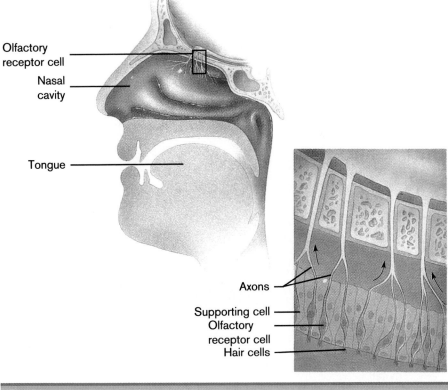

Figure 3.16

The olfactory system, showing its proximity to the brain and the transducers for smell—the hair cells.

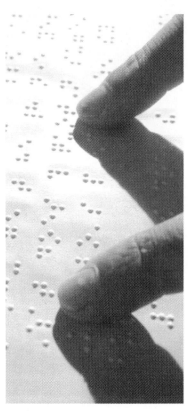

The fingertips contain many receptors for touch.

the opposite sex (Cutler et al., 1986; Wallace, 1977). If we do, the effect is no doubt very small, although people who advertise perfumes and colognes would like us to think otherwise (e.g., Doty, 1986).

Before You Go On

What are the stimuli and the receptors for the chemical senses of gustation and olfaction?

The Skin, or Cutaneous, Senses

Most of us take our skin for granted—at least we seldom think about it very much. We frequently abuse our skin by overexposing it to the sun's rays in summer and to excess cold in winter. We scratch it, cut it, scrape it, and wash away millions of its cells every time we shower or bathe.

Figure 3.17 is a diagram of some of the structures found in an area of skin from a hairy part of the human body. Each square inch of the layers of our skin contains nearly 20 million cells, including many special sense receptors. Some skin receptor cells have *free nerve endings,* whereas others have some sort of covering over them. We call these latter cells *encapsulated nerve endings,* of which there are many types. Our skin somehow gives rise to our psychological experience of touch or pressure, and of warmth and cold. It would be convenient if each of the various receptor cells within our skin gave rise to a different type of psychological sensation, but such seems not to be the case.

One of the problems in studying the cutaneous senses is trying to determine which cells in the skin give rise to different sensations of pressure and temperature. We can discriminate clearly between a light touch and a strong jab in the arm and between vibrations, tickles, and itches. A simple proposal is that there are different receptors in the skin responsible for each sensation, but this proposal is not supported by the facts. Although some types of receptor cells are more sensitive to some types of stimuli, current thinking is that our ability to discriminate among types of cutaneous sensation is due to the unique combination of responses the many receptor cells have to various types of stimulation.

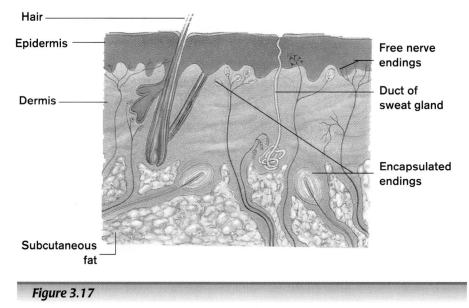

Figure 3.17

A patch of hairy skin, showing the layers of skin and several nerve cells.

By carefully stimulating very small areas of the skin, we can locate areas that are sensitive to temperature. We are convinced that warm and cold temperatures each stimulate specific locations on the skin. Even so, there is no consistent pattern of receptor cells found at these locations—or temperature spots, as they are called. That is, we have not yet located specific receptor cells for cold or hot. Actually, our experience of hot seems to come from the simultaneous stimulation of both warm and cold spots. A rather ingenious demonstration shows how this works. Cold water is run through one metal tube and warm water is run through another tube. The two tubes are coiled together (Figure 3.18). If you were to grasp the coiled tubes, your experience would be one of heat; the tubes would feel hot even if you knew they weren't.

Before You Go On

What are the cutaneous senses, and what are the transducers for each?

The Position Senses

Another sensory capacity we often take for granted is our ability to know how and where our bodies are positioned in space. Although we seldom worry about it, we can quickly become aware of how our bodies are positioned in regard to the pull of

Cold water

Warm water

Figure 3.18

A demonstration that our sense of what is hot can be constructed from sensations of what is warm and cold. Even if you know that the coiled tubes contain only warm and cold water, when you grasp the tubes they will feel very hot.

gravity. We also get sensory information about where various parts of our body are in relation to one another. We can tell if we are moving or standing still. And unless we are on a roller coaster, or racing across a field, we usually adapt to these sensory messages quickly and pay them little attention.

Most of the information about where we are in space comes through our sense of vision. If we want to know just how we are oriented in space, all we have to do is look around. But we can do the same sort of thing even with our eyes closed. We have two systems of position sense over and above what vision can provide. One, the **vestibular sense**, tells us about balance, about where we are in relation to gravity, and about acceleration or deceleration. The other, the **kinesthetic sense**, tells us about the movement or position of our muscles and joints.

The receptors for the vestibular sense are located on either side of the head, near the inner ears. Five chambers are located there: three semicircular canals and two vestibular sacs. Their orientation is shown in Figure 3.14. Each of these chambers is filled with fluid. When our head moves in any direction, fluid in the semicircular canals moves, drawn by gravity or the force of our head accelerating in space. The vestibular sacs contain very small solid particles that float around in the fluid within the sacs. When these particles are forced against one side of a sac, as happens when we move, they stimulate hair cells that start neural impulses. Overstim-

vestibular sense *the position sense that tells us about balance, about where we are in relation to gravity, and about acceleration or deceleration*

kinesthetic sense *the position sense that tells us the position of various parts of our bodies and what our muscles and joints are doing*

Acrobats generally have very keen vestibular and kinesthetic senses.

ulation of the receptor cells in the vestibular sacs or semicircular canals can lead to feelings of dizziness or nausea, reasonably enough called *motion sickness.*

Receptors for our kinesthetic sense are located primarily in our joints, but some information also comes from muscles and tendons. These receptors sense the position and movements of parts of the body—again, information to which we seldom attend. Impulses from these receptors travel to the brain through pathways in the spinal cord. They provide excellent examples of reflex actions. As muscles in the front of your upper arm (your biceps) contract, the corresponding muscles in the back of your arm (triceps) must relax if you are to bend your arm at the elbow successfully. How fortunate it is that our kinesthetic receptors, operating reflexively through the spinal cord, take care of these details without our having to consciously manipulate all of the appropriate muscular activity. In fact, about the only time we realize that our kinesthetic system is functioning is when it stops working well, such as when our leg "falls asleep" and we have trouble walking.

> *Before You Go On*
>
> **What are our position senses, and how do they operate?**

Pain: A Special Sense

The sense of pain is a curious and troublesome one for psychologists who are interested in sensory processes. Pain, or the fear of it, can be a strong motivator; we'll do all sorts of things to avoid it. Pain is surely unpleasant, but at the same time, it is very useful. Pain alerts us to problems occurring somewhere in our bodies, warning us that steps might need to be taken to remove the source of pain. It is the experience of pain that prompts more than 80 percent of all visits to the doctor's office (Turk, 1994). Feelings of pain are private sensations—difficult to share or describe (Verillo, 1975).

What *is* pain? What causes the experience of pain? What are its receptors? To these questions, we have only partial answers. Many stimuli can cause pain. Intense stimulation of any sense receptor can produce pain. Too much light, strong pressures on the skin, excessive temperatures, very loud sounds, and even very "hot" spices can all result in our experiencing pain. In the right circumstances, even a light pinprick can be painful. Our skin has many receptors for pain, but pain receptors can also be found deep inside our bodies; consider stomachaches, lower back pain, and headaches. Pain is experienced in our brains, and the thalamus seems to play an important role, but pain is the only "sense" for which we can find no one specific center in the cerebral cortex (Groves & Rebec, 1992, p. 265).

A theory of pain claims that pain is experienced within the central nervous system rather than in the periphery, and that a *gate control mechanism* (high in the spinal cord) opens to let pain messages race to the brain, or acts to block pain messages by "closing the gate" so that messages never get to the brain for processing (Melzack, 1973; Melzack & Wall, 1965). A *cognitive-behavioral theory* of pain also suggests that central mechanisms are important, noting that pain is influenced by a person's attitudes, expectations, and behaviors (Turk, 1994).

Even without a full understanding of how pain is sensed, there are techniques that can be used to minimize, or manage, the experience of pain. If pain is really experienced in the brain, what sorts of things can we do to keep pain messages from reaching those brain centers?

Drug therapy is one choice for pain management. Opiates such as morphine, when administered systematically, are believed to inhibit pain messages at the level of the spinal cord, as well as at the specific site of the pain (Bausbaum & Levine, 1991; Clinton, 1992; Randall, 1993; Richmond et al., 1993).

Hypnosis and cognitive self-control (trying very hard to convince yourself that the pain you're experiencing is not all that bad and will go away soon) can also be effective in lessening the experience of pain (Litt, 1988; Melzack, 1973).

That psychological processes can inhibit pain is reinforced by data on *placebo effects.* A **placebo** is a substance (perhaps in pill form) a person believes will be useful in treating some symptom, such as pain. When a person is given a placebo that he or she believes will alleviate pain, endorphins are released in the brain and effectively keep pain-carrying impulses from reaching the brain (Levine et al., 1979). This placebo effect is particularly strong when the health care provider is prestigious, empathic, and shows a positive attitude about the placebo (Turner et al., 1994). Another process that works to ease the feeling of pain, particularly pain from or near the surface of the skin, is called *counterirritation.* The idea is to forcefully (but not painfully, of course) stimulate an area of the body *near* the location of the pain. Dentists have learned that rubbing the gum near the spot of a Novocain injection significantly reduces the patient's experience of the pain of the needle.

The ancient Chinese practice of *acupuncture* can also be effective in the treatment of pain. We don't know yet why acupuncture works as well as it does. There are cases where it doesn't work at all, but these usually involve patients who are skeptics, which suggests that at least one of the benefits of acupuncture is its placebo effect. As many as 12 million acupuncture therapies for pain management are performed in the United States each year (George, 1992; Parson, 1993).

Individual responses to pain are unique and are influenced by many factors, such as prior experience, memory of those experiences, and how one feels about pain. It is clear that gender and cultural differences can be involved in the expression or display of pain. In Japan, for instance, individuals are socialized not to show pain—or any intense feeling, for that matter. In our Western culture, men are often socialized not to show pain, to "take it like a man," no matter what. Among other things, these socialization issues often create difficulties in the diagnosis and treatment of an illness or disease where pain is an informative symptom.

placebo *an inactive substance that has its effect because a person has come to believe it will be effective*

> *Before You Go On*

What produces the experience of pain, and how might this experience be reduced?

@@@@ **Thinking Critically** @@@@

What might be the consequences, both positive and negative, of reducing pain?

TOPIC 3A SUMMARY

In this Topic we have defined sensation as the transduction of environmental energy into the energy of the nervous system: neural impulses. For each of our senses we have looked at the stimulus and the receptor mechanisms that give rise to sensations. The stimulus for vision is light, which is transduced into neural impulses by the rods and cones of the retina of the eye. Cones respond best to high levels of illumination and give us the experience of color. Rods are more sensitive than cones, and respond in low levels of illumination. Objects in the left visual field are ultimately projected to one's right occipital lobe. The right visual field is represented in the left occipital lobe. Appreciating color is due to the interaction of cones in the retina and opponent-process structures beyond the retina itself.

Hearing, like vision, is stimulated by physical wave forms of energy, and the measurable characteristics of these waves (amplitude, frequency, and complexity) give rise to distinct psychological experiences of sounds (loudness, pitch, and timbre). Having noted the interrelationship between taste and smell, we reviewed the skin senses, as well as those senses (vestibular and kinesthetic) that inform us about our body's position in space. Finally, we've introduced some of the thinking about the sense of pain. It is clear that at any one time our brains are receiving a remarkable amount of information from our sensory receptors.

T O P I C 3 B Perceiving the World Around Us

Our senses are transducers. They receive information in the form of energy and convert that energy into neural impulses that are sent on to the brain. By and large, our senses can detect very small levels of stimulus intensity. Our senses, then, are constantly bombarding us with bits and pieces of information from the world around us. It is the process of perception that first selects incoming stimulus information to attend to and then organizes, interprets, and tries to make meaningful the data that sensation provides to us. In this Topic, we will examine some of what we know about the cognitive process called perception.

Paying Attention: A Process of Selection

Imagine you are at a party, engaged in a dreadfully boring conversation with someone you've just met. From time to time, it occurs to you that wearing your new shoes was not a good idea–your feet hurt. You are munching on some tasty appetizers. Music blares from a stereo at the other end of the room. Aromas of foods, smoke, and perfumes fill the air. Your senses are being bombarded simultaneously by all sorts of information: sights, sounds, tastes, smells, even pain. Suddenly, you hear someone speak your name. You redirect your attention, totally disregarding the person talking right in front of you.

   What determines which stimuli attract our attention and which get ignored? In fact, whether we perceive a stimulus depends on several factors, all acting at the same time. In this section, we'll discuss some of the important variables that influence what we attend to. These variables are of two general types: stimulus factors and personal factors. By *stimulus factors* I mean those characteristics that make some stimuli more compelling (attention-grabbing) than others, no matter who the perceiver is. By *personal factors* I mean those characteristics of the person, the perceiver, that influence which stimuli get attended to or perceived.

Stimulus Factors in Perceptual Selectivity

The most important stimulus factor in perceptual selection is **contrast**, the extent to which a stimulus is physically different from the other stimuli around it. One stimulus can contrast with other stimuli in a variety of ways. We are more likely to attend to a stimulus if its *intensity* is different from the intensities of other stimuli. Generally, the more intense a stimulus, the more likely we are to select it for further processing. A shout is more compelling than a whisper; a bright light is more attention-grabbing than a dim one; an extreme temperature is more likely to be noticed than a moderate one. This isn't always the case, however. Context can make a difference. A shout is more compelling than a whisper, unless everyone is shouting; then it may be the soft, quiet, reasoned tone that gets our attention. If we are faced with a barrage of bright lights, a dim one, because of its contrast, may be the one we process more fully.

   The same argument holds for the stimulus characteristic of physical *size*. In most cases, the bigger the stimulus, the more likely we are to attend to it. There is little point in building a small billboard to advertise your motel or restaurant. You'll want to construct the biggest billboard you can in hopes of attracting attention. Still, contrast effects are such that when we are faced with many large stimuli, one that is smaller may be the one to which we attend. The easiest player to spot on a football field is often the placekicker, who tends to be smaller and not wear as much protective padding as the other players.

contrast the extent to which a stimulus is in some physical way different from surrounding stimuli

One of the most compelling factors that determine which stimuli we attend to is contrast—the extent to which any stimulus is different from those around it.

A third dimension for which contrast is relevant is *motion*. Motion is a powerful factor in determining visual attention. Walking through the woods, you may nearly step on a chipmunk before you notice it, as long as it stays still—an adaptive camouflage that chipmunks do well. But when that chipmunk makes a dash to escape, it is easily noticed scurrying across the leaves. Again, the *contrast* created by movement is important. As you enter a nightclub, your attention is immediately drawn to the dance floor by the bright lights and the moving throng dancing to the loud music. How easy it is to spot the person on the dance floor, who, for whatever reason, is motionless against the background of moving bodies.

Although intensity, size, and motion are three characteristics of stimuli that readily come to mind, there are others. Indeed, any way in which two stimuli are different (i.e., contrast) can provide a dimension that determines which stimulus we attend to. (Even a small grease spot can easily grab one's attention if it's located in the middle of a solid yellow tie.) Because contrast guides attention, important terms are printed in **boldface** type throughout this book—so you'll notice them, attend to them, and then recognize them as important stimuli.

There is another stimulus characteristic that can determine attention, but for which contrast really is not relevant, and that is *repetition*. Simply put, the more often a stimulus is presented, the more likely it is that it will be attended to—everything else being equal. Note that I have to say "everything else being equal" or I start to develop contradictions. If stimuli are repeated too often, we adapt to them. They're no longer very novel. Even so, there are many examples that convince us of the value of repetition for getting someone to pay attention. Instructors who want to make an important point will seldom mention it just once, but will repeat it. This is why I repeat the definitions of important terms in the text, in the margin, and again in the glossary. The people who schedule commercials on television want you to attend to their messages, and obviously repetition is one of their main techniques.

There are many ways in which stimuli can differ. The greater the contrast between any stimulus and the others around it, the greater the likelihood that that stimulus will capture our attention. Everything else being equal, the more often a stimulus is presented, the greater the likelihood that it will be perceived and selected for further processing.

Before You Go On

Personal Factors in Perceptual Selectivity

Sometimes attention is determined not so much by the physical characteristics of the stimuli present but by personal characteristics of the perceiver. For example, imagine two students watching a football game on television. Both are being presented with identical stimulation from the same TV screen. One asks, "Wow, did you see that tackle?" The other responds, "No, I was watching the cheerleaders." The difference in perception here is hardly attributable to the nature of the stimuli, in that both students received exactly the same sensory information from the same TV. The difference is due to characteristics of the perceivers, or personal factors, which we can categorize as motivation, expectation, or past experience.

I go over my classroom quizzes in class as soon as I have collected all of the answer sheets. Many times I have announced the answer to an item on a quiz to be "D" only to have a student hear me say "B." As you can guess, that student had marked "B" as his answer, and he perceived that I was reinforcing his good choice. He heard not what was there to be heard, but what he wanted to hear. Our *motivation* affects the selection of our perceptions.

It is true that we often perceive what we want to perceive, and it is equally true that we often perceive what we *expect* to perceive. We may not notice stimuli when they are present simply because we did not "know" they were coming—we didn't expect them. When we are psychologically predisposed to perceive something, we have formed a **mental set**.

Take just a second and quickly glance at the message in Figure 3.19. What does the message say? (If you have seen this before, you'll have to try it with someone who hasn't.) Many people say the message is PARIS IN THE SPRING. In fact, there are two *THE*s in the triangle: PARIS IN THE THE SPRING. Most people familiar with the English language (and with this phrase) do not expect there to be two *THE*s next to each other. Following their mental set, they report seeing only one. Others may develop a different mental set. Their reasoning may go something like this: "This is a psychology text, so there's probably a trick here, and I'm going to find it." In this instance, such skeptics get rewarded. There *is* a trick, and if their mental set was to find one, they did so. We will see later (Chapter 7) that our inability to change a mentally set way of perceiving a problem may interfere with our finding a solution to that problem. What we call "creative" problem solving is often a matter of perceiving aspects of a problem in new or unexpected ways. Thus, even as complex a cognitive process as problem solving often hinges on basic perceptual processes.

When we say that what we attend to is due to motivation and expectation we are claiming that what we perceive is often influenced by our past experiences. Much of our motivation and many of our expectations develop from past experiences. We are likely to perceive, or be set to perceive, what we have perceived in the past. Perhaps a personal example will make clear what I mean. I once took a course in comparative psychology that examined the behaviors of nonhuman organisms. One of the co-teachers of the course was an ornithologist (a scientist who studies birds). A requirement of the course was to participate in an early-morning outing to go bird-watching. The memory is still vivid: Cold, tired, clutching my thermos of coffee, I slopped through the marshland looking for birds as the sun was just rising. After 20 minutes of this unpleasantness, our instructor had identified ten or eleven different birds. I wasn't certain, but I thought I had seen a duck. I didn't know what sort of duck it was, but I did think that I'd seen a duck. The differences in perception between my instructor and me that cold, wet morning could

mental set *a predisposed (set) way to perceive something; an expectation*

Figure 3.19

How we perceive the world is determined at least in part by our mental set or our expectations about the world. How many THEs did you see when you first glanced at this figure? Why?

be explained in terms of motivation (he *did* care more than I); but I suspect his ability to spot birds so quickly and surely reflected his past experience. He knew where to look and what to look for.

Our perception of stimuli is usually accomplished without conscious effort, and the process is influenced by several factors. Some depend on the stimuli themselves. The implication is that what we perceive is determined to some extent by the bits and pieces of information we receive directly from our senses. We may attend to a particular stimulus because it is significantly larger, smaller, more colorful, louder, or slower than the other stimuli around it. We then try to organize, identify, and store that stimulus in our memory. This sort of processing is called *bottom-up processing.* On the other hand, whether, or how, stimuli are perceived can also be influenced by the perceiver. In this case, selection of stimuli is a matter of applying concepts and information already processed. Examples include the use of motivation, mental set, and past experience to influence perceptual selectivity. When what one selects and perceives depends on what the perceiver already knows, we have an example of *top-down processing.*

Before You Go On

What personal factors are involved in perceptual selectivity?

Organizing Our Perceptual World

One of our basic perceptual reactions to the environment is to select certain stimuli from among all those that strike our receptors so they may be processed further. A related perceptual process is to organize and interpret the bits and pieces of experience given to us by our senses into meaningful, organized wholes. We do not really hear the individual sounds of speech; we perceive words, phrases, and sentences. Our visual experience is not one of bits of color and light and dark but of identifiable objects and events. We don't perceive a warm pat on the back as responses from hundreds of individual receptors in our skin.

gestalt *whole, totality, configuration; the gestalt is seen as more than the sum of its parts*

Perceptual organization was of considerable interest to the Gestalt psychologists. Perhaps you recall from Chapter 1 that **gestalt** is a German word that means something like "configuration" or "whole." You form a gestalt when you see the overall scheme of things. If you have a general idea of how something works or appreciate the general nature of something without overly attending to details, you've formed a gestalt.

figure-ground relationship *the Gestalt psychology principle that stimuli are selected and perceived as figures against a ground (background)*

A basic principle of Gestalt psychology is the **figure-ground relationship**. Of all the stimuli in your environment, those you attend to and group together are said to be *figures,* whereas all the rest become the *ground.* As you focus your attention on the words on this page, they form figures against the ground (or background, if you'd prefer) provided by the rest of the page. When you hear your instructor's voice during a lecture, that voice is the figure against the ground of all other sounds in the room. Figure 3.20 provides a couple of visual examples of the figure-ground relationship.

Gestalt psychologists were intrigued by how perception groups and organizes stimuli together to form meaningful gestalts. As was the case for perceptual selection, many factors influence how we organize our perceptual worlds. Again, it will be useful to consider both stimulus factors, or bottom-up processing, and personal factors, or top-down processing.

A   B

Figure 3.20

(A) A classic reversible figure-ground pattern. What do you see here? A white vase or two black pro-files facing each other? Can you see both figures clearly at the same time? (B) After a few moments' inspection, a small square should emerge as a figure against a ground of diagonal lines.

Grouping Stimuli with Bottom-Up Processing

Bottom-up processing refers to selecting stimuli as they enter our senses, process-ing those stimuli "higher" in our cognitive systems by organizing them, interpret-ing them, making them meaningful, and storing them in memory. When we talk about bottom-up processing in this context, we're talking about forming gestalts, putting stimuli together based solely on the characteristics of the stimuli them-selves. We've called these "stimulus factors." We'll consider five of the most influ-ential: proximity, similarity, continuity, common fate, and closure.

1. *Proximity.* Glance quickly at Figure 3.21(A). Without giving it much thought, what did you see there? A bunch of *X*s yes, but more than that, there were two identifiable groups of *X*s, weren't there? The group of *X*s on the left seems sep-arate from the group on the right, whereas the *X*s within each group seem to go together. This illustrates what the Gestalt psychologists called proximity, or *contiguity*—events occurring close together in space or time are perceived as belonging together as part of the same figure.

   Proximity operates on more than just visual stimuli. Sounds that occur to-gether (are contiguous) in speech are perceived as going together to form words or phrases. In written language there are physical spaces between words on the printed page. Thunder and lightning usually occur together, thunder following shortly after the lightning. As a result, it's difficult to think about one without also thinking about the other.

   proximity *the Gestalt principle of organization claiming that stimuli will be perceived as belonging together if they occur together in space or time*

2. *Similarity.* Now glance at Figure 3.21(B) and describe what you see there. Here we have a collection of *X*s and *O*s that are clearly organized into a simple pat-tern—as two columns of *X*s and two of *O*s. Perceiving rows of alternating *X*s and *O*s is difficult. This demonstrates the Gestalt principle of similarity. Stimuli that are alike, or have properties in common, tend to be grouped together in our perception—a "birds of a feather are perceived together" sort of thing. Most of us perceive Australian koalas as bears because they look so much like bears, when in fact, they are related more to kangaroos and wallabies than to bears.

   similarity *the Gestalt principle of organization claiming that stimuli will be perceived together if they share some common characteristics*

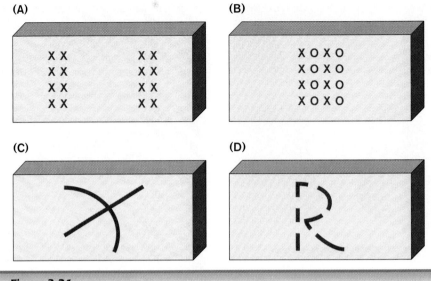

Figure 3.21

Four Gestalt psychology examples of grouping. (A) These *X*s are organized as two groups, not as four rows or four columns, because of *proximity*. (B) Here we see two columns of *O*s and two columns of *X*s because of *similarity*. (C) We tend to see this figure as two intersecting lines—one curved, the other straight—because of *continuity*. (D) This figure is perceived as the letter *R*, not because it is a well-drawn representation, but because of *closure*.

continuity *the Gestalt principle of organization claiming that a stimulus or a movement will be perceived as continuing in the same smooth direction as first established*

3. *Continuity.* The Gestalt principle of continuity (or good continuation) is operating when we see things as ending up consistent with the way they started off. Figure 3.21(C) illustrates this point with a simple line drawing. The clearest, easiest way to organize this drawing is as two separate but intersecting lines—one straight, the other curved. It's difficult to imagine seeing this figure any other way.

Continuity may account for how we organize some of our perceptions of people. Aren't we particularly surprised when a young man who was a hardworking, award-winning honor student throughout high school suddenly does poorly at college and flunks out? That's not the way we like to view the world working. We would not be as surprised to find that another student, who barely made it through high school, failed to pass at college. We want to see things continue as they started off; largely a matter of "as the twig is bent, so grows the tree."

common fate *the Gestalt principle of organization claiming that we group together, within the same figure, elements of a scene that move together in the same direction and at the same speed*

4. *Common fate.* Common fate describes our tendency to group together in the same figure those elements of a scene that appear to move together in the same direction and at the same speed. Common fate is not unlike continuity, but it applies to moving stimuli. Remember our example of a chipmunk sitting motionless on the leaves in the woods? As long as both the chipmunk and the leaves remain still, the chipmunk isn't noticed. When it moves, all of the parts of the chipmunk move together—sharing a common fate—and we see it scurrying away.

closure *the Gestalt principle of organization claiming that we tend to perceive incomplete figures as whole, as complete*

5. *Closure.* One of the most commonly encountered Gestalt principles of organization, or grouping, is called closure. This is our tendency to fill in gaps in our perceptual world. Closure provides an excellent example of what is meant by saying that perception is an active process. It underscores the notion that we constantly seek to make sense out of our environment, whether that environment presents us with sensible stimuli or not. This concept is illustrated by Figure 3.21(D). At a glance, anyone would tell you that this figure is the letter *R,*

but of course it is not. That's not the way you make an *R.* However, it is the way we *perceive* an *R* because of closure.

As an example of closure in audition, tape-record a casual conversation with a friend. Then write down exactly what was said during the conversation. A truly faithful transcription will reveal that many words and sounds were left out. Although they were not actually there as stimuli, they were not missed by the listener, because he or she filled in the gaps (closure) and understood what was being said.

A phenomenon that many psychologists believe is a special case of closure is the perception of **subjective contours**, in which arrangements of lines and patterns enable us to see figures that are not actually there. If that sounds a bit strange, look at Figure 3.22, in which we have an example of subjective contour. In this figure, you can "see" a solid triangle that is so clearly there it nearly jumps off the page. There is no accepted explanation for subjective contours (Bradley & Dumais, 1975; Coren, 1972; Kanizsa, 1976; Rock, 1986), but it seems to be another example of our perceptual processes filling in gaps in our perceptual world in order to provide us with sensible information.

Figure 3.22

An example of subjective contour.

subjective contours *the perception of a contour (a line or plane) that is not there, but is suggested by other aspects of a scene*

Grouping Stimuli with Top-Down Processing

Remember that when we refer to top-down processing, the implication is that one will take advantage of motivations, expectations, and previously stored memories in order to deal with incoming stimuli. In terms of perceptual organization, this means that we often perceive stimuli as going together, as part of the same gestalt or figure, because we want to, because we expect to, or because we have perceived them together in the past.

I can think of no better example in my experience than the one used to open this chapter. Six hundred students claimed to have seen something that did not happen. The problem was not one of perceptual selection. Everybody saw the gun. The problem was one of organization—with whom did they associate the gun? No one was *mentally set* for, or expected the professor to bring a gun to class. No one *wanted* to see the professor with a gun. And no one had *experienced* a professor with a gun in class before. (Seeing crazed students with guns is not a common experience either, but with television and movies, it is certainly a more probable one.)

How we organize our experience of the world depends on several factors. Our perception that some stimuli go together with other stimuli to form coherent figures is a process influenced in part by characteristics of the stimuli themselves (their proximity or similarity, for instance), and by our own motives, expectations, and past experiences.

Before You Go On

What factors can influence how we organize stimuli in perception?

Perceiving Depth and Distance

Perception is more complex and active than is the simple reception of information we call sensation. Perception requires that we select and organize stimulus information. One of the ways in which we organize a visual stimulus is to note not only what it is, but where it happens to be. We perceive the world for what it is—three-dimensional. As long as we are paying attention (surely a required perceptual process), we don't fall off cliffs or run into buildings. We know with considerable accuracy just how far we are from objects in our environment. What is remarkable about this ability is that light reflected from objects and events in our environment falls on two-dimensional retinas. The depth and distance in our world is not something we directly *sense;* it is something we *perceive.*

©©©© **Thinking Critically** ©©©©

For what sorts of professions might it be particularly important to understand how stimuli are organized in perception?

The ability to judge depth and distance accurately is an adaptive skill that plays an important role in determining many of our actions. Our ability to make such judgments reflects the fact that we are simultaneously responding to a large number of cues to depth and distance. Some cues are built into our visual systems and are referred to as *ocular cues.* What we call *physical,* or *pictorial cues,* have to do with our appreciation of the physical environment. We'll also see that one's culture plays a role in the perception of depth and distance.

Ocular Cues. Some of the cues we get about distance and depth reflect the way our eyes work. Cues that involve both eyes are called *binocular cues* (*bi* means "two").

When we look at a nearby three-dimensional object, each eye gets a somewhat different view of it. Hold a pen with a clip on it a few feet in front of your eyes. Rotate the pen until the clip can be viewed by the left eye, but not the right. (You check that by closing first one eye, then the other, as you rotate the pen.) Now each eye (retina) gets a different (disparate) view of the same object. This phenomenon is called **retinal disparity**. It is a cue that what we are looking at must be solid or three-dimensional. Otherwise, each eye would see the same image, not two disparate ones (Figure 3.23).

Another binocular cue to depth and distance is **convergence**—our eyes turning in, toward each other, when we view something up close. As we gaze off into the distance, our two eyes aim outward in almost parallel fashion. As we focus on objects close to us, our two eyes come together, or converge, and we interpret that convergence as an indication that what we are looking at is close to us. Convergence is illustrated in Figure 3.23.

The rest of the cues we'll consider are *monocular,* implying that they require only one eye to have their influence. (Even the physical cues that follow are monocular cues because they can be appreciated by persons who can see with but one eye.) A unique monocular cue, at least for relatively short distances, is **accommodation**. This process, you'll remember, is the changing of the shape of the lens, by the ciliary muscles, to focus images on the retina. When we focus on distant objects, accommodation flattens our lens, and when we focus on nearby objects, our lens gets rounder or fatter. Although the process is reflexive and occurs automatically, our brains react to the activity of our ciliary muscles in terms of the distance of an object from our eyes. Accommodation does not function well as a cue for distances beyond arm's length because the changes in the activity of the ciliary muscles in such cases are too slight to be noticed. But it is within arm's length that decisions about distance are often terribly critical.

Physical Cues. The physical cues to distance and depth are those we get from the structure of our environment. These are sometimes called *pictorial cues* because they are used by artists to create the impression of three-dimensionality on a two-dimensional canvas or paper. Here are some of the most important.

1. *Linear perspective* (see Figure 3.24): As you stand in the middle of a road, looking off into the distance, the sides of the road—which you know to be parallel—seem to come together in the distance. Using this pictorial cue in drawing takes some time and experience to develop.

2. *Interposition* (see Figure 3.25): This cue to distance reflects our appreciation that objects in the foreground tend to cover, or partially hide from view, objects in the background, and not vice versa. One of the reasons I know that people sitting in the back of a classroom are farther away from me than people sitting in the front row is the information that I get from interposition. People (and other objects) in the front partially block my view of the people sitting behind them.

retinal disparity *the phenomenon in which each retina receives a different (disparate) view of the same three-dimensional object*

convergence *the tendency of the eyes to move toward each other as we focus on objects close up*

accommodation *in vision, the process in which the shape of the lens is changed by the ciliary muscles to focus an image on the retina*

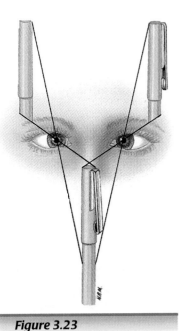

Figure 3.23

When looking at a three-dimensional object, such as a pen, the right eye sees a slightly different image than does the left eye—a phenomenon called *retinal disparity*. This disparity gives us a cue that the object we are viewing is three-dimensional. Here, we also note *convergence*—the fact that our eyes turn toward each other when we view an object that is close to us.

Figure 3.24

Although we know that the sides of a road are parallel, they appear to come together in the distance—an example of *linear perspective*.

3. *Relative size* (see Figure 3.26): This is a commonly used clue to our judgment of distance. Very few stimuli in this world change their size, but a lot of things get nearer to or farther away from us. So, everything else being equal, we tend to judge the object that produces the larger retinal image as being closer to us.

4. *Texture gradient* (see Figure 3.27): Standing on a gravel road, looking down at your feet, you can clearly make out the details of the texture of the roadway. You can see individual pieces of gravel. As you look on down the road, the texture gradually changes, details giving way to a smooth blend of a textureless surface. We interpret this gradual change (which is what *gradient* means) in texture as indicating a change in distance.

5. *Patterns of shading* (see Figure 3.28): Drawings that do not use shading look flat and two-dimensional. Children eventually learn that if they want their pictures to look lifelike, they should shade in tree trunks and apples and show them as casting shadows. Two-dimensional objects do not cast shadows, and how objects create patterns of light and shade can tell us a great deal about their shape and solidity.

6. *Motion parallax:* This rather technical label names something with which we are all familiar. The clearest example may occur when we are in a car, looking out a side window. Even if the car is going at a modest speed, nearby utility poles and fence posts seem to race by. Objects farther away from the car seem to be moving more slowly, and mountains or trees way off in the distance seem not to be moving at all. This difference in apparent motion is known as motion parallax. Observations of this phenomenon during a train ride in 1910 is what first got Max Wertheimer interested in what eventually evolved into Gestalt psychology.

Figure 3.25

Interposition occurs when objects in the foreground partially block or obscure objects that are farther away.

Figure 3.26

All of these hot air balloons are about the same size. Those in the distance project much smaller images on our retinas, however, demonstrating the importance of *relative size* as a cue to distance.

The Role of Culture. In Chapter 8, we will discuss the *development* of depth perception and the extent to which it is a learned or an innate process. But now, I need to note that even something so "natural" as perceiving depth and distance is susceptible to cultural constraints. Here are two classic examples. Turnbull (1961) reported that the Bambuti people of the African Congo live so much of their lives in the dense Ituri Forest that they seldom can see much farther than 100 feet. When Turnbull first took his Bambuti guide out of the forest onto the open plains, the guide, Kenge, was disoriented with regard to cues for distance. Kenge thought that buffalo grazing a few miles away were, in fact, tiny insects, responding more to retinal size than relative size as a cue to distance.

As a second example, take a look at Figure 3.29. If the man with the spear was trying to kill an animal, which animal would it be? Because you are responding to well-known pictorial depth cues such as relative size and interposition, the answer is obvious: the antelope. When pictures such as this one were shown to persons from remote areas of Africa, many failed to react to these "standard" cues and responded that the hunter was trying to kill the elephant (Deregowski, 1972, 1973; Hudson, 1960). In this example, the problem was not one of judging depth and distance in the real world but of interpreting physical cues as represented in a picture or a drawing (Serpell & Deregowski, 1980). With just a little training in how the real, physical world can be represented in pictures or drawings, most cultural differences in the perception of depth disappear (Mshelia & Lapidus, 1990).

Before You Go On

What are some of the cues that provide us with information about depth and distance?

Figure 3.27

Gradients of texture provide cues to distance because we can more clearly see the details of objects that are close to us.

The Constancy of Visual Perception

Perceptual constancies help us organize and interpret the stimulus input we get from our senses. Because of the constancy of perception, we recognize a familiar object as being the same regardless of how far away it is, the angle from which we view it, or the color or intensity of the light reflected from it. You can recognize

Figure 3.28

We see depth and distance in this image of sand dunes largely because patterns of *light and shadow* provide us with information about the three-dimensionality of objects in our environment.

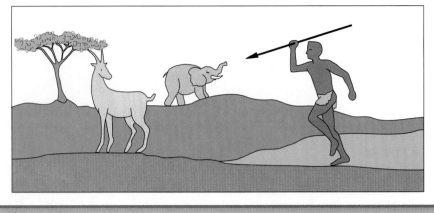

your textbook whether you view it from a distance or close up, straight on or from an angle, in a dimly or brightly lighted room, or in blue, red, or white light; it is still your textbook, and you will perceive it as such regardless of how your senses detect it. If it were not for perceptual constancy, every individual sensation might be perceived as a new experience and little would appear familiar to you.

Perceptual Constancy. *Size constancy* is the tendency to see objects as being of constant size regardless of the size of the retinal image. A friend standing close to you may fill your visual field. At a distance, the image of the same person may take up only a fraction of your visual field. The size of the image on your retina may be significantly different, but you know very well that your friend has not shrunk but has simply moved farther away. Our tendency to view objects as remaining the same size depends on several factors, most importantly the quality of the depth perception cues available to us and our familiarity with the stimulus object.

Shape constancy refers to our perception that objects maintain their shape even though the retinal image they cast may change. Shape constancy may be demonstrated with any familiar object—say, the nearest door in your field of view. As you look at that door from various angles, the shape of the image of the door on your retina changes radically. Straight on it appears to be a rectangle; partially open, the image is that of a trapezoid; from the edge, fully open, the retinal image is of a straight line. But, no matter what the retinal image, because of shape constancy, you still see that object as a door (see Figure 3.30.)

Figure 3.30

At the level of the retina, we experience four different images, yet we know we are looking at the same door because of *shape constancy*.

Because of *brightness constancy,* the apparent brightness of familiar objects is perceived as being the same regardless of the actual amount or type of light under which they are viewed. The white shirt you put on this morning may be *sensed* as gray when you pass through a shadow, or as black when night falls, but it is still *perceived* as a white shirt—in no way darker than it was in the morning. The same is true for color perception. If you know you put on a white shirt this morning, you would still perceive it as white even if I were to illuminate it with a red light. Most of the light waves reflected by the shirt would be associated with the experience of red (about 700 nm), and someone else, who didn't know any better, might perceive the shirt as red, but you'd perceive it as white because of color constancy.

When Constancy Fails: Geometric Illusions and Impossible Figures. By now you should appreciate that the relationship between the "real world" and our perception of that world is tenuous at best. What we come to perceive is often flavored by factors above and beyond any physical reality that impinges on our sense receptors. We have seen several applications of this theme. The interaction between physical reality and our psychological experience can be appreciated when we consider illusions and impossible figures. **Illusions** are experiences in which our perceptions are at odds with what we know as physical reality. In most cases, illusions occur when our usual reliance on perceptual constancies is challenged.

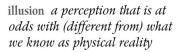
illusion *a perception that is at odds with (different from) what we know as physical reality*

Several simple and compelling geometrical illusions are presented in Figure 3.31. Figure 3.31(A) depicts the vertical-horizontal illusion. Figure 3.31(B) is the same illusion, but in slightly more meaningful terms. Are the lines in Figure 3.31(A) the same length? Yes, you know they are—we're talking about illusions here. Do they *appear* to be the same length? No, they do not. The vertical line seems much longer than the horizontal one. The hat in Figure 3.31(B) seems to be considerably

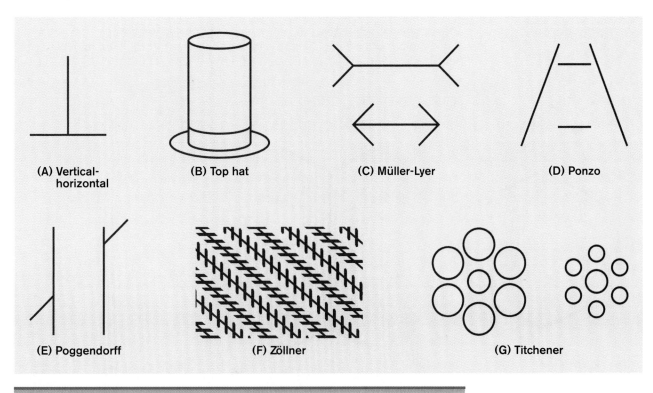

(A) Vertical-horizontal **(B) Top hat** **(C) Müller-Lyer** **(D) Ponzo**

(E) Poggendorff **(F) Zöllner** **(G) Titchener**

Figure 3.31

A few classic geometrical illusions. In each case, you know the answer, but the relevant questions are: (A) Are the vertical and horizontal lines the same length? (B) Is the brim of the hat as wide as the hat is tall? (C) Are the two horizontal lines the same length? (D) Are the two horizontal lines the same length? (E) Are the two diagonals part of the same line? (F) Are the long diagonal lines parallel? (G) Are the two center circles the same size?

taller than it is wide. Notice that the vertical-horizontal illusion works even after you have measured the two lines to confirm that they are the same length. They *still* don't look equal. This is one of three fundamental facts about illusions: they do not depend on our ignorance of the situation.

A second fact about illusions is that they do not occur at the retina. Figure 3.31(C) is the well-known Müller-Lyer illusion, named after the man who first drew it. The top line would continue to appear longer than the bottom one even if the two (equal) lines were presented to one eye, and the arrowlike vanes were presented to the other. A third fact about illusions is that their effects do not depend on eye movements. Illusions appear vividly even when they are flashed before the eyes so quickly that there is no opportunity to scan the presented image (Gillam, 1980).

Illusions of the sort presented in Figure 3.31 are not new. Scientists have been searching for reasonable explanations for illusions for well over a hundred years. How *do* geometrical illusions give rise to perceptions, to visual experiences that are at odds with the physical reality detected by the eyes? Frankly, we just can't say. Several factors seem to be working together to create illusions. A reasonable observation about illusions is that they provide evidence of our perceptual constancies being overapplied. Illusions largely depend on how we perceive and interpret clues to the size of objects in a three-dimensional world, and on inferences we make about the world, given our experience with it (Coren & Girgus, 1978; Gillam, 1980; Gregory, 1977; Hoffman, 1983).

Here's just one example. A reasonable-sounding explanation of the Müller-Lyer illusion is that the vanes of the arrows are taken to represent corners, as in a room. To see what I mean, refer to Figure 3.32(A). When corners are near to us or far away, we are presented with perspective cues to their distance. Hence, we see the arrows of the illusion as representing corners and edges. This view is known as the "carpentered world hypothesis" (e.g., Davidoff, 1975; Gregory, 1977). In fact, in those cultures such as the Zulu in Africa, who through most of their history have lived in circular houses with round doors and domed roofs—without all of our familiar corners and edges—the effects of the Müller-Lyer illusion are difficult to find (Segall et al., 1966). The carpentered world hypothesis sounds pretty good, doesn't

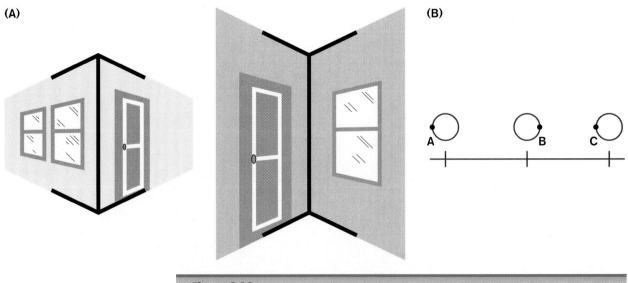

(A)   **(B)**

Figure 3.32

(A) One attempt to "explain" the Müller-Lyer illusion as the representation of edges and corners. (B) A variant of the Müller-Lyer illusion. The distance between the circles A and B is equal to the distance between circles B and C. An explanation in terms of edges and corners no longer seems reasonable.

it? Why, then in Figure 3.32(B) do we see the distance between circles *A* and *B* as greater than the distance between circles *B* and *C* when they are, in fact, equal?

The main instructional point of illusions is that they remind us that perception is a higher-level process than simple sensation; perception involves the organization and interpretation of the information we get from our senses, and things are not always as they seem. This point is made even more dramatically with what are called impossible figures (see Figure 3.33).

Before You Go On

What are the perceptual constancies?
What do the visual illusions teach us about perception?

TOPIC 3B SUMMARY

In this Topic we have focused on perception and how we begin to deal with all the information presented to us by our senses. We've seen that several factors—all working together and at the same time—operate to guide our attention to some stimuli as we ignore others. Some of these factors are inherent in the stimuli themselves, the extent to which they contrast with other stimuli in the environment, or the extent to which they are repeated, for instance. Attention and organization of stimulus inputs are also driven from the "top down" as our expectations, motivations, and past experiences influence what we attend to and how we group stimuli to form meaningful gestalts.

The fact that we organize the world as a three-dimensional environment is a good example of the difference between sensation (where visual stimuli are detected on a two-dimensional surface) and perception (where several interacting factors influence our judgments of depth and distance). We've also seen that without perceptual constancy, every new or different encounter with a stimulus would have to be interpreted as a new and different perceptual experience.

Figure 3.33

Impossible figures—examples of conflicting visual information.

CHAPTER SUMMARY

Topic 3A

Define sensation and perception. What is an absolute threshold, and how is it related to sensitivity?

Sensation is the first step in the processing of information. It involves the transduction of physical energy from the environment into the energy of the nervous system at our sense receptors. Perception is a cognitive process, involving the selection, organization, and interpretation of the information provided by the senses. An absolute threshold is the intensity of a stimulus that can be detected 50 percent of the time. The lower one's threshold for a sense, the more sensitive it is; thus, sensitivity and threshold are inversely related. */pp. 70–72*

What is the difference between a difference threshold and a j.n.d.? Briefly summarize signal detection theory.

A difference threshold is the difference between two stimuli (on any dimension) that can be detected 50 percent of the time. It is that point at which two stimuli are detected to be just noticeably different (j.n.d.). Signal detection theory considers threshold determination as a matter of detecting a signal (or stimulus) against a ground of shifting "noise," where the subjects' biases, motivation, and attention are also considered. */pp. 72–74*

How does sensory adaptation relate to thresholds?

Sensory adaptation is the process by which our sensory experience tends to decrease with continued exposure to a stimulus. In other words, as senses adapt, one's threshold value increases. */p. 74*

In what ways do the major physical characteristics of light affect our psychological experience of vision?

We can think of light as a wave form of radiant energy with three major characteristics: wave amplitude, which determines our experience of the light's brightness; wavelength, which determines our experience of hue; and wave purity, which determines a light's degree of saturation, from the extremes of a monochromatic light to the lowest saturation, white light. */pp. 74–77*

List the major structures of the eye, and describe the function of each.

Before light reaches the retina, it passes through several structures whose function is to focus an image on the retina. In order, light passes through the cornea, the

aqueous humor, the pupil (an opening in the iris), the lens (whose shape is controlled by ciliary muscles), and the vitreous humor. At the retina, after passing through layers of neural fibers that combine and integrate visual information, light reaches the photoreceptors (the rods and cones), the transducers for vision. Neural impulses that originate at the rods and cones are collected and leave the eye at the blind spot. */pp. 77–80*

Why can we claim that rods and cones provide us with two different kinds of visual experience?

Cones, which are concentrated in the fovea of the retina, respond best when stimulated by medium to high levels of illumination (e.g., as by daylight) and respond differentially to light of varying wavelength (or hue). Although rods, concentrated in the periphery of the retina, do not discriminate among hues, they do react to relatively low levels of illumination. Evidence for this point of view comes from common experience, the examination of the retinas of nocturnal animals, and data on adaptation to darkness. */pp. 80–83*

Briefly trace the path of neural impulses from each eye to the cerebral cortex.

Once nerve fibers leave the eye at the blind spot, they travel to the optic chiasma, where some are sent straight back and others cross to the opposite side of the brain. Images from the left visual field are processed in the right side of the brain, and images from the right visual field are processed in the left side of the brain. From the optic chiasma, impulses travel through the superior colliculi, the thalamus, and then to the occipital lobes of the cerebral cortex, where visual experiences are processed. */pp. 83–84*

Briefly summarize the trichromatic and the opponent-process theories of color vision.

These theories attempt to explain how the visual system codes wavelengths of light to give us the experience of color. Young and Helmholtz's trichromatic theory claims that there are three types of cones, each maximally sensitive to one of the three primary hues—red, green, and blue. Hering's opponent-process theory claims that there are three pairs of mechanisms involved in our experience of color: a blue-yellow processor, a red-green processor, and a black-white processor. Processors respond to either of the characteristics that give it its name, but not to both at the same time. There is evidence that supports both theories, some of which comes from our understanding of why some people have defects in color vision. */pp. 84–86*

What are the three physical characteristics of sound, and which psychological experiences do they produce?

Like light, sound may be represented as a wave form of energy with three major physical characteristics: wave amplitude, frequency, and purity. These in turn give rise to our experiences of loudness, pitch, and timbre. */pp. 87–89*

Summarize how sound wave pressures pass through the various structures of the ear.

Most of the structures of the ear (pinna, auditory canal, eardrum, malleus, incus, stapes, and oval window) intensify and transmit the pressure of sound waves to the fluid in the cochlea, which then vibrates the basilar membrane. The basilar membrane stimulates tiny hair cells to transmit neural impulses along the auditory nerve to the temporal lobes of the cerebral cortex. */pp. 89–91*

What are the stimuli and the receptors for the chemical senses of gustation and olfaction?

The senses of gustation (taste) and olfaction (smell) are interrelated, and are referred to as chemical senses because both respond to chemical molecules. The receptors for taste are cells in the taste buds located on the tongue; for smell, they are hair cells that line the upper regions of the nasal cavity. Taste appears to have four primary qualities: sweet, salt, sour, and bitter. */pp. 91–94*

What are the cutaneous senses, and what are the transducers for each?

The cutaneous senses are our skin senses: touch, pressure, warmth, and cold. Specific receptor cells for each of the skin senses have not yet been identified, although they no doubt include free nerve endings and encapsulated nerve endings, which most likely work in combination. */pp. 94–95*

What are our position senses, and how do they operate?

One of our position senses is the vestibular sense, which, by responding to the movement of small particles suspended in a fluid within our vestibular sacs and semicircular canals, can inform us about orientation with regard to gravity or accelerated motion. The other position sense is kinesthesis, which, through receptors in our tendons, muscles, and joints, informs us about the orientation of various parts of our bodies. */pp. 95–96*

What produces the experience of pain, and how might this experience be reduced?

A wide variety of stimuli can give rise to our experience of pain, from high levels of stimulus intensity, to light pinpricks, to internal stimuli of the sort that produce headaches. The central nervous system is involved in the experience of pain, perhaps as a gate-control mechanism in the spinal cord that either blocks or sends impulses carrying information about pain to the brain. Anything that can effectively block the passage of pain impulses— close the gate—can control our experience of pain. This is directly accomplished by the action of endorphins and counterirritation. The experience of pain can be controlled by hypnosis, placebo effects, self-persuasion, and acupuncture. */pp. 96–98*

Topic 3B

What stimulus factors influence the selection of stimuli to be perceived?

Of all the information that stimulates our receptors, only a small portion is attended to, or selected, for further processing. Characteristics of the stimuli themselves may determine which stimuli will be attended to. We are more likely to attend to a stimulus if it contrasts with others around it in terms of intensity, size, motion, novelty, or any other physical characteristic. The repetition of a stimulus also increases the likelihood that we will attend to it. */pp. 99–101*

What personal factors are involved in perceptual selectivity?

The selection of stimuli is partly based on characteristics of the perceiver. Such factors as motivation, expectation (or mental set), and past experience often determine which stimuli are attended to. When characteristics of the perceiver are influential, we say that information is processed from the top down, rather than from the bottom up. */pp. 101–102*

What factors can influence how we organize stimuli in perception?

The organization of stimuli depends in part on the characteristics of the available stimuli, such as proximity, similarity, continuity, common fate, and closure. When these factors influence organization, we have bottom-up processing again. The personal factors that affect perceptual organization are the same as those that influence attention: motivation, mental set, and past experience. */pp. 102–105*

What are some of the cues that provide us with information about depth and distance?

We are able to perceive three-dimensionality and distance even though we sense the environment on two-dimensional retinas because of the many cues with which we are provided. Some have to do with the visual system and are called *ocular cues,* such as retinal disparity (each eye gets a different view of three-dimensional objects), convergence (as we look at something up close our eyes move inward, toward each other), and accommodation (our lenses change shape to focus images as objects move toward or away from us). Cues also come from the environment, including many *physical cues* such as linear perspective (parallel lines seem to come together in the distance), relative size (everything else being equal, the smaller the stimulus, the farther away we judge it to be), interposition (near objects partially obscure our view of more distant objects), texture gradients (details of texture that we can see clearly up close are difficult to determine at a distance), patterns of shading, and motion parallax (as we move toward stationary objects, those close to us seem to move past us more rapidly than do objects in the distance). Reliance on some of these cues may depend on the culture in which one lives. */pp. 105–108*

What are the perceptual constancies? What do the visual illusions teach us about perception?

Constancies bring stability to our perceptual world. With size constancy, we perceive objects as being of the same size regardless of how the size of their retinal images may change. Similarly, shape constancy refers to the stability of our perception of an object's shape regardless of the shape of its retinal image. With brightness and color constancy, we perceive an object's true color and brightness regardless of the intensity or the wavelength of light reflected from it. The geometric illusions can be thought of as a distortion of normal perceptual constancy. They demonstrate the impact of one's culture on perception, and remind us of the difference between the world as we sense it and the world as we perceive it. */pp. 109–113*

PRACTICING PSYCHOLOGY

Sensory Terminology

A significant part of learning about psychology is learning the technical names of various structures and processes—a matter of vocabulary. In grade school, we may refer to the three small bones in the middle ear as the *stirrup, hammer,* and *anvil.* Now, we know them to be the *malleus, incus,* and *stapes;* collectively, the *ossicles.* For each of the following common human senses, provide the technical label for that sense, name the sense receptor, and name the receptor cell(s), or transducer(s)—if known. I've filled in the first one, just to get you started. [Suggested answers can be found on p. 572.]

	Technical Label	Sense Receptor	Receptor Cell(s)
Seeing:	vision	the eye	rods and cones
Hearing:			
Taste:			
Smell:			
Touch:			
Balance:			
Body Position:			

OUTLINE

*T*he National Commission on Sleep Disorder Research (NCSDR) titled its report to Congress *Wake Up America: A National Sleep Alert.* The Commission claimed that 40 million Americans suffer from chronic disorders of sleep and that another 20 to 30 million occasionally experience sleep-related problems. We'll review more of the NCSDR report in this chapter. For now here's a small sample of testimony presented to the commission.

I was experiencing constant daytime drowsiness. I would fall asleep for short periods during meetings, conversations, and public functions. At times, I could awaken and make a very inappropriate comment only to realize that I was commenting on a dream I had just experienced. My associates began to question my mental stability . . . It was my practice in those days to carry a large pin or pocket knife with which I would stab myself in the leg, arm or hand to stay awake at meetings and while driving. (p. 15)

To help you understand narcolepsy, set your alarm for every 90 minutes, and stay awake for ten minutes every time it goes off. Alternate that with periods of 48 hours without sleep. . . . Collapse on the floor each time you are angry, scared, surprised, laughing, or upset. Sleep for 1/2 hour before you drive anywhere; sleep again for 1/2 hour when you arrive. . . . Be late for everything. Fall asleep at every traffic light. . . . I figured out the difference between

4

Varieties of Consciousness

my life as a narcoleptic and dead people. The dead don't have to get up and go to work every day. (p. 35)

The Exxon Valdez, grounded in Prince William Sound, Alaska, in March, 1989, cost our nation billions of dollars: $25 million in damage to the vessel itself; $3.4 million in lost cargo; and $1.85 billion in cleanup costs. We continue to assess the impact of the long-term devastation upon an extremely productive and unique ecosystem, for generations an important resource for local fishermen and the state's tourist industry. The National Transportation Safety Board (NTSB) determined that "the probable cause of the grounding . . . was failure of the third mate to properly maneuver the vessel because of fatigue and excessive workload." The third mate was asleep on his feet and failed to respond to the warning light signaling Bligh Reef. (p. 16)

TOPIC 4A Consciousness: Awake and Asleep

Consciousness is such an integral part of our lives, we might argue that to be alive is to be conscious. Remember that the earliest psychologists (e.g., both Wilhelm Wundt and William James) actually *defined* psychology as the science of consciousness, or mental activity. Dealing with consciousness scientifically proved to be a very tricky business. After years of struggling with a science of consciousness, psychologists were more than happy to abandon consciousness altogether and turn their attention to observable behavior, as John B. Watson (and behaviorism) argued they should. But consciousness would not go away, and within the past 25 years, the scientific study of consciousness has reemerged, resuming its place in mainstream psychology.

consciousness *the awareness or perception of the environment and of one's own mental processes*

Consciousness is the awareness of the environment and of one's own mental processes. Normal, waking consciousness is the awareness of those thoughts, feelings, and perceptions that are active in our minds. With this as a working definition, we might ask how to best characterize consciousness. What are its aspects or dimensions?

Normal Waking Consciousness

We probably have no better description of consciousness than that provided by William James a hundred years ago (1890, 1892, 1904). According to James, there are four basic aspects of what we are calling our normal, waking consciousness. We should keep these four factors in mind—in our own consciousness—as we work through this chapter.

1. Consciousness is always *changing*. Consciousness doesn't hold still. It cannot be held before the mind for study. "No state once gone can recur and be identical with what was before," James wrote (1892, p. 152).

2. Consciousness is a very *personal* experience. Consciousness does not exist without an individual to have it. My consciousness and yours are separate and different. The only consciousness I can experience with certainty is mine. You may try to tell me about yours, but I will never be able to fully appreciate the state of mind that is your consciousness.

3. Consciousness is *continuous*. Our awareness of our environment and of our own mental processes cannot be broken into pieces. There are no gaps in our awareness. We can't tell where one thought begins and another leaves off. James wrote, "Consciousness, then, does not appear to itself chopped up in bits. Such words as 'chain' or 'train' do not describe it fitly as it presents itself in the first instance. It is nothing jointed; it flows. A 'river' or 'stream' is most naturally described. In talking of it hereafter, let us call it the stream of thought, of consciousness . . . " (1890, p. 243).

4. Consciousness is *selective*. Awareness is often a matter of making choices, of selectively attending to some aspect of experience while ignoring others. "We find it [consciousness] always doing one thing, choosing one out of several of the materials so presented to its notice, emphasizing and accentuating that and suppressing as far as possible all the rest" (James, 1890, p. 139). We had a good bit to say about the factors that influence the selective nature of consciousness in our last chapter.

You can appreciate that studying human consciousness scientifically, or experimentally, has been a challenge to psychologists over the years. An even more slippery notion is that consciousness is not an either-or proposition; that it functions to different degrees, or levels, of awareness. Let's now consider levels of consciousness and the possibility of subconscious mental processes.

> *Before You Go On*
>
> What is "consciousness," and what, according to William James, are its major features?

⊚⊚⊚ **Thinking Critically** ⊚⊚⊚

Defining consciousness as we have is fine, but can you generate an *operational definition* of normal waking consciousness?

Levels of Consciousness

The observation that levels or degrees of consciousness vary throughout the day seems intuitively obvious. At times we are wide awake, paying full attention to nearly everything around us. At other times our "minds wander," we're "unfocused," not paying attention to or processing much information of any sort from anywhere. And, of course, when we are asleep there are long periods when we are virtually unconscious, seemingly unaware of what is happening either in the environment or in our own minds.

Levels of consciousness—our awareness of our environment and our own mental processes—vary throughout the day: from being wide awake, to thoughtful daydreaming, to being half asleep, to being in deep sleep.

It also seems intuitively obvious that the higher the level of our consciousness, the better able we are to process (i.e., interpret, understand, recall, or react to) information. Is it not more likely that you will remember something said in class if your consciousness is focused; if you are attentive, wide awake, and straining your attention to understand what is being said? Are you not more likely to trip over something on the sidewalk if you are daydreaming about this weekend's plans rather than remaining fully conscious of the environment around you?

Now we come to the interesting question: Is it possible to process information without being aware of it? Is it possible to process information *unconsciously?* The idea of an unconscious aspect of mind has a long history in philosophy and psychology (Epstein, 1994; Greenwald, 1992; Hilgard, 1992; Kihlstrom, 1987; Whyte, 1960). In this section, we'll focus first on a classic view of the unconscious as proposed by Sigmund Freud, and then briefly consider some contemporary research.

The Freudian View of Levels of Consciousness

Sigmund Freud was trained in medicine, and can rightfully be called the Father of Psychiatry—where psychiatry refers to that subfield of medicine that studies, diagnoses, and treats mental disorders. Early in his career, Freud became intrigued by what were then called "nervous disorders." He was struck by how little was known about disorders wherein one's psychological experiences and mental life seemed to produce pain and suffering for which there was no medical explanation. Freud proposed an elaborate theory of personality (see Topic 9A), and put his ideas about human nature into practice by developing a new technique for treating mental disorders (see Topic 13B). So, you see, we shall be referring to Sigmund Freud again. For now, we are focusing on Freud's view of consciousness, a central aspect of both his theory and of his therapy.

Freud's vision of consciousness is often depicted as an iceberg nearly totally submerged in the sea (Figure 4.1). This iceberg analogy is one that Freud used himself. What does it imply?

Freud wrote that only a small portion of one's mental life was readily available to one's awareness at any given time. Ideas, memories, feelings, or motives of which we are actively aware are said to be *conscious.* It is hoped you are right now conscious of the words you are reading, what they mean, and how you can relate them to your own experience. Aspects of our experience that are not conscious at any one moment, but that can easily be brought to awareness, are stored at a *preconscious* level. Right now you may not be thinking about what you had for dinner last night or what you might have for dinner tonight, but with just a little effort these matters—now in your preconscious—can be brought into your conscious awareness.

Cognitions, feelings, or motives that are not available at the conscious or the preconscious level are said to be in the unconscious. At this level are ideas, desires, and memories of which we are not aware and cannot easily become aware. This is a strange notion: that there are thoughts and feelings stored away in our minds of which we are completely unaware. Freud theorized that the unconscious level of mind can and does influence us. Much of the content of our unconscious mind is there because if we were to think about or dwell on these issues we would experience anxiety and distress. A husband, for instance, who constantly forgets his wedding anniversary and occasionally cannot even remember his wife's name when he tries to introduce her may be having some unconscious conflict or doubts about being married in the first place. (There are, of course, other explanations.) Unconscious mental content—passing through the preconscious—can show itself in dreams, humor, and slips of the tongue. It might be significant that following a lively discussion of some issue, Nathan says to Heather, "Let's rape about this some more some time," when he *meant* to say, "Let's rap about this some more some time." As we'll see, many Freudian techniques of psychotherapy are aimed at helping the patient learn about the contents of his or her unconscious mind.

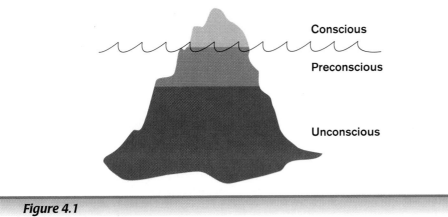

Figure 4.1

In the theories of Sigmund Freud, the mind is likened to an iceberg where only a small portion of one's mental life is available in normal waking consciousness; more is available, with some effort of retrieval, at a preconscious level; and most is stored away at an unconscious level from which intentional retrieval occurs only with great effort.

Demonstrating the reality of levels of consciousness as Freud proposed them has proven difficult in controlled laboratory research. Nonetheless, Freud's basic ideas about levels of consciousness have gained wide acceptance in psychology, particularly among practicing clinical psychologists (Epstein, 1994; Erdelyi, 1985; Greenwald, 1992; Lockhard & Paulus, 1988).

Contemporary Investigations of the Unconscious

Contemporary research is trying to bring the unconscious mind to the laboratory and to describe how (or if) information from the environment can be processed, and how it can influence our behaviors without our awareness. At the moment, virtually all conclusions on these matters are tentative, but we can summarize some of the research being done. A major stumbling block is the "lack of consensus on where the division between conscious and unconscious processes lies" (Loftus & Klinger, 1992, p. 763).

There are two ways in which psychologists assess unconscious processing. In one sense, you have processed information unconsciously if you were not actively attending to that information when it was presented (a matter of perception without awareness). In another sense, you have processed information unconsciously if you cannot verbally report that such information was presented, whether you were paying attention at the time or not (a matter of memory) (Erdelyi, 1992; Greenwald, 1992). In either sense, current research indicates that we sometimes do process things without awareness (Holyoak & Spellman, 1993; Loftus & Klinger, 1992). Let's look at an example of each type of "unconscious processing."

Picture this. You are sitting in a theater watching a movie. Suddenly, there on the screen, in big letters, is a message: BUY POPCORN. If this sort of interruption actually occurred, you'd probably be upset, leave the theater, and demand your money back. But what if the message embedded in the movie was so brief, or so dim that you were not consciously aware of it? If you did not realize the message was there, could it still influence you? Could it influence you to the point of actually going to the refreshment stand and placing an order for popcorn?

When we ask the question this way, the answer is clearly no. The issue here is known as **subliminal perception,** the process of perceiving and responding to stimuli presented at levels of intensity that are below our absolute threshold—below our level of conscious processing. In some ways, it is almost a shame that subliminal perception in this sense does not work. Wouldn't it be wonderful if we could increase our earning potential, or improve our study habits, or build our self-confi-

subliminal perception *the process of perceiving and responding to stimuli presented at levels below one's absolute threshold* dence simply by listening to audiotapes or watching videos into which subliminal messages have been inserted? But these tapes do not work—at least they do not work through subliminal, unconscious processing. Many people claim to have been helped by such tapes, and perhaps they have been. A better explanation is that when people genuinely believe the tapes will help, and have invested time and money in them, they can convince themselves that the tapes are of value (Balay & Shevrin, 1988; Dixon, 1971; Duncan, 1985; Vokey & Read, 1985).

One experiment on subliminal perception examined the changes that occurred when 237 motivated students listened to audiotapes that were supposed to either improve memory or enhance self-esteem through subliminal suggestion (Greenwald et al., 1991). What the students didn't know was that the labels on some of the tapes were switched so that some students who believed they were using the memory enhancement tapes were actually using the self-esteem tapes, and vice versa. Although there *was* some improvement in both memory and self-esteem for everyone, "neither the memory nor the self-esteem tapes produced their claimed effects" (p. 119). Even so, more than a third of the participants in this experiment had the illusion of improvement that the tape's label promised.

Is it true, then, that stimuli outside one's awareness or consciousness never have any effect? No, that's too strong a statement. Although messages directed only at your unconscious mind are not going to influence you to get up from your TV set and march down to the store to buy some new snack food, there is evidence that to some degree we may be sensitive to stimuli presented below our levels of immediate awareness. Here's one example of that sort of evidence.

A person sits in front of a small screen. A word is flashed on the screen so dimly and so quickly that the person does not report seeing the word. Let's say the word is STARS. Now two words are flashed on the screen that the subject can see clearly. The task is to choose the word related in some way to the word that was not seen. Let's say the words used in this example are STRIPES and PENCIL. Even when subjects claim they are only guessing, they choose STRIPES significantly more frequently than chance would predict. If the "unconscious prompt" were ERASER, not STARS, they would more likely choose PENCIL. It is as if the initially presented word influenced their choice (Cheesman & Merikle, 1984; Dixon, 1971, 1981; Fowler et al., 1981; Tulving & Schacter, 1990). For that matter, simply reading a list of words at one point in time increases the ability of subjects to read those words later when they are flashed very briefly on a computer screen, even if the subjects did not recognize that the words had been read previously (Jacoby & Dallas, 1981). We'll return to this issue when we discuss memory in Chapter 6.

So is there an unconscious mind, and if so, what is it like? There is little doubt that we can process some information without our full awareness—unconsciously, if you will. At present, the data suggest that the unconscious is unsophisticated and primitive in terms of the amount or type of information it can handle.

> A large body of research now suggests that the reality of unconscious processes is no longer questionable. Although there is not uniform agreement about how sophisticated these processes are, there seems to be a general consensus that the unconscious may not be as smart as previously believed. More important, there is absolute agreement that exciting times, both in research and theory, are ahead for the unconscious. (Loftus & Klinger, 1992, p. 764)

Before You Go On

How did Freud describe consciousness?

How may we characterize the unconscious processing of information?

Sleep and Dreaming

Sleep reduces our alertness, awareness, and perception of events occurring around us. Sleep is a normal process, yet it is one we do not understand well. We are seldom aware or conscious of our own sleeping, even though we may spend more than 200,000 hours of our lifetime asleep. Just as the level or degree of our awareness varies during the day, so does our sleep vary in its level or quality throughout the night and from night to night. The study of sleep and dreams has intrigued psychologists for many years. Here, we will examine some of what we know about the altered state of consciousness we call sleep.

The Stages of a "Good Night's Sleep"

How do we know when someone is asleep? Self-reports of sleeping are notoriously unreliable. A person who claims that he or she "didn't sleep a wink last night" may have slept soundly for many hours (Dement, 1974).

Our best indicators of sleep are measurements of brain activity and muscle tone. The **electroencephalogram (EEG)** is an instrument that measures and records the electrical activity of the brain. It does so by means of small electrodes pasted onto the scalp. Each of those electrodes is measuring the summation of the action potentials of hundreds of the neurons that lie below it. The process is slightly messy, but it is in no way painful. The **electromyogram (EMG)** similarly produces a record of a muscle's activity, tone, or state of relaxation.

When you are in a calm, relaxed state, with your eyes closed, but not yet asleep, your EEG pattern shows a rhythmic cycle of brain wave activity called **alpha activity**. In this presleep stage, we find smooth EEG waves cycling 8 to 12 times per second. If, as you lie still, you start worrying about an event of the day or try to solve a problem, the alpha waves become disrupted and are replaced by an apparently random pattern of heightened electrical activity typical of what we usually find in wakefulness.

As you drift from rest and relaxation into sleep, your brain waves change, as alpha waves give way to the stages of sleep. The EEG tracings of sleeping subjects reveal that sleep can be divided into four stages (Borbely, 1986). As I review these four stages, you can refer to Figure 4.2, which shows the EEGs of a person in each stage of sleep.

Stage 1: This is a very light sleep from which you can be easily aroused. The smooth, cyclical alpha pattern disappears, replaced by the slower theta waves (3–7 cycles per second). The amplitude, or magnitude, of the electrical activity also lessens considerably. At the same time, your breathing is becoming more regular, and your heart rate is slowing and blood pressure is decreasing. This stage does not last long—generally less than 10 minutes. Then you start to slide into stage 2 sleep.

Stage 2: In this stage, the EEG pattern is similar to stage 1—low amplitude, with no noticeable wavelike pattern. The difference is that we now see *sleep spindles* in the EEG record. These are brief, high-amplitude bursts of electrical activity that occur with regularity (about every 15 seconds). You're really getting off to sleep now, but still can be easily awakened.

Stage 3: You're getting into deep sleep now. There is a reduction in the brain's electrical activity. We can clearly make out *delta wave* activity in your EEG. Delta waves are high, slow waves (from 0.5 to 3 cycles per second). In this stage, delta waves constitute between 20 and 50 percent of your EEG pattern. Your internal functions (temperature, heart rate, breathing) are lowering and slowing. It's going to be difficult to wake you now.

electroencephalogram (EEG) *an instrument used to measure and record the electrical activity of the brain*

electromyogram (EMG) *an instrument used to measure and record muscle tension or relaxation*

alpha activity *an EEG pattern associated with quiet relaxation and characterized by slow wave cycles of 8 to 12 per second*

Stage 4: Now you're in deep sleep. Your EEG record is virtually filled with slow, recurring delta waves (as opposed to stage 3 sleep, where delta waves made up only a portion of your brain wave activity). Readings from an electromyogram indicate that your muscles have become totally relaxed. About 15 percent of your night's sleep will be spent in this stage of sleep.

It usually takes about an hour to go from stage 1 to stage 4, depending on such things as how tired you are and the physical conditions that surround you. We'll assume a quiet, dark room, with a comfortable and familiar bed. After an hour's passage through these four stages, the sequence begins to reverse itself. You go back through stage 3 to stage 2, but before going through the stages again, something remarkable happens. Your eyes move rapidly under closed eyelids.

Before You Go On

What are the EEG and the EMG?

Briefly describe the four stages of sleep.

REM and NREM Sleep

In the early 1950s, Nathaniel Kleitman and Eugene Aserinsky made quite a discovery. They noticed that as sleeping subjects began their second series of stages into

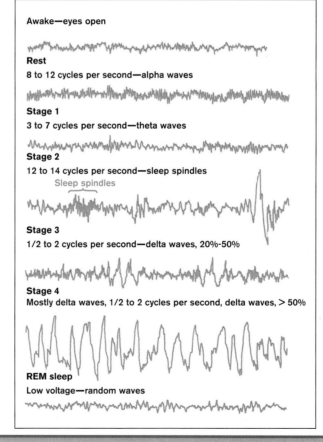

Awake—eyes open

Rest
8 to 12 cycles per second—alpha waves

Stage 1
3 to 7 cycles per second—theta waves

Stage 2
12 to 14 cycles per second—sleep spindles
Sleep spindles

Stage 3
1/2 to 2 cycles per second—delta waves, 20%-50%

Stage 4
Mostly delta waves, 1/2 to 2 cycles per second, delta waves, > 50%

REM sleep
Low voltage—random waves

Figure 4.2

EEG records showing the general electrical activity of the brain for a person at various stages of sleep and wakefulness.

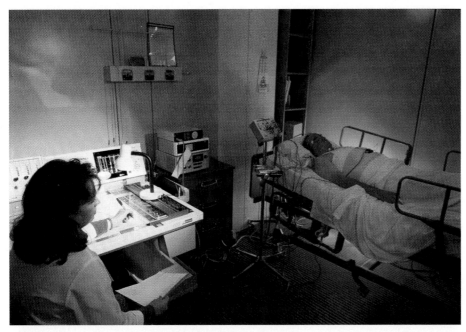

Volunteers (and patients with sleep disorders) in sleep laboratories provide scientists with information about human sleep patterns. Electrodes attached to the scalp provide an indication of brain activity with EEG records.

deeper levels of sleep, their eyes darted back and forth under their closed eyelids (Aserinsky & Kleitman, 1953; Kleitman, 1963b). This period of rapid eye movement is called **REM sleep**. A noteworthy aspect of this discovery is that when people are awakened during REM sleep, they usually (about 85 percent of the time) report that they are having a vivid, storylike dream. When awakened during sleep periods not accompanied by rapid eye movements—NREM (nonREM) sleep—people report fewer and much more fragmented dreams (Kleitman, 1963a; NCSDR, 1993). At first it was believed that eye movements during REM sleep were being made as the dreamer literally viewed, or scanned, images produced by the dream. It turns out that a dreamer's eye movements are unrelated to the content of his or her dream. Eye movements are produced instead by a cluster of cells in the brain stem near other clusters of cells that have been implicated in moving us in and out of REM and NREM sleep (Hobson, 1977; Kiester, 1980).

Periods of REM sleep occur throughout the night, normally lasting from a few minutes to half an hour, occupying about 20 to 25 percent of the sleep of adult humans. About 90 to 120 minutes each night are spent in REM sleep. During these REM periods, we are probably dreaming. As one goes through a night's sleep, REM episodes tend to become longer and dreams more vivid (NCSDR, 1993). The normal pattern of REM episodes is presented in Figure 4.3. Note that during the course of a night's sleep, one does not necessarily pass through all stages of sleep in an orderly fashion. Occasionally stage 3 may be passed over completely; later in the evening, stage 4 may be absent. Indeed, toward the end of our sleeping, we tend not to return to the deep sleep of stage 4 between REM episodes. If you refer to Figure 4.2, you will find an EEG tracing typical of the sort found during REM sleep. Note that it looks much like the tracing indicating wakefulness.

Everyone REMs. Everyone dreams. Some of us have difficulty remembering what we have dreamed when we awake in the morning, but we can be sure that in the course of a normal night's sleep, we have dreamed several times. There's no great mystery why we don't remember our dreams any better than we do. Most dreams are ordinary, boring, and forgettable. Unless we make some conscious effort to do so, we seldom try to store dream content in our memories so that it can be recalled later. That is, we are seldom motivated to remember our dreams.

REM sleep *rapid-eye-movement sleep, during which vivid dreaming occurs, as do heightened levels of physiological functioning*

Freud believed that dreams allow the unconscious mind the freedom to express itself without burdening the conscious mind with fears and anxieties. Many of the paintings of Salvador Dali (such as this image, titled *Solitude*) appear to be renderings of a mind in a dream state.

Although we're sure that everyone does dream, we're less sure *why* everyone dreams. Some theories have their basis in the writings of Freud (1900), who believed that dreaming allows us the opportunity to engage in fantasy and wish fulfillment of a sort that might cause us discomfort or embarrassment if we entertained such thoughts while we were awake. Freud saw dreams as a pathway (which he called the "royal road") to the discovery of the contents of our unconscious mind.

Modern theories about REM sleep and dreaming emphasize the physiological activity that occurs during this phase of sleep. One hypothesis is that REM sleep

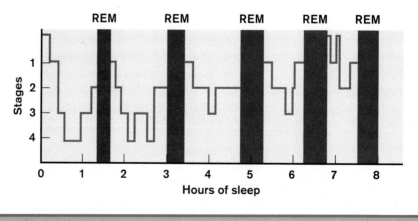

Figure 4.3

A typical sequence of sleep stages during a night's sleep for a young adult. Notice the recurring REM sleep throughout the night, and note that one does not need to enter each stage of sleep in the same order or sequence.

helps the brain form, or consolidate, memories of events that occurred during the day. In one study, for example, students were less able to recall stories they read before they went to bed if their REM sleep was interrupted during the night (Tilley & Empson, 1978).

Another hypothesis is that dreams (and our recall of them) represent convenient cognitive "explanations" for what may be the random activity of our brains. For example, if the area of the brain associated with the movement of our legs is active while we are asleep, our brain will "manufacture" a reasonable story—a dream—that involves kicking, running, or using our leg muscles (Hobson, 1988; Hobson & McCarley, 1977).

These theories are consistent with contemporary theories about why we sleep in the first place. One theory argues that there are several networks of neurons involved in falling asleep, not just one brain center that controls whether we are awake or asleep. Some of these groups of neurons are involved in critical, but infrequent, activities (such as informing us that our body temperature is too high). We sleep, then, to activate these seldom-used neuron groups in order to maintain their function (Krueger & Obal, 1993; Saunders & Sullivan, 1994).

Dreaming isn't all that happens during REM sleep. From the outside, someone in REM sleep seems quiet and calm, except for those barely noticeable eye movements. On the inside, however, is quite a different story. One change is a muscular immobility, called **atonia**, caused by the total relaxation of the muscles (Chase & Morales, 1990). It does seem adaptive to have the body lie still so that the dreamer does not react to the action of his or her dreams. This state of immobilization is occasionally interrupted by slight muscle "twitches" (which you may have seen if you've watched a sleeping dog that seems to be chasing an imaginary rabbit in a dream). Some people do not demonstrate normal atonia but thrash about wildly during REM sleep, a condition reasonably called *REM sleep disorder* (Mahowald & Schenck, 1989).

atonia muscular immobility, associated with REM sleep, caused by the total relaxation of the muscles

In many ways, the REM sleeper is very active even though not conscious of most external stimulation. During REM sleep there is often an excitement of the sex organs, males having a penile erection, females having a discharge of vaginal fluids (although this latter finding is not as common). Breathing usually becomes shallow and rapid. Blood pressure levels may skyrocket and heart rates increase, all while the person lies "peacefully" asleep. There does not appear to be very much that is peaceful or quiet about REM sleep. These changes occur no matter what the sleeper is dreaming about—whether lying on the beach getting a tan, having a sexual encounter, or engaging in hand-to-hand combat, physiologically, the reactions are the same. This marked increase in physiological activity during REM sleep has long been suspected to be related to heart attacks, strokes, and other cardiovascular problems that can develop "even though the patient was asleep" (King et al., 1973; Kirby & Verrier, 1989; Somers et al., 1993).

Before You Go On

What are REM and NREM sleep?

Sleep Deprivation and Disorders of Sleep

"Each year, the lives of millions of American men, women, and children are disturbed, disrupted, or destroyed by sleep deprivation, sleep disorders, or sleep disturbances." So begins the report of the National Commission on Sleep Disorders Research (NCSDR, 1993, p. 15). In this section, we'll consider some of the issues that have concerned this commission.

We are a nation in need of a good night's sleep. On average, Americans get about 1.5 hours less sleep each night than they need. This reflects an average re-

Thinking Critically

Choose one of the theories discussed above about why people REM, and describe an experiment that might test that theory, providing evidence either for or against the position.

According to the National Commission on Sleep Disorder Research (NCSDR), we are a nation badly in need of sleep. The commission reports that interstate truck drivers regularly get fewer than five hours of sleep a night.

duction in nightly sleep of nearly 20 percent over the last century—due to a myriad of factors, including demands of the workplace, school, home, and family. Interstate truck drivers, for instance, regularly get less than five hours of sleep a night (NCSDR, 1993). Each of us requires a specific amount of sleep in a 24-hour period to maintain optimal waking activity. "A good night's sleep" is the amount of sleep that will allow a person to awaken without the use of some device or environmental influence, such as an alarm clock. If a person does not get an adequate amount of sleep (yes, there are individual differences in terms of how much sleep is adequate), he or she will be less alert and less able to function well the next day. What is particularly troubling is that sleep loss accumulates from one night to the next as a "sleep debt." The more sleep lost each day, the greater the debt, and the more severe the consequences.

Most sleep deprivation studies—in which humans or animals are awakened so as to disrupt their sleep—show remarkably few long-term adverse side-effects (Horne, 1988; Martin, 1986; Webb & Cartwright, 1978). Even if sleep is disrupted over several nights, there are few lasting changes in a person's reactions, particularly if the person is in good physical and psychological health to begin with. If, after deprivation, a task is interesting enough and if it is not lengthy or time-consuming, there is little impairment of intellectual functioning (Dement, 1974; Webb, 1975). At least up to a point, we can adapt to deprivation, perhaps by taking little catnaps while we're awake. Very short episodes of sleep, called microsleeps, can be found in the EEG records of waking subjects, both animal and human. These microsleep episodes increase in number when normal sleep is disrupted.

That's not to say that there aren't any effects of being deprived of sleep. Some people show marked signs of depression and irritability when their sleep is interrupted (Moorecroft, 1987, 1989). People deprived of REM sleep for a few nights and then left alone will spend long periods REMing, as if to catch up on lost REMs. This REM rebound effect is generally found only for the first night after deprivation, then patterns return to normal. There is some evidence that NREM sleep (particularly stage 4 deep sleep) also rebounds (Agnew et al., 1964). When, in 1965, 17-year-old Randy Gardner set the world record by going without sleep for nearly 266 hours, he slept for 14 hours the first night after deprivation, but by the second night he returned to his normal 8 hours of sleep. The current record holder for sleeplessness, Maureen Weston, went nearly 19 days without sleep and similarly experienced no lasting effects once given the opportunity to reduce her sleep debt.

A good night's sleep is a wonderful and apparently necessary thing. Some people have no difficulty sleeping. Others experience problems, either in getting to sleep in the first place, or during sleep itself. As is the case for so many psychological processes, we often take sleep for granted until we experience problems with it.

insomnia *the inability to fall asleep or stay asleep*

Insomnia. At some time or another, each of us has suffered from a bout of **insomnia**—the inability to fall asleep or stay asleep when we want to. We may be excited or worried about something that is going to happen the next day. We may have overstimulated our autonomic nervous systems with drugs such as caffeine. However, most people who chronically (regularly) suffer from insomnia haven't the slightest idea why they are unable to get a good night's sleep. Chronic, debilitating insomnia afflicts nearly 30 million Americans, women more commonly than men, and the elderly about 1.5 times as often as younger adults (Fredrickson, 1987; NCSDR, 1993).

An interesting finding from the sleep laboratory is that many people who believe they are not getting enough sleep are, in fact, sleeping much more than they think. The phenomenon is called *pseudoinsomnia,* and one hypothesis is that such people spend several dream episodes each night dreaming that they are awake and trying to get to sleep. Then, in the morning, they remember their dreams and come to believe that they haven't slept at all (e.g., Dement, 1974). Pseudoinsomnia can usually be cured simply by demonstrating to patients that they really are getting a good night's sleep, as indicated by their EEG records.

Prescribing sleeping pills (common in nursing home settings) and using over-the-counter medications to treat insomnia may cause more problems than it solves. The medication (usually sedatives or depressants) may have a positive effect for a while, but eventually dosages have to be increased as tolerance builds. When the medications are discontinued, a rebound effect occurs that makes it more difficult to get to sleep than it had been before (Kales et al., 1979; Kripke & Gillin, 1985; Pal-fai & Jankiewicz, 1991).

Narcolepsy. **Narcolepsy** involves going to sleep, even during the day, without any intention to do so. Symptoms include excessive sleepiness, brief episodes of muscle weakness or paralysis precipitated by strong emotion, paralysis upon falling asleep, and dreamlike images that occur as soon as one goes to sleep (in a narcoleptic episode, one immediately goes into REM sleep). No one knows exactly what causes narcolepsy, and the disorder seems resistant to treatment. Although only 50,000 cases of the disorder have been diagnosed, nearly 350,000 Americans suffer from narcolepsy (NCSDR, 1993). The big problem with narcolepsy (in addition to the embarrassment it may cause) is the total relaxation of muscle tone that is associated with REM sleep (Dement, 1974; Lucas et al., 1979). The danger involved in suddenly going to sleep and losing muscle control during one's daily activities is obvious.

narcolepsy a disorder that involves unintentional sleeping, muscle paralysis, and immediate REM sleep; it is resistant to treatment

Sleep Apnea. Apnea means a sudden stoppage in breathing, literally "without breath." If we were to stop breathing when awake and conscious, we could do something about it. We can exercise conscious, voluntary control over our breathing. We cannot do so, however, when we are asleep. **Sleep apnea** involves patterns of sleep during which breathing stops entirely. Episodes are usually short, and long-term dangers are few. When apnea episodes are longer—say, a minute or two—carbon dioxide in the lungs builds to such a level that the sleeper is awakened, draws a few gasps of air, and returns to sleep, probably oblivious to what just happened. Potential consequences of sleep apnea include hypertension, coronary heart disease, stroke, psychiatric problems, impotence, and memory loss. The Commission on Sleep Disorders Research estimates that 38,000 cardiovascular deaths due to sleep apnea occur each year (1993, p. 33).

sleep apnea involves patterns of sleep during which breathing stops entirely

For reasons not clearly understood, sleep apnea appears most commonly in obese, middle-aged males. Sleep apnea is also a prime suspect in the search for a cause of Sudden Infant Death Syndrome, or SIDS. In this syndrome, young infants, apparently without any major illness, but sometimes with a slight cold or infection, suddenly die in their sleep. Such sudden death occurs at a rate of about two infants per thousand.

Before You Go On

What are the effects of sleep deprivation?
What are three common sleep disorders?

TOPIC 4A SUMMARY

Consciousness is the awareness of the environment and of one's own mental processes. Normal, waking consciousness is always changing, personal, continuous, and selective. Human consciousness occurs to differing degrees or differing levels of awareness. In fact, the processing of some information may occur without our awareness and is said to be unconscious. Freud argued that the information in our unconscious minds is (typically, at least) the sort of information that would cause us anxiety or distress if it were to be dealt with on a conscious level. Contemporary research suggests that there may be something to unconscious processing, but, so far, that processing seems very limited and simple.

We spend nearly one-third of our lives in that altered state of consciousness we call sleep. EEG tracings show us that sleep flows through four discernible stages. The distinction between REM and NREM sleep is made on the basis of involuntary rapid eye movements. REM sleep is associated with clear, vivid dreaming episodes and occupies about one-quarter of our sleeping time. During rapid eye movement (REM) sleep, we experience atonia and an activation of the sympathetic division of the ANS. Millions of people are afflicted by disturbances of sleep, many simply not getting enough sleep. Short-term consequences of sleep deprivation are not severe and can be rectified with just one or two nights of normal sleep. Long-term effects can be serious. Common disorders of sleep include insomnia (an inability to fall asleep and stay asleep when one wants to), narcolepsy (rapidly falling asleep, even in the daytime, without intention), and sleep apnea (patterns of sleep in which one stops breathing).

TOPIC 4B Voluntary Alterations of Consciousness

We have reviewed some of the evidence and theories that focus on how consciousness normally changes throughout the day when we are awake, and how it varies thoughout the night as we sleep. The changes in consciousness that we've addressed so far are quite automatic and involuntary. We don't really decide exactly when we'll go to sleep or when we'll REM and dream, or when we'll spontaneously awaken. These alterations in consciousness just "happen." Now we direct our attention to those altered states of consciousness that normally require some effort to attain. We'll consider three processes that alter consciousness: hypnosis, meditation, and the use of psychoactive drugs.

Hypnosis

hypnosis *an altered state of consciousness characterized by an increase in suggestibility, attention, and imagination*

Hypnosis is a state of consciousness that typically requires the voluntary cooperation of the person being hypnotized. Hypnosis is characterized by (1) a marked increase in suggestibility, (2) a focusing of attention, (3) an exaggerated use of imagination, (4) an unwillingness or inability to act on one's own, and (5) an unquestioning acceptance of distortions of reality (Hilgard & Hilgard, 1975). There is little truth to the belief that being hypnotized is like going to sleep. Few of the characteristics of sleep are to be found in the hypnotized subject. EEG patterns, for example, are significantly different.

Hypnosis has been used, with varying degrees of success, for several purposes. As you know, it is used as entertainment, as a show business routine where members of an audience are hypnotized—usually to do silly things in public. Hypnosis has long been seen as a method for gaining access to memories of events not in immediate awareness. It has been touted as a treatment for a wide range of psychological and physical disorders. In this section, we'll consider some common questions about hypnosis.

1. *Can everyone be hypnotized?* No, probably not. The susceptibility to hypnosis varies from person to person. Some people resist and cannot be hypnotized. Contrary to popular belief, you cannot be hypnotized against your will, which is one reason why I say that one enters a hypnotic state voluntarily (Some hyp-

Hypnosis has been used as a show business routine for many years. Typically, volunteers are hypnotized and then asked to do some pretty silly things in public.

notists claim that they can hypnotize anyone under the right conditions, which is why I hedged and said "probably" not) (e.g., Lynn et al., 1990).

2. *What predicts who can be easily hypnotized?* Although not everyone can be easily hypnotized, some people are excellent subjects, can readily be put into deep hypnotic states, and can easily learn to hypnotize themselves (Hilgard, 1975, 1978). A number of traits are correlated with one's hypnotizability. The most important factor seems to be the ability to engage easily in daydreaming and fantasy, to be able to "set ordinary reality aside for awhile" (Lynn & Rhue, 1986; Wilkes, 1986, p. 25). Other factors include suggestibility and a degree of passivity or willingness to cooperate, at least during the hypnotic session. An intriguing notion is that persons who were often punished in childhood, or are avid readers, runners, or actors, are good subjects for hypnosis. The logic is that these people have a history of self-induced trancelike states (to escape punishment, to focus and become absorbed in a task at hand, and so on), which makes them more likely to be hypnotizable (Hilgard, 1970).

3. *Can I be made to do things under the influence of hypnosis that I would be embarrassed to do otherwise?* Next to being unknowingly hypnotized, this seems to be the greatest fear associated with hypnosis. Again, the answer is probably no. Under the influence of a skilled hypnotist, you may do some pretty silly things and do them publicly. Under the right circumstances, you might do those same things without being hypnotized. It is unlikely you would do under hypnosis anything you would not do otherwise. However, under certain (unusual) circumstances, people can do outrageous–and dangerous–things, which is why hypnosis should be used with caution.

4. *Are hypnotized subjects simply more open to the suggestions of the hypnotist, or is their consciousness really changed?* This issue is in dispute. Some believe that hypnosis is really no more than a heightened level of suggestibility (Barber, 1972; Spanos & Barber, 1974), whereas others believe it to be a special state, separate from the compliance of a willing subject. When hypnotized subjects are left alone, they usually maintain the condition induced by their hypnosis. Subjects not hypnotized, but simply complying as best they can with an experimenter, revert quickly to normal behaviors when left alone (Hilgard, 1975; Orne, 1969).

5. *Can hypnosis be used to alleviate pain–real, physical pain?* Yes. It won't (can't) cure the underlying cause, but it can be used to control the feeling of pain. Hypnosis can be used to create hallucinations in the hypnotized subject. *Hallucinations* are perceptual experiences that occur without sensory input. Some hallucinations are said to be *positive* when a person perceives something that is not there. Pain reduction uses *negative* hallucinations: a failure to perceive something (e.g., pain) that is there. If a person is a good candidate for hypnosis, there is a significant chance that at least a portion of perceived pain can be blocked from conscious awareness (Hilgard & Hilgard, 1975; Long, 1986).

6. *Is a person in a hypnotic state in any sense aware of what he or she is doing?* Yes, but in a strange way. Within the hypnotized subject is what Hilgard calls a "hidden observer" who may be aware of what is going on. In one study (Hilgard & Hilgard, 1975), a person was hypnotized and told that he would feel no pain as his hand was held in a container of ice water (usually very painful). When asked, the person reported feeling little pain, just as expected. The hypnotic suggestion was working. The Hilgards then asked the person if "some part of him" was feeling any pain and to indicate the presence of such pain by using his free hand to press a lever (or to write out a description of what he was feeling). Although the person continued to verbally report no feeling of pain, the free hand (on behalf of the "hidden observer") indicated that it "knew" there was pain in the immersed hand.

7. *Can I remember things under hypnosis I couldn't remember otherwise?* No, probably not, although there is no more hotly contested issue related to hypnosis. In the sense of "Can you hypnotize me to remember psychology material better for the test next Friday?" the answer is an apologetic "Almost certainly not." I might be able to convince you under hypnosis that you'd better remember your psychology and lead you to want to remember your psychology, but there is no evidence that hypnotic suggestion can directly improve your ability to learn and remember new material. In the more restrictive sense of "I don't remember all the details of the accident and the trauma that followed. Can hypnosis help me recall those events more clearly?" the answer is less sure. When we get to our discussion of memory (Chapter 6), we'll see that distortions of memory in recollection can easily occur in normal states. In hypnotic states, the subject is suggestible and susceptible to distortions in recall fur-

nished by the hypnotist (even assuming that the hypnotist has no reason to cause distortions). To the extent that hypnosis can reduce feelings of anxiety and tension, it may help in the recollection of anxiety-producing memories. The evidence is neither clear nor convincing on this issue in either direction (Dywan & Bowers, 1983; Kihlstrom, 1985). What of the related questions, "Can hypnosis make me go back in time (regress) and remember what it was like when I was only 3 or 4 years old?" or "Can hypnosis help me recall past life experiences?" Here, we do have a clear-cut answer, and the answer is no. So-called age-regression hypnotic sessions have simply not proven valid (e.g., Nash, 1987; Spanos et al., 1991).

Hypnosis does alter one's consciousness, does open one to suggestions of the hypnotist, can be used to treat symptoms (if not their underlying causes), and can distort one's view of reality. However, we are learning that it is neither mystical nor magical; there are limits to what hypnosis can do.

Before You Go On

What is hypnosis and who can be hypnotized?

Meditation

Meditation is a self-induced state of altered consciousness characterized by a focusing of attention and relaxation. Meditation is usually associated with ancient, particularly Eastern, cultures and has been practiced for centuries. We tend to think of meditation in a religious context. Meditation became popular in North America in the 1960s. It was then that psychologists began to study the process seriously. In this section we'll first review the process of meditation and then look at some of the claims that have been made about its potential benefits.

There are several types of meditation, but the most popular are those that require mental focusing, or concentration. *Transcendental meditation (TM)* is a type of meditation of this sort (Maharishi, 1963). In TM, one begins meditating by assuming a comfortable position and becoming calm and relaxed. The meditator then directs his or her attention to one particular stimulus. This could be some simple bodily function, such as one's own breathing. Attention could be focused on some softly spoken or chanted word or phrase, or mantra, such as "oom," "one," or "calm." As attention is focused, other stimuli, either external (events in the environment) or internal (thoughts, feelings, or bodily processes), can be blocked from consciousness. The challenge is to stay relaxed, to remain peaceful and calm. A state of meditation cannot be forced. Its practitioners claim that reaching an altered state of awareness through meditation is not difficult (Benson, 1975).

Once a person is in a meditative state, measurable physiological changes do take place that allow us to claim meditation to be an altered state of consciousness. The most noticeable is a predominance of alpha waves in the EEG record (remember, such waves characterize a relaxed state of the sort experienced just before one enters into sleep). Breathing slows and becomes deeper. Oxygen intake is reduced, and the heart rate may decrease (Wallace & Benson, 1972).

There is no doubt that people enter meditative states of consciousness. Doubts that have arisen concerning meditation center on the claims of its benefits. One of the major claims for meditation is that it is a reasonably simple, very effective, even superior way to enter into a state of relaxation. The reduction of somatic (bodily) arousal is taken to be one of the main advantages of meditation. The claim is that by meditating, one can slow bodily processes and enter into a state of physical as

⊚⊚⊚ Thinking Critically ⊚⊚⊚

Why would anyone want to alter their state of consciousness? Are some reasons for doing so better than others? Why or why not?

meditation *a self-induced state of altered consciousness characterized by a focusing of attention and relaxation*

Meditation may not enable the mind to "transcend" the real world and open one to a "cosmic wholeness," but it *is* a very effective means of relaxation and reducing somatic arousal.

well as psychological calm. Researcher David Holmes (1984, 1985, 1987) has reviewed the evidence for somatic relaxation through meditation. On several measures of arousal and relaxation, including heart rate, respiration rate, muscle tension, and oxygen use, Holmes concluded that there were no differences between meditating persons and people who were "simply" resting or relaxing. After reviewing the data of dozens of experiments, he concluded:

> There is not a measure of arousal on which the meditating subjects were consistently found to have reliably lower arousal than resting subjects. Indeed, the most consistent finding was that there were not reliable differences between meditating and resting subjects. Furthermore, there appear to be about as many instances in which the meditating subjects showed reliably higher arousal as there are instances in which they showed reliably lower arousal than their resting counterparts. (1984, p. 5)

Another claim made for meditation is that those who practice it are better able to cope with stress, pressure, or threatening situations than are those who do not practice meditation. Once again, Holmes (1984, 1985) reports that he could find no evidence to support this claim. In fact, in four of the studies he reviewed, Holmes found that under mild threat, meditating subjects showed greater arousal than did nonmeditating subjects. I must add two important notes here: (1) Some psychologists have taken issue with Holmes's methods and conclusions, and argue that meditation does offer advantages over simply resting, suggesting also that "resting" is a difficult concept to define (e.g., Shapiro, 1985; Suler, 1985; West, 1985). (2) Holmes does not argue that meditation is useless. He simply says that with regard to somatic arousal there is no evidence that it is any better than resting.

Some of the claims made for meditation techniques go well beyond relaxation and somatic arousal reduction. Claims that meditation can raise one's consciousness to transcendental heights of new awareness and thus make one a better person are viewed with considerable skepticism in psychology. Some people claim that they have an incredible "openness" to ideas and feelings, that they have hallucinatory experiences, and that they can divorce themselves from their bodies and minds when they meditate. Such experiences might, in some instances, be true. The idea that a meditating person can exist apart from present experience and view life "as if from without" isn't far removed from Hilgard's concept of a "hidden observer" in hypnosis. Nonetheless, the majority of psychologists who have investigated meditation continue to question any claims for a heightened state of well-being that is achieved through such little effort and that relies more on testimonials of personal experience than on scientific evidence (Webb, 1981).

Before You Go On

What is meditation and what are its benefits?

Altering Consciousness with Drugs

In this final section, we will discuss some of the chemicals that alter consciousness by inducing changes in perception, mood, or behavior. Because of their ability to alter psychological processes, these chemicals are referred to as **psychoactive drugs**.

psychoactive drug *a chemical that affects psychological processes and consciousness*

Drugs have been used for centuries to alter consciousness. Psychoactive drugs are taken—at least initially—to achieve a state of consciousness the user considers to be positive, pleasant, even euphoric. No reasonable person would take a drug because he or she expected to have a negative, unpleasant experience. However, the use of drugs that alter our mood, perception, and behaviors often has seriously negative outcomes. In this regard, there are a few terms that will be relevant for our discussion. Although there is not total agreement on how these terms are used, for our purposes, we'll use the following definitions:

EXPERIENCING PSYCHOLOGY

Let's Try a Little Meditation

A reasonable meditation session usually lasts for about 20 minutes, but giving it a good try for five minutes will be long enough to provide you with an example of what the procedure is all about and long enough to realize how difficult it is to withdraw from normal waking consciousness and all of its demands for your attention. As best you can, follow these directions literally. (It would help if someone could read these directions to you slowly and softly.)

- Sit in a comfortable chair, with nothing on your lap or in your hands.
- Sit with your legs uncrossed. Cup one hand loosely inside the other on your lap, or even a bit higher if that is more comfortable.
- Close your eyes gently and relax. Begin with your feet, then your ankles, then the calves of your legs, and progress to your face, letting all your muscles relax.

- Breathe slowly through your nose. Each time you breathe, count slowly from 1 to 10, then take another breath.
- Focus on your breathing and your counting. The object is to exclude all other thoughts from your consciousness. When distracting thoughts occur, try to ignore them, thinking, "oh well," and continue with your breathing and your counting.

After 5 minutes, or so, open your eyes and return to normal consciousness. How did you do? Were you really able to exclude all other thoughts from your mind? What kind of thoughts interfered with your meditation? Thoughts about the past? Thoughts about the future? If you tried this every day, how long do you think it would be before you could meditate successfully—in the sense of keeping intruding thoughts to a minimum?

dependence *a state in which drug use is either necessary or believed to be necessary to maintain functioning at some desired level*

tolerance *in using a drug, a state in which more and more of the drug is required to produce the same desired effect*

withdrawal *a negative reaction that may occur when one stops taking a drug*

addiction *an extreme dependency, usually accompanied by symptoms of tolerance and painful withdrawal*

drug abuse *a lack of control, a disruption of interpersonal relationships or difficulties at work, and a history of maladaptive use for at least 1 month*

stimulants *drugs (such as caffeine, cocaine, and amphetamines) that increase nervous system activities*

1. *Dependence:* a state in which (a) the use of a drug is required to maintain bodily functioning (called physical dependence), or (b) continued use of a drug is *believed* to be necessary to maintain psychological functioning at some level (called psychological dependence). "I just can't face the day without my three cups of coffee in the morning."

2. *Tolerance:* a condition in which the use of a drug leads to a state in which more and more of it is needed to produce the same effect. "I used to get high with just one of these; now I need three."

3. *Withdrawal:* a strongly negative response, either physical or psychological (including reactions such as headaches, vomiting, and cramps), that results when one stops taking a drug. "When I take these, I don't feel real good, but it sure does hurt when I stop."

4. *Addiction:* an extreme dependency, physical or psychological, in which signs of tolerance and painful withdrawal are usually found (Schuckit, 1989). Addiction also implies seeking a short-term gain (say, a pleasurable feeling) at the expense of long-term negative consequences (Miller, 1992). "No way I'm gonna give it up; no matter what. It feels too good. And who cares if I lose my job?"

Another important distinction we should make is between drug use and **drug abuse**. We are dealing with abuse when we find (1) a lack of control, as evidenced by daily intoxication and continued use, even knowing that one's condition will deteriorate; (2) a disruption of interpersonal relationships or difficulties at work that can be traced to drug usage; and (3) indications that maladaptive drug use has continued for at least one month (American Psychiatric Association, 1987). Hidden in this distinction is the reality that although drug use may not have negative consequences, drug abuse will. There is no clear dividing line between drug use and drug abuse. For that matter, there are no clear dividing lines between drug use, dependency on drugs, and drug addiction. There is, instead, a continuum from total abstinence through heavy social use to addiction (Doweiko, 1993; Peele et al., 1991).

There are many psychoactive drugs. We'll focus on four types, or categories: stimulants, depressants, hallucinogens, and (as a separate category) marijuana.

Stimulants

Chemical **stimulants** do just that—they stimulate, or activate an organism, producing a heightened sense of arousal and an elevation of mood. Most of the time, these drugs also activate neural reactions, but at this level we have to be careful. For example, one stimulant administered directly to the reticular formation can awaken and arouse a sleeping cat, but if that same drug is administered to a different area of the reticular formation, the cat will go to sleep.

Caffeine is one of the most widely used stimulants. It is found in common foods and drinks (coffee, tea, and chocolate), as well as in several varieties of painkillers. It is an ingredient in many soft drinks, notably colas. In moderate amounts, it seems to have no life-threatening effects on the user. At some point, a mild dependence may develop. Caffeine temporarily increases cellular metabolism (the general process of converting food into energy), which then results in a burst of newfound energy. It also blocks the effects of some inhibitory neurotransmitters in the brain (Julien, 1985). Caffeine disrupts sleep, making it more difficult to get to sleep in the first place and more difficult to stay asleep.

After long or excessive use, giving up sources of caffeine may result in the pain of withdrawal. If you tend to drink a lot of coffee and cola during the week, but take a break from them during the weekend, you may experience headaches of caffeine withdrawal. You may drink coffee to help stay awake to withstand an all-night study session, but in a few hours after you stop drinking the caffeine, you may experience a streak of extreme mental and physical fatigue—perhaps right at exam time!

Nicotine is another popular stimulant, usually taken by smoking and absorption by the lungs. Nicotine is carried to the brain very quickly—in a matter of seconds. Nicotine *is* a stimulant of central nervous system activity, but it does relax muscle tone slightly, which may explain the rationalization of smokers who claim that they can relax by having a cup of coffee and a cigarette. Nicotine produces its effects by activating excitatory synapses in both the central and peripheral nervous systems (McKim, 1986).

Many individuals (but not all) develop a tolerance to nicotine, requiring more and more to reach a desired state of stimulation (Hughes et al., 1987). Indeed, beginning smokers generally cannot smoke more than one or two cigarettes without becoming ill. The drug often leads to dependency. In 1989, then Surgeon General C. Everett Koop declared cigarette smoking an addiction, calling it the single most preventable cause of death in our society, accounting for more than one-sixth of all deaths reported in 1985 (DeAngelis, 1989; Shiffman, 1992; Shiffman et al., 1990). More recent reports blame tobacco use for nearly half of all deaths in the United States. How addictive nicotine (or perhaps any other drug) becomes may depend primarily on how quickly it enters the brain. This means that people who take many quick deep puffs when smoking may become addicted more easily than will people who take slow, shallow puffs (Bennett, 1980). We'll return to issues of smoking and nicotine addiction in our discussion of health psychology in Chapter 11.

Cocaine is a stimulant derived from leaves of the coca shrub (native to the Andes Mountains in South America). The allure of cocaine and its derivative "crack" is the rush of pleasure and energy it produces when it first enters the bloodstream, either through the mucous membranes when inhaled as smoke ("free basing"), inhaled through the nose as a powder ("snorting"), or injected directly as a liquid. A cocaine "high" doesn't last very long; 15 to 20 minutes is average.

There are many physiological reactions that result from cocaine use. It elevates blood pressure and heart rate. Cocaine also blocks the reuptake of two important neurotransmitters (Julien, 1988). This means that once these neurotransmitters have entered a synapse, cocaine will prohibit their being taken back up into the neuron from which they have been released. The result is that, for a time at least, excessive amounts of the neurotransmitters are available in the nervous system. The two neurotransmitters in question are norepinephrine, which acts in both the central and peripheral nervous systems to provide arousal and the sense of extra energy, and dopamine, which acts in the brain to produce feelings of pleasure and euphoria.

Some of the effects of cocaine use are long-lasting, if not permanent, even though the psychological effects last but a few minutes. Not only is the rush of the psychological reaction to cocaine or "crack" short-lived, but it is followed by a letdown approaching depression. As users know, one way to combat letdown and depression is to take more of the drug—a vicious cycle that invariably leads to dependency and addiction. Cocaine is such a powerfully addictive drug that many individuals can become psychologically and physically dependent on its use after just one or two episodes. Determining the number of cocaine users or addicts is difficult (after all, the drug is illegal), but estimates range from slightly fewer than 2 million to over 6 million users in the United States alone (Doweiko, 1993, pp. 82–83). Cocaine addiction tends to run in families to such an extent that current research is exploring the hypothesis that there is a genetic basis for cocaine addiction. Cocaine is a drug that no one can handle safely.

Amphetamines are synthetically manufactured stimulants that usually come in the form of capsules or pills, and are known by many "street names," such as bennies, wake-ups, uppers, dexies, or jellie babies. In addition to blocking reuptake,

Only one or two episodes of use and most people will find themselves physically and psychologically dependent on cocaine. The use of cocaine is illegal. It is also very expensive.

amphetamines cause the release of excess dopamine and norepinephrine. However, their action is considerably slower and less widespread than that of cocaine. Once an amphetamine takes effect, users feel alert, awake, aroused, filled with energy, and ready to go. These results are short-lived. The drug does not create alertness so much as it masks fatigue, which will ultimately overcome the user when the drug wears off. These are not the only effects of amphetamine use; it has a direct effect on the heart and circulatory system, causing, for example, irregular heartbeat and increased blood pressure (McKim, 1986).

Before You Go On

What are stimulant drugs, and what are their effects?

Depressants

depressants *drugs (such as alcohol, opiates, heroin, and barbiturates) that slow or reduce nervous system activity*

In terms of their effects on consciousness, **depressants** are the opposite of stimulants. They reduce one's awareness of external stimuli, slow bodily functioning, and decrease levels of overt behavior. Predictably, one's reaction to depressant drugs depends largely on how much is taken. In small doses, they may produce relaxation, a sense of freedom from anxiety, and a loss of stifling inhibitions. In greater amounts, they may produce sedation, sleep, coma, or death.

Alcohol is the most commonly used of all depressants. It has been in use for thousands of years—perhaps since as long ago as 8000 B.C. (Ray & Ksir, 1987). Alcohol is a dangerous drug because of its popularity and widespread use, if for no other reason. It can be a deadly drug. Over 100,000 deaths a year in the United States are attributed to alcohol use. The devastating effects of alcohol consumption by pregnant women are also well documented. Alcohol use has been associated with a myriad of problems of the newborn (see Topic 8A, page 278).

Perhaps the first thing to remember about alcohol is that it is a depressant. Some folks may feel that they are entertaining and stimulating when drinking alcohol, but their nervous system activity is actually being slowed. Alcohol increases urination, leading to an overall loss of fluids. It raises visual thresholds, making it more difficult to detect dim lights. Alcohol affects mood, leading to friendly elation as levels rise, and to depression, anger, and fatigue as alcohol levels drop (Babor et al., 1983).

The specific effects of alcohol on the drinker reflect several interacting factors. Primary among them (again) is amount. What matters most is the amount of alcohol that gets into a person's bloodstream. Blood alcohol level (BAL) is affected by how much one drinks and by how fast the alcohol can get into the bloodstream, which in turn is affected by what else is in the stomach. Drinking on an empty stomach is more dangerous than drinking while or soon after eating, because the alcohol will be more quickly absorbed. One-tenth of 1 percent alcohol in the bloodstream is enough to declare someone legally drunk in most states. At this level, brain activity is so depressed that decision making is distorted and motor coordination is impaired (and both are skills required to drive safely). Drinking more than one mixed drink or one can of beer or glass of wine per hour will raise blood alcohol levels (Maguire, 1990).

Drug use and abuse are susceptible to *sociocultural* factors, including ethnic background, religion, and socioeconomic level, an observation especially relevant in the context of alcohol. For example, Europeans constitute about one-eighth of the world's population, but they consume nearly half of all the alcohol produced. Think about the impact of the social pressures derived from religious beliefs and attitudes toward alcohol. The use of alcohol is virtually nonexistent among Muslims and Mormons, and used sparingly—usually in religious settings—by the Chi-

Alcohol can lead to a minor alteration of consciousness in small doses, or a total loss of consciousness in high doses. Its use is forbidden to Muslims and Mormons, used sparingly—mostly in religious rituals by the Chinese and Orthodox Jews.

nese and Orthodox Jews. Alcoholism rates are very low among these groups. In the United States, Irish Americans are six times more likely to suffer alcoholism than are Greek Americans—*in general.* Remember, there *are* Irish Americans who do not use alcohol at all (Valliant, 1983). Adolescent Native Americans, especially those living on reservations, have much higher rates of alcohol use and abuse than any other American ethnic-racial population (Moncher et al., 1990; Swaim et al., 1993). Peer pressure, a major determining factor in drug and alcohol use for Anglo youths, is much less important in the culture of adolescent Native Americans (Oetting & Beauvais, 1987). Economics are also relevant. Research clearly demonstrates a relationship between alcohol use and economic indicators such as poverty, unemployment, and lack of opportunity (Beauvais et al., 1989; Gefou-Madianou, 1992; Ley, 1985).

Opiates, such as morphine and codeine, are called analgesics because they can be used to reduce or eliminate sensations of pain. They were first used for this purpose. In small doses, they create feelings of well-being and ease, relaxation, and a trancelike state. Unlike alcohol, they seem to have little effect on motor behavior. The catch, again, is that they produce dependence and addiction. Their removal results in extreme pain and depression.

Heroin is an opiate, originally (in the 1890s) derived from morphine, but thought not to be as addictive—a notion soon proven wrong. Strong dependency and addiction grow rapidly. Estimates suggest that more than 500,000 persons in the United States are addicted to heroin—and nearly half of them live in New York City. As with other drugs, we find that the addictive nature of heroin may be related to its rapid entry into the brain. Methadone, used in some treatment programs for long-term heroin users, is a drug with many of the chemical properties of heroin and many of the same effects. A difference is that methadone is slow to reach the brain and thus tends not to produce heroin's predictable "rush," which makes methadone somewhat less addictive.

The psychological effects of heroin (above whatever painkilling use it may have) are most related to one's emotional state and mood. Unlike alcohol or the opiates, there seldom are hallucinations or thought disturbances associated with heroin use. But as increased amounts of heroin become needed to produce the desired emotional states of pleasant euphoria, tolerance builds—and increased dosages of heroin can cause breathing to stop, often for long enough periods that death results.

Barbiturates are synthetically produced sedatives of which there are many varieties. Well over 2,500 barbiturate chemicals have been isolated in laboratories (Doweiko, 1993). All barbiturates slow nervous system activity—in small amounts producing a sense of calm and tranquility, in higher doses producing sleep or coma. They have this effect either by blocking receptor sites of excitatory synapses or by enhancing the effects of inhibitory neurotransmitters. Barbiturates also depress the cells and organs outside the central nervous system, slowing muscular responses and reducing respiration and heart rates. Some barbiturates are addictive, producing strong withdrawal symptoms when discontinued. All produce dependency if used with regularity. As is generally the case, once addiction develops, getting off these drugs is very difficult.

Before You Go On

What are depressant drugs, and what are their effects?

Hallucinogens

hallucinogens *drugs (such as LSD) whose major effect is the alteration of perceptual experience and mood*

The chemicals called **hallucinogens** have unpredictable effects on consciousness. One of the reactions to these drugs is the formation of hallucinations, usually visual. That is, users often report seeing things when there is nothing there to see, or they see things in ways that others do not. Hallucinations of hearing, smell, taste, and touch are possible, but are much less common.

There are nearly a hundred different types of hallucinogenic substances around the world, and many have been in use for centuries. In many cultures, the drugs are used in religious practices to induce trancelike states that may help the user communicate with the supernatural; in such settings, the drug may be given to young people by their elders. In such cases, "unauthorized" use of the drug, or abuse of the drug, is nearly unheard of (e.g., Chagnon, 1983; Grob & Dobkin de Rois, 1992).

A drug called *ebene,* for example, is used by the Yanomamö Indians, who live near the border between Brazil and Venezuela. They make a green pasty mixture from a powder derived from a tree that grows sparsely throughout the region.

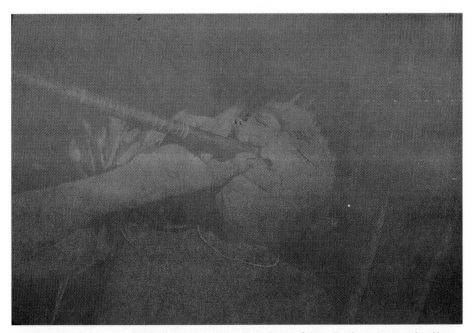

In some cultures, the use of hallucinogens is a sanctioned part of rites, rituals, or ceremonies. Here, a Yanomamö Indian is receiving a wad of *ebene*—a powerful hallucinogen—blown up his nose.

Wads of the mixture are place in 3-foot-long hollow tubes and forcefully blown into the nostrils of a recipient. The initial experience is painful, but eventually becomes pleasurable, and may bring the person face to face with the spirit world.

> Dry heaves are also very common, as is out-and-out vomiting. Within a few minutes, one has difficulty focusing and begins to see spots and blips of light. Knees get rubbery. . . . Soon spirits can be seen dancing out of the sky and from the mountain tops, rhythmically prancing down their trails to enter the chest of their human beckoner, who by now is singing to lure them into his body where he can control them—send them to harm enemies or help cure sick kinsmen. (Chagnon, 1983, pp. 50–51)

LSD (lysergic acid diethylamide), a potent and popular hallucinogen in most Western cultures, was introduced in the United States in the 1940s. LSD raises levels of emotionality that can produce profound changes in perception, usually vivid visual hallucinations. One of the first steps in discovering how LSD works was finding that levels of the neurotransmitter serotonin increased when LSD was given to animals (Jacobs, 1987; Jacobs & Trulson, 1979). In itself this was not surprising, because LSD and similar hallucinogens (such as mescaline) have a chemical composition much like that of serotonin. Serotonin has its effects, both excitatory and inhibitory, on many areas of the brain (Jacobs, 1987). Now we know that serotonin levels increase because LSD acts on serotonin receptor sites, much like a neurotransmitter. Small doses (measured in millionths of a gram) can produce major behavioral effects.

The changes in mood that take place with LSD are usually exaggerations of one's present mood. From the start this has been viewed as one of the dangers of the drug. Some people may be drawn to drugs such as LSD because things are not going well for them. Perhaps they are depressed and feeling hopeless. They think LSD might help cheer them up. In fact, it may worsen their mood, resulting in a "bad trip," by exaggerating their unpleasant feelings.

Hallucinations under the influence of LSD usually involve exaggerations of some actual perception. Colors seem more vivid, dimly lit stimuli take on a glow, stationary objects move, and otherwise unnoticed details become apparent. On some occasions, LSD gives rise to an experience of synesthesia, in which a stimulus of one modality is perceived in a different modality. For example, the individual may "hear" colored lights, "see" sounds, "feel" odors, and so forth.

Before You Go On

What are hallucinogenic drugs, and what are their effects?

Marijuana—A Special Case

Marijuana is a consciousness-altering drug that I'll consider a special case because it doesn't fit neatly into any of the three previous categories. Marijuana can act as a depressant. In small doses its effects are similar to those of alcohol: decreased nervous system activity and depression of thought and action. In greater doses, marijuana acts as if it were a hallucinogen, producing hallucinations and alterations in mood.

Marijuana is produced from the cannabis, or hemp plant—the source of most of the rope manufactured for sailing ships in the eighteenth century. It was an important crop in the American colonies, grown by George Washington, among other notables. The plants were farmed in great numbers throughout the Midwest during World War II. The cannabis plant is hardy, and many of the remnants of those farms of the early 1940s are still found in Illinois and Indiana, where every summer, adventurers come in search of a profitable—albeit illegal—harvest. More marijuana is grown in the United States than anywhere else in the world. Use of the drug is not uncommon, with estimates of Americans who have tried marijuana ranging from 40 to 60 million; as many as 3 to 6 million use the drug daily (Mirin et al., 1991).

The active ingredient in marijuana is the chemical tetrahydrocannabinol, or THC. THC is also the active ingredient in hashish, a similar but more potent drug also made from the cannabis plant. Although marijuana, in large doses, has been found to increase overall levels of some neurotransmitters, it is not known just how it produces this effect.

Marijuana is a difficult drug for society to deal with. In the United States, it is illegal to sell, possess, or use marijuana, yet it can be prescribed to reduce nausea associated with chemotherapy treatments for cancer. There is evidence that marijuana tolerance may develop rapidly, but little evidence that it is addictive. Is marijuana dangerous? Certainly, if for no other reason than that it is usually smoked, and smoking is a danger to one's health. But smoking marijuana is more dangerous than cigarette smoking in terms of causing cancers, lung disease, and respiratory problems. It is also dangerous in the sense that alcohol is dangerous. Excessive use leads to impaired judgment, impaired reflexes, unrealistic moods, poor physical coordination, and hallucinations (Bennett, 1982; Weil et al., 1968).

The most debatable aspect of marijuana use involves the results of moderate to heavy long-term use. The use of marijuana may have genetic implications (producing chromosomal abnormalities in nonhumans). It can adversely affect the body's immune system and white blood cells. It is partially responsible for lowering the sperm count of male users. It can impair memory function, affecting memories of recent events in particular. It has predictably negative effects when taken during pregnancy, resulting in smaller babies, increased numbers of miscarriages, and so on (Bloodworth, 1987; Doweiko, 1993; Grinspoon, 1977; Julien, 1985; McKim, 1986). One issue of genuine concern is the considerable variability in the potency and quality, or purity, of marijuana available on the street today.

Figure 4.4 summarizes much of our discussion of the psychoactive drugs.

@@@@ **Thinking Critically** @@@@

Once people realize that drugs are maladaptive, harmful, and could actually kill them, why don't they just stop?

Before You Go On

What is the active ingredient in marijuana, and what are its effects?

Figure 4.4
Psychoactive Drugs—A Few Examples

Type of Drug	Examples	Likely Effects
Stimulants	Caffeine	increases CNS activity and metabolism; disrupts sleep; rebound possible
	Nicotine	activates excitatory synapses in CNS and PNS; leads to tolerance or addiction
	Cocaine	15–20 min high; raises blood pressure and heart rate; blocks reuptake; powerfully addictive
	Amphetamines	release excess norepinephrine and dopamine; slower acting than cocaine; mask fatigue; lead to dependence
Depressants	Alcohol	decreases nervous system activity; releases inhibitions; impairs decision making; birth defects; dependency and addiction
	Opiates	reduce pain; feelings of calm and ease; dependency and addiction
	Heroin	"rush" of euphoria; reduces pain; very addictive
	Barbiturates	slow nervous system activity; from calm, to sleep, to coma; slow muscle response; reduce heart rate; addiction
Hallucinogens	LSD	hallucinations; increase serotonin levels; raise level of emotionality
Marijuana		slight depressant; hallucinations in high doses; alters mood; reduces nausea; lung disease; chromosomal abnormalities; impairs memory

TOPIC 4B SUMMARY

To be conscious is to be aware of one's own mental processes and one's environment. We can voluntarily, consciously, alter our consciousness, and in this Topic we examined three means of doing so: hypnosis, meditation, and using psychoactive drugs. What have we learned?

You cannot be hypnotized without your consent, nor is it likely that you can be made to do anything while under hypnosis that you wouldn't do otherwise. Some people are easier to hypnotize than others, and although hypnosis can be used to alleviate pain, you cannot be hypnotized to improve your memory. Meditation alters consciousness through relaxation and the focusing of one's attention. Although meditation may not be significantly different from several other techniques of relaxation, there are benefits to be gained from meditation, and there are measurable physiological changes that occur while one is in a meditative state.

Chemicals that alter consciousness are called psychoactive drugs, and they fall into three major categories, the names of which indicate the ultimate effect on one's nervous system activity. There are stimulants, including caffeine, nicotine, cocaine, and the amphetamines; depressants, including alcohol, the opiates (such as heroin), and the barbiturates; and hallucinogens, such as LSD. Marijuana is a special psychoactive drug because it can produce the effects of stimulants and depressants and can produce many of the effects of hallucinogens.

CHAPTER SUMMARY

Topic 4A

What is "consciousness," and what, according to William James, are its major features?

We define consciousness as the perception or awareness of our environment and our own mental processes. According to William James, human consciousness is (1) always changing, (2) personal, (3) continuous, and (4) selective. */pp. 120–121*

How did Freud describe consciousness? How may we characterize the unconscious processing of information?

Sigmund Freud proposed that consciousness could be classified into one of three levels. (1) What is in your *conscious* mind is that of which you are aware at the moment. (2) The *preconscious* holds memories, feelings, desires, and the like that are not immediately known, but that can be brought to attention, to consciousness, with relatively little effort. (3) Most of the contents of our minds are at an *unconscious* level of awareness. Feelings, information, and desires are stored at the unconscious level because becoming aware of these issues might lead to feelings of anxiety and distress. Although information stored at the unconscious level could influence our behaviors and could show itself in slips of the tongue and in our dreams, it can be retrieved only with considerable effort.

   Unconscious processing occurs when information is processed without one's awareness of it. For example, when people are shown words presented so quickly or dimly that they do not report seeing them, those words will still influence the choice of a word that is related to the word they claimed they did not see. At best, however, the unconscious processing of information appears simple, unsophisticated, and primitive. */pp. 121–125*

What are the EEG and the EMG? Briefly describe the four stages of sleep.

The EEG (electroencephalogram) measures the general pattern of electrical activity of the brain, the most common indicator of the stages of sleep. The EMG (electromyogram) measures muscle tone, another indicator of sleep. In addition to a state of relaxation characterized by EEG alpha waves, we say that there are four levels, or stages, of sleep: (1) light sleep with low-amplitude, slow theta waves, (2) sleep showing low-amplitude EEG waves with sleep spindles present, (3) a level where delta waves enter the EEG record, and (4) deep sleep, with more than 50 percent delta wave activity. */pp. 125–127*

What are REM and NREM sleep?

REM sleep is "rapid eye movement sleep," which constitutes about one-fourth of each night's sleep. Several events occur during REM, most noticeably vivid, story-like dreams. During REM sleep we find loss of muscle tone (atonia), excitement of the sexual organs, rapid breathing, and increased heart rate and blood pressure. NREM is "non-REM" sleep and, predictably, the eyes are still and there is little dream activity. */pp. 127–129*

What are the effects of sleep deprivation? What are three common sleep disorders?

People who have been deprived of sleep show a rebound effect, making up for lost sleep, usually in just one night. There is more certain to be a rebound effect for REM sleep than for NREM sleep. Millions of persons chronically get less sleep than they need. The effects of short-term deprivation are minimal and reversible; the effects of long-term deprivation are more negative. *Insomnia* is being unable to fall asleep and/or stay asleep when one wants to. Nearly 30 million Americans suffer from chronic insomnia. *Narcolepsy* involves going to sleep, even in the daytime, without any intention of doing so. It is an underdiagnosed sleep disorder. *Sleep apnea* involves patterns of sleep during which one suddenly stops breathing, often long enough to awaken the sleeping person, or cause serious medical consequences. */pp. 130–131*

Topic 4B

What is hypnosis, and who can be hypnotized?

Hypnosis is an altered state of consciousness into which one enters voluntarily. It is characterized by an increase in suggestibility, a focusing of attention, an exaggeration of imagination, a reduction of spontaneous activity, and an unquestioning acceptance of distortions in reality. Not everyone can be hypnotized. Those who most readily can be hypnotized easily engage in fantasy and daydreaming, show signs of suggestibility, and demonstrate a willingness to cooperate with the hypnotist. */pp. 132–135*

What is meditation, and what are its benefits?

Meditation is a self-induced state of consciousness characterized by an extreme focusing of attention and relaxation. There are many claims for the benefits of meditation. It *is* an effective means of relaxing and reducing levels of somatic activity, but it may not be significantly better in these regards than other relaxation techniques. */pp. 135–137*

What are stimulant drugs, and what are their effects?

Stimulants are psychoactive drugs such as caffeine, nicotine, cocaine, and the amphetamines. Their basic effect is to increase levels of arousal and elevate mood, often by affecting the neural synapse, or by increasing effective levels of norepinephrine and dopamine. With heavy or continued use, tolerance to stimulants may develop, as may dependence and addiction. */pp. 137–140*

What are depressant drugs, and what are their effects?

The depressants include such drugs as alcohol, the opiates (e.g., morphine, codeine, and heroin), and a variety of synthetically produced barbiturates. All depressants slow nervous system activity, reduce one's awareness of outside stimulation, and, in small doses, may alleviate feelings of nervousness and anxiety. In large doses, however, they produce sedation, sleep, coma, or death. Tolerance, dependence, and addiction may result from the use of these drugs. The use of these drugs (and virtually all others) is influenced to some degree by sociocultural factors. */pp. 140–142*

What are the hallucinogenic drugs, and what are their effects?

Hallucinogens (such as LSD) are drugs that alter mood or perceptions. They get their name from their ability to induce hallucinations, where a user may have experiences that are unrelated to what is going on in the user's environment. Hallucinogens may intensify already unpleasant moods. *Synesthesia,* a hallucinatory experience that crosses sense modalities ("hearing" lights, for example), may occur under the influence of LSD. */pp. 142–144*

What is the active ingredient in marijuana, and what are its effects?

The active ingredient in marijuana is the chemical compound THC. The use of marijuana through smoking is more dangerous to lungs and the respiratory system than is the smoking of regular cigarettes. Negative effects have been associated with long-term use: impaired judgment, unrealistic mood, impaired coordination, and hallucinations. Also, marijuana may have an adverse effect on the body's immune system and has been implicated in producing a range of negative consequences when taken before or during pregnancy. */pp. 144–145*

PRACTICING PSYCHOLOGY

Personalizing Consciousness

William James claimed that there are four major characteristics of normal, waking consciousness. Over the last 100 years, no one has seriously challenged James's description. For each of the four characteristics listed below, cite an example from your own experience. (Suggested answers can be found on p. 572.)

1. Consciousness is always *changing.*
2. Consciousness is *personal.*
3. Consciousness is *continuous.*
4. Consciousness is *selective.*

OUTLINE

I was an undergraduate in a large child psychology class. The instructor in that class had what we thought was a terribly boring style—he simply sat at his desk and read his notes to us for the 50-minute class period. About 25 of us had just left our psychology of learning lecture, where the professor suggested we try a "little experiment" and see if we could modify someone's behavior. Our choice was clear.

We decided to reward the child psychology instructor for doing what we wanted him to do by smiling, looking attentive, and appearing to take notes. Whenever he did what we didn't want him to, we'd appear bored, gaze around the room, and stop taking notes. We began our little experiment on a Wednesday. We didn't accomplish much. We weren't very well organized. We needed to agree on exactly which behaviors to reward and which to ignore. By the end of class on Friday, we had made progress. The instructor was looking up from his notes more frequently, and he was squirming about in his chair.

Monday's class brought a breakthrough: the instructor rose from his chair! From time to time he would sit back down again (only to be ignored), and would not give up physical contact with his notes. He was still reading, but occasionally he would stand to do so.

5

Learning

On the following Friday, about halfway through the class period, the instructor was standing in the corner of the room. Notes still on the desk, he was simply talking to us about child psychology.

Think about that. In just five class days 25 students had lifted their instructor out of his chair and stood him in the corner. We had no doubt that in another 10 minutes we could have moved him from one corner to the other. And all this was done by rewarding some behaviors with attention, and by ignoring other behaviors. The class was impressed, and so was I, although I am now more concerned about the ethical implications of what we had done than I was at the time.

In this chapter on learning we'll see that the child psychology class's "little experiment" provides a good example of one the most fundamental varieties of learning.

TOPIC 5A Classical Conditioning

Topic 5A begins by considering definitions of learning and conditioning. We'll focus on classical conditioning in this Topic, first by reviewing Pavlov's work with salivating dogs. Then we'll see why classical conditioning is so important to all of us and how it can be applied in our daily lives. We'll also see how contemporary psychology views the process, discovering that some of Pavlov's assumptions may not have been correct.

What Is Learning?

learning *demonstration of a relatively permanent change in behavior that occurs as the result of practice or experience*

Directly or indirectly, learning has an impact on every aspect of our being. The human organism is poorly suited to survive without learning. If we are to survive, much less prosper, we must profit from our experiences. **Learning** is demonstrated by a relatively permanent change in behavior that occurs as the result of practice or experience. This is a rather standard definition, and it raises some important points we should explore.

For one, when we say that learning is *demonstrated by* a change in behavior we are saying that learning (like many other psychological processes) cannot be observed directly. In a literal sense, there is no way that I can directly observe, or measure, what you have learned. All I can measure directly is your performance, or your behavior. To determine if you have learned something, I ask you to perform and then make inferences about your learning on the basis of your performance. And sometimes I may be wrong.

For example, you may learn everything there is to know about the psychology of learning for your next exam. But just days before that exam, someone you care about becomes seriously ill. As a result, you don't get much sleep. Then, with your resistance down, you catch the flu. When you come to class to take your exam, you have a high fever, feel miserable, and can't concentrate. You fail the exam. Your instructor may infer that you haven't learned very much about learning. On the other hand, there may be a student in class who hasn't studied at all and has actually learned very little. But the exam is of the multiple-choice type, and she correctly guesses the answers to 90 percent of the questions. Your instructor might infer (incorrectly again) that this student has learned a great deal.

Another way to make this point is to say that what is learned is a *potential,* or a predisposition, to respond. Because what is learned is just potential, we won't recognize that learning has taken place until that potential is realized in behavior.

A second aspect of our definition that takes a bit of explaining is that learned changes in behavior are *relatively permanent.* This means that they are not fleeting, short-lived, or cyclical changes, such as those due to fatigue or brief shifts in motivation. Consider, for example, the change in typing behavior that occurs—even for a skilled typist—between 8 and 10 A.M. on any given morning. There is likely to be a significant improvement in typing behavior that we ought not attribute to learning but to *warm-up.* That same skilled typist might not function as well at the end of the day—a change in behavior better attributed to fatigue than to forgetting. These are important changes in behavior, but they are not due to learning. Learned changes are relatively permanent.

Another term in our definition reminds us that there are other changes in behavior that do not result from learning. By definition, learned changes in behavior result from *practice or experience.* Some behavioral changes may be due to maturation. The fact that birds fly, that salamanders swim, or that humans walk probably has more to do with genes and physical development than with learning and experience. For another thing, some changes in our behaviors are due to automatic physiological reactions, such as sensory adaptation, and are not learned. When we enter a darkened theater we don't "learn" to see in the dark. Our vision improves and our behaviors change as our eyes adapt to the lighting.

One final point about learning: We often fall into the habit of thinking that learning is necessarily a good thing. Clearly, it isn't. We can learn bad, ineffective habits just as readily as we learn good, adaptive ones. No one I know honestly claims to have enjoyed the first cigarette that he or she smoked. Yet many people have learned the habit, which is hardly an adaptive one. Learning is simply reflected in a change in behavior, be it for better or worse.

When we put these ideas together, we come up with our definition: Learning is demonstrated by (or inferred from) a relatively permanent change in behavior that occurs as the result of practice or experience.

We now begin our discussion of learning by considering *classical conditioning*. Although *conditioning* and *learning* are not technically synonymous terms, they can be used interchangeably. For the sake of simplicity, we will follow common usage here and agree to call the most basic and fundamental types of learning "conditioning."

Before You Go On

How do we define learning?

Pavlov and a Classic Demonstration

When we think about learning, we typically think about such activities as memorizing the Bill of Rights, studying for an exam, or learning to do things, such as ice skate. But our study of learning begins nearly a hundred years ago in the laboratory of a Russian physiologist who taught dogs to salivate in response to tones. How salivating dogs could be relevant to college students may be difficult to imagine at first, but the relevance will soon become apparent.

Late in the nineteenth century, Ivan Pavlov, a physiologist, was studying the basic processes of digestion—work for which he was awarded a Nobel Prize in 1904.

> ꙮꙮꙮ **Thinking Critically** ꙮꙮꙮ
>
> How could you demonstrate that an observed behavior, say of a chicken pecking at a piece of grain, was learned or inherited?

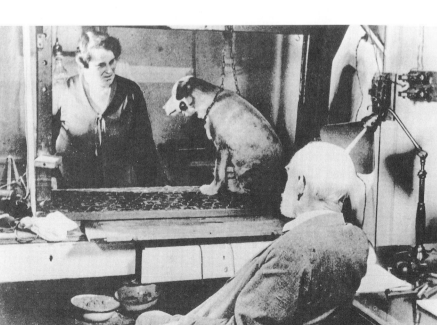

Russian physiologist Ivan Pavlov (seated) observes a dog in one of his laboratory's testing chambers.

reflex *an unlearned, automatic response that occurs in the presence of a specific stimulus*

Pavlov focused on the salivation reflex in dogs. He knew that he could get his dogs to salivate by forcing food powder into their mouths. A **reflex** is an unlearned, automatic response that occurs in the presence of a specific stimulus. Every time Pavlov presented the food powder, his dogs salivated.

Pavlov earned his reputation in psychology by pursuing something not as simple as reflexive responses. He noticed that sometimes his dogs would salivate *before* food was put in their mouths. They would salivate at the sight of the food or even at the sight of the laboratory assistant who usually delivered the food. With this observation, Pavlov went off on a tangent that he pursued for the rest of his life (Pavlov, 1927, 1928). The phenomenon he studied is now called **classical conditioning**—a type of learning in which an originally neutral stimulus comes to elicit a new response after having been paired with another stimulus that reflexively elicits that same response. In the abstract, that may not make much sense, but as we go through the process step by step, I believe that you will appreciate that the process *is* simple and straightforward.

classical conditioning *learning in which an originally neutral stimulus comes to elicit a new response after having been paired with a stimulus that reflexively elicits that same response*

To demonstrate classical conditioning, we first need a stimulus that reliably, or consistently, produces a predictable response. The relationship between this stimulus and the response it elicits is usually an unlearned, reflexive one. Given this stimulus, the same response always follows. Here is where the food powder comes in. If we present the food powder to a dog, the salivation response reliably follows. There is no learning involved in this association, so we call the stimulus an **unconditioned stimulus (UCS)** and the response an **unconditioned response (UCR)**. A UCS (food powder) produces a UCR (salivation).

unconditioned stimulus (UCS) *in classical conditioning, a stimulus (e.g., food powder) that reflexively and reliably evokes a response*

Now we need a *neutral stimulus* that, when presented, produces a minimal response, or a response of no particular interest. For this neutral stimulus, Pavlov chose a tone. At first, when a tone is sounded, a dog *will* respond. It will, among other things, perk up its ears and try to orient toward the source of the sound. We call this response an **orienting reflex**—a simple, unlearned response of attending to a new or unusual stimulus. After a while, however, the dog will get used to the tone and will ignore it. This process is called **habituation**, a form of learning in which an organism comes to ignore a stimulus of little or no consequence. Essentially, the dog learns not to orient toward the tone. We're ready to go. We have two stimuli: a tone that produces a minimal response, and food powder (UCS) that reliably produces salivation (UCR).

unconditioned response (UCR) *in classical conditioning, a response (e.g., salivation in response to food) reliably and reflexively evoked by a stimulus*

orienting reflex *the simple, unlearned response of orienting toward, or attending to, a new or unusual stimulus*

habituation *in classical conditioning, a simple form of learning in which an organism comes to ignore a stimulus of little or no consequence*

Neutral stimulus   ⟶   No response
(a tone)   (no salivation)

UCS   ⟶   UCR
(food powder)   (salivation)

Once we get our stimuli and responses straight, the rest is easy. The two stimuli are paired. That is, they are presented at about the same time—the tone first, then the food powder. The salivation then occurs automatically in response to the food powder. We have a neutral stimulus, then a UCS, followed by the UCR (or tone-food-salivation).

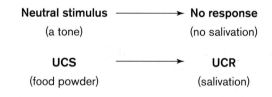

Neutral stimulus   +   UCS   ⟶   UCR
(a tone)   (food powder)   (salivation)

Each pairing of the two stimuli may be considered a conditioning *trial*. If we repeat this procedure several times—for several trials—conditioning, or learning, takes place. We find a relatively permanent change in behavior as a result of this experience. After a number of trials, when we present the tone by itself, the dog salivates, something it did not do before. Now the dog salivates not just in response to the food powder, but to the tone as well. The tone is no longer "neutral." Now it produces a response, so we call the tone a **conditioned stimulus (CS)**. To keep the salivation response that it elicits separate from the salivation in response to the food powder, we call it a **conditioned response (CR)**, indicating that it has been conditioned, or learned.

CS   ⟶   CR
(a tone)   (salivation)

Let's review: (1) We start with two stimuli: the neutral stimulus, which elicits no response, and the UCS, which elicits the UCR. (2) We repeatedly present the two stimuli together. (3) As a result, we find that when we present the CS alone, it now elicits a CR.

The same type of stimulus—a tone, for example—can be either a neutral stimulus (before learning occurs), or a conditioned stimulus (when it elicits a learned response). Similarly, the same type of response—say, salivation—can be either an unconditioned response (if it is elicited without learning) or a conditioned response (if it is elicited as the result of learning).

If you have a pet at home, you have seen this process in action. If you keep your pet's food in the same cabinet all the time, you may note a range of excited, anticipatory behaviors by your pet every time you open that cabinet door. The open door (CS) has been paired with the food within it (UCS), now producing the same sort of reaction (CR) that was originally reserved for the food (UCR).

Shortly we'll look at how classical conditioning influences human behaviors, but let me make it clear now that classical conditioning is not something that occurs only in dogs and cats. You demonstrate a classically conditioned salivation response when you see pictures or smell the aromas of your favorite foods (particularly if you're hungry). If you respond with anxiety at the sight of your instructor entering the classroom with exam papers, you're displaying a classically conditioned response.

There are two technical points I need to make. First, the CR seldom reaches the strength of the UCR no matter how many times the CS and the UCS are paired. For example, in salivation conditioning, we never get as much saliva in response to the tone (as a CR) as we originally got in response to the food powder alone (as a UCR). Second, *how* the conditioned stimulus and the unconditioned stimulus are paired does matter. If you think about it, you'll realize that there are many ways in which two stimuli can be presented at about the same time (e.g., simultaneously, or UCS then CS, or CS then UCS, with varying time intervals in between). Of all the alternatives, one method consistently works best: The CS comes first, followed shortly (within a second or so) by the UCS, or, again, tone-food-salivation. (I tell my classes that Pavlovian conditioning is basically a matter of "ding-food-slobber.")

> *Before You Go On*

What are the basic procedures of classical conditioning?

Classical Conditioning Phenomena

Now that we have the basics of classical conditioning in mind, we can turn to some of the details that go along with it—some of the procedures developed in Pavlov's laboratory. We'll first see how a classical conditioning experiment actually proceeds.

---

conditioned stimulus (CS) *in classical conditioning, an originally neutral stimulus (such as a tone) that, when paired with a UCS, comes to evoke a new response (a CR)*

conditioned response (CR) *in classical conditioning, the learned response (such as salivation in response to a tone) evoked by the CS after conditioning*

Acquisition

acquisition *the process in classical conditioning in which the strength of the CR increases with repeated pairings of the CS and UCS*

The stage of classical conditioning during which the strength of the CR increases—in which a dog acquires the response of salivating to a tone—is called **acquisition.** When conditioning begins, the conditioned stimulus (CS) does not produce a conditioned response (CR), which is why we refer to it as a neutral stimulus at this point. After a few pairings of the CS and UCS (conditioning trials), we can demonstrate the presence of a CR. To do that, of course, we'll have to present the conditioned stimulus (CS) by itself. We now discover that there is some saliva produced in response to the tone presented alone. The more trials of the CS and UCS together, the more the dog salivates in response to the tone when it is presented alone. Over repeated trials, the increase in CR strength (the amount of saliva in response to the tone) is rapid at first, but soon slows, and eventually levels off. The first part of Figure 5.1 illustrates the acquisition phase of classical conditioning.

Extinction and Spontaneous Recovery

extinction *the process in classical conditioning in which the strength of the CR decreases with repeated presentations of the CS alone (without the UCS)*

Assume we have a well-conditioned dog producing a good deal of saliva at the sound of a tone. Continuing to present the CS-UCS pair adds little to the amount of saliva we get when we present the tone alone. Now we go through a series of trials during which the CS (the tone) is presented but is not paired with the UCS (no more food powder). The result is that the CR will weaken. As we continue to present the tone alone, the dog provides less and less saliva. If we keep it up, the dog eventually will stop salivating to the tone. This is called **extinction**—the process in which the strength of a CR decreases with repeated presentations of the CS alone (without the UCS).

spontaneous recovery *the phenomenon in classical conditioning in which a previously extinguished CR returns after a rest interval*

It would appear that we're right back where we started. Because the CR has been extinguished, when we present the tone, our dog does nothing—at least it no longer salivates. Let's return our dog to the kennel and give it a rest. When the dog comes back to the laboratory and the tone is sounded, the dog salivates again! Not a lot, perhaps, but the salivation does return, or recover. It recovers automatically, or spontaneously, so we call this phenomenon **spontaneous recovery**. Extinction and spontaneous recovery are also illustrated in Figure 5.1.

Spontaneous recovery occurs after extinction and following a rest interval, which indicates two things. First, one series of extinction trials may not be sufficient to eliminate a conditioned response. Because of the possibility of spontaneous recovery, to get our dog to stop salivating altogether, we may have to run more

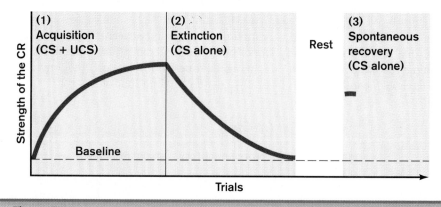

Figure 5.1

The stages of conditioning. (1) Acquisition is produced by the repeated pairing of a CS and a UCS. The strength of the CR increases rapidly at first, then slows, and eventually levels off. (2) Extinction is produced by presenting the CS without pairing it with the UCS. The strength of the CR then decreases. (3) After a rest interval (and following extinction), spontaneous recovery is demonstrated by a partial return of the CR.

than one series of extinction trials. Second, what is happening during extinction is not literally "forgetting"—at least not in the usual sense. The response is not forgotten so much as it is suppressed. That is, the learned salivation response is still there, but it is not showing up in performance during extinction, which is why it can (and does) return later, in spontaneous recovery.

Before You Go On

In classical conditioning, what are acquisition, extinction, and spontaneous recovery?

Generalization and Discrimination

During the course of conditioning, assume we consistently use a tone of a given pitch as the conditioned stimulus. After repeated pairings of this tone with food powder, a dog salivates when the tone is presented alone.

What will happen if we now present a different tone, one the dog has not heard before? Typically, the dog will salivate in response to it also. This response may not be as strong as the original CR (there may not be as much saliva). How strong it is depends on how similar the new tone is to the original CS. The more similar the new tone is to the original, the more saliva will be produced. This is **generalization**—a process by which a conditioned response is elicited by stimuli different from, but similar to, the CS.

This is a powerful process. It means that an unconditioned stimulus need not be paired with all possible conditioned stimuli. If you choose a mid-range CS, a conditioned response automatically generalizes to other, similar stimuli. Conditioning does not have to be applied over and over for separate stimuli. A graph of this process is presented in Figure 5.2. A young boy is bitten by a large black Labrador

generalization the phenomenon in classical conditioning in which a CR is elicited by stimuli different from, but similar to, the CS

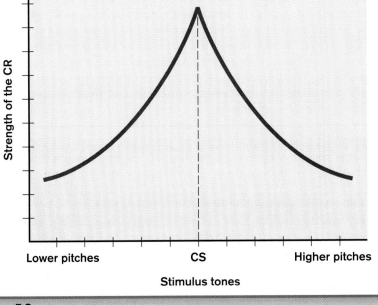

Figure 5.2

Generalization. Presenting stimuli other than the CS may produce a CR. How much conditioned response is produced depends on the similarity between the new stimulus and the original CS.

retriever. Originally, this dog was a neutral stimulus, but having been paired (associated) with the trauma and pain of a bite, the dog is now feared by the boy (a conditioned response). Is it not predictable that the boy's conditioned fear will generalize to other large black dogs—and, to a lesser extent, to small gray ones?

So, if a dog is conditioned to salivate to a tone of middle pitch, it also will salivate to higher and lower tones through generalization. What if we do not want it to? What if we want our dog to salivate to the CS alone and not to other tones? We would use a process called **discrimination** training, in which an organism learns to make a CR in response to only one CS but not to other stimuli. In a sense, discrimination is the opposite of generalization. To demonstrate discrimination training, we would present a dog with many tones, but would pair the UCS food powder with only one of them—the CS we want the dog to salivate to. We might, for example, pair food powder with a tone of middle C. A lower tone, say A, would also be presented to the dog, but *would not* be followed by food powder. At first there would be some saliva in response to the lower A tone (generalization), but eventually our subject would learn to discriminate and would no longer salivate to the lower tone of A.

discrimination *the phenomenon in classical conditioning in which an organism learns to make a CR in response to only one CS but not to other stimuli*

Before You Go On

In classical conditioning, what are generalization and discrimination?

ꙭꙭꙭ **Thinking Critically** ꙭꙭꙭ

Which of your own behaviors have been classically conditioned? Have they demonstrated either generalization or discrimination?

The Significance of Classical Conditioning for People

It is time to leave our discussion of dogs, tones, salivation, and Pavlov's laboratory and turn our attention to the practical application of classical conditioning. Once we start looking, we can find examples of classically conditioned human behaviors everywhere.

One of the significant aspects of classical conditioning is its role in the development of emotional responses to stimuli in our environment. There are few stimuli that naturally, or instinctively, produce an emotional response. Yet think of all those things that *do* directly influence how we feel.

For example, very young children seldom seem afraid of spiders, plane rides, or snakes. (Some children actually seem to enjoy them.) How many people do you know who *are* afraid of these things? There are many stimuli in our environments that cause us to be afraid. There are stimuli that produce feelings of pleasure, calm, and being at ease. What scares you? What makes you feel relaxed? Why? Might you feel upset in a certain store because you once had an unpleasant experience there? Might you fondly look forward to a vacation at the beach because of a very enjoyable vacation you had there as a child? Do you shudder at the sight of a police car, or smile at the thought of a payroll envelope? In each case, we are talking about classical conditioning. (Not all our learned emotional reactions are acquired through classical conditioning alone. As we shall see, there are other possibilities.)

When I was a senior in high school, I agreed to have surgery on my nose. (A not-very-well coordinated basketball player, I had broken it a number of times.) The surgery was done under local anesthetic, was painful, messy, and altogether unpleasant. For nearly twenty years after that surgery, whenever I visited a hospital, my nose ached! Now I knew better. I knew that the pain was just "in my head," but my nose hurt nonetheless. This is an example of some relatively permanent classical conditioning, isn't it? The CS of hospital sights, sounds, and odors was paired with the UCS of an operative procedure that caused a UCR of pain and discomfort. This pairing, which lasted for a few days, led to the establishment of a CR of discomfort associated with the CS of the hospital. My conditioned response obvi-

Early childhood experiences with particular dogs will generalize to other, similar, dogs, and may affect how one feels about dogs for many years.

ously generalized to many other hospitals, not just the one in which the surgery was performed. And the conditioned response took a very long time to extinguish.

An Example: The Case of "Little Albert"

In 1920, John B. Watson (the founder of behaviorism) and his student assistant, Rosalie Rayner, published a summary article about a series of experiments they performed with "Little Albert." Albert's experiences have become well known, and although Watson and Rayner's summary of their own work tended to oversimplify matters (Samuelson, 1980), the story of Little Albert provides a good model for the classical conditioning of emotional responses.

Eleven-month-old Albert was given many toys to play with. Among other things, he was allowed to play with a live white rat. Albert enjoyed the rat; at least he showed no sign of fearing it. Then conditioning began. One day, just as Albert reached for the rat, one of the experimenters (Rayner) made a sudden loud noise by striking a metal bar with a hammer. The loud noise frightened Albert. Two months earlier Watson and Rayner had established that a sudden loud noise frightened Albert—at least he behaved in a way that Watson and Rayner felt indicated fear.

After repeated pairings of the rat and the loud noise, Albert's reaction to the rat underwent a relatively permanent change. Albert would at first start to reach out toward the rat, but then would recoil and cry, often trying to bury his head in his

For a long time, advertisers have understood the value of pairing products with images of people having a good time. The hope is that, through classical conditioning, you will come to associate the product with having a good time. This ad for Seven-Up was published in 1950.

blanket. He was making emotional responses to a stimulus that did not elicit those responses before it was paired with a sudden loud noise. This sounds like classical conditioning: the rat is the CS and the sudden loud noise is the UCS that elicits the UCR of an emotional fear response. After repeated pairings of the rat and the noise (CS and UCS), the rat elicits the same sort of fear response (or CR). Figure 5.3 presents a diagram of the procedures used to condition Little Albert to be afraid of a white rat.

Watson and Rayner then went on to demonstrate that Albert's fear of the white rat generalized to all sorts of stimuli: a dog, a ball of cotton, even a Santa Claus mask with a white beard and mustache. In some cases, however, Watson and Rayner did not test for generalization as they should have. They occasionally paired the loud noise (UCS) with new stimuli before testing to see what the reaction might be (Harris, 1979).

Several issues have been raised concerning Watson and Rayner's demonstration of learned fear—not the least of which is the unethical treatment of Albert. It is unlikely that anyone would even attempt such a project today. Watson had previously argued (1919) that emotional experiences of early childhood can affect an individual for a lifetime, yet here he was purposely frightening a young child (and without the advised consent of the boy's mother). Albert's mother removed him

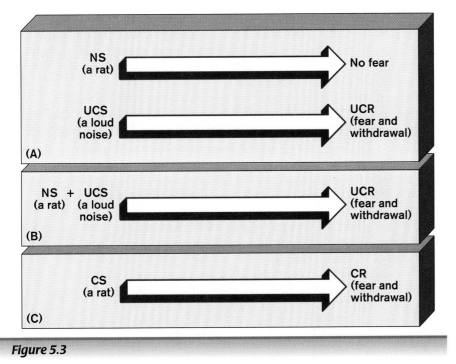

Figure 5.3

Conditioned fear in "Little Albert" as an example of classical conditioning.

from the hospital before Watson and Rayner had a chance to undo the conditioning. They were convinced that they could reverse Little Albert's fear, but as fate would have it, they never got the chance. A number of researchers who tried to replicate Watson and Rayner's experiment, despite ethical considerations, were not totally successful (Harris, 1979).

Even with these disclaimers, it is easy to see how the Little Albert demonstration can be used as a model for describing how fear or any other emotional response can develop. When the project began, Albert didn't respond fearfully to a rat, cotton, or a furry mask. After a few trials of pairing a neutral stimulus (the rat) with an emotion-producing stimulus (the loud noise), Albert appeared afraid of all sorts of white, fuzzy objects.

Before You Go On

What sorts of responses are most readily formed by classical conditioning?

@@@@ **Thinking Critically** @@@@

Describe the "Little Albert" demonstration.

An Application: Treating Fear with Classical Conditioning

There are many things in this world that are life-threatening and downright frightening. Being afraid of certain stimuli is often a wise, rational, adaptive reaction. Occasionally, however, some people experience distressing fears of stimuli that are not threatening in any real or rational sense.

Some people are intensely afraid of heights, spiders, the dark, riding on elevators, or flying. Psychologists say that these people are suffering from a **phobic disorder**—an intense, irrational fear of an object or event that leads a person to avoid contact with it. There are many explanations for how phobic disorders, or phobias, occur, but one clear possibility is classical conditioning.

Sadly, phobic disorders are far from rare. Estimates place prevalence at between 7 and 20 percent of the population, and that's tens of millions of people

phobic disorder *an intense, irrational fear of an object or event that leads a person to avoid contact with it*

(Kessler, 1994; Marks, 1986; Robins et al., 1984). Phobic reactions seldom extinguish on their own. Why don't they? There are many reasons, but one is that someone with a phobia is usually successful at avoiding the conditioned stimulus that elicits the fear. Someone with a fear of flying may simply get where he or she wants to go by driving or taking a bus or train.

Although there are a number of techniques that are used to treat phobic disorders (see Chapter 13), one of the most common is based on Pavlovian conditioning. The procedure, called *systematic desensitization,* was introduced by therapist Joseph Wolpe (1958, 1969, 1981). As an example, we'll consider a college student with an extreme fear of public speaking, who is now enrolled in a speech class.

In its standard form, there are three stages of systematic desensitization. First, the therapist instructs or trains the client to relax. There are several ways to go about such training. Some therapists use hypnosis, but most simply have the client relax one foot, then both feet, one leg, then both, and so on, until the entire body is relaxed. Whatever method is used, this stage generally doesn't take very long. After a few hours of training, the subject knows how to enter a relaxed state quickly.

The second stage is to construct an "anxiety hierarchy"—a listing of stimuli that gradually decrease in their ability to elicit anxiety. The most feared stimulus is placed at the top of the list (in our example that might be "Giving a formal speech to a large group," followed by "Being called on in class," "Talking to a small group of strangers," "Being introduced to two or more people," "Talking with friends," and so on).

Now treatment is ready to begin. The student relaxes completely and thinks about the stimulus lowest on the anxiety hierarchy. The student is then instructed to think about the next highest stimulus, and the next, and so on, all the while remaining as relaxed as possible. As progress is made up the list toward the anxiety-producing stimulus at the top, the therapist constantly monitors the student's level of tension or relaxation. When anxiety seems to be overcoming relaxation, the stu-

A phobic fear of heights, apparently not a problem for this daring snowboarder, may be a conditioned emotional response. If so, it can be lessened or relieved through systematic desensitization.

dent is told to stop thinking about that item on the hierarchy and to think about an item lower on the list.

Systematic desensitization is more than the simple extinction of a previously conditioned fear response. A new response (relaxation) is being acquired to "replace" an old one (fear). This process is called *counterconditioning*. The logic is that a person cannot be relaxed and anxious at the same time. These are incompatible responses. If I pair a stimulus (CS) with the feeling of being relaxed (UCS), through classical conditioning it will come to produce a reaction of calm (a CR), not the incompatible response of tension and anxiety (the old CR). For many people, this technique can be effective (e.g., Wilson, 1982). It works best for fears or anxieties associated with specific, easily identifiable stimuli; it works least well for a diffuse, generalized fear, for which hierarchies are difficult to generate.

Before You Go On

What is systematic desensitization?

Rethinking What Happens in Classical Conditioning

Pavlovian conditioning continues to be an active area of research. Psychologists today are interested in understanding precisely what happens in classical conditioning and what factors influence the effectiveness of the procedure (Adler & Cohen, 1993; Domjan, 1987; Lavond et al., 1993; Rescorla, 1987, 1988; Spear et al., 1990).

Pavlov believed, as did generations of psychologists who followed him, that any stimulus paired with an unconditioned stimulus could effectively serve as a conditioned stimulus. It's easy to see how psychologists came to this conclusion. A wide variety of stimuli *can* be paired with food powder and as a result come to elicit salivation. It was further understood that the time interval between the CS and the UCS had to be brief.

We now see classical conditioning in a broader light: as a process of learning about relationships among events in the world; as an active search for ways to represent the environment; as a search for information that one stimulus provides about another. We also recognize that there are biological constraints on which sorts of conditioning are likely to occur easily.

> Pavlovian conditioning is not a stupid process by which the organism willy-nilly forms associations between any two stimuli that happen to co-occur. Rather, the organism is better seen as an information seeker using logical and perceptual relations among events, along with its own preconceptions, to form a sophisticated representation of its world. (Rescorla, 1988, p. 154)

Can *Any* Stimulus Serve as a CS?

At least two lines of research suggest that one cannot pair just any stimulus with an unconditioned stimulus and expect conditioning to result. One is associated with Robert Rescorla and his colleagues, the other with Leon Kamin and his colleagues.

A rat can be conditioned to fear the sound of a tone by presenting that tone and consistently following it with an electric shock. It doesn't take many pairings of the tone and the shock for the conditioned response (fear of tone) to develop—a straightforward example of classical conditioning. Assume that we present a different rat with a tone and occasionally follow it with a mild shock. For this rat, we also present the shock from time to time, but *without the preceding tone.* This rat will end up with several shocks without a preceding tone, but it will have as many tone-shock pairings as our first rat. Will this rat demonstrate a conditional response to

⊚⊚⊚ **Thinking Critically** ⊚⊚⊚

Can you think of any risks that might be associated with systematic desensitization?

the tone when it is presented alone? No, it won't. Although this rat experienced the same number of tone-shock pairings, there will be no conditioning (Rescorla, 1968, 1987). Before I explain this failure of conditioning, let's consider Kamin's research.

In a demonstration of a phenomenon called *blocking,* rats are shocked (a UCS) at the same time a noise (the CS) is presented. Classically conditioned fear of the noise is readily established. The rats are then given several trials in which the noise *and* a light (a new "compound" CS) are paired with the UCS of a shock. Even though the light (now presented with the noise) is paired with the shock several times, no conditioned fear of the light will be found. That is, when the light is presented to these rats by itself, no fear reaction can be detected. The light remains a neutral stimulus. The rats had learned that the noise was a good predictor of the shock; presenting the light was redundant and not informative (Kamin, 1968, 1969).

In both of these cases (and in others; e.g., Miller & Spear, 1985; Pearce & Hall, 1980; Rescorla & Wagner, 1972), what matters most in determining whether a stimulus will act as a CS is the extent to which that stimulus provides information, or predicts the occurrence of another stimulus. In the original Pavlovian demonstration, the tone was highly informative. Every time the tone was presented, food powder followed, so the tone was an effective CS. In Rescorla's experiments, we see that if the tone does not reliably predict the presence of a shock (as when some shocks occur without the previous tone), that tone will not be an effective CS no matter how many times it is paired with the UCS. And in Kamin's experiments we see that because rats had already learned that the noise predicted the shocks, adding a light as a potential CS provided no additional information and hence was ineffective.

Let's recast this issue in human terms. If we can talk about rats representing their environments by learning which stimuli predict other stimuli, isn't it reasonable to think about classical conditioning in humans in a similar vein? We may experience a pleasant feeling when we see a picture of a mountain stream because it is associated with one of our best vacations. The fact that we happened to have left for that vacation on a Tuesday is not. Mountain streams predict fun and good times; Tuesdays do not. We have not been conditioned to associate a fireplace with the pain of being burned, even though we may have first been burned when we placed our hand into a fire there. Little Albert's fear of a rat generalized to many stimuli, but he developed no particular fear of blankets, even though he was sitting on a blanket every time Raynor created the loud noise that Albert did come to associate with the rat.

Now, let's consider an additional complication that has arisen in the search to understand the basic process of classical conditioning: the fact that the CS and the UCS do not have to be paired close together in time.

Before You Go On

Under what circumstances are stimuli likely to serve effectively as conditioned stimuli?

Taste aversion involves a classically conditioned association of nausea or an upset stomach with foods eaten earlier. Seldom is the nausea associated with stimuli such as the restaurant where the food was eaten, the server of the food, or others you may have eaten with.

Must the Time Interval Between the CS and UCS Always Be Brief?

Pavlov thought that the time interval between the CS and the UCS was a critical variable in classical conditioning. For nearly fifty years it was assumed that the most appropriate interval between the CS and UCS was a brief one—a few seconds, at most (Beecroft, 1966; Gormezano, 1972). The claim in most textbooks on learning was that the shorter the interval between the CS and UCS, the faster conditioning would be. It now appears that there is at least one excellent example of classical conditioning in which the CS-UCS interval may be much longer than a few seconds—even hours long. This example also reinforces the point that some stimuli make more effective conditioned stimuli than others. The example is found in the research on the formation of aversions (very strong dislikes) to certain tastes.

Many experiments have confirmed that rats and people (and many other animals) can be classically conditioned to avoid particular foods (Garcia et al., 1966; Gemberling & Domjan, 1982; Revulsky & Garcia, 1970). For example, rats eat or drink a food that has been given a distinctive taste. Then they are given a poison, or treated with X rays, so that they will develop nausea. However, the feelings of nausea do not occur until hours after the food has been eaten. (In a few days, the rats are perfectly normal and healthy again.) Even though there has been a long delay between the flavored food (CS) and the feelings of nausea (UCS), the rats learn to avoid the food, often in just one trial. Patients being treated for cancer may experience nausea as an unpleasant side effect of chemotherapy. Such patients will often show a strong taste aversion for whatever they ate hours before their treatment—even if what they ate was something pleasant, such as ice cream (Bernstein, 1978).

The time delay between the CS and UCS here is clearly at odds with the standard belief that to be effective the CS and UCS need to be presented together in time. A related question is why the *taste* of previously eaten food should so commonly serve as the CS for nausea that occurs hours later. That is, why is the nausea associated with the taste of food instead of some other stimulus event that could be paired with the nausea? Think of this experience happening to you. At a restaurant, you order a piece of pumpkin pie. Hours later, you suffer severe stomach cramps and nausea. Why should you then associate these physical symptoms with the pie and not the type of chair you sat on, or the car you drove to the restaurant, or the person you were with? Actually, we may have a predisposition, or bias, rooted in our biology for associating some things with others, particularly if they have a functional basis (Mackintosh, 1975, 1983; Revulsky, 1985). Food followed by nausea is an example of just such a predisposed association.

Before You Go On

What do taste aversion studies tell us about the CS and the UCS in classical conditioning?

TOPIC 5A SUMMARY

Learning is inferred from the observation of relatively permanent changes in behavior that occur as the result of practice or experience. In this Topic, we have reviewed the procedures of classical, or Pavlovian, conditioning. In this sort of conditioning, when one stimulus precedes another and predicts the occurrence of a second stimulus, that first stimulus comes to produce the response usually produced by the second one. One of the major applications of Pavlovian conditioning is in eliciting emotional behaviors. Many of the stimuli to which we respond emotionally do not elicit these responses naturally or reflexively; they do so through classical conditioning. There are other ways in which classical conditioning can have an impact on our daily lives. In Topic 5B, we consider another fundamental form of learning: operant conditioning.

TOPIC 5B Operant Conditioning and Cognitive Approaches

The premise of operant conditioning is that behaviors are shaped by the consequences they have produced in the past.

The Basics of Operant Conditioning

Most of the early research on operant conditioning was done by B. F. Skinner. Although we correctly associate operant conditioning with Skinner, he did not discover it in any literal sense. The techniques of operant conditioning had been in use for hundreds of years before Skinner was born. What Skinner did was bring that earlier work—most of it casual, some of it scientific—into the laboratory. There he studied the process of operant conditioning with a unique vigor that helped the rest of us realize the significance of the process.

Defining Operant Conditioning

operant *behavior(s) used by an organism to interact with or operate on its environment*

operant conditioning *a procedure that changes the rate of a response on the basis of the consequences that result from that response*

Skinner used the term **operant** to refer to a behavior or group of behaviors an organism uses to operate on its environment. Operants are controlled by their consequences: they will maintain or increase their rate if they are reinforced; they will decrease their rate if they are not reinforced or if they are punished. Thus, **operant conditioning** changes the rate, or probability, of responses on the basis of the consequences that result from those responses. We are not claiming here that the future governs what happens in the present, but that past experiences influence present ones. Skinner put it this way, ". . . behavior is shaped by its consequences, but only by consequences that lie in the past. We do what we do because of what *has* happened, not what *will* happen" (Skinner, 1989, p. 14).

Figure 5.4

After noting that cats became more and more proficient at escaping from his "puzzle box," E. L. Thorndike came to believe that they were demonstrating lawful behaviors. Those behaviors could be explained, Thorndike argued, in terms of his *law of effect*.

Actually, the first clear statement of operant conditioning came not from Skinner, but from E. L. Thorndike, a psychologist at Columbia University in the early twentieth century, who worked to discover the "laws of learning." In one experiment, he placed a cat inside a wooden box. The door of the box was latched with a wooden peg. If manipulated correctly, the peg could be moved and the latch opened, and the cat could go outside the box to eat a small piece of fish that Thorndike had placed there (Figure 5.4). When it was first placed in the box, the cat engaged in a wide range of behaviors: clawing, licking, biting, scratching, hissing, stretching, and so on. But eventually—and at first, by chance—the door was unlatched and the cat got to the food. The next time the cat was in Thorndike's "puzzle box," it exhibited many of the same behaviors, but it did unlatch the door and escape a bit sooner. Over a series of trials, Thorndike noted that his cat reduced its irrelevant behaviors and directly moved to open the door more and more quickly. After some experience, a cat placed in the box would go immediately to the latch, move the peg, open the door, and eat the fish provided by its trainer. Thorndike had discovered a law of learning—the *law of effect.*

The **law of effect** embodies the basics of operant conditioning, claiming that responses are learned ("stamped in," Thorndike said) when followed by a "satisfying state of affairs" (Thorndike, 1911, p. 245). On the other hand, if a response is not followed by a satisfying state of affairs, or if a response leads to "discomfort," an organism will tend not to make that response again. Thorndike seemed to be saying, "We tend to do, and continue to do, whatever makes us feel good." This seemingly simple observation is also a profound one, because it is true. Behaviors are shaped by their consequences.

law of effect (Thorndike's) *the observation that responses that lead to a "satisfying state of affairs" tend to be repeated; responses that do not lead to a satisfying state of affairs tend not to be repeated*

Examples of operant conditioning are all around us. You don't need any special apparatus to observe the principle. Imagine a father rushing through a supermarket with his toddler seated in a shopping cart. The youngster is screaming at the top of his lungs for a candy bar—over and over, echoing throughout the store, "I wanna candy bar! I wanna candy bar!" Father is doing a good (and an appropriate) job of ignoring this monstrous behavior until he spies a neighbor coming down the next aisle. The neighbor has her three children with her, all of whom are acting like perfect angels. What's a parent to do? He races by the checkout lanes, grabs a chocolate bar, and gives it to his child. Does one have to be an expert in child psychology (or operant conditioning) to predict what will happen on the next visit to the store? Screaming "worked" this time, so it will be tried again. Reinforced behaviors tend to recur.

Demonstrating Operant Conditioning

To demonstrate operant conditioning in the laboratory, Skinner built a special apparatus, which he called an operant chamber. Although Skinner never used the term, and said he didn't like it (Skinner, 1984), some psychologists call this device a "Skinner box." Figure 5.5 shows a standard operant chamber. The chamber pictured here is designed for rats. The box is empty except for a small lever that protrudes from one wall and a small cup that holds a piece of rat food. Food pellets are automatically dispensed through a tube into the food cup. They are released one at a time when the lever is pressed all the way down.

Now that we have our chamber, we need a subject. If we put a hungry rat into the chamber and do nothing else, the rat will occasionally press the lever. There's little else for it to do in there. Rats naturally explore their environments and tend to manipulate objects in it. The rate at which the rat freely presses the lever is called its *base rate* of responding. Typically, a rat will press the lever 8 to 10 times an hour.

After a period of observation, we activate the food dispenser so that a food pellet is delivered every time the lever is pressed. As predicted by Thorndike's law of effect, the rate of the lever-pressing response increases. The rat may reach the point of pressing the lever as many as 500 to 600 times an hour. Learning has

Figure 5.5

A drawing of a typical operant chamber.

taken place. There has been a relatively permanent change in behavior as a result of experience.

Here is a little subtlety: has the rat learned to press the lever? In any sense can we say that we have taught the rat a lever-pressing response? No. The rat "knew" how to press the lever and did so long before we introduced the food pellets as a reward for its behavior. What it did learn—the change in behavior that took place—was a change in *the rate* of the response, not in *the nature* of the response.

Before You Go On

What is operant conditioning?

@@@@ **Thinking Critically** @@@@

Identify two instances of operant conditioning in your own life.

The Course of Conditioning

Now that we have the basic principles of operant conditioning in mind, let's briefly review just how one goes about using the procedure.

A reality of operant conditioning is that before you can reinforce a response, you have to get that response to occur in the first place. If your rat never presses the lever, it will never get a pellet. What if you place your rat in an operant chamber and discover that after grooming itself, it stops, stares off into space, and settles down, facing away from the lever and the food cup? Your operant chamber is prepared to deliver a food pellet as soon as your rat presses the lever, but you may have a long wait.

shaping *a procedure of reinforcing successive approximations of a desired response until that desired response is made*

In such circumstances, you could use a procedure called **shaping**, reinforcing *successive approximations* of the response you ultimately want to condition. You have a button that delivers a pellet to the food cup of the operant chamber even though the lever is not pressed. When your rat turns to face the lever, you deliver a pellet, reinforcing that behavior. This isn't exactly the response you want, but at least the rat is facing in the correct direction. You don't give your rat another pellet until it moves toward the lever. It gets another pellet for moving even closer to the lever. The next pellet doesn't come until the rat touches the lever. Eventually the rat will press the lever to deliver a pellet by itself. Shaping is over, and the rat is on its own.

Once an organism emits the responses you wish to reinforce, the procedures of operant conditioning are simple. Immediately following the response, a reinforcer is provided. As responses produce reinforcers, those responses become more and more likely to occur. The increase in response rate that follows reinforcement will generally be slow at first, then become more rapid, and eventually will level off. This stage in which response rates increase is **acquisition**. Figure 5.6 is a curve showing the stages of operant conditioning. Note that the vertical axis is a measure of *rate of response,* not response strength, that is, what increases in acquisition for operant conditioning is the rate of a response.

acquisition *the process in operant conditioning in which the rate of a reinforced response increases*

Once an organism is responding at a high rate of response, what will happen if reinforcers are withheld? Let's say that because we have reinforced its lever pressing, a rat is pressing a lever at a rate of 550 presses an hour. From now on, however, it will receive no more pellets of food for its efforts—no more reinforcers. What happens is very predictable: the rate of lever-pressing response decreases gradually until it returns to the low base rate at which it began. That is, eventually the lever pressing returns to base rate (not to zero, because it didn't start at zero), and we say that **extinction** has taken place. In operant conditioning, extinction is the decrease in the rate of a response as reinforcers are withheld.

extinction *the process in operant conditioning in which the rate of a response decreases as reinforcers are withheld*

Now assume that extinction has occurred, and that the rat has been removed from the operant chamber and returned to its cage for a few days. When we again deprive it of food and return it to the chamber, what will it do? It will go to the lever and begin to press it again. Although the lever pressing has undergone extinction (the last time this rat was in the operant chamber, it was not pressing the

Operant conditioning techniques were used to train this dolphin.

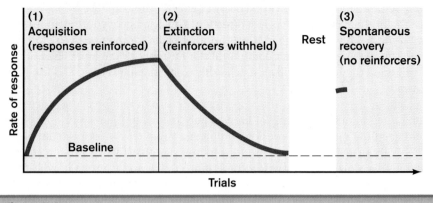

Figure 5.6

The stages of operant conditioning. (1) During acquisition, response rates increase as responses are reinforced. (2) In extinction, reinforcers are withheld and response rates return to their original baseline rates. In spontaneous recovery, an increase in response rate is noted following a rest interval after extinction. Note that the vertical axis indicates a measure of the *rate* of a response, not its strength.

spontaneous recovery *the phenomenon in operant conditioning in which a previously extinguished response returns after a rest interval*

lever), it will resume once the rat is given a rest interval. This return of an extinguished response following a rest interval is called **spontaneous recovery**. Figure 5.6 also shows extinction and spontaneous recovery for operant conditioning.

> ### Before You Go On
>
> Describe shaping, acquisition, extinction, and spontaneous recovery as they occur in operant conditioning.

⊚⊚⊚ Thinking Critically ⊚⊚⊚

Think again of one of the instances of operant conditioning in your own life that you identified earlier. How could you reconstruct the experience to include shaping, acquisition, extinction, and spontaneous recovery?

reinforcement *a process that increases the rate, or probability, of the response it follows*

reinforcers *stimuli that increase the rate, or probability, of the responses they follow*

Reinforcement

From what I've said so far, it is obvious that reinforcement is a crucial concept in operant conditioning. **Reinforcement** is a process that increases the rate, or probability, of the response it follows. It is the operation of administering a *reinforcer.*

Positive and Negative Reinforcers

What qualifies as an effective reinforcer? What creates that satisfying state of affairs that Thorndike claimed is necessary to increase response rate? For hungry rats in operant chambers, the answer seems simple. Here we can ensure that a rat is hungry and can confidently predict that receiving food will be reinforcing. For people, or for rats who are no longer hungry, the answer may not be as obvious.

Skinner and his students have long argued that we should define reinforcers only in terms of their effect on behavior. Reinforcers are stimuli. Stimuli that increase the rate, or probability, of the response they follow are **reinforcers**. This reasoning suggests that nothing is necessarily going to be reinforcing. Reinforcers are defined only after we have noted their effect on behavior. Thus, we do not know ahead of time what will or what will not produce an increased rate of response—or a satisfying state of affairs. We may have some strong suspicions, based on what has worked in the past, but we will not know for sure until we try.

For example, determining what will or will not be reinforcing is sensitive to cultural influences. In many cultures (mostly Eastern and African) the group is valued above the individual. In such cultures, reinforcing an individual's achievements will have less effect than in those cultures (mostly Western) in which individual effort and achievement are valued (e.g., Arnett, 1995; Brislin, 1993; Triandis,

Playing Pigeon: A Shaping Exercise

This activity works best in small groups—it's nearly a party game. The point is to select one "player" to be your pigeon. The others in the group are to shape the behavior of the pigeon by using a positive verbal reinforcer, like "good" or "right," as the pigeon successively approximates the desired behavior. Desired behaviors for your pigeon might include such things as:

Sit on the floor.
Put your thumb in your mouth.
Scratch your right leg.
Put your hands over your ears.
Stand on a chair.
Take off your left shoe.
Pull your hair.
Sit down and cross your legs.

Clap your hands.
Spin around in a circle (twice).

Obviously, the "shapers" must know the goal behavior, but the pigeon must not. When you begin, the pigeon should start emitting behaviors, and the group should begin to shape the pigeon's behaviors toward the goal (target behavior). Make sure that the pigeon receives no feedback other than the verbal reinforcer. See how long it takes to shape your pigeon. Anything less than 5 minutes is good.

Once your group has had some success shaping behaviors by using positive reinforcers, try to shape one of the above behaviors with a punisher—that is, by saying "bad" or "no." This is more difficult, isn't it? Can you make any progress in 5 minutes?

1990). In traditional Hawaiian culture, the sense of family is strong, and personal independence is not a sought-after goal. Thus, "the Hawaiian child may not be motivated by individual rewards (gold stars, grades) to the extent that his or her Caucasian counterpart may be" (Cushner, 1990, p. 107). The point is that we cannot tell

Reinforcers come in many forms, including awards, prizes, trophies, medals, and letter grades. Sometimes the respect and appreciation of others can be powerfully reinforcing.

whether a stimulus will be reinforcing until we try it. It is reinforcing only if it increases the rate or the likelihood of the response it follows (Kimble, 1981).

Now that we have a general idea of what a reinforcer is, we can get more specific. A **positive reinforcer** is a stimulus given to an organism that increases (or maintains) the rate of a response it follows. This sounds familiar, and even redundant: if something is positive, it ought to be reinforcing. Examples include such stimuli as food for hungry organisms, water for thirsty ones, high letter grades for well-motivated students, and money, praise, and attention for most of us. Remember: the intention of the person doing the reinforcing does not matter at all. Reinforcers are defined solely on the basis of their effect on behavior.

A **negative reinforcer** is a stimulus that increases (or maintains) the rate of a response that precedes its removal. In order to increase the rate of a response, one *removes* or *terminates* a negative reinforcer. *Negative reinforcer* is a strange term. If something is negative, how can it be a reinforcer? Part of the secret is to remember that the key word here is *reinforcer,* and reinforcers increase the rate of responses. In terms of the law of effect, negative reinforcement must produce some sort of satisfying state of affairs. It does. The reinforcement comes not from the delivery or presentation of negative reinforcers, but from their removal. (Another secret is to remember that reinforcement is a process. You may think of negative reinforcers as unpleasant stimuli, whereas negative reinforcement is a pleasant process, or outcome.)

So negative reinforcers are stimuli that increase the probability of a response when they are removed. They may include such stimuli as shocks, enforced isolation, or ridicule—exactly the sorts of things a person would work to avoid or escape. Although it may not sound like it, negative reinforcement is desirable. If one is offered negative reinforcement, "one should accept the offer. It is always good to have bad things terminated or removed" (Michael, 1985, p. 107).

Consider a few examples. A rat in an operant chamber is given a constant shock (through the metal floor of the chamber). As soon as the rat presses a lever, the shock is turned off. The lever press has been reinforced. Because an unpleasant, painful stimulus was terminated, this was negative reinforcement—the negative reinforcer was the shock. You take an aspirin when you have a headache and are reinforced: the pain stops. You will be likely to try aspirin the next time you have a headache. When Wayne says "uncle" to get Ken to stop twisting his arm, Ken does stop, thereby reinforcing Wayne's saying "uncle." If this negative reinforcement is effective, Wayne will be more likely to say "uncle" in the future when Ken asks him to. (Note that Ken could have used a positive reinforcer to get Wayne to say "uncle," perhaps by offering him 50 cents to do so.) When a prisoner is released from prison early, "for good behavior," the good behavior is being reinforced. The process is negative reinforcement.

Here's one more hint for you, suggested by a few of my colleagues. Don't think of positive and negative reinforcement in terms of good and bad, but in terms of plus (+) and minus (−). In using positive reinforcement, one adds (+) a stimulus, and in negative reinforcement one takes away, or subtracts (−), a stimulus.

positive reinforcer *a stimulus that increases the rate of a response it follows*

negative reinforcer *a stimulus that increases the rate of a response when that stimulus is removed after the response is made*

Before You Go On

Distinguish between positive and negative reinforcers.

Primary and Secondary Reinforcers

We've seen that reinforcers are defined in terms of their effects on behavior and that both positive and negative reinforcers increase response rate. When we distinguish between primary and secondary reinforcers the issue is the extent to which reinforcers are natural and unlearned, or acquire their reinforcing capability through learning or experience.

Primary reinforcers do not require previous experience to be effective. They are related to the organism's survival in some way, and are usually physiological or biological in nature. Food for a hungry organism or water for a thirsty one are common examples. Providing a warm place by the fire to a cold, wet, stray dog involves primary reinforcement.

Secondary reinforcers may be referred to as *conditioned, acquired,* or *learned* reinforcers. There is nothing about them that implies that they are inherently reinforcing in any biological sense, yet they operate to strengthen responses. Most of the reinforcers you and I work for are of this sort. Money, praise, high letter grades, and promotions are good examples. Money, in itself, is not worth much. But previous experiences have convinced most of us of the reinforcing nature of money, and it can serve to increase the rate of a variety of responses. Among other things, we have learned that money can give us access to many other reinforcers, such as food and clothing.

The use of secondary reinforcers—and operant conditioning—can be illustrated by a type of psychotherapy called *contingency contracting* (see page 484 in Topic 13B). Contingency contracting amounts to setting up a system—called a token economy—that provides secondary reinforcers for appropriate behaviors. For example, a child earns a check mark on the calendar for each day he or she makes the bed (or takes out the trash, walks the dog, or clears the table). The economy here hinges on the extent to which the check marks serve as tokens, as secondary reinforcers. The child must first learn that a certain number of check marks can be exchanged for something that already reinforces his or her behaviors (for example, an extra dessert, an hour of playing a video game, or a new toy). Techniques such as this, when applied consistently, can be very effective in modifying behaviors.

Perhaps because of their effectiveness, examples such as this one often disturb students and parents. "Why, this isn't psychology," they argue. "You're just bribing the child to behave." There are at least two reasons why we need not be overly concerned. First, bribery involves contracting to reward someone to do something that both parties view as inappropriate. People are bribed to steal, cheat, lie, change votes, or otherwise engage in behaviors they know they should not. Token economies reinforce behaviors judged in the first place to be appropriate. Second, as Skinner argued for many years, the long-term hope is that the child (in our example) will come to appreciate that having trash removed, or walking the dog, or having a clean room is a valued end in itself, and can be its own reward. The hope is that the use of reinforcers will no longer be needed as appropriate behaviors become reinforced by more subtle, intrinsic factors.

Before You Go On

Compare and contrast primary and secondary reinforcers.

Scheduling Reinforcers

In all of our discussions and examples so far, I have implied that operant conditioning requires that a reinforcer be provided after every desired response. In fact, particularly at the start, it may be best to reinforce each response as it occurs. But as response rates begin to increase, there is good reason for reinforcing responses intermittently.

The procedure of reinforcing each and every response after it occurs is called a **continuous reinforcement (CRF) schedule**. One problem with CRF schedules is that earning a reinforcer after each response may reduce the effectiveness of that reinforcer. For example, once a rat has eaten its fill, food pellets will no longer serve

primary reinforcers *stimuli (usually biologically or physiologically based) that increase the rate of a response with no previous experience required*

secondary reinforcers *stimuli that increase the rate of a response because of their having been associated with other reinforcers; also called conditioned, or learned, reinforcers*

continuous reinforcement (CRF) schedule *a reinforcement schedule in which every response is followed by a reinforcer* to reinforce its behavior, and the rat will have to be removed from the operant chamber until it becomes hungry again (Skinner, 1956). Another problem is that responses acquired under a CRF schedule tend to extinguish very quickly. Once reinforcement is withheld, response rates decrease drastically.

Alternatives to reinforcing every response are **intermittent reinforcement schedules**. Simply put, these are strategies for reinforcing a response less frequently than every time it occurs. There are several ways in which one might reinforce responses according to an intermittent schedule. We will review four: the fixed-ratio, fixed-interval, variable-ratio, and variable-interval schedules. These schedules were devised in the laboratory. In the world outside the laboratory, there are not many good examples of the precise, literal application of intermittent schedules. There are a few real-life examples that are fairly close, however, and they are instructive. Although intermittent schedules do influence the manner in which responses are acquired, their major effects are on extinction. These effects are depicted in Figure 5.7.

With a *fixed-ratio (FR)* schedule, one establishes (fixes) a ratio of reinforcers to responses. In an FR 1:5 schedule, for example, a reinforcer is delivered after every five responses. A 1:10 fixed-ratio schedule for a rat in an operant chamber means that the rat receives a pellet only after it presses the lever ten times. Piecework is an example of a fixed-ratio schedule: "I'll pay you 25 cents for every 12 gizmos you assemble," or "You'll earn 10 points of credit for every three book reports you hand in." Understandably, there is a high and steady rate of responding under a fixed-ratio schedule. After all, the more one responds, the more reinforcement there will be. For most organisms, there is a brief pause just after a reinforcement occurs. Responses acquired under an FR schedule are more resistant to extinction than those acquired under a CRF schedule.

With a *fixed-interval (FI)* schedule, time is divided into set (fixed) intervals. After each fixed interval, a reinforcer is delivered when the next response occurs. An FI 30-second schedule calls for the delivery of a food pellet for the first lever press a rat makes after each 30-second interval passes. With such a schedule, you know from the start that you won't be dispensing more than two pellets every minute. Note that the rat doesn't get a pellet just because 30 seconds has elasped; it gets a pellet for the first response it makes after the fixed interval. A commonly cited ex-

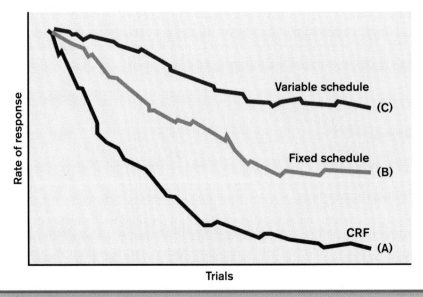

Figure 5.7

The effects of a schedule of reinforcement on extinction. These are three hypothetical extinction curves following operant conditioning on (A) continuous reinforcement (CRF), (B), a fixed schedule (FR or FI), and (C), a variable schedule (VR or VI).

ample is employees paid on a regular interval of, say, every Friday, or once a month. Under an FI schedule, response rates decrease immediately after a reinforcer, then increase as the time for the next reinforcer approaches. FI schedules also produce responses that are resistant to extinction.

There are two variable schedules of reinforcement: a *variable-ratio (VR)* schedule and a *variable-interval (VI)* schedule. From the learner's point of view, these schedules are very much alike. They differ from the perspective of the dispenser of reinforcers. With a VR schedule, one varies the ratio of reinforcers to responses. With a VR 1:5 schedule, the experimenter provides one reinforcer for every five responses *on the average,* but always in a different ratio. The first reinforcer may come after five responses, the next after six, the next after nine, the next after one, and so on. On the average, the ratio of reinforcers to responses is 1:5, but the patterning of actual ratios is variable. From the learner's point of view, this is a random schedule. The most commonly cited examples of VR reinforcement schedules are gambling devices, such as slot machines. They pay off (reinforce) on a variable-ratio schedule where the ratios are usually quite large. Not surprisingly, VR schedules produce high rates of responding and responses that are very resistant to extinction.

Variable-interval (VI) schedules follow the same logic as variable-ratio schedules. The difference is that for VI schedules, time intervals are established randomly. For a rat on a VI 30-second schedule, a food pellet comes following the first lever press response after a 30-second interval; the next follows the first response after a 50-second interval; then after a 10-second interval, and so on. For a VI 30-second schedule, the varied intervals *average* 30 seconds in length. An instructor who wants to keep a class studying regularly and attending class consistently may schedule quizzes on a variable-interval schedule. The students will learn that the quizzes are coming, but they never know when. What we find when VI schedules are used is a slower but very steady pattern of performance. If you know when your exams are coming, you may hold off studying until just before they occur. If they are scheduled to occur randomly throughout the semester, you'll keep your studying rate up just in case there's a test the next class period.

The terminology I have used here is standard, but it is somewhat technical. The main point to remember is that operant conditioning does not require that each response be reinforced. The scheduling of reinforcers will influence the pattern of the learned responses, and will affect their resistance to extinction.

Another point should be made regarding the scheduling of reinforcers. No matter whether one is using a continuous or an intermittent schedule, reinforcers should come immediately after the desired response is made. Delayed reinforcement is likely to be ineffective. I'm not saying that delaying reinforcement destroys the possibility of learning, but in most cases the more immediate the reinforcer, the better the learning. In one study, for example, rats were reinforced for entering a black box instead of a white one. The task was learned readily when reinforcers were delivered immediately. If the delivery of reinforcers was delayed only a second or two, very little learning took place; with a 10-second delay, there was no learning at all (Grice, 1948). Several experiments have demonstrated the same phenomenon with human subjects (Hall, 1976). This point has many practical applications. What if parents buy tickets to the circus to reinforce their son's behavior with the baby-sitter? But the circus is not until Saturday. When the family does go off to the circus Saturday afternoon, what is reinforced may not be the child's "good behaviors" of last Tuesday night but inappropriate behaviors of Wednesday, Thursday, Friday, and Saturday morning.

Before You Go On

What are fixed-ratio, fixed-interval, variable-ratio, and variable-interval schedules of reinforcement?

Punishment

punishment *the administration of a punisher, which is a stimulus that decreases the rate, or probability, of a response that precedes it*

We've talked about reinforcers—positive and negative, primary and secondary—and how they can be scheduled. Let's now consider punishment. **Punishment** occurs when a stimulus delivered to an organism *decreases* the rate, or probability, of the response that preceded it. In common usage, punishment is usually in some way hurtful or painful, either physically (a spanking) or psychologically (ridicule). It is a painful, unpleasant stimulus presented to an organism after some response is made. It may have occurred to you that if punishers are removed, the result will be reinforcing; in fact, we would have an example of negative reinforcement.

Determining ahead of time what stimulus will be punishing is as difficult to do as determining what stimulus will serve as a reinforcer. Once again, one's intentions are irrelevant. We'll know for sure that something is a punisher only after observing its effect on behavior. We may think we are punishing Jon by sending him to his room because he has begun to throw a temper tantrum. It may be that "in his room" is exactly where Jon would like to be. We may have reinforced Jon's temper tantrum behaviors simply by attending to them. The only way to know for certain is to note the effect on behavior. If Jon's tantrum-throwing behaviors become less frequent, sending him to his room may indeed have been a punishing thing to do.

We can think of punishers as being positive and negative in the same way that we explained positive and negative reinforcers. Positive punishment means delivering or giving (adding, +) a painful, unpleasant stimulus (e.g., a slap on the hand) following an inappropriate response. Negative punishment means removing (subtracting, −) a valued, pleasant stimulus (e.g., "No more TV for a week!") following an inappropriate response.

Is punishment an effective way of controlling behavior? Does punishment work? Yes, it does—sometimes. Punishment *can* be an impressive modifier of behavior. A rat has learned to press a lever to get food. Now you decide that you no longer want the rat to press the lever. You pass an electric current through the lever so that each time the rat touches the lever it receives a strong shock. What will happen? Actually, several things may happen, but—if your shock is strong enough—there's one thing of which we can be sure: the rat will stop pressing the

Punishment certainly need not mean physical abuse. Here we see an example of negative punishment—taking away something positive, or something of value. The child in the foreground ("sitting in the corner") is not allowed to participate in group activities with the others.

lever. If punishment is effective, why do psychologists argue against its use, particularly the punishment of children for their misbehavior?

There are many potential problems, or side-effects, of the use of punishment, even when it is used correctly. And often it is used incorrectly. Let's review some of what we know about the use of punishment (e.g., Axelrod & Apsche, 1983; Azrin & Holz, 1966; Walters & Grusec, 1977).

1. To be effective, punishment should be delivered immediately after the response. The logic here is the same as for the immediacy of reinforcement. Priscilla is caught in mid-afternoon throwing flour all over the kitchen. Father counts to ten in an attempt to control his temper (good), then says, "Just wait 'til your mother gets home" (not good). For the next three hours, Priscilla's behavior is angelic. When mother does get home, what is punished, Priscilla's flour tossing or the appropriate behaviors that followed?

2. For punishment to be effective, it needs to be administered consistently. If one chooses to punish a certain behavior, it should be punished whenever it occurs—and often that is difficult to do.

3. Punishment may decrease (suppress) overall behavior levels. Although an effectively punished response may end, so may other responses. That rat who has been shocked for pressing the bar not only will stop pressing the bar, but also cower in the corner, doing very little of anything.

4. When responses are punished, alternatives should be introduced. Think about your rat for a minute. The poor thing knows what to do when it is hungry: press the lever. Now it gets shocked for doing that very thing. With no alternative response to make in order to get food, the rat is in a conflict that has no solution. There is no way out. The result may be fear, anxiety, and even aggressiveness. One way to make this point is to say that punishment does not convey any information about what to do; it only communicates what not to do. Rubbing your puppy's nose in a "mess" it just made on the living room carpet doesn't give the dog much of a sense of what it is supposed to do when it feels a need to relieve itself; taking it outside will.

5. Among other things, spanking or hitting—physical approaches to punishment—provide a model for aggressive behavior. It conveys the message that when one is frustrated, to hit and to strike out is acceptable behavior—and it conveys the message that it's okay for "big" people to hit smaller people. As we will soon see, such a message, provided by important models, can easily be taken as a model for the behavior of youngsters.

Before You Go On

What are punishers, and how can they be used effectively?

Generalization and Discrimination

In classical conditioning, we saw that a response conditioned to one stimulus could be elicited by other, similar stimuli. We have a comparable process in operant conditioning, and again we call it **generalization**—a process in which responses conditioned in the presence of a specific stimulus appear in the presence of other, similar stimuli.

For example, little Leslie receives a reinforcer for saying "doggie" as a neighbor's poodle wanders across the front yard. "Yes, Leslie, good girl. That's a doggie."

⊚⊚⊚⊚ **Thinking Critically** ⊚⊚⊚⊚

Is effectiveness an adequate justification for the use of punishers? Why or why not?

generalization *the phenomenon in operant conditioning in which a response that was reinforced in the presence of one stimulus appears in response to other, similar stimuli*

Having learned that calling the poodle a "doggie" earns parental approval, the response is tried again, this time with a German shepherd. Leslie's operantly conditioned response of saying "doggie" in the presence of a poodle has generalized to the German shepherd. When it does, it will no doubt be reinforced again. The problem is, of course, that Leslie may overgeneralize "doggie" to virtually any furry, four-legged animal and start calling cats and raccoons "doggie" also. When a child turns to a total stranger and utters "Dada," generalization can (usually) be blamed for the embarrassing mislabeling.

The process of generalization can be countered with **discrimination** training. Discrimination conditioning is basically a matter of *differential reinforcement*. In other words, responses made to appropriate stimuli will be reinforced, while responses made to inappropriate stimuli will be ignored or extinguished (note: by withholding reinforcers, not by punishing the response).

To demonstrate how discrimination training works, consider a strange question. Are pigeons color blind? Disregarding for now why anyone would care, how might you go about testing the color vision of a pigeon? The standard tests we use for people certainly wouldn't work.

A pigeon can be readily trained to peck at a single lighted disk in order to earn a food reward. A pigeon in an operant chamber pecks at a lighted disk, and a few grains of food are delivered. Soon the pigeon pecks the disk at a high rate. Now let's present the pigeon with two lighted disks, one red, the other green. Otherwise, they are identical: the same shape, brightness, size, and so on. The question is whether the pigeon can tell the difference between red and green. We make the green disk the discriminative (positive) stimulus—pecking at it will earn a reinforcer. Pecks at the red disk will not be reinforced. The position of the colored disks is randomly altered, of course. We don't want simply to demonstrate that the pigeon can tell left from right.

The results of this sort of manipulation are depicted in Figure 5.8. At first the red and green lighted disks are responded to at an approximately equal rate. But in short order, the pigeon is ignoring the red disk and pecking only at the green one, for which it receives its reinforcer. In order to maintain such behavior, the pigeon must be able to discriminate between the two colored disks. We still don't know what red and green look like to a pigeon, but we may conclude that pigeons can tell the difference between the two. This is sensible because the eyes of pigeons contain cones in their retinas, and as you'll recall, cones are the receptors for color

discrimination *the process of differential reinforcement wherein one stimulus is reinforced while another stimulus is not*

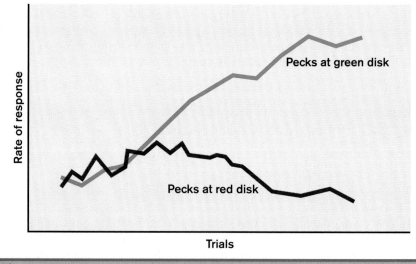

Figure 5.8

Discrimination training. Response rates for a pigeon presented with a green disk and a red disk. Pecks at the green disk are reinforced; those at the red disk are not.

vision. Some varieties of owls are virtually without cone receptor cells and thus are color blind. They cannot discriminate between red and green and appear frustrated in a discrimination learning task based on color.

Please don't think that generalization and discrimination learning are processes relevant only to young children, rats, and pigeons. A great deal of our own learning has involved learning to discriminate when behaviors are appropriate and are likely to be reinforced, and when they are inappropriate and likely to be ignored or punished. You have, I hope, learned that many of the behaviors that may be reinforced at a party are inappropriate responses to make in the classroom. You may have learned that it's okay to put your feet up on the coffee table at home, but not when you're at your boss's house or at Grandma's. Learning to interact with people from different cultures is also a matter of discrimination learning. In Saudi Arabia, for example, if two people approach a door at the same time, the person on the right always enters first. Being courteous by holding the door open for someone to the left of you and insisting that they enter is a generalized response that is simply not "proper" in all situations.

When a pigeon in an operant chamber is presented with both a red disk and a green disk, it will soon learn to discriminate between the two, pecking only at the disk for which pecking is reinforced.

Before You Go On

In operant conditioning, what are generalization and discrimination?

Cognitive Approaches to Learning

Cognitive approaches to learning accent changes that occur in an organism's system of cognitions—its mental representations of itself and its world. Cognitive learning involves the acquisition of knowledge or understanding and need not be reflected in behavior. I first alerted you to this issue when we discussed the definition of learning. We said that learning is demonstrated by, or inferred from, changes in behavior. The implication is that there may be something less than a perfect correspondence between what one has learned and what one does. We anticipated this issue with our coverage of the work of Rescorla and Kamin in Topic 5A, noting that a stimulus acted as an effective conditional stimulus only when it informed the organism about something happening in its world; as in, "When this tone sounds, food will follow it." Extracting useful information from one's experience in the world is largely a cognitive experience (Bolles, 1970, 1972, 1975). In this section, we'll review the work of two theorists who have stressed cognitive approaches to learning from the outset: Edward Tolman and Albert Bandura.

Latent Learning and Cognitive Maps

Do rats have brains? Of course they do. Their brains aren't very large, and the cerebral cortex of a rat's brain is small indeed, but they do have brains. A more intriguing question about rats is whether they form and manipulate cognitions. Can they figure things out? Can they understand? They can form simple associations. They can learn to associate a light with a shock and a lever-press response with a reinforcer, and they can modify their behaviors on the basis of these associations. Can they do more?

Consider a now-classic experiment performed over 60 years ago by Tolman and Honzik (1930). Even then, it was well established that a rat could learn to run through a complicated maze of alleyways and dead ends to get to a goal box, where it would find a food reward. Tolman and Honzik wanted to understand just what the rats were learning when they negotiated such a maze. They used three groups of rats with the same maze.

One group of hungry rats was given a series of exposures to the maze (i.e., trials). Each time the rats ran from the starting point to the goal box, they were given a food reward for their efforts. Over the course of 16 days, the rats in this group demonstrated a steady improvement in maze running. Their rate of errors dropped from approximately nine per trial to just two. Getting quickly and errorlessly from the start box to the goal box was just what had earned them their reinforcers.

A second group of rats was also given an opportunity to explore the maze for 16 days of test trials. However, they were not given a food reward for making it to the end of the maze. When they got to the goal box, they were simply removed from the maze. The average number of errors made by the rats in this group also dropped over the course of the experiment (from about nine errors per trial to about six). That the rats in this group did improve their maze-running skills suggests that simply being removed from the maze provided some measure of reinforcement. Even so, after 16 days, this group was having much more difficulty in their maze running than was the group being given a food reinforcer.

Now for the critical group. A third group of rats was allowed to explore the maze on their own for ten days. The rats were not given a food reward on reaching the goal box. But, beginning on day 11, a food reinforcer was introduced when they reached the goal box. The food was provided as a reinforcer on days 11 through 16. Introducing the food reward had a very significant effect on the rats' behaviors. Throughout the first ten days in the maze—without food—the group's performance showed only a slight improvement. Soon after the food was introduced, however, the rats' maze running improved markedly. In fact, on days 13 through 16, they made fewer errors than did the rats who received the food all along! Figure 5.9 shows the relative performance of these three groups.

What do you make of this experiment? Why did that third group of rats do so much better after the food reward was introduced? Could they have learned something about the pattern of that maze before they received reinforcement for getting to the goal box? Could they have "figured out" the maze early on, but failed to rush to the goal box until there was some good reason to do so?

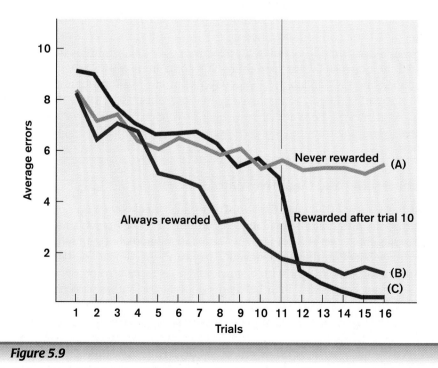

Figure 5.9

The performance of rats in a complicated maze where the rats were (A) never rewarded for reaching the end of the maze, (B) rewarded every time they reached the end of the maze, and (C) rewarded for reaching the end of the maze only on trials 11–16. (After Tolman & Honzik, 1930.)

Tolman thought they had. He argued that the food rewarded a change in the rats' performance, but that the actual learning had taken place earlier. This sort of learning is called **latent learning** because it is, in a sense, hidden and not shown in behavior until it is reinforced.

During those first ten days in the maze, the rats developed what Tolman called a **cognitive map** of the maze; they formed a mental picture, or representation, of their physical environment, noting significant landmarks when possible. The rats knew about the maze, but until food was provided at the goal box, there was no reason, or purpose, for getting there in a hurry. This logic led Tolman to refer to his approach as "purposive behaviorism" (Tolman, 1932). Introducing a distinction between performance and what was actually learned focused attention on what was happening to the learner during learning, which was one of Tolman's goals. If you stop and think for a minute about what Tolman's rats did, you have to be impressed. But cognitive maps learned by small birds that live in the Alps are even more impressive. These small birds spend most of the summer and early fall hiding seeds in the ground (about four or five at a time). During the winter, they find their hidden supplies of seeds with remarkable accuracy. Have they formed cognitive maps of their seed placements? Apparently they have. Making their judgments on the basis of nearby landmarks, these small birds, called Clark's nutcrackers, can remember the location of at least 2,500 hiding places (Vander Wall, 1982)!

You should be able to find examples from your own experiences that approximate latent learning and the formation of cognitive maps. You may take the same route home from campus every day. If one day an accident blocks your path, won't you be able to use your knowledge of other routes (a cognitive map) to get where you are going? When you park your car in a large new parking lot, what do you do as you walk away from your car? Do you look around, trying to develop a mental image, a cognitive representation, of the parking lot and some of its features? You are to meet a friend in a new classroom building on campus. You arrive early, so you stroll around the building for a few minutes. Isn't it likely that this unreinforced, apparently aimless behavior will be useful if you have to locate a room in that building for class the next semester?

Another setting in which we may find Tolman's purposive behaviorism at work is athletics. Before the big game, the coaching staff devises a perfect game plan—a set of ideas or cognitions dealing with what the team should do. The team members may learn the coaches' strategy and all of the new plays they are to use. They know what they are supposed to do to win (latent learning), but what will decide the contest is not their understanding but their performance. In sports, this is called execution. Knowing what to do and actually doing it are often different things.

> latent learning *hidden learning that is not demonstrated in performance until that performance is reinforced*
>
> cognitive map *a mental representation of the learning situation or physical environment*

Before You Go On

What is latent learning?

What is a cognitive map?

Social Learning and Modeling

Albert Bandura's approach to learning also is cognitive, but it adds a decidedly social flavor, and for that reason is referred to as **social learning theory** (Bandura, 1974, 1977, 1982). The central idea of this theory is that learning often takes place through the observation and imitation of models. What makes social learning theory *social* is the idea that we often learn from others. What makes it *cognitive* is that what is learned through observation or modeling are changes in one's cognitions that may never be expressed as behavior nor be directly reinforced.

> social learning theory *the theory that learning takes place through observation and imitation of models*

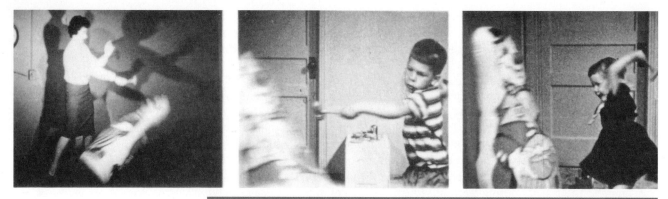

Figure 5.10

In Albert Bandura's classic study, children who watched others (either in person, on film, or in a cartoon version) behave aggressively toward a "Bobo" doll, displayed the same sort of behaviors themselves. Social learning theory claims that the children learned their aggressive behaviors through observation.

The classic study of observational learning was reported in 1963 by Bandura, Ross, and Ross. For this demonstration, 96 preschoolers were randomly assigned to one of four experimental conditions. One group of children observed an adult model act aggressively toward an inflated plastic "Bobo" doll toy (Figure 5.10). The adult model vigorously attacked the doll. Children in the second group watched the same aggressive behaviors directed toward the "Bobo" doll, but in a movie. The third group watched a cartoon version of the same aggressive behaviors, this time performed by a cat. Children in the fourth group constituted the control group and did not watch anyone—or anything—interact with "Bobo" dolls, either live or on film.

Then each child, tested individually, was given new and interesting toys to play with, but only for a brief time. The child was soon led to another room containing fewer, older, and less interesting toys, including a small version of the inflated "Bobo" doll. Each child was left alone in the room while researchers, hidden from view, watched the child's behavior.

The children who had seen the aggressive behaviors of the model—whether live, on film, or in a cartoon-were much more aggressive in their play than were the children who did not have the observational experience. Children in the first three experimental conditions attacked the "Bobo" doll the same way the model had.

According to social learning theory, the children had learned simply by observing. As with latent learning, the learning was separated from performance. The children had no opportunity to imitate (to perform) what they had learned until they had a "Bobo" doll of their own. The learning that took place during observation was cognitive. As Bandura puts it, "Observational learning is primarily concerned with processes whereby observers organize response elements into new patterns of behavior at a symbolic level on the basis of information conveyed by modeling stimuli" (Bandura, 1976, p. 395).

Later studies have shown that reinforcement and punishment play a major role in observational learning. For example, a twist was added to an experiment that replicated the one just described. The difference was that after attacking the "Bobo" doll, the adult models were either rewarded or punished for their behavior. Children who observed the model being punished for attacking the doll engaged in very little aggressive behavior toward their own "Bobo" dolls. Those who saw the model receive reinforcement for attacking the doll acted aggressively, imitating the model's behaviors in considerable detail (Bandura, 1965).

Learning about the consequences of one's own behavior by observing what happens to someone else is **vicarious reinforcement** or **vicarious punishment.**

The application of this sort of data is very straightforward. For example, Bandura's research suggests that children can learn all sorts of potential behaviors by

vicarious reinforcement (or punishment) *increasing the rate (with reinforcement) or decreasing the rate (with punishment) of responses due to observing the consequences of someone else's behaviors* watching TV. Our real concern should be reserved for occasions in which inappropriate behaviors are left unpunished. This logic suggests that it would be most unfortunate for one of a child's TV heroes to get away with murder, much less be rewarded for doing so. As it happens, reinforced behaviors of valued models are more likely to be imitated than punished behaviors of less valued models (Bandura, 1965).

Our own experiences speak to the usefulness of these concepts. Aren't you much more likely to imitate (as best you can) the behaviors of a person who is rewarded for his or her efforts than you are to imitate the behaviors of someone who gets punished? Doesn't it make more sense to model your behaviors after a top-notch student than after someone failing the course? A child does not have to burn her fingers in a fire to learn to avoid the fireplace. Just watching someone else getting burned (or pretending to get burned) will usually suffice (Domjan, 1987).

In fact, learning through observation and imitation is a common form of human learning. Your television on any Saturday provides many examples, particularly if you watch a PBS station. All day long there are people (role models) trying to teach us how to paint landscapes, build solar energy devices, do aerobic exercises, improve our golf game, remodel the basement, replace a carburetor, or prepare a low-calorie meal. The basic message is, "Watch me; see how I do it. Then, try it yourself."

Here, too, sociocultural variables may come into play. In one experiment, for example, when a model performed a task correctly and received reinforcement for doing so, Japanese students learned more than did American students. A possible explanation is that Japanese observers are more attentive to high-status others and are more likely to learn more from their actions (Haruki et al., 1984).

There is little doubt that the behaviors and mannerisms of children are in large measure a reflection of their attempts to imitate adult models.

Before You Go On

Summarize the basic concepts of social learning theory.

⊚⊚⊚⊚ Thinking Critically ⊚⊚⊚⊚

Some behaviors may be learned more effectively through modeling than other behaviors. What sorts of responses might *not* be learned effectively through exposure to models?

TOPIC 5B SUMMARY

In this Topic we explored the power of operant conditioning—a process by which an organism's rate of responding is altered by the consequences that follow that responding. Responses followed by reinforcers—be they positive or negative, primary or secondary, and regardless of how they are scheduled—will increase in their rate, or probability. The rate or probability of responses that are not reinforced, or are punished, will decrease. Additionally, we have seen that to be effective, reinforcers or punishers should be administered as soon after a response of interest as possible.

We have also looked at a few types of learning in which new cognitions—or changes in existing cognitions—are learned. Tolman's research show us that rats can gain considerable knowledge of the structure of a complicated maze even though they do not act on that knowledge (perform) until their performance is reinforced—a process called latent learning. In the process of latent learning, rats, and certainly people, can and do form cognitive maps that provide them with an internalized, mental representation of their surroundings. Bandura's research shows us that learning can take place through the observation of others, particularly when they are either reinforced or punished for their behaviors. These cognitive approaches remind us why we defined learning as being "demonstrated by or inferred from" relatively permanent changes in behavior that occur as the result of practice or experience.

But wait a minute! Here we are at the end of the chapter on learning, and we have not yet said anything about memorizing all of those definitions one needs to know when talking about classical conditioning. We haven't yet mentioned about how we go about learning concepts, theories, and academic sorts of things. What happened to "learning" as students generally think about human learning? Be assured I haven't forgotten about these concerns regarding human learning. Here are two points to keep in mind: (1) You should be convinced by now that classical conditioning, operant conditioning, and the cognitive approaches we have summarized do affect everyday human learning. (2) Psychologists have moved much of their discussion of human learning to their treatment of human memory—and to higher cognitive processes such as problem solving. You will find most of the discussion of human learning you're looking for in the next two chapters.

CHAPTER SUMMARY

Topic 5A

How do we define learning?

Learning is demonstrated by a relatively permanent change in behavior that occurs as the result of practice or experience. We can use the same definition for "conditioning," in that it is a simple, basic form of learning. /pp. 150–151

What are the basic procedures of classical conditioning?

In classical, or Pavlovian, conditioning, a neutral stimulus that originally does not elicit a response of interest is paired with an unconditioned stimulus (UCS), one that reliably and reflexively does produce a response—an unconditioned response (UCR). As a result, the once-neutral stimulus becomes a conditioned stimulus (CS) and elicits a conditioned response (CR) that is the same type of response as the original UCR. /pp. 151–153

In classical conditioning, what are acquisition, extinction, and spontaneous recovery?

In classical conditioning, acquisition is an increase in the strength of the CR as the CS and the UCS continue to be presented together. Extinction is a decrease in the strength of the CR that occurs when the CS is repeatedly presented alone (without being paired with the UCS). Spontaneous recovery is the return of a CR after extinction and a rest interval. /pp. 153–155

In classical conditioning, what are generalization and discrimination?

In generalization, a response (CR) conditioned to a specific stimulus (the CS) will also be elicited by other, similar stimuli. The more similar the new stimuli are to the original CS, the greater the resultant CR. In many ways, discrimination is the opposite of generalization. It is a case of learning to make a CR in response to a specific CS (paired with the UCS), while learning not to make the CR in response to other stimuli, which are not paired with the UCS. /pp. 155–156

What sorts of responses are most readily formed by classical conditioning? Describe the "Little Albert" demonstration.

Classical conditioning has its most noticeable effect on emotion or mood. Most of the stimuli to which we respond emotionally have probably been classically conditioned to elicit those responses, called conditioned emotional responses. In the Watson and Rayner 1920 "Little Albert" demonstration, a sudden loud noise (the UCS) was paired with the presentation of the neutral stimulus, a white rat. As a result of such pairings, Albert came to display a learned fear response (a CR) to the originally neutral rat (now the CS). The conditioned fear generalized to other, similar stimuli. The demonstration has been used to explain learned emotional reactions to events in our environments. /pp. 156–159

What is systematic desensitization?

Systematic desensitization involves counterconditioning—training a person to relax and stay relaxed while thinking about a hierarchy of stimuli that are more and more likely to elicit anxiety or fear. If relaxation can be conditioned to thoughts of anxiety-producing stimuli, the sense of calm and relaxation will come to replace the competing response of anxiety. The procedure is often used to treat phobic disorders. /pp. 159–161

Under what circumstances are stimuli likely to serve effectively as conditioned stimuli?

Pavlov and others believed that any stimulus could serve effectively as a conditioned stimulus if it was repeatedly paired with an unconditioned stimulus. We now believe that those stimuli that work most effectively as CSs are those that best or most reliably predict or signal the occurrence of the UCS. Stimuli are effective conditioned stimuli only if they provide useful information to the learner; for example, a shock is going to follow this tone. /*pp. 161–162*

What do taste aversion studies tell us about the CS and the UCS in classical conditioning?

Taste aversion studies, in which subjects develop strong dislikes and avoidance of particular foods or tastes, tell us that the time interval between the CS and the UCS may be very long. This result is in conflict with early conclusions that classical conditioning is most effective with very short CS-UCS intervals. These studies also provide evidence for the fact that some behaviors are more easily, or more naturally, conditioned than others, for example, associating nausea with the taste of food is more "natural" than associating nausea with other stimuli that may have been present when the nausea-inducing foods were eaten. /*pp. 162–163*

Topic 5B

What is operant conditioning?

Operant conditioning occurs when the probability, or rate, of a response is changed as a result of the consequences that follow that response. Reinforced responses increase in rate, while nonreinforced responses decrease in rate. /*pp. 164–166*

Describe shaping, acquisition, extinction, and spontaneous recovery as they occur in operant conditioning.

Shaping is used to establish a response, that is, it is used to get an organism to make a desired response in the first place. We shape a response by reinforcing successive approximations to the desired response. In operant conditioning, acquisition is produced by reinforcing a desired response so that its rate increases. Extinction decreases the rate of a response (to return to its original baseline rate) by withholding reinforcement. After a rest interval, a previously extinguished response will return at a rate above baseline; that is, in the same situation, it will spontaneously recover. /*pp. 166–168*

Distinguish between positive and negative reinforcers.

In general, a reinforcer is a stimulus that increases the rate, or probability, of a response it follows. A positive re-inforcer increases the rate of the response that precedes its presentation. Negative reinforcers increase the rate of the response that precedes their removal or termination. /*pp. 168–170*

Compare and contrast primary and secondary reinforcers.

Primary reinforcers are stimuli that are in some way biologically important or related to an organism's survival, such as food for a hungry organism or warm shelter for a cold one. Secondary reinforcers increase response rates because of the organism's previous learning history. That is, secondary reinforcers, such as praise, money, letter grades, and the like, are secondary, or acquired reinforcers. /*pp. 170–171*

What are fixed-ratio, fixed-interval, variable-ratio, and variable-interval schedules of reinforcement?

Intermittent schedules of reinforcement provide a reinforcer for less than every response. The FR (fixed-ratio) schedule calls for delivering one reinforcer after a set number of responses (e.g., one reinforcer after every five responses). The FI (fixed-interval) schedule calls for a reinforcer at the first response following a specified, or fixed, interval. A VR (variable-ratio) schedule randomly changes the ratio of reinforcers to responses, but maintains a given ratio as an average. A VI (variable-interval) schedule calls for a reinforcer for the first response after a time interval whose length is randomly varied. In general, responses reinforced with fixed schedules are more resistant to extinction than are responses that have been reinforced each time they occur (a CRF, or continuous reinforcement schedule). Responses acquired under variable schedules are even more resistant to extinction than are those acquired by fixed schedules. /*pp. 171–173*

What are punishers, and how can they be used effectively?

A punisher is a stimulus that decreases the rate of the response it follows. Punishers can be effective in suppressing a response when they are strong enough and are delivered immediately after the response to be punished. Fear, anxiety, aggression, and an overall suppression of behavior may accompany punishment, which, in itself, provides no information about what an organism should do in a given situation. Punishing one response should be paired with the reinforcement of another, more appropriate one. /*pp. 174–175*

In operant conditioning, what are generalization and discrimination?

Generalization has occurred when a response reinforced in the presence of one stimulus also occurs in the presence of other, similar stimuli. Discrimination involves differential reinforcement—reinforcing responses to some stimuli while extinguishing responses to other (inappropriate) stimuli. /pp. 175–177

map, one develops a cognitive representation (or picture) of one's surroundings—an appreciation of general location and where key objects are located. /pp. 177–179

What is latent learning? What is a cognitive map?

According to Tolman, latent learning is the acquisition of information (an internal, mental, cognitive process) that may not be demonstrated in performance until later, if at all. The formation of a cognitive map can be viewed as a type of latent learning. When one acquires a cognitive

Summarize the basic concepts of social learning theory.

Bandura's social learning theory emphasizes the role of the observation of others (models) and imitation in the acquisition of cognitions and behaviors. We often learn by imitating models through vicarious reinforcement and vicarious punishment. /pp. 179–181

PRACTICING PSYCHOLOGY

A Potpourri of Reinforcers and Punishers

There's no doubt that reinforcement and punishment are central processes in operant conditioning. The challenge, sometimes, is keeping the different kinds of reinforcers and punishers sorted out. Here are six brief scenarios. For each, indicate whether it is depicting positive reinforcement, negative reinforcement, primary reinforcement, or secondary reinforcement, positive punishment, or negative punishment. (Suggested answers can be found on p. 572.)

1. Billy brings home his school work and shows it to his parents. Each time he does so, he is told, "We don't care about that book learnin'" and that he should do his chores. His grades at school show a steady decline.
2. Susan has a terrible toothache. She needs a root canal. Dr. Patnik does the job and charges $445.00 for his services. At the next sign of a toothache, Susan immediately calls Dr. Patnik.
3. André enjoys drawing, but soon gives it up to do other things because his teacher keeps putting gold stars and writing "well done" comments on his drawings.
4. After doing badly on Exam One, Bruce buys a Study Guide and works on all the exercises. His score on the next exam is significantly higher. He continues to use the Study Guide to prepare for exams.
5. Kirsten often gets into fights with a few of the other girls at her play school. Now, whenever she instigates a fight, she is made to sit quietly in the corner. As a result, she is starting fewer fights.
6. Becky is an infant who can crawl around very quickly. Whenever she gets to an electrical cord or an extension cord, she puts it into her mouth. As a result, her parents jump up and pick her up to get her away from the cord. Her cord-chewing behaviors seem to be getting more common.

OUTLINE

was a fairly good student in high school. I can't re-member ever worrying very much about having to study. But I did attend a small school in a small town, and I didn't really experience much of a challenge. Per-haps you can imagine my surprise when I finished the first semester of my freshman year at college with two Fs, two Ds, and two Cs as final grades. Matters didn't get any better in my second semester, or in summer school. I didn't literally "flunk out" my freshman year, but let's say that when I told the dean I wouldn't be returning the following fall, he seemed pleased.

As you can imagine, I've reflected on that freshman year many times since then, and I have generated quite a list of reasons and excuses for why I did so poorly. I joined a frater-nity, which took up a lot of my time. I played on the basket-ball team, which took up even more time. If we had a one-hour break between classes, my friends and I would go to the student union to see how many hands of bridge we could play. With a two-hour break, I had enough time to get to the gym, change my clothes, and practice basketball.

One of the main reasons I did not do as well as I should have in my first year of college is that I scheduled my study time so poorly. I imagined that somehow I could get by at college with the same sort of study schedule that seemed to

Memory

work so well in high school: never studying during the week, and studying on the weekend only if absolutely necessary. By the end of my freshman year, I was pretty good at bridge and basketball. And I had the grades to prove it.

More than any other chapter, this one, on memory, will contain helpful advice about studying for your college courses. Some of this advice is tucked away in discussions of such issues as overlearning and elaborative rehearsal. Most is out in the open and obvious, including a discussion of the importance of distributing study time and taking advantage of breaks during the day for effective study.

TOPIC 6A How Can We Describe Human Memory?

Imagine what life would be like without memory. For one thing, this sentence in your text would make no sense. Without your memory, you would have no idea what a textbook is or why you had it open in front of you. The patterns of print you now recognize as words would appear as no more than random marks. We care about memory in an academic, study–learn–test sense, but the importance of memory goes well beyond classroom exams. All of those things that define us as individuals—our feelings, beliefs, attitudes, and experiences—are stored in our memories.

In Topic 6A, we'll formulate a working definition of memory. Then we will consider how information gets into memory and is stored there. We will explore the possibility that there are several types of memory, and see what these varieties of memory might be. We'll also take a moment to see what scientists can tell about the physiological changes that occur when new memories are formed.

Memory as Information Processing

One way to think about human memory is to consider it as a final step in a series of psychological activities that process information. As we first noted in Chapter 3, the processing of information begins when our sensory receptors are stimulated above threshold levels. The process of perception then selects and organizes the information provided by our senses. With memory, we form a record of that information.

memory *the cognitive capacity to encode, store, and retrieve information*

encoding *the active process of representing, or putting information into memory*

storage *the process of holding encoded information in memory*

retrieval *the process of locating, removing, and using information stored in memory*

Memory is the capacity to encode, store, and retrieve information. It is "the mental processes of acquiring and retaining information for later retrieval" (Ashcraft, 1994, p. 11). Using one's memory is a cognitive activity that involves three interrelated processes. The first is **encoding**, a process of putting information into memory—a matter of forming cognitive representations of information. Once those representations are in memory, we must keep them there—a process called **storage**. In order to use stored information, we need to get it out again. This process is **retrieval** (after Murdock, 1974).

Modern theories view memory as being complex and multidimensional. That is, not all of the information that gets into memory necessarily gets encoded or stored in the same way or even in the same place. As it happens, there is considerable disagreement over just how we should conceptualize human memory. Theories are plentiful, and often at odds with each other (Baddeley, 1992; Cowan, 1994; Loftus, 1991; Roediger, 1990; Schacter, 1992; Squire et al., 1993; Watkins, 1990).

Some psychologists argue that there are various memory storehouses, each with its own characteristics and mechanisms for processing information. Psychologists who talk about separate, distinct memories, or stores of information, support what are called *multistore models of memory* (Atkinson & Shiffrin, 1968; Cowan, 1993; Tulving, 1985; Waugh & Norman, 1965).

Other theorists claim that there is but one type of human memory, or storehouse of information, but that within that memory are various levels or depths to which information can be processed (Cermak & Craik, 1979; Craik, 1970; Craik & Lockhart, 1972; Crowder, 1993). Their claim is that information can get more (deep) or less (shallow) processing within the same memory. Depth of processing is seen as a function of work or effort and is related to the likelihood of retrieval. This position gives rise to what is called a *levels-of-processing model of memory.* Although it has wide support, it is but one theory that views memory as a single, unitary process.

So, which model shall we use? We can construct "our own" conceptualization of memory by combining major aspects of both of these dominant positions. Our model will include three stores, or levels, of memory: *sensory memory, short-term memory (STM), and long-term memory (LTM).* Sometimes I'll refer to sensory, short-term, and long-term memories as if they were memory stores, or structures—some-

more fully by moving it to short-term memory. **Short-term memory (STM)** is a level, or store, in human memory with a limited capacity and—without the benefit of rehearsal—a brief duration.

What I am here calling short-term memory is often referred to as *working memory* (Baddeley, 1982, 1990, 1992). It is viewed as something like a workbench or desk top on which we pull together, use, and manipulate the information to which we pay attention.

Figure 6.1 presents a schematic diagram of the model of memory we are building. At the top are stimuli from the environment affecting our senses and moving directly to sensory memory. In the middle is short-term memory. We see that information from sensory memory *or* from long-term memory can be moved into STM. To get material into short-term memory requires that we attend to it.

The Duration of STM

Interest in short-term memory can be traced to two experiments reported independently in the late 1950s (Brown, 1958; Peterson & Peterson, 1959). We'll review the Petersons' project.

A student is shown three consonants, such as KRW, for 3 seconds. Presenting the letters for a full 3 seconds ensures that they are attended to and encoded into STM. The student is then asked to recall the three letters after retention intervals ranging from 0 to 18 seconds. This doesn't sound like a difficult task, and it isn't.

short-term memory (STM) *a type of memory with limited capacity and limited duration; also called working memory*

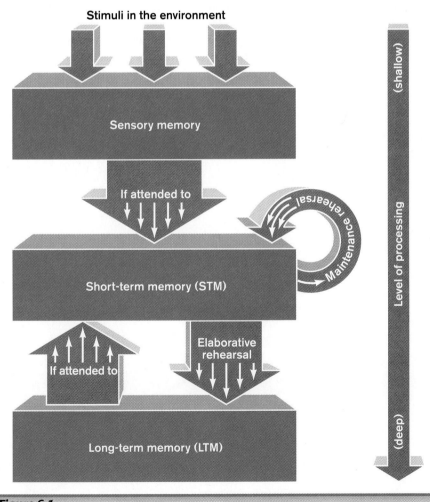

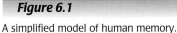
Figure 6.1

A simplified model of human memory.

Anyone can remember a few letters for 18 seconds. In this study, however, students are kept from rehearsing the letters during the retention interval. They are given a "distractor" task to perform right after they see the letters. They are to count backward, by threes, from a three-digit number.

If you were a participant in this sort of experiment, you would be shown a letter sequence—say, KRW—and then asked to immediately start counting backward from, say, 397, by threes, or "397, 394, 391, 388," and so forth. You would be instructed to do your counting out loud and as rapidly as possible. The idea is that the counting keeps you from rehearsing the three letters you were just shown.

Under these conditions, your correct recall of the letters will depend on the length of the retention interval. If you are asked to recall the letters after just a few seconds of counting, you'll do pretty well. If you have to count for as long as 15 to 20 seconds, your recall of the letters will drop to almost zero (see Figure 6.2). Distracted by the counting task, you cannot rehearse the letters, and they are soon unavailable to you.

This laboratory example isn't as abstract as it may appear. Consider this scenario. Having studied psychology for hours, you decide to reward yourself and have a pizza delivered. Never having called Pizza City before, you turn to the yellow pages to find the number: 555–5897. You repeat the number to yourself: 555–5897. You close the phone book, then dial the number without error. Buzzz-buzzz-buzzz-buzzz. Darn, the line's busy! Well, you'll call back in a minute.

Just as you hang up the phone, the doorbell rings. It's the paper boy. You owe him $11.60 for the past two weeks' deliveries. Discovering that you don't have enough cash on hand to pay for the paper and a pizza, you write a personal check. "Let's see, what is today's date? 10–15–98. How much did you say I owed you? Oh yes, $11.60, and a dollar and a half for a tip, comes to $13.10. This is check number 1079; I'd better write that down. There you go. Thanks a lot."

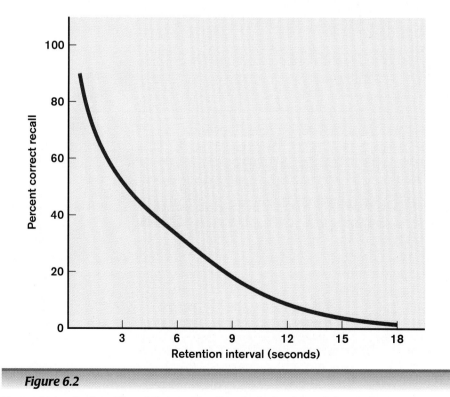

Figure 6.2

The recall of a stimulus of three letters as a function of retention interval when maintenance rehearsal is minimized. (After Peterson & Peterson, 1959.)

If we are not interrupted or distracted, we easily can hold a seven-digit telephone number in STM long enough to dial it.

The paper boy leaves, and you return to your studying. Then you recall that you were going to order a pizza. Only five or six minutes have passed since you got a busy signal from Pizza City. As you go to dial the phone now, you cannot remember the phone number. Back to the yellow pages. A number once attended to was active in your short-term memory. When you were kept from rehearsing it, and when other numbers entered as interfering information, that original telephone number was soon inaccessible.

We can increase the duration of short-term memory by rehearsing the information stored there. The rehearsal we use to keep material active in our short-term memory is **maintenance rehearsal**, or rote rehearsal, and amounts to little more than the simple repetition of the information already in our STM. To get material into STM (encoding), we have to attend to it. By repeating that material (as we might if we wanted to remember a telephone number until we could dial it), we are reattending to it with each repetition.

maintenance rehearsal *a process of rote repetition (reattending) to keep information in short-term memory*

The duration of STM *is* long enough for us to use it in many everyday activities. Usually all we want to do with a telephone number is remember it long enough to dial it. Few people feel the need to make a permanent record of every telephone number they dial. Using STM in mathematical computations is a good example, particularly when we do computations "in our head." Multiply 28 by 6 without paper and pencil: "Let's see. Six times 8 is 48. Now I have to keep the 8 and carry the 4." Stop right there. Where do you "keep the 8" and where do you store the 4 until they are needed? Right, in STM. For that matter, where did the notion that $6 \times 8 = 48$ come from in the first place? Where did the idea of what "multiply" means come from? Right, again. This is an example of information entering STM, not "from the outside," through our senses and sensory memory, but from long-term storage (see Figure 6.1).

Another example of STM in action is in the processing of language. As you read one of my longer sentences, such as this one, it is useful to have a short-term storage place to keep the beginning of the sentence in mind until you finally get to the end of the sentence, so that you can figure out the basic idea of the sentence before deciding whether anything in the sentence is worth remembering.

Having discussed the duration of short-term memory, let's now deal with its capacity. Just how much information can we hold in STM for that 15 to 20 seconds?

Before You Go On

How long is information stored in STM, and how does it get there?

The Capacity of STM

In 1956, George Miller wrote a charming paper about "the magical number seven, plus or minus two." In it, he argued that the capacity of our short-term memories is very small—limited to just 5 to 9 (or 7 ± 2) bits, or "chunks," of information.

chunk *an imprecise concept referring to a meaningful unit of information represented in short-term memory*

In the context of short-term memory, the concept of chunk is actually a technical, and at the same time an imprecise, term (Anderson, 1980). A **chunk** may be defined as the representation in memory of a meaningful unit of information. Thus, the claim is that we can store 7 ± 2 meaningful pieces of information in STM.

We can easily attend to, encode, and store five or six letters in STM. Holding the letters YRDWIAADEFDNSYE in short-term memory, however, would be a challenge. Fifteen randomly presented letters exceed the capacity of STM for most of us. What if I asked you to remember the words *Friday* and *Wednesday*? Keeping these two simple words in STM is easy—even though they contain (the same) 15 letters. Here you are storing just two chunks of meaningful information, not 15. In fact, you can easily store 50 letters in short-term memory if you recode them into the one meaningful chunk: "days of the week."

As we all know, we can readily store a telephone number in short-term memory. Adding an area code makes the task somewhat more difficult because the ten digits now come fairly close to the upper limit of our STM capacity. Notice, though,

Many mathematical calculations require that we briefly hold information in STM until we are ready to use it.

how we tend to cluster the digits of a telephone number into a pattern. The digit series 2195553661 is more difficult to deal with as a simple string than when it is seen and encoded as a telephone number: (219) 555–3661 (Bower & Springston, 1970). Grouping the digits this way lets us see them in a new, more meaningful, way.

At best, short-term memory works something like a leaky bucket. From the vast storehouse of information available in sensory memory, we scoop up some (not much, at that) by paying attention to it, and hold it for a while until we either use it, maintain it with maintenance rehearsal, move it along to long-term storage, or lose it. Before we go on to long-term memory, we'll consider how information is encoded and stored in STM.

Before You Go On

How much information can be stored in short-term memory?

How Information Is Represented in STM

The material or information stored in sensory memory is kept there in virtually the same form in which it was presented. Visually presented stimuli are held as visual images, auditory stimuli form auditory memories, and so on. Getting information into STM is not such an automatic process. We have to attend to the material to encode it into STM. How is that material stored, or represented, there?

Conrad (1963, 1964) was one of the first to argue that information is stored in STM with an acoustic code. This means that material is processed in terms of how it sounds. Conrad's conclusion was based on his interpretation of the errors people make in short-term memory experiments. In one experiment, he presented a series of letters visually, one at a time, and asked participants to recall the letters they had just seen. Many errors were made over the course of the experiment. What was surprising was that when people responded incorrectly, it was often with a letter that *sounded like* the correct one. For example, if participants were to recall the letter E and failed to do so, they would recall V, G, or T, letters that sound like the E they were supposed to recall. They rarely responded with F, which certainly looks more like the E they had just seen than do V, G, and T. (This was true whether recall was given orally or in writing.)

It seems that using STM is largely a matter of talking to ourselves. Regardless of how it is presented, we tend to encode information acoustically, the way it sounds. At least that's what the early evidence suggested. Psychologists still believe that acoustic coding is the most important means of representing information in STM, but some may be encoded in STM in other ways—e.g., visually or spatially (Cooper & Shepard, 1973; Martindale, 1981; Shulman, 1971, 1972; Squire et al., 1993; Wickens, 1973). Perhaps the most we can say is that there is a tendency to rely heavily on the acoustic coding of information in STM, but that other codes may also be used.

Before You Go On

How is information represented in STM?

Long-Term Memory

Long-term memory (LTM) is memory as you and I usually think of it: memory for large amounts of information that is held for long periods. Our own experience

long-term memory (LTM) *a type of memory with virtually unlimited capacity and very long, if not limitless, duration* tells us that the capacity of long-term memory is huge—virtually limitless. At times we even impress ourselves with the amount of material we have stashed away in LTM (for instance, when we play Trivial Pursuit or TV game shows). How much can be stored in human memory may never be measured, but we can rest assured there is no way we will ever learn so much that there won't be room for more. (Getting that information out again when we want it is another matter, which we'll get to in Topic 6B.)

How Long Do Long-Term Memories Last?

On an experiential basis, we can again impress ourselves with the duration of some of our own memories. Assuming you remain free from disease or injury, you're likely never to forget some information, such as your own name or the words to "Happy Birthday."

At the moment, it is difficult to imagine an experiment that could tell us with any certainty how long information or experiences remain stored in LTM. One thing we know for a fact is that we often cannot remember things we once knew. We do tend to forget things. The issue is *why*. Do we forget because the information is no longer available to us in our long-term memories, just not there any more? Or do we forget because we are unable to get the information out of LTM, which implies that it is still available but now somehow not accessible? "How can we ever be sure that a memory failure is due to the relevant information being unavailable and hence inaccessible under all conceivable conditions rather than just merely being inaccessible under the prevailing conditions?" (Watkins, 1990, p. 330).

An article by Elizabeth and Geoffry Loftus (1980) focused on the issue of the duration of long-term memories. They concluded: "The evidence in no way confirms the view that all memories are permanent and thus potentially recoverable" (p. 409). They claim that the bulk of such evidence is neither scientific nor reliable, and that when we think we recall specific events of the long-distant past, we may be reconstructing a reasonable facsimile of that information from bits and pieces of our past. In other words, when we do remember something that happened to us a long time ago, we don't recall the events as they actually happened. Instead, we recall a few specific details and then actively reconstruct a reasonable story. But even if we do reconstruct recollections of our past experiences, that would not necessarily mean that our original memory was no longer available. It might only suggest that we can maintain several versions of the same event in long-term memory (e.g., McCloskey & Zaragoza, 1985). This discussion gives rise to our next question.

The capacity of our long-term memories is so large that sometimes we surprise ourselves with how much information we have stored there.

How Accurate Are Long-Term Memories?

When we try to remember a fact we learned in school many years ago, it is often easy to determine the accuracy of our recall. As on many classroom tests, we are either right or wrong. Note that if we learned something many years ago that was wrong and recalled that incorrect information now, it might still be wrong, even though our memory would be accurate.

Determining the accuracy of our memories for real past experiences is difficult at best, and sometimes simply impossible. Do we really remember all the details of that vacation we took with our family when we were 6 years old, or are we recalling bits and pieces of what actually happened, bits and pieces of what we have been told happened, and adding in other details to reconstruct a likely story? Most of the time the accuracy of our recollection of experiences from the distant past is of little or no consequence. In some situations, the accuracy of the report of one's long-term memory for events can be of critical importance.

Repressed Memories. One example of the importance of accuracy in the retrieval of information from long-term storage involves what are called "repressed memories." We discussed the Freudian concept of repression in Chapter 4 (page 122). Repression is said to have occurred when extremely unpleasant or traumatic events of one's life are pushed deep into the unconscious corners of one's memory, from which retrieval is at best very difficult. The notion that repression—or in more modern terms, "motivated forgetting"—can help us forget unpleasant events of the past has gained wide acceptance in psychology (Baddeley, 1990; Byrd, 1994; Erdelyi, 1985; Erdelyi & Goldberg, 1979; Gold et al., 1994; Loftus, 1993a, 1994).

In recent years, thousands of persons have come forward with accusations that they were sexually abused as children, usually by members of their own family (Jaroff, 1993). Some among the rich and famous—TV star Roseanne, and former Miss America Marilyn Van Derbur, to name just two—have gone public with the stories of the recovery of once-repressed memories of terrible child abuse (Garry & Loftus, 1994). The trauma of child abuse (sexual or not) seems to be a likely event to be repressed—to be put out of one's conscious awareness.

Without questioning the enormity of the problem of child abuse or challenging reports of its prevalence, Elizabeth Loftus (1993a, 1993b) has recently challenged the authenticity of the repressed memories of some adults who "remember" events that may never have happened in the first place. Loftus has never argued that child abuse is not a real phenomenon. It may be, however, that *some* people genuinely come to believe that they were abused as children in order to help make sense of the difficulties they are now encountering as adults (Frankel, 1993; Gardner, 1993; Powell & Boer, 1994; Wakefield & Underwager, 1992; Yapko, 1993). In some cases, the notion that a person has been abused may come from a therapist who says something such as, "You know, I've seen many cases like yours and often find that the person was abused or molested as a child. Do you suppose anything like that ever happened to you?"

In May 1994, a jury in Napa, California, awarded Gary Ramona $500,000 in a civil trial. Ramona's daughter, Holly, had entered psychotherapy in 1989 for treatment of bulimia, an eating disorder (see page 372). Shortly thereafter, Holly began accusing her father of dozens of incidents of rape and abuse. The incidents reportedly happened when Holly was between 8 and 12 years old. They had been "repressed" until they were uncovered in the course of therapy. We will probably never know what happened to Holly as a child, or what brought on the symptoms of her disorder, but at least this jury agreed with her father that the therapist had planted ideas of abuse in her memory.

Whether repressed memories of child abuse and trauma are real is obviously not just an academic question. The American Psychiatric Association, the American Medical Association, and the American Psychological Association have each formed "study groups" and committees to explore the issue and bring it to some resolution. Interestingly enough, although there are opinions galore, the one thing on which all agree is that there is virtually no sound, empirical research currently available that can resolve this question (Byrd, 1994; Gleaves, 1994; Gold et al., 1994; Loftus, 1994; Olio, 1994).

Before You Go On

What are repressed memories, and what do they tell us about LTM?

Eyewitness Testimony. Another area in which the accuracy of long-term memory is of critical importance is eyewitness testimony. If, in fact, memories may not be permanent and they can be distorted or replaced by events processed later, we may have to reconsider the weight given to eyewitness testimony—eyewitness identification in particular (Buckhout, 1975; Clifford & Lloyd-Bostock, 1983; Loftus, 1984; MacLeod & Ellis, 1986; Ross et al., 1993; Wells et al., 1994).

Let's review a classic study in this area (Loftus & Zanni, 1975). Students view a short film showing the collision of two cars. Later, the viewers are asked about what they had seen, and were asked to estimate the speed of the cars at the time of the collision. Actually, some were asked about the cars "colliding," some were asked about the cars "hitting" each other, and others were asked about cars "contacting," "bumping," or "smashing" each other. Estimates of the speeds of the cars varied according to the verb used in the question. The cars were reported to be going nearly 41 mph when they "smashed" together, but only about 31 mph when they "contacted" each other. Although these are laboratory studies—and there is danger in trying to generalize too much from the laboratory to the real world (Bekerian, 1993; Yuille, 1993)—the relevance for eyewitness testimony is fairly obvious.

What do the "experts" say about eyewitness testimony? On what issues would psychologists be willing to go to court and claim that valid, scientific evidence exists? Just this question was put to 113 researchers who had published data on eye-

There are several reasons why some people are more reliable eyewitnesses than others. Just because someone says that he or she can clearly recall what happened does not mean that his or her retrieval is accurate.

witness testimony (Kassin et al., 1989). Statements that these experts claim are reliable and accurate are presented in Figure 6.3. The first statement on this list is the most reliable (agreed to by 96.8 percent of the respondents) and even the tenth statement was judged reliable by 79.4 percent of the respondents.

A review article by Gary Wells of Iowa State University, who has done research on eyewitness identification for years, claims that there *are* steps that can be taken (asking the right questions, structuring lineups, properly instructing witnesses, and so on) that can improve the accuracy of eyewitness identification (Wells, 1993; Wells et al., 1994). Other researchers remain more pessimistic, arguing that we still know too little about either the real-world process of eyewitness testimony or the nature of witnesses (particularly those who are crime victims) to be able to determine if the recollections of eyewitnesses are or are not accurate (Bekerian, 1993; Egeth, 1993; Yuille, 1993).

Before You Go On

What does eyewitness testimony tell us about LTM?

How Does Information Get into Long-Term Memory?

Simple repetition (maintenance rehearsal) can be used to keep material active in short-term memory. This type of rehearsal is also one way to move information from STM to LTM. Within limits, the more one repeats a bit of information, the

©©©© **Thinking Critically** ©©©©

What sorts of factors might affect the reliability of eyewitness testimony?

Figure 6.3

Statements About Eyewitness Testimony with Which the "Experts" Agree

1. An eyewitness's testimony about an event can be affected by how the questions put to the witness are worded.
2. Police instructions can affect an eyewitness's willingness to make an identification and/or the likelihood that he or she will identify a particular person.
3. Eyewitnesses' testimony about an event often reflects not only what they actually saw but information they obtained later on.
4. An eyewitness's confidence is not a good predictor of his or her identification accuracy.
5. An eyewitness's perception and memory for an event may be affected by his or her attitudes and expectations.
6. The less time an eyewitness has to observe an event, the less well he or she will remember it.
7. Eyewitnesses sometimes identify as a culprit someone they have seen in another situation or context.
8. The use of a one-person showup instead of a full lineup increases the risk of misidentification.
9. The rate of memory loss for an event is greatest right after the event, and then levels off with time.
10. White eyewitnesses are better at identifying other white people than they are at identifying black people.

From Kassin 1989, pp. 1089–1098.

more likely it will be remembered—beyond the limits of short-term memory. However, the simple repetition of information is seldom sufficient to process it into long-term storage. Simply attending to information—the essence of repetition—is an inefficient means of encoding information in long-term memory.

To get information into long-term memory we need to think about it, organize it, form images of it, make it meaningful, or relate it to something already in our long-term memories. In other words, to get information into LTM we need to use **elaborative rehearsal**, a term proposed by Craik and Lockhart (1972). Elaborative rehearsal is not an either-or process. Information can be elaborated to greater or lesser degrees.

Do you see how the distinction between maintenance rehearsal and elaborative rehearsal fits the levels-of-processing model of memory we discussed earlier? When we do no more than attend to an item, as in maintenance rehearsal, our processing is fairly minimal, or shallow, and that item is likely to remain in memory for a relatively short time. The more we are able to rehearse an item elaboratively, the deeper into memory it is processed. And, as the model claims, the more we elaborate on it, the easier it will be to remember.

Consider a hypothetical experiment in which students are asked to respond to a list of words in different ways. In one instance they are asked to count the number of letters in each word on the list. In another they are to generate a word that rhymes with each one they read. In a third they are asked to use each word in a sentence. The logic is that in each case, the words are processed at an increasingly "deeper" level as students focus on (1) the simple, physical structure of the words, (2) the sounds of the words as they are said aloud, and (3) the meaning of the words and their role in sentence structure. In such an experiment, as processing increases, so does recall of the words being processed (Cermak & Craik, 1979; Craik & Tulving, 1975).

elaborative rehearsal a means of processing information into LTM that involves thinking about information, organizing it, and making it meaningful

---

Before You Go On

Contrast elaborative rehearsal with maintenance rehearsal.

Are There Different Types of Long-Term Memories?

Our own experiences tell us that what we have stored in LTM can be retrieved in various forms. We can remember the definitions of words. We can visualize people and events from the past. We can recall the melodies of songs. We can recall how our bodies moved when we first tried to rollerskate or ski. Could it be that distinct types of information in our long-term memories are held in different subsystems, or types, of LTM? Can information be encoded in LTM in various ways? The notion of multiple long-term memory systems is a relatively new one in psychology, and as you might expect, there is little agreement on just what the systems within LTM might be, how to label them, or even how many there may be (Johnson & Hasher, 1987). We'll briefly review three possible LTM subsystems (Tulving, 1972, 1983, 1985, 1986). All three interact, but they are basically different.

procedural memory a subsystem of LTM, in which stimulus-response associations and skilled patterns of responses are stored

One type of long-term memory is **procedural memory**. In this memory, we have stored recollections of learned responses, or chains of responses. Stored here are the patterned responses we have learned well, such as how to ride a bicycle, type, shave, or apply makeup. Simply, stored in procedural memory are the basic procedures of our lives. What we have stored here is retrieved and put into use with little or no effort. At one time in your life handwriting was difficult, as you strained to form letters and words correctly. But by now, your writing skills, or "procedures," are so ingrained that you can retrieve the processes involved almost without thinking. John Anderson (1986, 1987) calls the information in this subsystem

Basic activities or procedures, such as those acquired when one learns how to swim, are stored in *procedural memory*. Words, facts, meanings, and rules are stored in *semantic memory*. Life experiences, both mundane and dramatic, are stored in *episodic memory*.

procedural knowledge, or "knowing how." The other types of LTM hold what Anderson calls *declarative knowledge,* or "knowing that."

In **semantic memory** we store all our vocabulary, simple concepts, and rules (including the rules that govern our use of language). Here we have stored our concepts and knowledge of the world in which we live. Our semantic memories are crammed with facts, both important and trivial. Can you answer the following questions?

> *Who opened the first psychology laboratory in Leipzig in 1879?*
>
> *How many stripes are there on the American flag?*
>
> *Is "Colorless green ideas sleep furiously" a well-formed, grammatically correct sentence?*
>
> *What do dogs eat?*

If you can, you found the answers in your long-term semantic memory.

Information in semantic memory is stored there in an organized fashion. We're not yet sure how to characterize the (no doubt) complex structure of semantic

semantic memory *a subsystem of LTM, in which vocabulary, facts, simple concepts, and rules are stored* memory, but there have been several ideas put forward. At the very least, concepts seem to be related in terms of their ability to elicit each other as associates. If I ask you to say the first thing that comes to mind when I say a word, and then I say "hot," are you not likely to say "cold" in response? When people are asked to recall a list of randomly presented words from various categories (e.g., pieces of furniture, men's names, fruits, sports, and colors), they do so by category, recalling first furniture pieces, then names, then fruits, and so on (e.g., Bousfield, 1953). In fact, when people recall lists of words that are not from distinct categories, they still produce recall lists that reflect their own associative organization (Tulving, 1962).

Over the past twenty years, several *network models* have been proposed to describe the structure of semantic LTM. Each theory is somewhat different, but they all propose that the concepts (e.g., "animal," "bird," "canary," "yellow") or propositions ("birds are animals," "birds can fly," "canaries are birds," "canaries are yellow") stored in semantic memory are interrelated in highly structured, predictable ways (Anderson, 1976, 1983a, 1983b; Collins & Loftus, 1975; Collins & Quillian, 1969).

Semantic long-term memory is also abstract. By that I mean that although we may know how many stripes there are on the American flag, and although we have a general idea of the sorts of things that dogs eat, we have difficulty remembering how, why, or when we ever acquired that tidbit of information. The information in semantic memory is not tied in any real way to our memories of our own life experiences—which sets it apart from the third variety of LTM.

The third type or subsystem of memory proposed by Tulving is called **episodic memory**. Here we store the memories of our life events and experiences. It is a time-related memory, and the experiences stored there are laid down in chronological order. Episodic memory operates something like a video camera that simply registers, or catalogues, all of our life's events on one continuous videotape. In other words, episodic memories are memories of specific events, not abstract events. For example:

> *What did you have for lunch yesterday?*
> *Did you have a good night's sleep?*
> *How did you spend last summer's vacation?*
> *What did your dog eat yesterday?*

The answers to these sorts of questions are stored in our episodic memories.

Some researchers claim that there is a separate category of episodic memory that they call *autobiographical memory* (e.g., Baddeley, 1990; Berscheid, 1994). Episodic memory contains things that have happened to us, but the events in autobiographical memory are particularly significant. What I had for lunch last Monday may be in my episodic memory, but the experience of teaching my first class in introductory psychology as a graduate student at the University of Tennessee is probably in my autobiographical memory as well. One's autobiographical memory does not seem to develop until about the age of 3 to 31/2 years, or until we are old enough to be able to talk to ourselves and to others about the events of our lives (Nelson, 1993; Pillemer & White, 1989).

episodic memory *a subsystem of LTM, in which personal experiences are stored*

Before You Go On

Describe three possible subsystems of LTM.

Where and How Are Memories Formed in the Brain?

We may safely assume that memories of our experiences are stored in our brains. Logic suggests that as information is encoded, stored, and retrieved, reliable changes occur in the central nervous system. Trying to discover where and how memories are formed in the nervous system is not a new line of research, but over the last decade it has become one of the most exciting and most promising.

Where Are Memories Formed?

Karl Lashley (1890–1958), a student of John B. Watson, spent over 30 years trying to find the particular part of the brain in which memories are stored. Lashley taught rats, cats, and monkeys to negotiate all sorts of complex mazes. Then he systematically removed or lesioned (cut) portions of the learner's cerebral cortex. Once he destroyed a part of the brain, Lashley tested his subject's memory for the previously learned task. What Lashley found was quite unexpected (Lashley, 1950). He discovered that specific memories do not have a specific location in the brain. When he went looking for a memory in the brain to lesion, he could not find one. What he did find was that, in general, the more brain tissue he destroyed, the more impaired the organism's performance, but *it seemed to matter very little where the damage occurred.*

A rabbit can be conditioned to close the nictitating membrane of its eyes when a tone is sounded. That response, once learned, is at least partially stored in the rabbit's cerebellum.

We now recognize a few of the limitations of Lashley's studies. For one thing, he studied mostly maze learning, a rather complex set of procedures that involves the interaction of many senses and many muscle groups. Lashley may have been correct about memories for mazes: They are probably not stored in one location. But some types of memories do seem to be found in certain predictable locations. Individual experiences of sight, sound, or touch may very well be stored in–or near–the relevant sensory area of the cerebral cortex, and memories for the images of faces and for images of animals may have storage places of their own (e.g., Squire, 1986, 1987, 1992).

Another "problem" we see in Lashley's work is that it focused only on the cerebral cortex. Some evidence suggests that many lower brain centers are intimately involved in encoding and storing information (Gluck & Myers, 1995; McCormick et al., 1982; Mishkin & Appenzeller, 1987; Thompson, 1969, 1981, 1986). For example, we know that rabbits can be classically conditioned to close the protective tissue (nictitating membrane) that covers their eyes in response to the sound of a tone. Once this response has been learned, the only way to destroy the association is to make small lesions in areas of the cerebellum. For rabbits, then, we know that there is at least one conditioned response stored in the cerebellum (Thompson, 1990).

Scientists do assume that most human memories are stored in the cerebral cortex, but also argue that other, lower structures are involved. As we noted in Chapter 2, it is the *hippocampus* that seems most necessary for memory formation. Much of what we know about the role of the hippocampus we have learned from observations of a few unfortunate individuals for whom at least one aspect of memory had been stolen away by illness or disease (Baddeley, 1990; Corkin, 1984; Milner, 1959, 1965; Milner et al., 1968; Squire, 1992).

A patient known to us only as "H. M." suffered from epilepsy. For nearly 11 years he experienced an average of one major convulsive attack and several partial seizures every day. Finally it was decided that drastic treatment was called for. Parts of the temporal lobe would be severed, and the hippocampus would be removed from both sides of H. M.'s brain. The surgery was successful. Epileptic seizures became rare. Sensory, perceptual, and most intellectual functioning were left intact.

However, there were disastrous effects on H. M.'s memory. He could not form new long-term memories. Failure to recall events before his surgery would have meant a diagnosis of **retrograde** (backward-acting) **amnesia**–the loss of memory of events that occurred before the onset of the amnesia. No, this was not the problem. H. M. could remember all that had happened to him *before* his surgery, but he could not form memories of events that happened after the surgery. H. M. had **anterograde** (forward-acting) **amnesia**. If asked what year it was, H. M. would say, "1953"–the year the surgery was performed. If you were to interact with H. M. and

retrograde amnesia *the loss of the memory of events stored before the onset of the loss*

anterograde amnesia *the inability to form or retrieve new memories* then leave for a few minutes, he would have no idea who you were when you returned.

Consider the fate of Clive Wearing, a bright musician who contracted encephalitis, which ultimately damaged his brain. He, too, was left after treatment with an inability to form new, lasting memories. "If his wife left the room for a few minutes, when she returned he would greet her with great joy, declaring that he had not seen her for months and asking how long he had been unconscious. Experienced once, such an event could be intriguing and touching, but when it happens repeatedly day in, day out, it rapidly loses its charm" (Baddeley, 1990, p. 5). Unlike H. M.'s experience, Mr. Wearing also had signs of retrograde amnesia. His recollections for events that preceded his illness were spotty and seldom included detail. One marvelous exception is that throughout all of his memory problems, his memory for making beautiful music remains.

From other similar cases, we find that if damage is localized to the hippocampus, and the rest of the brain is unscathed, the degree of amnesia (retrograde or anterograde) is considerably less than that of either H. M. or Mr. Wearing, each of whom had damage to the temporal lobes as well (Squire, 1992).

How Are Memories Formed?

So when human memories are formed, changes occur in the cerebral cortex that are, at least in part, influenced by the action of the hippocampus. *That* sounds simple enough, but what sorts of changes take place as memories are stored? Exactly what is changed, and in what ways? Answers to these questions are not yet available, and what hints we do have tell us that the processes involved are incredibly complex. If the nervous system is in some way altered as memories are formed, that alteration must be at the level of the neuron or the synapse. Given the recency of most of the research in this area, the story changes regularly, but here is some of what psychologists suspect.

First, let's make sure we understand what does *not* happen. We do not develop or grow new neurons as a function of experience. Recall from our discussion in Chapter 2 that we are born with about as many neurons as we'll ever have. Learning and memory have to take advantage of existing neurons. Experience may not provide us with new neurons, but it does increase the number of axon endings, dendrites, and synapses in the brain (Greenough, 1984; Rosenzweig et al., 1972).

By the late 1970s, the best guess was that evidence for memory formation could be found by examining changes at the synapse (Bartus et al., 1982; Kandel & Schwartz, 1982; Lavond et al., 1993; Matthies, 1989; McNaughton & Morris, 1987). The argument that emerges from the research—most of it done with simple, nonhuman animals—is that with repetition or experience, the flow of impulses across synapses becomes easier and easier. It is as if synapses become more efficient with practice.

If memories are formed because repetition, experience, or practice allows some neurotransmitters to work more effectively at the synaptic level, what would happen if something disrupted or blocked the action of those neurotransmitters? You would predict that memories formed at synapses that used those neurotransmitters would be disrupted as well. This is essentially what happens. The neurotransmitters most often involved in studies such as these are acetylcholine (ACh) and serotonin.

A slightly different line of research claims that experience does not increase (or alter in any way) the neurotransmitter released at synapses. What matters are changes in the postsynaptic membrane. The most common changes are thought to be increases in the number of effective or useful receptor sites (Lynch & Baudry, 1984). As synapses are used and used again, the number of receptor sites increases, and this is what makes for more efficient use of the synapse.

In brief, the formation of memories involves making some synaptic transmissions easier than they once were. What remains to be seen is whether changes at the synapse involve the amount of neurotransmitter present or produce physical changes in the neuronal membranes to allow existing neurotransmitters to function more effectively.

Before You Go On

What parts of the brain are most involved in memory formation?

At the level of the neuron, what changes take place when memories are formed?

TOPIC 6A SUMMARY

In this Topic I have tried to show that human memory is not just a simple receptacle for information that passively enters through our senses and gets dumped where we can get it out whenever we wish. Multistore models of memory claim that to encode and store information requires a series of steps needed to move that information through distinct memory stores. Levels-of-processing models claim that there is but one memory store where information is processed at various levels. What I've tried to do is present a model of memory that borrows heavily from a multistore viewpoint, but that also acknowledges the usefulness of a levels-of-processing approach. Our model included sensory memory, short-term memory, and long-term memory components.

There may be various types of long-term memory, and information in long-term memory may be stored in an organized fashion, although we do not yet fully appreciate all of the patterns of organization that can best characterize our memory systems. Human memories seem to be produced when synaptic transmission is somehow made easier. Memories may be stored throughout the brain, mostly in the cerebral cortex, and seem to need the hippocampus to be consolidated as long-term memories.

It is still true, however, that on a practical level, what matters most to us, day in and day out, is whether we can get information out of our memory systems when we want to. We consider this process of retrieval in Topic 6B.

TOPIC 6B Improving Memory: Factors Affecting Retrieval

In this Topic we turn to the practical matter of accounting for why we forget things. In the terminology we've been developing, forgetting is a matter of retrieval failure. Our focus, then, will be on factors that affect the retrieval of information from memory. Whether we are talking about a simple, well-learned habit stored in procedural memory, a precise definition stored in semantic memory, a personal experience stored in episodic memory, or a telephone number temporarily stored in short-term memory, if retrieval fails at a critical time, that information will be of no use to us.

What factors influence whether information can be retrieved on demand? What can be done to increase the likelihood that retrieval will succeed? In truth, the list is *not* a very long one. I have organized this discussion around four different but related factors: (1) how memory is measured, (2) how encoding strategies influence later retrieval, (3) how encoding is scheduled, and (4) how interference can affect retrieval. Throughout this Topic we will assume that the to-be-remembered information is actually stored in memory. That is, we will focus on problems of retrieval, not retention. Occasionally we may feel that we have "forgotten" something when it was never really stored in memory in the first place.

How We Measure Retrieval

One factor affecting the retrieval of information from memory is how one is asked to go about retrieving it. This is a factor over which you and I seldom have much control. For instance, unless you have an unusually democratic instructor, you will not be allowed to vote on what type of exams will be given in class. Students are usually asked to retrieve information in one of a number of standard exam formats chosen by their instructor. In this section, we'll see how retrieval is influenced by the choice of measuring technique.

Direct, Explicit Measures of Memory

Measures of retrieval are called *direct,* or *explicit,* when someone must consciously, or purposively, retrieve specified information from his or her memory (as on a classroom exam). Both recall and recognition qualify as direct measures.

Let's design an example to work with. We have students come to the laboratory on a Tuesday to learn a list of 15 randomly chosen words. Some students take longer than others, but all eventually demonstrate that they have learned the list. The students report back to the laboratory two weeks later, when our basic question is: "How many of the words that you learned two weeks ago do you still remember?" How could we find out?

One thing we could do is simply ask each student to recall the list of words. **Recall** asks someone to produce information to which he or she has been previously exposed. To use recall as a measure of memory, we need only give the students a blank sheet of paper and ask them to write, in any order, as many words from the previously learned list as they can. (Technically, this is "free recall." If we asked the students to recall the list in the order in which it was presented, we would be asking for "serial recall.") For recall, we provide the fewest cues to aid the retrieval. We merely specify the information we want and essentially say, "Go into your long-term memory, locate that information, get it out, and write it down." Let's assume that one student correctly recalls six words.

Now suppose that we furnish our student with a list of 50 words that includes those on the previously learned list. We instruct her to "circle the words on this list that you recognize from the list you learned two weeks ago." In this case, we're not asking for recall, but for **recognition,** a task that requires someone to identify material previously experienced. Isn't it likely that our student will do better on this task? She was able to recall 6 words of the original 15, so let's say she recognizes 11 words. In a way, we have a small dilemma. Do we say that our student remembered 6 words or 11 words? The answer is, both or either. Whether our student remembered 6 or 11 words depends on how we asked her to go about remembering.

In virtually every case, retrieval by recognition is superior to retrieval by recall (Bahrick, 1984; Brown, 1976; Schacter, 1987). Figure 6.4 provides some clear-cut data of this point. Over a two-day period, tests of retrieval by recognition are superior to tests of retrieval by recall. Most students I know would rather take a multiple-choice exam, in which they only have to recognize the correct response from among a few alternatives, than a fill-in-the-blank test (or an essay test), which requires recall.

Recall and recognition are similar in that they both involve the retrieval of material usually stored in semantic memory (possibly in episodic memory) (Hayman & Tulving, 1989; Tulving, 1983), and seem to involve the same physiological underpinnings in the brain (Haist et al., 1992; Squire et al., 1993).

recall *a measure of retrieval in which one is given the fewest possible cues to aid retrieval and must produce information to which he or she has been previously exposed*

recognition *a measure of retrieval in which an individual is required to identify material previously learned*

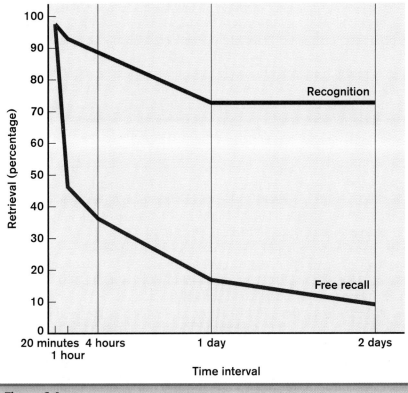

Figure 6.4

Differences in retrieval scores for the memory of nonsense syllables over a 2-day period. In one case retrieval is measured with a test for recall, whereas in the other case, retrieval is measured with a test for recognition. (From Luh, 1922.)

Indirect, Implicit Measures of Memory

Measures of memory classified as *indirect,* or *implicit,* are more subtle than either recall or recognition. With indirect measures, someone demonstrates that information is stored in memory when he or she can take advantage of previous experiences without consciously trying to do so.

What if one of the students in our example experiment came back to the laboratory two weeks after memorizing a list of words and could neither recall nor recognize any of the items? I suspect that we'd be a bit surprised, but we might be wrong if we assumed that nothing was retained from the learning experience two weeks earlier. What if we ask this student to relearn the list of 15 words? Two weeks ago it took ten presentations of the list, or trials, before the words were learned. Now, relearning the same list, takes only seven trials. This is a common finding in memory research.

Relearning—the change in performance that occurs when one is required to learn material for a second time—almost always requires fewer trials, or less time, than did original learning. The difference is attributed to the benefit provided by one's memory of the original learning. Because relearning does not require the direct, conscious retrieval of information from memory, it qualifies as an indirect, or implicit, test of memory retention (Graf & Schacter, 1985; Schacter, 1987, 1992).

The importance of relearning as a measure of memory dates back to 1885 and the research of Hermann Ebbinghaus. To minimize the impact of experience, Ebbinghaus designed "nonsense syllables"—such as *dax, wuj, lep, pib, loz*—to use in his research. [As it happens, not all syllables are equally nonsensical; some *are* more meaningful (e.g., *tix, luv, bot*) than others (e.g., *wuj, xyg, keq*).] Ebbinghaus memorized list after list of nonsense syllables under various conditions of practice.

relearning the change in performance that occurs when one is required to learn material for a second time

Later, he assessed his memory for what he had learned. He noted that even when recall was poor, he could *relearn* a list of syllables in just a few trials.

Implicit tests of memory have become an active area of research in cognitive psychology (Richardson-Klavehn & Bjork, 1988; Roediger, 1990). Among other things, this research supports the hypothesis that information is stored in various types of long-term memory. Although we may think of the relearning of verbal materials, such as words or nonsense syllables, as an indirect measure of memory, many implicit tests of retention focus on *procedural memories,* or procedural knowledge. You'll recall from our last Topic that procedural memories include the storage of "knowing how to go about doing things," such as tying a shoelace, typing, speaking, or riding a bicycle. Remembering how to do such things is virtually automatic, or unconscious. When we specifically try to recall how to do them—when we really pause and think about what we're doing—our performance often deteriorates. "In some sense, these performances reflect prior learning, but seem to resist conscious remembering" (Roediger, 1990, p. 1043).

Implicit memory tests provide some intriguing data about amnesia. As we noted in Topic 6A, some people with amnesia (such as H. M.) are unable to transfer information from STM to LTM. What is learned today is forgotten by tomorrow. In one study, persons with amnesia and control subjects learned a list of words. Retention of the list was tested. In two direct, explicit measures, recall and recognition, the control subjects were superior to the amnesic subjects, who predictably scored poorly (Warrington & Weiskrantz, 1968, 1970). Then the subjects were given two implicit tests. Neither test was presented as a test of memory, but as a guessing game. In one, subjects were shown a few letters (such as *tab*) and were asked to identify a word that began with those letters. In the other test, they were to identify words that had been mutilated so that they were very difficult to read. How many words from the previously learned list would be identified in either task? It turned out that words from the list learned previously were easier to identify than "new" words, and there were *no differences* between the amnesic and non-amnesic subjects on these implicit tests of memory. These findings have been replicated many times (Bowers & Schacter, 1990; Graf & Mandler, 1984; Shimamura, 1986).

What this means is that in even the worst amnesia cases, some memory processing may be saved. Some long-term memories—those in procedural memory in

Information stored in procedural long-term memory (such as knowing how to ride a bicycle) can be tapped by implicit tests of memory. "Recalling" how to ride a bicycle is nearly an automatic process. You just get up on the bike and ride away, essentially without thinking about it.

particular—may be maintained. Remember the last time you heard about someone with amnesia? Typically, we hear about some adult found wandering about, totally unaware of who he is, where he came from, or how he got there. There seems to be no direct recollection of any long-term memories. But note that such amnesia patients usually do demonstrate all sorts of long-term memories. They remember how to talk, how to eat, and how to get dressed. They remember, in short, behaviors stored in their procedural memories.

Before You Go On

What is the difference between recall and recognition?

What do implicit measures tell us about long-term memory?

How We Encode Information

Encoding, storage, and retrieval are interrelated memory processes. The issue is simple: If you do not encode information properly, you will have difficulty retrieving it. You cannot recall my mother's maiden name simply because you never knew it in the first place. You have never heard my mother's maiden name before, but you have had countless encounters with pennies. Can you draw a picture of a penny, locating all of its features? Can you recognize an accurate drawing of a penny (Figure 6.5)? In fact, few of us can, and even fewer can recall all of its essential features, nearly 90 percent forgetting that the word *Liberty* appears right behind Lincoln's shoulder (Nickerson & Adams, 1979; Rubin & Kontis, 1983). These retrieval failures do not result from a lack of experience but from a lack of proper encoding. We'll cover four encoding issues: context effects, meaningfulness, mnemonic devices, and schemas.

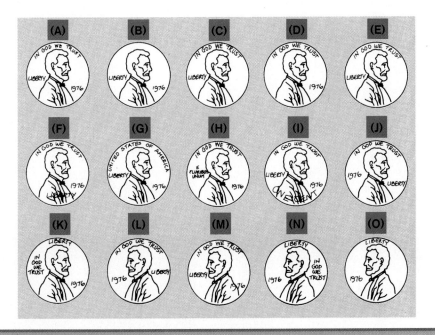

Figure 6.5

Fifteen drawings of the head of a penny. The fact that we cannot easily identify the correct rendition emphasizes that simple exposure to a stimulus does not guarantee that it will be adequately encoded in long-term memory. (After Nickerson & Adams, 1979.)

The Power of Context

encoding specificity principle *the hypothesis that we can retrieve only what we have stored and that retrieval is enhanced to the extent that retrieval cues match encoding cues*

Retrieval is best when the situation, or context, in which retrieval takes place matches the context that was present at encoding. When cues present at encoding are also present at retrieval, retrieval is enhanced. This observation reflects the main point of the **encoding specificity principle**, which asserts that how we retrieve information depends on how it was encoded in the first place (Flexser & Tulving, 1982; Newby, 1987; Tulving & Thompson, 1973). Not only do we encode and store particular items of information, we also note and store the context in which those items occur. The encoding specificity principle is as valid for animals as it is for humans. "Ease of retrieval . . . is quite strongly influenced by the context in which the animal is asked to retrieve it. The closer the test context is to training conditions and the more unique the context is for specific memories, the better the retrieval" (Spear et al., 1990, pp. 190–191).

Here's a hypothetical experiment that demonstrates encoding specificity (based on Tulving & Thompson, 1973). Students are asked to learn a list of 24 common words. Half the students are given cue words to help them remember each item on the list. For the stimulus word *wood,* the cue word is tree; for *cheese,* the cue is *green,* and so on for each of the 24 words. The other students receive no such cue during their memorization (i.e., while encoding). Later, students are asked to recall as many words from the list as they can. What we discover is that presenting the cue at recall helps those students who had seen it during learning, but *decreases* the recall for those who had not seen it during learning. If learning takes place without a cue, recall will be better without it.

Research on the relationship between encoding and retrieval tells us that the best place to study for an exam is in the room in which the exam will be given. The greater the difference between the context available at study time and the context available at retrieval, the poorer the retrieval will be.

How-to-study-in-college books often recommend that you choose one place for studying. Your kitchen table is not likely to be a good choice because it is associated with eating experiences (and many others). In other words, the context of a kitchen is not a good one for encoding information unless you expect to be tested for retrieval in that same context—which seems highly unlikely. This advice was reaffirmed by a series of experiments by Steven Smith (1979). He had students learn some material in one room, and then tested their recall for that material in either the same room or a different one. When a new room—a different context, with different cues—was used, retrieval scores dropped substantially. Simply instructing students to try to remember and think about the room in which learning took place helped recall considerably.

These context effects may be related to what has been called **state-dependent memory**. The idea here is that, to a degree, retrieval depends on the extent to which a person's *state of mind* at retrieval matches the person's state of mind at encoding (Leahy & Harris, 1989, p. 146). If learning takes place while a person is under the influence of a drug, for example, being under the influence of that drug at retrieval often has beneficial effects (Eich et al., 1975; Goodwin et al., 1969; Parker et al., 1976). Intriguing research by Gordon Bower (Bower, 1981; Bower et al., 1978; Bower & Mayer, 1989) suggests that mood may also predict retrieval. Using moods (sad or happy) induced by posthypnotic suggestion, Bower found that retrieval was best when mood at retrieval matched mood at learning. This effect is more pronounced for females than for males (Clark & Teasdale, 1985). Unfortunately, this "mood-dependent memory" effect has proven to be somewhat unreliable. Neither the circumstances under which it occurs nor the mechanisms that produce it are well understood (Eich, 1995; Eich et al., 1994). There is, however, considerable evidence that a given mood or frame of mind tends to evoke memories that are consistent with that mood (e.g., Blaney, 1986). Simply put: when you are in a good mood, you tend to remember pleasant things, and when you are in a bad or depressed mood, you tend to remember unpleasant, depressing things.

Furthermore, our memories for emotionally arousing experiences are likely to be easier to recall than memories of emotionally neutral events (Thompson, 1982). This may be because emotional arousal increases the levels of certain hormones that, in turn, help form vivid memories associated with the emotional arousal (Gold, 1987; McGaugh, 1983). That emotional arousal may help to form particularly vivid memories may help us understand what Brown and Kulik (1977) call **flashbulb memories**—memories that are unusually clear and vivid. You probably

state-dependent memory *the hypothesis that retrieval can be enhanced by the extent to which one's state of mind at retrieval matches one's state of mind at encoding*

flashbulb memory *a particularly clear and vivid (although not necessarily accurate) recollection from one's past*

EXPERIENCING PSYCHOLOGY

Tapping into Flashbulb Memories

We have defined *flashbulb memories* as memories stored in long-term memory that are particularly clear and vivid and easy to retrieve. Most likely, these memories are stored in episodic memory, and although their recollections are easy and vivid, they may not be at all accurate.

By and large, flashbulb memories vary from one generation to another. To explore flashbulb memories in more detail, you might try a few things. First, ask someone in their twenties, their forties, and their sixties for the two or three flashbulb memories that most easily come to their minds. To what extent was there

any overlap in the sorts of events that constitute flashbulb memories for people of different ages? Can you assess the extent to which the flashbulb memories you noted were accurate representations of the events recalled? Did you note any distortions? Did you note any consistent ways in which these memories were distorted? Were there any differences in the *kinds* of events that people recalled? Even though they may have recalled different flashbulb memory events, were there any similarities in the sorts of things that people recalled, that is, did they mention what they were doing, how they felt, who was with them, etc.?

have flashbulb memories of several events: your high school graduation; the funeral of a close friend; or how you learned about some significant news event. Although flashbulb memories *are* particularly clear and vivid, there is little reason to believe that they are necessarily any more complete or accurate than any other memories. Although we seem to recall these events in vivid detail, much of that detail may be totally wrong or may never have really happened (McCloskey et al., 1988; Neisser, 1982, 1991).

Before You Go On

How does the context in which one encodes information affect the retrieval of that information?

The Usefulness of Meaningfulness

I have a hypothesis. I believe I can determine the learning ability of students by noting where they sit in a classroom. The best, brightest students choose seats farthest from the door. Poorer students sit by the door, apparently interested in getting easily into and out of the room. (There may be some truth to this, but I'm not serious.) To make my point, I do an experiment. Students seated away from the door are asked to learn a list of words I read aloud only once. I need a second list of words for the students seated by the door because they've already heard my first list. The list my "smart students" hears contains words such as *university, registrar, automobile, environmental, psychology,* and so forth. As I predicted, they have little problem recalling this list after just one presentation. The students huddled by the door get my second list: *insidious, tachistoscope, sophistry, flotsam, episcotister,* and so forth. Needless to say, my hypothesis will be confirmed.

This obviously is not a fair experiment. Those students sitting by the door will yell foul. My second list of words is clearly more difficult to learn and recall than the first. The words on the first list *are* more familiar, and they are easier to pronounce. However, the major difference between these lists is the **meaningfulness** of the items—the extent to which they elicit existing associations in memory. The *university, registrar, automobile* list is easy to remember because each word in it is meaningful. Each word makes us think of many other things, or produces many associations. These items are easy to elaborate. Words like *episcotister* are more difficult because they evoke few, if any, associations.

Meaningfulness is not a characteristic or feature built into materials to be learned. Meaningfulness resides in the learner. *Episcotister* may be a meaningless collection of letters for many, but for others it is a word rich in meaning, a word with which they can readily form many associations. What is or is not meaningful is a function of individual experiences. (An episcotister, by the way, is a type of apparatus used in psychology. To make this word meaningful for you, you might want to do some research on episcotisters.)

It follows, then, that one of your tasks as a learner is to do whatever you can to make the material you are learning as meaningful as possible. You need to seek out and form associations between what you are learning and what you already know. You need to elaboratively rehearse what you are encoding so that you can retrieve it later. You need to ask about what you are studying. What does this mean? What does it make me think of? Does this remind me of something I already know? How can I make this more meaningful? Perhaps you now see a reason for including "Before You Go On" questions within each chapter.

meaningfulness *the extent to which new information evokes associations with information already in memory*

⊚⊚⊚⊚ **Thinking Critically** ⊚⊚⊚⊚

How can you make what you've learned about meaningfulness more meaningful to you?

Before You Go On

How is "meaningfulness" related to retrieval?

The Value of Mnemonic Devices

Retrieval is enhanced when we elaborate on the material we are learning—when we organize it and make it meaningful during the encoding process. Now we'll look at a few specific encoding techniques, **mnemonic devices**, that can aid our retrieval by helping us to organize and add meaningfulness to new material.

Research by Bower and Clark (1969) shows us that we can improve the retrieval of otherwise unorganized material if we weave that material into a meaningful story—a technique called *narrative chaining*. A group of college students was asked to learn a list of 10 simple nouns in order. This is not a difficult task, and students had little trouble with it. Then they were given another list of 10 nouns to learn, and then another—12 lists in all. These students were given no instructions other than to remember each list of words in order.

A second group of students was given the same 12 lists of 10 nouns each to learn. They were asked to make up little stories that used each of the words on the list in order. After each list was presented, both groups were asked to recall the list of words they had just heard. At this point, there was no difference in the recall scores for the two groups. Then came a surprise. After all 12 lists had been recalled, the students were tested again on their recall for each of the lists. Students were given a word from one of the 12 lists, and were asked to recall the other nine words from that list. Now the difference in recall between the two groups of students was striking (see Figure 6.6). Those who used a narrative-chaining technique recalled

mnemonic devices *strategies for improving retrieval that take advantage of existing memories in order to make new material more meaningful*

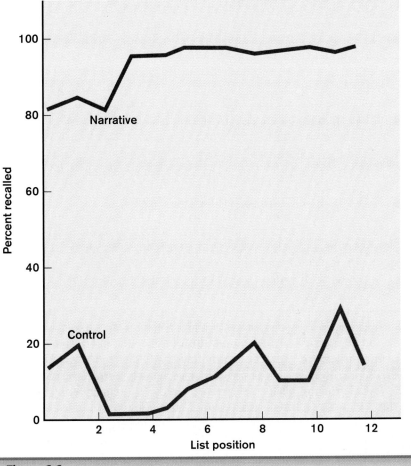

Figure 6.6

Percent correct recall for words from 12 lists learned under two study, or encoding, conditions. In the narrative condition, students made up short stories to relate the words meaningfully, whereas in the control condition, simple memorization without any specified mnemonic device was used. (After Bower & Clark, 1969.)

93 percent of the words (on average), whereas those who did not organize the words recalled only 13 percent of them. The message is clear and consistent with what we've learned so far: organizing unrelated words into sensible stories helps us remember them.

Forming *mental images* can also improve memory. Using imagery at encoding to improve retrieval has proven to be very helpful in many different circumstances (Begg & Paivio, 1969; Marschark et al., 1987; Paivio, 1971, 1986). It is Paivio's contention that visual images provide a unique way of encoding meaningful information; that is, we are at an advantage when we can encode not only what a stimulus means, but also what it looks like. Imagery helps us retrieve words such as *horse, rainbow,* and *typewriter* more readily than words such as *treason, session,* and *effort*–even when the frequency and meaningfulness of the words are equated.

Assume that you have to learn the meanings of a large number of Spanish words. You could use simple rote repetition, but this technique is tedious and not very efficient. Atkinson (1975) suggested that to improve memory for foreign language vocabulary, it is useful to imagine some connection visually tying the two words together. He calls this the *key word method* of study. The Spanish word for "horse," for example is *caballo,* which is pronounced *cab-eye-yo.* To remember this association, you might choose *eye* as the key word and picture a horse actually kicking someone in the eye. Or, if you are not prepared to be that gruesome, you might imagine a horse with a very large eye. The Spanish word for "duck" is *pato.* Here your key word might be *pot,* and you'd picture a duck wearing a pot on its head (Figure 6.7) or sitting in a large pot on the stove. This may sound strange, but research suggests that it works very well (Pressley et al., 1982).

The same basic technique works whenever you need to remember any paired items. Gordon Bower (1972), for example, asked students to learn lists of pairs of English words. Some students were instructed to form a mental image that showed an interaction between the two words. One pair, for instance, was *piano-cigar.* Recall for word pairs was much better for those students who formed mental images than it was for those who did not. As it happens common, interactive images are more useful than strange and bizarre ones (Bower, 1970; Wollen et al., 1972). That is, to remember the *piano–cigar* pair, it is more useful to picture a cigar placed on a piano than to picture a piano actually smoking a cigar (Figure 6.8). If you wanted to remember that it was Bower and Clark who did the experiment on narrative chaining, picture two storytellers chained together, holding a Clark Bar in their hands as they take a bow on a stage. It may sound silly, but it works.

The last imagery-related mnemonic device I'll mention may be the oldest. It is attributed to the Greek poet Simonides and is called the *method of loci* (Yates, 1966). The idea here is to get in your mind a well-known location (loci are locations); say, the floor plan of your house or apartment. Visually place the material you are trying to recall in various places throughout your house in a sensible order. When the time comes for you to retrieve the material, mentally walk through your chosen locations, recalling the information you have stored at each place.

Mnemonic devices don't have to be formal techniques with special names. You used a mnemonic trick to learn which months of the year had 30 days and which had 31 when you learned the ditty "Thirty days hath September, April, June, and November. All the rest have. . . . " Some students originally learned the colors of the rainbow (we called it the visible spectrum) in order by remembering the name "ROY G. BIV," which I grant you isn't terribly meaningful, but it does help us remember "red, orange, yellow, green, blue, indigo, and violet." My guess is that you can think of several mnemonic devices you have used to organize and make meaningful material to be learned. In each case, the message is that when we can organize otherwise unrelated material in a meaningful way, retrieval will be enhanced.

Before You Go On

Describe narrative chaining, mental imagery, and the method of loci as mnemonic devices.

Figure 6.7

An illustration of how the key word method can be used to help foreign language retrieval. The Spanish word for "duck" is *pato,* pronounced "pot-oh." (After Atkinson, 1975.)

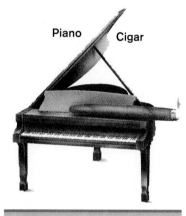

Figure 6.8

The key word method and the use of visual imagery can also be used to help us remember pairs of English words. (After Wollen et al., 1972.)

Having a complex, complete schema for chess makes it easier to recall the position of pieces on a chess board—so long as the position of the pieces reflects a true game situation. If pieces are placed randomly on a board, the chess-playing schema will be of little value.

The Role of Schemas

The encoding specificity hypothesis tells us that how we retrieve information is affected by how we have encoded it. One of the processes that influences how we encode and retrieve information is our use of schemas (sometimes referred to as scripts). A **schema** is an organized, general knowledge system stored in long-term memory (Mayer, 1983). Sir Frederic Bartlett, who first used the term in the context of memory, saw schemas as an organized part of our memories that held what we knew about some aspect of the world and guided our expectations about it (Bartlett, 1932). Schemas give us a general framework to understand new information and to remember or retrieve that information later (Alba & Hasher, 1983; Lord, 1980).

> schema *a system of organized, general knowledge, stored in long-term memory, that guides the encoding and retrieval of information*

I've never learned to play chess. I know what a chessboard looks like and I can probably name most of the pieces. I realize that there are restrictions on how pieces can be moved in a chess game, but I don't know what those restrictions are. In other words, I have a very sketchy schema for chess. If you were to show me a chessboard with the pieces positioned as if in the midst of a game and then later ask me to reconstruct what I had seen, I'm afraid I would do very poorly. When chess experts are shown the board and are later asked to reconstruct the positions of the pieces from memory, they do very well (DeGroot, 1965, 1966). Part of the explanation for their success is that they have a complete, detailed schema for chess games, which helps them encode and later retrieve the positions of the pieces on the board. When chess pieces are positioned *randomly* on a chessboard (not consistent with the rules of the game), the memory of chess experts for the location of the pieces is no better than mine or that of other novices (Chase & Simon, 1973). This is because the randomly positioned pieces don't fit the experts' schemas for chess, taking away their advantage. A detailed schema is not necessarily going to help one's retrieval unless the retrieval task takes advantage of the information stored in that schema (Brewer & Nakamura, 1984). This result has been found for expertise in several areas, including computer programming (Adelson, 1984) and medicine (Norman et al., 1989).

The role of prior knowledge in the form of schemas was nicely demonstrated by an experiment by Anderson and Pichert (1978). All participants read a story about a couple of boys playing alone in a house. The story contained several details about the house and its contents. One group was asked to read the story from the perspective of a potential buyer of the home, while a second group was asked to read the story from the point of view of a burglar who is planning to rob the house. When recalling the story from the buyer's perspective, people remembered details such as a leaky roof and a large living room. Those who took the burglar's point of view remembered where jewelry was kept and that the house contained a large television set. Think in terms of your memory. If I ask you to tell me all of the details of your last trip to the dentist, won't you rely heavily on your knowledge of what it is like to go to the dentist in general—your schema? Then you'll supplement the recall of your last specific visit by adding whatever details you can.

So, what's the bottom line? When to-be-remembered information is consistent with prior, existing information (such as schemas), retrieval is enhanced. When to-be-remembered material is at odds with existing schemas, those schemas may actually inhibit retrieval.

Before You Go On

What are schemas, and how do they affect retrieval?

How We Schedule Practice

As we've seen repeatedly, retrieval, no matter how it is measured, depends on how one goes about encoding, rehearsing, or practicing information in the first place. Retrieval is a function of the *amount* of practice and how that practice is spaced or *distributed*. One of the reasons some students do not do as well on classroom exams as they would like is that they simply do not have (or make) enough time to study or practice the material covered on exams. Another reason is that some students do not schedule wisely what time they do have.

Overlearning

What you and I often do once we decide to learn something is to read, practice, and study the material until we know it. We study until we are satisfied that we have encoded and stored the information in our memories, and then we quit. In other words, we often fail to engage in **overlearning**, the process of practicing or rehearsing material over and above what is needed to learn it. Consider this fictitious example, and see if you can extend this evidence to your own study habits.

overlearning *the practice, or rehearsal, of material over and above what is needed to learn it*

A student comes to the laboratory to learn a list of syllables such as *dax, wuj, pib,* and *zuw.* There are 15 items on the list, and the material has to be presented repeatedly before our student can recall all of the items correctly. Having correctly recalled the items once, our student is dismissed with instructions to return two weeks later for a test of his recall of the syllables. Not surprisingly, he does not fare very well on the retrieval task.

What do you think would have happened if we had continued to present the list of syllables at the time of learning, well beyond the point at which it was first learned? Let's say the list was learned in 12 trials. We have the student practice the list for 6 additional presentations (50-percent overlearning—practice that is 50 percent over and above that required for learning). What if we required an additional 12 trials of practice (100-percent overlearning), or an additional 48 trials of practice (400-percent overlearning)?

The effects of overlearning are well documented and very predictable. The recall data for this imaginary experiment might look like those in Figure 6.9. Note three things about these data: (1) If we measure retrieval at various times after learning, forgetting is rather impressive and quite sudden. (This is one of the re-

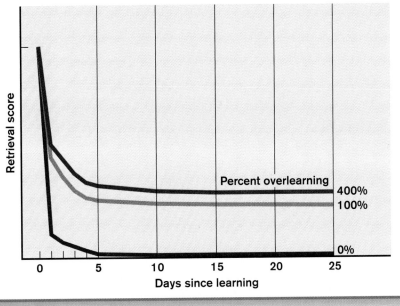

Figure 6.9

Idealized data showing the short-term and long-term advantages of overlearning. Note the "diminished returns" with additional overlearning. (From Krueger, 1929.)

sults of his research on memory reported by Ebbinghaus in 1885.) (2) Overlearning improves retrieval, having its greatest effects with longer retention intervals. (3) There is a "diminishing returns" phenomenon present; that is, 50-percent overlearning is much more useful than no overlearning; 100-percent overlearning is somewhat better than 50 percent; and 400 percent is better than 100 percent, but not by very much. For any learning task, or individual, there is probably an optimum amount of overlearning. How one *schedules* one's practice or learning time is also an important factor in determining the likelihood of retrieval, and it is to this issue we turn next.

Scheduling, or Spacing, Practice

Some of the oldest data in psychology tell us that retrieval will be improved if practice (encoding) is spread out over time, with rest intervals spaced in between. The data in Figure 6.10 are fairly standard. In fact, this experiment, first performed in 1946, provides such reliable results that it is commonly used as a student project in psychology classes. The task is to write the letters of the alphabet, upside down and from right to left. (If you think that sounds easy, give it a try.)

Subjects are given the opportunity to practice the task under four conditions. The *massed-practice* group works with no break between trials. The three *distributed-practice* groups receive the same amount of practice, but get rest intervals interspersed between each 1-minute trial. One group gets a 3- to 5-second break between trials, a second group receives a 30-second rest, and a third group gets a 45-second rest between trials.

As we can see in Figure 6.10, subjects in all four groups begin at about the same (poor) level of performance. After 20 minutes of practice, the performance of all groups shows improvement, but by far, the massed-practice (no rest) group does the poorest, and the 45-second-rest group does the best.

The conclusion from years of research is that almost without exception distributed practice is superior to massed practice. There are exceptions, however. Some tasks may suffer from having rest intervals inserted in practice time. In general, whenever you must keep track of many things at the same time, you should mass your practice until you have finished what you are working on. If, for example, you

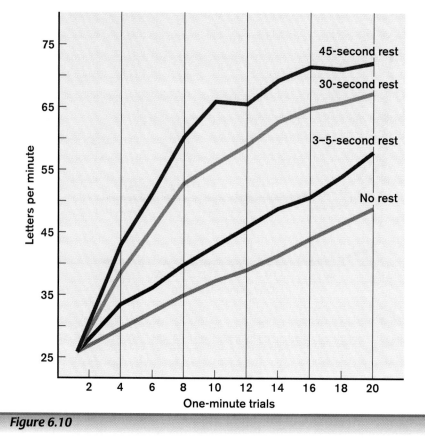

Figure 6.10

Improvement in performance as a function of the distribution of practice time. The task involved was printing the letters of the alphabet upside-down and backward with twenty 1-minute trials separated by rest intervals of various lengths (After Kientzle, 1946.)

are working on a complex math problem, you should work it through until you find a solution, whether it's time for a break or not. And, of course, you should not break up your practice in such a way as to disrupt the meaningfulness of the material you are studying.

What we're talking about here is the scheduling of study time. The message is always the same: short (and meaningful) study periods with rest periods interspersed are more efficient than study periods massed together. There may be times when cramming is better than not studying at all, but as a general strategy, cramming is inefficient.

Before You Go On

How does overlearning affect retrieval?

How does distributing one's practice affect retrieval?

ⓔⓔⓔ **Thinking Critically** ⓔⓔⓔ

How would you design a study strategy for this course that took advantage of overlearning and distributed practice?

How We Overcome Interference

Think back to when you were in third grade. Can you remember the name of the student who sat behind you at school? I know I can't. I can guess who it might have been, but there seems to be no way I can directly access and retrieve that piece of information from my long-term memory with certainty. One possibility is that that information is simply no longer there. It may, in some literal sense, be lost forever. Perhaps I never encoded that name in a way that would allow me to retrieve it effectively. Another possibility is that the name of that student *is* available in memory, but inaccessible at the moment because I have been in so many classes since third grade. So much has happened and entered my memory since third grade that the material I am looking for is "covered up" and being interfered with by information that entered later.

How about your most recent class? Can you recall who sat behind you in your last class? That may be a little easier, but remembering that name with confidence is still not easy. Again, our basic retrieval problem may be one of interference. Assuming that what we are searching for is still there, we may not be able to retrieve it because so many previous experiences are getting in the way, interfering with retrieval.

Retroactive Interference

The idea that interference can account for retrieval failure is an old one in psychology. Some early experiments, for example, demonstrated that subjects who were active for a period after learning remembered what they had learned less well than did subjects who used the intervening period for sleep (Jenkins & Dallenbach, 1924). The graphs in Figure 6.11 show reasonably comparable data from two experiments, one with college students who had learned a list of nonsense syllables, and the other with cockroaches that had learned to avoid an area of their cage. In both cases, subjects who engaged in normal waking activity did more poorly on tests of retrieval over all retention intervals.

When interfering activities come *after* the learning that is to be remembered or retrieved, we have **retroactive interference**. Let's go back into the laboratory. (You can follow along with the summary diagram in Figure 6.12). We need students randomly assigned to either a control group or an experimental group. Students in both groups are required to learn something (almost anything will do; we'll assume it's a list of nonsense syllables). Having learned their lists, the groups are treated differently. Students in the experimental group are now required to learn something else, perhaps a new list of nonsense syllables. At the same time, control group

retroactive interference *the inhibition of retrieval of previously learned material caused by material learned later*

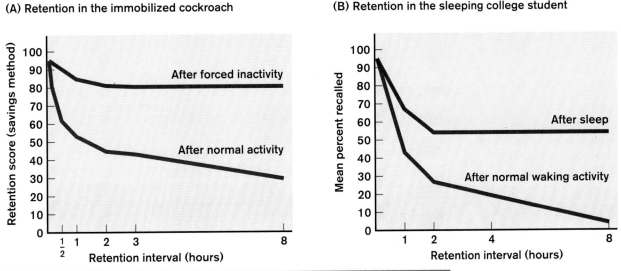

(A) Retention in the immobilized cockroach

(B) Retention in the sleeping college student

Figure 6.11

These graphs illustrate how activity following learning can interfere with the retrieval of the learned behavior or materials. In both cases, normal waking activity caused more interference than did forced inactivity (for cockroaches) or sleeping (for college students). (After Minami & Dallenbach, 1946.)

> **Figure 6.12**
>
> Designs of Experiments to Demonstrate Retroactive Interference and Proactive Interference
>
> **(A) Retroactive interference**
>
> | | **Learn** | **Learn** | **Test** |
> |---|---|---|---|
> | Experimental group | Task A | Task B | Retrieval of Task A |
> | Control group | Task A | Nothing | Retrieval of Task A |
>
> **(B) Proactive interference**
>
> | | **Learn** | **Learn** | **Test** |
> |---|---|---|---|
> | Experimental group | Task A | Task B | Retrieval of Task B |
> | Control group | Nothing | Task B | Retrieval of Task B |
>
> Note: If interference is operating, the control group will demonstrate better retrieval than will the experimental group.

subjects are asked to do nothing (which is impossible, of course, in a literal sense). They might be asked to rest quietly or to play some simple game.

Now for the test. Both groups are asked to remember whatever was presented in the first learning task. Students in the control group will show a higher retrieval score than students in the experimental group. For the experimental group, the second set of learned material interferes with the retrieval of the material learned first. Figure 6.12(A) summarizes this research design.

Most of us are familiar with retroactive interference from our own experiences. A student who studied French in high school takes a few Spanish courses in college and now can't remember very much French. The Spanish keeps getting in the way. I have two students who are scheduled to take a psychology test tomorrow morning at 9:00. Both are equally able and equally well motivated. One is taking only one class—mine. She studies psychology for two hours, watches TV for two hours, and goes to bed. She comes in the next morning to take the test. The second student also studies psychology for two hours, but then must read a chapter and a half from her sociology text, just in case she is called on in class. After reading sociology, she goes to bed, comes to class, and takes the test. Everything else being equal, this student will be at a disadvantage. The sociology she studied will retroactively interfere with her retrieval of the psychology she learned previously. What is this student to do? She has to study psychology, and she knows that she had better read her sociology, too. About all she can do is to set herself up for proactive interference.

proactive interference *the inhibition of retrieval of recently learned material caused by material learned earlier*

Proactive Interference

Proactive interference occurs when *previously* learned material interferes with the retrieval of material learned later. First follow along in Figure 6.12(B), then we'll get back to our student and her studying problem. We have two groups of students, experimental and control. The experimental group again starts by learning something-that same list of syllables, perhaps. This time the control group students begin by resting quietly while the experimental group goes through the learning task. Both groups then learn a new list of syllables. We test for retrieval, but this time we test for the retrieval of the more recently learned material. Again, the control group students have an advantage. They have none of that first list in their memories to interfere with retrieval. However, the advantage is not as great as it was in the case of retroactive interference. Proactive interference is not as detrimental as retroactive interference, which is why I would advise our student to study what she thinks is her most important assignment last.

Americans learn to drive on the right side of a road. If they find themselves in a country where one must drive on the left side of the road, interference effects from previous learning can be very powerful.

Although both retroactive and proactive interference are well documented, there are many factors that influence the extent of such interference (Underwood, 1957). For example, meaningful, well-organized material is less susceptible to interference than is less meaningful material, such as nonsense syllables. As a rule, the more similar the interfering material is to the material being retrieved, the greater will be the interference (e.g., McGeoch & McDonald, 1931). My student who had to study for a psychology test and read a sociology text will experience more interference (retroactive or proactive) than will a student who has to study for the psychology test and work calculus problems. In this context, I might suggest that working on calculus is rather like "doing nothing." I would make such a suggestion only in the sense that there is little about calculus to get in the way, or interfere, with the psychology lesson.

Before You Go On

Briefly describe retroactive interference and proactive interference.

TOPIC 6B SUMMARY

The most practical aspect of human memory is our ability to retrieve information stored there. Retrieval depends on how it is measured, as well as the number and quality of the retrieval cues available to us. The quality of learning (how well we have elaborated new information by making it meaningful and organizing it, aided by mnemonic devices or existing schema) and the quantity of learning (the extent to which we have overlearned and distributed practice) influence memory retrieval. To improve our chance of retrieving information from memory, we need to spend time with the material we are learning, encoding that information in a meaningful and well-organized way. Whenever possible, we should match cues available at retrieval with those present at encoding. We also need to do what we can to avoid the effects of interference.

CHAPTER SUMMARY

Topic 6A

How shall we characterize human memory?

Memory refers to the interrelated cognitive processes of actively representing information in memory (encoding), keeping it there (storage), and bringing it out again at some later time (retrieval). There are many theories about the nature of human memory. One, the multistore model, claims that there are a number (usually three) of distinct memories, or storehouses of information, each with its own mechanisms for processing information. A levels-of-processing model contends that there is but one memory store, but various depths, levels, or degrees to which new information is processed into that memory store. */pp. 188–189*

What are the characteristics of sensory memory?

Sensory memory provides storage for large amounts of information for very brief periods. We cannot manipulate or encode information in sensory memory, but have to deal with it as it is presented to us by our senses. The length of storage in this memory store, or level of memory, is measured in fractions of a second to a maximum of just a few seconds. */pp. 189–190*

How long is information stored in STM, and how does it get there?

Information will be held in short-term memory for several seconds (occasionally up to 1 minute) before it fades or is replaced. Encoding information into this memory requires that we attend to it. Information may enter short-term storage from sensory memory or be retrieved from long-term memory. We keep material in STM by reattending to it, a process called maintenance rehearsal. */pp. 190–194*

How much information can be stored in short-term memory?

The capacity of short-term memory is approximately 7 ± 2 "chunks of information," where a chunk is an imprecise

measure of a unit of meaningful material. Organizing information into meaningful clusters or units can expand the apparent capacity of STM. */pp. 194–195*

How is information represented in STM?

Information in our short-term memories may be encoded in several forms, but acoustic coding seems to be the most common. */p. 195*

What are repressed memories, and what do they tell us about LTM?

Repressed memories are events presumed to be in one's long-term memory, but that cannot be retrieved because to do so would be anxiety-producing. Some psychologists have challenged the reality of some repressed memories, as when people remember only as adults incidents of abuse when they were children. It may be that our recall of events long past has been influenced by events that have occurred since. */pp. 197–198*

What does eyewitness testimony tell us about LTM?

Eyewitness testimony is another example of how one's recollection of events can be influenced or distorted by factors other than the events themselves. Steps can be taken to improve the validity of eyewitness testimony. See Figure 6.3. */pp. 198–199*

Contrast elaborative rehearsal with maintenance rehearsal.

Although maintenance rehearsal (rote repetition) may sometimes be sufficient to move information from STM to LTM, the best way is elaborative rehearsal; that is, to think about the material, organize the material, and form associations with or images of the material to relate it to something already stored in LTM. The more one elaborates, or the "deeper" the elaboration, the better retrieval will be. */pp. 199–200*

Describe three possible subsystems of LTM.

Information can be stored in any one of three subtypes of LTM. One of the most basic is procedural memory, where we retain connections between stimuli and responses—how we perform simple, well-learned behaviors. Semantic long-term memory holds concepts and knowledge—the facts, vocabulary, and rules one has accumulated. One's episodic memories record life events and experiences. They are tied to a specific time and place. */pp. 200–202*

What parts of the brain are most involved in memory formation? At the level of the neuron, what changes take place when memories are formed?

In ways yet unknown, human memories are probably stored throughout the cerebral cortex. The hippocampus is surely involved in the consolidation of long-term memories, as studies of patients with amnesia have shown. At the neural level, synaptic pathways that are used repeatedly become more and more efficient in their ability to transmit neural impulses. */pp. 202–205*

Topic 6B

What is the difference between recall and recognition? What do implicit measures tell us about long-term memory?

Retrieving information from LTM is a function of how we ask for that retrieval. When we ask for retrieval by recall, we provide the fewest possible retrieval cues, only identifying which information is to be retrieved. With recognition, we actually provide the information to be retrieved and ask that it be identified as familiar. Retrieval measured by recognition is generally superior to retrieval measured by recall. Implicit tests of memory assess the extent to which previously experienced material is helpful in subsequent tasks. For example, relearning shows us that even when information can be neither recalled nor recognized, it will be easier to relearn than it was to learn in the first place. Even though people do not recall being shown a word, it will be easier to identify when subsequently mutilated or masked. These tests show us that even material that appears inaccessible through conscious effort may be available and useful in LTM. */pp. 206–209*

How does the context in which one encodes information affect the retrieval of that information?

The greater the extent to which the cues or context available at retrieval match the cues or context available at encoding, the better retrieval will be. Even matching a person's state of mind at encoding and retrieval may improve retrieval. Heightened emotionality at encoding may also produce memories that seem more vivid than others, even if they are not more accurate. */pp. 209–211*

How is "meaningfulness" related to retrieval?

Meaningfulness reflects the extent to which material is associated with, or related to, information already stored in memory. In general, the more meaningful the material, the easier it will be to retrieve. Meaningfulness resides in the individual and not in the material to be learned. */pp. 211–212*

Describe narrative chaining, mental imagery, and the method of loci as mnemonic devices.

In general, mnemonic devices are strategies used at encoding to organize and increase the meaningfulness of material to be retrieved. Narrative chaining involves making up a story that meaningfully weaves together otherwise unorganized words or information. Forming mental images, or "pictures in one's mind," of to-be-remembered information is also helpful. Sensible, interactive images seem to work best. The method of loci is an imagery method in which one "places" pieces of information at various locations (loci) in a familiar setting and then retrieves those pieces of information while mentally traveling through the setting. */pp. 212–214*

What are schemas, and how do they affect retrieval?

Schemas are organized, general knowledge systems stored in LTM. Based on past experiences, schemas summarize the essential features of common events or situations. They are used to guide the organization of and give meaning to new information. The more relevant one's available schemas for to-be-remembered information, the better will be encoding and retrieval. */pp. 214–216*

How does overlearning affect retrieval? How does distributing one's practice affect retrieval?

Overlearning is the rehearsal or practice of material above and beyond that necessary for immediate recall. Within limits, the more one overlearns, the greater the likelihood of accurate retrieval. In massed practice, study or rehearsal continues without intervening rest intervals. Distributed practice uses shorter segments of rehearsal interspersed with rest intervals. In almost all cases, distributed practice is superior to massed practice. */pp. 216–218*

Briefly describe retroactive interference and proactive interference.

Retroactive interference occurs when material or information cannot be retrieved because it is inhibited or blocked by material or information learned later. Proactive interference occurs when information cannot be retrieved because it is inhibited or blocked by material or information learned earlier. Retroactive interference is typically more detrimental to retrieval than is proactive interference. */pp. 219–221*

A Memory Experiment You Can Do

You'll need a volunteer for this project, one who will take a few minutes to try to memorize a short list of words. Not only will you act as "experimenter" and present the words, but you can also predict which words your "subject" is likely to remember. (Suggested answers can be found on p. 573.)

Read the following list of words slowly:

1. Bed
2. Silence
3. Snoring
4. Tired
5. Turn
6. Quilt
7. Fatigue
8. Night
9. Night
10. Night
11. Dark
12. Clock
13. Toss
14. Artichoke
15. Rest
16. Dream

On a list of 16 unrelated words, the usual recall rate is about 7 words, but on a list of related words like this one, recall should be close to 10 words, even with just one presentation. Can you predict which words form this list are most likely to be recalled correctly?

OUTLINE

He was the most intelligent person I have ever known. His colleagues in the psychology department called him "Ted," but because his initials were E. E., we also called him "E². " We meant no disrespect; it somehow seemed fitting. His teaching specialty was "multivariate statistical analysis," an advanced course in correlational methods. There was no text for this class. Every day, E² wrote out the text in class on the blackboards he had installed to encircle the room. In truth, few of us followed all of his reasoning as he derived formulas from one blackboard to another. From time to time his eyes would sparkle, and he seemed to no longer notice where he was. We would hear him mutter something to himself: "No, that shouldn't be *r*, it should be capital *R*. No, no. It should be *R'*! Yes, that's it, *R'*!" And off he'd go writing on the board faster than we could copy—much less comprehend—his equations.

Over his 60-year career, he authored scores of scientific articles and wrote several books. None of us who were his students will ever forget his brilliance. Nor will we tire of telling "E² stories." Such as the time he and his wife (also a well-respected psychologist) traveled to a psychology convention two states away. When the meetings were over, E² got in their car and drove home, apparently forgetting that his wife had accompanied him. Or the times when he would

Intelligence, Language, and Problem Solving

"get lost" in his equations, toss a lighted cigarette into the trash, start a fire in the wastebasket, and continue without pause, as one of us carried the flaming receptacle out of the room. I spent an academic year as E^2's graduate student assistant. One dreary, misty morning I arrived on campus to find that he had left his car lights on, and had locked the car doors. When I told him what I'd discovered, he thanked me, put on his topcoat, and left the office. Forty-five minutes later, his phone rang and I answered it. It was E^2, telling me that he was at home, but that he could not remember why. Did I have any clue? You see, when E^2 put on his coat, left his office, and got in his car, he went home. Now he was confused because it was only 9:00 in the morning.

I cannot think of a better example from my own experiences of an "absentminded professor." My memories of E^2, and the stories about him, also reinforce the point that intelligence is a multifaceted concept.

As a species, we humans are not particularly fast, nor are we very strong. We cannot swim far or deep. Unaided, we cannot fly at all. Still, we survive and thrive, largely because of the use of our intelligence, our languages, and our skills or problem solving, the cognitive abilities that are covered in this chapter.

TOPIC 7A Intelligence

For the last few chapters we have been discussing cognitive processes: perception, consciousness, learning, and memory. In Topic 7A we focus on the most complex of all cognitive processes: intelligence. We will find that defining the concept of intelligence is difficult. We'll look at how intelligence is measured, and we'll end the Topic by examining group and individual differences in measured intelligence.

Just What *Is* Intelligence?

Intelligence is a troublesome concept in psychology. We all know what we mean when we use the word, but we have a terrible time trying to define intelligence concisely. We wonder if John's failure in school is due to his lack of intelligence or to some other factor. You may argue that locking my keys in my car was not very intelligent. I may argue that a student with any intelligence can see the difference between positive and negative reinforcement. In this section, we'll develop a working definition of intelligence, and then we'll review some of the ways in which psychologists have described the concept.

To guide our study through this Topic, I propose that we accept two definitions of *intelligence,* one academic and theoretical, the other operational and practical. For our theoretical definition of intelligence, we will use the one offered by David Wechsler: "The capacity of an individual to understand the world about him [or her] and his [or her] resourcefulness to cope with its challenges" (1975, p. 139). This definition, and others like it, sounds sensible at first, but it does present some ambiguities. What does "capacity" mean in this context? What is meant by "understand the world"? What if the world never really challenges one's "resourcefulness"? Would such people be considered less intelligent?

In Chapter 1, I suggested that defining concepts operationally helps us deal with conceptually abstract concepts. We have to be careful here, but, as E. G. Boring put it in 1923, "Intelligence is what the intelligence tests measure" (Hunt, 1995, p. 356). Before we get to a discussion of intelligence tests, it will be helpful to spend a bit of time reviewing some of the ways in which psychologists have described intelligence.

Classic Models of Intelligence

Theoretical models of intelligence are attempts to categorize and organize cognitive or intellectual abilities into sensible groupings. In a way, they are sophisticated attempts to provide a definition for "intelligence."

British psychologist *Charles Spearman* was one of the pioneers of mental testing and the inventor of many statistical procedures that could be used to analyze test scores. Spearman's image of intelligence came from his inspection of scores earned by people on a wide range of psychological tests designed to measure cognitive skills. What impressed Spearman was that no matter what cognitive ability a specific test was designed to measure, some people always seemed to do better than others. People who scored high on some tests tended to score high on all the tests. It seemed as if there was an intellectual power that facilitated performance in general, whereas variations in performance reflected strengths and weaknesses for specific tasks.

Spearman (1904) concluded that intelligence consists of two things: a general intelligence, called a **g-factor**, and a collection of specific cognitive skills, or **s-factors**. Spearman believed that "g" was independent of knowledge, of content—it went beyond knowing facts. It involved the ability to understand and apply relationships in all content areas. In this view, everyone has some degree of general in-

g-factor (g) *general intelligence; a global measure of intellectual abilities*

s-factors *specific cognitive, or intellectual skills; in Spearman's theory, part of intelligence in addition to g* telligence (which Spearman thought was inherited), and everyone has specific skills that are useful in some tasks but not in others. A controversy remains over the extent to which "g" is an all-important, sometimes-important, or never-important factor in intelligence (Barrett & Depinet, 1991; Helms, 1992; Hunt, 1995; Ree & Earles, 1992; Sternberg & Wagner, 1993; McClelland, 1973, 1993). Still, looking at intelligence in terms of what a variety of tests measure, and how such measures are interrelated, became a popular way to think about intelligence.

When *L. L. Thurstone* examined correlations among various tests of cognitive abilities he administered, he found something different from what Spearman had found. Thurstone (1938) saw little or no evidence to support the notion of a general g-factor of intellectual ability. Instead, he claimed that abilities fall into seven categories, which he called the seven **primary mental abilities** (Figure 7.1). Thurstone argued that each factor in his model is independent, and to know one's intelligence requires that you know how one fares on all seven factors.

With the model of *J. P. Guilford* (1967), matters get more complicated than with either Spearman's or Thurstone's theory. Guilford claimed that intelligence can be analyzed as three intersecting dimensions. Guilford said that any intellectual task can be described in terms of the mental *operations* used in the task, the *content* of the material involved, and the *product* or outcome of the task. Each of these three dimensions has a number of possible values. There are five operations, four contents, and six possible products. The three dimensions of this model, and their values, are found in Figure 7.2.

If you study Figure 7.2, you will see that there are 120 possible combinations of content, operations, and products in Guilford's model. (In 1988, Guilford increased the possible number of combinations to 150 by coming up with two memory operations. His basic logic remained the same.) Just to give you an idea of how

primary mental abilities *in Thurstone's model, the seven distinct abilities that constitute intelligence*

Figure 7.1
Thurstone's Seven Primary Mental Abilities

Verbal comprehension (V)	The ability to understand ideas, concepts, and words, as in a vocabulary test.
Number (N)	The ability to use numbers to solve problems quickly and accurately.
Spatial relations (S)	The ability to visualize and manipulate patterns and forms in space, as in the ability to recognize an object viewed from a different perspective.
Perceptual speed (P)	The ability to determine quickly and accurately whether or not two complex stimuli are identical or in some way different.
Word fluency (W)	The ability to use words quickly and fluently, as in the ability to solve anagrams and produce rhymes.
Memory (M)	The ability to remember lists of materials, such as digits, letters, or words presented previously.
Inductive reasoning	The ability to discover a general rule from presented information, to discover relationships, as in, "what number comes next? 2, 4, 6, 8, –."

After Thurstone, 1938.

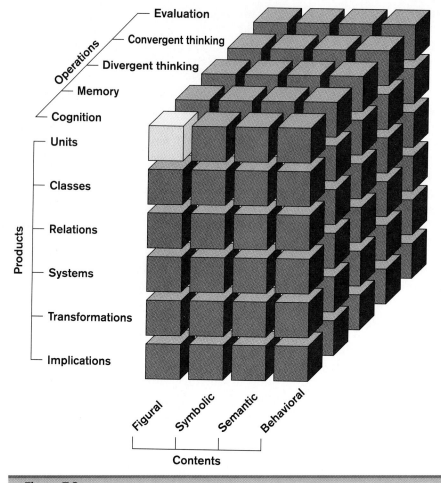

Figure 7.2

Guilford's model of intelligence. In this model there are three major divisions (contents, products, and operations), each with its own subdivisions. Each subdivision may interact with all others, yielding 120 specific intellectual skills or abilities. (After Guilford, 1967.)

this system works, let's choose one of the "cells" depicted in Figure 7.2—where cognition, figural, and units intersect (the little "block" in the uppermost left corner). What would this intellectual skill be like? Guilford says it's a matter of recognizing (cognitive) diagrams or pictures (figural) of simple, well-defined elements (units). To test this ability, one might be shown an incomplete drawing of a simple object and asked to identify it as quickly as possible.

Philip Vernon (1960, 1979) suggests we think of intelligence as a collection of skills and abilities arranged in a hierarchy (Figure 7.3). At the top is a general cognitive ability similar to Spearman's "g." Under it are two factors; one is a verbal, academic sort of intelligence, whereas the other is a mechanical, practical sort. Either of these in turn is thought of as consisting of yet more specific intellectual skills. The verbal-academic skill, for example, consists of numerical and verbal abilities, among others. Each of these can be broken down further (verbal skills include word usage and vocabulary, for instance); and then further still because vocabulary includes knowing synonyms and antonyms. Seeing intelligence as including a general factor and a structured set of specific factors gives us a model that combines some of the thinking of Spearman, Thurstone, and Guilford.

Before You Go On

Briefly describe Spearman's, Thurstone's, Guilford's, and Vernon's models of intelligence.

Contemporary Models of Intelligence

Over the last decade, theories about intelligence have taken a different approach than those we've reviewed so far. First, they assume that intelligence is a multidimensional concept (remember E^2?). Second, they view intelligence as an active processing of information rather than a "thing" that one either has or doesn't have to some degree.

Robert Sternberg, a cognitive psychologist, sees intelligence as multifaceted, and focuses on how one uses intellectual abilities rather than on trying to describe those abilities. Sternberg sees one sort of intelligent behavior as a reflection of three different processes, or components (1979, 1981, 1985, 1988, 1990). He calls this *componential intelligence,* which includes: (1) skills we bring to bear when we set about to solve a problem. "Just what is the problem here?" "How shall I get started?" "What will I need to see this through?" "How will I know when I've succeeded?"; (2) the skills we actually use in our attempt to solve problems—for example, when we work on a math problem and realize that two numbers must be multiplied, this component of our cognitive abilities gets the job done; and (3) the techniques or strategies for collecting and assimilating new information. Being intelligent is demonstrating that one can profit from experience.

In addition to this view of intelligence, Sternberg adds two others. *Experiential intelligence* is related to behaviors that reflect creative thinking. It is a measure of the extent that one can combine elements in new, unusual, and useful ways and is reflected in how well one reacts to new situations. Successful artists, writers, actors, and scientists display experiential intelligence. *Contextual intelligence* is commonly referred to as "street smarts" in today's slang. People with this sort intelligence are very good at getting along with others, figuring out how to "get by" in difficult situations. It is a practical, nitty-gritty set of cognitive skills. This intelligence is a measure of the extent to which one can manage to adapt and make the most of a situation. Quite clearly, how one demonstrates contextual intelligence varies widely from culture to culture—and from one situation to the next. Experiential and contextual varieties of intelligence are not the sorts of things that are measured on most intelligence tests.

Another model that refers to multiple types of intelligence has been proposed by *Howard Gardner* (1983, 1993a, 1993b; Gardner & Hatch, 1989). Gardner suggests that people can display intelligence in any one of seven different ways (or in a combination of these seven). First, he acknowledges that there is a scholastic, academic intelligence, made up of both (1) *mathematical/logical* and (2) *verbal/linguistic abilities.* To these he adds (3) *spatial* intelligence—needed to be a successful architect or designer; (4) *musical* intelligence—needed not only to produce, but also to appreciate pitch, rhythm, tone, and the subtleties of music; (5) *body/kinesthetic* in-

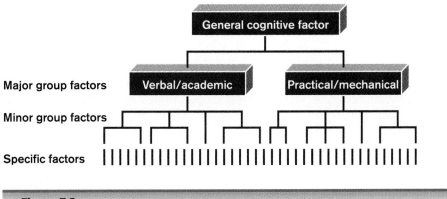

Figure 7.3

According to Philip Vernon, intellectual abilities may be represented in a hierarchy from very general intellectual skills at the top to very specific abilities at the bottom. (After Vernon, 1960.)

Contemporary theories of intelligence (such as that proposed by Gardner) suggest that there are several ways in which intelligence can be manifested, including interpersonal intelligence (the ability to get along with others), intrapersonal intelligence (the ability to introspect and understand one's self), and kinesthetic intelligence (the ability to control one's body).

telligence—reflected in the ability to control one's body and to handle objects, as one finds in skilled athletes and dancers; (6) *interpersonal* intelligence—the ability to get along with others, and to "read other people" (Rosnow et al., 1995), and (7) *intrapersonal* intelligence—required to understand one's own self, to realize one's strengths and weaknesses. Obviously, a person can find success in life with any one (or more) of these multiple intelligences, but which are valued the most depends on the demands of one's culture. Highly technological societies, such as ours, value the first two types of intelligence. In cultures where one must climb tall trees or hunt wild game for food, body/kinesthetic skills are valued. Interpersonal skills are valuable in cultures that emphasize family and group activities.

What we have reviewed here is only a sampling of the theoretical approaches to intelligence that have been proposed over the years. None of these models has been tested fully enough to evaluate the extent to which it characterizes human intelligence. As is often the case when we are faced with multiple descriptions or explanations (as we will be again when we look at theories of personality [pp. 324–340] and of motivation [pp. 358–365]), it is important to keep an open mind and to select from each approach aspects that are best supported by the evidence and that make the most sense.

Now that we have an idea of the sorts of theoretical issues psychologists have struggled with, we can turn our attention to tests of intelligence.

Before You Go On

Briefly describe Sternberg's and Gardner's models of intelligence.

Psychological Tests of Intelligence

Just as there are several ways to define intelligence, so are there several ways to measure it. Most involve psychological tests. Although the focus of our discussion here is intelligence, we must recognize that psychological tests have been devised to measure the full range of human traits and abilities. For that reason, we start with a few words about tests in general.

Testing the Tests

A **psychological test** is an objective, standardized measure of a sample of behavior (Anastasi, 1988; Dahlstrom, 1993). A psychological test measures *behavior* because that is all we can measure. We cannot directly measure feelings, aptitudes, or abilities. We can and do make inferences about such things on the basis of our measure of behavior, but we cannot measure them directly. Psychological tests can only measure a *sample* of one's behaviors. If I want to know about your tendency to be aggressive, I cannot very well ask you everything that relates to aggression in your life. What I can do is to sample (identify a portion of) the behaviors in which I am interested. Then I assume that your responses to my sample of items predict, or are similar to, responses to questions I have not asked. Even a classroom final exam only asks you about a sample of the material you have learned.

A psychological test should also be *objective*. The objectivity of tests refers to the evaluation of the behaviors being measured. Several examiners (at least those with the same level of expertise) should give the same interpretation and evaluation to a test response. If the same responses to a psychological test lead one psychologist to say that a person is perfectly normal, a second to consider the person a mass of inner conflict, and a third to wonder why this person is not now in a psychiatric institution, we have a problem, and it is probably with the objectivity of our test.

As a consumer, and as a student of psychology, you should be able to assess the value or quality of a psychological test. The quality of a psychological test depends on the extent to which it has three characteristics: reliability, validity, and adequate norms.

In the context of psychological testing, **reliability** means the same thing it means in other contexts: consistency or dependability. Suppose someone gives you a test, and on the basis of your responses claims that you have an IQ slightly below average—94, let's say. Three weeks later, you retake the same test and are told that your IQ is now 127—nearly in the top 3 percent of the population. We haven't yet discussed IQ scores, but we recognize that one's IQ—as a measure of intelligence—does not change by 33 points in a matter of three weeks.

When people worry about the usefulness of a test, their concern is usually with **validity**. Measures of validity tell us the extent to which a test actually measures what it claims to be measuring. It is the extent to which there is agreement be-

psychological test *an objective, standardized measure of a sample of behavior*

reliability *in psychological testing, the extent to which a test measures whatever it measures consistently*

validity *in psychological testing, the extent to which a test measures what it claims to be measuring* tween a test score and the quality or trait that the test is believed to measure (Kaplan & Saccuzzo, 1989).

There is one more issue that we need to address: the adequacy of test norms. Suppose you have filled out a long paper-and-pencil questionnaire designed to measure the extent to which you are outgoing. You know that the test is a reliable and valid instrument. You are told that you scored a 50 on the test. So what? What does *that* mean? It does not mean that you answered 50 percent of the items correctly—on this test there are no correct or incorrect answers. The point is that if you don't have a basis of comparison, one test score by itself is meaningless. You need to compare your score with the scores of other people like yourself who have also taken the test. Results of a test taken by a large group of people whose scores are used to make comparisons are called **norms**. You may discover by checking the norms that a score of 50 is average, or it might indicate a very high or a very low level of extroversion.

As we review some of the psychological tests used to measure intelligence, keep in mind the many ways in which psychologists have described intelligence. Given the difficulty that psychologists have coming to any agreement on the nature of intelligence, you won't be surprised to learn that not all psychologists are pleased with the currently available intelligence tests.

norms *in psychological testing, scores on a test taken by a large number of persons that can be used for making comparisons*

Before You Go On

What determines the quality of psychological tests?

The Stanford-Binet Intelligence Scale

Alfred Binet (1857–1911) was the leading psychologist in France early in the twentieth century. Of great concern in those days were children in the Paris school system who seemed unable to profit from the educational experiences they were being given. Binet and his collaborator, Théodore Simon, wanted to identify students who should be placed in special (remedial) classes, where their education could proceed more efficiently than it had in the standard classroom.

Binet's first test appeared in 1905 and was an immediate success. It caught the attention of Lewis M. Terman at Stanford University, who supervised a translation and revision of the test in 1916. Since then, the test has been called the *Stanford-Binet* and has undergone subsequent revisions, the most recent of which was published in 1986. This edition, the fourth, made several significant changes in the test and in its scoring. So, what is this test like?

The test follows what its authors call a three-level, hierarchical model of cognitive ability (Thorndike et al., 1986). As did Binet's original test, the current edition yields an overall test score that reflects *g,* or general intellectual ability, which the authors describe as "what an individual uses when faced with a problem that he or she has not been taught to solve" (Thorndike et al., 1986, p. 3). Underlying g are three second-level factors (Figure 7.4). *Crystallized abilities* represent those skills needed for acquiring and using information about verbal and quantitative concepts. These abilities are influenced by schooling and can be called an academic ability factor. *Fluid-analytic abilities* are those needed to solve problems that involve figural or nonverbal types of information. They involve the ability to see things in new and different ways, and are less tied to formal schooling. The third factor at this level of the model is *short-term memory.* Items that test one's ability to hold information in memory for short periods can be found on Binet's original test.

The next level of abilities tested by the new Stanford-Binet provides more specific, content-oriented definitions of the factors from level two. As you can see from Figure 7.4, at this level, crystallized abilities are divided into verbal and quantitative reasoning, fluid-analytic abilities are seen as abstract/visual reasoning, and

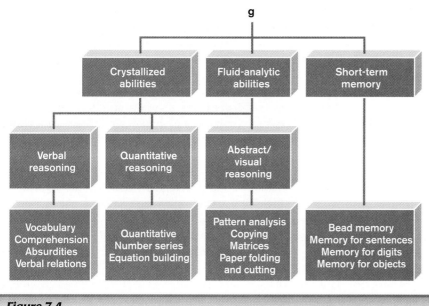

Figure 7.4

The factors tested by the Stanford-Binet Intelligence Scale, Fourth Edition, arranged in three levels below "g," or general intellectual ability. Each subtest is noted at the lowest level. (After Thorndike et al., 1986.)

there is no ability at this level that corresponds to short-term memory. At the base of the hierarchy are the 15 subtests that constitute the actual Stanford-Binet test.

What all of this means is that the authors of the 1986 revision of the Stanford-Binet acknowledge that a person's measured intelligence should be reflected in more than just one test score. Not only can we determine an overall g score (the only score available from earlier editions) but we can calculate scores for each factor at each level. There are also scores for the 15 subtests by themselves. Figure 7.5 shows the way g scores on the Stanford-Binet are distributed for the general population.

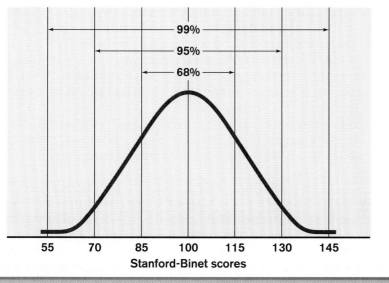

Figure 7.5

An idealized curve that shows the distribution of scores on the Stanford-Binet Intelligence Scale taken by a very large sample of the general population. The numbers at the top of the curve indicate the percentages of the population expected to score within the range of scores indicated; that is, 68 percent earn scores between 85 and 115, 95 percent score between 70 and 130, and 99 percent earn scores between 55 and 145.

IQ *intelligence quotient; a measure of general intelligence that results from dividing one's mental age by one's chronological age and multipying the result by 100*

Before we go on, let's take a minute to discuss what has happened to the concept of IQ. **IQ** is an abbreviation for the term *intelligence quotient.* As you know, a quotient is the result you get when you divide one number by another. In dividing 8 by 6, the quotient is 1.33. For the early versions of the Stanford-Binet, the examiner's job was to determine a person's mental age (or *MA*), the age level at which the person functioned in terms of intellectual abilities. A person with the intellectual abilities of an average 8-year-old would have an MA of 8. IQ was determined by dividing the person's mental age by his or her actual age (called chronological age, or *CA*). This quotient was then multiplied by 100 to determine IQ, or IQ = (MA/CA) × 100. If an 8-year-old girl had a mental age of 8, she would be average, and her IQ would equal 100 (or (8/8) × 100 = 1 × 100). If the 8-year-old were above average, with the intellectual abilities of an average 10-year-old, her IQ would be 125 (10/8 × 100, or 1.25 × 100). If she were below average, say with the mental abilities of an average 6-year-old, her computed IQ would be 75. Because it is a term ingrained in our vocabulary, we will continue to use "IQ" as a measure of general intelligence, even though we now use established norm groups, and no longer calculate MAs or compute quotients.

Before You Go On

Briefly describe the Stanford-Binet Intelligence Scale.

The Wechsler Tests of Intelligence

David Wechsler published his first intelligence test in 1939. Unlike the Stanford-Binet that existed at the time, it was designed for use with adult populations and to reduce the heavy reliance on verbal skills that characterized Binet's tests. With a major revision in 1955, the test became known as the *Wechsler Adult Intelligence Scale (WAIS),* and a revision, the *WAIS-R,* was published in 1981. The WAIS-R is appropriate for persons between 16 and 74 years of age and is reported to be the most commonly used of all psychological tests (Lubin et al., 1984).

A natural extension was the *Wechsler Intelligence Scale for Children (WISC),* originally published 11 years after the WAIS. With updated norms and several new items (among other things, designed to minimize bias against any ethnic group or gender), the *WISC-III* appeared in 1991. It is appropriate for children ages 6 to 16 (there is some overlap with the WAIS-R). A third test in the series is for younger children, between the ages of 4 and 6. It is called the *Wechsler Preschool and Primary Scale of Intelligence, or WPPSI.* It was published in 1967, was revised in 1989, and is now the *WPPSI-R.* There are some subtle differences among the three Wechsler tests, but each is based on the same logic. Therefore, we will consider only one, the WAIS-R, in detail.

The WAIS-R consists of 11 subtests organized in two categories. Six subtests define the *verbal scale,* and five subtests constitute a *performance scale.* Figure 7.6 lists the subtests of the WAIS-R and describes some of the types of items found on each.

Each item on each subtest is scored. (Some of the performance items have time limits that affect scoring.) You now have 11 scores earned by your subject. As is now the case with the Stanford-Binet, each subtest score is compared to a score provided by the test's norms. How your subject's earned score compares to the score earned by subjects in the norm group determines the subject's standard score for each Wechsler subtest. In addition to one overall score, the Wechsler tests provide verbal and performance scores, which can tell us something about a person's particular strengths and weaknesses.

There has been controversy for many years, about individually administered intelligence tests such as the Wechsler and the Stanford-Binet. The extent to which the tests are culturally biased, thus favoring one group of subjects over an-

Figure 7.6
The Subtests of the Wechsler Adult Intelligence Scale, Revised (WAIS-R)

Verbal scales

Information	(29 items) Questions designed to tap one's general knowledge about a variety of topics dealing with one's culture; for example, "Who wrote *Huckleberry Finn?*" or "How many nickels in a quarter?"
Digit span	(7 series) Subject is read a series of three to nine digits and is asked to repeat them; then a different series is to be repeated in reverse order.
Comprehension	(16 items) A test of judgment, common sense, and practical knowledge; for example, "Why is it good to have prisons?"
Similarities	(14 pairs) Subject must indicate the way(s) in which two things are alike; for example, "In what way are an apple and a potato alike?"
Vocabulary	(35 words) Subject must provide an acceptable definition for a series of words.
Arithmetic	(14 problems) Math problems must be solved without the use of paper and pencil; for example, "How far will a bird travel in 90 minutes if it flies at the rate of 10 miles per hour?"

Performance scales

Picture completion	(20 pictures) Subject must identify or name the missing part or object in a drawing; for example, a truck with only three wheels.
Picture arrangement	(10 series) A series of cartoonlike pictures must be arranged in an order that tells a story.
Block design	(9 items) Using blocks whose sides are either all red, all white, or diagonally red and white, subject must copy a designed picture or pattern shown on a card.
Object assembly	(4 objects) Free-form jigsaw puzzles must be put together to form familiar objects.
Digit symbol	In a key, each of nine digits is paired with a simple symbol. Given a random series of digits, the subject must provide the paired symbol within a time limit.

other, whether they truly measure intelligence and not just academic success, and whether test results can be used for political purposes, perhaps as a basis for racial discrimination, are just some of the concerns that keep surfacing. Although experts allow that the tests may be somewhat biased on racial and socioeconomic grounds, they "believe that such tests adequately measure more important elements of intelligence" (Snyderman & Rothman, 1987, p.143).

Before You Go On

What are the major features of the Wechler intelligence scales?

Group Tests of Intelligence

There are advantages of individually administered tests such as the Wechsler tests and the Stanford-Binet. Both have demonstrated considerable reliability and validity at least with respect to predicting academic or scholastic achievement. One of the most important advantages is that the examiner has the opportunity to interact with the person taking the test. The examiner can develop opinions about the examinee and observe how he or she goes about responding to test items. A disadvantage of the individually administered tests is that they are time consuming and expensive. There are alternatives. Group IQ tests are generally paper-and-pencil tests that can be administered to many individuals at one time.

By the beginning of World War I, Binet's test had gained wide approval, and the basic notion of using psychological methods to measure intellectual abilities had been generally accepted. There was good reason to know the intellectual capabilities of the recruits who were entering the armed services, but obviously not all could be individually tested. A committee of psychologists was charged with the task of creating a group test of intelligence. The result, published in 1917, was the *Army Alpha Test,* a paper-and-pencil test that made rough discriminations among examinees on the basis of intelligence. In the same year, the committee published the *Army Beta Test,* designed for illiterates who could not read the Army Alpha. It was a performance test, the instructions of which were given orally or acted out.

The military continues to be a major publisher and consumer of group intelligence tests. The U.S. Army now uses the *Armed Forces Qualification Test (AFQT),* and anyone who goes through military induction will have firsthand experience with this test.

When psychological tests of cognitive ability are used to predict future behaviors, we call them **aptitude tests**. Many of the aptitude tests used in the context of education are tests of general intellectual ability. The difference is in the use to which the score is put: predicting future academic success. The two most com-

aptitude tests *psychological tests of cognitive abilities used to predict future behaviors*

An advantage of group testing is that many people can be tested in a given period of time. Group tests of intelligence, however, are not as reliable or as valid as individually administered tests.

monly used college entrance tests are the *ACT (American College Testing Program)* and the *SAT (Scholastic Aptitude Test),* which yields verbal and mathematics scores as well as an overall score. In 1994, a major revision of the test, the SAT-I was published. The SAT-I includes math items that are not in the usual multiple-choice format, and the verbal section places more emphasis on reading comprehension. A new, optional SAT-II is also available. The SAT-II includes a written essay section, language proficiency tests for native speakers of Japanese and Chinese, and tests for nonnative English speakers.

Before You Go On

What is the difference between a paper-and-pencil intelligence test and an aptitude test?

Group Differences in Measured Intelligence

For the remainder of this Topic, we'll be focusing on IQ scores. Please keep in mind that IQ is simply a convenient abbreviation for intelligence as it is measured by psychological tests. *We should not take IQ to equal one's intelligence.* IQ scores reflect only a particular measure of intelligence.

Recognizing that there are individual differences in intelligence, can we make any statements about differences in IQ in general? Who are smarter, women or men? Do we become less intelligent with age? Are there differences in intelligence among ethnic groups? As you are aware, simple answers to such questions are often misleading and, if interpreted incorrectly, can be harmful to some groups of people.

Reported average differences in IQ test scores are often misleading. Let's imagine that I have tested two large groups of people: 1,000 Alphas and 1,000 Thetas. On the average, the IQ score for Alphas is 95, and for Thetas, it is 110. An appropriate statistical analysis tells me that this difference of 15 points is too large to have been expected by chance. Are Thetas smarter than Alphas? Yes, on the average they are—that's exactly what I just discovered.

Now look at Figure 7.7. Here are two curves that represent the IQ scores from my study. We can see the difference in the averages (means) of the two groups.

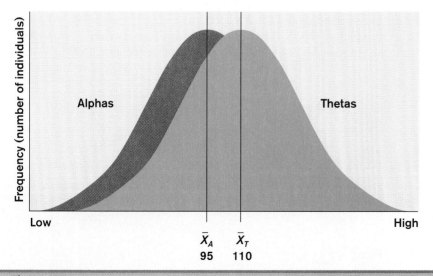

Figure 7.7

Hypothetical distributions of IQ scores for two groups (ALPHAs and THETAs). The average IQ for THETAs is higher than that for ALPHAs, but there is considerable overlap between the two distributions. That is, some ALPHAs have IQs higher than the average for THETAs (110), and some THETAs have IQs lower than the average for ALPHAs (95).

However, there *are* Thetas whose IQs are below the average IQ of Alphas. And there *are* Alphas with IQs above that of the average Thetas. We may draw conclusions about average IQs, but making definitive statements about individual Thetas and Alphas is not possible.

Being able to demonstrate a significant difference between the average IQs of two groups in itself tells us nothing about *why* those differences exist. Are Thetas genetically superior to Alphas? Maybe, maybe not. Have Alphas had equal access to the sorts of experiences that IQ tests ask about? Maybe, maybe not. Are the tests biased to provide Thetas with an advantage? Maybe, maybe not. And so on. Learning that two groups of persons have different average IQ scores usually raises more questions than it answers.

Gender Differences in IQ

Here's a question to which we have a reasonably definitive answer: Is there a difference between the IQs of males and females? Answer: no. At least there are very few studies that report any differences between men and women on any test of general intelligence of the sort represented by an IQ score; and, what small differences have been found seem to be getting smaller over the past two decades (Aiken, 1984; Halpern, 1986; Hyde et al., 1990; Maccoby & Jacklin, 1974). Note that there may be no measured differences between the IQs of men and women because IQ tests are constructed to minimize or eliminate any such differences. Usually, if an item on an intelligence test discriminates between women and men, it is dropped from consideration.

When we look beyond global measures of IQ, however, there are signs of gender differences on specific intellectual skills (which offset each other on general IQ tests). For example, males score significantly higher than do females on tests of spatial relations—particularly on tests that require one to visualize what a three-dimensional object would look like when rotated in space (Eagly, 1995; Masters & Sanders, 1993). What is curious about this rather specialized ability is that males perform better than females on such tasks from an early age, widening the gap through the school years, even though this particular ability is only marginally related to academic course work (Linn & Peterson, 1985; McGee, 1979). This suggests that these sex differences cannot be easily attributed to differences in educational opportunity.

On the other hand, educational experiences may be related to some differences in mathematical ability. Scores on tests of mathematics skills are well correlated with the number and type of math classes taken while a student is in high

Some psychologists argue that males generally outperform females on tests of mathematics and spatial relations because of the courses they are encouraged to take in school. As more females are drawn to classes in math and science, differences in test scores most likely will continue to decline.

school (Kimball, 1989; Welch et al., 1982). For many reasons, males enroll in more advanced math courses than do females. It is not surprising, then, that by the time they leave high school, there are differences between men and women on tests of mathematical ability (particularly for those that assess mathematical reasoning and problem solving). There is evidence that average differences between males and females on tests of mathematical abilities have been declining steadily over the past 25 years (Hyde, 1994; Hyde et al., 1990; Jacklin, 1989). Other researchers argue that although average differences may be small and shrinking, there remain significant differences in the respective proportions of males and females who score at the very top or the very bottom of ability tests (Feingold, 1993, 1994, 1995). Still other researchers, noting the higher scores males have earned on the math portion of the SAT over the past 17 years, suspect genetic factors are at work (Benbow, 1987, 1990).

A recent analysis by Larry V. Hedges and Amy Nowell of the University of Chicago examined the performances of male and female teenagers on tests of mental ability over the past 30 years (Hedges & Nowell, 1995). In every case, *average differences* were small. However, on some tests there were disproportionally larger numbers of boys at the top or the bottom of the distributions of scores. For example, seven times as many boys as girls scored in the top 5 percent on science tests, and twice as many boys as girls scored in the top 5 percent on math tests. On the other hand, boys were much more likely than girls to score near the bottom of the distribution on tests of perceptual speed and reading comprehension. Boys also showed an "alarming" disadvantage on tests of writing skills. A significant aspect of this study was that differences in the scores of males and females showed remarkably little change between 1960 and 1992, the dates of testing sessions used in the research. Although their research in no way addressed the cause of any observed differences, Dr. Hedges felt compelled to state that he believes that "the sex differences in abilities are caused by social constraints rather than biology."

Some adults worry that they cannot learn many new things "at their age." That part of intelligence that reflects general information and vocabulary—basic to much academic school work—does not show a decline until very late in adulthood.

Before You Go On

Are there gender differences in IQ?

Age Differences in IQ

You know a great deal more now than you did when you were 12 years old. You knew more when you were 12 than you did when you were 10. Many 12-year-olds think they know more than their parents do. *What* we know changes with age, even *how much* we know changes with age, but neither provides a measure of intelligence. IQ scores are computed so that, by definition, they remain consistent with age. The IQ of the average 12-year-old is 100, the same as the IQ of the average 30-year-old and the average 60-year-old, regardless of which test is used. But what about the IQ of any one individual? If Kim's IQ is 112 at age 4, will it still be 112 at age 14, or age 40?

Infant and preschool IQ tests are poor predictors of IQ at older ages (Baumeister, 1987; Bayley & Schaefer, 1964). IQ test scores of children younger than 7 simply do not correlate well with IQs measured later. This does not mean that testing young children is without purpose. Having even a rough idea of the intellectual abilities of young children is often useful, particularly if there is concern about retardation or some thought that the child may be exceptional. The resulting scores may not predict adult intelligence well, but they may help in assessing the development of the child compared to other children.

What about intellectual changes throughout the life span? Does IQ decrease with old age? You may have guessed the answer: yes, no, and it depends. Most of the data on age differences in IQ scores have been gathered using a *cross-sectional method,* in which tests are given, at about the same time, to many people of varied ages. When this is done, the results indicate that overall IQ peaks in the early twenties, remains stable for about 20 years, and then declines sharply (e.g., Schaie, 1983; Wechsler, 1958, 1981). A different approach is to test the same individuals repeatedly, over a period of time. This is the *longitudinal method.* With this method, things don't look quite the same, showing IQ scores rising until the mid-fifties and then very gradually declining (Schaie, 1974; Schaie & Strother, 1968).

So far we have qualified "yes" and "no" answers to our question about age and IQ. Probably the best answer is "it depends." Studies of cognitive abilities demonstrate that we should ask about specific intellectual skills because they do not all decline at the same rate, and some do not decline at all. For example, tests of vocabulary often show no drop in scores with increasing age (Blum et al., 1970), whereas tests of verbal fluency often show steep declines beginning at age 30 (Schaie & Strother, 1968). A longitudinal study of more than 300 bright, well-educated adults showed a slight *increase* in general intellectual performance throughout adulthood (ages 18 to 54) on the Wechsler Adult Intelligence Scale (Sands et al., 1989). A closer look at scores on the Wechsler subtests for people between the ages of 40 and 61 showed improvement on the Information, Comprehension, and Vocabulary subtests, but a decline in scores on Digit Symbol and Block Design (see Figure 7.6).

Another "it depends" answer surfaces when we consider what are called fluid and crystallized intelligence (Cattell, 1963; Horn, 1982, 1985; Horn & Cattell, 1966). **Fluid intelligence**—abilities related to speed, adaptation, flexibility, and abstract reasoning—includes the skills that show the greatest decline with age. **Crystallized intelligence**—abilities depending on acquired knowledge, accumulated experiences, and general information—remains constant or even increases throughout one's lifetime (Horn, 1976, 1985; Vernon, 1979). If the concepts of fluid and crystallized intelligence sound familiar, you may be reminded of two of the dimensions the Stanford-Binet Intelligence Scale measures (see pages 234–235). With age, the ability to acquire new information or to solve new and different types of problems may decline, but there is no reason to expect a decline in those intellectual abilities already acquired (Salthouse, 1989, pp. 19–20). Recent research supporting this idea comes from the National Institute on Aging (Grady et al., 1995). Older volunteers (average age, *69*) had greater difficulty than younger volunteers (average age, 25) recognizing pictures of faces they had been shown 15 minutes earlier. Using PET scan imaging techniques that show the brain centers that are active in a given task, the researchers noted many fewer areas of the brains of the older subjects were active when they tried to memorize the faces. They could not remember the faces because they had not encoded them effectively.

fluid intelligence *abilities related to speed, adaptation, flexibility and abstract reasoning*

crystallized intelligence *abilities related to acquired knowledge, accumulated experiences, and general information*

Before You Go On

Does intelligence increase, decrease, or remain the same with increasing age?

Racial and Ethnic Differences in IQ

That there are significant differences between the IQ test scores of black and white Americans is not a new discovery. It was one of the conclusions drawn from the testing of army recruits during World War I. Since then, many studies have reconfirmed the fact that—on average—white people score about 15 points higher on general intelligence (IQ) tests than do black people. Black people earn lower scores on performance tests and on tests designed to minimize the influence of one's cultural backgound (so-called culture-fair tests) (Helms, 1992; Jensen, 1980; Rushton, 1988). At the same time, Japanese children between the ages of 6 and 16 score higher on IQ tests—about 11 points on the average—than do American white children of the same age (e.g., Lynn, 1982, 1987). The superiority of Japanese children on mathematics tests is even greater (Stevenson, et al., 1986). Curiously, there are no real differences in math abilities or in general intelligence between Asian and white American children at ages 4 or 5—*before* formal schooling begins (Geary, 1995). Asian American students score higher on the SAT than other students in math (e.g., average math scores on the SAT of 525 compared to 476) (Caplan, 1989; College Board, 1989; Hsia, 1988; Lynn, 1991; Sue & Okasaki, 1990). The nagging question, of course, is why? Why do these differences appear?

The proposed answers have been controversial and point to several possibilities: (1) The *tests are biased* and unfair. Current IQ tests may reflect mainstream life and the experiences of white Americans to a greater extent than they reflect the experiences of most black people or Hispanics. (2) Differences in IQ scores can be attributed to *environmental factors,* such as available economic or educational opportunities, or the extent to which one is exposed to a wide range of stimuli. (3) There are *genetic factors* that place some groups at a disadvantage. (4) There are *cultural differences in motivation* and attitudes about performance on standardized tests. In most Western cultures, poor performance on an academic test is typically attributed to factors other than one's effort: "The test was bad; my teachers were lousy, and I had the flu." In some cultures, including most Asian cultures, failure is more likely to be attributed to lack of effort: "I didn't work hard enough to prepare and should try harder next time."

Test bias may account for some of the differences in IQ scores, but assume for the moment that available techniques for assessing general intelligence are as valid as they can be. First, let's remind ourselves that even the best and fairest of tests only measure one, or a few, of the various possible dimensions of intelligence. What then?

In the 1950s and 1960s, social scientists were confident that most if not all of the difference between the average IQ scores of white people and black people could be accounted for in terms of environmental, sociocultural, and motivational factors. There may not have been a lot of research to support the position, but the logic was compelling and was consistent with prevailing attitudes. Black people were at a disadvantage on standard IQ tests because they were often denied access to enriching educational opportunities. Their generally lower socioeconomic status deprived blacks of many of the sorts of experiences that could raise their IQ scores.

In 1969, Arthur Jensen shocked the scientific community with an article published in the *Harvard Educational Review.* Jensen argued that there was insufficient evidence to justify the conclusion that the environment alone produced such large differences in IQ scores. The alternative was obvious to Jensen: differences were attributable to genetic factors. Many readers took Jensen's claim to mean that black people are genetically inferior to white people. Jensen says that his argument was meant only as a reasonable hypothesis, intended to provoke scientific efforts to explore such a possibility (Jensen, 1981).

Perhaps you can imagine the furor created by Jensen's article. Researchers took up the challenge to find convincing evidence to demonstrate that the environment is the cause of lower black IQ scores. After reviewing the body of evidence that accumulated from these efforts, one scientist, Brian Mackenzie, asserted that "what is finally clear from such research is that environmental factors have not been identified that are sufficient to account for all or even most of the 15-point mean difference in IQ between blacks and whites in the United States. Jensen's conclusion that one-half to two-thirds of the gap remains unaccounted for by any proposed combination of environmental influences is still unrefuted" (Mackenzie, 1984, p. 1217). Now what does *that* mean? Does it mean that racial differences in IQ *are* caused by genetic factors? *Are* black people genetically less able than white people? *Of course not.* There is not sufficient evidence to support such a conclusion (Mackintosh, 1986).

Just as many were coming to believe that the debate over racial differences in IQ was settling down, the controversy was reignited late in 1994 with the publication of a book titled, *The Bell Curve.* (The "bell curve" refers to the symmetrical curve of IQ scores we saw in Figure 7.5.) The book, by psychologist Richard Herrnstein and political analyst Charles Murray, raises several points about intelligence and IQ testing. Relevant to our discussion are their assertions that intelligence (1) is largely inherited (up to 60 percent inherited, they claim), (2) is virtually unchangeable from very early childhood on, (3) accounts for the "winners and losers" in today's society, and (4) is possessed in varying degrees by members of different races. Murray and Herrnstein predict the emergence of one class of "cognitive elite" and an impoverished low-IQ class, the former being white, the latter mostly black. Objections to nearly every aspect of *The Bell Curve* were loud and immediate (Bower, 1995; Jacoby & Glauberman, 1995; Kamin, 1995).

To understand why the issue of the inheritance of IQ has not yet been resolved requires that we understand three points: (1) Any evidence that genetic factors may affect differences in intelligence *within* races does not imply that genetic factors influence differences in intelligence *between* races. (2) A failure to identify specific environmental causes of racial differences in IQ is insufficient reason to drop the environmental-factors argument. (3) Just because we have not identified the specific environmental factors that can cause racial differences in IQ does not mean we must accept genetic explanations.

So where do we stand on the issue of racial-ethnic differences in IQ? We stand in a position of considerable uncertainty. For one thing, even the very concept of race is being challenged as a meaningful descriptor of persons. As we have seen, there are data that underscore the contributions of both genetic and environmental influences on intelligence. We would do well to keep in mind the following: "whether intelligence is largely genetically or largely environmentally determined is actually irrelevant in the context of group differences. The real issue is whether intelligence can be changed, an issue that does not go hand in hand with the issue of heritability" (Angoff, 1988, p. 713).

Before You Go On

Briefly summarize the data on racial differences in IQ scores.

Extremes of Intelligence

When we look at the IQ scores earned by large random samples of people, we find that they are distributed in a predictable pattern. The most frequently occurring score is the average score, 100. Most other earned scores are close to this average. In fact, about 95 percent of all IQ scores fall between 70 and 130 (see Figure 7.5, page 235). We'll end this Topic by considering those people who score at the extremes.

The Mentally Gifted

There are several ways in which a person can be gifted. The United States Office of Education (1972) defines giftedness as a demonstrated achievement or aptitude for excellence in any one of six areas. These categories are similar to those proposed by Gardner's model of intelligence (pages 231–232).

1. *Psychomotor ability:* An overlooked area in which some people clearly excel. We are dealing with people of outstanding abilities in behaviors or skills that require agility, strength, speed, quickness, coordination, and so forth.

2. *Visual and performing arts:* Some people, even as children, demonstrate an unusual talent for art, music, drama, or writing.

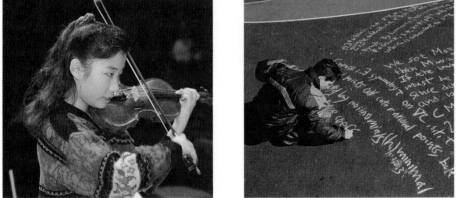

Consistent with the notion that there may be many kinds of "intelligence," so may there be many ways in which one can demonstrate giftedness—in leadership, musical ability, or mathematical skills, for example.

3. *Leadership ability:* Leadership skills are valued in most societies, and there are individuals who are particularly gifted in this area, even as very young children. Youngsters with good leadership skills tend to be bright, but they are not necessarily the smartest of the group.

4. *Creative or productive thinking:* Here we are talking about individuals who may be intellectually or academically above average, but not necessarily. Scores on measures of creativity typically are unrelated to measures of general intelligence (e.g., Horn, 1976; Kershner & Ledger, 1985). Among other things, people with this type of giftedness are able to generate unique and different, but useful, solutions to problems. Persons with exceptional creative talents in one area (art, math, or language, for instance) usually show no special creativity in other areas (Amabile, 1985; Weisberg, 1986).

5. *Specific academic aptitude:* In this case we are talking about people who have a special ability in a particular subject or two. Someone who is a whiz in math,

history, or laboratory science, without necessarily being outstanding in other academic areas, would fit this category.

6. *Intellectually gifted:* Inclusion in this group is based on scores earned on a general intelligence test. It is likely that when people use the term *mentally gifted,* they are referring to individuals who fit this category—people of exceptionally high IQ. (IQ scores of 130 or above usually qualify for this category. Some reserve the label for those with IQs above 135. In either case, we are dealing with a very small portion of the population: fewer than 3 percent.)

How can we describe intellectually gifted individuals? Actually, there have been few large-scale attempts to understand mental giftedness or the cognitive processing of people at the upper end of the IQ distribution (Horowitz & O'Brien, 1985; Reis, 1989). A lot of what we do know about the mentally gifted comes from a classic study begun by Lewis M. Terman in the early 1920s (the Lewis Terman who revised Binet's IQ test in 1916). Terman supervised the testing of more than 250,000 children throughout California. His research group at Stanford University focused on those children who earned the highest scores—1,528 in all, each with an IQ above 135.

Lewis Terman died in 1956, but the study of those mentally gifted individuals, who were between the ages of 8 and 12 in 1922, continues. Ever since their inclusion in the study, and at regular intervals, they continue to be retested, surveyed, interviewed, and polled by psychologists and others (Friedman et al., 1995; Goleman, 1980; Oden, 1968; Sears & Barbee, 1977).

The Terman study has its drawbacks. Choosing a narrow definition of gifted in terms of IQ alone is one. Failing to account for the educational or socioeconomic level of each child's parents is another. The researchers also may have excluded from the sample any children who showed signs of psychological disorders or problems, whether their IQ scores were high enough or not. Nonetheless, the study is an impressive one for having continued for more than 60 years, if nothing else. What can this longitudinal analysis tell us about people with very high IQs?

Most of Terman's results fly in the face of the classic stereotype of the bright child as skinny, anxious, clumsy, sickly, and a wearer of thick glasses (Sears & Barbee, 1977). In fact, if there is any overall conclusion to be drawn from the Terman-Stanford study it is that, in general, gifted children experience advantages in virtually everything. They are taller, faster, better coordinated, have better eyesight and fewer emotional problems, and tend to stay married longer than average. These findings have been confirmed by others with different samples of subjects (Holden, 1980). Many obvious things are also true: the mentally gifted received more education; found better, higher-paying jobs; and had brighter children than did people of average intelligence. By now, we know better than to overgeneralize. Not all of Terman's children (sometimes referred to as "Termites") did not grew up to be rich and famous or live happily ever after. Many did, but not all.

Before You Go On

What defines the mentally gifted?

@@@@ **Thinking Critically** @@@@

What factors would you add to the six listed above that define dimensions on which one may demonstrate "giftedness"?

The Mentally Retarded

Our understanding of mental retardation has changed markedly over the past 25 years. We've seen changes in treatment and care, and great strides in prevention. There have been significant changes in how psychology defines mental retardation (Baumeister, 1987; Landesman & Ramey, 1989).

Intelligence as measured by IQ tests is often used to confirm suspected cases of mental retardation. As is true for the mentally gifted, however, there is more to retardation than IQ alone. The American Association of Mental Deficiency (AAMD) cites three factors in its definition of **mental retardation**: "subaverage general intellectual functioning which originated during the developmental period and is associated with impairment in adaptive behavior" (Grossman, 1973). Let's look at each of these three points.

The IQ cutoff for mental retardation is usually taken to be 70, with IQs between 70 and 85 considered "borderline" or "slow" (Zigler & Hodapp, 1991). Standard IQ cutoff scores for the four major degrees of retardation are:

IQ 50–69: mildly mentally retarded (approximately 80% of all cases of retardation)

IQ 35–49: moderately mentally retarded (approximately 12% of all cases of retardation)

IQ 20–34: severely mentally retarded (approximately 8% of all cases of retardation)

IQ less than 19: profoundly mentally retarded (less than 1% of all cases of retardation) (American Psychiatric Association, 1994)

As you review this list, keep two things in mind. First, these scores are suggested limits. Given what we know about IQ tests, it is ridiculous to claim after one administration of a test that a person with an IQ of *69* is mentally retarded, while someone else with an IQ of *71* is not. Second, a diagnosis of mental retardation is not (should not be) made on the basis of IQ score alone. Of late there has been much controversy over where to place the upper limit of mental retardation, with some (e.g., the American Association of Mental Retardation) arguing that it should be at 75 rather than 70.

To fit the AAMD definition of mental retardation, the cause or the symptoms of the below-average intellectual functioning must show up during the period of intellectual development (up to age 18). In many circles the term *developmentally delayed* is beginning to replace the narrower term *mentally retarded.* Diagnosis may come only after the administration of an IQ test, but initial suspicions generally come from perceived delays in developmental or adjustive patterns of behavior.

By making "impairment in adaptive behavior" a part of their definition of mental retardation, the AAMD is acknowledging that there is more to getting along in this world than the intellectual and academic sorts of skills IQ tests emphasize. Being mentally retarded does not mean being helpless, particularly for those at borderline or mild levels of retardation. Of major consideration is the ability to adapt to one's environment. In this regard, such skills as the abilities to dress oneself, follow directions, make change, or find one's way home from a distance become relevant (Coulter & Morrow, 1978).

Even without a simple definition of retardation based solely on IQ, the population of mentally retarded or developmentally delayed citizens is large. Estimates indicate that approximately 3 percent of the population at any one time falls within the IQ range for retardation. Two other relevant estimates are that nearly 900,000 children and young adults with mental retardation between the ages of 3 and 21 years are being served in the public schools (Schroeder et al., 1987) and that nearly 200,000 mentally retarded persons are found in community residential facilities: state and county mental hospitals, and nursing homes (Landesman & Butterfield, 1987). Let's now turn to a brief discussion of the causes, treatment, and prevention of mental retardation.

The Causes of Mental Retardation. We cannot explain the causes of all types of mental retardation, but we have some good ideas. Psychologists suspect that there are hundreds of causes. The list of known or highly suspected causes exceeds 200 (Grossman, 1983). The more we learn about the sources of mental retardation, the better able we will be to treat it or even prevent it.

mental retardation *a condition indicated by an IQ score below 70 that begins during development and is associated with an impairment in adaptive functioning*

Approximately one-fourth of all cases of mental retardation reflect a problem that developed before, during, or just after birth. Between 15 and 20 percent of those persons referred to as mentally retarded were born prematurely—at least three weeks before the due date or at a weight below 5 pounds, 8 ounces.

We appreciate that the health of the mother during pregnancy—and the health of the father at conception—can affect the health of the child. Many prenatal conditions can cause developmental delays, including hypertension, exposure to X rays, low oxygen intake, rubella, maternal syphilis, and the mother's use of drugs, from powerful narcotics to the frequent use of aspirin, alcohol, or nicotine. To greater and lesser degrees, all of these can be linked to mental retardation. In addition, some cases stem from difficulties or injuries during the birth process itself.

As we've seen, the extent to which normal levels of intelligence are inherited is open to debate. Some types of mental retardation, however, are clearly genetic in origin. One of the clearest examples of such a case is the intellectual retardation accompanying **Down syndrome**, first described in 1866. We don't know exactly why it happens, but occasionally a fetus develops with 47 chromosomes instead of the usual 46, or 23 pairs. We do know that Down syndrome is more likely to occur as the age of *either* parent increases. The physical signs are well known: small, round skull; flattened face; large tongue; short, broad nose; broad hands; and short, stubby fingers. During childhood, behavioral development is delayed. A Down syndrome child may fall into any level of retardation. Many are educable and lead lives of considerable independence, although even as adults many will require supervision at least some of the time.

Fragile X syndrome is a variety of mental retardation with a genetic basis that was discovered more recently—in the late 1960s (Bregman et al., 1987). Although it can occur in females, it is found primarily in males. Males with Fragile X syndrome usually have long faces, big ears, and, as adults, large testes (Zigler & Hodapp, 1991). Individuals with this form of retardation have difficulty processing sequences of events, or events in a series, which means that they have problems with

Down syndrome *a condition of several symptoms, including mental retardation, caused by an extra (47th) chromosome*

Down syndrome children can benefit from from special education programs and individualized instruction. Many flourish in a standard classroom environment.

language skills. One curiosity is that whereas males with Down syndrome show a gradual but steady decrease in IQ scores with age, males with Fragile X syndrome show their most noticeable declines during puberty.

Most cases of mental retardation do not have obvious causes. About one-half to three-quarters of cases of mental retardation do not have known biological or genetic causes (Zigler & Hodapp, 1991).

Dealing effectively with mental retardation has been difficult. Special-education programs have helped, but not all have been successful (Zigler & Hodapp, 1991). Preparing teachers and mental health professionals to be sensitive to the wide range of behaviors and feelings of which mentally retarded persons are capable has also helped. Impressive changes *can* be made in raising the IQs of some mildly retarded and a few moderately retarded children (Landesman & Ramey, 1989). For severely and profoundly retarded persons, the outlook is not bright—at least in terms of raising IQ points (Spitz, 1986). But we always need to remind ourselves that quality of life is not necessarily a function of IQ. The emphasis in recent years has been less on overall intellectual growth and more on those specific skills and abilities that can be improved.

There is greater hope in the area of prevention. As we continue to appreciate the influences of the prenatal environment on the development of cognitive abilities, we can educate mothers and fathers about how their behaviors can affect their child even before it is born. An excellent example of how mental retardation can be prevented concerns a disorder called *phenylketonuria,* or *PKU.* This disorder is genetic in origin, and over fifty years ago it was found to be a cause of mental retardation. PKU results when a child inherits genes that fail to produce an enzyme that normally breaks down chemicals found in many foods. Although a newborn with PKU usually appears normal, a simple blood test that can detect the disorder soon after birth has been developed. Once PKU has been detected, a prescribed diet (which must be maintained for about four years) can reduce or eliminate any of the retardation effects of the disorder.

Unfortunately, most cases (about 70 percent) of mental retardation cannot be detected at birth, which means that preventive or therapeutic intervention also has to wait until the child is older (Scott & Carran, 1987).

Before You Go On

How do we define mental retardation?

What causes it?

TOPIC 7A SUMMARY

In this Topic, we soon found that generating a complete, adequate definition of intelligence is not easily done. We looked at a few theoretical approaches and moved on to consider intelligence in operational terms—in terms of how it is typically measured. We reviewed two individual tests of intelligence (the Stanford-Binet and the Wechsler tests) in some detail. These tests yield g-scores, or total scores, which are taken to indicate general intellectual abilities.

Our ability to measure general intellectual abilities (which we continue to call IQ) is not without limitation. Nonetheless, IQ tests have raised controversial and intriguing questions. We examined differences in measured intelligence as a function of gender, age, and race. General, overall IQ scores are stable as a function of age, although some types of intelligent behaviors may be lost with advancing years. Differences in IQ scores between males and females are slight at best, although, again, there are cognitive skills for which gender differences have been found. There are some significant differences in measured intelligence when we look at various racial or ethnic groups, but accounting for these differences remains an elusive goal. Finally, in this Topic we considered individuals with extreme IQ scores. In every instance, we're confronted with the issue of the extent to which intelligence—as it is measured by our tests—is a function of one's nature or one's nurture.

TOPIC 7B Language and Problem Solving

In Topic 7B we consider two examples of human intelligence in action: the use of language as a means of communication and problem solving.

Language

Language is a social process, a means of communication, which reflects a marvelously complex cognitive activity. The philosopher Suzanne Langer put it this way:

> Language is, without a doubt, the most momentous and at the same time the most mysterious product of the human mind. Between the clearest animal call of love or warning or anger, and a man's least, trivial word, there lies a whole day of Creation—or in modern phrase, a whole chapter of evolution. (1951, p. 94)

Let's Talk: What Is Language?

How shall we characterize this mysterious product of the human mind called language? **Language** is a large collection of arbitrary symbols that have a shared significance for a language-using community, and that follow certain rules of combination (Morris, 1946). Now let's pull apart this definition and examine the points it raises.

First, language consists of a large number of *symbols*. The symbols that constitute language are commonly referred to as words—labels we have assigned to concepts, or our mental representations. When we use the word *chair* as a symbol, we don't use it to label just one specific instance of a chair. We use the word as a symbol to represent our concept of chairs. As symbols, words need not stand for real things in the real world. We have words to describe objects or events that cannot be perceived, such as *ghost* or, for that matter, *mind*. With language we can communicate about owls and pussycats in teacups and a four-dimensional, time-warped hyperspace. Words stand for cognitions, or concepts, and we have a great number of them.

It is important that we define the symbols of language as being *arbitrary*. By doing so we imply that there is no requirement for using the particular symbol we do. You call what you are reading a book (or a textbook, to use a more specific symbol). We have all agreed (in English) that *book* is the appropriate symbol for what you are reading. But we don't have to. We could agree to call it a *relm*. Or a *poge*. The symbols of a language are arbitrary, but once established by common use or tradition, they become part of one's language and must be learned and applied consistently by each new language user.

To be part of a language, at least in a practical sense, language symbols need to have shared *significance for a language-using community*. That is, people have to

language *a large collection of arbitrary symbols that have a shared significance for a language-using community and that follow certain combinatorial rules*

Language use is a social process, a means of communicating our understanding of events to others.

agree on both the symbols used in a language and what those symbols mean. This is another way of saying that language use is a social enterprise. You and I might decide to call what you are now reading a *relm,* but then you and I would be in a terribly small language-using community.

The final part of our definition tells us that the symbols of a language must follow certain *rules of combination.* What this means is that language is structured, or rule-governed. It is used to communicate ideas, to share our thoughts and feelings with others. Of course, there are ways of communicating that do not involve language. What makes language use a special form of communication is the fact that it is governed by rules of combination. For one thing, there are rules about how we can and cannot string symbols together in language. In English, we say, "The small boy slept late." We do not say, "Slept boy late small the." Well, we could say it, but no one will know for sure exactly what we mean by it. The utterance violates the combinatorial rules of English. When the rules of language are violated, utterances lose their meaning, and the value of language as a means of communication is lost.

Even with this complex definition of language a few points are left out. For one, using language is a remarkably *creative, generative process.* Nearly everything we say is something we've never said before. It's unlikely, for example, that you have ever before read a sentence just like this one. Almost every time we use language, we use it in a new and creative way, which emphasizes the importance of the underlying rules, or structure, of language. Another point: language allows displacement—the ability to communicate about the "not here and the not now." We can use language to talk about yesterday's lunch and tomorrow's class schedule. We can talk about things that are not here, never were, and never will be. Language is the only form of communication that allows us to do so.

Finally: Language and speech are not synonymous terms. Speech is but one way in which language is expressed as behavior. There are others, including writing, coding (as in Morse code), or signing (as in American Sign Language).

Before You Go On

What are the defining characteristics of language?

ⓔⓔⓔⓔ **Thinking Critically** ⓔⓔⓔⓔ

What are the similarities and differences between a page of written language and a page of written music?

Describing the Structure in Language

Psycholinguistics is a hybrid discipline consisting of scientists trained in psychology *and* linguistics. When psycholinguists analyze a language, they usually do so at three levels. The first level involves the sounds that are used when we express language as speech. The second level deals with the meaning of words and sentences, and the third involves the rules used for combining words and phrases to generate sentences. At each of these three levels we can see structure and rules at work.

Individual speech sounds of a language are called **phonemes**. They are the sounds we make when we talk to each other. Phonemes by themselves have no meaning, but when put together in the proper order, result in a meaningful utterance. For example, the word *cat* consists of three phonemes: an initial consonant sound (a "k" sound here), the vowel sound of "a," and a consonant sound, "t." How phonemes are combined to form words and phrases is rule-governed. If we were to interchange the consonant sounds in *cat* we would have an altogether different utterance, *tack,* with an altogether different meaning. To use a language requires that one know which speech sounds are part of that language and how they may be combined to form larger language units. There are approximately 45 phonemes in English. (Because those 45 sounds are represented by only 26 letters in our alphabet, it is little wonder many of us have problems spelling.)

phoneme *the smallest distinguishable unit of sound in the spoken form of a language*

Describing a language's phonemes, noting which sounds are relevant and which combinations are possible, is only a small part of a complete description of a language. Another level of analysis involves *meaning* in the language. The study of meaning is called **semantics**. Researchers interested in semantics take the morpheme as their unit of analysis. A **morpheme** is the smallest unit of *meaning* in a spoken language. A morpheme is a collection of phonemes that means something. In most cases, *morpheme* and *word* are synonymous, but in addition to words, morphemes include the prefixes and suffixes of a language. For example, *write* is a morpheme and a word; it has meaning, and it is not possible to subdivide it into smaller, meaningful units. *Rewrite* is also a word and has meaning, but it consists of two morphemes, *write* and *re,* which in this context means roughly, "do it again." *Tablecloth* is a word composed of two morphemes, *table* and *cloth.*

semantics *the study of the meaning of words and sentences*

morpheme *the smallest unit of meaning in a language*

Notice that how we generate morphemes is governed by rules. For example, we cannot go around making nouns plural in any old way. The plural of ox is oxen, not oxes. The plural of mouse is mice, not mouses, mousen, or meese. If I want to write something over again, I have to rewrite it, not write-re it. Note how morphemes are verbal labels for concepts (mental representations). Asking you to rewrite something would make no sense if we did not share the concepts of "writing" and of "doing things over again."

The aspect of our language that most obviously uses rules is the generation of sentences—stringing words (or morphemes) together to create meaningful utterances (Hörmann, 1986). The rules that govern how sentences are formed (or structured) in a language are referred to as the **syntax** of a language.

syntax *the rules that govern how the morphemes of a language are to be combined in order to form meaningful utterances*

To know the syntax, or syntactic rules, of one's language involves a peculiar sort of knowledge or cognitive ability. We all know the rules of English in the sense that we can and do use them, but few of us know what those rules are in the sense that we can tell anyone else what they are. We say that people have a *competence,* a cognitive skill that governs language use. That skill allows us to judge the extent to which an utterance is a meaningful, well-formed sentence (Howard, 1983; Slobin, 1979). We know that "The dog looks terrifying" fits the rules of English and that "The dog looks barking" does not, and somehow we recognize that "The dog looks watermelon" is downright absurd. At the same time, we recognize that "Colorless green ideas sleep furiously" *does* fit the rules of English, even though it doesn't make sense (Chomsky, 1957). It may be a silly thing to say, but we realize that it is an acceptable thing to say.

We also know that these two utterances communicate the same message, even though they look (and sound) quite different:

The student read the textbook.

The textbook was read by the student.

In either case, we know who is doing what. Another linguistic intuition that demonstrates our competence with the rules of our language is in our ability to detect ambiguity. Look at these two sentences:

They are cooking apples.

They are cooking apples.

There is no doubt that they appear to be identical, but upon reflection we can see that they may be communicating different (ambiguous) ideas. In one case we may be talking about what some people are cooking (apples as opposed to spaghetti). In another we may be identifying a variety of apple (those best suited for cooking as opposed to those best suited for eating). In yet another case, we may be describing what is being done to the apples (cooking them as opposed to eating them). You may be able to think of yet other ways in which this simple sentence can be interpreted. This is not an isolated example of ambiguity in language. There are many: "The shooting of the policemen was terrible," or "Flying airplanes can be dangerous."

Before You Go On

How are rules and structure reflected in the use of phonemes, morphemes, and syntax?

Language Use as a Social Process

The main purpose to which language is put is communication. Language helps us share our thoughts, feelings, intentions, and experiences with others. Language use is social behavior. **Pragmatics** is the study of how language is related to the social context in which it occurs. Our understanding of sarcasm (as in "Well, it certainly is a beautiful day!" when in fact it is rainy, cold, and miserable), or simile (as in "Life is like a sewer . . . "), or metaphor (as in "His slam dunk to start the second half was the knockout blow"), or cliché (as in "It rained cats and dogs") depends on many things, including an appreciation of the context of the utterance and the intention of the speaker.

Pragmatics involves decisions based on the perception of the social situation at the moment. Think how you modify your language use when you talk to your best friend, a preschool child, a professor in her office, or a driver who cuts you off at an intersection. Contemporary concerns about "political correctness" seem relevant

pragmatics *the study of how social contexts affect the meaning of linguistic events*

Taken literally, the notion of "singing in the rain" would seem silly at best. In the context of the motion picture, starring Gene Kelly, Debbie Reynolds, and Donald O'Connor, we can use our pragmatic understanding of language to interpret the phrase "singing in the rain" differently.

here, don't they? In most contexts, words such as *pig, Uncle Tom, boy,* and *girl* are reasonable and proper; in other contexts they can evoke angry responses. In some American Indian cultures, periods of silence—even lengthy periods of silence—during conversation are common and acceptable. Someone not familiar with this pragmatic reality could become anxious and upset about long pauses in the midst of a conversation (e.g., Basso, 1970; Brislin, 1993, pp. 217–221). As you can imagine, translations from one language to another can cause huge changes in meaning as cultural contexts change. Two of my favorites (from Berkowitz, 1994) are the translation of the slogan "Finger Lickin' Good" into Chinese, yielding, "Eat Your Fingers Off," and in Taiwan, the slogan "Come alive with the Pepsi Generation" becomes "Pepsi will bring your ancestors back from the dead."

Before You Go On

What is the study of "pragmatics," and what does it tell us about language use?

Language Acquisition

One of the most significant achievements of childhood is the acquisition of language. Few, if any, cognitive skills can compare to language use in complexity and utility. The process seems nearly magical: gooing, cooing, babbling one day, then a word or two, then "Why is the sky blue, Daddy, why is the sky blue?"—and all in the span of just a few months' time. At best we have tentative theories and hypotheses. We are getting close to adequately describing *what* happens. Describing *how* it happens will take longer.

What Happens in Language Acquisition

Infants create speech sounds spontaneously. They come into the world with a cry and make noise with regularity forever after. At about the age of 6 months, random cries and noises are replaced by the more regular sounds of babbling. **Babbling** is the production of speech phonemes, often in repetitive, rhythmic patterns, such as "ma-ma-ma" or "lu-lu-nah-nah" All babies babble in the same way (Nakazima, 1962; Oller, 1981). An adult cannot distinguish the babbling of a Chinese infant from that of a Greek or an American infant. Deaf infants produce babbling sounds that are indistinguishable from those of hearing children (Lenneberg et al., 1965). Deaf babies also "babble" with their fingers and hands. These motions are meaningless, but are the basis for what will later become (for many of them) their native (sign) language.

babbling *speech phonemes produced in rhythmic, repetitive patterns*

The acquisition of vocabulary follows soon after babbling begins. In all cases, comprehension, or understanding, comes before production. Children understand and respond appropriately to the meaning of utterances long before they are able to produce those utterances themselves. A child's first word or two usually appears at about the age of 1 year (parents often argue that the onset of speech is earlier, but independent observers often fail to confirm what may be parental wishful thinking). Once begun, word acquisition is remarkable. A 1-year-old may produce only two or three words. By the age of 2 years, word production is up to about 50. In terms of comprehension, by age 2, a child understands 200 to 300 words; by age 3, over 1,000; and by age 6, between 8,000 and 14,000 words (Benedict, 1979; Brown, 1973; Carey, 1978).

Describing the development of syntactic rules in children has proven difficult. As linguists began to understand the rules of adult language, it seemed reasonable to look for these same rules in the language of children. What soon became apparent was that the syntax of adult forms of language do not emerge until long after children have begun stringing words and morphemes together in utterances. Even though we do not find adult structure or rules in the language use of young children, they still use language in a rule-governed way. In other words, children do not speak adult language badly; instead, their language follows its own rules (e.g., Radford, 1990).

The first use of vocalization as language is called **holophrastic speech**—the use of just one word to communicate a range of intentions and meanings dependent on gestures, intonation, and so on. Before this stage a child may produce words, but only as a naming exercise. Words are used as labels for concepts and nothing else. With holophrastic speech, individual words are used to communicate a range of possibilities. Imagine it yourself. Picture a young child sitting in a high chair. Can't you just see how the utterance *milk* could be used to communicate such things as "I want my milk!" or "Uh-oh, I dropped my milk," or "Oh yea! here's my milk," or "Yuck, not milk again."

holophrastic speech *the use of one word to communicate several meanings*

About the age of 2 years, we note the appearance of two-word utterances. When carefully analyzed, these utterances are very regular, as if they were being put together according to strict rules. Given an understanding of the words *big* and *little* and many nouns, a child may say, "big ball," "big plane," "big doggie," "little stick," "little cup," and so on. What is interesting is that this child will never reverse this word order. He or she will not say "ball big" or "cup little" (Braine, 1976).

From this point on, language development is extremely rapid. From the two-word utterance stage there is a period typified by **telegraphic speech**—spoken language consisting of nouns, verbs, and adjectives, but hardly any function words such as articles or prepositions. We hear children say such things as "Daddy go store" or "Billy draw pictures." Then, at roughly 2 1/2 years of age, language use expands at an explosive rate. There really is no noticeable three-word or four-word stage of development. Phrases are lengthened, noun phrases first, so that "Billy's ball" becomes "Billy's red ball," which soon becomes "Billy's red ball that Mommy

telegraphic speech *utterances characterized by the use of nouns, verbs, and adjectives, and few function words* got at the store." When children are ready to begin grade school, at age 5 or 6, they demonstrate both the understanding and the production of virtually every acceptable type of sentence structure in their language.

Before You Go On

What are some of the landmark events that occur during language acquisition?

Theories of Language Acquisition

How is language acquired? If you studied a foreign language in high school or are studying one now, did it occur to you that there were children somewhere in the world who were easily acquiring the same language you were struggling with? Acquiring one's language is a cognitive feat at which all (normal) humans succeed.

I have avoided the phrase "language learning," and have referred to language "acquisition" or "development" instead. This was intentional because I do not want to imply that acquiring language is simply a matter of learning. On the other hand, language is not innate or instinctive in the usual sense, or everyone would speak the very same language. Some of language acquisition can be accounted for by learning (in ways discussed in Chapter 5), but most aspects of language acquisition defy explanation in terms of learning and suggest an inherited basis for the process.

Theories of language development as learning (e.g., Skinner, 1957; Whitehurst, 1982) certainly have their place. No one will claim that language emerges free of the influence of learning, experience, conditioning, reinforcement, and the like. We can be most comfortable with learning approaches when we try to account for the acquisition of phonemes and morphemes. Acquiring the phonemes of one's language seems to be a straightforward process, albeit slightly backward. The infant

Language acquisition may have a biological foundation, but it requires the interaction of language users and language learners to progress normally.

spontaneously produces phonemes from all languages, but learns, through imitation and reinforcement, which sounds need to be "saved" for use in his or her language. Sounds not appropriate for the child's language are simply not used and disappear from the child's repertoire (deVillers & deVillers, 1978).

There are several varieties of learning involved in word acquisition. Some of the meaning of words comes from classical conditioning. The use of some morphemes or words is reinforced and the use of others is not, as operant conditioning predicts. Some growth in vocabulary results from observational learning–using words that others use. Some word meanings develop through direct instruction. Yes, learning seems to handle morpheme acquisition rather nicely, but there are a few problems.

For one thing, as children acquire morphemes that change the meaning of a word (called bound morphemes), they do so with a disturbing regularity. For no good reason that learning theory can account for, children learn to add *-ing* to words before they learn to form possessives (by adding *-'s*), which they learn before they learn to form the past tense of verbs (by adding *-ed*). When asked what he is doing, a child may be expected first to respond, "I draw." Later will come "I drawing." Only later may we expect "That Billy's picture." Still later we'll hear something like "I drawed it yesterday." In short, there is a predictable sequence in which many morphemes are acquired. This sequencing may reflect limits set by the child's genetic constitution or by the child's cognitive growth (i.e., he or she may not understand the basic concept of past tense until the concept of possessive is acquired), but in either case, simple learning theory is strained.

Another problem for learning theory is called **overregularization**–the continued application of an acquired language rule (e.g., for forming plurals or past tense) in a situation for which it is not appropriate. A child might say, "I have two foots," "I saw four mans," or "I goed to the store," even after using the words *feet, men,* and *went* appropriately in similar contexts. What accounts for overregularization? Biologically oriented theories (e.g., Chomsky, 1965, 1975, 1986; Lenneberg, 1967; McNeil, 1970, Pinker, 1995) say that there must be some innate, "prewired" biological mechanism that compels the child to seek out and apply rules during acquisition. This mechanism, often called a *language acquisition device,* or *LAD,* becomes active when we are about 1 year old, and usually turns off by the time we are 5 or 6 years old. The child is so predisposed to find and use rules that she or he will do so consistently, even when a particular application of the rule is wrong. Actually, "two foots" is a more reasonable construction than "two feet," even though "two foots" is not likely to have been heard in adult speech (Anisfeld, 1984).

Reliance on some sort of innate LAD is even more sensible when we consider the acquisition of rules reflected in the generation of sentences. The argument for an innate predisposition for the acquisition of language rules comes once again from the orderliness of language development. The ages are not always the same, but with uncanny regularity, children everywhere go about acquiring their different languages in virtually the same pattern. Holophrastic speech, the stability of the two-word utterance, the expansion of noun phrases, and the ordered acquisition of bound morphemes have been noted over and over as a consistent pattern– a pattern much more consistent than we could ever expect of the learning histories of the children being observed (Slobin, 1979).

Another point often raised against the learning approach is that when it comes to the rules of syntax, most adults cannot begin to tell us what the rules of their language *are.* How, then, can you teach something to someone else if you don't have any idea what it is you're teaching? The argument is sensible. Yet as adults, we do have certain linguistic intuitions. We can tell when an utterance is correctly formed, even if we can't specify why. Perhaps we use these intuitions to reinforce proper use and to correct improper use? The problem is that when we carefully watch adults interacting with young children, we find that they are much more likely to correct the *content* of what the child says than the *form* in which it is said. If a child says,

overregularization *the excessive application of an acquired language rule (e.g., for forming plurals) in a situation in which it is not appropriate*

"Me no like cereal," a parent is likely to respond with a statement such as, "Sure you do; you eat it all the time" (Brown, 1973; Brown et al., 1969). "Explicit language teaching from adults is not necessary. In fact, if adults try to structure and direct a child's language learning, the outcome may be interference . . ." (Rice, 1989, p. 153).

So, when it comes to explaining language acquisition, where are we? We seem to be where we commonly are when faced with two theoretical positions—particularly when one position favors learning (nurture) and the other favors innate factors (nature). Some aspects of language are learned. For most language acquisition processes, however, learning, reinforcement, and imitation provide unsatisfactory explanations. A reasonable position, for now, is an interactionist position: humans are born with a predisposition to acquire certain aspects of language. But which language they acquire will reflect their experiences in their language-using community.

Before You Go On

Briefly summarize the theories of language acquisition.

@@@@ **Thinking Critically** @@@@

Are there any other skills or behaviors that you think you may have acquired in the same general way that you acquired language?

Problem Solving

Our daily lives are filled with problems of various sorts. Some are simple, straightforward, or trivial; others are complex and very important to us. Here we'll focus on cognitive, or intellectual, problems: those that require the manipulation of cognitions for their solution. The first thing to do is define what a problem is, and then we can consider how to go about solving one.

Just What *Is* a Problem?

Sometimes our goals are obvious, our present situation is clear, and the way to get from where we are to where we want to be is also obvious. In such cases, we don't have a problem, do we? Say you want to have a nice breakfast. You have eggs, bacon, bread, and butter available. You also have the implements needed to prepare these foods, and you know how to use them. You know that, for you, a nice breakfast would be two eggs over easy, three strips of fried bacon, and a piece of buttered toast. With little hesitation, you engage in the appropriate behaviors and reach your goal.

problem *a discrepancy between one's present state and one's goal state with no apparent way to get from one to the other*

A **problem** exists when there is a discrepancy between one's present state and one's perceived goal state and no readily apparent way to get from one to the other. In situations in which the path to goal attainment is not clear a problem exists, and you need to engage in problem-solving behaviors—as might be the case if halfway through the preparation of breakfast you discover you have no butter or margarine.

A problem has three major components: (1) an *initial state*—the situation as it is, or is perceived to exist, at the moment; (2) a *goal state*—the situation as the problem solver would like it to be, or the end product; and (3) possible *routes or strategies* for getting from the initial state to the goal state.

Psychologists also distinguish between well-defined and ill-defined problems. *Well-defined problems* are those in which both the initial state and the goal state are clearly defined. We know what the current situation is, what the goal is, and we may even know some of the possible ways to go about getting from one to the other. "What English word can be made from the letters *teralbay*?" We see that this question presents a problem. We understand what the question is asking, have some ideas about how we might go about answering it, and will surely know when we have succeeded. "How do you get home from campus if you discover that your car, which is in the campus parking lot, won't start?" Again, we know our initial state (on campus with a car that won't start), and we'll know when we have reached our goal (we're at home), but we have to find a different way to get there.

Most of the problems you and I face every day are *ill-defined.* In such cases, we do not have a clear idea of what we are starting with, nor are we able to clearly identify or define any ideal solution. "What should my college major be?" Many high school seniors (and some college seniors) don't even know what their options are. They have few ideas about how to find out about college majors. And once they have selected a major, they are not at all sure that their choice was the best one—which may explain why so many college students change their majors so often. Ill-defined problems usually involve many variables that are difficult to define (much less control), so psychologists usually study problems that are at least reasonably well defined.

Before You Go On

What are well-defined and ill-defined problems?

Problem Representation

Once we realize we're facing a problem, the first thing we should do is put it in some form that allows us to think about it in familiar terms. We need to *represent* the problem in our own minds, interpreting the problem so that the initial state and the goal state are clear to us. We also need to note if there are any restrictions on how we can go about seeking solutions. In short, we need to understand the nature of the problem, and should try to make it meaningful by relating it to information we have available in our memories.

By examining a few problems of the sort that have been used in the psychology laboratory, we can see that how we represent a problem can be critical. Consider the following classic (from Duncker, 1945):

> One morning, exactly at sunrise, a Buddhist monk began to climb a tall mountain. A narrow path, only a foot or two wide, spiraled around the mountain to a glittering temple at the summit. The monk ascended at varying rates of speed, stopping many times along the way to rest and eat dried fruit which he carried with him. He reached the temple shortly before sunset. After days of fasting and meditation, he began his journey back down along the same path, starting at sunrise again and walking at variable speeds, with many pauses along the way. His average speed going down was, of course, greater than his average climbing speed. Show that there is a spot along the path that the monk occupied on both trips at precisely the same time of day.

Thinking about this problem as it is presented—in words—can be maddening. As is often the case with real-life problems, this statement contains a lot of irrelevant information. Useful problem representation often involves sorting out what matters and what doesn't. The fact that we're dealing with a monk is not relevant, nor are the temple, the dried fruit, the fact that the path is a narrow one, or that the trip was made on two different days.

You might represent this problem in terms of just one climber making the trip in one day. Or, better still, imagine that there are two climbers: one starting from the top of the mountain, the other starting from the bottom. Because they both take the same path, surely they will meet somewhere on that mountain trail sometime during the day (see Figure 7.8). When you represent the problem this way, the solution is readily apparent. So it might help to represent the mountain-climbing problem visually, drawing out the ascending and descending pathways on a sheet of paper.

As it happens, representing the following problem visually would not be wise:

Imagine that you have a very large sheet of paper, 1/100 of an inch thick. Imagine folding it over on itself so that now you have two layers of paper. Fold it again so that there are four layers. It is impossible to actually fold a sheet of paper 50 times, but imagine that you could. About how thick would the paper be if it were folded over on itself 50 times? (From Adams, 1974)

On the one hand, it sounds so simple: imagine what it would be like to fold a piece of paper over and over. Unfortunately, picturing just what a piece of paper folded 50 times really would look like is very difficult. Some people guess a few inches. Some say that the folded paper would be a few feet thick. Many have no idea at all. Representing this problem in visual terms is of little help. If one recognizes this as a mathematics problem, involving exponents, a correct solution is more likely. Actually, 50 folds will increase the paper's thickness by a factor of 2^{50}. That comes to 1,100,000,000,000,000 inches, and the resulting paper would be so thick it would nearly reach from the earth to the sun!

Problem representation often provides *the* stumbling block to problem solution (Bourne et al., 1983). Once you realize you're faced with a problem, your first step should be to represent it in a variety of ways. Eliminate nonessential information. Try to relate the problem to other problems you have solved before. Having done so, if the solution is still not obvious you may have to develop some strategy to move from your representation of the problem to its solution. We now turn to how one might go about generating possible problem solutions.

Before You Go On

In the context of problem solving, what is meant by problem representation?

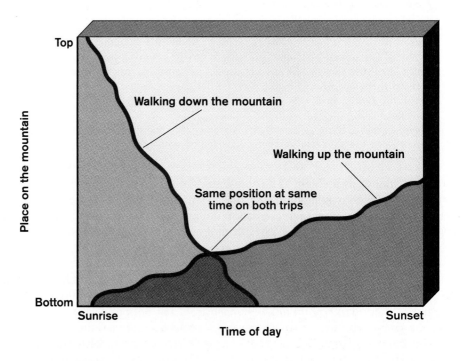

Figure 7.8

One way to pictorially represent the problem of the mountain-climbing monk in order to make its solution more accessible.

Some problems—where should I go to college? or where should I get a job?—are *ill-defined* in the sense that we often have no clear idea where we are starting, or how we should progress toward our goal of making a good choice.

Problem-Solving Strategies

Once you have represented the initial state of a problem and have a clear idea of what an acceptable goal state might be, you still have to figure out how to get to that goal. You might spend a few minutes guessing wildly at a solution, but soon you'll have to settle on some strategy. In this context, a **strategy** is a systematic plan for generating possible solutions that can be tested to see if they are correct. The main advantage of cognitive strategies is that they permit the problem solver to exercise some degree of control over the task at hand. They allow solvers to choose the skills and knowledge they will bring to bear on any particular problem at any time (Gagné, 1984). There are several strategies one might choose to try. We'll consider two types of strategies: algorithms and heuristics.

> **strategy** *in problem solving, a systematic plan for generating possible solutions that can be tested to see if they are correct*

    Algorithms. An **algorithm** is a strategy that guarantees that eventually you will arrive at a solution if the strategy is correctly applied. Algorithms systematically explore and evaluate all possible solutions until the correct one is found. It is sometimes referred to as a *generate-test strategy,* in which one generates hypotheses about solutions and then tests each one in turn. Given their speed of computation, most computer programs designed to solve problems use algorithmic strategies.

> **algorithm** *a problem-solving strategy in which all possible solutions are generated and tested until an acceptable solution appears*

    Simple anagram problems (letters of a word shown in a scrambled fashion) can be solved using an algorithmic strategy. "What English word has been scrambled to make *uleb*?" With sufficient patience, you can systematically rearrange these four letters until you hit on a correct solution: *leub, lueb, elub, uleb, buel, beul, blue.* There it is, *blue.* With only four letters to deal with, finding a solution generally doesn't take very long; there are only 24 possible arrangements of four letters ($4 \times 3 \times 2 \times 1 = 24$).

On the other hand, consider the eight-letter anagram *teralbay*. In fact, there are 40,320 possible combinations of these eight letters: $8 \times 7 \times 6 \times 5 \times 4 \times 3 \times 2 \times 1 = 40,320$ (Reynolds & Flagg, 1983). Unless your system for moving letters around just happens to start in a good place, you could spend a lot of time trying to come up with a combination that produces an English word. If we were dealing with a ten-letter word, there would be 3,628,800 possible combinations to check!

Imagine that you go to the supermarket to buy a jar of horseradish. You're quite sure the store has horseradish, but you have no idea where to find it. One plan would be to go up and down every aisle of the store, checking first the top shelf, then the second, then the third, until you spied the horseradish. This (algorithm) strategy would work if the store carried horseradish and if you searched carefully enough. There must be a better way to solve such problems. Here's where heuristic strategies come in.

heuristic *an informal, economical, yet reasonable, method of testing problem solutions without the guarantee of success*

Heuristics. A **heuristic** is an informal, rule-of-thumb strategy of generating and testing problem solutions. Heuristics are more economical for solving problems than are algorithms, but when one uses a heuristic, there is no guarantee of success. On the other hand, heuristics are usually much less time consuming than algorithm strategies and do lead searches for goals in a logical, sensible way.

A heuristic strategy for finding horseradish in a supermarket might take you to various sections in the store in the order you believed to be most reasonable. You might start with spices, but you would be disappointed. Next, you might look among the fresh vegetables. Then, upon recalling that horseradish needs to be refrigerated, you go next to the dairy case, and there you'll find the horseradish. You would not have wasted time searching the cereal aisle or the frozen food section—real possibilities if you tried an algorithmic strategy. Another, more reasonable, heuristic would be to ask an employee where the horseradish is kept.

If you tried the *teralbay* anagram problem, it is likely you used a heuristic strategy. To do so, you rely on your experience with the English language. You seriously consider only those letter combinations you know occur frequently. You generate and test the most common combinations first. You just don't worry much about the possibility that the solution may contain a combination such as *brty*. Nor do you search for a word with an *aae* string in it. You explore words that end in *able* because you know these to be fairly common. But that doesn't work. What about *br* words? No, that doesn't work. How about words with *tray* in them? *Traybeal*? No. *Baletray*? No. "Oh! Now I see it: *betrayal*." This heuristic strategy is a

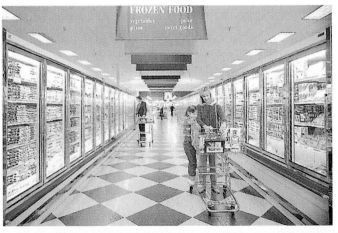

The problem of searching a large supermarket to find a specific item would not be solved quickly if one employed an algorithmic strategy. Although finding a solution is not guaranteed, heuristic strategies are typically less time consuming.

means-ends analysis, a strategy in which one always keeps the final goal in mind, but first works toward reaching subgoals (Newell & Simon, 1972). In the *teralbay* example, subgoals are letter combinations that make sense or are commonly found. Once subgoals are reached, they are manipulated in an attempt to reach the final goal. The example of the search for horseradish also involved a means-ends analysis: first find the right section of the store, then search for the specific product.

Before You Go On

How are algorithmic and heuristic strategies used to solve problems?

Barriers to Effective Problem Solving

It is difficult, often impossible, to solve problems without relying heavily on one's memory. If you couldn't remember the recipe for something you wanted for dinner, you'd have a hard time buying the correct ingredients when you went to the store. Regardless of the type of problem or the strategy employed to solve it, solving problems effectively requires that we use our memories. There are times, however, when previous experiences (and memories of them) create difficulties in problem solving. We'll look at three such cases.

Mental Set and Functional Fixedness

In Topic 3B, we saw that our perceptions can be influenced by expectations, or mental set. We said that we often perceive what we are set to perceive. The concept of mental set is also very relevant in problem solving. A **mental set** is a tendency to perceive or respond to something in a given, or set, way. It is, in essence, a cognitive predisposition. We may have or develop expectations that interfere with effective problem solving.

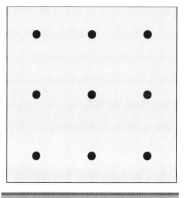

Figure 7.9

Without lifting your pen or pencil from the page, connect these nine dots with four (4) straight lines. (From Scheerer, 1963).

mental set *a predisposed (set) way to perceive or respond to something; an expectation*

EXPERIENCING PSYCHOLOGY

By Their Label Shall Ye Know Them

Here are four simple drawings.

a Hat, a Four, a Table, and a Trowel

Reproduce them on 3 × 5 inch index cards. The task here is to ask several people to try to remember and then reproduce, as best they can, the images that you show them. For half your subjects, hand them a card and, in order, name the objects as:

a Bee Hive, a Seven, an Hourglass, and a Pine Tree

For the other half of your subjects do exactly the same thing, except identify the objects as:

Once you've presented each card, wait for about 2 minutes, then provide your subjects with blank cards and ask them to reproduce the four drawings as best they can. To what extent did your verbal label of the image influence the drawings that were reproduced from memory?

Figure 7.9 provides an example of how an inappropriate mental set can interfere with problem solving. When first presented with this problem, most people make an assumption (form a mental set). They assume the nine dots form a square and that their lines somehow must stay within that square. Only when this mental set is "broken" can the problem be solved. Figure 7.13 at the end of this Topic provides one solution to the nine-dot problem.

Mental sets do not necessarily interfere with problem solving. The appropriate mental set can be facilitating. For example, if I were to have told you to look beyond the confines of any imagined square when attempting the nine-dot problem, that mental set—which seems strange out of context—could have made the problem easier to solve.

Functional fixedness is a type of mental set defined by Duncker (1945) as the inability to discover an appropriate new use for an object because of experience using the object in some other function. The problem solver fails to see a solution to a problem because he or she has "fixed" some "function" to an object that makes it difficult to see how it could help with the problem at hand.

A standard example is one used by Maier (1931). Two strings are hung from the ceiling. The problem is that they are so far apart a subject cannot reach both of them at the same time. The goal is to do just that: to hold on to both strings at once. If there were nothing else in the room, this problem might never get solved. However, there are other objects in the room that the subject can use, including a pair of pliers (see Figure 7.10). One solution to this problem is to tie the pliers to one string and start the pliers swinging like a pendulum. As the person holds the other string, the string with the pliers attached can be grasped as it swings over to the person. Because many people fail to see pliers as useful (functioning) for anything but turning nuts and bolts, they fail to see the pliers as a potential pendulum weight and thus may fail to solve the problem. They have "fixed" the "function" of the pliers in their mind.

Another famous example that demonstrates functional fixedness was reported by Duncker (1945). Here, someone is provided with a box of tacks, a candle, and some matches. The task is to use these materials to mount the candle on the wall and light it. Obviously one cannot just tack a candle to the wall. The solution to

functional fixedness *a type of mental set that interferes with the discovery of a new use for an object because of the experience of using that object for some other function*

Figure 7.10

Maier's two-string problem. The person is to manage to get both strings in his grasp. They are separated so that when one string is held, the other cannot be reached. See text for solution. (After Maier, 1931.)

Figure 7.11

The materials provided in the candle problem—and one solution. (After Duncker, 1945.)

this problem requires breaking the mental set of functional fixedness for the box containing the tacks, seeing it as a potential candleholder, tacking it to the wall, and mounting the candle on it (Figure 7.11).

A number of experiments (e.g., Glucksberg & Danks, 1968) have shown that some subtle changes in the way in which the materials are presented have an effect on solving this problem. When the box of tacks is labeled *tacks,* the problem is much more difficult to solve. Using an empty box and having the tacks scattered about increases the likelihood that subjects will overcome the functional fixedness of seeing the box as something that holds things.

Before You Go On

How might mental sets or functional fixedness hinder problem solving?

Biased Heuristics and Decision Making

For some of the problems we encounter in real life, we are provided with possibilities from which we must choose a correct or "best" alternative. Looked at this way, we see that some decision-making tasks are much like the problems we have been considering in this Topic. We've seen that problem solving requires us to use our past experience to devise strategies for reaching goal states. Occasionally our heuristic strategies—those rules of thumb used to guide problem solving—are biased because of perceptions of past experience. Such biases create a barrier to effective problem solving.

Some strategies we use to make decisions require us to estimate the probability of events, and many of these strategies are notoriously poor (Hastie & Park, 1986; Payne et al., 1992). Most of the research on judging probabilities and frequencies has been reported by Daniel Kahneman and Amos Tversky (1973, 1979, 1984; Tversky & Kahneman, 1974).

The **availability heuristic** is the assumption that things that readily come to mind are more common, or frequently occurring, than things difficult to recall or think of. For example, I show you a list that includes the names of 19 famous women and 20 less famous men. Later, you will almost certainly overestimate the number of women on the list, because those famous names were more available to you. The media (newspapers, TV, radio, and so on) often draw our attention to events (make them available) in such a way that we tend to overestimate their frequency of occurrence. When reports of terrorist bombings at foreign airports make

⊚⊚⊚⊚ **Thinking Critically** ⊚⊚⊚⊚

What connections can you make between mental sets and functional fixedness and the obstacles to memory retrieval discussed in the previous chapter?

availability heuristic *the assumption that whatever comes to mind readily must be more common or probable than what does not easily come to mind* the news, many Americans cancel their plans for European vacations, overestimating the risk of flying to Europe. Even without terrorists, most people will overestimate the number of airplane crashes that occur each year compared to the number of automobile crashes that occur, simply because we tend to hear more about the airplane accidents; they are more available in our memories.

representativeness heuristic *the assumption that judgments made about a very typical member of some category will hold for all members of that category*

The **representativeness heuristic** is the assumption that any judgments made about the most prototypic member of a category will hold for all members of the category. You know that a group of men consists of 70 percent lawyers and 30 percent engineers. You are told that one of the men, chosen at random, has hobbies that include carpentry, sailing, and mathematical puzzles. Is this man an engineer or a lawyer? Because you believe these hobbies to be representative of engineers, not lawyers, you may say that the man is an engineer, even though (by chance) the likelihood that he is a lawyer is more than twice (7 to 3) the chance that he is an engineer.

Which group includes more tobacco chewers, professional baseball players, or college students? The answer is college students (because there are so many of them, even though a smaller percentage uses chewing tobacco). If I flip a coin (it's a fair coin) and it turns up heads five times in a row, what is the chance of getting tails on the next flip? The probability is no better than it's been all along, 50–50 (the fact that heads have appeared the previous five times is of absolutely no consequence to the coin).

positive test strategy *the heuristic of sticking with an acceptable decision or solution, even if better ones may exist*

There are other heuristics that can bias our decision making and interfere with problem solving. A multiple-choice test item is the sort of problem that requires you to decide which of a number of alternatives best answers a question. A problem-solving heuristic that may cause trouble is called the **positive test strategy**—the strategy that claims that if something works, don't drop it to try something else (Klayman & Ha, 1987). This is the heuristic that suggests "If it isn't broken, don't fix it." This approach is often a sensible one, but there are instances when even better solutions—more useful decisions—could be found if only one continued to look. Have you fallen into the "trap" of saying that alternative A was the correct answer to a multiple-choice item simply because it was correct, only to discover later that alternatives B and C were also correct, thus making alternative D, "all of the above," the best answer to the question?

Successful problem solving requires that we break out of the restraints imposed by improper mental sets, functional fixedness, and some heuristic strategies. To be able to overcome these barriers reflects an ability to solve problems creatively, and it is to this subject that we turn next.

Before You Go On

Which heuristics actually hinder problem solving?

Overcoming Barriers with Creative Problem Solving

Creative solutions to problems are new, innovative, and useful. In the context of problem solving, creative means more than unusual, rare, or different. Someone may generate a very original plan to solve a given problem, but unless that plan works, we shouldn't view it as creative (Newell et al., 1962; Vinacke, 1974). Creative solutions should be put to the same test as more ordinary solutions: do they solve the problem at hand?

Creative solutions generally involve a reorganization of problem elements. As I mentioned earlier, it is often at the stage of problem representation that creativity is most noticeable. Seeing a problem in a new light, or combining elements of a problem in a new and different way, can lead to creative solutions.

Creative problem solutions must be more than unusual or different—they must provide a workable solution to the problem at hand. (Rube Goldberg/Reprinted with special permission of King Features Syndicate.)

There is virtually no correlation between creative problem solving and intelligence (Barron & Harrington, 1981; Horn, 1976; Kershner & Ledger, 1985). At least there are virtually no significant correlations between tests for creativity and tests for intelligence.

We say that creative problem solving often involves **divergent thinking**; that is, starting with one idea and generating from it a number of alternative possibilities and new ideas (Dirkes, 1978; Guilford, 1959b). When we engage in **convergent**

divergent thinking *the creation of many ideas or possible solutions from one idea*

convergent thinking *the reduction or focusing of many ideas or solutions into one, or a few*

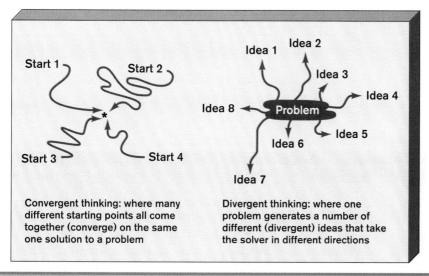

Figure 7.12

A schematic representation of convergent and divergent thinking in the context of problem solving.

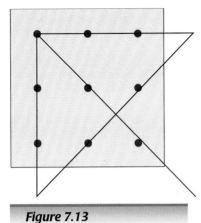

Figure 7.13

A possible solution to the nine-dot problem. Note that one has to break the "mental set" that the four lines must remain inside the rectangle defined by the dots.

thinking, we take many ideas, or bits of information, and try to reduce them to just one possible solution (Figure 7.12). Obviously, convergent thinking has its place in problem solving. But for creative problem solving, divergent thinking is generally more useful because many possibilities are explored. Remember, however, that all these new possibilities for a problem's solution need to be judged ultimately in terms of whether or not they really solve the problem.

Creative problem solving can be divided into four interrelated stages. This view of the problem-solving process is an old one in psychology, but it has held up rather nicely over the years (Wallas, 1926).

1. *Preparation:* This is not unlike problem representation. The basic elements of the problem are considered. Past experience is relevant, but should not become restrictive. At this stage of problem solving, it is important to overcome negative effects of mental set and functional fixedness. Various ways of expressing the problem are considered, but a solution is not found.

2. *Incubation:* In this stage, the problem is "put away" and not thought about. Perhaps fatigue that developed during failed efforts can then dissipate. Perhaps inappropriate strategies can be forgotten. Perhaps unconscious processes can be brought to bear on the problem. Why setting aside a problem may lead to its creative solution we cannot say for sure. We do know, however, that it is often very useful (Koestler, 1964; Yaniv & Meyer, 1987).

3. *Illumination:* This is the most mysterious stage of the process. Like insight, a potential solution to a problem seems to materialize as if from nowhere. A critical analogy becomes apparent, as does a new path to the problem's solution (Glass et al., 1979; Metcalfe & Wiebe, 1987).

4. *Verification*: Now the proposed solution must be tested, or verified, to see if it does in fact provide an answer to the question posed by the problem.

You have probably noted that there is really nothing extraordinary about Wallas's description of the creative problem-solving process. It sounds very much like the sort of thing anyone should do when faced with a problem to solve. The truth is, however, that we often fail to go through these stages in any systematic fashion. To do so consciously often helps problem solving. Good problem solvers show more conscious awareness of what they are doing during the course of problem solving than do poor problem solvers (Glaser, 1984).

Before You Go On

What is involved in creative problem solving?

TOPIC 7B SUMMARY

In this Topic we have examined two complex cognitive processes: language use and problem solving. Language use is an excellent example of structured, rule-governed behavior at three levels of analysis: sound (phonemes), meaning (morphemes), and morpheme or word order (syntax). All language users demonstrate a knowledge—a competence—of the rules of their language, whether or not they can state explicitly what those rules are. It is this competence, this implicit knowledge of the structure of one's language, that is most difficult to account for when one considers how language is acquired.

Problem solving is also a complex cognitive process requiring that we rely on our perceptions, learning, and memories. To solve a problem necessitates that we understand a situation as it exists, understand the situation as we would like it to be, and then discover some way to reach this desired goal state. To do so effectively often requires that we represent the nature of the problem correctly, generate an appropriate problem-solving strategy, and overcome inhibiting influences of mental set, functional fixedness, or the choice of a misleading heuristic strategy.

CHAPTER SUMMARY

Topic 7A

Briefly describe Spearman's, Thurstone's, Guilford's, and Vernon's models of intelligence.

Spearman viewed intelligence as consisting of one general factor ("g") and a number of specific abilities ("s"). Thurstone saw intelligence as a combination of seven unique and primary mental abilities. Guilford argued that there are as many as 120 cognitive skills that constitute one's intelligence. Vernon suggested that intellectual skills or cognitive abilities can be arranged in a hierarchy from general at the top to specific at the bottom. */pp. 228–231*

Briefly describe Sternberg's and Gardner's models of intelligence.

Sternberg argues that intelligence should be conceptualized as an organized set of three cognitive processes: (1) a componential, "academic" type of intelligence, (2) an experiential, "creative" type of intelligence, and (3) a contextual, "practical" type of intelligence. Gardner also proposes multiple intelligences: mathematical, verbal, spatial, musical, bodily, interpersonal, and intrapersonal. */pp. 231–233*

What determines the quality of psychological tests?

Psychological tests are objective, standardized measures of samples of behaviors. To be a "good," quality test, an instrument must demonstrate (1) reliability—that it measures something consistently, (2) validity—that it measures what it says it's measuring, and (3) adequate norms that can be used to assign meaning to an individual score. */pp. 233-234*

Briefly describe the Stanford-Binet Intelligence Scale.

The Stanford-Binet is the oldest of the tests of general intelligence (commonly called IQ tests). Its most recent (1986) revision yields an overall score ("g") as well as subscores for a number of abilities assumed to underlie general intelligence. The test consists of 15 subtests—each assessing a specific cognitive task. Scores on the test compare the performance of an individual to that of others of the same age level. */pp. 234–236*

What are the major features of the Wechsler intelligence scales?

The three Wechsler scales are individually administered tests of general intelligence, each appropriate for a specific age group. Each scale consists of verbal or performance subtests of varied content. Hence, three scores can be determined: an overall score, a score on the verbal subtests, and a score on the performance subtests. Scores on the Wechsler tests are standard scores that compare one's abilities to those of others of the same age. */pp. 236–237*

What is the difference between a paper-and-pencil intelligence test and an aptitude test?

Most educational aptitude tests (such as the SAT or ACT) are essentially paper-and-pencil tests of general intellectual abilities that are used to make predictions about future academic performance. That is, the difference between the two types lies in how the scores are used. */pp. 238–239*

Are there gender differences in IQ?

No and yes. There are no significant differences between men and women on virtually any test that yields a general IQ score. There are some specific skills and abilities that demonstrate sex differences, but the differences are "on the average" and quite slight. Exceptions are spatial relations skills and advanced math (males score higher) and verbal fluency and writing skills (females score higher). */pp. 240–241*

Does intelligence increase, decrease, or remain the same with increasing age?

Overall intelligence does tend to decline slightly as one approaches the age of 50 or 60. Various skills and abilities are differentially affected by age. Fluid intelligence declines with age, whereas crystallized intelligence remains constant or even increases slightly with age. Although with advanced age one may have a more difficult time encoding new information, there is little reason to believe that other intellectual skills will be diminished. */pp. 241–242*

Briefly summarize the data on racial differences in IQ scores.

There are reliable differences between the IQs of blacks and whites, with most studies putting the average difference at about 15 points, in favor of whites, whereas Asian American students, on average, perform better on tests of academic achievement, mathematics in particular. The data on group differences tell us nothing, however, about their source. Arguments have been made favoring genetic and environmental causes, including different emphases put on testing in different cultures. */pp. 242–244*

What defines the mentally gifted?

Giftedness can mean several things in addition to overall intellectual ability as measured by IQ tests (usually an IQ over 130). Other abilities in which individuals may be gifted include psychomotor skills, the visual and performing arts, leadership, creativity, and abilities in specific academic areas. The Terman-Stanford research tells us that persons who are mentally gifted experience other physical, educational, social, and economic advantages. */pp. 244–246*

How do we define mental retardation? What causes it?

Mental retardation is indicated by below-average intellectual functioning (IQ scores less than 70), originating during the developmental period (within 18 years) and associated with impairment in adaptive behavior (as well as academic behaviors). In addition to genetic causes (as in Down syndrome and Fragile X syndrome), most known causes of mental retardation involve the health of the parents at conception and the care of the mother and fetus during pregnancy and delivery. Drugs, lack of oxygen, poor nutrition, and the like have been implicated in mental retardation. In other words, many causes of mental retardation appear to be preventable. */pp. 246–249*

Topic 7B

What are the defining characteristics of language?

Language is a complex and creative cognitive skill used for communication. A language consists of a large number of arbitrary symbols, usually words, that stand for, or label, our conceptualization of objects and events, that have meaning for users of that language, and that are combined in accordance with certain rules. The use of language is a generative process that, among other things, allows us to communicate about the "not here and the not now." */pp. 250–252*

How are rules and structure reflected in the use of phonemes, morphemes, and syntax?

A phoneme is the smallest unit of sound in the spoken form of a language, i.e., a speech sound. How phonemes can be combined in a language follows strict rules. Morphemes are the smallest units of meaning in a language, including words, prefixes, and suffixes. How morphemes are ordered, or structured, in language affects their meaning. Syntax refers to the rules that govern the way morphemes are ordered, or structured, to produce sentences. Language speakers are competent in the use of these rules even though they may not be able to state them explicitly. We can determine intuitively (without being able to explain why) when utterances are syntactically correct and when they are not. We can tell when two sentences that take different forms are communicating the same idea or message. We can identify ambiguous sentences and can often remove that ambiguity, but only when we are aware of a larger context in which the utterance occurred. */pp. 252–253*

What is the study of "pragmatics," and what does it tell us about language use?

Pragmatics is the study of how the social situation, or context, in which language is used influences the meaning of what is being said. An appreciation of that context allows us to recognize the use of sarcasm, simile, metaphors, and the like. Differences in language use as a function of gender are very small and are related to pragmatics. The language of women tends to be less assertive, more self-disclosing, and contains more qualifiers than does the language of men, who, in most situations, tend to be more talkative and interrupt others more than women do. */pp. 253–254*

What are some of the landmark events that occur during language acquisition?

Although infants cry and babble, the first linguistic utterances are found in holophrastic speech, which occurs when one word is used to communicate a range of feelings, intentions, and meanings. A two-word stage of development shows structure in word ordering–a syntax that is not merely a copy of adult language structure. From the two-word utterance on, language development is extremely rapid. By the time a child is 5 years old, he or she will know thousands of words (will understand more than she or he will produce) and be able to combine

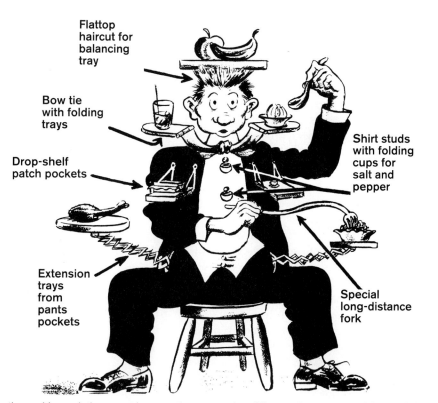

Flattop
haircut for
balancing
tray

Bow tie
with folding
trays

Drop-shelf
patch pockets

Extension
trays
from
pants
pockets

Shirt studs
with folding
cups for
salt and
pepper

Special
long-distance
fork

Creative problem solutions must be more than unusual or different—they must provide a workable solution to the problem at hand. (Rube Goldberg/Reprinted with special permission of King Features Syndicate.)

There is virtually no correlation between creative problem solving and intelligence (Barron & Harrington, 1981; Horn, 1976; Kershner & Ledger, 1985). At least there are virtually no significant correlations between tests for creativity and tests for intelligence.

We say that creative problem solving often involves **divergent thinking**; that is, starting with one idea and generating from it a number of alternative possibilities and new ideas (Dirkes, 1978; Guilford, 1959b). When we engage in **convergent**

divergent thinking *the creation of many ideas or possible solutions from one idea*

convergent thinking *the reduction or focusing of many ideas or solutions into one, or a few*

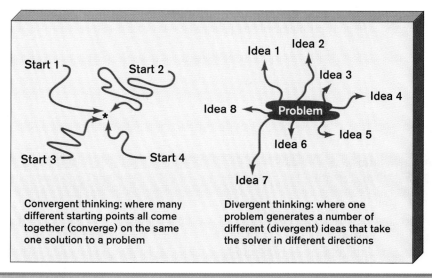

Idea 1   Idea 2

Start 1   Start 2   Idea 3

Idea 8 ← Problem   Idea 4

Idea 5

Start 3   Start 4   Idea 6

Idea 7

Convergent thinking: where many different starting points all come together (converge) on the same one solution to a problem

Divergent thinking: where one problem generates a number of different (divergent) ideas that take the solver in different directions

Figure 7.12

A schematic representation of convergent and divergent thinking in the context of problem solving.

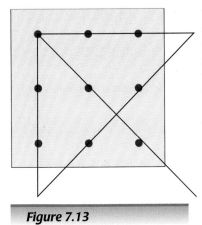

Figure 7.13

A possible solution to the nine-dot problem. Note that one has to break the "mental set" that the four lines must remain inside the rectangle defined by the dots.

thinking, we take many ideas, or bits of information, and try to reduce them to just one possible solution (Figure 7.12). Obviously, convergent thinking has its place in problem solving. But for creative problem solving, divergent thinking is generally more useful because many possibilities are explored. Remember, however, that all these new possibilities for a problem's solution need to be judged ultimately in terms of whether or not they really solve the problem.

Creative problem solving can be divided into four interrelated stages. This view of the problem-solving process is an old one in psychology, but it has held up rather nicely over the years (Wallas, 1926).

1. *Preparation:* This is not unlike problem representation. The basic elements of the problem are considered. Past experience is relevant, but should not become restrictive. At this stage of problem solving, it is important to overcome negative effects of mental set and functional fixedness. Various ways of expressing the problem are considered, but a solution is not found.

2. *Incubation:* In this stage, the problem is "put away" and not thought about. Perhaps fatigue that developed during failed efforts can then dissipate. Perhaps inappropriate strategies can be forgotten. Perhaps unconscious processes can be brought to bear on the problem. Why setting aside a problem may lead to its creative solution we cannot say for sure. We do know, however, that it is often very useful (Koestler, 1964; Yaniv & Meyer, 1987).

3. *Illumination:* This is the most mysterious stage of the process. Like insight, a potential solution to a problem seems to materialize as if from nowhere. A critical analogy becomes apparent, as does a new path to the problem's solution (Glass et al., 1979; Metcalfe & Wiebe, 1987).

4. *Verification*: Now the proposed solution must be tested, or verified, to see if it does in fact provide an answer to the question posed by the problem.

You have probably noted that there is really nothing extraordinary about Wallas's description of the creative problem-solving process. It sounds very much like the sort of thing anyone should do when faced with a problem to solve. The truth is, however, that we often fail to go through these stages in any systematic fashion. To do so consciously often helps problem solving. Good problem solvers show more conscious awareness of what they are doing during the course of problem solving than do poor problem solvers (Glaser, 1984).

Before You Go On

What is involved in creative problem solving?

TOPIC 7B SUMMARY

In this Topic we have examined two complex cognitive processes: language use and problem solving. Language use is an excellent example of structured, rule-governed behavior at three levels of analysis: sound (phonemes), meaning (morphemes), and morpheme or word order (syntax). All language users demonstrate a knowledge—a competence—of the rules of their language, whether or not they can state explicitly what those rules are. It is this competence, this implicit knowledge of the structure of one's language, that is most difficult to account for when one considers how language is acquired.

Problem solving is also a complex cognitive process requiring that we rely on our perceptions, learning, and memories. To solve a problem necessitates that we understand a situation as it exists, understand the situation as we would like it to be, and then discover some way to reach this desired goal state. To do so effectively often requires that we represent the nature of the problem correctly, generate an appropriate problem-solving strategy, and overcome inhibiting influences of mental set, functional fixedness, or the choice of a misleading heuristic strategy.

CHAPTER SUMMARY

Topic 7A

Briefly describe Spearman's, Thurstone's, Guilford's, and Vernon's models of intelligence.

Spearman viewed intelligence as consisting of one general factor ("g") and a number of specific abilities ("s"). Thurstone saw intelligence as a combination of seven unique and primary mental abilities. Guilford argued that there are as many as 120 cognitive skills that constitute one's intelligence. Vernon suggested that intellectual skills or cognitive abilities can be arranged in a hierarchy from general at the top to specific at the bottom. */pp. 228–231*

Briefly describe Sternberg's and Gardner's models of intelligence.

Sternberg argues that intelligence should be conceptualized as an organized set of three cognitive processes: (1) a componential, "academic" type of intelligence, (2) an experiential, "creative" type of intelligence, and (3) a contextual, "practical" type of intelligence. Gardner also proposes multiple intelligences: mathematical, verbal, spatial, musical, bodily, interpersonal, and intrapersonal. */pp. 231–233*

What determines the quality of psychological tests?

Psychological tests are objective, standardized measures of samples of behaviors. To be a "good," quality test, an instrument must demonstrate (1) reliability—that it measures something consistently, (2) validity—that it measures what it says it's measuring, and (3) adequate norms that can be used to assign meaning to an individual score. */pp. 233–234*

Briefly describe the Stanford-Binet Intelligence Scale.

The Stanford-Binet is the oldest of the tests of general intelligence (commonly called IQ tests). Its most recent (1986) revision yields an overall score ("g") as well as subscores for a number of abilities assumed to underlie general intelligence. The test consists of 15 subtests—each assessing a specific cognitive task. Scores on the test compare the performance of an individual to that of others of the same age level. */pp. 234–236*

What are the major features of the Wechsler intelligence scales?

The three Wechsler scales are individually administered tests of general intelligence, each appropriate for a specific age group. Each scale consists of verbal or performance subtests of varied content. Hence, three scores can be determined: an overall score, a score on the verbal subtests, and a score on the performance subtests. Scores on the Wechsler tests are standard scores that compare one's abilities to those of others of the same age. */pp. 236–237*

What is the difference between a paper-and-pencil intelligence test and an aptitude test?

Most educational aptitude tests (such as the SAT or ACT) are essentially paper-and-pencil tests of general intellectual abilities that are used to make predictions about future academic performance. That is, the difference between the two types lies in how the scores are used. */pp. 238–239*

Are there gender differences in IQ?

No and yes. There are no significant differences between men and women on virtually any test that yields a general IQ score. There are some specific skills and abilities that demonstrate sex differences, but the differences are "on the average" and quite slight. Exceptions are spatial relations skills and advanced math (males score higher) and verbal fluency and writing skills (females score higher). */pp. 240–241*

Does intelligence increase, decrease, or remain the same with increasing age?

Overall intelligence does tend to decline slightly as one approaches the age of 50 or 60. Various skills and abilities are differentially affected by age. Fluid intelligence declines with age, whereas crystallized intelligence remains constant or even increases slightly with age. Although with advanced age one may have a more difficult time encoding new information, there is little reason to believe that other intellectual skills will be diminished. */pp. 241–242*

Briefly summarize the data on racial differences in IQ scores.

There are reliable differences between the IQs of blacks and whites, with most studies putting the average difference at about 15 points, in favor of whites, whereas Asian American students, on average, perform better on tests of academic achievement, mathematics in particular. The data on group differences tell us nothing, however, about their source. Arguments have been made favoring genetic and environmental causes, including different emphases put on testing in different cultures. */pp. 242–244*

What defines the mentally gifted?

Giftedness can mean several things in addition to overall intellectual ability as measured by IQ tests (usually an IQ over 130). Other abilities in which individuals may be gifted include psychomotor skills, the visual and performing arts, leadership, creativity, and abilities in specific academic areas. The Terman-Stanford research tells us that persons who are mentally gifted experience other physical, educational, social, and economic advantages. */pp. 244–246*

How do we define mental retardation? What causes it?

Mental retardation is indicated by below-average intellectual functioning (IQ scores less than 70), originating during the developmental period (within 18 years) and associated with impairment in adaptive behavior (as well as academic behaviors). In addition to genetic causes (as in Down syndrome and Fragile X syndrome), most known causes of mental retardation involve the health of the parents at conception and the care of the mother and fetus during pregnancy and delivery. Drugs, lack of oxygen, poor nutrition, and the like have been implicated in mental retardation. In other words, many causes of mental retardation appear to be preventable. */pp. 246–249*

Topic 7B

What are the defining characteristics of language?

Language is a complex and creative cognitive skill used for communication. A language consists of a large number of arbitrary symbols, usually words, that stand for, or label, our conceptualization of objects and events, that have meaning for users of that language, and that are combined in accordance with certain rules. The use of language is a generative process that, among other things, allows us to communicate about the "not here and the not now." */pp. 250–252*

How are rules and structure reflected in the use of phonemes, morphemes, and syntax?

A phoneme is the smallest unit of sound in the spoken form of a language, i.e., a speech sound. How phonemes can be combined in a language follows strict rules. Morphemes are the smallest units of meaning in a language, including words, prefixes, and suffixes. How morphemes are ordered, or structured, in language affects their meaning. Syntax refers to the rules that govern the way morphemes are ordered, or structured, to produce sentences. Language speakers are competent in the use of these rules even though they may not be able to state them explicitly. We can determine intuitively (without being able to explain why) when utterances are syntactically correct and when they are not. We can tell when two sentences that take different forms are communicating the same idea or message. We can identify ambiguous sentences and can often remove that ambiguity, but only when we are aware of a larger context in which the utterance occurred. */pp. 252–253*

What is the study of "pragmatics," and what does it tell us about language use?

Pragmatics is the study of how the social situation, or context, in which language is used influences the meaning of what is being said. An appreciation of that context allows us to recognize the use of sarcasm, simile, metaphors, and the like. Differences in language use as a function of gender are very small and are related to pragmatics. The language of women tends to be less assertive, more self-disclosing, and contains more qualifiers than does the language of men, who, in most situations, tend to be more talkative and interrupt others more than women do. */pp. 253–254*

What are some of the landmark events that occur during language acquisition?

Although infants cry and babble, the first linguistic utterances are found in holophrastic speech, which occurs when one word is used to communicate a range of feelings, intentions, and meanings. A two-word stage of development shows structure in word ordering—a syntax that is not merely a copy of adult language structure. From the two-word utterance on, language development is extremely rapid. By the time a child is 5 years old, he or she will know thousands of words (will understand more than she or he will produce) and be able to combine those words in virtually every acceptable sentence structure in the language. */pp. 254–256*

Briefly summarize the theories of language acquisition.

Neither learning nor biological theories can totally account for language acquisition. One's learning history does have an impact on language development, particularly in the formation of words and morphemes (we do not all speak the same language in the same way). At the same time, learning theory is challenged by the cross-cultural regularities that occur in language acquisition—by the fact that all children of all languages develop their languages in the same general, patterned way. The complex process seems too rapid and too regular not to have a strong biological basis. */pp. 256–258*

What are well-defined and ill-defined problems?

A problem has three components: (1) an initial state—the situation as it exists, (2) a goal state—the situation as the problem solver would like it to be, and (3) routes or strategies for getting from the initial state to the goal state. Whether a problem is well defined or ill defined is a matter of the extent to which the elements of the initial state and goal state are well delineated and clearly understood by the problem solver. An example of a well-defined problem might be that which you face when a familiar route home from campus is blocked. An example of an ill-defined problem might be that which you face when you have to write a term paper on the topic of your choice. */pp. 258–259*

In the context of problem solving, what is meant by problem representation?

Problem representation involves the mental activity of thinking about a problem and putting it into familiar terms. */pp. 259–261*

How are algorithmic and heuristic strategies used to solve problems?

Algorithms and heuristics are types of strategies, or systematic plans, we use to solve problems. Algorithms involve a systematic search of all possible solutions until the goal is reached; with algorithms, a solution is guaran-

teed. A heuristic strategy—of which there are many—is a more informal, rule-of-thumb approach that involves generating and testing hypotheses that may lead to a problem solution in a sensible, organized way. */pp. 261–263*

How might mental sets or functional fixedness hinder problem solving?

A mental set is a predisposition to perceive or respond in a particular way. Mental sets develop from past experience and involve the continued use of strategies that have been successful in the past. Because those ways of perceiving or solving a problem that have worked in the past may no longer be appropriate for the problem at hand, mental sets can hinder effective problem solving. Functional fixedness is a type of mental set in which an object is seen as serving only a few fixed functions. */pp. 263–265*

Which heuristics actually hinder problem solving?

We tend to judge as more likely or more probable those events more readily available to us in memory—the "availability heuristic." We also tend to overgeneralize about events that are prototypic representatives of a category or concept—the "representativeness heuristic." Additionally, "positive test strategy" may have us accept a successful solution that is still not the best solution to a problem. */pp. 265–266*

What is involved in creative problem solving?

Divergent thinking in which a large number of alternative possibilities are generated to be tested for usefulness is seen as a useful technique in problem solving. Convergent thinking involves taking a large number of ideas or possibilities and reducing them to one or a few. Problem solving in general, and creative problem solving in particular, has four interrelated stages: (1) preparation (the problem is represented mentally), (2) incubation (the problem is put aside for a while), (3) illumination (a potential solution becomes known), and (4) verification (the potential solution is tested to see if it does solve the problem at hand). */pp. 266–268*

PRACTICING PSYCHOLOGY

Assessing Creativity

As you know, *creativity*, either in the context of problem solving or as an aspect of human intelligence, is a difficult term to define precisely. It is also a difficult term to define operationally. If you were to ask several people the following questions, do you think that you could use their responses to generate an indication of their creativity?

- List all the uses you can think of for a paper clip.
- List all the means of transportation you can think of.
- Make as many four-word sentences as you can in which *all four words* start with the letter *h*. Do not use the same word twice in the same sentence.

- Imagine that you are going camping in the wilderness for a month. What would you take, *excluding* food and clothing?
- How would you explain the word "infinity" to a person who is unfamiliar with the word?
- Imagine that you own an extremely valuable gold coin and that you are going out of town for a month. Where would you hide the coin?

Obviously, there are no right or wrong answers to these questions, thus, none are provided at the back of the book. Can you generate a scheme for scoring answers in terms of creativity?

OUTLINE

've only done one experiment that involved children: a study of word associations. The procedure was simple: present a stimulus word and have a child respond with the first thing that came to mind.

Two undergraduate research assistants went to a local nursery school to collect data. I couldn't go with them that first day because I had a class to teach. When I met the assistants upon their return, they were upset. One said, "It was just awful! The kids won't do it. It was a mess!" I became very paternalistic and reassured the assistants, "Now, now, don't worry, I'll go with you tomorrow and everything will be fine." It wasn't. My assistants were absolutely right. The kids wouldn't do it; they wouldn't play our game.

I approached a 4-year-old. "Hi. How are you? Let's play a game, okay? Would you like to play a game with words?" My first discovery was that 10 percent of the children did not want to play. They simply walked away, back to the sandbox or some other activity. When children did agree to "play," they did some peculiar things. I gave my instructions: "I'm going to say a word, and then you tell me the first word you think of when you hear my word. Okay? My first word is *black.*" After a moment's pause, a child looked up and responded, "My Mommy has a black dress and she wears it to church sometimes."

Human Development

"Okay, that's fine," I'd say, "but next time tell me just one word. Do not tell me a story. If *black* makes you think of your Mommy's dress, just say, 'dress,' okay?" I gave the next word. "The word is *happy*." "Dress," the child quickly responded. "No. No. You have to tell me what happy makes you think of." "I'm happy when we have ice cream."

Some children demonstrated that they were learning the alphabet. "What's the first thing you think of when I say *black?*" The response: "Bee." To *man,* the response was "Em," and so on. Some children came up with sounds I didn't even know how to record. In response to *black,* one child responded with a series of "buh-buh-buh" noises. To *happy,* the response was "hap-hap-puh-puh-puh."

I eventually included more than 300 children in this study, just to see how they would respond to my "word game." By far, most of the responses produced by the young children were not words at all.

The word association task is one of the most straightforward techniques in all of psychology. But some children will "play the game" with their own set of rules, and some may not be ready to play the game at all. I had failed to take into account the cognitive level of my research participants. Doing simple experiments with children is often not as easy as it may sound. To study the behavior of children scientifically requires that we be particularly clever—and very patient. Experimental techniques may not work, so other methods, such as naturalistic observation, may be needed. To varying degrees, similar problems arise throughout our study of human development.

TOPIC 8A   The Development of Children

From conception to death, human beings share certain developmental events that unite us as one species. As I have noted several times, it is also true that each of us is unique. Developmental psychologists are interested in both the common patterns of our growth and development and the ways in which we differ as we grow and develop throughout our lives. We tend to think that a person's development begins at birth. In fact, growth and development begin earlier—at conception, and with the first division of one cell into two, so that is where we will start.

The Stages of Prenatal Development

conception *when the father's sperm cell unites with the mother's ovum to produce a new cell*

zygote *the one-celled product of the union of sperm and ovum at conception*

Human development begins at **conception**, when the father's sperm cell unites with the mother's ovum. At that time, all of the genes on the 23 chromosomes from each parent pair off within a single cell: the **zygote**. We have in that one action the transmission of all inherited characteristics. Within the next 30 hours, the one-celled zygote will divide and become two. In three days, there may be about 10 to 15 cells; after five days, there will be slightly more than 100 (Moore, 1982; Torrey & Feduccia, 1979). No one knows how many cells the human organism has at birth, and few are willing to even hazard a guess; "more than a trillion" is a conservative estimate (Moore, 1982).

prenatal period *the period of development from conception to birth*

The time from conception to birth is the **prenatal period**. Many events that can have lifelong consequences occur during this very sensitive period.

Throughout this discussion I will use *growth* and *development* to mean different things. Growth refers to simple enlargement—getting bigger. Development refers to a differentiation of structure or function. Something develops when it appears for the first time and remains. Thus, we say that the nervous system *develops* between week 2 and week 8 after conception.

Prenatal development is divided into three stages: the *zygote,* the *embryo,* and the *fetus.* Each stage is characterized by its own landmarks of development.

stage of the zygote *prenatal developmental period from conception to the age of 2 weeks*

The **stage of the zygote** is the shortest of the prenatal stages—from conception until approximately two weeks later, when the zygote becomes implanted in the wall of the uterus. At this point, the zygote includes hundreds of cells, and for the first time it is clear that not all of the cells are exact replicas of each other. That is, there is now some differentiation among the cells in the zygote. For example, some cells develop to form the protective placenta, whereas others form the umbilical cord that will supply nourishment to the developing organism.

stage of the embryo *the second prenatal developmental period; from 2 to 8 weeks*

The **stage of the embryo** lasts about six weeks. During this period, the embryo develops at a rapid rate. At the beginning of this stage, we can identify only three types of cells: (1) those that will become the nervous system, the sense organs, and the skin; (2) those that will become the internal organs; and (3) those that will become the muscles, skeleton, and blood vessels. By the end of the embryonic stage we can identify the face, eyes, ears, fingers, and toes.

During this stage—conservatively, within the first three months—the unborn is most sensitive to external or environmental influences. If prenatal problems (i.e., birth defects) occur, they are most likely to develop during this stage. For example, if the heart, eyes, and hands do not differentiate and develop during this embryonic period, there will be no way to compensate later. The central nervous system is at risk throughout the prenatal period—particularly in weeks 3 through 6.

Two months after conception, the stage of the embryo draws to a close. The 1-inch-long embryo now has enough of a primitive nervous system to respond to a light touch, exhibiting a simple reflex movement.

stage of the fetus *the third prenatal developmental period; from week 8 until birth*

The final stage of prenatal development is the longest, the **stage of the fetus**. It includes months 3 through 9. Not only do the organs of the body continue to in-

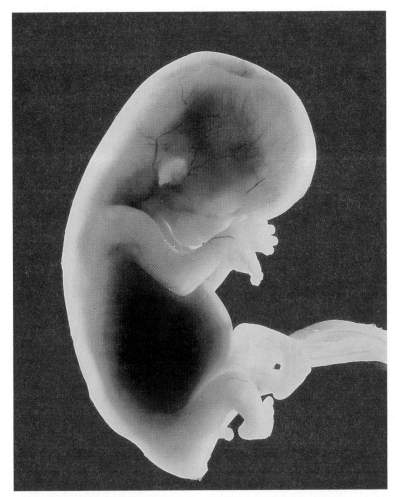

A human fetus at about eleven weeks. At this point the fetus weighs about 35 grams, and begins moving about—these movements can seldom be detected by the mother, however.

crease in complexity and size, but they begin to function. The arms and legs move spontaneously by the end of the third month. In two more months, these movements will be substantial enough for the mother to feel them. At the end of the fifth month, the fetus is 10 inches long. Internal organs have developed, but not to the point of sustaining life outside the uterus. The brain has developed, but neurons within it have not formed many synapses.

Development and growth continue through the last few months of pregnancy. The most noticeable change—at least to the mother—is the significant increase in weight and overall movement of the fetus. Sometime during the seventh month, most fetuses have reached the point of **viability**—the point at which, if they were forced to do so, they could survive, without interference or medical intervention, if they were born. During its last few weeks in the uterus, the fetus grows more slowly. Its movements may be more powerful, but overall activity is slowed because of the cramped quarters in which the fetus finds itself. After nearly 270 days, the fetus is ready to enter the world as a newborn.

viability *the ability to survive without medical interference or intervention*

Before You Go On

Describe the stages of prenatal development.

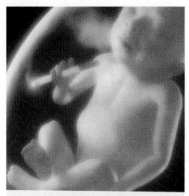

WOULD YOU GIVE A CIGARETTE TO YOUR UNBORN CHILD?
YOU DO EVERY TIME YOU SMOKE!

AMERICAN CANCER SOCIETY

Women who smoke when they are pregnant significantly increase their chances of having miscarriages, stillbirths, low-weight babies, and babies who die shortly after birth.

fetal alcohol syndrome (FAS) *a cluster of symptoms (e.g., low birth weight, poor muscle tone, and intellectual retardation) associated with a child born to a mother who was a heavy drinker of alcohol during pregnancy*

Environmental Influences on Prenatal Development

In most cases, the growth and development of the human organism from zygote to fetus progresses according to the blueprint laid down in the genes, but in the prenatal stage, the human organism is not immune to influences from the environment. Most external influences on prenatal development have negative consequences.

Nourishment

Never meant to be taken literally, the old expression, "You are what you eat" does have some truth to it. By the same token, before we are born, we are what our mothers eat. Maternal malnutrition often leads to increases in miscarriages, stillbirths, and premature births. At best, we can expect the newborn child of a malnourished mother to be similarly malnourished (e.g., Lozoff, 1989).

Deficiencies in specific vitamins and minerals affect the prenatal organism (Bratic, 1982). For example, a mother's calcium deficiencies affect the development of bones and teeth in the fetus. As is the case for many nutrients, it may very well be the mother who suffers more. If there are inadequate supplies of calcium in the mother's system, "the fetal need for calcium will be met at the expense of the mother" (Hughes & Noppe, 1985, p. 140). Taking vitamins *can* be overdone. Overdosing some vitamins (vitamins A and D, in particular) can be toxic, with negative effects for both mother and unborn child. What works best is a balanced, sensible diet.

Smoking, Drinking, and Drugs

There is ample evidence that smoking has harmful effects on the smoker. Research also shows that smoking by pregnant women has harmful effects on their unborn children (Frazier et al., 1961; Fribourg, 1982; Jacobson, 1984; Vorhees & Mollnow, 1987). Exactly how smoking affects the fetus is not known. It may be a matter of reducing the oxygen or the blood supply to the fetus. It may be that the tar and nicotine of the smoke act directly as poisons. What we do know is that cigarette smoking is a cause of retarded prenatal growth (Golbus, 1980). Mothers who smoke during pregnancy give birth to children who are more likely to have hearing defects, and the more the mother smokes, the more serious the defects are likely to be (Fried, 1993). Smoking mothers have many more miscarriages, stillbirths, and babies who die soon after birth than do mothers who do not smoke (Frazier et al., 1961; Golbus, 1980).

Alcohol is a drug that can be injurious to unborn children. Alcohol is quickly and directly passed through the umbilical cord from the mother to the fetus. Heavy drinking (three drinks or more per day) significantly increases the chance of having smaller babies with retarded physical growth, poor coordination, poor muscle tone, intellectual retardation, and other problems, collectively referred to as **fetal alcohol syndrome (FAS)** (Jones et al., 1973; Mattson et al., 1988). In the United States, fetal alcohol syndrome is the leading preventable cause of birth defects that produce mental retardation (Streissguth et al., 1991). The Centers for Disease Control and Prevention estimate that 8,000 babies with FAS are born in the United States every year. In the summer of 1995, the CDC released a report that the rate of babies born with fetal alcohol syndrome increased *sixfold* from 1979 to 1993. Back in the 1970s, it was believed that an occasional drink or two had no lasting effect on prenatal development. Now experts agree that the best advice is total abstinence (Abel, 1981, 1984; Barr et al., 1990).

Mothers who use or abuse psychoactive drugs such as heroin, cocaine, or "crack" during pregnancy cause considerable complications for their unborn children. At best, such children enter the world with low birth weights, difficulty regulating their sleep-wake cycles, and many symptoms of fetal alcohol syndrome, perhaps because their mothers also used or abused alcohol (Finnegan, 1982; Zuckerman & Bresnahan, 1991). At worst, they are born addicted themselves, suffer the pains of withdrawal, and require a hospital stay averaging 42 days (Adler, 1989; Chasnoff et al., 1989; Finnegan, 1982).

Even common aspirin has become suspect as a cause of prenatal complications (Briggs et al., 1986; Govoni & Hayes, 1988; Sibai et al., 1993). Caffeine has been implicated, too. One study involved 1,324 women, of whom 331 had a miscarriage during the fetal stage of their pregnancy, and confirmed what animal studies had previously indicated: "The incidence of fetal loss was strongly associated with caffeine intake during pregnancy, and moderately associated with caffeine use before pregnancy" (Infante-Rivard et al., 1993, p. 2943).

What About Dad?

As you read through the last sections on nourishment and drugs, did it sound at all sexist to you? All of what we've covered puts the focus on mothers—what mothers should and should not do. Eat a balanced diet. Don't drink. Don't do drugs. Don't smoke. There has been little concern expressed about the father's role in the process. A review of the literature on factors that influence the pathological development of children and adolescents found that only 1 percent of the 577 studies cited focused on the role of fathers (Phares & Compas, 1993).

This situation is changing. Researchers are now looking at the role of the father in determining the quality of life of the prenatal child. The main issue revolves around factors affecting the quality of the father's sperm at the moment of conception. As one example, consider the known causes of Down syndrome, a collection of birth defects associated with mental retardation (see page 248). Down syndrome is the result of a child being born with 47 chromosomes per cell instead of the standard 23 pairs. From the beginning, it was assumed that a problem with the mother's ovum caused this syndrome. This was because the likelihood of having a child with Down syndrome increases as the mother's age increases (much beyond the age of 35 to 40).

We now recognize that the age of *the father* matters just as much as the age of the mother, that as many as one-third of all Down syndrome cases reflect difficulties with the father's sperm, and that the syndrome is more likely in children whose fathers have jobs that subject them to toxic chemicals. Alcohol use by fathers has also been implicated as a probable cause of prenatal and birth abnormalities, but nearly all of this research has been on rats and mice (Hood, 1990). Obviously, some difficulties of pregnancy, birth, and development are due to the condition of the father at or near the time of conception (Brown, 1985; Soyka & Joffee, 1980).

Before You Go On

What effects do diet and drugs have on prenatal development?

Motor Development: Getting from Here to There

Now we turn our attention to development in *childhood,* that period between birth and adolescence. We'll begin by considering the orderly sequence of the development of the motor responses of children—their ability to do things with their bodies.

The Neonate

When a baby is first born, it looks like it can't do much of anything. Mostly it just sleeps. In fact, newborns *do* sleep a lot, about 15 to 17 hours a day. But as parents are quick to find out, that sleep occurs in short naps, seldom lasting more than a few hours at a time. A careful examination of **neonates**—newborns through the first two weeks of life—reveals that they are capable of a wide range of behaviors.

⊚⊚⊚ **Thinking Critically** ⊚⊚⊚

How would we increase our understanding of the impact of the environment on prenatal development by examining the practices of other countries and other cultures?

neonate *the newborn, from birth through the first 2 weeks*

Most of the behaviors of the neonate are *reflexive*–simple, unlearned, involuntary reactions to specific stimuli. Many of the neonate's reflexes serve a purpose, helping the child respond to the demands of its environment. Some do not seem to have any survival value, but they are important because they can be used as diagnostic indicators of the quality of the neonate's development. More than a dozen reflexes can be observed and measured (e.g., for strength and duration) in the newborn child.

The Motor Development of Children

Parents trying to keep their young children in properly fitting clothes know how quickly children grow. In their first three years, children's height and weight normally increase at a rate never again equaled. Although changes in size and motor skills are rapid, they do tend to be orderly and well sequenced.

No two children can be expected to grow at the same rate or to develop control over their bodies at the same time. Joan may walk at the age of 10 months. Bill may not venture forth until he's 13 months old. The rate of motor development in early childhood is largely unrelated to adult characteristics, such as intelligence or physical coordination.

Regardless of the *rate* of one's motor development, there are regularities in the *sequence* of motor development. No matter when Joan does walk, she will first sit, then crawl. Figure 8.1 summarizes the development of common motor skills. There are two important things for you to notice about this figure: first, the sequence of events is regular, and second, *when* each stage develops includes a wide range of ages that should be considered normal. It is also true that the sequence and timing of the events listed in this figure hold equally for boys and girls. That is, in the development of these basic motor skills there are no significant sex differences.

Whether a child begins to walk at 10 months or 13 months, he or she will still follow the age-old patterns of sitting, crawling, and then walking. Although walking may not be learned in the usual sense, it is an accomplishment that often brings pleasure to parents.

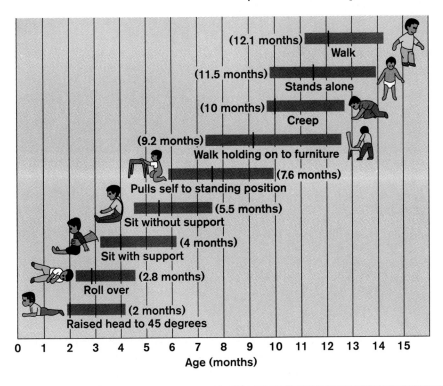

Figure 8.1

The sequence of human motor development. Each bar represents the ages at which between 25 percent of children (left end) and 90 percent of children (right end) engage in a given behavior. The short vertical line though the bar indicates the age at which 50 percent of children exhibit that behavior.

The regularity of physical growth and development is guided by two "principles": (1) *Cephalocaudal sequencing* refers to the fact that a child's growth and bodily control proceed from top to bottom, or from head to upper torso to lower body. Children's heads and upper torsos develop before their trunks and lower bodies; hands and arms can be manipulated before feet and legs can. (2) *Proximodistal sequencing* refers to the fact that a child's growth and bodily control proceed from the center core to the extremities; from the internal organs to the arms and legs, then to the hands and feet, then to the fingers and toes.

Before You Go On

What general observations can we make about physical growth and motor control in childhood?

Sensory and Perceptual Development

Neonates can respond to a wide range of stimuli. To some degree, all human senses are functioning at birth, having developed in order: touch, body position, balance, taste, smell, hearing, and finally, vision (Gibson, 1987, 1988; Hall & Oppenheim, 1987).

The neonate's ability to sense even subtle changes is remarkable. However, there are limitations. The ability of the eyes to focus on an object, for example, does not fully develop until the child is about 4 months old. The neonate can focus well on objects held 1 to 2 feet away, but everything nearer or farther appears out of focus. This means that even newborns can focus on the facial features of the persons cradling or feeding them. Visual acuity—the ability to discern detail—shows a threefold to fourfold improvement in their first year (Aslin & Smith, 1988). Newborns can detect differences in brightness, and soon develop the ability to detect surfaces, edges, borders, and the differences among colors (Cohen et al., 1978; Termine et al., 1987).

When does the perception of depth and distance develop? Even newborns show some reactions to distance. They will close their eyes and squirm away if you rush an object toward their face (Bower et al., 1971). In the late 1950s, two Cornell University psychologists, Eleanor Gibson and Richard Walk (1960), built an apparatus to test the depth perception of young children. The *visual cliff,* as it is called, is a deep box covered by a sheet of thick, clear Plexiglas. It is divided into two sides, one shallow, the other deep, separated by a center board (Figure 8.2). Gibson and Walk found that 6-month-old children would not leave the center board to venture out over the deep side of the box, even to get to their mothers. By crawling age, the child seems able to perceive depth and to make an appropriate response to it.

It seems likely that the perception of depth develops before the age of 6 months. When neonates (who obviously can't crawl) are placed on the Plexiglas over the deep side of the visual cliff, their heart rates *decrease,* indicating that at least they notice the change in visual stimulation (Campos et al., 1978). When 7-month-old infants are placed over the deep side of the visual cliff, their heart rates *increase.* The increase in heart rate is taken as indicating fear—a response that develops after the ability to discriminate depth (Bertenthal & Campos, 1989; Campos, 1976). There is also ample evidence that retinal disparity (the discrepancy in images received by the retinas of the two eyes) does not develop until the fourth month after birth (Birch et al., 1983; Fox et al., 1980). So, in some rudimentary form,

Figure 8.2

The visual cliff was designed to determine if depth perception is learned or innate. By the time infants can move about, most will avoid the "deep" side of the apparatus.

even neonates sense depth, but reacting appropriately to depth requires experiences and learning that come later.

What about the other senses? Newborn infants can hear very well, directing their attention to the source of a sound, even a faint one. Wertheimer (1961) reports a study demonstrating sound localization in a newborn between 3 and 10 *minutes* after birth. (The child moved her eyes to the left or right in response to a loud clicking sound.) Sounds probably don't mean much to neonates, but they can respond differently to sounds of varied pitch and loudness. Even 3-day-old newborns are able to discriminate the sound of their mother's voice from other sounds (DeCasper & Fifer, 1980; Kolata, 1987; Martin & Clark, 1982).

Newborns also respond to differences in taste and smell. They can discriminate among the four basic taste qualities of salt, sweet, bitter, and sour. They display a distinct preference for sweet-tasting liquids. Although they are unable to use it then, the sense of smell is established before birth. Immediately after birth, neonates respond predictably—drawing away and wrinkling their noses—to a variety of strong odors (e.g., Bartoshuk & Beauchamp, 1994).

In summary, a wide range of sensory and perceptual capabilities appears to be available to the newborn child. The neonate may require some time to learn what to do with the sensory information it acquires from its environment, but many of its senses are operational. What the newborn makes of the sensations it receives will depend on the development of its mental, or cognitive, abilities. This is the subject we turn to now.

Before You Go On

Summarize the sensory capacities of the neonate.

Cognitive and Social Development

Cognitive processes are those that enable us to know and understand ourselves and the world around us. Now we'll examine how these skills develop throughout childhood, beginning with a summary of the cognitive capacities of the newborn infant.

Cognitive Abilities of the Neonate: What Does the Newborn Know?

Reflex reactions can help neonates survive, but for long-term survival, they must learn to adapt to their environments and profit from their experiences. Neonates have to form memories of their experiences and learn to make discriminations among the stimuli with which they are presented. Are these cognitive processes possible in a baby just a couple of days or weeks old? In several specific ways, the answer seems to be yes.

First, we can note that newborns can engage in simple learning tasks. A neonate (only two hours old!) is stroked on the forehead and seems not to respond. This stimulus is then paired with a sugar solution delivered to the infant's lips. The unconditioned stimulus of the sugar solution elicits the unconditioned response of turning the head and making sucking movements. After several trials of pairing the stroking of the forehead and the sugar solution, the baby makes sucking and head movements simply when its forehead is touched (Blass et al., 1984). This is an example of classical conditioning (for a review, see Topic 5A, pages 151–153).

Head-turning and sucking movements of neonates can also be brought under the control of operant conditioning (see Topic 5B). The rates of these responses increase when they are followed by (reinforced by) sugar solutions, the sound of mother's voice, or the recorded sound of the mother's heartbeat (DeCasper & Sigafoos, 1983; Moon & Fifer, 1990; Sameroff & Cavanaugh, 1979).

Friedman (1972) reported a demonstration of memory in neonates only 1 to 4 days old. Babies were shown a picture of a simple figure—say, a checkerboard pattern—for 60 seconds. Experimenters recorded how long the baby looked at the stimulus. After the same pattern was shown over and over again, the baby appeared to be bored and gave it less attention. (You should recognize this as "habituation," which, in Topic 5A, we characterized as a simple form of learning.) When a new stimulus pattern was presented, the baby stared at it for the full 60 seconds of its exposure. So what does this have to do with memory? The argument is that for the neonate to stare at the new stimulus, it must have formed some memory of the old one. How else would it recognize the new pattern as being new or different? In fact, if the new stimulus pattern was very similar to the old one, the baby would not give it as much attention as it would if it were totally different.

In this context, I should mention the classic research of Robert Fantz (1961, 1963). Fantz presented newborn children with pairs of visual stimuli. In most pairs, one stimulus was more complex than the other. As the babies looked up at the stimuli, the researchers could note which of the two stimuli received more attention from the child. In nearly every case, the babies showed a preference for the more complex stimulus pattern.

The major finding of Fantz's studies is that newborns can discriminate between two stimuli. That attention equals "preference" is more of an assumption than a research finding. Fantz also discovered that even newborn infants show a preference for (choose to attend to) drawings of a human face. They chose the face pattern as the focus of their attention no matter what it was paired with. Newborns just a few hours old can recognize a picture of their own mother's face, and prefer to look at it over any other face paired with it (Bushnell et al., 1989; Walton et al., 1992; Walton & Bower, 1993). Young infants can also discriminate among facial expressions of emotions, and spend more time looking at facial expressions of joy than of anger, for instance (Malatesta & Isard, 1984).

Before You Go On

What cognitive abilities can be demonstrated by a neonate?

Piaget's Theory of Cognitive Development

The physical growth and development of a child is remarkable. Even more impressive are the increases in cognitive or intellectual abilities that occur during childhood. By the time the human reaches adolescence, he or she has acquired an enormous stockpile of information. More than just learning facts, the child comes to appreciate how to learn.

Accounting for *how* children's intellectual skills change is a difficult business. It is important to be able to describe the changes that occur, but it is more important to be able to specify the principles that underlie cognitive development (Siegler, 1989; Wellman & Gelman, 1992). The theory that has attracted the most attention in this regard is that of the Swiss psychologist Jean Piaget (1896–1980). Although there are others, Piaget's theory of cognitive development has been so influential that it will be the focus of our discussion (Piaget, 1932/1948, 1954, 1967).

In Piaget's theory, cognitive development relies on the formation of **schemas**, or organized mental representations of the world that have predictable behavioral consequences. For example, children develop a schema for "daddy," for "mommy," for "eating breakfast," and for "bedtime." Schemas aid the child in adapting to the demands and pressures of the environment and are formed by experience. Organizing the world into schemas is, according to Piaget, a process found in all children the world over.

⊚⊚⊚⊚ **Thinking Critically** ⊚⊚⊚⊚

How would you define "thinking" in a neonate, and what evidence would you have to generate to demonstrate that neonates think?

schemas *organized mental representations of the world that are adaptive and formed by experience*

Jean Piaget's observations about the cognitive development of children are the most comprehensive and influential. Nonetheless, some of Piaget's ideas have been challenged.

Forming mental representations of the environment involves two processes, assimilation and accommodation. **Assimilation** involves taking on new information and fitting it into an existing schema. For example, children develop a complex schema for mealtime. When they are taken to a fast-food restaurant for the first time, new information will have to be added to the mealtime schema: that a stranger prepares the meal, that meals may come in cardboard boxes, and that others will be eating in the same room.

Accommodation is a matter of changing or revising existing schemas in the face of new experiences, not just adding to them. As children are shifted away from the bottle to strained foods, to chunkier foods, to regular food, they must make accommodations in their schemas for efficient feeding. What used to work in the past may not work in the future. Learning that mommy or daddy won't necessarily come running when one cries may require accommodation.

Piaget proposed that as children assimilate new ideas into existing schemas and make accommodations to old ones, they progress through four stages of development: a *sensorimotor stage,* a *preoperational stage,* a *concrete operations stage,* and a *formal operations stage.* Determining precisely when each stage begins or ends is not always possible, in that adjacent stages may overlap and blend for a while. Even

assimilation *in Piaget's theory, the process of adding, and "fitting in," new material or information to an existing schema*

accommodation *in Piaget's theory, the process of changing or revising an existing schema as a result of new experiences* so, each stage is characterized by its own schemas, cognitive methods, insights, and abilities.

Sensorimotor Stage. (Ages birth to 2 years.) For children younger than age 2, language is not an effective means of finding out about the world. Children of this age are unable to discover much about their world by asking questions about it or by trying to understand long-winded explanations. Trying to explain to a 10-month-old baby *why* it shouldn't chew on an electrical cord is likely to be an unrewarding piece of parental behavior. In the **sensorimotor stage**, children discover by sensing (sensori-) and by doing (motor). A child may come to appreciate, for example, that a quick pull on a dog's tail (a motor activity) reliably produces a loud yelp (a sensory experience), perhaps followed in turn by parental attention.

sensorimotor stage in Piaget's theory, from ages birth to 2 years, when a child learns by sensing and doing

One of the most useful schemas to develop in the sensorimotor stage is that of *causality*. Infants gradually come to realize that events may have knowable causes and that some behaviors cause predictable reactions. Pushing a bowl of oatmeal off the high chair causes a mess and gets mommy's attention: if A, then B—a very practical insight. Another important discovery that occurs during this developmental stage is that objects may exist even when they are not immediately in view. Early in this stage, an object that is out of sight is more than out of mind. The object ceases to exist for the child. By the end of the sensorimotor period, children have learned that objects can and do still exist even if they are not physically present, and that their reappearance can be anticipated. This awareness is called **object permanence** (see Figure 8.3).

object permanence the appreciation that an object no longer in view can still exist and reappear later

Another useful skill that characterizes the sensorimotor period is imitation. As long as it is within its range of abilities, a baby will imitate almost any behavior it sees. A cognitive strategy has developed, one that will be used for a lifetime: trying to imitate the behaviors of a model.

Preoperational Stage. (Ages 2 to 6 years.) By the end of the sensorimotor stage, a child recognizes that he or she is a separate, independent person. Throughout most of the **preoperational stage**, a child's thinking is self-centered, or *egocentric*. According to Piaget, the child has difficulty understanding life from someone else's perspective. In this stage, the world is very much *me-, mine-,* and *I-*oriented.

preoperational stage in Piaget's theory, from ages 2 to 6 years, characterized by egocentrism and the beginning of symbol development

In the preoperational stage, children begin to develop symbols, usually in the form of words to represent concepts. At this stage, children do not know how to manipulate symbols in a consistent, rule-governed way (remember my difficulties with preschoolers and a simple word association task). It's not until the end of this period that they can play word games or understand why riddles about rabbits throwing clocks out of windows in order to "see time fly" are funny. It is similarly true that children at this stage have great difficulty with many "abstract" concepts, such as those involved with religious beliefs.

Concrete Operations Stage. (Ages 7 to 12 years.) Children in the **concrete operations stage** begin to develop many concepts *and* show that they can manipulate those concepts. For example, they can organize objects into categories of things: balls over here, blocks over there, plastic soldiers in a pile by the door, and so on. Each of these items is recognized as a toy, ultimately to be put away in the toy box and not in the closet, which is where clothes are supposed to go. It is in this period that rule-governed behavior begins. The concrete, observable objects of the child's world can be classified, ranked, ordered, or separated into more than one category, according to rules.

concrete operations stage in Piaget's theory, from ages 7 to 12 years, when concepts can be manipulated, but not in an abstract fashion

A sign of the beginning of the concrete operations stage is the ability to solve *conservation problems*. **Conservation** involves the awareness that changing the form or the appearance of something does not change what it really is. Many experiments convinced Piaget that conservation marked the end of the preoperational stage. Figure 8.4 shows a test for conservation of volume. We can show size conservation by giving two equal-size balls of clay to a 4-year-old. One ball is then

conservation in Piaget's theory, an appreciation that changing the physical properties of an object does not necessarily change its essence

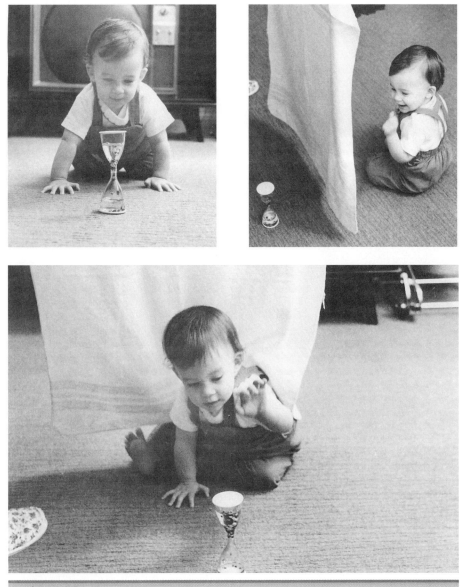

Figure 8.3

By the end of the sensorimotor stage of development, a child comes to appreciate that simply because an object is no longer in view does not mean that the object ceases to exist. Here an infant sees a toy, and even when it is blocked from view, realizes that it is still there and crawls under the blanket to get it, thus demonstrating "object permanence."

rolled into a long cigar shape, and the child will now assert that it has more clay in it than the ball does. A 7-year-old will seldom hesitate to tell you that each form contains the same amount of clay. The 7-year-old has moved on to the next stage of cognitive development.

As its name suggests, in the concrete operations stage children begin to use and manipulate (operate on) concepts and ideas. Their manipulations are still very concrete, however—tied to real objects in the here and now. An 8-year-old can be expected to find her way to and from school, even if she throws in a side trip along the way. What she will have a difficult time doing is telling you with any precision just how she gets from one place to another. Drawing a sensible map is difficult for her. If she stands on the corner of Maple Street and Oak Avenue, she knows where to go next to get home. Dealing with the concrete reality, here and now, is easy. Dealing with such knowledge in abstract terms is tough.

Figure 8.4

In a demonstration of the concept of conservation of volume, a child in Piaget's preoperational stage of cognitive development will claim that there is more liquid in the taller glass than in the shorter, wider glass, even though the liquid was just poured from the short glass into the tall glass.

formal operations stage *in Piaget's theory, ages older than 12 years, when one can generate and test abstract hypotheses and manipulate symbolic concepts*

Formal Operations Stage. (Ages over 12 years.) The logical manipulation of abstract, symbolic concepts appears in the last of Piaget's stages: **formal operations**. The key to this stage, usually begun in adolescence, is abstract, symbolic reasoning. By the age of 12 years, most children can develop and mentally test hypotheses—they can work through problems in their mind. Problem-solving strategies of the sort that we discussed in Topic 7B develop at this stage.

In the stage of formal operations, youngsters can reason through hypothetical problems: "What if you were the only person in the world who liked rock music?" "If nobody had to go to school, what would happen?" Similarly, children are now able to deal with questions that are literally contrary to fact: "What if John F. Kennedy or Ronald Reagan were still president of the United States?" The stages of Piaget's theory and the cognitive milestones associated with each are summarized in Figure 8.5.

Before You Go On

What characterizes each of the four stages of cognitive development proposed by Piaget?

Reactions to Piaget

There can be no doubt of the significance of Piaget's influence. His observations and insights about intellectual development spanned decades. Considerable research has supported many of these insights. Finding evidence of Piagetian stages is one of the success stories of cross-cultural research. That evidence tells us that the stages we have just reviewed can be identified in children around the world (Brislin, 1993; Dasen & Heron, 1981; Dasen & de Ribaupierre, 1987; Segall et al., 1990). There will be some individual differences, of course. Remember my example of conservation that involved estimating the amount of clay one has when it is

Figure 8.5
Piaget's Stages of Cognitive Development

1. Sensorimotor stage (ages birth to 2 years)
   "Knows" through active interaction with environment
   Becomes aware of cause-effect relationships
   Learns that objects exist even when not in view
   Imitates crudely the actions of others

2. Preoperational stage (ages 2 to 6 years)
   Begins by being very egocentric
   Language and mental representations develop
   Objects are classified on just one characteristic at a time

3. Concrete operations stage (ages 7 to 12 years)
   Develops conservation of volume, length, mass, etc.
   Organizes objects into ordered categories
   Understands relational terms (e.g., bigger than, above)
   Begins using simple logic

4. Formal operations stage (ages over 12)
   Thinking becomes abstract and symbolic
   Reasoning skills develop
   A sense of hypothetical concepts develops

rolled into varied shapes? Sons and daughters of potters understand the conservation of sizes of clay with great ease (Price-Williams et al., 1969). In other words, experience does matter.

The two major criticisms of Piaget's theory are that (1) the borderlines between his proposed stages are much less clear-cut than his theory suggests, and (2) Piaget underestimated the cognitive talents of preschool children (Flavell, 1982, 1985; Gelman, 1978; Wellman & Gelman, 1992).

For example, the egocentrism said to characterize the preoperational child may not be as flagrant as Piaget believed. In one study (Lempers et al., 1977), children were shown a picture pasted inside a box. They were asked to show the picture to someone else. In showing the picture, they turned it so that it would be right side up to the viewer. Every child over 2 years of age indicated such an appreciation of someone else's point of view. More than that, recent research makes it clear that young children (18 months old) readily ascribe goals and intentions to the action of others. That is, preschoolers can observe someone else doing something, and appreciate what it is they are tryng to do (Meltzoff, 1995).

Similarly, object permanence may be neither universal nor consistently found in any one child; it depends on how you test for it (Harris, 1983). For example, psychologist Renée Baillargeon (1993, 1995) reports that even "infants aged 2.5 to 3.5 *months* are aware that objects continue to exist when masked by other objects, that objects cannot remain stable without support, that objects move along spatially continuous paths, and that objects cannot move through the space occupied by other objects" (p. 133, emphasis added). Piaget's theory tells us that these sorts of abilities do not appear until a child is about 2 years old.

Piaget's notion of conservation may not be such an obvious indicator of cognitive development either. When experimenters pour liquid from a short beaker into a tall one, a 5-year-old will probably say that the taller beaker now holds more liquid—evidence of preoperational stage thinking. If the child does the pouring from one beaker to the other, as opposed to just watching, 5-year-olds show conservation and recognize that the amount of liquid is the same in both containers (Rose & Blank, 1974).

A further criticism is that Piaget's theory, focusing on a stage approach, gives little attention to the impact of language development. Nor did Piaget have much to say about the smooth and gradual increase in the capacity of a child's memory.

So, some of Piaget's observations and assumptions have come under attack. This is to be expected in science. One of the most important contributions of Jean Piaget is that he developed a theory of cognitive development in children that was so detailed, so thought-provoking, that it will continue to challenge researchers for years to come.

Before You Go On

Cite two criticisms of Piaget's theory.

Kohlberg's Theory of Moral Development

How children learn to reason about and make judgments about what is right and wrong is an aspect of cognitive development that has received considerable attention (Darley & Schultz, 1990; Vitz, 1990). Piaget included the study of moral development in his theory, arguing that morality is related to cognitive awareness, and that children are unable to make moral judgments until they are at least 3 or 4 years old (Piaget, 1932/1948).

Lawrence Kohlberg (1963, 1969, 1981, 1985) has offered a theory that focuses on moral development. Like Piaget's approach, Kohlberg's is a theory of stages, of moving from one stage to another in an orderly fashion. Kohlberg's database comes from the responses made by young boys who were asked questions about stories that involve a moral dilemma. A commonly cited example concerns whether a man should steal a drug in order to save his wife's life after the pharmacist who invented the drug refuses to sell it to him. Should the man steal the drug; why or why not?

On the basis of responses to such dilemmas, Kohlberg proposed three levels of moral development, with two stages (or "orientations") at each level. The result is the six stages of moral development summarized in Figure 8.6. For example, a child who says that the man should not steal the drug because "he'll get caught and be put in jail" is at the first, *preconventional,* level of reasoning because the prime interest of the child is simply with the punishment that comes from breaking a rule. A child who says the man should steal the drug because "it will make his wife happy, and most people would do it anyway" is reflecting a type of reasoning at the second, *conventional,* level because the judgment is based on an accepted social convention, and social approval matters as much as or more than anything else. The argument that, "no, he shouldn't steal the drug for a basically selfish reason, which in the long run would promote more stealing in the society in general" is an example of moral reasoning at the third, or *postconventional,* level because it reflects complex, internalized standards. Notice that what matters is not the choice the child makes, but the reasoning behind that choice.

Research tells us that the basic thrust of Kohlberg's theory has merit (Rest, 1983). It also has cross-cultural application. To varying degrees, Kohlberg's descriptions are valid for several cultures, including Israel, Turkey, India, and Nigeria (Edwards, 1977, 1981; Magsud, 1979; Nisan & Kohlberg, 1982; Snarey, 1987; Snarey et al., 1985).

Problems with the theory also exist. For one thing, few people (including adults) operate at the higher stages of moral reasoning described by the theory (Colby & Kohlberg, 1984). This is particularly true in cultures that emphasize communal or group membership—such as the Israeli kibbutz or tribal groups in New Guinea—more than individuality (Snarey, 1987).

This observation brings us to a key concept in cross-cultural psychology: the dimension of individualism-collectivism (Bhawuk & Brislin, 1992; Erez & Early,

---

Figure 8.6
Kohlberg's Stages of Moral Development

Level 1	**Preconventional morality**
1. Obedience and punishment orientation	Rules are obeyed simply to avoid punishment; "If I take the cookies, I'll get spanked."
2. Naive egotism and instrumental orientation	Rules are obeyed simply to earn rewards; "If I wash my hands, will you let me have two desserts?"
Level 2	**Conventional (conforming) morality**
3. Good boy/girl orientation	Rules are conformed to in order to avoid disapproval and gain approval; "I'm a good boy 'cause I cleaned my room, aren't I?"
4. Authority-maintaining orientation	Social conventions blindly accepted to avoid criticism from those in authority; "You shouldn't steal because it's against the law, and you'll go to jail if the police catch you."
Level 3	**Postconventional morality**
5. Contractual-legalistic orientation	Morality is based on agreement with others to serve the common good and protect the rights of individuals; "I don't like stopping at stop signs, but if we didn't all obey traffic signals, it would be difficult to get anywhere."
6. Universal ethical principle orientation	Morality is a reflection of internalized standards; "I don't care what anybody says, what's right is right."

1993; Triandis, 1990, 1993; Triandis et al., 1988). People in some cultures are socialized from early childhood to take others (the family, the tribe, the neighborhood, the society) into account when setting goals or making decisions. Such a tendency toward **collectivism** is found more commonly in Asia and South America. People in many other cultures are socialized to think mostly about themselves and their own individual behaviors, a sort of "pull yourself up by your own boot straps; make it on your own; you'll get what you deserve" sort of mentality. This tendency toward **individualism** is common in North America and Western Europe. We are talking about a dimension of comparison here; even within the same culture, individualism and collectivism exist to varying degrees. This discussion relates to Kohlberg's theory because most measures of moral reasoning put a high value on the sort of thinking found in individualistic (largely Western) cultures, and devalue the sorts of thinking typical of collective cultures. This does not mean that Kohlberg was wrong, of course. It just means that what is true for one culture may not be for another, and neither is necessarily any "better" or more moral.

A similar argument has been raised about Kohlberg's theory as it applies to females (Ford & Lowery, 1986; Gilligan, 1982). All of Kohlberg's original data came from the responses of young boys, remember. Later, when girls were tested, some studies seemed to suggest that the girls showed slower moral development when compared to boys. Carol Gilligan's argument is that the moral reasoning of females

collectivism *in cross-cultural psychology, the tendency to set goals and make decisions based on a concern for the group or the common good*

individualism *in cross-cultural psychology, the tendency to set goals and make decisions based on a concern for one's self or the individual*

Judgments concerning what constitutes moral reasoning need to take into account gender and cultural differences. Members of some cultures in Japan for instance, or other Asian or South American countries, place a strong emphasis on collectivism, on adherence to the values and goals of the group, the family, the tribe, or the society.

is neither slower nor faster but is simply *different* from the reasoning of males. Males (at least in Western cultures) are concerned with rules, justice, and an individual's rights. As a result, they approach moral dilemmas differently than do females, who are characteristically more concerned with caring, personal responsibility, and interpersonal relationships (Gilligan, 1982). The issue is not a judgmental one in the sense of determining if men are more or less moral in their thinking than women. The question is whether women and men develop different styles of moral reasoning. So far, most studies have shown that any differences between men and women in resolving moral conflicts are insignificant (Darley & Schultz, 1990; Donneberg & Hoffman, 1988; Mednick, 1989; Walker, 1989).

Before You Go On

Summarize Kohlberg's theory of moral development.

Erikson's Psychosocial Theory of Development

Erik Erikson (1902–1994) was a psychologist who, like Piaget, proposed a stage theory of human development (Erikson, 1963, 1965, 1968). Unlike Piaget, his theory focuses on more than cognitive development, although this aspect is included. Erikson's theory is based on his observations of a wide range of peoples of various ages. As we will see, his theory extends from childhood through adolescence into adulthood and has a cross-cultural basis. Erikson was born in Germany, studied with Anna Freud (Sigmund Freud's daughter) in Vienna, and then came to the United States to do his research. Erikson's views were influenced more by Freud than by Piaget. Unlike Freud, Erikson focused on the social environment, which is why his theory is called *psychosocial*.

Erikson lists eight stages of development through which a person passes. These stages are not so much time periods as they are a series of conflicts, or crises, that need to be resolved. Each of the eight stages is referenced by a pair of terms

Erik Erikson (1902–1994)

that indicates the nature of the conflict that needs to be resolved in this period of development. As a stage theory, Erikson's implies that we naturally go through the resolution of each conflict in order and that facing any one type of crisis usually occurs at about the same age for all of us. Figure 8.7 is a summary of each of Erikson's eight stages of development.

As you can see, only the first four stages are relevant for children. In fact, a major strength of Erikson's view of development is that it covers the entire life span. For now, we'll describe Erikson's first four crises, but we will return to his theory in Topic 8B.

During one's first year of life, according to Erikson, one's greatest struggle centers around the establishment of a sense of *trust or mistrust*. There's not much a newborn can accomplish on its own. If its needs are met in a reasonable fashion, the child will develop a basic sense of safety and security, optimistic that the world is a predictable place. If a child's needs aren't adequately met, what develops is a sense of mistrust—feelings of frustration and insecurity.

During the period of *autonomy versus self-doubt,* from ages 1 1/2 to 3 years, what emerges most plainly is a sense of self-esteem. The child begins to act independently; to dress and feed him- or herself, for example. Physically more able, the child strikes off on its own, exploring ways of assuming personal responsibility. Frustration at this level of development leads to feelings of inadequacy and doubts of one's self-worth.

From ages 3 years to 6 years is Erikson's period of *initiative versus guilt.* Now the challenge is to develop as a contributing member of social groups, particularly the family. If the child is encouraged to do so, he or she should develop a strong sense of initiative, a certain joy of trying new things. How reinforcing it is to a 5-year-old to be asked for an opinion on what the family should do this evening. Without such encouragement, a child is likely to feel guilty and resentful.

Figure 8.7
Erikson's Eight Stages of Development

Approximate age	Crisis	Adequate resolution	Inadequate resolution
0–1 1/2	Trust vs. mistrust	Basic sense of safety	Insecurity, anxiety
1 1/2–3	Autonomy vs. self-doubt	Perception of self as agent capable of controlling own body and making things happen	Feelings of inadequacy to control events
3–6	Initiative vs. guilt	Confidence in oneself as initiator, creator	Feeling of lack of self-worth
6–puberty	Competence vs. inferiority	Adequacy in basic social and intellectual skills	Lack of self-confidence, feelings of failure
Adolescent	Identity vs. role confusion	Comfortable sense of self as a person	Sense of self as fragmented; shifting, unclear sense of self
Early adult	Intimacy vs. isolation	Capacity for closeness and commitment to another	Feeling of aloneness, separation; denial of need for closeness
Middle adult	Generativity vs. stagnation	Focus on concern beyond oneself to family, society, future generations	Self-indulgent concerns; lack of future orientation
Later adult	Ego-integrity vs. despair	Sense of wholeness, basic satisfaction with life	Feelings of futility, disappointment

The final childhood period, *competence versus inferiority,* lasts from about age 6 years to puberty. During this period of choices, the child is challenged to move beyond the safety and comfort of the family unit. The main focus of development is "out there" in the neighborhood and the school. Children have to begin to acquire those skills that will enable them to become fully functioning adults in society. If the child's efforts of industry are constantly belittled or ignored, the child may develop a sense of inadequacy and inferiority and thus remain dependent on others even into adulthood.

Before You Go On

Briefly describe the first four stages (crises) of development according to Erikson.

Developing Gender Identity

The theories of Piaget, Kohlberg, and Erikson deal with how (and when) children develop concepts or cognitions about themselves and the world in which they live.

Adults often reinforce gender differences in children at a very young age, dressing girls in pink and boys in blue. This phenomenon is not a new one. These two works of art are often hung together. "Pinkie," by Sir Thomas Lawrence, was painted about 1795, and "The Blue Boy," by Thomas Gainsborough, was painted in 1770.

In this section we'll focus on the concept of **gender**—one's maleness or femaleness, as opposed to one's sex, which is a biological term. Gender has been defined as "the socially ascribed characteristics of females and males, their roles and appropriate behaviors" (Amaro, 1995, p. 437), and "the meanings that societies and individuals ascribe to female and male categories" (Eagly, 1995, p. 145).

One of the first proclamations made upon the birth of a baby is "It's a girl!" or "It's a boy!" Parents then wrap up little girls in pink, boys in blue, and dress an infant or small child in clothes that clearly label the child as a boy or a girl.

One question we might ask is what differences do we find between boys and girls in childhood? Let me give you the general answer first, then I'll fill in some of the details. Differences between male and female infants and children are few and subtle. They are more likely to be in the eye of the beholder than in the behaviors of children.

As infants, boys do develop a bit more slowly than girls, have a little more muscle tissue than girls, and are somewhat more active, but even these differences are slight (e.g., Eaton & Enns, 1986). During the first year of life there are virtually no differences in temperament or "difficulty" between boys and girls (Thomas & Chess, 1977). Adults often believe that there ought to be differences between the sexes (Paludi & Gullo, 1986) and choose toys, clothing, and playmates based on what they believe is acceptable (Schau et al., 1980). However, when averaged over many studies, there are few areas in which parents consistently treat their sons and daughters differently (Lytton & Romney, 1991).

gender *one's maleness or femaleness; socially ascribed characteristics of males and females, as opposed to their biological characteristics*

The only area in which North American parents show significant differentiation is in the encouragement of different sex-typed activities for girls and boys. For example, in one study (Snow et al., 1983), fathers were more likely to give dolls to 1-year-old girls than to boys. However, even at this age, children themselves already have their own toy preferences; when offered dolls, boys are less likely to play with them than are girls. In the first few years of elementary school, girls have a different view of areas of their own competence and activities of value than boys do. Girls tend to value (and see themselves as competent in) reading and instrumental music, for example, whereas boys value math and sports activities (Eccles et al., 1993.)

Children's peer groups provide significant experiences for both girls and boys (Maccoby, 1988, 1990; Maccoby & Jacklin, 1987). By the age of 3 or 4, girls and boys gravitate toward playmates of the same sex—a pattern that is shown cross-culturally. Girls tend to be dominated in mixed-sex interactions (Jacklin & Maccoby, 1978). Boys develop the tendency to use direct commands to influence others, whereas girls tend to use polite suggestions, which are effective with other girls but not with boys (Serbin et al., 1984). Girls develop more intensive friendships than boys and are more distressed when those friendships end. Maccoby (1990) has suggested that the interactive styles that develop in same-sex groups in childhood lay the foundation for differences in social relationships of adult men and women, with more supportive, intimate relationships among women and more direct, hierarchical relationships among men.

Here's a different, but related, question: At what age do boys and girls begin to see each other as "different"? When do children develop gender identity, the basic sense or self-awareness of one's maleness or femaleness? Even 5-month-old infants are able to distinguish gender in faces shown to them in pictures (Fagan & Singer, 1979). Most of us develop a sense of gender identity by the time we are 2 or 3 years old (Money, 1972; Paludi & Gullo, 1986). By the age of 4, most children demonstrate gender stereotypes, showing that they believe that certain occupations, activities, or toys go better with males and some go better with females. By the time they are ready to start school, most children have a notion of associating various personality traits with men and women. This pattern has been found in several cultures (Williams & Best, 1990). Once gender identity is established, it remains quite invulnerable to change (Bem, 1981; Spence, 1985).

Cognitive psychologists believe that once children can discriminate between the sexes, they develop schemas for gender-related information (Martin, 1991).

Reinforcing the notion of gender identity. It's recess time at school. Notice that every girl is wearing a dress; every boy is wearing pants.

You'll recall that a schema is an organized system of general information, stored in one's memory, that guides the processing of new information. For example, children show more interest in and a better memory for new toys when those toys are labeled as appropriate for their own sex than appropriate for the other sex (Bradbard & Endsley, 1983). If information is inconsistent with the gender schema the child has developed, that information is likely to be distorted in memory. Children shown a picture of a female doctor tend to remember her as a nurse (Cordua et al., 1979). Children shown a girl sawing wood may remember a boy sawing wood. As Martin (1991) has pointed out, such distortions in memory may serve to perpetuate gender stereotypes, because information that does not fit the child's schema regarding gender is simply changed so that it conforms to the stereotype.

Before You Go On

What conclusions may we draw about the development of gender identity in children?

Developing Social Attachments

To a large degree, we adapt and thrive in this world to the extent that we can profit from interpersonal relationships (Hartup, 1989). The roots of social development can be found in early infancy—in the formation of attachment. **Attachment** is a strong, two-way emotional bond, usually referring to the relationship between a child and his or her mother or primary caregiver (Bowlby, 1982). Attachment has survival value, "increasing the chances of an infant being protected by those to whom he or she keeps proximity" (Ainsworth, 1989). Well-formed attachment provides a child with freedom to explore the environment, curiosity, adaptive problem solving, and competence when interacting with peers (Collins & Gunnar, 1990).

attachment *a strong two-way emotional bond, usually between a child and parent, or primary caregiver*

Forming an attachment between infant and mother (for example) involves regular interaction and active give-and-take between the two. Strong attachments are most likely to be formed if the mother is sensitive to the needs of the child, picking up the baby when he or she cries, changing the diaper as soon as it is soiled, feeding on a regular basis, and so on. Simply spending time with an infant is seldom enough to produce successful attachment. Attachment is promoted by spontaneous hugging, smiling, eye contact, and vocalizing (Lamb et al., 1982; Stern, 1977). It is fostered by qualities such as warmth and gentleness (Londerville & Main, 1981). When the process is successful, we say that the children are "securely attached." Forming an attachment is a two-way street. Attachment will be most secure when the baby reciprocates by smiling, cooing, and clinging to mother when attended to (Ainsworth, 1979; Pederson et al., 1990). About 65 percent of American children become securely attached by the age of 1 year—a percentage close to that found in seven other countries (van Ijzendorn & Koonenberg, 1988).

Are there long-term benefits of becoming securely attached in infancy? Yes. Secure attachment in infancy tends to lead to (1) sociability (less fear of strangers, better relationships with peers, more popularity, and more friends), (2) higher self-esteem, (3) better relationships with siblings, (4) fewer tantruming or aggressive behaviors, (5) less concern by teachers over controlling behaviors in the classroom, (6) more empathy and concern for the feelings of others, (7) fewer behavioral problems at later ages, and (8) better attention spans (from Bee, 1992, p. 433). Securely attached children also show greater persistence at problem solving, and are less likely to seek help from adults when injured or disappointed (Goldsmith & Harman, 1994).

I need to make it clear that infants can and do form attachments with persons other than their mothers. Father-child attachments are quite common and are beneficial for the long-term development of the child (Lamb, 1977, 1979; Lynn, 1974). One researcher found that she could predict the extent to which a child showed

Social attachments between parents and children are a two-way street in which signs of mutual interest and affection are exchanged. Studies tell us that early father-child attachments are beneficial later in life.

signs of attachment to its father simply by knowing how often Dad changed the baby's diaper (Ross et al., 1975). There is no evidence that fathers are less sensitive to the needs of their children than are mothers (Parke, 1981), although they may be a little more physical and a little less verbal in their interactions (Parke & Tinsley, 1987).

Finally, we need to consider attachment formation for those children who spend time—occasionally a lot of time—in day care facilities. In the United States more than half the mothers of children younger than three are employed, and the care of those children is at least in part taken over by others. How do these children fare? It depends to a large extent on the quality of the care the children are given—no matter where they get it. Children who receive warm, supportive, attentive care, adequate stimulation, and opportunities for exploration demonstrate secure attachment (Howes, 1990; Phillips et al., 1987). The impact of day care depends on the likelihood that the child would have received good, warm, supportive, loving care at home (Scarr & Eisenberg, 1993). In addition, the impact of day care is a function of the extent the mother has a challenging job that she enjoys and is excited about. Related to this point is the fact that women who are now 60 years old or older who worked in challenging jobs outside the home while their children were young now have higher self-esteem and suffer less depression than those mothers who stayed home with their children (Woodruff, 1994).

The benefits or harm of nonparental child care may also depend on the age of the child. "There is little dispute about the conclusion that children who enter day care at 18 months, 2 years, or later show no consistent loss of security of attachment to their parents" (Bee, 1992, p. 510). The debate centers on children less than one year old, and there is some evidence that secure attachment is less likely among those children who are not cared for at home during their first year (Belsky, 1990; Belsky & Rovine, 1988; Hennessy & Melhuish, 1991; Lamb & Sternberg, 1990).

It may tentatively be concluded that forming secure attachments is important for the later development of the human infant. There are long-term benefits (ranging from improved emotional stability to improved problem-solving skills) to be derived from the development of strong attachments formed early in childhood (Ainsworth, 1989; Bowlby, 1982; Etaugh, 1980; Schwartz, 1983). Further, attachments formed with the father or other caregivers seem as useful for long-term development as do attachments to the mother.

Before You Go On

In child development, what is "attachment," and what are the consequences of developing secure attachments?

TOPIC 8A SUMMARY

Human development begins at conception when genes from the father's sperm cell unite with the genes from the mother's ovum to form a zygote. For the next nine months, the human organism grows and develops in the mother's uterus. This prenatal period has three stages: zygote, embryo, and fetus, during which development is governed largely by genetics. Most environmental influences on prenatal development result in negative consequences, which leads us to advise pregnant women to eat well, to avoid smoking and drinking alcohol, and to use any drug with extreme care. Recent interest has also reinforced the notion that the father's physical condition at the time of conception may be related to the health and development of his child.

With birth, the neonatal period begins. Several useful reflexes and sensory capacities are available to the newborn, but interaction with the environment shapes the developmental process. Throughout childhood we find that motor development varies from child to child, but usually progresses in the same, orderly sequence.

Piaget argued that children go through a sequence of stages in their efforts to find out about the world in which they live, thus developing new schemas along the way. Few theories have generated the sort of research activity as has Piaget's. There are problems with some of the particular points of Piaget's theory, but we also saw that his theory has found support in cross-cultural research efforts. Kohlberg's theory of the development of moral reasoning is a six-stage theory. There is support for this theory, too, but it seems that support is mostly to be found in Western, individualistic cultures particularly among males. Erikson's theory of psychosocial development is also a stage theory, but unlike Piaget's, it considers developmental stages throughout adolescence and adulthood as well as childhood. Erikson's stages are defined in terms of conflicts that need to be resolved at various times in one's life.

We also learned that although adults may treat boys and girls differently, their behavior as infants and young children provides no basis for doing so. Most children become aware of gender differences by the age of 4 years. We examined the lasting importance of the early development of social attachments. These bidirectional, largely emotional bonds are established between young children and their primary caregivers. We continue our story of human development now by considering that span that falls between childhood and adulthood: adolescence.

TOPIC 8B Development in Adolescence and Adulthood

What Are Adolescents Really Like?

Adolescence is a period of transition from the dependence of childhood to the independence of adulthood. It is difficult, however, to specify exactly when adolescence begins and it ends. In biological terms, adolescence begins with **puberty**—sexual maturity and a readiness to reproduce—and ends with the end of physical growth, which is usually late in the teen years.

A more psychological perspective emphasizes the development of the cognitions, feelings, and behaviors that characterize adolescence. Such approaches emphasize the development of problem-solving skills and an increased reliance on the use of symbols, logic, and abstract thinking. Such perspectives stress the importance of identity formation and the appreciation of self and self-worth.

A social perspective looks at the role of adolescents in their societies, and defines adolescence in terms of being in between: not yet an adult, but no longer a child. In this context, adolescence usually lasts from the early teen years through one's highest educational level, when one is thought to enter the adult world.

Actually, whether we accept a biological, psychological, or social perspective, we are usually talking about people who, in our culture, are between the ages of 12 and 20. For purposes of our discussion, **adolescence** will be defined as the period of development begun at puberty and lasting through the teen years—essentially the second decade of life. An intriguing issue in the psychology of adolescence today is how to characterize this stage of development in a general way. Is it a time of personal growth, independence, and positive change? Or is adolescence a period of rebellion, turmoil, and negativism?

The view that adolescence can be described in terms of turmoil, storm, and stress is actually the older of the two, attributed to G. Stanley Hall (who wrote the first textbook on adolescence in 1904) and to Anna Freud (who applied psychoanalytic theory to adolescents). This position claims that normal adolescence involves many difficulties of adjustment. "To be normal during the adolescent period is by itself abnormal" (Freud, 1958, p. 275). In this view, "Adolescents may be expected to be extremely moody and depressed one day and excitedly 'high' the next. Explosive conflict with family, friends, and authorities is thought of as commonplace" (Powers et al., 1989, p. 200).

As we'll see, the teen years often do present conflicts and pressures that require difficult choices, and some teenagers do react to the pressures of their adolescence in maladaptive ways (Larson & Ham, 1993; Quadrel et al., 1993; Takanishi, 1993). In 1992 alone, 1,738,180 juveniles under age 18 were arrested in the United States, and arrests for violent crimes increased by 82 percent over 1982. And, although the physical health and general well-being of the North American population has consistently improved over recent decades, it has declined sharply for adolescents (Hamburg, 1992).

Yes, adolescence does require changes and adjustments, *but* those adjustments and changes are usually made in psychologically healthy ways (Feldman & Elliott, 1990; Jessor, 1993; Manning, 1983; Millstein et al., 1993; Peterson & Ebata, 1987; Rutter et al., 1976). As adolescents struggle for independence and for means of self-

puberty *the stage of physical development at which one becomes capable of sexual reproduction*

adolescence *the developmental period between childhood and adulthood, often begun at puberty and ending with full physical growth; generally between the ages of 12 and 20* expression, some engage in behaviors that may be considered reckless. Such behaviors are often a reflection of the socialization process of the teenagers' culture (Arnett, 1995; Compas et al., 1995). "While many adolescents face occasional periods of uncertainty and self-doubt, loneliness and sadness, and anxiety and concern for the future, they are also likely to experience joy, excitement, curiosity, a sense of adventure, and a feeling of competence as they master new challenges" (Conger, 1991, p. 24). Here we have a theme we've seen before: There is a "wide variability that characterizes psychological development during the second decade of life" (Compas et al, 1995, p. 271).

Before You Go On

How might adolescence be defined, and how might the period be characterized?

Some of the Challenges of Adolescence

In this section, we'll examine a few of the challenges faced by an adolescent: puberty, identity formation, drug use, and adolescent sexuality.

The Challenge of Puberty

The onset of adolescence is marked by two biological changes. First, there is a marked increase in height and weight, known as a growth spurt, and second, there is sexual maturation.

The *growth spurt* of adolescence usually occurs in girls at an earlier age than it does in boys. Girls begin their growth spurt as early as age 9 or 10, and then slow down at about age 15. Boys generally show increased rates of growth between the ages of 12 and 17 years. Males usually don't reach adult height until their early twenties; females generally attain maximum height by their late teens (Roche & Davila, 1972; Tanner, 1981).

At least some of the challenge of early adolescence is a direct result of the growth spurt. It is not uncommon to find increases in weight and height occurring so rapidly that they are accompanied by real, physical growing pains, particularly in the arms and legs. The spurt of adolescent growth seldom affects all parts of the body uniformly, especially in boys. Thirteen- and 14-year-old boys often appear incredibly clumsy and awkward as they try to coordinate their large hands and feet with the rest of their body. One of the most noticeable areas of growth in boys is that of the larynx and vocal cords. As the vocal cords lengthen, the pitch of the voice lowers. This transition is seldom a smooth one, and a teenage boy may suffer through weeks of a squeaking, cracking change of pitch in the middle of a serious conversation (Adams, 1977; Adams & Gullotta, 1983).

Puberty occurs when one becomes physically capable of sexual reproduction. With the onset of puberty, there is a marked increase in levels of the sex hormones, androgens in males and estrogens in females. (All of us have androgens and estrogens in our bodies. Males simply have more androgens; females have more estrogens.) Boys seldom know when their own puberty begins. For some time they have experienced penile erections and nocturnal emissions of seminal fluid. Puberty in males begins with the appearance of live sperm in the semen, and most males have no idea when that happens; such determinations require a laboratory test. In females, puberty is noticeable. It is indicated by the first menstrual period, called **menarche**.

⊚⊚⊚ **Thinking Critically** ⊚⊚⊚

Having been an adolescent, what do your own experiences tell you about that stage of development in terms of the "abnormal being normal"?

---

menarche *a female's first menstrual period, a sure sign of the beginning of adolescence*

For some young teens, the fact that girls generally have their growth spurt before boys do may cause some embarrassment or discomfort.

With puberty, adolescents are biologically ready to reproduce. Dealing with that readiness and making the adjustments that we associate with psychological maturity, however, do not come automatically with sexual maturity.

Many boys and girls reach puberty before or after most of their age mates, and are referred to as *early* or *late bloomers.* Reaching puberty well before or after others of the same age may have some psychological effects, although few are long-lasting. Let's first get an idea of what early and late puberty means. Figure 8.8 shows the age ranges during which the major developments associated with puberty may be expected to occur. In some cases, the age range is quite large. Many of the ages in this figure are subject to change. For example, in the United States 150 years ago, the average age of menarche was 16; now it's close to 12 (Hamburg & Takanishi, 1989). The age of puberty varies around the world. African girls, for example, experience menarche at a much younger age than do European girls (Eveleth & Tanner, 1978).

What are the advantages and disadvantages of early maturation? A girl who enters puberty early will probably be taller, stronger, faster, and more athletic than other girls (and many boys) in her class at school. She is more likely to be approached for dates, have more early sexual encounters, and marry at a younger age than her peers. She may have self-image problems, particularly if she puts on weight and shows marked breast development (Conger & Peterson, 1984; Crockett & Peterson, 1987).

Because of the premium put on physical activity in boys, the early-maturing boy is at a greater advantage than the early-maturing girl. He will have more dating and sexual experiences than his age mates, which will raise his status among his peers. He'll also have a better body image and higher self-esteem (Peterson, 1988).

For teens of both sexes, being a late bloomer is more negative in its impact (at the time) than is being an early bloomer (Gross & Duke, 1980). Late-maturing boys

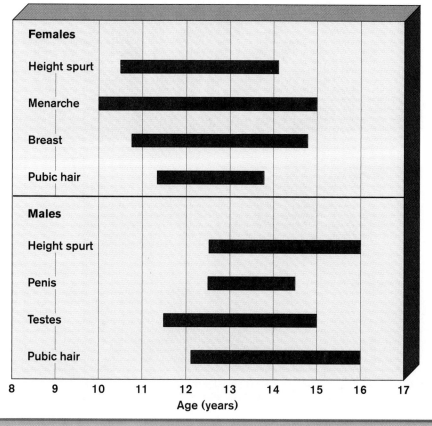

Figure 8.8

The ages at which certain physical changes occur in the average male and female during puberty. (Adapted from "Growing Up" by J. M. Tanner, *Scientific American*, September, 1973, Volume 229, Number 3. Copyright © 1973 by *Scientific American*. All rights reserved. Reprinted by permission.)

may carry a sense of inadequacy and poor self-esteem into adulthood (Jones, 1957). Late maturity for girls has virtually no long-term negative consequences. Some feel, at least in retrospect, that being a late bloomer was an advantage because it allowed them to develop other, broadening interests, rather than becoming "boy-crazy" like so many of their peers in early adolescence (Tobin-Richards et al., 1984).

Before You Go On

What physical changes accompany early adolescence?

The Challenge of Identity Formation

Adolescents around the world give the impression of being great experimenters. They experiment with hairstyles, music, religions, drugs, sexual outlets, fad diets, part-time jobs, part-time relationships, and part-time philosophies of life. It often appears that most of a teenager's commitments are made on a part-time basis. Teens are busy trying things out, doing things their own way, off on a grand search for Truth.

This perception of adolescents as experimenters is not without foundation. It is consistent with the view that one of the major tasks of adolescence is the resolution of an **identity crisis**—the struggle to define and integrate the sense of who one is, what one is to do in life, and what one's attitudes, beliefs, and values should be. As I noted in Topic 8A, the concept of identity formation is associated with Erik

identity crisis *the effort to define and integrate one's sense of self and what one's attitudes, beliefs, and values should be*

One of the challenges of adolescence is identity formation. Who am I? What kind of a person am I to be? What shall be my values? What will I do with my life as I give up my dependence on my parents?

Erikson (1963), where the search for identity is the fifth stage of psychosocial development and occurs during the adolescent years (see Figure 8.7). During adolescence we come to grips with questions like: "Who am I?" "What am I going to do with my life?" "What is the point of it all?" Needless to say, these are not trivial questions.

For many young people, resolving one's identity crisis is a relatively simple and straightforward process. In such cases, the adolescent years bring very little confusion or conflict in terms of attitudes, beliefs, or values. Many teenagers are able and willing to accept the values and sense of self they began to develop in childhood. For many teenagers, however, the conflict of identity formation is quite real. They have a sense of giving up the values of parents and teachers in favor of new ones— their own. Physical growth, physiological changes, increased sexuality, and the perception of societal pressures to decide what they want to be when they "grow up" may lead to what Erikson calls role confusion, in which wanting to be independent, to be one's own self, does not fit in with the values of the past, of childhood. As a result, the teenager experiments with various possibilities in an attempt to see what works best, often to the dissatisfaction of bewildered parents.

Before You Go On

Summarize the adolescent's search for identity as described by Erikson.

The Challenge of Drug Use

There simply is no doubt that many adolescents experiment with drugs. Many use drugs on a regular basis, and many abuse drugs. Smoking (79 percent) and drinking alcohol (65 percent) lead the list of drug-related activities teenagers have tried at least once by the ninth grade (Gans & Blyth, 1990). The Centers for Disease Control (CDC) estimate that at least 600,000 adolescents began to smoke between 1985

One of the most serious challenges of adolescence is dealing with the attraction of alcohol and drugs. After a gradual decline, marijuana use among teenages has recently been on the rise.

and 1989 and that if they continue, about 50 percent will die from smoking-related diseases. The same CDC study showed that cigarette company expenditures for promoting their product rose from $771 million in 1982 to over $6 billion in 1993.

Drug use among teens rose steadily during the 1970s, dropped slowly during the 1980s, and is on the increase again in the 1990s. A survey by the University of Michigan Institute for Social Research showed a significant rise in drug use by secondary school students between 1993 and 1994, reporting that over 45 percent of 12th graders (and over 25 percent of 8th graders) admitted to using illegal drugs—most often marijuana. In September 1995 the Substance Abuse and Mental Health Services Administration released the results of their survey of 22,181 teens between the ages of 12 and 17. In this group, marijuana use had *doubled* since 1992. On the basis of this survey, we may estimate that nearly 1.3 million teenagers use marijuana on a monthly basis. There are no racial differences in drug use among adolescents (Oetting & Beauvais, 1990). Perceptions to the contrary, there are no differences in the rates of drug use between adolescents and adults (Warner et al., 1995).

Researchers have looked at the relationship between adolescent drug use and psychological health (Shedler & Block,1990). Participants in this investigation were 18-year-olds who had been under study since they were 3 years old. Based on their level of drug use, they were divided into one of three groups: (1) *abstainers* (N = 29), who had never tried any drug; (2) *experimenters* (N = 36), who had used marijuana "once or twice, or a few times," and who tried no more than one other drug; and (3) *frequent users* (N = 20), who used marijuana frequently and tried at least one other drug. There were no socioeconomic or IQ differences among the groups.

The researchers found that *frequent users* were generally maladjusted, alienated, deficient in impulse control, and "manifestly" distressed. The *abstainers* were overly anxious, "emotionally constricted," and lacking in social skills. These same results were apparent when the researchers examined records from when the same subjects were 7 and 11 years old. Generally, the *experimenters* were better adjusted and psychologically "healthier" than either of the other two groups. The authors of this study are concerned that their data will be misinterpreted—that their data might be taken to indicate "that drug use might somehow improve an adolescent's psychological health" (p. 628). Clearly this interpretation would be in error. You recognize these as correlational data from which no conclusion regarding cause and effect is justified.

While drug use among adolescents is a matter of great concern, there is evidence that we need not get hysterical about infrequent drug use among teenagers. In a review of substance use among teenagers, Newcomb and Bentler (1989, p. 247) put it this way:

> Not all drug use is bad and will fry one's brain (as the commercials imply). Such claims as reflected in the national hysteria and depicted in media advertisements for treatment programs repeat the failed scare tactics of the past. All drug abuse is destructive and can have devastating consequences for individuals, their families, and society. The difference or distinction lies in the use versus abuse of drugs.

Before You Go On

Summarize the data on drug use in adolescence.

The Challenge of Sexuality

For the adolescent, puberty is an intensely personal, private, and potentially confusing process. Under the direction of the hypothalamus and the pituitary gland, large doses of sex hormones enter the bloodstream, stimulating the development of secondary sex characteristics. In males, the neck and shoulders expand, hips narrow, facial and body hair begins to sprout, and the voice crackles and then lowers in pitch. In females, the breasts begin to develop, hips broaden and become more rounded, and the shoulders narrow. All of this takes time, but then, puberty is more of a process than a single event. It is during this process that sex hormones give rise to sex drives, which are expressed in sexual behaviors. With puberty, sexual behaviors can lead to pregnancy.

As you might imagine, collecting data on the sexual behaviors of adolescents isn't easy. Many surveys are biased because samples are small or not representative

In many cases, sexual intercourse among adolescents is unplanned and spontaneous. Unfortunately, this may lead to pregnancy and childbirth. It has become standard practice in many high schools to set aside a room for the care of the children of their high school students.

of the general population. Truthfulness can be a problem with survey data, even if anonymity is ensured. This is particularly the case when we are asking young people about an issue as sensitive as their own sexual behaviors. Some respondents stretch reality with tales of numerous sexual exploits, whereas others, perhaps somewhat anxious or guilt-ridden, tend to minimize reports of their sexual activities. Still, quality data can be found, and they tell us that adolescents are a sexually active group.

A report from the CDC released in 1991 tells us that the incidence of premarital sex has risen sharply in the last two decades. Nearly twice as many female teenagers (51.5 percent) had engaged in premarital sex by their late teens, compared to 1970 (28.6 percent). The largest relative increase occurred among girls 15 years old. A 1995 CDC report tells us that 53 percent of their sample was sexually active.

Most teens do not "plan" to be sexually active; it "just happens" (Chilman, 1983). The implication is that there is little consideration of short- and long-term consequences when behaviors "just happen." There are gender differences in how sexual activity is evaluated. One study (Coles & Stokes, 1985) tells us that about 60 percent of the males, but only 23 percent of the females, "felt glad" about their first intercourse (34 percent of the males and 61 percent of the females reported feeling "ambivalent"). A similar study reports that 67.4 percent of the males in their survey were "psychologically satisfied after their first sexual experience," whereas only 28.3 percent of the females shared in that satisfaction (Darling & Davidson, 1986).

With all of this sexual activity among adolescents, it is not surprising that teenage pregnancy has become a significant social problem. There are statistics to review. Each year more than half a million babies are born to adolescent mothers, of whom 66 percent of the white mothers and 97 percent of the black mothers are single (Furstenberg et al., 1989). A study released by the Alan Guttmacher Institute in 1995 tells us that half the fathers of babies born to mothers between 15 and 17 years old are adults—20 years or older. "Adolescent women in the United States have a higher risk of pregnancy than adolescents in any other developed Western country, with 4 out of 5 pregnancies unintended" (Ambuel, 1995, p. 1). Girls in the United States younger than 15 are five times more likely to give birth than are girls from any other developed country (Landers, 1987b). Between 1973 and 1987, pregnancy among teenagers *between the ages of 10 and 14* increased 23 percent (Moore, 1992). In 1989 alone, there were an estimated 9,000 births and 14,000 abortions among *girls age 14 and under* (Ambuel, 1995). Hayes (1987) estimates that approximately 400,000 teenage pregnancies end in abortion each year. Fortunately, America's teenage birthrates are slowly dropping—at the rates of 2 percent from 1992–1993, and another 2 percent from 1993–1994. Unfortunately, all of this decrease occurred in teens 18 and 19 years old; for girls 15 to 17, the birthrate was unchanged.

The physical, psychological, and financial costs of teenage pregnancy are high. Seventy percent of teenage mothers are not married. The child of a teenage mother is certainly a baby at risk. Teenage mothers face innumerable hurdles: they are much more likely to drop out of school, to be on welfare, to have inadequate access to health care, and to suffer economic hardships (Hayes, 1987; Hofferth & Hayes, 1987). But, remember, most adolescents do not plan to become pregnant. Teenage pregnancy may reflect a poor understanding of sexuality. For example, a significant number of adolescents do not believe they can become pregnant the first time they have intercourse, and teenagers generally hold negative attitudes about the use of contraceptives (Morrison, 1985).

What can we conclude about adolescents on the basis of the statistics we have reviewed here? Millions of adolescents are sexually active, and many are ignorant of the consequences of their own sexual behaviors. Those for whom sexual activity results in pregnancy may exceed a million each year. But let's not lose sight of the fact that most teenagers are not involved with unwanted pregnancies. Many adolescents know a great deal about sex. Dealing with one's sexuality effectively may not be easy, but it is just one of the challenges that must be addressed as one passes through adolescence. Adolescence is a developmental stage of challenge, and for some it is a stage of risk and danger. On the other hand, adolescence is a stage of growth, newfound freedom, responsibility, and independence.

Before You Go On

Summarize the data on adolescent sexuality and teenage pregnancy.

Early Adulthood

The changes that occur during our adult years may not seem as striking or dramatic as those that typify our childhood and adolescence, but they are no less real. Many of the adjustments we make as adults go unnoticed as we accommodate physical changes and psychological pressures. As an adult, one's health may become a concern for the first time. Psychological adjustments need to be made to marriage, parenthood, career, the death of friends and family, retirement, and, ultimately, one's own death.

Following the lead of Erikson (1968) and Levinson (1978, 1986), we will consider adulthood in terms of three overlapping periods, or seasons: *early adulthood* (roughly ages 18 to 45), *middle adulthood* (ages 45 to 65), and *late adulthood* (over age 65). Presenting adult development in this way can be misleading, so we'll have to be careful. Although there is support for developmental stages in adulthood, these stages may be better defined by the individual adult than by the developmental psychologist (Datan et al., 1987). Some psychologists find little evidence of orderly transitions in adulthood (Costa & McCrae, 1980; McCrae & Costa, 1984), while others find that there are sex differences in what determines the stage of one's adult life (Reinke et al., 1985).

If anything marks the transition from adolescence to adulthood it is choice and commitments made independently. The sense of identity fashioned in adolescence now needs to be put into action. In fact, the achievement of a sense of self by early adulthood is a good predictor of the success of intimate relationships later in adulthood (Kahn et al., 1985). With adult status, there are new and often difficult choices to be made. Advice may be sought from elders, parents, teachers, or friends, but as adults, individuals make their own choices. Should I get married? Which job should I pursue? Do I need more education? What sort? Where? Should we have children? How many? Many of these issues are first addressed in adolescence, during identity formation. But for the adult, these questions are no longer abstract. They are real questions that demand a response.

Levinson calls early adulthood the "era of greatest energy and abundance and of greatest contradiction and stress" (1986, p. 5). In terms of our physical development, we are at something of a peak during our twenties and thirties, and we are apparently willing to work hard to maintain that physical condition (McCann & Holmes, 1984). On the one hand, young adulthood is a season for finding our niche, for working through aspirations of our youth, for raising a family. On the other hand, it is a period of stress, finding the "right" job, taking on parenthood, and maintaining a balance among self, family, job, and society at large. Let's take a look at two important decision-making processes of young adulthood: the choice of mate and family, and the choice of job or career.

Marriage and Family

Erikson (1963) claims that early adulthood revolves around the choice of *intimacy or isolation*. Failure to establish close, loving, intimate relationships may result in loneliness and long periods of social isolation. Marriage is not the only source of interpersonal intimacy, but it is the first choice of most Americans. More young adults than ever before are postponing marriage plans, but fully 95 percent of us marry (at least once). In 1950, the average (median) age at the time of first marriage was 20.3 years for women and 22.8 years for men. By 1989, the age of women at their first marriage was 23.8 and the age of men was 26.2 years (U.S. Bureau of the Census, 1991). Americans claim that happiness in adulthood depends more on a successful marriage than any other factor, including friendship, career, community activities, and hobbies (Glenn & Weaver, 1981).

Young adults may value marriage, but the choice of whom to marry is of no small consequence. We've learned over the past 30 years that mate selection is a complex process. At least three factors influence the choice of a marriage partner

One of the markers of early adulthood is independence from one's parents. At the same time, early adulthood is marked by dependence—often in the form of marriage and the beginning of a new family.

(Newman & Newman, 1984). The first deals with *availability*. Before we can develop an intimate relationship with someone, we need the opportunity to develop the relationship in the first place. Availability is one thing, *eligibility* is a second. Here, matters of age, religion, race, politics, and background come into play. Available and eligible, a third factor enters the picture: *attractiveness*. Attractiveness in this context means physical attractiveness, but as we all know, judgments of physical beauty depend on who's doing the judging. Attractiveness also involves psychological characteristics such as understanding, emotional supportiveness, and similarity in values and goals.

Psychologist David Buss reviewed the evidence on mate selection with a focus on the question of whether opposites attract. He concluded that, in marriage, they do not. He found that "we are likely to marry someone who is similar to us in almost every variable" (Buss, 1985, p. 47). Most important (in order) are age, education, race, religion, and ethnic background, followed by attitudes and opinions, mental abilities, socioeconomic status, height, weight, and even eye color. Buss and his colleagues found that men and women are in nearly total agreement on the characteristics they seek in a mate (Buss, 1985; Buss & Barnes, 1986). Figure 8.9 presents 13 such characteristics ranked by men and women. There is a significant difference in ranking for only two: good earning potential and physical attractiveness.

Let's pause here and remind ourselves of two points that have come up before. (1) The conclusions of the studies cited above are true only in general, on the average. There may be happy couples that have few of the traits listed in Figure 8.9 in common. (2) These conclusions only hold in Western, largely Anglo, North American cultures. Buss and many others are studying preferences in selecting mates around the world. In one report of their efforts (Buss et al., 1990), people from 33 countries on six continents were studied. There were some similarities among all of the cultures studied, but cultures tended to show significantly different rankings of preferences for mates. The trait that varied most across cultures was *chastity*.

> Samples from China, India, Indonesia, Iran, Taiwan, and Arab Palestine placed great importance on chastity in a potential mate. Samples from Ireland and Japan placed moderate importance on chastity. In contrast, samples from Sweden, Finland, Norway, the Netherlands, and West Germany generally judged chastity to be irrelevant or unimportant. (Buss et al., 1990, p. 16)

Figure 8.9
Characteristics Sought in Mates

Rank (most important)	Male choices	Female choices
1	Kindness and understanding	Kindness and understanding
2	Intelligence	Intelligence
3	Physical attractiveness	Exciting personality
4	Exciting personality	Good health
5	Good health	Adaptability
6	Adaptability	Physical attractiveness
7	Creativity	Creativity
8	Desire for children	Good earning capacity
9	College graduate	College graduate
10	Good heredity	Desire for children
11	Good earning capacity	Good heredity
12	Good housekeeper	Good housekeeper

From Buss & Barnes, 1986.

You'll note that chastity is nowhere to be found on the list of preferred characteristics presented in Figure 8.9.

Choosing a marriage partner is not always a matter of making sound, rational decisions, regardless of one's culture. Several factors, including romantic love and the realities of economic hardship, sometimes affect such choices. As sound and sensible as choices at the time of marriage may seem, approximately 50 percent of all first marriages end in divorce (75 percent of second marriages suffer the same fate) (Gottman, 1994). In the United States, 9.4 years is the average life span of a first marriage (U.S. Bureau of the Census, 1991). In 1993, there were 10.9 million single parents rearing children in the United States, and over 4.7 million children lived with their grandparents, and not with either parent (U. S. Bureau of the Census, 1994).

Just as men and women tend to agree on what matters in choosing a mate, so do they agree on what matters in maintaining a marriage, listing such things as liking one's spouse as a friend, agreeing on goals, and a mutual concern for making the marriage work (Lauer & Lauer, 1985). Typically, men are more satisfied with their marriage than are women (Rhyne, 1981). One of the best predictors of a successful marriage is the extent to which marriage partners were able to maintain close relationships (such as with parents) *before* marriage (Wamboldt & Reiss, 1989). We'll return to this discussion in Chapter 14 when we consider interpersonal relationships in general.

Beyond establishing an intimate relationship, becoming a parent is often taken as a sure sign of adulthood. For many couples, parenthood is more a matter of choice than ever before because of more available means of contraception and new treatments for infertility. Having a family fosters the process of *generativity,* which Erikson associates with middle adulthood. **Generativity** reflects a concern for family and for one's impact on future generations. Although such concerns may not become central until one is over age 40, parenthood usually begins much sooner.

generativity a concern in adulthood for one's family and for one's impact on future generations

There is no doubt that having a baby around the house significantly changes established routines. Few couples have a realistic vision of what having children will do to their lives. The freedom for spontaneous trips, intimate outings, and privacy is in large measure given up in trade for the joys of parenthood. As parents, men and women take on the responsibilities of new social roles—of father and mother. These new adult roles add to the already established roles of being male or female, son or daughter, husband or wife, and so on. It seems that choosing to have children (or at least choosing to have a large number of children) is becoming less and less popular. Although many people see the decision not to have children as selfish, irresponsible, and immoral (Skolnick, 1978), there is no evidence that such a decision leads to a decline in well-being or satisfaction later in life (Beckman & Houser, 1982; Keith, 1983).

Career Choice

By the time a person has become a young adult, it is generally assumed that he or she has chosen a vocation or life's work. One's choice of occupation, and one's satisfaction with that choice, go a long way toward determining self-esteem and identity. For women in early adulthood, being employed outside the home is a major determinant of self-worth (Stein et al., 1990). These days, "dual-career" families, in which both the woman and the man are pursuing lifelong careers, are becoming quite common (Gilbert, 1994; Wisensale, 1992). Women now constitute about 39 percent of the professional labor force in this country.

Selection of a career is driven by many factors; family influence and the potential for earning money are just two (Rhodes, 1983; Shertzer, 1985). Choosing a career path involves several stages (Turner & Helms, 1987).

1. *Exploration:* There is a general concern that something needs to be done; a choice needs to be made, but alternatives are poorly defined, and plans for making a choice are not yet developed.

2. *Crystallization:* Some real alternatives are being weighed, pluses and minuses are associated with each possibility, and although some are eliminated, a choice is not yet made.

3. *Choice:* For better or worse, a decision is made. There is a sense of relief that at least one knows what one wants, and an optimistic feeling develops that everything will work out.

4. *Career clarification:* The person's self-image and career choice become intertwined. Adjustments and accommodations are made. This is a matter of fine-tuning one's initial choice: "I know I want to be a teacher; but what do I want to teach, and to whom?"

5. *Induction:* The career decision is implemented, presenting a series of potentially frightening challenges to one's own values and goals. "Is this really what I want to do?"

6. *Reformation:* One discovers that changes need to be made if one is to fit in with fellow workers and do the job as one is expected to do it. "This isn't going to be as simple as I thought it would be. I'd better take a few more classes."

7. *Integration:* The job and one's work become part of one's self, and one gives up part of one's self to the job. This is a period of considerable satisfaction.

Occasionally a person makes a poor career decision. This is most likely to occur, of course, in the third stage of choosing a career path, but probably won't be recognized until the fourth or fifth stage. In such cases, there is little to do but begin again and work through the process, seeking the self-satisfaction that comes at the final stage.

Before You Go On

What developments characterize early adulthood?

Middle Adulthood

As the middle years of adulthood approach, many aspects of one's life have become settled. By the time most people reach the age of 40, their place in the framework of society is fairly set. They have chosen their lifestyle and have grown accustomed to it. They have a family (or have decided not to). They have chosen their life work. "Most of us during our 40s and 50s become 'senior members' in our own particular worlds, however grand or modest they may be" (Levinson, 1986, p. 6). By and large, the notion of a *mid-life crisis* is mostly a myth (Costa & McCrae, 1980; Farrell & Rosenberg, 1981; Hunter & Sundel, 1989).

There are several tasks that one must face in the middle years. For starters, one must adjust to the physiological changes of middle age. Middle-aged persons can surely engage in many physical activities, but they may have to be selective or modify the vigor with which they attack such activities. Heading out to the backyard for pickup basketball with the neighborhood teenagers is something a 45-year-old may have to think twice about.

By middle adulthood, most people have chosen their career paths and have developed lifestyles that allow for more leisure time. At least this is presented as part of the American dream.

While career choices have been made, in middle age one comes to expect satisfaction with one's job. If career satisfaction is not attained, one may attempt a mid-career job change. Of course, there are also situations in which changing jobs in middle age is more a matter of necessity than choice. In either case, the potential for crisis and conflict or for growth and development exists.

A major set of challenges that middle-aged persons face is dealing with family members. At this stage in life, parents are often in the throes of helping their teenagers adjust to adolescence and prepare to "leave the nest," while at the same time caring for their own parents. Adults in this situation have been referred to as "the sandwich generation" (Brody, 1981; Neugarten & Neugarten, 1989). Individual responsibility and concern for the care of the elderly has not deteriorated in recent years. In fact, 80 percent of all day-to-day health care for the elderly is provided by family members.

One task of middle adulthood is similar to Erikson's crisis of generativity versus stagnation. People shift from thinking about all they have done with their life to thinking about what they will do with what time is left for them, and how they can leave a mark on future generations (Erikson, 1963; Harris, 1983).

Although all of the "tasks" I've noted so far are interdependent, this is particularly true of these last two: relating to one's spouse as a person, and developing leisure-time activities. As children leave home and financial concerns diminish, there may be more time for one's spouse and for leisure. In the eyes of adults, these tasks can amount to enjoying each other, enjoying one's status, enjoying one's retirement, vacations, and travel. In truth, taking advantage of these opportunities in meaningful ways provides a challenge for some adults whose lives have previously been devoted to children and career.

Before You Go On

What are some of the tasks typically faced during the middle years of adulthood?

⊚⊚⊚⊚ **Thinking Critically** ⊚⊚⊚⊚

If there is no such thing as a "mid-life crisis," why do so many people seem to act as if there were?

Late Adulthood

The transition to *late adulthood* generally occurs in our early to mid-sixties. Perhaps the first thing to acknowledge is that persons over the age of 65 constitute a sizable and growing proportion of the population. More than 30.4 million Americans were in this age bracket in 1988, and the numbers are increasing by an average of 1,400 per day (Fowles, 1990). By the year 2020, Americans over 65 will constitute nearly 20 percent of the population, compared to the current 12 percent (Cavenaugh & Park, 1993). Because of the coming of age of the "baby boom" generation, by the year 2030 there will be about *66 million* older persons in the United States (Fowles, 1990). According to a Census Bureau report, by the year 2050, the number of persons of age 65-plus years will be *78.9 million*—with an average life span of 82.1 years (AARP, 1993). The data also tell us that "aging is disproportionally a women's issue." The vast majority of those over age 80 are women, and the number of older ethnic minority adults is increasing more rapidly than for the population in general (Cavenaugh & Park, 1993).

What It Means to Be Old

ageism *discrimination or prejudice against someone formed solely on the basis of age*

Ageism is the name given to discrimination and prejudice against a group on the basis of age. Ageism is particularly acute in our attitudes about the elderly (Kimmel, 1988). One misconception about the aged is that they live in misery. We cannot ignore some of the difficulties that come with aging, but matters may not be as bad as many believe they are. Sensory capacities, for example, are not what they used to be. But as Skinner (1983) suggested, "If you cannot read, listen to book recordings. If you do not hear well, turn up the volume of your phonograph (and wear headphones to protect your neighbors)." Some cognitive abilities decline with age, but others develop to compensate for most losses (Salthouse, 1989). Some apparent memory loss may reflect more of a choice of what one wants to remember than an actual loss. Mental speed is reduced, but the accumulated experience of living often outweighs any advantages of speed (Meer, 1986).

Children have long since left the nest, but they're still in touch, and now there are grandchildren with whom to interact. Further, the children of the elderly have reached adulthood themselves, and are more able and likely to provide support for aging parents. Most older adults live in family settings. In fact, only about 5 percent of Americans over the age of 65 live in nursing homes (Fowles, 1990; Harris, 1983). Even among those elderly in the United States classified as "poor" or "near poor," almost two-thirds own and live in their own homes—a percentage higher than that for their children (USGAO, 1992).

Some individuals dread retirement, but most welcome it as a chance to do things they have planned on for years (Haynes et al., 1978). Many people over the age of 65 become *more* physically active after retiring, perhaps from a job in which they sat at a desk all day long.

We often assume that old age necessarily brings with it the curse of poor health, but in 1987, only 31 percent of respondents to a survey over age 65 claimed poor health to be a serious problem (Fowles, 1990). That compares to 7 percent in the 18-to–54 age range and 18 percent in the 55-to–65 age range. So, although health problems are more common in the elderly, they are not as widespread or as devastating as we might think.

One scheme developmental psychologists are finding useful is to divide those over age 65 into two groups: *the young-old* and *the old-old*. This distinction is not made on the basis of one's actual age, but on the basis of psychological, social, and health characteristics (Committee on an Aging Society, 1986; Neugarten & Neugarten, 1986). This distinction reinforces the notion that aging is not some sort of disease. The young-old group is the large majority of those over 65 years of age (80 to 85 percent). They are "vigorous and competent men and women who have re-

One of the benefits of late adulthood is that there should be time to become involved in one's community. Many older adults derive great satisfaction from volunteering to serve as aides in hospitals, helping out with newborn babies.

duced their time investments in work or homemaking, are relatively comfortable financially and relatively well educated, and are well-integrated members of their families and communities" (Neugarten & Neugarten, 1989).

The concept of *successful aging* is one that, until recently, seldom got much attention. Most research on the elderly has focused on *average* age-related losses. John Rowe and Robert Kahn (1987) argue "that the role of aging per se in these losses has often been over-stated and that a major component of many age-associated declines can be explained in terms of life-style, habits, diet, and an array of psychosocial factors extrinsic to the aging process" (p. 143). The argument is that the declines, deficits, and losses of the elderly are not the result of advanced age but of factors over which we all can exercise some degree of control (Schaie, 1993). The major contributors to decline in old age include such things as poor nutrition, smoking, alcohol use, inadequate calcium intake, failure to maintain a sense of autonomy or control over one's life circumstances, and lack of social support (as long as the support does not erode self-control). Attention to these factors may not lengthen the life span, but should extend what Rowe and Kahn call the "health span, the maintenance of full function as nearly as possible to the end of life" (1987, p.149). Research suggests, for example, that close family relationships and involvement in effective exercise programs predict successful aging (Clarkson-Smith & Hartley, 1989; Valliant & Valliant, 1990). If it comes from the initiative of the individual, a growing dependency on others can be a positive, adaptive strategy for successful aging (Baltes, 1995; Baltes & Baltes, 1990).

Death and Dying

Of the two sure things in life, death and taxes, the former is the surer. There are no loopholes. Dealing with the reality of our own death is the last major crisis we face in life. Many people never have to deal with their own death in psychological

---

EXPERIENCING PSYCHOLOGY

An Ageism Survey

Ageism is a discriminatory practice or negative stereotype formed solely on the basis of age. Although ageism can occur with regard to persons of any age, it is most often directed against the elderly. Here is a simple, 10-item true or false quiz about the elderly. Use it to see if you can detect any signs of ageism in the responses.

Indicate whether each of the following statements is "true" or "false." Consider "younger" to refer to persons under 65 years of age and "older" to refer to those over 65 years of age.

1. Older people are more likely than younger people to attend church.
2. Older people are more cautious and less likely to make risky decisions than are younger people.
3. As people age, they tend to become more like each other.
4. Older people have more difficulty than younger people in adapting to a changing environment.
5. A decrease in life satisfaction is usually experienced by older persons.
6. The majority of persons over 65 live in nursing home type institutions.
7. Mental disorders occur more frequently among older people than among younger people.
8. Depression is more common in older people than in younger people.
9. Decreasing intelligence as measured by IQ tests and other measures of cognitive functions is one of the inevitable changes that occur with age.
10. Aging of the brain leads the way for deterioration of other bodily systems and functions.

Scoring this "quiz" is very easy because each item is worded so that it is false.

The one sure thing about life is death. In old age, people do think about and talk about death more than when they were younger, but they are no more morbid about or afraid of death than younger adults. This scene is a New Orleans funeral procession, "celebrating" the passing of a loved one.

terms. These are the people who die young or suddenly. Many individuals *do* have time to contemplate their own death, and this usually takes place in late adulthood.

Much attention was focused on the confrontation with death in the popular book *On Death and Dying,* by Elisabeth Kübler-Ross (1969, 1981). Her description of the stages one goes through when facing death was based on hundreds of interviews with terminally ill patients who were aware that they were dying. Kübler-Ross suggests that the process takes place in five stages: (1) *denial*–a firm, simple avoidance of the evidence; a sort of "No, this can't be happening to me" reaction; (2) *anger*–often accompanied by resentment and envy of others, along with a realization of what is truly happening; a sort of "Why me? Why not someone else?" reaction; (3) *bargaining*–a matter of dealing, or bartering, usually with God; a search for more time; a sort of "If you'll just grant me a few more weeks, or months, I'll go to church every week; no, every day" reaction; (4) *depression*–a sense of hopelessness that bargaining won't work, that a great loss is imminent; a period of grief and sorrow over both past mistakes and what will be missed in the future; and (5) *acceptance*–a rather quiet facing of the reality of death, with no great joy or sadness; simply a realization that the time has come.

Kübler-Ross's description may be idealized. Many dying patients do not fit this pattern at all (Butler & Lewis, 1981; Katenbaum & Costa, 1977). Some may show behaviors consistent with one or two of the stages, but seldom all five (Schultz & Alderman, 1974). There is some concern that this pattern of approaching death may be viewed as the "best" or the "right'" way to go about it. The concern is that caretakers may try to force dying people into and through these stages, instead of letting each face the inevitability of death in his or her own way (Kalish, 1976, 1985).

Although elderly people have to deal with dying and death, they are less morbid about it than are adolescents (Lanetto, 1980). In one study (Kalish, 1976), adults over age 60 did more frequently think about and talk about death than did the younger adults surveyed. However, of all of the adults in the study, the oldest group expressed the least fear of death, some even saying they were eager for it.

Before You Go On

Summarize what we know about the elderly.

☾☉☉☾ **Thinking Critically** ☾☉☉☾

How do different cultures view and treat the elderly in their societies?

TOPIC 8B SUMMARY

Adolescence begins with a growth spurt and puberty—the processes that bring one to full sexual maturity. Reaching puberty before or after most of one's peers can have implications for both boys and girls, although the consequences of early or late blooming are seldom long-lasting, especially for girls. We briefly explored three challenges of the teen years: (1) identity formation, in which one struggles to define one's self and to find how he or she will fit into the world; (2) drug use, which is again on the increase, but still no more common in adolescence than in adulthood and (3) sexuality, where we noted that a large percentage of adolescents are sexually active. A consequence of adolescent sexual activity is a rising rate of pregnancy and parenthood, especially among very young teens—children having children.

Adulthood is characterized by both independence (largely from parents) and interdependence (on new family ties). Development throughout adulthood is slower than in other stages, but choices still need to be made and crises resolved, both often involving marriage, family, and career.

Having read this chapter, you might now be impressed with the orderliness and predictability of human development. Ova and sperm cells unite to form zygotes. Zygotes become embryos, fetuses, and, through birth, neonates. Neonates are born with a range of adaptive reflexes and sensory capabilities. Motor development progresses through a series of identifiable stages. Depending on the theory, cognitive development passes through four stages, psychosocial development progresses through eight stages, and moral development through six. Many of the conflicts of adolescence are predictable. Adulthood moves from choice to commitment to preparation for death. As easy as it is to be impressed with the orderliness of human development, please remember not to take this too literally. Orderly sequences of development emerge from examining averages and progressions in general. Developmental trends and stages are like so many other things: if one looks hard enough, they can be found. But the individual differences we see around us constantly remind us that for any individual—child, adolescent, or adult—many of our observations may not hold true. The orderliness of development may exist only in the eyes of the observer. The picture we have drawn in this chapter is one of general conclusions to which there will always be exceptions.

CHAPTER SUMMARY

Topic 8A

Describe the stages of prenatal development.

Prenatal development begins at conception and ends at birth. The period is divided into three stages: the stage of the zygote (conception to 2 weeks), during which the organism becomes implanted in the uterus; the stage of the embryo (week 2 to week 8), during which there is rapid growth and differentiation of developing cells; and the stage of the fetus (month 3 until birth), during which the organs begin to function. /pp. 276–277

What effects do diet and drugs have on prenatal development?

A mother's diet and use of drugs can have profound effects on prenatal development. Malnutrition in the mother, or deficiencies of specific vitamins or minerals, are usually shared by the embryo or the fetus. Smoking and alcohol use during pregnancy have well-documented negative effects. Even aspirin and caffeine use should be curtailed during pregnancy. Although most attention is focused on the health and behaviors of the pregnant mother, the health and behavior of the father at or about the time of conception are not irrelevant in predicting the birth of a healthy child. /pp. 278–279

What general observations can we make about physical growth and motor control in childhood?

The neonate is born with several reflexes that have survival value. Other reflexes seem to serve no particular function for the neonate but can be used to confirm normal physical development. The age at which motor skills develop varies from child to child, but the sequence is predictable. Review Figure 8.1. Growth and development follow two patterns: (1) cephalocaudal, from head to torso to feet, and (2) proximodistal, from center to extremities. /pp. 279–281

Summarize the sensory capacities of the neonate.

The neonate's senses function reasonably well from birth. The eyes can focus at arm's length, although they will require a few months to focus over a range of object distances. Rudimentary depth perception seems to be present even in the neonate, but improves considerably within the first year. Hearing and auditory discrimination are quite good, as are the senses of taste, smell, and touch. /pp. 281–283

What cognitive abilities can be demonstrated by a neonate?

Newborns just a few hours old give evidence of learning through classical and operant conditioning. Neonates (in one study only 1 to 4 days old) demonstrate memory. They will attend to a new visual pattern after ignoring a familiar one, showing an appreciation of the difference between familiar and new. They show preferences for complex visual patterns over simple ones, and prefer (attend to) visual representations of the human face, the mother's face in particular. /pp. 283–284

What characterizes each of the four stages of cognitive development proposed by Piaget?

During the sensorimotor stage a baby develops schemas (assimilating new information and accommodating old concepts) through an interaction with the environment—by sensing and doing. The baby begins to appreciate cause-and-effect relationships, imitates the actions of others, and by the end of the period, develops a sense of object permanence. Egocentrism is found in the preoperational stage of development. The child becomes me- and I-oriented, unable to appreciate the world from anyone else's perspective. In addition, children begin to develop and use symbols, in the form of words to represent concepts.

In the concrete operations stage, a child organizes concepts into categories, begins to use simple logic and to understand relational terms. Conservation involves coming to understand that changing something's form does not change its nature or quantity. The essence of the formal operations stage is the ability to think, reason, and solve problems symbolically, or in an abstract rather than a concrete, tangible form. /pp. 284–288

Cite two criticisms of Piaget's theory.

Piaget's theory of cognitive development has been very influential and has received support from cross-cultural studies, but it has not escaped criticism. Two criticisms of the theory are that (1) there is little evidence that cognitive abilities develop in a series of well-defined stages (that is, the borders between stages are poorly defined), and (2) preschool children seem to have more cognitive abilities than Piaget suggested. /pp. 288–290

Summarize Kohlberg's theory of moral development.

Kohlberg claims that moral reasoning develops through three levels of two stages each. First, one decides between right and wrong on the basis of avoiding punishment and gaining rewards (preconventional morality), then on the basis of conforming to authority or accepting social convention (conventional morality), and finally on the basis of one's understanding of the common good, individual rights, and internalized standards (postconventional morality). Although much of the theory has been supported, there is little evidence that many individuals reach the higher levels of moral reasoning. Also, there may be serious deficiencies in applying the theory equally to both sexes or to all cultures, wherein what is "moral," or "right" may vary. /pp. 290–292

Briefly describe the first four stages (crises) of development according to Erikson.

Of Erikson's eight stages of development, four occur during childhood. These stages are described in terms of crises that need resolution, and include (1) trust versus mistrust (whether the child develops a sense of security or anxiety), (2) autonomy versus self-doubt (whether the child develops a sense of competence or doubt), (3) initiative versus guilt (whether the child gains confidence in his or her own ability or becomes guilty and resentful), and (4) competence versus inferiority (whether the child develops confidence in intellectual and social skills or develops a sense of failure and lack of confidence.) /pp. 292–294

What conclusions may we draw about the development of gender identity in children?

Gender identity is the sense or self-awareness of one's maleness or femaleness and the roles that males and females traditionally play in one's culture. Most children have a sense of their own gender by the age of 2 to 3 years, with gender identity most strongly reinforced by peer groups and play activities. A child's cognitive sense of gender stereotypes may flavor how new information is accommodated. /pp. 294–297

In child development, what is "attachment," and what are the consequences of developing secure attachments?

Attachment is a strong, two-way emotional bond, formed early in childhood between the child and primary caregiver(s). It has survival value in an evolutionary sense, keeping the child in proximity to those who can best care for him or her. Secure attachment in childhood has been associated with improved self-esteem later in life. Fathers, as well as mothers, demonstrate appropriate attachment-related behaviors, and to date, most evidence is that day care for children (at least those older than 2 years) need

not have negative consequences (depending mostly on the quality of care). /pp. 297–299

Topic 8B

How might adolescence be defined, and how might the period be characterized?

Physically, adolescence begins with puberty (attainment of sexual maturity) and lasts until the end of one's physical growth. Psychologically, it is defined in terms of cognitions and feelings that characterize the period, searching for identity, and abstract thinking. Socially, it is a period of transition, coming between childhood and adulthood, reflecting how the adolescent is viewed by others. Historically, the period has been seen as one of stress, distress, and abnormality. More contemporary views see adolescence as a period of challenges, but a period that most survive with no lasting negative consequences. /pp. 300–301

What physical changes accompany early adolescence?

Two significant physical developments mark adolescence: a spurt of growth, seen at an earlier age in girls than in boys, and the beginning of sexual maturity, a period called puberty. As adolescents, individuals are for the first time physically prepared for sexual reproduction and begin to develop secondary sex characteristics. The consequences of reaching puberty early are a bit more positive for males than females, although the long-term consequences for both are few and slight. /pp. 301–303

Summarize the adolescent's search for identity as described by Erikson.

The search for one's identity—a sense of who one is and what one is to do with one's life—is, for Erikson, the major crisis of adolescence. Most do develop such a sense of identity, but some do enter adulthood in a state of what Erikson calls role confusion. /pp. 303–304

Summarize the data on drug use in adolescence.

Most teenagers have experimented with drugs, and many use drugs frequently. One study showed that among frequent users, experimenters, and abstainers, adolescents classified as experimenters evidenced the fewest psychological problems as 18-year-olds. Drug use among teenagers is no worse (but no better) than among the adult population. After declinng slightly in the 1980s, drug use is on the rise again. /pp. 304–306

Summarize the data on adolescent sexuality and teenage pregnancy.

About half of all adolescent females and males report being sexually active. Teens' first sexual encounters most often just "happen," which may help to explain why so many become pregnant each year. Slightly over half of all teenage pregnancies result in live births. About two-thirds of white teenage mothers are unmarried, and virtually all black teenage mothers are single; most of the fathers are adults (older than 20). In 1989 alone, there were 14,000 abortions among girls age 14 and younger. */pp. 306–308*

What developments characterize early adulthood?

Early adulthood (ages 18 to 45) is characterized by choices and commitments made independently. One assumes new responsibilities and is faced with decisions about career, marriage, and family. For Erikson, the period is marked by the conflict between intimacy and social relationships on the one hand and social isolation on the other. Many marriages do fail, but most young adults list a good marriage as a major source of happiness in their lives. Many factors determine one's selection of a mate. There is little support for the notion that opposites attract. Characteristics of desired mates vary among cultures. Choosing one's career or occupation is a decision of early adulthood. It is a process that goes through several stages, and often initially fails. */pp. 308–312*

What are some of the tasks typically faced during the middle years of adulthood?

Middle adulthood (ages 45 to 65) may be troublesome for some, but most find middle age a period of great satis-faction and opportunity. The individual comes to accept his or her own mortality in several ways. Tasks of middle age involve adapting to one's changing physiology, occupation, aging parents and growing children, social and civic responsibilities, and the use of leisure time. */pp. 312–313*

Summarize what we know about the elderly.

There are more than 30 million Americans over age 65, and the number of elderly is growing rapidly. Although there may be sensory, physical, and cognitive limits forced by old age, only 31 percent of elderly people rate health problems as a major concern. Although some elderly are isolated and lonely, fewer than 5 percent live in nursing homes. Older people may be concerned about death, but they are neither consumed by it nor morbid about it. With good nutrition and diet, the development of a healthy lifestyle, proper social support, and the maintenance of some degree of autonomy and control over one's life, "successful aging" can become even more common than it is today. This is another way of saying that we can increase the already large percentage (now 80 to 85 percent) of those over the age of 65 who have been characterized as young-old, as opposed to old-old. */pp. 314–317*

PRACTICING PSYCHOLOGY

Testing the Reality of Stages of Development

In this chapter we've had much to say about stages of development in childhood—cognitive development, psychosocial development, and moral development. Here is a list of these various stages, grouped by theorist. Your task is to devise a means of assessing the development of any particular person in terms of these stages. That is, what characterizes a person in Piaget's preoperational stage or in Erikson's stage of initiative vs. guilt or Kohlberg's conventional morality? (Suggested answers can be found on p. 573.)

Piaget's Stages of Cognitive Development

   Sensorimotor stage:
   Preoperational stage:
   Concrete operations stage:
   Formal operations stage:

Erikson's Psychosocial Stages of Development

   Trust versus mistrust:
   Autonomy versus self-doubt:
   Initiative versus guilt:
   Competence versus inferiority:
   Identity versus role confusion:
   Intimacy versus isolation:
   Generativity versus stagnation:
   Ego-identity versus despair:

Kohlberg's Stages of Moral Development

   Preconventional morality:
   Conventional (conforming) morality:
   Postconventional morality:

OUTLINE

J have been teaching introductory psychology for many years. By now, I feel I understand the basic personalities of most introductory psychology students quite well. Some of my observations are listed below. To test their accuracy, go through the list and indicate the extent to which each statement applies to you. If you think the statement is an accurate appraisal, mark it with a 1. If you think it is only partially accurate, or true only some of the time, give it a 2. If you think the statement does not apply to you at all, give it a 3.

_____ You have a rather strong need for other people to like you and for them to admire you.

_____ You have a tendency to be critical of yourself.

_____ You feel somewhat uncomfortable when called on in class, even if you know the answer to the question.

_____ While you have some personality weaknesses, you generally are able to compensate for them.

_____ Disciplined and controlled on the outside, you tend to be a bit insecure and worrisome on the inside.

_____ You prefer a certain amount of change and variety, and become dissatisfied when hemmed in by restrictions.

Personality

_____ You have found it unwise to be too frank in revealing yourself to others.

_____ At times you are extroverted, easy-going, and sociable, while at other times you are introverted, wary, and reserved.

_____ Some of your aspirations tend to be pretty unrealistic.

_____ Your sexual adjustments have presented some problems for you.

_____ At times you have serious doubts as to whether you have made the right decision or done the right thing.

Add up the scores so that we can see how well I've done. A low score means I did fairly well; a score of 11 indicates that I was accurate with every observation. When I do this exercise in class, nearly 90 percent of my students have a score of 18 or less. That's pretty good, isn't it? But wait a minute! How could I possibly have any insight about the personalities of the students in my class, most of whom I hardly know at all? How could I describe your personality accurately, when we've never met?

This little "test" is a version of a demonstration that dates back at least to 1956 (Munn, 1956). Ten of these items come from the Generalized Personality Test (or GPT) described in an article by Ulrich, Stachnick, and Stainton in 1963. The truth is that these statements are so general that they are virtually meaningless, and could be applied to nearly everyone. Also note that these "test items" are very similar to the statements one commonly finds in daily horoscopes.

Psychology has valued the concept of personality throughout its history. Over the years, many theories have sought to describe the nature of personality. In Topic 9A, we'll examine some of those theories, each of which has added to our understanding of personality. In Topic 9B, we consider three issues related to personality: the extent to which personality or the situation determines our behaviors, the extent to which there are gender differences in personality, and how personality is measured or assessed.

TOPIC 9A Theories of Personality

The major task of this Topic is to describe some of the theories of personality. We'll organize this discussion of specific personality theories into four basic approaches. But, before we do, let's see what we mean by *theory* and *personality* in this context.

A theory is a series of assumptions; in our particular case, these assumptions are about people and their personalities. The ideas or assumptions that constitute a theory are based on observations, and are reasonably and logically related to each other. The ideas of a theory should lead, through reason, to specific, testable hypotheses. In short, a **theory** is an organized collection of testable ideas used to explain a particular subject matter.

What, then, is personality? Few terms have been as difficult to define. Actually, each of the theoretical approaches we will study in this Topic generates its own definition of personality. We'll say that **personality** includes the affects, behaviors, and cognitions of people that characterize them in a number of situations over time. (Here again is our *ABC* mnemonic from Topic 1A.) Personality also includes those dimensions we can use to judge people to be different from one another. So, with personality theories we are looking for ways that allow us to describe how people remain the same over time and circumstances, and to describe differences we know exist among people (R. F. Baumeister, 1987). Note that personality somehow resides *inside* the person; it's something a person brings to his or her interactions with the environment. Here's another way of saying the same thing: "Personality refers to the enduring, inner characteristics of individuals that organize their behaviors" (Derlega et al., 1991, p. 2).

theory *an organized collection of ultimately testable ideas used to explain a particular subject matter*

personality *those affects, behaviors, and cognitions that characterize a person in a variety of situations*

The Psychoanalytic Approach

psychoanalytic *the approach to personality associated with Freud and his followers that relies on instincts and the unconscious as explanatory concepts*

We begin our discussion of personality with the **psychoanalytic** approach, associated with Sigmund Freud and his students. We begin with Freud because he was the first to present a unified theory of personality.

Freud's theory of personality has been one of the most influential and, at the same time, most controversial in all of science. There are many facets to Freud's theory (and those of his students), but two basic premises characterize the approach: (1) a reliance on innate drives as explanatory concepts for human behavior, and (2) an acceptance of the power of unconscious forces to mold and shape behavior.

Freud's Theory

Freud's ideas about personality arose from his reading of the works of philosophers, his observations of his patients, and intense self-examination. His private practice provided Freud with experiences from which he proposed a general theory of personality and a technique of therapy, which is discussed in Topic 13B. Here we review some of Freud's basic ideas about the structure and dynamics of human personality.

Levels of Consciousness. Central to Freudian personality theory is the notion that information, feelings, wants, drives, desires, and the like can be found at various levels of awareness, or consciousness. Topic 4A centered on a discussion of levels of human consciousness—and Freud's views about such levels. Let's quickly review that discussion. (You might want to check Figure 4.1 on page 123 again.)

Mental events of which we are actively aware at the moment are *conscious,* or "in consciousness." Aspects of our mental life of which we are not conscious at any moment, but that can be easily brought to awareness, are stored at a *preconscious* level. When you shift your awareness to think about something you may do this evening, those plans were probably already there, in your preconscious mind.

Cognitions, feelings, motives, and the like that are not available at the conscious or preconscious level are said to be in the *unconscious*. Here we keep ideas, memories, and desires of which we are not aware and cannot easily become aware. Remember the significance of the unconscious level of the mind: even though thoughts and feelings are stored there so that we are completely unaware of them, the contents of the unconscious mind still influence us. Unconscious content, passing through the preconscious, may show itself in slips of the tongue, humor, neurotic symptoms, and dreams. Freud believed that unconscious forces could explain behaviors that otherwise seemed irrational and beyond description.

Before You Go On

What are the three levels of consciousness proposed by Freud?

Basic Instincts. According to Freudian theory, our behaviors, thoughts, and feelings are largely governed by innate biological drives, referred to as *instincts* in this context. These are inborn impulses or forces that rule our personalities. There may be many separate drives or instincts, but they can be grouped into two categories.

On the one hand are **life instincts (eros),** or impulses for survival, including those that motivate sex, hunger, and thirst. Each instinct has its own energy that compels us into action (drives us). Freud called the energy through which the sexual instincts operate **libido**. Opposed to life instincts are **death instincts (thanatos)**. These are largely impulses of destruction. Directed inward, they give rise to feelings of depression or suicide; directed outward, they result in aggression. In large measure, life (according to Freud) is an attempt to resolve conflicts between these two natural but diametrically opposed instincts.

The Structure of Personality. As we have seen, Freud believed that the mind operates on three interacting levels of awareness: conscious, preconscious, and unconscious. Freud proposed that personality also consists of three separate, though interacting, structures or subsystems: the id, ego, and superego. Each of these structures or subsystems has its own job to do and its own principles to follow.

The **id** is the totally inborn or inherited portion of personality. It resides in the unconscious level of the mind, and it is through the id that basic instincts develop. The driving force of the id is *libido,* or sexual energy, although it may be more fair to say "sensual" rather than "sexual" so as not to imply that Freud was always talking about adult sexual intercourse. The id operates on the **pleasure principle**, indicating that the major function of the id is to find satisfaction for basic pleasurable impulses. Although the other divisions of personality develop later, our id remains with us always and is the basic energy source in our lives.

The **ego** is the part of the personality that develops through one's experience with reality. In many ways, it is our self, the rational, reasoning part of our personality. The ego operates on the **reality principle**. One of the ego's main jobs is to try to find satisfaction for the id, but in ways that are reasonable and rational. The ego may delay gratification of some libidinal impulse or may need to find an acceptable outlet for some need. Freud said that "the ego stands for reason and good sense while the id stands for untamed passions" (Freud, 1933).

The last of the three structures to develop is the **superego**, which we can liken to one's sense of morality, or conscience. It reflects our internalization of society's rules. The superego operates on the **idealistic principle**. One problem we have with our superegos is that they, like our ids, have no contact with reality and therefore often place unrealistic demands on the individual. The superego demands that

life instincts (eros) *inborn impulses, proposed by Freud, that compel one toward survival; they include hunger, thirst, and sex*

libido *the energy that activates the sexual instincts*

death instincts (thanatos) *the inborn impulses, proposed by Freud, that compel one toward destruction; they include feelings of depression and aggression*

id *the instinctive aspect of personality that seeks immediate gratification of impulses; it operates on the pleasure principle*

pleasure principle *the impulse of the id to seek immediate gratification to reduce tensions*

ego *the aspect of personality that encompasses the sense of "self"; it is in contact with the real world and operates on the reality principle*

reality principle *the force that governs the ego, arbitrating between the demands of the id and the realities of the world*

superego *the aspect of personality that refers to ethical or moral considerations; it operates on the idealistic principle*

idealistic principle *the force that governs the superego; opposed to the id, it seeks adherence to standards of ethics and morality* we do what *it* deems right and proper, no matter what the circumstances. Failure to do so may lead to guilt and shame. Again, it falls to the ego to try to maintain a realistic balance between the conscience of the superego and the libido of the id.

This isn't as complicated as it may sound. Suppose a bank teller discovers an extra $20 in her cash drawer at the end of the day. She certainly could use an extra $20. "Go ahead. Nobody will miss it. The bank can afford a few dollars here and there. Think of the fun you can have with an extra $20," is the basic message from her id. "The odds are that you'll get caught if you take this money. If you are caught, you may lose your job; then you'll have to find another one," reasons her ego. "You shouldn't even think about taking that money. Shame on you! It's not yours. It belongs to someone else and should be returned," the superego protests. Clearly, the interaction of the three components of one's personality isn't always this simple and straightforward, but this example illustrates the general idea.

Before You Go On

Describe the three structures of personality as Freud saw them.

The Defense Mechanisms. If the ego cannot find acceptable ways to satisfy the drives of the id, or if it cannot deal with the demands of the superego, conflict and anxiety result. Then ways must be found to combat the resulting anxiety. It

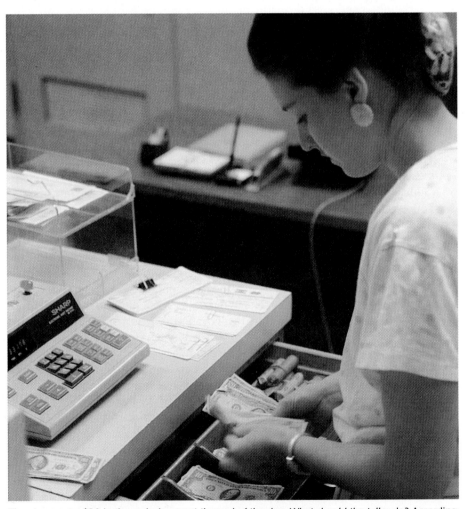

There's an extra $20 in the cash drawer at the end of the day. What should the teller do? According to Freudian theory, her id may tell her one thing, her ego may tell her something else, and her superego may give her a third message to consider.

was for this purpose that Freud proposed **defense mechanisms**—unconsciously applied techniques that protect the self (ego) against strong feelings of anxiety. What follows is a list of some of the more common ego defense mechanisms, with an example of each.

Repression is the most basic defense mechanism. It is sometimes referred to as *motivated forgetting,* which gives you a good idea of what is involved. Repression is a matter of (conveniently) forgetting about some anxiety-producing event or desire. Paul had a teacher with whom he did not get along. After spending an entire semester trying to do his best, Paul failed the course. The following summer, while Paul was walking with his girlfriend, the teacher approached Paul, and Paul could not remember the instructor's name. He had repressed it. Forgetting about everything and everyone who ever caused you anxiety is not an adaptive response, but pushing some anxiety-producing memories into the depths of the unconscious can protect us from dwelling on unpleasantness.

Denial is a mechanism of defense in which a person refuses to acknowledge the realities of an anxiety-producing situation. When a physician first tells a patient that he or she has a terminal illness, a common reaction is denial; the patient refuses to believe or accept that the diagnosis is accurate.

Rationalization amounts to making up excuses for one's behaviors rather than facing the (anxiety-producing) real reasons for them. The real reason Kevin failed his psychology midterm is that he didn't study for it and had missed several classes. Kevin hates to admit, even to himself, that he could have been so stupid as to flunk this exam because of his own actions or inactions. So he rationalizes: "It really wasn't my fault. I had a terrible instructor. The test was grossly unfair. We used a lousy textbook. And I've been fighting the flu all semester."

Fantasy provides an escape from anxiety through imagination or daydreaming. It is a defense mechanism commonly used by college students. After a week of exams and term paper deadlines, isn't it pleasant to sit back in a comfortable chair and fantasize about graduating from college with honors? To engage in fantasy from time to time is a normal and acceptable reaction to stress and anxiety. On the other hand, there are potential dangers here. One needs to be able to keep separate those activities that are real and those that occur in fantasies. Fantasy in itself will not solve the problems or resolve the conflicts that caused the anxiety in the first

defense mechanisms *unconsciously applied techniques that protect the self (ego) from feelings of anxiety*

repression *a defense mechanism referring to motivated forgetting of an anxiety-producing event or desire*

denial *a defense mechanism wherein one refuses to believe the realities of an anxiety-producing situation*

rationalization *a defense mechanism that excuses one's behaviors rather than facing the anxiety-producing reasons for them*

fantasy *a defense mechanism that involves the imagination or daydreaming as a reaction to stress and anxiety*

Fantasy is a common anxiety defense mechanism, often used by college students. You are frustrated with traffic and parking problems on campus. Wouldn't it be fun to imagine that you were at the controls of a sports car, racing down the open road?

projection *a defense mechanism that involves seeing one's own unacceptable, anxiety-producing characteristics in others*

regression *a defense mechanism that involves returning to earlier, more primitive levels of behavior that were once effective*

displacement *a defense mechanism in which one's behaviors or motives (usually aggressive) are directed at a substitute rather than the real object of those behaviors or motives*

place. Daydreaming about academic success may help one feel better for a while, but it is not likely to make anyone a better student.

Projection is a matter of seeing in others one's own unacceptable, anxiety-producing thoughts, motives, or traits. Under enormous pressure to do well on an exam, Kirsten decides to cheat. But at exam time, her conscience (superego) won't let her. Because of projection, Kirsten may think that she sees cheating going on all around her. Projection is a defense mechanism often used in conjunction with aggression or hostility. When people feel uncomfortable with their own hostility, they often project their aggressiveness onto others, coming to believe that others are "out to do me harm," or "I'm only protecting myself."

To employ the defense of **regression** is to return to earlier, more primitive, even childish levels of behavior that were once effective. We often see regression occurring in children. Imagine a 4-year-old who until recently was an only child; Mommy has just returned from the hospital with a new baby sister. The 4-year-old is no longer the "center of attention." He reverts to earlier behaviors and starts wetting the bed, screaming for a bottle of his own, and crawling on all fours. He is regressing.

The defense mechanism of **displacement** is usually discussed in the context of aggression. It's a matter of directing one's motives or behaviors at a substitute person or object rather than expressing them directly—which would be anxiety-producing. Dorothy expects to get promoted at work, but someone else gets the new job she wanted. She's upset and angry at her boss, but feels, perhaps correctly, that blowing her top at her boss will do more harm than good, so she displaces her hostility toward her husband, the children, or the family cat.

This list of defense mechanisms is not an exhaustive one. These are among the more common, however, and should give you an idea of what Freud had in mind. There are two points that deserve special mention. (1) Using defense mechanisms is a normal reaction. You shouldn't be alarmed if you find that some of these mechanisms sound like reactions you have used. In moderation they help us to cope with the anxieties and conflicts of everyday life. (2) Although they are normal, these mechanisms can become maladaptive. As long as defense mechanisms are successful in easing the unpleasant feelings of anxiety, we may no longer feel a need to search for the true sources of anxiety and thus will be less likely to resolve the conflicts that produced the anxiety in the first place. We'll have more to say about this point when we discuss effective and ineffective strategies for dealing with stress and anxiety in Chapter 11.

Before You Go On

Define seven defense mechanisms.

The Psychosexual Stages of Personality Development. Freud put a lot of stock in the biological bases of personality, relying on concepts such as drive and instinct. This same orientation flavored his view of personality development. According to Freud, personality develops naturally, in a biologically based series of overlapping stages. The events that occur in early stages have the potential to produce profound effects on later development.

One of Freud's most controversial assumptions about human behavior was that even infants and young children were under the influence of the sexual strivings of the id and its libidinal energy. The outlet for the sexual impulses (again, "sensual" may be a better term in today's usage) of young children is not the reproductive sex act. But Freud thought that much of the pleasure derived by children *is* essentially sexual; hence, we refer to Freud's stages of development as *psychosexual*. Freud claimed that there are five such stages.

1. *Oral Stage* (Birth to 1 year). Pleasure and satisfaction come from oral activities: feeding, sucking, and making noises. The mouth continues to be a source of pleasure for many people long into adulthood, as demonstrated by overeating, fingernail biting, smoking, or talkativeness.

2. *Anal Stage* (Age 1 to 3 years). Sometime in their second year, children develop the ability to control their bladder and bowel habits. At this time, the anus becomes the focus of pleasure. Satisfaction is gained through bowel control. Aggression (the id again) can be displayed (particularly against parents) by either having bowel movements at inappropriate times or by refusing "to go" when placed on the potty chair. Here we clearly can see the thoughtful, reasoning ego emerging and exercising some control. After all, the parents can't make the child do what they want it to. The child is in control, and that can lead to great satisfaction.

3. *Phallic Stage* (Age 3 to 5 years). Here there is an awareness of one's sexuality. The genitals become more important than the mouth and the anus as the source of pleasure, and masturbation or fondling of the genitals may become a common practice. Freud admitted that he did not understand women or the psychology of women very well (Fadiman & Frager, 1994, p. 18). He often offended the feminists of his day. (Yes, there were feminists at that time, and Freud was well aware of their criticisms.) One of the things that got him in trouble was suggesting that in the phallic stage, girls come to realize that they do not have a penis, and feel inferior, "lacking," and jealous as a result (Freud, 1933, p. 126). Freud said that such "penis envy" led mature women to desire children—a male child in particular, who will bring the "longed-for penis" with him. During this stage of development children tend to form close (sexually based) attachments to the parent of the opposite sex, and feelings of jealousy or fear of the same-sex parent may arise. This pattern of reaction is called the *Oedipus complex* in boys and the *Electra complex* in girls. It is in the phallic stage that the superego begins to develop.

4. *Latency Stage* (Age 6 years until puberty). At this stage, sexual development gets put on hold. Now the ego is developing very rapidly. There is much to be learned about the world and how it operates. Sexual development can wait. Sexuality is suppressed. Friends tend to be of the same sex. You have no doubt heard the protestations of a 9-year-old boy, "Oh, yuck; kiss a girl? No way! Yuck!" And you counsel, "Just wait; soon girls won't seem so 'yucky.'"

5. *Genital Stage* (After puberty). With puberty, there is a renewal of sexual impulses, a reawakening of desire, and an interest in matters sexual and sensual.

Before You Go On

Briefly review Freud's psychosexual stages of development.

The Psychoanalytic Approach After Freud

Sigmund Freud was a persuasive communicator. His ideas were challenging, and they attracted many students. Freud founded a psychoanalytic society in Vienna. There was an inner circle of colleagues and friends who shared his ideas, but some did not entirely agree with all aspects of his theory. Among other things, they were bothered by the very strong emphasis on biological instincts and libido, and what they perceived as a lack of concern for social influences. Some of these analysts proposed theories of their own. They became known as **neo-Freudians**. Because

@@@@ **Thinking Critically** @@@@

No matter what its hypotheses, proposals, or predictions, to what extent is it reasonable to think that any theory of personality can emerge from the study of persons with psychological disorders?

neo-Freudians *theorists (including Adler, Jung, and Horney) who supported the basics of psychoanalytic theory, but differed from Freud*

According to Freud, from the age of 6 until puberty, children are in a latency period and tend to associate with other children of the same sex.

they had their own ideas, they had to part from Freud; he would not tolerate disagreement with his theory. One had to accept all of Freudian theory, or one had to leave Freud's inner circle.

Since a theory consists of logically interrelated, testable assumptions, I really cannot do justice to someone's theory of personality in a short paragraph or two. What I can do is sketch the basic idea(s) behind the theories of a few neo-Freudians.

Alfred Adler (1870–1937). As the psychoanalytic movement was beginning to take shape, Adler was one of Freud's closest friends. However, Adler left Freud and, in 1911, founded his own version of a psychoanalytic approach to personality. Two things seemed most to offend Adler: the negativity of Freud's views (e.g., the death instinct) and the idea of sexual libido as the prime impulse in life.

Alfred Adler founded his own version of a psychoanalytic approach to personality. Rejecting the negativity of Freud's death instinct and the idea of sexual libido as a prime impulse, Adler focused instead on goal-motivated behavior and the achievement of success or superiority. This photo of the Adlers is dated September 1935.

Adler argued that we are a product of the social influences on our personality. We are motivated not so much by drives and instincts as by goals and incentives. The future and one's hope for what it holds are often more important than one's past. For Adler, our goal in life is the achievement of success or superiority. This goal is fashioned in childhood when, because we are then weak and vulnerable, we develop an **inferiority complex**—the feeling that we are less able than others to solve life's problems and get along in the world. Although we may seem inferior as children, with the help of social support and our own creativity, we can overcome and succeed.

inferiority complex *the feeling that we are less able than others to solve life's problems and get along in the world*

Carl Jung (1875–1961). Another student and colleague of Freud, Carl Jung left the inner circle in 1913. Jung was chosen by Freud to be his successor, but several disagreements developed, mostly about the role of sexuality and the nature of the unconscious—two central themes in psychoanalysis. Jung was more mystical in his approach to personality and, like Adler, certainly was more positive about one's ability to control one's own destiny. He believed the major goal in life is to unify all of the aspects of our personality, conscious and unconscious, introverted (inwardly directed) and extroverted (outwardly directed). Libido was energy for Jung, but not sexual energy; it was energy for personal growth and development.

Jung accepted the idea of an unconscious mind and expanded on it, claiming that there are two types of unconscious: the *personal unconscious,* which is very much like Freud's view of the unconscious, and the *collective unconscious,* which contains very basic ideas that go beyond an individual's own personal experiences. The ideas of the collective unconscious are common to all of humanity and are inherited from all past generations. The contents of our collective unconscious include what Jung called *archetypes*—universal forms and patterns of thought. These are basic "ideas" that transcend generations and all of history. They include certain themes that repeatedly show up in myths: motherhood, opposites, good, evil, masculinity, femininity, and the circle as a symbol representing travel from a beginning back to where one started, or the complete, whole self.

Karen Horney (1885–1952). Trained as a psychoanalyst in Germany, Karen Horney (pronounced "horn-eye") came to the United States in 1934. She held onto

For Carl Jung, who, like Adler, broke away from Freud's inner circle, libido was energy for personal growth and development. Jung expanded on Freud's idea of the unconscious mind.

Psychoanalytically trained, Karen Horney developed the concepts of basic anxiety and basic hostility. By emphasizing styles of social interaction, how does her approach differ from that of Freud?

a few Freudian concepts, but changed most of them significantly. Horney believed that the idea of levels of consciousness made sense, as did anxiety and repression, but she theorized that the prime impulses that motivate behavior are not biological and inborn or sexual and aggressive. A major concept for Horney was *basic anxiety,* which grows out of childhood when the child feels alone and isolated in a hostile environment. If proper parental nurturance is forthcoming, basic anxiety can be overcome. If parents are overly punishing, inconsistent, or indifferent, however, children may develop *basic hostility* and may feel very hostile and aggressive toward their parents. However, young children cannot express hostility toward their parents openly so the hostility gets repressed (into the unconscious), building even more anxiety.

Horney did emphasize early childhood experiences, but from a perspective of social interaction and personal growth. Horney claimed that there are three distinct ways in which people interact with each other. In some cases, people *move away from others,* seeking self-sufficiency and independence. The idea here is something like, "If I am on my own and uninvolved, you won't be able to hurt me." On the other hand, some move toward others, and are compliant and dependent. This style of interaction shields against anxiety in the sense of "If I always do what you want me to do, you won't be upset with me." Horney's third interpersonal style involves *moving against others,* where the effort is to be in control, to gain power and dominate: "If I am in control, you'll have to do what I want you to." The ideal, of course, is to maintain a balance among these three styles, but Horney argued that many people have just one style that predominates their dealings with others.

Horney also disagreed with Freud's position regarding the biological basis of differences between men and women. Freud's theories have been taken to task several times for their male bias (Fisher & Greenberg, 1977; Jordan et al., 1991). Karen Horney was one of the first to do so.

Evaluating the Psychoanalytic Approach

Given that we have reviewed only a few major ideas from a very complex approach to personality, can we make any value judgments about its contribution? I suspect that you can anticipate my answer. There are critics and supporters of each of the theoretical approaches summarized in this Topic. Each can tell us something about ourselves and about human personality in general. So long as we realize that our evaluations are going to be somewhat superficial, let's take a moment and reflect on the strengths and weaknesses of each approach as we go along.

The psychoanalytic approach, particularly as modified by the neo-Freudians, is the most comprehensive and complex of the theories we'll review. Psychologists have debated the relative merits of Freud's works for decades, and the debate continues. On the positive side, Freud and other psychoanalytically oriented theorists must be credited for focusing our attention on the importance of the childhood years and for suggesting that some (even biologically determined) impulses may affect our behaviors even though they are beyond our immediate awareness. Although Freud may have overstated the matter, drawing our attention to the impact of sexuality and sexual impulses as influences on personality and human behavior is also a significant contribution. Freud's concept of defense mechanisms has generated considerable research and has found general acceptance (Feshbach et al., 1996).

On the other hand, many psychologists have been critical of several aspects of psychoanalytic theory. We've seen how the neo-Freudians tended to downplay innate biological drives and take a more social approach to personality development than did Freud. One of the major criticisms of the psychoanalytic approach is that so many of its insights appear to be untestable. Freud thought of himself as a scientist, but he tested none of his ideas about human nature experimentally. Some seem beyond testing. Just what *is* libidinal energy? How can it be measured? How would we recognize it if we saw it? Concepts such as id, ego, and superego may sound sensible, but how can we prove or (more importantly) disprove their existence? Such a heavy reliance on instincts, especially with sexual and aggressive overtones, as explanatory concepts goes beyond where most psychologists are willing to venture.

Before You Go On

Summarize the contributions of Adler, Jung, and Horney to the psychoanalytic approach to personality.

The Behavioral-Learning Approach

Many American psychologists in the early twentieth century did not think much of the psychoanalytic approach, regardless of its form or who happened to propose it. From its beginnings, American psychology was oriented toward the laboratory and theories of learning. Explaining personality in terms of learning and observable behaviors seemed a reasonable course of action. In this section we'll briefly review some of the behavioral approaches to personality.

Learning Theorists

John B. Watson (1878–1958) and his followers in behaviorism argued that psychology should turn away from the study of consciousness and the mind because the contents of mental life were unverifiable and ultimately unscientific. They argued that psychologists should study observable behavior. Yet here were Freud and the psychoanalysts arguing that *un*conscious and *pre*conscious forces are determiners of behavior. "Nonsense," the behaviorist would say. "We don't even know what we mean by consciousness, and you want to talk about levels of unconscious influence!"

Watson emphasized the role of the environment in shaping one's behaviors. Behaviorists could not accept the Freudian notion of inborn traits or impulses, whether called id or libido or anything else. What mattered was *learning*. A personality theory was not needed. A theory of learning would include all of the details about personality that one would ever need.

Who we are is determined by our learning experiences, and early experiences count heavily; on this point Watson and Freud would have agreed. Even our fears are conditioned (remember Watson's "Little Albert" study?). So convinced was Watson that instincts and innate impulses had little to do with the development of behavior that he could write, albeit somewhat tongue in cheek: "Give me a dozen healthy infants, well-formed, and my own specified world to bring them up in and I'll guarantee to take any one at random and train him to become any type of specialist I might select—doctor, lawyer, artist, merchant, chief, and yes, even beggarman and thief, regardless of his talents, penchants, tendencies, abilities, vocations, and race of his ancestors" (Watson, 1925).

B. F. Skinner (1904–1990) should be mentioned in this context. Skinner's variety of behaviorism simply refuses to refer to any internal variables to explain behavior—which is, essentially, what personality is taken to mean. Look at observable stimuli and observable responses, and for relationships among these; do not go meddling about in the mind of the organism, Skinnerians argue. Behavior is shaped by its consequences. Some behaviors result in reinforcement and, thus, are repeated. Other behaviors are not reinforced and thus tend *not* to be repeated. Consistency in behavior simply reflects the consistency of one's reinforcement history. The question is, how shall external conditions be manipulated to produce the consequences we want?

John Dollard (1900–1980) and *Neal Miller* (b. 1909) tried to see if they could use the principles of learning theory to explain personality and how it developed. What matters for one's personality, they argued, was the system of habits one developed in response to cues in the environment. Behavior was motivated by *primary drives* (upon whose satisfaction survival depended) and *learned drives,* which developed through experience. Motivated by drives, habits that get reinforced tend

Learning theorists see no particular need for a separate theory of personality. Who we are is determined by our learning experiences, and early childhood experiences count heavily. Bandura, for example, argued that much of who we are is learned by imitating others.

to be repeated and, thus, become part of the stable collection of habits that constitute personality. For example, repression into the unconscious is simply a matter of learned forgetfulness: forgetting about some anxiety-producing experience is reinforcing and, consequently, tends to be repeated. It was Miller (1944) who proposed that conflict can be explained in terms of tendencies (habits) to approach or avoid goals and has little to do with the id, ego, and superego or with unconscious impulses of any sort.

Albert Bandura (b. 1925) is one learning theorist more than willing to consider the internal cognitive processes of the learner. He claims that many aspects of personality are learned, but often through observation and social influence. For Bandura, learning is more than forming connections between stimuli and responses or between responses and resulting reinforcers; it involves a cognitive rearrangement and representation of the world. In simpler terms, this approach argues that you may learn to behave honestly, for example, through the observation of others. If you view your parents as being honest and see their behaviors being reinforced, you may acquire similar responses.

Evaluating the Behavioral-Learning Approach

Many critics of the behavioral-learning approach to personality argue that Watson, Skinner, and others dehumanize personality, and that even the social learning theory of Bandura is too deterministic. The impression is that virtually everything a person does, thinks, or feels is in some way determined by his or her environment or learning history. This leaves nothing for the person, for personality, to contribute. Behavioral-learning approaches to personality often are not theories at all—at least not very comprehensive theories. To their credit, they demand that theoretical terms be carefully defined and that hypotheses be verified experimentally. It is also undeniable that many of the concepts of the behaviorist psychologists have found application in the many forms of behavior therapy, which we discuss in Chapter 13.

Before You Go On

Specify a contribution to the concept of personality made by Watson, Skinner, Dollard and Miller, and Bandura.

The Humanistic-Phenomenological Approach

To some degree, the humanistic-phenomenological approach to personality contrasts with both the psychoanalytic and behavioral approaches. It claims that people have the ability to shape their own destiny and to chart and follow their own course of action, and that biological, instinctive, or environmental influences can be overcome or minimized. The humanistic view may be thought of as more optimistic than either the Freudian approach (with its death instincts and innate impulses) or the learning approach (with its emphasis on control exerted by forces of the environment). It tends to focus more on the "here and now" than on early childhood experiences as important molders of personality. The humanistic-phenomenological point of view emphasizes the wholeness or completeness of personality, rather than focusing on its structural parts. What matters most is how people view themselves and others, which is essentially what *phenomenological* means.

Humanistic Theorists

Carl Rogers' (1902–1986) approach to personality is referred to as a *person-centered* or self theory. Like Freud, Rogers developed his views of human nature through the observation of clients in a clinical setting. (Rogers preferred the term *client* to *patient* and preferred the term *person-centered* to *client-centered* to describe his approach.) Rogers believed that the most powerful of human drives is the one to become fully functioning.

To be *fully functioning* implies that the person has become all that he or she can be. To be fully functioning is to experience "optimal psychological adjustment, optimal psychological maturity, complete congruence, complete openness to experience . . ." (Rogers, 1959, p. 235). People who realize this drive can be described as living in the present, getting the most from each experience, not moping around over opportunities lost or anticipating events to come. As long as we act only to please others, we are not fully functioning. To be fully functioning involves an openness to one's own feelings and desires, an awareness of one's inner self, and a positive self-regard.

Helping children to become fully functioning requires that we offer more of what Rogers calls *unconditional positive regard.* When we are children, some things we do brings reward, but other things do not. How we are regarded by those we care about is often conditional on how we behave. That is, we tend to receive only conditional positive regard. *If* we do what is expected or desired, *then* we get rewarded. As a result, we try to act in ways that bring rewards and avoid punishment; we try to act in ways that please others. Feelings of self and self-worth are thus dependent on the actions of others who either reward us, don't reward us, or punish us. Rogers also argued that we should separate the child's behaviors from the child's self. That means that we may punish a child for doing a bad thing, but never for being a bad child (e.g., "I love you very much, but what you have done is inappropriate and, therefore, will be punished"). Helping people achieve positive self-regard is one of the major goals of Carl Rogers' person-centered therapy.

Note that what matters here is not so much what *is,* but what is *felt* or *perceived.* One's true self (whatever it may be) is less important than one's *image* of oneself. How the world is experienced is what matters—a clearly phenomenological point of view. You may be an excellent piano player (better, perhaps, than 98 percent of all of us), but if you feel you are a poor piano player, that perception or self-regard is what matters most.

Abraham Maslow's (1908–1970) basic criticism of the psychology he had studied was that it was altogether too pessimistic and negative. The person was seen as being battered about by either a hostile environment or by depraved instincts, many of which propelled the person on a course of self-destruction.

There must be more to living than this, thought Maslow. He preferred to attend to the positive side of human nature. Maslow felt that people's needs are not low and base, but are positive, or, at worst, neutral (Maslow, 1954). Our major goal in life is to realize and put into practice those needs, or to *self-actualize.*

Let's look, Maslow argued, at the very best among us. Let's focus our attention on the characteristics of those who have realized their fullest positive potential and have become self-actualized (see Figure 9.1). In his search for such individuals, Maslow could not find many. Most were historical figures, such as Thomas Jefferson and Eleanor Roosevelt. We'll look at Maslow's self-actualization again in our discussion of motivation in Topic 10A.

Evaluating the Humanistic-Phenomenological Approach

Like the others, the humanistic-phenomenological approach has a number of strengths. For one, it reminds us of the *wholeness* of personality and of the danger in analyzing something so complex in artificial segments. That the approach, stressing as it does personal growth and development, is positive and upbeat in its flavor serves to inform us that at least such views are possible. As we shall see in our discussion of psychotherapy (Topic 13B), the humanistic-phenomenological approach has had a significant impact on many therapists and counselors. A major problem with this approach is much like the basic problem with Freud's theory. It

Figure 9.1

Some of the Characteristics or Attributes or Self-Actualizers

1. They tend to be realistic in their orientation.
2. They accept themselves, others, and the world for what they are, not for what they should be.
3. They have a great deal of spontaneity.
4. They tend to be problem-centered rather than self-centered.
5. They have a need for privacy and a sense of detachment.
6. They are autonomous, independent, and self-sufficient.
7. Their appreciation of others (and of things of the world) is fresh, free, and not stereotyped.
8. Many have spiritual or mystical (although not necessarily religious) experiences.
9. They can identify with humankind as a whole and share a concern for humanity.
10. They have a number of interpersonal relationships, some of them very deep and profound.
11. They tend to have democratic views in the sense that all are created equal and should be treated equally.
12. They have a sense of humor that tends more to the philosophical than the hostile.
13. They tend to be creative in their approach.
14. They are hard working.
15. They resist pressures to conform to society.

After Maslow, 1954.

seems to make sense, but how does one go about *testing* any of the observations and statements made by proponents of the approach? Many of the key terms are defined in general, fuzzy ways. What is self-image? How do we really know when someone is "growing"? How can one document the advantages of unconditional positive regard? In many ways, what we have here is a blueprint for living, a vision for the nature of personality, not a scientific theory. There are also critics who claim that the notions of striving to become fully functioning or self-actualized are both naive and far from universal.

Before You Go On

Summarize the humanistic-phenomeno-logical approach to personality as epitomized by Rogers and Maslow.

The Trait Approach

Trait theories of personality have a markedly different flavor from any of the approaches we have looked at. Trait theories are more concerned with the adequate *description* of personality than with the *explanation* of personality. Arnold Buss put it this way: "Trait psychologists typically seek to reveal the psychological dimensions along which people differ and ways in which traits cluster within individuals" (1989, p. 1379). We may define a **trait** as "any distinguishable, relatively enduring way in which one individual differs from others" (Guilford, 1959a, p. 5).

Traits are descriptive *dimensions*. In other words, any trait (e.g., friendliness) is not a simple either-or proposition. Friendliness falls on a continuum, ranging from

trait *a distinguishable, relatively enduring way in which individuals may be described and in which they may differ* extremely unfriendly to extremely friendly, with many possibilities in between. To be useful, traits need to be measurable so we can assess the extent to which people may differ on those traits (Hogan & Nicholson, 1988; Ozer & Reise, 1994; Wiggins & Pincus, 1992).

The main issue focus for psychologists who have taken this approach has been to try to determine which traits are the important ones. Which dimensions best characterize a person and how she or he is different from everyone else? How can personality traits be organized? The various answers to these and related questions have given rise to several trait theories. We'll briefly summarize two classic trait theories and then look at a contemporary trait theory.

Two Classic Examples

For *Gordon Allport* (1897–1967), personality traits exist within a person and can help to explain the consistency in that person's behavior. In various situations, a personality trait of friendliness might produce a range of specific responses, but those responses would be, in their essence, very much alike.

Allport proposed that there are two types of personality traits: *common traits* and *personal traits* (or personal dispositions) (Allport, 1961). By common traits Allport means those dimensions of personality shared by almost everyone—to greater or lesser degrees perhaps, but shared in common with nearly everyone. Aggressiveness is an example of a common trait, as is intelligence. These are traits we can use to make comparisons among people. Personal dispositions, on the other hand, are traits unique to just some persons. How one displays a sense of humor (sharp wit, cutting sarcasm, philosophical puns, dirty jokes, and so on) is usually thought of as being a unique disposition.

Allport went on to claim that personal traits are of three subtypes: cardinal, central, and secondary. A *cardinal trait* is so overwhelming that it influences virtually everything a person does. The personalities of few of us are ruled by cardinal traits. Allport could imagine only a few examples (Don Quixote, the Marquis de Sade, Mohandas Gandhi, and Don Juan among them). No, what influences your behaviors and mine are not likely to be cardinal traits, but *central traits,* or dispositions. These can usually be described in just one word. They are the five to ten traits that best characterize someone (e.g., honest, friendly, neat, outgoing, fair, and kind). Finally, each of us is occasionally influenced by *secondary traits.* These traits (dispositions) seldom govern many of our reactions, but may be found in specific circumstances. For example, people who are basically very calm and easygoing, even when threatened (reflecting their central traits), may be very aggressive and excited when threatened in their own home (by intruders, let's say).

Another classic approach is that of *Raymond Cattell* (b. 1905). Cattell's is an empirical approach, relying on psychological tests, questionnaires, and surveys. Talking about personality traits without talking about how they are measured makes little sense to Cattell. Cattell used a technique called *factor analysis*—a correlational procedure that identifies groups of highly related variables that may be assumed to measure the same underlying factor (here, a personality trait). The logic is that if you know that some people are outgoing, you don't need to test them to see if they are sociable or extroverted; such information would be redundant.

Cattell argues that there are two major types of personality traits (1973, 1979). *Surface traits* are clusters of behaviors that go together, like those that make up curiosity, trustworthiness, or kindliness. These traits are easily observed and can be found in many settings. More important than surface traits are the fewer number of underlying traits from which surface traits develop. These are called *source traits.* One's pattern of source traits determines which surface traits get expressed in behavior. Source traits are not as easily measured as surface traits because they are not directly observable. Cattell's source traits are listed in Figure 9.2.

Figure 9.2
Sixteen Source Traits as Identified by Cattell
(Each trait is a dimension)

Reserved ↔ **Outgoing**	**Trusting** ↔ **Suspicious**
(detached, aloof) (participating)	(accepting) (circumspect)
Less intelligent ↔ **More intelligent**	**Practical** ↔ **Imaginative**
(dull) (bright)	(down-to-earth) (absentminded)
Affected by feelings ↔ **Emotionally stable**	**Forthright** ↔ **Shrewd**
(easily upset) (calm)	(unpretentious) (astute, worldly)
Submissive ↔ **Dominant**	**Self-assured** ↔ **Apprehensive**
(obedient, easily led) (assertive)	(secure, complacent) (insecure, troubled)
Serious ↔ **Happy-go-lucky**	**Conservative** ↔ **Experimenting**
(sober, taciturn) (enthusiastic)	(disinclined to change) (experimenting)
Expedient ↔ **Conscientious**	**Group-dependent** ↔ **Self-sufficient**
(disregards rules) (moralistic, staid)	(a joiner) (resourceful)
Timid ↔ **Venturesome**	**Uncontrolled** ↔ **Controlled**
(shy, restrained) (socially bold)	(follows own urges) (shows will power)
Tough-minded ↔ **Sensitive**	**Relaxed** ↔ **Tense**
(rejects illusions) (tender-minded)	(tranquil, composed) (frustrated, driven)

Before You Go On

What are the major personality traits according to Allport and Cattell?

A Contemporary Perspective: The Big Five

We've taken a brief look at just two theories that have tried to identify relatively enduring personality traits, and we've generated quite a list. Allport named common traits and personal dispositions, and Cattell found many surface traits and a smaller number of source traits. Which scheme is right? Which set is most reasonable? Is there even a set of personality traits that is acceptable?

It may surprise you to learn that personality theorists are coming to a consensus concerning which traits have the most research support to best qualify as descriptors of personality. This model is referred to as the *Five-Factor Model* (Digman, 1990; McCrae & Costa, 1986, 1987; McCrae & John, 1992; Ozer & Reise, 1994; Wiggins & Pincus, 1992). What are the dimensions of personality that are now being referred to as the "Big Five"?

Although there may be some consensus that five major dimensions will suffice to characterize human personality, there is disagreement on exactly how to describe these five. The following dimensions are from Digman (1990) and Goldberg (1993):

Dimension I, called "Extroversion/Introversion," embodies such things as assurance, talkativeness, openness, self-confidence, and assertiveness on the one hand, and silence and passivity on the other.

Dimension II is "Agreeableness" or "Friendliness," with altruism, caring, and emotional support at one end and hostility, indifference, selfishness, and distrust on the other.

Dimension III is called "Conscientiousness," and amounts to a "will to achieve" (or simply a "will"). It includes self-control, dependability, planning, thoroughness, and persistence paired with carelessness, negligence, and unreliability. It is well correlated with educational achievement.

Dimension IV is an "Emotionality" dimension. In many ways, this is the extent to which one is emotionally stable or in some way psychologically disordered. It includes such things as nervousness and moodiness.

Dimension V is "Intellect," "Intelligence," or "Openness to Experience and Culture." (In this context, "culture" refers to aspects of experience such as art, dance, literature, music, and the like.) This factor includes such characteristics as curiosity, imagination, and creativity.

The recurrent finding that all personality traits can be reduced to just five, with these names (or names like these), is remarkable. Each of these five traits represents a dimension of possible habits and individual responses that a person may bring to bear in any given situation.

These five traits have emerged from nearly 50 years of research in many cultures (Paunonen et al., 1992; Stumpf, 1993; Wiggins & Pincus, 1992). They have emerged regardless of the individuals being assessed, and "the Big Five have appeared now in at least five languages, leading one to suspect that something quite fundamental is involved here" (Digman, 1990, p. 433). On the other hand, Revelle (1987) notes that "the agreement among these descriptive dimensions is impressive, [but] there is a lack of theoretical explanation for the how and the why of these dimensions" (p. 437).

Evaluating the Trait Approach

As I've already mentioned, trait approaches to personality are different from the others, even in their basic intent. Trait theories have a few obvious advantages. They provide us not only with descriptive terms, but with means of measuring the important dimensions of personality. They give us an idea of how measured traits are related to one another. On the other hand, as theories, they offer little more than description. To say that someone acted in a certain way "because he is introverted" does not go far to explain that action. It functions merely as a label. And even with the so-called Big Five traits, there continues to be disagreement about how to define or characterize the most basic traits that describe personality.

The basic relevance or value of personality traits also varies from one culture to another. The notion of individual personality traits seems to be relevant and sensible to people in individualistic societies, such as ours, and most Western cultures. In these cultures, people are viewed as individual actors, and knowing about the characteristics of those actors is viewed as helpful. If people are viewed in terms of their membership in a group or a collective (as in collectivistic cultures, such as are found in Asia and South America), then their individual traits will be of less interest than their roles, duties, group loyalties, and responsibilities, for example (Miller, 1984; Shwedler & Sullivan, 1993).

So, as we might have predicted, when we try to evaluate overall various approaches to or theories of personality, there are no real winners or losers. Each approach has its shortcomings, but each adds something to our appreciation of the complex concept of human personality.

⊚⊚⊚⊚ Thinking Critically ⊚⊚⊚⊚

Can you generate examples of how each of the Big Five dimensions of personality shows up in observable behaviors? Can you judge where you might fall on each of these five proposed dimensions?

Before You Go On

What are the Big Five personality dimensions?

TOPIC 9A SUMMARY

We've covered a lot of ground in this Topic. We began with the realization that although we regularly talk about "personality," describing its nature is not easily done. What we did was briefly outline a few approaches to personality, examining a sample of theories.

Psychoanalytic approaches, following the lead of Freud, emphasize unconscious influences, early childhood experiences, and sexual and aggressive instincts. The neo-Freudians placed more concern on social issues and less on biologically based drives and strivings. Some psychologists prefer to talk about personality in terms derived from learning theories. In these cases, there is much less emphasis on what may be inside a person and much more on how the environment molds the apparent consistency we see in behavior. The humanistic-phenomenological approach was characterized as being "optimistic," stressing such factors as personal growth and self-actualization. Trait approaches to personality have been more inclined to care about generating adequate descriptions of personality traits than about explaining where these traits may come from. A consensus seems to be building among trait theorists that human personality can be described adequately by five clusters, or factors, of personality traits.

When we ask which of these approaches is the best, we are asking a question with no answer. Each approach is qualitatively different from the others and emphasizes different aspects of personality. In its own way, each has a contribution to make.

TOPIC 9B   Issues Related to Personality

Not all psychologists who claim "personality" as one of their areas of interest are actively involved in trying to devise a grand theory to describe or explain human nature. Many are involved in research that focuses on one or a few aspects of the complex concept we call personality. In this section we'll look at three areas: the extent to which personality is a useful concept when trying to explain behavior, gender differences in personality, and personality assessment or measurement.

Is There a Personality?

Each approach to personality that we reviewed in Topic 9A brings its own perspective to the study of personality. There is one theme, however, that they have in common: all address the *consistency* of personality. Someone with an "overdeveloped superego" should be consistently conscientious and feel guilty whenever established standards are not met. Someone who has learned to behave aggressively should behave aggressively in a range of settings. Someone trying to "grow personally and to self-actualize" should be consistently open to a wide variety of new opinions and ideas. Someone with a trait of extraversion should appear outgoing and extroverted most of the time.

About 30 years ago, this very basic assumption about personality was challenged by Walter Mischel (1968). One problem with arguing for the consistency of personality is that personality just may not be consistent at all (Council, 1993; Epstein, 1979; Mischel, 1968, 1979; Mischel & Peake, 1982). Think carefully about your own behavior and your own personality. Assume for the moment you think of yourself as easygoing. Are you *always* easygoing, easy to get along with? Are there some situations in which you would be easygoing, but others in which you might fight to

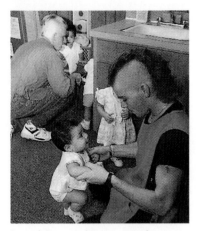

Part of the complex concept of personality is that one's behaviors are generally consistent with previous behaviors. Sometimes, however, the situation may overwhelm internal, personal dispositions and determine how one acts.

have your way? Are there some situations in which you tend to be social and outgoing, yet different situations in which your preference is to be alone and not mix in? Such was the thrust of Mischel's challenge: personality characteristics appear to be consistent only when they are viewed in similar or consistent situations.

We may observe consistency in the personality of others for two reasons: (1) It is convenient. We like to think that we can quickly and accurately categorize people. If we see someone do something dishonest—pick up change left as a tip for a waiter-we find it convenient to label that person as basically dishonest. It's easy to assume that the mean, aggressive football player will probably be mean and aggressive off the field as well. Such assumptions may not be true, but they make it easy to form judgments about others. (2) We tend to see others only in a restricted range of situations, where their behaviors and attitudes may very well be consistent. The real test would be to see those people in varied situations on many occasions (Epstein, 1979; Kendrick & Funder, 1991).

As you might suspect, arguments challenging the very definition of personality created quite a stir. Since Mischel raised it, there has been an exciting barrage of research and debate on this issue. We now see that things may not be as unstable and situation-bound as Mischel suggested. One analysis, using methodology borrowed from the field of behavior genetics, argues that most of the variability we see in behaviors does reflect individual differences even more than the pressures of the situation (Rowe, 1987; see also Digman, 1990; McCrae & Costa, 1994; Wiggins & Pincus, 1993).

In fact, most personality theorists today are ready and willing to declare the debate of "personality traits versus the situation as determinants of behavior" resolved (Carson, 1989; Digman, 1990; Kendrick & Funder, 1988, 1991). Depending on how you look at it, neither side or both sides won. By and large, research supports the position that, indeed, there are some person-related characteristics that show remarkable stability over a wide range of time and situations. The research also supports the notion that it is folly not to take into account the situation in which behaviors occur.

One outcome of the debate triggered by Mischel is a view of personality and situational variables known as *interactionism,* or the *transactional* approach (Bandura, 1978; Magnusson, 1990; Magnusson & Edler, 1977; Mischel, 1981). This approach says that how one behaves is a function of an interaction of stable personality characteristics *and* the individual's perception of the situation. Neither personality characteristics (inside the person) nor the situation (external environment) can be fully relied on to explain an individual's reaction.

Let's say that Ken agrees to a friendly racquetball game, just for the exercise. At first all goes well and Ken, a superior player, takes it easy on his opponent. After all, they are just playing for the exercise. In the second game, Ken's opponent makes a few good shots and moves ahead in the score. Ken now notices that a small group of spectators is watching them play. As the situation changes, so does Ken's perception of it. "This is no longer fun and games," he thinks to himself, as he starts smashing low line drives off the front wall. Within just a few minutes, Ken's behavior is considerably different. The situation has been altered, and now his behavior is aggressive and forceful. As the situation changed, it brought about a change in Ken's behavior: a perceived challenge to his ability brought out competitive reactions. Ken's personality also brought about a change in the situation: to some degree, his competitiveness turned a friendly game into an athletic contest. With interactionism we have an approach that acknowledges the impact of the environment but also allows for the influence of stable, internal personality traits.

@@@@ **Thinking Critically** @@@@

What situations can you think of in which you did not act in ways that are generally characteristic of your personality?

Before You Go On

Summarize the debate concerning personality versus situational influences on behavior.

Gender and Personality

Personality traits give us reasonable ways to describe people and to express differences we observe among them. We can note Kathy's assertiveness and Juan's sociability. We can say that Chick is friendlier than Steve or that Melissa is more impulsive than Jesse. An issue that intrigues personality psychologists is the extent to which personality traits can be used to characterize groups of people, and if there are consistent differences, in general, among groups. The two groups that have been studied most closely in this regard are men and women.

What do you think about the following statements? Boys have higher self-esteem than girls. Girls are more social than boys. Men are more analytical than women. Men are better at rote learning, whereas women are more creative. Women are more open to suggestion and influence than are men.

These assertions might sound sensible, but there is no research evidence to support any of them. There are no gender differences in self-esteem, sociability, analytic skills, rote learning, creativity, or suggestibility.

These were the findings of the first large-scale exploration of gender differences, reported by Eleanor Maccoby and Carol Jacklin in 1974. Maccoby and Jacklin's work was not the first to ask whether there are differences between males and females (theirs was a re-analysis of data that existed at the time). It did, however, stimulate others to join in the search for ways in which gender could be used to predict how one might behave in a range of situations. That search has turned up little. The research tells us that gender differences tend to be insignificant and inconsistent (Huston, 1985; Hyde, 1984, 1986; Maccoby, 1990). "There appear to be relatively few basic psychological differences between the sexes, although members of the two sexes are socialized to behave in different ways" (Feshbach et al., 1996).

There is one glaring exception, and that is overt, physical aggression, which has consistently been found more commonly in males than in females (Eagly, 1987; Eagly & Steffen, 1986; Hyde, 1986; Maccoby, 1990). The difference in aggression found between males and females seems to be there (to varying degrees) at all ages and in all cultural settings (Ashmore, 1990; Maccoby & Jacklin, 1980; Rushton et al., 1986; Whiting & Edwards, 1973). Although we may claim that males are more

As adults, there are few significant differences in the personalities of men and women. There are several observable differences in the behaviors and preferences of young boys and girls, however.

aggressive than females, there are two necessary cautions: (1) This is a generality made "on the average" for groups of persons. Any one female might be significantly more aggressive in all regards than any one male. (2) We have no evidence that this difference is necessarily genetic or biologically based.

On the assumption that you will not overinterpret them, we can list instances, other than aggression, in which small gender differences have occasionally been found.

1. *Communication style.* Men seem to be more talkative in a variety of settings and are more likely to interrupt others (Key, 1975), but in some situations, females are more likely to "self-disclose" and share their inner ideas and feelings (Cozby, 1973). Girls may also be somewhat more compliant to the demands of parents, teachers, and other (older) authority figures (Cowan & Avants, 1988; Macoby, 1988).

2. *Body language.* Women may be better at decoding or interpreting the body language of others (Eagly, 1987; Hall, 1978), but there are no differences in the display of postures or gestures associated with dominance in nonverbal social situations (Halberstadt & Saitta, 1987).

3. *Altruism.* Women report that they are more willing to engage in self-sacrifice for the good of others, but whether their behaviors are actually more altruistic than that of men is not clear (Rushton et al., 1986; Sennecker & Hendrick, 1983).

4. *Empathy.* As with altruism, when we rely on self-reports, women appear to be more empathic than men, more able to appreciate and understand another's feelings. But when we look at laboratory or real-life evidence, differences disappear (Eisenberg & Lennon, 1983).

5. *Self-confidence.* Particularly when they are asked to do something usually associated with a male role (e.g., take a test on sports figures), women tend to be less self-confident in their performance than men—even when performances are equivalent (Beyer, 1990; Lenney, 1977). This difference occurs only in social situations, in which females may be acting in accord with their perception of what is expected (Daubman et al., 1992).

Well, then, where are we on the issue of personality differences as a function of one's gender? There are gender differences in physical aggression, and there may be gender differences on a few other traits, but even these differences are not found with consistency. On most personality traits, there simply are no differences between females and males.

Before You Go On

Briefly summarize what we know about gender differences in personality traits.

Personality Measurement or Assessment

As we know, personality is a difficult concept to define. Common to most definitions is the idea that there are characteristics of an individual that remain fairly consistent over time and over many (if not all) situations. It would be very useful, then, to *reliably* and *validly* measure personal characteristics. At this point, you might want to review the discussion of reliability and validity in Topic 7A. There we were talking about tests of intelligence. Here we are talking about measuring aspects of personality, but the issues are still the same.

Why do psychologists engage in personality assessment in the first place? There are three goals that lie behind the measurement of personality. One is related to mental illness and psychological disorders. One question that a psychologist may ask in a clinical setting is, "What is wrong with this person?" In fact, the first question is often, "Is there anything wrong with this person?" (Burisch, 1984). Thus, adequate and proper diagnosis is one aim of personality measurement.

A second use for personality assessment is theory building, where there are a number of interrelated questions (Ozer & Reise, 1994): Which personality traits can be measured? How may traits be organized within the person? Which traits are the most important for describing someone's personality? For trait theorists, this is obviously the major purpose for constructing personality measurement devices.

The third goal involves the extent to which knowledge of personality traits can be used to predict some target behavior or behaviors. This concern is a practical one—particularly in vocational placement. For example, if we know that Joe is dominant and extroverted, what does that knowledge tell us about his leadership potential? Or the likelihood that he will succeed as a sales manager? For that matter, what personality traits best describe a successful astronaut, police officer, or secretary?

In brief, personality assessment has three goals: diagnosis, theory building, and behavioral prediction. These goals often interact. A clinical diagnosis made in the context of some theoretical approach is often used to predict possible outcomes, such as which therapy is most appropriate for a given patient.

Now let's consider a few of the assessment techniques that are used to discover the nature of someone's personality.

Behavioral Observations

As you and I develop our impressions of the personalities of friends and acquaintances, we usually do so by relying on **behavioral observation**, which, as its name suggests, involves drawing conclusions about someone's personality on the basis of observations of his or her behaviors. We judge Dan to be bright because he was the only one who knew the answer to a question in class. We feel that Maria is submissive because she always seems to do whatever her husband demands.

As helpful as our observations may be, there may be problems with the casual, unstructured observations you and I normally make. Because we have observed only a small range of behaviors in a limited range of settings, we may be overgeneralizing when we assume that those same behaviors will show up in new, different situations. Dan may never again know the answer to a question in class. Maria may give in to her husband only because we are there. That is, the behaviors that we observe may not be typical at all.

Nonetheless, behavioral observation can be an excellent source of information, particularly when the observations being made are purposeful, careful, and structured, as opposed to the casual observations you and I usually make, or when steps are taken to make the observations reliable and valid and to ensure our sample is representative. Among other things, the accuracy of one's observations are related to the degree of acquaintance between the observer and the person being observed (Paulus & Bruce, 1992). Behavioral observations are commonly a part of a clinical assessment. The clinical psychologist may note several behaviors of a client as potentially significant—the style of dress, manner of speaking, gestures, postures, and so on.

Consider an example. A child is reportedly having trouble at school, behaving aggressively and generally being disruptive. One thing a psychologist may do is visit the school and observe the child's behaviors in the natural setting of the classroom. It may be that the child does behave aggressively and engage in fighting behavior, but only when the teacher is in the room. Otherwise, the child is pleasant

behavioral observation *the assessment technique of drawing conclusions about one's personality based on observations of that person's behaviors*

Behavioral observation involves drawing conclusions about an individual's personality on the basis of his or her behaviors. Using rating scales and several observers adds to the reliability and the validity of behavioral observations.

and passive. It may be that the child's aggressive behaviors reflect a ploy to get the teacher's attention.

In an attempt to add to her observations, a psychologist may use *role-playing* as a means to collect information. Role-playing is a matter of acting out a given life situation. "Let's say that I'm a student, and that you're the teacher, and that it's recess time," the psychologist says to a child. "Let's pretend that somebody takes a toy away from me, and I hit him on the arm. What will you do?"

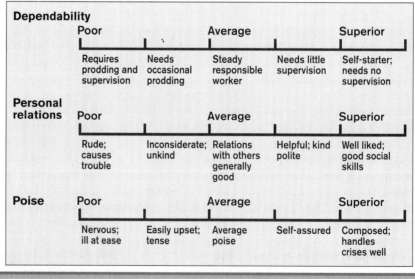

Dependability				
Poor		**Average**		**Superior**
Requires prodding and supervision	Needs occasional prodding	Steady responsible worker	Needs little supervision	Self-starter; needs no supervision
Personal relations				
Poor		**Average**		**Superior**
Rude; causes trouble	Inconsiderate; unkind	Relations with others generally good	Helpful; kind polite	Well liked; good social skills
Poise				
Poor		**Average**		**Superior**
Nervous; ill at ease	Easily upset; tense	Average poise	Self-assured	Composed; handles crises well

Figure 9.3

A graphic rating scale such as this might be used by an employer evaluating current or potential employees.

Observational techniques can be supplemented with a rating scale (Figure 9.3). Rating scales provide many advantages over casual observation. For one thing, they focus the attention of the observer on a set of specified behaviors to be observed. Rating scales also yield a more objective measure of behavior. With rating scales, one can have behaviors observed by several raters. If several raters are involved in the observation of the same behaviors (say, children at play in a nursery school), you can check on the reliability of the observations. If all five of your observers agree that Timothy engaged in hitting behavior on the average of six times per hour, the consistency of that assessment adds to its usefulness.

Before You Go On

What are the goals of personality assessment?

How are behavioral observations used to assess personality?

Interviews

We can learn some things about people just by watching them. We can also gain insight about some aspects of their personality by simply asking them about themselves. In fact, the interview is "one of the oldest and most widely used, although not always the most accurate, of the methods of personality assessment" (Aiken, 1984, p. 296). Its popularity is largely due to its basic simplicity and flexibility.

The data of the **interview** are what people say about themselves, rather than what they do. Interview results are usually impressionistic and not easily quantifiable (although some interview techniques are clearly more structured and objective than others). The interview is a technique of discovering more generalities than specifics.

A major advantage of the interview is its flexibility. The interviewer may decide to drop a certain line of questioning if it is producing no useful information, to pursue some other area of interest. Unfortunately, there is little evidence that unstructured interviews have very much reliability or validity (Tenopyr, 1981).

As is the case for observational techniques, there is variation in the degree to which interviews are unstructured or structured. In the latter type of interview, there is a specific set of questions to be asked in a prescribed order. The structured interview, then, becomes more like a psychological test to the extent that it is objective and standardized and asks about a particular sample of behavior. Analyses of structured interviews show that their validity can be high (Landy et al., 1994). We'll focus on this issue again in Topic 15A when we discuss means of evaluating candidates for employment.

interview *the assessment technique involving a conversational interchange between an interviewer and another in order to gain information about the latter's personality*

Before You Go On

Cite one advantage of the interview as a technique of personality assessment.

Paper-and-Pencil Tests

Observational and interview techniques barely qualify as psychological tests. (You might want to review our coverage of psychological tests back in Topic 7A.) In this section, we'll focus on one of the most often used paper-and-pencil personality tests, the **Minnesota Multiphasic Personality Inventory**, or **MMPI** for short. The test is called *multiphasic* because it measures several personality dimensions with the same set of items.

Minnesota Multiphasic Personality Inventory (MMPI) *a paper-and-pencil personality test designed to assess several dimensions of personality and to indicate the presence of a psychological disorder*

Although the data from casual, unstructured interviews are seldom very reliable or valid, psychologists can gain useful insights about personality by using formal, structured interviews.

The MMPI was designed to aid in the diagnosis of persons with mental disorders and, hence, is not a personality test in the sense of identifying personality traits. The test is the most researched test in psychology and remains one of the most commonly used (Lubin et al., 1984). In 1989, a revision of the MMPI (the MMPI-2) became available. The revision made two major changes and several lesser ones. Antiquated and offensive items (having to do with religion or sexual practices) were replaced. The norm group for the MMPI-2 was much larger (2,600 subjects) than for the MMPI (about 700 subjects) and is supposed to reflect a more representative sample of the population in regard to cultural background, ethnicity, and the like (Ben-Porath & Butcher, 1989). The intent of the authors of the MMPI-2 was to update and improve, but *not change,* the basic design or meaning of test scores. The extent to which the revision has succeeded remains to be seen (Adler, 1990a; Edwards & Edwards, 1991).

The MMPI-2 consists of 567 true-false questions that ask about feelings, attitudes, physical symptoms, and past experiences. It is a *criterion-referenced test,* which means that items on the test are referenced to one of the criterion groups—either normal persons or patients with a diagnosis of a particular mental disorder. Some of the items appear sensible. "I feel like people are plotting against me" seems like the sort of item someone with paranoia would call "true," whereas normals would tend to respond "false." Many items, however, are not as obvious. "I like to visit zoos," is not an MMPI-2 item, but it might have been if subjects of one diagnostic group responded to the item differently from other subjects. What the item *appears* to be measuring is irrelevant. What matters is whether subjects of different groups respond differently to the item. I need also mention that no one will make even a tentative diagnosis of a psychological disorder on the basis of a person's response to just a few items. What matters is not just the simple scores or even the pattern of scores on any set of items, but the *interpretation* of those scores by a trained, experienced psychologist.

The MMPI-2's *validity scales* consist of items from among the 567 that assess the extent to which the subject is attending to the task at hand, or is trying to present herself or himself in a favorable light instead of responding truthfully to the items. For example, responding "true" to several statements such as "I always smile at everyone I meet" would lead an examiner to doubt the validity of the subject's responses.

Although the MMPI-2 is commonly used, it is not the only paper-and-pencil test of personality. The *California Personality Inventory,* or CPI, was written using only normal people, not those who were diagnosed as having a psychological problem or disorder. It assesses 18 personality traits, including self-acceptance, dominance, responsibility, and sociability. Because it is designed to measure several traits, it can also be referred to as a multiphasic test.

Some multiphasic tests were designed in conjunction with a particular personality theory. For example, Cattell's trait theory approach investigated a number of potential personality traits. These traits are what are measured with *Cattell's 16 PF Questionnaire* (in which PF stands for personality factors). Analysis of responses on this test results in a personality profile that can be compared to one gathered from a large norm group.

Finally, many personality questionnaires or inventories are designed to measure just one trait and thus are not multiphasic. One example is the *Taylor Manifest Anxiety Scale.* Taylor began with a large pool of items, many of them from the MMPI, and then asked psychologists to choose those items they thought would best measure anxiety. The 50 items most commonly chosen as indicators of anxiety constitute this test, which has gained wide acceptance. A more recent test, the *Endler Multidimensional Anxiety Scale,* not only assesses anxiety levels, but also claims to distinguish between anxiety and depression (Endler et al., 1992).

Before You Go On

How was the MMPI-2 constructed?

Projective Techniques

A **projective technique** asks a person to respond to ambiguous stimuli. The stimuli can be any number of things, and there are no clearly right or wrong answers. Projective procedures are unstructured and open-ended. The idea is that because there is, in fact, so little content in the stimulus being presented, the person will project some of his or her own self into the response. In many ways, projective techniques are more like aids to interviewing than they are psychological tests (Korchin & Scheldberg, 1981).

Some projective techniques are very simple. The *word association technique,* introduced by Galton in 1879, is a projective procedure. "I will say a word, and I want you to say the first thing that pops into your head. Do not think about your response; just say the first thing that comes to mind." There are no right answers. The hope is that the psychologist can gain some insight, perhaps into the problems of a patient, by using this technique.

A similar technique is the *unfinished sentences,* or sentence completion, test. For example, a sentence is begun, "My greatest fear is . . . " The subject is asked to

<hr>

ꙮꙮꙮ **Thinking Critically** ꙮꙮꙮ

Test reliability is the extent to which a test measures whatever it measures dependably, or consistently. How would we assess the reliability of a test designed to measure a trait like anxiety which itself changes from day to day, and is thus "unreliable"?

projective technique *an assessment technique requiring a person to respond to ambiguous stimuli in the hopes that the person will reveal aspects of his or her personality*

Assessing One Aspect of Your Personality

Humanistic approaches to personality emphasize the analysis of the factors that enter into a person's perceptions and evaluations of his or her life experiences. Carl Rogers refers to these perceptions as the *self-concept*. Mark Snyder (*The Many Me's of the Self-Monitor*, Belmont, CA: Brooks/Cole, 1980) has prepared a *Self-Monitoring Scale* that indicates the extent to which one is aware of one's own wants, needs, and traits, that is, is aware of one's own "self." Complete the following questionnaire.

These statements concern personal reactions to a number of different situations. No two statements are exactly alike, so consider each statement carefully before responding.

If a statement is true, or mostly true, as applied to you, circle the T. If a statement is false, or usually not true, as applied to you, circle the F.

T F   1. I find it hard to imitate the behavior of other people.

T F   2. I guess I put on a show to impress or entertain people.

T F   3. I would probably make a good actor.

T F   4. I sometimes appear to others to be experiencing deeper emotions than I actually am.

T F   5. In a group of people, I am rarely the center of attention.

T F   6. In different situations and with different individuals, I often act like very different people.

T F   7. I can only argue for ideas I already believe.

T F   8. In order to get along and be liked, I tend to be what people expect me to be more than anything else.

T F   9. I may deceive people by being friendly when I really dislike them.

T F   10. I'm not always the person I appear to be.

Scoring: Give yourself 1 point for each of the questions 1, 5, and 7 that you answered F, and give yourself 1 point for each of the remaining questions that you answered T. If your total points are 7 or more, you are probably a high-monitoring individual; 3 or below, and you are probably low on self-monitoring.

Three points to ponder: (1) To what extent does the situation determine the extent to which one acts openly and honestly in the presence of others? (2) Can you think of any behaviors or characteristics that should be correlated with one's degree of self-monitoring? (3) How would you proceed to assess the reliability and validity of this scale, and to create adequate norms for it?

Rorschach inkblot test *a projective technique in which a person is asked to say what he or she sees in a series of inkblots*

complete the sentence. Although there are published tests available (e.g., the *Rotter Incomplete Sentences Blank*), many psychologists prefer to make up their own forms. Again, there are no right or wrong responses, and interpreting responses is subjective, but a skilled examiner can use these procedures to gain new insights about a subject's personality.

Of the projective techniques, none is as well known as the **Rorschach inkblot test**. This technique was introduced in 1921 by Hermann Rorschach, who believed that people respond differently to inkblot patterns (see Figure 9.4). There are 10 cards in the Rorschach test: 5 are black on white, 2 are red and gray, and 3 are multicolored. People are asked to tell what they see in the cards or what the inkblot represents.

Scoring Rorschach test responses has become controversial. Standard scoring procedures require attending to many factors: what the person says (content), where the person focuses attention (location), mention of detail versus global features, reacting to color or open spaces, and how many distinct responses there are. Many psychologists have questioned the efficiency of the Rorschach as a diagnostic instrument. Much of what it can tell an examiner may be gained directly. For example, Rorschach responses that include many references to death, sadness, and dying are indicative of a depressed person. One wonders if inkblots are really needed to

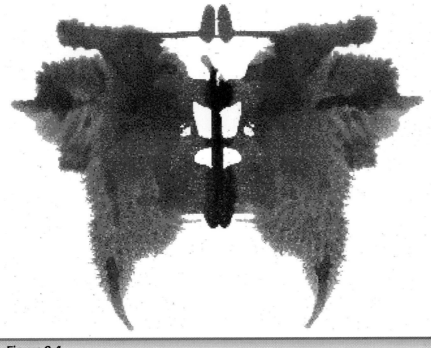

Figure 9.4

A sample Rorschach-like inkblot. The subject is asked what the inkblot represents and what she or he sees in it.

discover such depression. As a psychological test, the Rorschach seems neither reliable nor valid, yet it is still popular. It is used primarily as an aid to assessment.

A projective test we'll see again in Chapter 10 (in the context of achievement motivation), is the **Thematic Apperception Test**, or **TAT**, devised by Henry Murray in 1938. This test is a series of ambiguous pictures about which a person is asked to tell a story. The person is asked to describe what is going on, what led up to this situation, and what the outcome is likely to be. The test is designed to provide a mechanism to discover a person's hidden needs, desires, and emotions, which will be projected into his or her stories. The test is a *thematic* test because scoring depends largely on the interpretation of the themes of the stories told. Although scoring schemes are available, scoring and interpretation are usually subjective and impressionistic. It's likely the TAT is popular for the same reason that the Rorschach is: psychologists are used to it, comfortable with the insights it provides, and willing to accept any source of additional information they can use to make a reasonable assessment or diagnosis.

Thematic Apperception Test (TAT) *a projective technique in which a person is asked to tell a series of short stories about a set of ambiguous pictures*

Before You Go On

Describe projective techniques, the Rorschach and the TAT in particular.

TOPIC 9B SUMMARY

In this Topic, we explored a few of the issues in which personality psychologists are interested. We found an interactionist's position emerging that claims that both internal personality traits (dispositions) and the environment (or perception of the

⊚⊚⊚ **Thinking Critically** ⊚⊚⊚

If you were to take the logic of projective techniques seriously, what could you conclude about someone who viewed all of the inkblots in the Rorschach series and said for each card, "It just looks like an inkblot to me"?

environment) interact to produce a person's behaviors. We saw that with the exception of only physical aggression, there are few significant differences between males and females on traits of personality. Finally, we looked at some of the techniques psychologists use to assess personality: behavioral observations, interviews, paper-and-pencil tests, and projective techniques. Although none of these, in itself, provides a full picture of one's personality, each contributes to our understanding of the complex fabric we call human personality.

CHAPTER SUMMARY

Topic 9A

What are the three levels of consciousness proposed by Freud?

Freud proposed that at any given time we are only aware, or *conscious,* of a few things. With a little effort, some ideas or memories can be accessed from our *preconscious,* whereas others–those in our unconscious mind–may be accessed only with great difficulty. /*pp. 324–325*

Describe the three structures of personality as Freud saw them.

The three structures of personality according to Freud are the instinctive *id,* operating on the *pleasure principle* and seeking immediate gratification; the *ego,* or sense of self, which operates on the *reality principle,* mediating needs in the context of the real world; and the superego, or sense of morality or conscience, which operates on the *idealistic principle,* attempting to direct one to do what is right and proper. /*pp. 325–326*

Define seven defense mechanisms.

Defense mechanisms are unconscious devices employed to defend the ego against the feelings of anxiety. They include *repression,* or motivated forgetting, in which anxiety-producing ideas or experiences are forced into the unconscious; *denial,* in which one refuses to acknowledge the reality of anxiety-producing situations; *rationalization,* in which one generates excuses for anxiety-producing behaviors rather than facing the real reasons for those behaviors; *fantasy,* in which a person uses daydreaming to escape the anxieties of daily living; *projection,* in which one sees in others those traits or desires that would make one anxious if seen in oneself; *regression,* in which one retreats to earlier, primitive levels of behavior that were once effective as a means of dealing with anxiety; and *displacement,* in which one's anxiety-producing motives or behaviors are directed at some "safe" object or person rather than the person for whom they are intended. /*pp. 326–328*

Briefly review Freud's psychosexual stages of development.

Freud believed that personality developed in stages, each related to some expression of sexuality, or sensuality, beginning with an *oral stage,* in which pleasure and satisfaction derive from oral activities such as sucking, feeding, and noise making; to an *anal stage,* in which the control of bladder and bowel movements become a source of satisfaction and pleasure; to a *phallic stage,* in which one becomes aware of one's sexuality and forms a close attachment with the opposite sex parent; to a *latency stage,* in which sexuality is "put on hold" during a period of rapid ego development; to a *genital stage,* which follows puberty and wherein there is a reawakening of sexual, sensual desires. /*pp. 328–329*

Summarize the contributions of Adler, Jung, and Horney to the psychoanalytic approach to personality.

Adler, Jung, and Horney each parted with Freud on theoretical grounds, while remaining basically psychoanalytic in their respective approaches to personality. For Adler, social influences and *inferiority complexes* mattered much more than did innate drives. Jung was less biological, more positive, and expanded on Freud's view of the unconscious mind, adding the notion of the *collective unconscious.* Horney rejected the notion of instinctual impulses and discussed instead the concept of *basic anxiety* and how one reacts to it as the sculptor of one's personality. /*pp. 330–333*

Specify a contribution to the concept of personality made by Watson, Skinner, Dollard and Miller, and Bandura.

Many psychologists have argued that personality can be explained using learning principles and observable behavior. Watson emphasized behavior and argued that psychology should abandon mental concepts. Skinner emphasized the notion of operant conditioning and the consequences of one's behavior. Dollard and Miller tried to explain personality development in terms of learning and habit formation. Bandura stressed the role of observation and social learning in the formation of personality. */pp. 333–335*

Summarize the humanistic-phenomenological approach to personality as epitomized by Rogers and Maslow.

The theories of Rogers and Maslow are alike in many ways, emphasizing the integrity of the self and the power of personal development. Both theorists deny the negativity and biological bias of psychoanalytic theory as well as the environmental determinism of behaviorism. */pp. 335–336*

What are the major personality traits according to Allport and Cattell?

A personality trait is a characteristic and distinctive way in which an individual may differ from others. According to Allport, there are two varieties of traits: *common traits* and *personal dispositions.* The former is found in virtually everyone, and the latter is unique to some individuals. Cattell also feels that there are two varieties of traits: *surface traits,* which are readily observable, and *source traits,* from which surface traits develop. */pp. 337–338*

What are the Big Five personality dimensions?

Recent research in personality trait theory suggests that from all of those traits that have been proposed, five emerge most regularly, although there is as yet no agreement on what to call these dimensions. One version calls them (1) Extroversion-Introversion, (2) Agreeableness or Friendliness, (3) Will or Conscientiousness, (4) Stability-Instability, and (5) Intelligence. */pp. 338–340*

Topic 9B

Summarize the debate concerning personality versus situational influences on behavior.

An issue of interest among psychologists who study personality is the extent to which we can claim that there are internal, individual traits that are consistent over time and over situations. One's personal characteristics should be discernible at least within a range of situations. The debate over the stability or consistency of personality variables begun in the late 1960s is essentially over. A point of view, called *interactionism,* has emerged that says that predicting how a person will respond in a certain situation is determined by the interaction of stable personality characteristics and that person's perception of the situation. */pp. 341–342*

Briefly summarize what we know about gender differences in personality traits.

As much as our stereotypes would like to convince us that there are differences in the personalities of men and women, research continues to remind us that actual differences are few, and slight at best. The one personality trait that does seem to be more common in males than in females is aggression—at least as expressed in overt physical acts. On other personality traits the data are mixed, but some possibilities include differences in communication style, body language, altruism, empathy, and self-confidence. */pp. 342–344*

What are the goals of personality assessment? How are behavioral observations used to assess personality?

We would like to be able to reliably and validly measure or assess an individual's personality so that we may (1) make a proper diagnosis of any psychological disorder, (2) construct reasonable theories of personality, or (3) use measurements or assessments to predict future behaviors of that person. Conclusions about personality can be inferred from the observation of that person's behaviors. Behaviors should be observed in a large number of settings. Observations should be as objective as possible and may involve the use of behavioral rating scales to check reliability. */pp. 344–3477*

Cite one advantage and one disadvantage of the interview as a technique of personality assessment.

The major advantages of the interview are its ease and flexibility of administration, as it allows the interviewer to pursue certain avenues of interest and abandon lines of questioning that are not informative. Unfortunately, unstructured interviews lack demonstrated validity. */p. 347*

How was the MMPI-2 constructed?

Multiphasic instruments attempt to measure several characteristics or traits with the same set of items. The MMPI was designed (in the early 1940s and revised, as the MMPI-2, in 1989) as an aid to diagnosis. The test includes items that discriminate between persons of differing diagnostic categories (including "normal") and that assess the extent to which the subject is doing a thorough and honest job of answering the 567 true-false questions. Paper-and-pencil tests can serve as screening devices to indicate which traits or patterns of traits are likely to be found within a given individual. */pp. 347–349*

Describe projective techniques, the Rorschach and the TAT in particular.

With a projective technique, the assumption is that in responding to an ambiguous stimulus (describing what is indicated in a series of inkblots with the Rorschach, or telling short stories about a set of pictures with the TAT), a person will project aspects of him- or herself into his or her responses. /pp. 349–351

Three Faces of Personality

Imagine that three psychologists are having lunch together, and that you are eavesdropping on their conversation. There is a psychoanalyst (P), a behaviorist (B), and a humanistic psychologist (H) at the table. Which of the three is most likely to have made each of the following statements? (Suggested answers can be found on p. 574.)

_____ 1. I think people in our profession should put more effort into trying to understand mentally healthy people and positive, prosocial growth experiences.

_____ 2. Aggression is a human instinct. Society can control it to some extent, but we will never eliminate aggressive behavior.

_____ 3. Your student may be under a lot of pressure from his parents, but that is no excuse for cheating. We are responsible for what we do.

_____ 4. If you want to understand why she did it, look to the environment for clues instead of at inferred internal forces like impulses and motives.

_____ 5. We humans are products of evolutionary forces that have preserved selfishness, pleasure-seeking, and a tendency to deceive ourselves.

_____ 6. It doesn't seem to me that you need to dig into a person's past to understand the person's current problems and concerns.

_____ 7. There aren't any values inherent in human nature. Values are acquired in the same way we learn to say "please" and "thank you."

_____ 8. If we wanted to improve the character of people in our society, we would need to start when they are very young. By the time a kid is 5 years old, it's probably too late.

_____ 9. You may think your choice of chili and ice cream for lunch was freely made, but your perception of free choice is an illusion. Choosing chili and ice cream is predictable from the consequences of your past behaviors.

_____ 10. General laws of behavior and experience that apply to all people are not very helpful if you want to understand a particular individual.

_____ 11. You say people are inherently good, and she says they are inherently pretty bad. I don't think people are inherently either good or bad.

_____ 12. The sex drive is with us at birth. People just don't want to believe that infants get sexual pleasure from sucking and exploring anything they get in their hands with their mouths.

OUTLINE

Y ou had a great time. You and your friends spent the day backpacking in the mountains. The signs of spring were everywhere to be found, and you enjoyed every minute spent searching for them.

After a full day in the fresh mountain air, no one was terribly choosy about what to have for dinner. Large, heaping piles of beef stew and baked beans right from the can were enjoyed by everyone. You even found room for dessert—toasted marshmallows and a piece of chocolate squeezed between two graham crackers.

As your friends settle around the campfire, darkness just beginning to overtake the campsite, you excuse yourself. You need to "walk off" some of that dinner, so you head off to stroll down a narrow trail that leads away from the camp-site.

As you meander down the trail, you feel totally relaxed, at peace with the world. When you are about 200 yards from the campsite you think you hear a strange noise in the woods, off to your left. Looking back down the trail, you notice that you can barely see the campfire's glow through the trees and underbrush, even though their leaves are not yet fully formed. Well, maybe you'd better not venture too much farther, perhaps just over that ridge, and then you'd better . . .

10

Motivation and Emotion

suddenly, from behind a dense thicket, a large growling black bear appears. It takes one look at you, bares its teeth, and lets out a mighty roar. *What will you do now?*

In this situation, and in many similar, but less dramatic ones, we can be sure of one thing: Your reaction will involve motivational and emotional states. You certainly will become emotional. Encountering a bear in the woods is not something that one does with reason and intellect alone. You will be motivated to do something; getting away from that bear seems reasonable. We will return to this meeting-a-bear-in-the-woods story several times throughout this chapter as we explore what psychologists know about motivation and emotion.

TOPIC 10A   Issues of Motivation

In this Topic, we'll address some important practical issues. For the first time, our focus is on questions that begin with *why*. "Why did she *do* that (as opposed to doing nothing)?" "Why did she do *that* (as opposed to doing something else)?" "Why does she *keep* doing that (as opposed to stopping)?" As you can see, the study of motivation gets us involved with attempts to explain the causes of certain behaviors.

Motivation involves two subprocesses. First, motivation involves *arousal*—one's level of activation or excitement. Here we are using "motivation" to describe a force that initiates behaviors, that gets an organism going, energized to do something and to keep doing it. The second subprocess provides *direction,* or focus, to one's behaviors. More than being simply aroused and active, a motivated organism's behavior is in some way goal-directed or purposeful. Thus, **motivation** is the process that arouses, directs, and maintains behavior.

motivation *the process that arouses, directs, and maintains behavior*

How Shall We Characterize Motivation?

From its earliest days, psychology has tried to find some systematic theory to summarize and organize what various motivational states have in common. Psychologists have struggled to find one general pattern or scheme that could be used to account for why organisms tend to do what they do. In this section, we will review some of these theories in a somewhat chronological order. As you might predict, no one approach to motivation will satisfactorily answer all of our questions. I'd also like to draw your attention to Topic 15A, on industrial-organizational psychology, which includes a section on approaches to motivation, specifically those related to work motivation.

Instincts

instincts *unlearned, complex patterns of behavior that occur in the presence of certain stimuli*

In the psychology of the 1880s, behaviors were often explained in terms of **instincts**—unlearned, complex patterns of behavior that occur in the presence of certain stimuli. Why do birds build nests? A nest-building instinct. When conditions are right, birds build nests. Why do salmon swim upstream to mate? Instinct. Swimming upstream at mating season is part of what it means to be a salmon. Yes, these behaviors can be modified by the organisms' experiences, but the force behind them is unlearned, or instinctive.

Instinct may explain some of the behaviors of birds and salmon, but what about people? William James (1890) reasoned that because they are more complex, humans had to have more instincts that did the "lower" animals. William McDougall championed the instinctual explanation of human behaviors (McDougall, 1908). He said that human behaviors were motivated by 11 basic instincts: repulsion, curiosity, flight, reproduction, gregariousness, acquisitiveness, parenting, construction, self-assertion, self-abasement, and pugnacity. Soon McDougall had to extend his list to include 18 instincts. As different behaviors required explanation, new instincts were devised to explain them.

As lists of human instincts got longer and longer, the problem with this approach became obvious. Particularly for humans, "explaining" behavior patterns by alluding to instinct only relabeled them and didn't explain anything. Even so, the psychologists who argued for instincts did introduce and draw attention to an idea very much with us today: We may engage in some behaviors for reasons that are basically physiological, and more inherited than learned.

Why do salmon swim upstream when it is time to mate? Why do birds build nests? We may "explain" these behaviors by referring to instincts, but the concept of instinct has not been useful for explaining human behaviors.

Needs and Drives

An approach that provided an alternative to explaining behavior in terms of instincts was one that attempted to explain the whys of behavior in terms of needs and drives. We will look at two theories that incorporate these concepts.

Clark Hull. Clark Hull's ideas about motivation were dominant in the 1940s and 1950s (e.g., Hull, 1943). In Hull's system, a **need** is a lack or shortage of some biological essential required for survival. A need arises from deprivation. When an organism is kept from food, it develops a need for food. Needs give rise to drives. A **drive** is a state of tension, arousal, or activation. If an organism is in a drive state, it is aroused and directed to engage in some behavior to satisfy the drive by satisfying the underlying need. Needs produce tensions (drives) that the organism seeks to reduce; hence, this approach is referred to in terms of *drive reduction.*

Whereas instincts are tied to specific patterns of behavior, needs and drives are not. They are concepts that can be used to explain why we do what we do, and still allow for the influence of experience and the environment. Going without food may give rise to a need, which in turn gives rise to a drive, but *how* that drive is expressed in behavior is influenced by one's experiences and learning history.

One problem with a drive reduction approach centers on the biological nature of needs. To claim that needs result only from biological deprivations seems restrictive. It may be that not all of the drives that activate a person's behavior are based on biological needs. Humans often engage in behaviors to satisfy *learned drives.* Drives derived from one's learning experience are called **secondary drives**, as opposed to *primary drives,* which are based on unlearned, physiological needs. Most of the drives that arouse and direct our behavior have little to do with physiology. You may feel you "need" a new car this year. I may convince myself I "need" a new set of golf clubs, and we'll both work very hard to save the money to buy what we "need." We may say we are "driven" to work for money, but it's difficult to imagine how your car or my golf clubs could be satisfying a biological need. A lot of advertising is directed at trying to convince us that we need many products and services that will in fact have very little impact on our survival.

need *a lack or shortage of some biological essential resulting from deprivation*

drive *a state of tension resulting from an unlearned need that arouses and directs an organism's behavior*

secondary drive *a state of tension resulting from a learned, or acquired, need that motivates an organism's behavior*

Why does one climb a mountain? Because it is there. Psychologists have argued that we all have needs to explore our environments, needs that are particularly strong in childhood.

A related complication is that organisms often continue to behave even after their biological needs are met. Drives are states of arousal, or tension. This position claims that we behave as we do in order to reduce tension or arousal. Yet we know that sky divers jump out of airplanes, mountain climbers risk life and limb to scale sheer cliffs of stone, monkeys play with mechanical puzzles even when solving those puzzles leads to no other reward, and children explore the pots and pans in kitchen cabinets even when repeatedly told not to. These actions do not appear to be reducing tension, do they? We might suggest, as some psychologists have, that these organisms are trying to satisfy an exploration drive, or a manipulation drive, or a curiosity drive. But then we run the risk of trying to explain why people behave as they do by generating longer and longer lists of drives—the same problem we have when we try to explain behavior in terms of instinct.

So what do these complications mean? It seems that people often do behave in ways that reduce drives and thereby satisfy needs. How drives are satisfied, or reduced, may reflect each organism's learning history. The concept of drive reduction is a useful one and is still very much with us in psychology, but it cannot be accepted as a complete explanation for motivated behaviors.

Abraham Maslow. Abraham Maslow is one of the persons we associate with the humanistic movement in psychology. *Humanistic psychologists* emphasize the person and his or her psychological growth. Maslow combined his concern for the person with Hull's drive reduction theory and proposed that human behavior does, in fact, respond to needs. Not all of those needs are physiological. Maslow believed that the needs that motivate human action are few, and are arranged hierarchically (Maslow, 1943, 1970). Figure 10.1 summarizes this hierarchy of needs.

Maslow's is basically a stage theory. It proposes that what motivates us first are *physiological needs*. These include the basic needs related to survival—for food, water, and shelter. Until these needs are met, there is no reason to suspect that an individual will be concerned with anything else. Once one's physiological needs are under control, a person is still motivated, now by *safety needs:* the need to feel secure, protected from dangers that might arise in the future. We are now motivated to see to it that the cupboard has food for later, that we won't freeze this winter, and that there's enough money saved to protect against sudden calamity. The hier-

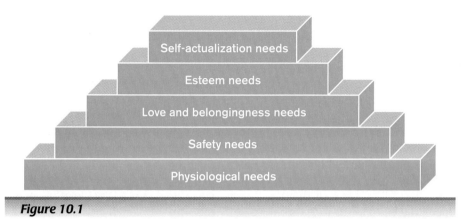

Figure 10.1

Maslow's hierarchy of needs.

archical nature of this theory is already clear. We are not going to worry about what we'll be eating tomorrow if there's not enough to eat today; but if today's needs are taken care of, we can then focus on the future.

Once safety needs are met, concern shifts to *love and belongingness:* a need for someone else to care about us, to love us. If these needs are satisfied, our concern shifts to *esteem.* Our aim is to be recognized for our achievements, our efforts. These needs are not physiological, but social. Now our behaviors are motivated by our awareness of others and a concern for their approval. One moves higher in the hierarchy, on to higher stages, only if needs at lower stages are met. Ultimately, we may reach the highest stage in Maslow's hierarchy: *self-actualization* needs. We self-actualize when we become the best we can be, taking the fullest advantage of our potential as human beings. We are self-actualizing when we strive to be as creative or productive as possible.

In many ways, Maslow's arrangement of needs in a hierarchical fashion reflects the values of Western culture, particularly those that reflect the notion of the individual working hard to overcome obstacles and achieve. We can hardly expect people to be motivated to grow and to achieve "success" when they are concerned about their very survival on a day-to-day basis. When people's needs for safety, belonging, and esteem are reasonably fulfilled, they don't just die, unmotivated to do anything else. It should be clear to you, as it was to Maslow, that many people never make it to the self-actualization stage in the hierarchy of needs. There are millions of people in this world who have great difficulty dealing with the very lowest stages and who never have the time, energy, or opportunity to be concerned with such issues as self-esteem or belongingness, much less self-actualization.

As a comprehensive theory of human motivation, Maslow's hierarchy has some difficulties. Perhaps the biggest stumbling block is the idea that one can assign ranks to needs and put them in a neat order, regardless of what that order may be. Some persons are motivated in ways that violate the stage approach of this theory. Individuals will, for example, freely give up satisfying basic survival needs for the sake of "higher" principles (as in hunger strikes). For the sake of love, people may abandon their own needs for safety and security. The truth of the matter is, there is little empirical research support for Maslow's approach to ranking needs in a hierarchy. It remains the case, however, that because of its intuitive appeal, Maslow's theory of human motivation has found favor both within and outside psychology.

Incentives

One alternative to a drive reduction approach to motivation focuses on the *end state,* or goal, of behavior, not needs or drives within the organism. In this view, external stimuli serve as motivating agents, or **incentives**, for behavior. Incentives are **incentives** *external stimuli an organism may be motivated to approach or avoid* external events that act to *pull* our behavior from without, as opposed to drives, which are internal events that *push* our behavior from within.

When a mountain climber says she climbs a mountain "because it is there," she is indicating that she is being motivated by an incentive. After enjoying a large meal, we may order a piece of cherry cheesecake, not because we need it in any physiological sense, but because it's there on the dessert cart and looks so good (and because previous experience tells us that it is likely to taste very good).

Some parents want to know how to "motivate their child to clean up his room." We can interpret this case in terms of establishing goals or incentives. What those parents really want to know is how they can get their child to value, work for, and be reinforced by a clean room. What they want is a clean room, and they'd like to have the child clean it. If they want the child to be motivated to clean his or her room, the child needs to learn the value or incentive of having a clean room. How to teach a child that a clean room is a thing to be valued is another story, involving other incentives the child does value. For now, let's just acknowledge that establishing a clean room as a valued goal is the major task at hand, and having a clean room is not an innate, inborn need.

If you think this all sounds like our discussion of operant conditioning (Topic 5B), you're right. Remember, the basic tenet of operant conditioning is that behaviors are controlled by their consequences. We tend to do (are motivated to do) what leads to reinforcement (positive incentives), and we tend not to do what leads to punishment or failure of reinforcement (negative incentives).

Before You Go On

How have the concepts of instincts, needs, drives, and incentives been used to explain motivated behaviors?

Balance, or Equilibrium

A concept that has proven useful in understanding motivation is *balance,* or *equilibrium.* The idea is that we are motivated to maintain a state of balance. What are we motivated to balance? Sometimes balance involves physiological processes that need to be kept at some level, or a restricted range, of activity. Sometimes equilibrium is required among our thoughts or cognitions. We'll review three approaches

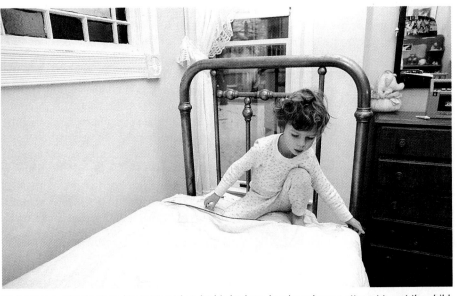

Motivating a child to clean his room and make his bed can be viewed as an attempt to get the child to share some of the incentives that are valued by his parents.

to motivation that emphasize maintaining a state of balance, equilibrium, or optimum level of functioning.

Homeostasis. One of the first references to a need for equilibrium is found in the work of Walter Cannon (1932). Cannon was concerned with our internal physiological reactions, and the term he used to describe a state of balance within those reactions was **homeostasis**. The idea is that each of our physiological processes has a balanced set point of operation. One's *set point* is a level of activity that is "normal" or "most suitable." When anything upsets this balance, we become motivated, driven to do whatever we can to return to our set point, our optimum, homeostatic level. If we drift only slightly from our set point, our physiological mechanisms return us to homeostasis without our intention or awareness. If these automatic processes are not successful, we may have to take action, motivated by the drive to maintain homeostasis.

homeostasis a state of balance, or equilibrium, among internal, physiological conditions

Everyone has normal set levels for body temperature, blood pressure, heart rate, basal metabolism (the rate at which energy is used by bodily functions), and so on. If any of these processes deviate from their set point, homeostatic level, we become motivated to do something that will return to our state of balance. Cannon's concept of homeostasis was devised to explain physiological processes, but the ideas of balance and optimum level of operation have been applied to psychological processes as well.

Arousal. **Arousal** is defined in terms of overall level of activation or excitement. A person's level of arousal may change from day to day and within the same day. After a good night's sleep and a brisk morning shower, your arousal level may be high. (It also may be high as your instructor moves through class handing out exams.) Late at night, after a busy day at school, your level of arousal may be quite low. Your arousal level is at its lowest when you are in the deepest stages of sleep.

arousal one's level of activation or excitement

Arousal theories of motivation (Berlyne, 1960, 1971; Duffy, 1962; Hebb, 1955) claim that there is an optimal level of arousal (an "arousal set point") that organisms are motivated to maintain. Drive reduction theories, remember, argue that we are motivated to *reduce* tension or arousal by satisfying the needs that give rise to drives. Arousal theories argue that sometimes we seek out ways to *increase* arousal in order to maintain our optimal arousal level. If we find ourselves bored and in a rut, the idea of going to an action-adventure movie may seem like a good one. On the other hand, if we've had a very busy, hectic day, just staying at home doing nothing may sound appealing.

This approach is like Cannon's idea of homeostasis, but in more general terms than specific physiological processes. It suggests that for any situation there is a "best," or most efficient, level of arousal. To do well on an exam, for example, requires that a student have a certain level of overall arousal. If a student is tired, bored, or just doesn't care one way or the other about the exam, we can expect a poor performance. If, on the other hand, a student is so worried and anxious that she or he can barely function, we can also expect a poor exam score. The relationship between arousal and the efficiency of performance is depicted in Figure 10.2.

Arousal theory also takes into account the difficulty or complexity of the activity in which a person is engaged. For simple tasks, a high level of arousal may be optimal, whereas that same high level of arousal would be disastrous for difficult, complex tasks (Brehm & Self, 1989). For example, students who were judged to be poorly, moderately, or highly motivated tried a series of difficult anagram problems (identifying a word whose letters have been scrambled). The most highly motivated subjects did significantly worse than did the moderately motivated subjects (Ford et al., 1985). The notion that optimum levels of arousal vary with the difficulty of a task can be traced to an article published in 1908 by Yerkes and Dodson,

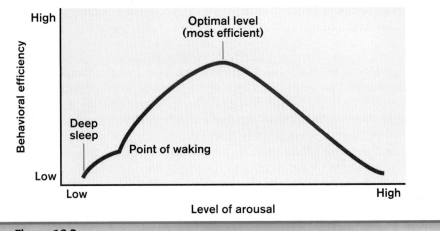

Figure 10.2

For each task we attempt, there is an optimal level of arousal. What that level is depends on several factors, including the difficulty of the task. In other words, it is possible to be *too* aroused (motivated), just as it is possible to be underaroused. (After Hebb, 1955.)

even though the concept of "arousal" did not appear in psychology until many decades later (Winton, 1987).

An interesting twist on the theory of arousal is that for some reason optimum levels of arousal vary widely from individual to individual. Some people seem to

For many of us, jumping off into space held only by a bungee cord attached to our ankles would be overly arousing, to say the least. For "sensation seekers," however, bungee jumping may provide a near optimum level of arousal.

need and seek particularly high levels of arousal and excitement in their lives. Marvin Zuckerman calls such people "sensation seekers" (Zuckerman et al., 1978, 1980). They enjoy skydiving or mountain climbing and look forward to the challenge of driving in heavy city traffic. Some recent evidence suggests that there may be a genetic basis for individual differences in sensation-seeking, or risk-taking (Ebstein et al., 1996).

Cognitive Dissonance. There is also a point of view that we are motivated to maintain a state of balance among our ideas or beliefs (our cognitions) as well as among our physiological processes and levels of arousal. That is, we are motivated to maintain what Leon Festinger (1957) calls a *state of consonance* among our cognitions.

You believe yourself to be a good student. You study hard for an exam in biology and think you're prepared. You judge the exam to be a fairly easy one. But when you get your exam paper back, you discover you failed the test! Now that's hard to accept. You believe you studied adequately and that the test wasn't difficult. But you also know you failed the test. Here are cognitions that do not fit together. They are not consonant; they are not balanced. You are experiencing **cognitive dissonance**, a state of tension or discomfort that exists when we hold and are aware of inconsistent cognitions. When this occurs, Festinger argues, we are motivated to bring about a change in our system of cognitions. You may come to believe you're not such a good student after all. Or you may come to believe your paper was unfairly graded. Or you may come to believe you are a poor judge of an exam's difficulty. This theory doesn't predict *what* will happen, but it does predict that cognitive dissonance produces motivation to return to a balanced state of cognitive consonance.

These days, almost all smokers experience cognitive dissonance. They know that smoking is a very dangerous habit, and yet they continue to smoke. Some reduce their dissonance by convincing themselves that although smoking is bad for one's health in general, it really isn't bad for them in particular, at least not when compared to perceived "benefits." We'll return to cognitive dissonance when we discuss attitude change (Topic 14A).

cognitive dissonance *a motivating discomfort or tension caused by a lack of balance or consonance among one's cognitions*

Before You Go On

How has the concept of balance, or equilibrium, been used to explain motivated behaviors?

Summing Up: Applying Motivational Concepts

Let's go back now to the story about meeting a bear in the woods with which I opened this chapter. Granted that the example is somewhat far-fetched, and that we'll have to oversimplify a bit, but can we apply the theoretical approaches we've been discussing to explain your behavior in the circumstances of the story? Let's say that upon seeing the bear you throw your arms straight up in the air, scream at the top of your lungs, and race back to camp as fast as you can. Your friends, still sitting around the campfire, can see and hear you coming. How might they explain your behaviors?

(1) "Clearly, it's a matter of instinct. Humans have a powerful and useful instinct for avoiding large animals in the wild. In this instance, running away is just an unlearned, natural, instinctive reaction." (2) "No, I think that the fear that arose upon seeing the bear created a tension—a drive—that needed to be relieved. There were several options available, but in your need to reduce your fear, you chose to

⊚⊚⊚⊚ **Thinking Critically** ⊚⊚⊚⊚

What are instructors really trying to do when they say they want to "motivate their students" to do as well as they can?

run away." (3) "Why do you folks keep relying on all this internal instinct-need-drive nonsense? Previous learning experience, even if it was secondhand, or vicarious, taught you that bears in the wild are incentives to be avoided. They are negative goals. You ran back here simply to reach the goal of safety with us, your friends." (4) "I see your reaction as an attempt to maintain a state of equilibrium or balance. Seeing that bear was an emotional experience that increased many physiological functions. Your running away was just one way to try to return those physiological functions to their normal, homeostatic levels." (5) "Why get so complicated with physiological functions? Why not just say that your overall arousal level was much higher than normal—higher than you wanted it to be—so you ran away from the bear simply in need of lowering your level of arousal?" (6) "The same argument can be made for your cognitions—and cognitive dissonance reduction. You know that you like being safe and free of pain. You believe that bears in the woods can be very hurtful, and there's one in front of you. These two ideas are in conflict. You will do something. In this case, you chose to run away. If you believed that a bear in the woods would be afraid of you and of no potential harm, then there wouldn't have been any dissonance, and you wouldn't have run away."

Temperature Regulation

Now that we've reviewed a few theoretical approaches to motivation, we can turn to a few specific examples. As we go through this discussion, I will follow convention and use the term *drive* when talking about activators of behavior that have a known biological or physiological basis (e.g., a hunger drive) and the term *motive* for those that do not (e.g., a power motive).

Most of us seldom give our body temperature much thought beyond the fuzzy notion that 98.6° F is "normal." That body temperature has anything to do with motivation is sensible in the context of homeostasis. Whenever anything happens to raise or lower our body temperature above or below its homeostatic set point range, we become motivated. We become driven to return our body temperature to its normal, balanced 98.6° F. (In passing, research confirms the observation that body temperature normally fluctuates throughout the day, and suggests that 98.2° F is a better estimate of "normal," average body temperature than is 98.6° F [Mackowiak et al., 1992].)

Let's say you are outside on a bitterly cold day, and are improperly dressed for the low temperature and high wind. Your body temperature starts to drop. Automatically your body responds to elevate your temperature back to its normal level: blood vessels in the hands and feet constrict, forcing blood back to the center of the body to conserve heat (as a result, your lips turn blue); you shiver (those involuntary muscle movements create small amounts of heat energy); you get "goose bumps" as the skin thickens to insulate against the cold. These are just the sorts of automatic physiological reactions Cannon had in mind when he wrote about homeostasis.

Imagine that you are fully dressed, and walking across a desert at noon on a hot day in August. Your temperature rises. Automatically, blood is diverted to the surface of your body, and your face becomes flushed. You perspire, and as moisture on the surface of the skin evaporates, the skin is cooled, as is the blood now near the surface—all in an attempt to return your body's temperature to its homeostatic level.

There are two centers in your brain that act as a thermostat and initiate attempts at temperature regulation. Both are located in the **hypothalamus**, a mid-brain structure near the limbic system that is involved in several physiological drives (see Figure 10.3). One center is particularly sensitive to elevated body temperatures, the other to lowered temperatures. Together they act to mobilize the internal environment when normal balance is upset. If these automatic reactions are not successful, you may be driven to take some voluntary action. You may have to get

hypothalamus *a small structure near the limbic system in the center of the brain, associated with temperature regulation, feeding, drinking, and sex*

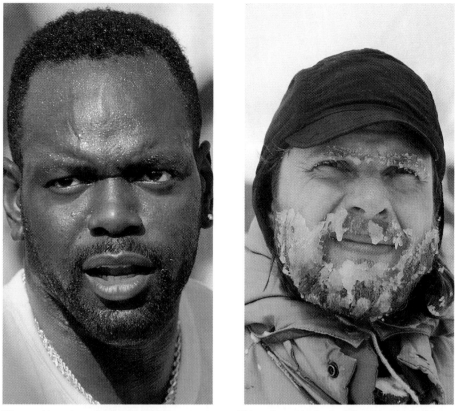

We are driven to maintain our body temperatures within rather strict limits. When our autonomic nervous systems cannot deal adequately with temperature extremes, we may be driven to do something that will lower or raise our body temperatures.

inside, out of the cold or heat. You may need to turn on the furnace or the air conditioner. Over and above what your brain and body do automatically, you may have to engage in learned behaviors in order to maintain homeostasis.

Before You Go On

How is temperature regulation a physiological drive?

The Thirst Drive and Drinking Behaviors

We need water for survival. If we don't drink, we die. As the need for water increases, it gives rise to a thirst drive. The intriguing issue is not so much that we need to drink, but how we *know* we're thirsty. What actually causes us to seek liquid and drink it?

Internal, Physiological Cues

For a long time, psychologists thought that we drank to relieve the discomfort caused by the dryness of our mouths and throats. No doubt, the unpleasantness of a dry mouth and throat *can* cause one to drink, but there must be more to drinking behavior than this. Animals with no salivary glands, whose mouths and throats are constantly dry, drink no more than normal animals (they drink more frequently but not more in terms of quantity). Normal bodily processes (such as urination, exhaling, and perspiration) cause us to lose about 2 liters of water a day (Levinthal, 1983). That water needs to be replaced, but what motivates us to do so?

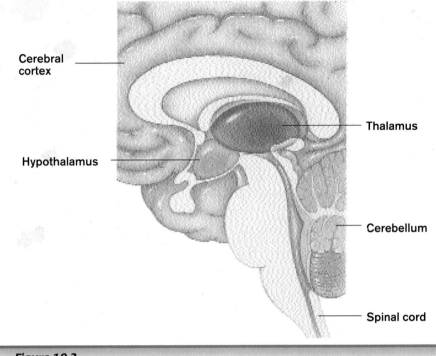

Cerebral cortex

Hypothalamus

Thalamus

Cerebellum

Spinal cord

Figure 10.3

A section of the human brain, showing the location of the hypothalamus.

About two-thirds of the fluid in our bodies is contained *within* our body's cells (intracellular); the remaining one-third is held in the spaces *between* cells (extracellular). There seem to be two mechanisms sensitive to losses of fluid. Intracellular fluid loss is monitored by the hypothalamus. One small center acts to "turn on" the thirst drive when fluid levels are low, and another center "turns off" the thirst drive when fluid levels are adequate. Thirst that stems from extracellular loss is also monitored in the brain, through a complex chain of events involving the kidneys, which stimulate the production of a hormone that leads to a thirst drive.

External, Psychological Cues

Drinking behavior may be motivated by a physiological drive arising from a physiological need for water. Sometimes, however, our drinking behavior is influenced by external factors, or incentives. For example, the aroma of freshly brewed coffee may stimulate us to order a second (unneeded) cup. A frosty glass of iced tea may look too good to refuse. We may drink a cold beer or a soda simply because it tastes good, whether we *need* the fluid it contains or not.

Notice also that once we are motivated in terms of being aroused, *what* we drink will be influenced by our previous learning experiences. Choices for what we drink are also shaped by availability. Even with such an obvious physiological drive as thirst, and such an obvious physiological need as ours for water, psychological factors can be very relevant.

Before You Go On

What are some of the internal and external factors that influence drinking behavior?

The Hunger Drive and Eating Behaviors

Our need for food is as obvious as our need for water. If we don't eat, we die. Again, the interesting question is, what gives rise to the hunger drive? As it happens, many factors motivate a person to eat. Some are physiological. Some are psychological and reflect learning experiences. Some involve social pressures.

Internal, Physiological and Genetic Cues for Hunger and Eating

People and animals with no stomachs eat the same amounts of food as do people and animals with intact stomachs. Cues from our stomachs, then, don't seem to be very important in producing a hunger drive. The two structures that seem most involved in the hunger drive are the hypothalamus (again) and the liver, which is involved in the production and breakdown of fat.

Theories of hunger that focus on the role of the hypothalamus are referred to as *dual-center theories,* because there are two regions there that regulate food intake. One (the ventromedial hypothalamus) is an "eat" center that gives rise to feelings of hunger, while the other (the lateral hypothalamus) is a "no-eat" center that lets us know when we've had enough. Removing or lesioning the eat center (and leaving the no-eat center intact) in rats, leads to starvation, whereas lesioning the no-eat center (and leaving the eat center intact) leads to extreme overeating. Electrically stimulating the no-eat center will cause even a food-deprived rat to stop eating (Friedman & Stricker, 1976).

Although the hypothalamus is involved in hunger, normal eating patterns are not under the influence of electrical stimulation and brain lesioning procedures. What, then, activates the brain's hunger-regulating centers in a normal organism? Here we are at the level of hypothesis and conjecture, and there are several hypotheses to consider. One proposal is that the body responds to levels of blood sugar, or glucose, that can be metabolized, or converted into energy, for the body's use. When levels of glucose are low, which they are when we haven't eaten for a while, we are stimulated to eat. When glucose levels are adequate, we will stop eating. It may be that our liver most closely monitors such blood chemistry for us.

Another view holds that we respond, through a complex chain of events, to levels of fat stored in our bodies. When fat stores are adequately filled, we feel no hunger. If fat supplies are depleted, a hunger drive arises. Once again, it is the liver that is involved in the cycle of storing and depleting fat supplies.

Another hypothesis that emphasizes the role of internal, physiological cues also relies heavily on the concept of set point, or homeostasis. This position claims that a person's *overall body weight,* like blood pressure or body temperature, is regulated (Nisbett, 1972). "Being so regulated, weight normally is maintained at a particular level or set-point, not only by the control of food intake, as is often assumed, but also by complementary adjustments in energy utilization and expenditure" (Keesey & Powley, 1986). An implication is that if body weight decreases significantly, through dieting or exercise, or both, the organism will be driven to return to the set point level. The result may be to abandon the diet, cut down on exercise, or both. Conversely, if one eats too much—more than is necessary to keep a homeostatic level of energy consumption and storage—one will be motivated to expend energy to return to set point levels. Still to be determined are the mechanisms involved in establishing one's set point body weight and energy utilization levels to begin with. There is evidence that these body weight set points are influenced by both genetic factors (Nisbett, 1972) and feeding behaviors during infancy (Knittle, 1975).

We are learning that there are powerful genetic forces at work that may determine one's body size and the distribution of fat within the body (Stunkard, 1988; Stunkard et al., 1986). One experiment (Bouchard et al., 1990) looked at the effects of overeating on 12 pairs of adult (ages 19 to 27) male identical twins. After eating normally for two weeks, the men were required to consume 1,000 excess calories of food each day for 6 days a week over a 100-day period. Weight gains *between* twin pairs varied considerably by the end of the study. Significantly, there were virtually no differences in weight gain *within* each pair of twins! In addition, *where* the excess weight was stored (e.g., the waist or hips) also varied between pairs, but not within twin pairs. The researchers concluded that "the most likely explanation for the intrapair similarity . . . is that genetic factors are involved" (p. 1477). A related correlational study looked at the body weights of twins reared together or apart and found that regardless of where or how the twins were reared, there was a significant relationship between genetic similarity and body mass (Stunkard et al., 1990). Even early childhood environments had little or no effect. Such data tell us that genetic factors are important in both the ultimate determination of body weight and size and the distribution of fat within the body. But they do not tell us that the only factors involved in determining body size are genetic (Brownell & Rodin, 1994; Sobal & Stunkard, 1989).

There is one other series of studies to consider before we leave this discussion. In 1994, a group of researchers at the Howard Hughes Medical Institute of Rockefeller University led by Dr. Jeffrey Friedman announced that they had isolated a specific gene related to eating and obesity. They called it the *obese gene,* or the *ob gene* (Baringa, 1995). This gene controls the amount of a hormone the researchers named *leptin* (after the Greek word for *thin*) in the bloodstream. This hormone is a protein–called *ob protein*–that directly or indirectly tells the brain how much fat is stored in the body. When something goes wrong with the gene, insufficient amounts of *ob protein* are available, and the organism continues to eat, "unaware" that it already has adequate (or more than adequate) fat stored away. The obvious result is an overweight organism. In the summer of 1995 Friedman and his colleagues reported on three independent studies in which *ob protein* was injected into mice that were either obese or of normal weight (Campfield et al., 1995; Halaas et al., 1995; Pelleymounter, 1995). The results were astounding. In just two weeks, the mice ate less and burned energy faster. Obese mice lost about 30 percent of their body weight and had about 9 grams of body fat, compared to 38 grams of body fat in control mice who were not given the protein. Normal mice given *ob protein* injections lost almost all of their body fat–about 12 percent of their weight.

Lest those of us who would like to lose weight get too excited, note two things: (1) all experiments to date have been on mice, and whether the same effects will be found on humans remains to be determined, and (2) present results are only for the relative short term–we do not know yet what the long-term results of *ob protein* injections will be.

External, Psychological Cues for Hunger and Eating

As we know, eating behaviors are influenced by factors beyond our physiology. We often respond to external cues. Sometimes, the stimulus properties of foods–aroma, taste, or appearance–are enough to get us to eat. You may not want any dessert after a large meal until the waitress shows you a piece of chocolate cake. Eating that cake has nothing to do with your internal physiological conditions (reminding us of the "incentive approach" to motivation described earlier.)

Sometimes people eat more from habit than from need. "It's 12 o'clock. It's lunch time; so let's eat." We may fall into habits of eating at certain times, tied more to the clock than to internal cues from our bodies. Some people seem unable to watch television without poking food into their mouths, a behavioral pattern motivated more by learning than by physiology.

Occasionally we eat simply because others around us are eating. Such "socially facilitated" eating has been noted in several species (Harlow, 1932; Tolman, 1969). If a caged chicken is allowed to eat its fill of grain, it eventually stops eating. When other hungry chickens are placed in the cage and begin to eat, the "full" chicken starts right in eating again. Its behaviors are not noticeably different from those of the chickens just added to the cage.

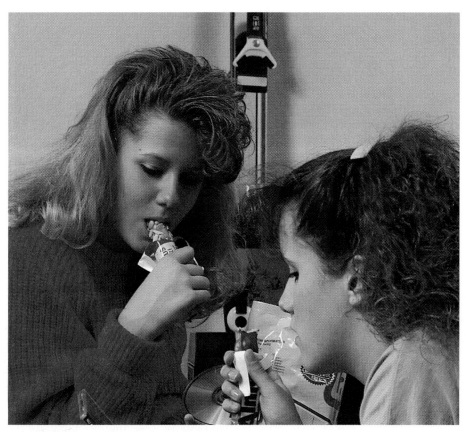

We eat for many reasons, not all of them physiological. Sometimes we eat simply because others around us are eating. Sometimes we have developed eating habits, such as munching on snack foods while listening to CDs.

Overweight people may be less sensitive to internal hunger cues and more sensitive to external eating cues from the environment (Schacter, 1971), although there is evidence that this logical analysis is not always true (Rodin, 1981). We know that many people who are overweight tend to underestimate the amount of food (calories) they eat each day—even when they are in a controlled weight-loss program. They fail to lose weight because they really aren't dieting, even though they believe they are. They also overestimate their level of exercise and physical activity (Lightman et al., 1992).

For those people who are overweight, it would be nice if there were some simple, foolproof way to lose weight. Indeed, 31 percent of all men and 24 percent of all women in this country are overweight (National Academy of Sciences, 1989), and most of them support a $30 *billion* a year weight-loss industry (Brownell & Rodin, 1994; Horm & Anderson, 1993). About 15 percent of teenagers were deemed to be overweight through the 1970s, but that percentage jumped to 21 by 1991 (Centers for Disease Control, 1994). We find considerable disagreement among experts over whether dieting can ever be effective (Brownell, 1993; Brownell & Rodin, 1994; Lee et al., 1993). "Fully 95 percent of those starting a weight-loss program will return to their original weight within five years" (Martin et al., 1991, p. 528). Our society's preoccupation with weight and body size may help to explain the increasing rates of eating disorders that have occurred in the last decade (e.g., Fairburn & Wilson, 1993). It is to this issue that we turn next.

Before You Go On

What are some of the internal and external cues that motivate eating behaviors?

◎◎◎◎ **Thinking Critically** ◎◎◎◎

Think about your own experiences. Why do you eat what you eat, when you eat?

Eating Disorders

Eating well is something few of us do all the time. Some of us simply eat too much—too many saturated fats in particular. There are those, however, whose problems with eating go beyond eating too much, or eating the wrong types of food. These are people who suffer from two disorders of eating: anorexia nervosa and bulimia. These disorders are independent of each other, but there are many cases in which an individual shows the symptoms of both at the same time.

anorexia nervosa *an eating disorder characterized by the reduction of body weight through self-starvation and/or increased activity*

Anorexia nervosa is characterized by an inability (or refusal) to maintain one's body weight. It is essentially a condition of self-starvation, accompanied by a fear of becoming fat and a feeling of being overweight in spite of the fact that the person is considerably underweight (more than 15 percent below normal) (APA, 1987; Yates, 1989). The person with anorexia nervosa maintains a reduced body weight by severely reducing food intake, by increasing levels of physical activity, or both. The disorder is surprisingly common, particularly among females. Nearly 1 percent of adolescent girls and females of college age suffer from anorexia (Edmands, 1993). Only about 10 to 15 percent of anorexic patients are males (Yates, 1990). Incidence rates are increasing in this country and in diverse cultural settings around the world (Pate et al., 1992).

bulimia *an eating disorder characterized by recurrent episodes of binge eating and then purging to remove the just-eaten food*

Bulimia is characterized by episodes of binge eating followed by purging—usually self-induced vomiting or the use of laxatives to rapidly rid the body of just-eaten food (APA, 1987; Yates, 1989). The binge eating episodes are often well planned, anticipated with a great deal of pleasure, and involve rapidly eating large amounts of high-calorie, sweet-tasting food. Like the anorexic patient, the person with bulimia is very likely to be female, from an upper socioeconomic class, and usually shows concern about weight. Unlike a person with anorexia nervosa, a bulimic patient need not be well below normal body weight. Another difference in-

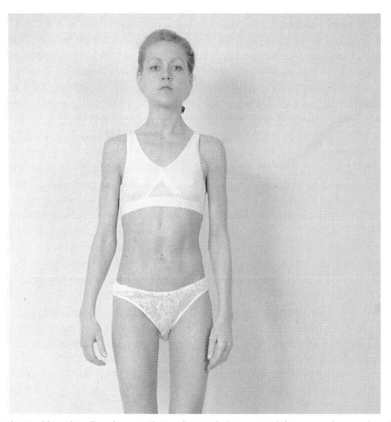

Many patients with eating disorders see themselves as being overweight—even obese—when in fact their body weights are below normal.

volves denial: "the anorexic denies to others and herself that any problem or abnormal eating behavior exists, whereas the bulimic usually denies the existence of a problem to others, but clearly recognizes that her eating is abnormal" (Sherman & Thompson, 1990, p. 4). Nearly 4 percent of female college freshmen suffer from bulimia, compared to only 0.4 percent of male freshmen. An estimated 15 percent of female medical students report having an eating disorder sometime in their lives (Yates, 1989).

What causes eating disorders, and what can be done to treat them effectively? Eating disorders have a number of interacting causes. The value that Western cultures place on thinness is certainly one. We are constantly being bombarded with messages that communicate the same theme: "To be thin is good; to be fat is bad." Role models for many young girls include super-thin fashion models, dancers, and entertainers. More than 75 percent of adolescent girls desire to weigh less than they do (Brownell & Rodin, 1994; Yates, 1989). The cultural emphasis on feminine thinness likely contributes to the greater dissatisfaction among women than men with their weight and body shape (Rolls et al., 1991). One study found that women eat less in the presence of a desirable male partner than when they are with a less desirable partner (Mori & Pliner, 1987).

When we look for specific behavioral or personality traits that might predict the development of an eating disorder, we find little. There is a tendency for adolescent girls with eating disorders to have rather strong needs for achievement and approval. Patients with eating disorders often show relatively high rates of depression, but such depression may be a response to an eating disorder rather than a cause (Garner et al., 1990). Some psychologists have examined parenting and family style as contributors. Anorexia nervosa patients *do* tend to come from very rigid, rule-governed, overprotecting families. And bulimic patients often experienced inordinate blame and rejection in childhood (Bruch, 1980; Yates, 1990). You know by now not to overinterpret findings like these; there are many exceptions.

Obviously, researchers have considered physiological processes as causes of eating disorders. One significant line of scientific detective work stems from the often-confirmed observation that bulimic patients do not "feel full" after they eat, even after they binge (Pyle et al., 1981; Walsh et al., 1989). This may be due to the fact that the hormone *cholecystokinin* (CCK) is found in very low levels in bulimic patients. This is significant because CCK is a hormone, normally produced in the small intestine, that signals that one is full and need eat no more. When drug treatment elevates CCK levels in bulimic patients, they often show fewer symptoms of the disorder.

The **prognosis**, or prediction of the course of a disorder, for anorexia nervosa is particularly poor. Nearly 50 percent of those who are released from treatment relapse within one year (Yates, 1990). About 5 percent of patients with anorexia actually die from excessive weight loss (Hsu, 1986). At first, treatment will be medical, in response to nourishment needs. Hospitalization may be required. Virtually all forms of psychotherapy (see Topic 13B) have been tried, but with little consistent success, and no one form of therapy is significantly more effective than any other. The best predictor of the success of psychotherapy is the extent to which the family gets involved. If all members of the family participate in therapeutic interventions, prognosis is much better than if the patient is left on her (or his) own.

The outlook for bulimia is usually much better. If nothing else, bulimic patients are seldom malnourished and for that reason do not require hospitalization. For persons with bulimia, the prognosis is better with family-oriented therapy than with individual therapy (e.g., Fairburn et al., 1993). With bulimic patients there has been some short-lived success with antidepressant medications (Geracioti & Liddle, 1988; Pope et al., 1985; Pope & Hudson, 1986), but when one looks at long-term success, the data are not as encouraging (Pyle et al., 1990; Walsh et al., 1991). A recently reported study (Fairburn et al., 1995) looked at the long-term condition (3 to 11 years after diagnosis) of 89 persons who had been diagnosed with bulimia.

prognosis *the prediction of the course of an illness or disorder*

Nearly one in five was still bulimic at the time of the follow-up, and about one-quarter had a different eating disorder. These researchers found that having a father who was overweight was a significant predictor of a negative outcome. They also found that prognosis was best for those patients who had been treated with a form of cognitive therapy (see Topic 13B).

Before You Go On

Describe anorexia nervosa and bulimia.

The Sex Drive and Human Sexual Behaviors

Sex can be an important motivator for humans and nonhumans alike. Sexual motivation varies considerably, not only among individuals, but also among species. We begin with a discussion of sex drives and then go on to consider a few aspects of human sexuality.

The Sex Drive

As a physiologically based drive, the sex drive is unique in many ways. First, the survival of the individual does not depend on satisfying the sex drive. If we do not drink, we die; if we do not regulate our body temperatures, we die; if we do not eat, we die. If we do not have sex—well, we don't die. The survival of a species requires an adequate number of its members to respond successfully to a sex drive, but an individual member can get along without doing so.

Second, most physiologically based drives, including thirst and hunger, provide mechanisms that ultimately replenish or maintain the body's energy. When it is satisfied, the sex drive depletes bodily energy. In fact, the sex drive motivates the organism to seek tension, as opposed to most drives, which seek to reduce tension in order to return to homeostasis.

A third point about the sex drive that makes it different from other drives is that it is not present—in the usual sense—at birth, but requires maturation (puberty) before it is apparent. The other drives are present, and most critical, early in life.

A fourth unique quality of the sex drive is the extent to which internal and external forces have differing degrees of impact on sexual behaviors, depending on the species involved. Internal, physiological states are much more important in "lower" species than they are in humans. For rats, for example, matters of sex are simple and straightforward. If adequate testosterone (the male sex hormone) is

In so-called lower animals, engaging in sexual behaviors is biologically driven. There is little evidence of any concern over the "quality" of one's "performance."

present, and if the opportunity presents itself, a male rat will respond to its hormone-induced sex drive and will engage in sexual behaviors. If adequate levels of estrogen (a female sex hormone) are present, and if the opportunity arises, the female rat will engage in sexual behaviors. For rats, learning or experience has little to do with sexual behaviors—they are tied closely to physiology, to hormone level. There is little difference between the mating behaviors of sexually experienced rats—those that have mated once or twice—and virgin rats. What we find, then, is that the sex drive in "lower" species is tied to a hormonal, physiological base.

No one would get far arguing that sex is not an important human motivator, but it is easy to lose sight of the fact that it is a *physiologically based* drive. Learning seems to be very important. Among other things, sex may not be as all-consuming as many believe. For example, one-third of Americans have sex twice a week or more, one-third have sex "a few times a month," and one-third only a few times in a year, if at all (Laumann et al., 1994). In societies such as ours, one could come to believe that sex drives are learned through experience alone. Hormones may provide humans with an arousing force to do something, but what to do, how to do it, and when to do it are shaped by society, religion, family, and personal experience. Sex manuals of a "how to" nature sell well, and sex therapy has become a standard practice for many psychologists trying to help people cope with pressures that external forces put on their "natural" sexual motivation.

Before You Go On

In what ways is the sex drive a unique physiologically based drive?

Sexual Dysfunctions

Sexual drives and behaviors, which seem so natural and virtually automatic in lower species, are often the source of considerable distress for humans. **Sexual dysfunction** is the name given to any chronic (long-term) problem, disturbance, or inadequacy of sexual functioning. It is difficult to determine the number of persons who experience sexual dysfunctions. Part of the problem is the commonly held belief that everyone else's sex life is perfect, and that other couples constantly engage in sexual activities. People don't like to talk about their sex life if they think they are having problems. Physicians and therapists who ask their patients about sexual problems report many more cases than do those who wait for patients to volunteer such information. Most experts agree that about 50 percent of all married couples have experienced some sexual dysfunction (Hyde, 1994; McCarthy et al., 1975). That's a lot of people, and when you add in people with sexual problems who happen not to be married, the number is even more impressive. Once someone openly admits to having sexual problems, treatment is usually successful (Zilbergeld & Evans, 1980). Masters and Johnson (1979) claim sex therapy failure for fewer than 20 percent of their patients. We'll review some of the most common sexual dysfunctions, three that occur in males and three that occur in females.

sexual dysfunction *any one of a number of chronic difficulties or problems with sexual functioning*

Sexual Dysfunctions in Males. *Erectile dysfunction* is the inability to attain or maintain an erection long enough to experience intercourse. It is the preferred term for what many still refer to as "impotence." Impotence literally means "without power," and power is not what sex or sexual dysfunctions are all about. Erectile dysfunction is the most commonly reported dysfunction among men seeking treatment. It can be found in men of any age. In most cases there has been success at achieving an erection in the past (APA, 1994). Psychological reactions to erectile dysfunction can be severe. Self-esteem is often involved. Embarrassment, depression, fear of future failures, and guilt often accompany erectile dysfunction. Unfortunately, when left untreated, these reactions almost ensure that achieving an erection will be less likely in the future.

There are many causes of erectile dysfunction. Failure to attain or maintain an erection may be associated with short-term physical problems such as fatigue, drinking too much alcohol, being in a strange situation, or stress, but an occasional episode or two does not constitute a dysfunction. There *are* physical causes of erectile dysfunction, including underlying disorders or diseases such as heart disease or diabetes, injury to the spinal cord, infection in the testes or prostate, and some prescribed medications (Richardson, 1991). On the other hand, at least half of the cases of erectile dysfunction seen by therapists have psychological causes, usually involving such factors as fear of failure, anxiety about the quality of one's "performance," guilt about having sex, or lack of adequate communication with one's partner (Gendel & Bonner, 1988).

Two dysfunctions of male sexual responsiveness involve the timing of ejaculation during vaginal intercourse (or coitus). *Premature ejaculation* is difficult to define. The implication is that the male ejaculates too soon, but what determines what is too soon? The most generally accepted definitions have to do with the male's voluntary control over ejaculation, rather than with time per se (Kaplan, 1974). Premature ejaculation is usually self-defined by the person (or his partner) as a condition in which ejaculation chronically occurs too early to provide satisfaction. A less common problem is *retarded ejaculation,* in which the male has difficulty ejaculating at all during coitus, although he may have little difficulty doing so while masturbating or when he is with a new sex partner. When this dysfunction occurs, we tend to find frustration on the part of the male, and a sense of rejection in his partner. As with all the sexual dysfunctions, retarded ejaculation occurs to varying degrees, with partial failure to ejaculate more common than total failure.

Occasionally sexual dysfunctions in men that involve the timing or adequacy of ejaculation have physical causes (e.g., infections or neurological problems), but almost all cases are caused by psychological factors (Hyde, 1994; Kaplan, 1974; Masters et al., 1992). The main issues, again, involve fear and anxiety over one's performance, and a lack of intimate communication with one's partner. Ejaculation control problems often lead to erectile dysfunctions. The male, concerned about his performance, starts to think about distracting, nonsexual issues, starts to evaluate his own performance and worry about when he might ejaculate, and all in the midst of sexual intercourse. In such a case, he has taken on what Masters and Johnson call a *spectator role,* and has become more concerned about his own performance than about the needs and desires of his partner (Masters & Johnson, 1979; Masters et al., 1992).

Sexual Dysfunctions in Females. *Female sexual unresponsiveness* is the term that psychiatrist Helen Kaplan used to describe what used to be known as "frigidity" (Kaplan, 1974, 1975). In severe forms of female sexual unresponsiveness, a fear or loathing of sexual activities may develop. This dysfunction is usually self-diagnosed, because what may be "acceptably responsive," or pleasurable, varies from person to person. What matters is the extent to which a woman and her partner feel satisfied with the woman's ability to be sexually aroused. The causes of female sexual unresponsiveness are almost always psychological, involving feelings of shame and guilt, accompanied by a belief that sex is somehow "dirty." The dysfunction can lead to related problems, such as a lack of self-esteem and depression.

Orgasmic dysfunction is the inability to experience an orgasm. In many cases there may have been an occasional orgasm, perhaps not as forceful or timely as desired. This sexual dysfunction is the one most often mentioned by women seeking therapy for sexual problems (Wincze & Carey, 1992). Part of the problem may be the mystique that has been associated with orgasm through coitus. Many women who experience orgasm through masturbation, for example, and seldom experience orgasm through intercourse, come to believe that they are sexually inadequate, or a disappointment to their partners. Sex partners may experience guilt if orgasm is not reached. Although most women (nearly 90 percent) can and do experience orgasm, fewer than half do so with only the stimulation from vaginal intercourse (Kaplan, 1974; Wilcox & Hager, 1980).

Orgasmic dysfunction in women may have a biological basis. Orgasmic problems may be related to illness, alcohol consumption, or extreme fatigue. Most cases, however, can be traced to many of the same psychological factors that disrupt sexual functioning in males: anxiety, fear of failure, becoming a "spectator," and—most commonly—poor communication with one's partner. Sex therapists have noted that women are even more reluctant than men to share with their partners the behaviors, touches, actions, and so on that would bring them pleasure, or orgasm, during sexual intercourse.

Vaginismus is the powerful, spasmodic, and occasionally painful contraction of the muscles surrounding the opening to the vagina. In some cases, the contractions are severe enough to prohibit the penis from entering the vagina. This is a relatively rare dysfunction, accounting for fewer than 10 percent of women treated for sexual problems (Masters et al., 1992). Hypotheses about why women develop vaginismus usually refer to a reflexlike reaction of the woman against pain—either the anticipated pain of coitus not yet achieved or pain experienced in the past.

There are other difficulties associated with sexual behaviors, to be sure. I've only covered those most commonly encountered by sex therapists. Many adults will suffer the distress caused by one or more of these dysfunctions during their sexually active years. Most sexual dysfunctions are amenable to treatment and therapy, and there are steps that can be taken to help prevent these dysfunctions in the first place: (1) Communicate, communicate, communicate. Try to make sure, using whatever means you can, that your partner understands those things that "turn you on," and those things you do not like, or find painful. What does your partner like and dislike? Communication also means saying "no" when that is how you feel. Trust in your partner and in yourself. (2) Do not believe everything you hear and read about the sexual exploits of others. Your aim should be to find pleasure with your sexual partner, not surpass some imagined "goal." (3) Avoid playing the role of "spectator." Do not spend time and energy assessing how well you're doing, worrying about exactly what you're supposed to do next. Don't evaluate; enjoy. (4) Choose the times and situations for engaging in sex with some care. Try to avoid those times when you are rushed, or when you are likely to be interrupted. (5) Be ready to seek and accept help if engaging in sexual behaviors becomes difficult, a chore, or a bore.

Before You Go On

Briefly describe some common sexual dysfunctions, and comment on their causes.

Homosexuality

The complexities of human sexuality are no more apparent than when we consider **homosexuals**—individuals sexually attracted to and sexually aroused by members of their own sex, as opposed to heterosexuals, who seek outlets for their sexual drives among members of the opposite sex. Psychologists argue that homosexuality should be referred to as an orientation, not as a sexual preference. Like handedness or language, sexual orientation is not chosen voluntarily (Committee on Lesbian and Gay Concerns, 1991; Money, 1987).

Homosexuality and heterosexuality are not mutually exclusive categories, but are endpoints of a dimension of sexual orientations. Alfred Kinsey and his colleagues (1948, 1953) first brought the prevalence of homosexuality to the attention of the general public. Kinsey devised a seven-point scale of sexual orientation, with those who are exclusively heterosexual at one end and persons who are exclusively homosexual at the other (see Figure 10.4). Kinsey found that about half the males

homosexuals *persons who are sexually attracted to and aroused by members of their own sex* who responded to his surveys fell somewhere between the two endpoints. Even though homosexuality is now more openly discussed than it was in the 1940s and 1950s, it is still difficult to get accurate estimates of the numbers of persons who are exclusively or predominantly homosexual. Estimates suggest that about 2 percent of North American males are exclusively homosexual, and that 8 to 10 percent have had more than an occasional homosexual encounter (e.g., Billy et al., 1993). A survey from researchers at the University of Chicago tells us that when asked if they are sexually attracted to persons of the same gender, 6.2 percent of the men and 4.4 percent of the women responded affirmatively. When asked about having an actual sexual encounter with someone of the same gender *within the past year,* 2.7 percent of the men and 1.3 percent of the women responded "yes." When this question was rephrased to read *since puberty,* comparable figures were 7.1 percent and 3.8 percent, respectively (Laumann et al., 1994).

There is little difference between persons with homosexual and heterosexual orientations in the pattern of their sexual responsiveness. Most homosexuals have experienced heterosexual sex. They simply find same-sex relationships more satisfying. In fact, homosexual couples are often more at ease and comfortable with their sexual relationship than most heterosexual couples (Masters & Johnson, 1979).

We have no generally accepted theory of the causes of homosexuality. What we do know is that the matter is not simple, and probably involves an interaction of genetic, hormonal, and environmental factors (Money, 1987). There is now ample evidence that homosexuality tends to "run in families" (Bailey & Pillard, 1991; Diamond & Karlen, 1980; Pool, 1993; Whitam et al., 1993). A team of researchers has claimed they have located a segment of the X chromosome that seems certain to be the site for genes that influence the development of homosexual orientation in males (Hamer et al., 1993). This is only the first step. These results have not yet been confirmed, and there is much to learn about which genes are found there and how such genes have their effects.

There are no differences in sex hormone levels of adult heterosexuals and adult homosexuals (Gladue, 1994). Providing gay males and lesbians with extra amounts of sex hormones may increase overall sex drive, but it has virtually no effect on sexual orientation. One hypothesis with research support suggests that prenatal hormonal imbalances may affect one's sexual orientation in adulthood (Money, 1987). This hypothesis claims that embryos (genetically male or female) exposed to above-average concentrations of female hormones will develop into adults attracted to persons having masculine characteristics (Ellis & Ames, 1987; Gladue et al., 1984).

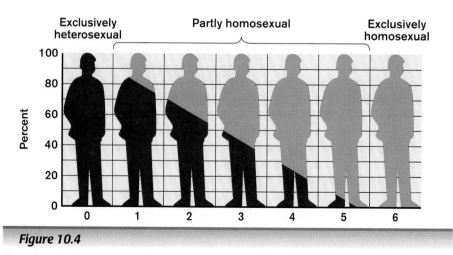

Figure 10.4

Kinsey's scale of sexual orientation.

Although homosexual men and women are now able to be more free and open about their sexual orientation, homosexuality is still a controversial issue.

In 1991, Simon LeVay of the Salk Institute in San Diego published an article on his research that became headline news (LeVay, 1991). LeVay performed a post-mortem examination of the brains of 19 gay males, 16 males with heterosexual orientation, and 6 women with heterosexual orientation. He found an area in the hypothalamus that was significantly smaller in the gay men. In gay men, this area was precisely the same size as that found in the hypothalamus of women. Note that LeVay has not claimed he located the cause of homosexual orientation. His observations lead us only to an association from which a cause-and-effect conclusion is unwarranted. But as one brain scientist, Dennis Landis of Case Western Reserve University, said of LeVay's work, "It would begin to suggest why male homosexuality is present in most human populations, despite cultural constraints. It suggests it's a biological phenomenon" (Barinaga, 1991).

As the biological evidence accumulates, psychologists remain unwilling to totally abandon hypotheses that emphasize environmental influences. One thing, however, is clear: sexual orientation cannot be attributed to any one early childhood experience. We cannot yet discount them, but environmental, experiential causes of sexual orientation are mostly of theoretical interest, with little research evidence to support them. "With a larger data base . . . we may be able to construct a biosocial model in which different events—genetic, hormonal, and environmental—occurring at critical times are weighted for their impact on the development of sexual orientation. Associated with this model would be the idea that not all men and women arrive at their sexual orientation following the same path" (Gladue, 1994, p. 154).

Before You Go On

What is homosexuality, and what causes it?

Psychologically Based Motives

From time to time, you may be able to analyze your behaviors in terms of physiologically based needs and drives. That you had breakfast this morning soon after you got up may have reflected your response to a hunger drive. That you got dressed may have been your attempt to do what you could to control your body temperature, which also may have influenced your choice of clothes. Some sexual motivation may also have affected what you chose to wear today.

On the other hand, many of our behaviors are aroused and directed (motivated) by forces that are not clearly biological in origin. In this section we'll review a few of the motivators that reflect learned or social influences on our behaviors. We'll consider three motives often used for "explaining" human behavior: achievement, power, and affiliation motivation.

Achievement Motivation

The hypothesis that people are motivated to varying degrees by a need to achieve was introduced to psychology in 1938 by Henry Murray. The **need to achieve (nAch)** is the acquired need to meet or exceed some standard of excellence in one's behaviors. Measuring nAch and determining its implications have been the major work of David McClelland and his associates (McClelland, 1985; McClelland et al., 1953; Smith, 1992).

Although there are short paper-and-pencil tests for the purpose, nAch is usually assessed by means of the **Thematic Apperception Test (TAT)**. This is a projective test (see Topic 9B) in which people are asked to tell short stories about a series of rather ambiguous pictures depicting people in various settings (see Figure 10.5). Stories are interpreted and scored according to a series of objective criteria that note references to attempting difficult tasks, succeeding, being rewarded for one's efforts, setting short- and long-term goals, and so on. There are no right or wrong responses. Judgments are made about the references to achievement a person "projects" into the pictures.

One of the first things McClelland and his colleagues found was that there *were* consistent differences in measured levels of nAch. A reliable finding about people with high needs for achievement is that when given a choice, they attempt tasks in which success is not guaranteed (otherwise, there is no challenge), but in which there still is a reasonable chance of success. Both young children (McClelland, 1958) and college students (Atkinson & Litwin, 1960) who were high in nAch were observed playing a ring-toss game, in which the object was to score points by tossing a small ring over a peg from a distance. The farther away from the peg one stood, the more points one could earn successfully. High nAch subjects in both studies stood at a moderate distance from the peg. They didn't stand so close as to guarantee success, but they didn't choose to stand so far away that they would almost certainly fail. People with low nAch scores tended to go to either extreme—very close, earning few points for their successes, or so far away they rarely succeeded.

People with high achievement needs are not always interested just in their own success, or in personal achievement at the expense of others. Particularly in collectivist societies, people may work very hard to achieve goals that are available only to the group of which they are a part (Brislin, 1993).

McClelland would argue that you are reading this text at this moment because you are motivated by a need to achieve. You want to do well on your next exam. You want to get a good grade in this course, and you have decided that to do so you need to study the assigned text material. Some students, however, may read assignments not because they are motivated by a need to achieve, but because they are motivated by a *fear of failure* (Atkinson & Feather, 1966). In such a case, the incentive is negative (avoid an F), rather than positive (earn an A). Individuals motivated by a fear of failure tend to take few risks. They either choose tasks they are bound to do well or tasks that are virtually impossible (if the task is impossible they don't have to blame themselves for failures).

It seems that the need to achieve is learned, usually in childhood. Children who show high levels of achievement motivation are those who have been encouraged in a positive way to excel ("Leslie, that grade of B is very good. You must feel

need to achieve (nAch) *the learned need to meet or exceed some standard of excellence in one's behaviors*

Thematic Apperception Test (TAT) *a projective personality test requiring a subject to tell a series of short stories about a set of ambiguous pictures*

Figure 10.5

The administration of the TAT. The subject is shown a series of ambiguous pictures and is asked such questions as "What is going on here? What led up to this situation? What is likely to happen now?"

proud!" versus "What! only a B?"). High-nAch children are generally encouraged to work things out for themselves, perhaps with parental support and encouragement ("Here, Leslie, see if you can do this" as opposed to "Here, dummy, let me do it; you'll never get it right!"). Also, McClelland is convinced that achievement motivation can be acquired by almost anyone, of any age, and he has developed training programs to increase achievement motivation levels (e.g., McClelland & Winter, 1969).

Before You Go On

What is achievement motivation, and how is it measured?

Power Motivation

Some people are motivated not only to excel, but to be in control, to be in charge of both the situation and others. In such cases, we speak of a **need for power** (McClelland, 1982; Winter & Stewart, 1978). Power needs are also measured by the interpretation of stories generated with the Thematic Apperception Test. Note that a high need for power is, in itself, neither good nor bad. What matters is the end to which one uses one's power.

People with high power needs like to be admired. They prefer situations in which they can control the fate of others, usually by manipulating access to information. They present an attitude of "If you want to get this job done, you'll have to come to me to find out how to do it." People with low power needs tend to avoid

need for power *the learned need to be in control of events or persons* situations in which others would have to depend on them, and tend to be some-what submissive in interpersonal relationships. Even though the situation is chang-ing slowly in Western cultures, men are more commonly to be found in positions of power than are women (Darley & Fazio, 1980; Falbo & Peplau, 1980; Mulac et al., 1985). At the same time, there are no reliable differences between men and women in measured *needs* for power (Winter, 1988).

Affiliation Motivation

need for affiliation *the need to be with others and to form relationships*

Another psychologically based motivator is the **need for affiliation**—a need to be with others, to work with others toward some end, and to form friendships and as-sociations.

One interesting implication of having a high need for affiliation is that it is of-ten at odds with a need for power. Logic suggests that if you are simultaneously motivated to be in control and to be with others in a truly supportive way, conflicts may arise. It is more difficult to exercise power over people whose friendship you value than it is to exercise power and control over people whose friendship is of lit-tle concern to you. It remains the case, however, that there are circumstances in which we find people who are high on both power and affiliation needs. These are often politicians who enjoy the exercise of power, but who also value being public figures and being surrounded by aides and advisors (e.g., Winter, 1987). Affiliation and achievement motives are also somewhat independent. Success can be earned either with others (high affiliation) or on one's own (low affiliation).

Although we might be quite confident that achievement and power motives are learned, and culturally determined, we are less confident about the sources of affiliation motivation. There is a reasonable argument that the need to affiliate and be with others is at least partly biologically based. We are social animals for whom social isolation is difficult, particularly when we are young (you might want to re-view our discussion of attachment in Topic 8A). On the other hand, some of the de-gree to which we value affiliation relationships can be attributed to our learning experiences.

Before You Go On

Define the needs for power and for affiliation.

@@@@ **Thinking Critically** @@@@

What motivated you to take this class in psychology? How do you feel about it now?

Many politicians would rate high on both a need for power and a need for affiliation. Other people are strongly influenced by a need for affiliation: to be with others, socializing, perhaps working together for common goals.

TOPIC 10A SUMMARY

Psychologists have generated several concepts to explain why organisms do what they do: (1) instinct (some complex patterns of behavior are triggered in response to particular stimuli without the benefit of learning or experience); (2) drive and need (an organism is aroused and directed by drives from within that are responses to biological (primary) needs or learned (secondary) needs, wherein a need is a real or perceived shortage of something); (3) incentives (an organism is not pushed by internal states, but pulled by valued goals or events in the environment); (4) homeostasis (an organism is motivated to maintain a state of balance or equilibrium among internal, physiological conditions); (5) arousal (equilibrium is sought for one's overall level of activation; varied levels of arousal are most fitting for tasks of differing difficulty); and (6) cognitive dissonance (one is motivated to maintain consonance or balance among cognitive states). Each of these approaches has added to our understanding of motivation.

We examined in some detail temperature regulation, thirst, hunger, and sex as examples of drives rooted in our physiology, yet still under the influence of learning and social pressures. Along the way we examined two eating disorders, anorexia nervosa and bulimia, and considered the nature and causes of sexual dysfunctions. We saw that there is an increasing body of evidence that sexual orientation may be rooted in one's physiology as well. Finally, we touched on three psychological motives for which no underlying biological basis has yet been found: the needs to achieve, to gain power, and to affiliate with others.

TOPIC 10B The Psychology of Emotion

Since its emergence in the late 1800s, psychology has included emotion as part of its subject matter. Psychologists have learned a great deal about emotional reactions, but answers to some critical questions have remained elusive. We wish that psychologists could tell us just what emotions are and where they come from. We want to know how to increase the pleasant emotions and decrease our experience of the unpleasant ones. Some emotional reactions seem quite unpleasant: fear, shame, jealousy, rage, and so on. Just the same, we would not want to give up our ability to experience emotions. To do so would be to surrender the likes of love, joy, satisfaction, and ecstasy. We'll begin this Topic as we have begun many others—trying to generate an acceptable working definition of "emotion." You ought to give that a try yourself before you go on. How would you define *emotion?*

Defining and Classifying Emotions

In this section, we'll consider two interrelated issues: defining emotion and classifying primary emotions. The goal for this section is simple: to describe human emotions as best we can.

Defining Emotion

Try to recall the last time you experienced an emotion of some significance—perhaps the fear of going to the dentist, the joy of receiving an A on a classroom exam, the sadness at the death of a friend, or the anger at being unable to register for a class you wanted to take. You may be able to identify four components to your emotional reaction. (1) You experience a *subjective feeling,* or *affect,* which you may label fear, joy, sadness, anger, or the like. (2) You have a *cognitive reaction;* you recognize, or "know," what happened. (3) You have an internal, *physiological reaction,* involving glands, hormones, and internal organs. (4) You engage in an overt *behavioral reaction.* You tremble as you approach the dentist's office. You run down the hallway, a broad smile on your face, waving your exam over your head. You cry at the news of your friend's death. You shake your fist and yell at the registrar when you find you can't enroll in the class of your choice.

Note that when we add an overt behavioral component to emotions, we can see how emotions and motivation are related. Emotions are motivators (Greenberg & Safran, 1989; Lang, 1985; Lazarus, 1991a, 1991b, 1993). To be motivated is to be aroused to action. Emotional experiences also arouse behaviors. Theorist Richard Lazarus put it this way: "Without some version of a motivational principle, emotion makes little sense, inasmuch as what is important or unimportant to us determines what we define as harmful or beneficial, hence emotional" (1991a, p. 352).

There has been considerable debate in psychology concerning how best to define emotion. As one researcher puts it, "Despite the obvious importance of emotion to human existence, scientists concerned with human nature have not been able to reach a consensus about what emotion is and what place emotion should have in a theory of mind and behavior" (LeDoux, 1995, p. 209). For now, however, we need a working definition, and we'll say that an **emotion** is an experience that includes a subjective feeling, a cognitive interpretation, a physiological reaction, and a behavioral expression. With this definition in mind, we turn to the related issue of how to classify emotions.

emotion *an experience that includes a subjective feeling, a cognitive interpretation, a physical reaction, and a behavioral expression*

Before You Go On

What are the four components of an emotional reaction?

Classifying Emotions

Although cognitions, physiology, and overt behavior are involved in an emotion, there is little doubt that a very important aspect is the "subjective feeling" component. Perhaps it would help if we had a scheme or plan that described and classified various emotional reactions or feelings in a systematic way.

Emotions give flavor and coloring to our lives. If nothing else, emotions can be classified as pleasant or unpleasant. Here we see joy and sadness.

In fact, there are several ways to classify emotional responses. Wilhelm Wundt, in that first psychology laboratory in Leipzig, was concerned with emotional reactions. He believed that emotions could be described in terms of three intersecting dimensions: pleasantness-unpleasantness, relaxation-tension, and calm-excitement. Let's look at a few more recent attempts to classify emotions.

Carroll Izard (1972, 1977, 1993) has proposed a classification scheme calling for nine primary emotions. From these, he claims, all others can be constructed. Izard's nine primary emotions are fear, anger, shame, contempt, disgust, distress, interest, surprise, and joy. Izard calls these nine emotions primary because he believes that they cannot be dissected into simpler, more basic emotions and because each is thought to have its own underlying physiological basis. Other emotions are some combination of any two or more of these nine.

Robert Plutchik (1980a,1980b) argues for eight basic emotions. What makes these emotions primary, Plutchik claims, is that each is directly tied to some adaptive pattern of behavior; they are emotions related to survival. Plutchik's eight primary emotions, and their adaptive significance, are listed in Figure 10.6. Plutchik believes that emotions in addition to these eight are variants of the primary emotions. While rage, for example, may be an extreme emotion, it is viewed as being essentially the same as anger. Anger in a weaker form is annoyance (Plutchik, 1980b).

Richard Lazarus (1991a, 1991b, 1993) proposes a theory of emotion that stresses the motivational role of emotionality. He claims that emotion is the result of specific relationships or interactions between people and their environments. Some relations are perceived as (potentially) harmful to one's well-being and yield negative emotions, such as anger, anxiety, fear, shame, or guilt. These are emotions we are motivated to avoid. Some relations are (potentially) beneficial, give rise to positive emotions, such as joy, pride, gratitude, and love, and are emotions we are motivated to seek, or approach. Lazarus's list of basic emotions and their relational themes is presented in Figure 10.7.

I'm sure you won't be surprised to learn that none of the approaches to classifying emotions I have listed so far has proven completely satisfactory. Psychologists continue to propose theories to account for the nature of an emotional reaction (e.g., Berkowitz, 1990; Buck, 1985; Ekman, 1993; Frijda, 1988; Greenberg & Safron, 1989; Mathews & MacLeod, 1994; Oatley & Jenkins, 1992; Ortony et al., 1988; Ortony & Turner, 1990).

Whether there are eight or nine primary emotions (or more or fewer) and how they might be combined to form other emotions depends on one's theoretical perspective. A review by Ortony and Turner (1990) lists more than a dozen theoretical

---

Figure 10.6
Plutchik's Eight Primary Emotions and How They Relate to Adaptive Behaviors

Emotion or feeling	Common stimulus	Typical behavior
1. Anger	Blocking of goal-directed behavior	Destruction of obstacle
2. Fear	A threat or danger	Protection
3. Sadness	Loss of something valued	Search for help and comfort
4. Disgust	Something gruesome or loathsome	Rejection; pushing away
5. Surprise	A sudden, novel stimulus	Orientation; turning toward
6. Curiosity	A new place or environment	Explore and search
7. Acceptance	A member of own group; something of value	Sharing; taking in; incorporating
8. Joy	Potential mate	Reproduction; courting; mating

Figure 10.7
Basic Emotions and Their Relational Themes

Emotion	Relational theme
Anger	A demeaning offense against me and mine
Anxiety	Facing an uncertain, existential threat
Fright	An immediate, concrete, and overwhelming physical danger
Guilt	Having transgressed a moral imperative
Shame	Failing to live up to an ego ideal
Sadness	Having experienced an irrevocable loss
Envy	Wanting what someone else has
Jealousy	Resenting a third party for the loss of, or a threat to, another's affection or favor
Disgust	Taking in or being too close to an indigestible (metaphorically speaking) object or idea
Happiness	Making reasonable progress toward the realization of a goal
Pride	Enhancement of one's ego-identity by taking credit for a valued object or achievement, either one's own or that of some group with which one identifies
Relief	A distressing goal-incongruent condition that has changed for the better or gone away
Hope	Fearing the worst but wanting better
Love	Desiring or participating in affection, usually but not necessarily reciprocated
Compassion	Being moved by another's suffering and wanting to help

From Lazarus, 1993. Reproduced, with permission, from the *Annual Review of Psychology,* Volume 44, © 1993 by Annual Reviews, Inc.

versions of basic, or primary, emotions. A similar review by Plutchik (1994) lists sixteen, and *none is in complete agreement with any other.* The only issue on which there appears to be a consensus is that emotions are *valenced states,* meaning that emotions can be classified as being either positive (relief, happiness, and the like) or negative (fear, anger, shame, and the like). Unfortunately, there isn't even complete agreement on how to distinguish between positive and negative emotions. Fear, for example, seems like a reasonable candidate for a list of negative emotions. Yet it is clear that fear can be useful and can serve to guide one's behavior in positive or adaptive ways.

So, where does this leave us? As sensible as it may sound to try to construct a system of basic, primary emotions—particularly if such a system had a physiological or evolutionary foundation—such an attempt will prove difficult at best. One problem is that there is less than total agreement on just what *basic* or *primary* means when we are talking about emotions. "Thus, the question 'Which are the basic emotions?' is not only one that probably cannot be answered, it is a misdirected question, as though we asked, 'Which are the basic people?' and hoped to get a reply that would explain human diversity" (Ortony & Turner, 1990, p. 329).

If there is one conclusion regarding emotion with which all theorists agree, it is that part of being emotional is a physiological, visceral response. To put it plainly, being emotional is a gut-level reaction. To be emotional involves more than our thinking, reasoning cerebral cortex. We turn next to discuss the physiological aspects of emotion.

Before You Go On

Can emotions be classified?

⊚⊚⊚ **Thinking Critically** ⊚⊚⊚

If you were to make up a list of the basic, primary emotions, which would be on your list?

Physiological Aspects of Emotion

Let's return once again to our opening story about meeting a bear while walking in the woods. One question I asked then was, "What will you do now?" We agreed that, if nothing else, your reaction would be an emotional one. You will experience

EXPERIENCING PSYCHOLOGY

Joy To The World

This is a little exercise that demonstrates just how complex emotions can be—particularly for those who would like to organize or categorize "basic" human emotions.

Joy or *happiness* is commonly considered to be a basic emotion. There are a great many words in our language that are somehow related to the idea of joy or happiness. Here is a list of some of them:

bliss	amusement	cheerfulness	gaiety
glee	jolliness	joviality	delight
gladness	enthrallment	enjoyment	happiness
jubilation	elation	satisfaction	ecstasy
euphoria	enthusiasm	zest	excitement
thrill	pleasure	contentment	triumph
pride	exhilaration	eagerness	optimism
hope	joy	rapture	
mirth	levity	relief	

Write each of these (and any others you can think of) on a sheet of paper. Read each of the following statements to others and ask them to indicate which of the above words best describes the situation being described. For which item(s) was there the most and the least agreement? Did you notice any sex differences in terms of which terms were chosen?

1. Colleen didn't think that she would be accepted at the college she most wanted to attend, but she has just received notification that she has been accepted.
2. Tom's uncle told Tom that he was sending Tom a check. Tom was expecting a check for about $100. He has just opened the envelope from his uncle and found a check for $3000.
3. One of Juanita's professors has just read her paper to the class as an example of a thoughtful and well-written paper.
4. An instructor who usually dresses very conservatively has just walked into class wearing an oversized T-shirt with a picture of Mickey Mouse on the front.
5. A male student that Mary admires very much has just asked her if she will meet with him and help him with his math assignment.
6. Sam's mother had a brain tumor surgically removed two days ago. Sam has just received word from his father that the tumor was not malignant.
7. Jan's best friend has just told her that she and Jack, whom Jan admires and likes a lot, are planning to get married at the end of the term.
8. Julio worked hard campaigning for Alice Hawkins for student body president. He has just learned that she was elected with 71 percent of the votes.
9. It is Father's Day. The picnic is over, and Ralph is thinking about what great kids he and Evelyn have and how beautiful the six grandchildren are.
10. Gail went to visit her friend Margaret. When she arrived, 17 of her friends were there to give her a surprise birthday party.
11. The party Judy worked so hard to plan and give was a great success. The guests have all gone home, and Judy is exhausted. She is thinking about the party as she settles herself in bed.
12. Joe's favorite team just won the Super Bowl.

affect (call it fear, if not panic). You will have a *cognitive reaction* (realizing you've just encountered a bear and that you'd rather you hadn't). You will engage in some *overt behavior* (either freezing in your tracks or racing back to the campfire). A significant part of your reaction in this situation (or one like it) will be internal, *physiological,* and "gut-level." Responding to a bear in the wild is not something people would do in a purely intellectual sort of way. When we are emotional, we respond with our insides, our viscera.

Our biological reaction to emotional situations takes place at several levels. Of primary interest is the autonomic nervous system, or ANS (see Topic 2A). The brain has a role to play in emotion, but first we'll consider the autonomic response.

The Role of the Autonomic Nervous System

As you recall, the *autonomic nervous system (ANS)* consists of two parts that serve the same organs but have nearly the opposite effect on those organs. The *parasym-*

pathetic division is actively involved in maintaining a relaxed, calm, and unemotional state. As you strolled down the path into the woods, the parasympathetic division of your ANS actively directed your digestive processes to do the best they could with the meal you'd just eaten. Blood was diverted from the extremities to the stomach and intestines. Saliva flowed freely. With your stomach full, and with blood diverted to it, you felt somewhat sleepy as your brain responded to the lower levels of blood supply. Your breathing was slow, deep, and steady, as was your heart rate. Again, all of these activities were under the control of the parasympathetic division of your autonomic nervous system.

Suddenly, there's that bear! Now the *sympathetic division* of your ANS takes over. Automatically, many physiological changes take place—changes that are usually quite adaptive.

1. The pupils of your eyes dilate, letting in as much of what light is available, increasing your visual sensitivity.

2. Your heart rate and blood pressure are elevated (energy needs to be mobilized as fast as possible).

3. Blood is diverted away from the digestive tract toward the limbs and brain, and digestion stops; you've got a bear to deal with; dinner can wait until later. Let's get the blood supply out there to the arms and legs where it can do some good (with what is called the fight-or-flight response).

4. Respiration increases, becoming deeper and more rapid; you'll need all the oxygen you can get.

5. Moisture is brought to the surface of the skin in the form of perspiration; as it evaporates, the body is cooled, thus conserving energy.

6. Blood sugar levels increase, making more energy readily available.

7. Blood will clot more readily than usual—for obvious but, it is hoped, unnecessary reasons.

The sympathetic system makes some of these changes directly (e.g., stopping salivation and stimulating the cardiac muscle). Others are made indirectly through the release of hormones into the bloodstream, mostly epinephrine and norepinephrine from the adrenal glands. Because part of the physiological aspect of emotion is hormonal, it takes a few seconds for the effect to be experienced. If you were, in fact, confronted by a bear in the woods, you would probably not have the presence of mind to notice, but the reactions of sweaty palms, gasping breaths, and "butterflies in your stomach" take a few seconds to develop.

Is the autonomic and endocrine system reaction the same for every emotion that we experience? That's a very difficult question. There may be slight differences. There appears to be a small difference in the hormones produced during rage and fear reactions. There may be differences in the biological bases of emotions that prepare us for defense or for retreat—fight or flight (Blanchard & Blanchard, 1988). Consistent differences in physiological reactions for the various emotional states are, at best, very slight indeed. This issue has been controversial in psychology for many years and is likely to remain so (Blanchard & Blanchard, 1988; Plutchik, 1994; Selye, 1976).

The Role of the Brain

When we become emotional, our sympathetic nervous system does not just spring into action on its own. Autonomic nervous system activity is related to, and coordinated by, central nervous system activity.

The two brain structures most intimately involved in emotionality are the *limbic system* and the *hypothalamus,* that small structure in the middle of the brain centrally involved with physiological drives. The limbic system is a "lower" center in the brain consisting of a number of small structures (the amygdala may be the most important for emotionality). These centers are "lower" in the sense of being well below the cerebral cortex, and in the sense of being present (and important) in the brains of "lower" animals, such as rats and cats.

The limbic system (you may want to refer to Figure 2.9, page 55) is most involved in emotional responses that call for defensive or attacking responses–those emotions stimulated by threat. Electrical stimulation or destruction of portions of the limbic system reliably produces a variety of changes in emotional reaction.

It is to be expected that the hypothalamus would play a role in emotionality. It is involved in many motivational states. Hypothalamic stimulation can produce strong emotional reactions, including those that lead to attacking and killing any nearby prey (Flynn et al., 1970). Precisely how the limbic system and hypothalamus are coordinated in the normal experience and expression of emotion is not yet fully understood.

The role of the *cerebral cortex* in emotionality is also poorly understood. It seems to be largely inhibitory. That is, the limbic system and hypothalamus seem to act as the sources for extreme and rather poorly directed emotional reactions. The cortex *interprets* impulses from these lower centers and other information available to it and then modifies and directs the emotional reaction accordingly.

The clearest involvement of the cerebral cortex in emotionality is in the cognitive aspect of an emotion. It is the cerebral cortex that is involved in the interpretation and memory of emotional events. When you get back to camp, having just been frightened by a bear, you will use your cortex to tell the emotional details of your story. Emotional reactions tend to be processed in the right hemisphere of the brain: the left hemisphere is usually rather unemotional (Borod, 1992; LeDoux, 1995; Sperry, 1982; Tucker, 1981).

To review, along with the autonomic nervous system, the limbic system and the hypothalamus are centers of emotion. These centers are coordinated by higher centers in the cerebral cortex, which, among other things, provides the cognitive interpretation of emotional responses.

Before You Go On

What physiological changes occur when one becomes emotional?

Outward Expressions of Emotion

An aspect of emotion that has long intrigued psychologists is how inner emotional states are communicated to others. Charles Darwin was one of the first to popularize the idea that facial expressions provide indicators of an organism's emotional state. More than a hundred years later, psychologists are discovering new evidence that suggests that Darwin was correct.

It is very useful for one organism to let another know how it is feeling. As one wild animal approaches a second, the second better have a good idea about the emotional state of the first. Is it angry? Does it come in peace? Is it just curious, or is it looking for dinner? Is it sad, looking for comfort, or is it sexually aroused, looking for a mate? An inability to make such determinations can quickly be disastrous. Animals need to know the emotional state of other animals if they are to survive for long.

Nonhuman animals have many instinctive and ritualistic patterns of behavior to communicate aggressiveness, interest in courtship, submission, and other emotional states. Humans also express their emotional states in a variety of ways, in-

⊚⊛⊚⊛ **Thinking Critically** ⊚⊛⊚⊛

In this chapter I used the rather dramatic example of meeting a bear in the woods to discuss approaches to motivation and physiological reactions to emotion-producing stimuli. Can you recast this discussion with a more reasonable example, such as a big exam coming up tomorrow?

Because they cannot verbalize how they feel, it is particularly important for animals to be able to convey their emotions through posture and facial expressions.

cluding verbal report. Surely if I am happy, sad, angry, or jealous, I can try to tell you how I feel. In fact, the ability to communicate with language often puts humans at an advantage. Research now tells us that emotional states are reflected in *how* we speak, even if our message is not related to emotion at all (Bachorowski & Owren, 1995; Scherer, 1986). Even without verbal language, there is a school of thought that suggests that the human animal, like the nonhuman, uses a *body language* to communicate its emotional condition (e.g., Birdwhistell, 1952; Fast, 1970). Someone sitting quietly, slumped slightly forward with head down, may be viewed as feeling sad, even from a distance. We similarly interpret postural cues and gestures as being associated with fear, anger, happiness, and so on. Such expressions often result from learning and may be modified by cultural influences.

Darwin recognized facial expression as a common cue to emotion in animals, especially mammals. Might facial expression provide the key to underlying emotions in humans, too? Are there facial expressions of emotional states that are universal among the human species, just as there appear to be among nonhumans? A growing body of evidence supports the hypothesis that facial expressions of emotional states are innate responses, only slightly sensitive to cultural influence (Kelmann & Zajonc, 1989; Andrews, 1963; Buck, 1980; Gellhorn, 1964; Oatley & Jenkins, 1992; Tomkins, 1962).

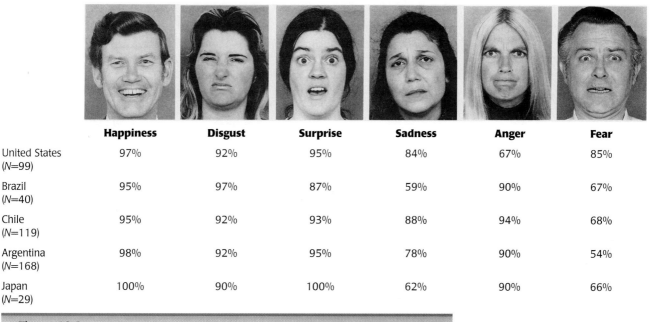

	Happiness	Disgust	Surprise	Sadness	Anger	Fear
United States (*N*=99)	97%	92%	95%	84%	67%	85%
Brazil (*N*=40)	95%	97%	87%	59%	90%	67%
Chile (*N*=119)	95%	92%	93%	88%	94%	68%
Argentina (*N*=168)	98%	92%	95%	78%	90%	54%
Japan (*N*=29)	100%	90%	100%	62%	90%	66%

Figure 10.8

Photos displaying facial expressions like these were shown to subjects from the United States, Brazil, Chile, Argentina, and Japan. (The subjects were asked to identify the emotions being displayed. The percentage of subjects who identified the photos with emotion labels is indicated.)

Paul Ekman and his colleagues have conducted several studies trying to find a reliable relationship between emotional state and facial expression across cultures (Ekman, 1972, 1992, 1993; Ekman et al., 1987). In one large study (Ekman et al., 1973) college students were shown six pictures of people's faces. In each picture, a different emotion was displayed: happiness, disgust, surprise, sadness, anger, or fear. When students from the United States, Argentina, Japan, Brazil, and Chile were asked to identify the emotion experienced by the people in the photographs, their agreement was remarkable (see Figure 10.8). One problem with this study is that all of the subjects did have many shared experiences, even though they were from basically different cultures. They were, after all, college students and had many experiences in common (perhaps they had seen the same movies, watched the same TV shows, and so on). Even though Ekman's subjects came from different countries, their agreement could be explained in terms of the similarities of their experiences rather than some innate tendency to express emotions through facial expression.

An argument against this line of reasoning is found in another project by Ekman (Ekman, 1972; Ekman & Friesen, 1971). Here, natives of a remote New Guinea tribe were asked to make faces showing various emotional reactions (e.g., "A friend has come and you are happy"). No one in any other culture would have much difficulty identifying the emotion the subjects were trying to display (see Figure 10.9). These New Guinea tribesmen had little contact with persons outside New Guinea, and virtually no contact with magazines, television, or movies that could have introduced them to the facial expressions of people from other cultures. Distinctive, universal facial expressions have been identified for anger, fear, disgust, sadness, and happiness (Ekman, 1993).

Another study of facial expression (Ekman et al., 1983) has shown that simply moving one's facial muscles into the positions associated with emotional expression can cause distinctive physiological changes associated with an emotional state (see also, Adelmann & Zajonc, 1989; Laird, 1984; Matsumoto, 1987; Schiff & Lamon, 1989). As bizarre as it sounds, the idea is that if you raise your eyebrows, open your

Figure 10.9

Paul Ekman and his colleagues went to New Guinea to study the relationships between facial expressions and emotions. The man on the left was told to look happy because a friend was coming. The man in the second picture was told to respond to the news that his child had died. The man in the third picture was told that he should act angry and about to fight. The man in the fourth photo was told to respond to the sight of a dead pig that had been lying in one place for a long time. People from any country or culture would have little difficulty identifying the emotional state displayed in these facial expressions.

eyes widely, and raise the corners of your mouth, you will produce an internal physiological change not unlike that which occurs when you are happy, and you will smile as a result!

Before You Go On

What is the relationship, if any, between facial expression and emotion?

TOPIC 10B SUMMARY

In this Topic, we summarized some of what we know about emotions. When we discuss emotion, our focus is on the subjective experience or feeling of affect—the *A* of our *ABC* model first introduced in Chapter 1. We began by struggling with a definition of emotion. We saw that it consists of four aspects: a subjective feeling, a cognitive interpretation, a visceral or physiological response, and some outward expression in overt behavior. We saw that there is little consensus on which emotional states are the most basic, or primary. This reflects, among other things, one's vision of the role emotions play in our lives. We then moved on to a couple of issues for which there is more certainty: the nature of the physiological changes that occur with emotional states, and how facial expressions are related to experienced emotion.

"I don't sing because I am happy. I am happy because I sing."

Drawing by Frascino © 1991. The New Yorker Magazine, Inc.

CHAPTER SUMMARY

Topic 10A

How have the concepts of instincts, needs, drives, and incentives been used to explain motivated behaviors?

Instincts are complex patterns of unlearned behavior that occur in the presence of certain stimuli. Instinct approaches to explaining why humans do what they do have not proven to be satisfactory. Needs are shortages of some biological necessity. Deprivation leads to a need, which gives rise to a drive, which arouses and directs an organism's behavior. Many drives are more learned than biologically based. Maslow said that needs can be placed in a hierarchy, from survival needs to a need to self-actualize. Focusing on incentives explains behaviors in terms of goals and outcomes rather than internal driving forces. These approaches are not mutually exclusive. */pp. 358–362*

How has the concept of balance, or equilibrium, been used to explain motivated behaviors?

The basic idea is that organisms are motivated to reach and maintain a state of balance—a set point level of activity. Homeostasis is a drive to maintain a state of equilibrium among internal physiological conditions such as blood pressure, metabolism, and heart rate. Others argue for a general drive to maintain a balanced state of arousal, with an optimal level of arousal being best suited for any given task or situation. Festinger claims that we are motivated to maintain consonance, or balance, among cognitive states, thereby reducing cognitive dissonance. */pp. 362–365*

How is temperature regulation a physiological drive?

Temperature regulation can be viewed as a physiological drive because we have a need (are driven) to maintain our body temperatures within certain strict (homeostatic) levels. Doing so involves voluntary as well as involuntary, autonomic, responding. */p. 366–367*

What are some of the internal and external factors that influence drinking behavior?

We are motivated to drink for several reasons, including a need to relieve dryness in our mouths and throats and to maintain a homeostatic level of fluid within our bodies (which is monitored by the hypothalamus). We also engage in drinking behavior in response to external cues (incentives), such as taste, aroma, or appearance, and by our previous learning experiences. */pp. 367–368*

What are some of the internal and external cues that motivate eating behaviors?

Several factors affect eating behaviors. Internal factors include cues mediated by the hypothalamus, which may be responding to stored fat levels, blood sugar levels, or other indicators that our normal homeostatic balance has been disrupted. Associated with this view is the position that body weight is maintained at a set point by both food intake and exercise levels. Awareness of being full may be stimulated by a hormone (*ob protein*) produced under the control of an *obese gene*. There is evidence that body size may be significantly determined by genetic factors. The stimulus properties of foods may motivate eating, as may habit patterns and social pressures. */pp. 369–371*

Describe anorexia nervosa and bulimia.

Anorexia nervosa and bulimia are eating disorders most commonly found in females. The anorexic patient is essentially engaged in self-starvation, significantly reducing body weight. Bulimia involves recurrent episodes of binging and purging of large amounts of sweet, high-calorie foods. We do not know what causes eating disorders, but cultural, family, and hormonal influences have been implicated. All sorts of psychotherapy have been tried as treatments for eating disorders. The prognosis for anorexia is poor. Family-oriented therapy and cognitive therapies seem most effective for bulimia. Antidepressant medication is occasionally effective in the treatment of bulimia, at least for the short term, particularly when paired with psychotherapy. */pp. 372–374*

In what ways is the sex drive a unique physiologically based drive?

The sex drive is an unusual physiological drive because: (1) individual survival does not depend on its satisfaction; (2) the drive involves seeking tension rather than relief from tension; (3) it is not fully present at birth, but matures-later; and (4) the extent to which it is influenced by learned or external influences varies among species. */pp. 374–375*

Briefly describe some common sexual dysfunctions, and comment on their causes.

Sexual dysfunctions are chronic problems in sexual functioning. The most commonly reported by males is *erectile dysfunction,* an inability to attain or maintain an erection long enough to experience intercourse. *Premature ejacu-*

lation and *delayed ejaculation* are self-diagnosed, and have to do with the timing of ejaculation during intercourse, the former being more common than the latter. *Female sexual unresponsiveness* is said to occur when a woman gains little or no satisfaction or pleasure from sexual activities. *Orgasmic dysfunction* is the inability to experience an orgasm to one's satisfaction. It is the dysfunction most commonly reported by women. *Vaginismus* refers to the powerful, spasmodic contraction of the muscles surrounding the opening to the vagina. These sexual dysfunctions, in men and women, may, in turn, create additional problems, such as loss of self-esteem, guilt, anxiety, or depression. There may be a physiological cause (illness, fatigue, alcohol use, medication, injury) for sexual dysfunctions, but most often they are caused by psychological factors. */pp. 375–377*

What is homosexuality, and what causes it?

Homosexuals are persons who are attracted to and sexually aroused by members of their own sex. There is a continuum that extends from exclusively homosexual on the one extreme to exclusively heterosexual on the other. Kinsey found that about half his sample of males fell somewhere between these two endpoints. Recent surveys indicate that about 2 percent of North American males are exclusively homosexual. We do not know what "causes" homosexual orientation, but strongly suspect a genetic basis, the influence of prenatal hormone levels, and the involvement of the hypothalamus. */pp. 377–379*

What is achievement motivation, and how is it measured?

Achievement motivation, based on the need to achieve (nAch), is a need to attempt and succeed at tasks so as to meet or exceed a standard of excellence. Achievement needs are usually assessed through the interpretation of short stories generated in response to the Thematic Apperception Test, or TAT, in which one looks for themes of striving and achievement. */pp. 380–381*

Define the needs for power and for affiliation.

The need for power is the need to be in charge, to be in control of a situation. Affiliation needs involve being motivated to be with others, to form friendships and interpersonal relationships. */pp. 381–382*

Topic 10B

What are the four components of an emotional reaction?

There are four possible components of an emotional reaction: (1) the experience of a subjective feeling, or affective component; (2) a cognitive appraisal or interpretation; (3) an internal, visceral, physiological reaction; and (4) an overt behavioral response. */pp. 383–384*

Can emotions be classified?

There have been several attempts to categorize emotional reactions, dating back to Wundt in the late 1800s. Izard has a theory that calls for nine primary emotions. Plutchik argues that there are eight basic emotions and many combinations and degrees of them. Other theorists have proposed as few as two or as many as dozens of primary emotions. The inconsistency among theories leads some psychologists to wonder if the attempt to classify basic emotions is misguided. */pp. 384–386*

What physiological changes occur when one becomes emotional?

Among the changes that take place when we become emotional are those produced by the sympathetic division of the autonomic nervous system. Occurring to varying degrees and depending on the situation, these reactions include dilation of the pupils, increased heart rate and blood pressure, cessation of digestive processes, deeper and more rapid breathing, increased perspiration, and elevated blood sugar levels. The cerebral cortex is involved in the cognitive interpretation of emotional events and acts as an inhibitory mechanism, exerting some control over the activity of lower brain centers for emotionality (largely the limbic system and the hypothalamus). The brain coordinates physiological aspects of emotionality. */pp. 386–388*

What is the relationship, if any, between facial expression and emotion?

Facial expressions indicate the internal, emotional state of an individual. What leads us to believe that facial expression of emotion is unlearned (innate) is that there is universal reliability in the interpretation of facial expressions, even across widely different cultures. Additionally, the relationship appears to be two-way; data indicate that one can actually change one's subjective emotional state by changing one's facial expression. */pp. 389–391*

Why, Oh Why?

In this chapter we discussed several theories, or approaches to motivation, several ways of trying to explain *why* organisms do what they do. Here is a summary list of some of the terms used in those approaches:

1. Instinct
2. Primary drive
3. Secondary drive
4. Incentive
5. Homeostasis
6. Arousal
7. Cognitive dissonance

For each of the following statements, identify the motivational concept to which the speaker is alluding. (Suggested answers can be found on p. 574.)

_____ 1. "Fish gotta swim, birds gotta fly . . . "

_____ 2. "After four days cooped up inside the house because of the blizzard, I was having cabin fever—I just had to get out and do something."

_____ 3. "No, I really didn't want the popcorn, but when I walked in it just smelled so good."

_____ 4. "You'll get your promotion if you keep your nose to the grindstone and your back to the wheel."

_____ 5. "I just thought I'd get frostbite if I didn't start a fire."

_____ 6. "I didn't think I'd like this show, but after I watched it at Jodie's house last month, I haven't missed an episode."

_____ 7. "You go skiing, I'm just gonna sit here."

_____ 8. "Hey, look. The first robin of spring!"

_____ 9. "If we had a better textbook, I'd have gotten an 'A' on that exam."

_____ 10. "More than anything else, I just want to get to graduation!"

OUTLINE

*I*t's Friday, and you have a chance to get away for the weekend. Unfortunately, you have two big exams scheduled for Monday and need the weekend to study.

—Lindsay is just about through typing a term paper on her word processor when suddenly the power goes out. Having failed to save her work as she went along, she will have to redo it all.

—Cindy and Jerry have known each other since grade school. They dated throughout high school and college. Next week, family and friends will join in the celebration of their marriage.

—Doug wants to make the basketball team, but the coach informs him that despite his best efforts, Doug is just too short to make the team.

—Marian is excited to be in Germany in a student-exchange program, but she's also very nervous about getting along in a new country.

—After 11 years on the road as a salesman, Wayne is being promoted to district sales manager—an office job with a substantial raise in pay.

—Jake had cut back his smoking to one pack a day, and was thinking about starting an exercise program. Now he

11

Psychology, Stress, and Physical Health

finds himself in a coronary intensive care unit, having just suffered a heart attack.

—Three-year-old Trudy keeps asking her mother for a cookie. Mother steadfastly refuses because it's almost dinner time. Trudy returns to her room and promptly pulls an arm off her favorite doll.

—You are late for class, driving down a two-lane road, when someone pulls out in front of you and drives along 10 miles an hour below the speed limit.

—Felicia has just learned that, like 100,000 other women in the United States, she is unable to have children because she contracted chlamydia when she was a teenager and was "sleeping around."

Life is filled with stress, frustration, and conflict. This list provides only a very small sample of the types of stressful events people encounter every day. We'll return to each of these examples throughout this chapter, where our focus is the role of psychological factors as they affect one's physical health and well-being. Here we encounter a familiar theme: biological and psychological processes interact; body and mind are interrelated.

TOPIC 11A Stress, Stressors, and How to Cope

Our study of stress is divided into two main sections. First we'll see, at least in general terms, where stress comes from. What are the common stressors in our lives? Second we'll examine the complex patterns of responses we make when we experience stress. We begin by trying to understand the causes of stress.

Stressors: The Causes of Stress

stress *a complex set of reactions to real or perceived threats to one's well-being that motivates adaptation*

Although each of us is familiar with stress and how it feels, psychologists have struggled with how to characterize stress for nearly sixty years (Hobfoll, 1989). We will define **stress** as a complex set of reactions made by an individual under pressure to adapt. In other words, stress is a response one makes to real or perceived threats to one's sense of well-being. Stress is something that happens inside people. There are physiological reactions and unpleasant feelings (e.g., distress and anxiety) associated with stress.

stressors *the sources or stimuli for stress, which include frustration, conflict, and life events*

There are many circumstances or events that can produce stress. *The sources of stress are called* **stressors**. We'll consider three types of stressors: frustration, conflict, and life events. As we go along, I'll provide examples as a reminder that stress is not necessarily a reaction to some overwhelming, catastrophic event, such as the death of a loved one or a natural disaster. Once we see where stress comes from, we'll consider techniques people use to cope with it.

Frustration-Induced Stress

As we saw in Topic 10A, we can characterize motivated behaviors as *goal-directed*. Whether by internal processes (drives) or external stimuli (incentives) we are pushed or pulled toward positive goals and away from negative goals. Now let me introduce an assumption: Organisms don't always reach all of their goals. Have you always gotten everything you've ever wanted? Have you always been able to avoid unpleasantness, pain, or sorrow? Do you know anyone who has?

frustration *a stressor; the blocking or thwarting of goal-directed behavior*

Sometimes we are totally prohibited from ever reaching a particular goal. At other times our progress may be slower or more difficult than we would like. In either case, we are frustrated. **Frustration** is the blocking or thwarting of goal-directed behavior—blocking that may be total and permanent or partial and temporary (see Figure 11.1).

Stress that results from frustration is a normal, commonplace reaction. Frustration is a stressor, and the stress it produces is a fact of life. In no way does it imply weakness, pathology, or illness. What matters is how individuals react to the stressors in their lives.

To someone who is frustrated, the actual source of stress may be of little consequence. However, in order to respond adaptively to frustration-induced stress, it may be helpful to recognize the source of the blocking—the particular stressor—keeping us from our goals. There are two basic types of frustration: environmental and personal.

Environmental frustration implies that the blocking or thwarting of one's goal-directed behavior is caused by something or somebody in the environment. (Note that we talk about the *source* of frustration, not *fault* or *blame*, which are evaluative terms.)

Remember Lindsay, who lost her term paper when the power went out? This is an example of environmental frustration. Lindsay wanted to get her paper typed. Her goal-directed behavior led her to use her word processor. Something in her environment—a momentary power outage—kept her from reaching her goal. And remember Trudy? She wanted a cookie, but her mother said, "No, it's almost dinner-

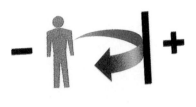

Figure 11.1

A depiction of frustration, the blocking or thwarting of goal-directed behavior.

Stress resulting from frustration occurs when our goal-directed behaviors are blocked or thwarted. On some days, being stuck in a traffic jam can be very frustrating.

time." Trudy is also being frustrated by her environment, but in a slightly different way. She wants a cookie, and her mother is blocking that motivated behavior. This type of environmental frustration, in which the source of the blocking is another person, is sometimes called *social frustration.*

Occasionally we are frustrated not because something in our environment blocks our progress, but because of an internal or personal reason. This is *personal frustration.* Doug fails to make the basketball team simply because he is too short. Shirley, who wants to be a concert pianist, may be frustrated in her attempt to do so simply because she doesn't have sufficient talent. Shirley's frustration and resulting stress are not her *fault* (fault and blame are just not relevant), but if she persists in this goal-directed behavior, she will be frustrated. Some of us are learning that simply getting older can be stressful. I know I am often frustrated when I find I have difficulty doing things now that at one time I was able to do easily. The stress we experience is frustration-induced, and this type of frustration is personal.

Before You Go On

What is meant by frustration-induced stress?

Conflict-Induced Stress

Sometimes we are unable to satisfy a particular drive or motive because it is in **conflict** with other motives that are influencing us at the same time. Stress may result from conflicts within our own motivational system.

With motivational conflicts, there is the implication of a decision or choice to be made. Sometimes the choice is relatively easy, and the resulting stress will be

◎◎◎◎ **Thinking Critically** ◎◎◎◎

This is the second time I've mentioned the assumption that all behaviors are goal-directed. Can you think of any behaviors for which this might not be true?

conflict *a stressor in which some goals can be satisfied only at the expense of others*

Figure 11.2

A diagram of an approach-approach conflict. In such a conflict, a person is faced with two (or more) attractive, positive goals, and must choose between or among them.

slight; sometimes decision making is difficult, and the resulting stress will be greater. When discussing conflicts, we talk about positive goals or incentives that one wishes to approach, and negative goals or incentives one wishes to avoid. There are four major types of stress-inducing motivational conflicts.

(1) *Approach-Approach Conflicts.* Conflicts are necessarily unpleasant, stress-producing situations, and will be so even when the goals involved are positive. In an approach-approach conflict, an organism is caught between two (or more) alternatives, and each of them is positive, or potentially reinforcing (Figure 11.2). If alternative A is chosen, a desired goal will be reached. If B is chosen, a different desirable goal will be attained. What makes this a conflict is that both goals or alternatives are not available at the same time. It has to be one or the other.

Once an approach-approach conflict is resolved, the person does end up with something positive no matter which alternative is chosen. If Carla enters an ice cream shop with only enough money to buy one dip of ice cream, she may experience a conflict when faced with all of the flavors from which she could choose. Typical of conflict, we'll probably see some swaying back and forth among alternatives. We can assume that this conflict will be resolved with a choice, and Carla will at least walk out of the store with an ice cream cone of some flavor she likes. Her life might have been easier (less stressful) if the store had just one flavor in the first place and she didn't have to make such choices, but she'll contemplate that possibility with an ice cream cone.

Sometimes the choices we are called on to make are much more serious than those involving ice cream flavors. What will be your college major? On the one hand, you'd like to go to medical school and be a surgeon (that's a positive incentive or goal). On the other hand, you'd like to study composition and conducting at a school of music (also a clear positive goal). At the moment, you can't do both. The courses you would take as a premed student are different from those you'd take if you were to follow music as a career path. Both are constructive, desirable alterna-

Even if the choices that one has to make are positive (which casino shall I visit next?), the very process of making those choices can put one in a conflict and produce stress.

tives; but now, at registration, you have to make a choice, one that may have long-lasting repercussions. The consequences of such a conflict qualify it as a stressor.

(2) *Avoidance-Avoidance Conflicts.* Perhaps the most stress-inducing of all the motivational conflicts are the avoidance-avoidance conflicts (Figure 11.3). In this type of conflict, a person is faced with several alternatives, and each of them is negative or in some way punishing. To be in an avoidance-avoidance conflict is, in a way, to be boxed in so that no matter what you do, the result will be punishing or unpleasant.

This sort of conflict is not at all unusual in the workplace. Imagine that you are a supervisor in charge of a reasonably large department. Your department has been doing well, making a profit, but word comes from management that you must cut your operating budget by 20 percent by next month. There are ways you can reduce expenses—limit travel, cut down on supplies, reduce pay, eliminate expense accounts, and so on—but each involves an action you'd rather not take. If you do nothing at all, you may lose your job. The result may be stress, and the stressor is an avoidance-avoidance conflict.

(3) *Approach-Avoidance Conflicts.* With approach-avoidance conflicts, a person is in the position of considering only one goal (Figure 11.4). What makes this situation a conflict is that the person would very much like to reach that goal, but at the same time would very much like not to. It's a matter of "Yes, I'd love to . . . Well, I'd rather not . . . Maybe I would . . . No, I wouldn't . . . yes . . . no." Consider the possibility of entering into a relationship with someone you think of as special. On the one hand, such a relationship might turn out to be wonderful and rewarding. On the other hand, such a relationship might put you in the position of being rejected. Typical of conflict, we'll find vacillation between alternatives—motivated to approach and, at the same time, motivated to avoid. Like Marian in our opening examples, you might find yourself in an approach-avoidance conflict if you want to interact with people who are culturally different, perhaps to show that you are open-minded. At the same time, you may be reluctant to initiate such an interaction for fear that your behaviors will be inappropriate or misinterpreted.

(4) *Multiple Approach-Avoidance Conflicts.* Multiple approach-avoidance conflicts may be the most common of the conflicts experienced by adults (see Figure 11.5). This type of conflict arises when an individual is faced with a number of alternatives, each one of which is in some way both positive and negative.

Perhaps you and some friends are out shopping on a Saturday morning. You realize that it's getting late, and you're all hungry. Where will you go to lunch? You may have a multiple approach-avoidance conflict here. "We could go to Bob's Diner, where the food is cheap and the service is fast, but the food is terrible. We could go to Cafe Olé, where the food is better, but service is a little slower, and the food is more expensive. Or we could go to The Grill, where the service is elegant and the food is superb, but the price is very high." Granted this is not an earth-shaking dilemma, but in each case there is a plus and a minus to be considered in making the choice. The more difficult the choice, the greater the induced stress.

Life is filled with such conflicts, and some of them can cause extreme stress. They may encompass questions of the "What shall I do with the rest of my life?" sort. "Should I stay at home with the children (+ and –), or should I have a career (+ and –)?" "Should I get married or stay single, or is there another way (+ and– in each case)?" "Should I work for company A (+ and –), or should I work for company B (+ and –)?" Clearly, such lists could go on and on. You might want to reflect on the conflicts you have faced during the past few weeks. You should be able to categorize each of them into one of the four types I have listed here.

Before You Go On

Describe four types of motivational conflict.

Figure 11.3

A diagram of an avoidance-avoidance conflict. In such a conflict, a person is faced with two (or more) unattractive, negative goals, and must choose between or among them. This is sometimes referred to as a "no-win" situation.

Figure 11.4

A diagram of an approach-avoidance conflict. Here, a person is faced with but one goal. What makes this a conflict is that the goal has both positive and negative aspects or features.

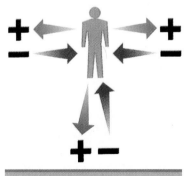

Figure 11.5

A diagram of a multiple approach-avoidance conflict. In such a conflict, a person is faced with two (or more) alternatives, each of which has both positive and negative aspects or features, and a choice must be made between or among the alternatives.

Life-Induced Stress

Frustration and conflict are potent sources of stress and often are simply unavoidable consequences of being a motivated organism. Psychologists have also considered sources of stress that do not fit neatly into our descriptions of either conflict or frustration. One useful approach has been to look at certain events and changes that occur in one's life as potential sources of stress.

In 1967, Thomas Holmes and Richard Rahe published the first version of their *Social Readjustment Rating Scale,* or *SRRS* (Holmes & Holmes, 1970). The basic idea of this scale is that stress results whenever life situations change. The scale provides a list of life events that might be potentially stressful. The original list of such events was drawn from the reports of patients suffering from moderate to high levels of stress in their lives. Marriage was arbitrarily assigned a value of 50 stress points, or *life-change units.* With "marriage = 50" as their guide, the patients rated a number of other life changes in terms of the amount of stress they might provide. The death of a spouse got the highest rating (100 units), followed by divorce (rated at 73 units). Pregnancy (40 units), trouble with the boss (23 units), changing to a new school (20 units), and minor violations of the law (11 units) are some other stress-inducing life-change events on the scale. In a rather direct way, the *SRRS* gives us a way to measure the stress in our lives.

There is a positive correlation between scores on the SRRS and the incidence of physical illness and disease (Rahe & Arthur, 1978). People with SRRS scores between 200 and 299 have a 50–50 chance of developing symptoms of physical illness within the next two years, whereas 80 percent of those with scores above 300 develop symptoms within the same time period. Several studies that have looked at correlations between SRRS scores and physical health problems have found the correlations to be positive (e.g., Adler et al., 1994; Brett et al., 1990; and McCrae, 1984). The logic is that stress predisposes one to physical illness. But remember what we learned in Chapter 1 about correlations: They do not tell us about cause and effect. Some of the SRRS items are worded to include mention of a physical illness, or are health related. It is not much of a surprise, then, to find scores on this scale are related to levels of physical illness. We'll return to the relationship between stress (and other psychological factors) and physical health in our next Topic.

Sometimes life events that are evaluated as being positive, such as going on a long-anticipated cruise, can be stressors.

Socioeconomic status, or **SES**, is a measure that reflects income, educational level, and occupation. Sensibly, there is a negative correlation between socioeconomic status and experienced stress. SES is related to stress in at least two ways. (1) Persons of higher socioeconomic status are less likely than persons of low SES to encounter negative life events, such as unemployment, poor housing, and less access to quality health care (McLeod & Kessler, 1990). (2) Persons of low SES have fewer resources to deal with stressful life events when they do occur (Adler et al., 1994).

Richard Lazarus (1981, 1991c, 1993) argues that psychologists ought to focus more attention on those causes of stress that are less dramatic than major life changes such as the death of a family member or marriage. What often matters most are life's little hassles—the traffic that goes too slowly, the toothpaste tube that splits, ants at a picnic, the cost of a pizza compared to what it was just a few years ago, and so on. Part of this argument is that big crises or major life-change events are too large to have an impact on us directly. What causes us to feel stressed are the ways in which big events produce little, irritating changes in our lives (hassles). Being retired may mean a lack of access to friendly conversation at coffee-break time. A spouse who starts to work may make life more difficult; the other spouse may have to cook dinner for the first time. Thus, stress is not so much a reaction to an event itself, but to the hassles it creates.

Lazarus and his colleagues have a scale to assess the extent to which hassles enter peoples' lives (Kanner, Coyne, Schaefer, & Lazarus, 1981). Respondents to the *Hassles Scale,* as it is called, indicate which hassles have happened to them and rate the severity of the experienced stress. The ten most commonly cited daily hassles for college students and for middle-aged adults are listed in Figure 11.6. The Hassles Scale is a better predictor of problems with physical health and a better predictor of symptoms such as anxiety and depression than is the Social Readjustment Rating Scale (e.g., DeLongis et al., 1988).

Other scales have been designed to assess the stressors people encounter. One, the *Comprehensive Scale of Stress Assessment* (Sheridan & Smith, 1987), has been revised for use with teenagers (Sheridan & Perkins, 1992). Significant stressors for teens include such things as "having thoughts of losing your parents or someone else dear to you," "being bombarded by questions and requests," "experiencing high-level noise at school or home," "being around angry people," and "having someone call something you have said or done 'stupid.'"

socioeconomic status (SES) *a measure that reflects one's income, education and occupation*

Figure 11.6

Ten Common Stressors in the Lives of Middle-aged Adults and College Students

For middle-aged adults:
1. Concerns about weight
2. Health of a family member
3. Rising prices of common goods
4. Home maintenance (interior)
5. Too many things to do
6. Misplacing or losing things
7. Yard work or outside home maintenance
8. Property, investments, or taxes
9. Crime
10. Physical appearance

For college students:
1. Troubling thoughts about the future
2. Not getting enough sleep
3. Wasting time
4. Inconsiderate smokers
5. Physical appearance
6. Too many things to do
7. Misplacing or losing things
8. Not enough time to do the things you need to do
9. Concerns about meeting high standards
10. Being lonely

From Kanner, Coyne, Schaefer, & Lazarus, 1981.

One final note about life-induced stressors: the events in our lives we talk about as stressors do not have to be negative or unpleasant events. Many events we look forward to, that we judge to be changes for the better, can bring with them the hassles associated with stress. For example, everybody is happy about Cindy and Jerry getting married, no doubt a pleasant, positive life event. At the same time—as anyone who has ever gone through the process will attest—wedding preparations are stressors. They may produce new conflicts. If Aunt Sarah is invited, does that mean that Aunt Louise must be invited as well? Cindy and Jerry are planning an outdoor reception. What if it rains? And there's Wayne the experienced salesman, now a sales manager. Wayne may have gotten used to being on the road and setting his own hours. Now that he has a promotion—"good news"—his daily routine may be drastically altered by his being confined to an office, which may produce new stress.

Before You Go On

In what ways might life events produce stress?

Reacting to the Stressors in Our Lives

So far we have defined stress and reviewed a number of potential stressors. Now we need to consider what someone might do when he or she experiences stress. We often hear about people trying to "cope with the stress in their lives." Consistent with the terminology we've been using, it would be more correct to speak of "coping with, or dealing with, the *stressors* in one's life." Stress is a reaction to stressors (frus-

EXPERIENCING PSYCHOLOGY

Log in Those Stressors

As a college student—no matter what your age—you are no stranger to stress. Stress is a universal experience, and it is one that is very common among college students. Granted that stress cannot be avoided, perhaps some of the stressors in your life can be. A preliminary step to reducing one's stressors is to identify them honestly. The basic question of this exercise is, "What events or situations in your life, *right now*, are causing you stress?"

For three days in a row, keep a log of those things that you find stressful. At least one of the three days should be a class day and one should be a weekend day when you have no classes scheduled. From the minute you get up, and at one-hour intervals all day long, pause and reflect: "What aggravated you within the last hour?" "What hassles did you encounter?" "What made your blood pressure rise?" "What made you angry?" "What did you find upsetting?" "What conflicts or frustrations did you encounter?"

With any luck, there may be several hours in each day when the honest answer to these questions is "nothing." We may experience stress regularly, but we don't necessarily experience new stressors every hour. Actually, stopping every hour to consider one's stressors can in itself be quite an annoying hassle, but it will be for only three days, and it may be very revealing.

After three days of self-observation, look back over your list of stressors and hassles very carefully. Do any patterns emerge? Are there any particular situations in which you are most likely to experience stress? Are these situations avoidable? Do any particular people trigger a stress response for you? Are these people avoidable? Can you classify the stressors of your three-day log as being primarily frustrations, conflicts, or just life events? What can you change to minimize these stressors in your life?

This is an exercise that you can repeat throughout the semester. It might be interesting to compare your log with that of one of your friends. How does your log of stressors in mid-semester compare to one you construct at finals time? or when you are at home for the holidays? or on vacation?

tration, conflict, or life events). Stress may motivate us, but it motivates us to do something about the perceived threats to our well-being we are calling stressors.

Individual Differences in Responding to Stressors

As with so many other things, there are large individual differences in how one responds to stressors. What consitutes a stressor and what someone may do when he or she experiences stress can vary considerably from person to person. Some people fall apart at weddings; others find them only mildly stressful. For some people, simple choices are difficult to make; for others, choices are not enough, they seek challenges. The variability in stress we see among different people can usually be found within any one person at different times. For example, on one day, being caught in slow-moving traffic might drive you up the wall. In the very same situation a few days later, you find you couldn't care less. So we need to remember that reactions to stressors vary from time to time and from person to person. The amount of stress one experiences and the means of coping with stress *do not* appear to be different for men and women (e. g., Baum & Grunberg, 1991; Lazarus, 1993). For example, in one study comparing men and women who were married and employed full-time, no gender difference was found in the degree to which work-related concerns contributed to individual levels of stress (Barnette et al., 1993).

Some people seem so generally resistant to the negative aspects of stress that they have been labeled as having *hardy personalities* (e.g., Kobasa, 1979, 1982, 1987; Maddi & Kobasa, 1984; Neubauer, 1992). Hardiness in this context is related to three things: (1) *challenge* (being able to see difficulties in one's life as an opportunity for change and growth, not threats to one's status); (2) *control* (being in charge of what is happening in one's life and believing that one is the master of one's fate); and (3) *commitment* (being engaged and involved with one's life and one's circumstances, not just watching life go by from the sidelines).

Here's another observation about how we deal with stress: some responses are more effective or adaptive than others. Stress often follows as a natural consequence of being alive, motivated in the real world. What is unfortunate is that we occasionally develop ineffective or maladaptive strategies for dealing with the stress we experience. By that I mean that one's reaction will not, in the long run, be successful in reducing stress. Before we consider strategies for dealing with stress, let's look more closely at the reaction to stressors that we call stress.

Before You Go On

What does it mean to say that there are individual differences in reactions to stressors?

Stress as a Physiological Reaction: Selye's GAS

No matter how we ultimately cope with stress, stressors produce a series of physiological reactions within us. In this way, stress is much like other reactions to emotion-producing stimuli in our environments. When we experience stress, demands are made on the physiological systems of our bodies.

The most widely accepted description of the physiological reactions one makes to stressors is described by Hans Selye's **general adaptation syndrome**, or **GAS**. According to Selye (1956, 1974), the reaction to stressors occurs in three stages: alarm, resistance, and exhaustion (see Figure 11.7).

The first response to the perception of a stressor is *alarm*. Any perceived threat produces rapid and noticeable changes in the sympathetic division of the autonomic nervous system. There will be an increase in blood pressure and heart rate, pupillary dilation, a cessation of digestion, and a rerouting of the blood supply to the extremities of the body. The adrenal glands enlarge and secrete norepinephrine

⊚⊚⊚ Thinking Critically ⊚⊚⊚

Do you see any general gender differences in the manner in which people you know deal with the stressors in their lives?

general adaptation syndrome (GAS) *Selye's description of physiological reactions made to stressors, which include the three stages of alarm, resistance, and exhaustion*

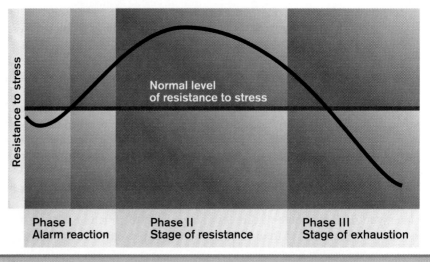

Resistance to stress

Normal level
of resistance to stress

Phase I
Alarm reaction

Phase II
Stage of resistance

Phase III
Stage of exhaustion

Figure 11.7

The general adaptation syndrome (GAS) as proposed by Hans Selye calls for three identifiable, largely physiological, reactions to stressors. In the first stage (alarm reaction), resources are quickly mobilized as the sympathetic division of the ANS springs into action. If the stressor persists, the organism shows a defensive reaction (resistance stage) in an attempt to react to the continuing stressor. Following a prolonged exposure to stress, the energy necessary for adaptation may become depleted (exhaustion stage).

into the bloodstream mobilizing the body's resources, and providing increased levels of blood sugar. These reactions are similar to those we experience in any emotional situation. This strong, dramatic reaction cannot last very long. We usually maintain high levels of sympathetic activity for no more than several minutes, a few hours at the most.

Let's start an illustrative example. Imagine Pam, a college student in the midst of an important semester. Pam is strongly motivated to do well in her courses. It is just past midterm and she gets word from home that her father has had a massive heart attack. She leaves school and drives straight home, a 16-hour drive, and rushes to the hospital. Her father has never been seriously ill before; now he's in coronary intensive care. The shock and disbelief are nearly overwhelming during Pam's initial alarm-stage reaction.

In *resistance,* the second stage of the general adaptation syndrome, the cause of one's stress remains present, and Pam's body continues to fight off the challenge of the stressor. Pam's father begins to show some signs of recovery, but he will be in intensive care for another three days and will be hospitalized well beyond that. There's little Pam can do to help her father, but she feels she can't leave and go back to school right now. Every day she stays at home, she gets further behind in her classes.

Pam's bodily resources were mobilized in the alarm stage of the GAS. Now she has discovered that there is no means of escaping or lessening the source of her stress. The drain on her body's resources continues as she maintains a high level of arousal. If new stressors appear, Pam will be less able to deal with them effectively. More than that, she will be more sensitive to stressors that she otherwise might have ignored. She will become vulnerable to physical illness and infection to a greater degree than she would without the constant stress she is experiencing. High blood pressure, ulcers, skin rashes, or respiratory difficulties may develop. Pam may appear to be in control, but the reality of her father's condition and the approach of her final exams continue to eat away at her, intruding into her awareness.

If Pam cannot find some useful way to deal with the stress she is experiencing, her physical reaction to the still-present stressors may be *exhaustion.* In this stage, her bodily resources become nearly depleted. She is running out of energy and out of time. Pam may break down—psychologically or physically, or both. Depression is

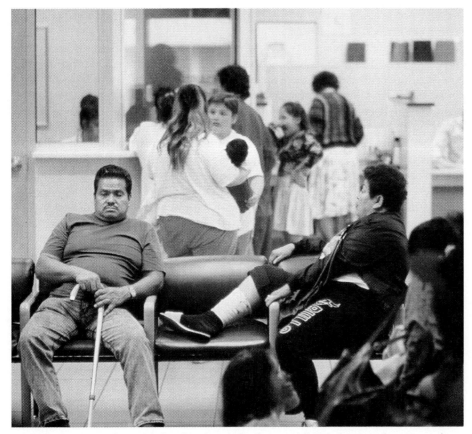

If stressors persist—as they might in a long hospitalization—one's initial alarm reaction may evolve into a reaction of resistance, or even exhaustion, according to Selye's general adaptation syndrome.

a real possibility. Although the resistance stage may last for several months, eventually one's resources become expended. In extreme cases, the exhaustion stage of the general adaptation syndrome may result in death.

For Selye, stress is a three-stage mobilization of the body's resources to combat real or perceived threats to our well-being. In that sense the process *is* "adaptive"—at least through the stage of resistance. Unfortunately, we have a limited supply of adaptive resources. Repeated exposure to stressors has cumulative effects. Dire consequences can result when someone is faced with several stressful situations at about the same time. Selye's model focuses on the physiological aspects of responding to stressors. It does not take into account just how a person can respond to stressors in more cognitive and behavioral ways. Let's first consider effective strategies for dealing with stress and stressors, and then look at some common ineffective strategies.

Before You Go On

What are the three stages of Selye's general adaptation syndrome?

Effective Strategies for Coping with Stressors

In the long run, the most effective way to deal with stress is to make relatively permanent changes in our behaviors as a result of the experience of stress. You will recall that we defined learning as a relatively permanent change in behavior that occurs as the result of practice or experience. To respond to a stressor with learning makes particularly good sense for frustration-induced stress. In a frustrating situation, our pathway to a goal is being blocked. An adaptive way to handle such a

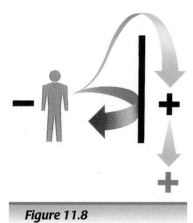

Figure 11.8

Reacting to frustration with learning is the most effective long-term reaction to stressors. That is, when one's goal-directed behaviors are continually blocked or thwarted, one should consider bringing about a relatively permanent change in those behaviors, or consider changing one's goals altogether.

stressor is to find a new way to reach our goal or to learn to modify our goal (see Figure 11.8).

In fact, much of our everyday learning is motivated by frustration-induced stress. We've had to learn many new responses as a means of coping with frustration. Having been frustrated once (or twice) by locking yourself out of your house or car, you learn to hide another set of keys somewhere where you can easily find them. Having been caught at home in a blizzard with no cookies in the house, you have learned to bake them yourself. Having discovered he's too short to make the basketball team, Doug has learned to play tennis. You may have learned as a child to get what you wanted from your parents by smiling sweetly and asking politely. In each of these cases, what prompted, or motivated, the learning of new responses or the establishment of new goals was the stress resulting from frustration.

Learning motivated by stress may also have taught you the value of escape and avoidance. You now know how to avoid getting into many motivational conflicts. You may have learned that a sensible thing to do once you are in a conflict is to escape or to make major changes in what is motivating you. This is one way in which stress can be seen as a positive force in our lives. If we were never challenged, if we never set difficult goals, if we never faced stressful situations, we would miss out on many opportunities for personal growth and learning. The stress we experience is unpleasant at the time, but it may produce positive consequences.

To say that we should respond to stressful situations by learning new, effective behaviors is sensible enough, but are there any specific measures we can take to help alleviate the unpleasantness of stress in our lives? Indeed, there are many specific steps we can take. Here we'll review eight such strategies.

Identify the Stressor. Remember that stress is a reaction to any one of several types of stressors. If you are experiencing stress in your life, the first thing you should ask is, "Where is it coming from?" Are you having difficulty resolving a motivational conflict? What positive or negative goals are involved? Is your goal-directed behavior being blocked? If so, what is the source of your frustration? What recent changes or events in your life are particularly upsetting or problematic? Any successful strategy for coping with stress will require change—and effort—on your part. The first thing to do is to make sure your efforts are well directed.

Efforts for dealing with stress can be categorized as being either emotion-focused or problem-focused (Lazarus & Folkman, 1984). The difference is self-evident. Strategies that are *emotion focused* deal with how you feel, and with finding ways to feel differently. This is often one's first reaction to stressors. "I feel miserable, stressed out; how can I feel better?" Real progress usually requires that you look beyond how you feel at the moment to discover the underlying situation causing your present feelings—a *problem-focused* strategy. "Where did this stress come from, and how can I make it go away?"

Remove or Negate the Stressor. Once a stressor has been identified, the next logical question is, "Can anything be done about it?" Do I *have* to stay in this situation, or can I bring about a change? If a particular interpersonal relationship has become a constant, nagging source of stress, might this be the time to think about breaking off the relationship? If the stress you experience at work has become overwhelming, might this be a good time to consider a different job? The issue is one of taking control, of trying to turn a challenge into an opportunity. Perhaps you recall that a tendency to take control of potentially stressful situations is one of the characteristics of people with the so-called "hardy personality" who usually manage to avoid many of the negative consequences of stress. Even people with a terminal illness fare much better if they take control, find out everything there is to know about their illness, seek second and third opinions, make the most of what time they have left, and so on (Folkman, 1984).

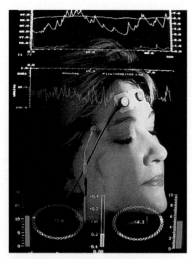

Biofeedback is an "emotion-focused" strategy for dealing with stressors. Even when it is effective, it will not remove the source of one's stress, but it can help one feel better.

Reappraise the Situation. We should assess whether the stressors in our lives are real or (even partially) imagined threats to our well-being. Making this determination is part of what is called a cognitive reappraisal of one's situation (e.g., Schultz & Decker, 1985). In the context of stress management, *cognitive reappraisal* means rethinking a situation to put it in the best possible light. Is that co-worker really trying to do you out of a promotion? Do you really care if you are invited to the party? Must you earn an A on the next test in order to pass the course? Are things really as bad as they seem? Lazarus sees this as realizing that "people should try to change the noxious things that can be changed, accept those that cannot, and have the wisdom to know the difference"—a paraphrase of an ancient Hebrew prayer (1993, p. 9).

Meichenbaum (1977) argues that we can deal with a lot of stress simply by talking to ourselves, replacing negative statements (such as, "Oh boy, I'm really in trouble now. I'm sure to be called on and I'll embarrass myself in front of the whole class") with coping statements (such as, "I'll just do the best I can. I'm as prepared as anybody in here, and in a little while this will all be over"). This cognitive approach does take a bit of practice, but it can be very effective.

Inoculate Against Future Stressors. Among other things, this strategy involves accepting and internalizing much of what we have been saying about the universality of stress and stressors. It's a matter of convincing yourself that stress has occurred before, will occur again, and that this too will pass. It's a matter of anticipation and preparation—truly coming to accept the reality that "worrying about this won't make it any better," or "no matter how bad things look, I'll be able to figure out some plan to deal with it." We know that surgery patients recover faster and with fewer postsurgical complications if they are fully informed before their surgery of what they can expect, how they are likely to feel, and what they can do to aid in their own recovery (MacDonald & Kuiper, 1983).

Inoculating oneself against future stressors amounts to trying to develop a sense of optimism—the belief that good things, as opposed to bad things, will generally happen in one's life. People with this sort of optimistic outlook "routinely maintain higher levels of subjective well-being during times of stress than do people who are less optimistic" (Scheier & Carver, 1993, p. 27). Optimism also predicts such things as better adjustment in one's first year away at college, less depression among mothers following childbirth, and rate of recovery from heart surgery (Aspinwall & Taylor, 1992; Carver & Gaines, 1987; Scheier & Carver, 1992, 1993; Scheier et al., 1989).

Take Your Time with Important Decisions. Stress often accompanies the process of making tough decisions. You're frustrated. A goal-directed behavior is being blocked. You have to decide if you will pursue a different course of action. Which course of action? Would it be wiser to change your goal? Do you want to do this (+ and −) or do you want to do that (+ and −)? We make matters worse by rushing a decision "just to have it over with." Occasionally we are faced with deadlines by which final decisions must be made. We often add to an already stressful situation by racing to conclusions before we have all of the facts, before we have explored all of the costs and benefits associated with the alternatives we are contemplating (e.g., Hogan, 1989). For example, if you can't make up your mind about a new car you're thinking about buying, why not rent one for a few days to see if you'd be happy with it in the long run?

The strategies I've listed above make suggestions for dealing with the stressor that has caused the stress in one's life. As I've said before, being problem focused—as these strategies are—is the only effective, long-term way to deal with stressors. In the short term, there *are* some things you can do to combat the unpleasant feelings or affects that accompany stress (i.e., emotion-focused strategies). We'll look at three.

Learn Techniques of Relaxation. Learning effective ways to relax may not be as easy as it sounds, but the logic is simple: feeling stressed and being relaxed are not compatible responses. If you can become relaxed, the experience (feelings) of stress will be diminished (e.g., Lehrer & Woolfolk, 1984). Hypnosis may help. Meditation may help. So may relaxation training.

A variety of operant conditioning called *biofeedback* can provide relief from the tension associated with stress (Kamiya et al., 1977; Shirley et al., 1992; Yates, 1980). Biofeedback is "the process of providing information to an individual about his [or her] bodily processes in some form which he [or she] might be able to use to modify those processes" (Hill, 1985, p. 201). One's heart rate, let us say, is constantly monitored, and the rate is fed back to the person, perhaps in the form of an audible tone. As heart rate increases, the pitch of the tone becomes higher. As heart rate decreases, the tone gets lower. Once the learner knows (through the feedback) what his or her heart rate (or blood pressure, or muscle tension, and so on) is doing, a certain degree of control over that response is possible. The reinforcement involved here is simply the newly gained knowledge that a desired change is being made. As a result of being reinforced, the stress-fighting responses increase in their frequency (Kaplan, 1991; Kimmel, 1974; Miller, 1978; Thackwray-Emerson, 1989).

Engage in Physical Exercise. There is a good deal of evidence that claims that physical exercise is a useful agent in the battle against stress (Brown, 1991; Crews & Landers, 1987; McCann & Holmes, 1984; Wheeler & Frank, 1988). Physical exercise is helpful once stress is experienced, but when it does help, it is difficult to say if exercise combats stress directly, or does so indirectly by improving physical health, stamina, self-esteem, and self-confidence. And of course, one must be careful. Deciding that tomorrow you'll start running five miles a day, rain or shine, may be a decision that in itself will create more stress than it will reduce. One needs an exercise program that is enjoyable, not overly strenuous, and that helps one feel better about oneself.

Seek Social Support. Finally, I should mention the advantage of social support for persons who are experiencing stress. Stress is a common phenomenon. Perhaps no one else knows precisely how you feel, or has experienced exactly the same situation in which you find yourself, but all of us have known stress, and we are all aware of the types of situations that give rise to it. Social support from friends and relatives, or from others, such as physicians, clergy, therapists, or counselors, can be very helpful (Adler & Matthews, 1994; Coyne & Downey, 1991; Gottlieb, 1981; Hobfall, 1986; Rook, 1987). If at all possible, one should not face stress alone.

Now that we've reviewed some of the steps one can take to help alleviate the unpleasantness of stress, let's consider some reactions stress can produce that are not as adaptive.

Before You Go On

What are some adaptive ways of dealing with stress?

Ineffective Strategies for Coping with Stressors

Coping effectively with stress is a matter of bringing about change. Not to change is to *fixate,* accepting the same stress from the same stressor. Fixation is seldom an adequate reaction to stress. Don't get me wrong here. "If at first you don't succeed, try, try again." Why, of course; this is sound advice. But, again, and again, and again? At some point we must be ready and able to give up a particular course of action to try something else.

In a way, *procrastination* is a form of fixation, isn't it? A student has a term paper due in two weeks and just can't seem to get going on it, deciding to "put if off until this weekend." This weekend may not bring any progress either, but the stress of dealing with the paper is momentarily postponed. The catch is that there's going to be a price to pay. Eventually, the paper will have to be done, and then, with very little time before the deadline, the experienced stress will probably be greater than ever before. In addition to not changing one's behavior or one's goals, or simply not doing anything at all, there are two other reactions to stressors that are clearly maladaptive: aggression and anxiety.

There are many causes of aggression, and one source of aggressive behavior is stress; in particular, stress that results from frustration. Remember our example of Trudy, who was frustrated because she couldn't have a cookie, and tore the arm off her doll? At one time, it was proposed that frustration was the only cause of aggression, the so-called **frustration-aggression hypothesis** (Dollard et al., 1939). This point of view claimed that frustration could produce a number of reactions, including aggression, but that aggression was always caused by frustration. We now recognize that there are other sources of aggression (some view it as innate or instinctive, whereas others see it as a response learned through reinforcement or modeling that need not be stimulated by frustration). It is true, however, that frustration remains a prime candidate as the cause of aggression. It usually doesn't do much good in the long run, but a flash of aggressive behavior often follows stress (Berkowitz, 1978, 1982, 1989, 1990).

There you are in the parking lot, trying to get home from class, and your car won't start. Over and over you crank the ignition. Continuing to turn the key without success is a good example of fixation—it's not doing you any good, but you keep at it, perhaps until you run down the battery. Still frustrated, you swing open the door, get out, kick the front left fender, throw up the hood, and glower at the engine. You're mad! Having released a bit of tension, you might feel better for a few seconds, but being angry and kicking at the car, or yelling at someone who offers to assist, won't help you solve your problem.

Another negative consequence of stress is **anxiety**—a general feeling of tension, apprehension, and dread that involves predictable physiological changes. Anxiety is a very difficult concept to define precisely, but everyone "knows" what you're talking about when you refer to anxiety. It is a reaction we have all experienced. Often, it is a reaction that accompanies stress. We can think of anxiety as an

frustration-aggression hypothesis *the view (now discredited) that all aggression stems from frustration*

anxiety *a general feeling of tension, apprehension and dread that involves predictable physiological changes*

Aggression, even verbal aggression, often follows from frustration. It does nothing to remove the stressor, however, and is therefore an ineffective reaction to stress.

Physical exercise seldom can remove stressors, but it has been found helpful in combating the negative consequences of stress.

unpleasant emotional component of the stress response. As much as anything else, we want to rid ourselves of stress in order to minimize our anxiety.

Sometimes the amount of stress and anxiety in one's life becomes more than one can cope with effectively. Feelings of anxiety start to interfere with normal adaptations to the environment and to other people. Such feelings may become the focus of one's attention. More anxiety follows, and then more distress, and more discomfort, and more pain. For many people–tens of millions of people in the United States and Canada–the anxiety that results from stress is so discomforting and so maladaptive that we say they are suffering from a psychological disorder. In Chapter 12 we will discuss psychological disorders, starting with the anxiety disorders. When you get to that discussion, recall just how commonplace stress and anxiety are–and where most of that anxiety comes from.

Before You Go On

What are some maladaptive reactions to stressors?

⊚⊚⊚⊚ **Thinking Critically** ⊚⊚⊚⊚

Recall Freud's defense mechanisms, discussed in Chapter 9. Where do these fit in our discussion of stressors, stress, and reactions to them?

TOPIC 11A SUMMARY

In this Topic, we've dealt with stress, stressors, and reactions to both. On the one hand, stress is a response to stressors, real or perceived threats to our sense of well-being or to our resources. At the same time, stress is a motivator, stimulating us to engage in behaviors that reduce (at least) the felt negative aspects of stress.

Stressors can be either frustration (the blocking of goal-directed behavior), conflict (motives and drives that cannot all be satisfied at the same time), or simply life events, particularly changes in our lives. Hans Selye saw stress as a physiological reaction to stressors involving three stages: alarm, resistance, and exhaustion. We now recognize that dealing with stress encompasses a cognitive component as well, and we can talk about effective and ineffective means of dealing with stress. Remember, stress cannot be avoided; successful reactions are aimed at the stressor that causes the stress.

Successful problem-oriented strategies include identifying the stressor, removing or negating that stressor, engaging in cognitive reappraisal, inoculating oneself against future stressors, and taking one's time with important decisions. Emotion-oriented strategies include learning techniques of relaxation, engaging in physical exercise, and seeking social support. Ineffective strategies include fixation, aggression, and anxiety.

T O P I C 1 1 B Health Psychology

Health psychology became a division of the American Psychological Association in 1978 (Division 38) and now has approximately 3,000 members—an increase of 200 percent over 1980 membership. **Health psychology** is the study of psychological or behavioral factors affecting physical health and illness. As applied psychologists, or practitioners, health psychologists help people cope with physical diseases and illnesses, and are involved in efforts to try to prevent health problems from occurring in the first place. As researchers, health psychologists seek to better understand the relationships between psychological functioning and physical health.

health psychology *the field of applied psychology that studies psychological factors affecting physical health and illness*

The involvement of psychologists in the medical realm of physical health and well-being is based on four assumptions:

1. Certain behaviors increase the risk of certain chronic diseases.

2. Changes in behaviors can reduce the risk of certain diseases.

3. Changing behaviors is often easier and safer than treating many diseases.

4. Behavioral interventions are comparatively cost-effective (Kaplan, 1984).

In this Topic we'll examine two major thrusts of health psychology. We'll look at the relationships between psychological variables and physical health, an issue anticipated in Topic 11A when we saw that stress—a psychological reaction—can have serious physical consequences. Then we'll consider how psychologists are joining the fight against illness and disease.

Psychological Factors That Influence Physical Health

Is there a relationship between aspects of one's personality and one's state of physical health? Can psychological evaluations of an individual predict physical disease as well as psychological disorders? Is there such a thing as a disease-prone personality? "Why do some people get sick and some stay well?" (Adler & Matthews, 1994, p. 229). Our response is tentative, and not all of the data are supportive, but we can respond, "Yes, there is a positive correlation between some personality variables and physical health."

One meta-analysis of 101 published research articles looked for relationships between personality measures and physical disease (including coronary heart disease, asthma, ulcers, arthritis, and headaches). The strongest associations were those that predicted coronary heart disease (CHD), although depression, anxiety, and anger or hostility were each associated with the physical disorders studied (Friedman & Booth-Kewley, 1987). These researchers argued that there are sufficient data linking some personality variables to some physical diseases to "argue for a key role for psychological research on the prevention and treatment of disease" (p. 539). Recognizing that psychologists can help in the battle to prevent disease and to promote good health, the Centers for Disease Control and the American Psychological Association have begun discussions on how to best work together on these issues (Cavaliere, 1995, p.1).

When we talk about relating personality to physical diseases, what first comes to mind is the **Type A behavior pattern (TABP)** and coronary heart disease. As it was *originally defined,* the Type A individual was a competitive, achievement-oriented, impatient person who typically works at many tasks at the same time, is easily aroused, and is often hostile or angry (Friedman & Rosenman, 1959; Rosenman et al., 1964). Coronary heart disease is a label given to several physical symptoms, including chest pains and heart attacks, caused by a buildup of substances (e.g., cholesterol) that block the supply of blood to the heart. People who show none of the characteristics of the TABP and who are relaxed and easy-going are said to have a *Type B behavior pattern.*

For nearly 20 years—from the early 1960s to the early 1980s—many studies found a clear, positive relationship between CHD and behaviors typical of the Type A personality (Jenkins, 1976; Rosenman et al., 1975; Wood, 1986). The National Institutes of Health declared the Type A behavior pattern to be an independent risk factor for heart disease (National Institutes of Health, 1981). The Type A personal-

Type A behavior pattern (TABP) *a collection of behaviors (in which one is competitive, achievement-oriented, impatient, easily aroused, often hostile or angry) commonly associated with coronary heart disease*

Logan Wright claims that one important aspect, or "active ingredient," of the Type A behavior patterrn is *multiphasia*—having several things going on all at the same time.

ity pattern profile was implicated in hypertension (chronic high blood pressure) even when no other signs of coronary heart disease are present (Irvine et al., 1991). It all seemed clear. Find people with a Type A behavior pattern, intervene to change their behaviors, and watch coronary heart disease rates decline. By now you know to be suspicious when complex problems seem to have simple solutions.

Data began to surface that failed to show a clear relation between TABP and CHD (Fishman, 1987; Hollis et al., 1990; Krantz & Glass, 1984; Matthews, 1982, 1988; Wright, 1988). Perhaps Type A people were no more at risk for heart disease than anyone else. Perhaps studies that failed to find a relation between TABP and CHD were flawed. Both of these hypotheses seem valid. For one thing, the Type A behavioral pattern is complex and difficult to assess. It is likely that simple paper-and-pencil inventories—which have been used in many studies—fail to identify a large number of people with the TABP.

It also may be that the TABP, as originally defined, is simply too global a pattern of behaviors (Adler & Matthews, 1994; Dembroski & Costa, 1987). Perhaps there is a set of behaviors within the constellation of Type A behaviors that *does* predict coronary heart disease. This is a hypothesis being investigated by many psychologists, including Logan Wright, a self-confessed Type A personality who needed surgery to relieve blockage of a coronary artery. "If certain so-called active ingredients, or subcomponents of the TABP are what is really responsible for coronary-prone risk, one would expect to find them to correlate more highly with CHD than does the global Type A pattern itself" (Wright, 1988, p. 3).

What are Wright's candidates for the active ingredients of the Type A personality?

1. *Time urgency:* concern over wasting precious, small bits of time; shifting lanes while in traffic to gain a car length

2. *Chronic activation:* the tendency to stay alert and aroused and ready all of the time; being "fired up" for everything, no matter how mundane

3. *Multiphasia:* the tendency to have several projects all going at once, having many irons in the fire; doing homework and eating while watching TV.

Some research suggests that these components, taken together, predict coronary heart disease, but the evidence is not conclusive. Other research tells us that the potent ingredients of Type A personality are *anger* or *hostility* (Barefoot et al., 1983; Dembroski et al., 1985; Friedman et al., 1994; Houston & Vavak, 1991; Smith, 1992).

A meta-analysis by Scott Lyness tells us that there is a correlation between the global Type A behavior pattern and both heart rate and blood pressure levels (Lyness, 1993). What may be most significant about these findings is that there were virtually no differences between Type A and Type B persons *on baseline measures.* Differences did appear, however, when people with these "personality types" were exposed to stressful situations. When responding to stressors, the Type A individuals showed the significant increase in blood pressure and heart rate, and Type B individuals did not.

Lyness found no gender differences in Type A and Type B patterns. This finding is consistent with data from others who have found women with Type A or Type B behavior patterns equally at risk for nonfatal heart attacks (Shekelle & Gale, 1985). Lynda Powell and her associates have found gender differences, but in a curious way (Powell et al., 1993). These researchers found that after one has a first heart attack, women with a Type B behavior pattern are *more likely* to have cardiovascular problems and additional heart attacks than are other women. For reasons yet unknown, there is a survival advantage for women with Type A behavior patterns following a heart attack. According to Powell's research, women with Type B personality profiles, and whose aspirations to a traditional family lifestyle go unfulfilled, appear to be at greatest risk for subsequent cardiovascular disease (see also Eaker et al., 1988; Eaker et al., 1992).

Much more work needs to be done. We need research on adequately diagnosing Type A behavior patterns and on the mechanisms that underlie whatever relationships there may be between TABP and CHD. We also need research on how to bring about psychological changes in "Type A" persons that would reduce the likelihood of their contracting physical disease (see Winett, 1995). The ingredients of TABP appear to be precisely the characteristics many people in our society learn to value and to imitate in their quest to "get ahead." How can psychologists intervene to help people change those behaviors that directly and indirectly impact on their state of health? It is to matters of intervention that we now turn.

Before You Go On

Summarize the relationship, if any, between the Type A behavior pattern and coronary heart disease.

⊚⊚⊚ Thinking Critically ⊚⊚⊚

How do you think that you would be classified—a Type A or a Type B person?

Promoting Healthy Behaviors

At the very least, it is possible that some personality characteristics have an impact on one's physical health. The specific traits involved and the nature of that impact are the subject of debate and ongoing research. There is no debate and no doubt, however, that certain behaviors put people at risk for physical disease and death. One role of the health psychologist is to help change potentially dangerous behaviors (Kirscht, 1983; Levine et al., 1993; Matarazzo, 1980; Miller, 1983).

There is now considerable evidence that many deaths in the United States could be postponed if people were to change their behaviors—that is, give up their "unhealthy lifestyles."

Why Do People Die?

Obviously, people die for an almost infinite number of reasons. Ultimately, death is unavoidable. On the other hand, many deaths are "premature," and preventable.

Let's review a few gruesome statistics. The leading causes of death in this country are cardiovascular disorders and cancers, diseases caused by and maintained by the interaction of several factors—genetic, biological, social, environmental, and behavioral. Among the latter, such variables as cigarette smoking, nutrition, obesity, and stress have been identified as important risk factors (Krantz et al., 1985). This means that millions of people engage in what may be referred to as a deadly lifestyle. Here are some more numbers from a review article in the *Journal of the American Medical Association.*

> In 1990 there were 2,148,000 deaths in the United States. Of these, 400,000 deaths could be traced to tobacco use; diet and activity patterns accounted for 300,000 deaths, alcohol use accounted for 100,000 deaths, microbial agents (bacteria and viruses) 90,000 deaths, toxic agents 60,000 deaths, firearms 35,000 deaths, sexual behaviors 30,000 deaths, motor vehicles 25,000 deaths, and illegal drug use 20,000 deaths. (McGinnis & Foege, 1993, p. 2207)

In many of these cases, there was probably little or nothing that could have been done to prevent or delay death. In many other cases, bringing about changes in behavior in a timely fashion might have reduced these numbers.

Notice that a deadly lifestyle may involve behaviors that directly lead to death; for instance, failing to wear safety belts or knowingly engaging in other unsafe behaviors at work or play. The Department of Health and Human Services and the Centers for Disease Control tell us that deaths by gunfire have surpassed deaths by traffic accidents. Nearly 50,000 children and teenagers were killed by firearms between 1979 and 1991—a number nearly equal to the American casualties in the Vietnam War. By early 1995, the leading cause of death among Americans ages 25–44 years was AIDS.

Interventions designed to prevent health problems from arising in the first place have been applied to a wide range of behaviors and situations, including smoking and the misuse of alcohol. Programs have tried to change nutrition, physical fitness and exercise, controlling stress and high blood pressure, immunization, and unsafe sexual behaviors (Jeffery, 1989; McGinnis, 1985; Rodin & Salovey, 1989; Winett et al., 1993). Psychologists also use behavioral techniques in attempts to promote healthy and safe behaviors, such as the wearing of car safety belts (Geller et al., 1987; Geller et al., 1990). Many psychologists argue that we should be doing all we can to help promote healthy environments (smoke-free spaces, safe work places, opportunities for exercise at work, the installation of air bags in cars) while working to change individual behaviors (e.g., Aldwin & Stokals, 1988; Fielding & Phenow, 1988; Geller et al., 1982; Stokals, 1992; Winett, 1995).

For the remainder of this Topic we will examine two areas in which psychologists have been particularly active: helping people to stop smoking, and helping people deal with or prevent sexually transmitted diseases.

Helping People to Stop Smoking

Although efforts to bring about behavioral change have been moving forward on many fronts, few have received as much attention as those to discourage young people from smoking. One reason for the special efforts in this area is that smoking is so deadly, accounting for about one-third of all cancer deaths and nearly 400,000 of all deaths each year in the United States (Jeffery, 1989), and about 2 million deaths worldwide (Peto et al., 1992). According to a 1994 estimate of the World Health Organization, smoking is *the* leading cause of premature death in the industrialized world, killing one person every 10 seconds! Cigarettes are viewed as one of

Antismoking ads, such as this one from the American Cancer Society, are focusing on trying to keep young people from smoking in the first place.

the most addictive of substances, and among the most deadly (Fiore et al., 1989; Schelling, 1992; Surgeon General, 1988). Concern now includes the impact of "secondhand smoke," as we see evidence that the children of parents who smoke are significantly at risk for lung cancer even if they, as adults, have never smoked. A 1994 analysis of data collected in 1985 claims that secondhand smoke caused enough heart disease in nonsmokers to kill 62,000 Americans and to bring on 200,000 nonfatal heart attacks.

Of particular concern is the fact that an estimated 2.2 million American children ages 12 to 17 smoke cigarettes, and 9 million children under age 5 live with smokers, according to the American Heart Association. Each day an estimated 3,000 children begin smoking, claims Dr. James Moller, president of the American Heart Association. In the summer of 1995 the *Journal of the American Medical Association* (Editorial, July 19, 1995) published an editorial supported unanimously by its editorial board. In part the editorial said, "The evidence is unequivocal—the U. S. public has been duped by the tobacco industry. No right-thinking individual can ignore the evidence. We should all be outraged, and we should force the removal of this scourge from our nation."

Yet another reason for concern among health psychologists is that success rates of programs to persuade smokers to quit have not been encouraging: nearly 80 percent of "quitters" relapse within a year (Cohen et al., 1989; Glasgow & Lichtenstein, 1987; Leventhal & Cleary, 1980). This statistic isn't as depressing as it may first appear when we consider that a person who finally does give up smoking permanently has quit, on the average, five times before. Quitters who can cope with other stressors in their lives are significantly more likely to stay off cigarettes than are those who experience additional stress (Cohen & Lichtenstein, 1990). A good predictor of whether an attempt to stop smoking will be successful is the absence of negative affect–unpleasant feelings, including anxiety and depression (Brandon, 1994). Most smokers who quit permanently do so without any special program of intervention. And, in fact, the total number of adult smokers in the United States and Canada is decreasing, albeit at a rather slow rate (Hugick & Leonard, 1991).

Psychologists have been marginally successful in designing programs aimed at getting people–teenagers in particular–to refrain from smoking in the first place. Given the pressures of national advertising campaigns by the tobacco industry, the effort has not been an easy one. As more and more facilities declare themselves to be "smoke-free environments," the more difficult it is for people to begin or continue smoking. The use of role models and peers to teach specific skills to be used to resist pressures to begin smoking in the first place has been successful, when the focus is on short-term benefits derived from not smoking, such as freedom from coughing and bad breath, and positive factors such as improved appearance (e.g., Murray et al., 1984). Increasing the taxes on, and hence the price of, a pack of cigarettes also provides a negative incentive.

Some hope came late in 1995, when researchers at the Columbia-Presbyterian Medical Center in New York reported that they had found an area of the limbic system in the mid-brain that responds directly to nicotine (McGehee et al., 1995). It seems that nicotine speeds up and intensifies the flow of *glutamate,* a neurotransmitter in the brain. This, in turn, increases the rate of neural firing in the limbic area, which is experienced as an increase in pleasant mood and alertness. If a drug can be found to block this effect, much of the addictive nature of smoking would be negated.

Before You Go On

Why are psychologists concerned about smoking?

Sexually Transmitted Diseases

Sexually transmitted diseases (STDs) are contagious diseases usually passed on through sexual contact. Sexually transmitted diseases affect millions of individuals each year, and for every person we know of with an STD, there may be two to five others with the disease, but in a nonsymptomatic stage, not yet diagnosed. We will begin with a description of the more common STDs, and then consider psychological interventions aimed at controlling the spread of AIDS, the most deadly of the STDs.

Chlamydia is one of the most common STDs in North America. Chlamydia is caused by a bacterial infection. It is usually diagnosed in sexually active persons younger than 35. Its incidence is soaring; about 4 million Americans have the disease. Symptoms include burning urination in both men and women. Men may experience a penile discharge; women may experience a disruption in their menstrual cycle. Left untreated in women, chlamydia can lead to *pelvic inflammatory disease (PID),* which can cause infertility (in about 100,000 women a year). When diagnosed, treatment with an antibiotic, usually *erythromycin,* is generally effective within one week.

⊚⊚⊚⊚ **Thinking Critically** ⊚⊚⊚⊚

What would be the consequences of simply passing a law banning the use, sale, or possession of cigarettes in this country?

sexually transmitted diseases (STDs) *contagious diseases that are usually transmitted through sexual contact*

chlamydia *a common STD caused by a bacterial infection that can lead to PID and infertility in women if untreated*

gonorrhea *an STD caused by a bacterial infection of moist tissues in the genital area*

Gonorrhea is a disease of the young and sexually active. Of the more than 1.8 million cases that will be diagnosed this year, most will be men between the ages of 20 and 24. It is a bacterial infection that affects the moist tissue areas around the genitals. The bacteria that produce the symptoms of gonorrhea can live for only a few seconds outside the human body, so there is little likelihood of contracting the disease from toilet seats, utensils, towels, or drinking fountains. One may be infected with the gonorrhea bacteria and not even know it. This is particularly true for women, most of whom remain relatively free of symptoms. When symptoms do develop, they are like those experienced with chlamydia: frequent, painful urination, vaginal discharges, and a reddening of the genital area. In men, there is a milky discharge from the penis and painful, frequent urination. Treatment for this STD–*penicillin* or *tetracycline*–is usually successful, although drug-resistant strains have been noted.

syphilis *an STD caused by a bacterial infection; the disease may pass through four stages, ultimately resulting in death*

Syphilis is caused by the bacterium *spirochete.* If left untreated, the disease may run its course through four known stages, from relatively simple and painless sores all the way to the infection of other, nonsexual organs, which can lead to death. Ten years ago it was believed that syphilis had become a disease of the past. Then, in the fall of 1990, the Centers for Disease Control (CDC) released figures indicating that since 1985, the number of syphilis cases had skyrocketed. Rates were up 60 percent (132 percent among the black population) to levels not seen since 1949. Nearly 85,000 new cases can be expected this year. Treatment for syphilis is simple, once a diagnosis has been confirmed. Penicillin (or tetracycline) is used, and the prognosis is related to length of infection. The sooner treatment begins, the better the prognosis.

genital herpes (herpes type II) *the most common STD; a skin infection in the form of a rash or blisters in the genital area*

Genital herpes (herpes type II) is a skin disease that affects the genital area, producing small sores and blisters. It is not caused by bacteria, but by a virus that was virtually unknown until the mid–1960s. Now, genital herpes is one of the most common of the STDs. Some estimates place incidence rates as high as 40 million Americans, with 500,000 new cases each year. At the moment, herpes has no cure, although medication can reduce the occasionally painful symptoms. A person with genital herpes is most infectious when the sores and blisters are active and erupting. There may be periods during which the infected person remains symptom free, only to have the reddening and sores recur. Levels of stress in one's life are related to the onset of herpes symptoms (VanderPlate et al., 1988). There are no life-threatening complications of the disease in males, but genital herpes in females increases the risk of contracting cervical cancer. Another complication arises when pregnant women contract genital herpes. The herpes virus can be passed along during childbirth, which can cause considerable damage, even death, to the newborn.

acquired immune deficiency syndrome (AIDS) *a deadly disease caused by a virus (the HIV) that destroys the body's natural immune system; can be transmitted by an interchange of blood or semen*

No other STD has attracted as much public attention as has **acquired immune deficiency syndrome**, or **AIDS**. AIDS was virtually unknown in the United States before 1981. Just 12 years later, over 250,000 cases and more than 160,000 deaths had been reported. Of those deaths, 31,000 were in 1990 alone. Recently, AIDS has risen to be among the most common (fifth) killer of women. In 1982, 18 American women died of AIDS; in 1988, 1,430 died, and by 1993, more than half of the women with AIDS had been infected through heterosexual contact. Globally, the World Health Organization estimates that nearly 20 million men and women will be infected by the year 2000. Just what is AIDS?

AIDS is caused by a virus called the *human immunodeficiency virus,* or *HIV.* The HIV almost always enters the body through sexual contact or by the use of contaminated needles in intravenous (IV) drug use. About 1 infant in 3 born to an HIV-positive mother will also be infected. Each year, about 2,000 babies are born HIV-positive. In infected persons, concentrations of the virus are highest in the blood, semen, and vaginal fluids. An infected person may experience few symptoms other than those usually associated with the common cold. Then the person enters a *carrier state.* He or she may pass the virus on to others, yet remain symptom free. What is not clear is just how many persons infected with the HIV will de-

AIDS is a physical disease with many psychological ramifications. At the time this photo was taken at a rally in Washington, D.C., more than 20,000 names had been added to the "AIDS Quilt," memorializing those who have died from AIDS.

velop AIDS, or how long the process takes. Of those with a diagnosis of AIDS (not just HIV-positive), virtually all will die within four years.

The HIV directly attacks the body's immune system, which normally fights off infections. With a weakened or nonfunctioning immune system, someone with AIDS does not have the resources to defend against other infections that otherwise would not be life-threatening. In other words, patients do not die of AIDS directly, but from other diseases or opportunistic infections (e.g., pneumonia or cancer) against which the body cannot defend.

Whereas other sexually transmitted diseases cause discomfort and pain, AIDS will be fatal. There is no vaccine to prevent it. There is no cure for AIDS, and it is unlikely that one will be discovered soon. The only reasonable way to avoid AIDS is through the monitoring of one's behaviors. Psychological interventions aimed at preventing the spread of AIDS is where we now turn.

Interventions to Decrease the Incidence of AIDS

"Behavior change remains the only means for primary prevention of HIV disease. Psychology should take a leading role in efforts to curtail the epidemic, but has not contributed to HIV prevention at a level proportionate to the urgency of the crisis" (Kelly et al., 1993, p. 1023). Attempts to prevent AIDS, or at the very least, to reduce its spread, have met with mixed results. Successful interventions are multifaceted, involving education, the changing of attitudes, increasing motivation to engage in safe (or safer) sexual practices, and providing people with the "negotiating skills (e.g., to say 'no' or 'please wear a condom')" to avoid high-risk situations in the first place (Brigham, 1991, p. 617). Successful interventions are those that attend to larger issues, such as the environment in which targeted behaviors occur, the culture in which the audience resides, and marketing strategies (Winett, 1995).

Attempts to educate have been reasonably successful. For example, in 1987, the Surgeon General's Office mailed a pamphlet describing AIDS and what could be done to avoid the HIV infection to every household in the United States. The effort was well received and has been credited for helping increase the sales of condoms (Gerbert & Maguire, 1989; Moran et al., 1990). By and large, most Americans *are* aware of AIDS, *do* have a reasonable idea of what causes the disease, and are aware of what can be done to avoid it (e.g., Levine et al., 1993; Sheridan et al., 1990).

On the assumption that many adolescents and adults will not abstain from sex, many experts counsel "safe sex," but there is disagreement on just what safe sex is. In general, the advice seems reasonable. The fewer sexual contacts one has, the less the probability of encountering someone infected with the HIV. The more selective one is in choosing a partner, the less the risk. The use of condoms reduces (does not eliminate) the likelihood of infection. Engaging in sexual behaviors in which there is no exchange of bodily fluids (such as mutual masturbation) also contributes to lower-risk sex (Masters et al., 1987). What is discouraging is that even with considerable knowledge about AIDS, few people, teenagers in particular, seem willing to change their sexual practices (e.g., Klepinger et al., 1993). Many teenagers believe that they simply will not get AIDS, and most do not use condoms (Hansen et al., 1990).

Some programs that go beyond providing information and actively seek to change behaviors have been effective—particularly those aimed at small groups identified as members of "high-risk" populations, such as gay men and IV drug users (e.g., DeJarlais & Friedman, 1988; Kelly et al., 1993; Stall et al., 1988). What works best are long-term, small-group sessions that present information and provide social support for changing high-risk behaviors (Kelly et al., 1989; Sorensen et al., 1991). Although short-term gains (in changing attitudes and behaviors) have been noted, maintaining those gains for the long term has proven more difficult (Kelly et al., 1991). The "enormous challenge posed by HIV infection suggests that multiple approaches will be necessary to have the largest and most lasting effects" (Levine et al., 1993, p. 549).

AIDS *is* a physical disease, but it is a disease with unprecedented psychological complications. Patients diagnosed with HIV, but who have not yet developed AIDS tend to be more depressed and disturbed than those who have developed the full-blown and fatal symptoms of the disease (Chuang et al., 1989). As you might expect, people with a diagnosis of AIDS experience significant levels of stress, depression, anger, anxiety, and denial (Herek & Glunt, 1988; Kelly & St. Lawrence, 1988; Namir et al., 1987). Males with AIDS are almost *7.5 times* more likely to commit suicide than are men in the general population (Coté et al., 1992). Because AIDS can be such a devastating disease, AIDS patients are often shunned—by loved ones and even by health care professionals. In 1987, the American Medical Association issued a statement that it is unethical for a physician to refuse treatment to an AIDS patient. In 1994, the U.S. Public Health Service published a 196-page "clinical practice guideline" on how to diagnose and manage patients in the early stages of infection by HIV. The Health Service's concern was that too many primary care, general practice physicians were unnecessarily referring suspected HIV patients to "specialists." The fear, alienation, and stress experienced by AIDS patients (and their friends and families) are in many ways as painful as the disease itself and often require psychological treatment (Knapp & VandeCreek, 1989).

☻☻☻ Thinking Critically ☻☻☻

Many argue that the incidence of AIDS would be reduced if more people simply practiced abstinence. What can you say for and against such an argument?

Before You Go On

Describe five sexually transmitted diseases.

What roles can psychologists play in the fight against AIDS?

TOPIC 11B SUMMARY

In this Topic we've reviewed some of the activities that concern health psychologists. The basic message is that there are many ways in which psychological factors affect the state of one's physical health. There are at least some personality variables, part of the "Type A behavior pattern," associated with physical disease, coronary heart disease in particular.

A major contention of health psychology is that many physical diseases or illnesses are at least partially caused by psychological or behavioral factors—that the incidence of many, often deadly, diseases can be significantly reduced if people would change some of their behaviors. We looked at two examples of interventions aimed at promoting healthy behaviors: helping people to stop smoking, and helping people change their risky sexual practices in order to avoid STDs. On each front, progress has been made; there are success stories, but there is still a long way to go.

CHAPTER SUMMARY

Topic 11A

What is meant by frustration-induced stress?

Frustration, a stressor, is the blocking or thwarting of goal-directed behaviors. If someone or something in one's environment blocks goal-directed behaviors, we have *environmental* frustration. There are many examples: your car won't start; your pen runs out of ink during an exam; your dog eats your term paper. If the source of the frustration is a characteristic of the person him- or herself, we have *personal* frustration. Examples include someone doing poorly in a physics class because of a poor math background, or someone who agrees to go mountain climbing even though inexperienced and out of shape. */pp. 398–399*

Describe four types of motivational conflict.

Motivational conflicts are stressors. They are situations in which we find ourselves faced with difficult choices to make with regard to our motivated behaviors. In an *approach-approach conflict,* one is faced with two (or more) attractive (positive) goals and must choose between them. In an *avoidance-avoidance conflict,* a choice must be made between or among unpleasant (negative) alternatives. In an *approach-avoidance conflict,* there is but one goal under consideration; in some ways that goal is positive, in others it is negative (it attracts and repels at the same time). In a *multiple approach-avoidance conflict,* one faces a number of alternatives, each of which has its strengths and its weaknesses, and a choice must be made between or among them. */pp. 399–401*

In what ways might life events produce stress?

Many psychologists argue that life events, particularly changes in one's life situation, can act as stressors. The Social Readjustment Rating Scale (SRRS) is one example of an instrument that measures the amount of stress in one's life by having the person indicate recent life-change events. High scores on such scales are associated with an above-average incidence of physical illness. Some psychologists claim that the little hassles of life can be more stressful in their effects than large-scale life events. Socioeconomic status is correlated with stress and health. Life-change events do not have to be negative or unpleasant events to act as stressors. */pp. 402–404*

What does it mean to say that there are individual differences in reactions to stressors?

People often respond differently when presented with the same stressor. What some find merely challenging, others may find overwhelmingly stressful. One's reaction to stressors varies over time: events that do not seem stressful today may be very stressful tomorrow. Some people are particularly resistant to stressors, and have been called "hardy personalities." Such people tend to see difficulties as opportunities, have a sense of being in control of their lives, and are fully engaged in and committed to life. */pp. 404–405*

What are the three stages of Selye's general adaptation syndrome?

According to Hans Selye, a prolonged stress reaction progresses through three stages, collectively referred to as the *general adaptation syndrome.* First there is the mobilization of the sympathetic nervous system of the ANS in the *alarm stage* as the body prepares to cope with the stressor. If the stressor is not removed, the body goes into a *stage of resistance,* in which resources continue to be mobilized but new stressors are difficult to deal with, and in which physical illness becomes more and more likely. If the stressor remains, one may eventually enter an *exhaustion stage,* in which the body's resources become depleted, adaptation breaks down, and serious illness or death may result. */pp. 405–407*

What are some adaptive ways of dealing with stress?

The most effective means of dealing with stress is to deal with the stressors that caused it, and to do so by using the experience to bring about a relatively permanent change in one's behaviors—which is to say to learn new behaviors that will help one cope with stressors. There are two approaches to dealing with stress. One is *problem focused,* and includes such things as identifying the specific stressor causing one's stress, removing or minimizing the stressor, reappraising the situation, inoculating oneself against future stressors, and taking one's time in making difficult decisions. Battling the feelings or affect associated with stress, called *emotion-focused* approaches, includes learning relaxation techniques, engaging in physical exercise, and seeking social support. */pp. 407–410*

What are some maladaptive reactions to stressors?

Maladaptive reactions to stressors are those that interfere with attempts to change one's behaviors as a result of experiencing stress. *Fixation* is the term we use to describe a pattern of behaviors in which a person tries over and over again to deal with stressors, is unsuccessful, but does not try anything new or different. *Aggression* often results from stress, particularly frustration. Although aggression may yield a momentary release of tension, in itself, it usually does not remove the original stressor. *Anxiety* is yet another maladaptive response to stress. This general feeling of apprehension and dread is often the aspect of experienced stress that motivates us to do something about it. */pp. 410–412*

Topic 11B

Summarize the relationship, if any, between the Type A behavior pattern and coronary heart disease.

There is a relationship between some personality variables and physical health; that is, some psychological traits put one at risk for disease. Beginning in the 1950s, evidence accumulated showing a strong positive relationship between a Type A behavior pattern, or TABP (a person who is competitive, achievement-oriented, impatient, easily aroused, often angry or hostile, and who tends to have many projects going at once) and coronary heart disease (blockage of major arteries). The picture, it now seems, is a little less clear as psychologists seek to identify the "active ingredients" of the TABP. Some claim that time urgency, chronic activation, and multiphasia are the main culprits, whereas others have focused on the influence of anger and hostility as best correlated with physical health. */pp. 414–416*

Why are psychologists concerned about smoking?

Of the leading causes of death in this country, most could be reduced by behavioral change. Smoking is a central part of what has been called a "deadly lifestyle." Smoking may account for as many as 400,000 deaths each year. Health psychologists continue to look for effective means of helping people to stop smoking. By and large, efforts have not met with much success. Most smokers who do quit on a permanent basis do so on their own. But overall, the number of adult smokers is decreasing. Current efforts focus on attempts to get children and teens to avoid smoking in the first place. */pp. 417–419*

Describe five sexually transmitted diseases. What roles can psychologists play in the fight against AIDS?

Sexually transmitted diseases (STDs) are common. Among them are (1) *Chlamydia,* a bacterial infection of the genitals that results in painful urination and fluid discharge. Left untreated in women, it may lead to pelvic inflammatory disease (PID) and infertility. (2) *Gonorrhea,* a bacterial infection of the moist tissues around the genitals, is passed on only by sexual contact. If left untreated, its symptoms increase in severity. Penicillin is an effective treatment. (3) *Syphilis,* a bacterial infection, may progress through four stages as symptoms increase in severity. Left untreated, it may result in death. Again, penicillin is an effective treatment. (4) *Genital herpes,* a viral infection that affects tissue around the genitals, is a very common STD and has no known cure. (5) *Acquired immune deficiency syndrome (AIDS)* is a viral (HIV) infection transmitted through the exchange of bodily fluids, usually semen or blood. Once infected, a person may stay symptom-free (but capable of infecting others) in a "carrier state" until full-blown AIDS appears. Virtually all persons with AIDS die within four years.

There is no vaccine or treatment for AIDS. For this very reason, health psychologists have been involved in helping people change their risky sexual behaviors or their IV drug use. Awareness of AIDS and understanding of the disease have increased markedly, but many people at risk—largely sexually active, heterosexual adolescents—have made few changes in their sexual practices. Some groups at risk–largely gay men and IV drug users–have made changes. Psychologists are also involved in helping AIDS sufferers (and their friends and families) deal with the emotionally charged nature of the disease. /*pp. 419–422*

Name That Stressor

Coping effectively with the stress in one's life is usually a matter of coping with stressors. The text identifies several potential stressors:

a. environmental frustration
b. personal frustration
c. approach-approach conflicts
d. avoidance-avoidance conflicts
e. approach-avoidance conflicts
f. multiple approach-avoidance conflicts
g. life events and hassles

For each of the following situations, identify the type of stressor involved. (Suggested answers can be found on p. 574.)

_____ 1. Just as Tamara is about to leave, her shoe lace breaks, and another cannot be found.

_____ 2. Anthony wants to take a class in abnormal psychology and he wants to take a beginning class in astronomy. Unfortunately, the only available sections of these classes are both scheduled for Tuesdays and Thursdays at 10:00 A.M.

_____ 3. Brett gets cut from the roster of his Little League team.

_____ 4. Arden has three final exams scheduled for the same day.

_____ 5. After making three attempts at a required statistics course, Kayle's advisor won't sign his registration card as Kayle tries for the fourth time.

_____ 6. The party has been over for nearly an hour. Angela will have to accept a ride with Ryan, whom she really dislikes, or walk home.

_____ 7. Colleena can't decide if she should live at home, save money, and go to the local junior college, or borrow money now and leave home for State U.

_____ 8. As Jared is sitting in the library studying his psychology, Nicole comes up and asks him to join the Student Activities Board. On the one hand, Jared really wants to be a member of the SAB, but on the other hand, he knows that it will require a lot of extra time.

_____ 9. Sylvia got a gift certificate from the local CD-video store. The problem is that Sylvia wants more CDs than the certificate will pay for.

_____ 10. Yolanda was planning on studying at the library this afternoon, but has just discovered that the building has been evacuated and closed because of a bomb scare.

_____ 11. With her baccalaureate degree in hand, Natessa has scheduled her first job interview for tomorrow morning.

_____ 12. Because his parents were recently divorced, Brad is dreading the up-coming holiday vacation.

OUTLINE

When I was a graduate student, I took a course on psychological testing. One of the requirements of this class was to administer tests at various agencies in the surrounding area. I was excited, and more than a little nervous about the prospect of giving psychological tests to patients at a nearby psychiatric institution.

I need to tell you a bit about this institution and the patients it housed. It was a state hospital, built in the late 1800s, and badly in need of repair. Most of the patients there were elderly and had spent the greater part of their adult lives in one state institution or another. These were the hard core, chronically mentally ill.

I was surprised by the appearance of my first patient. He seemed to me very well groomed, reasonably well dressed, and generally quite pleasant. His chart said he was 61 years old, but he looked younger. As I began the testing, it was clear that my "subject" was much more at ease than I was. He was more familiar with the tests I was trying to administer than I.

My initial surprise at the appearance of my patient soon turned to real concern. He seemed to be answering every test item in a perfectly normal way. His responses to each of my questions struck me as reasonable, sensible, and in no

The Psychological Disorders

way "disordered." In response to my standard interview question, "Why are you here?" my subject said, "Because I'm crazy I guess. I can't think of any other reason." "Oh no," I thought, "you're not crazy. Someone's made an awful mistake! You shouldn't be here in this terrible place."

I ended the testing session a little early and went running off to find the clinical director of the hospital floor I was on. As soon as I found him, I began my protest: "A terrible error has been made. My patient is as sane as the day is long. There's absolutely nothing wrong with him! We've got to get him out of here!"

The clinical director nodded, and muttered something like "Sure, sure; we'll look into it." I was concerned that nothing was going to be done to help this man I had genuinely gotten to like in the course of our three-hour testing session.

A week later I returned to the same floor to test another patient. The clinical director met me at the head of the stairs and said he had something he wanted to show me. We walked down a hallway, and he asked me to look in the small window in the door of one of the patient's rooms. There was my testing subject from the week before. He was sitting on the hard tile floor, naked, staring off into space, attending to nothing at all in the world around him, and muttering strange guttural sounds.

One point of this story is that even the most severely disordered people are not always in a state of total disorder. One of the painful realities of the psychological disorders is that people with psychological disorders usually know there is a problem; that things just aren't right.

TOPIC 12A Anxiety, Somatoform, Dissociative, and Personality Disorders

This chapter begins our discussion of psychological disorders, a discussion that will be continued in the next chapter, in which we consider techniques of treatment, or therapy. Psychological disorders have an impact on us all. I will spare you a lengthy recitation of the statistics on incidence and prevalence here. For now, we need only note that as you read this sentence, approximately 28 percent of U.S. adults, nearly 50 million men and women, are suffering from some sort of psychological disorder. Fewer than one-third of these people are seeking help (National Institute of Mental Health, 1984, 1993; Offord et al., 1987). In their lifetimes, nearly half of all Americans will suffer from a psychological disorder (Kessler et al., 1994). Statistics such as these are astounding and frightening; they are also impersonal. It is difficult to conceptualize what it really means to say that tens of millions of people are suffering from psychological disorders. What we can say is that it is unlikely any of us can be exempt from personally experiencing, or having someone close to us experience, the pain and suffering of a psychological disorder.

Just What *Is* "Abnormal"?

abnormal *in psychology: maladaptive cognitions, affect, or behaviors at odds with social expectations that result in stress or discomfort*

We all have a basic idea of what is meant by such terms as *abnormal, mental illness,* or *psychological disorder.* The more we think about abnormality, however, the more difficult it becomes to define. The concept of abnormal as it is used in psychology is not a simple one. We'll use this definition: **Abnormal** refers to maladaptive cognitions, affect, and/or behaviors that are at odds with social expectations and result in distress or discomfort. That is lengthy, but to be complete, our definition must include each of these aspects.

Literally, abnormal means "not of the norm" or "not average." Therefore, behaviors or mental processes that are rare could be considered abnormal; in a literal sense, of course, they are. The problem with this statistical approach is that it would categorize the behaviors of Michael Jordan, Barbara Walters, Dave Letterman, and Meg Ryan as abnormal. Statistically, they *are* abnormal. There are very few others who do what these people do. But, as far as we know, none of these people has a psychological disorder. Psychological disorders are not determined solely by the statistical averages.

The reactions of people with psychological disorders are *maladaptive.* This is a critical part of our definition. Thoughts, feelings, and behaviors are such that the person does not function as well as he or she could without the disorder. To be different, or to be strange, does not in itself mean that someone has a psychological disorder. There must be some impairment, some self-defeating interference with one's growth and functioning (Carson & Butcher, 1992, p. 8).

Another observation reflected in our definition is that abnormality may show itself in a number of ways. A person with a psychological disorder may experience abnormal *affect,* engage in abnormal *behaviors,* have abnormal *cognitions,* or any combination of these. Once again we see our *ABCs* from Chapter 1.

Any definition of psychological abnormality should acknowledge *social and/or cultural expectations.* What may clearly be abnormal and disordered in one culture may be viewed as quite normal or commonplace in another. In some cultures, loud crying and wailing at the funeral of a total stranger is considered strange or deviant; in others, it is common and expected. In some cultures, to claim you have been communicating with dead ancestors would be taken as a sign of mental disturbance; in others, it would be treated as a great gift. What may at first seem like extreme examples are the disorders listed in Figure 12.1. These sets of symptoms

What is considered abnormal or deviant in one culture may be viewed as quite normal and acceptable in another. One simple example is how people of various cultures dress.

(and twenty others) are listed in the *DSM-IV* as patterns of behavior indicative of abnormality in their culture of origin and that "may be encountered in clinical practice in North America" (p. 845). Even in your own culture, behaviors that are appropriate, or at least tolerated, in one situation, say a party, may be judged as inappropriate in another context, say a religious service.

One additional issue needs to be addressed: psychological disorders involve *distress or discomfort.* People we consider abnormal are suffering or are the source of suffering in others. Psychological disorders cause emotional distress, and individuals with such disorders are often the source of distress and discomfort to others—friends and family who care and worry about them.

Figure 12.1
Culture Specific Syndromes

(Forms of disorders that have no counterpart in Western cultures)

Syndrome	Culture	Symptoms
amok	Malaysian	acute indiscriminate homicidal mania
koro	Chinese S.E. Asian	fear of retraction of penis into abdomen with the belief that this will lead to death
latah	S.E. Asian	startle-induced disorganization, hypersuggestibility, automatic obedience
piblokto	Inuit (Eskimo)	attacks of screaming, crying, and running naked through the snow
windigo	Canadian Indians	delusions of being possessed by a cannibalistic monster (Windigo), attacks of agitated depression, oral sadistic fears and impulses

From The American Psychiatric Association's *Psychiatric Glossary,* 1984, p. 25 (Published and distributed by the American Psychiatric Press, Inc.; 1400 K Street, Washington, D.C., and the *DSM-IV,* 1994, pp. 843–851.

As complex as it is, I hope you can see that there is a reason for each point in our definition of abnormal: behaviors or mental processes that are maladaptive, at odds with social expectations, and resulting in distress or discomfort.

Before You Go On

How do we define psychological abnormality?

Classifying Abnormal Reactions—The DSM

One way of dealing with the broad concept of psychological abnormality is to consider each psychological disorder separately, in terms of how that disorder is to be diagnosed. **Diagnosis** is the act of recognizing a disorder on the basis of specified symptoms. Once individual disorders have been identified, it would be helpful if they were organized in a systematic way.

diagnosis *the act of recognizing a disorder on the basis of the presence of particular symptoms*

Systems of classification are common in science and are not new to psychology. In 1883, Emil Kraepelin published the first classification scheme for what he called the "mental disturbances." His system was based on the idea that each disorder had its own collection of symptoms (a syndrome) and its own biological cause.

In 1952, the American Psychiatric Association published its system for classifying psychological disorders, the *Diagnostic and Statistical Manual of Mental Disorders,* which became known as the *DSM.* In 1987, a revised version of the third edition, the *DSM-III-R,* was published. Even before the *DSM-III-R* was available, work began on its revision, the *DSM-IV,* published in 1994.

DSM-IV *the fourth edition of the Diagnostic and Statistical Manual of Mental Disorders; the most common system for classifying psychological disorders*

The *DSM-IV* is the system of classification most widely used in all mental health fields. I've used the *DSM-IV* as a major source of information for this chapter. Figure 12.2 presents a partial list of the disorders contained in the *DSM-IV.* The *DSM-IV* lists 297 different diagnostic categories, compared to 265 in the *DSM-III,* 182 in the *DSM-II,* and only 106 in the original *Diagnostic and Statistical Manual* (Clark et al., 1995).

The *DSM-IV* is more than just an organized list of disorders in terms of symptoms. The *DSM-IV* recommends that a diagnosis of a disorder be sensitive to (1) any physical illnesses or ailments present, (2) the amount of stress the individual has recently been under, and (3) the level of adaptive functioning the individual has managed over the past three years. Except for cases for which there are known biological factors, the manual attempts to avoid any reference to the **etiology**, or causes, of disorders. It is meant to be objective, based on research evidence, describe as completely as possible, and theorize as little as possible. The *DSM-IV* also contains more material and reference to ethnic and cultural issues than did its predecessors, thanks largely to a 3-year effort of the "Group on Culture and Diagnosis," sponsored by the National Institute of Mental Health (DeAngelis, 1994).

etiology *the cause or predisposing factors of a disorder*

There are several advantages of having a classification system for psychological disorders. The major advantage, of course, is communication. If I mean one thing when I use the term *phobia* and you mean something else, we cannot hold a very reasonable conversation about your patient's problem. If we both agreed on the *DSM-IV*'s definition, at least we'd be using the term in the same way. A related advantage is that a reliable way of classifying disorders allows one to think in terms of how to prescribe appropriate treatment or therapy most effectively. I cannot leave the impression that there is only one treatment for each of the diagnostic categories of the *DSM-IV.* As we'll see in Chapter 13, on treatment and therapy, this is far from the case, but it does make sense that we be able to classify disorders before we treat them. At the same time, classification can cause difficulties.

Problems with Classification and Labeling

Assigning labels to people may be useful for purposes of communication, but it can also be dehumanizing. It is occasionally difficult to remember that Sally Jane is a

Figure 12.2
A Sample of Psychological Disorders Listed in the *DSM-IV*

Types of disorder	Subtypes (examples)
Disorders usually first diagnosed in infancy, childhood, or adolescence	a. Mental retardation b. Learning disorders c. Autistic disorder
Delirium, dementia, amnestic and other cognitive disorders	a. Dementia of the Alzheimer's type
Substance-related disorders	a. Alcohol use disorders b. Amphetamine use disorders c. Cocaine use disorders d. Hallucinogen disorders
Schizophrenia and other psychotic disorders	a. Schizophrenia
Mood disorders	a. Depressive disorders b. Dysthymic disorder c. Bipolar disorder
Anxiety disorders	a. Panic disorder b. Specific phobia c. Obsessive-compulsive disorder d. Posttraumatic stress disorder e. Generalized anxiety disorder
Somatoform disorders	a. Conversion disorder b. Hypochondriasis
Dissociative disorders	a. Dissociative amnesia b. Dissociative fugue c. Dissociative identity disorder
Eating disorders	a. Anorexia nervosa b. Bulimia
Personality disorders	a. Paranoid personality disorder b. Schizoid personality disorder c. Antisocial personality disorder d. Histrionic personality disorder e. Narcissistic personality disorder

complex and complicated human being with a range of feelings, thoughts, and behaviors, not just a "paranoid schizophrenic." In response to this concern, the *DSM-IV* refers only to disordered behaviors and to patterns of behaviors, not to disordered people. That is, it refers to paranoid reactions, not to individuals who are paranoid; to persons with anxiety, not anxious persons.

A second problem inherent in classification and labeling is that it is so easy to fall into the habit of believing that labels *explain,* when clearly they don't. Diagnosing and labeling a pattern of behaviors does not explain those behaviors. It does not tell us why such a pattern of behaviors developed or what we can or should do about them now.

Third, labels can create unfortunate and lasting stigmas of negative attitudes about people. To learn that someone is "psychologically disordered" or is "mentally ill" may carry with it a wide range of negative reactions, and the label often sticks long after the disorder has been treated and the symptoms are gone.

Another consequence of diagnostic labeling is that the brunt of the problem tends to fall on the individual. It is the individual who has a psychological disorder, not the group, the family, or the society of which the person is a part. Classification schemes focus on the person and not on the context in which the person lives

(Gorenstein, 1984; Szasz, 1960, 1982). This issue is complex and has been debated within psychology for many years. Here's an example of this difficulty: Mary Beth, a third-grader, is referred to the school psychologist because she is withdrawn, often appears to be on the verge of tears, will not talk about her home life, and is doing poorly in her academic work. Without going into the particulars, doesn't it seem misguided to focus all of our attention on Mary Beth, disregarding her family or the demands of the school, when we try to diagnose her problems? Is it proper to diagnose and label the person without attending to the larger social networks of which that person is a part?

comorbidity *the co-occurrence of two or more disorders in the same individual*

Yet another potential problem is **comorbidity**—the occurrence of two or more disorders in the same individual (Clark et al., 1995). Comorbidity has been described as "the premier challenge facing mental health professionals in the 1990s" (Kendall & Clarkin, 1992, p. 833). The 1994 National Comorbidity Survey found that psychological disorders were much more common than previously believed. This study suggested that of the people who experience a disorder in their lifetime, most (79 percent) will have two or more disorders. Although 52 percent of those surveyed never had a psychological disorder, 14 percent had a history of three or more disorders (Kessler et al., 1994). The problem is particularly acute in high-risk samples. A study of one group of incest victims showed an average of nearly two different diagnoses per person (Pribor & Dinwiddie, 1992). A study of combat veterans found an average of 3.1 disorders per person in their sample (Mellman et al., 1992), and an average of 4.0 current disorders per person was found in a sample of suicidal patients (Rudd et al., 1993).

On "Insanity"

In common practice, the terms *psychological disorder, mental disorder,* and *behavior disorder* are often used interchangeably. There is one term, however, with which we need to exercise particular care, and that is *insanity*. Insanity is not a psychological term. It is a legal term. It relates to problems with psychological functioning, but in a restricted sense. Definitions of **insanity** vary from state to state, but to be judged insane usually requires evidence that a person did not know or fully understand the consequences of his or her actions at a given time, could not discern the difference between right and wrong, and was unable to exercise control over his or her actions.

insanity *a legal term for diminished capacity, inability to tell right from wrong, and inability to exercise control over one's actions*

A related issue has to do with whether a person is in enough control of his or her mental and intellectual functions to understand courtroom procedures and aid in his or her own defense. If one is not, one may be ruled "not competent" to stand trial for his or her actions, whatever those actions may have been.

A Caution

For the remainder of this chapter, we will consider a variety of psychological disorders. As we do so, there are several important points you need to keep in mind.

1. "Abnormal" and "normal" are not two distinct categories. They may be thought of as end points on some dimension we can use to describe people, but there is a large gray area between the two in which distinctions get fuzzy.

2. Abnormal does not mean dangerous. True, some people diagnosed as having mental disorders *may* cause harm to themselves or to others, but most people with psychological disorders are not dangerous at all. Even among persons who have been in jail for violent crimes, those with psychological disorders have no more subsequent arrests than do persons without disorders (Teplin et al., 1994).

3. Abnormal does not mean bad. People diagnosed with psychological disorders are not "bad" people, or weak people, in any evaluative sense. They may have

Insanity is not a psychological concept so much as it is a legal term. Defense attorneys considered entering an insanity plea for Susan Smith, who admitted to killing her two young sons by strapping them into their car seats and directing her car into a pond.

done bad things, and bad things may have happened to them, but it is certainly not in psychology's tradition to make moral judgments about good and bad.

4. Most of our depictions of psychological disorders will be made in terms of extreme and obvious cases. Psychological disorders, like physical disorders, may occur in mild or moderate forms. As we have seen repeatedly, no two people are exactly alike; there are individual differences in psychological functioning. Such is also the case here. No two people, even with the same diagnosis of a psychological disorder, will be exactly alike in all regards. Remember the introductory story—no one will be disordered to the same degree 24 hours a day, every day.

Unless I specify otherwise, diagnostic criteria for the disorders discussed below are taken from the *DSM-IV*, and statistics on the prevalence of the disorders are from the National Institute of Mental Health (Freedman, 1984) or the National Comorbidity Survey (Kessler et al., 1994).

Before You Go On

Cite advantages and disadvantages of classifying psychological disorders.

Anxiety Disorders

In Topic 11A we defined **anxiety** as a feeling of general apprehension or dread accompanied by predictable physiological changes: increased muscle tension; shallow, rapid breathing; cessation of digestion; increased perspiration; and drying of the mouth. Thus, anxiety involves two levels of reaction: subjective feelings (e.g., fear or dread) and physiological responses (e.g., rapid breathing). The major symptom of *anxiety disorders* is felt anxiety, often coupled with "avoidance behavior," or attempts to resist or avoid any situation that seems to produce anxiety.

⊚⊚⊚ **Thinking Critically** ⊚⊚⊚

Why do you think that someone who is willing to tell us all about his or her physical illness (e.g. the gory details of a recent surgery) will probably be unwilling to share his or her experiences with psychological disorders?

anxiety *a general feeling of apprehension or dread accompanied by predictable physiological changes*

What Do People Believe About Psychological Disorders?

There are misconceptions about many different areas in psychology, but none more so than in abnormal psychology. This simple 10-item, true-false survey will give you an idea of some of the mistaken ideas that many people have about psychological disorders. It might be interesting to compare the responses of persons who have had a psychology class with the responses of those who have not.

T F   1. Most violent crimes are committed by persons who are mentally ill.

T F   2. People with psychological disorders always behave in some bizarre way.

T F   3. This week, more people will be diagnosed with psychological disorders than with cancer and cardiovascular disease combined.

T F   4. Except in rare cases, a clear distinction can be drawn between "normal" and "abnormal" behaviors.

T F   5. Geniuses are particularly prone to emotional disorders.

T F   6. Psychological disorders are more prevalent in highly technical, advanced societies.

T F   7. Most mental disorders are incurable.

T F   8. People with mental illness hardly ever realize that they are ill.

T F   9. Mental illness is about as common among children and adolescents as it is among adults.

T F 10. If a person is diagnosed with one psychological disorder he or she almost certainly will not have another, different disorder as well.

As you know, items number 3, 6, and 9 are true, all the others are false.

Anxiety disorders are the most common of all the psychological disorders. The National Institute of Mental Health reports high rates: within a six-month period, from 7 to 15 percent of the population can be diagnosed with one or more of the several anxiety diagnoses. The National Comorbidity Survey claims that 17 percent of its sample had some sort of anxiety disorder in the year before the survey was taken, and 25 percent had an anxiety disorder at some time in their lives. Anxiety disorders are two to three times more likely to be diagnosed in women than in men (Kessler et al., 1994; Roth & Argyle, 1988). Percentages of this sort do not convey the enormity of the problem. We're talking about real people here—people like you and me. In this section, we will consider five anxiety disorders: generalized anxiety disorder, panic disorder, phobic disorders, obsessive-compulsive disorder, and post-traumatic stress disorder.

Generalized Anxiety Disorder

generalized anxiety disorder
persistent, chronic, and distressingly high levels of unattributable and uncontrollable anxiety or worry

The major symptom of **generalized anxiety disorder** is distressing, felt anxiety. With this disorder we find unrealistic, excessive, persistent worry. People with generalized anxiety disorder report that the anxiety they experience causes substantial interference with their lives and that they need a significant dosage of medications to control their symptoms (Wittchen et al., 1994). The *DSM-IV* adds the criterion that people with this disorder find it difficult to control worry or anxiety.

The experienced anxiety may be very intense, but it is also diffuse, meaning that it is not brought on by anything specific in the person's environment; it just seems to come and go (or come and stay) without reason or warning. People with this disorder are usually in a state of uneasiness and seldom have any clear insight or ideas about what exactly is causing their anxiety. The self-reports of persons with generalized anxiety disorder show that their major concerns are an inability to relax, tenseness, difficulty concentrating, feeling frightened, being afraid of losing control, and so on (Beck & Emery, 1985). Clearly, this is a distressing and disruptive disorder that brings with it considerable pain. Although people with this disorder can often continue to function in social situations and on the job, they may be particularly prone to drug and alcohol abuse—the comorbidity problem I alluded to earlier (Brown & Barlow, 1992; Wittchen et al., 1994).

Before You Go On

Describe the symptoms of generalized anxiety disorder.

Panic Disorder

In the generalized anxiety disorder, the experience of felt anxiety may be characterized as *chronic,* implying that the anxiety is always present, albeit sometimes more so than at other times. For a person suffering from **panic disorder**, the major symptom is more *acute*—a recurrent, unpredictable, unprovoked onset of sudden, intense anxiety, or a "panic attack." These attacks may last for a few seconds or for hours. Significantly, there is no one particular stimulus to bring it on. The panic attack is unexpected. It just happens. The *DSM-IV* points out that panic attacks do occur in conjunction with other disorders—not just panic disorders. With panic disorder, however, there is a recurrent pattern of attacks and a building worry about future attacks.

panic disorder *a disorder in which anxiety attacks suddenly and unpredictably; there may be periods free from anxiety*

At some time in their lives, between 1.5 and 3.5 percent of the population will experience panic disorder. (That doesn't sound very significant until we realize that that's 4 to 9 million people!) The age of onset for this disorder is usually between adolescence and the mid-twenties (Hayward et al., 1992; Markowitz et al., 1989). Initial panic attacks are often associated with stress, particularly from the loss of an important relationship (Ballenger, 1989). A complication of panic disorder is that it can be accompanied by feelings of depression—another example of comorbidity (Noyes et al., 1990). This may be why the rate of suicide and suicide attempts is so high for persons with this diagnosis (20 percent), which is higher than that for persons diagnosed with depression alone (15 percent) (Johnson et al., 1990; Weissman et al., 1989).

Before You Go On

What is a panic disorder?

Phobic Disorders

The essential feature of **phobic disorders** (or phobias) is a persistent and excessive fear of some object, activity, or situation that consistently leads a person to avoid that object, activity, or situation. Implied in this definition is the notion that the fear is intense enough to be disruptive. Also implied is the fact that there is no real or significant threat involved in the stimulus that gives rise to a phobia; that is, the fear is unreasonable, exaggerated, or inappropriate.

phobic disorder *an intense, irrational fear that leads a person to avoid the feared object, activity, or situation*

Many things are life-threatening or downright frightening. For example, if you were driving down a rather steep hill and suddenly realized the brakes on your car were not working, you would be likely to feel an intense reaction of fear. Such a reaction would not be phobic because it is not *irrational.* Similarly, there are few of us who really enjoy the company of bees. Just because we don't like bees and would rather they not be around does not qualify us as having a phobic disorder. What is missing here is *intensity* of response. People who do have a phobic reaction to bees (called *mellissaphobia*) may refuse to leave the house in the summer for fear of encountering a bee and may become genuinely anxious at the buzzing sound of any insect, fearing it to be a bee. People with this disorder may become uncomfortable simply reading a paragraph, such as this one, about bees.

A job as a steel worker, laboring high above the city, would be out of the question for someone suffering from acrophobia, the fear of high places. An intense irrational fear of public speaking is quite common among college students.

social phobia *a significant, persistent fear of social or performance situations in which one may be embarrassed*

There are many phobias. The two main categories of phobic disorder are *specific phobias* and *social phobias.* The former involve the fear of (a) animals; (b) the physical environment (storms, heights, water, etc.); (c) blood, injection, or injury; or (d) a specific situation (tunnels, elevators, airplanes, etc.). Of these, the most common are phobias that involve animals (Costello, 1982). **Social phobias** are significant and persistent fears of social or performance situations in which embarrassment may occur. Fears of eating in public, of public speaking, or of being in large crowds qualify as social phobias.

prognosis *the prediction of the future course of an illness or disorder*

Within 1 year, about 15 percent of the population experiences some type of phobic disorder. In any 6-month period, social phobias adversely affect over 10 percent of the population (Davidson et al., 1994). In some cases, a person with a phobia can avoid the source of his or her fear and, as a result, does not seek treatment. Sometimes, avoiding the source of one's phobia is impossible. The **prognosis** (the prediction of the future course of a disorder) is good for phobic disorders. That is, therapy for persons with a phobia is likely to be successful.

agoraphobia *a phobic fear of being in public places from which escape might be difficult*

A commonly treated phobic disorder is **agoraphobia**, which literally means "fear of open places." This diagnosis is for people with an exaggerated fear of venturing forth into the world alone. People with this disorder avoid crowds, streets, stores, and the like. They establish a safe base for themselves and may, in extreme cases, refuse to leave it altogether. It is common to find agoraphobia as an associated complication of panic disorder (comorbidity again). This is not unreasonable, is it? After experiencing several panic attacks—brought on by no particular stimulus, remember—one finds it more and more difficult to venture out in the world, for fear of having yet another panic attack in some public place.

> *Before You Go On*
>
> **What characterizes a phobic disorder?**

ⓔⓔⓔⓔ **Thinking Critically** ⓔⓔⓔⓔ

Phobias are characterized as an intense, irrational fear. What is the difference, if any, between "fear" and "anxiety"?

Obsessive-Compulsive Disorder (OCD)

The **obsessive-compulsive disorder (OCD)** is an anxiety disorder characterized by a pattern of recurrent obsessions and compulsions. **Obsessions** are ideas or thoughts that involuntarily and constantly intrude into awareness. Generally speaking, obsessions are pointless, or groundless thoughts, most commonly of violence, disease, danger, or doubt (Swedo et al., 1989a). Many of us have experienced mild, obsessivelike thoughts. Worrying throughout the first few days of a vacation if you really did turn off the stove would be an example. To qualify as part of OCD, obsessions must be disruptive; they must interfere with normal functioning. They are also time consuming and are the source of anxiety and distress.

Compulsions are constantly intruding, repetitive behaviors. The most commonly reported compulsions are hand washing, grooming, and counting or checking behaviors, such as checking over and over again to be sure that the door is really locked (Swedo et al., 1989a). Have you ever checked an answer sheet to see that you've really answered all of the questions and then checked it again, and again, and again? To do so is a compulsive sort of response. It serves no real purpose, and it provides no real sense of satisfaction, although it is done very conscientiously in an attempt to reduce anxiety or stress. The people with OCD recognize that their behaviors serve no useful purpose, but cannot stop them. It is as if such a person engages in these compulsive behaviors to prevent some other (even more anxiety-producing) behaviors from taking place.

In many cases, an obsession or compulsion can exert an enormous influence on a person's life. For example, consider the case of a happily married accountant, the father of three. For reasons he cannot explain, he has become obsessed with the fear of contracting AIDS. There is no reason for him to be concerned: his sexual activities are entirely monogamous; he has never used drugs; he has never had a blood transfusion. Still, he is overwhelmed with the idea that he will contract this deadly disease. We find ritualized, compulsive behaviors associated with his obsessive thoughts: he washes his hands vigorously at every opportunity and becomes anxious if he cannot change his clothes at least three times a day (all in his effort to avoid contact with the dreaded AIDS virus). You can imagine how distressing this must be, and you can also appreciate that OCD involves more than checking responses on an answer sheet or concern over a stove you may not have turned off. Figure 12.3 lists some of the common obsessions and ritualized compulsions found in persons with OCD.

Notice that we are using *compulsive* in an altogether different way when we refer to someone being a compulsive gambler, a compulsive eater, or a compulsive practical joker. What's different about the use of the term in such cases is that although the person engages in habitual patterns of behavior, he or she gains pleasure from doing so. The compulsive gambler enjoys gambling; the compulsive eater loves to eat. Such people may not enjoy the ultimate, long-term consequences of their actions, but they feel little discomfort about the behaviors themselves. To be diagnosed as compulsive in the context of an anxiety disorder requires that behaviors be recognized as senseless and not be the source of pleasure.

Obsessive-compulsive disorder is much more common than once believed. It afflicts nearly 1 of every 200 teenagers (OCD is commonly diagnosed in childhood

obsessive-compulsive disorder (OCD) *a combination of constantly intruding thoughts and constantly intruding behaviors*

obsessions *ideas or thoughts that involuntarily and constantly intrude into awareness*

compulsions *constantly intruding, repetitive, and essentially involuntary behaviors*

Figure 12.3
Common Obsessions and Compulsions in OCD

Common obsessions
Fear of getting dirty, contaminated, or infected by people or things in the environment
Fear of AIDS
Disgust over body wastes or secretions
Concern that a task or assignment has been done poorly or incorrectly, even when the person knows this is not the case
Extreme concern with order, symmetry, or exactness
Fear of thinking evil or sinful thoughts that go against one's religion
Fear of losing important things that will be needed later
Recurring thoughts about harming or killing others or oneself
Fear of comitting a crime, such as theft
Recurring thoughts or images of a sexual nature
Extreme concern with certain sounds, images, words, or numbers
Fear of blurting out obscenities or insulting others
Fear that some disaster will occur

Common compulsive rituals
Cleaning and grooming behaviors such as washing hands, showering, and brushing teeth in particular ways
Touching certain objects in a specific way
Repeatedly cleaning items in the house
Ordering or arranging things in a certain way
Checking locks, electrical outlets, light switches, and the like repeatedly
Repeatedly putting clothes on, then taking them off
Repeating certain actions, such as going through a doorway
Counting over and over again to a certain number
Hoarding items such as old newspapers, mail, and containers
Checking to see that no one has been hurt or killed, or no other disaster has occurred because of something the person with OCD has done
Constantly seeking approval (especially children)

From CIBA-GEIGY, 1991, pp. 6–7.

or adolescence), and as many as 5 million Americans in total (CIBA-GEIGY, 1991; Flament et al., 1988). It is a disorder with a high rate of comorbidity, often found in conjunction with another disorder (Galbaud du Fort et al., 1993).

Research suggests that obsessive-compulsive disorder has a biological basis. The most likely candidate for the source of the problem is the frontal lobes, particularly the pathways used for communication between the frontal lobes and the basal ganglia. The neurotransmitter *serotonin* is also directly implicated (Hollander et al., 1992; Swedo et al., 1989b). Support for the biological basis of OCD comes from the observation that drug treatment (using antidepressant medications) is often successful in eliminating many of the symptoms of OCD (Flament et al., 1985). Unfortunately, the prognosis for OCD is generally not very good. One study found that even after as many as seven years of treatment, only 6 percent of a sample of patients with obsessive-compulsive disorder could be considered totally symptom-free, and 43 percent still met the diagnostic criteria for the disorder (Leonard et al., 1993).

Before You Go On

What characterizes the obsessive-compulsive disorder?

Posttraumatic Stress Disorder (PTSD)

An anxiety disorder that has been the subject of much public discussion over the past decade is **posttraumatic stress disorder (PTSD)**. This disorder involves distressing symptoms that arise some time *after* the experience of a highly traumatic event. *Trauma* is defined by the *DSM-IV* as one that meets two criteria: (1) the person has experienced, witnessed, or been confronted with an event that involves actual or threatened death or serious injury, and (2) the person's response involves intense fear, helplessness, or horror. There are three clusters of symptoms that further define PTSD: (1) *reexperiencing* the traumatic event (e.g., in flashbacks or nightmares), (2) *avoidance* of any possible reminders of the event (including people who were there), and (3) *increased arousal* that was not present before the trauma (e.g., irritability, insomnia, difficulty concentrating).

The traumatic events that trigger this disorder are many, ranging from natural disasters (e.g., floods or hurricanes), to life-threatening situations (e.g., kidnapping, rape, assault, or combat), to the loss of property (e.g., the house burns down; the car is stolen). Nearly 1.7 million veterans—nearly half of all who served in Southeast Asia—have suffered from PTSD at some time since discharge from military service (True et al., 1993).

Posttraumatic stress disorder was not recognized as a distinct diagnostic category of anxiety disorder until 1980. Defining PTSD has made it possible to identify those who suffer from it, who, according to current estimates, constitute about 2 percent of the population (Robb-Nicholson, 1995). Of those who experience a severe trauma, nearly 15 percent will experience the symptoms of posttraumatic stress disorder (Helzer et al., 1987). Within two weeks, 94 percent of rape victims and 76 percent of female victims of physical assault evidence the symptoms of PTSD. Nine weeks later, comparable figures are 47 percent and 22 percent, respectively (Foa & Riggs, 1995; Resnick et al., 1993; Rothbaum et al., 1992).

posttraumatic stress disorder (PTSD) *an anxiety disorder in which disruptive recollections, distressing dreams, flashbacks, and felt anxiety occur well after the experience of a traumatic event*

Posttraumatic stress disorder (PTSD) can be expected in some survivors of trauma or catastrophe. Here we see some of the families of the victims of the bombing of the federal building in Oklahoma City in April 1995.

We often find comorbidity with PTSD. It is commonly associated with alcohol and substance abuse or depression. In fact, the prognosis for posttraumatic stress disorder is related to the extent to which there are comorbid disorders (e.g., alcoholism) attending it, the extent to which the patient experienced psychological problems before the traumatic event, and the extent to which social support is available (Jordan et al., 1992). Some recent research suggests that there are genetic factors that may predispose someone to develop symptoms of the disorder (Charney et al., 1993; True et al., 1993).

Before You Go On

Describe the symptoms of posttraumatic stress disorder.

Somatoform Disorders

somatoform disorders
psychological disorders reflecting physical or bodily symptoms or complaints for which there is no known physical cause

Soma means "body." Hence, all of the **somatoform disorders** in some way involve physical, bodily symptoms or complaints. What makes these *psychological* disorders is that there is no known medical or biological cause for the symptoms. We'll consider just two somatoform disorders: one common, *hypochondriasis,* and the other rare but very dramatic, *conversion disorder.*

Hypochondriasis

hypochondriasis *a mental disorder involving the fear of developing some serious disease or medical illness*

Hypochondriasis is the diagnosis for someone preoccupied with the fear of having or developing a serious disease. Persons with this disorder are unusually aware of every ache and pain. They often read popular magazines devoted to health issues, and feel free to diagnose their own ailments. The catch is that they have no medical disorder or disease. Nonetheless, they constantly seek medical attention and will not be convinced of their good health despite the best of medical opinion and reassurance.

A man with occasional chest pains, for example, diagnoses his own condition as lung cancer. Even after many physicians reassure him that his lungs are perfectly fine and that he has no signs of lung cancer, the man's fears are not put to rest. "They are just trying to make me feel better by not telling me, but they know, as I do, that I have lung cancer and am going to die soon."

It's not terribly difficult to imagine why someone would develop hypochondriasis. If a person believes he or she (hypochondriasis is found equally in men and women) has contracted some serious disease, three problems might be solved. (1) The person now has a way to explain otherwise unexplainable anxiety: "Well, my goodness, if you had lung cancer, you'd be anxious, too." (2) The illness may be used to excuse the individual from activities that he or she finds anxiety-producing: "As sick as I am, you don't expect me to go to work, do you?" (3) The illness may be used to gain attention or sympathy: "Don't you feel sorry for me, knowing that I have such a terrible disease?"

Conversion Disorder

conversion disorder *the display of a severe physical disorder for which there is no medical explanation; often accompanied by an apparent lack of concern on the part of the patient*

Conversion disorder is now rare (accounting for less than 5 percent of the anxiety-based disorders). The *DSM-IV* tells us that it is likely to be more common in rural areas or in undeveloped countries. Indeed, in some cultures, some of the symptoms of the disorder are considered quite normal. The symptoms of **conversion disorder** are striking. Here we find a loss or altering of physical function that suggests a physical disorder. The symptoms are not intentionally produced and cannot be explained by any physical disorder. The loss of functioning is typically of great significance; paralysis, blindness, and deafness being classic examples. As difficult as it may be to believe, the symptoms are real in the sense that the person cannot feel, see, or hear.

What makes the disorder psychological is that there is no medical explanation for the symptoms. In some cases, medical explanations run contrary to the symptoms. One type of conversion disorder is *glove anesthesia,* a condition in which the hands lose feeling and become paralyzed from the wrist down. As it happens, it is physically impossible to have such a paralysis and loss of feeling in the hands alone; there would have to be some paralysis in the forearm, upper arm, and shoulder as well. Paralysis, of course, must follow neural pathways.

One remarkable secondary symptom of this disorder (which occurs only in some patients) is known as *la belle indifference*—a seemingly inappropriate lack of concern over one's condition. Some persons with this disorder seem to feel comfortable with and accepting of their infirmity. Here are people who are blind, deaf, or paralyzed, and who show very little concern over their condition.

This disorder holds an important position in psychology's history. This was the disorder that most intrigued Sigmund Freud and ultimately led him to develop a new method of therapy (see Topic 13B). The disorder was known to the Greeks, who named it *hysteria,* a label still occasionally used, as in "hysterical blindness." They believed the disorder was found only in women and was a disorder of the uterus, or *hysterium,* hence the name *hysteria.* The ancient logic was that the disease would leave the uterus, float through the body, and settle in the eyes, hands, or whatever part of the body was affected. Of course, this idea is no longer considered valid, although the potential sexual basis for the disorder was one of the aspects that caught Freud's attention.

Before You Go On

Describe hypochondriasis and conversion disorder.

Dissociative Disorders

To *dissociate* means to become separate from or to escape. The underlying theme of the **dissociative disorders** is that a person seeks to escape from some aspect of life or personality seen as the source of stress, discomfort, or anxiety. These disorders can be dramatic and are often the subject of novels, movies, and television shows.

dissociative disorder *a disorder in which one escapes from aspects of one's life or personality seen as the source of discomfort*

Dissociative Amnesia

Dissociative amnesia is the inability to recall important personal information—an inability too extensive to be explained by ordinary forgetfulness. Before the publication of the *DSM-IV* in 1994, this disorder was called psychogenic amnesia, where *psychogenic* means "psychological in origin," and *amnesia* refers to a loss of memory. What is forgotten is usually some traumatic incident and some or all of the experiences that led up to or followed the incident. As you may suspect, there is no medical explanation for the loss of memory. There is a large range of the extent of the forgetting associated with dissociative amnesia. In some cases, a person may "lose" entire days and weeks at a time; in other cases, only specific details cannot be recalled. Not surprisingly, cases of this disorder tend to be more common in wartime, when traumatic experiences are more common. The disorder is related to the issue of "repressed memories" we discussed in Topic 6A.

dissociative amnesia *a psychologically caused inability—too extensive to be caused by ordinary forgetfulness—to recall important personal information*

Dissociative Fugue

Occasionally, amnesic forgetfulness is accompanied by a change of location—seemingly pointless travel. The person finds himself or herself in a strange and different place, with no reasonable explanation for how he or she got there. When this dimension is added, we have a disorder known as **dissociative fugue**. A typical story would be that of "Carol," found wandering around in the business district of a large eastern city, inappropriately dressed for the cold winds and low temperatures. Her behaviors seemed aimless, and she was stopped by a police officer, who asked if he could be of assistance. It became apparent that Carol did not know where she was, so the officer took her to a nearby hospital. It was soon discovered that she had no memory of where she had been or what she had been doing for the last two weeks. She had no idea how she got to the city in which she was found, 350 miles from home.

Both dissociative amnesia and fugue disorder are, in their own ways, like the somatoform disorders in that they involve escape from stressful situations. In conversion disorders, for example, a person may escape from stress by taking on the symptoms of a major physical disorder. With amnesia and fugue, escape is more literal. People escape by forgetting, or they avoid stress by psychologically or physically running away.

Dissociative Identity Disorder

This disorder is still commonly known as *multiple personality disorder,* as it was called until the publication of the *DSM-IV.* Perhaps the most important fact to recognize about the disorder is that it is listed here as a dissociative disorder and not as schizophrenia. I say that because the media quite consistently give the impression that these are one and the same. They are not. Schizophrenia is a different disorder, which we'll discuss shortly.

The major symptom of **dissociative identity disorder** is the existence within the same person of two or more distinct personalities or personality traits. The disorder has been very rare, although for unknown reasons its incidence is increasing markedly (Carson & Butcher, 1992).

The very idea of two or more personalities inhabiting the same person is difficult to imagine. Perhaps it would help to contrast this disorder with a pattern of behavior typical of all of us. We all change our behaviors, and in a small way, our personalities change every day, depending on the situation in which we find ourselves. We do not act, think, or feel exactly the same way at school as we do at work, at a party, or at a house of worship. We modify our behaviors to fit the circumstances in which we find ourselves. But these changes do not qualify as an identity disorder. What's the difference?

The difference is one of degree and quality. For someone with a dissociative identity disorder, the change in personality is dramatic and extreme. We are not dealing with a person who slightly alters his or her behaviors; we are dealing with two or more distinct personalities, implying a change in underlying consciousness, not just a change in behaviors. Another difference is that when we change our behaviors, we do so in response to cues in the situation in which we find ourselves. Such is not the case for a person with this dissociative disorder, whose changes in personality can take place without warning or provocation. The third major difference has to do with control. When we change our behaviors, we do so intentionally. Persons with a multiple personality disorder can seldom control or predict which of their personalities will be dominant at any one time. Persons diagnosed with dissociative identity disorder have often been the victim of child abuse or sexual abuse (Putnam et al., 1986; Ross, 1989). The significantly higher incidence of multiple personality disorder in women than in men might be partially understood when we consider that girls and women are much more likely to be sexually or

dissociative fugue *a condition of amnesia accompanied by unexplained travel or change of location*

dissociative identity disorder *the existence within one individual of two or more distinct personalities, each of which is dominant at a particular time*

Dissociative identity disorder used to be called "multiple personality." It is a disorder characterized by evidence of two or more distinct personalities within the same person.

physically abused than are boys and men (Ross, 1989). Females also tend to have a greater number of separate identities, averaging 15 or more, to the male average of 8 identities.

Before You Go On

What are the defining symptoms of the dissociative disorders?

Personality Disorders

The psychological disorders we have reviewed so far are disorders that seem to af-flict people who at one time were normal and undisturbed. In most cases, we can re-member when the person did not show the symptoms of his or her disorder. That is more difficult to do with the personality disorders because persons with these dis-orders have a long-standing history of symptoms. **Personality disorders** are *long-lasting* patterns of perceiving, relating to, and thinking about the environment and oneself that are maladaptive and inflexible and cause either impaired functioning

personality disorders *enduring patterns of perceiving, relating to, and thinking about the environment and oneself that are inflexible and maladaptive* or distress. The problems associated with personality disorders are usually identifiable by the time an individual is an adolescent, but a diagnosis of a personality disorder is not appropriate for anyone younger than 18 years of age. The *DSM-IV* cautions that these disorders should not be associated with the sorts of problems that immigrants may have when they arrive in the midst of a new culture.

The Major Clusters of Personality Disorders

The *DSM-IV* lists eleven personality disorders (PD), clustered in three groups. Group 1 includes disorders in which the person can be characterized as odd or eccentric. People with disorders from this cluster are often difficult to get along with. Group 2 includes those disorders in which the person seems overly dramatic, emotional, or erratic, and where behaviors are impulsive. Group 3 includes disorders that add the dimension of anxiety or fearfulness to the standard criteria for personality disorder. Note that it is only for those personality disorders in Group 3 that we find any reports of fear, anxiety, or depression.

Rather than attempting to deal with all of the personality disorders in detail, I'll list some of the common PDs, and then discuss one, the antisocial personality disorder, in a bit more detail. Keep in mind that to be a personality disorder, the symptoms must be relatively long-standing, generally beginning in childhood or adolescence.

Cluster I: Disorders of odd or eccentric reactions:

Paranoid personality disorder: an extreme sensitivity, suspiciousness, envy, and mistrust of others; the actions of other people are interpreted as deliberately demeaning or threatening. The attitude of suspicion is not justified. A person with this disorder shows a restricted range of emotional reactivity, is humorless, and rarely seeks help. Example: A person who continuously, and without justification, accuses a spouse of infidelity, and believes that every wrong number was really a call from the spouse's lover. More than any other, this personality disorder includes symptoms that could readily describe many people in a new cultural setting. Imagine a newly arrived Vietnamese immigrant living in the inner city of a large metropolitan area. A little sensitivity, suspiciousness, and mistrust in such an instance probably does not indicate a disorder.

Schizoid personality disorder: an inability to form, and an indifference to, interpersonal relationships. A person with schizoid personality disorder seems "cold and aloof," and often engages in excessive daydreaming. Example: A person who lives, as she has for years, in a one-room flat in a poor part of town, venturing out only to pick up a social security check and a few necessities at the corner store.

Cluster II: Disorders of dramatic, emotional, or erratic reactions:

Histrionic personality disorder: overly dramatic, reactive, and intensely expressed behaviors. A person with this disorder is emotionally very lively, tending to draw attention to him- or herself, overreacting to matters of little consequence. Example: A woman who spends an inordinate amount of time on her appearance, calls everyone "Darling!," seems to be constantly asking for feedback about how she looks, describing most of her experiences as "wonderful!" and "vastly outstanding!" even when such an experience is no more than finding a detergent on sale at the grocery store.

Narcissistic personality disorder: a grandiose exaggeration of self-importance, a need for attention or admiration, and a tendency to set unrealistic goals. Someone with this personality disorder maintains few lasting relationships and in many ways engages in a "childish" level of behavior. Example: A person who always wants to be the topic of conversation, and shows a lack of interest in saying anything positive about anyone else. Someone who believes that no one else has ever taken a vacation as stupendous as his or hers, or understood an issue as clearly as he or she, and who will do whatever it takes to be complimented.

Cluster III: Disorders involving anxiety and fearfulness:

Avoidant personality disorder: an oversensitivity to the possibility of being rejected by others and an unwillingness to enter into relationships for fear of being rejected. A person with this disorder is devastated by disapproval, but holds out a desire for social relationships. Example: A man with few close friends who almost never dates, and only talks to women who are older and less attractive than he. He has worked for years at the same job, never seeking a job change or promotion, rarely speaks in public, and may attend meetings and public gatherings but without actively participating.

Dependent personality disorder: allowing and seeking others to dominate and assume responsibility for one's actions; a poor self-image and lack of confidence. A person with this disorder sees himself or herself as stupid and helpless, thus deferring to others. Example: A woman whose husband commonly abuses her. Although she has from time to time reported the abuse, she refuses to take an active role in finding help or treatment for her husband, saying it is "her place" to do as he says, and that if she does not please him, it is her fault.

Because personality disorders are difficult to diagnose accurately, estimates of their prevalence tend to be inexact. Most cases of personality disorder first come to the attention of mental health professionals on referral from the courts (or family members), or because of related problems such as child abuse or alcoholism. What we do find is that "while the overall rate of PD may be between 10% and 20%, the rates of specific disorders are very low" (Zimmerman & Coryell, 1989). About one-fourth of those with symptoms of a personality disorder fit more than one diagnostic category—another example of comorbidity (Blashfield & Breen, 1989; Zimmerman & Coryell, 1989). Several studies tell us that "relatively few people meet the criteria for a given personality disorder without also meeting criteria for one or more other *DSM* diagnoses" (Clark et al., 1995).

The prognosis for the personality disorders is poor. The maladaptive patterns of behavior that characterize personality disorders have usually taken a lifetime to develop. Changing them is very difficult. This makes understanding the causes of these disorders all the more important. What hypotheses are now under investigation? (1) There is a biologically based lack of adequate emotional arousal (Eysenck, 1960; Lykken, 1982; Raine et al., 1990). (2) There is an unusually high need to seek stimulation (i.e., persons with some personality disorders tend to be "sensation seekers") (Quay, 1965; Zuckerman, 1978). (3) There is a genetic basis for at least some of the personality disorders (Kendler & Gruenberg, 1982; Mednick et al., 1987; Nigg & Goldsmith, 1994). (4) There is a high incidence of parental loss. Many adults with personality disorders were abandoned in their childhood by at least one parent, usually the father (Greer, 1964; Hare, 1970). (5) There is a significantly high level of abuse in childhood (Ogata et al., 1990). (6) There was inappropriate, or a lack of, emotional "bonding" or attachment with parents in childhood (Buss, 1966; Magid, 1988).

As we have noted before and will see again, no one of these hypotheses adequately explains why a particular individual will develop a personality disorder. The key, no doubt, is the interaction of two or more of these factors in the life of the individual.

Before You Go On

What are the defining characteristics of the personality disorders?

Persons with antisocial personality disorder often come to the attention of society when they violate the law.

An Example: The Antisocial Personality Disorder

antisocial personality disorder *an exceptional lack of regard for the rights and property of others accompanied by impulsive, often criminal, behaviors*

The **antisocial personality disorder** is characterized by an exceptional lack of regard for the rights and property of others. Someone with this disorder often engages in impulsive behaviors with little or no regard for the consequences of those behaviors. One of the things that makes this diagnosis difficult is that, by definition, the symptoms of the disorder include deceit and the manipulation of others. "Lacking in conscience and in feelings for others, they cold-bloodedly take what they want and do as they please, violating social norms and expectations without the slightest guilt or regret" (Hare, 1995, p. 4). Many still refer to people with antisocial PD with the outdated terms "psychopath" or "sociopath." The disorder is included, with the histrionic and the narcissistic personality disorders, in Cluster II in the *DSM-IV.*

Remember, as is the case for all PDs, the antisocial personality disorder is not an appropriate diagnosis for anyone younger than 18 years old. Still, there is usually a history of "getting into trouble" long before the diagnosis is made. Persons with antisocial personality disorder are impulsive. They change jobs, residences, and relationships frequently. At best, they are irresponsible. At worst, their behaviors are criminal. A person who has committed a crime does not necessarily have antisocial personality disorder. Many criminals, in fact, show genuine sadness and remorse over the crime they have committed. If nothing else, they show remorse for the fact that they were caught and punished. An individual with antisocial personality disorder is likely to be indifferent about their actions, their victims, or even their apprehension. "Well, that's the way it goes." "He shouldn't have been carrying that much money with him." "A few more months in jail won't bother me much." Fifteen to 20 percent of the American prison population is composed of psychopaths.

The antisocial personality disorder is much more likely to be found among those who are of low socioeconomic status, live in an urban setting, and have a history of antisocial behaviors beginning before age 10 years. It is also much more likely to be diagnosed in males than in females. Estimates put the disorder at about 3 percent of the population for males and about 1 percent of the population for females. Like many of the other personality disorders, antisocial personality disorder is resistant to treatment. The main problem is that most psychotherapy is designed for people who recognize they have a problem and want to change. Persons with antisocial personality disorder usually enter treatment programs because they have been court-ordered to do so (Hare, 1995). Court-ordered therapy programs are ineffective for the 25 to 35 percent of spouse abusers who are psychopaths.

Unlike the other personality disorders, there is evidence of a "burnout factor" for antisocial personality disorder (Weiss, 1973). That is, some persons with the disorder have a spontaneous remission of symptoms in their early 40s. In one study, for example, prisoners with antisocial personality disorder were most likely to be in prison when they were between the ages of 31 and 35 (90 percent of the sample), and much less likely to be in prison when they were between the ages of 41 and 45 (less than 60 percent of the sample) (Hare et al., 1988).

Before You Go On

Describe the antisocial personality disorder.

TOPIC 12A SUMMARY

In psychology, the concept of abnormality is a complex one, encompassing the notions of maladaptations of affects, behaviors, and/or cognitions, defined in a sociocultural context, and implying distress and discomfort. Psychological disorders may be defined in terms of their symptoms, and are classified in a system published as the *Diagnostic and Statistical Manual of Mental Disorders (DSM),* now in its fourth edition. The advantage of a system of classification, such as the *DSM-IV,* is that it fosters better communication. Disadvantages include the fact that naming or classifying disorders does not explain them in any way, may put undue focus on the person rather than the group of which the person is a member, and may foster negative attitudes toward those who are labeled disordered. Insanity is a legal term, not a psychological one.

Psychological disorders are much more common than any of us would like to think, afflicting tens of millions of Americans. We began with the anxiety disorders, each of which manifests high levels of anxiety in one form or another. We discussed the somatoform and dissociative disorders. The former disorders involve some aspect of physical health when there is no reason to believe that there is a medical problem, while the latter involve the separation, or disconnection, of aspects of one's personality. We then looked at the personality disorders, which are characterized by lifelong patterns of inflexible and maladaptive behaviors. These disorders are difficult to diagnose and equally difficult to treat.

TOPIC 12B Alzheimer's Dementia, Mood Disorders, and Schizophrenia

In this Topic we continue our discussion of individual psychological disorders. It may be inappropriate and in a sense unfair to classify some disorders as being more severe or debilitating than others. To the person who is experiencing a disorder, and to those who care about that person, any disorder can seem severe and debilitating. It is nonetheless the case that the disorders in this Topic do tend to be more disruptive and discomforting than those we've covered so far. Most of the disorders we'll look at in this Topic cause great difficulties in meeting the demands of everyday life and a loss of contact with the real world as the rest of us know it. As a result, persons with these diagnoses frequently require hospitalization.

Alzheimer's Dementia

dementia *a marked loss of intellectual abilities in which memory is poor and deteriorates and judgment is adversely affected*

Alzheimer's disease *a dementia caused by the premature death of brain cells because of the accumulation of plaques and tangles*

By definition, **dementia** is a condition characterized by the marked loss of intellectual abilities. One's attention may be intact, but use of memory is poor and deteriorates. Judgment and impulse control may be adversely affected.

A slow deterioration of one's intellectual functioning is the most common symptom associated with **Alzheimer's disease** (Katzman, 1987). Problems of recent memory mark the early stages of the disease: "Did I take my pills this morning?" Mild personality changes—apathy, less spontaneity, withdrawal—soon follow, perhaps in an attempt to hide one's symptoms from others. Figure 12.4 is from a summary table recently prepared by the Alzheimer's Association.

This dementia was first described in 1907 by Alois Alzheimer and was thought to be an inevitable process of aging (often incorrectly referred to as *senile psychosis*). The symptoms associated with dementia of the Alzheimer's type are *not* normal, natural, or a necessary part of growing old, but a general acceptance of this reality did not occur until the early 1970s. Alzheimer's disease has been diagnosed in persons younger than age 65. In such cases, we have what is called an *early onset* form of the disease, but some researchers are coming to conclude that age of onset, by itself, does not define different forms of the disease (Bondareff et al., 1993).

Approximately 4 million Americans are afflicted with Alzheimer's disease. A female born in 1994 who lives to an average life expectancy will have a one in six chance of developing Alzheimer's disease, and a male, a one in 16 chance. Each year 11,000 people in the United States die of the disease (Fackelman, 1992; Hostetler, 1987; Mace & Rabins, 1981; Wurtman, 1985). Deaths attributed to Alzheimer's disease have increased nearly 1,000 percent since the late 1970s, which can be attributed to several factors, including a greater awareness and willingness to diagnose the disease and an increasing number of people living to advanced ages, when Alzheimer's is more likely to occur. Given this, an estimated 14 million Americans will have the disease by the year 2050.

Although the symptoms of Alzheimer's disease are psychological, it *is* a physical disease caused by abnormal changes in brain tissue. Reliable diagnostic tests may be on the horizon, but today Alzheimer's dementia is diagnosed with certainty only after an autopsy of the brain. There are four signs of Alzheimer's disease: (1) a mass of *tangles,* a "spaghetti-like jumble of abnormal protein fibers" (Butler & Emr,

Alzheimer's dementia involves the premature death of brain cells. Early symptoms include mild disorientation and memory loss.

Figure 12.4

The 10 Warning Signs of Alzheimer's Disease

Normal	Possible Alzhemier's
1. Temporarily forgetting a colleague's name	Not being able to remember the name later
2. Forgetting the carrots on the stove until the meal is over	Forgetting that a meal was ever prepared
3. Unable to find right word, but using a fit substitute	Uttering incomprehensible sentences
4. Forgetting for a moment where you're going	Getting lost on your own street
5. Talking on the phone, temporarily forgetting to watch a child	Forgetting there is a child there
6. Having trouble balancing a checkbook	Not knowing what the numbers mean
7. Misplacing a wristwatch until steps are retraced	Putting a wristwatch in the sugarbowl
8. Having a bad day	Having rapid mood shifts
9. Gradual changes in personality with age	Drastic changes in personality
10. Tiring of housework, but getting back to it	Not knowing or caring that housework needs to be done

From *Is It Alzheimer's? Warning Signs You Should Know;* a pamphlet by the Alzheimer's Association, 919 North Michigan Avenue, Suite 1000, Chicago, IL 60611-1676.

1982); (2) the presence of *plaques*—waste material, degenerated nerve fibers that wrap around a core of protein; (3) the presence of small *cavities* filled with fluid and debris; (4) *atrophy*—some structures in the brain are reduced in size. Two problems with these observations are that these signs can sometimes be found in a normal brain (seldom more than one at a time, however), and we don't know what causes these signs in the first place.

Scientists are beginning to understand the etiology, or causes, of Alzheimer's, but we're still at the level of discussing hypotheses, though some do seem more promising than others. The basic issue is that nerve cells in the brains of Alzheimer's patients start to die off sooner than they should, resulting in the tangles, plaques, and other signs we see at autopsy. The crucial question is, how and why do these brain cells die?

As is so often the case with psychological functioning, there is a genetic basis for Alzheimer's disease, although no one yet is claiming that it is directly inherited. There is no doubt that the disease runs in families. This is particularly true for cases in which the age of onset is younger than 60 (Marx, 1990). A breakthrough occurred in 1993, when a team of researchers at Duke University isolated a gene that might be part of the cause of Alzheimer's. By the summer of 1995, two other genes associated with Alzheimer's were discovered. *How* these genes are involved is another story, yet to be understood.

Another hypothesis about the cause of Alzheimer's dementia is related to the role of a particular protein molecule. This protein is a major component of the plaques found in the brains of Alzheimer's patients. Scientists now know the specific type and structure of the protein involved (Marx, 1990; Selkoe, 1990). Another model involves levels of the neurotransmitter acetylcholine; patients with Alzheimer's dementia often have low levels of acetylcholine (Coyle et al., 1983). We've already noted that acetylcholine is involved in memory, so a belief that it is involved in memory deficit is quite reasonable. There is the possibility that Alzheimer's is the result of a poison, or toxin (aluminum salts have been shown to produce similar symptoms). At present, there seems to be at least a shred of truth in each of these hypotheses, reminding us of a theme from Chapter 1: for many questions in psychology, there are no simple answers.

⊚⊚⊚ **Thinking Critically** ⊚⊚⊚

If there were a test available that could tell you whether you would get Alzheimer's dementia when you were older, would you opt to have the test? Under what conditions?

Before You Go On

What is Alzheimer's dementia?

Mood Disorders

mood disorders *disorders of affect or feeling; usually depression; less frequently mania and depression occurring in cycles*

The **mood disorders** (called *affective disorders* until the publication of the *DSM-III-R*) clearly demonstrate a disturbance in one's emotional reactions or feelings. We have to be a little careful here. Almost all psychological disorders have an impact on one's mood or affect. With mood disorders, however, the intensity or extreme nature of one's mood is the major symptom.

Types of Mood Disorder

Listed under the classification *mood disorder* are several specific disorders differentiated in terms of such criteria as length of episode and severity.

major depression *a mood disorder characterized by inexplicable moods of sadness and hopelessness, accompanied by a loss of pleasure or interest in usual activities*

Major depression is the diagnosis for a constellation of symptoms that includes feeling sad, low, and hopeless, coupled with a loss of pleasure or interest in almost all normal activities. Associated with major depression are such factors as poor appetite, loss of energy, insomnia, decrease in sexual activity, and feelings of worthlessness.

This mood disorder is diagnosed about two times more often in women than in men; during any 6-month period, approximately 6.6 percent of women and 3.5 percent of men will have an episode of major depression. This ratio of nearly two women to every man developing major depression holds across nationalities and ethnic groups (Cross-National Collaborative Group, 1992; McGrath et al., 1990). Worldwide, major depression is on the increase, with current rates at more than 100 million persons (Gotlib, 1992; Weissman & Klerman, 1992). Unfortunately, re-

Major depression is a mood disorder characterized by inexplicable feelings of sadness and hopelessness accompanied by a loss of pleasure in common activities.

lapse and reoccurrence are common for those who have ever had a depressive episode (Belsher & Costello, 1988; Klerman, 1990; Lewinsohn et al., 1989). Major depression seldom occurs as just one episode of illness, but rather is a fairly chronic condition (Frank et al., 1990).

Dysthymia [diss-thigh'-me-a'] is essentially a mild case of major depression. The disorder is also chronic, with recurrent pessimism, low energy level, and low self-esteem. Whereas major depression tends to occur in a series of extremely debilitating episodes, dysthymia is a more continuous sense of being depressed and sad.

As in the case of major depression, there is no identifiable event that precipitates the depressed mood of dysthymia. That is, to feel even overwhelmingly depressed upon hearing of the death of a dear friend is not enough to qualify as a disorder of any sort. We all feel periods of depression from time to time, but when we do, there is some sensible reason for that depressed mood. With these two disorders, a distressing, debilitating mood seems to be present for no good reason.

In **bipolar disorder**, episodes of depression are occasionally interspersed with episodes of mania. This disorder is still often referred to as "manic depression." **Mania** is characterized as an elevated mood with feelings of euphoria or irritability. In a manic state one shows an increase in activity, is more talkative than usual, and seems to get by with less sleep than usual. Mania is a condition of mood that cannot be maintained for long. It is too tiring to stay manic for an extended time. As is true for depression, mania seldom occurs as an isolated episode. Follow-up studies show that recurrences of manic reactions are common. Relapse is found in approximately 40 percent of those who have been diagnosed as having a manic episode (Harrow et al., 1990; Tohen et al., 1990). People are rarely manic without also showing interspersed periods of depression. Approximately 2 million Americans presently suffer from bipolar disorder.

dysthymia a mood disorder that is basically a mild form of major depression; it is chronic, with recurrent pessimism, low energy level, and low self-esteem

bipolar disorder a mood disorder characterized by depression with intermittent periods of mania

mania heightened euphoria and increased activity; typically occurs between episodes of depression

Observations on the Causes of Depression

The answers we find to the question "What causes depression?" depend largely on how and where we look for such answers. It seems most likely that depression is caused by several different, but potentially interrelated, causes—both biological and psychological.

Biological Factors. Bipolar mood disorder isn't very common. An individual chosen at random has less than a one-half of 1 percent chance of developing the symptoms of the disorder. The chances of developing the symptoms rise to 15 percent if a brother, a sister, or either parent ever had the disorder. This 15 percent figure holds for fraternal twins. If, however, one member of a pair of identical twins has bipolar mood disorder, the chances that the other twin will be diagnosed as having the disorder jump to more than 70 percent (Allen, 1976). What all this means, of course, is that there is excellent evidence for a genetic, or inherited, predisposition to the bipolar mood disorder. The data are not quite as striking for the unipolar mood disorder (depression only), for which the equivalent figures are 40 percent for identical twins and 11 percent for fraternal twins. We suspect, however, that there is some sort of genetic basis for major depression as well (Hammen et al., 1990; Kendler et al., 1993). A recent study of twins confirmed the influence of heredity in major depression and ruled out early childhood experiences as a causative factor. The study found that no evidence that growing up at the same time, in the same home with the same parents, in the same neighborhood, or in the same school was related to the development of the symptoms of depression (Kendler et al., 1994).

There was much excitement generated by reports in 1987 that a specific gene that was the cause of bipolar mood disorder had been localized in a community of Old Order Amish living in Pennsylvania (Egeland et al., 1987). Follow-up research has made it clear that the original reports were premature and overly optimistic

(Baron et al., 1993). Although there may be some "linkage" between the disorder and specific sites on certain chromosomes, we realize that there are too many exceptions to claim that we know the genetic basis of bipolar mood disorder (e.g., Berrettini et al., 1990).

Even if we did know the site of a specific gene, or two, or three, that provided the basis for a disorder, researchers would still be challenged to specify the mechanisms that produce the symptoms of that disorder. For the mood disorders, attention has been focused on neurotransmitters that appear to influence mood directly. Collectively they are referred to as *biogenic amines* and include such neurotransmitters as serotonin, dopamine, and norepinephrine. The major breakthrough in this research came when it was discovered that a drug (reserpine) used to treat high blood pressure also produced symptoms of depression. It was then discovered that reserpine lowered the brain's level of norepinephrine, and the search for neurotransmitter involvement in affective disorders was on (Bennett, 1982).

One theory holds that depression is caused by a shortage of biogenic amines, and that mania is caused by an excess of these chemicals. It remains to be seen why these biochemical imbalances occur in some people and not others. Perhaps they reflect an inherited predisposition. Another argument follows from the observation that stress causes changes in the neurotransmitters in the brain—including an increase in biogenic amines (Anisman & Zacharko, 1982). If the biogenic amines are stimulated by prolonged stress, perhaps their supply becomes depleted, leading to symptoms of depression. In cases of depression that seem to occur without any striking or unusual stressors, we may suspect that a genetic predisposition makes some people highly susceptible to the biochemical changes that accompany stress in any degree. The theory is logical, but as yet there is insufficient evidence for us to draw any firm conclusions. Recent studies of the brains of persons with mood disorders have found that such persons have some of the same structural abnormalities that are associated with schizophrenia, a disorder we discuss next. In particular, persons with mood disorders have abnormally large ventricles (openings in the brain that contain cerebrospinal fluid) although the abnormality is not as large as in persons with schizophrenia (Elkis et al., 1995; Van Horn & McManus, 1992). Patients with bipolar mood disorder have abnormally high levels of white matter in the brain, and tend to have larger thalamuses than control subjects, while patients with major depression have smaller thalamuses than normal (Dupont et al., 1995).

Psychological Factors. Learning theorists have attributed depression to experiential phenomena, including a lack of effective reinforcers. Someone with a history of making responses without earning reinforcement may just stop responding altogether and become quiet, withdrawn, passive, and depressed (Seligman, 1975). Some people, lacking the ability to earn reinforcers, simply respond less often to environmental cues. They enter into a long, generalized period of extinction, ultimately leading to depression. On the other hand, certain research suggests that the ineffectiveness of reinforcers in some people's lives is more a result of depression than a cause of it. Because they are depressed, they may find less reinforcement for their responses to the world about them (Carson & Carson, 1984).

Other theorists, most notably psychiatrist Aaron Beck (1967, 1976), argue that although depression is a disorder of affect, its causes are largely cognitive. Some people, the argument goes, tend to think of themselves in a poor light; they believe that they are, in many ways, ineffective people. They tend to blame themselves for many of their failures, whether deservedly so or not. Facing life every day with these negative attitudes about oneself tends to foster even more failures and self-doubt, and such cycles then lead to feelings of depression.

To be sure, there are other views about the causes of depression, including the psychoanalytic view that depression is a reflection of early childhood experiences that lead to anger that is directed inward. In brief, we can conclude that depression probably stems from a combination of genetic predispositions, biochemical influences, learning experiences, situational stress, and cognitive factors. Which of these is more, or most, important remains to be seen.

Before we go on, let's briefly consider the data on mood disorders that tell us they are twice as likely to be diagnosed in women than in men. Why should this be so? Several hypotheses have been proposed. (1) Perhaps the genetic basis of depression is located on X chromosomes (males carry an XY pair of chromosomes, whereas women have XX pairs). There are little data to support this hypothesis. (2) Perhaps women, given their roles in our culture, feel more free and open to discuss their feelings—their negative feelings in particular—than do men. More open to sharing their sad, unhappy moods, women may be diagnosed more often as being depressed. In contrast, men are more likely to abuse alcohol: it's a male response to feelings of sadness and depression. Again, this hypothesis may sound good, but there are not much data to support it. Among other things, remember, mood disorders are more common in women than in men in every culture that has been studied. (3) Perhaps women are more exposed to the types of stressors (less education, poorer employment, lower pay, child-rearing responsibilities, and so on) that would lead one to become depressed. This may be a valid observation, but when such factors are controlled for (when men and women are matched for such stressors), the sex difference in diagnosis remains. Even when factors such as self-esteem are controlled for, the sex difference remains. As you might guess, there are several other hypotheses, including the notion that mental health professionals (males in particular) are simply following a cultural expectation and diagnosing the disorder more commonly in women. Once again, a common theme emerges: sex differences in depression reflect a complex interaction of genetic, biological, psychological, and cultural factors (McGrath et al., 1990; Strickland, 1992).

Before You Go On

What are the mood disorders?

Schizophrenia

Schizophrenia is a diagnosis for what may be several different disorders, which have in common a distortion of reality and a retreat from other people, accompanied by disturbances in affect, behavior, and cognition (our ABC again). Schizophrenia can impair every aspect of living. The range of symptoms is so great that it is nearly impossible to specify just which are fundamental and which are secondary.

schizophrenia *a complex family of disorders characterized by impairment of cognitive functioning, delusions and hallucinations, social withdrawal, and inappropriate affect*

Incidence and Types of Schizophrenia

Schizophrenia was originally thought to be confined to North America and Western Europe. We now understand that the disorder (or varieties of the disorder) can be found around the world at the same rate: about 1 percent of the population (Adler & Gielen, 1994; Bloom et al., 1985). People in developing countries tend to have a more acute (intense, but short-lived) course—and a better outcome—of the disorder than do people in industrialized nations. In the United States, schizophrenia accounts for 75 percent of all mental health expenditures (Carpenter & Buchanan, 1994). Schizophrenia occurs at the same rate for both sexes, but symptoms are likely to show up earlier in males, and males are more likely to be disabled by the disorder (Grinspoon, 1995).

No matter how we state the statistics, we are talking about very large numbers of people. The prognosis for schizophrenia is not very encouraging. About 25 percent recover fully from their first episode of the disorder and have no recurrences;

One of the defining symptoms of schizophrenia is disordered or disorganized thoughts and perceptions.

in about 50 percent of all cases of schizophrenia, there is a recurrent illness with periods of remission in between, and in about 25 percent of the cases there are no signs of recovery and a long-term deterioration in functioning. In one study, only 10 to 17 percent of patients with schizophrenia showed complete remission of symptoms in a follow-up 5 years after initial diagnosis (Carone et al., 1991). Prognosis is related to when intervention begins. If treatment begins immediately after an initial episode, the prognosis is fairly good, with as many as 83 percent recovering (Lieberman et al., 1993). Here is a picture we also see with many physical ailments: the sooner treatment begins, the better the likelihood of recovery.

I've already indicated that schizophrenia is a label that applies to several specific disorders. In this way, the term *schizophrenia* is not unlike the term *cancer*. To say that one has cancer communicates only a general diagnosis. We then want to know what *sort* of cancer. Classifying varieties of schizophrenia has been motivated by an attempt to better understand what causes the disorder, which might then lead to more effective treatment. There have been several attempts at "typing" schizophrenia. Only recently has a consensus begun to develop for a system for classifying the disorder into types on the basis of *positive and negative symptoms*.

In 1919, Emil Kraepelin claimed there were two types of schizophrenia depending on the symptoms found at diagnosis. Recent research indicates that schizophrenia has three dimensions of symptoms (Andreasen, 1982; Andreasen et al., 1990; Andreasen et al., 1995; Arndt et al., 1995; Brown & White, 1992; Eaton et al., 1995; Kay & Singh, 1989). One dimension of schizophrenia is typified by **negative symptoms**—emotional and social withdrawal, reduced energy and motivation, apathy, and poor attention.

The other two dimensions of schizophrenia are typified by *positive symptoms*. The **positive psychotic symptoms** include hallucinations and delusions. *Hallucinations* are false perceptions; perceiving that which is not there or failing to perceive that which is. Schizophrenic hallucinations are often auditory, taking the form of "hearing voices inside one's head." **Delusions** are false beliefs; ideas that are firmly held regardless of evidence to the contrary. Delusions of someone with

negative symptoms *emotional and social withdrawal, reduced energy and motivation, apathy, and poor attention*

positive psychotic symptoms *hallucinations and delusions; false perceptions and false beliefs*

delusions *false beliefs; ideas that are firmly held regardless of evidence to the contrary* schizophrenia are inconsistent and unorganized. **Positive disorganized symptoms** of schizophrenia include disorders of thinking and speech, bizarre behaviors, and inappropriate affect. A person displaying positive disorganized symptoms may say something like, "When you swallow in your throat like a key it comes out, but not a scissors, a robin too, it means spring" (Marengo & Harrow, 1987, p. 654), or may giggle and laugh or sob and cry for no apparent reason, or may stand perfectly still for hours at a time.

The usefulness of this negative-positive distinction is that there may be differences in both the causes and the most effective treatment plans for the three types. In brief, we find the correlates of negative symptoms to include structural abnormalities in the brain (as seen on CAT scans, for example), a clearer genetic basis, more severe complications at birth, a lower educational level, poorer adjustment patterns before onset, and a poorer prognosis given the relative ineffectiveness of medications. Correlated with both types of positive symptoms are excesses of the neurotransmitter dopamine, relatively normal brain configuration, severe disruptions in early family life, overactivity and aggressiveness in adolescence, and a relatively good response to treatment (Andreasen et al., 1990; Breier et al., 1991; Brown & White, 1992; Cannon et al., 1990; Eaton et al., 1995; Lenzenweger et al., 1989; McGlashan & Fenton, 1992).

As is always the case in such matters, we need to be cautious. Not all of the data on typing schizophrenia have been supportive (Kay, 1990; Pogue-Geile & Zubin, 1988). The distinctions described here are quite new, only time and further research will tell us how useful they will be in the long run.

I need to make two things clear before we go on. First, as unsettling as these symptoms may be, the average patient with schizophrenia does not present the picture of the crazed, wild lunatic that is often depicted in movies and on television. Day in and day out, the average schizophrenic patient is quite colorless, socially withdrawn, and of very little danger. Although there are exceptions to this rule of thumb, it is particularly true when the patient with schizophrenia is medicated or in treatment. Their "differentness" may be frightening, but people with schizophrenia are seldom any more dangerous than anyone else. Second, when literally translated, *schizophrenia* means "splitting of the mind." This term was first used by a Swiss psychiatrist, Eugen Bleuler, in 1911. The split Bleuler was addressing was a split of the mind of the patient from the real world and social relationships as the rest of us experience them. The term has never been used to describe multiple or split personalities of the Jekyll and Hyde variety. Such disorders do occur, but as we have seen, they are classified as dissociative identity disorders.

positive disorganized symptoms *disorders of thinking and speech, bizarre behaviors, and inappropriate affect*

Before You Go On

What is schizophrenia, and what distinguishes among its positive and its negative symptoms?

What Causes Schizophrenia?

Schizophrenia is a complex family of disorders, and as you may suspect, any bottom-line conclusion on the causes of schizophrenia will be tentative and multidimensional. We may not know what causes the disorder, but we do have several interesting hypotheses.

Schizophrenia has a genetic basis (Gottesman & Bertelsen, 1989; Kessler, 1980; Rosenthal, 1970). The data are not as striking as they are for the mood disorders, but one is at a higher risk of being diagnosed as having schizophrenia if there is a history of the disorder in one's family. A child of two parents with schizophrenia has about a 40 percent chance of developing the disorder. Schizophrenia occurs at a 30 to 50 percent rate among the identical twins of schizophrenics, but at only a 10 to 15 percent rate in fraternal twins (Grinspoon, 1995; Kety et al., 1994; Kendler et al., 1994). It is reasonable to say that one may inherit a predisposition to develop

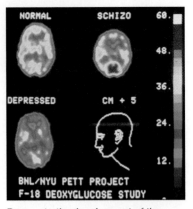

Demonstrating involvement of the brain in psychological disorders, these PET scans show brain images of someone diagnosed with schizophrenia and someone in a depressed state. A normal brain image is also shown for comparison.

schizophrenia, but lest we get too committed to a genetic hypothesis on the causes of schizophrenia, we must consider that 89 percent of persons diagnosed with schizophrenia have no known relative with the disorder (Cromwell, 1993; Plomin, 1988).

There is no doubt that schizophrenia is a disease of the brain, and for some time, the focus has been on the neurotransmitter dopamine. The role of dopamine has come to light from several lines of research. We know that the abuse of amphetamines can lead to many of the symptoms also found in schizophrenia. We know that amphetamines are chemically very similar to dopamine and actually cause an increase in dopamine levels in the brain. Logic leads researchers to wonder if schizophrenic symptoms (in particular those we have recognized as positive symptoms) are caused by excess amounts of dopamine. Although dopamine is found in all human brains, it is present at high levels in late adolescence, which is when schizophrenia usually first appears (Grinspoon, 1995).

Further support for the dopamine hypothesis comes from examining the action of drugs that reduce schizophrenic symptoms. Some of the drugs that ease schizophrenic symptoms commonly block receptor sites for dopamine in the brain (Snyder, 1980). If reducing the effectiveness of dopamine by blocking its activity at the synapse can control schizophrenic symptoms, might these symptoms have been caused by dopamine in the first place (Schooler & Keith, 1993; Tandon & Greden, 1989)?

The arguments for this hypothesis appear compelling, but are far from certain. For one thing, there is little evidence that persons with schizophrenia have elevated levels of dopamine in their brains (Karoum et al., 1987). Even so, there may be a heightened sensitivity in the brains of schizophrenics to whatever levels of dopamine *are* present (i.e., perhaps there are more dopamine receptor sites). This may sound reasonable, but not all medications used to treat schizophrenia block dopamine receptor sites. It is also troublesome that when such drugs are effective, their effects generally take a few weeks to develop. If the effect of the drugs on receptor sites is immediate, why isn't the effect on symptoms immediate also?

Additionally, we have a "chicken-and-egg" problem with the dopamine hypothesis. If dopamine were shown to be related to schizophrenic symptoms, we would still have to ask if there was a causal relationship. That is, do increased levels of dopamine cause schizophrenic symptoms, or does schizophrenia cause elevated dopamine levels? Or does some other factor—perhaps stress—cause elevated dopamine levels *and* the symptoms of schizophrenia? In summary, "schizophrenia may be a dopamine-related illness, but this relationship has not yet emerged as the neurological key to the disorder" (Heinrichs, 1993, p. 225).

We have some of the same chicken-and-egg problem with findings concerning brain structure and schizophrenia. Many patients with schizophrenia, mostly those with positive symptoms, have abnormally large ventricles in their brains (cavities or openings that contain cerebrospinal fluid) (Andreasen et al., 1982, 1990b), and evidence suggests a lack of balance between the two hemispheres of the brain (Gur et al., 1987; Reveley et al., 1987). There are other differences between the brains of persons with schizophrenia and persons without the disorder, although they tend to be less dramatic. Persons with the disorder tend to have a loss of tissue in and around the limbic system (related to the regulation of emotion, remember), larger crevices in the surface of the cerebral cortex, and a smaller thalamus (the structure that relays information between the cerebral cortex and the rest of the brain). Even if these differences in the brain are confirmed, we still don't know if we're dealing with causes or effects.

Perhaps genetic or biochemical factors, or both, predispose a person to develop the symptoms of schizophrenia. What sorts of events then turn such predispositions into reality? To this question, answers are very sketchy.

One view is that schizophrenia develops as a response to early experiences in the family (e.g., Lidz, 1973). The childhood experiences of people who later develop schizophrenic symptoms sometimes seem different from those who do not develop the disorder. In truth, however, very few mental health professionals put much stock in the notion that family lifestyle has much to do with the development of schizophrenia.

There is evidence that in some people, the symptoms of schizophrenia remain dormant, or unexpressed, until the individual is subjected to environmental stressors (Gottesman & Bertelsen, 1989; Johnson, 1989; Ventura et al., 1989). The theory here is that some people are genetically prone to develop the symptoms of schizophrenia when they are exposed to stressors. Other people faced with the same type or amount of stress might develop ulcers, might become excessively anxious, or might show no particular symptoms at all. So it is possible that some life experiences do bring on the symptoms of schizophrenia or tend to make those symptoms worse than they would otherwise be. The consensus, however, is that with schizophrenia we are dealing with a complex disease of the brain, not a "disorder of living" (Johnson, 1989). "How the environment interacts with genetic risk to trigger the development of schizophrenia remains unknown" (Iacono & Grove, 1993).

Before You Go On

What are some of the possible causes of schizophrenia?

TOPIC 12B SUMMARY

In this Topic, we continued our discussion of the psychological disorders, focusing on disorders that produce a loss of contact with reality and cause great difficulty in responding to the demands of daily living. This was surely the case with our example of Alzheimer's disease.

We saw that it is a distortion of affect, usually extreme depression, that marks the mood disorders—disorders (bipolar disorder in particular) that have a genetic foundation. Schizophrenia is a set of disorders that to some degree involves impairment of all areas of functioning: affect, cognition, and behavior. Current thinking is that there are three dimensions of schizophrenia, defined in terms of positive symptoms, either (1) psychotic or (2) disorganized, and (3) negative symptoms.

Again, the prevalence of psychological disorders is staggering. Millions of people are, at this moment, suffering from one of the disorders we've discussed in this chapter. It is now time to consider what can be done to help and to provide relief to those who suffer the pain of the psychological disorders.

CHAPTER SUMMARY

Topic 12A
How do we define psychological abnormality?

In the context of psychological disorders, "abnormal" refers to maladaptive behaviors, cognitions, and/or affect that are at odds with social expectations and that result in distress or discomfort. */pp. 428–430*

Cite advantages and disadvantages of classifying psychological disorders.

The *DSM-IV* is the revised fourth edition of the *Diagnostic and Statistical Manual of Mental Disorders,* the standard system of classification for the psychological disorders. The major advantage of this system is that it provides one standard label and cluster of symptoms for each disorder that all mental health practitioners can use; as such, it is a basis for improved communication. It does have its limitations, however. Many persons have more than one disorder at a time, a phenomenon called comorbidity. Schemes of classification can confuse description with explanation; classifying and labeling persons as having psychological disorders may overlook the larger group or society of which that individual is a part. */pp. 430–433*

Describe the symptoms of generalized anxiety disorder.

The defining characteristic of generalized anxiety disorder is a high level of anxiety that cannot be attributed to any particular source. With generalized anxiety disorder, the anxiety is chronic, persistent, and diffuse. */pp. 434–435*

What is a panic disorder?

The defining symptom of a panic disorder is a sudden, often unpredictable, attack of intense anxiety, called a panic attack, which may last for seconds or for hours. There is no particular stimulus that prompts the attack. It has a high rate of comorbidity, often being coupled with depression */p. 435*

What characterizes a phobic disorder?

By definition, a phobic disorder is typified by an intense, persistent fear of some object, activity, or situation that is in no real sense a threat to the individual's well-being; in brief, an intense, irrational fear. Phobias imply attempts to avoid the phobic object. Social phobias are significant, persistent fears of social or performance situations. Most phobias have a reasonably good prognosis. */pp. 435–437*

What characterizes the obsessive-compulsive disorder?

Obsessions and compulsions are the main symptoms in the obsessive-compulsive disorder, or OCD. An obsession is a thought or an idea that constantly intrudes on one's awareness. A compulsion, on the other hand, is a repeated and stereotyped behavior or act that constantly intrudes on one's behavior. OCD is a relatively common disorder with a biological basis. */pp. 437–438*

Describe the symptoms of posttraumatic stress disorder.

Posttraumatic stress disorder, or PTSD, is an anxiety disorder in which the symptoms of high levels of anxiety, recurrent and disruptive dreams, and recollections of a highly traumatic event (e.g., rape, combat, or natural disaster) occur well after the danger of the event has passed. We often find persons with PTSD also have alcohol or drug abuse problems or suffer from depresssion. */pp. 439–440*

Describe hypochondriasis and conversion disorder.

By definition, somatoform disorders reflect a physical or bodily symptom or complaint. In every case, there is no known biological cause for the complaint. In hypochondriasis, a person lives in fear and dread of contracting some serious illness or disease, when there is no medical evidence that such fears are well founded. In conversion disorder, there is an actual loss or alteration in physical functioning—often dramatic, such as blindness or deafness—not under voluntary control, suggesting a physical disorder, but without medical basis. */pp. 440–441*

What are the defining symptoms of the dissociative disorders?

Dissociative disorders are marked by a retreat or escape from (dissociation with) some aspect of one's personality. It may be a matter of an inability to recall some life event (amnesia), sometimes accompanied by unexplained travel to a different location (fugue state). In some rare cases, aspects of one's personality become so separated that the person suffers from dissociative identity disorder, where two or more personalities are found in the same individual. */pp. 441–443*

What are the defining characteristics of the personality disorders?

Personality disorders (PDs) are enduring patterns of perceiving, relating to, and thinking about the environment and oneself that are inflexible and maladaptive. They are lifelong patterns of maladjustment and may be classified as belonging to one of three groups, or clusters. Cluster 1 includes those PDs involving odd or eccentric reactions, such as the paranoid and schizoid personality disorders. Cluster 2 includes disorders of dramatic, emotional, or erratic reactions, such as the narcissistic and histrionic personality disorders. Cluster 3 includes disorders involving fear and anxiety, such as the avoidant and dependent personality disorders. */pp. 443–445*

Describe the antisocial personality disorder.

In the antisocial PD, we find an individual with an exceptional lack of regard for the rights and property of others who engages in impulsive behaviors with little or no thought to the consequences of those behaviors. These persons are usually found in the criminal justice system—about 15 to 20 percent of prisoners are diagnosed with antisocial personality disorder. Most people with the disorder are male. It seems to "burn out" in many as they reach their mid-40s. */pp. 446–447*

Topic 12B

What is Alzheimer's dementia?

Alzheimer's disease is a form of degenerative dementia associated with abnormalities in the brain—among other things, the formation of tangles and plaques. There is a strong likelihood of a genetic basis for the disease. Research is also focusing on the formation of certain brain proteins and the neurotransmitter acetylcholine. */pp. 447–450*

What are the mood disorders?

In the mood disorders, a disturbance in affect or feeling is the prime, and perhaps only, symptom. Most commonly we find the disorder to be one of depression alone; less commonly we find mania and depression occurring in cycles (bipolar mood disorder). In any case, whether the major symptom be depression or mania, there is no reason for the observed mood. Major depression affects about twice as many women as men. Mood disorders have a strong hereditary basis. Neurotransmitters (biogenic amines) such as serotonin and dopamine have been implicated. Psychological theories of depression focus on the learned ineffectiveness of reinforcers and cognitive factors, such as a poor self-image, as models for explaining the causes of depression. */pp. 450–453*

What is schizophrenia, and what distinguishes among its positive and negative symptoms?

Schizophrenia is a label applied to disorders that involve varying degrees of impairment. It occurs in about one percent of the population world wide. Many believe that there are three distinct types of schizophrenia, depending on the cluster of symptoms found. *Negative symptoms* include emotional and social withdrawal, reduced energy and motivation, apathy, and poor attention. There are two types with positive symptoms: *psychotic positive symptoms,* which includes hallucinations and delusions, and *disorganized psychotic symptoms,* which includes disorders of thinking and speech, bizarre behaviors, and inappropriate affect. */pp. 453–455*

What are some of the possible causes of schizophrenia?

Although we do not know the causes of schizophrenia, three lines of investigation have produced hopeful leads. (1) There is a genetic predisposition for the disorder. Although schizophrenia is not inherited, it runs in families. (2) Research on biochemical correlates have localized the neurotransmitter dopamine as being involved in the production of schizophrenia-like symptoms, although dopamine's role in the disorder is now being questioned. (3) Some psychological experiences, or stressful events, may bring on symptoms or make them worse. A reasonable position is that for some individuals, environmental events, such as extreme stress, trigger biochemical and structural changes in the brain that result in the symptoms of schizophrenia. */pp. 455–457*

What Is Your Diagnosis?

Here are a few very brief case studies. As best you can, identify the most likely diagnosis for each. Each case involves a disorder discussed in this chapter. (Suggested answers can be found on p. 574.)

1. M.Y. and her husband are with friends at a psychology convention. Before going out for dinner, it is suggested that everyone go to the revolving restaurant at the top of the hotel for a cocktail. M.Y. cannot be convinced to enter the elevator for the ride to the restaurant.

2. G.F. is convinced that he hears voices in the night that warn him about the terrible consequences that would result if he ever had a sexual thought about any woman.

3. P.L. is a 44-year-old male who apparently is suffering from amnesia. He was found living in a large city almost 600 miles from his home, where he had assumed a new identity. His wife identified him on the basis of a photo.

4. Without warning, and for no apparent reason, C.G. became debilitated by a series of severe attacks of anxiety. The attacks nearly immobilized her. Having now had four or five such attacks, C.G. refuses to leave her home and venture out into public places.

5. C.R. feels dirty unless she bathes and changes her clothes at least four times a day. Every room in her house is scrubbed at least twice a week and the bathroom is cleaned twice daily.

6. Although he was not personally injured, H.R. has had problems ever since the earthquake. He is listless and quarrelsome and sleeps fitfully, reliving the quake in nightmarish dreams.

7. For reasons neither he nor anyone else can determine, J.T. feels exceedingly sad, blue, and melancholy. He often sits with his head in his hands, sobbing and muttering general threats about suicide.

8. B.H. has always been something of a loner. He's a hard worker, but seldom interacts with anyone on the job. Occasionally, he talks about wanting a girl friend, but he doesn't seem to do anything to get one.

9. Ever since the armed robbers broke into her home, 14-year-old S.S. has been blind. She seems oddly unconcerned about her loss of sight.

10. One morning J.A. wakes up and says, "This just isn't right. I know life is tough, but there's something wrong here. I'm tired all the time but I have trouble getting to sleep. I'm yelling at the kids and my husband all the time, not doing a good job at work, and my grades at school are a D and an F, and I know I can do better. And sometimes, I just feel like I want to cry—and I don't know why. I've got to call somebody."

OUTLINE

*B*arbara is an 18-year-old freshman at City Community College. Living at home with her parents and two younger brothers, she is having difficulty dealing with demands on her time. She has a job as a waitress and is taking four classes at CCC. Lately, Barbara has become uncharacteristically anxious and depressed. She is falling behind in her school work, doing poorly at her job, and finding life at home almost unbearable. Barbara has been seeing a counselor at the Student Services Center.

Psychotherapist: Good morning, Barbara; how do you feel today?
Barbara: [snapping back] Can't you ever say anything but "how do you feel today?" I feel fine, just fine.
P.: You sound angry.
B.: [in a sarcastically mocking tone] "You sound angry."
P.: [silence]
B.: Well, I'm not angry, so there.
P.: Um. Hmm.
B.: So I'm angry. So big deal! So what of it? Is there something wrong with being angry?
P.: Of course not.
B.: You'd be angry too.

13

Treatment and Therapy

P.: Oh?

B.: My father threatened to throw me out of the house last night.

P.: He threatened you?

B.: He said that if I didn't get my act together and shape up, he'd send me packing. I don't know where I'd go, but if he pulls that crap on me one more time I'll show him. I will leave.

P.: Would you like to leave?

B.: Yes! No! No, I don't really want to. Nobody cares about me around there. They don't know how hard it is trying to work and go to school and everything, ya' know?

P.: [nods]

B.: *They* never went to college. What do *they* know? They don't know what it's like.

P.: You feel that your parents can't appreciate your problems?

B.: You got that right! What do they know? They've never tried to work and go to college at the same time.

P.: They don't know what it's like.

B.: No, they don't. Of course, I suppose it's not all their fault. They've never been in this situation. I suppose I could try to explain it to them better.

P.: So it would be helpful to share with them how you feel?

B.: Yeah. Maybe that's a good idea, I'll do that. At least I'll try. I don't want to just whine and complain all the time, but

maybe I can get them to understand what it's like. Boy that would help—to have somebody besides you understand and maybe be on my side once in awhile instead of on my case all the time.

Things seldom go as smoothly as depicted here, but this idealized dialogue does reflect several of the principles of psychotherapy we will be discussing in this chapter. We will begin with a brief look at the history of treatment for psychological disorders. In Topic 13A, we'll also consider treatment techniques that fall outside of the realm of psychology. Topic 13B is devoted to varieties of psychotherapy.

TOPIC 13A History and Biomedical Treatments

Mental illness is not a new phenomenon. Among the earliest written records from the Babylonians, Egyptians, and ancient Hebrews are descriptions of what we now know as psychological disorders (Murray, 1983). How individuals with disorders were treated was consistent with the prevailing view of what caused the disorder. Let's take a brief look at some of that history.

A Historical Perspective

The history of treating psychological disorders in the Western world isn't a pleasant one. By today's standards, *therapy*—in the sense of active, humane intervention to improve the condition of persons in psychological distress—doesn't even seem to be the right term to describe how most disordered persons were dealt with in the past.

The ancient Greeks and Romans believed that individuals who were depressed, manic, irrational, or intellectually retarded, or who had hallucinations or delusions, had in some way offended the gods. In some cases, persons were viewed as temporarily out of favor with the gods, and it followed that their condition could be improved through prayer and religious ritual. More severely disturbed patients were seen as physically possessed by evil spirits. These cases were more difficult, often impossible, to cure. The goal of treatment was to exorcise the evil spirits and demons inhabiting the minds and souls of the mentally deranged. Many unfortunates died as a result of their treatment or were killed outright when treatment failed. Treatment was left to the priests, who were, after all, thought to be skilled in the ways and means of spirit manipulation.

There *were* those in ancient times who had a more enlightened, or reasonable, view of psychological disorders. Among them was Hippocrates (460–377 B.C.), who believed that mental disorders had physical causes, not spiritual ones. He saw epilepsy as being a disorder of the brain, for example. Some of his views were wrong (e.g., that hysteria is a disorder of the uterus), but at least he tried (without success) to demystify psychological disorders.

During the Middle Ages (1000–1500), the oppression and persecution of the disordered were at their peak. During this period, the prevailing view continued to be that psychologically disordered people were "bad people," under the spell of devils and evil spirits. They had brought on their own grief, and there was no hope for them, except that they save their immortal souls and confess their evil ways.

For hundreds of years, well into the eighteenth century, the prevailing attitude toward the mentally ill continued to be that they were in league with the devil or that they were being punished by God for sinful thoughts and deeds. They were witches who could not be cured except by confession. When such confessions were not forthcoming, the prescribed treatment was torture. If torture failed to evoke a confession, death was the only recourse—often death by being burned at the stake. Between the fourteenth and mid-seventeenth centuries, nearly 200,000 to 500,000 "witches" were put to death (Ben-Yehuda, 1980).

When the disordered (or those who were severely intellectually retarded) were not tortured or immediately put to death, they were usually placed in asylums for the insane. The first insane asylum, opened in 1547, was St. Mary of Bethlehem Hospital in London, to house "fools" and "lunatics." The institution became known as Bedlam (a cockney pronunciation of Bethlehem). It was a terrible place. Inmates were tortured, poorly fed, or starved to death. To remove the "bad blood" from their systems, thought to be a cause of their melancholy or delirium, patients were regularly led to bleeding chambers, where a small incision was made in a vein in the calf of their legs so that their blood would ooze into leather buckets. There was no real professional staff at Bedlam. The "keepers," as they were called, could make extra

This painting by William Hogarth depicts a scene of the "Fools of Bedlam."

money by putting their charges on view for the public. Viewing the lunatics of Bedlam became an entertainment for the nobility. Inmates who were able were sent into the streets to beg, wearing a sign that identified them as "fools of Bedlam." Even today we use the word *bedlam* to describe a condition of uproar and confusion.

It would be comforting to think that Bedlam was an exception, an aberration. It was not. In the eighteenth and nineteenth centuries, similar institutions were commonplace. Against this backdrop of misery and despair, the names of a few enlightened individuals deserve mention. One is Philippe Pinel (1745–1826), a French physician who, in the midst of the French Revolution (on April 25, 1793), was named director of an asylum for the insane in Paris. We know of Pinel today largely because of an act of compassion and courage. The law of the day required that asylum inmates be chained and confined. On September 2, 1793, Pinel ordered the chains and shackles removed from about fifty of the inmates of his "hospital." He allowed them to move freely about the institution and its grounds. This humane gesture produced surprising effects: the symptoms of the patients, in many cases, improved markedly. A few patients were even released from the asylum. Unfortunately, Pinel's "humane therapy," as he called it, did not spread to other asylums. Yet Pinel's unchaining of the insane and his belief in moral treatment for the mentally ill can be seen as the beginning of a gradual enlightenment concerning mental illness, even if Pinel's success did not lead to broad, sweeping reforms.

There are a few other pioneers whose efforts deserve mention here. Benjamin Rush (1745–1813) was the founder of American psychiatry. He published the first text on mental disorders in the United States. Although some of the treatments recommended by Rush seem barbaric by today's standards (he believed in bleeding, for example), his general attitudes were very humane. He argued vehemently and successfully, for example, that the mentally ill should not be put on display to satisfy the curiosity of onlookers.

Dorothea Dix (1802–1887) was an American nurse. In 1841 she took a position in a women's prison and was appalled at what she saw there. Among the prisoners were hundreds of women who clearly were mentally retarded or psychologically disordered. Despite her slight stature and her own ill health, she entered upon a crusade of singular vigor. She traveled from state to state, campaigning for reform in prisons, mental hospitals, and asylums.

Clifford Beers, a graduate of Yale University, had been institutionalized in a series of hospitals and asylums. It seems likely that he was suffering from what we now call a bipolar mood disorder. Probably in spite of his treatment rather than because of it, Beers recovered and was released—in itself an unusual occurrence. In 1908, he wrote a book about his experience, *A Mind That Found Itself.* The book became a best seller—William James and Theodore Roosevelt were said to be very impressed with Beers and his story. Clifford Beers's book was read by people in power, and is often cited as one of the main stimuli for the beginning of what we now call the "mental health movement."

Since the early 1900s, progress in providing help for the mentally ill has been both slow and unsteady. World War I and the Great Depression reduced the monies available to support state institutions for mental patients. Within the past 50 years, conditions have improved immeasurably, but there's still a long way to go. We continue to fight a prejudice against persons suffering from psychological disorders.

Before You Go On

Briefly trace the history of the treatment of persons with psychological disorders.

Biomedical Treatments of Psychological Disorders

As we have seen, biological and medical approaches to mental illness can be traced to ancient times. Psychologists today cannot use medical treatments. Currently, performing surgery, administering shock treatments, and prescribing medication require a medical degree. Psychologists are often involved in biomedical treatments, however. They may recommend a medical treatment or refer a client to the care of a physician or psychiatrist (a person with a medical degree who specializes in mental disorders). The approaches psychologists use, the psychotherapies, will be the subject of Topic 13B.

Here we'll review three types of biomedical intervention: psychosurgery, which was common just 50 years ago, but is now rare; electroconvulsive therapy, which is far from uncommon; and drug therapy, one of the newest and most promising developments in the treatment of mental illness.

Psychosurgery

psychosurgery *a surgical procedure designed to affect one's psychological or behavioral reactions*

Psychosurgery is the name we give to surgical procedures, usually directed at the brain, designed to affect psychological reactions. Psychosurgical techniques today are largely experimental, and are aimed at making rather minimal lesions in the brain.

We have already noted that the surgical destruction of the corpus callosum (in the so-called "split-brain" procedure) can alleviate symptoms in extreme cases of epilepsy. Small surgical lesions in the limbic system have been effective in reducing or eliminating violent behaviors. A surgical technique, a *cingulectomy,* has been used successfully to reduce extreme anxiety and the symptoms of obsessive-compulsive disorders. This is a treatment of last resort that involves cutting a bundle of nerve fibers that connects the very front of the frontal lobe with parts of the limbic system (Baer et al., 1995; Sachdev et al., 1992). And, as we've already noted in Chapter 2, surgical techniques are being used to treat some cases of Parkinson's disease.

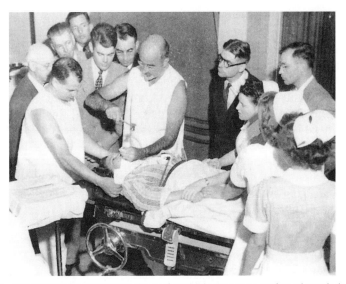

During the late 1940s and the 1950s, the prefontal lobotomy was perfomed regularly. Although psychosurgeons understood that the procedure was irreversible, it took many years before viable alternatives were available.

Of all of the types of psychosurgery, none has ever been used as commonly as a procedure called a prefrontal lobotomy or, simply, **lobotomy** (Valenstein, 1980, 1986). This surgery severs the major neural connections between the prefrontal lobes (the area at the very front of the cerebral cortex) and lower brain centers.

A lobotomy was first performed in 1935 by a Portuguese psychiatrist, Egas Moniz. For developing the procedure, Moniz was awarded the Nobel Prize in 1949. (The next year, in an ironic twist of fate, Moniz was shot by one of his lobotomized patients. He was rendered paraplegic and was confined to a wheelchair for the rest of his life.) The logic behind a lobotomy was that the prefrontal lobes influence the more basic emotional centers, lower in the brain (e.g., in the limbic system). Severely disturbed patients were thought to have difficulty exercising cerebral cortex control over those lower parts of the brain. It was reasoned that if these areas of the brain were separated surgically, the more depressed, agitated, or violent patients could be brought under control.

The operation often appeared to be successful. Always used as a measure of last resort, stories of the changes it produced in chronic mental patients circulated widely. For example, in its November 30, 1942 issue, *Time* magazine called the surgical procedure "revolutionary," claiming that at that time, "some 300 people in the United States have had their psychoses surgically removed." *Life* magazine, in a graphic photo essay titled "Psychosurgery: Operation to Cure Sick Minds Turns Surgeon's Blade into an Instrument of Mental Therapy," called the results of lobotomy procedures "spectacular," claiming that "about 30% of the lobotomized patients were able to return to everyday productive lives" (*Life*, 3/3/47, p. 93).

In the 1940s and 1950s, prefrontal lobotomies were performed regularly. *Time* reported (September 15, 1952) that neurologist Walter Freeman was performing about a hundred lobotomies a week. It is difficult to estimate how many lobotomies were performed in these two decades, but certainly they numbered in the tens of thousands.

Treating severely disturbed patients had always been difficult. Perhaps we should not be surprised that this relatively simple surgical technique was accepted so widely at first. The procedure was done under local anesthetic in a physician's office and took only 10 minutes. An instrument that looks very much like an ice pick was inserted through the eye socket, on the nasal side, and pushed up into the brain. A few movements of the instrument and the job was done—the lobes were

lobotomy *a psychosurgical technique in which the prefrontal lobes of the cerebral cortex are severed from lower brain centers* cut loose from the lower brain centers. Within a couple of hours, the patient would be ready to return to his or her room.

It was always appreciated that the procedure was an irreversible one. What took longer to realize was that it often brought terrible side effects. Between 1 and 4 percent of patients receiving prefrontal lobotomies died (Carson & Butcher, 1992, p. 610). Many who survived suffered seizures, memory loss, an inability to plan ahead, and a general listlessness and loss of affect. Many acted childishly and were difficult to manage within institutions. By the late 1950s, lobotomies had become rare. Contrary to common belief, a prefrontal lobotomy is not an illegal procedure, although the conditions under which it might even be considered are very restrictive. Prefrontal lobotomies are not done today for the very simple reason that they are no longer needed. Psychoactive drugs, which have fewer side effects, produce similar results more safely and reliably.

Before You Go On

What is psychosurgery?
Is it still in use today?

Electroconvulsive Therapy

electroconvulsive therapy (ECT) *a treatment, usually for severe depression, in which an electric current passed across a patient's head causes a seizure*

As gruesome as the procedures of psychosurgery can be, many people find the very notion of **electroconvulsive therapy (ECT)**, or shock treatments, even more difficult to appreciate. This technique, introduced in 1937, involves passing an electric current of between 70 and 150 volts across a patient's head for a fraction of a second. The patient has been given a fast-acting general anesthetic and is thus unconscious when the shock is delivered. As soon as the anesthetic is administered, the patient receives a muscle relaxant to minimize muscular contractions, which were quite common—and potentially dangerous—in the early days of ECT. The electric shock induces a reaction in the brain not unlike an epileptic seizure. The entire procedure takes about five minutes. One of the side effects of ECT is a loss of memory for events just preceding the administration of the shock and for the shock itself.

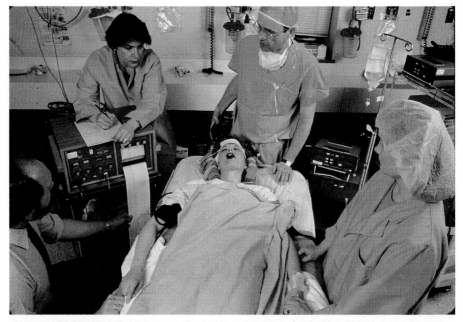

Electroconvulsive shock therapy is not pleasant to watch. There is considerable concern that we do not yet fully understand why the procedure has the beneficial effects that it does.

At first the treatment was used to help calm agitated schizophrenics, but it soon became clear that its most beneficial results were for those patients suffering from major depression. It often alleviates the symptoms of depression and, in some cases, has beneficial effects on other symptoms. In fact, the group of patients best suited to the ECT procedure are those for whom depression is a major symptom, but for whom other symptoms (such as hallucinations or delusions) are also present (Joyce & Paykel, 1989).

Virtually all patients (97 percent) give their consent to the procedure, and negative side effects are rare. The most commonly reported side effects are memory loss and a general mental confusion. In nearly all cases, these effects disappear in a few days or weeks. In one study of 99,425 treatments given to 18,627 patients, only two deaths were reported. The death rate for childbirth in the United States is nearly six times greater (Kramer, 1985). Once they have experienced the procedure, most ECT patients are far from terrorized by the notion of having an electrical shock sent through their brain. In one study, 82 percent of 166 patients surveyed rated ECT as no more upsetting than a visit to the dentist (Sackeim, 1985). The beneficial effects of ECT are reasonably long-lasting. After only 10 to 12 treatments, many patients remain free of symptoms for months.

The poor reputation ECT has among the general population, and among some psychologists and psychiatrists as well, did not develop without foundation. There are horror stories of the negative side effects that can follow abuse of the procedure. (At first, the seizures of the shock treatment were induced by drugs, not electricity, and it is largely from these drug-induced treatments we have the stories of convulsions so massive as to result in broken bones.) It is now recommended that no more than a dozen treatments be given and that they be administered over an extended period. Some patients in the past received hundreds of ECT treatments. In such cases, there were reports of brain damage and permanent memory loss.

Just why ECT produces the benefits it does is not fully understood. Researchers are looking at the action of neurotransmitters in the brain for explanations. The effects, if not the amounts, of some neurotransmitters—GABA, serotonin, and norepinephrine, in particular—are increased by ECT. Even though we do not understand fully how ECT works, and even though it is a treatment that must be used with extreme care, ECT is very much in practice today. Although the numbers declined during the late 1970s, the National Institute of Mental Health estimates that 110,000 American patients receive shock treatments each year. The introduction of antidepressant medications has reduced the need for ECT. But drug treatment is not always successful, and even when it is, it often takes six to eight weeks for the drugs to produce their results. Researchers have found that in many cases electroconvulsive therapy is a more effective treatment than are antidepressant medications (Small et al., 1988). ECT is now reserved for (1) patients for whom drug therapies seem ineffective, (2) patients with acute suicidal tendencies (because drugs take so long to have an effect), and (3) depressed patients who also suffer from delusions.

Administering a shock to just one side of the brain, called a *unilateral ECT,* may be a safer yet equally effective procedure with fewer side effects. More success has been found by creating seizures in the right hemisphere of the cerebral cortex (which is more associated with emotional reactions) than in the left hemisphere (Squire & Slater, 1978).

Before You Go On

What is ECT, and why is it still being used?

Drug Therapy

Chemicals that have their effect on a person's affect, behavior, or cognitions are referred to as *psychoactive drugs.* As we've seen, there are many of them, and most are

©©©© **Thinking Critically** ©©©©

What ethical considerations are involved in asking a person with a severe psychological disorder to give his or her informed consent to a procedure like ECT or psychosurgery?

used to produce an altered state of consciousness or awareness. Using chemicals to improve the condition of the mentally disordered is a much more recent development and has been hailed as one of the most significant scientific achievements of the latter half of the twentieth century (Snyder, 1984). In this section we'll examine the three main types of medication used as therapy: the antipsychotic, antidepressant, and antianxiety drugs.

antipsychotic drugs *chemicals, such as chlorpromazine, effective in reducing psychotic symptoms*

Antipsychotic Drugs. As their name implies, the **antipsychotic drugs** alleviate or eliminate psychotic symptoms. *Psychotic symptoms* are those that signal loss of contact with reality, such as delusions and hallucinations, and a gross impairment of functioning. Inappropriate affect, or total loss of affect, is also a psychotic symptom. Antipsychotic medications are primarily designed to treat schizophrenia, although they are also used with other disorders, including cases of substance abuse disorders.

The breakthrough in the use of antipsychotic drugs came with the introduction of *chlorpromazine* in the early 1950s. A French neurosurgeon, Henri Laborit, was looking for a drug that would calm his patients before surgery. Laborit wanted to help them relax because he knew that if they did, his patients' postsurgical recovery would be improved. A drug company gave Laborit chlorpromazine. It worked even better than anyone had expected, producing relaxation and calm in the patients. Laborit convinced some of his colleagues to try the drug on their more agitated patients, some of whom were suffering from psychological disorders. The experiments met with great success, and by the late 1950s the drug was widely used in both North America and Europe. Not only did "Laborit's tranquilizer" produce a calm and relaxed state in his patients, it also significantly reduced psychotic symptoms in other patients.

The drug revolution had begun. With the success of chlorpromazine, the search for other chemicals that could improve the plight of the mentally ill began in earnest. By 1956, more than half a dozen antipsychotic medications were available. From 1976 to 1985, the use of antipsychotic medication remained stable overall, with between 19 and 21 million prescriptions being written (Wysowski & Baum, 1989).

Chlorpromazine is one of many drugs currently being used with success to treat psychotic symptoms. Although there are many types of antipsychotic drugs, most work in essentially the same way: by blocking receptor sites for the neurotransmitter dopamine. Antipsychotic drugs are most effective in treating the positive symptoms of schizophrenia: delusions, hallucinations, and bizarre behaviors. Clozapine (trade name *Clozaril*) seems to be an exception, because it is effective in reducing negative symptoms, such as social withdrawal, as well as positive ones. Unfortunately, clozapine carries with it the risk of serious side effects, some of which can be fatal. As a result, the use of this drug is very carefully monitored.

The effects of the antipsychotic drugs are remarkable and impressive. They have revolutionized the care of psychotic patients, but they are not the ultimate solution for disorders such as schizophrenia. With high dosages or prolonged use, side effects emerge that are unpleasant at best: dry mouth and throat, sore muscles and joints, sedation, sexual impotence, and muscle tremors. About 30 percent of patients with schizophrenia do not respond to antipsychotic medication (Kane, 1989). These drugs are most effective when they are used early on, with patients who have recently been diagnosed with schizophrenia, as opposed to those who have exhibited symptoms of the disease for some time (Carpenter & Buchanan, 1994; Lieberman et al., 1993).

Although antipsychotic drugs can suppress symptoms, the question remains: Are they in any sense curing the disorder? In the usual sense of the word *cure,* they are not. Symptom-free patients, who are often released from institutional care to the outside world, soon stop using their medication, only to find that their psychotic symptoms return. A review of 66 studies of 4,365 patients found that relapse was highly associated with sudden withdrawal from antipsychotic medication. Recognizing the unpleasantness and even the danger of the prolonged use of such medications, the authors of this review recommended a slow tapering off of the drugs being used (Gilbert et al., 1995).

Antidepressant Drugs. The **antidepressant drugs** elevate the mood of persons who are feeling depressed. Some antidepressant medications may be useful in treating disorders other than depression, e.g., panic disorder and generalized anxiety disorder (Rickels et al., 1993). An antidepressant drug that has little or no effect on one person may cause severe, unpleasant side effects in another, and yet have markedly beneficial effects for a third person. Antidepressant drugs can elevate the mood of many depressed individuals, but they have no effect on people who are not depressed. That is, they do not produce a euphoric high in people who are already in a good mood.

Antidepressant medications typically take 10 to 14 days to show any effect. Their full effect may take six weeks and they need to be taken on a long-term basis to prevent a recurrence of the depression (Maxman, 1991). As you might have guessed, most antidepressant medications produce unfortunate side effects in some patients, including intellectual confusion, increased perspiration, and weight gain. Some have been implicated as a cause of heart disease. A major problem with some antidepressant drugs is that they require adherence to a strict diet and carefully monitored dosages to be most effective.

antidepressant drugs *chemicals that reduce the symptoms of depression*

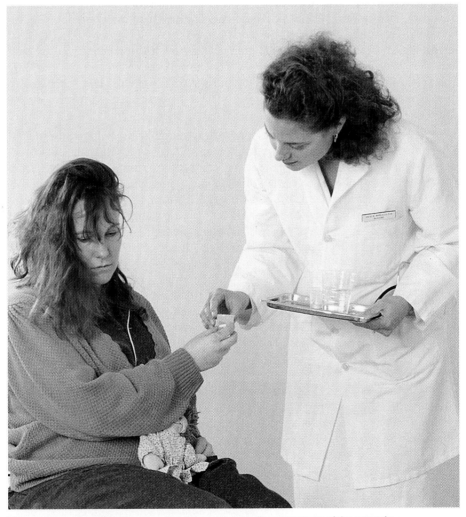

The use of psychoactive drugs to suppress, or manage, the symptoms of the severely psychologically disordered has been hailed as one of the most significant scientific achievements of the twentieth century.

Fluoxetine (trade name *Prozac*) was introduced in 1987. It now is the single most prescribed antidepressant, with about 650,000 prescriptions written each month. By 1996, sales of Prozac will exceed $5 billion. Chemically, *Prozac* is unrelated to most of the other antidepressants, although it, too, affects a brain neurotransmitter (serotonin). Often an effective medication, its main advantage is that it produces fewer negative side effects. It seems to be an effective treatment for many women who suffer from the irritability and tension of premenstrual syndrome, or PMS (Steiner et al., 1995). A newer drug, *Effexor,* was approved for use in 1993. So far, *Effexor* shows great promise, and with few side effects. Like *Prozac,* it targets levels of the neurotransmitter serotonin in the brain, but does so with slightly more precision, and also regulates norepinephrine levels.

This is an appropriate context in which to mention *lithium,* or lithium salts, such as lithium carbonate. Lithium salts are referred to as "mood stabilizers" (Maxman, 1991). They have been used with success in treating major depression, but are most useful in controlling the manic stage of bipolar disorders. A major benefit of lithium treatments is that they are often effective in preventing or reducing the occurrence of future episodes of mood disorder (NIMH, 1981, 1989). There are those for whom the drug has no beneficial effects, and its prolonged use can cause convulsions, kidney failure, and other serious reactions. In the summer of 1995, the Food and Drug Administration approved a medication commonly used to treat epilepsy for use in treating bipolar disorder as well. The drug, *Depakote,* seems to be as effective as lithium salts, has fewer side effects, and is faster acting.

Unlike antipsychotic medications, when antidepressant drugs are effective, they may actually bring about long-term cures rather than just symptom suppression. In other words, the changes in mood caused by the drugs may outlast use of the drug itself. The plan, in fact, is to gradually reduce the dosage of the drug over time. For persons with mood disorders who do not respond to drugs presently available, other types are being tested, and for such patients, electroconvulsive therapy may be indicated.

antianxiety drugs *chemicals that alleviate the symptoms of anxiety; also known as tranquilizers*

Antianxiety Drugs. The **antianxiety drugs** (tranquilizers) help reduce the felt aspect of anxiety. Some antianxiety drugs, e.g., *Miltown* or *Equanil,* are muscle relaxers. When muscular tension is reduced, the patient often reports feeling calm and at ease. The other major variety of antianxiety drug is the group of chemicals called *benzodiazepines* (e.g., *Librium, Valium,* and *Xanax*). These are the most commonly prescribed of all drugs. They act directly on the central nervous system, and their impact is significant. They help anxious people feel less anxious. Initially, the only negative side effects appear to be a slight drowsiness, blurred vision, and a slight impairment of coordination.

Unfortunately, the tranquilizing effect of the drugs is not long-lasting. Patients can fall into a pattern of relying on the drugs to alleviate even the slightest fears and worries. A dependency and addiction can develop from which withdrawal can be difficult. In fact, a danger of the antianxiety medications is the very fact that they are so effective. As long as one can avoid the unpleasant feelings of anxiety simply by taking a pill, there is little to motivate one to seek out and deal with the actual cause of one's anxiety.

A curiosity is that these drugs are much more likely to be prescribed for women, especially women over age 45, than they are for men (Travis, 1988). This may very well be the result of a tendency on the part of physicians to see women as more likely to be anxious in the first place (Unger & Crawford, 1992).

Before You Go On

What are antipsychotic, antidepressant, and antianxiety drugs?
Describe any side effects of each.

Deinstitutionalization: Blessing or Curse?

As I mentioned earlier, the first institution for the mentally ill was St. Mary of Bethlehem Hospital, so designated in 1547. Despite many well-intentioned efforts to promote mental health (rather than just house the disordered), not much changed for nearly 400 years after "Bedlam" opened. By the mid-twentieth century, large government-supported institutions were the commonplace residences of the mentally retarded and the mentally ill. Lack of public support, leading to a lack of adequate funding for staff and facilities, resulted in what amounted to a national disgrace.

Within the last 40 years, there has been a truly revolutionary shift in mental health care. For several seemingly sound and sensible reasons, many patients with mental disorders have experienced **deinstitutionalization**. They have been released from the large mental institutions to return to family and community. The drop in institutional patient population has been dramatic. The number of patients in state and county mental hospitals reached a peak of nearly 560,000 in the mid-1950s and has dropped over 80 percent since then to hold steady at just over 100,000 for the last ten years. Interestingly, although the population of patients in mental, or psychiatric, hospitals at any one time continues to decrease, the number of admissions is again on the rise. It seems that once admitted, a patient is spending much less time in the hospital, but is much more likely to be readmitted soon after release. One psychiatric hospital in Boston found that in 1994, 21 percent of the patients it released were readmitted to the hospital within one month. What brought about this change, and has it been a change for the better or the worse?

There are several reasons for deinstitutionalization we might list. I have already alluded to some of them. Let's consider just three. (1) *A concern for the rights of the patient* arose. The overcrowded and nearly inhumane conditions that existed

deinstitutionalization *the practice, begun in the mid–1950s, of releasing patients from mental institutions and returning them to their home communities*

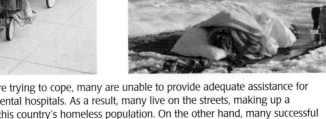

Although communities are trying to cope, many are unable to provide adequate assistance for patients released from mental hospitals. As a result, many live on the streets, making up a significant proportion of this country's homeless population. On the other hand, many successful programs are in place that meet patients' needs after they are deinstitutionalized.

in many institutions simply became more than society was willing to bear. The courts entered the picture, and in 1971, ruled that patients either receive adequate and proper treatment or be released. (2) *Symptoms can be managed with drugs.* We've already touched on this matter. The introduction of effective drugs that suppressed psychotic symptoms made it more reasonable for patients who no longer displayed unusual or bizarre behaviors to be released from institutional care. (3) *Community mental health centers were to be established.* In 1963, Congress passed the Community Mental Health Act, which included a provision for establishing a large number of mental health centers in local communities rather than centralized in one or two state institutions. The plan was for there to be one easily accessible mental health center for every 50,000 people. These centers were to accommodate people on an outpatient basis and were to provide other services, such as short-term inpatient care, as well as consultation, education, and prevention programs.

Has the system of deinstitutionalization worked? There are those who applaud the change (Braun et al., 1981), and argue that "continued optimism about community care seems warranted" (Shadish, 1984).

On the other hand, many see deinstitutionalization as trading one set of problems for a host of others. Many patients released from mental hospitals are, quite literally, "dumped" back into their home communities, where resources to assist them are often minimal. Many require the support of the welfare system and there is seldom adequate housing for those who have been released. Patients often end up in nursing homes, boarding houses, and other settings ill-prepared to care for their needs (Bellack & Mueser, 1986; Smith et al., 1993). Frequently, negative attitudes get involved, as in, "We don't want 'those people' living in our neighborhood." Many released patients become homeless "street people," particularly in large cities. The National Institute of Mental Health estimates the percentage of homeless persons with psychological disorders at 30 to 35 percent; others place the percentage at closer to 50 percent (Bellack, 1986; Levine et al., 1993; Toro et al., 1991).

No matter how capable a community mental health center and its staff may be (assuming there is a center nearby), if patients do not seek its support, it will do them little good. The notion of social support—both seeking it and offering it—varies from culture to culture. It is one of the landmark differences between cultures we have characterized as individualistic or collectivistic. It may be that some of our negative experiences with deinstitutionalization are reflections of the individualistic nature of American society (see, for example, Lin & Kleinman, 1988).

As we have noted, most of the antipsychotic medications patients require do not have lasting effects. When patients stop taking their medication (because of its expense or its side effects), symptoms return, and they will likely need to return once again to the institution. Indeed, as many as one-half to two-thirds of released patients do stop taking their medication (Gilbert et al., 1995; McGrath et al., 1990).

The trend to reduce the population of patients in institutions is likely to continue. Effective community programs and more resources are needed to assist those released from these institutions to ensure that discharge is appropriate both for the patients and for the communities to which they return. Mental health professionals view the treatment of the chronically mentally disordered as a national health concern of high priority (e.g., Levine et al., 1993; Smith et al., 1993; Youngstrom, 1991).

Before You Go On

What is deinstitutionalization, and has it been successful?

TOPIC 13A SUMMARY

This chapter began with a brief synopsis of the history of the treatment of psychological disorders. The idea of intervening on behalf of persons with psychological disorders—particularly the most bizarre or most chronic disorders—is a relatively new direction. We began our discussion of therapy by considering biomedical treatments. We first considered a technique—the lobotomy—that now is more of a historical curiosity than anything else. Then we considered electroconvulsive therapy, or ECT. Although we still do not know exactly why ECT has the effects that it does (largely, relieving the symptoms of major depression), it remains a common treatment option.

We saw in our discussion of the use of psychoactive drugs that there is reason to be optimistic about using biochemical means to suppress, if not eliminate, many of the symptoms associated with psychological disorders. At the moment, however, we should remain somewhat cautious. Remember that only thirty-five years ago it was widely held that lobotomies would be the ultimate treatment for persons with severe psychological disorders. Scientists do continue to learn about the delicate balance between brain and behavior, and we can now be more cautiously optimistic than ever before that real cures for psychological disorders will be found.

T O P I C 1 3 B The Psychotherapies

The major goal of the various techniques of psychotherapy is to help a person to think, feel, or act more effectively. Additionally, different types of therapy have different specific subgoals. In this Topic, we will focus on five types of psychotherapy and see that each approaches the therapeutic interaction a bit differently. Before we get to our discussion of specific techniques, let's see what sorts of professionals provide treatment or therapy for persons with psychological disorders.

Who Provides Psychotherapy?

Just 30 years ago, only 13 percent of the population sought psychotherapy at any time in their lives (Meredith, 1986). Now we find that 30 percent will have some experience in psychotherapy in their lifetime. Each year, about 3 percent of the population seeks professional help for a psychological problem—that's about 80 million visits (Olfson & Pincus, 1994). People seek help from mental health professionals twice as often as they visit internists (Hunt, 1987, p. 2).

What follows is a list of generalities; my descriptions will not hold true for everyone within a given category. Remember also that because of their experience and training, some mental health professionals develop specialties within their fields. That is, some therapists specialize in working with children or adolescents; some work primarily with adults; some prefer to work with families; and some devote their efforts to people with substance and alcohol abuse problems.

Some psychotherapists have special training in dealing with clients from various cultures or ethnic groups (Sue & Sue, 1990). This can be useful. In this country, "most mental health workers come from middle-class backgrounds and expect their clients to be open, verbal, and psychologically minded. They tend to value verbal, emotional, and behavioral expressiveness" (Koslow & Salett, 1989, p. 3).

Adler and Gielen (1994) tell the story of an African American woman of Bahamian descent who was complaining of depression. It seems the woman believed that another girlfriend of her lover had placed a "hex" on her. The depressed woman sought treatment from a Haitian spiritual healer who, among other things, took the woman to a cemetery at midnight, placed her in an open grave, and sprinkled some dirt on her before retrieving her. Shortly after this "treatment," the woman was free of her depression, received a raise at her job, and had sent her lover packing. I suspect that most American therapists would judge this treatment plan to be as bizarre and troubling as the symptoms that prompted it. But in this

Regardless of the specifics involved, all forms of psychotherapy are designed to help a person think, feel, or act differently.

woman's cultural framework, the ritualistic, symbolic burial allowed her to bury her evil spirits at the cemetery—their source—and come away cleansed. This may be an extreme example, but it is true that members of other cultures and ethnic minorities state a strong preference for "ethnically similar" therapists (e.g., Coleman et al., 1995).

With these cautions in mind, the following may be considered psychotherapists:

1. The *clinical psychologist* usually has earned a Ph.D. in psychology, a program that provides practical, applied experience, as well as an emphasis on research. The Ph.D. clinician has completed a one-year internship, usually at a mental health center or psychiatric hospital. The clinical psychologist has extensive training in psychological testing (in general, psychodiagnostics). Some clinical psychologists have a Psy.D. (pronounced "sigh-dee"), which is a Doctor of Psychology, rather than the Doctor of Philosophy degree. Psy.D. programs take as long to complete as Ph.D. programs, but tend to emphasize more practical, clinical work.

2. Psychiatry is a specialty area in medicine. In addition to course work required for an M.D., the *psychiatrist* spends an internship (usually one year) and a residency (usually three years) in a mental hospital, specializing in the care of psychologically disturbed patients. At the moment, the psychiatrist is the only type of psychotherapist permitted to use the biomedical treatments reviewed in Topic 13A. (There is a campaign under way to get some medical privileges for Ph.D. psychologists.)

3. The *counseling psychologist* usually has a Ph.D. in psychology. The focus of study (and required one-year internship), however, is generally with patients with less severe psychological problems. For instance, rather than spending one's internship in a psychiatric hospital, a counseling psychologist would more likely spend time at a university counseling center.

4. A *licensed professional counselor* will have a degree in counselor education and will have met state requirements for a license to practice psychotherapy. Coun-

EXPERIENCING PSYCHOLOGY

Designing Your Own Mental Health Directory

Given the statistics on the prevalence of psychological disorders, it is very unlikely that any of us can go very long without the need of some sort of psychotherapy or treatment for psychological disorders—either for ourselves, or for someone close to us. When the need arises, there are many options available to you. You may contact your psychology instructor, family doctor, or clergy person. You may contact the student services office on your campus, or a local, community mental health center. You may ask family, friends, or the local office of the Mental Health Association for a referral.

It will only take a few minutes now to explore the possibilities for therapy, counseling, or treatment in your current situation. Look through your campus directory, or the yellow pages of your telephone directory for names, addresses, and telephone numbers. Make a list of resources or agencies that you could call if you encounter a need for mental health services. Put the list some place handy—in with your notes, in your address book, wherever. The need for psychotherapy seldom arises in an emergency situation, where seconds count. On the other hand, it makes good sense to be prepared, to have a course of action ready should the need arise.

selors are found in school settings, but also work in mental health settings, specializing in family counseling and drug abuse.

5. *Psychoanalyst* is a special label given to a clinical psychologist or a psychiatrist who has also received intensive training (and certification) in the particular methods of Freudian psychoanalysis.

6. The terminal degree for *clinical social workers* is generally the master's degree, although Ph.D.s in social work are becoming more common. Social workers engage in a variety of psychotherapies, but their traditional role has been involvement in family and group therapy.

Some people with a master's degree in psychology provide psychotherapy, but because of certification laws in many states, they cannot advertise themselves as "psychologists." *Occupational therapists* usually have a master's degree (less frequently, a bachelor's degree) in occupational therapy, which includes many psychology classes and internship training in aiding the psychologically and physically handicapped. *Psychiatric nurses* often work in mental hospitals and clinics. In addition to their R.N., psychiatric nurses have training in the care of mentally ill patients. *Pastoral counseling* is a specialty of those with a religious background and a master's degree in psychology or educational counseling. The *mental health technician* usually has an associate degree in mental health technology (MHT). MHT graduates seldom provide unsupervised therapy, although they may be involved in the delivery of many mental health services.

Now that we have an idea of who may offer psychotherapy services, let's consider the types of techniques or approaches they may employ.

Before You Go On

Who may offer psychotherapy?

Psychoanalytic Techniques

Psychoanalysis began with Sigmund Freud near the end of the nineteenth century. This means of therapy did not really evolve from Freudian personality theory (see

⊚⊚⊚ **Thinking Critically** ⊚⊚⊚

If you felt that you had problems and could profit from some form of therapy, how would you go about getting in contact with a therapist? Where would you start?

Topic 9A). If anything, the reverse is true. Freud was a therapist first, a personality theorist second. But his techniques of therapy and theory of personality sprang forth from the same mind, and are thus related.

psychoanalysis *the form of psychotherapy associated with Freud, aimed at helping the patient gain insight into unconscious conflicts*

Psychoanalysis is based on several assumptions, most of them having to do with conflict and the unconscious mind. For Freud, one's life is often a struggle to resolve conflicts between naturally opposing forces. The biological, sexual, aggressive strivings of the id are often in conflict with the superego, associated with over-cautiousness and guilt. The strivings of the id also can be in conflict with the rational, reality-based ego, which may be called upon to mediate between the id and the superego. Anxiety-producing conflicts that go unresolved are repressed; they are forced out of awareness into the unconscious mind. Conflicts and anxiety-producing traumas of childhood can be expected to produce symptoms of psychological disturbance later in life.

According to Freud, the way to rid oneself of anxiety is to enter the unconscious, identify the details of the repressed, anxiety-producing conflict, bring it out into the open, and then resolve it as well as possible. The first step is to gain insight into the true nature of one's problems; only then can problem solving begin. Thus the goals of Freudian psychoanalysis are insight and resolution of repressed conflict. The process should be very gradual as old, repressed experiences are integrated in one's current life situation (Kaplan & Sadock, 1991).

Sigmund Freud died in 1939, but his approach to psychotherapy did not die with him. It has been modified (as Freud himself modified it over the years), but it remains true to the basic thrust of Freudian psychoanalysis. Before we consider how it has changed, let's examine Freudian analysis as Freud practiced it.

Freudian Psychoanalysis

Psychoanalysis with Sigmund Freud was a time-consuming (up to five days per week for as many as ten years), often tedious process of self-examination and introspection. The major task for the patient was to talk openly and honestly about all aspects of his or her life, from early childhood memories to the dreams of the present. The main task of the therapist, or analyst, was to interpret what was being expressed by the patient, always on the lookout for clues to possible repressed con-

Classic Freudian psychoanalysis required the use of a couch, where the patient could lie down, relax, and try to uncover unconscious conflicts under the direction of the analyst. Can you think of any disadvantage to the use of a couch?

flict. Once identified, the patient and the analyst could try together to resolve the conflict(s) that brought the patient to analysis in the first place. Several procedures and processes were used in the search for repressed conflicts.

Free Association. In 1881, Freud graduated from the University of Vienna Medical School. From the start, he was interested in what were then called nervous disorders. He went to France to study the technique of hypnosis, which many were claiming to be a worthwhile treatment for psychological disorders. Freud was not totally convinced, but when he returned to Vienna, he and a colleague, Josef Breuer, tried hypnosis to treat nervous disorders, conversion reaction (hysteria) in particular. Both became convinced that hypnosis itself was of little benefit. What mattered more, they believed, was to have the patients talk—about anything and everything—which is what they were encouraged to do under hypnosis. Freud and Breuer's method became known as the "talking cure."

The method of **free association** became a standard procedure. Patients were to say out loud whatever came into their minds. Sometimes the analyst would provide a stimulus word to get a chain of freely flowing associations going. To free-associate the way Freud would have wanted is not an easy task. It often required many sessions for patients to learn the technique. Patients were not to edit their associations. They were to be completely honest and say whatever they thought. Many people are uncomfortable, at least initially, sharing their private, innermost thoughts and desires with anyone, much less a stranger. Here is where the Freudian couch came in. To help his patients relax, Freud would have them lie down, be comfortable, and avoid eye contact with him. The job of the analyst through all this was to try to interpret the apparently free-flowing and random verbal responses, always looking for expressions of unconscious desires and conflicts.

free association *the procedure in psychoanalysis in which the patient is to express whatever comes to mind without editing responses*

Resistance. During the course of psychoanalysis, the analyst listens very carefully to what the patient says. The analyst also carefully listens for what the patient does not say. Freud believed **resistance**—the unwillingness or inability to discuss freely some aspect of one's life—was a significant process in analysis. Resistance can show itself in many ways, from simply avoiding the mention of some topic, to joking about matters as being inconsequential, to disrupting a session when a particular topic comes-up for discussion, to missing appointments altogether.

resistance *in psychoanalysis, the inability or unwillingness to discuss freely some aspect of one's life*

Let's say, for example, that over the last six months in psychoanalysis a patient has talked freely about a wide variety of subjects, including early childhood memories and all the members of her family—all, that is, except her older brother. She has talked about all sorts of private experiences, some of them sexual, some of them pleasant, some unpleasant. But after six months of talking, she has not had anything to say about her older brother. Her analyst, noting this possible resistance, suggests that during the next visit, he would like to hear about this older brother. Then, for the first time since analysis began, the patient misses her next appointment. She comes to the following appointment, but 10 minutes late. The analyst may now suspect that there is a problem with the relationship between the patient and her older brother, a problem that may have begun in childhood and has been repressed ever since. Of course, *there may be no problem at all,* but for psychoanalysis to be successful, potential resistance needs to be broken down and investigated.

Dream Interpretation. Analyzing a patient's dreams is an important aspect of psychoanalysis. Freud referred to dreams as the "royal road" to the unconscious level of the mind. Freud often trained his patients to recall and record their dreams in great detail. He analyzed dreams at two levels: *manifest content,* the dream as re-

Before You Go On

Describe the features of Freudian psychoanalysis.

called and reported, and *latent content,* the dream as a symbolic representation of the contents of the unconscious. Symbolism hidden in the latent content of dreams has been one of the most controversial aspects of Freud's theories. The idea was that true feelings, motives, and desires might be camouflaged in a dream. For example, someone who reports a dream about suffocating under a huge pile of pillows might be expressing feelings about parental overprotectiveness. Someone who dreams about driving into an endless tunnel and becoming lost there might be expressing fears or concerns of a sexual nature. The job for the analyst, Freud argued, was to interpret dreams in terms of whatever insights they could provide about the true nature of the patient's unconscious mind.

transference *in psychoanalysis, the situation in which the patient comes to feel about the analyst in the same way he or she once felt about some other important person*

Transference. Another controversial aspect of Freudian psychoanalysis is his concept of transference. **Transference** occurs when the patient unconsciously comes to view and feel about the analyst in much the same way he or she feels about another important person in his or her life, usually a parent. As therapy progresses over a long period, the relationship between analyst and patient often does become a complex and emotional one. If feelings once directed toward someone else of significance become directed toward the analyst, they are more accessible, more easily observed, and more readily dealt with. Therapists have to guard against doing the same thing themselves—letting their own feelings and experiences interfere with their objective interactions with their patients. Failure to do so is called *countertransference.*

Post-Freudian Psychoanalysis

Early in this century, Freudian psychoanalysis was the only form of psychotherapy. In the 1940s and 1950s, it was the therapy of choice. "Psychoanalytic theory was the dominant force in psychiatry in the postwar period and was embraced by a large number of clinical psychologists. To a certain extent, and for all practical purposes, there was no rival orientation" (Garfield, 1981, p. 176). In recent years, psychoanalysis has become much less common, and strict, Freudian psychoanalysis has become rare indeed.

Let's see how the Freudian system of therapy has changed. First, however, we should note what hasn't changed: to qualify as a psychoanalytic approach, the basic aim of therapy must be the uncovering of deep-seated, unconscious conflict, perhaps caused by childhood experiences, and the removal of defenses so that such conflicts can be resolved (Luborsky et al., 1993; Sandler, Dare, & Holder, 1992).

Probably the most significant change since Freud's practice is the concern for shortening the length of analysis (Strupp & Binder, 1984). Now we talk about time-limited and short-form psychoanalytic therapy (Binder, 1993; Koss & Butcher, 1986). Today's analyst will take a more active role than did Freud, using interviews and discussions, and relying less on free association. The couch as a requirement is gone; the comfort of the patient is what matters, and some patients feel more comfortable pacing or sitting than they do lying on a couch. Modern psychoanalysts, although not insensitive to the impact of childhood experiences, tend to spend more time exploring the present. For example, a patient may come for analysis complaining of feelings of depression and anger to the point where the analyst believes there is a real and present danger that the patient might harm himself or herself, or even commit suicide. The thrust of therapy is going to be in the here and now, dealing with the patient's current anger and depression until the analyst is convinced the patient is no longer in danger of harming himself or herself.

Carl Rogers gave us client-centered therapy, which aims at helping a person grow and self-actualize.

Before You Go On

How is psychoanalysis different today from when it was practiced by Freud?

Humanistic Techniques

There are many different types of humanistic psychotherapy and their allied cousins, the *existential therapies*. What they all have in common is a concern for self-examination, personal growth, and development. The goal of these therapies is not to uncover deep-seated conflicts, but to foster psychological growth, helping a person take full advantage of life's opportunities. Based on the premise that we can take charge of ourselves and our futures, grow and change, therapy is directed at assisting us with these processes.

Client-centered therapy, also called Rogerian therapy after its founder, Carl Rogers, is the therapy that best typifies the humanistic approach. As its name suggests, the client is the center of the therapeutic interaction. Note that, given his medical training, Freud called the people he dealt with *patients*. Rogers never used the term *patient*, and before his death in 1987 began using the term *person-centered* rather than *client-centered* to describe his approach to therapy.

For Rogers, therapy provides a special opportunity for a person to engage in self-discovery. Another way to express this is to say that a goal of client-centered therapy is to help the individual self-actualize. We discussed self-actualization in Chapter 9 when we covered humanistic approaches to personality (see page 335).

What are the characteristics of client-centered therapy? Again, there are variants, but the following ideas characterize a client-centered approach. The focus is on the *present*, not the past or childhood. The focus is on one's *feelings* or affect, not beliefs or cognitions; that is, you are more likely to hear, "How do you feel about that?" than "What do you think about that?" The therapist will attempt to *reflect* or mirror, not interpret, how a client is feeling (using statements such as, "You seem angry about that," or "Does that make you feel sad?"). Assessing and reflecting the true nature of a client's feelings is not necessarily easy to do. To do so requires that the therapist be an active listener and be **empathic**, or able to understand and share the essence of another's feelings.

Throughout each session, the therapist will try to express *unconditional positive regard*. This is the expression of being accepting and noncritical. "I will not be critical. If that is the way you feel, that is the way you feel. Anything you say in here is okay, so long as you are being honest; honest with yourself." The exchange that opened this chapter is meant to reflect a client-centered approach.

Gestalt therapy is associated with Fritz Perls (1893–1970) and shares many of the same goals as Rogers's person-centered approach (Perls, 1967, 1971; Perls et al., 1951). You may recall that we've used the term *gestalt* before (in Chapters 1 and 3), and that it means (roughly) "whole" or "totality." Thus, the goal of gestalt therapy is to assist a person to integrate his or her thoughts, feelings, and actions—to assist in increasing the person's self-awareness, self-acceptance, and growth. The therapy is aimed at helping the person become aware of his or her whole self—including conflicts and problems- and to begin establishing ways to deal with conflicts and problems.

What we have here is "getting in touch with one's feelings," acknowledging them as valid, and moving to get on with one's life. Although the focus of gestalt therapy is the individual, sessions are often convened in small group settings. Clients may be given role-playing exercises in which they have to play several parts. They may be asked to act out how they feel in a given situation and then act out how they wish they could respond in that situation.

client-centered therapy *the humanistic psychotherapy associated with Rogers, aimed at helping a person grow and self-actualize*

empathic *able to understand and share the essence of another's feelings, or to view from another's perspective*

Fritz Perls. How is his therapy similar to Rogers? How does it differ?

Before You Go On

What are the characteristics of client-centered and gestalt therapy?

Behavioral Techniques

behavior therapy *techniques of psychotherapy founded on principles of learning established in the psychological laboratory and aimed at changing one's behaviors*

systematic desensitization *classical conditioning procedures, used to alleviate anxiety, in which anxiety-producing stimuli are paired with a state of relaxation*

There is no one **behavior therapy**; it is a collection of several techniques. What unites these techniques is that they are "methods of psychotherapeutic change founded on principles of learning established in the psychological laboratory" (Wolpe, 1981, p. 159). There are many principles of learning and many psychological disorders to which such methods and principles can be applied. We've already discussed two types of behavior therapy in Chapter 5. In this section, I will list a few of the applications of learning theory that have become part of behavior therapy.

Systematic desensitization, applying classical conditioning to alleviate feelings of anxiety, particularly those associated with phobic disorders, is one of the first applications of learning theory to meet with success. It was introduced by Joseph Wolpe in the late 1950s (Wolpe, 1958, 1982), although others had used similar procedures earlier. You'll recall from our discussion in Topic 5A that systematic desensitization is basically a matter of teaching a person first to relax totally and then to remain relaxed as he or she thinks about or is exposed to stimuli that produce anxiety at ever-increasing levels. If the person can remain calm and relaxed, that response can be conditioned to replace the anxious or fear response previously associated with a particular stimulus.

A relatively new form of behavior therapy, *exposure and response prevention,* has shown promise as a treatment for obsessive-compulsive disorder (OCD), a disorder that is usually resistant to psychotherapy. In one clinic, patients are exposed for two hours, five days a week, for three weeks to whatever stimulus situation evokes their obsessional thinking. They are asked to vividly imagine the consequences they fear *without* engaging in their usual compulsive routine. The procedure is repeated in homework assignments. This is followed by a maintenance program of phone calls or clinic visits. For example, a patient who is obsessed with dirt

Behavior therapy techniques, such as systematic desensitization, are particularly useful in treating phobic disorders. A common disorder is agoraphobia, an intense, irrational fear of being alone in public places from which escape might be difficult.

Aversion therapy, though not a commonly used technique, is one way to help problem drinkers stop drinking. For a series of sessions, each time a person takes a drink, a drug added to that drink will make him or her nauseous. Eventually, drinking becomes less desirable and the person will quit the habit—at least for a short while.

and germs is told to sit on the floor and imagine that she has become ill because of insufficient washing and cleaning. For the first two weeks she must not wash her hands (at all) and can only take a shower for 10 minutes every other day. In the third week she can wash her hands for 30 seconds, five times a day. This program claims that 75 to 83 percent of the patients who have completed the regimen show significant and lasting improvement (Foa, 1995).

Aversion therapy is another example of learning applied to solving psychological problems. In **aversion therapy**, a stimulus that may be harmful but that produces a pleasant response is paired with an aversive, painful stimulus until the original stimulus is avoided. Every time you put a cigarette in your mouth, I deliver a painful shock to your lip. Every time you take a drink of alcohol, you get violently sick to your stomach from a nausea-producing drug. Every time a child molester is shown a picture of a young child, he gets an electric shock.

None of these situations sounds like the sort of thing anyone would agree to voluntarily. Many people do, however. They volunteer for such treatments for two reasons: (1) aversion therapy is very effective at suppressing a specific behavior, at least for a while, and (2) it is seen as the lesser of two evils (shocks and nausea-producing drugs are not much fun, but people see the continuation of their inappropriate, often self-destructive behaviors as even more dangerous in the long run). Still, aversion therapy, in any form, is not commonly practiced, and when it is, it tends to suppress behaviors for only a relatively short time. During that time, other techniques may be used in an attempt to bring about a more lasting change in behavior. In other words, aversion therapy is seldom effective when used alone; it is usually used in conjunction with some other form(s) of therapy.

Contingency management and contingency contracting (introduced in Topic 5B) borrow from the learning principles of operant conditioning. The basic idea is

aversion therapy *a technique of behavior therapy in which an aversive stimulus, such as a shock, is paired with an undesired behavior* to have a person appreciate the consequences of his or her behaviors. Appropriate behaviors lead to rewards and the opportunity to do valued things, whereas inappropriate behaviors do not lead to reinforcement and provide fewer opportunities.

In many cases, these basic procedures work very well. As operant conditioning would predict, their effectiveness is a function of the extent to which the therapist can effect control over the situation. If the therapist can manage the control of rewards and punishments, called **contingency management**, he or she stands a good chance of modifying the client's behavior. For example, in an institutional setting, if a patient (e.g., a severely disturbed, hospitalized person with schizophrenia) engages in the appropriate response (leaving her room to go to dinner), then the patient gets something she really wants (a chance to watch TV for an extra hour). In an outpatient setting, the therapist tries to arrange the situation so that the client learns to reinforce his or her own behaviors when they are appropriate.

contingency management *bringing about changes in one's behaviors by controlling rewards and punishments*

Contingency contracting amounts to establishing a contract with a client so that exhibiting certain behaviors (you prepare dinner) will result in certain rewards (then you can watch TV). In many cases, contingency contracting involves establishing a *token economy*. What this means is that the person is first taught that some token—a checker, a poker chip, or just a check mark on a pad—can be saved. When enough tokens are accumulated, they are cashed in for something of value to the person. With contracting, the value of a token for a specific behavior is spelled out ahead of time. Because control over the environment of the person/ learner is most complete in such circumstances, this technique is particularly effective in institutions and with young children. (Again, we went through examples of token economies in Topic 5B, page 164.)

contingency contracting *establishing an agreement (contract) with one to reinforce appropriate behaviors; often involving token economies*

Recognizing that not all learning can be explained in terms of classical or operant conditioning, it should be no surprise that some types of behavior therapy use learning principles other than those from simple conditioning. **Modeling**, a term introduced by Albert Bandura, involves the acquisition of an appropriate response through the imitation of a model. As we saw in Topic 5B, modeling can be an effective means of learning. In a therapy situation, modeling amounts to having patients watch someone else perform an appropriate behavior, perhaps earning a reward for it (called vicarious reinforcement).

modeling *the acquisition of new responses through the imitation of another who responds appropriately*

Some phobias, particularly those in children, can be overcome through modeling. A child who is afraid of dogs, for example, may profit from watching another child (which would be more effective than using an adult) playing with a dog. Modeling is also a part of what is called *assertiveness training*, which involves helping individuals stand up for their rights and come to the realization that their feelings and opinions matter and should be expressed. Such training involves many processes, including direct instruction, group discussion, role-playing, and contingency management, but often relies on modeling to help someone learn appropriate ways to express how they feel and what they think in social situations.

Before You Go On

Describe some of the methods of behavior therapy.

Cognitive Techniques

Psychotherapists who use cognitive techniques do not deny the importance of a person's behaviors (these therapies are often called *cognitive-behavioral*). Rather, they believe that what matters most are a client's beliefs, thoughts, perceptions, and attitudes about himself or herself and the environment. The major principle is that to change how one feels and acts, therapy should first be directed at changing how one thinks. As we've seen with other approaches to psychotherapy, there are several types of cognitive-behavioral therapy. One survey identified nearly two dozen types (Dobson, 1988). We'll examine just two: rational-emotive therapy and cognitive restructuring therapy.

Rational-Emotive Therapy

Rational-emotive therapy (RET) is associated with Albert Ellis (1970, 1973, 1991). Its basic premise is that psychological problems arise when people try to interpret what happens in the world (a cognitive activity) on the basis of irrational beliefs. "Rational-emotive therapy (RET) hypothesizes that people largely disturb themselves by thinking in a self-defeating, illogical, and unrealistic manner—especially by escalating their natural preferences and desires into absolutistic, dogmatic musts and commands on themselves, others, and their environmental conditions" (Ellis, 1987, p. 364).

rational-emotive therapy (RET) a form of cognitive therapy, associated with Ellis, aimed at changing a person's irrational beliefs or maladaptive cognitions

When compared to person-centered techniques, RET is quite directive. Ellis takes exception with techniques of psychotherapy designed to help a person *feel* better without providing useful strategies by which the person can *get* better (Ellis, 1991). In rational-emotive therapy, the therapist takes an active role interpreting the client's system of beliefs and encourages active change. Therapists often act as role models and make homework assignments that help clients bring their expectations and perceptions in line with reality.

To give a very simplified example, refer to the dialogue between Barbara and her client-centered therapist that I used to begin this chapter. A cognitive therapist might see several irrational beliefs operating in this scene, including two that Ellis (1970) claims are very common: (1) people should always be loved for everything they do, and (2) it's better to avoid problems than to face them. These, claims Ellis, are exactly the sort of cognitions that create psychological difficulties (others are listed in Figure 13.1). Rather than waiting for self-discovery, which might never come, a rational-emotive therapist would point out to Barbara that her irrational thoughts gave rise to her feelings of anger. Viewing the situation differently might lead to a homework assignment of attempting a more reasoned, effective interaction with her parents.

Figure 13.1

Some Irrational Beliefs That Lead to Maladjustment and Disorder. The More Rational Alternative to These Beliefs Should Be Obvious.

1. One should be loved by everyone for everything one does.
2. Because I strongly desire to perform important tasks competently and successfully, I absolutely must perform them well at all times.
3. Because I strongly desire to be approved of by people I find significant, I absolutely must always have their approval.
4. Certain acts are wicked and people who perform them should be severely punished no matter what.
5. It is horrible when things are not the way we want them to be.
6. It is better to avoid life's problems, if possible, than to face them.
7. One needs something stronger or more powerful than oneself to rely on.
8. One must have perfect and certain self-control.
9. Because I strongly desire people to treat me considerately and fairly, they must absolutely do so.
10. Because something once affected one's life, it will always affect it.

From Ellis, 1970, 1987.

Sometimes people become very upset if they are not included, or liked by everyone. Both Albert Ellis and Aaron Beck, as cognitive therapists, would argue that such is an irrational belief, and so long as it is held, the person will experience distress.

Cognitive Restructuring Therapy

cognitive restructuring therapy *a form of cognitive therapy, associated with Beck, in which an individual is led to overcome negative self-images and pessimistic views of the future*

Similar to rational-emotive therapy is **cognitive restructuring therapy**, associated with Aaron Beck (1976, 1991). Although the goals are similar, cognitive restructuring therapy is much less confrontational and direct than RET.

Beck's assumption is that considerable psychological distress stems from a few simple, but misguided, beliefs (cognitions). According to Beck, people with psychological disorders (particularly those related to depression, for which cognitive restructuring was first designed) share certain characteristics. For example:

1. They tend to have very negative self-images. They do not value themselves or what they do.
2. They tend to take a very negative view of life experiences.
3. They overgeneralize. For example, having failed one test, a person comes to believe that there is no way he or she can do college work, withdraws from school and looks for a job, even though he or she believes that no one would offer a job to someone who is such a failure and a college dropout.
4. They actually seek out experiences that reinforce their negative expectations. The student in the above example may apply for a job as a stockbroker or a law clerk. Lacking even minimal experience, he or she will not be offered either job and, thus, will confirm his or her own worthlessness.
5. They tend to hold a rather dismal outlook for the future.
6. They tend to avoid seeing the bright side of any experience.

In cognitive restructuring therapy, the patient is given opportunities to test or demonstrate his or her beliefs. The patient and therapist make up a list of hypotheses based on the patient's assumptions and beliefs and then actually go out and test these hypotheses. Obviously, the therapist tries to exercise enough control over the situation so that the experiments do not confirm the patient's beliefs about himself or herself, but will lead instead to positive outcomes. Given the hypothesis "Nobody cares about me," the therapist need only find one person who does care to refute it. This approach, of leading a person to the self-discovery that negative attitudes directed toward oneself are often inappropriate, has proven very successful in the treatment of depression, although it has been extended to cover a wide range of psychological disorders (Beck, 1985, 1991; Beck & Freeman, 1990; Zinbarg et al., 1992).

Before You Go On

Summarize the logic of rational-emotive therapy and cognitive restructuring therapy.

Group Approaches

Many patients profit from some type of *group therapy*. Group therapy is a label applied to a variety of situations in which a number of people are involved in a therapeutic setting at the same time. If nothing else, group therapy provides an economic advantage over individual psychotherapy: one therapist can interact with several people at once.

In standard forms of group therapy, clients are brought together at the same time, under the guidance of a therapist, to share their feelings and experiences. Most groups are quite informal, and no particular form of psychotherapy is dominant. In other words, meeting with people in groups is something a psychotherapist with any sort of training or background may do from time to time.

There are several possible benefits that can be derived from group meetings, including an awareness that "I'm not the only one with problems." The sense of support that one can get from someone else with problems occasionally may be even greater than that afforded by a therapist alone—a sort of "she really knows from experience the hell that I'm going through" logic. And there is truth in the notion that getting involved in helping someone else with a problem is, in itself, a therapeutic process. Yet another advantage of group therapy situations is that the person may learn new, more effective ways of "presenting" himself or herself to others.

A group approach that has become popular is **family therapy**, which focuses on the roles, interdependence, and communication skills of family members. Fam-

family therapy *a type of group therapy focusing on the roles, interdependence, and communication skills of family members*

Group approaches are particularly helpful when there are communication problems within the family system.

ily therapy is often begun after one member of a family enters psychotherapy. After discussing the person's problems for a while, other members of the family are invited to join in the therapy sessions. There is evidence that getting the family unit involved in therapy has benefit for patients with a wide range of disorders, from alcoholism and agoraphobia to depression and schizophrenia (Bloch & Simon, 1982; Feist, 1993; Goldfried et al., 1990).

Two related assumptions underlie a family therapy approach. One is that each family member is a part of a system (the family unit), and his or her feelings, thoughts, and behaviors necessarily impact on other family members (Minuchin & Fishman, 1981; Thomas, 1992). Bringing about a change (even a therapeutic one) in one member of the family system without involving the other members of the system will not last long. This is particularly true when the initial problem appears to be with a child or adolescent. I say "appears to be" because we can be confident that other family members have at least contributed to the troublesome symptoms of the child or adolescent. A therapist will have a difficult time bringing about significant and lasting change in a child whose parents refuse to become involved in therapy.

A second assumption often relevant in family therapy sessions is that difficulties arise from improper methods of family communication (e.g., Satir, 1967). Quite often, individuals develop false beliefs about the feelings and/or needs of family members. The goal of therapy in such situations, then, is to meet with the family in a group setting to foster and encourage open expressions of feelings and desires. It may be very helpful for an adolescent to learn that her parents are upset and anxious about work-related stress and financial affairs. The adolescent has assumed all along that her parents yelled at her and at each other because of something she was doing. And the parents didn't want to share their concerns over money with the adolescent for fear that it would upset her.

Before You Go On

What are some advantages of group therapy?

Describe two assumptions underlying family therapy.

Evaluating Psychotherapy

Evaluating psychotherapy has proven to be a difficult task. Is psychotherapy effective? Compared to what? Is any variety of psychotherapy better than any other? These are obviously important questions, but the best we can do is offer partial answers. Yes, psychotherapy is certainly effective when compared to doing nothing. "By about 1980 a consensus of sorts was reached that psychotherapy, as a generic treatment process, was demonstrably more effective than no treatment" (Vanden-Bos, 1986, p. 111; see also Gelso & Fassinger, 1990; Goldfried et al., 1990; Kingsbury, 1995).

More treatment appears to be better than less treatment, with most improvement made early on (Howard et al., 1986). More recent research indicates that there are limits to this observation, however. In one study, time-limited therapy that actively involved the family in dealing with problems of children was as effective as therapy that used an unlimited number of sessions (Smyrnios & Kirby, 1993). Whether short-term or long-term intervention will be best is often a function of known variables, such as the client's awareness of his or her problems, a willingness to change, and the extent to which the client lives in a supportive environment (Steenbarger, 1994).

Research also confirms the logical assertion that the sooner one begins therapy, the better the prognosis (Kupfer, Frank, & Perel, 1989). There is also evidence that some therapists are more effective than others, regardless of what type of therapy is practiced (Beutler et al., 1986; Lafferty et al., 1989).

At this point, I need to mention just a few of the problems encountered when doing research on the effectiveness of psychotherapy. First, we have little data on how people might have responded without treatment. In other words, we often do not have a baseline for comparison. We know that sometimes there is a *spontaneous remission of symptoms.* Sometimes people "get better" without the formal intervention of a therapist. To say that people get better on their own is seldom literally true. There are many factors that can contribute to improve one's mental health, even if one is not "officially" in psychotherapy (Erwin, 1980). Perhaps the source of one's stress is removed; a nagging parent moves out of state, an aggravating boss gets transferred, or an interpersonal relationship begins that provides needed support.

Second, we can't seem to agree on what we mean by recovery, or cure. For some, it is simply the absence of observable symptoms for a specified period. For others, the goal of psychotherapy is something different: the self-report of "feeling better," personal growth, a relatively permanent change in behavior, insight into deep-seated conflicts, or a restructuring of cognitions.

Finally, even when we can agree on criteria for recovery there is often concern about how to measure or assess therapy outcomes. It hardly seems realistic to expect unbiased responses from therapists *or* their patients if we were to ask them to report if therapy has been a helpful experience.

These are three commonly cited problems with designing studies to evaluate the outcome of psychotherapy. Even so, quality studies have been done. Most have focused on just one technique, and the results have generally been very positive (Erwin, 1980; Eysenck, 1952; Greenberg & Safran, 1987; Kazdin et al., 1987; Lipsey & Wilson, 1993; Marziali, 1984; Miller & Berman, 1983; Scogin & McElreath, 1994; Wolpe, 1981).

A meta-analysis of 475 published research articles showed positive results for psychotherapy and has become a commonly cited study of its effectiveness (Smith, Glass, & Miller, 1980). A more recent meta-analysis of 302 studies of psychotherapy outcomes came to the same conclusion: what psychotherapy provides is beneficial, and "the magnitude of the effects for a substantial portion of those treatments is in a range of practical significance by almost any reasonable criterion" (Lipsey & Wilson, 1993).

What about comparing psychotherapy methods? In general, there are very few differences. There is no evidence that any one type of therapy is universally better than any other (Stiles et al., 1986). There *is* evidence that some types of therapy are better suited for some types of problems than for others, but the evidence is still sketchy. Which therapy is best suited for which disorder is one of the most active areas of research in psychotherapy (Deffenbacher, 1988; Goldfried et al., 1990; Lipsey & Wilson, 1993).

Each variety of psychotherapy has its strengths and weaknesses. Psychoanalytic approaches can be time-consuming and expensive. Client-centered approaches require an introspective, nondependent client to be most useful. Group approaches may not be useful for clients who need personal attention. Behavioral methods work well with phobic disorders, and cognitive therapies appear to be well suited to patients with depression. A combination of behavioral and cognitive approaches seems particularly effective for the obsessive-compulsive disorders. No variety of psychotherapy is effective, by itself, for persons with bipolar disorder or schizophrenia. Many studies indicate that even when the primary treatment option is medical (say, an antidepressant drug), psychotherapy and medication together yield the best prognosis (Frank et al., 1990; Klerman, 1990). "Psychotherapy alone is not a good treatment for schizophrenia, but schizophrenic patients who take antipsychotic drugs can benefit from social skills training and related therapies" (Kingsbury, 1995, p. 8).

Evaluating group therapy techniques is particularly difficult, and few good reviews of outcome studies are available. In general, there seems to be support for the sorts of approaches outlined here, and there is some indication that family therapy is a better approach for some problems than is individual treatment

(Gurman et al., 1986; Opalic, 1989; Yalom, 1985). One large study recently found significant beneficial effects of marital and family therapies (Shadish et al., 1993).

Before You Go On

Is there evidence that psychotherapy is effective?

@@@@ **Thinking Critically** @@@@

Psychotherapists often claim that it is inadvisable—even dangerous—for persons without formal training in psychology and therapy to engage in "amateur psychotherapy." Why do they make this claim?

TOPIC 13B SUMMARY

Psychotherapy is an attempt, using psychological means, to bring about a change in the way a person thinks, feels, or acts. As Freud characterized it, it is "talking therapy," but it involves careful, interpretive listening as well. There are hundreds of such techniques, and in this Topic we've reviewed only a few of the classic or mainstream approaches.

Approaches to psychotherapy can be distinguished in terms of their major goals. Psychoanalytic techniques try to uncover and resolve repressed conflicts or problems; the humanistic approaches tend to focus on feelings, dealing with them realistically to help a person grow and flourish; behavioral approaches take their foundation from the learning laboratory, and aim to change a person's behaviors in the hopes that changes in feelings and cognitions will follow; cognitive therapies help people form more realistic, rational cognitions about themselves and the world in which they live; and group therapies build on the support that the interactions of several people in a therapeutic setting can provide.

Research tells us that psychotherapy is effective in helping people suffering from psychological distress and discomfort.

CHAPTER SUMMARY

Topic 13A

Briefly trace the history of the treatment of persons with psychological disorders.

In ancient times and throughout the Middle Ages, the prevailing view of the mentally ill was that they were possessed by evil spirits. As a result, treatment was often harsh, involving torture and placement in dungeon-like asylums for the insane. It was common for the mentally ill, who were often viewed as witches, to be put to death for their unusual behaviors. Throughout history, there have been attempts by compassionate persons to provide humane treatment to the disordered. It wasn't until the twentieth century that what we now call the mental health movement began with an aim of treating the mentally ill in the most humane way possible. */pp. 464–466*

What is psychosurgery? Is it still in use today?

Psychosurgery is any surgical technique, usually directed at the brain, designed to bring about a change in a patient's affects, behaviors, or cognitions. A *prefrontal lobotomy* is a psychosurgical technique that severs connections between the prefrontal lobes and lower brain centers. It was a common treatment in the 1940s and 1950s, used because it was often successful in alleviating the worst of psychotic symptoms. It also produced mild to severe side effects—occasionally even death. Because of its inherent danger, and because safer, reversible treatments such as drug therapy are available today, it is no longer used. There are, however, psychosurgical techniques that *are* used, including the split-brain procedure as a treatment for epilepsy and the cingulectomy as a treatment for anxiety and obsessive-compulsive disorder. */pp. 466–468*

What is ECT, and why is it still being used?

ECT stands for electroconvulsive, or shock, therapy. In this treatment, a brain seizure is produced with an electric current. Upon regaining consciousness, the patient has no memory of the procedure. Although there may be negative side effects, particularly with prolonged or repeated use, the technique is demonstrably useful for many patients as a means of reducing or even eliminating severe depression and other symptoms usually associated with schizophrenia. */pp. 468–469*

What are antipsychotic, antidepressant, and antianxiety drugs? Describe any side effects of each.

Antipsychotic drugs are used to reduce or control psychotic symptoms, characterized by a loss of contact with reality and a gross impairment of functioning. Chlorpromazine was the first. Introduced in 1950, chlorpromazine was used to suppress symptoms associated with psychosis: delusions, hallucinations, disordered thought, and inappropriate affect. Although these drugs do reduce psychotic symptoms in many patients, those symptoms often return when the drugs are discontinued. When they are effective, *antidepressant drugs* reduce episodes of depression. Lithium salts not only reduce depressive symptoms, but are useful in treating bipolar disorders. Unlike the antipsychotic drugs, these often have long-term beneficial effects (alleviating feelings of depression), even after the patient stops taking them. They often take weeks to produce their effects, however, and do not work for all patients. Long-term use of the drugs may produce a number of potentially harmful or unpleasant side effects. The most common *antianxiety drugs,* or tranquilizers, are the benzodiazepines, including Valium and Librium, which are among the most commonly prescribed of all drugs in the world. These drugs are effective in reducing felt levels of anxiety. There is evidence that some patients who use antianxiety drugs develop addictions to them. Like antipsychotic drugs, they suppress symptoms; they do not cure the underlying anxiety, and even small overdoses can lead to dependency and addiction. */pp. 470–472*

What is deinstitutionalization, and has it been successful?

Deinstitutionalization refers to the policy of taking measures to release patients from publicly supported mental institutions. Deinstitutionalization is a response to factors that became apparent in the United States by the mid-1950s: (1) conditions in mental hospitals generally were very bad, (2) antipsychotic medications significantly reduced many troublesome psychotic symptoms, and (3) community-based mental health centers were to be created to care for patients after they were released back to the community. The blessing is mixed. Some patients are better off living at home and visiting their community mental health centers. Others are less fortunate. They may have no nearby mental health facility, or not visit it

if they do, and soon stop taking their medication, so their psychotic symptoms return. */pp. 473–474*

Topic 13B

Who may offer psychotherapy?

Many different mental health professionals can provide psychotherapy. These include clinical psychologists (Ph.D.s or Psy.D.s with graduate training in psychology and a one-year internship), psychiatrists (M.D.s with an internship and residency in a mental hospital), counseling psychologists (Ph.D.s in psychology specializing in less severe disorders and with an internship in a counseling setting), licensed counselors (perhaps with degrees in education), psychoanalysts (who specialize in Freudian therapy), clinical social workers (usually with a master's degree), and others, including pastoral counselors and mental health technicians. */pp. 475–477*

Describe the features of Freudian psychoanalysis.

Freudian psychoanalysis is aimed at uncovering repressed conflicts (often developed in childhood) so that they can be resolved. The process involves (1) free association, in which the patient is to say anything and everything that comes to mind, without editing; (2) resistance, in which a patient seems unable or unwilling to discuss some aspect of his or her life, suggesting that the resisted experiences may be anxiety producing; (3) dream interpretation, in which one analyzes both the manifest and the latent content for insights into the nature of the patient's unconscious mind; and (4) transference, in which feelings once directed at a significant person in the patient's life become directed toward the analyst. */pp. 477–479*

How is psychoanalysis different today from when it was practiced by Freud?

Although the principles of psychoanalysis have remained unchanged since Freud's day, some changes have evolved. There is now more effort to shorten the duration of analysis; there is less emphasis on childhood experiences and more concern with the here and now. Present-day analysis is also more directive than it was in Freud's day. */p. 480*

What are the characteristics of client-centered and gestalt therapy?

Client-centered or person-centered therapy, associated with Carl Rogers, is based on the belief that people can control their lives and solve their own problems if they can be helped to understand the true nature of their feelings. It promotes self-discovery and personal growth. The therapist reflects or mirrors the client's feelings, focuses on the here and now, and tries to be empathic, actively listening to and relating to the patient's feelings.

Throughout therapy, the therapist provides unconditional positive regard for the client. Gestalt therapy, associated with Fritz Perls, has many of the same goals, but is more directive and challenging, striving to integrate a person's thoughts, feelings, and behaviors. */pp. 480–481*

Describe some of the methods of behavior therapy.

Behavior therapies have evolved from the learning laboratory. Based on classical conditioning, systematic desensitization is a technique used for the treatment of phobic reactions. Exposure and response prevention therapy is used to treat obsessive-compulsive disorder. It amounts to having a patient vividly imagine the consequences of not performing his or her compulsive ritual. Aversion therapy pairs an unwanted behavior with a negative stimulus, such as shock or a nausea-producing drug. It can be an effective means of reducing unwanted behaviors, at least temporarily. Contingency management is a matter of exercising control over the pattern of rewards a person may receive. Contingency contracting often involves a token economy system in which a client agrees (by contract) to engage in certain behaviors in order to earn specified rewards. Modeling suggests that people can acquire appropriate behaviors through the imitation of models, particularly when the model's behavior is reinforced. */pp. 481–484*

Summarize the logic of rational-emotive therapy and cognitive restructuring therapy.

Cognitive therapies are designed to alter the way a person perceives and thinks about himself or herself and the environment. Rational-emotive therapy (RET) works on the premise that people with problems are operating on irrational assumptions about the world and themselves. RET is directive in its attempts to change people's cognitions. Cognitive restructuring therapy is somewhat less directive, but is based on the same sort of idea as RET. The underlying premise here is that people with psychological disorders have developed negative self-images and negative views (cognitions) about the future. The therapist provides opportunities for the patient to test those negative cognitions and discover that everything is not as bad as it may seem. */pp. 484–486*

What are some advantages of group therapy? Describe two assumptions underlying family therapy.

There are several potential advantages to group therapy. (1) The basic problem may be an interpersonal one, and will be better understood and dealt with in an interpersonal situation. (2) There is value in realizing that one is not the only person in the world with a problem and that there are others who may have an even more difficult problem of the same nature. (3) There is therapeutic value in providing support for someone else. (4) The dynamics of intragroup communication can be analyzed and changed in a group setting. Family therapy is based on the assumptions that (1) family members can be seen as part of a system in which one member (and one member's problem) affects all of the others, and that (2) psychological problems often arise because of faulty communication, and that this is particularly critical within a family. */pp. 486–488*

Is there any evidence that psychotherapy is effective?

Scientifically evaluating the appropriateness and effectiveness of psychotherapy has been very difficult. Nonetheless, in general, psychotherapy is effective. It is significantly better than leaving disorders untreated. There are data that suggest that some therapies may be better suited to some clients and to some disorders than they are to others. There is evidence that psychotherapy provides an advantage when offered with appropriate drug therapy. On the other hand, there is no evidence that, in general, any one type of therapy is better than any other. */pp. 488–489*

What Sort of Therapist Are You?

Imagine that you overhear each of the following statements while attending a convention of psychotherapists. Can you identify the type of psychotherapist who might have made each comment? Assume that the convention is attended by (a) psychoanalytic, (b) client-centered, (c) behavioral, (d) cognitive, (e) Gestalt, and (f) family therapists only. (Suggested answers can be found on p. 575.)

_____ 1. "The therapy I use has the name that it does because it reflects the reality that good mental health involves integration of aspects of self. Our goal is to make people whole again."

_____ 2. "As soon as she began relating to me in the way she related to her mother, it became clear that she perceived her mother as a rival for her father's affection."

_____ 3. "Now that child has a serious behavioral problem. It wasn't difficult to understand how he got to be that way after I had a few sessions with his parents and siblings."

_____ 4. "She has the worst case of agoraphobia I've ever seen. A peer counselor is stopping by every day to work with her. It took a week to get her out the front door, and more than a week to get her off the porch. They're working on walking out to the mailbox now. We're making progress, but it's slow."

_____ 5. "I had to refer a patient to another therapist last week. I just couldn't seem to identify with the guy; couldn't accept the way he acted. Feeling as I did about him, I didn't think I could help him."

_____ 6. "The theme of hostility toward authority figures occurs over and over again in his dreams and free associations, yet he claims that he and his father had a close and affectionate relationship."

_____ 7. "I asked her to list the reasons why she thinks she is unable to get through a job interview. She gave me three typewritten pages enumerating more fears, apprehensions, self-criticisms, and negative self-evaluations than I would have believed possible for one person to have. Her thinking about herself has really gotten off track."

_____ 8. "He needs to convince himself that his past failures are not elements of a pattern that will govern his future. And he needs to convince himself that he is in charge of his life, and that he can choose paths that will lead him to accomplishment and satisfaction."

_____ 9. "We have this voluntary program at the state penitentiary for men who have been convicted of child molestation. We are currently trying a method in which we pair electric shock with pictures of attractive children."

_____ 10. "I think that depression is frequently the result of a misperception of environmental events—a tendency to attribute failures to the self and accomplishments to things like luck, fate, or the help of other people."

Over 30 years ago, a New York City cocktail waitress named Kitty Genovese was brutally murdered in front of her apartment building as she returned from work about 3:30 in the morning. What made this particular murder noteworthy was that so many of Kitty Genovese's neighbors watched as she was bludgeoned and stabbed to death. Here is the account of the incident:

> For more than half an hour, thirty-eight respectable law-abiding citizens in Queens watched a killer stalk and stab a woman in three separate attacks in Kew Gardens.
>
> Twice the sound of their voices and the sudden glow of their bedroom lights interrupted him and frightened him off. Each time he returned, sought her out and stabbed her again. Not one person telephoned the police during the assault; one witness called after the woman was dead. (*New York Times*, March 27, 1964)

This story has become a classic example in the social psychology of violence and bystander behaviors. Still, I was concerned that because the incident took place so many years ago, it might have lost some of its relevance. Then, I read this newspaper story:

> Cheering bystanders spur on woman's killer. Oakland, Calif. (AP)—A dozen people who chanted "Kill her, kill her,"

14

Social Psychology

as a 32-year-old woman was stabbed to death could face murder charges, authorities say.

Police said Friday they were looking for members of the crowd who egged on the woman's attacker. The people could be charged with aiding and abetting a killing. "Usually, you hear of people who stand by, watch and do nothing," police Sergeant John McKenna said, "but this is the other end of things, where the people watched and participated, apparently for a thrill—to watch the kill." *The Toronto Times,* August 15, 1993).

Then I ran across this story:

Tourists watched woman drown. Mont Saint-Michel, France—Dozens of tourists at the medieval Mont Saint-Michel abbey impassively watched and even videotaped a woman drown as she tried to save her child.

Victorine Guillernée, 6, and her mother, Marie-Noëlle, 42, were walking along the base of the hill when the girl fell into a water hole. As the mother tried to save her, tourists apparently watched without trying to intervene.

Residents reported hearing one tourist say, "I got the whole thing on videotape." (*The Fort Wayne, IN Journal Gazette,* August 29, 1994).

Yes, the murder of Kitty Genovese occurred over 30 years ago. No, sadly, the story is not dated; nor is it irrelevant.

In yet another updating, and reminder, the convicted murderer of Kitty Genovese, Winston Mosley, now 61 years old, appeared before a parole board in August 1995, appealing to be released. Transcripts quote Mosley as saying, "There were worse murders, and more serious—or ones that are just as serious." He argued the suffering of his victim was only "a one-minute affair, but for the person who gets caught, it's forever."

Social psychology deals with people as they live and as they die: in a social world, influencing and being influenced by others. In this chapter, we will consider two major content areas in social psychology: (1) in Topic 14A, social cognition, or the perception and evaluation of oneself and others in social situations, and (2) in Topic 14B, social influence, or how others affect the reactions of the individual.

T O P I C   1 4 A Social Cognitions: Attitudes, Attributions, and Attractions

social psychology *the field of psychology concerned with how others influence the thoughts, feelings, and behaviors of the individual*

Social psychology is the field of psychology concerned with how others influence the thoughts, feelings, and behaviors of the individual. Social psychologists focus on the person or the individual in a group setting, and not on the group *per se* (which is more likely to be the focus of sociologists). Because we are social organisms, we are familiar, each in our own way, with many of the concerns of social psychology.

To claim that we are familiar with the concerns of social psychology has certain implications. On the one hand, it means that social psychology is perceived as relevant because it deals with everyday situations that affect us all. On the other hand, it means that we are often willing to accept common sense and our personal experiences as the basis for our explanations about social behavior. Although common sense and personal experience may sometimes be valid, they are not acceptable for a scientific approach to understanding social behavior. Social psychology relies on experimentation and other scientific methods as sources of knowledge about social behavior.

Over the last 25 years, much of social psychology has taken on a cognitive flavor. That is, social psychologists are attempting to understand social behavior by examining the mental structures and processes reflected in such behavior. A basic premise of this approach, and of this Topic, is that we do not view our social environment solely on the basis of the stimulus information it presents us (Baldwin, 1992; Berscheid, 1994; Higgins & Bargh, 1987). Instead, the argument goes, we have developed cognitive structures or processes (e.g., attitudes and schemas) that influence our interpretation of the world around us. "Discovering how people mentally organize and represent information about themselves and others has been a central task of social cognition research" (Berscheid, 1994, p. 84). Social cognition involves two related questions: What information about the social nature of the world do we have stored in memory? How does that information influence social judgments, choices, attractions, and behaviors (Sherman et al., 1989)? We will see these questions underlying each of the three major sections of Topic 14A. We begin with attitudes.

Attitudes

attitude *a relatively stable evaluative disposition directed toward some object or event; it consists of feelings, behaviors, and beliefs*

Since the 1920s, a central concern in social psychology has been the nature of attitudes. We'll define **attitude** as a relatively stable disposition to evaluate an object or event. An attitude has consequences for influencing one's beliefs, feelings, and behaviors toward that object or event (Olson & Zanna, 1993).

The concept of *evaluation* in this definition refers to a dimension of attitudes that includes such notions as being for or against, pro or con, positive or negative (Eagly & Chaiken, 1992). By *disposition* I mean a tendency, or a preparedness, to respond to the object of an attitude (actual responding isn't necessary). Note that, by definition, attitudes have *objects*. We do not have attitudes in general; we have attitudes about some object or event. I recognize that the word *attitude* is occasionally used differently in common speech. We may hear that someone has a "bad attitude" or "an attitude" in general, as in, "Boy, does he have an attitude!" In psychology, however, an attitude requires an object.

Anything can be the object of an attitude, whether it be a person, an object, or an idea (Fazio, 1990; Petty & Cacioppo, 1986). You may have attitudes about this course, the car you drive, your father, the president, or the corner fast-food restaurant where you eat lunch. Some of our attitudes are more important than others, of course, but the fact that we have attitudes about so many things is precisely why the study of attitudes is so central in social psychology.

The Components of Attitudes

Although many definitions of attitude have been proposed over the years, most of them suggest that an attitude consists of three components (Chaiken & Stangor, 1987). When we use the term in everyday conversation, we are most likely referring to the *affective component,* which consists of our feelings about the attitudinal object (Zanna & Rempel, 1988). The *behavioral component* consists of our response tendencies toward the object of our attitude. This component includes our actual behaviors and our intentions to act, should the opportunity arise. The *cognitive component* includes our beliefs about the attitudinal object. Any of these three may be primary. We form a positive attitude toward a particular beverage because we know it is good for us (cognitive), because it is very convenient to buy (behavioral), or because we like the way it tastes (affective). By now, these three components of affect, behavior, and cognition, or ABC, ought to be familiar.

Most of the time, the cognitive, affective, and behavioral components of attitudes are consistent. We think that classical music is relaxing and like to listen to it, so we buy classical music recordings. You believe that knowledge of psychology will be an asset in your career, you are enjoying your introductory psychology class, and you plan to take more psychology classes in the future. There are occasions, however, when behaviors are not consistent with beliefs and feelings (Ajzen & Fishbein, 1980). For example, we may have very strong, unfavorable beliefs and very negative feelings about someone, yet when we encounter that person at a social gathering, we smile, extend our hand, and say something pleasant. The social situation may "overpower" the cognitive and affective components of our attitudes. In other words, the components of an attitude may lack consistency, and it is the behavioral component that is most often inconsistent with the other two.

The components of an attitude are not always consistent. You may regard someone as shiftless and dishonest, yet when you meet that person in a social situation, you extend your hand in a pleasant greeting. Indeed, the behavioral component of an attitude is the one component most likely to be inconsistent with the other two.

Because our actual behaviors may not reflect our true feelings or beliefs, some social psychologists (e.g., Fazio, 1989; Fishbein & Ajzen, 1975) exclude the behavioral component from their definition, reserving the term *attitude* to refer only to the basic like or dislike for the attitudinal object. Others argue that *attitude* is a two-dimensional concept involving affect and cognition, but not behavior (Bagozzi & Burnkrant, 1979; Zajonc & Markus, 1982).

Before You Go On

What is an attitude, and what are its components?

⊚⊚⊚ **Thinking Critically** ⊚⊚⊚

Can you indentify the affective, behavioral, and cognitive components in any of the attitudes that you have?

Attitude Formation

As it happens, we have formed many attitudes about a wide range of objects and events. Where did they came from? Most experts agree that attitudes are learned, and that simple conditioning processes go a long way toward explaining attitude formation.

Some attitudes are acquired through the simple associative process of *classical conditioning*. As shown in Figure 14.1, pleasant events (unconditioned stimuli) can be paired with an attitudinal object (conditioned stimulus). As a result of this association, the attitudinal object comes to elicit the same good feeling (a positive evaluation) originally produced by the unconditioned stimulus. The good feeling, originally an unconditioned response elicited by a pleasant event, now becomes a conditioned response elicited by the attitudinal object. Of course, negative attitudes can be acquired in the same way (e.g., Cacioppo et al., 1992).

Some advertising tries to work in this way by taking an originally neutral object (the product) and trying to create positive associations for it. For instance, a soft drink advertisement may depict attractive young people having a great time playing volleyball, dancing, or enjoying a concert while drinking a particular soft drink. The obvious intent is that you and I will associate the product with good times and having fun. That sports figures often wear brand name logos or trademarks on their uniforms also suggests that manufacturers want us to learn to associate their

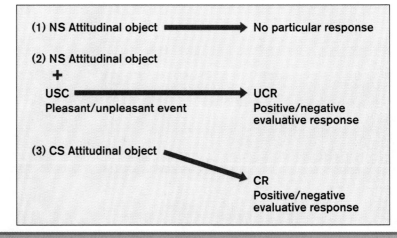

Figure 14.1

A schematic diagram of how attitudes may be formed through classical conditioning. At first, the attitudinal object is a neutral stimulus (NS), eliciting no particular response or interest. When it is paired with a stimulus (the unconditioned stimulus, or UCS) that naturally produces an evaluative response (the unconditioned response, or UCR), the attitudinal object becomes a conditioned stimulus (CS) that elicits a learned, or conditioned, response (CS).

An example of classical conditioning in attitude formation. Products that are endorsed by celebrities become associated with those celebrities—to the benefit of the products.

product with the skills of the athlete we are watching. Advertisements with sexual themes operate along the same lines.

Attitudes can also be formed as a result of the direct reinforcement of behaviors consistent with an attitudinal position, a matter of *operant conditioning.* Several studies have shown that verbal reinforcement (saying "good" or "that's right") when people agree with attitudinal statements leads to the development of attitudes consistent with the position expressed in those statements (Insko, 1965).

As we discussed in Topic 5C, people often imitate behaviors that they have seen reinforced in others (called vicarious reinforcement). To the extent we perceive others gaining reinforcers for having and expressing some attitude, we are likely to adopt that attitude ourselves. Advertising that relies on the testimonials of satisfied customers is appealing to this sort of *observational learning* (Figure 14.2). The consumer is shown that someone has used a certain product with success (received reinforcement), and the advertiser hopes that this will lead the observer to develop a favorable evaluation of the product. Obviously, the advertiser is going to show us only those people who are happy with their product or service. We seldom stop to think about how many people may have used the product or service and are unhappy with it.

Before You Go On

Briefly describe three ways in which attitudes might be acquired.

Attitude Change and Persuasion

Much of the research on attitudes has been concerned with the practical questions of when and how attitudes change. This research has dealt largely with conscious, planned attempts to change someone's attitude(s) by exposing them to information—a process called **persuasion** (Olson & Zanna, 1993). In this section we will examine a few factors involved in attitude change.

persuasion *a planned, conscious attempt to change someone's attitude*

Figure 14.2

Observational learning is demonstrated in advertising that uses personal testimony of satisfied customers to promote a product or service.

Cognitive Dissonance. It seems reasonable that one's attitudes will help to mold one's behaviors; that attitude change will lead to behavior change. In 1957, Leon Festinger proposed just the reverse: that attitudes follow behavior. Festinger's theory involves a concept he called **cognitive dissonance**. Cognitions are ideas, thoughts, beliefs, and the like. Dissonance means discord, discomfort, or distress due to things being out of balance or inconsistent. Cognitive dissonance often arises when we realize (a cognition) we have behaved in a way inconsistent (dissonant) with other cognitions. (You may recall that cognitive dissonance was introduced in Topic 10A, on motivation.)

cognitive dissonance *a state of tension or distress that occurs when there is a lack of balance, or equilibrium, between or among one's cognitions*

One of the best examples of how cognitive dissonance might work is found in one of the original demonstrations of the phenomenon (Festinger & Carlsmith, 1959). Participants in the research were asked to perform an extremely boring task of rotating row after row of small wooden knobs. Following a lengthy knob-turning session, the experimenter explained that the research really had to do with the effects of motivation on such a task. Further, the subject was told that the person in the waiting area was to be the next subject in the project. This person was to be led to believe that the knob-turning task was interesting, fun, and educational. The experimenter explained that his assistant, who usually told these "lies" to the waiting subject, was absent. Would the subject do this "selling" job? The subject would be paid for his or her help. Subjects invariably agreed and worked very hard to convince the next subject the project was fun and educational. Weeks later, at the end of the semester, all participants filled out a questionnaire that asked about their reactions to the knob-turning experiment.

The only experimental manipulation was a simple one: some of the subjects were paid $20 for trying to convince the waiting person (who was really not a subject, but was in on the experiment) the obviously boring task was fun and interesting, whereas others were paid only $1. In all other respects, everyone was treated in

Cognitive dissonance occurs when you find yourself test-driving and considering buying a car that you previously have been reluctant to buy.

the very same way. Remember that this was the late 1950s, and for college students, $20 was a lot of money.

At the end of the semester, which subjects do you suppose expressed more positive attitudes about the project, the ones paid $20 or those paid $1? Doesn't it seem logical that those college students paid $20 would remember the task as being fun and enjoyable and indicate a willingness to participate in similar projects? Festinger and Carlsmith predicted just the opposite. They reasoned that students paid only $1 would feel that their behavior had not been sufficiently justified. They had told a "lie" and had been given only a trivial amount of money for doing so. They would experience a great deal of tension or discomfort—cognitive dissonance would have been created. "I lied for a lousy dollar." One way to resolve this dissonance would be to change their attitude about the project so that it fit better with their behavior—a sort of, "Well, I didn't really lie, because the experiment wasn't all that bad; in fact, it was kinda fun at that."

Subjects paid $20, on the other hand, had plenty of justification for their actions. Sure, they lied, but they had good reason to do so, and would experience little cognitive dissonance. They should not be expected to change their attitude about the experiment. "Yeah, I lied, but I got paid twenty bucks." The results of this experiment are presented in Figure 14.3. Seldom do we find differences in an experiment as clear-cut as these.

The results of this experiment (and numerous others) suggest that one way to change people's attitudes is to get them to change their behaviors first. Not only that, but there is a clear advantage in offering as little incentive as possible to bring about that change in behavior. Simply "buying one off" to change his or her behavior may get you compliance, but it will not produce the cognitive dissonance needed to bring about lasting attitude change.

You should be able to generate other examples of cognitive dissonance bringing about attitude change. Consider those students who have changed their attitude about a course, or a discipline, because they were required to take a course in that discipline. I know that as a chemistry major, my (quite negative) attitudes

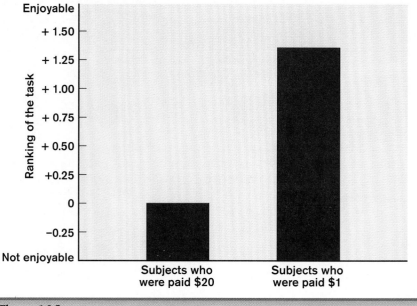

Figure 14.3

After being paid either $1 or $20 to "lie" about their participation in a boring task, subjects were later asked to rate the task in terms of enjoyment, interest, and educational value. As can be seen in the graph above, those paid $1 (those with cognitive dissonance) gave the task much higher ratings than did subjects paid $20. (From Festinger & Carlsmith, 1959.)

about psychology changed because of the dissonance created when I was required to take a (very enjoyable and informative) course in introductory psychology.

Extensions of Festinger's work tell us that what matters most in producing attitude change is the perception of responsibility for unpleasant outcomes—whether those outcomes are consistent with other cognitions or not (Cooper & Scher, 1992; Scher & Cooper, 1989). In other words, when we feel our behaviors have led to some unfortunate consequence, we are more likely to end up convincing ourselves that the consequence, or outcome, really wasn't that bad after all. For example, I once bought a car I thought I really wanted to have (even though friends and relatives advised me not to). In fact, the car was a lemon, hardly ever ran properly, and spent most of its life in the shop being repaired. Nonetheless, I was continually heard to claim that "when that car is running, it's the best car I've ever had." I was responsible for an "unpleasant outcome" and I tried to resolve my dissonance by convincing myself I really had not made a mistake.

Before You Go On

How is cognitive dissonance related to attitude change?

The Source of Persuasive Communication. One theory of attitude change claims that there are two factors, or routes, involved in changing one's attitudes (Petty & Cacioppo, 1986; Tesser & Shaffer, 1990). One factor is the *central route:* the nature and quality of the persuasive message itself. Here what matters most is a strong message—who delivers it, or how it is delivered is not terribly important. The other factor is the *peripheral route:* issues above and beyond the content of the message. This route is of greater concern when one has a weak message to convey, and the research tells us that a highly credible (believable) source will be more persuasive than will a less credible source. There are several factors involved in source credibility, including vocal pleasantness and facial expressiveness (Burgoon, Birk, & Pfau, 1990), but the two that seem especially important are perceived *expertise* and *trustworthiness.*

The greater the perceived expertise of the communicator, the greater the resulting persuasion (e.g., Aronson et al.,1963; Hovland & Weiss, 1951). People convinced that they are listening to an expert are much more likely to be persuaded than they would be if they thought the speaker knew little about the subject matter—even if the messages were exactly the same. For example, I am much more likely to be persuaded by Garth Brooks if he were trying to change my mind about a guitar I was thinking about buying than I would be if he were trying to sell me a toaster oven or spaghetti sauce. (Celebrities without apparent expertise *are* used to promote products on the following logic: First, you will recognize them and attend to what they say. Second, their credibility and expertise in some other area, which has brought about their fame, will transfer to the product they are selling.)

Another factor likely to enhance a communicator's credibility is a high degree of trustworthiness (Cooper & Croyle, 1984). Studies by Walster and Festinger (1962), for example, demonstrated that more attitude change results when someone overhears a persuasive communication than when they believe the communication is directed at them. Trustworthiness and credibility are enhanced by a perceived lack of intent to persuade ("Why should they lie; they don't even know I can hear them?").

Before You Go On

What communicator characteristics have an impact on attitude change?

Attribution Theory

Another facet of the cognitive orientation we find in social psychology is called *attribution theory.* Social psychologists working with attributions are interested in understanding the cognitions we use when we try to explain the causes or sources of behavior (Jones, 1990). One question here is, "Do we tend to attribute behaviors or events we observe in the world around us to internal or to external sources—to personal dispositions or to environmental factors?" You may recognize this question as related to issues we raised in the Topic on personality when we discussed the extent to which one's behaviors are determined by personality (dispositional) factors or environmental (situational) factors.

Internal attributions explain the source of a person's behavior in terms of some characteristic of the person, often a personality trait or disposition, and for this reason are sometimes called dispositional attributions. **External attributions** explain the sources of a person's behavior in terms of the situation or context outside the individual, and are referred to as situational attributions.

We tend to rely on different types of information when making judgments about the sources of behavior. Imagine, for example, that your best friend shows his temper only when he is with his girlfriend. That information is useful because of its *distinctiveness* (his bad temper shows up only when he's with his girlfriend). As a result, you may take it as a signal of a troubled relationship.

Imagine you have just received an A on a test in a history class. In this case, you could (and probably would) use information about how well everyone else did on the test before you decide about your own superiority. This type of information is concerned with *consensus.* If you discover that everyone else also received an A, your explanation of your own behavior (and theirs) might be different from a situation in which you discover that yours is the only A in the class. Before you get excited about your accomplishment, you might wait for some sign of *consistency* over

⊚⊚⊚⊚ Thinking Critically ⊚⊚⊚⊚

Imagine that you want to change a friend's attitude about abortion (in either direction). How would you do so?

internal attribution *an explanation of behavior in terms of something (a trait) within the person; a dispositional attribution*

external attribution *an explanation of behavior in terms of something outside the person; a situational attribution*

We observe someone clearly behaving kindly toward an animal. Are we likely to attribute this behavior to "the way the person is" (an internal attribution) or to the situation as it exists at the moment (an external attribution)?

time lest this one exam be just a fluke. Using information about distinctiveness, consensus, and consistency is important in determining the kinds of attributions we make about our own behaviors and about the behaviors of others (Kelley, 1967, 1973, 1992; Kelley & Michela, 1980).

One focus of research is how people go about making inferences about the behaviors of others. Current thinking is that there are two basic processes involved, the *trait inference process* and the *situational inference process* (Krull & Erickson, 1995). In some cases we are interested in knowing about a particular person ("Just what kind of a guy is he, really?"). Our tendency then is to (1) note the person's behavior, (2) draw an inference about the presence of some trait the person has that led to that behavior, and (3) revise or modify that inference or attribution as we consider the situation more fully. In other cases, we are interested in knowing about a particular situation ("Just what kind of a party is this, really?"). In this case, we may reverse steps (2) and (3). First we (1) note a person's behaviors, then we (2) infer that the situation has caused these behaviors, and then we (3) revise or modify our inferences on the basis of what we know—or find out—about the person we first observed. In brief: Using internal or external attributions will depend on whether one is interested in another person or the situation.

Another area of research deals with the errors we make in our social thinking. In general terms, we make attribution errors because preexisting cognitive biases influence our judgments of causality. An example of such a bias is the **fundamental attribution error**—the tendency to favor internal, or personal, attributions for behaviors rather than external, situational explanations (Jones, 1979; Ross, 1977) . We see a man pick up a wallet that has been dropped on the pavement and race half a block to return it to its owner. We say to ourselves, "Now there's an honest man." (And we predict that that man will act honestly in a variety of situations.) The truth is, however, that the fellow returned the wallet only because he knew that we (and others) saw him pick it up. If no one else was around, the wallet may not have been returned. The fundamental attribution error is the tendency to disregard, or discount, situational factors in favor of internal, dispositional factors when we make inferences about the causes of behaviors. There is evidence that biases such as the fundamental attribution error are more common in Western cultures. People from India, for example, particularly adults, make fewer dispositional attributions than do American subjects (Miller, 1984). They are much more likely to explain behavior in terms of the situation or the environment than in terms of personality traits, abilities, or inabilities. That is, they are more likely to use a situational inference process.

There are other biases that lead us to make incorrect attributions about ourselves or others. One is called the **just world hypothesis**, in which people believe that we live in a world where good things happen only to good people and bad things happen only to bad people (Lerner, 1965, 1980). It's a sort of "everybody gets what they deserve" mentality. We see this bias (or fallacy) when we hear people claim that victims of rape often "ask for it by the way they dress and act." In fact, even the victims of rape sometimes engage in self-blame in an attempt to explain why in the world they were singled out for a crime in which they were the victim quite by chance (Janoff-Bulman, 1979; McCaul et al., 1990).

Another bias that affects our attributions is the **self-serving bias**. It occurs when we attribute successes or positive outcomes to personal, internal sources and failures or negative outcomes to situational, external sources (Harvey & Weary, 1984; Miller & Ross, 1975). We tend to think that when we do well it is because we're able, talented, and work hard, whereas when we do poorly it is the fault of someone or something else. "Boy, I did a great job of painting that room" versus "The room looks so shoddy because the paint was cheap and the brush was old" would be an example. The same process works even when extended to the social groups of which we feel a part. If someone of *our group* (be it an ethnic group, cultural group, social group, or gender) succeeds, we're likely to attribute that success to internal, personal effort or an ability. If we perceive someone *not in our group* succeeding, we are likely to attribute that success to the situation (see, for example, Finchilescu, 1994).

Recall from our discussion of depression in Topic 12B that cognitive theorists argue that depression can be explained as a failure to apply the self-serving bias. That is, some people may get into the habit of blaming themselves for failures and negative outcomes regardless of where the real blame resides or regardless of whether there even is any blame to attribute.

Yet another attribution error is the **actor-observer bias** (Jones & Nisbett, 1971; Monson & Snyder, 1977). Here we find a discrepancy between the way we explain our behavior (as actor) and the way we explain someone else's (as observer). What usually happens is that we use external attributions when we talk about why we do things. When we explain someone else's behaviors we are more likely to use internal attributions and refer to characteristics of the person. "I took that class because the instructor is excellent," versus "He took that class because he's so lazy." "I am dating Bill because he's so caring and considerate," versus "She's dating him only

fundamental attribution error *the tendency to overuse internal attributions when explaining behavior*

just world hypothesis *the belief that the world is just and that people get what they deserve*

self-serving bias *the tendency to attribute our successes to our own effort and abilities, and our failures to situational, external sources*

actor-observer bias *the overuse of internal attributions to explain the behaviors of others and external attributions to explain our own behaviors* because she wants to be seen with an athlete." "I went there because the rates were lower than anyplace else," versus "He went there because he wanted to show off."

That we explain our own behaviors in ways that are different from the ways we explain the behaviors of others should not be surprising. For one thing, we have more information about ourselves and our own past experiences than we do about anyone else. In fact, the more information we have about someone else, the less likely we are to use internal attributions to explain his or her behaviors. Also, in any situation, the actor gets a different view of what is happening than does the observer—that is, actors and observers attempt to attribute the causes of behavior on the basis of different information.

Before You Go On

What are attributions, and what sorts of errors do we find when people make attributions?

Interpersonal Attraction

Interpersonal attraction can be seen as an attitude toward another person—a favorable and powerful attitude at that. Interpersonal attraction reflects the extent to which a person has formed positive feelings and beliefs about another person and is prepared to act on those affects and cognitions.

Theories of Interpersonal Attraction

Social psychologists have put forth several theoretical models to explain the bases of interpersonal attraction. Let's briefly review four such theories.

Probably the simplest theory is one we can call the *reinforcement model* (Clore & Byrne, 1974; Lott & Lott, 1974). This model claims that we are attracted to (have positive attitudes toward) those people we associate with rewarding experiences. It also follows that we will tend not to be attracted to those we associate with punishment. One implication of this point of view is that you're going to like your instructor more, and seek him or her out for other classes in the future, if you get (or earn) a high grade in his or her class than you will if you get a low grade.

Another popular theory of interpersonal attraction is not quite as direct. It is called the *social exchange model* (Kelley & Thibault, 1978; Thibault & Kelley, 1959). According to this model, what matters most is a comparison of the costs and benefits of establishing or maintaining a relationship. For example, Leslie may judge that John is attractive, but that entering into a relationship with him is not worth the grief she would get from friends and family, who believe John to be lazy and untrustworthy. On the other hand, if Leslie has recently gone through a series of failed relationships with other men who were not physically attractive, she might take a chance on John, judging (in her frustration) that he was "worth it." This theory takes into account a series of comparative judgments made in social situations. Being attracted to someone else is not just a matter of "Is this a good thing?" It's a matter of, "Is the reward I might get from this relationship worth the cost, and what other alternatives exist at the moment?"

A third theoretical approach to interpersonal attraction is an *equity model*, which is more of an extension of social exchange theory than a departure from it (Greenberg & Cohen, 1982; Walster et al.,1978). Equity theory adds the appraisal of rewards and costs for *both* parties of a social relationship. That is, you may feel a relationship is worth the effort you have been putting into it, but if your partner in that relationship does not feel likewise, the relationship is in danger. What matters, then, is that both (or all) members of a relationship feel they are getting a fair deal (equity). Notice two things about this model: (1) Both members of a relationship do not have to share rewards equally. What matters is that the ratio of costs to rewards

There are many reasons why some persons are attracted to others, and physical attractiveness is surely a relevant one.

be equitable for both members. (2) If one person were to feel that he or she is getting more from a relationship than is deserved (on the basis of costs and compared to the other's rewards), the relationship would not be equitable and would be jeopardized. The best relationships are those in which all members receive an equal ratio of rewards to costs.

A more recent approach to understanding interpersonal relationships is based on feelings or affect more than on cognitions. This model is referred to as *attachment theory* (Berscheid, 1994; Feeney & Noller, 1990; Hazan & Shaver, 1987). It suggests that interpersonal relationships can be classified into one of three types depending on the attitudes one has about such relationships (from Shaver, Hazan, & Bradshaw, 1988, p. 80):

Secure: "I find it relatively easy to get close to others and am comfortable depending on them and having them depend on me. I don't often worry about being abandoned or about someone getting too close to me."

Avoidant: "I am somewhat uncomfortable being close to others; I find it difficult to trust them completely, difficult to allow myself to depend on them. I get nervous when anyone gets too close, and partners often want me to be more intimate than I feel comfortable being."

Anxious/ambivalent: "I find that others are reluctant to get as close as I would like. I often worry that my partner doesn't really love me or won't stay with me. I want to merge completely with another person, and this desire sometimes scares people away."

One of the things that makes attachment theory appealing is the evidence that suggests that one's "style" of forming attachments with others is remarkably stable throughout the life span. It may be that the types of interpersonal relationships we form as adults are influenced by the types of attachments we developed as very young children.

Finally, I should remind you of a point we first discussed in the context of mate selection (Topic 8B): few people enter into relationships having carefully considered all of the factors these models imply. That is, assessments of reinforcement, exchange, or equity value are seldom made at a conscious level; nor do we purposively seek out relationships that mirror those we had in childhood (e.g., Bargh, 1993).

Before You Go On

Summarize four approaches that account for interpersonal attractions.

Factors Affecting Interpersonal Attraction

Having reviewed four general models of interpersonal attraction, let's now look at some empirical evidence related to attraction. What determines who you will be attracted to? What factors tend to provide the rewards, or the positive reward/cost ratios, that serve as the basis for strong relationships? We'll consider four common determinants of attraction.

Reciprocity, our first principle, is perhaps the most obvious: we tend to value and like people who like and value us (Backman & Secord, 1959; Curtis & Miller, 1986). We have already noted, when discussing operant conditioning (Topic 5B), that the attention of others can be a powerful reinforcer. This is particularly true if the attention is positive, supportive, or affectionate. The value of someone else caring for us is particularly strong when that someone else initially seemed to have neutral or negative attitudes toward us (Aronson & Linder, 1965). In other words, we are most attracted to people who like us now, but who didn't originally.

Our second principle, *proximity,* suggests that physical closeness yields attraction. Sociologists, as well as your own experience, will tell you that people tend to establish friendships (and romances) with others with whom they have grown up, worked, or gone to school. Residents of apartments or dormitories, for example, tend to become friends with those other residents living closest to them (Festinger et al., 1950). Being around others gives us the opportunity to discover just who does provide those interpersonal rewards we seek in friendship.

There may be a social-psychological phenomenon at work here called the **mere exposure phenomenon**. Research, pioneered by Robert Zajonc (1968), has shown with a variety of stimuli that liking tends to increase with repeated exposure. Examples of this phenomenon are abundant in everyday life. Have you ever bought a CD you had not heard previously, assuming you would like it because you have liked all the other CDs made by this performer? The first time you listen to your new CD, however, your reaction is lukewarm at best, and you are disappointed with your purchase. Not wanting to feel you've wasted your money, you play the CD a few more times. What often happens is that you soon realize you like this CD. The mere exposure effect has occurred. This also commonly happens in our formation of attitudes about other people. Familiarity is apt to breed attraction, not contempt. Although there is ample evidence that the mere exposure phenomenon is real, there remains considerable disagreement about *why* familiarity and repeated interactions breed attraction (e.g., Birnbaum & Mellers, 1979; Kunst-Wilson & Zajonc, 1980). I also have to add that there are limits. Too much exposure may lead to boredom and to devaluation (Bornstein, 1989; Bornstein, Kale, & Cornell, 1990).

mere exposure phenomenon *the tendency to increase our liking of people and things as a result of recurring contact*

Proximity leads to liking and attracting, which is one reason why teenagers who go to the same school and live in the same neighborhood are likely to form friendships.

Physical attractiveness is related to interpersonal attraction. The power of physical attractiveness in the context of dating has been demonstrated experimentally in a classic study directed by Elaine Walster (Walster et al., 1966). University of Minnesota freshmen completed several psychological tests as part of an orientation program. Students were then randomly matched for dates to an orientation dance, during which they took a break and evaluated their assigned partners. The researchers hoped to uncover intricate, complex, and subtle facts about interpersonal attraction, such as which personality traits might mesh in such a way as to produce attraction. As it turned out, none of these factors was important. The impact of physical attractiveness was so powerful it wiped out all other effects. For both men and women, the more physically attractive their date, the more they liked that date and the more they wanted to date her or him again. Numerous studies of physical attractiveness followed this one. Some of these studies gave subjects a chance to pick a date from a group of several potential partners (using descriptions or pictures). Not surprisingly, subjects almost invariably selected the most attractive person to be their date (Reis et al., 1980).

In real life we seldom have the luxury of asking for a date without the possibility of being turned down. When experiments added the possibility of rejection, an interesting effect emerged: people no longer chose the most attractive candidate, but selected partners whose level of physical attractiveness was more similar to their own. This behavior is called the **matching phenomenon**, and has been verified by naturalistic observation studies (Walster & Walster, 1969). Even when we consider relationships between or among friends of the same sex, we find that such friends tend to be similar when rated for physical attractiveness (Cash & Derlega, 1978).

Our fourth determinant of interpersonal attraction is *similarity.* There is a large body of research on similarity and attraction, but the findings are consistent, and

matching phenomenon *the tendency to select partners whose level of physical attractiveness matches our own*

The more similar another person is to you, the more you will tend to like that person. Our friends usually share our attitudes and enjoy doing the same things that we enjoy.

we can summarize them briefly. Much of this research has been done by Donn Byrne and his colleagues (Byrne, 1971; Smeaton et al., 1989). Simply put, the more similar another person is to you, the more you will tend to like that person—and the more you are likely to believe that that person likes you (Buss, 1985; Davis, 1985; Gonzales et al., 1983; Rubin, 1973). We also tend to be repelled, or put off, by persons we believe to be dissimilar to us (Rosenbaum, 1986). Opposites may occasionally attract, but similarity is probably the glue that over the long haul holds together romances and friendships. It is this principle that makes it unusual, or difficult, for people to form significant interpersonal relationships with persons of other cultures or other ethnic groups (e.g., Stephan, 1985).

Before You Go On

What are four determinants of interpersonal attraction?

@@@@ **Thinking Critically** @@@@

Can you explain your own attraction to any of your friends in terms of the theories or factors presented above?

TOPIC 14A SUMMARY

In this Topic, we've addressed important issues related to social cognition. We spent most of our time on attitudes, which are largely cognitive, at least to the extent that they involve mental representations stored in memory, but which also involve affect and action tendencies directed toward some object or event. We have reviewed ways in which we develop cognitions about the sources of the behaviors we see around us. In many instances, we make erroneous attributions based on biased expectations. We ended with a discussion of interpersonal attraction, searching for explanations for why some people get along so well with each other and some do not. Although the impact of group influence can be found in each of the issues we covered in this Topic, social influence and group processes will be the major focuses of Topic 14B.

TOPIC 14B Social Influence

So far, we have reviewed some of the ways in which our social nature has an impact on our cognitions—our perceptions and beliefs about ourselves and others. Now it is time to consider more direct influences of the social world on our everyday behaviors. We'll deal with the processes of conformity and obedience, and consider bystander apathy and intervention. We'll end by reviewing a few other situations in which social influence is a potent force in our lives.

Conformity

One of the most direct forms of social influence occurs when we modify our behavior, under perceived pressure to do so, so that it is consistent with the behavior of others, a process referred to as **conformity**. Although we often think of conformity in a negative way, to conform is natural and often desirable. Conformity helps make social behaviors efficient and, at least to some degree, predictable.

conformity *the changing of one's behavior, under perceived pressure, so that it is consistent with the behavior of others*

When he began his research on conformity, Solomon Asch believed people are not that susceptible to social pressure when the situation in which they find themselves is clear-cut and unambiguous. Asch thought people would behave independently of group pressure when there was little doubt their own judgments were accurate. He developed an interesting technique for testing his hypothesis (Asch, 1951, 1956).

A subject in Asch's procedure joined a group seated around a table. In his original study, the group consisted of seven people. Unknown to the subject, six of the people in the group were confederates of the experimenter; they were "in on" the experiment. A real subject was told that the study dealt with the ability to make perceptual judgments. The participant had to do nothing more than decide which of three lines was the same length as a standard line (Figure 14.4). The experimenter showed each set of lines to the group and collected responses, one by one,

Conformity is said to occur whenever one changes his or her behaviors in response to the perceived pressure of others to make that change.

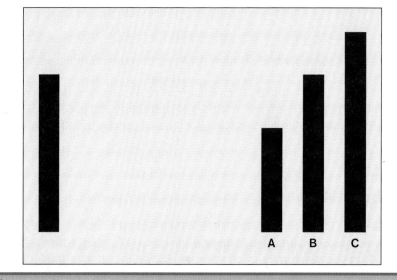

Figure 14.4

The type of stimuli used in Asch's conformity experiments. Subjects are to say which of the three lines on the right (A, B, or C) equals the line on the left. Associates of the experimenter will occasionally make incorrect choices, even though the correct choice is always as obvious as this one.

from each member of the group. There were 18 sets of lines to judge, and the only real subject was always the last one to respond.

Each judgment involved unambiguous stimuli: the correct answer was obvious. On 12 of the 18 trials, however, the confederates gave a unanimous but *incorrect* answer. What would the subjects do? How would they resolve this conflict? Their eyes were telling them what the right answer was, but the group was saying something else.

The results of his initial study surprised Asch, because they did not confirm his hypothesis. When confederates gave "wrong" answers, conformity occurred 37 percent of the time. Subjects responded with an incorrect answer that agreed with the majority on more than one-third of the trials. Moreover, three-quarters of Asch's subjects conformed to the group pressure at least once.

In subsequent studies, Asch tried several variations of his original procedure. In one experiment, he varied the size of the unanimous, incorrect majority. As you might expect, the level of conformity increased as the size of the majority increased, leveling off at three or four people (Asch, 1956; Knowles, 1983). Subjects gave incorrect judgments only 4 percent of the time when just one other incorrect judgment preceded their own. In another study, Asch found that subjects gave an erroneous judgment only 10 percent of the time when there was but one dissenter among the six confederates who voiced an accurate judgment before the subjects gave theirs. In other words, when the subjects had any social support for what their eyes had told them, they tended to trust their own judgment. Other researchers have demonstrated that the minority opinion (say, even one dissenter) can have significant effects on conformity, especially if the minority position is held with any consistency (Moscovici et al., *1969*, 1985; Nemeth, 1986).

Conformity involves yielding to the perceived pressure of a group. In most cases, it is assumed, group members are peers, or at least similar to the conformer. When one yields to the pressure of a perceived authority, the result is obedience. It is to the issue of obedience we turn next.

Before You Go On

Describe the methods and findings of Asch's conformity studies.

Norms and Compliance

We live in a social world in which we have all formed expectations about the acceptability of behaviors in given situations. That is, we have learned how one is "expected to act," or "supposed to act," in a social context. These expectations are called norms. This exercise asks that you see what happens when you violate those social norms. Can you get anyone else to change his or her behaviors just by violating a few common social norms? Please be very careful here. Some people become very upset when social norms are violated. Try these activities in good humor and be sensitive to the feelings of others, quickly explaining what you are doing at any sign of discomfort.

1. While others can watch you, try eating a banana by peeling back only part of the peel, and eat it as you would an ear of corn. Or, eat a chocolate bar with a knife and fork, cutting the chocolate into small, bite-sized pieces. (This violation of social norms became a running gag in the *Seinfeld* television program for weeks.)

2. Dress in a manner that is radically different from how you usually do when going to classes. How long does it take for your friends and acquaintances to comment on your choice of clothes?

3. Note the reactions you get if you simply walk across campus holding hands with a friend of the same sex.

4. Here's a classic (from the old television program *Candid Camera*). Enter an elevator and ride up and down for a while facing the rear. Does anyone enter and join in facing the rear? Now try the same thing with some friends. What is the reaction of someone entering an elevator to find four of you facing the rear?

5. As you stand at a pay phone with a one dollar bill in your hand, see how many people will respond to your request for change.

6. You should get the permission of your instructor for this one. Enter a class a bit early, go to a seat, but simply stand there–do not sit down, even as the class begins. Try the same thing with the aid of five or six classmates–and the permission of the instructor. How do people react when they come into a classroom and find six of you standing?

7. Here's another situation that requires the help of some friends–five or six will do. In the library, or in a hallway, approach a student and ask if you can borrow a sheet of notebook paper. Then, a minute or so later, have a friend make the same request of the same student. Then a second friend, and a third, and so on, make the same request. Be sure to explain what you were up to, and ask the student how he or she felt as more and more people asked for a sheet of paper.

Obedience to Authority

The participants in Asch's studies took the procedures seriously, but the consequences of either conforming or maintaining independence were rather trivial. At worst, subjects might have experienced some discomfort as a result of voicing independent judgments. There were no external rewards or punishments for their behavior, and there was no one telling them how to respond. Stanley Milgram (1933–1984), a social psychologist at Yale University, went beyond Asch's procedure. Milgram's research has become among the most famous and controversial in all of psychology. His experiments pressured subjects to comply with the demand of an authority figure. The demand was both unreasonable and troubling (Milgram, 1963, 1965, 1974).

All of Milgram's studies involved the same basic procedure. Subjects arrived at the laboratory to find that they would be participating with a second person (again, a confederate of the experimenter). The experimenter explained that the research dealt with the effects of punishment on learning and that one participant would serve as a "teacher," while the other would act as a "learner." The roles were assigned by a rigged drawing in which the actual subject was always assigned the role of teacher, while the confederate was always the learner. The subject watched as the learner was taken into a room and wired to electrodes to be used for delivering punishment in the form of electric shocks.

The teacher then received his instructions. First, he was to read to the learner a list of four pairs of words. The teacher was then to read the first word of one of the pairs, and the learner was to supply the second word. The teacher sat in front of a rather imposing electric "shock generator" (Figure 14.5) that had 30 switches. From left to right, the switches increased by increments of 15 volts, ranging from 15 volts to 450 volts. Labels were printed under the switches on the generator, ranging from "Slight" to "Moderate" to "Extreme Intensity" to "Danger: Severe Shock." The label at the 450-volt end read "XXX."

As the task proceeded, the learner periodically made errors according to a pre-arranged schedule. The teacher had been instructed to deliver an electric shock for every incorrect answer. With each error, the teacher was to move up the scale of shocks, giving the learner a more potent shock with each new mistake. (The learner, remember, was part of the act, and no one was actually receiving any shocks.)

Whenever the teacher hesitated or questioned whether he should continue, the experimenter was ready with a verbal prod: "Please continue," or "The experiment requires that you continue." If the subject protested, the experimenter became more assertive and offered an alternative prod, such as, "You have no choice; you must go on." Milgram was astonished by the results of his own study, and the results still amaze us. Twenty-six of Milgram's 40 subjects—65 percent—obeyed the demands of the experimenter and went all the way to the highest shock and closed all of the switches. In fact, no subject stopped prior to the 300-volt level, the point at which the learner pounded on the wall in protest. One later variation of this study added vocal responses from the learner, who delivered an increasingly stronger series of demands to be let out of the experiment. The level of obedience

Figure 14.5

A shock generator apparatus of the sort the "teacher" used to punish the "learner" in Stanley Milgram's study of obedience.

in this study was still unbelievably high, as 25 of 40 subjects (62.5 percent) continued to administer shocks to the 450-volt level.

The behavior of Milgram's subjects indicated that they *were* concerned about
the learner. All subjects claimed that they experienced genuine and extreme stress
in this situation. Some fidgeted, some trembled, many perspired profusely. Several
giggled nervously. In short, the people caught up in this situation showed obvious
signs of conflict and anxiety. Nonetheless, they continued to obey the orders of the
experimenter even though they had good reason to believe they might be harming
the learner.

Milgram's first study was performed with male subjects ranging in age from 20
to 50. A later replication with adult women produced precisely the same results: 65
percent obeyed fully. Other variations of the procedure, however, uncovered several factors that could reduce the amount of obedience. Putting the learner and
teacher in the same room, or having the experimenter deliver his orders over the
telephone, reduced levels of obedience markedly. When the shocks were delivered
by a team consisting of the subject and two confederates who refused to give the
shocks, full-scale obedience dropped to only 10 percent.

Attribution Errors and a Word of Caution

Upon first hearing about these distressing results, many people tend to think of
Milgram's obedient subjects as unfeeling, unusual, or even downright cruel and
sadistic people (Safer, 1980). Nothing could be further from the truth. The participants were truly troubled by what was happening. If you thought Milgram's subjects must be strange or different, perhaps you were a victim of what we identified
in our last Topic as an *attribution error.* You were willing to attribute the subjects'
behavior to internal personality characteristics instead of recognizing the powerful
situational forces at work.

Attributing negative personality characteristics to the "teachers" is particularly
understandable in light of the unexpected nature of the results. In commenting on
this research, many psychologists have suggested, in fact, that the most significant
aspect of Milgram's findings is that they are so surprising. As part of his research,
Milgram asked people, including a group of psychiatrists and a group of ministers,
to predict what they would do under these circumstances, and asked them to predict how far others would go before refusing the authority. Respondents predicted
very little obedience, expecting practically no one to proceed all the way to the final switch on the shock generator.

A Reminder About Ethics in Research

In reading about Milgram's research, it should have occurred to you that putting
people in such a stressful situation could be considered ethically objectionable.
Milgram himself was concerned with the welfare of his subjects. He took great care
to debrief them fully after each session. He informed them that they had not really
administered any shocks and explained why deception had been used. It is, of
course, standard practice in psychological experiments to conclude the session by
disclosing the true purpose of the study and alleviating any anxiety that might
have arisen.

Milgram reported that after debriefing, the people in his studies were not upset
at having been deceived. Their principal reaction was one of relief when they
learned that no electric shock had been used. Milgram indicated that a follow-up
study performed a year later with some of the same subjects showed that no long-
term adverse effects had been created by his procedure. Despite his precautions,
Milgram was severely criticized for placing people in such an extremely stressful

situation. One of the effects of his research was to establish in the scientific community a higher level of awareness of the need to protect the well-being of human research subjects.

Before You Go On

Briefly describe Milgram's demonstrations of obedience.

⊚⊚⊚⊚ **Thinking Critically** ⊚⊚⊚⊚

Now that you know all about the results of his project, how do you think that you would have reacted if you had been one of Milgram's "teachers"? (Don't forget attribution errors.)

Bystander Intervention

Remember the story of Kitty Genovese with which I started this chapter? Here was a young woman brutally slain in full view of (at least) 38 witnesses, none of whom came to her aid. This tragic event stimulated public concern and sparked much commentary in the media. People wondered how all those witnesses could have shown such a lack of concern for another human being. *Apathy* and *alienation* were terms used to describe what had happened.

Bibb Latané and John Darley, two social psychologists who at the time were at universities in New York City, were not satisfied that terms such as *bystander apathy* or *alienation* adequately explained what happened in the Genovese case. They were not willing to attribute people's failure to help to internal, dispositional, or personality factors. They were convinced that situational factors make such events possible. Latané and Darley (1970) pointed out that there are logical reasons people should not be expected to offer help in an emergency. Emergencies tend to happen quickly and without advance warning. Except for medical technicians, firefighters, and a few other select categories of individuals, people are not prepared to deal with emergencies when they do arise. In fact, one good predictor of who will intervene in an emergency turns out to be previous experience with similar emergency situations (Cramer et al., 1988; Huston et al., 1981).

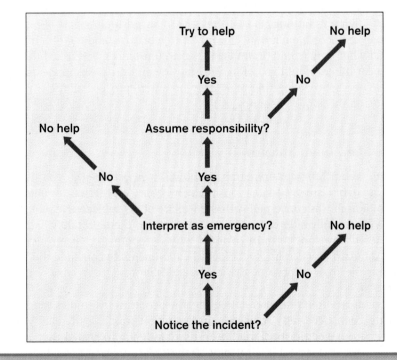

Figure 14.6

Some of the decisions and outcomes involved as a bystander considers intervening in an emergency situation. (After Latané & Darley, 1968.)

A Cognitive Model of Bystander Intervention

Latané and Darley (1968) suggest that a series of cognitive events must occur before a bystander can intervene in an emergency (Figure 14.6). First, the bystander must *notice* what is going on. A person who is window shopping and fails to see someone collapse on the opposite side of the street cannot be expected to rush over and offer assistance. Second, if the bystander does notice something happen, he or she still must *interpret* the situation as an emergency; perhaps the person who has collapsed is simply drunk or tired and not really having a stroke or a heart attack. The third step involves the decision that it is the bystander's (and not someone else's) *responsibility* to do something.

Even if the bystander has noticed something happening, has interpreted the situation as one calling for action, and has assumed responsibility for helping, he or she still faces the decision of what form of assistance to offer. Should he or she try to give first aid? Should he or she try to find the nearest telephone, or simply start shouting for help? As a final step, then, the person must decide how to *implement* his or her decision to act. What is the best first aid under these circumstances? Just where can a phone be found? Thus, we can see that intervening on behalf of someone else in a social situation involves a series of cognitive choices.

A negative outcome at any of these steps will lead to a decision to not offer assistance. When one considers the cognitive events necessary for helping, it becomes apparent that the deck is stacked against the victim in an emergency. Ironically, it is the very presence of others that leads to this social-psychological

Crossing the village, Mowaka is overpowered by army ants. (Later, bystanders were all quoted as saying they were horrified, but "didn't want to get involved.")

phenomenon (Cunningham, 1984; Shotland, 1985). Perhaps we should be surprised that bystanders ever *do* offer help. There seem to be several psychological processes that account for what is called the *social inhibition of helping,* or *bystander effect.* Let's review just three (Latané & Darley, 1970; Latané & Nida, 1981).

Audience Inhibition. **Audience inhibition** refers to our tendency to be hesitant to do things in front of others, especially strangers. We tend to be concerned about how others will evaluate us. In public, no one wants to do anything that might appear to be improper, incompetent, or silly. The bystander who intervenes risks embarrassment if he or she blunders, and that risk increases as the number of people present increases. People who are particularly sensitive to becoming embarrassed in public are most likely to be inhibited (Tice & Baumeister, 1985).

Pluralistic Ignorance. Emergencies tend to be ambiguous: is the man who has collapsed on the street ill or drunk? Is the commotion in a neighboring apartment an assault or a family quarrel that's just a little out of hand? When social reality is not clear, we often turn to others for clues. While someone is in the process of getting information from others, he or she will probably try to remain calm, cool, and collected, behaving as if there is no emergency. Everyone else, of course, is doing the very same thing, showing no outward sign of concern. The result is that each person is led by the others to think that the situation is really not an emergency after all, a phenomenon called **pluralistic ignorance** (Miller & McFarland, 1987). What pluralistic ignorance amounts to is the belief on the part of the individual that only she or he is confused and doesn't know what to do in an emergency, whereas everyone else is standing around doing nothing for a good reason. The group becomes paralyzed by a type of conformity—conformity to the inaction of others.

This process was demonstrated in a classic experiment by Latané and Darley (1968, 1970). Columbia University students reported to a campus building to participate in an interview. They were sent to a waiting room where they were to fill out some forms. While they did so, smoke began to billow through a vent in the wall. After six minutes (the point at which the procedure was terminated if the "emergency" had not been reported), there was enough smoke in the room to interfere with breathing and prevent seeing across the room.

When subjects were alone in the waiting room, 75 percent of them came out to report the smoke. However, when two passive confederates were in the room with the subject, only 10 percent responded. Those people who reported the smoke did so quickly. Those from the groups who failed to do so generated all sorts of explanations for the smoke: steam, vapors from the air conditioner, smog introduced to simulate an urban environment, even "truth gas." In short, subjects who remained unresponsive had been led by the inaction of others to conclude almost anything but the obvious—that something was very wrong.

Diffusion of Responsibility. In the Kitty Genovese murder, it was terribly clear that an emergency was in progress. There was little ambiguity about what was going on. Further, the 38 witnesses in the Genovese case were not in a face-to-face group that would allow social influence processes such as pluralistic ignorance to operate. Latané and Darley suggested that a third process is necessary to complete the explanation of bystander behavior.

A single bystander in an emergency situation must bear the full responsibility for offering assistance, but the witness who is part of a group shares that responsibility with other onlookers. The greater the number of other people present, the smaller is each individual's perceived obligation to intervene, a process referred to as **diffusion of responsibility**.

Latané and Darley devised a clever demonstration of this phenomenon. College students arrived at a laboratory to take part in a group discussion of some of the personal problems they experienced as students at an urban campus. To re-

audience inhibition *reluctance to intervene and offer assistance in front of others*

pluralistic ignorance *a condition in which the inaction of others leads each individual in a group to interpret a situation as a nonemergency, thus leading to general inactivity*

diffusion of responsibility *the tendency to allow others to share in the obligation to intervene* duce embarrassment of talking about such matters in public, each group member was isolated in his or her own cubicle and could communicate with the others only through an intercom system. Actually, there were no other group members, only tape-recorded voices. Thus, there really was only one student in each group, and the perceived size of the group could be manipulated to see if diffusion of responsibility would occur.

The first person to "speak" mentioned that he was prone to seizures when under stress, such as when studying for an exam. The others, including the actual subject, then took turns talking about their problems. A second round of discussion began again with the seizure-prone student who, as he started talking, began to suffer one of his seizures. Clearly, something was wrong. As the "victim" began stammering, choking, and pleading for help, the typical subject became nervous—some trembled. The study had another feature in common with the Genovese episode: subjects could not be sure if any other bystanders (members of the group) had taken any action. (In fact, remember, there were no others.)

As expected, the likelihood of helping decreased as the perceived size of the group increased. Eighty-five percent of those in two-person groups (just the subject

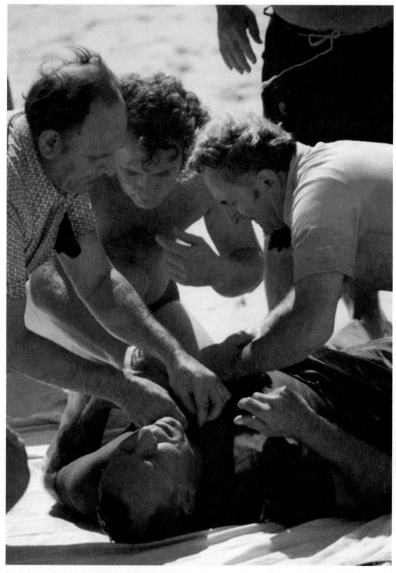

Researchers have found several reasons to explain why people should not be expected to get involved in a perceived emergency situation. Nonetheless, some bystanders will choose to intervene, particularly if they have experience from previous similar emergencies.

and victim) left the cubicle to report the emergency. When the subject thought he or she was in a three-person group, 62 percent responded. Only 31 percent of the students who believed they were in a six-person group took any step to intervene. The responsibility for reporting the seizure was divided (diffused) among those thought to be present.

Incidentally, diffusion of responsibility does come in forms less serious in their implications. Those of you with a few siblings can probably recall times at home when the telephone rang five or six times before anyone made a move to answer it, even though the entire family was home at the time. Some of you probably have been at parties where the doorbell went unanswered with everyone thinking that "someone else" would get it.

The Bystander Effect: A Conclusion

The situational determinants of helping behavior continued to be a popular research topic for social psychologists throughout the 1970s. Many of these studies manipulated the size of the group witnessing the event that created the need for help in the first place. Latané and Nida (1981) reviewed nearly 50 studies involving nearly 100 helping–not-helping situations. Although they involved a wide range of settings, procedures, and participants, the social inhibition of helping (the bystander effect) occurred in almost every instance. Latané and Nida combined the data from all of these studies in a meta-analysis. Their conclusion: A person is more likely to help when he or she is alone rather than in a group. The bystander effect is a remarkably consistent phenomenon, perhaps as predictable as any phenomenon in social psychology.

Now let's look at a few other situations in which we can see the impact of group influence on the behavior of the individual.

Before You Go On

What effect does the presence of others have on a person's willingness to help in an emergency?

◎◎◎◎ **Thinking Critically** ◎◎◎◎

To what extent can you observe "bystander apathy" on your campus? When there is a student government election, what percentage of the student body actually votes?

social loafing *the tendency to decrease one's individual work effort as the size of the group in which one is working increases*

Social Loafing and Facilitation

Latané, Williams, and Harkins (1979) have identified a process of social influence they call **social loafing**: the tendency to work less (to decrease individual effort) as the size of the group in which one is working becomes larger. Their studies had participants shout or clap as loud as possible, either in groups or alone. If people were led to believe their performance could not be identified, they invested less and less effort in the task as group size increased. Other studies (e.g., Harkins & Petty, 1983; Karou & Williams, 1993; Weldon & Gargano, 1988; Williams & Karou, 1991) have used different, more cognitive tasks, such as evaluating poetry. The results tend to be consistent: when people can hide in the crowd, their effort (and hence their productivity) declines.

Although social loafing is a widespread phenomenon, it is not always predicted when one works in a group setting. Remember our earlier discussions of cultures that can be described in terms of the extent to which they exhibit collectivist or individualist characteristics? As you might predict, social loafing is significantly less likely in those (collectivist) cultures—such as in Japan, China, and other Asian countries—that place a high value on participation in group activities (e.g., Early, 1989; Gabrena et al., 1985). In individualist cultures, such as in the United States, and most Western countries, social loafing can be virtually eliminated if group members believe their effort is special and required for the group's success, or if group members believe that their performance can be identified and evaluated individually (Harkins, 1987; Harkins & Syzmanski, 1989; Williams et al., 1981, 1989). Indeed, there are situations in which social influence actually facilitates behavior.

Many years ago, psychologist Norman Triplett observed that bicycle riders competing against other cyclists outperformed those racing against a clock. He then performed what is considered the first laboratory experiment in social psychology (Triplett, 1898). Triplett had children wind a fishing reel as rapidly as they could. They engaged in this task either alone or with another child alongside doing the same thing. Just as he had noticed in his records of bicycle races, Triplett found that the children worked faster when another child was present. We now know that such an effect sometimes occurs not only with coactors (others engaged in the same task), but if a person performs before an audience. For example, joggers, both male and female, pick up the pace and run faster when going past a woman sitting on a park bench (Worringham & Messick, 1983). When the presence of others improves an individual's performance on some task, we have evidence of what is called **social facilitation**.

Numerous studies of these phenomena were performed early in the twentieth century, but with a puzzling inconsistency in results. Sometimes social facilitation would occur, but on other occasions, just the opposite would happen. Sometimes people performed more poorly in the presence of others than they did alone, an effect social psychologists called **social interference**. The inconsistency in these findings was so bewildering that psychologists for the most part eventually gave up investigating social facilitation.

In 1965, Robert Zajonc resurrected the topic of social facilitation by providing a plausible interpretation for the lack of consistency in social facilitation effects. In his examination of the research, Zajonc noticed that social facilitation occurred whenever the behavior under study was simple, routine, or very well learned (e.g., bicycle riding or winding a fishing reel). Social interference, on the other hand, tended to occur whenever the behavior involved was complex or not well practiced. Zajonc's insight was that the presence of others creates increased arousal,

social facilitation *improved performance due to the presence of others*

social interference *impaired performance due to the presence of others*

Because of social facilitation, we tend to perform better when we are in the presence of others—at least when we are engaged in a simple or well-rehearsed task. Bicycle riders, for example, ride faster when racing against each other than they do when they are racing against the clock.

which in turn energizes the dominant (most likely) response under the circumstances. When the dominant response is correct, as with a simple, well-practiced task, facilitation occurs. When the dominant response is incorrect, as with a complex task or one with which we have had little practice, the result is interference (Levine et al., 1993).

You may have experienced this effect yourself if you have ever tried to acquire a skill at a sport totally new to you. Whereas skilled athletes often perform better in front of audiences, the novice tends to do better when alone. (Even skilled athletes don't always perform better in front of audiences, sometimes "choking" in front of home crowds during important games [Baumeister, 1985].) You may have experienced—as a novice, that is—the frustration of finding it difficult to even make contact with a golf ball or tennis ball when there are others standing nearby, watching you.

As an overall conclusion, we may safely assume that social interference and social loafing are more common phenomena than is social facilitation. Although there are occasions in which coworkers or an audience may enhance an individual's performance, the presence of others is more likely to inhibit it.

Before You Go On

What may we conclude concerning the effects of social influence on the quality of an individual's performance?

Decision Making in Groups

Many of the decisions we face in our daily lives are the sort that are made in group settings. Committees, boards, family groups, and group projects for a class are only a few examples. There is logic in the belief that group efforts to solve problems should be superior to the efforts of individuals. Having more people available should mean having more talent and knowledge available. It also seems logical that the cohesiveness of the group might contribute to a more productive effort (for some groups and some problems, this is exactly the case). But by now we know better than to assume that just because a conclusion is logical it is necessarily true.

When he was an MIT graduate student in industrial management, James Stoner gave subjects in his research a series of dilemmas to grapple with (Stoner, 1961). The result of each decision was to be a statement of how much risk the fictitious character in the dilemma should take. Much to his surprise, Stoner found that the decisions rendered by groups were much riskier than those individual group members had made prior to the group decision. Stoner called this move away from conservative solutions a *risky shift*. For example, doctors, if asked individually, might claim that a patient's problem (whatever it might be) could be handled with medication and a change in diet. If these same doctors were to get together to discuss the patient's situation, they might very well end up concluding that what was called for here was a new and potentially dangerous (risky) surgical procedure.

group polarization *the tendency for members of a group to give more extreme judgments following a discussion than they gave initially*

Several hundred experimental studies later, we now know that this effect occurs in the opposite direction (Levine & Moreland, 1990; Moscovici et al., 1985). In other words, the risky shift is simply a specific case of a more general **group polarization** effect—that group participation will make an individual's reactions more extreme, or polarized. Group discussion usually leads to an enhancement of the beliefs and attitudes of the group members that existed before the discussion began. One explanation for group polarization is that open discussion gives group members an opportunity to hear persuasive arguments they have not previously considered, leading to a strengthening of their original attitudes (Isenberg, 1986). Another possibility is that after comparing attitudinal positions with one another, some group members feel pressure to catch up with other group members who have more extreme attitudes (Hinsz & Davis, 1984).

Irving Janis (1972, 1983a) has described a related phenomenon of influence he calls **groupthink**, an excessive concern for reaching a consensus in group decision making to the extent that critical evaluations are withheld. Janis maintains that this style of thinking emerges when group members are so interested in maintaining harmony in the group that differences of opinion or alternative courses of action are suppressed. Groupthink is most likely to occur in cohesive groups. By analyzing several key historical events such as responding to the Pearl Harbor invasion in terms of groupthink, Janis found that such situations involved a cohesive decision-making group that was relatively isolated from outside judgments, a directive leader who supplied pressure to conform to his position, and an illusion of unanimity (see also, McCauley, 1989). When, for example, decisions about women or minorities are made by a group of white males, we might at least suspect that groupthink could be at work.

There are circumstances in which groups *are* more efficient than individuals working alone. Groups are useful when problems are complex and require skills and abilities more likely to be found in a number of different individuals working together. Group decision making can also serve to identify errors individuals might not identify.

groupthink an excessive concern for reaching a consensus in group decision making to the extent that critical evaluations of input are withheld

Before You Go On

How does social influence affect decision making in groups?

TOPIC 14B SUMMARY

We are social animals. Our behaviors, feelings, and cognitions are influenced by those around us in our social environments. In this Topic, we discussed some of the processes of group influence, and many of them seem unfavorable, leading people to avoid helping someone else in need of assistance, to actually harm someone in obedient response to an authority figure, to exert less effort, to perform

Many of the decisions that we face every day are the sort made in groups, whether committees, boards, families, or friends.

poorly, or to think inefficiently. At the same time, groups are a major part of social life, and many of our individual goals simply cannot be reached alone, without group membership. It is hoped that an awareness of the potentially negative consequences of group activity and the conditions that produce them will enable us to counter obstacles to group productivity.

CHAPTER SUMMARY

Topic 14A

What is an attitude, and what are its components?

An attitude is a relatively stable evaluative disposition (positive or negative) directed toward some object or event. An attitude consists of feelings (affects), behaviors (or action tendencies), and beliefs (cognitions). Although the affective and cognitive components of attitudes are often consistent with each other, behavior—influenced by many situational variables—may be inconsistent with the other two major components. /pp. 496–498

Briefly describe three ways in which attitudes might be acquired.

Attitudes may be acquired through classical conditioning: after positive or negative experiences are associated with an attitudinal object, the object by itself comes to produce a positive or negative evaluation. Attitudes may develop as a result of direct reinforcement (operant conditioning), or they may be formed when they are vicariously reinforced (observational learning). /pp. 498–499

How is cognitive dissonance related to attitude change?

Cognitive dissonance is an unpleasant state of tension between or among cognitions that may occur when we behave in a fashion inconsistent with our attitudes. Because we are motivated to reduce dissonance, we may do so by changing our attitudes so that they become consistent with the way we behave. /pp. 499–502

What communicator characteristics have an impact on attitude change?

The quality of the arguments in a persuasive communication will influence the degree of persuasion the communication produces—the "central route" to attitude change. Concern with communicator characteristics and other situational variables reflects a focus on "peripheral routes" to attitude change. Those communicators perceived as being expert or trustworthy are seen as credible sources of information and are hence more persuasive. /pp. 502–503

What are attributions, and what sorts of errors do we find when people make attributions?

Attributions are cognitions we use to explain the sources of the behaviors we see in our social worlds. *Internal attributions* identify the source of behavior as within the person and are also called dispositional attributions. *External attributions* find the source of behaviors to be outside the person and are also called situational attributions. The *fundamental attribution error* leads us to overuse internal, or personal, attributions when explaining behaviors. Those persons who hold to the *just world hypothesis* are likely to believe that good things happen to good people only and that bad things happen to bad people only, who in some way deserve their misfortune. The *self-serving bias* has us tend to attribute our successes to our own efforts and actions and our failures to other, external factors. The *actor-observer bias* is the tendency to use external attributions to explain our own (as actor) behaviors, and internal attributions to explain the behaviors of others (as observer). /pp. 503–506

Summarize four approaches that account for interpersonal attraction.

The *reinforcement model* claims that we are attracted to those persons we associate with rewards or reinforcers. The *social exchange model* adds cost to the equation, claiming that what matters in interpersonal relationships is the ratio of the benefits received to the costs invested in that relationship. The *equity model* suggests that both or all members of a relationship assess a benefit/cost ratio, and the best, most stable relationships are those in which the ratio is nearly the same (equitable) for both or all parties, no matter what the value of the benefits for any one member of the relationship. *Attachment theory* tells us that there are only a few relationship styles, and that each individual is consistent over his or her lifetime in the style used when relating to others. /pp. 506–508

What are four determinants of interpersonal attraction?

The principle of *reciprocity* states that we tend to like people who like us back. This is the most straightforward example of interpersonal attraction being based on a system of rewards. *Proximity* promotes attraction, in part, by means of the mere exposure effect: being near another person on a frequent basis gives us the opportunity to see what that other person has to offer. We also tend to be attracted to people we judge physically attractive. Finally, the principle of *similarity* suggests that we tend to be attracted to those we believe similar to ourselves. */pp. 508–510*

Topic 14B

Describe the methods and findings of Asch's conformity studies.

In Asch's studies, people made judgments about unambiguous perceptual stimuli: the length of lines. On some trials, confederates gave judgments that were clearly incorrect before the actual subject had a chance to respond. Although there were situations in which yielding to perceived group pressure could be lessened, many of Asch's subjects followed suit and conformed. */pp. 511–512*

Briefly describe Milgram's demonstrations of obedience.

Subjects in Milgram's experiments were led to believe they were administering more and more potent shocks to another person in a learning task. Whenever they hesitated to deliver shocks, an authority figure, the experimenter, prodded them to continue. All subjects obeyed to some degree, and nearly two-thirds delivered what they thought was the most intense shock, even over the protests of the learner. Those who obeyed in Milgram's experiments were neither cruel nor inhumane. Rather, the experimenter created a powerful social situation that made it difficult to refuse the authority figure's orders. */pp. 513–516*

What effect does the presence of others have on a person's willingness to help in an emergency?

The likelihood that someone will intervene on behalf of another in an emergency is lessened as a function of how many others (bystanders) are present at the time. Several factors have been proposed to account for this phenomenon. *Audience inhibition* is the term used to describe the hesitancy to intervene in front of others, perhaps for fear of embarrassing oneself. *Pluralistic ignorance* occurs when others lead one to think (by their inactivity) that nothing is wrong in an ambiguous emergency situation. *Diffusion of responsibility* causes a member of a group to feel less obligated to intervene (less responsible) than if he or she were alone. Each of these processes tends to discourage helping and is more likely to operate as the number of persons present increases. */pp. 516–520*

What may we conclude concerning the effects of social influence on the quality of an individual's performance?

The data suggest that as group size increases, *social loafing* increases. That is, one is less likely to invest full effort and energy in the task at hand as a member of a group than he or she would if working alone (at least in Western, individualist cultures). It is also the case that the quality of one's performance tends to suffer when one works in a group, a phenomenon called *social interference.* On the other hand, when tasks are simple or well rehearsed, performance may be enhanced, a process called *social facilitation. /pp. 520–522*

How does social influence affect decision making in groups?

There are some advantages to problem solving in a group setting. The combined efforts and expertise present in a group may provide better solutions and provide a better check on errors than we might find if individuals worked independently. On the other hand, *group polarization,* the tendency of group discussion to solidify and enhance preexisting attitudes, and *groupthink,* an excessive concern for reaching a consensus within the group, operate to detract from group decision making. */pp. 522–523*

Identify the Concept

Each of the following is intended to provide an example of one of the important concepts introduced in this chapter. See if you can identify (at least) one concept being exemplified. Each concept was printed in **boldface** type in the text. (Suggested answers can be found on p. 575.)

1. "I don't believe that any of us thought that it was a very good idea at first, but we were so anxious to come up with *something* that everybody could live with, we decided on this course of action."
2. "I didn't think I liked ice hockey. I've always thought that it was too rough and violent. But after seeing the game last Saturday, I think I may go again."
3. "I thought that there might have been a serious problem, but I wasn't sure, and I assumed that no one else was helping because they knew better."
4. "He picked up that wallet and returned it because he's an honest man."
5. "He picked up that wallet and returned it because he saw us watching him and he knew we'd report him to the police if he didn't."
6. "I subscribe to *The New Yorker* because I'm intellectually curious and read of all the fine articles, but he gets it because someone bought him a subscription as a gift."
7. "I've known this guy all my life, and I'd rather have him on my team, even if you do think that the other fellow is more talented."
8. "At first I thought the movie was pretty stupid, but everyone else seemed to like it so much I changed my mind."
9. "I thought that there might be a problem, but there were so many people around, I didn't want to say anything for fear of being embarrassed."
10. "I really like the Independent candidate running for mayor. I think that she has some good ideas, and I intend to vote for her this fall."
11. "Why should I break my back and do this work, if they will do it for me?"
12. "It's a shame to see that child being punished, but I'm sure he's only getting what he deserves."

OUTLINE

ack Farwell is plant manager for Acme Flange Fabrication, Inc., a manufacturing company in the Midwest that is experiencing several problems. Pressure from foreign imports and a reduced demand for the high-quality flanges that AFF makes have reduced profits severely.

Jack sees the need for increased productivity as an opportunity to introduce some changes at AFF. He wants to use some of the new technology that has revolutionized flange manufacturing. He also realizes that to return Acme Flange to its highly respected status in the industry, management will have to take a new look at techniques to motivate a group of talented but discouraged factory workers.

Installing new equipment and restructuring the organization means retraining at all levels of the company. In some cases, retraining will be directed at the acquisition of new skills; in others, it will mean fostering changes in attitudes and communication styles. To complicate matters, contract negotiations with the local union begin soon. Farwell wants to be sure the changes he is proposing can be implemented while enhancing job satisfaction among AFF employees. He

Industrial/Organizational, Environmental, and Sport Psychology

will have to address concerns about day care, flexible time schedules, and pregnancy leaves.

Two other realities are on the mind of the plant manager, including visits from two government agencies. Inspectors will be by soon to check the plant for safety violations. More troublesome is the visit from the Environmental Protection Agency. There has been concern about waste water from the plant polluting area streams and well water.

Although Jack Farwell is the plant manager of a manufacturing firm, many of the tasks he has before him are psychological in nature. Farwell's challenges have more to do with affect, behavior, and cognition than with steel and flanges. His challenges reflect many of the concerns of industrial-organizational psychology.

Topic 15A looks at industrial/organizational, or I/O, psychology. Psychologists in this field are concerned with applying psychological principles in order to improve the effectiveness and efficiency of business and industrial organizations.

The second Topic of this chapter focuses on two subfields of applied psychology. First, we'll sample some of the work of psychologists concerned about interactions between the physical environment and one's psychological state of well-being. Then we'll examine the notions of space and territory, using life in a big city as an example. Finally, we'll look at a few ways in which psychologists apply their knowledge to the world of sports and athletics.

TOPIC 15A Industrial/Organizational Psychology

industrial/organizational (I/O) psychologist *one who uses scientific methods to study the affects, cognitions, and behaviors of persons in work settings*

Industrial/organizational (I/O) psychologists specialize in the scientific study of affect, behavior, and cognition in work settings. Industrial/organizational psychology is one of the fastest growing areas of specialization in psychology (Zedeck, 1987). We will examine two major thrusts of I/O psychology. First, we'll discuss how best to fit the right person to a given job. This will entail a discussion of what is meant by "doing a good job," followed by a consideration of how we can select, train, and motivate someone to do that job well. Then, we'll examine how best to fit a job to the person, which will involve examining such matters as the quality of work life, job satisfaction, and worker safety. Each of these issues is meaningful to anyone who has ever entered the world of work.

Fitting the Person to the Job

It is to everyone's advantage to have the best available person assigned to do any job. Employers benefit from having workers who are well qualified and well motivated to do their work. Employees also benefit from being assigned tasks that they enjoy and that are within the scope of their talents and abilities. When I was a college student, a summer job required that I fill in for another employee and drive a large truck loaded with milk from a dairy in upstate New York to various locations in New York City. That I ever got that milk delivered had more to do with good luck and youthful enthusiasm than anything else. It took me twice as long as the regular driver to make the deliveries, and, to say the least, I did not enjoy spending a summer's day being lost in New York City with a truck filled with milk. I was clearly not the best worker for the task.

What is involved in getting the best person to do a job? The relevant issues from the perspective of the I/O psychologist are *personnel selection, training,* and *motivation.* One way to get a person to do good work is to select and hire a person who already has the ability and the motivation to do that work. On the other hand, we may choose to train people to do good work. We may also have to face the task of motivating people with ability to do good work. But before we can select, train, or motivate someone to do a job, we need to understand the nature of the job itself.

Defining "Good Work": The Job Analysis

Assume you are an industrial/organizational psychologist hired by a company to help select a manager for one of its retail stores in a local shopping center. You cannot begin to tell your employers what sort of person they were looking for until you had a complete description of the job this new manager was to do. You would have to know the duties and responsibilities of a store manager in this company. Then, you could translate that job description into measurable characteristics a successful store manager should have. That is, you would begin with a **job analysis**, "the systematic study of the tasks, duties, and responsibilities of a job and the knowledge, skills, and abilities needed to perform it" (Riggio, 1990, p. 59).

job analysis *a complete and specific description of a job, including the qualities and behaviors required to do it well*

A job analysis may be written by someone who is presently in the job in question, or a supervisor of that job position. What matters is that the person doing the job analysis have knowledge of the skills required (Fleishman & Mumford, 1991; Landy et al., 1994). Typically, writing a complete job analysis is a two-step process. The first step involves compiling a complete description of what a person in that job is expected to do. There are several sources of information one might use to generate such a description. Most companies have job descriptions for their employees, but these are usually stated in very general terms, such as "supervise workers in the store; maintain acceptable levels of sales; prepare payrolls; monitor

One of the most important roles of industrial/organizational psychologists is to help employers make the best possible personnel decisions. The first step in doing a job analysis is to get a complete description of the job.

inventory; schedule workloads," and the like. To be useful, a job analysis must be specific and describe the actual *behaviors* engaged in by someone in a given position. Does a store manager have to know how to operate the cash register and inventory control devices? Does the manager deal with the sales staff on a one-to-one basis or in groups? Are interactions with employees informal, or are there scheduled, formal meetings that need to be organized? This list of questions can be a long one. The underlying concern at this level of analysis is, "On a daily basis, just what does a store manager do?"

Once duties and responsibilities are specified, the second step requires that these be translated into terms of measurable personal characteristics. That is, one determines the **performance criteria** required to do a job well. What are the characteristics a person in this position needs in order to do that job as well as possible?

performance criteria *specific behaviors or characteristics a person should have in order to do a job as well as possible*

To be useful, a job description must include a complete, detailed description of the personal qualities and behaviors required to do that job well.

There are several areas that might be explored at this point. Smith (1976), for example, distinguishes between what she calls "hard" (or objective) criteria and "soft" (or subjective) criteria. The former come from available data—salary, number of units sold, number of days absent, and the like. Soft criteria require a degree of judgment—sense of humor, congeniality, creativity, and so on. Let's use an academic example. Suppose your psychology department wants to give an award to its "outstanding senior." Some of the criteria that determine which student has done a good job and is worthy of the award may be hard data—senior standing, a certain grade point average, and a minimum number of psychology classes. Other criteria may be subjective, or soft. The department may want to give this award to a student only if he or she is known to many members of the faculty, has impressive communication skills, or has been active in the Psychology Club. These criteria require the judgment of those who are making the award. Most job analyses involve considering both hard (objective) and soft (subjective) criteria.

Remember, the basic task is to find the best available person to do a job as well as possible. If we are not fully aware of the demands of a job and have not translated those demands into specific performance criteria, we will have difficulty determining if we have found the right person. In other words, we need to build in procedures early on by which our selection program can be evaluated (Dunnette & Borman, 1979). Once a job analysis has been completed—once we know what an applicant will be expected to do on the job and once we have translated those tasks into measurable criteria—we are ready to begin designing an assessment process.

Before You Go On

What is involved in doing a job analysis?

ⓔⓔⓔ **Thinking Critically** ⓔⓔⓔ

Consider your most recent job. Could you write a complete job analysis for it? What might the analysis include?

Selecting People Who Can Do Good Work

Personnel selection involves not only devising procedures to help one decide which of many applicants to hire, but also making decisions relating to retention, promotion, and termination (Guion & Gibson, 1988). If the job analysis has been done properly, the I/O psychologist has a full list of those duties and characteristics in which the employer is interested. The task now is to find the individual who has those characteristics.

Useful information can be gleaned from a well-constructed application form. A *job application form* can serve three useful functions. (1) It can be used as a rough screening device. Some applicants may be denied simply because they do not meet some basic requirement for the job, such as a minimal educational level or specified job experience. (2) It can supplement or provide cues for interviewing. Bits of data from application forms can be pursued later, during in-depth interviews. (3) It provides biographical data (called *biodata*), including educational and work history, that may be useful in making direct predictions about a candidate's potential. Some industrial/organizational psychologists list biographical information of the sort that can be uncovered on application forms as the best source of data for predicting success on the job (Baley, 1985; Drakeley et al., 1988; Muchinsky, 1987; Mumford et al., 1992; Rothstein et al., 1990). Although one cannot rule out the possibility of faking responses, people generally give honest answers when completing biodata forms (Shaffer et al., 1986).

An integral part of many personnel selection procedures is the *employment interview.* I have already commented (Topic 9B) on the dangers of relying too heavily on information gained through interviews. Unstructured interviews in particular are subject to error. Interviews, by their nature, involve the interaction of two people: the interviewer and the person being interviewed. Among other things, the biases of the interviewer, conscious or unconscious, may influence the results of an interview (Cash & Kilcullen, 1985). In addition, there are considerable individual

The interview remains an integral part of the employee selection process, although research has shown the unstructured interview to be of questionable value.

differences in interviewer skill. Some interviewers consistently obtain more useful (or valid) information than do others (Thayer, 1983; Zedeck et al., 1983). Training interviewers to be sensitive to biases can improve the validity of the technique.

Over the last few years, the outlook for the interview has become more positive and optimistic. In large measure, this is because of the increased use of the *structured interview* (Harris, 1989; Weisner & Cronshaw, 1988). As the name implies, structured interviews consist of a carefully prescribed series of questions asked of all applicants in the same order. Structured interviews take away some of the interviewer's latitude in exploring various issues, but they are much more valid than are unstructured interviews (Landy et al., 1994; Schmitt & Robertson, 1990; Weisner & Cronshaw, 1988).

In addition to the job application form and the interview, personnel selection often involves the administration and interpretation of psychological tests (Topic 7A). Many tests are designed to assess only one specific characteristic of the applicant (e.g., finger dexterity, which a job analysis may indicate to be relevant for an assembly line worker in an electronics plant). Others are more general, assessing a number of skills and abilities. Tests of intelligence or personality traits may be called for, particularly when evaluating candidates for managerial or supervisory positions. There are literally hundreds of published paper-and-pencil tests designed to measure a variety of characteristics, from typing skills, to mechanical aptitude, to leadership style, to motivation for sales work, to critical thinking skills. Some popular tests of general traits or abilities are being modified to focus more sharply on work-related applications (e.g., Gough, 1985).

In general, the most useful of all psychological tests are those that assess some sort of cognitive function, such as ability or achievement tests (Campbell et al., 1990; Guion & Gibson, 1988). One of the most controversial questions in all of psychology (not just I/O) is whether tests of general intelligence are better predictors of job performance than are tests of specific cognitive ability or aptitude (Ackerman, 1992; Ackerman & Kanfer, 1993; Hunt, 1995; Landy et al., 1994; McClelland, 1993; Ree & Earles, 1992, 1993; Schmidt & Hunter, 1993; Sternberg & Wagner, 1993). At this point, the best answer seems to be "it depends." It depends on which tests of which behaviors are used whether general measures are superior or equal to specific measures.

From time to time, it may be necessary to construct one's own test to assess some unique or special ability not measured by available instruments. A form of testing found in employment settings is called *situational testing,* in which applicants are given the opportunity to role-play the task they may be hired to do (Lin, Dobbins, & Farh, 1992; Weekley & Gier, 1987). If you were going to hire someone to work at the counter of your dry cleaning business, for instance, you might ask an applicant how he or she would respond to an irate customer whose suit was damaged in cleaning. Role-playing the part of an angry customer while the applicant plays the part of employee might provide very useful information.

An important issue when using psychological tests for personnel decisions is the demonstrated *validity* of such tests. What is particularly crucial in employee testing is that the employer be able to demonstrate that performance on a test is actually related to performance on the job (e.g., Landy et al., 1994; Schmidt et al., 1992).

Some corporations use what is called an *assessment center approach* to select management personnel (both for initial hiring and promotion decisions). This approach gives evaluators opportunities to observe applicants in various social situations and under stress. An assessment center involves an intensive period of evaluation, typically for three or four days. Several applicants (usually 6 to 12 at a time) are brought together with executives of the company and a team of psychologists. In addition to batteries of standard paper-and-pencil tests and interviews, the applicants are given situational tests in which their behaviors in situations similar to those they might encounter on the job can be observed. One method is called the *in-basket technique.* Applicants are given a variety of tasks, memos, and assignments of the sort they might encounter in a typical day at the office (as previously determined through a job analysis). They are then observed as they attempt to sort out and deal with the imaginary issues they find in their in-baskets.

Assessment centers are popular, and their usefulness is virtually taken for granted (Gaugler et al., 1987; Hinrichs, 1976; Saal & Knight, 1988; Schmidt et al., 1992; Schmitt, Schneider, & Cohen, 1990). Although the technique can be useful for predicting general outcomes, such as who is likely to get promoted or get larger salaries, it does not seem very useful in making specific predictions regarding specific behaviors (Hunter & Hunter, 1984; McEvoy & Beatty, 1989; Pynes & Bernardin, 1989). "The research question seems not to be whether to use assessment centers but how to understand what goes on in them, how to evaluate the results, and how to make them better" (Guion & Gibson, 1988).

It may not always be practical or possible to find people who have the abilities, characteristics, and motivation for doing the type of work we have in mind. It may be that the major personnel issues involve training and motivating existing workers to do good (or better) work. Let's first look at training.

Before You Go On

What are some of the sources of information that can be used in making personnel decisions?

Training People to Do Good Work

Training employees is one of the major concerns of business, industry, and government. The cost of such training runs into billions of dollars every year. Training or retraining present employees will become even more critical in the years ahead as the number of people entering the work force decreases (Offermann & Gowing, 1990; Tannenbaum & Yukl, 1992). Additional training needs stem from the move of many businesses to open operations overseas. Training concerning cultural issues in foreign countries is seen as essential for such businesses (e.g., Brislin, 1990,

1993; Erez & Early, 1993; Tung, 1988). For that matter, training aimed at increasing sensitivity and communication when dealing with employees from a variety of ethnic and cultural backgrounds is also becoming more common and more necessary (e.g. Dadler & Gustavson, 1992).

In industrial/organizational psychology, **training** means "a systematic intentional process of altering behavior of organizational members in a direction which contributes to organizational effectiveness" (Hinrichs, 1976). Training is a systematic intervention, as opposed to a hit-or-miss approach to instruction. Training programs have been found successful in many organizational settings, with various types of personnel, and as indicated by a number of productivity criteria, including quantity and quality of work, cost reduction, turnover, accident reduction, and absenteeism (Katzell & Guzzo, 1983). In the spring of 1995, the American Association of Retired Persons (AARP) released results of a survey of 400 human resources executives that showed that older workers may be an exception. Only 24 percent of the firms surveyed were offering skill training to their older employees, down from 30 percent in 1989 (AARP, 1995).

Developing a successful training program is a complex, multifaceted enterprise. Let's review the steps involved in designing and implementing a training program. Our discussion is based on a system proposed by Goldstein (1986, 1989) and is summarized in Figure 15.1. Assume for the moment you are an I/O psychologist in charge of training and development for Acme Flange.

Assessing Training Needs. Training programs are designed to address a need within the organization. So one of the first things you have to do is an assessment of instructional needs. A complete needs assessment in this context is very much like a job analysis in personnel selection. There are several questions to be answered at this critical stage. What is the problem training is supposed to solve? Is production falling? Is there a new product that salespeople need to know about? Is the accident rate getting too high? Is the company reducing the number of employees? At this point, a difficult question to face is whether a training program is the best solution for a given problem. In fact, the most crucial decision to be made about training is if it is really needed (Latham, 1988; Saari et al., 1988).

training *a systematic and intentional process of altering the behaviors of employees to increase organizational effectiveness*

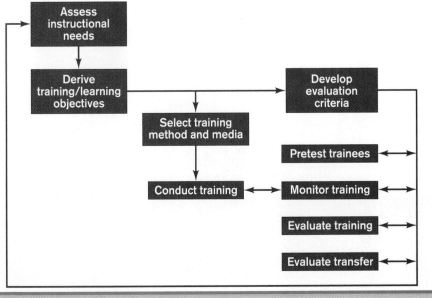

Figure 15.1

The steps involved in planning, conducting, and evaluating a training program. (From Goldstein, 1986.)

A second step requires translating general goals into actual training objectives. At this stage, general statements of outcomes will no longer suffice. Now you need *specific* statements of what you expect the training program to accomplish. Just precisely what do you want trainees to know (or be able to do) at the end of the training session that they do not know (or do not do) now? Your training program will usually be evaluated in terms of these specific learning or behavioral objectives. Indeed, even before you begin actual training, you will want to specify criteria by which your training can be evaluated when it is over. You might want to design a pretest procedure to assess your trainees in terms of their present skill or information levels.

Training Techniques. After you have determined the criteria for assessing outcomes, you have to decide how you will go about the actual training. Given what you know about your needs, objectives, and employees, what will be the most efficient type of training mechanism you can use to reach your specified goals?

There are many methods that might be used in a training program. In some cases, bringing workers together for classroom instruction works well. On the other hand, there are situations in which assembling large numbers of workers would be unrealistic. For example, automobile manufacturers can hardly be expected to have all car salespeople report to the home office for instruction on improvements in the new models of cars they will be selling. Occasionally, training has to go to the worker—in the form of printed material, audiocassettes, videotaped programs, or live presentations by a trainer—rather than having the worker go to the training.

As a designer of a training program, you will have many decisions to make about the methods you will use. Should you use "live" instructors, or should information be presented in the form of some media: print, audiotapes, videotapes, videodisks, and the like? Should training be formalized and time-limited, or can trainees be allowed to work individually, at their own pace? Will there need to be hands-on experience? Will training be held in groups, or be individually oriented? Will on-the-job training be efficient or disruptive? Can the job be simulated for the purposes of training?

Your options are many, and all should be considered, because some are clearly more effective than others for certain types of training. Many trainers fall into the habit of using only one or two techniques for a range of needs and objectives. For

Training—and retraining—employees to learn new skills and procedures helps keep worker motivation high and helps companies stay abreast of new technologies.

example, televised instruction may be useful to point out a few new features of an automobile to a salesperson, but ineffective for describing the details of a new health insurance program. By and large, presenting information is less effective than demonstrating it, and involving one's audience as participants (a hands-on, or simulation, approach) is most effective. In general terms, there is no research that tells us that any particular training technique is superior to others in all circumstances. What is needed is a "fit" between present training needs and available training techniques (Campbell, 1988; Tannenbaum & Yukl, 1992; Thornton & Cleveland, 1990).

Having decided on a training technique, you are ready to begin. You will have to monitor the effectiveness of the training program as it runs its course (review Figure 15.1). Even the best of plans sometimes need to be adjusted during actual training.

Measuring Training Effectiveness. When you have finished your training program, you are ready to reconsider what may be the most difficult aspect of training and development. You must evaluate the success of your training. Now you need some measure of the extent to which your training transfers to the actual job in the workplace, thus meeting the needs that prompted the training in the first place. There are several difficulties involved in doing quality evaluations of training programs, and we need not review them all here. I will make only three observations:

1. Training programs can be evaluated at various levels. You may ask participants to rate how they feel about or evaluate the program. You may assess the extent to which the training has produced behavioral changes. You may measure how much has been learned, perhaps with a formal testing before and after training. (Do you recognize our *ABC* here?) Or you may go right to the bottom line and ask about increases in productivity or profit (Kirkpatrick, 1976).

2. Training programs that do not include ways of evaluating both short-term and long-term effectiveness will generally be of little value. Sadly enough, very few training programs are well evaluated. Many seem to be taken simply on faith or face value because of their logical appeal (Brinkerhoff, 1989; Saari et al., 1988; Schultz & Schultz, 1990).

3. The greater the effort put into the assessment of organizational needs, job analysis, performance criteria, and the establishment of training objectives at the beginning of a training project, the easier it will be to evaluate the program when it is over.

Before You Go On

List some of the factors that need to be considered in the design, implementation, and evaluation of a training program.

Motivating People to Do Good Work

Let's review for a moment. Our major concern in this section is fitting the person to the job—finding someone to do good work. The first step in this process involves carefully delineating just what is meant by a good job. To this end, one does a job analysis and lists specific performance criteria for the job. An employer can go through the process of selection, trying to find the best person for the job—someone who already has all of the skills to do the job well. Another possibility is to train a present employee to do good (or better) work. There remains an important consideration. There may still be something missing: the motivation to do good work. Being able to do a job well and wanting to do a job well are different matters. Notice, too, that issues of training and motivation are both ongoing concerns. People change and jobs change. Seldom will one training program or one attempt to motivate employees be sufficient over the long term.

As you can imagine, I/O psychologists have been interested in how to motivate employees to do their best work. When we talk about work motivation, we are referring to three interrelated processes: *arousing* (getting the worker to do a task), *directing* (getting the worker to do the task we want done), and *sustaining* (keeping the worker at the task). As you can also imagine, there is no one answer to questions of how to motivate workers to do a job and stick with it. We'll briefly review a few of the more popular approaches.

Values and Expectations. The expectancy theory of work motivation has been around for years and has been modified by many theorists, but it is best associated with Victor Vroom (1964). It is highly cognitive in its orientation. **Expectancy theory** says that workers behave rationally and logically, making work-related decisions based on their beliefs, judgments, and expectations.

Vroom's expression of his theory is quite complex, but what it amounts to is that we are motivated to do good work if (1) we expect rewards to be contingent on levels of performance, and (2) we value the rewards that are being offered. We must also believe that rewards are attainable, that we can actually do the work to a level of performance that will earn those valued rewards.

There are several implications here for employers concerned about motivating employees. For one thing, employers should see if the outcomes that follow good

expectancy theory *the view that workers make logical choices to do what they believe will result in their attaining outcomes of highest value*

For rewards to be valuable in motivating, employees must see the rewards they are being given as worth their efforts.

work are truly valued by the workers. For example, in one company, good work is rewarded by recognition with a plaque and a free trip awarded at the annual company dinner. (The dinner is viewed by management as a reward for a profitable year.) What if most of the work force found company dinners a huge bore, plaques an embarrassment, and trips a nuisance (arranging for transportation, baby-sitters, and so on)? What if the employees would rather have a cash bonus or longer coffee breaks? That is, what if the employees actually believed there was little value in what the company thought were rewards?

Another implication of expectancy theory is that workers must understand the relationship between their behaviors and outcomes (e.g., Ilgen & Klein, 1989). Simply, workers need to know what to expect if they behave in a certain way. Which behaviors lead to positive outcomes, and which lead to negative outcomes? Why should any employee work very hard, put in overtime, and take work home on the weekend if he or she has little or no reason to believe that such behaviors will lead to valued rewards? In fact, fewer than one-third of workers believe their compensation is based on their work performance (Plawin & Suied, 1988).

Fair Rewards. Another approach to work motivation, called **equity theory**, is associated with J. Stacy Adams (1965). Equity theory is also cognitive, claiming that what matters most to workers is their perception of the extent to which they are being treated fairly compared to fellow workers in similar work situations.

> **equity theory** *the view that workers are motivated to match their inputs and outcomes with those of fellow workers in similar positions*

In Adams's view, workers make a number of social comparisons (or cognitive judgments). They judge how much they are getting from the organization compared to what they are putting into it. That is, the worker judges the extent to which effort, skill, education, experience, and so on (inputs) are being rewarded by salary, praise, fringe benefits, awards, and the like (outcomes). Then this ratio of inputs and outcomes is compared with a ratio from some other, similarly placed employee. If the relationship is perceived as being about the same—or equitable—the worker will not be motivated to change. If, however, there is a perceived inequity when compared to the inputs and outcomes of a fellow worker, changes can be predicted. The worker may increase or decrease inputs (work longer or shorter hours; take fewer or more breaks) or try to effect a change in outcomes. What matters most here is not the actual value of what a worker gains for his or her efforts. What matters is the *perception* of equity. A worker will be more willing to maintain effort (input) and take a cut in pay (outcome) if he or she believes that everyone else in the company is taking a similar cut in pay (Locke, 1976; Middlemist & Peterson, 1976; Mowday, 1983).

Goal Setting. How work-related goals are set has been the centerpiece of a number of approaches to worker motivation, particularly that of Edwin Locke (1968; Locke & Latham, 1984). This approach has a cognitive basis, assuming that workers are motivated to perform a task for which goals are clearly and specifically detailed. In order for goal setting to have a positive influence on a worker's behavior on a task, two things are necessary. First, the goal must be clear. The employee must be perfectly aware of just what he or she is working for. Second, the employee must accept the goal as worth the effort.

Goal setting is the approach to motivating workers that is presently receiving the most research interest (Smithers, 1994). Here are some general conclusions.

1. Difficult but achievable goals tend to increase productivity more than easy goals. The issue here seems to hinge on the acceptance of goals as being worthwhile. Goals that are too easy may simply fail to require any change in performance. On the other hand, goals that are perceived as being too difficult and beyond the abilities of workers are not likely to be very useful (Erez & Zidon, 1984).

2. Specific, focused, goals are better than general ones. Simply telling workers to "do better" or "do your best" provides little information about what behaviors are expected.

3. Feedback informing workers of their progress toward established goals is important in maintaining motivated behaviors. Feedback delivered soon after an appropriate response is made is more effective than delayed feedback (e.g., Geller et al., 1985; Geller et al., 1987).

4. Although it may seem reasonable to predict that goals set by employers and employees working together are more effective than goals established by employers alone, the evidence suggests that this is not necessarily the case. What matters most is that the employee be aware of specific goals and accept those goals as reasonable (Locke et al., 1981).

5. Cultural concerns are also relevant here. The more one is used to working together (as in collectivist cultures), the more important it is to be involved in goal setting. In most Western (individualistic) cultures, involvement in goal setting is less critical (e.g., Early, 1986; Erez & Early, 1987).

There are other useful approaches to work motivation. Some refer to motivational concepts we introduced in Topic 10A, where we discussed motivation in general. That is, some approaches stress the importance of workers' needs (as in Maslow's theory about a hierarchy from basic physiological needs to needs to self-actualize). Some stress the importance of operant conditioning procedures and attending to the consequences of behavior (an aproach called organizational behavior management when applied in work environments).

Here's a brief summary of our discussion. Workers will tend to be motivated to do a good job if:

1. Clear and specific goals are established and accepted.

2. The goals employers set match workers' expectations and needs.

3. Workers see clearly the relationship between their work performance and accepted outcomes.

4. Workers judge the outcomes that follow from their efforts as being in line with those earned by fellow workers making similar efforts.

5. Workers are given feedback about the nature of their work (Katzell & Thompson, 1990).

Now let's shift our emphasis slightly from a concern about finding and fitting the person to the job to the issue of fitting the job to the person. In large measure, our interest is in what we call job satisfaction. What can be done to make jobs more satisfying? What are the consequences of doing so?

Before You Go On

Briefly summarize some of the factors that affect the motivation of workers to do a good job.

Fitting the Job to the Person

We have considered what employers can do to find the best person for a given task. For the remainder of this Topic, we'll change our perspective just a bit and focus on some of the issues relevant to the person on the job in the workplace. There are two issues here. The first has to do with job satisfaction. We'll define the concept, and see if it is correlated with job performance. The second issue has to do with safety in the workplace. How can jobs be designed to maximize employee safety and health?

Job Satisfaction

Job satisfaction refers to the attitude one holds toward one's work: "a pleasurable or positive emotional state resulting from the appraisal of one's job or job experiences" (Locke, 1976). It amounts to an employee's emotional responses toward his or her job (Hui, 1990). We may refer to job satisfaction in general terms (a "global" approach), but an employee's degree of satisfaction can vary considerably for various aspects of the job itself (a "facet" approach) (Riggio, 1990). As you know from your own work experience, you might be reasonably happy with your physical working conditions, unhappy with the base salary, pleased with your fringe benefits, satisfied with the challenge provided by the job, very dissatisfied with relationships with coworkers, and so on. In fact, there may be as many facets of job satisfaction or dissatisfaction as there are aspects to the job.

A great deal of research has looked for relationships between job satisfaction and characteristics of workers. Let's summarize some of that research very briefly.

1. There is a positive correlation between global job satisfaction and age. Younger workers tend to be most dissatisfied with their jobs (Rhodes, 1983), but there also is evidence that older employees develop dissatisfaction with their jobs toward the end of their careers (Kacmar & Ferris, 1989).

2. Data on gender differences in job satisfaction tend to be inconsistent. Gender differences are small (Sauser & York, 1978) and virtually nonexistent when pay, tenure, and education are controlled (Hulin & Smith, 1964).

3. Racial differences in job satisfaction have consistently been shown to be small—in the United States—with white people having more positive attitudes about their jobs than black people (Weaver, 1980), and Mexican Americans showing more satisfaction than whites.

job satisfaction *an attitude toward, or a collection of positive feelings about, one's job or job experiences*

Although it seems logical that job satisfaction be a useful predictor of job performance, the relationship between satisfaction and productivity is tenuous at best.

4. Satisfaction is positively related to the perceived level or status of one's job or occupation, wherein jobs of lowest rank tend to be filled by the least satisfied workers (King et al., 1982).

5. The data are few, but there appear to be some cultural differences in job satisfaction. In one survey of ten countries, Sweden had the largest proportion of satisfied workers (63 percent), whereas Japan had the fewest (20 percent) (de Boer, 1978). The low level of job satisfaction in Japan has been reported by others (Azumi & McMillan, 1976; Lincoln & Kalleberg, 1985). Accounting for the low job satisfaction ratings in Japan, researchers cite strong commitment and motivation for success, and unrealistically high expectations (Cole, 1979).

Of course, the real challenge for I/O psychologists is to determine *why* any of these differences in job satisfaction do or do not occur.

Before You Go On

What is meant by job satisfaction?

Job Satisfaction and Work Behaviors

It may seem reasonable to assert that "a happy worker is a productive worker"—that an increase in job satisfaction will be reflected in increased worker productivity. For the last 50 years, many managers and executives have assumed, pretty much without question, a causal relationship between satisfaction and productivity. In many ways, satisfaction and productivity *are* related, but the relationship is not a simple one and is at best a weak one (Iaffaldano & Muchinsky, 1985). Research often refutes the contention that increased performance necessarily results from increased satisfaction (Howell & Dipboye, 1982; Staw, 1984). Over and over, we find contradictory evidence. The only conclusion we can draw about these two variables is that in some instances they may be correlated. Cause-and-effect statements are out of the question.

The lack of a consistent relationship between satisfaction and productivity may not be that difficult to explain. Some workers may hate their present jobs but work hard at them nonetheless so they can be promoted to another position they believe they will prefer. Some workers may be very satisfied with their present positions simply because expectations for productivity are low; if demands for productivity increase, satisfaction may decrease. *Increasing productivity may increase satisfaction,* rather than vice versa. Well-motivated employees, who want to do their best, will be pleased to enter a training program to improve on-the-job efficiency. Doing the job better leads to pride and an overall increase in satisfaction for this worker; for another, the same training program may be viewed as a ploy on the part of management to make his or her life miserable.

I should not give the impression that job satisfaction is totally unrelated to work behaviors. Job satisfaction measures can be used to aid the prediction of which workers are likely to be absent from work and which are likely to quit. Job satisfaction is not the best predictor of absenteeism, however (marital status, age, and size of one's work group are better [Watson, 1981]), but the positive correlations are at least consistent (Porter & Steers, 1973). The relationship between dissatisfaction with one's job and turnover is even stronger, although this relationship may not be direct. That is, dissatisfaction may be an important contributing factor, but it is only one of several variables that can be used to explain why one leaves a job. (Many times people are forced to quit their jobs for reasons that have nothing to do with the job or the employer; illness and family concerns, for example.) Still, the logic that persons who are most unhappy with their work are the ones most likely to leave it does have research support (Mobley, 1977; Muchinsky & Tuttle, 1979).

Before You Go On

Summarize the relationship between job satisfaction and job productivity.

Worker Safety

In this final section, we review one of the oldest concerns of I/O psychologists: safety in the workplace. The statistics are impressive. In 1994, Labor Secretary Robert B. Reich observed that "the workplace is still a dangerous environment." The Labor Department reported 6,271 job-related deaths in 1993, up from 6,217 the previous year. During the peak years of the Vietnam War (1966–1970), more Americans were killed in industrial accidents than in combat (Schultz & Schultz, 1990, p. 445). From a different perspective: accidents in the workplace cost the United States over $100 billion a year in lost wages, insurance and medical expenses, and property loss (Riggio, 1990). The Occupational Safety and Health Administration (OSHA) is the federal government's job-safety agency. Unfortunately, they often do not get to inspect and intervene in potentially dangerous situations. For example, in 1994 and the first four months of 1995, there were 1,835 job-related deaths at U. S. work sites that had never been inspected. The challenge is clear: increase the safety of the workplace. But how?

One of the oldest approaches to worker safety is based on the popular notion that some people are simply more "accident prone" than others, or that at least there are a few personality traits consistently related to high incidences of accidents. If this were true, safety could be improved by not hiring those applicants who are prone to accidents. The problem is that there just don't seem to be people who are, in general, more accident prone than anyone else. (Which may reflect our inability to adequately assess such a trait.) Still, there is some obvious sense to this approach. The less well qualified a person is for a job, the less well trained, or the less well motivated, the more likely that person will have an accident—particularly if the job is a dangerous one. Workers younger than 25 or older than 55 do have more accidents than do other workers (Smither, 1994).

For employees to work safely, two things are required. For one, the employee must understand that safe work habits are expected and will be reinforced, and for another, the employee may need to be trained in safe working procedures.

A position consistent with our discussion of worker motivation is that workers often need to be motivated to work safely. At first you might think that anyone in his or her right mind would want to work safely and avoid being in an accident. You might be right. But does the worker *know specifically* what constitutes safe behavior? Does the worker know that the employer *values* safe work and that safe work will be rewarded? If such is not the case, workers may cut corners, working too quickly—and too dangerously—if they think that rewards are only for amount of work and output. A long, detailed warning label, for instance, may be so long and so detailed that the worker for whom it was intended won't even bother reading it. In short, employers must see to it that workers are trained in safe ways to do their job (Levine, 1983) and realize that safe behaviors are valued (Zohar, 1980). What matters most, as we have seen before, is clearly establishing safety goals, providing feedback to workers, and reinforcing those behaviors that lead to attaining stated goals.

What Landy (1989) calls the "engineering approach" to worker safety attempts to reduce accidents by designing safer equipment and implementing safer procedures. Over the years, this approach has been the most successful in a range of applications. Examples abound. All automobiles now sold in this country are required to have a (third) stop light positioned at eye level. This requirement evolved from a safety study done with taxicabs in San Francisco in an attempt to reduce rear-end collisions (Voevodsky, 1974). Complex control panels are engineered with safety in mind so that the most important dials, meters, buttons, and switches are in clear view and easy to read and interpret (e.g., Wickens, 1992). Work areas are designed so that there is adequate illumination and sufficient space, and so that scrap materials and trash can be easily removed. Heavy equipment is designed so that it can be operated in a reasonably safe way. Computer screens have shields to protect against glare and radiation, and keyboards are now engineered to reduce physical damage to the wrist that may result from spending hours at the keyboard.

Engineering approaches to accident prevention may involve matters such as the scheduling of work time. There is ample evidence of a positive relationship between fatigue and accidents. Scheduling work time (by reducing overtime work, for example) to minimize fatigue seems to improve safety (Dunham, 1979).

Before You Go On

What steps can be taken to improve worker safety?

TOPIC 15A SUMMARY

In this Topic, we have only scratched the surface of what industrial/organizational psychologists do in their attempt to apply principles of psychology to the world of work. We've focused on two interrelated issues. First, we considered how employers can best fit a person to a given job. This process involves several subprocesses, such as doing a job analysis, specifying performance criteria by which personnel can be evaluated for a given job, and using devices such as application forms, interviews, and psychological tests, to select the best person for a job. We saw that even with a qualified workforce, it will be necessary from time to time to consider programs for training or motivating that workforce to do the best possible job.

Then we turned our attention to the worker in an organization, looking at job satisfaction and how it is related to productivity. We found that although enhancing workers' satisfaction with their jobs may be a noble goal, there is little evidence that improved job satisfaction will lead to increased productivity. We reviewed some of the approaches that I/O psychologists have taken to improve the safety of the workplace.

In Topic 15B, we look at two more areas of applied psychology: environmental psychology and sport psychology.

TOPIC 15B Environmental and Sport Psychology

One of the major goals of psychology is to apply what we have learned about our subject matter in the real world. Generally, we first think of applying psychology in the context of diagnosis and therapy for the psychological disorders. We often think about applying principles of learning and memory to improve education. In Topic 15A, we saw how our understanding of affect, behavior, and cognition can be applied in the workplace. In this Topic, we'll briefly examine two more areas in which psychological principles are being applied.

Psychology and the Environment

Environmental psychology is the study of how the general environment (as opposed to specific stimuli) affects the behavior and mental processes of those living in it, and how people, in turn, affect their environments. It is an interdisciplinary endeavor in which environmental psychologists work with urban planners, economists, sociologists, clinical psychologists, architects, interior decorators, landscape architects, builders, and others.

environmental psychology *the field of applied psychology that studies how the general environment affects the behavior and mental processes of individuals and how individuals affect their environments*

The range of specific interest areas within environmental psychology is large. Some psychologists are interested in such factors as how color and lighting might affect workers' productivity, students' learning, or nursing home patients' mental and physical health. Some are concerned with behavioral and psychological reactions to the poisons, or toxins, that are present in our environments. Some are interested in the design and construction of physical space that maximizes the functions for which that space is constructed. Some seek efficient means of changing behaviors in order to influence the natural environment in positive ways, through antilittering campaigns, for example. Others focus on crowding, territoriality, and adjustment to the demands of city living. Of course, many of these issues are interrelated.

Environmental psychologists recognize that what may influence behavior most is one's *perception* of the physical environment. A room with ten persons in it can appear to be terribly small and crowded if it is perceived as an office. The same space can seem large and uncrowded if it is perceived as a waiting area. In fact, two rooms of the same area, one square and the other rectangular, are often perceived differently; the square room will appear smaller than the rectangular room (Sadalla & Oxley, 1984). Let's begin our discussion of environmental psychology by considering some of the issues involved in the perception of space and distance.

Space and Territory

Imagine you are seated in the library, studying at a large table. There is no one else at the table. Then another student enters the room and sits right next to you. Although there are seven other chairs, she chooses to sit in the one just to your left. Or imagine that you are in the process of buying a car. While you are examining a new car, a salesperson approaches, stands right in front of you (not more than 8 inches away), and begins to tell you about the features of the car you are looking at. Or imagine that in your psychology class you always sit in the same seat. The semester is about over, and you have gotten to know some of the people who habitually sit near you. The next time you go to class, you find there is someone else

EXPERIENCING PSYCHOLOGY

Too Close for Comfort

We usually take our personal space for granted. We seldom think about the limits to our own personal space unless it is invaded, entered into without invitation. When our personal space *is* invaded, we often feel uncomfortable, a bit defensive, or even aggressive. Because reactions to the invasion of personal space are usually negative—and occasionally even openly hostile—**extreme care** (and good judgment) need to be exercised if you try this project.

The basic goal of this activity is simple: to note the reactions of individuals when you intentionally invade their personal space. Encroaching on another's personal space amounts to moving very close to someone (generally within arm's length) without explicit permission to do so.

There are many independent variables that you can manipulate here. For example, you might look for differences in reaction as a function of (a) the sex of your subject, (b) the age of your subject, (c) whether your subject was sitting or standing, (d) the specific environmental locale of your encounter, (e) whether your subject was alone or with others, and so on.

What will be your dependent variable(s)? As is usually the case in a study of this sort, there are many possibilities. What did the other person do when you entered his or her personal space? It would be wise to have a checklist of possible reactions made up ahead of time so that you can simply note reactions with a check mark. Such a checklist might include such items as: "Moved Away" (allow a space to indicate how far), "Looked Down," "Looked Away," "Looked Me in the Eye," "Said . . . (leaving space to record any verbal response)." As you go along, you may want to extend your checklist. Of course, you can ask your subject how he or she felt about your "invasion."

Whether or not you engage your subject in conversation about his or her reaction to your behaviors, it would be well to at least explain yourself, and what you were doing, and why, before you leave (i.e., debrief your subject).

---

in "your seat." Or imagine you are a homeowner who has spent years getting your backyard to look just the way you want it to. Then neighborhood children discover that going through your rose garden makes a great shortcut for them on their way to school.

In each of these scenarios, and in hundreds of others, you will probably feel a sense of discomfort. Your personal space, or territory, has been invaded without your invitation. The study of the effects of invading personal space and territory has been an active research area for environmental psychologists.

personal space *the mobile "bubble" of space around you reserved for intimate relationships and into which others may enter only by invitation*

Personal space is mobile. It goes with you where you go. It is an imaginary "bubble" of space that surrounds you and into which others may enter comfortably by invitation only. The extent of your personal space depends on the situation, as well as on other factors, including your age (Aiello & Aiello, 1974), gender (Evans & Howard, 1973), cultural background (Pandey, 1990), and who the "intruder" happens to be. You will be more likely to allow an invasion of your personal space by someone you know well, by someone about your age, or by an attractive member of the opposite sex (Hayduk, 1983). Personal space also seems to be a bit smaller for females than for males (Heshka & Nelson, 1972). The anthropologist Edward Hall (1966) claimed that personal space is also determined in part by one's culture. Westerners, for example, are said to require more personal space than people of Arab, Japanese, or Latin cultures (Sommer, 1969). These stereotypes may be overgeneralized. Evidence of cultural differences in personal space is not compelling; too many other situational factors are more powerful (Hayduk, 1983).

Hall (1966) also claimed that personal space can be subdivided into four different distances, each relevant for different types of social interaction, and relevant for Western cultures.

1. *Intimate distance* is defined as being between actual contact and about 18 inches. This space tends to be reserved for very special, intimate communica-

Intimate distance is reserved for interactions with good friends, as illustrated in the picture above (top left). Personal distance is reserved for day-to-day interactions with acquaintances (top right). Social distance is appropriate for persons we do not know well (middle). Public distance minimizes personal contact, although communication is still possible (bottom).

tions: displays of affection by lovers, offerings of comfort, and the like. This space is usually reserved only for people you know well and care about, and you will feel uncomfortable if someone else is in it.

2. *Personal distance,* according to Hall, is reserved for day-to-day interactions with acquaintances and friends. It extends from about 18 inches to approximately 4 feet, or just beyond arm's length. This space can be seen clearly in social gatherings, in which clusters of persons gather around to share in conversation. Actual physical contact in this sort of situation is unusual and unwelcomed. We typically keep our bubble of personal space adjusted to this size.

3. Hall refers to the distance of 4 to 12 feet as *social distance.* This distance is used for social interactions with persons we do not know well. It commonly includes some sort of physical barrier, such as a desk or table, between us and others around us. Within this space, communication can continue, but there is an implied message of lack of intimacy. This is the distance used for conducting routine business or for formal meetings.

4. Finally, there is *public distance,* in which personal contact is minimized, though communication remains possible. This distance is defined as being between 12 and 25 feet. Formal lectures in large classrooms, performances from a stage, and after-dinner talks presented from behind the head table are examples. Because of the distances involved, communication in these settings tends to flow in only one direction.

We will feel pressured or uncomfortable whenever these distances are violated. When that perfect stranger sits next to you in the library, she is violating your personal space. The salesperson with his or her nose almost touching yours is violating your intimate space. When a lecturer leaves the podium and begins to wander through the audience, we feel strange because our defined public space is being invaded.

territoriality *the setting off and marking of a piece of territory (a location) as one's own*

Territoriality is also related to the use of space. It involves the setting off and marking of a piece of a geographical location as one's own. It is the tendency to want to declare that "this space is mine; it's my turf and someone else can enter here only at my request or with my permission."

Territoriality was first studied extensively in nonhumans (e.g., Lorenz, 1969). Many species of animals establish, mark, and defend geographical areas that they use for finding and hunting food, for mating or for rearing their young. These territories are often defended vigorously—with ritualistic posturing and threats of aggression, but seldom with actual combat (Leger, 1992).

People, too, establish territories as their own, not to be entered without invitation. Altman (1975) noted that like personal space, territories vary in their value. Some are *primary territories,* defined by us as ours and no one else's. "This is my room, and you'd better stay out of it." We often invest heavily in our primary territories. We decorate our homes, yards, dormitory rooms, or apartments to mark our space. Primary territories are well marked, claimed for the long term, and staunchly defended. By controlling primary territory, we maintain a sense of privacy and a sense of identity.

Altman suggests that we are sensitive to two other types of territory: secondary and public. *Secondary territories* are more flexible and less well defined. They are areas set aside for social gatherings, not so much for personal privacy. Members of the faculty may stake out a room in a college building as a faculty lounge and may be unnerved to discover students using it, even if they are using it to study. Secondary territories are not "owned" by those who use them and tend not to be used for expressing personal identity. There may be a sign on the door that says Faculty Lounge, but the area can be used for other functions, and occasional intrusions by nonfaculty may be tolerated.

One's "territory" can take on different dimensions. We have primary territories (above right) that we think of as ours alone. We also have secondary territories (above left) that we see as primarily ours, and may mark as ours, but that are used by others. And we have a certain claim on some public territories (bottom) that we occupy only for a short time and then relinquish to others.

Public territories are those we occupy for only a short time. They are not ours in any literal sense, and we will not feel much distress if these territories are violated. While waiting for a plane, you sit in a seat in the airport terminal and place your luggage at your feet. You get up for a minute to buy a newspaper, and when you return, you discover that someone has claimed your seat. In such a situation, you may be momentarily annoyed, but you will have less difficulty in finding another seat than in starting a major battle.

Personal space and territories we claim as our own serve many functions. They provide a sense of structure and continuity in what otherwise may seem to be a complex and ever-changing environment. They help us claim a sense of identity. They help us set ourselves apart from others. They regulate and reinforce needs for privacy. Although expressed differently from culture to culture, these needs appear to be universal (Lonner, 1980). When space and territory are violated, we can predict negative outcomes: anxiety, distress, and sometimes even aggressive attempts of reclamation.

Before You Go On

Define the concepts of personal space and territoriality.

@@@@ **Thinking Critically** @@@@

List examples of occasions when your personal space or territory has been invaded. How did you feel about such invasions?

Life in the City: An Example

In the fall of 1994, the World Bank held a meeting of about 900 urban leaders from around the world. Some of the statistics from that session underscore the importance of understanding the dynamics of people living in small areas of space. The world's biggest cities are growing at a rate of 1 million people *a week* (combined), and will be home to more than half the world's population soon after the turn of the twenty-first century. By the year 2000, there will be 391 cities with more than 1 million residents, and 26 will be "mega-cities," home to over 10 million each. Concern about city living, overcrowding, and the consequences of urbanization has been a part of environmental psychology for over 30 years. Curiously, it was a series of experiments involving rats that sparked that initial concern.

In 1962, John B. Calhoun published the results of his studies of the overcrowding of rats. The data were impressive and intriguing. Calhoun raised colonies of rats in a number of environments. In some, population density was allowed, even encouraged, to increase to the point that overcrowding began to affect the behavior of the rats in the colony. Male rats became aggressive. Newborn rats were often cannibalized or ignored and left to die. Females became unreceptive to sexual advances from male rats, and if mating did occur, litter size decreased, apparently in response

Living in the big city may have its drawbacks and hazards, but it also provides unique opportunities. A perceived degree of control over one's life situation (i.e., "I can move if I wanted to") is a good predictor of satisfaction with city life.

to the pressures of colony overpopulation. It did not take long for some psychologists to look for parallels between Calhoun's rat studies and life in modern cities.

Early investigations found correlations between population density and negative behavioral consequences, such as mental illness, crime, stress, and delinquency (Altman, 1975; Freedman, 1975; Schmitt, 1966). As psychologists looked more closely at the lives of people in urban environments, however, it became clear that the translation of the data from Calhoun's rats to residents of our metropolitan centers was not all that straightforward.

The first thing we need to do is distinguish between two easily confused terms (Stokols, 1972). The first is **population density**, which refers to the number of persons (or animals) per unit of area. Density is an objective, descriptive measure. **Crowding**, on the other hand, is a psychological concept. It is a *subjective feeling* of discomfort or distress produced by a perceived lack of space. Crowding may be independent of how many persons are involved. You might feel very crowded and uncomfortable if you have to sit in the back seat of a small car with two other people, and not at all crowded when you get to the stadium and are jammed together with 60,000 others to watch a football game (Freedman, 1975).

Crowding is a negative condition that tends to produce negative consequences. It is not correct, however, to conclude that living in a densely populated city necessarily produces negative consequences. Potential stressors such as noise, pollution, and the threat of crime that we commonly associate with city life may be more than offset by better medical care, better sanitation, and systems for handling emergencies of all types (Creekmore, 1985). One's perception of control also matters (Rodin, 1976). Ruback and Pandey (1988) looked at the role of perceived control for married couples in the United States and in India, and they found striking similarities. In both cultures, low levels of perceived control were associated with high levels of mental distress and physical symptoms. Among other things, people who believe they can leave the city whenever they so choose will have more positive attitudes about living in that city than will people who feel "trapped" there.

There is evidence to support the claim that living in the city can be healthier, in a variety of physical and psychological ways, than living in the country (Creekmore, 1985; Krupat, 1985; Milgram, 1970, 1977). Many of the advantages of city living are simply not available to residents of smaller communities. Few cities with populations of less than 50,000 can support large symphony orchestras, opera companies, museums, and art galleries (for residents who can afford them), parks and playgrounds (for those who want them), or fully staffed emergency rooms or trauma centers (for those who need them) such as those found in much larger urban areas. Small communities can seldom afford stadiums or arenas for professional sports. A challenge for environmental psychologists is to help urban planners and architects design living spaces in areas of high population density that minimize the subjective experience of crowding, maintain privacy, and that allow for expressions of individual territoriality.

population density *a quantitative measure of the number of persons (or animals) per unit of area*

crowding *the subjective feeling of discomfort caused by a sense of lack of space*

Before You Go On

What are some of the positive and negative aspects of life in the city?

Noise, Temperature, and Environmental Toxins

In this section, we'll review some evidence that suggests that the physical environment can have profound effects on behavior. We'll consider noise, temperature, and toxins (poisons) and how they affect human performance.

Noise is defined as an intrusive, unwanted, or excessive experience of sound. Almost any environment will provide some level of background noise, and sound

noise *an intrusive, unwanted, or excessive experience of sound* *per se* need not be disruptive or stressful. In fact, the total absence of sound can induce stress. Noise becomes most stressful when it is loud, high-pitched, and unpredictable (Glass & Singer, 1972). Continued exposure to high-intensity sound can produce lasting deafness (Scharf, 1978), although prolonged exposure to high levels of noise seems to produce few other serious physical problems directly (Matlin, 1983). Prolonged exposure to noise increases levels of stress, anxiety, and aggressive behaviors (Bell et al., 1978; Smith & Stansfield, 1986).

Noise levels have predictable effects on the performance of cognitive tasks, such as problem solving and school work. Sheldon Cohen and his associates (1980, 1986), for example, have shown that children who attended schools near the busy Los Angeles airport were more easily distracted from their work than children who attended schools in quieter neighborhoods. Glass and Singer (1972) claim that the absolute level of background noise is not the major determiner of disruption. What matters more in the disruption of performance is the *predictability* of the noise and the degree of *control* over that noise. The results of one experiment demonstrating this phenomenon are presented in Figure 15.2.

Students were given the task of trying to solve problems that in fact had no solutions. Students worked on these puzzles under three levels of background noise. In one condition, there was no unusual noise; in a second condition, a relatively soft (68-decibel) noise was presented; in the third condition, a loud (110-decibel) noise was introduced. In the two treatments using background noise, the predictability of the noise was also manipulated. That is, in one condition, the onset of the noise was regular and predictable; in the other, the noise was introduced on a random schedule. Introducing predictable noise–soft or loud–did not significantly alter the students' persistence in working on problems. Unpredictable noise, however, reduced the number of trials students were willing to invest in the problem task. Glass and Singer (1972) reported that when students were able to exercise control over the occurrence of noise, their problem-solving tasks were unaffected. When noise is uncontrollable, performance levels drop, and performance often remains poor even after the stimulus noise has been removed.

Extremes of temperature can also have adverse effects on behavior. Probably any task can be accomplished most effectively within a range of moderate environmental temperatures (Baron, 1977). It is important, for example, to try to keep the

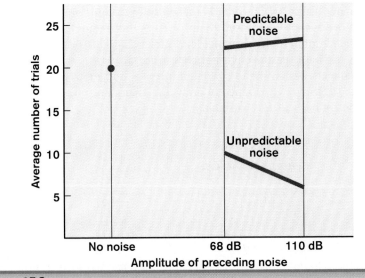

Figure 15.2

The effects of the unpredictability of noise as a distractor during a cognitive task. When noise occurred unpredictably, students spent fewer trials attempting to solve unsolvable puzzles. (From Glass et al., 1969.)

temperature of a workplace within reasonable limits. If temperatures become excessively high or low, performance will deteriorate, although the specific effects of temperature on performance depend in large measure on the type of task being performed.

Environmental psychologists have been concerned with the effects that extremely high temperatures have on social interactions, particularly on aggression. There is a common perception that riots and other more common displays of violent behaviors are more frequent during the long, hot days of summer. This observation is largely supported by research evidence (Anderson, 1989; Anderson & Anderson, 1984; Rotton & Frey, 1985). C. A. Anderson (1987, 1989) reported on a series of studies showing that violent crimes are more prevalent in hotter quarters of the year and in hotter years, although nonviolent crimes were less affected. Anderson also concluded that differences in crime rates between cities are better predicted by temperature than by social, demographic (age, race, education), and economic variables. Baron and Ransberger (1978) point out that riots are most likely to occur when the outside temperature is only moderately high, between about 75° and 90° F. But when temperatures get much above 90°F, energy (even for aggression) becomes rapidly depleted, and rioting is less likely to occur.

As societies become more heavily invested in technological advancement, an accompanying side effect is that increased levels of toxins or pollutants find their way into the environment. Psychologists concerned with quality of life issues are becoming increasingly involved in issues concerning the quality of the natural environment (Daniel, 1990; Fischhoff, 1990; Kaplan, 1987; Stern, 1992; Stokols, 1990).

Of the nearly 100,000 chemicals in use in this country's industries, more than 600 have been declared dangerous in large doses by the federal government. Many of the chemicals that pollute the natural environment are called **neurotoxins** because they have their poisonous effects on the human nervous system. Even in small doses, some can cause detectable behavioral and emotional changes in individuals.

neurotoxins chemicals (poisons) that affect psychological processes through the nervous system

Environmental psychologists are involved in research on neurotoxins at several levels. On the one hand, there is education: workers and consumers need to know about the short-term and long-term effects of contact with chemical toxins and how to deal with such materials. Because many of the effects of pollutants are psychological (behavioral irregularities, disorientation, impairment of cognitive abilities), and particularly because these chemicals affect the behaviors of young children (and the unborn), psychologists are becoming more involved in the actual diagnosis of the effects of toxins (Fein et al., 1983). Exposure to neurotoxins may be more readily diagnosed through behavioral or psychological means than through medical diagnosis.

Before You Go On

What are some of the effects that noise, extreme temperature, and neurotoxins have on behavior?

Changing Behaviors That Impact on the Environment

Psychologists have long been active in helping to establish programs aimed at changing the behaviors of people in such a way as to benefit the environment. Finding solutions to environmental problems is one of the goals of **applied behavior analysis (ABA)**. The techniques of applied behavior analysis are derived from the work of B. F. Skinner and the procedures of operant conditioning (Topic 5B), and can be used to modify a range of behaviors. In the present context, ABA attempts to (1) operationally define some target behavior to be modified (e.g., the

applied behavior analysis (ABA) an approach, based on operant conditioning, that attempts to find solutions to human environment problems in the real world conservation of energy or water, or the reduction of roadside litter), (2) determine the antecedent environmental conditions that set the occasion for, or that prompt the behavior, and (3) determine the consequences that increase, decrease, or maintain the targeted behavior (Geller, 1986; Geller & Nimmer, 1985). Programs of this sort have had a positive effect in many environmentally sensitive areas, such as energy conservation in general (Geller, 1989, 1992; Stern, 1992), conservation of natural gas (Shippee & Gregory, 1982), home-based energy conservation (Winett et al., 1985), gasoline conservation (Hake & Foxx, 1978), home weatherization projects (Pavlovich & Greene, 1984), and paper recycling (Witmer & Geller, 1976).

Let's look at one example: motivating waste management behavior (Geller, 1985; Geller & Lehman, 1986). We recognize that waste management *is* a problem. Millions of tons of solid waste are disposed of daily, often in ways that threaten environmental quality. The first step is to develop a precise, operational definition of target behaviors. Just what behavior does one want to change? Do you want to increase the use of trash receptacles? Do you want to have litter removed from roadsides? Do you want to increase solid waste recycling? What waste materials do you want to emphasize?

Once you have decided which behavior is to be modified, attention shifts to antecedent strategies, or prompting procedures. Here, you have to let people know just what it is that you want done. This is an educational component of the program. Prompts may be general ("Please dispose of properly!") or specific ("Leave your old newspapers here"). Prompts may also communicate possible consequences of one's actions ("Fine for Littering: $50" or "Bring your own container and receive a 5% discount"). Securing a behavioral commitment to a waste management program can be an effective means of prompting participation. People who sign pledges or engage in discussions of waste management alternatives are more likely to follow through.

As we learned in our study of operant conditioning, behaviors will change and be maintained to the extent that those behaviors produce certain consequences. Programs designed to modify behaviors that impact on the environment are often successful to the extent that consequences are tied to a person's response, not to some potentially long-term outcome. For example, scouts who pick up trash from the side of a highway should be rewarded immediately with a few cents for each bag of litter they collect rather than given an award (or reward) for providing a lit-

Environmental pollutants pose a serious threat not only to people's health but also to their very way of life. Psychologists use applied behavior analysis techniques to try to change people's interactions with their physical environments.

ter-free roadway. Positive consequences for desired actions (thanking someone for picking up trash) typically are more effective than negative consequences (fining someone for leaving a soda can on a public beach). Intervention programs should be designed so that they can be maintained by an agency or institution within the community once the program is underway.

Before You Go On

How can applied behavior analysis programs be adapted to change behaviors that affect the environment?

Psychology and Sport

Sports psychology is another new and exciting area of applied psychology. Although it has had a long history in Europe, sports psychology has become an organized focus of attention in this country only within the last 20 to 25 years. **Sport psychology** is "the application of psychological principles to sport and physical activity at all levels of skill development" (Browne & Mahoney, 1984, p. 605). There are many potential applications of psychology to sports and athletes. We'll review just two: analyzing the psychological characteristics of athletes and maximizing athletic performance.

The Psychological Characteristics of Athletes

Psychology's history is filled with research on the measurement of individual differences. Wouldn't it be useful to be able to predict who might become a world-class athlete on the basis of psychological testing? There are physiological differences between athletes and nonathletes—amount of muscle, muscle type, height, weight, lung capacity, and so on. Are there any differences between athletes and nonathletes on personality measures?

Generally, research in this area has been disappointing and results often confirm the obvious. Differences tend to be small, but athletes usually score higher than nonathletes on tests of assertion, dominance, aggression, and need for achievement; they score lower on anxiety level, depression, and fatigue (Browne & Mahoney, 1984; Cox, 1990; Morgan, 1980). This is particularly true when the athletes are at a high skill level. Athletes in some sports, such as hockey and football, are more tolerant of pain than are athletes in other sports, such as golf and bowling (e.g., Ryan & Kovacic, 1966). Tolerance of pain, however, may be more of an outcome (result of their activity) for some athletes than a determinant of their success.

This point raises a problem that has plagued research on the personality of the athlete: Just how shall we define *athlete*? Given the differences among hockey players, golfers, long-distance runners, pocket billiards players, cowboys, bowlers, rock climbers, gymnasts, and so on, it is surprising that research can find *any* significant differences between athletes and nonathletes. In fact, when general trends are sought, they often are not found (e.g., Fisher, 1977).

Maximizing Athletic Performance

Of practical importance to coaches and athletes is the performance of the athlete in competition, and what can be done to maximize that performance.

One area of interest focuses on manipulating the arousal level of the athlete. The athlete in competition surely needs to be aroused and motivated to perform— "psyched up" to his or her best. Psychologists also know that too much arousal can

⊚⊚⊚⊚ Thinking Critically ⊚⊚⊚⊚

One slogan of environmentalists is "Think globally and act locally." What are the psychological implications of such a challenge?

sport psychology *the application of psychological principles to sport and physical activity at all levels of skill development* interfere with athletic performance—that optimum levels of arousal can vary as a function of the task at hand. For example, making a long putt in golf requires a low level of arousal, blocking a shot in volleyball requires a slightly higher level, making a tackle in football a higher level, and a bench press in weight lifting requires a very high level of arousal (e.g., Cox, 1990, p. 98). (We addressed some of these issues of arousal when we discussed motivation in Topic 10A.) Psychologists can help athletes be sensitive to appropriate levels of arousal while maintaining concentration on the task at hand. This often involves training athletes to be sensitive to such indicators as their own blood pressure, respiration and heart rates, muscle tension, and the like (Harris, 1973; Landers, 1982).

Sports psychologists have tried to find evidence for a performance phenomenon many athletes and nonathletes take for granted: the notion of developing a "hot hand," or being "in a groove," or "in the zone." The concept is not well defined, but is assumed to be demonstrated by a string or cluster of successful performances (e.g., made shots) greater than chance or past history would predict (Vallerand et al., 1988). As it happens, evidence for a "hot hand" phenomenon is virtually nonexistent. It doesn't seem to occur at all in team sports such as basketball (Adams, 1992; Gilovich et al., 1985), and occurs only minimally in individual sports such as tennis or racquetball (Iso-Ahola & Blanchard, 1986; Silva et al., 1988).

Bob Adams, of Eastern Kentucky University, may have found an exception: professional pocket billiards (Adams, 1995). Adams found that in nine-ball tournaments, there was evidence that a player could get on a "hot streak," make significantly more shots, and win more games than usual. Adams asserts that there are two reasons why pocket billiards is different from other sports and susceptible to streaks or "hot hands": (1) there is not much time between opportunities to shoot (as opposed to basketball, for instance), and (2) once a player starts shooting, the opponent can do nothing to affect outcomes (as opposed to tennis, for instance).

In a similar vein, psychologists now claim that the so-called home field advantage (Varca, 1980) often may be exaggerated, particularly in important games (Baumeister, 1985; Baumeister & Steinhilber, 1984). The argument is that frenzied, yelling, screaming hometown fans may raise arousal levels of the home team beyond the point of maximum efficiency. The negative effect of fans' reactions is more potent when teams are on offense than when they are playing defense, and it is clearly more potent in end-of-season playoff and championship games.

Being "in a groove," "on a hot streak," or "in the zone" probably does not occur in any team sport, no matter the extent to which many athletes believe that it does. Research does suggest, however, that the phenomenon may exist in very personal sports, such as pocket billiards—at least at the professional level.

One sports psychologist, Michael Mahoney, commenting on Olympic athletes, has said, "At this level of competition, the difference between two athletes is 20 percent physical and 80 percent mental" (quoted in Kiester, 1984a, pp. 20–21). To the extent that this observation is accurate, psychologists have tried to help athletes to do their best—to give what is called their *peak performance*. Mental practice or "imagery" combined, of course, with physical practice has proven beneficial (e.g., Smith, 1987). In addition to manipulating acceptable levels of arousal, mental practice is useful in the following:

1. Mentally rehearsing a particular behavioral pattern. (Think about—mentally picture—that golf swing and the flight of the ball before you step up to the tee.)

2. Reducing negative thoughts that may interfere with performance. (Forget about an earlier error and focus on positive experiences, perhaps past victories.)

3. Rehearsing one's role in a team sport. (Mentally practice what you are supposed to do and when you are supposed to do it in various game situations.)

4. Setting realistic goals. (Don't get tense worrying about a competitor in this race, simply try to better your last performance; e.g., Creekmore, 1984; Fenker & Lambiotte, 1987; Kiester, 1984a, 1984b; Ogilvie & Howe, 1984; Scott & Pelliccioni, 1982; Smith, 1987; Suinn, 1980.)

Obviously, using mental imagery is not a simple matter, nor is it the only way in which athletes can improve their performances. It's just one technique with which sports psychologists can help.

Before You Go On

What are some of the ways in which psychologists become involved in sports and athletics?

TOPIC 15B SUMMARY

In this Topic, we've reviewed two areas in which psychological understanding can be applied to real-life situations. We have seen how the physical environment can have sweeping effects on our affects, cognitions, and behaviors, and how sports and athletics can benefit from our knowledge of human behavior.

Environmental psychologists face many challenges as they try to accommodate physical space to suit the needs of those who occupy that space. We looked in some detail at issues of crowding and population density, particularly as these concepts relate to life in large cities. We also considered some of the ways in which psychologists can help bring about the sorts of changes in behavior that will be necessary to save and refurbish the natural environment.

When considering some of the things sports psychologists do, we found that attempts to find personality traits or variables that would predict athletic ability in general terms have been largely unsuccessful—as have attempts to find data to support the notion that athletes can develop a "hot hand" (except in professional pocket billiards). On the other hand, there is evidence that psychological techniques can help athletes raise their overall levels of performance.

CHAPTER SUMMARY

Topic 15A

What is involved in doing a job analysis?

Doing a proper job analysis involves two stages: (1) constructing a complete and specific description of the activities performed by someone in a given position (i.e., a listing of the behaviors required to do the job) and (2) developing ways of evaluating the performance of a person in that job (performance criteria). */pp. 530–532*

What are some of the sources of information that can be used in making personnel decisions?

Personnel selection may use several assessment tools including application forms, interviews, psychological tests, situational tests, and assessment center approaches, to measure relevant characteristics of employees and potential employees. Of these, the casual, unstructured interview seems to be of least value. The assessment center is one location where many applicants (or present employees) can be brought together for a period of intense evaluation. In most instances, assessment centers can simulate actual job situations and give evaluators a sense of how someone will perform on the job, in social situations, and under stress. */pp. 532–534*

List factors that need to be considered in the design, implementation, and evaluation of a training program.

Several factors need to be considered in designing and implementing employee training programs. These include an assessment of the organization's instructional needs (what training, if any, is required?), the development of specific training objectives, the means by which training will be evaluated, and the selection of media and methods for actual training. Once training has begun, it should be monitored constantly to see if objectives are being met. After training has been completed, the program itself should be evaluated in the short and long term, as should the transfer of information and skills from training to actual on-the-job performance. */pp. 534–537*

Summarize some of the factors that affect the motivation of workers.

Even workers with ability may not do a good job unless they are motivated to do so. We looked at three approaches to worker motivation. Vroom's *expectancy theory* says that workers develop expectations concerning the relationship between their work behaviors and the likelihood of certain outcomes. They also assign values to outcomes. They will be most highly motivated to behave in ways that earn valued rewards. Adams's *equity theory* says that what matters most is the perception of fairness or equal reward for equal effort when one's work behaviors are compared with those of someone else at the same level. Locke's *goal-setting* approach says that what matters most is that workers be aware of just what they are working for and that they accept that goal as worth the effort. */pp. 537–540*

What is meant by job satisfaction?

Job satisfaction is an attitude, a measure of an employee's evaluation of his or her position in an organization. There are as many facets to job satisfaction as there are aspects of one's job. */pp. 540–542*

Summarize the relationship between job satisfaction and job productivity.

Although job satisfaction and productivity may be related, there is little evidence that the relationship is a strong one, and no evidence that one causes the other. Interventions designed to increase job satisfaction sometimes have a positive impact on productivity, but interventions designed to improve productivity may also increase job satisfaction. Job satisfaction seems most closely related to employee turnover and somewhat less related to absenteeism. */pp. 542–543*

What steps can be taken to improve worker safety?

I/O psychologists have long been interested in making the workplace as accident-free as possible. We looked at a few ways of approaching work safety: (1) seeing to it that only qualified persons are assigned to a job—particularly if the job is a dangerous one, (2) motivating workers to work more safely by providing training in safe behaviors and convincing them that safety is valued in the organization, and (3) engineering the job and equipment to be as safe as possible. */pp. 543–544*

Topic 15B

Define the concepts of personal space and territoriality.

Personal space is the imaginary bubble of area around a person into which others enter only by invitation or in specified situations. It is mobile and goes with the person. There are several types of personal space defined for various situations. *Territoriality,* on the other hand, is one's claim to certain areas in the environment. Territories may be defended against intrusion and are often used as statements of self-expression. Intrusion into one's personal space or territory without invitation may lead to tension, stress, and even aggression. */pp. 545–550*

What are some of the positive and negative aspects of life in the city?

Although city life necessarily involves population density, it need not involve crowding. *Population density* is a physical, quantitative measure of the number of units (e.g., people) occupying a given geographical area, while crowding is a psychological reaction of distress that occurs when individuals perceive a lack of adequate space. City living increases the probability of living with crowding, noise, and other pollutants, but these stressors may be offset by the advantages of a wide range of opportunities not found outside large population centers, such as health care, and access to the arts and entertainment. */pp. 550–551*

What are some of the effects that noise, extreme temperature, and neurotoxins have on behavior?

Noise, extreme temperatures, and neurotoxins may be seen as environmental pollutants and harmful to physical and psychological well-being. Noise *per se* is less stressful than is unexpected, unpredictable, or uncontrollable noise. High temperatures may lead to aggressive, violent reactions, but extremely high (or low) temperatures tend to decrease all levels of behavior. Many chemicals found in the environment have potentially negative consequences for behavior and mental activities; those that directly affect the nervous system are called neurotoxins. */pp. 551–553*

How can applied behavior analysis programs be adapted to change behaviors that affect the environment?

Environmentalists work to conserve natural resources and to restore the environment to its natural and unspoiled state. Programs associated with an approach called *applied behavior analysis,* or ABA, target specific behaviors, identify antecedent conditions that prompt these target behaviors, and attempt to control consequences of relevant behavior to increase the rate of appropriate responses. */pp. 553–555*

What are some of the ways in which psychologists become involved in sports and athletics?

Psychologists have become involved in sports and athletics in several ways, including trying to discover how athletes are different from nonathletes, attempting to improve an athlete's peak performance, and studying the effects of audience reactions on athletic performance. */pp. 555–557*

Manager for a Day

This chapter opened with a brief story about Jack Far-well, plant manager for Acme Flange Fabrication, Inc., and some of the problems he was having. Now that you've been through this chapter, provide a suggestion for what Jack should do for each of the following. Be as brief and specific as possible. (Suggested answers can be found on p. 575.)

1. Jack needs to hire an assistant plant manager. What is one of the first things that Jack has to do?

2. In selecting a new assistant manager from a list of candidates, what are some of the sources of information that Jack can use to choose the best one?

3. If Jack sent his current supervisors to an assessment center, in hopes of finding one who could function as assistant manager, what sorts of things could the supervisors expect to find at the assessment center?

4. Once Jack hires a new assistant, he feels that the supervisors and salespeople need training to effectively deal with new production techniques and the new products being developed. What are some of the questions Jack needs to ask with regard to his plans for a training program?

5. Jack also wants to motivate his employees to do their best work. For each of the following approaches to worker motivation, what issues will Jack have to address? (a) Expectancy theory, (b) Equity theory, (c) Goal setting.

6. No matter what, Jack has to improve plant productivity. To what extent does Jack need to concern himself with issues of worker satisfaction?

Statistical Appendix

Doing research in psychology, or applying psychology, often involves measuring some aspect of behavior or mental processes. When we measure the affects, cognitions, or behaviors of organisms, the result of our measurement is a set of numbers. Assuming that we have adequately measured what we are interested in, we now have to deal with the numbers we have accumulated. That's where statistics come in.

It's one thing to be able to measure a psychological characteristic and something else again to make sense out of those measurements once they've been made. This is particularly true when we have a large number of measurements, made repeatedly on the same individual or on many different individuals. After making our measurements, we need to be able to summarize and describe our data. We may want to make decisions based on the measurements we have made. **Statistics** are arithmetic manipulations of a set of measurements that help us to summarize, describe, and make judgments about those measurements. How they do so will be the subject of this appendix.

Before we go on, I'd like to insert a word of caution. In this appendix, we are going to deal with numbers and a few simple formulas. Please don't let the numbers make you anxious. Some students find dealing with numbers difficult and think that statistics are not really relevant for psychology students. Always keep in mind that statistics are tools—necessary tools—to help us understand our subject matter. At this level at least, you don't need mathematical sophistication to appreciate statistics. What is required is a positive attitude and a few arithmetic skills, such as addition, subtraction, multiplication, and division.

statistics *values computed from a set of scores or measurements that help us to summarize, describe, and make judgments about those measurements*

An Example to Work With

When we observe or measure the affects, behaviors, or cognitions of organisms, the result of observations is often a set of numbers. Let's generate some numbers to work with for a while. Let's say that you become enthralled with the notion that where students sit in a classroom can be related to their performance in that class. You hypothesize that students who sit in the front of the room earn higher scores than those who sit at the rear. You find a psychology class that has twelve rows of seats in it. You eliminate the middle two rows and get exam scores (anonymously, of course) for students who sit in the first five rows and for students who sit in the rear five rows. As it happens, there were 30 students in the first five rows and 30 in the last five rows. Their scores were as follows:

Front of the Class						Rear of the Class					
82	64	84	92	72	96	100	74	76	84	76	68
92	78	100	86	82	82	86	84	78	82	66	64
80	76	80	64	86	68	70	80	82	86	80	90
98	88	100	94	82	82	82	82	82	82	82	78
98	86	96	72	64	66	74	80	76	78	70	78

Well, now what do you make of that? Just looking at these numbers, as they are arranged here, doesn't tell much. To answer your original question (Is there a difference in test performance depending on where one sits?), you're going to have to manipulate these numbers somehow.

Graphic Representations

One thing that might help is to get a pictorial view of how these numbers are distributed for each of your two groups. Graphs that depict the frequency with which scores occur are among the most common in psychology. For such graphs, our scores (referred to in general as *X-scores*) are plotted on the horizontal (*x*) axis of the graph, and frequencies (*f*) are plotted on the vertical (*y*) axis.

Figure A.1 shows one way to graph frequencies. This sort of bar graph is called a **histogram**. The frequency of each *X*-score is indicated by the height of the bar above that score. When we don't have many *X*-scores, and when frequencies aren't too large, histograms provide clear depictions of our data. We can see some potential differences between our two groups of exam scores in Figure A.1.

Figure A.2 shows the same data in a simple line graph. The advantage of this sort of graph is obvious: We can easily show both distributions of exam scores on the same axes. As is the case with histograms, scores are plotted on the *x* axis, and frequencies are indicated on the *y* axis. With line graphs it is important to indicate which line represents which set of scores or data.

histogram *a bar graph, an indication of the frequency with which X-values occur, where the height of a bar indicates the frequency of an X-value, or score*

Descriptive Statistics

So far we've collected some numbers, and have made them presentable by displaying them in the form of graphs. We still want to know if there is any difference in exam scores between students sitting in the front and in the rear of the class. There are other steps we can take. When describing sets of data, our concern is usually with measures of central tendency and variability. **Central tendency** measures are statistics that tell us where our scores tend to center; in general terms we often refer to them as "averages." Measures of **variability** are statistics that tell us about the extent of dispersion, or the spread of scores in a distribution. Are scores grouped or clustered closely around the average, or are they more variable, deviating widely from the center?

central tendency *a measure of the middle, or average, score of a set of scores*

variability *the extent of spread or dispersion in a set or distribution of scores*

Measures of Central Tendency

There are three statistics we can use to represent the central tendency of a distribution of numbers. The most commonly used is the mean.

The **mean** of a set of scores is the scores' total divided by the number of scores in the set. It's what most people refer to as an "average." For example, if Max is 6

mean *the sum of all X-scores divided by the number of X-scores*

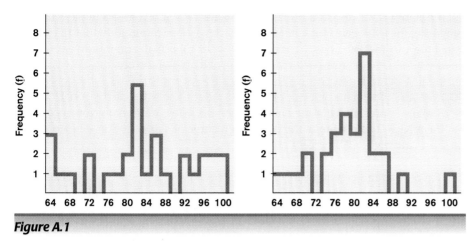

Figure A.1

Histograms showing the frequency with which exam scores (*X*-scores) were earned by students seated at the front (first five rows) and the rear of the classroom (last five rows).

feet tall and Ruth is 4 feet tall, their mean height is 5 feet. Four inches of snow today and 2 inches yesterday yields a mean snowfall of 3 inches for the two days (4″ + 2″ = 6″ ÷ 2 = 3″). To compute the mean scores for the students in our example who sit at the front of the class, we'd add up all their the scores and divide by 30—because there are 30 scores in each set. We'd find the mean score for the students sitting at the rear of the class by adding up their scores and dividing by 30 again because there are also 30 students in that group. The total of the scores for the group at the front of the class is 2,490, so their mean is *83*. The total of scores for students at the rear of the class is 2,370, so their mean is *79,* four points lower.

Although the mean is generally the measure of choice, there are occasions where it may not be appropriate, such as when a distribution contains a few extreme scores. As a simple example, the mean of the numbers 2, 3, 3, 5, and 7 is 4 (the total is 20; there are 5 numbers, so the mean is 20 ÷ 5 = 4). Even by inspection, 4 looks right; it is a value at or near the middle of the set. Now consider the numbers 2, 3, 3, 5, and 37. What is their mean? The sum of these five numbers is 40, so their mean is 10. Here, it seems by inspection that the score of 37 is adding too

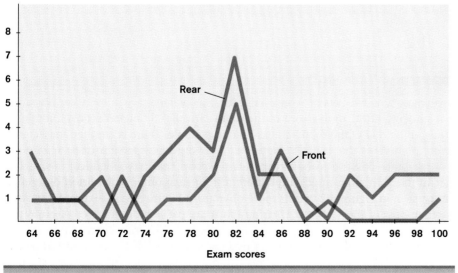

Figure A.2

Line graphs showing the frequency with which exam scores were earned by students seated at the front of the (Front) and the rear of the classroom (Rear).

much weight to our measure of central tendency. For a real-life example, imagine computing the average income of a small, working-class community that happened to include two millionaires. The mean income of this small community would be unfairly influenced by two persons with unusually high incomes.

In such cases, we might use the median as our measure of central tendency. The **median** is the value of a set of numbers that divides it exactly in half. There are as many scores above a median as there are below it. Perhaps you recognize that the median is the same as the fiftieth percentile of a distribution—50 percent of the scores are higher; 50 percent are lower.

Don't fall for this trick: "What is the median of the numbers: 42, 58, 37, 62, and 55?" There is a tendency to want to say "37" because it is in the middle of the list, with two numbers on the left and two on the right. But "37" certainly isn't at the center of these scores; it's the lowest of the five! Before you choose a median, the scores must be in order: 37, 42, 55, 58, 62. *Now* the score in the middle, 55, is the median. Whenever we have an even number of scores, there won't be one value in the center, will there? What is the median of these numbers: 3, 6, 8, 10, 14, and 18? What we do is calculate the mean of the two numbers in the middle (here 8 and 10). So the median of these numbers is *9*. When we have a large number of scores to deal with, the computation becomes a little more complicated, but the logic is the same, and there are simple formulas that tell us what steps to take to calculate the median. In our example, the median exam score for students sitting at the front of the room is 82.6 and the median score for students sitting at the rear of the room is 79.7.

The easiest measure of central tendency to calculate is the mode. The **mode** is simply the most frequently occurring score in a set or distribution of scores. The mode is seldom used as a measure of central tendency. For one thing, the mode disregards all of the other values in the distribution of scores. For another, there is no guarantee that the most frequently occurring number will be at (or even near) the middle. And it is also quite possible for one set of numbers to have two modes (be "bimodal"), or three modes, or more. For many psychological characteristics measured for a large number of people, the mode often does fall at or near the center of the distribution of scores. For both of the groups in our example, the mode is 82.

Before You Go On

Define three measures of central tendency.

Measures of Variability

If we know how two sets of scores differ "on the average," we know a lot. We know that students sitting in the front of the room earn slightly higher scores than those sitting at the rear of the room, at least in our example. There is another characteristic of number sets that can also be useful: their spread, dispersion, or *variability*.

It is quite possible to have two sets of scores that have identical means but that, at the same time, are clearly different from each other. This sort of difference can be seen in Figure A.2, and is more obvious in Figure A.3. In Figure A.3 we can see that most of the scores of Distribution A are packed, or clustered, around the mean of the distribution. The scores of Distribution B are more spread out or variable, even though the means of the two distributions are the same. So knowing about the variability of a set of scores can provide some useful information. How shall we represent this variability?

One way to measure the spread of a set of scores is with a statistic called range. It is one of the easiest statistics to calculate. The **range** of a distribution is found by

---

median *the score of an ordered set above and below which fall half of the scores*

mode *the most frequently occurring score in a set or distribution of scores*

⊚⊚⊚ **Thinking Critically** ⊚⊚⊚
How many times in the last week did you hear about, or were you asked to deal with "averages" or means?

range *the highest score in a distribution minus the lowest score*

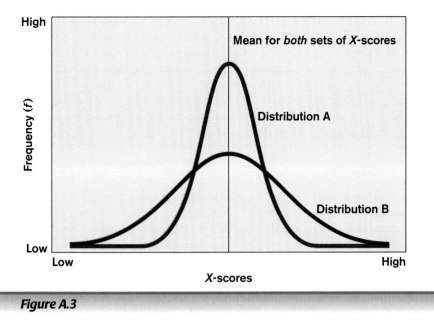

Figure A.3

Two distributions of X-scores (A and B) that have identical means but clearly different variabilities.

subtracting the lowest score from the highest. Unfortunately, the range disregards all the other values in the set, so if there are just a couple of extreme scores, the range will be very large. Range would be an inappropriate measure of variability for the distributions represented in Figure A.3, because both appear to have the same highest and the same lowest scores, even though we've already agreed that their variability is different.

A measure of variability that takes into account *all* of the scores of a distribution is **standard deviation**, which amounts to a kind of average of the extent to which scores in a distribution are different from (deviate from) the mean value of that distribution. We needn't go though the procedures for calculating standard deviations here. (Many hand-held calculators come with a button that yields a standard deviation value once you've entered in all the X-values.) We'll see this statistic in use later, however, so you do need to appreciate that what it does is to provide a measure—with just one number—of the extent to which scores in a distribution deviate, or are spread from the distribution's mean. In our example, the standard deviation of the scores of students sitting in the front of the class is 11.01 and it's 7.15 for students sitting at the rear of the class. This fits our impression of the variability of the scores in the two distributions that we can get from an inspection of the graphs of the data in either Figure A.1 or Figure A.2.

standard deviation *a type of average of the extent to which each X-score in a distribution is different from (deviates from) the mean of that distribution*

Before You Go On

What are two ways of indicating the variability of a distribution of measurements?

Drawing Inferences with Statistics

Not only can statistics be used to help us organize and summarize data, they can also be used to guide our decision making concerning the data we have collected in the process of making our observations. That is, statistics can allow us to make inferences about our data. **Inferential statistics** tell us about the *significance* of the results of our data collection. In general, they tell us the likelihood that the data we have collected might have occurred by chance.

inferential statistics *statistical tests that tell us about the significance of the results of experimental or correlational studies*

Let's stick with our working example. Imagine that where one sits in class really has no effect whatsoever on test scores. If you tested 30 students at the rear of a room and 30 at the front, would you expect their scores to be identical? No. You'd expect some chance variation in the scores. If you repeated your observations a week later, would you expect the scores to be exactly the same? No, again. We generally anticipate that simply because of chance factors alone there will be some difference between the scores of two groups of people—even if they are doing the very same thing under the same conditions. So if mean scores, for example, for two groups of students are found to be different, how can we tell if the observed difference is due to chance factors or due to the ways in which the two groups were treated? This is where inferential statistics come in.

Inferential statistics allow us to make probability statements. They help us to determine the likelihood that observed differences in our descriptive statistics (such as means) are differences due to chance and random factors or reflect some true difference between the groups we have measured. Observed differences that are not likely to have occurred by chance are said to be **statistically significant differences**. If the difference between two calculated means is found to be statistically significant, that difference may or may not be meaningful, but we can claim that the difference is not likely to have occurred by chance.

statistically significant differences *differences between descriptive statistics not likely to have occurred by chance if those statistics were describing the same group*

In our example, students sitting at the front of the room earned a mean score of 83 points, while those at the rear earned a mean score of 79 points. Are these means due to random effects, or is it likely, statistically, that they reflect real differences? There are three factors that influence a test of statistical significance. One, of course, is the size of the observed difference, here 4 points. *Everything else being equal,* the larger the observed difference, the more likely it reflects a real difference and not chance factors. A second factor is the number of observations involved. *Everything else being equal,* differences based on large numbers of observations are more likely to be significant than are differences based on fewer scores. The third factor is the variability of the observations. *Everything else being equal,* observed differences are more likely to be significant as the variability of the observations is less. As it happens, even though the actual mean difference is not very large, and the number of observations is not great, because the variability of the scores of the groups in our example is small, the difference of 4 points between the means is statistically significant.

Before You Go On

How can statistics help us determine if observed differences between measures are "real?"

Some Normal Curve Statistics

As I suggested in our topics on personality assessment and intelligence, many of the measurements in psychology tend to fall into a similar pattern. Particularly when those measurements are made on large numbers of subjects, we commonly find that they fall into a distribution we call the normal curve (see Figure A.4). The normal curve is a frequency distribution that is symmetrical and bell shaped. As you can see, scores that are normally distributed tend to bunch around the mean and become infrequent at the extreme values of X (whatever the X-scores may be). Because this normal distribution of scores does occur so often, we tend to know a lot about the nature of this curve.

The normal curve is simply a graphical representation of a collection of numbers. As such, we can compute the mean and the standard deviation of the scores that make up the distribution. Because the normal distribution is symmetrical, the mean always falls in the middle of the distribution and is coincident with the me-

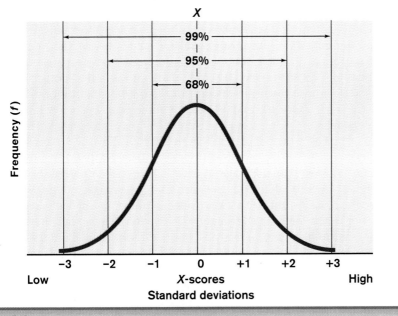

Figure A.4

The percentage of cases in a normal distribution falling between ±1 standard deviation around the mean (68%) and between ±2 and ±3 standard deviations around the mean (95% and 99%). The curve is symmetrical, and the mean divides it exactly in half.

dian and the mode. That is, there are just as many scores above the mean as there are below it. We also know how many scores, or what proportion of scores, fall within standard deviation units around the mean. For example, we know that 68 percent of all the scores fall between 1 standard deviation below the mean and 1 standard deviation above the mean (Figure A.4). It is also the case that 95 percent of the cases fall between ±2 standard deviations around the mean. Almost all the cases (about 99 percent) in a normal distribution fall between _3 and +3 standard deviations around the mean. What good is this sort of information? Let's look at an example problem.

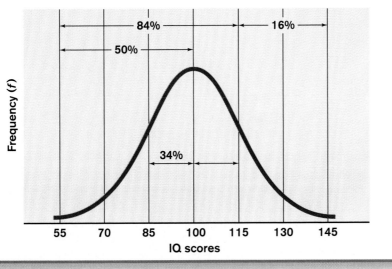

Figure A.5

A theoretical normal curve of IQ scores. With the mean equal to 100, and the standard deviation equal to 15, 84 percent of the population has an IQ of 115 or less [50% to the mean, and 34% from the mean to +1 standard deviation above the mean]. Thus, only 16 percent has an IQ above 115.

When many people are measured, IQ scores tend to fall in distributions that we may consider to be normal distributions. Figure A.5 depicts a theoretical IQ distribution where, by definition, the mean equals 100 and the standard deviation is equal to 15 IQ points. We might want to know, for instance, what percentage of the population has an IQ score above 100. Well, that's an easy one. Because the mean equals 100, and because the mean divides the distribution exactly in half, 50 percent of the cases fall above 100 and 50 percent of the cases fall below it, so the answer is 50 percent.

What percentage of the population has an IQ score above 115? This takes a little more effort, and following along with Figure A.5 might help. We might work backward. If we know the percentage of cases in the shaded portion of the curve (up to IQ = 115) then the difference between that percentage and 100 will be the percentage who have IQs above 115. We can't determine the shaded percentage by inspection, but we can do so in a few easy steps. Up to the mean fall one-half, or 50 percent, of the cases (this we've already established). Now what about that segment between 100 and 115? What we do know (check Figure A.4 again) is that 68 percent of the cases fall between _1 standard deviation and +1 standard deviation. In a normal distribution, the mean divides this segment exactly in half, so that between the mean and 1 standard deviation above the mean are included 34 percent of the cases. (Note that IQ = 115 is 1 SD above the mean.) So now we have 50 percent to the mean of 100, and 34 percent from the mean to 115. We add the two together and determine that 84 percent of the cases fall below an IQ of 115, so 16 percent must fall above it.

Using the same logic, we can convert any score to a percentage or a proportion, if we are dealing with a normal curve. To do so for scores that do not fall right on standard deviation units above or below the mean involves a slight complication, but the general method is the same as we have indicated here. What percentage of the population (in accord with Figures A.4 and A.5) has earned IQ scores above 130? (The answer is 2.5 percent. Can you see where that comes from?)

Before You Go On

What is a normal curve?

A P P E N D I X   S U M M A R Y

Define three measures of central tendency.

There are three measures of central tendency, or average: (1) *mean,* the sum of X-scores divided by the number of scores; (2) *median,* the score above and below which fall 50 percent of the scores; and (3) *mode,* the most frequently occurring score in the distribution. */pp. 562–564*

What are two ways of indicating the variability of a distribution of measurements?

Variability refers to the extent to which scores in a distribution are dispersed, or spread out. The *range* of a distribution is simply the difference between the largest value or score in the set and the smallest. The *standard devia-*

tion is (essentially) the average of the extent to which each score in the distribution deviates from its mean. */pp. 564–565*

How can statistics help us determine if observed differences between measures are "real?"

A test of *statistical significance* tells us about the likelihood that an observed descriptive statistical difference might have occurred by chance. To say that the difference between the two means is "statistically significant at the 0.01 level" means that if there were no real difference between the groups from which the means came, the likelihood of finding a mean difference as large as the one observed is less than 1 in 100. */pp. 565–566*

What is a normal curve?

The normal curve depicts data often encountered in psychology when large numbers of measurements are made. It is a graph of frequencies of scores that is symmetrical and bell shaped. Within 1 standard deviation above the mean and 1 standard deviation below the mean fall 68 percent of all the cases measured. Between ± 2 SDs around the mean fall 95 percent of all cases, and 99 percent of all cases fall between _3 SDs and +3 SDs around the mean. */pp. 566–568*

Suggested Answers to "Practicing Psychology" Questions

Chapter 1—Understanding Correlations

The answers provided here are to be taken as suggestions only; there are other reasonable explanations for each of the correlations described.

1. Positive. Mutual influence. Similar life experiences.
2. Negative. Orphanage environment has an adverse effect on cognitive development. More intelligent children are more likely to be adopted out of the orphanage sooner.
3. Positive. Violent pornography stimulates violent behaviors. Both violent crime and the number of stores are related to the size of the cities. Violent criminals are attracted to violent pornography.
4. Negative. Absent students miss information presented in class not available elsewhere. Students with jobs or other responsibilities find it difficult to get to class or to find time to study.
5. Positive. The money appropriated to fight crime was poorly spent. The city grew during the time period, resulting in more crime and more tax revenues.
6. Positive. Both variables are related to socioeconomic factors—children from affluent homes have both intellectual and physical advantages over children from substandard home environments. Age is a third variable that affects scores on both variables—older children have larger vocabularies and are also stronger and better coordinated.
7. Positive. Smoking causes lung cancer. People who are cancer-prone are those who are likely to smoke. A third variable, perhaps alcohol consumption, increases the risk of cancer and the tendency to smoke.

Chapter 2—Damage to the CNS: What Happens If?

1. There would be paralysis and loss of feeling from the waist down.
2. There would be paralysis and loss of feeling for the entire body below the neck.
3. With the centers for respiration and heart rate destroyed, death would result.
4. Major pathways between the brain and the body below the neck would be lost, resulting in the loss of voluntary movement and feeling.
5. There would be a disruption of all smooth, coordinated behaviors; for example, speech would be slurred, movements would be jerky.
6. There would be few noticeable effects of such a split-brain procedure except in the laboratory, where one could note how the two hemispheres of the cerebral cortex operate independently.
7. The last relay station for sensory impulses would be lost, resulting in a loss of all sensory processing.
8. If the cut were total, coma would result, because the reticular formation regulates one's level of arousal or activation.
9. The individual would be blind.
10. There would be a loss of feeling from the right side of the body.

Chapter 3—Sensory Terminology

Seeing: vision, the eye, rods and cones

Hearing: audition, the ear, hair cells in the cochlea

Taste: gustation, the tongue, gustatory cells in the taste buds

Smell: olfaction, the nose, hair cells

Touch: the cutaneous sense, the skin, free and encapsulated nerve endings

Balance: the vestibular sense, semicircular canals and vestibular sacs, hair cells

Body Position: the kinesthetic sense; unspecified receptors in joints, muscles, and tendons

Chapter 4—Personalizing Consciousness

By definition, I cannot provide you with examples about your own consciousness. I can, however, provide examples from my own. You might see how much our experiences are alike.

1. Consciousness is *changing*. Although I can focus on a given task, like preparing these exercises, I cannot hold any one idea still. It is almost immediately replaced by another idea, then another, perhaps on the same topic, maybe not. Right now I'm thinking about food and being hungry—not very productive, but such is the nature of consciousness. Not only does it change, but sometimes, it just goes where it wants.

2. Consciousness is *personal*. I can tell you about these thoughts I'm having concerning this exercise and about my being hungry, but these thoughts, ideas, and images (I'm now picturing the inside of my refrigerator) are very much mine alone, and there is no way that you can experience them directly.

3. Consciousness is *continuous*. I went to bed last night thinking about the end of Chapter 4 and what I might put there. After a good night's sleep, I awoke, still me, still thinking about Chapter 4 and what to put at the end of the chapter. I may have slept soundly or I may have slept poorly, and I may have had several dreams during the night, but my personal, changing consciousness just kept on going and going.

4. Consciousness is *selective*. As it happens, today is a busy day, and there are many things I need to be thinking about and several things that I need to do (with luck, I've written down the most important on my list). But at any one time I can only focus on and think about one thing at a time. I can't imagine what it would be like to literally "think about two or more things at once."

Chapter 5—A Potpourri of Reinforcers and Punishers

1. Simple, positive punishment.
2. Again, a painful stimulus was removed, thus creating negative reinforcement.
3. This is punishment again, exactly like example #2.
4. Bruce's use of the Study Guide was reinforced. This example (and many others, by the way) can be seen as negative reinforcement (the use of the Study Guide removed the "painful" low grades), or positive reinforcement (the use of the Study Guide led to the joy of high grades).
5. Kirsten's fighting behaviors are becoming less frequent because they are being punished—not by hitting or shocking or hurting, but by taking away play time; thus, we have negative punishment.
6. The parental attention (jumping up and holding) is clearly acting as a positive reinforcer in addition to the intrinsic pleasure derived from chewing on the cool plastic cord.

Chapter 6—A Memory Experiment You Can Do

There certainly will be individual differences, but your "Subject" should recall:

a. BED because it is the first word on the list and receives the most rehearsal (the so-called primacy effect)
b. DREAM because it is the last word on the list and is still in STM (the so-called recency effect)
c. NIGHT because it is presented three times and should profit from the extra rehearsal
d. ARTICHOKE because it is so different from the other words (the so-called distinctiveness effect)
e. TOSS and TURN consecutively because they are commonly associated
f. SLEEP as a superordinate, organizing term, although it is *not* on the list

Chapter 7—Assessing Creativity

[No answers are provided for this exercise.]

Chapter 8—Testing the Reality of Stages of Development

Sensorimotor Stage: learns through active interaction with environment; starts to appreciate cause-and-effect; demonstrates object permanence; imitates others

Preoperational Stage: becomes egocentric; language development begins; can categorize objects into simple classifications

Concrete Operations Stage: demonstrates conservation; understands relational terms; begins to use simple logic

Formal Operations Stage: develops abstract and symbolic cognitions; begins to reason and understand the hypothetical

Trust Versus Mistrust: develops sense of security and safety, or anxiety and insecurity

Autonomy Versus Self-Doubt: develops a view of being in control of one's body and making things happen, or feelings of inadequacy to control events

Initiative Versus Guilt: develops self-confidence as one who can create things, or feelings of a lack of self-worth

Competence Versus Inferiority: develops adequacy in social and intellectual skills, or a lack of self-confidence and feelings of failure

Identity Versus Role Confusion: develops a comfortable sense of self, or has a fragmented, unclear sense of self

Intimacy Versus Isolation: develops a capacity for closeness and commitment to others, or feelings of aloneness and separation

Generativity Versus Stagnation: develops a focus beyond one's self to family, society, or future generations, or self-indulgent concerns with a lack of future orientation

Ego-Identity Versus Despair: develops a sense of wholeness and a basic satisfaction with life, or feelings of futility and disappointment

Preconventional Morality: rules are obeyed simply to avoid punishment or to earn rewards

Conventional (Conforming) Morality: rules are conformed to in order to avoid disapproval and gain approval, with social conventions accepted blindly in order to avoid criticism

Postconventional Morality: morality based on agreement with others to serve the common good and as a reflection of internalized standards

Chapter 9—Three Faces of Personality

1. Humanist
2. Psychoanalyst
3. Humanist
4. Behaviorist
5. Psychoanalyst
6. Humanist (or behaviorist)
7. Behaviorist
8. Psychoanalyst
9. Behaviorist
10. Humanist
11. Behaviorist
12. Psychoanalyst

Chapter 10—Why, Oh Why?

1. Instinct
2. Arousal
3. Incentive
4. Secondary drive
5. Primary drive (or homeostasis)
6. Cognitive dissonance
7. Arousal
8. Instinct
9. Cognitive dissonance
10. Incentive (or secondary drive)

Chapter 11—Name That Stressor

1. Environmental frustration
2. Approach-approach conflict
3. Personal frustration
4. Life events and hassles
5. Personal frustration
6. Avoidance-avoidance conflict
7. Multiple approach-avoidance conflict
8. Approach-avoidance conflict
9. Approach-approach conflict
10. Environmental frustration
11. Life events and hassles
12. Life events and hassles

Chapter 12—What Is Your Diagnosis?

1. phobic disorder
2. schizophrenia
3. dissociative fugue
4. panic disorder with comorbid agoraphobia
5. obsessive-compulsive disorder
6. posttraumatic stress disorder
7. major depression
8. avoidant personality disorder

9. conversion disorder
10. generalized anxiety disorder

Chapter 13—What Sort of Therapist Are You?

1. Gestalt
2. Psychoanalytic
3. Family
4. Behavioral
5. Client-centered
6. Psychoanalytic
7. Cognitive
8. Client-centered
9. Behavioral
10. Cognitive

Chapter 14—Identify the Concept

1. Group think
2. Cognitive dissonance
3. Pluralistic ignorance
4. Internal attribution
5. External attribution
6. Actor-observer bias
7. Mere exposure phenomenon
8. Conformity
9. Audience inhibition or diffusion of responsibility
10. An attitude
11. Social loafing
12. Just world hypothesis

Chapter 15—Manager for a Day

1. Write a job analysis with a detailed set of performance criteria.
2. An application form (for biodata), a structured interview, reliable and valid psychological tests, situational tests, assessment centers.
3. Assessment centers provide opportunities to observe a person in a range of situations similar to those found on the job, for example, a situation using the "in-basket" technique.
4. (a) Do I really need a program? (b) What do I want to accomplish? (c) Which training techniques should I use? (d) How shall I assess the short-term and long-term effectiveness of my program?
5. (a) Do workers know that rewards follow from their behaviors, and do workers value these rewards? (b) Do workers perceive that their efforts are being rewarded in ways that are equal to the rewards being earned by other workers in similar positions? (c) Are goals clear and specific? Do workers see the relation between their work and their goals? Are goals achievable? Are workers given feedback on their progress?
6. Jack need not be overly concerned; there appears to be little correlation between job satisfaction and productivity levels.

Glossary

ablation the process of surgically removing tissue from living organisms to study the effects of that removal (p. 15)

abnormal in psychology: maladaptive cognitions, affect, or behaviors at odds with social expectations that result in stress or discomfort (p. 428)

absolute threshold the physical intensity of a stimulus that one can detect 50 percent of the time (p. 71)

accommodation in Piaget's theory, the process of changing or revising an existing schema as a result of new experiences (p. 285)

accommodation in vision, the process in which the shape of the lens is changed by the ciliary muscles to focus an image on the retina (pp. 78, 106)

acquired immune deficiency syndrome (AIDS) a deadly disease caused by a virus (the HIV) that destroys the body's natural immune system; can be transmitted by an interchange of blood or semen (p. 420)

acquisition the process in classical conditioning in which the strength of the CR increases with repeated pairings of the CS and UCS (p. 154)

acquisition the process in operant conditioning in which the rate of a reinforced response increases (p. 167)

action potential the short-lived electrical burst caused by the sudden reversal of electric charges inside and outside a neuron, such that the inside becomes positive (about +40 mV) (p. 41)

actor-observer bias the overuse of internal attributions to explain the behaviors of others and external attributions to explain our own behaviors (p. 505)

addiction an extreme dependency, usually accompanied by symptoms of tolerance and painful withdrawal (p. 138)

adolescence the developmental period between childhood and adulthood, often begun at puberty and ending with full physical growth; generally between the ages of 12 and 20 (p. 300)

adrenal glands endocrine glands that release adrenalin, or epinephrine, into the bloodstream to activate the body in times of stress or danger (p. 48)

affect one's feelings, mood, or emotional state (p. 7)

ageism discrimination or prejudice against someone formed solely on the basis of age (p. 314)

agoraphobia a phobic fear of being in public places from which escape might be difficult (p. 436)

algorithm a problem-solving strategy in which all possible solutions are generated and tested until an acceptable solution appears (p. 261)

all-or-none principle the fact that a neuron will either produce a full impulse, or action potential, or will not fire at all (p. 41)

alpha activity an EEG pattern associated with quiet relaxation and characterized by slow wave cycles of 8 to 12 per second (p. 1251)

Alzheimer's disease a dementia caused by the premature death of brain cells because of the accumulation of plaques and tangles (p. 448)

anorexia nervosa an eating disorder characterized by the reduction of body weight through self-starvation and/or increased activity (p. 372)

anterograde amnesia the inability to form or retrieve new memories (p. 203)

antianxiety drugs chemicals that alleviate the symptoms of anxiety; also known as tranquilizers (p. 472)

antidepressant drugs chemicals that reduce the symptoms of depression (p. 471)

antipsychotic drugs chemicals, such as chlorpromazine, effective in reducing psychotic symptoms (p. 470)

antisocial personality disorder an exceptional lack of regard for the rights and property of others accompanied by impulsive, often criminal, behaviors (p. 446)

anxiety a general feeling of apprehension or dread accompanied by predictable physiological changes (pp. 411, 433)

applied behavior analysis (ABA) an approach, based on operant conditioning, that attempts to find solutions to human environment problems in the real world (p. 553)

aptitude tests psychological tests of cognitive abilities used to predict future behaviors (p. 238)

aqueous humor watery fluid found in the space between the cornea and the lens that nourishes the front of the eye (p. 79)

arousal one's level of activation or excitement (p. 363)

assimilation in Piaget's theory, the process of adding, and "fitting in," new material or information to an existing schema (p. 285)

association areas those areas of the frontal, temporal, and parietal lobes in which mental processes (planning, thinking, problem-solving memory) occur; where incoming sensory information is integrated with outgoing motor responses (p. 60)

atonia muscular immobility, associated with REM sleep, caused by the total relaxation of the muscles (p. 129)

attachment a strong two-way emotional bond, usually between a child and parent, or primary caregiver (p. 297)

attitude a relatively stable evaluative disposition directed toward some object or event; it consists of feelings, behaviors, and beliefs (p. 496)

audience inhibition reluctance to intervene and offer assistance in front of others (p. 518)

autonomic nervous system (ANS) neurons in the PNS that activate smooth muscles and glands (p. 47)

availability heuristic the assumption that whatever comes to mind readily must be more common or probable than what does not easily come to mind (p. 265)

aversion therapy a technique of behavior therapy in which an aversive stimulus, such as a shock, is paired with an undesired behavior (p. 482)

axon a long, tail-like extension of a neuron that carries impulses away from the cell body and to other cells (p. 38)

axon terminals the set of branching end points of an axon; where neurons begin to communicate with adjacent neurons (p. 38)

babbling speech phonemes produced in rhythmic, repetitive patterns (p. 255)

basal ganglia a collection of structures in front of the limbic system involved in the control of large, slow movements; a source of much of the brain's dopamine (p. 56)

baseline design a method in which a participant's performance with an (p. 29)

basilar membrane a structure within the cochlea that vibrates and thus stimulates the hair cells of the inner ear (p. 91)

behavior what organisms do; their actions and reactions (p. 7)

behavior therapy techniques of psychotherapy founded on principles of learning established in the psychological laboratory and aimed at changing one's behaviors (p. 481)

behavioral observation the assessment technique of drawing conclusions about one's personality based on observations of that person's behaviors (p. 345)

behaviorism associated with John Watson, the approach to psychology that argues for the scientific study of observable behavior alone, not mental processes (p. 13)

bipolar disorder a mood disorder characterized by depression with intermittent periods of mania (p. 451)

blind spot the small region of the retina, containing no photoreceptors, where the optic nerve leaves the eye (p. 80)

brain stem the lowest part of the brain, just above the spinal cord, consisting of the medulla and the pons (p. 52)

brightness the psychological experience associated with a light's intensity, or wave amplitude (p. 75)

bulimia an eating disorder characterized by recurrent episodes of binge eating and then purging to remove the just-eaten food (p. 372)

case history method the technique of studying (observing) one person (or a few persons) in depth, using interviews, tests, and the like (p. 23)

cell body the largest concentration of mass of a neuron; contains the cell's nucleus (p. 381)

central nervous system (CNS) neurons and supporting cells in the spinal cord and the brain (p. 46)

central tendency a measure of the middle, or average, score of a set of scores (p. 562)

cerebellum a spherical structure at the rear base of the brain that coordinates fine and rapid muscular movements (p. 53)

cerebral cortex the large convoluted outer covering of the brain that is the seat of voluntary action and cognitive functioning (p. 57)

chemical ions electrically charged (+ or –) chemical particles in solution (p. 40)

chlamydia a common STD caused by a bacterial infection that can lead to PID and infertility in women if untreated (p. 419)

chunk an imprecise concept referring to a meaningful unit of information represented in short-term memory (p. 194)

ciliary muscles small muscles attached to the lens that control its shape and focusing capability (p. 78)

classical conditioning learning in which an originally neutral stimulus comes to elicit a new response after having been paired with a stimulus that reflexively elicits that same response (p. 152)

client-centered therapy the humanistic psychotherapy associated with Rogers, aimed at helping a person grow and self-actualize (p. 480)

closure the Gestalt principle of organization claiming that we tend to perceive incomplete figures as whole, as complete (p. 104)

cochlea part of the inner ear where sound waves become neural impulses (p. 91)

cognitions mental events such as perceptions, beliefs, thoughts, ideas, and memories (p. 7)

cognitive dissonance a state of tension or distress that occurs when there is a lack of balance, or equilibrium, between or among one's cognitions (pp. 365–500)

cognitive map a mental representation of the learning situation or physical environment (p. 179)

cognitive restructuring therapy a form of cognitive therapy, associated with Beck, in which an individual is led to overcome negative self-images and pessimistic views of the future (p. 485)

collectivism in cross-cultural psychology, the tendency to set goals and make decisions based on a concern for the group or the common good (p. 291)

common fate the Gestalt principle of organization claiming that we group together, within the same figure, elements of a scene that move together in the same direction and at the same speed (p. 104)

comorbidity the co-occurrence of two or more disorders in the same individual (p. 432)

compulsions constantly intruding, repetitive, and essentially involuntary behaviors (p. 437)

conception the act of the father's sperm cell unites with the mother's ovum to produce a new cell (p. 276)

concrete operations stage in Piaget's theory, from ages 7 to 12 years, when concepts can be manipulated, but not in an abstract fashion (p. 286)

conditioned response (CR) in classical conditioning, the learned response (such as, salivation in response to a tone) evoked by the CS after conditioning (p. 153)

conditioned stimulus (CS) in classical conditioning, an originally neutral stimulus (such as, a tone) that, when paired with a UCS, comes to evoke a new response (a CR) (p. 153)

cones photosensitive cells of the retina that operate best at high levels of illumination and that are responsible for color vision (p. 79)

conflict a stressor in which some goals can be satisfied only at the expense of others (p. 399)

conformity the changing of one's behavior, under perceived pressure, so that it is consistent with the behavior of others (p. 511)

consciousness the awareness or perception of the environment and of one's own mental processes (p. 120)

conservation in Piaget's theory, an appreciation that changing the physical properties of an object does not necessarily change its essence (p. 286)

contingency contracting establishing an agreement (contract) with one to reinforce appropriate behaviors; often involving token economies (p. 483)

contingency management bringing about changes in one's behaviors by controlling rewards and punishments (p. 483)

continuity the Gestalt principle of organization claiming that a stimulus or a movement will be perceived as continuing in the same smooth direction as first established (p. 104)

continuous reinforcement (CRF) schedule a reinforcement schedule in which every response is followed by a reinforcer (p. 171)

contrast the extent to which a stimulus is in some physical way different from surrounding stimuli (p. 99)

control group participants in an experiment who do not receive a treatment or manipulation (p. 29)

convergence the tendency of the eyes to move toward each other as we focus on objects close up (p. 106)

convergent thinking the reduction or focusing of many ideas or solutions into one, or a few (p. 267)

conversion disorder the display of a severe physical disorder for which there is no medical explanation; often accompanied by an apparent lack of concern on the part of the patient (p. 440)

cornea the outermost structure of the eye that protects the eye and begins to focus light waves (p. 78)

corpus callosum the network of nerve fibers that connects the two hemispheres of the cerebral cortex (p. 61)

correlation a statistical procedure used to assess the degree to which sets of observed responses are associated (co-related) with each other (p. 23)

correlation coefficient a number that indicates the nature (+ or −) and the degree (0.00 to +1.00 or −1.00) of the relationship between measured responses (p. 24)

cross-laterality the arrangement of nerve fibers crossing from the left side of the body to the right side of the brain, and from the right side of the body to the left side of the brain (p. 53)

crowding the subjective feeling of discomfort caused by a sense of lack of space (p. 551)

crystallized intelligence abilities related to acquired knowledge, accumulated experiences, and general information (p. 242)

dark adaptation the process by which our eyes become more sensitive to light as we spend time in the dark (p. 74)

death instincts (thanatos) the inborn impulses, proposed by Freud, that compel one toward destruction; they include feelings of depression and aggression (p. 325)

debrief the process of informing participants of the true and complete nature of an experiment after the experiment is over (p. 32)

decibel scale a scale of our experience of loudness in which 0 represents the absolute threshold and 120 is sensed as pain (p. 87)

defense mechanisms unconsciously applied techniques that protect the self (ego) from feelings of anxiety (p. 327)

deinstitutionalization the practice, begun in the mid–1950s, of releasing patients from mental institutions and returning them to their home communities (p. 473)

delusions false beliefs; ideas that are firmly held regardless of evidence to the contrary (p. 454)

dementia a marked loss of intellectual abilities in which memory is poor and deteriorates and judgment is adversely affected (p. 448)

dendrites extensions from a neuron's cell body that receive impulses (p. 38)

denial a defense mechanism wherein one refuses to believe the realities of an anxiety-producing situation (p. 327)

dependence a state in which drug use is either necessary or believed to be necessary to maintain functioning at some desired level (p. 138)

dependent variable the event or situation measured by an experimenter to see if it has changed upon manipulation of an independent variable (p. 27)

depressants drugs (such as alcohol, opiates, heroin, and barbiturates) that slow or reduce nervous system activity (p. 140)

diagnosis the act of recognizing a disorder on the basis of the presence of particular symptoms (p. 430)

difference threshold differences in a stimulus attribute that can be detected 50 percent of the time (p. 72)

diffusion of responsibility the tendency to allow others to share in the obligation to intervene (p. 518)

discrimination the phenomenon in classical conditioning in which an organism learns to make a CR in response to only one CS but not to other stimuli (p. 156)

discrimination the process of differential reinforcement wherein one stimulus is reinforced while another stimulus is not (p. 176)

displacement a defense mechanism in which one's behaviors or motives (usually aggressive) are directed at a substitute rather than the real object of those behaviors or motives (p. 328)

dissociative amnesia a psychologically caused inability—too extensive to be caused by ordinary forgetfulness—to recall important personal information (p. 441)

dissociative disorder a disorder in which one escapes from aspects of one's life or personality seen as the source of discomfort (p. 441)

dissociative fugue a condition of amnesia accompanied by unexplained travel or change of location (p. 442)

dissociative identity disorder the existence within one individual of two or more distinct personalities, each of which is dominant at a particular time (p. 442)

divergent thinking the creation of many ideas or possible solutions from one idea (p. 266)

Down syndrome a condition of several symptoms, including mental retardation, caused by an extra (47th) chromosome (p. 248)

drive a state of tension resulting from an unlearned need that arouses and directs an organism's behavior (p. 359)

drug abuse a lack of control, a disruption of interpersonal relationships or difficulties at work, and a history of maladaptive use for at least one month (p. 138)

DSM-IV the fourth edition of the *Diagnostic and Statistical Manual of Mental Disorders;* the most common system for classifying psychological disorders (p. 430)

dysthymia a mood disorder that is basically a mild form of major depression; it is chronic, with recurrent pessimism, low energy level, and low self-esteem (p. 451)

eardrum the outermost membrane of the ear; set in motion by the vibrations of a sound; transmits vibrations to the ossicles (p. 91)

ego the aspect of personality that encompasses the sense of "self"; it is in contact with the real world and operates on the reality principle (p. 325)

elaborative rehearsal a means of processing information into LTM that involves thinking about information, organizing it, and making it meaningful (p. 200)

electroconvulsive therapy (ECT) a treatment, usually for severe depression, in which an electric current passed across a patient's head causes a seizure (p. 468)

electroencephalogram (EEG) an instrument that measures and records the electrical activity of the brain, indicative of arousal (pp. 16, 125)

electromyogram (EMG) an instrument used to measure and record muscle tension or relaxation (p. 125)

emotion an experience that includes a subjective feeling, a cognitive interpretation, a physical reaction, and a behavioral expression (p. 384)

empathic able to understand and share the essence of another's feelings, or to view from another's perspective (p. 481)

empiricists those who credit experience and observation as the source of mental life (p. 9)

encoding the active process of representing, or putting information into memory (p. 188)

encoding specificity principle the hypothesis that we can retrieve only what we have stored and that retrieval is enhanced to the extent that retrieval cues match encoding cues (p. 210)

endocrine system a network of glands that secrete hormones directly into the bloodstream (p. 47)

environmental psychology the field of applied psychology that studies how the general environment affects the behavior and mental processes of individuals and how individuals affect their environments (p. 545)

episodic memory a subsystem of LTM, in which personal experiences are stored (p. 202)

equity theory the view that workers are motivated to match their inputs and outcomes with those of fellow workers in similar positions (p. 539)

etiology the cause or predisposing factors of a disorder (p. 430)

expectancy theory the view that workers make logical choices to do what they believe will result in their attaining outcomes of highest value (p. 538)

experiment a series of operations used to examine possible cause-and-effect relations between manipulated events and measured events (p. 26)

experimental group participants in an experiment who receive a treatment or manipulation (p. 29)

external attribution an explanation of behavior in terms of something outside the person; a situational attribution (p. 503)

extinction the process in classical conditioning in which the strength of the CR decreases with repeated presentations of the CS alone (without the UCS) (p. 154)

extinction the process in operant conditioning in which the rate of a response decreases as reinforcers are withheld (p. 167)

extraneous variables those events or situations in an experiment that must be controlled or eliminated so as not to affect one's dependent variable (p. 27)

family therapy a type of group therapy focusing on the roles, interdependence, and communication skills of family members (p. 487)

fantasy a defense mechanism that involves the imagination or daydreaming as a reaction to stress and anxiety (p. 327)

fetal alcohol syndrome (FAS) a cluster of symptoms (e.g., low birth weight, poor muscle tone, and intellectual retardation) associated with a child born to a mother who was a heavy drinker of alcohol during pregnancy (p. 278)

figure-ground relationship the Gestalt psychology principle that stimuli are selected and perceived as figures against a ground (background) (p. 102)

flashbulb memory a particularly clear and vivid (although not necessarily accurate) recollection from one's past (p. 211)

fluid intelligence abilities related to speed, adaptation, flexibility and abstract reasoning (p. 242)

formal operations stage in Piaget's theory, ages older than 12 years, when one can generate and test abstract hypotheses and manipulate symbolic concepts (p. 288)

fovea the region at the center of the retina, consisting solely of cones, where acuity is best in daylight (p. 79)

free association the procedure in psychoanalysis in which the patient is to express whatever comes to mind without editing responses (p. 478)

frustration a stressor; the blocking or thwarting of goal-directed behavior (p. 398)

frustration-aggression hypothesis the view (now discredited) that all aggression stems from frustration (p. 411)

functional fixedness a type of mental set that interferes with the discovery of a new use for an object because of the experience of using that object for some other function (p. 264)

functionalism the approach to psychology that emphasized the utilitarian, adaptive functions of the human mind, or consciousness (p. 12)

fundamental attribution error the tendency to overuse internal attributions when explaining behavior (p. 505)

g-factor (g) general intelligence; a global measure of intellectual abilities (p. 228)

gender one's maleness or femaleness; socially ascribed characteristics of males and females, as opposed to their biological characteristics (p. 294)

general adaptation syndrome (GAS) Selye's description of physiological reactions made to stressors, which include the three stages of alarm, resistance, and exhaustion (p. 405)

generalization the phenomenon in classical conditioning in which a CR is elicited by stimuli different from, but similar to, the CS (p. 155)

generalization the phenomenon in operant conditioning in which a response that was reinforced in the presence of one stimulus appears in response to other, similar stimuli (p. 175)

generalized anxiety disorder persistent, chronic, and distressingly high levels of unattributable and uncontrollable anxiety or worry (p. 434)

generativity a concern in adulthood for one's family and for one's impact on future generations (p. 311)

genital herpes (herpes type II) the most common STD; a skin infection in the form of a rash or blisters in the genital area (p. 420)

gestalt whole, totality, configuration; the gestalt is seen as more than the sum of its parts (p. 102)

Gestalt psychology the approach to psychology that emphasizes perception; in particular, the selection and organization of information (p. 14)

gonorrhea an STD caused by a bacterial infection of moist tissues in the genital area (p. 420)

group polarization the tendency for members of a group to give more extreme judgments following a discussion than they gave initially (p. 522)

groupthink an excessive concern for reaching a consensus in group decision making to the extent that critical evaluations of input are withheld (p. 523)

habituation in classical conditioning, a simple form of learning in which an organism comes to ignore a stimulus of little or no consequence (p. 152)

hair cells the receptor cells for hearing, located in the cochlea, stimulated by the vibrating basilar membrane; they send neural impulses to the temporal lobe of the brain (p. 91)

hallucinogens drugs (such as LSD) whose major effect is the alteration of perceptual experience and mood (p. 142)

health psychology the field of applied psychology that studies psychological factors affecting physical health and illness (p. 413)

hertz (Hz) the standard measure of sound wave frequency that is the number of wave cycles per second (p. 88)

heuristic an informal, economical, yet reasonable, method of testing problem solutions without the guarantee of success (p. 262)

histogram a bar graph, an indication of the frequency with which X-values occur, where the height of a bar indicates the frequency of an X-value, or score (p. 562)

holophrastic speech the use of one word to communicate several meanings (p. 255)

homeostasis a state of balance, or equilibrium, among internal, physiological conditions (p. 363)

homosexuals persons who are sexually attracted to and aroused by members of their own sex (p. 377)

hue the psychological experience of color associated with a light's wavelength (p. 76)

humanistic psychology the approach to psychology that emphasizes the person, or the self, and personal growth and development (p. 14)

hypnosis an altered state of consciousness characterized by an increase in suggestibility, attention, and imagination (p. 132)

hypochondriasis a mental disorder involving the fear of developing some serious disease or medical illness (p. 440)

hypothalamus a small structure in the middle of the brain involved in feeding, drinking, temperature regulation, sex, and aggression (pp. 56, 366)

hypothesis a tentative explanation of some phenomenon that can be tested and either supported or rejected (p. 4)

id the instinctive aspect of personality that seeks immediate gratification of impulses; it operates on the pleasure principle (p. 325)

idealistic principle the force that governs the superego; opposed to the id, it seeks adherence to standards of ethics and morality (p. 325)

identity crisis the effort to define and integrate one's sense of self and what one's attitudes, beliefs, and values should be (p. 303)

illusion a perception that is at odds with (different from) what we know as physical reality (p. 111)

incentives external stimuli an organism may be motivated to approach or avoid (p. 36)

independent variable the event or situation manipulated by an experimenter to see if it will have a predicted effect on some other event or situation (p. 27)

individualism in cross-cultural psychology, the tendency to set goals and make decisions based on a concern for one's self or the individual (p. 291)

industrial/organizational (I/O) psychologist one who uses scientific methods to study the affects, cognitions, and behaviors of persons in work settings (p. 530)

inferential statistics statistical tests that tell us about the significance of the results of experimental or correlational studies (p. 565)

inferiority complex the feeling that we are less able than others to solve life's problems and get along in the world (p. 331)

insanity a legal term for diminished capacity, inability to tell right from wrong, and inability to exercise control over one's actions (p. 432)

insomnia the inability to fall asleep or stay asleep (p. 130)

instincts unlearned, complex patterns of behavior that occur in the presence of certain stimuli (p. 358)

intermittent reinforcement schedule a schedule in which responses are not reinforced every time they occur (p. 172)

internal attribution an explanation of behavior in terms of something (a trait) within the person; a dispositional attribution (p. 503)

interneurons neurons within the spinal cord or brain (p. 50)

interview the assessment technique involving a conversational interchange between an interviewer and another in order to gain information about the latter's personality (p. 347)

IQ intelligence quotient; a measure of general intelligence that results from dividing one's mental age by one's chronological age and multipying the result by 100 (p. 236)

iris the colored structure of the eye that reflexively opens or closes the pupil (p. 78)

job analysis a complete and specific description of a job, including the qualities and behaviors required to do it well (p. 530)

job satisfaction an attitude toward, or a collection of positive feelings about, one's job or job experiences (p. 541)

just noticeable difference (j.n.d.) the minimal change in a stimulus attribute, such as intensity, that can be detected (p. 72)

just world hypothesis the belief that the world is just and that people get what they deserve (p. 505)

kinesthetic sense the position sense that tells us the position of various parts of our bodies and what our muscles and joints are doing (p. 95)

language a large collection of arbitrary symbols that have a shared significance for a language-using community and that follow certain combinatorial rules (p. 250)

latent learning hidden learning that is not demonstrated in performance until that performance is reinforced (p. 179)

law of effect (Thorndike's) the observation that responses that lead to a "satisfying state of affairs" tend to be repeated; responses that do not lead to a satisfying state of affairs tend not to be repeated (p. 165)

learning demonstration of a relatively permanent change in behavior that occurs as the result of practice or experience (p. 150)

lens the structure behind the iris that changes shape to focus visual images in the eye (p. 78)

libido the energy that activates the sexual instincts (p. 325)

life instincts (eros) inborn impulses, proposed by Freud, that compel one toward survival; they include hunger, thirst, and sex (p. 325)

light a radiant form of energy that can be represented in wave form with wavelengths between 380 and 760 nanometers (p. 75)

limbic system a collection of structures near the middle of the brain involved in emotionality (amygdala and septum) and long-term memory storage (hippocampus) (p. 55)

lobotomy a psychosurgical technique in which the prefrontal lobes of the cerebral cortex are severed from lower brain centers (p. 467)

long-term memory (LTM) a type of memory with virtually unlimited capacity and very long, if not limitless, duration (p. 195)

loudness the psychological experience correlated with the intensity, or amplitude, of a sound wave (p. 87)

maintenance rehearsal a process of rote repetition (reattending) to keep information in short-term memory (p. 193)

major depression a mood disorder characterized by inexplicable moods of sadness and hopelessness, accompanied by a loss of pleasure or interest in usual activities (p. 450)

malleus, incus, and stapes (collectively, *ossicles*) three small bones that intensify sound vibrations and transmit them from the eardrum to the oval window (p. 91)

mania heightened euphoria and increased activity; typically occurs between episodes of depression (p. 451)

matching phenomenon the tendency to select partners whose level of physical attractiveness matches our own (p. 509)

mean the sum of all *X*-scores divided by the number of *X*-scores (p. 562)

meaningfulness the extent to which new information evokes associations with information already in memory (p. 212)

median the score of an ordered set above and below which fall half of the scores (p. 564)

meditation a self-induced state of altered consciousness characterized by a focusing of attention and relaxation (p. 135)

medulla the structure in the brain stem where cross laterality begins; it contains centers that monitor reflex functions such as heart rate and respiration (p. 521)

memory the cognitive capacity to encode, store, and retrieve information (p. 188)

menarche a female's first menstrual period, a sure sign of the beginning of adolescence (p. 301)

mental retardation a condition indicated by an IQ score below 70 that begins during development and is associated with an impairment in adaptive functioning (p. 247)

mental set a predisposed (set) way to perceive or respond to something; an expectation (pp. 101, 263)

mere exposure phenomenon the tendency to increase our liking of people and things as a result of recurring contact (p. 508)

meta-analysis the statistical procedure of combining the results of many studies or experiments to determine if any commonalities exist (p. 30)

Minnesota Multiphasic Personality Inventory (MMPI) a paper-and-pencil personality test designed to assess several dimensions of personality and to indicate the presence of a psychological disorder (p. 347)

mnemonic devices strategies for improving retrieval that take advantage of existing memories in order to make new material more meaningful (p. 212)

mode the most frequently occurring score in a set or distribution of scores (p. 564)

modeling the acquisition of new responses through the imitation of another who responds appropriately (p. 484)

monochromatic literally *one-colored;* a pure light consisting of light waves all of the same wavelength (p. 77)

mood disorders disorders of affect or feeling; usually depression; less frequently mania and depression occurring in cycles (p. 450)

morphemes the smallest unit of meaning in a language (p. 252)

motivation the process that arouses, directs, and maintains behavior (p. 358)

motor areas those areas at the rear of the frontal lobes that control voluntary muscular movement (p. 60)

motor neurons neurons that carry impulses away from the CNS to muscles and glands (p. 50)

myelin a white, fatty covering found on some axons that insulates and protects them and speeds impulses along (p. 38)

nanometer (nm) one-millionth of a millimeter; the unit of measurement for the wavelength of light (p. 75)

narcolepsy a disorder that involves unintentional sleeping, muscle paralysis, and immediate REM sleep; it is resistant to treatment (p. 131)

naturalistic observation the careful, systematic observation of behaviors as they occur, without any involvement by the observer (p. 21)

need a lack or shortage of some biological essential resulting from deprivation (p. 359)

need for affiliation the need to be with others and to form relationships (p. 382)

need for power the learned need to be in control of events or persons (p. 381)

need to achieve (nAch) the learned need to meet or exceed some standard of excellence in one's behaviors (p. 380)

negative reinforcer a stimulus that increases the rate of a response when that stimulus is removed after the response is made (p. 170)

negative symptoms emotional and social withdrawal, reduced energy and motivaton, apathy, and poor attention (p. 454)

neo-Freudians theorists (including Adler, Jung, and Horney) who supported the basics of psychoanalytic theory, but differed from Freud (p. 329)

neonate the newborn, from birth through the first 2 weeks (p. 279)

neural impulse a rapid and reversible change in the electrical charges inside and outside a neuron; it travels from dendrite to axon terminal of a neuron (p. 40)

neural threshold the minimum amount of stimulation necessary to get a neuron to fire (p. 42)

neuron a nerve cell that transmits information, in the form of neural impulses, from one part of the body to another (p. 38)

neurotoxins chemicals (poisons) that affect psychological processes through the nervous system (p. 553)

neurotransmitters chemical molecules released at the synapse that, in general, will either excite or inhibit a reaction in the cell on the other side of the synapse (p. 43)

noise an intrusive, unwanted, or excessive experience of sound (p. 551)

norms in psychological testing, scores on a test taken by a large number of persons that can be used for making comparisons (p. 234)

object permanence the appreciation that an object no longer in view can still exist and reappear later (p. 286)

observer bias a situation in which one's motives, expectations, and previous experiences interfere with the objectivity of observations (p. 21)

obsessions ideas or thoughts that involuntarily and constantly intrude into awareness (p. 437)

obsessive-compulsive disorder (OCD) a combination of constantly intruding thoughts and constantly intruding behaviors (p. 437)

operant behavior(s) used by an organism to interact with or operate on its environment (p. 164)

operant conditioning a procedure that changes the rate of a response on the basis of the consequences that result from that response (p. 164)

operational definition a definition of a concept given in terms of the procedures used to measure or create that concept (p. 7)

optic chiasma the location in the brain where impulses from light in the left visual field cross to the right side of the brain, and impulses from light in the right visual field cross to the left side of the brain (p. 84)

optic nerve the fiber, consisting of many neurons, that leaves the eye and carries impulses to the occipital lobe of the brain (p. 79)

orienting reflex the simple, unlearned response of orienting toward, or attending to, a new or unusual stimulus (p. 152)

overlearning the practice, or rehearsal, of material over and above what is needed to learn it (p. 216)

overregularization the excessive application of an acquired language rule (e.g., for forming plurals) in a situation in which it is not appropriate (p. 257)

panic disorder a disorder in which anxiety attacks suddenly and unpredictably; there may be periods free from anxiety (p. 435)

perception the cognitive process of selecting, organizing, and interpreting stimuli (p. 70)

performance criteria specific behaviors or characteristics a person should have in order to do a job as well as possible (p. 53)

peripheral nervous system (PNS) neurons not found in the brain and spinal cord, but in the periphery of the body (p. 46)

personal space the mobile "bubble" of space around you reserved for intimate relationships and into which others may enter only by invitation (p. 546)

personality those affects, behaviors, and cognitions that characterize a person in a variety of situations (p. 324)

personality disorders enduring patterns of perceiving, relating to, and thinking about the environment and oneself that are inflexible and maladaptive (p. 443)

persuasion a planned, conscious attempt to change someone's attitude (p. 499)

phenomenology the study of events, not as they occur, but as they are experienced by the individual (p. 18)

pheromones chemicals that produce an odor used as a method of communication between organisms (p. 93)

phobic disorder an intense, irrational fear of an object or event that leads a person to avoid contact with it (pp. 159, 435)

phoneme the smallest distinguishable unit of sound in the spoken form of a language (p. 252)

phrenology the now discredited notion that one could relate personal traits to the location of bumps on the skull (p. 15)

pinna the outer ear, which collects and funnels sound waves into the auditory canal toward the eardrum (p. 90)

pitch the psychological experience that corresponds to sound wave frequency and gives rise to high (treble) or low (bass) sounds (p. 88)

pituitary gland the "master gland" of the endocrine system that influences many others, controls such processes as body growth rate, water retention, and the release of milk from the mammary glands (p. 47)

placebo an inactive substance that has its effect because a person has come to believe it will be effective (p. 98)

pleasure principle the impulse of the id to seek immediate gratification to reduce tensions (p. 325)

pluralistic ignorance a condition in which the inaction of others leads each individual in a group to interpret a situation as a nonemergency, thus leading to general inactivity (p. 518)

pons a brain stem structure that forms a bridge, organizing fibers from the spinal cord to the brain and vice versa (p. 53)

population density a quantitative measure of the number of persons (or animals) per unit of area (p. 551)

positive disorganized symptoms disorders of thinking and speech, bizarre behaviors, and inappropriate affect (p. 455)

positive psychotic symptoms hallucinations and delusions; false perceptions and false beliefs (p. 454)

positive reinforcer a stimulus that increases the rate of a response it follows (p. 170)

positive test strategy the heuristic of sticking with an acceptable decision or solution, even if better ones may exist (p. 266)

posttraumatic stress disorder (PTSD) an anxiety disorder in which disruptive recollections, distressing dreams, flashbacks, and felt anxiety occur well after the experience of a traumatic event (p. 439)

pragmatics the study of how social contexts affect the meaning of linguistic events (p. 253)

prenatal period the period of development from conception to birth (p. 276)

preoperational stage in Piaget's theory, from ages 2 to 6 years, characterized by egocentrism and the beginning of symbol development (p. 286)

primary hues red, green, and blue; those colors of light from which all others can be produced (p. 84)

primary mental abilities in Thurstone's model, the seven distinct abilities that constitute intelligence (p. 229)

primary reinforcers stimuli (usually biologically or physiologically based) that increase the rate of a response with no previous experience required (p. 171)

proactive interference the inhibition of retrieval of recently learned material caused by material learned earlier (p. 220)

problem a discrepancy between one's present state and one's goal state with no apparent way to get from one to the other (p. 258)

procedural memory a subsystem of long-term memory, in which stimulus-response associations and skilled patterns of responses are stored (p. 200)

prognosis the prediction of the course of an illness or disorder (pp. 373, 436)

projection a defense mechanism that involves seeing one's own unacceptable, anxiety-producing characteristics in others (p. 328)

projective technique an assessment technique requiring a person to respond to ambiguous stimuli in the hopes that the person will reveal aspects of his or her personality (p. 349)

proximity the Gestalt principle of organization claiming that stimuli will be perceived as belonging together if they occur together in space or time (p. 103)

psychoactive drug a chemical that affects psychological processes and consciousness (p. 137)

psychoanalysis the form of psychotherapy associated with Freud, aimed at helping the patient gain insight into unconscious conflicts (p. 477)

psychoanalytic the approach to personality associated with Freud and his followers that relies on instincts and the unconscious as explanatory concepts (p. 324)

psychoanalytic psychology associated with Sigmund Freud, the approach to psychology that emphasizes the role of innate strivings and the unconscious mind (p. 13)

psychological test an objective, standardized measure of a sample of behavior (p. 233)

psychology the science of behavior and mental processes (p. 4)

psychophysics the study of the relationship between the physical attributes of stimuli and the psychological experiences they produce (p. 70)

psychosurgery a surgical procedure designed to affect one's psychological or behavioral reactions (p. 466)

puberty the stage of physical development at which one becomes capable of sexual reproduction (p. 300)

punishment the administration of a punisher, which is a stimulus that decreases the rate, or probability, of a response that precedes it (p. 174)

pupil the opening of the iris, which changes size in relation to the amount of light available and to emotional factors (p. 78)

random assignment the selection of members of a population such that each participant has an equal chance of being in any of the study groups (p. 29)

range the highest score in a distribution minus the lowest score (p. 564)

rational-emotive therapy (RET) a form of cognitive therapy, associated with Ellis, aimed at changing a person's irrational beliefs or maladaptive cognitions (p. 484)

rationalization a defense mechanism that excuses one's behaviors rather than facing the anxiety-producing reasons for them (p. 327)

reality principle the force that governs the ego, arbitrating between the demands of the id and the realities of the world (p. 325)

recall a measure of retrieval in which one is given the fewest possible cues to aid retrieval and must produce information to which he or she has been previously exposed (p. 206)

recognition a measure of retrieval in which an individual is required to identify material previously learned (p. 206)

reflex an unlearned, automatic response that occurs in the presence of a specific stimulus (p. 152)

regression a defense mechanism that involves returning to earlier, more primitive levels of behavior that were once effective (p. 328)

reinforcement a process that increases the rate, or probability, of the response it follows (p. 168)

reinforcers stimuli that increase the rate, or probability, of the responses they follow (p. 168)

relearning the change in performance that occurs when one is required to learn material for a second time (p. 207)

reliability in psychological testing, the extent to which a test measures whatever it measures consistently (p. 233)

REM sleep rapid-eye-movement sleep, during which vivid dreaming occurs, as do heightened levels of physiological functioning (p. 129)

representativeness heuristic the assumption that judgments made about a very typical member of some category will hold for all members of that category (p. 266)

repression a defense mechanism referring to motivated forgetting of an anxiety-producing event or desire (p. 327)

resistance in psychoanalysis, the inability or unwillingness to discuss freely some aspect of one's life (p. 479)

resting potential the electrical tension resulting from the difference in electrical charge of a neuron where the inside is negatively charged and the outside is positively charged (about −70mV) (p. 41)

reticular formation a network of nerve fibers extending from the base of the brain to the cerebrum that controls one's level of arousal (p. 55)

retina layers of cells at the back of the eye that contain the photosensitive rod and cone cells (p. 79)

retinal disparity the phenomenon in which each retina receives a different (disparate) view of the same three-dimensional object (p. 106)

retrieval the process of locating, removing, and using information stored in memory (p. 188)

retroactive interference the inhibition of retrieval of previously learned material caused by material learned later (p. 219)

retrograde amnesia the loss of the memory of events stored before the onset of the loss (p. 203)

rods photosensitive cells of the retina that are most active in low levels of illumination and do not respond differentially to various wavelengths of light (p. 79)

Rorschach inkblot test a projective technique in which a person is asked to say what he or she sees in a series of inkblots (p. 349)

s-factors specific cognitive, or intellectual skills; in Spearman's theory, part of intelligence in addition to g (p. 228)

sample a subset, or portion, of a larger population that has been chosen for study (p. 22)

saturation the psychological experience associated with the purity of a light wave; the most saturated lights are monochromatic, and the least saturated are white light (p. 77)

schema a system of organized, general knowledge, stored in long-term memory, that guides the encoding and retrieval of information (p. 214)

schemas organized mental representations of the world that are adaptive and formed by experience (p. 284)

schizophrenia a complex family of disorders characterized by impairment of cognitive functioning, delusions and hallucinations, social withdrawal, and inappropriate affect (p. 453)

science an organized body of knowledge gained through application of scientific methods (p. 4)

scientific methods a series of systematic procedures involving observation, description, control, and replication (p. 4)

secondary drive a state of tension resulting from a learned, or acquired, need that motivates an organism's behavior (p. 359)

secondary reinforcers stimuli that increase the rate of a response because of their having been associated with other reinforcers; also called conditioned, or learned, reinforcers (p. 171)

self-serving bias the tendency to attribute our successes to our own effort and abilities, and our failures to situational, external sources (p. 505)

semantic memory a subsystem of long-term memory, in which vocabulary, facts, simple concepts, and rules are stored (p. 201)

semantics the study of the meaning of words and sentences (p. 252)

sensation the process of receiving information from the environment and changing that input into nervous system activity (p. 70)

sensorimotor stage in Piaget's theory, from ages birth to 2 years, when a child learns by sensing and doing (p. 286)

sensory adaptation the process in which our sensory experience tends to diminish with continued exposure to a stimulus (p. 74)

sensory areas those areas of the cerebral cortex that ultimately receive neural impulses from sense receptors (p. 58)

sensory memory a type of memory that stores large amounts of information for very brief periods (a few seconds or less) (p. 188)

sensory neurons neurons that carry impulses from the sense receptors to the CNS (p. 50)

sexual dysfunction any one of a number of chronic difficulties or problems with sexual functioning (p. 375)

sexually transmitted diseases (STDs) contagious diseases that are usually transmitted through sexual contact (p. 419)

shaping a procedure of reinforcing successive approximations of a desired response until that desired response is made (p. 166)

short-term memory (STM) a type of memory with limited capacity and limited duration; also called working memory (p. 191)

signal detection theory the view that signal detection is a matter of decision making, of separating a signal from ground (background) noise (p. 73)

similarity the Gestalt principle of organization claiming that stimuli will be perceived together if they share some common characteristics (p. 103)

sleep apnea involves patterns of sleep during which breathing stops entirely (p. 131)

social facilitation improved performance due to the presence of others (p. 521)

social interference impaired performance due to the presence of others (p. 521)

social learning theory the theory that learning takes place through observation and imitation of models (p. 179)

social loafing the tendency to decrease one's individual work effort as the size of the group in which one is working increases (p. 520)

social phobia a significant, persistent fear of social or performance situations in which one may be embarrassed (p. 436)

social psychology the field of psychology concerned with how others influence the thoughts, feelings, and behaviors of the individual (p. 496)

socioeconomic status (SES) a measure that reflects one's income, education and occupation (p. 403)

somatic nervous system sensory and motor neurons outside the CNS that serve the sense receptors and the skeletal muscles (p. 46)

somatoform disorders psychological disorders reflecting physical or bodily symptoms or complaints for which there is no known physical cause (p. 440)

spinal cord a mass of interconnected neurons within the spinal column that transmits impulses to and from the brain and is involved in spinal reflex behaviors (p. 50)

spinal reflexes involuntary responses to a stimulus that involve sensory neurons, the spinal cord, and motor neurons (p. 51)

split-brain procedure the surgical lesioning of the corpus callosum which separates the functions of the left and right hemispheres of the cerebral cortex; a treatment of last resort for epilepsy (p. 61)

spontaneous recovery the phenomenon in classical conditioning in which a previously extinguished CR returns after a rest interval (p. 154)

spontaneous recovery the phenomenon in operant conditioning in which a previously extinguished response returns after a rest interval (p. 168)

sport psychology the application of psychological principles to sport and physical activity at all levels of skill development (p. 555)

stage of the embryo the second prenatal developmental period; from 2 to 8 weeks (p. 276)

stage of the fetus the third prenatal developmental period; from week 8 until birth (p. 276)

stage of the zygote prenatal developmental period from conception to the age of 2 weeks (p. 276)

standard deviation a type of average of the extent to which each *X*-score in a distribution is different from (deviates from) the mean of that distribution (p. 565)

state-dependent memory the hypothesis that retrieval can be enhanced by the extent to which one's state of mind at retrieval matches one's state of mind at encoding (p. 210)

statistically significant differences differences between descriptive statistics not likely to have occurred by chance if those statistics were describing the same group (p. 566)

statistics values computed from a set of scores or measurements that help us to summarize, describe, and make judgments about those measurements (p. 561)

stimulants drugs (such as caffeine, cocaine, and amphetamines) that increase nervous system activities (p. 138)

storage the process of holding encoded information in memory (p. 188)

strategy in problem solving, a systematic plan for generating possible solutions that can be tested to see if they are correct (p. 261)

stress a complex set of reactions to real or perceived threats to one's well-being that motivates adaptation (p. 398)

stressors the sources or stimuli for stress, which include frustration, conflict, and life events (p. 398)

structuralism associated with Wilhelm Wundt, the approach to psychology that seeks to understand the structure and operation of consciousness, or the human mind (p. 11)

subjective contours the perception of a contour (a line or plane) that is not there, but is suggested by other aspects of a scene (p. 105)

subliminal perception the process of perceiving and responding to stimuli presented at levels below one's absolute threshold (p. 124)

superego the aspect of personality that refers to ethical or moral considerations; it operates on the idealistic principle (p. 325)

survey the process of asking a large sample of persons a small set of questions (p. 22)

synapse the location where one neuron communicates with other cells via neurotransmitters (p. 43)

synaptic cleft the actual space between a neuron and the next cell at a synapse (p. 43)

syntax the rules that govern how the morphemes of a language are to be combined in order to form meaningful utterances (p. 252)

syphilis an STD caused by a bacterial infection; the disease may pass through four stages, ultimately resulting in death (p. 420)

systematic desensitization classical conditioning procedures, used to alleviate anxiety, in which anxiety-producing stimuli are paired with a state of relaxation (p. 481)

taste buds the receptors for taste located on the tongue (p. 92)

telegraphic speech utterances characterized by the use of nouns, verbs, and adjectives, and few function words (p. 255)

territoriality the setting off and marking of a piece of territory (a location) as one's own (p. 548)

thalamus just below the cerebral cortex, the last sensory relay station; projects sensory impulses to the appropriate areas of the cerebral cortex (p. 57)

Thematic Apperception Test (TAT) a projective personality test requiring a subject to tell a series of short stories about a set of ambiguous pictures (pp. 350, 380)

theory an organized collection of ultimately testable ideas used to explain a particular subject matter (p. 324)

thyroid gland endocrine gland that releases thyroxine, the hormone that regulates the pace of the body's functioning (p. 48)

timbre the psychological experience of wave purity by which we differentiate the qualities of tones (p. 89)

tolerance in using a drug, a state in which more and more of the drug is required to produce the same desired effect (p. 138)

training a systematic and intentional process of altering the behaviors of employees to increase organizational effectiveness (p. 535)

trait a distinguishable, relatively enduring way in which individuals may be described and in which they may differ (p. 337)

transducer a mechanism that converts energy from one form to another—a basic process common to all of our senses (p. 70)

transference in psychoanalysis, the situation in which the patient comes to feel about the analyst in the same way he or she once felt about some other important person (p. 479)

tremors involuntary trembling movements (p. 54)

Type A behavior pattern (TABP) a collection of behaviors (in which one is competitive, achievement-oriented, impatient, easily aroused, often hostile or angry) commonly associated with coronary heart disease (p. 414)

unconditioned response (UCR) in classical conditioning, a response (e.g., salivation in response to food) reliably and reflexively evoked by a stimulus (p. 152)

unconditioned stimulus (UCS) in classical conditioning, a stimulus (e.g., food powder) that reflexively and reliably evokes a response (p. 152)

validity in psychological testing, the extent to which a test measures what it claims to be measuring (p. 233)

variability the extent of spread or dispersion in a set or distribution of scores (p. 562)

vesicles small containers concentrated in a neuron's axon terminals that hold neurotransmitter molecules (p. 43)

vestibular sense the position sense that tells us about balance, about where we are in relation to gravity, and about acceleration or deceleration (p. 95)

viability the ability to survive without medical interference or intervention (p. 277)

vicarious reinforcement (or punishment) increasing the rate (with reinforcement) or decreasing the rate (with punishment) of responses due to observing the consequences of someone else's behaviors (p. 180)

vitreous humor the thick fluid behind the lens of the eye that helps keep the eyeball spherical (p. 79)

wavelength the distance between any point on a wave and the corresponding point on the next cycle of the wave (p. 75)

white light a light of the lowest possible saturation, containing a mixture of all visible wavelengths (p. 77)

white noise a sound made up of a random mixture of audible sound wave frequencies (p. 89)

withdrawal a negative reaction that may occur when one stops taking a drug (p. 138)

zygote the one-celled product of the union of sperm and ovum at conception (p. 276)

References

AARP. (1995). Negative stereotypes still plague older workers on the job. *AARP Bulletin, 36,* April, p. 3.

Abel, E. L. (1981). Behavioral teratology. *Psychological Bulletin, 90,* 564–581.

Ackerman, P. L. (1992). Predicting individual differences in complex skill acquisition: Dynamics of ability determinants. *Journal of Applied Psychology, 77,* 598–614.

Ackerman, P. L., & Kanfer, R. (1993). Integrating laboratory and field study for improving selection: Development of a battery for predicting air traffic controller success. *Journal of Applied Psychology, 78,* 413–432.

Adams, G. R. (1977). Physical attractiveness, personality, and social reactions to peer pressure. *Journal of Psychology, 96,* 287–296.

Adams, G. R., & Gullotta, T. (1983). *Adolescent life experiences.* Monterey, CA: Brooks/Cole.

Adams, J. L. (1974). *Conceptual blockbusting.* Stanford, CA: Stanford Alumni Association. Cited in A. L. Glass, K. J. Holyoak, & J. L. Santa (1979). *Cognition.* Reading, MA: Addison-Wesley.

Adams, J. S. (1965). Inequity in social exchange. In L. Berkowitz (Ed.), *Advances in experimental social psychology.* New York: Academic Press.

Adams, R. M. (1992). The "hot hand" revisited: Successful basketball shooting as a function of intershot interval. *Perceptual and Motor Skills, 74,* 934.

Adams, R. M. (1995). Momentum in the performance of professional tournament pocket billiards players. *International Journal of Sport Psychology, 26,* 580–587.

Adelmann, P. K., & Zajonc, R. B. (1989). Facial efference and the experience of emotion. *Annual Review of Psychology, 40,* 249–280.

Adelson, B. (1984). When novices surpass experts: The difficulty of a task may interfere with expertise. *Journal of Experimental Psychology, 10,* 483–495.

Adler, L. L., & Gielen, U. P. (1994). *Cross-cultural topics in psychology.* Westport, CT: Praeger.

Adler, N., & Matthews, K. (1994). Health psychology: Why do some people get sick and some stay well? *Annual Review of Psychology, 45,* 229–259.

Adler, N. E., Boyce, T., Chesney, M. A., Cohen, S., Folkman, S., Kahn, R. L., & Syme, S. L. (1994). Socioeconomic status and health: The challenge of the gradient. *American Psychologist, 49,* 15–24.

Adler, N. E., & Stone, G. (1984). Psychology in the health system. In J. Ruffini (Ed.). *Advances in medical social science.* New York: Gordon & Breach.

Adler, R., & Cohen, N. (1993). Psychoneuroimmunology: Conditioning and stress. *Annual review of Psychology, 44,* 23–51.

Adler, T. (1989). Cocaine babies face behavior deficits. *APA Monitor, 20,* 14.

Adler, T. (1990). Does the "new" MMPI beat the "classic"? *APA Monitor, 21,* 18–19.

Agnew, H. W., Webb, W. W., & Williams, R. L. (1964). The effects of stage 4 sleep deprivation. *Electroencephalography and Clinical Neurophysiology, 17,* 68–70.

Aiello, R. R., & Aiello, T. D. (1974). The development of personal space: Proxemic behavior of children 6 through 16. *Human Ecology, 2,* 177–189.

Aiken, L. R. (1984). *Psychological testing and assessment* (4th ed.). Boston: Allyn & Bacon.

Ainsworth, M. D. S. (1979). Infant–mother attachment. *American Psychologist, 34,* 932–937.

Ainsworth, M. D. S. (1989). Attachments beyond infancy. *American Psychologist, 44,* 709–716.

Ajzen, I., & Fishbein, M. (1980). *Understanding attitudes and predicting social behavior.* Englewood Cliffs, NJ: Prentice-Hall.

Alba, J. W., & Hasher, L. (1983). Is memory schematic? *Psychological Bulletin, 93,* 201–231.

Aldwin, C., & Stokals, D. (1988). The effects of environmental change on individuals and groups: Some neglected issues in stress research. *Journal of Environmental Psychology, 8,* 57–75.

Allen, J. L., Walker, L. D., Schroeder, D. A., & Johnson, D. E. (1987). Attributions and attribution-behavior relations: The effect of level of cognitive development. *Journal of Personality and Social Psychology, 52,* 1099–1109.

Allen, M. G. (1976). Twin studies of affective illness. *Archives of General Psychiatry, 33,* 1476–1478.

Allport, G. W. (1961). *Pattern and growth in personality.* New York: Holt, Rinehart & Winston.

Altman, I. (1975). *The environment and social behavior.* Monterey, CA: Brooks/Cole.

Amabile, T. M. (1985). Motivation and creativity. *Journal of Personality and Social Psychology, 48,* 393–399.

Amaro, H. (1995). Love, sex, and power: Considering women's realities in HIV prevention. *American Psychologist, 50,* 437–447.

Ambuel, B. (1995). Adolescents, unintended pregnancy, and abortion: The struggle for a compassionate social policy. *Current Directions in Psychological Science, 4,* 1–5.

American Association of Retired Persons. (1993). Census Bureau ups 65+ population estimates. *AARP Bulletin, 34,* 2.

American Psychiatric Association. (1987). *Diagnostic and statistical manual of mental disorders* (3rd rev. ed.). Washington, DC: American Psychiatric Association.

American Psychiatric Association. (1994). *Diagnostic and statistical manual of mental disorders* (4th ed.). Washington, DC: American Psychiatric Association.

American Psychological Association. (1992). Ethical principles of psychologists and code of conduct. *American Psychologist, 47,* 1597–1611.

Amoore, J. E. (1970). *Molecular basis of odor.* Springfield, IL: Thomas.

Anastasi, A. (1988). *Psychological testing* (6th ed.). New York: Macmillan.

Anderson, C. A. (1987). Temperature and aggression: Effects on quarterly, yearly, and city rates of violent and nonviolent crime. *Journal of Personality and Social Psychology, 52,* 1161–1173.

Anderson, C. A. (1989). Temperature and aggression: Ubiquitous effects of heat on occurrence of human violence. *Psychological Bulletin, 106,* 74–96.

Anderson, C. A., & Anderson, D. C. (1984). Ambient temperature and violent crime: Tests of the linear and curvilinear hypotheses. *Journal of Personality and Social Psychology, 46,* 91–97.

Anderson, J. R. (1976). *Language, memory, and thought.* Hillsdale, NJ: Erlbaum.

Anderson, J. R. (1983a). *The architecture of cognition.* Cambridge, MA: Harvard University Press.

Anderson, J. R. (1983b). A spreading activation theory of memory. *Journal of Verbal Learning and Verbal Behavior, 22,* 261–295.

Anderson, J. R. (1986). Knowledge compilation: The general learning mechanism. In R. Michalski, J. Carbonnell, & T. Mitchell (Eds.), *Machine learning II.* Palo Alto, CA: Tioga Press.

Anderson, J. R. (1987). Skill acquisition: Compilation of weak-method problem solutions. *Psychological Review, 94,* 192–210.

Anderson, R., & Nida, S. A. (1978). Effect of physical attractiveness on opposite- and same-sex evaluations. *Journal of Personality, 46,* 401–413.

Anderson, R. C., & Pichert, J. W. (1978). Recall of previously unrecallable information following a shift in perspective. *Journal of Verbal Learning and Verbal Behavior, 17,* 1–12.

Andreasen, N. C. (1982). Negative versus positive schizophrenia: Definition and validation. *Archives of General Psychiatry, 39,* 789–794.

Andreasen, N. C., Arndt, S., Alliger, R., Miller, D., & Flaum, M. (1995). Symptoms of schizophrenia: Methods, meanings, and mechanisms. *Archives of General Psychiatry, 52,* 341–351.

Andreasen, N. C., Ehrhardt, J. C., Swayze, V. W., Alliger, R. J, Yuh, W. T. C., Cohen, G., & Ziebell, S. (1990a). Magnetic resonance imaging of the brain in schizophrenia. *Archives of General Psychiatry, 47,* 35–44.

Andreasen, N. C., Flaum, M., Swayze, V. W., Tyrrell, G., & Arndt, S. (1990). Positive and negative symptoms in schizophrenia. *Archives of General Psychiatry, 47,* 615–621.

Andreasen, N. C., Olsen, S. A., Dennert, J. W., & Smith, M. R. (1982). Ventricular enlargement in schizophrenia: Definition and prevalence. *American Journal of Psychiatry, 139,* 292–296.

Andrews, R. J. (1963). Evolution of facial expression. *Science, 142,* 1034–1041.

Angoff, W. H. (1988). The nature-nurture debate, aptitudes, and group differences. *American Psychologist, 43,* 713–720.

Anisfeld, M. (1984). *Language development from birth to three.* Hillsdale, NJ: Erlbaum.

Anisman, H., & Zacharko, R. M. (1982). Depression: The predisposing influence of stress. *The Behavioral and Brain Sciences, 5,* 89–137.

Arndt, S., Andreasen, N. C., Flaum, M., Miller, D., & Nopoulos, P. (1995). A longitudinal study of symptom dimensions in schizophrenia. *Archives of General Psychiatry, 52,* 352–360.

Arnett, J. (1995). The young and the restless: Adolescent reckless behavior. *Current Directions in Psychological Science, 4,* 67–71.

Aronson, E., & Linder, D. (1965). Gain and loss of esteem as determinants of interpersonal attractiveness. *Journal of Personality and Social Psychology, 1,* 156–171.

Aronson, E., Turner, J. A., & Carlsmith, J. M. (1963). Communicator credibility and communication discrepancy as a determinant of opinion change. *Journal of Abnormal and Social Psychology, 67,* 31–36.

Arvey, R. D., & Campion, J. E. (1982). The employee interview: A summary and review of recent research. *Personnel Psychology, 35,* 281–322.

Arvey, R. D., Miller, H. E., Gould, R., & Burch, P. (1987). Interview validity for selecting sales clerks. *Personnel Psychology, 40,* 1–12.

Asch, S. E. (1951). The effects of group pressure upon the modification and distortion of judgment. In H. Guetzkow (Ed.), *Groups, leadership, and men.* Pittsburgh: Carnegie Press.

Asch, S. E. (1956). Studies of independence and conformity: I. A minority of one against a unanimous majority. *Psychologal Monographs: General and Applied, 70* (Whole No. 416), 1–7.

Aserinsky, E., & Kleitman, N. (1953). Regularly occurring periods of eye mobility and concomitant phenomena during sleep. *Science, 18,* 273–274.

Ashcraft, M. H. (1994). *Human Memory and Cognition* (2nd ed.). New York: HarperCollins.

Ashmore, R. D. (1990). Sex, gender, and the individual. In L. A. Pervin (Ed.), *Handbook of personality.* New York: Guilford.

Aslin, R. N., & Smith, L. B. (1988). Perceptual development. *Annual Review of Psychology, 39,* 435–473.

Aspinwall, L. G., & Taylor, S. E. (1992). Modeling cognitive adaptation: A longitudinal investigation of the impact of individual differences and coping on college adjustment and performance. *Journal of Personality and Social Psychology, 63,* 989–1003.

Atkinson, J. W., & Feather, N. T. (1966). *A theory of achievement motivation.* New York: Wiley.

Atkinson, J. W., & Litwin, G. H. (1960). Achievement motive and test anxiety conceived as motive to approach success and motive to avoid failure. *Journal of Abnormal and Social Psychology, 60,* 27–36.

Atkinson, R. C. (1975). Mnemotechnics in second-language learning. *American Psychologist, 30,* 821–828.

Atkinson, R. C., & Shiffrin, R. M. (1968). Human memory: A proposed system and its control processes. In K. W. Spence & J. T. Spence (Eds.), *The psychology of learning and motivation: Advances in research and theory.* New York: Academic Press.

Atwood, M. E., & Polson, P. G. (1976). A process model for water jug problems. *Cognitive Psychology, 8,* 191–216.

Auletta, K. (1984). Children of children. *Parade Magazine, 17,* 4–7.

Axelrod, S., & Apsche, J. (1983). *The effects of punishment on human behavior.* New York: Academic Press.

Azrin, N. H., & Holz, W. C. (1966). Punishment. In W. K. Honig

(Ed.), *Operant behavior: Areas of research and application.* Englewood Cliffs, NJ: Prentice-Hall.

Azumi, K., & McMillan, C. J. (1976). Worker sentiment in the Japanese factory: Its organizational determinants. In L. Austin (Ed.), *Japan: The paradox of progress.* New Haven, CT: Yale University Press.

Babor, T. F., Berglas, S., Mendelson, J. H., Ellinboe, J., & Miller, K. (1983). Alcohol, effect and the disinhibition of behavior. *Psychopharmacology, 80,* 53–60.

Bachorowski, J., & Owren, M. J. (1995). Vocal expression of emotion: Acoustic properties of speech are associated with emotional intensity and context. *Psychological Science, 6,* 219–224.

Backman, C. W., & Secord, P. F. (1959). The effect of perceived liking on interpersonal attraction. *Human Relations, 12,* 379–384.

Baddeley, A. (1990). *Human memory: Theory and practice.* Boston: Allyn & Bacon.

Baddeley, A. (1992). Working memory. *Science, 25,* 556–559.

Baddeley, A. D. (1982). Domains of recollection. *Psychological Review, 89,* 708–729.

Baer, L., Rauch, S. L., Ballantine, T., Martoza, R., Cosgrove, R., Cassem, E., et al. (1995). Cingulotomy for intractable obsessive-compulsive disorder. *Archives of General Psychiatry, 52,* 384–392.

Bagozzi, R. P., & Burnkrant, R. E. (1979). Attitude organization and the attitude-behavior relationship. *Journal of Personality and Social Psychology, 37,* 913–929.

Bahrick, H. P. (1984). Semantic memory content in perma-store. *Journal of Experimental Psychology: General, 13,* 1–29.

Bailey, J. M., & Pillard, R. C. (1991). A genetic study of male sexual orientation. *Archives of General Psychiatry, 48,* 1089–1096.

Baillargeon, R. (1993). The object concept revisited: New directions in the investigation of infants' physical knowledge. In C. E. Granrud (Ed.), *Visual perception and cognition in infancy.* Hillsdale, NJ: Lawrence Erlbaum Associates.

Baillargeon, R. (1995). How do infants learn about the physical world? *Current Directions in Psychological Science, 4,* 133–140.

Balay, J., & Shevrin, H. (1988). The subliminal psychodynamic activation method: A critical review. *American Psychologist, 43,* 161–174.

Baldwin, M. W. (1992). Relational schemas and the processing of social information. *Psychological Bulletin, 112,* 461–484.

Baley, S. (1985). The legalities of hiring in the 80s. *Personnel Journal, 64,* 112–115.

Ballenger, J. C. (1989). Toward an integrated model of panic disorder. *American Journal of Orthopsychiatry, 9,* 284–293.

Baltes, M. M. (1995). Dependency in old age: Gains and losses. *Current Directions in Psychological Science, 4,* 14–19.

Baltes, P. B., & Baltes, M. M. (1990). Selective optimization with compensation. In P. B. Baltes & M. M. Baltes (Eds.), *Successful aging: Perspectives from the behavioral sciences.* New York: Cambridge University Press.

Bandura, A. (1965). Influence of models' reinforcement contingencies on the acquisition of imitative responses. *Journal of Personality and Social Psychology, 1,* 589–595.

Bandura, A. (1974). Behavior theory and the models of man. *American Psychologist, 29,* 859–869.

Bandura, A. (1976). Modeling theory: Some traditions, trends and disputes. In W. S. Sahakian (Ed.), *Learning: Systems,*

models, and theories. Skokie, IL: Rand McNally.

Bandura, A. (1977). *Social learning theory.* Englewood Cliffs, NJ: Prentice-Hall.

Bandura, A. (1978). The self-system in reciprocal determinism. *American Psychologist, 33,* 344–358.

Bandura, A. (1982). Self-efficacy mechanism in human agency. *American Psychologist, 37,* 122–147.

Bandura, A., Ross, D., & Ross, S. A. (1963). Imitation of film-mediated aggressive models. *Journal of Abnormal and Social Psychology, 66,* 3–11.

Barber, T. F. X. (1972). Suggested (hypnotic) behavior: The trace paradigm vs. an alternative paradigm. In E. Fromm & R. E. Shorr (Eds.), *Hypnosis: Research developments and perspectives.* Chicago: Aldine-Atherton.

Barefoot, J. C., Dahlstrom, W. D., & Williams, R. B. (1983). Hostility, CHD incidence, and total mortality: A 25-year follow-up study of 255 physicians. *Psychosomatic Medicine, 45,* 59–63.

Bargh, J. A. (1993). The four horsemen of automaticity: Awareness, intention, efficiency and control in social cognition. In R. S. Wyer & T. K. Srull (Eds.), *Handbook of social cognition.* Hillsdale, NJ: Erlbaum.

Barinaga, M. (1991). Is homosexuality biological? *Science, 253,* 956–957.

Barinaga, M. (1995). "Obese" protein slims mice. *Science, 269,* 475–476.

Barker, R. (1968). *Ecological psychology.* Stanford, CA: Stanford University Press.

Barnette, R. C., Marshall, N. L., Raudenbush, S. W., & Brennan, R. T. (1993). Gender and the relationship between job experiences and psychological distress: A study of dual-earner couples. *Journal of Personality and Social Psychology, 64,* 794–806.

Baron, M., Freimer, N. F., Risch, N., Lerer, B., Alexander, J. R., et al. (1993). Diminished support for linkage between manic depressive illness and X-chromosome markers in three Israeli pedigrees. *Natural Genetics, 3,* 49–55.

Baron, R. A. (1977). *Human aggression.* New York: Plenum.

Baron, R. A., & Ransberger, V. M. (1978). Ambient temperature and the occurrence of collective violence: The "long hot summer" revisited. *Journal of Personality and Social Psychology, 36,* 351–360.

Barr, H. M., Streissguth, A. P., Darby, B. L., & Sampson, P. D. (1990). Prenatal exposure to alcohol, caffeine, tobacco, and aspirin: Effects on fine and gross motor performance in 4-year-old children. *Developmental Psychology, 26,* 339–348.

Barrett, G. V., & Depinet, R. L. (1991). A reconsideration of testing for competence rather than for intelligence. *American Psychologist, 46,* 1012–1024.

Barron, F., & Harrington, D. M. (1981). Creativity, intelligence, and personality. *Annual Review of Psychology, 32,* 439–476.

Barsalou, L. W. (1983). Ad hoc categories. *Memory and cognition, 11,* 211–227.

Barsalou, L. W. (1989). Intra-concept similarity and its implications for inter-concept similarity. In S. Vosniadou & A. Ortony (Eds.), *Similarity and analogical reasoning.* New York: Cambridge University Press.

Bartlett, F. C. (1932). *Remembering.* Cambridge: Cambridge University Press.

Bartoshuk, L. M., & Beauchamp, G. K. (1994). Chemical senses. *Annual Review of Psychology, 45,* 419–449.

Bartus, R. T., Dean, R. L., Beer, B., & Lippa, A. S. (1982). The cholinergic hypothesis of geriatric memory dysfunction. *Science, 217,* 408–417.

Basso, K. (1970). To give up words: Silence in Western Apache culture. *Southwestern Journal of Anthropology, 26,* 213–230.

Baum, A., & Grunberg, N. E. (1991). Gender, stress, and health. *Health Psychology, 10,* 80–85.

Baumeister, A. A. (1987). Mental retardation: Some conceptions and dilemmas. *American Psychologist, 42,* 796–800.

Baumeister, R. F. (1985). The championship choke. *Psychology Today, 19,* 48–52.

Baumeister, R. F. (1987). How the self became a problem: A Psychological review of historical research. *Journal of Personality and Social Psychology, 52,* 163–176.

Baumeister, R. F., & Steinhilber, A. (1984). Paradoxical effects of supportive audiences on performance under pressure: The home field disadvantage in sports championships. *Journal of Personality and Social Psychology, 47,* 85–93.

Bausbaum, A. I., & Levine, J. D. (1991). Opiate analgesia: How central is a peripheral target? *New England Journal of Medicine, 325,* 1168–1169.

Bayley, N. & Schaefer, E. S. (1964). Correlations of maternal and child behaviors with the development of mental abilities: Data from the Berkeley Growth Study. *Monographs of the Society for Research in Child Development, 29,* 1–80.

Beauvais, F., Oetting, E. R., Wolf, W., & Edwards, R. W. (1989). American Indian youth and drugs: 1975–1987, a continuing problem. *American Journal of Public Health, 79,* 634–636.

Beck, A. T. (1967). *Depression: Clinical, experimental, and theoretical aspects.* New York: HarperCollins.

Beck, A. T. (1976). *Cognitive therapy and the emotional disorders.* New York: International University Press.

Beck, A. T. (1985). Theoretical perspectives in clinical anxiety. In A. H. Tuma & J. D. Master (Eds.), *Anxiety and the anxiety disorders.* Hillsdale, NJ: Erlbaum.

Beck, A. T. (1991). Cognitive therapy: A 30-year retrospective. *American Psychologist, 46,* 368–375.

Beck, A. T., & Emery, G. (1985). *Anxiety disorders and phobias: A cognitive perspective.* New York: Basic Books.

Beck, A. T., & Freeman, A. (1990). *Cognitive therapy of personality disorders.* New York: Guilford.

Beckman, L. J., & Houser, B. B. (1982). The consequences of childlessness on the social-psycholagal well-being of older women. *Journal of Gerontology, 37,* 243–250.

Bee, H. (1995). *The developing child* (7th ed.). New York: HarperCollins.

Beecroft, R. (1966). *Classical conditioning.* Goleta, CA: Psychonomic Press.

Beer, M., & Walton, A. E. (1987). Organization change and development. *Annual Review of Psychology, 38,* 339–367.

Begg, I., & Paivio, A. (1969). Concreteness and imagery in sentence meaning. *Journal of Verbal Learning and Verbal Behavior, 8,* 812–817.

Bekerian, D. A. (1993). In search of the typical eyewitness. *American Psychologist, 48,* 574–576.

Bell, P. A., Fisher, J. D., & Loomis, R. J. (1978). *Environmental psychology.* Philadelphia: Saunders.

Bellack, A. S. (1986). Schizophrenia: Behavior therapy's forgotten child. *Behavior Therapy, 17,* 199–214.

Bellack, A. S., & Mueser, K. T. (1986). A comprehensive treatment program for schizophrenia and chronic mental illness. *Community Mental Health Journal, 22,* 175–189.

Belsher, G., & Costello, C. G. (1988). Relapse after recovery from unipolar depression: A critical review. *Psychological Bulletin, 104,* 84–96.

Belsky, J. (1990). The "effects" of infant day care reconsidered. In N. Fox & G. G. Fein (Eds.), *Infant day care: The current debate.* Norwood, NJ: Ablex.

Belsky, J., & Rovine, M. (1988). Nonmaternal care in the first year of life and the security of infant–parent attachment. *Child Development, 59,* 157–167.

Bem, S. (1981). Gender schema theory: A cognitive account of sex typing. *Psychological Review, 88,* 354–364.

Ben-Porath, Y. S., & Butcher, J. N. (1989). The comparability of MMPI and MMPI-2 scales and profiles. *Psychological Assessment, 1,* 345–347.

Ben-Yehuda, N. (1980). The European witch craze. *American Journal of Sociology, 86,* 1–31.

Benbow, C. P. (1987). Possible biological correlates of precocious mathematical reasoning ability. *Trends in Neuroscience, 10,* 17–20.

Benbow, C. P. (1990). Gender differences: Searching for facts. *American Psychologist, 45,* 988.

Benedict, H. (1979). Early lexical development: Comprehension and production. *Journal of Child Language, 6,* 183–200.

Bennett, T. L. (1982). *Introduction to physiological psychology.* Monterey, CA: Brooks/Cole.

Bennett, W. (1980). The cigarette century. *Science, 80,* 36–43.

Benson, H. (1975). *The relaxation response.* New York: Morrow.

Berkowitz, L. (1978). What ever happened to the frustration-aggression hypothesis? *American Behavioral Scientist, 21,* 691–708.

Berkowitz, L. (1982). Aversive conditions as stimuli to aggression. *Advances in Experimental Social Psychology, 15,* 249–288.

Berkowitz, L. (1989). Frustration-aggression hypothesis: Examination and reformulation. *Psychological Bulletin, 106,* 59–73.

Berkowitz, L. (1990). On the formation and regulation of anger and aggression. *American Psychologist, 45,* 494–503.

Berkowitz, H. (1994). U. S. Firms Trip Over Their Tongues in Wooing the World. *The Journal Gazette,* June 21, Fort Wayne, IN.

Berlyne, D. E. (1960). *Conflict, arousal, and curiosity.* New York: McGraw-Hill.

Berlyne, D. E. (1971). *Aesthetics and psychobiology.* Englewood Cliffs, NJ: Prentice-Hall.

Bernstein, I. (1978). Learned taste aversion in children receiving chemotherapy. *Science, 200,* 1302–1303.

Bernstein, R. (1981). The Y chromosome and primary sexual differentiation. *Journal of the American Medical Association, 245,* 1953–1956.

Berrettini, W. H., Golden, L. R., Gelernter, J., Gejman, P. V., Gershon, E. S., & Datera-Wadleigh, S. (1990). X-chromosome markers and manic-depressive illness. *Archives of General psychiatry, 47,* 366–374.

Berry, J., Poortinga, Y., Segall, M., & Dasen P. (1992). *Cross-cultural psychology: Research and applications.* New York: Cambridge University Press.

Berscheid, E. (1994). Interpersonal relationships. *Annual Review of Psychology, 45,* 79–129.

Bertenthal, B. I., & Campos, J. J. (1989). A systems approach to the organizing effects of self-produced locomotion during infancy. In C. Rovee-Collier & L. P. Lipsett (Eds.), *Advances in infancy research.* Norwood, NJ: Ablex.

Beutler, L. E., Crago, M., & Arizmendi, T. G. (1986). Therapist variables in psychotherapy process and outcome. In S. L. Garfield & A. E. Bergin (Eds.), *Handbook of psychotherapy and behavior change* (3rd ed.). New York: Wiley.

Beyer, S. (1990). Gender differences in the accuracy of self-evaluation and performance. *Journal of Personality and Social Psychology, 59,* 960–970.

Bhawuk, D. P. S., & Brislin, R. (1992). The measurement of intercultural sensitivity using the concepts of individualism and collectivism. *International Journal of Intercultural Relations, 16,* 413–436.

Billy, J. O. G., Tanfer, K., Grady, W. R., & Klepinger, D. H. (1993). The sexual behavior of men in the United States. *Family Planning Perspectives, 25,* 52–60.

Binder, J. L. (1993). Research findings on short-term psychodynamic therapy techniques. *Directions in Clinical Psychology, 3,* 10.3–10.13.

Birch, E. E., Gwiazda, J., & Held, R. (1983). The development of vergence does not account for the onset of stereopsis. *Perception, 12,* 331–336.

Birdwhistell, R. L. (1952). *Introduction to kinesics.* Louisville, KY: University of Louisville Press.

Birnbaum, M. H., & Mellers, B. A. (1979). Stimulus recognition may mediate exposure effects. *Journal of Personality and Social Psychology, 37,* 391–394.

Bjorklund, A., Dunnett, S. B., & Stenevi, U. (1980). Reinnervation of the denervated striatum by substantia nigra transplants: Functional consequences as revealed by pharmacological and sensorimotor testing. *Brain Research, 199,* 307–333.

Blanchard, D. C., & Blanchard, R. J. (1988). Ethoexperimental approaches to the biology of emotion. *Annual Review of Psychology, 39,* 43–68.

Blaney, P. H. (1986). Affect and memory: A review. *Psychological Bulletin, 99,* 229–246.

Blashfield, R. K., & Breen, M. J. (1989). Face validity of the DSM-III-R personality disorders. *American Journal of Psychiatry, 146,* 1575–1579.

Blass, E. M., Ganchow, J. R., & Steiner, J. E. (1984). Classical conditioning in newborn human infants 2–48 hours of age. *Infant Behavior and Development, 7,* 223–235.

Bleier, R., Houston, L., & Byne, W. (1987). Can the corpus callosum predict gender, age, handedness, or cognitive differences? *Trends in Neuroscience, 9,* 391–394.

Bloch, D., & Simon, R. (Eds.). (1982). *The strength of family therapy: Selected papers of Nathan Ackerman.* New York: Brunner/Mazel.

Block, J. (1965). *The challenge of response sets.* Englewood Cliffs, NJ: Prentice-Hall.

Bloodworth, R. C. (1987). Major problems associated with marijuana abuse. *Psychiatric Medicine, 3,* 173–184.

Bloom, F. E., Lazerson, A., & Hotstadter, L. (1985). *Brain, mind, and behavior.* San Francisco: Freeman.

Blum, J. E., Jarvik, L. F., & Clark, E. T. (1970). Rate of change on selective tests of intelligence: A twenty-year longitudinal study. *Journal of Gerontology, 25,* 171–176.

Bolles, R. C. (1970). Species-specific defense reactions and avoidance learning. *Psychological Review, 7,* 32–48.

Bolles, R. C. (1972). Reinforcement, expectancy, and learning. *Psychological Review, 79,* 394–409.

Bolles, R. C. (1975). Learning, motivation, and cognition. In W. K. Estes (Ed.), *Handbook of learning and cgnitive processes* (Vol. 1). Hillsdale, NJ: Erlbaum.

Bondareff, W., Mountjoy, C. Q., Wischik, C. M., Hauser, D. L., LaBree, L. D., & Roth, M. (1993). Evidence of subtypes of Alzheimer's disease and implications for etiology. *Archives of General Psychiatry, 50,* 350–356.

Bootzin, R. R., & Accella, J. R. (1984). *Abnormal psychology: Current perspectives* (4th ed.). New York: Random House.

Boraod, J. C. (1992). Interhemispheric and introhemispheric control of emotion: A focus on unilateral brain damage. *Journal of Consulting and Clinical Psychology, 60,* 339–348.

Borbely, A. (1986). *Secrets of sleep.* New York: Basic Books.

Bordens, K. S., & Abbott, B. B. (1991). *Research design and methods: A process approach.* Mountain View, CA: Mayfield.

Bornstein, R. F. (1989). Exposure and affect: Overview and meta-analysis of research 1968–1987. *Psychological Bulletin, 106,* 265–289.

Bornstein, R. F., Kale, A. R., & Cornell, K. R. (1990). Boredom as a limiting condition of the mere exposure effect. *Journal of Personality and Social Psychology, 58,* 791–800.

Bouchard, C., Tremblay, A., Després, J., et al. (1990). The response to long-term overfeeding in identical twins. *The New England Journal of Medicine, 322,* 1477–1482.

Bourne, L. E. (1992). Cognitive psychology: A brief verview. *Psychology Science Agenda, 5(5),* 5, 20.

Bourne, L. E., Dominowski, R. L., & Loftus, E. F. (1983). *Cognitive process.* Englewood Cliffs, NJ: Prentice-Hall.

Bousfield, W. A. (1953). The occurrence of clustering in the free recall of randomly arranged associates. *Journal of General Psychology, 49,* 229–240.

Bower, B. (1995). IQs evolutionary breakdown: Intelligence may have more facets than testers realize. *Science News, 147,* 220–222.

Bower, G. H. (1970). Imagery as a relational organizer in associative learning. *Journal of Verbal Learning and Verbal Behavior, 9,* 529–533.

Bower, G. H. (1972). Mental imagery and associative learning. In L. W. Gregg (Ed.), *Cognition in learning and memory.* New York: Wiley.

Bower, G. H. (1981). Mood and memory. *American Psychologist, 36,* 129–148.

Bower, G. H., & Clark, M. C. (1969). Narrative stories as mediators for serial learning. *Psychonomic Science, 14,* 181–182.

Bower, G. H., & Mayer, J. D. (1989). In search of mood-dependent retrieval. *Journal of Social Behavior and Personality, 4,* 133–168.

Bower, G. H., Monteiro, K. P., & Gilligan, S. G. (1978). Emotional mood as a context for learning and recall. *Journal of Verbal Learning and Verbal Behavior, 17,* 573–587.

Bower, G. H., & Springston, F. (1970). Pauses as recoding points in letter series. *Journal of Experimental Psychology, 83,* 421–430.

Bower, T. G. R., Broughton, J. M., & Moore, M. K. (1971). Infant responses to approaching objects: An indicator of response to distal variables. *Perception and Psychophysics, 9,* 193–196.

Bowers, J. S., & Schacter, D. L. (1990). Implicit memory and test awareness. *Journal of Experimental Psychology: Learning, Memory, and Cognition, 16,* 404–416.

Bowlby, J. (1982). *Attachment and loss: Vol. 1. Attachment* (2nd ed.). New York: Basic Books.

Bradbard, M. R., & Endsley, R. C. (1983). The effects of sex-typed labelling on preschool children's information seeking and retention. *Sex Roles, 9,* 247–260.

Bradley, D. R, & Dumais, S. T. (1975). Ambiguous cognitive contours. *Nature, 257,* 582–584.

Bradshaw, J. L., & Nettleton, N. C. (1983). *Human cerebral asymmetry.* Englewood Cliffs, NJ: Prentice-Hall.

Braine, M. D. S. (1976). Children's first word combinations. *Monographs for the Society for Research in Child Development, 4* (Serial No. 164).

Brandon, T. H. (1994). Negative affect as motivation to smoke. *Current Directions in Psychological Sciences, 3,* 33–37.

Bransford, J. D., & Johnson, M. K. (1972). Contextual prerequisites for understanding: Some investigations of comprehension and recall. *Journal of Verbal Learning and Verbal Behavior, 11,* 717–720.

Bratic, E. B. (1982). Healthy mothers, healthy babies coalition. *Prevention, 97,* 503–509.

Braun, P., Kochansky, G., Shapiro, R., Greenberg, S., Gudeman, J. E., Johnson, S., & Shore, M. (1981). Overview: Deinstitutionalization of psychiatric patients, a critical review of outcome studies. *American Journal of Psychiatry, 138,* 736–749.

Bray, D. W., Campbell, R. J., & Grant, D. L. (1974). *Formative years in business: A long-term AT&T study of managerial lives.* New York: Wiley.

Bregman, J., Dykens, E. Watson, M., & Leckman, J. (1987). Fragile X syndrome: Variability in phenotype expression. *Journal of the American Academy of Child and Adolescent Psychiatry, 26,* 463–471.

Brehm, J. W., & Self, E. A. (1989). The intensity of motivation. *Annual Review of Psychology, 40,* 109–131.

Breier, A., Schreiber, J. L., Dyer, J., & Pickar, D. (1991). National Institute of Mental Health longitudinal study of chronic schizophrenia: Prognosis and predictors of outcome. *Archives of General Psychiatry, 48,* 239–246.

Breland, K., & Breland, M. (1961). This misbehavior of organisms. *American Psychologist, 16,* 681–684.

Brett, J. F., Brief, A. P., Burke, M. J., George, J. M., & Webster, J. (1990). Negative affectivity and the reporting of stressful events. *Health Psychology, 9,* 57–68.

Brewer, W. F., & Nakamura, G. V. (1984). The nature and function of schemas. In R. S. Wyler and T. K. Sroll (Eds.), *Handbook of social cognition.* Hillsdale, NJ: Erlbaum.

Briggs, G. G., Freeman, R. K, & Yaffe, S. J. (1986). *Drugs in pregnancy and lactation* (2nd ed.). Baltimore: Williams & Wilkins.

Brigham, J. C. (1991). *Social psychology* (2nd ed.). New York: HarperCollins.

Brinkerhoff, R. O. (1989). *Evaluating training programs in business and industry.* San Francisco: Jossey-Bass.

Brislin, R. W. (1990). *Applied cross-cultural psychology.* Newbury Park, CA: Sage.

Brislin, R. W. (1993). *Understanding culture's influence on behavior.* Fort Worth, TX: Harcourt Brace.

Brody, E. M. (1981). Women in the middle and family help to older people. *Gerontologist, 21,* 471–480.

Brody, E. M. (1985). Parent care as a normative family stress. *Gerontologist, 25,* 19–29.

Brown, J. (1958). Some tests of the decay theory of immediate memory. *Quarterly Journal of Experimental Psychology, 10,* 12–21.

Brown, J. (1976). An analysis of recognition and recall and of

problems in their comparison. In J. Brown (Ed.), *Recall and recognition.* New York: Wiley.

Brown, J. D. (1991). Staying fit and staying well. *Journal of Personality and Social Psychology, 60,* 555–561.

Brown, J. I. (1973). *The Nelson-Denny reading test.* Boston: Houghton Mifflin.

Brown, K. W., & White, T. (1992). Syndromes of chronic schizophrenia and some clinical correlates. *British Journal of Psychiatry, 161,* 317–322.

Brown, N. A. (1985). Are offspring at risk from their father's exposure to toxins? *Nature, 316,* 110.

Brown, R. (1973). *A first language: The early stages.* Cambridge, MA: Harvard University Press.

Brown, R., Cazden, C. B., & Bellugi, U. (1969). The child's grammar from 1 to 3. *Symposia on child language* (Vol. 2). Minneapolis: University of Minnesota Press.

Brown, R., & Kulik, J. (1977). Flashbulb memories. *Cognition, 5,* 73–99.

Brown, T. A., & Barlow, D. H. (1992). Comorbidity among anxiety disorders: Implications for treatment and *DSM-IV. Journal of Consulting and Clinical Psychology, 60,* 835–844.

Browne, M. A., & Mahoney, M. J. (1984). Sport psychology. *Annual Review of Psychology, 35,* 605–626.

Brownell, K. D. (1993). Whether obesity should be treated. *Health Psychology, 12,* 339–341.

Brownell, K. D., & Rodin, J. (1994). The dieting maelstrom: Is it possible and advisable to lose weight? *American Psychologist, 49,* 781–791.

Bruch, H. (1980). Preconditions for the development of anorexia nervosa. *American Journal of Psychoanalysis, 40,* 169–172.

Bruner, J. S. & Goodman, C. C. (1947). Value and need as organizing factors in perception. *Journal of Abnormal and Social Psychology, 42,* 33–44.

Bruner, J. S., Goodnow, J. J., & Austin, G. A. (1956). *A study of thinking.* New York: Wiley.

Buck, R. (1980). Nonverbal behavior and the theory of emotion: The facial feedback hypothesis. *Journal of Personality and Social Psychology, 38,* 811–824.

Buck, R. (1985). Prime theory: An integrated view of motivation and emotion. *Psychological Review, 92,* 389–413.

Buckout, R. (1975). Nearly 2000 witnesses can be wrong. *Social Action and the Law, 2,* 7.

Burgoon, J. K., Birk, T., & Pfau, M. (1990). Non-verbal behaviors, persuasion, and credibility. *Human Communication Research, 17,* 140–169.

Burisch, M. (1984). Approaches to personality inventory construction. *American Psychologist, 39,* 214–227.

Bushnell, I. W. R., Sai, F., & Mullin, J. T. (1989). Neonatal recognition of the mother's face. *British Journal of Developmental Psychology, 7,* 3–15.

Buss, A. H. (1966). *Psychopathology.* New York: Wiley.

Buss, D. M. (1984). Evolutionary biology and personality psychology. *American Psychologist, 39,* 1135–1147.

Buss, D. M. (1985). Human mate selection. *American Scientist, 73,* 47–51.

Buss, D. M. (1989). Personality as traits. *American Psychologist, 44,* 1378–1388.

Buss, D. M., Abbott, M., Angleitner, A., Asherian, A., Biaggio, A., Blanco-Villasenor, A., et al. (1990). International preferences in mate selection: A study of 37 cultures. *Journal of Cross-Cultural Psychology, 21,* 5–47.

Buss, D. M., & Barnes, M. (1986). Preferences in human mate selection. *Journal of Personality and Social Psychology, 50,* 559–570.

Butler, R., & Emr, M. (1982). SDAT research: Current trends. *Generations, 7,* 14–18.

Butler, R., & Lewis, M. (1981). *Aging and mental health.* St. Louis: Mosby.

Byrd, K. R. (1994). The narrative reconstruction of incest survivors. *American Psychologist, 49,* 439–440.

Byrne, D. (1971). *The attraction paradigm.* New York: Academic Press.

Cacioppo, J. T., Marshall-Goodell, B. S., Tassinary, L. G., & Petty, R. E. (1992). Rudimentary determinants of attitudes: Classical conditioning is more effective when prior knowledge about the attitude stimulus is low than high. *Journal of Experimental Social Psychology, 28,* 207–233.

Cacioppo, J. T., & Petty, R. E. (1989). Effects of message repetition on argument processing, recall, and persuasion. *Basic Applied Social Psychology, 10,* 3–12.

Calhoun, J. B. (1962). Population density and social pathology. *Scientific American, 206,* 139–148.

Campbell, J. P. (1988). Training design for performance improvement. In J. P. Campbell & R. J. Campbell (Eds.), *Productivity in organizations.* San Francisco: Jossey-Bass.

Campbell, J. P., McHenry, J. J., & Wise, L. L. (1990). Modeling job performance in a population of jobs. *Personnel Psychology, 43,* 313–333.

Campfield, L. A., Smith, F. J., Guisez, Y., Devos, R., & Burn, P. (1995). Recombinant mouse OB protein: Evidence for a peripheral signal linking adiposity and central neural networks. *Science, 269,* 546–549.

Campos, J. J. Heart rates: A sensitive tool for the study of emotional development. In L. Lipsett (Ed.), *Developmental psychobiology: The significance of infancy.* Hillsdale, NJ: Erlbaum.

Campos, J. J., Hiatt, S., Ramsey, D., Henderson, C., & Svejda, M. (1978). The emergence of fear on the visual cliff. In M. Lewis & L. A. Rosenbaum (Eds.), *The development of affect.* New York: Plenum.

Cannon, T. D., Mednick, S. A., & Parnas, J. (1990). Antecedents of predominantly negative- and predominantly positive-symptom schizophrenia in a high-risk population. *Archives of General Psychiatry, 47,* 622–632.

Cannon, W. B. (1932). *The wisdom of the body.* New York: Norton.

Caplan, N. (1989). *The boat people and achievement in America: A study of family life, hard work, and cultural values.* Ann Arbor: University of Michigan Press.

Carey, S. (1978). The child as word learner. In M. Halle, J. Bresnan, & G. A. Miller (Eds.), *Linguistic theory and psychological reality.* Cambridge, MA: MIT Press.

Carlson, N. R. (1991). *Physiology of behavior* (4th ed.). Boston: Allyn & Bacon.

Carone, B. J., Harrow, M., & Westermeyer, J. F. (1991). Posthospital course and outcome in schizophrenia. *Archives of General Psychiatry, 48,* 247–253.

Carpenter, W. T., Jr., & Buchanan, R. W. (1994). Medical progress: Schizophrenia. *New England Journal of Medicine, 330,* 681–690.

Carson, R. C. (1989). Personality. *Annual Review of Psychology, 40,* 227–248.

Carson, R. C., & Butcher, J. N. (1992). *Abnormal psychology and modern life* (9th ed.). New York: HarperCollins.

Carson, R. L. (1962). *Silent spring.* Boston: Houghton Mifflin.

Carson, T. P., & Carson, R. C. (1984). The affective disorders. In H. E. Adams & P. B. Sutker (Eds.), *Comprehensive handbook of psychpathology.* New York: Plenum.

Carver, C. S., & Gaines, J. G. (1987). Optimism, pessimism, and postpartum depression. *Cognitive Therapy and Research, 11,* 449–462.

Cash, T. F., & Derlega, V. J. (1978). The matching hypothesis: Physical attractiveness among same-sexed friends. *Personality and Social Psychology Bulletin, 4,* 240–243.

Cash, T. F., & Kilcullen, R. N. (1985). The eye of the beholder: Susceptibility to sexism and beautyism in the evaluation of managerial applicants. *Journal of Applied Social Psychology, 15,* 591–605.

Cattell, R. (1963). Theory of fluid and crystallized intelligence: A critical experiment. *Journal of Educational Psychology, 54,* 1–22.

Cattell, R. B. (1973). *Personality and mood by questionnaire.* San Francisco: Jossey-Bass.

Cattell, R. B. (1979). *The structure of personality in its environment.* New York: Springer.

Cavaliere, F. (1995). APA and CDC join forces to combat illness. *The PA Monitor, 26,* 1, 13.

Cavanaugh, J. C., & Park, D. C. (1993). Vitality for life: Psychological research for productive aging. *APS Observer,* Special Issue: December.

Cermak, L. S., & Craik, F. I. M. (Eds.). (1979). *Levels of processing in human memory.* Hillsdale, NJ: Erlbaum.

Chagnon, N. A. (1983). *Yanomamö: The fierce people* (3rd ed.). New York: Holt, Rinehart & Winston.

Chaiken, S., & Stangor, C. (1987). Attitudes and attitude change. *Annual Review of Psychology, 38,* 575–630.

Charney, D. S., Deutch, A. Y., Krystal, J. H., Southwick, S. M., & Davis, M. (1993). Psychobiological mechanisms of posttraumatic stress disorder. *Archives of General Psychiatry, 50,* 294–305.

Chase, M. H., & Morales, F. R. (1990). The atonia and myoclonia of active (REM) sleep. *Annual Review of Psychology, 41,* 557–584.

Chase, W. G., & Simon, H. A. (1973). The mind's eye in chess. In W. G. Chase (Ed.), *Visual information processing.* New York: Academic Press.

Chasnoff, I. J., Griffith, D. R., MacGregor, S., Dirkes, K., & Burns, K. (1989). Temporal patterns of cocaine use in pregnancy. *Journal of the American Medical Association, 261,* 1741–1744.

Cheesman, J., & Merikle, P. M. (1984). Priming with and without awareness. *Perception and Psychophysics, 36,* 387–395.

Chi, M. T. H., & Glaser, R. (1985). Problem solving ability. In R. J. Sternberg (Ed.), *Advances in the psychology of human intelligence.* San Francisco: Freeman.

Chilman, C. S. (1980). Parent satisfactions, concerns, and goals for their children. *Family Relations, 29,* 339–346.

Chilman, C. S. (1983). *Adolescent sexuality in a changing American society: Social and psychological perspectives for the human services profession* (2nd ed.). New York:Wiley.

Chomsky, N. (1957). *Syntactic structures.* The Hague: Mouton.

Chomsky, N. (1965). *Aspects of a theory of syntax.* Cambridge, MA: Harvard University Press.

Chomsky, N. (1975). *Reflections on language.* New York: Pantheon Books.

Chomsky, N. (1986). *Knowledge of language: Its nature, origin, and use.* New York: Praeger.

Chuang, H. T., Devins, G. M., Hunsley, J., & Gill, M. J. (1989). Psychosocial distress and well-being among gay and bisexual men with immunodeficiency virus infection. *American Journal of Psychiatry, 146,* 876–880.

CIBA-GEIGY. (1991). *OCD: When a habit isn't just a habit.* Pine Brook, NJ: CIBA-GEIGY Corporation.

Clark, D. M., & Teasdale, J. D. (1985). Constraints on the effects of mood on memory. *Journal of Personality and Social Psychology, 48,* 1595–1608.

Clark, L. A., Watson, D., & Reynolds, S. (1995). Diagnosis and classification of psychopathology: Challenges to the current system and future directions. *Annual Review of Psychology, 46,* 121–153.

Clarkson-Smith, L., & Hartley, A. A. (1989). Relationships between physical exercise and cognitive abilities in older adults. *Psychology and Aging, 4,* 183–189.

Clifford, B. R., & Lloyd-Bostock, S. (Eds.). (1983). *Evaluating witness evidence: Recent psychological research and new perspectives.* Norwood, NJ: Ablex.

Clifford, M. M., & Hatfield, E. (1973). The effect of physical attractiveness on teacher expectation. *Sociology of Education, 46,* 248–258.

Clinton, J. J. (1992). Acute pain management can be improved. *The Journal of the American Medical Association, 267,* 2580.

Clore, G. L., & Byrne, D. (1974). A reinforcement-affect model of attraction. In T. L. Huston (Ed.), *Foundations of interpersonal attraction.* New York: Academic Press.

Cohen, G. D. (1980). *Fact sheet: Senile dementia (Alzheimer's disease).* [No. ADM 80-929]. Washington, DC: Center for Studies of the Mental Health of the Aging.

Cohen, L. R., DeLoach, J., & Stauss, M. (1978). Infant visual perception. In J. Osofky (Ed.), *The handbook of infant development.* New York: Wiley.

Cohen, S., Evans, G. W., Krantz, D. S., Stokols, D., & Kelly, S. (1980). Aircraft noise and children: Longitudinal and cross-sectional evidence on the adaptation to noise and the effectiveness of noise abatement. *Journal of Personality and Social Psychology, 40,* 331–345.

Cohen, S., Evans, G. W., Stokols, D., & Krantz, D. S. (1986). *Behavior, health, and environmental stress.* New York: Plenum.

Cohen, S., & Lichtenstein, E. (1990). Perceived stress, quitting smoking, and smoking relapse. *Health Psychology, 9,* 466–478.

Cohen, S., Lichtenstein, E., Prochaska, J. O., Rossi, J. S., Gritz, E. R., Carr, C. R., et al. (1989). Debunking myths about self-quitting: Evidence from 10 prospective studies of persons who attempt to quit smoking by themselves. *American Psychologist, 44,* 1355–1365.

Colby, A., & Kohlberg, L. (1984). Invariant sequence and internal consistency in moral judgment stages. In W. M. Kurtines & J. L. Gewitz (Eds.), *Morality, moral behavior, and moral development.* New York: Wiley.

Cole, J. O. (1988). Where are those new antidepressants we were promised? *Archives of General Psychiatry, 45,* 193–194.

Cole, R. E. (1979). *Work, mobility, and participation.* Berkeley: University of California Press.

Coleman, H. L. K., Wampold, B. E., & Casali, S. L. (1995). Ethnic minorities' ratings of ethnically similar and European-American counselors: A meta-analysis. *Journal of Counseling Psychology, 42,* 55–64.

Coles, R., & Stokes, G. (1985). *Sex and the American teenager.*

New York: HarperCollins.

College Board. (1989). *College-bound seniors: 1989 SAT profile.* New York: College Entrance Examination Board.

Collins, A. M., & Loftus, E. F. (1975). A spreading activation theory of semantic processing. *Psychological Review, 82,* 407–428.

Collins, A. M., & Quillian, M. R. (1960). Retrieval time from semantic memory. *Journal of Verbal Learning and Verbal Behavior, 8,* 240–247.

Collins, W. A., & Gunnar, M. R. (1990). Social and personality development. *Annual Review of Psychology, 41,* 387–416.

Committee on an Aging Society. (1986). *America's aging: Productive roles in an older society.* Washington, DC: National Academy Press.

Committee on Lesbian and Gay Concerns. (1991). Avoiding heterosexual bias in language. *American Psychologist, 46,* 973–974.

Compas, B. E., Hinden, B. R., & Gerhardt, C. A. (1995). Adolescent development: Pathways and processes of risk and resilience. *Annual Review of Psychology, 46,* 265–293.

Conger, J. J. (1991). *Adolescence and youth* (4th ed.). New York: HarperCollins.

Conger, J. J., & Peterson, A. C. (1984). *Adolescence and youth: Psychological development in a changing world.* New York: HarperCollins.

Conrad, R. (1963). Acoustic confusions and memory span for words. *Nature, 197,* 1029–1030.

Conrad, R. (1964). Acoustic confusions in immediate memory. *British Journal of Psychology, 55,* 75–84.

Cooper, J., & Croyle, R. T. (1984). Attitudes and attitude change. *Annual Review of Psychology, 35,* 395–426.

Cooper, J., & Scher, S. J. (1992). Actions and attitudes: The role of responsibility and aversive consequences in persuasion. In T. Brock & S. Shavitt (Eds.), *The psychology of persuasion.* San Francisco: Freeman.

Cooper, L. A., & Shepard, R. N. (1973). Chronometric studies of the rotation of mental images. In W. G. Chase (Ed.), *Visual information processing.* New York: Academic Press.

Cordua, G. D., McGraw, K. O., & Drabman, R. S. (1979). Doctor or nurse: Children's perception of sex typed occupations. *Child Development, 50,* 590–593.

Coren, S. (1972). Subjective contours and apparent depth. *Psychological Review, 79,* 359–367.

Coren, S., & Girgus, J. S. (1978). *Seeing is deceiving: The psychology of visual illusions.* Hillsdale, NJ: Erlbaum.

Corkin, S. (1984). Lasting consequences of bilateral medial temporal lobectomy: Clinical course and experimental findings in H. M. *Seminars in Neurology, 4,* 249–259.

Cornblatt, B. A., & Erlenmeyer-Kimling, L. (1985). Global attention deviance as a marker of risk for schizophrenia: Specificity and predictive validity. *Journal of Abnormal Psychology, 94,* 470–486.

Costa, P. T., & McCrae, R. R. (1980). Still stable after all these years: Personality as a key to some issues in adulthood and old age. In P. B. Baltes & O. G. Brim, Jr. (Eds.), *Life-span development and behavior.* New York: Academic Press.

Costello, C. G. (1982). Fears and phobias in women: A community study. *Journal of Abnormal Psychology, 91,* 280–286.

Coté, T. R., Biggar, R. J., & Dannenberg, A. L. (1992). Risk of suicide among persons with AIDS: A national assessment. *Journal of the American Medical Association, 268,* 2066–2068.

Coulter, W. A., & Morrow, H. W. (Eds.). (1978). *Adaptive behavior:*

Concepts and measurements. New York: Grune & Stratton.

Council, J. R. (1993). Context effects in personality research. *Current Directions in Psychological Science, 2,* 3–34.

Cowan, G., & Avants, S. K. (1988). Children's influence strategies: Structure, sex differences, and bilateral mother-child influences. *Child Development, 59,* 1303–1313.

Cowan, N. (1984). On short and long auditory stores. *Psychological Bulletin, 96,* 341–370.

Cowan, N. (1993). Activation, attention, and short-term memory. *Memory and Cognition, 21,* 162–167.

Cowan, N. (1994). Mechanisms of verbal short-term memory. *Current Directions in Psychological Science, 3,* 185–189.

Cowan, W. M. (1979). The development of the brain. In *The brain* (pp. 56–69). San Francisco: Freeman.

Cox, R. H. (1990). *Sport psychology: Concepts and applications.* Dubuque, IA: Brown.

Coyle, J. T., Price, D. L., & DeLong, M. H. (1983). Alzheimer's disease: A disorder of central cholinergic innervation. *Science, 219,* 1184–1189.

Coyne, J. C., & Downey, G. (1991). Social factors and psychopathology: Stress, social support, and coping processes. *Annual Review of Psychology, 42,* 401–425.

Cozby, P. C. (1973). Self-disclosure: A literature review. *Psychological Bulletin, 79,* 73–91.

Craik, F. I. M. (1970). The fate of primary memory items in free recall. *Journal of Verbal Learning and Verbal Behavior, 9,* 143–148.

Craik, F. I. M., & Lockhart, R. S. (1972). Levels of processing: A framework for memory research. *Journal of Verbal Learning and Verbal Behavior, 11,* 671–684.

Craik, F. I. M., & Tulving, E. (1975). Depth of processing and the retention of words in episodic memory. *Journal of Experimental Psychology: General, 104,* 268–294.

Cramer, R. E., McMaster, M. R., Bartell, P. A., & Dragna, M. (1988). Subject competence and minimization of the bystander effect. *Journal of Applied Social Psychology, 18,* 1133–1148.

Creekmore, C. R. (1984). Games athletes play. *Psychology Today, 19,* 40–44.

Creekmore, C. R. (1985). Cities won't drive you crazy. *Psychology Today, 19,* 46–53.

Crews, D. J., & Landers, D. M. (1987). A meta-analytic review of aerobic fitness and reactivity to psychosocial stressors. *Medicine and Science in Sport and Exercise 19,* 114–120.

Crockett, L. J., & Peterson, A. C. (1987). Pubertal status and psychosocial development: Findings from the Early Adolescence Study. In R. M. Lerner & T. T. Foch (Eds.), *Biological-psychosocial interactions in early adolescence: A life-span approach.* Hillsdale, NJ: Erlbaum.

Cromwell, R. L. (1993). Searching for the origins of schizophrenia. *Psychological Science, 4,* 276–279.

Cross-National Collaborative Group. (1992). The changing rate of major depression: Cross-national comparisons. *Journal of the American Medical Association, 268,* 3098–3105.

Crow, T. J. (1980). Molecular pathology of schizophrenia: More than one disease process? *The British Medical Journal, 280,* 66–68.

Crowder, R. G. (1993). Short-term memory: Where do we stand? *Memory and Cognition, 2,* 142–145.

Cunningham, S. (1984). Genovese: 20 years later, few heed stranger's cries. *APA Monitor, 15,* 30.

Curtis, R. C., & Miller, K. (1986). Believing another likes or dislikes you: Behaviors making the beliefs come true. *Journal of Personality and Social Psychology, 51,* 284–290.

Cushner, K. (1990). Cross-cultural psychology and the formal classroom. In R. W. Brislin (Ed.), *Applied cross-cultural psychology.* Newbury Park, CA: Sage.

Cutler, W. B., Preti, G., Krieger, A., Huggins, G. R., Ramon Garcia, C., & Lawley, H. J. (1986). Human axillary secretions influence women's menstrual cycles: The role of donor extract from men. *Hormones and Behavior, 20,* 463–473.

Dadler, H., & Gustavson, P. (1992). Competition by effective management of cultural diversity in the case of international construction projects. *International Studies of Management and Organizations, 22,* 81–93.

Dahlstrom, W. G. (1993). Tests: Small samples, large consequences. *American Psychologist, 48,* 393–399.

Daniel, T. C. (1990). Measuring the quality of the natural environment: A psychophysical approach. *American Psychologist, 45,* 633–637.

Darley, J. M., & Fazio, R. H. (1980). Expectancy confirmation processes arising in the interaction sequence. *American Psychologist, 35,* 861–866.

Darley, J. M., & Schultz, T. R. (1990). Moral rules: Their content and acquisition. *Annual Review of Psychology, 41,* 525–556.

Darling, C. A., & Davidson, J. K. (1986). Coitally active university students: Sexual behaviors, concerns, and challenges. *Adolescence, 21,* 403–419.

Darwin, C. T., Turvey, M. T., & Crowder, R. G. (1972). An auditory analogue of the Sperling partial report procedure: Evidence for brief auditory storage. *Cognitive Psychology, 3,* 255–267.

Dasen, P., & Heron, A. (1981). Cross-cultural tests of Piaget's theory. In H. C. Triandis & A. Heron (Eds.), *Handbook of cross-cultural psychology: Vol. 4. Developmental Psychology.* Boston: Allyn & Bacon.

Dasen, P. R., & de Ribaupierre, A. (1987). Neo-Piagetian theories: Cross-cultural and differential perspectives. *International Journal of Psychology, 22,* 793–832.

Datan, N., Rodehever, D., & Hughes, F. (1987). Adult development and aging. *Annual Review of Psychology, 38,* 153–180.

Daubman, K. A., Heatherinton, L., & Ahn, Alicia (1992). Gender and the self-presentation of academic achievement. *Sex Roles, 27,* 187–204.

Davidoff, J. B. (1975). *Differences in visual perception: The individual eye.* New York: Academic Press.

Davidson, J. M., Smith, E. R., Rodgers, C. H., & Bloch, G. J. (1968). Relative thresholds of behavioral and somatic responses to estrogen. *Physiology and Behavior, 3,* 227–229.

Davidson, J. R. T., Hughs, D. C., George, L. K., & Blazer, D. G. (1994). The boundary of social phobia: Exploring the threshold. *Archives of General Psychiatry, 51,* 975–983.

Davis, K. (1985). Near and dear: Friendship and love compared. *Psychology Today, 19,* 22–30.

Davis, L. E., & Cherns, A. B. (1975). *The quality of working life: Vol. I. Problems, prospects and the state of the art.* New York: Free Press.

de Cuevas, J. (1990, September/October). "No, she held them loosely." *Harvard Magazine,* pp. 60–67.

DeAngelis, T. (1989). Behavior is included in report on smoking. *APA Monitor, 20,* 3–4.

DeAngelis, T. (1994). Ethnic-minority issues recognized in *DSM-IV. Monitor,* November, p. 36.

deBoer, C. (1978). The polls: Attitudes toward work. *Public Opinion Quarterly, 42,* 414–423.

DeBono, K. G., & Harnish, R. J. (1988). Source expertise, source attractiveness, and the processing of persuasive information: A functional approach. *Journal of Personality and Social Psychology, 55,* 541–546.

DeCasper, A. J., & Fifer, W. P. (1980). Of human bonding: Newborns prefer their mother's voice. *Science, 208,* 1174–1176.

DeCasper, A. J., & Sigafoos, A. D. (1983). The intrauterine heartbeat: A potent reinforcer for newborns. *Infant Behavior and Development, 6,* 19–25.

Deffenbacher, J. L. (1988). Some recommendations and directions. *Counseling Psychology, 35,* 234–236.

DeGroot, A. D. (1965). *Thought and chance in chess.* The Hague: Mouton.

DeGroot, A. D. (1966). Perception and memory versus thought: Some old ideas and recent findings. In B. Kleinmuntz (Ed.), *Problem solving.* New York: Wiley.

DeJarlais, D. C., & Friedman, S. R. (1988). The psychology of preventing AIDS among intravenous drug users: A social learning conceptualization. *American Psychologist, 43,* 865–870.

DeLongis, A., Folkman, S., & Lazarus, R. S. (1988). The impact of daily stress on health and mood: Psychological and social resources as mediators. *Journal of Personality and Social Psychology, 54,* 486–495.

Dembroski, T. M., & Costa, P. T., Jr. (1987). Coronary prone behavior: Components of the Type A pattern and hostility. *Journal of Personality, 55,* 211–235.

Dembroski, T. M., MacDougall, J. M., Williams, R. B., Haney, T. I., & Blumenthal, J. A. (1985). Components of Type A, hostility, and anger in relationship to angiographic findings. *Psychosomatic Medicine, 47,* 219–233.

Dement, W. C. (1974). *Some must watch while some must sleep.* San Francisco: Freeman.

Deregowski, J. B. (1972). Pictorial perception and culture. *Scientific American, 83.*

Deregowski, J. B. (1973). Illusion and culture. In R. L. Gregory & G. H. Gombrich (Eds.), *Illusion in nature and art.* New York: Scribner's (pp. 161–192).

Derlega, V. J., Winstead, B. A., & Jones, W. H. (1991). *Personality: Contemporary theory and research.* Chicago: Nelson-Hall.

Deutsch, J. A. (1973). The cholinergic synapse and the site of memory. In J. A. Deutsch (Ed.), *The physiological basis of memory.* New York: Academic Press.

deVilliers, J. G., & deVilliers, P. A. (1978). *Language acquisition.* Cambridge, MA: Harvard University Press.

Diamond, M., & Karlen, A. (1980). *Sexual decisions.* Boston: Litte, Brown.

Diamond, M. C., Lindner, B., Johnson, R., Bennett, E. L., & Rosenzweig, M. R. (1975). Differences in occipital cortical synapses from environmentally enriched, impoverished, and standard colony rats. *Journal of Neuroscience Research, 1,* 109–119.

Digman, J. M. (1990). Personality structure: Emergence of the five-factor model. *Annual Review of Psychology, 41,* 417–440.

DiMatteo, M. R., & Friedman, H. S. (1988). *Social psychology and medicine.* Cambridge, MA: Oeleschlager, Gunn & Hain.

Dion, K. K. (1972). Physical attractiveness and evaluation of children's transgressions. *Journal of Personality and Social Psychology, 24,* 207–213.

Dion, K. K., Berscheid, E., & Walster (Hatfield), E. (1972). What is beautiful is good. *Journal of Personality and Social Psychology, 24,* 285–290.

Dirkes, M. A. (1978). The role of divergent production in the learning process. *American Psychologist, 33,* 815–820.

Dixon, N. F. (1971). *Subliminal perception: The nature of a controversy.* New York: McGraw-Hill.

Dixon, N. F. (1981). *Preconscious processing.* New York: Wiley.

Dobson, K. S. (1988). *Handbook of cognitive-behavioral therapies.* New York: Guilford.

Doll, R., & Peto, R. (1981). *The causes of cancer.* New York: Oxford University Press.

Dollard, J. Doob, L., Miller, N., Mowrer, O. H., & Sears, R. R. (1939). *Frustration and aggression.* New Haven, CT: Yale University Press.

Domjan, M. (1987). Animal learning comes of age. *American Psychologist, 42,* 556–564.

Donnenberg, G. R., & Hoffman, L. W. (1988). Gender differences in moral development. *Sex Roles, 18,* 701–717.

Doty, R. Y. (1986). Gender and endocrine-related influences on human olfactory perception. In H. Meiselman & R. S. Rivlin (Eds.), *Clinical measurement of taste and smell.* New York: Macmillan.

Doweiko, H. E. (1993). *Concepts of chemical dependency* (2nd ed.). Pacific Grove, CA: Brooks/Cole.

Drakeley, R. J., Herriot, P., & Jones, A. (1988). Biographical data, training success and turnover. *Journal of Occupational Psychology, 61,* 145–152.

Duffy, E. (1962). *Activation and behavior.* New York: Wiley.

Duncan, J. (1985). Two techniques for investigating perception without awareness. *Perception and Pychophysics, 38,* 296–298.

Dunham, R. B. (1979). Job design and redesign. In S. Kerr (Ed.), *Organizational behavior.* Columbus, OH: Grid.

Dunker, K. (1945). On problem solving. *Psychological Monographs, 58* (Whole No. 27).

Dunnette, M. D., & Borman, W. C. (197). Personnel selection and classification systems. *Annual Review of Psychology, 30,* 477–525.

Dupont, R. M., Jernigan, T. L., Heindel, W., Butters, N., Shafer, K., Wilson, T., Hesselin, J., & Gillin, C. (1995). Magnetic resonance imaging and mood disorders: Localization of white matter and other subcortical abnormalities. *Archives of General Psychiatry, 52,* 747–755.

Dweck, C. S. (1986). Motivational processes affecting learning. *American Psychologist, 41,* 1040–1048.

Dywan, J., & Bowers, K. (1983). The use of hypnosis to enhance recall. *Science, 222,* 184–185.

Eagly, A. H. (1987). *Sex differences in social behavior: A social-role interpretation.* Hillsdale, NJ: Lawrence Erlbaum Associates.

Eagly, A. H. (1995). The science and politics of comparing women and men. *American Psychologist, 50,* 145–158.

Eagly, A. H., & Chaiken, S. (1992). *The psychology of attitudes.* San Diego: Harcourt Brace Jovanovich.

Eagly, A. H., & Steffen, V. J. (1986). Gender and aggressive behavior: A meta-analytic review of the social psychological literature. *Psychological Bulletin, 100,* 309–330.

Eaker, E. D., Packard, B., Wenger, N. K., et al. (1988). Coronary heart disease in women. *American Journal of Cardiology, 61,* 641–644.

Eaker, E. D., Pinsky, J., & Castelli, W. P. (1992). Myocardial infarction and coronary death among women: Psychosocial predictors from a 20-year follow-up on women in the Framingham study. *American Journal of Epidemiology, 135,* 854–864.

Early, P. C. (1986). Supervisors and shop stewards as sources of contextual information in goal-setting: A comparison of the U.S. with England. *Journal of Applied Psychology, 71,* 111–118.

Early, P. C. (1989). Social loafing and collectivism: A comparison of the United States and the People's Republic of China. *Administrative Science Quarterly, 34,* 555–581.

Eaton, W. O., & Enns, L. R. (1986). Sex differences in human motor activity level. *Psychological Bulletin, 100,* 19–28.

Eaton, W. W., Thara, R., Federman, B., Melton, B., & Liang, K. (1955). Structure and course of positive and negative symptoms in schizophrenia. *Archives of General Psychiatry, 52,* 127–134.

Ebbinghaus, H. E. (1885/1964). *Memory: A contribution to experimental psychology.* New York: Dover.

Ebstein, R. P., Novick, O., Umansky, R., Priel, B., et al. (1996). Dopamine D4 Receptor (D4DR) Exon III polymorphism associated with the human personality trait of novelty seeking. *Nature Genetics, 12,* 78–80.

Eccles, J., Wigfield, A., Harold, R. D., & Blumenfeld, P. (1993). Age and gender differences in children's self- and task perceptions during elementary school. *Child Development, 64,* 830–847.

Edelman, G. (1992). *Bright air, brilliant fire: On the matter of mind.* New York: Basic Books.

Edmands, M. S. (1993). Caring for students with eating disorders on college and university campuses. *Advances in Medical psychotherapy, 6,* 59–75.

Edwards, C. P. (1977). The comparative study of the development of moral judgment and reasoning. In R. L. Munroe, R. Munroe, & B. B. Whiting (Eds.), *Handbook of cross-cultural human development.* New York: Garland.

Edwards, C. P. (1981). The development of moral reasoning in cross-cultural perspective. In R. H. Munroe, R. L. Munroe, & B. B. Whiting (Eds.), *Handbook of cross-cultural human development.* New York: Garland.

Edwards, L. K., & Edwards, A. L. (1991). A principal components analysis of the Minnesota Multiphasic Personality Inventory Factor Scales. Journal of Personality and Social Psychology, 60, 766–772.

Egeland, J. A., Gerhard, D. S., Pauls, D. L., Suddex, J. N., Kidd, K. K., Allen, C. R., Hostetter, A. M., & Housman, D. E. (1987). Bipolar affective disorders linked to DNA markers on chromosome 11. *Nature, 325,* 783–787.

Egeth, H. E. (1993). What do we *not* know about eyewitness identification? *American Psychologist, 48,* 577–580.

Eich, E. (1995). Searching for mood dependent memory. *Psychological Science, 6,* 67–75.

Eich, E., MacCauley, D., & Ryan, L. (1994). Mood dependent memory for events of the personal past. *Journal of Experiemental Psychology: General, 123,* 201–215.

Eich, J. E., Weingartner, H., Stillman, R. C., & Gillan, J. C. (1975). State-dependent accessibility of retrieval cues in the retention of a categorized list. *Journal of Verbal Learning and Verbal Behavior, 14,* 408–417.

Eisenberg, N. & Lennon, R. (1983). Sex differences in empathy and related capacities. *Psychological Bulletin, 94,* 100–131.

Ekman, P. (1972). Universals and cultural differences in facial expression of emotion. In J. K. Cole (Ed.), *Nebraska symposium on motivation.* Lincoln: University of Nebraska Press.

Ekman, P. (1973). Cross-cultural studies in facial expression. In P. Ekman (Ed.), *Darwin and facial expressions: A century of research in review.* New York: Academic Press.

Ekman, P. (1992). Facial expression and emotion: New findings, new questions. *Psychological Science, 3,* 34–38.

Ekman, P. (1992a). An argument for basic emotions. *Journal of Cognition and Emotion, 6,* 169–200.

Ekman, P. (1993). Facial expression and emotion. *American Psychologist, 48,* 384–392.

Ekman, P., & Friesen, W. V. (1971). Constants across cultures in the face and emotion. *Journal of Personality and Social Psychology, 17,* 124–129.

Ekman, P., Friesen, W. V., O'Sullivan, M., Diacoyanni-Tarlatzis, I., Krause, R., et al. (1987). Universals and cultural differences in the judgment of facial expressions of emotion. *Journal of Personality and Social Psychology, 53,* 712–717.

Ekman, P., Levenson, R. W., & Friesen, W. V. (1983). Autonomic nervous system activity distinguishes among emotions. *Science, 221,* 1208–1210.

Elkis, H., Friedman, L., Wise, A., & Meltzer, H. Y. (1995). Meta-analysis of studies of ventricular enlargement and cortical sulcal prominence in mood disorders. *Archives of General Psychiatry, 52,* 735–746.

Ellis, A. (1970). *Reason and emotion in psychotherapy.* Secaucus, NJ: Stuart.

Ellis, A. (1973). *Humanistic psychotherapy: The rational-emotive approach.* New York: McGraw-Hill.

Ellis, A. (1987). The impossibility of achieving consistently good mental health. *American Psychologist, 42,* 364–375.

Ellis, A. (1991). How can psychological treatment aim to be briefer and better? The rational-emotive approach to brief therapy. In K. N. Anchor (Ed.), *Handbook of medical psychotherapy.* Toronto: Hogrefe & Huber.

Ellis, L., & Ames, M. A. (1987). Neurohormonal functioning and sexual orientation: A theory of homosexuality-heterosexuality. *Psychological Bulletin, 101,* 233–258.

Endler, N. S., Cox, B. J., Parker, J. D. A., & Bagby, R. M. (1992). Self-reports of depression and state-trait-anxiety: Evidence for differential assessment. *Journal of Personality and Social Psychology, 63,* 832–838.

Epstein, L. H., & Cluss, P. A. (1982). A behavioral medicine perspective on adherence to long-term medical regimes. Journal of Consulting and Clinical Psychology, 50, 950–971.

Epstein, S. (1979). The stability of behavior: On predicting most of the people much of the time. *Journal of Personality and Social Psychology, 37,* 1097–1126.

Epstein, S. (1994). Integration of the cognitive and the psychodynamic unconscious. *American Psychologist, 49,* 709–724.

Erdelyi, M. H. (1985). *Psychoanalysis: Freud's cognitive psychology.* New York: Freeman.

Erdelyi, M. H. (1992). Psychodynamics and the unconscious. *American Psychologist, 47,* 784–787.

Erdelyi, M. H., & Goldberg, B. (1979). Let's not sweep repression under the rug: Toward a cognitive psychology of repression. In J. F. Kihlstrom & F. J. Evans (Eds.), *Functional disorders of memory.* Hillsdale, NJ: Erlbaum.

Erez, M., & Early, P. C. (1987). Comparative analysis of goal-setting strategies across cultures. *Journal of Applied Psychology, 72,* 658–665.

Erez, M., & Early, P. C. (1993). *Culture, self-identity, and work.* New York: Oxford University Press.

Erez, M., & Zidon, I. (1984). Effect of goal acceptance on the relationship of goal difficulty to performance. *Journal of Applied Psychology, 69,* 69–78.

Ericsson, K. A., & Chase, W. G. (1982). Exceptional memory.

American Scientist, 70, 607–615.

Erikson, E. H. (1963). *Childhood and society.* New York: Norton.

Erikson, E. H. (1965). *The challenge of youth.* Garden City, NY: Doubleday (Anchor Books).

Erikson, E. H. (1968). *Identity: Youth and crisis.* New York: Norton.

Erlenmeyer-Kimling, L. (1968). Studies on the offspring of two schizophrenic parents. In D. Rosenthal & S. S. Kety (Eds.), *The transmission of schizophrenia.* Elmsford, NY: Pergamon Press.

Erwin, E. (1980). Psychoanalytic therapy: The Eysenck argument. *American Psychologist, 35,* 435–443.

Etaugh, C. (1980). Effects of nonmaternal care on children. *American Psychologist, 35,* 309–316.

Evans, G. W., & Howard, R. B. (1973). Personal space. *Psychological Bulletin, 80,* 334–344.

Evans, R. I., Rozelle, R. M., Maxwell, S. E., Raines, B. E., et al. (1981). Social modeling films to deter smoking in adolescents: Results of a three-year field investigation. *Journal of Applied Psychology, 66,* 399–414.

Eveleth, P., & Tanner, J. (1978). *Worldwide variations in human growth.* New York: Cambridge University Press.

Eysenck, H. J. (1952). The effects of psychotherapy.: An evaluation. *Journal of Consulting Psychology, 16,* 319–324.

Eysenck, H. J. (1960). *Behavior therapy and neurosis.* London: Pergamon.

Fackelman, K. A. (1992). Anatomy of Alzheimer's: Do immune proteins help destroy brain cells? *Science News, 142,* 394–396.

Fadiman, J., & Frager, R. (1994). *Personality and personal growth* (3rd ed.). New York: HarperCollins.

Fagan, J. F., & Singer, L. T. (1979). The role of single feature differences in infant recognition of faces. *Infant Behavior and Development, 2,* 39–45.

Fahn, S. (1992). Fetal-tissue transplants in Parkinson's disease. *The New England Journal of Medicine, 327,* 1589–1590.

Fairburn, C. G., Jones, R. Peveler, R. C., Hope, R. A., & O'Conner, M. (1993). Psychotherapy and bulimia nervosa. *Archives of General Psychiatry, 50,* 419–428.

Fairburn, C. G., & Wilson, G. T. (Eds.). (1993). *Binge eating: Nature, assessment and treatment.* New York: Guilford.

Fairburn, C. G., Norman, P. A., Welch, S. L., O'Conner, M. E., Doll, H. A., & Peveler, R. C. (1995). A prospective study of outcome in bulimia nervosa and the long-term effects of three psychological treatments. *Archives of General Psychiatry, 52,* 304–312.

Falbo, T., & Peplau, L. A. (1980). Power strategies in intimate relationships. *Journal of Personality and Social Psychology, 38,* 618–628.

Fantz, R. L. (1961). The origin of form perception. *Scientific American, 204,* 66–72.

Fantz, R. L. (1963). Pattern vision in newborn infants. *Science, 140,* 296–297.

Farrell, M. P., & Rosenberg, S. D. (1981). *Men at midlife.* Boston: Auburn House.

Fast, J. (1970). *Body language.* New York: M. Evans.

Fazio, R. H. (1989). On the power and functionality of attitudes: The role of attitude accessibility. In A. R. Pratkanis, S. J. Breckler, & A. G. Greenwald (Eds.), *Attitude structure and function.* Hillsdale, NJ: Erlbaum.

Fazio, R. H. (1990). Multiple processes by which attitudes guide behavior. The MODE model as an integrative framework. *Advances in Experimental Psychology, 23,* 75–109.

Feeney, J. A., & Noller, P. (1990). Attachment style as a predictor of adult romantic relationships. *Journal of Personality and Social Psychology, 58,* 281–291.

Fein, G. G., Schwartz, P. M., Jacobson, S. W., & Jacobson, J. L. (1983). Environmental toxins and behavior development. *American Psychologist, 38,* 1188–1197.

Feingold, A. (1993). Cognitive gender differences: A developmental perspective. *Sex Roles, 29,* 91–112.

Feingold, A. (1994). Gender differences in personality: A meta-analysis. *Psychological Bulletin, 116,* 429–456.

Feingold, A. (1995). The additive effects of differences in central tendency and variability are important in comparisons between groups. *American Psychologist, 50,* 5–13.

Feist, S. C. (1993). Marriage and family therapy: Theories and applications. *Directions in Clinical Psychology, 3,* 4.3–4.24.

Feldman, S. S., & Elliott, G. R. (Eds.). (1990). *At the threshold: The developing adolescent.* Cambridge, MA: Harvard University Press.

Fenker, R. M., & Lambiotte, J. G. (1987). A performance enhancement program for a college football team: One incredible season. *The Sport Psychologist, 1,* 224–236.

Feshbach, S., Weiner, B., & Bohart, A. (1996). *Personality* (4th ed.). Lexington, MA: D. C. Heath & Co.

Festinger, L. (1957). *A theory of cognitive dissonance.* Stanford, CA: Stanford University Press.

Festinger, L., & Carlsmith, J. M. (1959). Cognitive consequences of forced compliance. *Journal of Abnormal and Social Psychology, 58,* 203–210.

Festinger, L., Schachter, S., & Back, K. (1950). *Social processes in informal groups: A study of human factors in housing.* New York: HarperCollins.

Fielding, J. E., & Phenow, K. J. (1988). Health effects of involuntary smoking. *The New England Journal of Medicine, 319,* 1452–1460.

Finchilescu, G. (1994). Intergroup attributions in minimal groups. *Journal of Social Psychology, 2,* 1–3.

Finnegan, L. P. (1982). Outcome of children born to women dependent upon narcotics. In B. Stimmel (Ed.), *The effects of maternal alcohol and drug abuse on the newborn.* New York: Haworth.

Fiore, M. C., Novotny, T. E., Pierce, J. P., Hatzlandreu, E. J., Patel, K. M., & Davis, R. M. (1989). Trends in cigarette smoking in the United States: The changing influence of gender and race. *Journal of the American Medical Association, 261,* 49–55.

Fischhoff, B. (1990). Psychology and public policy: Tool or toolmaker? *American Psychologist, 45,* 647–653.

Fishbein, M., & Ajzen, I. (1975). *Belief, attitude, intention, and behavior: An introduction to theory and research.* Reading, MA: Addison-Wesley.

Fisher, A. C. (1977). Sport personality assessment: Facts, fallacies, and perspectives. *Motor Skills: Theory into Practice, 1,* 87–97.

Fishman, J. (1987). Type A on trial. *Psychology Today, 21,* 42–50.

Fitzgerald, L. (1993). Sexual harassment: Violence against women in the workplace. *American Psychologist, 48,* 1070–1076.

Flament, M. F., Rapoport, J. L., Berg, C. J., Sceery, W., Kilts, C., Mellstrom, B., & Linnoila, M. (1985). Clomipramine treatment of childhood obsessive-compulsive disorder: A double-blind study. *Archives of General Psychiatry, 42,* 977–983.

Flament, M. F., Whitaker, A., Rapoport, J. L., Davies, M., Berg, C.

Z., Kalikow, K., Sceery, W., & Shaffer, D. (1988). Obsessive-compulsive disorder in adolescence: An epidemiologic study. *Journal of the American Academy of Child and Adolescent Psychiatry, 27,* 289–296.

Flavell, J. H. (1982). On cognitive develpment. *Child Development, 53,* 1–10.

Fleishman, E. A., & Mumford, M. D. (1991). Evaluating classifications of job behavior: A construct of the ability requirement scales. *Personnel Psychology, 44,* 523–575.

Flexser, A. J., & Tulving, E. (1982). Priming and recognition failure. *Journal of Verbal Learning and Verbal Behavior, 21,* 237–248.

Flynn, J. P., Vanegas, H., Foote, W., & Edwards, S. (1970). Neural mechanisms involved in a cat's attack on a rat. In R. E. Whalen, R. F. Thompson, M. Verzeano, & N. M. Weinberger (Eds.), *The neural control of behavior.* New York: Academic Press.

Foa, E. B. (1995). How do treatments for obsessive-compulsive disorder compare? *The Harvard Mental Health Letter, 12,* 8.

Foa, E. B., & Riggs, D. S. (1995). Posttraumatic stress disorder following assault: Theoretical considerations and empirical findings. *Current Directions in Psychological Science, 4,* 61–65.

Folkman, S. (1984). Personal control and stress and coping processes: A theoretical analysis. *Journal of Personality and Social Psychology, 46,* 839–852.

Folstein, S. E., & Rutter, M. L. (1977). Genetic influences and infantile autism. *Nature, 265,* 726–728.

Folstein, S. E., & Rutter, M. L. (1988). Autism: Familial aggregation and genetic implications. *Journal of Autism and Development Disorders, 18,* 3–30.

Ford, C. E., Wright, R. A., & Haythornwaite, J. (1985). Task performance and magnitude of goal valence. *Journal of Research in Personality, 19,* 253–260.

Ford, M. R., & Lowery, C. R. (1986). Gender differences in moral reasoning: A comparison of justice and care orientations. *Journal of Personality and Social Psychology, 4,* 777–783.

Fowler, C. A., Wolford, G., Slade, R., & Tassinary, L. (1981). Lexical access with and without awareness. *Journal of Experimental Psychology: General, 110,* 341–362.

Fowler, R. D. (1992). Report to the Chief Executive Officer: A year of building for the future. *American Psychologist, 47,* 876–883.

Fowles, D. G. (1990). *A profile of older Americans: 1989.* Washington, DC: American Association of Retired Persons.

Fox, R., Aslin, R. N., Shea, S. L., & Dumais, S. T. (1980). Stereopsis in human infants. *Science, 207,* 323–324.

Frank, E., Kupfer, D. J., Perel, J. M., Cornes, C., Jarrett, D. B., et al. (1990). Three-year outcomes for maintenance therapies in recurrent depression. *Archives of General Psychiatry, 47,* 1093–1099.

Frankel, F. H. (1993). Adult reconstruction of childhood events in the multiple personality literature. *American Journal of Psychiatry, 150,* 954–958.

Frankenburg, W. K., & Dodds, J. B. (1967). The Denver Developmental Screening Test. *Journal of Pediatrics, 71,* 181–191.

Frazier, T. M., David, G. H., Goldstein, H., & Goldberg, I. D. (1961). Cigarette smoking and prematurity. *American Journal of Obstetrics and Gynecology, 81,* 988–996.

Frederickson, P. A. (1987). The relevance of sleep disorders medicine to psychiatric practice. *Psychiatric Annals, 17,* 91–100.

Free, M. L., & Oei, T. P. S. (1989). Biological and psychological processes in the treatment and maintenance of depression. *Clinical Psychology Review, 9,* 653–688.

Freed, C. R., Breeze, R. E., Rosenberg, N. L., et al. (1992). Survival of implanted fetal dopamine cells and neurologic improvement 12 to 46 months after transplantation for Parkinson's disease. *The New England Journal of Medicine, 327,* 1549–1555.

Freedman, D. X. (1984). Psychiatric epidemiology counts. *Archives of General Psychiatry, 41,* 931–934.

Freedman, J. L. (1975). *Crowding and behavior.* New York: Viking Press.

Freud, A. (1958). *Adolescence: Psychoanalytic study of the child.* New York: Academic Press.

Freud, S. (1900). *The interpretation of dreams.* In J. Strachey (Ed.), *The complete psychological works of Sigmund Freud.* London: Hogarth Press.

Freud, S. (1933). *New introductory lectures on psychoanalysis: Standard edition.* New York: Norton.

Fribourg, S. (1982). Cigarette smoking and sudden infant death syndrome. *Journal of Obstetrics and Gynecology, 142,* 934–941.

Fried, P. A. (1993). Prenatal exposure to tobacco and marijuana: Effects during pregnancy, infancy, and early childhood. *Clinical Obstetrics and Gynecology, 36,* 319–337.

Friedman, H. S., & Booth-Kewley, S. (1987). The "disease-prone personality": A meta-analytic review of the construct. *American Psychologist, 42,* 539–555.

Friedman, H. S., Hawley, P. H., & Tucker, J. S. (1994). Personality, health and longevity. *Current Directions in Psychological Science, 3,* 37–41.

Friedman, H. S., Tucker, J. S., Schwartz, J. E., Tomlinson-Keasey, C., Martin, L. R., Wingard, D. L., & Cirqui, M. H. (1995). Psychosocial and behavioral predictors of longevity: The aging and death of the "Termites." *American Psychologist, 50,* 69–78.

Friedman, M., & Rosenman, R. (1959). Association of specific overt behavior patterns with blood and cardiovascular findings. *Journal of the American Medical Association, 169,* 1286.

Friedman, M. I., & Stricker, E. M. (1976). The physiological psychology of hunger: A physiological perspective. *Psychological Review, 83,* 409–431.

Friedman, S. (1972). Habituation and recovery of visual response in the alert human newborn. *Journal of Experimental Child Psychology, 13,* 339–349.

Frijda, N. H. (1988). The laws of emotion. *American Psychologist, 43,* 349–358.

Furstenberg, F. F., Brooks-Gunn, J., & Chase-Lansdale, L. (1989). Teenaged pregnancy and childbearing. *American Psychologist, 44,* 313–320.

Furumoto, L., & Scarborough, E. (1986). Placing women in the history of psychology: The first American women psychologists. *American Psychologist, 41,* 35–42.

Gabrena, W., Wang, Y., Latané, B. (1985). Social loafing on an optimizing task: Cross-cultural differences among Chinese and Americans. *Journal of Cross-cultural Psychology, 16,* 223–242.

Gagné, R. M. (1984). Learning outcomes and their effects: Useful categories of human performance. *American Psychologist, 39,* 377–385.

Galanter, E. (1962). Contemporary psychophysics. In R. Brown et al. (Eds.), *New directions in psychology.* New York: Holt, Rinehart & Winston.

Galbaud du Fort, G., Newman, S. C., & Bland, R. C. (1993). Psychiatric comorbidity and treatment seeking: Sources of selection bias in the study of clinical populations. *Journal of Nervous and Mental Disorders, 181,* 467–474.

Gallagher, J. J., & Ramey, C. T. (1987). *The malleability of children.* Baltimore: Paul H. Brooks.

Galton, F. (1879). *Hereditary genius: An inquiry into its laws and consequences.* Englewood Cliffs, NJ: Prentice-Hall.

Gans, J. E., & Blyth, D. A. (1990). *American adolescents: How healthy are they?* AMA Profiles of Adolescent Health series. Chicago: American Medical Association.

Garbarino, J. (1985). *Adolescent development: An ecological perspective.* Columbus, OH: Merrill.

Garcia, J., Ervin, F. R., & Koelling, R. A. (1966). Learning with prolonged delay of reinforcement. *Psychonomic Science, 5,* 121–122.

Gardner, H. (1983). *Frames of mind: The theory of multiple intelligences.* New York: Basic Books.

Gardner, H. (1993a). *Multiple intelligences: The theory in practice.* New York: Basic Books.

Gardner, H. (1993b). *Creating minds.* New York: Basic Books.

Gardner, H., & Hatch, T. (1989). Multiple intelligences go to school: Educational implications of the theory of multiple intelligences. *Educational Researcher, 18,* 6.

Gardner, M. (1993). The false memory syndrome. *Skeptical Inquirer, 17,* 370–375.

Garfield, S. L. (1981). Psychotherapy: A 40-year appraisal. *American Psychologist, 36,* 174–183.

Garner, D. M., Olmsted, M. P., Davis, R., Rockert, W., Goldbloom, D., & Eagle, M. (1990). The association between bulimic symptoms and reported psychopathology. *International Journal of Eating Disorders, 9,* 1–15.

Garry, M., & Loftus, E. F. (1994). Repressed memories of childhood trauma: Could some of them be suggested? *USA Today,* January, *22,* 82–84.

Gaugler, B. B., Rosenthal, D. B., Thornton, G. C., & Bentson, C. (1987). Meta-analysis of assessment center validity. *Journal of Applied Psychology, 72,* 493–511.

Gazzaniga, M. S., & Ledoux, J. E. (1978). *The integrated mind.* New York: Plenum.

Geary, D. C. (1995). Reflections of evolution and culture in children's cognition: Implications for mathematical development and instruction. *American Psychologist, 50,* 24–37.

Gefou-Madianou, D. (1992). *Alcohol, gender and culture.* New York: Routledge, Chapman Hall.

Geller, E. S. (1985). The behavior change approach to litter management. *Journal of Resource Management, 14,* 117–122.

Geller, E. S. (1986). Prevention of environmental problems. In B. A. Edelstein & L. Michelson (Eds.), *Handbook of prevention.* New York: Plenum.

Geller, E. S. (1989). Applied behavioral analysis and social marketing: An integration to preserve the environment. *Journal of Social Issues, 45,* 17–36.

Geller, E. S. (1992). It takes more than information to save energy. *American Psychologist, 47,* 814–815.

Geller, E. S., Berry, T. D., Ludwig, T. D., Evans, R. E., Gilmore, M. R., & Clarke, S. (1990). A conceptual framework for developing and evaluating behavior change interventions for injury control. *Health Education Research, 5,* 125–137.

Geller, E. S., Bruff, C. D., & Nimmer, J. G. (1985). "Flash for life": Community-based prompting for safety belt promotion. *Journal of Applied Behavioral Analysis, 18,* 309–314.

Geller, E. S., & Lehman, G. R. (1986). Motivating desirable waste management behavior: Applications of behavioral analysis. *Journal of Resource Management, 15,* 58–68.

Geller, E. S., & Nimmer, J. G. (1985). *Social marketing and applied behavior analysis: An integration for quality of life intervention.* Blacksburg: Virginia Polytechnic Institute and State University.

Geller, E. S., Rudd, J. R., Kalsher, M. J., Sreff, F. M., & Lehman, G. R. (1987). Employer-based programs to motivate safety belt use: A review of short-term and long-term effects. *Journal of Safety Research, 18,* 1–17.

Geller, E. S., Winett, R. A., & Everett, P. B. (1982). *Preserving the environment: New strategies for behavior change.* New York: Pergamon Press.

Gellhorn, E. (1964). Motion and emotion: The role of proprioception in the physiology and pathology of the emotions. *Psychological Review, 71,* 457–472.

Gelman, D., Doherty, S., Joseph, N., & Carroll, G. (1987, Spring). How infants learn to talk. *Newsweek: On Health.*

Gelman, R. (1978). Cognitive development. *Annual Review of Psychology, 29,* 297–332.

Gelso, C. J., & Fassinger, R. E. (1990). Counseling psychology: Theory and research on interventions. *Annual Review of Psychology, 41,* 355–386.

Gemberling, G. A., & Domjan, M. (1982). Selective associations in one-day-od rats: Taste toxicosis and texture-shock aversion learning. *Journal of Comparative and Physiological Psychology, 96,* 105–113.

Gendel, E. S., & Bonner, E. J. (1988). Sexual dysfunction. In H. H. Goldman (Ed.), *Review of general psychiatry* (2nd ed.). Norwalk, CT: Appleton and Lange.

George, L. (1992). Acupuncture: Drug free pain relief. *American Health, 11,* 45.

George, M. S., Ketter, T. A., Parekh, P. I., Horwitz, B., Herscovitch, P., & Post, R. M. (1995). Brain activity during transient sadness and happiness in healthy women. *American Journal of Psychiatry, 152,* 341–351.

Geracioti, T. D., & Liddle, R. A. (1988). Impaired cholecystokinin secretion in bulimia nervosa. *New England Journal of Medicine, 319,* 683–688.

Gerbert, B., & Maguire, B. (1989). Public acceptance of the Surgeon General's brochure on AIDS. *Public Health Report, 104,* 130–133.

Gerow, J. R., & Murphy, D. P. (1980). The validity of the Nelson-Denny Reading Test as a predictor of performance in introductory psychology. *Educational and Psychological Measurement, 40,* 553–556.

Gibson, E. J. (1987). Introductory essay: What does infant perception tell us about theories of perception? *Journal of Experimental Psychology: Perception and Performance, 13,* 515–523.

Gibson, E. J. (1988). Exploratory behavior in the development of perceiving, acting, and the acquiring of knowledge. *Annual Review of Psychology, 39,* 1–41.

Gibson, E. J., & Walk, R. D. (1960). The visual cliff. *Scientific American, 202,* 64–71.

Gilbert, L. A. (1994). Current perspectives on dual-career families. *Current Directions in Psychological Science, 3,* 101–104.

Gilbert, P. A., Harris, M. J., McAdams, L. A., & Jeste, D. (1995). Neuroleptic withdrawal in schizophrenic patients. *Archives of General Psychology, 52,* 173–188.

Gillam, B. (1980). Geometrical illusions. *Scientific American, 242,* 102–111.

Gilligan, C. (1982). *In a different voice.* Cambridge, MA: Harvard University Press.

Gilovich, T. Vallone, R., & Tversky, A. (1985). The hot hand in basketball: On the misperception of random sequences. *Cognitive Psychology, 17,* 295–314.

Gladue, B. A. (1994). The biopsychology of sexual orientation. *Current Directions in Psychological Science, 3,* 150–154.

Gladue, B. A., Green, R., & Hellman, R. E. (1984). Neuroendocrine response to estrogen and sexual orientation. *Science, 225,* 1496–1499.

Glaser, R. (1984). Education and thinking. *American Psychologist, 39,* 93–104.

Glasgow, R. E., & Lichtenstein, E. (1987). Long-term effects of behavioral smoking cessation interventions. *Behavior Therapy, 18,* 297–324.

Glass, A. L., Holyoak, K. J., & Santa, J. L. (1979). *Cognition.* Reading, MA: Addison-Wesley.

Glass, D. C., & Singer, J. E. (1972). *Urban stress.* Hillsdale, NJ: Erlbaum.

Glass, D. C., Singer, J. E., & Friedman, L. N. (1969). Psychic cost of adaptation to an environmental stressor. *Journal of Personality and Social Psychology, 12,* 200–210.

Gleaves, D. H. (1994). On "the reality of repressed memories." *American Psychologist, 49,* 440–441.

Glenn, N. D., & Weaver, C. N. (1981). The contribution of marital happiness to global happiness. *Journal of Marriage and the Family, 43,* 161–168.

Glickstein, M., & Yeo, C. (1990). The cerebellum and motor learning. *Journal of Cognitive Neuroscience, 2,* 69–80.

Gluck, M. A., & Myers, C. E. (1995). Representation and association in memory: A neurocomputational view of hippocampal function. *Current Directions in Psychological Science, 4,* 23–29.

Glucksberg, S., & Danks, J. H. (1968). Effects of discriminative labels and of nonsense labels upon the availability of novel function. *Journal of Verbal Learning and Verbal Behavior, 7,* 72–76.

Golbus, M. S. (1980). Teratology for the obstetrician: Current status. *American Journal of Obstetrics and Gynecology, 55,* 269.

Gold, P. E. (1987). Sweet memories. *American Scientist, 75,* 151–155.

Gold, S. N., Hughes, D., & Hohnecker, L. (1994). Degrees of repression of sexual abuse memories. *American Psychologist, 49,* 441–442.

Goldberg, L. R. (1993). The structure of phenotypic personality traits. *American Psychologist, 48,* 26–34.

Goldfried, M. R., Greenberg, L. S., & Marmar, C. (1990). Individual psychotherapy: Process and outcome. *Annual Review of Psychology, 41,* 659–688.

Goldsmith, H. H., & Harman, C. (1994). Temperament and attachment; individuals and relationships. *Current Directions in Psychological Science, 3,* 53–57.

Goldstein, I. L. (1986). *Training in organizations.* Monterey, CA: Brooks/Cole.

Goldstein, I. L. (1989). *Training and development in organizations.* San Francisco: Jossey-Bass.

Goleman, O. (1980). 1,528 little geniuses and how they grew. *Psychology Today, 14,* 28–53.

Gonzales, M. H., Davis, J. M., Loney, G. L., Lukens, C. K., & Junghans, C. M. (1983). Interactional approach to interpersonal attraction. Journal of Personality and Social Psychology, 44, 1192–1197.

Gooden, D., & Baddeley, A. D. (1975). Context-dependent memory in two natural environments: On and and under water. *British Journal of Psychology, 66,* 325–331.

Goodwin, D. W., Powell, B., Bremer, D., Hoine, H., & Stein, J. (1969). Alcohol and recall: State dependent effects in man. *Science, 163,* 1358–1360.

Gordon, C. T., State, R. C., Nelson, J. E., Hamburger, S. D., & Rapoport, J. L. (1993). A double-blind comparison of clomipramine, desipramine, and placebo in the treatment of autistic disorder. *Archives of General Psychiatry, 50,* 441–447.

Gorenstein, E. E. (1984). Debating mental illness. *American Psychologist, 39,* 50–56.

Gormezano, I. (1972). Investigations of defense and reward conditioning in the rabbit. In A. H. Black & W. F. Prokasy (Eds.), *Classical conditioning II: Current theory and research.* Englewood Cliffs, NJ: Prentice-Hall.

Gotlib, I. H. (1992). Interpersonal and cognitive aspects of depression. *Current Directions in Psychological Science, 1,* 149–156.

Gottesman, I. I., & Bertelsen, A. (1989). Confirming unexpressed genotypes for schizophrenia. *Archives of General Psychiatry, 46,* 867–872.

Gottesman, I. I., & Shields, J. (1982). *Schizophrenia: The epigenetic puzzle.* Cambridge, UK: Cambridge University Press.

Gottlieb, B. H. (1981). *Social networks and social support.* Beverly Hills, CA: Sage.

Gottlieb, G. (1970). Conceptions of prenatal development. In L. R. Aronson, E. Robach, D. S. Lehrman, & J. S. Rosenblatt (Eds.), *Development and evolution of behavior.* San Francisco: Freeman.

Gottman, J. (1994). Why marriages fail. *Networker, 18,* 41–48.

Gough, H. G. (1985). A work orientation scale for the California Psychological Inventory. *Journal of Applied Psychology, 70,* 505–513.

Govoni, L. E., & Hayes, J. E. (1988). *Drugs and nursing implications* (6th ed.). Norwalk, CT: Appleton & Lange.

Gracely, R. H., Lynch, S., & Bennett, G. J. (1991). *The central process responsible for A_LTM-medicated allodynia in some patients with RSD is sensitive to perfusion of the microenvironment of nociceptr terminals.* Paper presented at the 21st Annual Meeting of the Society for Neuroscience. New Orleans.

Grady, C. L., McIntosh, A. R., Horowitz, B., Maisog, J. M., Ungerleider, L. G., Mentis, M. J., Pietrini, P., Schapiro, M. B., & Haxby, J. V. (1995). Age-related reductions in human recognition memory due to impaired encoding. *Science, 269,* 218–221.

Graf, P., & Mandler, G. (1984). Activation makes words more accessible, but not necessarily more retrievable. *Journal of Verbal Learning and Verbal Behavior, 23,* 553–568.

Graf, P., & Schachter, D. A. (1985). Implicit and explicit memory for new associations in normal and amnesic subjects. *Journal of Experimental Psychology: Learning, Memory, and Cognition, 11,* 501–518.

Graziano, A. M., & Raulin, M. L. (1993). *Research methods: A process of inquiry.* New York: HarperCollins.

Green, D. M., & Swets, J. A. (1966). *Signal detection theory and psychophysics.* New York: Wiley.

Greenberg, J., & Cohen, R. L. (1982). *Equity and justice in social behavior.* New York: Academic Press.

Greenberg, L. S., & Safran, J. D. (1987). *Emotion in psychotherapy.*

New York: Guilford.

Greenberg, L. S., & Safran, J. D. (1989). Emotion in psychotherapy. *American Psychologist, 44,* 19–29.

Greeno, J. G. (1978). Natures of problem-solving abilities. In W. K. Estes (Ed.), *Handbook of learning and cognitive processes* (Vol. 5). Hillsdale, NJ: Erlbaum.

Greeno, J. G. (1989). A perspective on thinking. *American Psychologist, 44,* 134–141.

Greenough, W. T. (1984). Structural correlates of information storage in mammalian brain. *Trends in Neurosciences, 7,* 229–233.

Greenwald, A. G. (1992). New look 3: Unconsciousness reclaimed. *American Psychologist, 47,* 776–779.

Greenwald, A. G., Spangenberg, E. R., Pratkais, A. R., & Eskenazi, J. (1991). Double-blind tests of subliminal self-help audio tapes. *Psychological Science, 2,* 119–122.

Greer, S. (1964). Study of parental loss in neurotics and sociopaths. *Archives of General Psychiatry, 11,* 177–180.

Gregory, R. L. (1977). *Eye and brain: The psychology of seeing* (3rd ed.). New York: New World Library.

Grice, G. R. (1948). The relation of secondary reinforcement to delayed reward in visual discrimination learning. *Journal of Experimental Psychology, 38,* 1–16.

Grinspoon, L. (1977). *Marijuana reconsidered* (2nd ed.). Cambridge, MA: Harvard University Press.

Grinspoon, L. (1995). Schizophrenia update–Part I. *The Harvard Mental Health Letter, 11,* 1–4.

Grob, C., & Dobkin de Rois, M. (1992). Adolescent drug use in cross-cultural perspective. *Journal of Drug Issues, 22,* 121–138.

Gross, R. T., & Duke, P. M. (1980). The effect of early and late maturation on adolescent behavior. *The Pediatric Clinics of North America, 27,* 71–77.

Grossman, H. J. (Ed.). (1973). *Manual on terminology and classification in mental retardation.* Washington, DC: American Association on Mental Deficiency.

Groves, P. M., & Rebec, G. V. (1992). *Introduction to biological psychology* (4th ed.). Dubuque, IA: Brown.

Guilford, J. P. (1959a). *Personality.* New York: McGraw-Hill.

Guilford, J. P. (1959b). Traits of creativity. In H. H. Anderson (Ed.), *Creativity and its cultivation.* New York: HarperCollins.

Guilford, J. P. (1967). *The nature of human intelligence.* New York: McGraw-Hill.

Guilford, J. P. (1988). Some changes in the structure-of-intellect model. *Educational and Psychological Measurement, 48,* 1–4.

Guion, R. M., & Gibson, W. M. (1988). Personnel selection and placement. *Annual Review of Psychology, 39,* 349–374.

Gur, R. E., Resnick, S. M., Alavi, A., Gur, R. C., Caroff, S., Dann, R., et al. (1987). Regional brain function in schizophrenia. *Archives of General Psychiatry, 44,* 119–125.

Gurman, A. S., Kniskern, D. P., & Pinsof, W. M. (1986). Research on the process and outcome of marital and family therapy. In S. L. Garfield & A. E. Bergin (Eds.), *Handbook of psychotherapy and behavior change* (3rd ed.). New York: Wiley.

Haist, F., Shimamura, A. P., & Squire, L. R. (1992). On the relationship between recall and recognition memory. *Journal of Experimental Psychology: Learning, Memory and Cognition, 18,* 691–702.

Hake, D. F., & Foxx, R. M. (1978). Promoting gasoline conservation: The effects of reinforcement schedules, a leader, and self-recording. *Behavior Modification, 2,* 339–369.

Halaas, J. L., Gajiwala, K. S., Maffei, M., Cohen, S. L., Chait, B. T., et al. (1995). Weight-reducing effects of the plasma protein encoded by the *obese* gene. *Science, 269,* 543–546.

Halberstadt, A. G., & Saitta, M. B. (1987). Gender, nonverbal behavior, and perceived dominance: A test of the theory. *Journal of Personality and Social Psychology, 53,* 257–272.

Hall, E. T. (1966). *The hidden dimension.* Garden City, NY: Doubleday.

Hall, G. S. (1904). *Adolescence.* Englewood Cliffs, NJ: Prentice-Hall.

Hall, J. A. (1978). Gender effects in decoding nonverbal cues. *Psychological Bulletin, 85,* 845–857.

Hall, J. F. (1976). *Classical conditioning and instrumental conditioning: A contemporary approach.* Philadelphia: Lippincott.

Hall, W. G., & Oppenheim, R. W. (1987). Developmental psychology. *Annual Review of Psychology, 38,* 91–128.

Halpern, D. F. (1986). *Sex differences in cognitive abilities.* Hillsdale, NJ: Erlbaum.

Hamburg, D. A. (1992). *Today's children: Creating a future for a generation in crisis.* New York: New York Times Books.

Hamburg, D. A., & Takanishi, R. (1989). Preparing for life: The critical transition of adolescence. *American Psychologist, 44,* 825–827.

Hamer, D. H., Hu, S., Magnuson, V. L., Hu, N., & Pattatucci, A. M. L. (1993). A linkage between DNA markers on the X chromosome and male sexual orientation. *Science, 261,* 321–327.

Hammen, C., Burge, D. Burney, E., & Adrian, C. (1990). Longitudinal study of diagnoses in children of women with unipolar and bipolar affective disorder. *Archives of General Psychiatry, 47,* 1112–1117.

Hansen, W. B., Hahn, G. L., & Wolkenstein, J. (1990). Perceived personal immunity: Beliefs about susceptibility to AIDS. *Journal of Sex Research, 27,* 622–628.

Harding, C. M. (1988). Course types in schizophrenia: An analysis of European and American studies. *Schizophrenia Bulletin, 14,* 633–642.

Hare, R. D. (1970). *Psychopathology: Theory and research.* New York: Wiley.

Hare, R. D. (1995). Psychopaths: New trends in research. *The Harvard Mental Health Letter, 12,* 4–5.

Hare, R. D., McPherson, L. M., & Forth, A. E. (1988). Male psychopaths and their criminal careers. *Journal of Consulting and Clinical Psychology, 56,* 710–714.

Harkins, S. (1987). Social loafing and social facilitation. *Journal of Experimental Social Psychology, 23,* 1–18.

Harkins, S. G., & Petty, R. E. (1982). Effects of task difficulty and task uniqueness on social loafing. *Journal of Personality and Social Psychology, 43,* 1214–1229.

Harkins, S. G., & Petty, R. E. (1983). Social context effects in persuasion: The effects of multiple sources and multiple targets. In P. B. Paulus (Ed.), *Basic group processes.* New York: Springer-Verlag.

Harkins, S. G., & Szymanski, K. (1989). Social loafing and group evaluation. *Journal of Personality and Social Psychology, 56,* 934–941.

Harlow, H. F. (1932). Social facilitation of feeding in the albino rat. *Journal of Genetic Psychology, 41,* 211–221.

Harlow, H. F. (1959). Love in infant monkeys. *Scientific American, 200,* 68–74.

Harlow, H. F., Harlow, M. K., & Suomi, S. J. (1971). From thought to therapy: Lessons from a private library. *American Scientist, 59,* 536–549.

Harris, B. (1979). What ever happened to Little Albert? *American Psychologist, 34,* 151–160.

Harris, D. V. (1973). *Involvement in sport: A somatopsychic rationale for physical activity.* Philadelphia: Lea & Febiger.

Harris, L., & Associates. (1975, 1981, 1983). *The myth and reality of aging in America.* Washington, DC: The National Council on Aging.

Harris, M. M. (1989). Reconsidering the employment interview: A review of recent literature and suggestions for future research. *Personnel Psychology, 42,* 691–726.

Harris, P. L. (1983). Infant cognition. In P. H. Mussen (Ed.), *Handbook of child psychology* (Vol. 2). New York: Wiley.

Harrow, M., Goldberg, J. F., Grossman, L. S., & Meltzer, H. Y. (1990). Outcome in manic disorders. *Archives of General Psychiatry, 47,* 665–671.

Hartman, S., Grigsby, D. W., Crino, M. D., & Chokar, J. (1986). The measurement of job satisfaction by action tendencies. *Educational and Psychological Measurement, 46,* 317–329.

Hartup, W. W. (1989). Social relationships and their developmental significance. *American Psychologist, 44,* 120–126.

Haruki, T., Shigehisa, T., Nedate, K., Wajima, M., & Ogawa, R. (1984). Effects of alien-reinforcement and its combined type of learning behavior and efficacy in relation to personality. *International Journal of Psychology, 19,* 527–545.

Harvey, J. H., & Weary, G. (1984). Current issues in attribution theory. *Annual Review of Psychology, 35,* 427–459.

Hastie, R., & Park, B. (1986). The relationship between memory and judgment depends on whether the judgment task is memory-based or on-line. *Psychological Review, 93,* 258–268.

Hastorf, A. H., & Cantril, H. (1954). They saw a game: A case study. *Journal of Abnormal and Social Psychology, 49,* 129–134.

Hatfield, E., & Sprecher, S. (1986). *Mirror, mirror . . . The importance of looks in everyday life.* Albany: State University of New York Press.

Havighurst, R. J. (1972). *Developmental tasks and education* (3rd ed.). New York: McKay.

Hayduk, L. A. (1983). Personal space: Where we now stand. *Psychological Bulletin, 94,* 293–335.

Hayes, C. D. (1987). *Risking the future* (Vol. 1). Washington, DC: National Academy Press.

Hayman, C. A. G., & Tulving, E. (1989). Contingent dissociation between recognition and fragment completion: The method of triangulation. *Journal of Experimental Psychology: Learning, Memory, and Cognition, 15,* 220–224.

Haynes, S. G., McMichael, A. J., & Tyroler, H. A. (1978). Survival after early and normal retirement. *Journal of Gerontology, 33,* 872–883.

Hayward, C., Killan, J. D., Hammer, L. D., Litt, I. F., Wilson, D. M., Simmonds, B., & Taylor, C. B. (1992). Pubertal stage and panic attack history in sixth- and seventh-grade girls. American Journal of Psychiatry, 149, 1239–1243.

Hazan, C. & Shaver, P. (1987). Romantic love conceptualized as an attachment process. Journal of Personality and Social Psychology, 52, 511–524.

Hebb, D. O. (1955). Drives and the C.N.S. (conceptual nervous system). *Psychological Review, 62,* 243–254.

Hecht, S. (1934). Vision: II. The nature of the photoreceptor process. In C. Murchison (Ed.), *Handbook of general experimental psychology.* Worcester, MA: Clark University Press.

Hedges, L. V., & Newell, A. (1995). Sex differences in mental test scores, variability, and numbers of high-scoring individuals. *Science, 269,* 41–45.

Heffernan, J. A., & Albee, G. W. (1985). Prevention perspectives. *American Psychologist, 40,* 202–204.

Heidbreder, E. (1946). The attainment of concepts. *Journal of General Psychology, 24,* 93–108.

Heinrichs, R. W. (1993). Schizophrenia and the brain: Conditions for a neuropsychology of madness. *American Psychologist, 48,* 221–233.

Hellige, J. B. (1990). Hemispheric assymetry. *Annual Review of Psychology, 41,* 55–80.

Hellige, J. B. (Ed.). (1983). *Cerebral hemisphere asymmetry: Method, theory, and application.* New York: Praeger.

Helms, J. E. (1992). Why is there no study of cultural equivalence in standardized cognitive ability testing? *American Psychologist, 47,* 1083–1101.

Helzer, J. E., Robins, L. N., & McEnvoy, L. (1987). Posttraumatic stress disorder in the general population. *New England Journal of Medicine, 317,* 1630–1634.

Henley, T. B., Johnson, M. G., Jones, E. M., & Herzog, H. A. (1989). Definitions of psychology. *The Psychological Record, 39,* 143–152.

Hennessy, J., & Melhuish, E. C. (1991). Early day care and the development of school-age children. *Journal of Reproduction and Infant Psychology, 9,* 117–136.

Herek, G. M., & Glunt, E. K. (1988). An epidemic of stigma: Public reactions to AIDS. *American Psychologist, 43,* 886–891.

Herrnstein, R. J., & Murray, C. (1994). *The bell curve: Intelligence and class structure.* New York: Free Press.

Heshka, S., & Nelson, Y. (1972). Interpersonal speaking distance as a function of age, sex, and relationship. *Sociometry, 35,* 491–498.

Hetherington, E. M., & Parke, R. D. (1993). *Child psychology: A contemporary viewpoint.* New York: McGraw-Hill.

Higgins, E. T, & Bargh, J. A. (1987). Social cognition and social perception. *Annual Review of Psychology, 38,* 369–426.

Hilgard, E. R. (1975). Hypnosis. *Annual Review of Psychology, 26,* 19–44.

Hilgard, E. R. (1978, January). Hypnosis and consciousness. *Human Nature,* pp. 42–49.

Hilgard, E. R. (1992). Divided consciousness and dissociation. *Consciousness and Cognition, 1,* 16–31.

Hilgard, E. R., & Hilgard, J. R. (1975). *Hypnosis in the relief of pain.* Los Altos, CA: W. Kaufman.

Hilgard, J. R. (1970). *Personality and hypnosis: A study of imaginative involvement.* Chicago: University of Chicago Press.

Hill, W. F. (1985). *Learning: A survey of psychological interpretations* (4th ed.). New York: HarperCollins.

Hinrichs, J. R. (1976). Personnel training. In M. Dunnette (Ed.), *Handbook of industrial and organizational psychology.* Skokie, IL: Rand McNally.

Hinsz, V. B., & Davis, J. H. (1984). Persuasive arguments theory, group polarization, and choice shifts. *Personality and Social Psychology Bulletin, 10,* 260–268.

Hobfoll, S. E. (1986). *Stress, social support, and women.* Washington, DC: Hemisphere.

Hobfoll, S. E. (1988). *The ecology of stress.* Washington, DC: Hemisphere.

Hobfoll, S. E. (1989). Conservation of resources: A new attempt at conceptualizing stress. *American Psychologist, 44,* 513–524.

Hobson, J. A. (1977). The reciprocal interaction model of sleep cycle control: Implications for PGO wave generation and dream amnesia. In R. R. Drucker-Colin & J. L. McGaugh (Eds.), *Neurobiology of sleep and memory.* New York: Academic Press.

Hobson, J. A. (1988). *The dreaming brain.* New York: Basic Books.

Hobson, J. A., & McCarley, R. W. (1977). The brain as a dream state generator: An activation-synthesis hypothesis of the dream process. *American Journal of Psychiatry, 134,* 1335–1348.

Hofferth, S. L., & Hayes, C. D. (Eds.). (1987). *Risking the future: Adolescent sexuality, pregnancy, and childbearing.* Washington, DC: National Academy Press.

Hoffman, D. D. (1983). The interpretation of visual illusions. *Scientific American, 245,* 154–162.

Hogan, J. (1989). Personality correlates of physical fitness. *Journal of Personality and Social Psychology, 56,* 284–288.

Hogan, R., & Nicholson, R. A. (1988). The meaning of personality test scores. *American Psychologist, 43,* 621–626.

Holden, C. (1980). A new visibility for gifted children. *Science, 210,* 879–882.

Hollander, E., DeCaria, C. M., Nitescu, A., Gully, R., Suckow, R. F., et al. (1992). Serotonergic function in obsessive-compulsive disorder. *Archives of General Psychiatry, 49,* 21–28.

Hollis, J. F., Connett, J. E., Stevens, V. J., & Greenlick, M. R. (1990). Stressful life events, Type A behavior, and the prediction of cardiovascular and total mortality over six years. *Journal of Behavioral Medicine, 13,* 263–281.

Holman, B. L., & Tumeh, S. S. (1990). Single-photon emission computed tomography (SPECT): Applications and potential. *Journal of the American Medical Association, 263,* 561–564.

Holmes, D. (1994). *Abnormal psychology* (2nd ed.). New York: HarperCollins.

Holmes, D. S. (1984). Meditation and somatic arousal reduction: A review of the experimental evidence. *American Psychologist, 39,* 1–10.

Holmes, D. S. (1985). To meditate or simply rest, that is the question: A response to the comments of Shapiro. *American Psychologist, 40,* 722–725.

Holmes, D. S. (1987). The influence of meditation versus rest on physiological arousal: A second examination. In M. West (Ed.), *The psychology of meditation.* Oxford: Oxford University Press.

Holmes, T. S., & Holmes, T. H. (1970). Short-term intrusions into the life-style routine. *Journal of Psychosomatic Research, 14,* 121–132.

Holyoak, K. J., & Spellman, B. A. (1993). Thinking. *Annual Review of Psychology, 44,* 265–315.

Hood, R. D. (1990). Paternally mediated effects. In R. D. Hood (Ed.), *Developmental toxicology: Risk assessment and the future.* New York: Van Nostrand Reinhold.

Hoppock, R. (1935). *Job satisfaction.* New York: HarperCollins.

Hörmann, H. (1986). *Meaning and context.* New York: Plenum.

Horn, J., & Anderson, K. (1993). Who in America is trying to lose weight? *Annals of Internal Medicine, 119,* 672–676.

Horn, J. L. (1976). Human abilities: A review of research and theories in the early 1970s. *Annual Review of Psychology, 27,* 437–485.

Horn, J. L. (1982). The aging of human abilities. In J. Wolman, (Ed.), *Handbook of developmental psychology.* Englewood Cliffs, NJ: Prentice-Hall.

Horn, J. L. (1985). Remodeling old models of intelligence. In B. B. Wolman (Ed.), *Handbook of intelligence.* New York: Wiley.

Horn, J. L., & Cattell, R. B. (1966). Refinement and test of the theory of fluid and crystallized intelligence. *Journal of Educational Psychology, 57,* 253–276.

Horne, J. A. (1988). *Why we sleep: The function of sleep in humans and other mammals.* Oxford: Oxford University Press.

Horner, M. S. (1969). Women's will to fail. *Psychology Today, 3,* 36.

Horowitz, F. D., & O'Brien, M. (Eds.). (1985). *The gifted and talented: Developmental perspectives.* Washington, DC: American Psychological Association.

Hoshmand, T. L., & Polkinhorne, D. E. (1992). Redefining the science-practice relationship and professional training. *American Psychologist, 47,* 55–66.

Hostetler, A. J. (1987). Alzheimer's trials hinge on early diagnosis. *APA Monitor, 18,* 14–15.

Houston, B. K., & Vavak, C. R. (1991). Cynical hostility: Developmental factors, psycho-social correlates, and health behaviors. *Health Psychology, 10,* 9–17.

Houston, J. P. (1986). *Fundamentals of learning and memory* (3rd ed.). New York: Harcourt Brace Jovanovich.

Hovland, C. I., & Weiss, W. (1951). The influence of source credibility on communication effectiveness. *Public Opinion Quarterly, 15,* 635–650.

Howard, D. V. (1983). *Cognitive psychology.* New York: Macmillan.

Howard, K. I., Kopata, S. M., Krause, M. S., & Orlinsky, D. E. (1986). The dose-effect relationship in psychotherapy. *American Psychologist, 41,* 159–164.

Howell, W. C., & Dipboye, R. L. (1982). *Essentials of industrial and organizational psychology.* Homewood, IL: Dorsey Press.

Howes, C. (1990). Can the age of entry into child care and the quality of child care predict adjustment in kindergarten? *Developmental Psychology, 26,* 292–303.

Hsia, J. (1988). Limits on affirmative action: Asian American access to higher education. *Educational Policy, 2,* 117–136.

Hsu, L. K. G. (1986). The treatment of anorexia nervosa. *American Journal of Psychiatry, 143,* 573–581.

Hubel, D. H. (1979). The brain. *Scientific American, 241,* 45–53.

Hubel, D. H., & Wiesel, T. N. (1979). Brain mechanisms of vision. *Scientific American, 241,* 150–162.

Hudson, W. (1960). Pictorial depth perception in subcultural groups in Africa. *Journal of Social Psychology, 52,* 183–208.

Hughes, F. P., & Noppe, L. D. (1985). *Human development.* St. Paul, MN: West.

Hughes, J. Smith, T. W., Kosterlitz, H. W., Fothergill, L. A., Morgan, G. A., & Morris, H. R. (1975). Identification of two related peptides from the brain with potent opiate agonist activity. *Nature, 258,* 577–579.

Hughes, J. R., Gust, S. W., & Pechacek, T. F. (1987). Prevalence of tobacco dependence and withdrawal. *American Journal of Psychiatry, 144,* 205–208.

Hugick, L., & Leonard, J. (1991). Despite increasing hostility, one in four Americans still smokes. *Gallup Poll Monthly, 315,* 2–10.

Hui, C. H. (1990). Work attitudes, leadership styles, and managerial behaviors in different cultures. In R. W. Brislin (Ed.), *Applied cross-cultural psychology.* Newbury Park, CA: Sage.

Hulin, C. L., & Smith, P. C. (1964). Sex differences in job satisfaction. *Journal of Applied Psychology, 48,* 88–92.

Hull, C. L. (1943). *Principles of behavior.* Englewood Cliffs, NJ: Prentice-Hall.

Hunt, E. (1995). The role of intelligence in modern society. *American Scientist, 83,* 356–368.

Hunt, M. (1987, August 30). Navigating the therapy maze. *The New York Times Magazine,* pp. 28–31, 37, 44, 46, 49.

Hunter, J. E. (1986). Cognitive ability, cognitive aptitudes, job knowledge, and job performance. *Journal of Vocational Behavior, 29,* 340–362.

Hunter, J. E., & Hunter, R. F. (1984). Validity and utility of alternative predictors of job performance. *Psychological Bulletin, 96,* 72–98.

Hunter, S., & Sundel, M. (Eds.). (1989). *Midlife myths.* Newbury Park, CA: Sage.

Huston, A. C. (1985). The development of sex-typing: Themes from recent research. *Developmental Review, 5,* 1–17.

Huston, T. L., Ruggiero, M., Conner, R., & Geis, G. (1981). Bystander intervention into crime: A study based on naturally occurring episodes. *Social Psychology Quarterly, 44,* 14–23.

Hyde, J. S. (1984). How large are gender differences in aggression? A developmental meta-analysis. *Developmental Psychology, 20,* 697–706.

Hyde, J. S. (1986). *Understanding human sexuality* (3rd ed.). New York: McGraw-Hill.

Hyde, J. S. (1994a). *Understanding human sexuality* (5th ed.). New York: McGraw-Hill.

Hyde, J. S. (1994b). Can meta-analysis make feminist transformations in psychology? *Psychology of Women Quarterly, 18,* 451–462.

Hyde, J. S., Fennema, E., & Lamon, S. J. (1990). Gender differences in mathematics performance: A meta-analysis. *Psychological Bulletin, 107,* 139–155.

Iacono, W. G., & Grove, W. M. (1993). Schizophrenia reviewed: Toward an integrative genetic model. *Psychological Science, 4,* 273–276.

Iaffaldano, M. T., & Muchinsky, P. M. (1985). Job satisfaction and job performance: A meta-analysis. *Psychological Bulletin, 97,* 251–273.

Ilgen, D. R., & Klein, H. J. (1989). Organizational behavior. *Annual Review of Psychology, 40,* 327–351.

Infante-Rivard, C., Fernandez, A., Gauthier, R., David, M., & Rivard, G. (1993). Fetal loss associated with caffeine intake before and during pregnancy. *Journal of the American Medical Association, 270,* 2940–2943.

Insko, C. A. (1965). Verbal reinforcement of attitude. *Journal of Personality and Social Psychology, 2,* 621–623.

Irvine, J., Garner, D. M., Craig, H. M., & Logan, A. G. (1991). Prevalence of Type A behavior in untreated hypertensive individuals. *Hypertension, 18,* 72–78.

Isenberg, D. J. (1986). Group polarization: A critical review and meta-analysis. *Journal of Personality and Social Psychology, 50,* 1141–1151.

Iso-Ahola, S. E., & Blanchard, W. J. (1986). Psychological momentum and competitive sport performance: A field study. *Perceptual and Motor Skills, 62,* 763–768.

Istvan, J. (1986). Stress, anxiety, and birth outcomes: A critical review of the evidence. *Psychological Bulletin, 100,* 331–348.

Izard, C. E. (1972). *Patterns of emotion: A new analysis of anxiety and aggression.* New York: Academic Press.

Izard, C. E. (1977). *Human emotions.* New York: Plenum.

Izard, C. E. (1993). Four systems for emotional activation: Cognitive and metacognitive processes. *Psychological Review, 100,* 68–90.

Jackaway, R., & Teevan, R. (1976). Fear of failure and fear of success: Two dimensions of the same motive. *Sex Roles, 2,* 283–294.

Jacklin, C. N. (1989). Female and male: Issues of gender. *American Psychologist, 44,* 27–133.

Jacklin, C. N., & Maccoby, E. E. (1978). Social behavior at 33 months in same-sex and mixed-sex dyads. *Child Development, 49,* 557–569.

Jacobs, B. L. (1987). How hallucinogenic drugs work. *American Scientist, 75,* 386–392.

Jacobs, B. L., & Trulson, M. E. (1979). Mechanisms of action of LSD. *American Scientist, 67,* 396–404.

Jacobson, D. S. (1984). Neonatal correlates of prenatal exposure to smoking, caffeine, and alcohol. *Infant Behavior and Development, 7,* 253–265.

Jacoby, L. L., & Dallas, M. (1981). On the relationship between autobiographical memory and perceptual learning. *Journal of Experimental Psychology: General, 3,* 306–340.

Jacoby, R., & Glauberman, N. (Eds.), *The bell curve debate.* New York: Time Books/Random House.

James, W. (1890). *Principles of psychology.* New York: Holt, Rinehart & Winston.

James, W. (1892). *Psychology: Briefer course.* New York: Holt, Rinehart & Winston.

James, W. (1904). Does consciousness exist? *Journal of Philosophy, 1,* 477–491.

Janis, I. L. (1972). *Victims of groupthink.* Boston: Houghton Mifflin.

Janis, I. L. (1983a). *Groupthink: Psychological studies of policy decisions and fiascos* (2nd ed.). Boston: Houghton Mifflin.

Janis, I. L. (1983b). The role of social support in adherence to stressful decisions. *American Psychologist, 38,* 143–160.

Janoff-Bulman, R. (1979). Characterological versus behavioral self-blame: Inquiries into depression and rape. *Journal of Personality and Social Psychology, 37,* 1798–1809.

Jaroff, L. (1993). Lies of the mind. *Time,* November 29, 52–59.

Jeffery, R. W. (1989). Risk behaviors and health: Contrasting individual and population perspectives. *American Psychologist, 44,* 1194–1202.

Jenkins, C. D. (1976). Recent evidence supporting psychological and social risk factors for coronary disease. *New England Journal of Medicine, 294,* 1033–1038.

Jenkins, J. G., & Dallenbach, K. M. (1924). Oblivescence during sleep and waking. *American Journal of Psychology, 35,* 605–612.

Jensen, A. R. (1969). How much can we boost IQ and scholastic achievement? *Harvard Educational Review, 39,* 1–123.

Jensen, A. R. (1980). *Bias in mental testing.* New York: Free Press.

Jensen, A. R. (1981). *Straight talk about mental tests.* London: Methuen.

Jessor, R. (1993). Successful adolescent development among youth in high-risk settings. *American Psychologist, 48,* 117–126.

Johnson, D. L. (1989). Schizophrenia as a brain disease. *American Psychologist, 44,* 553–555.

Johnson, E. H. (1978). Validation of concept-learning strategies. *Journal of Experimental Psychology, 107,* 237–265.

Johnson, J., Weissman, M. M., & Klerman, G. L. (1990). Panic disorder, comorbidity, and suicide attempts. *Archives of General Psychiatry, 47,* 805–808.

Johnson, M. K., & Hasher, L. (1987). Human learning and memory. *Annual Review of Psychology, 38,* 631–668.

Jones, E. E. (1979). The rocky road from acts to dispositions.

American Psychologist, 34, 107–117.

Jones, E. E. (1990). *Interpersonal perception.* New York: Macmillan.

Jones, E. E., & Nisbett, R. E. (1971). *The actor and the observer: Divergent perceptions of behavior.* Morristown, NJ: General Learning Press.

Jones, K. L., Smith, D. W., Ulleland, C. N., & Streissgoth, A. P. (1973). Patterns of malformation in offspring of chronic alcoholic mothers. *Lancet, 3,* 1267–1271.

Jones, M. C. (1957). The careers of boys who were early or late maturing. *Child Development, 28,* 113–128.

Jordan, B. K., Marmar, C. R., Fairbank, J. A., Schlenger, W. E., Kulka, R. A., Hough, R. L., & Weiss, D. S. (1992). Problems in families of male Vietnam veterans with posttraumatic stress disorder. *Journal of Consulting and Clinical Psychology, 60,* 916–926.

Jordan, J., Kaplan, A., Miller, J., Striver, I., & Surrey, J. (1991). *Women's growth in connection.* New York: Guilford.

Journal of the American Medical Association (1995). Editorial. The Brown and Williamson Documents: Where do we go from here? July 19, *274,* 256–258.

Joyce, P. R., & Paykel, E. S. (1989). Predictors of drug response in depression. *Archives of General Psychiatry, 46,* 89–99.

Julien, R. M. (1985). *A primer of drug action* (4th ed.). San Francisco: Freeman.

Julien, R. M. (1988). *A primer of drug addiction* (5th ed.). New York: Freeman.

Kacmar, K. M., & Ferris, G. R. (1989). Theoretical and methodological considerations in the age-job satisfaction relationship. *Journal of Applied Psychology, 74,* 201–207.

Kagan, J. (1988). The meanings of personality predicates. *American Psychologist, 43,* 614–620.

Kahn, S., Zimmerman, G., Csikzentmihalyi, M., & Getzels, J. W. (1985). Relations between identity in young adulthood and intimacy at midlife. *Journal of Personality and Social Psychology, 49,* 1316–1322.

Kahneman, D., & Tversky, A. (1973). On the psychology of prediction. *Psychological Review, 80,* 237–251.

Kahneman, D., & Tversky, A. (1979). On the interpretation of intuitive probability: A reply to Jonathan Cohen. *Cognition, 7,* 409–411.

Kahneman, D., & Tversky, A. (1984). Choices, values, and frames. *American Psychologist, 39,* 341–350.

Kalat, J. W. (1984). *Biological psychology* (2nd ed.). Belmont, CA: Wadsworth.

Kales, A., Scharf, M. B., Kales, J. D., & Sodatos, C. R. (1979). Rebound insomnia: A potential hazard following withdrawal of certain benzodiazepines. *Journal of the American Medical Association, 241,* 1692–1695.

Kalish, R. A. (1976). Death and dying in a social context. In R. H. Binstock & E. Shanas (Eds.), *Handbook of aging and the social sciences.* New York: Van Nostrand Reinhold.

Kalish, R. A. (1982). *Late adulthood: Perspectives on human development.* Monterey, CA: Brooks/Cole.

Kamin, L. (1968). Attention-like processes in classical conditioning. In M. Jones (Ed.), *Miami symposium on the prediction of behavior: Aversive stimulation.* Miami: University of Miami Press.

Kamin, L. (1969). *Predictability, surprise, attention, and conditioning. In R. Church & B. Campbell (Eds.),* Punishment and aversion behaviors. Englewood Cliffs, NJ: Prentice-Hall.

Kamin, L. J. (1995). Behind the curve. *Scientific American, 272,*

99–103.

Kamiya, J., Barber, T. X., Miller, N. E., Shapiro, D., & Stoyva, J. (1977). *Biofeedback and self-control.* Chicago: Aldine.

Kandel, E. R., & Schwartz, J. H. (1982). Molecular biology of learning: Modulation of transmitter release. *Science, 218,* 433–443.

Kane, J. (1989). The current status of neuroleptics. *Journal of Clinical Psychiatry, 50,* 322–328.

Kanizsa, G. (1976). Subjective contours. *Scientific American, 234,* 48–52.

Kanner, A. D., Coyne, J. C., Schaefer, C., & Lazarus, R. S. (1981). Comparison of two modes of stress measurement: Daily hassles and uplifts versus major life events. *Journal of Behavioral Medicine, 4,* 1–39.

Kanner, L. (1943). Autistic disturbances of affective contact. *Nervous Child, 2,* 217–250.

Kaplan, G. M. (1991). The use of biofeedback in the treatment of chronic facial tics: A case study. *Medical Psychotherapy, 4,* 71–84.

Kaplan, H. S. (1974). *The new sex therapy: Active treatment of sexual dysfunction.* New York: Quadrangle.

Kaplan, H. S. (1975). *The illustrated manual of sex therapy.* New York: Quadrangle.

Kaplan, H. S., & Sadock, B. J. (1991). *Synopsis of psychiatry.* Baltimore: Williams & Wilkins.

Kaplan, R. M. (1984). The connection between clinical health promotion and health status. *American Psychologist, 39,* 755–765.

Kaplan, R. M., & Saccuzzo, D. P. (1989). *Psychological testing* (2nd ed.). Monterey, CA: Brooks/Cole.

Kaplan, S. (1987). Aesthetics, affect and cognition: Environmental preference from an evolutionary perspective. *Environment and Behavior, 19,* 3–32.

Karou, S. J., & Williams, K. D. (1993). Social loafing: A meta-analytic review and theoretical integration. *Journal of Personality and Social Psychology, 65,* 681–706.

Karoum, F., Karson, C. N., Bigelow, L. B., Lawson, W. B., & Wyatt, R. J. (1987). Preliminary evidence of reduced combined output of dopamine and its metabolites in chronic schizophrenia. *Archives of General Psychiatry, 44,* 604–607.

Kassin, S. M., Ellsworth, P. C., & Smith, V. L. (1989). The "general acceptance" of psychological research on eyewitness testimony: A survey of experts. *American Psychologist, 44,* 1089–1098.

Kastenbaum, R., & Costa, P. (1977). Psychological perspectives on death. *Annual Review of Psychology, 28,* 225–249.

Katzell, R. A., & Guzzo, R. A. (1983). Psychological approaches to productivity improvement. *American Psychologist, 38,* 468–472.

Katzell, R. A., & Thompson, D. E. (1990). Work motivation: Theory and practice. *American Psychologist, 45,* 144–153.

Katzman, R. (1987). Alzheimer's disease. *New England Journal of Medicine, 314,* 964–973.

Kay, S. R. (1990). Significance of the positive-negative distinction in schizophrenia. *Schizophrenia Bulletin, 16,* 635–652.

Kay, S. R., & Singh, M. M. (1989). The positive-negtive distinction in drug-free schizophrenic patients. *Archives of General Psychiatry, 46,* 711–717.

Kazdin, A. E., Esveldt-Dawson, K., French, N. H., & Unis, A. S. (1987). Problem-solving skills training and relationship therapy in the treatment of antisocial child behavior. *Journal of Consulting and Clinical Psychology, 55,* 76–85.

Keating, D. P. (1980). Thinking processes in adolescents. In J. Adelson (Ed.), *Handbook of adolescent psychology.* New York: Wiley.

Keesey, R. E., & Powley, T. L. (1975). Hypothalamic regulation of body weight. *American Scientist, 63,* 558–565.

Keesey, R. E., & Powley, T. L. (1986). The regulation of body weight. *Annual Review of Psychology, 37,* 109–133.

Keith, P. M. (1983). A comparison of the resources of parents and childless men and women in very old age. *Family Relations, 32,* 403–409.

Kelley, H. H. (1967). Attribution theory in social psychology. In D. Levine (Ed.), *Nebraska symposium on motivation.* Lincoln: University of Nebraska Press.

Kelley, H. H. (1973). The process of causal attribution. *American Psychologist, 28,* 107–128.

Kelley, H. H. (1992). Common-sense psychology and scientific psychology. *Annual Review of Psychology, 43,* 1–24.

Kelley, H. H., & Michela, J. L. (1980). Attribution theory and research. *Annual Review of Psychology, 31,* 457–501.

Kelley, H. H., & Thibault, J. W. (1978). *Interpersonal relations: A theory of interdependence.* New York: Wiley.

Kelley, K. (1985). Sex, sex guilt, and authoritarianism: Differences in responses to explicit heterosexual and masturbatory slides. *The Journal of Sex Research, 21,* 68–85.

Kelly, J. A., Kalichman, S. C., Kauth, M. R., Kilgore, H. G., Hood, H. V., et al. (1991). Situational factors associated with AIDS risk behavior lapses and coping strategies used by gay men who successfuly avoid lapses. *American Journal of Public Health, 81,* 1335–1338.

Kelly, J. A., Murphy, D. A., Sikkema, K. J., & Kalichman, S. C. (1993). Psychological interventions to prevent HIV infection are urgently needed. *American Psychologist, 48,* 1023–1034.

Kelly, J. A., & St. Lawrence, J. S. (1988). *The AIDS health crisis.* New York: Plenum.

Kelly, J. A., St. Lawrence, J. S., Hood, H. V., & Brasfield, T. L. (1989). Behavior intervention to reduce AIDS risk activities. *Journal of Consulting and Clinical Psychology, 57,* 60–67.

Kempler, D., & Van Lanker, D. (1987). The right turn of phrase. *Psychology Today, 21,* 20–22.

Kendall, P. C., & Clarkin, J. F. (1992). Introduction to special section: Comorbidity and treatment implications. *Journal of Consulting and Clinical Psychology, 60,* 833–834.

Kendler, K. S., & Gruenberg, A. M. (1982). Genetic relationship between paranoid personality disorder and the "schizophrenic" spectrum disorders. *American Journal of Psychiatry, 139,* 1185–1186.

Kendler, K. S., Gruenberg, A. M., & Kinney, D. K. (1994). Independent diagnoses of adoptees and relatives as defined by the *DSM-III-R* in the Provincial and National Samples of the Danish Adoption Study of Schizophrenia. *Archives of General Psychiatry, 51,* 456–468.

Kendler, K. S., Neale, M. C., Kessler, R. C., Heath, A. C., & Eaves, L. J. (1993). A longitudinal twin study of 1-year prevalence of major depression in women. *Archives of General Psychiatry, 50,* 843–852.

Kendler, K. S., Walters, E. E., Truett, K. R., et al. (1994). Sources of individual differences in depressive symptoms: Analysis of two samples of twins and their families. *American Journal of Psychiatry, 51,* 1605–1614.

Kendrick, D. T., & Funder, D. C. (1988). Profiting from controversy: Lesson from the person-situation debate. *American Psychologist, 43,* 23–34.

Kendrick, D. T., & Funder, D. C. (1991). The person-situation debate: Do personality traits really exist? In V. J. Derlega et al. (Eds.), *Personality: Contemporary theory and research.* Chicago: Nelson-Hall.

Kermis, M. D. (1984). *The psychology of human aging.* Boston: Allyn & Bacon.

Kershner, J. R., & Ledger, G. (1985). Effect of sex, intelligence, and style of thinking on creativity: A comparison of gifted and average IQ children. *Journal of Personality and Social Psychology, 48,* 1033–1040.

Kessler, R. C., McGonagle, K. A., Zhao, S., Nelson, C. P., et al. (1994). Lifetime and 12-month prevalence of DSM-III-R psychiatric disorders in the United States: Results from the National Comorbidity Survey. *Archives of General Psychiatry, 51,* 18–19.

Kessler, S. (1980). The genetics of schizophrenia: A review. In S. J. Keith & L. R. Mosher (Eds.), *Special report: Schizophrenia.* Washington, DC: U.S. Government Printing Office.

Kett, J. F. (1977). *Rites of passage: Adolescence in America from 1790 to the present.* New York: Basic Books.

Kety, S. S., Wender, P. H., Jacobsen, B., Ingraham, L. J., Jansson, L., Faber, B., & Kinney, D. K. (1994). Mental illness in the biological and adoptive relatives of schizophrenic adoptees. *Archives of General Psychiatry, 51,* 442–455.

Key, M. R. (1975). *Male/female language.* Metuchen, NJ: Scarecrow Press.

Kientzle, M. J. (1946). Properties of learning curves under varied distributions of practice. *Journal of Experimental Psychology, 36,* 187–211.

Kiester, E. (1984a). The playing fields of the mind. *Psychology Today, 18,* 18–24.

Kiester, E. (1984b). The uses of anger. *Psychology Today, 18,* 26.

Kiester, E., Jr. (1980). Images of the night: The physiological roots of dreaming. *Science 80, 1,* 36–43.

Kihlstrom, J. F. (1985). Hypnosis. *Annual Review of Psychology, 26,* 557–591.

Kihlstrom, J. F. (1987). The cognitive unconscious. *Science, 327,* 1445–1452.

Kimball, M. M. (1989). A new perspective on women's math achievement. *Psychological Bulletin, 105,* 198–214.

Kimble, G. A. (1981). Biological and cognitive constraints on learning. In L. Benjamin (Ed.), *The G. Stanley Hall Lecture Series* (Vol. 1). Washington, DC: American Psychological Association.

Kimble, G. A. (1989). Psychologist from the standpoint of a generalist. *American Psychologist, 44,* 491–499.

Kimmel, D. C. (1988). Ageism, psychology, and public policy. *American Psychologist, 43,* 175–178.

Kimmel, H. D. (1974). Instrumental conditioning of autonomically-mediated responses in human beings. *American Psychologist, 29,* 325–335.

King, M., Murray, M. A., & Atkinson, T. (1982). Background, personality, job characteristics, and satisfaction with work in a national sample. *Human Relations, 35,* 119–133.

King, M. J., Zir, L. M., Kaltman, A. J., & Fox, A. C. (1973). Variant angina associated with angiographically demonstrated coronary artery system spasm and REM sleep. *American Journal of Medical Science, 265,* 419–422.

Kingsbury, S. J. (1995). Where does research on the effectiveness of psychotherapy stand today? *The Harvard Mental Health Letter, 12(3),* 8.

Kinsbourne, M. (1982). Hemispheric specialization and the growth of human understanding. *American Psychologist, 37,* 411–420.

Kinsey, A. C., Pomeroy, W. B., & Martin, C. E. (1948). *Sexual behavior in the human male.* Philadelphia: Saunders.

Kinsey, A. C., Pomeroy, W. B., Martin, C. E., & Gebhard, P. H. (1953). *Sexual behavior in the human female.* Philadelphia: Saunders.

Kirby, D. A., & Verrier, R. L. (1989). Differential effects of sleep stage on coronary hemodynamic function during stenosis. *Physiology and Behavior, 45,* 1017–1020.

Kirkpatrick, D. L. (1976). Evaluation of training. In R. L. Craig (Ed.), *Training and development handbook* (2nd ed.). New York: McGraw-Hill.

Kirscht, J. P. (1983). Preventive health behavior: A review of research and issues. *Health Psychology, 2,* 277–301.

Klayman, J., & Ha, Y-W. (1987). Confirmation, disconfirmation, and information in hypothesis testing. *Psychological Review, 94,* 211–228.

Kleitman, N. (1963a). Patterns of dreaming. *Scientific American, 203,* 82–88.

Kleitman, N. (1963b). *Sleep and wakefuless.* Chicago: University of Chicago Press.

Klepinger, D. H., Billy, J. O. G., Tanfer, K., & Grady, W. R. (1993). Perceptions of AIDS risk and severity and their association with risk-related behavior among U.S. men. *Family Planning Perspectives, 25,* 74–82.

Klerman, G. L. (1990). Treatment of recurrent unipolar major depressive disorder. *Archives of General Psychiatry, 47,* 1158–1162.

Knapp, S., & VandeCreek, L. (1989). What psychologists need to know about AIDS. *The Journal of Training and Practice in Professional Psychology, 3,* 3–16.

Knittle, J. L. (1975). Early influences on development of adipose tissue. In G. A. Bray (Ed.), *Obesity in perspective.* Washington, DC: U.S. Government Printing Office.

Knowles, E. S. (1983). Social physics and the effects of others: Tests of the effects of audience size and distance on social judgments and behavior. *Journal of Personality and Social Psychology, 45,* 1263–1279.

Kobasa, S. C. (1979). Stressful life events, personality, and health: An inquiry into hardiness. *Journal of Personality and Social Psychology, 37,* 1–11.

Kobasa, S. C. (1982). The hardy personality: Toward a social pychology of stress and health. In G. S. Sanders & J. Suls (Eds.), *Social psychology of health and illness.* Hillsdale, NJ: Erlbaum.

Kobasa, S. C. (1987). Stress responses and personality. In R. C. Barnette, L. Beiner, & G. K. Baruch (Eds.), *Gender and stress.* New York: Free Press.

Kocel, K. M. (1977). Cognitive abilities: Handedness, familial sinistrality, and sex. *Annals of the New York Academy of Sciences, 299,* 233–243.

Koestler, A. (1964). *The act of creation.* New York: Macmillan.

Kohlberg, L. (1963). Moral development and identification. In H. W. Stevenson (Ed.), *Child psychology.* Chicago: University of Chicago Press.

Kohlberg, L. (1969). *Stages in the development of moral thought and action.* New York: Holt, Rinehart & Winston.

Kohlberg, L. (1981). *Philosophy of moral development.* New York: HarperCollins.

Kohlberg, L. (1985). *The psychology of moral development.* New York: HarperCollins.

Köhler, W. (1969). *The task of Gestalt psychology.* Princeton, NJ: Princeton University Press.

Kolata, G. (1987). What babies know, and noises parents make. *Science, 237,* 726.

Kolb, B. (1989). Brain development, plasticity, and behavior. *American Psychologist, 44,* 1203–1212.

Korchin, S. J., & Scheldberg, D. (1981). The future of clinical assessment. *American Psychologist, 36,* 1147–1158.

Kornhuber, H. H. (1974). Cerebral cortex, cerebellum, and basal ganglia: An introduction to their motor function. In F. O. Schmitt & F. G. Worden (Eds.), *The neurosciences: Third study program.* Cambridge: MIT Press.

Koslow, D. R., & Salett, E. P. (1989). *Crossing cultures in mental health.* Washington, DC: SIETAR International.

Koss, M. P., & Butcher, J. N. (1986). Research on brief psychotherapy. In S. L. Garfield & A. E. Bergin (Eds.), *Handbook of psychotherapy and behavior change* (3rd ed.). New York: Wiley.

Kosslyn, S. M. (1987). Seeing and imagining in the cerebral hemispheres: A computational approach. *Psychological Review, 94,* 148–175.

Kraepelin, E. (1883). *Compendium der psychiatrie.* Leipzig: Abel.

Kramer, B. A. (1985). The use of ECT in California, 1977–1983. *The American Journal of Psychiatry, 142,* 1190–1192.

Krantz, D. S., & Glass, D. C. (1984). Personality, behavior patterns, and physical illness: Conceptual and methodological issues. In W. D. Gentry (Ed.), *Handbook of behavioral medicine.* New York: Guilford.

Krantz, D. S., Grunberg, N. E., & Braum, A. (1985). Health psychology. *Annual Review of Psychology, 36,* 349–383.

Kripke, D. F., & Gillin, J. C. (1985). Sleep disorders. In J. O. Cavenar (Ed.), *Psychiatry.* Philadelphia: Lippincott.

Krueger, J. M., & Obal, F. (1993). A neuronal group theory of sleep function. *Journal of Sleep Research, 2,* 63–69.

Krueger, W. C. F. (1929). The effect of overlearning on retention. *Journal of Experimental Psychology, 12,* 71–78.

Krull, D. S., & Erickson, D. J. (1995). Inferential hopscotch: How people draw social inferences from behavior. *Current Directions in Psychological Science, 4,* 35–38.

Krupat, E. (1985). *People in cities: The urban environment and its effects.* New York: Cambridge University Press.

Kübler-Ross, E. (1969). *On death and dying.* New York: Macmillan.

Kübler-Ross, E. (1981). *Living with death and dying.* New York: Macmillan.

Kunst-Wilson, W. R., & Zajonc, R. B. (1980). Affective discrimination that cannot be recognized. *Science, 207,* 557–558.

Kupfer, D. J, Frank, E., & Perel, J. M. (1989). The advantage of early treatment intervention in recurrent depression. *Archives of General Psychiatry, 46,* 771–775.

Labov, W. (1973). The boundaries of words and their meaning. In C. J. N. Bailey & R. W. Shuy (Eds.), *New ways of analyzing variations in English.* Washington, DC: Georgetown University Press.

Lafferty, P., Beuter, L. E., & Crago, M. (1989). Differences between more and less effective psychotherapists: A study of select therapist variables. *Journal of Consulting and Clinical Psychology, 57,* 76–80.

Laird, J. (1984). The real role of facial response in the experience of emotion: A reply to Tourangeau and Ellsworth, and others. *Journal of Personality and Social Psychology, 47,* 909–917.

Laird, J. M. A., & Bennett, G. J. (1991). *Dorsal horn neurons in rats with an experimental peripheral mononeuropathy.* Paper presented at the 21st Annual Meeting of the Society for Neuroscience, New Orleans.

Lakoff, R. (1975). *Language and women's place.* New York: HarperCollins.

Lamb, M. E. (1977). Father-infant and mother-infant interaction in the first year of life. *Child Development, 48,* 167–181.

Lamb, M. E. (1979). Paternal influences and the father's role: A personal perspective. *American Psychologist, 34,* 938–943.

Lamb, M. E., Hwang, C. P., Frodi, A. M., & Frodi, M. (1982). Security of mother and father infant attachment and its reaction to sociability with strangers in traditional and nontraditional Swedish families. *Infant Behavior and Development, 5,* 355–368.

Lamb, M. E., & Sternberg, K. J. (1990). Do we really know how day care affects children? *Journal of Applied Developmental Psychology, 11,* 499.

Landers, D. M. (1982). Arousal, attention, and skilled performance: Further considerations. *Quest, 33,* 271–283.

Landers, S. (1987). Panel urges teen contraception. *APA Monitor, 18,* 6.

Landesman, S., & Butterfield, E. C. (1987). Normalization and de-institutionalization of mentally retarded individuals. *American Psychologist, 42,* 809–816.

Landesman, S., & Ramey, C. (1989). Developmental psychology and mental retardation: Integrating scientific principles with treatment practices. *American Psychologist, 44,* 409–415.

Landy, F. J. (1989). *Psychology of work behavior* (2nd ed.). Homewood, IL: Dorsey Press.

Landy, F. J., Shankster, L. J., & Köhler, S. S. (1994). Personnel selection and placement. *Annual Review of Psychology, 45,* 261–296.

Lanetto, R. (1980). *Children's conceptions of death.* New York: Springer.

Lang, P. J. (1985). The cognitive psychophysiology of emotion: Fear and anxiety. In A. H. Tuma & J. D. Maser (Eds.), *Anxiety and the anxiety disorders.* Hillsdale, NJ: Erlbaum.

Langer, S. K. (1951). *Philosophy in a new key.* New York: New American Library.

Larson, R., & Ham, M. (1993). Stress and "storm and stress" in early adolescence: The relationship of negative events with dysphoric affect. *Developmental Psychology, 29,* 130–140.

Larson, R., & Lampman-Petraitis, R. (1989). Daily emotional states as reported by children and adolescents. *Child Development, 60,* 1250–1260.

Lashley, K. S. (1950). In search of the engram. *Symposia for the Society for Experimental Biology, 4,* 454–482.

Lasky, R. E., & Kallio, K. D. (1978). Transformation rules in concept learning. *Memory and Cognition, 6,* 491–495.

Latané, B., & Darley, J. M. (1968). Group inhibition of bystander intervention in emergencies. *Journal of Personality and Social Psychology, 10,* 215–221.

Latané, B., & Darley, J. M. (1970). *The unresponsive bystander: Why doesn't he help?* Englewood Cliffs, NJ: Prentice-Hall.

Latané, B., & Nida, S. (1981). Ten years of research on group size and helping. *Psychological Bulletin, 89,* 308–324.

Latané, B., Williams, K., & Harkins, S. (1979). Many hands make light work: The causes and consequences of social loafing. *Journal of Personality and Social Psychology, 37,* 822–832.

Latham, G. P. (1988). Human resource training and development. *Annual Review of Psychology, 39,* 545–582.

Lattal, K. A. (1992). B. F. Skinner and psychology: Introduction to the special issue. *American Psychologist, 47,* 1269–1272.

Lauer, J., & Lauer, R. (1985). Marriages made to last. *Psychology Today, 19,* 22–26.

Laumann, E. O., Michael, R., Michael, S., & Gagnon, J. (1994). *The social organization of sexuality.* Chicago: University of Chicago Press.

Lavond, D. G., Kim, J. J., & Thompson, R. F. (1993). Mammaliam brain substrates of aversive classical conditioning. *Annual Review of Psychology, 44,* 317–342.

Lawler, E. E. (1982). Strategies for improving the quality of work life. *American Psychologist, 37,* 486–493.

Lazarus, R. S. (1981). Little hassles can be hazardous to your health. *Psychology Today, 15,* 58–62.

Lazarus, R. S. (1991a). Cognition and motivation in emotion. *American Psychologist, 46,* 352–367.

Lazarus, R. S. (1991b). Progress on a cognitive-motivational-relational theory of emotion. *American Psychologist, 46,* 819–834.

Lazarus, R. S. (1991c). *Emotion and adaptation.* New York:

Lazarus, R. S. (1993). From psychological stress to the emotions: A history of changing outlooks. *Annual Review of Psychology, 44,* 1–21.

Lazarus, R. S., & Folkman, S. (1984). *Stress, appraisal, and coping.* New York: Springer.

Leahey, T. H., & Harris, R. J. (1989). *Human learning* (2nd ed.). Englewood Cliffs, NJ: Prentice-Hall.

LeDoux, J. E. (1995). Emotion: Clues from the brain. *Annual Review of Psychology, 46,* 209–235.

Lee, I. M., Manson, J. E., Hennekens, C. H., & Paffenbarger, R. S. (1993). Body weight and mortality: A 27-year follow-up of middle-aged men. *Journal of the American Medical Association, 270,* 2823–2828.

Leger, D. W. (1992). *Biological foundations of behavior: An integrative approach.* New York: HarperCollins.

Lehrer, P. M., & Woolfolk, R. L. (1984). Are stress reduction techniques interchangeable, or do they have specific effects? A review of the comparative empirical literature. In L. Woolfolk & P. M. Lehrer (Eds.), *Principles and practice of stress management.* New York: Guilford.

Lempers, J. D., Flavell, E. R., & Flavell, J. H. (1977). The development in very young children of tactile knowledge concerning visual perception. *Genetic Psychology Monographs, 95,* 3–53.

Lenneberg, E. H. (1967). *Biological foundations of language.* New York: Wiley.

Lenneberg, E. H., Rebelsky, F. G., & Nichols, I. A. (1965). The vocalizations of infants born to deaf and hearing parents. *Human Development, 8,* 23–27.

Lenzenweger, M. F., Dworkin, R. H., & Wethington, E. (1989). Models of positive and negative symptoms in schizophrenia: An empirical evaluation of latent structures. *Journal of Abnormal Psychology, 98,* 62–70.

Leon, G. R., & Roth, L. (1977). Obesity: Psychological causes, correlations and speculations. *Psychological Bulletin, 84,* 117–139.

Leonard, H. L., Swedo, S. E., Lenane, M. C., Rettew, D. C., Hamburger, S. D., et al. (1993). A 2- to 7-year follow-up study of 54 obsessive-compulsive children and adolescents. *Archives of General Psychiatry, 50,* 429–439.

Lerner, M. J. (1965). The effect of responsibility and choice on a partner's attractiveness following failure. *Journal of Personality, 33,* 178–187.

Lerner, M. J. (1980). *The belief in a just world.* New York: Plenum.

Lerner, R. M. (1978). Nature, nurture, and dynamic interactionism. *Human Development, 21,* 1–20.

LeVay, S. (1991). A difference in hypothalamic structure between heterosexual and homosexual men. *Science, 253,* 1034–1037.

Leventhal, H., & Cleary, P. D. (1980). The smoking problem: A review of the research and theory in behavioral risk modification. *Psychological Bulletin, 88,* 370–405.

Levine, H. Z. (1983). Safety and health programs. *Personnel, 3,* 4–9.

Levine, J. D., Gordon, N. C., & Fields, H. L. (1979). Naloxone dose dependently produces analgesia and hyperalgesia in postoperative pain. *Nature, 278,* 740–741.

Levine, J. M., & Moreland, R. L. (1990). Progress in small group research. *Annual Review of Psychology, 41,* 585–634.

Levine, J. M., Resnick, L. B., & Higgins, E. T. (1993). Social foundations of cognition. *Annual Review of Psychology, 44,* 585–612.

Levine, M., Toro, P. A., & Perkins, D. V. (1993). Social and community interventions. *Annual Review of Psychology, 44,* 525–558.

Levine, M. F., Taylor, J. C., & Davis, L. E. (1984). Defining quality of work life. *Human Relations, 37,* 81–104.

Levine, M. W., & Shefner, J. M. *Fundamentals of sensation and perception* (2nd ed.). Pacific Grove, CA: Brooks/Cole.

Levinson, D. J. (1978). *The seasons of a man's life.* New York: Ballantine Books.

Levinson, D. J. (1986). A conception of adult development. *American Psychologist, 41,* 3–13.

Levinson, D. J., Darrow, C. M., Klein, E. B., Levinson, M. H., & McKee, B. (1974). *The seasons of a man's life.* New York: Knopf.

Levinthal, C. F. (983). *Introduction to physiological psychology* (2nd ed.). Englewood Cliffs, NJ: Prentice-Hall.

Lewinsohn, P. M., Zeiss, A. M., & Duncan, E. M. (1989). Probability of relapse after recovery from an episode of depression. *Journal of Abnormal Psychology, 98,* 107–116.

Ley, B. W. (1985). Alcohol problems in special populations. In J. H. Mendelson & N. K. Mello (Eds.), *The diagnosis and treatment of alcoholism* (2nd ed.). New York: McGraw-Hill.

Ley, P. (1977). Psychological studies of doctor-patient communication. In S. Rachman (Ed.), *Contributions to medical psychology* (Vol. 1). Elmsford, NY: Pergamon Press.

Lidz, T. (1973). *The origin and treatment of schizophrenic disorders.* New York: Basic Books.

Lieberman, J., Jody, D., Geisler, S., Alvir, J., Loebel, A., et al. (1993). Time course and biological correlates of treatment response in first-episode schizophrenia. *Archives of General Psychiatry, 50,* 369–376.

Lieberman, M. A. (1983). The effects of social support on response to stress. In L. Goldbert & D. S. Breznitz (Eds.), Handbook of stress management. New York: Free Press.

Lightman, S. W., Pisarska, K., Berman, E. R., Pestone, M., et al. (1992). Discrepancy between self-reported and actual caloric intake in obese subjects. *The New England Journal of Medicine, 327,* 1893–1898.

Lin, E., & Kleinman, A. (1988). Psychotherapy and clinical course of schizophrenia: A cross-cultural perspective. *Schizophrenia Bulletin, 14,* 555–567.

Lin, T. R., Dobbins, G. H., & Farh, J. L. (1992). A field study of race and similarity effects on interview ratings in conventional and situational interviews. *Journal of Applied Psychology,* 77, 363–371.

Lincoln, J. R., & Kalleberg, A. L. (1985). Work organization and workforce commitment: A study of plants and employees in the U.S. and Japan. *American Sociological Review, 50,* 738–760.

Lindsley, D. B., Bowden, J., & Magoun, H. W. (1949). Effect upon EEG of acute injury to the brain stem activating system. *Electroencephalography and Clinical Neurophysiology, 1,* 475–486.

Link, S. W. (1995). Rediscovering the past: Gustav Fechner and signal detection theory. *Psychological Science, 5,* 335–340.

Linn, M. C., & Peterson, A. C. (1985). Emergence and characterization of sex differences in spatial ability: A meta-analysis. *Child Development, 56,* 1479–1498.

Lipsey, M. W., & Wilson, D. B. (1993). The efficacy of psychological, educational, and behavioral treatment: Confirmation from meta-analysis. *American Psychologist, 48,* 1181–1209.

Litt, M. D. (1988). Self-efficacy and perceived control: Cognitive mediators of pain tolerance. *Journal of Personality and Social Psychology, 54,* 149–160.

Locke, E. A. (1968). Toward a theory of task motivation and incentives. *Organizational Behavior and Human Performance, 3,* 157–189.

Locke, E. A. (1976). The nature and causes of job satisfaction. In M. D. Dunnette (Ed.), *Handbook of industrial and organizational psychology.* Skokie, IL: Rand McNally.

Locke, E. A., & Latham, G. P. (1984). *Goal setting: A motivational technique that works.* Englewood Cliffs, NJ: Prentice-Hall.

Locke, E. A., Shaw, K. N., Saari, L. M., & Latham, G. (1981). Goal-setting and task performance: 1969–1980. *Psychological Bulletin, 90,* 124–152.

Lockhard, J. S., & Paulus, D. L. (Eds.). (1988). *Self-deception: An adaptive mechanism? Englewood Cliffs, NJ: Prentice-Hall.*

Lockyer, L., & Rutter, M. L. (1969). *A five- to fifteen-year follow-up study of infantile psychosis.* British Journal of Psychiatry, 115, 865–882.

Loftus, E. F. (1984). The eyewitness on trial. In B. D. Sales & A. Alwork (Eds.), *With liberty and justice for all.* Englewood Cliffs, NJ: Prentice-Hall.

Loftus, E. F. (1991). The glitter of everyday memory . . . and the gold. *American Psychologist, 46,* 16–18.

Loftus, E. F. (1993a). The reality of repressed memories. *American Psychologist, 48,* 518–537.

Loftus, E. F. (1993b). *Therapeutic memories of early childhood abuse: Fact or fiction.* Paper presented at the Annual Meeting of the American Psychological Association, Toronto.

Loftus, E. F. (1994). The repressed memory controversy. *American Psychologist, 49,* 443–445.

Loftus, E. F., & Klinger, M. R. (1992). Is the unconscious smart or dumb? *American Psychologist, 47,* 761–765.

Loftus, E. F., & Loftus, G. R. (1980). On the permanence of stored information in the human brain. *American Psychologist, 35,* 409–420.

Loftus, E. F., Miller, D. G., & Burns, H. J (1978). Semantic integration of verbal information into a visual memory. *Journal of Experimental Psychology: Human Learning and Memory, 4,* 19–31.

Loftus, E. F., & Zanni, G. (1975). Eyewitness testimony: The influence of wording on a question. *Bulletin of the Psychonomic Society, 5,* 86–88.

Londerville, S., & Main, M. (1981). Security of attachment and compliance in maternal training methods in the second year of life. *Developmental Psychology, 17,* 289–299.

Long, P. (1986). Medical mesmerism. *Psychology Today, 20*(1), 28–29.

Lonner, W. J. (1980). The search for psychological universals. In H. C. Triandis & W. W. Lambert (Eds.), *Handbook of cross-cultural psychology* (Vol. I). Boston: Allyn & Bacon.

Lord, C. G. (1980). Schemas and images as memory aids. *Journal of Personality and Social Psychology, 38,* 257–269.

Lorenz, K. (1969). *On aggression.* New York: Bantam Books.

Lott, A. J., & Lott, B. E. (1974). The role of reward in the formation of positive interpersonal attitudes. In T. L. Huston (Ed.), *Foundations of interpersonal attraction.* New York: Academic Press.

Lovaas, O. I. (1987). Behavioral treatment and normal educational and intellectual functioning in young autistic children. *Journal of Consulting and Clinical Psychology, 55,* 3–9.

Lovaas, O. I., & Smith, P. (1988). Intensive behavioral treatment for young autistic children. In B. Lahey & A. Kazdin (Eds.), *Advances in clinical child psychology* (Vol. 2). New York: Plenum.

Lozoff, B. (1989). Nutrition and behavior. *American Psychologist, 44,* 231–236.

Lubin, B., Larsen, R. M., & Matarazzo, J. D. (1984). Patterns of psychological test usage in the United States: 1935–1982. *American Psychologist, 39,* 451–454.

Luborsky, I., Barber, J. P., & Beutler, L. (Eds.). (1993). Curative factors in dynamic psychotherapy. *Journal of Consulting and Clinical Psychology, 61,* 539–610.

Lucas, E. A., Foutz, A. S., Dement, W. C., & Mittler, M. M. (1979). Sleep cycle organization in narcoleptic and normal dogs. *Physiology and Behavior, 23,* 325–331.

Lugaresi, E., R., Montagna, P., Baruzzi, A., Cortelli, P., Lugaresi, A., Tinuper, P., Zucconi, M., & Gambetti, P. (1986). Fatal familial insomnia and dyautonomia with selective degeneration of the thalamic nuclei. *New England Journal of Medicine, 315,* 997–1003.

Luh, C. W. (1922). The conditions of retention. *Psychological Monographs* (Whole No. 142).

Lykken, D. T. (1957). A study of anxiety in sociopathic personality. *Journal of Abnormal and Social Psychology, 55,* 6–10.

Lykken, D. T. (1982). Fearlessness: Its carefree charm and deadly risk. *Psychology Today, 16,* 20–28.

Lykken, D. T., McGue, M., Tellegen, A., & Bouchard, T. J., Jr. (1992). Emergenesis: Genetic traits that may not run in families. *American Psychologist, 47,* 1565–1577.

Lynch, G., & Baudry, M. (1984). The biochemistry of memory: A new and specific hypothesis. *Science, 224,* 1057–1063.

Lyness, S. A. (1993). Predictors of differences between Type A and B individuals in heart rate and blood pressure reactivity. *Psychological Bulletin, 114,* 266–295.

Lynn, D. (1974). *The father: His role in child development.* Monterey, CA: Brooks/Cole.

Lynn, R. (1977). The intelligence of the Japanese. *Bulletin of the British Psychological Society, 30,* 69–72.

Lynn, R. (1982). IQ in Japan and the United States shows a greater disparity. *Nature, 297,* 222–223.

Lynn, R. (1987). The intelligence of the Mongoloids: A psychometric, evolutionary, and neurological theory. *Personality and Individual Differences, 8,* 813–844.

Lynn, R. (1991). Educational achievements of Asian Americans. *American Psychologist, 46,* 875–876.

Lynn, S. J., & Rhue, J. W. (1986). The fantasy-prone person: Hyp-

nosis, imagination, and creativity. *Journal of Personality and Social Psychology, 51,* 404–408.

Lynn, S. J., Rhue, J. W., & Weekes, J. R. (1990). Hypnotic involuntariness: A social cognitive analysis. *Psychological Review, 97,* 69–184.

Lytton, H., & Romney, D. M. (1991). Parents' differential socialization of boys and girls: A meta-analysis. *Psychological Bulletin, 109,* 267–296.

Maccoby, E. E. (1988). Gender as a social category. *Developmental Psychology, 24,* 755–765.

Maccoby, E. E. (1990). Gender and relationships: A developmental account. *American Psychologist, 45,* 513–520.

Maccoby, E. E., & Jacklin, C. N. (1974). *The psychology of sex differences.* Stanford, CA: Stanford University Press.

Maccoby, E. E., & Jacklin, C. N. (1980) Sex differences in aggression: A rejoinder and reprise. *Child Development, 51,* 964–980.

Maccoby, E. E., & Jacklin, C. N. (1987). Gender segregation in childhood. In E. H. Reese (Ed.), *Advances in child development and behavior* (Vol. 23). New York: Academic Press.

MacDonald, M. R., & Kuiper, N. A. (1983). Cognitive behavioral preparations for surgery: Some theoretical and methodological concerns. *Clinical Psychology Review, 3,* 27–39.

Mace, N. L., & Rabins, P. V. (1981). *The 36-hour day.* Baltimore: Johns Hopkins University Press.

Mackenzie, B. (1984). Explaining race differences in IQ: The logic, the methodology, and the evidence. *American Psychologist, 39,* 1214–1233.

Mackintosh, N. J. (1975). A theory of attention: Variations in the associability of stimuli with reinforcement. *Psychological Review, 82,* 276–298.

Mackintosh, N. J. (1986). The biology of intelligence? *British Journal of Psychology, 77,* 1–18.

Mackowiak, P. A., Wasserman, S. S., & Levine, M. M. (1992). A critical appraisal of 98.6F, the upper limit of the normal body temperature, and other legacies of Carl Reinhold August Wunderlich. *Journal of the American Medical Association, 268,* 1578–1580.

MacMillan, J., & Kofoed, L. (1984). Sociobiology and antiocial personality: An alternative perspective. *Journal of Mental Disorders, 172,* 701–706.

Maddi, S. R., & Kobasa, S. C. (1984). *The hardy executive: Health and stress.* Homewood, IL: Dorsey Press.

Magid, K. (1988). *High Risk: Children Without a Conscience.* New York: Bantam.

Madigan, S., & O'Hara, R. (1992). Short-term memory at the turn of the century. Mary Whiton Calkin's memory research. *American Psychologist, 47,* 170–174.

Magnusson, D. (1990). Personality development from an interactional perspective. In L. A. Pervin (Ed.), *Handbook of personality.* New York: Guilford.

Magnusson, D., & Edler, N. S. (Eds.). (1977). *Personality at the crossroads: An international perspective.* Hillsdale, NJ: Erlbaum.

Magsud, M. (1979). Resolution and moral dilemmas by Nigerian secondary school pupils. *Journal of Moral Education, 7,* 40–49.

Maguire, J. (1990). *Care and feeding of the brain.* New York: Doubleday.

Maharishi, Mahesh Yogi. (1963). *The science of living and art of being.* London: Unwin.

Mahowald, M. W., & Schenck, C. H. (1989). REM sleep behavior disorder. In M. H. Krygr, T. Roth, & W. C. Dement (Eds.), *Principles and practice of sleep medicine.* Philadelphia: Saunders.

Maier, N. R. F. (1931). Reasoning in humans: II. The solution of a problem and its appearance in consciousness. *Journal of Experimental Psychology, 105,* 181–194.

Malatesta, C. A., & Isard, C. E. (1984). The ontogenesis of human social signals: From biological imperative to symbol utilization. In N. A. Fox & R. J. Davidson (Eds.), *The psychobiology of affective development.* Hillsdale, NJ: Erlbaum.

Mandler, G. (1980). Recognizing: The judgment of previous occurrence. *Psychological Review, 87,* 252–271.

Manning, M. L. (1983). Three myths concerning adolescence. *Adolescence, 18,* 823–829.

Marengo, J. T., & Harrow, M. (1987). Schizophrenic thought disorder at follow-up. *Archives of General Psychiatry, 44,* 651–659.

Markowitz, J. S., Weissman, M. M., Ouellete, R., Lish, J. D., & Klerman, G. L. (1989). Quality of life in panic disorder. *Archives of General Psychiatry, 46,* 984–992.

Marks, I. M. (1986). Epidemiology of anxiety. *Social Psychiatry, 21,* 167–171.

Marschark, M., Richmond, C. L., Yuille, J. C., & Hunt, R. R. (1987). The role of imagery in memory: On shared and distinctive information. *Psychological Bulletin, 102,* 28–41.

Martin, B. J. (1986). Sleep deprivation and exercise. In K. B. Pandolf (Ed.), *Exercise and sport sciences review* (pp. 213–229). New York: Macmillan.

Martin, C. L. (1991). The role of cognition in understanding gender effects. In H. W. Reese (Ed.), *Advances in child development and behavior* (Vol. 23). New York: Academic Press.

Martin, G. B., & Clark, R. D. (1982). Distress crying in neonates: Species and peer specificity. *Developmental Psychology, 18,* 3–9.

Martin, R. J., White, B. D., & Hulsey, M. G. (1991). The regulation of body weight. *American Scientist, 79,* 528–541.

Martindale, C. (1981). *Cognition and consciousness.* Homewood, IL: Dorsey Press.

Marx, J. (1990). Alzheimer's pathology explored. *Science, 249,* 984–986.

Marziali, E. (1984). Prediction of outcome of brief psychotherapy from therapist interpretive interactions. *Archives of General Psychiatry, 41,* 301–304.

Maslow, A. H. (1943). A theory of human motivation. *Psychological Review, 50,* 370–396.

Maslow, A. H. (1954). *Motivation and personality.* New York: Harper.

Maslow, A. H. (1970). *Motivation and personality.* (2nd ed.). New York: HarperCollins.

Massaro, D. W. (1975). *Experimental psychology and information processing.* Skokie, IL: Rand McNally.

Masters, M. S., & Sanders, B. (1993). Is the gender difference in mental rotation disappearing? *Behavior Genetics, 23,* 337–341.

Masters, W., & Johnson, V. (1970). *Human sexual inadequacy.* Boston: Little, Brown.

Masters, W., & Johnson, V. (1979). *Homosexuality in perspective.* Boston: Little, Brown.

Masters, W., Johnson, V., & Kolodny, R. C. (1987). *Human sexuaity* (3rd ed.). Glenview, IL: Scott, Foresman/Little, Brown.

Masters, W. H., Johnson, V. E., & Kolodny, R. C. (1992). *Human sexuality* (4th ed.). New York: HarperCollins.

Matarazzo, J. D. (1980). Behavioral health and behavioral medicine: Frontiers for a new health psychology. *American Psychologist, 35,* 807–817.

Matarazzo, J. D. (1990). Psychological assessment versus psychological testing: Validation from Binet to the school, clinic, and courtroom. *American Psychologist, 45,* 999–1017.

Mathews, A., & MacLeod, C. (1994). Cognitive approaches to emotion and emotional disorders. *Annual Review of Psychology, 45,* 25–50.

Matlin, M. W. (1983). *Perception.* Boston: Allyn & Bacon.

Matsumoto, D. (1987). The role of facial response in the experience of emotion: More methodological problems and a meta-analysis. *Journal of Personality and Social Psychology, 52,* 769–774.

Matthews, K. A. (1982). Psychological perspectives on the Type A behavior pattern. *Psychological Bulletin, 91,* 293–323.

Matthews, K. A. (1988). Coronary heart disease and Type A behavior: Update on an alternative to the Booth-Kewley and Friedman (1987) quantitative review. *Psychological Bulletin, 104,* 373–380.

Matthies, H. (1989). Neurobiological aspects of learning and memory. *Annual Review of Psychology, 40,* 381–404.

Mattson, S. N., Barron, S., & Riley, E. P. (1988). The behavioral effects of prenatal alcohol exposure. In K. Kuriyama, A. Takada, & H. Ishii (Eds.), *Biomedical and social aspects of alcohol and alcoholism.* Tokyo: Elsevier.

Maxman, J. S. (1991). *Psychotropic drugs: Fast facts.* New York: Norton.

Mayer, R. E. (1983). *Thinking, problem solving, cognition.* San Francisco: Freeman.

Mayo, E. (1933). *The human problems of an industrial civilization.* Cambridge, MA: Harvard University Press.

McAdoo, W. G., & DeMyer, M. K. (1978). Personality characteristics of parents. In M. Rutter & E. Schopler (Eds.), *Autism: A reappraisal of concepts and treatment.* New York: Plenum.

McCann, I. L., & Holmes, D. S. (1984). Influence of aerobic exercise on depression. *Journal of Personality and Social Psychology, 46,* 1142–1147.

McCarthy, B. W., Ryan, M., & Johnson, F. (1975). *Sexual awareness.* San Francisco: Boyd & Fraser.

McCaul, K. D., Veltum, L. G., Boyechko, V., & Crawford, J. J. (1990). Understanding attributions of victim blame for rape: Sex, violence, and foreseeability. *Journal of Applied Social Psychology, 20,* 1–26.

McCauley, C. (1989). The nature of social influence in groupthink: Compliance and internalization. *Journal of Personality and Social Psychology, 57,* 250–260.

McClelland, D. C. (1958). Risk-taking in children with high and low need for achievement. In J. W. Atkinson (Ed.), *Motives in fantasy, action, and society.* New York: Van Nostrand Reinhold.

McClelland, D. C. (1973). Testing for competence rather than for "intelligence." *American Psychologist, 28,* 1–14.

McClelland, D. C. (1982). The need for power, sympathetic activation, and illness. *Motivation and Emotion, 6,* 31–41.

McClelland, D. C. (1985). *Human motivation.* Glenview, IL: Scott, Foresman.

McClelland, D. C. (1993). Intelligence is not the best predictor of job performance. *Current Directions in Psychological Science, 2,* 5–6.

McClelland, D. C., Atkinson, J. W., Clark, R. A., & Lowell, E. L. (1953). *The achievement motive.* Englewood Cliffs, NJ: Prentice-Hall.

McClelland, D. C., & Winter, D. G. (1969). *Motivating economic development.* New York: Free Press.

McClintock, M. K. (1971). Menstrual synchrony and suppression. *Nature, 229,* 244–245.

McClintock, M. K. (1979). Estrous synchrony and its mediation by airborne chemical communication. *Hormones and Behavior, 10,* 264.

McCloskey, M., & Egeth, H. (1983). Eyewitness identification: What can a psychologist tell a jury? *American Psychologist, 38,* 550–563.

McCloskey, M., Wible, C., & Cohen, N. J. (1988). Is there a special flashbulb-memory mechanism? *Journal of Experimental Psychology: General, 117,* 171–181.

McCloskey, M., & Zaragoza, M. (1985). Misleading postevent information and memory for events: Arguments and evidence against memory impairment hypotheses. *Journal of Experimental Psychology: General, 114,* 1–16.

McCormick, D. A., Clark, G. A., Lavond, D. G., & Thompson, R. F. (1982). Initial localization of the memory trace for a basic form of learning. *Proceedings, National Academy of Sciences, 79,* 2731–2735.

McCrae, R. (1984). Situational determinants of coping responses: Loss, threat, and challenge. *Journal of Personality and Social Psychology, 46,* 919–928.

McCrae, R. R., & Costa, P. T. (1984). *Emerging lives, enduring dispositions: Personality in adulthood.* Boston: Little, Brown.

McCrae, R. R., & Costa, P. T. (1986). Clinical assessment can benefit from recent advances in personality psychology. *American Psychologist, 41,* 1001–1002.

McCrae, R. R., & Costa, P. T. (1987). Validation of the five-factor model of personality across instruments and observers. *Journal of Personality and Social Psychology, 52,* 81–90.

McCrae, R. R., & Costa, P. T. (1994). The stability of personality: Observations and evaluations. *Current Directions in Psychological Science, 3,* 173–175.

McCrae, R. R., & John, O. P. (1992). An introduction to the five-factor model and its applications. *Journal of Personality, 60,* 175–215.

McDougall, W. (1908). *An introduction to social psychology.* London: Methuen.

McEvoy, G. M., & Beatty, R. W. (1989). Assessment centers and subordinate appraisals of managers: A seven-year examination of predictive validity. *Personnel Psychology, 42,* 37–52.

McGaugh, J. L. (1984). Hormonal influences on memory. *Annual Review of Psychology, 34,* 297–323.

McGee, M. G. (1979). Human spatial abilities: Psychometric studies and environmental, genetic, hormonal, and neurological influences. *Psychological Bulletin, 86,* 889–918.

McGehee, D. S., Heath, M. J. S., Gelber, S., Devay, P., & Role, L. W. (1995). Nicotine enhancement of fast excitatory synaptic transmission in CNS by presynaptic receptors. *Science, 269,* 1692–1696.

McGeoch, J. A., & McDonald, W. T. (1931). Meaningful relation and retroactive inhibition. *American Journal of Psychology, 43,* 579–588.

McGinnis, J. M. (1985). Recent history of federal initiatives in prevention policy. *American Psychologist, 40,* 205–212.

McGinnis, J. M., & Foege, W. H. (1993). Actual causes of death in the United States. *Journal of the American Medical Association, 270,* 2207–2212.

McGlashen, T. H., & Fenton, W. S. (1992). The positive-negative distinction in schizophrenia: Review of natural history indicators. *Archives of General Psychiatry, 49,* 63–72.

McGlone, J. (1977). Sex differences in the cerebral organization of verbal functions in patients with unilateral lesions. *Brain, 100,* 775–793.

McGlone, J. (1978). Sex differences in functional brain asymmetry. *Cortex, 14,* 122–128.

McGlone, J. (1980). Sex differences in human brain asymmetry: A critical survey. *The Behavioral and Brain Sciences, 3,* 215–227.

McGrath, E., Keita, G. P., Strickland, B., & Russo, N. F. (Eds.). (1990). *Women and depression: Risk factors and treatment issues.* Washington, DC: American Psychological Association.

McGraw, K. O. (1987). *Developmental psychology.* San Diego: Harcourt Brace Jovanovich.

McGue, M., & Lykken, D. T. (1992). Genetic influence on risk of divorce. *Psychological Science, 3,* 368–373.

McGuire, W. J. (1985). Attitudes and attitude change. In G. Lindzey & E. Aronson (Eds.), *Handbook of social psychology.* New York: Random House.

McKim, W. A. (1986). *Drugs and behavior.* Englewood Cliffs, NJ: Prentice-Hall.

McLeod, M. D., & Ellis, H. D. (1986). Modes of presentation in eyewitness testimony research. *Human Learning Journal of Practical Research and Applications, 5,* 39–44.

McLeod, J. D., & Kessler, R. C. (1990). Socioeconomic status and differences in vulnerability to undesirable life events. *Journal of Health and Social Behavior, 31,* 162–172.

McNaughton, B. L., & Morris, R. G. M. (1987). Hippocampal synaptic enhancement and information storage within a distributed memory system. *Trends in Neuroscience, 10,* 408–415.

McNeil, D. (1970). *The acquisition of language: The study of developmental psycholinguistics.* New York: HarperCollins.

Medin, D. L. (1989). Concepts and concept structure. *American Psychologist, 44,* 1469–1481.

Mednick, M. T. (1989). On the politics of psychological constructs: Stop the bandwagon, I want to get off. *American Psychologist, 44,* 1118–1123.

Mednick, M. T. S. (1979). The new psychology of women: A feminist analysis. In J. E. Gullahorn (Ed.), *Psychology and women: In transition.* New York: Wiley.

Mednick, S. A., Moffitt, T. E., & Stack, S. (1987). *The causes of crime: New biological approaches.* New York: Cambridge University Press.

Meer, J. (1986). The reason of age. *Psychology Today, 20,* 60–64.

Meichenbaum, D. (1977). *Cognitive-behavior modification: An integrative approach.* New York: Plenum.

Meichenbaum, D., & Turk, D. C. (1987). *Facilitating treatment adherence.* New York: Plenum.

Mellman, T. A., Randolph, C. A., Brawman-Mintzer, O., Fores, L. P., & Milanes, F. J. (1992). Phenomenology and course of psychiatric disorders associated with combat-related post-traumatic stress disorder. *American Journal of Psychiatry, 149,* 1568–1574.

Meltzoff, A. N. (1995). Understanding the intentions of others: Re-enactment of intended acts by 18-month-old children. *Developmental Psychology, 31,* 838–850.

Meltzoff, A. N., & Moore, M. K. (1977). Imitation of facial and manual gestures by human neonates. *Science, 198,* 75–78.

Meltzoff, A. N., & Moore, M. K. (1989). Imitation in newborn infants: Exploring the range of gestures imitated and the underlying mechanism. *Developmental Psychology, 25,* 954–962.

Melzack, R. (1973). *The puzzle of pain.* Baltimore: Penguin Books.

Melzack, R., & Wall, P. D. (1965). Pain mechanisms: A new theory. *Science, 150,* 971–979.

Meredith, N. (1986). Testing the talking cure. *Science 86, 7(5),* 30–37.

Mervis, J. (1986). NIMH data points the way to effective treatment. *APA Monitor, 17,* 1, 13.

Metcalfe, J., Funnell, M., & Gazzaniga, M. S. (1995). Right-hemisphere memory superiority: Studies of a split-brain patient. *Psychological Science, 6,* 157–164.

Metcalfe, J., & Wiebe, D. (1987). Intuition and insight and noninsight problem solving. *Memory and Cognition, 15,* 238–246.

Michael, J. L. (1985). Behavior analysis: A radical perspective. In B. L. Hammonds (Ed.), *Psychology and learning.* Washington, DC: American Psychological Association.

Middlemist, R. D., & Peterson, R. B. (1976). Test of equity theory by controlling for comparison of workers' efforts. *Organizational Behavior and Human Performance, 15,* 335–354.

Milgram, S. (1963). Behavioral studies of obedience. *Journal of Abnormal and Social Psychology, 67,* 371–378.

Milgram, S. (1965). Some conditions of obedience and disobedience to authority. *Human Relations, 18,* 57–76.

Milgram, S. (1970). The experience of living in cities. *Science, 167,* 1461–1468.

Milgram, S. (1974). *Obedience to authority.* New York: HarperCollins.

Milgram, S. (1977). *The individual in a social world.* Reading, MA: Addison-Wesley.

Miller, D. T., & McFarland, C. (1987). Pluralistic ignorance: When similarity is interpreted as dissimilarity. *Journal of Personality and Social Psychology, 53,* 298–305.

Miller, D. T., & Ross, M. (1975). Self-serving biases in the attribution of causality: Fact or fiction? *Psychological Bulletin, 82,* 213–225.

Miller, J. G. (1984). Culture and the development of everyday social explanation. *Journal of Personality and Social Psychology, 46,* 961–978.

Miller, N. E. (1944). Experimental studies of conflict. In J. M. Hunt (Ed.), *Personality and the behavior disorders.* New York: Ronald Press.

Miller, N. E. (1978). Biofeedback and visceral learning. *Annual Review of Psychology, 29,* 373–404.

Miller, N. E. (1983). Behavioral medicine: Symbiosis between laboratory and clinic. *Annual Review of Psychology, 34,* 1–31.

Miller, R. C., & Berman, J. S. (1983). The efficacy of cognitive behavior therapies: A quantitative review of the research evidence. *Psychological Bulletin, 94,* 39–53.

Miller, R. R., & Spear, N. E. (Eds.). (1985). *Information processing in animals: Conditioned inhibition.* Hillsdale, NJ: Erlbaum.

Miller, W. R. (1992). Client/treatment matching in addictive behaviors. *The Behavior Therapist, 15,* 7–8.

Millstein, S. G. (1989). Adolescent health: Challenges for behavioral scientists. *American Psychologist, 44,* 837–842.

Millstein, S. G., Peterson, A. C., & Nightingate, E. O. (Eds.). (1993). *Promoting the health of adolescents: New directions for the twenty-first century.* New York: Oxford University Press.

Milner, B. (1959). The memory deficit in bilateral hippocampal lesions. *Psychiatric Research Reports, 11,* 43–52.

Milner, B. (1965). Memory disturbances after bilateral hippocampal lesions. In B. Milner & S. Glickman (Eds.), *Cognitive processes and the brain.* New York: Van Nostrand Reinhold.

Milner, B., Corkin, S., & Teuber, H. L. (1968). Further analysis of the hippocampal amnesic syndrome: 14-year follow-up study of H. M. *Neuropsychologica, 6,* 215–234.

Minami, H., & Dallenbach, K. M. (1946). The effect of activity upon learning and retention in the cockroach. *American Journal of Psychology, 59,* 682–697.

Minuchin, S., & Fishman, H. C. (1981). *Family therapy techniques.* Cambridge, MA: Harvard University Press.

Mirin, S. M., Weiss, R. D., & Greenfield, S. F. (1991). Psychoactive substance abuse disorders. In A. J. Galenberg, E. L. Bassuk, & S. C. Schoonover (Eds.), *The practitioner's guide to psychoactive drugs.* New York: Plenum.

Mischel, W. (1968). *Personality and assessment.* New York: Wiley.

Mischel, W. (1979). On the interface of cognition and personality. *American Psychologist, 34,* 740–754.

Mischel, W. (1981). *Introduction to personality* (3rd ed.). New York: Holt, Rinehart & Winston.

Mischel, W., & Peake, P. K. (1982). Beyond déja vu in the search for cross-situational consistency. *Psychological Review, 89,* 730–755.

Mishkin, M., & Appenzeller, T. (1987). The anatomy of memory. *Scientific American, 256,* 80–89.

Mobley, W. H. (1977). Intermediate linkages in the relationship between job satisfaction and employee turnover. *Journal of Applied Psychology, 62,* 237–240.

Moncher, M. S., Holden, G. W., & Trimble, J. E. (1990). Substance abuse among Native American youth. *Journal of Consulting and Clinical Psychology, 58,* 408–415.

Money, J. (1972). *Man woman/boy girl.* Baltimore: Johns Hopkins University Press.

Money, J. (1987). Sin, sickness, or status? Homosexual gender identity and psychoneuroendocrinology. *American Psychologist, 42,* 384–399.

Monson, T. C., & Snyder, M. (1977). Actors, observers, and the attribution process. *Journal of Experimental Social Psychology, 13,* 89–111.

Moon, C., & Fifer, W. P. (1990). Syllables as signals for 2-day old infants. *Infant Behavior and Development, 13,* 377–390.

Moore, K. (1992). *Facts at a glance.* Washington, DC: Childtrends.

Moore, K. L. (1982). *The developing human* (3rd ed.). Philadelphia: Saunders.

Moorecroft, W. H. (1987). An overview of sleep. In J. Gackenback (Ed.), *Sleep and dreams.* New York: Garland.

Moorecroft, W. H. (1989). *Sleep, dreaming, and sleep disorders.* Latham, MD: University Press of America.

Moran, J. S., Janes, H. R., Peterman, T. A., & Stone, K. M. (1990). Increase in condom sales following AIDS education and publicity, United States. *American Journal of Public Health, 80,* 607–608.

Morgan, W. P. (1980). The trait psychology controversy. *Research Quarterly for Exercise and Sport, 51,* 50–76.

Mori, D., & Pliner, P. L. (1987). "Eating lightly" and the self-presentation of femininity. *Journal of Social and Personality Psychology, 53,* 693–702.

Morris, C. W. (1946). *Signs, language, and behavior.* Englewood Cliffs, NJ: Prentice-Hall.

Morris, L. A., & Halperin, J. (1979). Effects of written drug information on patient knowledge and compliance: A literature review. *American Journal of Public Health, 69,* 47–52.

Morrison, D. M. (1985). Adolescent contraceptive behavior: A review. *Psychological Bulletin, 98,* 538–568.

Moruzzi, G. (1975). The sleep-wake cycle. *Reviews of Psychology, 64,* 1–165.

Moruzzi, G., & Magoun, H. W. (1949). Brain stem reticular formation and activation of the EEG. *Electroencephalography and Clinical Neurophysiology, 1,* 455–473.

Moscovici, S., Lage, E., & Naffrechoux, M. (1969). Influences of a consistent minority on the response of a majority in a color perception task. *Sociometry, 32,* 365–380.

Moscovici, S., Mugny, G., & Van Avermaet, E. (1985). *Perspectives on minority influence.* New York: Cambridge University Press.

Mowday, R. T. (1983). Equity theory prediction of behavior in organizations. In R. M. Steers & L. W. Porter (Eds.), *Motivation and work behavior* (3rd ed.). New York: McGraw-Hill.

Mshelia, A. Y., & Lapidus, L. B. (1990). Depth picture perception in relation to cognitive style and training in non-Western children. *Journal of Cross-Cultural Psychology, 21,* 414–433.

Muchinsky, P. M. (1987). *Psychology applied to work* (2nd ed.). Homewood, IL: Dorsey Press.

Muchinsky, P. M., & Tuttle, M. L. (1979). Employee turnover: An empirical and methodological assessment. *Journal of Vocational Behavior, 14,* 43–77.

Mulac, A., Incontro, C. R., & James, M. R. (1985). Comparison of gender-linked language effect and sex role stereotypes. *Journal of Personality and Social Psychology, 49,* 1098–1109.

Mumford, M. D., Uhlman, C. E., & Kilcullen, R. N. (1992). The structure of life history: Implications for the construct validity of background data scales. *Human Performance, 5,* 109–137.

Munn, N. L. (1956). *Introduction to psychology.* Boston: Houghton Mifflin.

Murdock, B. B. (1974). *Human memory: Theory and data.* New York: Wiley.

Murray, D. J. (1983). *A history of Western psychology.* Englewood Cliffs, NJ: Prentice-Hall.

Murray, D. M., Johnson, C. A., Leupker, R. R., & Mittlemark, M. B. (1984). The prevention of cigarette smoking in children: A comparison of four strategies. *Journal of Applied Social Psychology, 14,* 274–288.

Murray, H. A. (1938). *Explorations in personality.* New York: Oxford University Press.

Nakazima, S. (1962). A comparative study of the speech developments of Japanese and American English in children. *Studies in Phonology, 2,* 27–39.

Namir, S., Wolcott, D. L., Fawzy, F. I., & Alumbaugh, M. J. (1987). Coping with AIDS: Psychological and health implications. *Journal of Applied Social Psychology, 17,* 309–328.

Nash, M. (1987). What, if anything, is regressed about hypnotic age regression? *Psychological Bulletin, 102,* 42–52.

National Academy of Sciences, National Research Council. (1989). *Diet and health: Implications for reducing chronic disease risk.* Washington, DC: National Academy Press.

National Commission on Sleep Disorders Research (NCSDR). (1993). *Wake up America: A national sleep alert.* Washington, DC: Department of Health and Human Services.

National Institute of Mental Health (NIMH). (1981). Depressive disorders: Causes and treatment (DHEW Publication No. ADM 81–108). Washington, DC: U.S. Government Printing Office.

National Institute of Mental Health. (1984). The NIMH epidemiologic catchment area program. *Archives of General Psychi-*

atry, 41, 931–1011.

National Institute of Mental Health. (1989). *Information on lithium.* Rockville, MD: U.S. Department of Health and Human Services.

National Institute of Mental Health. (1990). *Bipolar disorder: Manic-depressive illness.* Washington, DC: U.S. Government Printing Office.

National Institute of Mental Health. (1991). *Information about D/Art and depression.* Rockville, MD: U.S. Department of Health and Human Services.

National Institute of Mental Health. (1993). The NIMH epidemiologic catchment area program. *Archives of General Psychiatry, 50.*

National Institute on Drug Abuse. (1987). National household survey on drug abuse: Population estimates 1985. Rockville, MD.

National Institutes of Health, Review Panel on Coronary Prone Behavior and Coronary Heart Disease. (1981). Coronary-prone behavior and coronary heart disease: A critical review. *Circulation, 63,* 1199–1215.

Neisser, U. (1982). *Memory observed.* San Francisco: Freeman.

Neisser, U. (1991). A case of misplaced nostalgia. *American Psychologist, 46,* 34–36.

Nelson, K. (1993). The psychological and social origins of autobiographical memory. *Psychological Science, 4,* 7–14.

Nemeth, C. (1986). Differential contributions of majority and minority influence. *Psychological Review, 93,* 23–32.

Neubauer, P. J. (1992). The impact of stress, hardiness, home and work environment on job satisfaction, illness, and absenteeism in critical care nurses. *Medical Psychotherapy, 5,* 109–122.

Neugarten, B. L., & Neugarten, D. A. (1986). Changing meanings of age in the aging society. In A. Piter & L. Bronte (Eds.), *Our aging society: Paradox and promise.* New York: Norton.

Neugarten, B. L., & Neugarten, D. A. (1989). Policy issues in an aging society. In M. Storandt & G. R. VandenBos (Eds.), *The adult years: Continuity and change.* Washington, DC: American Psychological Association.

Newby, R. W. (1987). Contextual areas in item recognition following verbal discrimination learning. *Journal of General Psychology, 114,* 281–287.

Newcomb, M. D., & Bentler, P. M. (1989). Substance abuse among children and teenagers. *American Psychologist, 44,* 242–248.

Newcomb, N., & Dubas, J. S. (1987). Individual differences in cognitive ability: Are they related to timing of puberty? In R. M. Lerner & T. T. Foch (Eds.), *Biological-psychosocial interactions in early adolescence: A life-span approach.* Hillsdale, NJ: Erlbaum.

Newell, A., Shaw, J. C., & Simon, H. A. (1962). The process of creative thinking. In H. E. Gruber, G. Terrell, & M. Wertheimer (Eds.), *Contemporary approaches to creative thinking.* New York: Atherton Press.

Newell, A., & Simon, H. A. (1972). *Human problem solving.* Englewood Cliffs, NJ: Prentice-Hall.

Newman, B. M., & Newman, P. R. (1984). *Development through life: A psychosocial approach.* Homewood, IL: Dorsey Press.

Nickerson, R. S., & Adams, M. J. (1979). Long-term memory for a common object. *Cognitive Psychology, 11,* 287–307.

Nigg, J. T., & Goldsmith, H. H. (1994). Genetics of personality disorders: Perspectives from personality and psychopathology research. *Psychological Bulletin, 115,* 346–380.

Nisan, M., & Kohlberg, L. (1982). Universality and variation in moral judgement: A longitudinal and cross-sectional study in Turkey. *Child Development, 53,* 865–876.

Nisbett, R. E. (1972). Hunger, obesity, and the ventromedial hypothalamus. *Psychological Review, 79,* 433–453.

Norcross, J. C. (1986). *Handbook of eclectic psychotherapy.* New York: Brunner/Mazel.

Norman, G. R., Brooks, L. R., & Allen, S. W. (1989). Recall by expert medical practitioners and novices as a record of processing attention. *Journal of Experimental Psychology: Learning, Memory, and Cognition, 15,* 1166–1174.

Noyes, R., Reich, J., Christiansen, J., Suelzer, M., Pfohl, B., & Coryell, W. A. (1990). Outcome of panic disorder. *Archives of General Psychiatry, 47,* 809–818.

Oatley, K., & Jenkins, J. M. (1992). Human emotions: Function and dysfunction. *Annual Review of Psychology, 43,* 55–85.

Oden, G. C. (1987). Concept, knowledge, and thought. *Annual Review of Psychology, 38,* 203–227.

Oden, M. H. (1968). The fulfillment of promise: 40-year follow-up of the Terman gifted group. *Genetic Psychology Monographs, 77*(1), 3–93.

Oetting, E. R., & Beauvais, F. (1987). Peer cluster theory, socialization characteristics and adolescent drug use: A path analysis. *Journal of Counseling Psychology, 34,* 205–213.

Oetting, E. R., & Beauvais, F. (1990). Adolescent drug use: Findings of national and local surveys. *Journal of Consulting and Clinical Psychology, 58,* 385–394.

Offer, D., & Offer, J. (1975). *From teenage to young manhood: A psychological study.* New York: Basic Books.

Offermann, L. R., & Gowing, M. K. (1990). Organizations of the future: Changes and challenges. *American Psychologist, 45,* 95–108.

Offord, D. R., Boyle, M. H., Szatmari, P., Rae-Grant, N. I., Links, P. S., et al. (1987). Ontario child health study. Archives of General Psychiatry, 44, 832–836.

Ogata, S. N., Silk, K. R., Goodrich, S., Lohr, N. E., & Hill, E. M. (1990). Childhood sexual and physical abuse in patients with borderline personality. *American Journal of Psychiatry, 147,* 1008–1013.

Ogilvie, B. C., & Howe, M. A. (1984). Beating slumps at their game. *Psychology Today, 18,* 28–32.

Olfson, M., & Pincus, H. A. (1994). Outpatient psychotherapy in the United States, I: Volume, costs, and user characteristics. *American Journal of Psychiatry, 151,* 1281–1288.

Olio, K. A. (1994). Truth in memory. *American Psychologist, 49,* 442–443.

Oller, D. K. (1981. Infant vocalization. In R. E. Stark (Ed.), *Language behavior in infancy and early childhood.* New York: Elsevier.

Olson, J. M., & Zanna, M. P. (1993). Attitudes and attitude change. *Annual Review of Psychology, 44,* 117–154.

Olton, D. S. (1978). Characteristics of spatial memory. In S. H. Hule, H. F. Fowler, & W. K. Honig (Eds.), *Cognitive processes in animal behavior.* Hillsdale, NJ: Erlbaum.

Olton, D. S. (1979). Mazes, maps, and memory. *American Psychologist, 34,* 583–596.

Opalic, P. (1989). Existential and psychopathological evaluation of group psychotherapy of neurotic and psychotic patients. *International Journal of Group Psychotherapy, 39,* 389–422.

Orne, M. (1969). Demand characteristics and the concept of quasi-controls. In R. Rosenthal & R. Rosnow (Eds.), *Artifact in behavioral research.* New York: Academic Press.

Ortony, A., Clore, G. L., & Collins, A. (1988). *The cognitive structure of emotions.* New York: Cambridge University Press.

Ortony, A., & Turner, T. J. (1990). What's basic about basic emotions? *Psychological Review, 97,* 315–331.

Ozer, D. J., & Reise, S. P. (1994). Personality assessment. *Annual Review of Psychology, 45,* 357–388.

Paivio, A. (1971). *Imagery and verbal processes.* New York: Holt, Rinehart & Winston.

Palfai, T., & Jankiewicz, H. (1991). *Drugs and human behavior.* Dubuque, IA: Brown.

Paludi, M. A., & Gullo, D. F. (1986). The effect of sex labels on adults' knowledge of infant development. *Sex Roles, 16,* 19–30.

Pandey, J. (1990). The environment, culture, and behavior. In R. W. Brislin (Ed.), *Applied cross-cultural psychology.* Newbury Park CA: Sage.

Parke, R. D. (1981). *Fathers.* Cambridge, MA: Harvard University Press.

Parke, R. D., & Tinsley, B. J. (1987). Family interaction in infancy. In J. D. Osofsky (Ed.), *Handbook of infant development* (2nd ed.). New York: Wiley.

Parker, E. S., Birnbaum, I. M., & Noble, E. P. (1976). Alcohol and memory: Storage and state dependency. *Journal of Verbal Learning and Verbal Behavior, 15,* 691–702.

Parson, A. (1993). Getting the point. *Harvard Health Letter, 18,* 6–9.

Pate, J. E., Pumariega, A. J., Hester, C., & Garner, D. M. (1992). Cross-cultural patterns in eating disorders: A review. *Journal of the American Academy of Child and Adolescent Psychiatry, 31,* 802–809.

Paulus, D. L., & Bruce, M. N. (1992). The effect of acquaintance-ment on the validity of personality impressions: A longitudinal study. *Journal of Personality and Social Psychology, 63,* 816–824.

Pauly, I. B., & Goldstein, S. G. (1970, November). Prevalence of significant sexual problems in medical practice. *Medical Aspects of Human Sexuality,* pp. 48–63.

Paunonen, S. P., Jackson, D. N., Trzebinski, J., & Fosterling, F. (1992). Personality structures across cultures: A multimethod evaluation. *Journal of Personality and Social Psychology, 62,* 447–456.

Pavlov, I. (1927). *Conditioned reflexes.* New York: Oxford University Press.

Pavlov, I. (1928). *Lectures on conditioned reflexes: The higher nervous activity of animals* (Vol. I) (H. Gantt, Trans.). London: Lawrence and Wishart.

Pavlovich, M., & Greene, B. F. (1984). A self-instructional manual for installing low-cost/no-cost weatherization material: Experimental validation with scouts. *Journal of Applied Behavior Analysis, 17,* 105–109.

Payne, J. W., Bettman, J. R., & Johnson, E. J. (1992). Behavioral decision research: A constructive processing perspective. *Annual Review of Psychology, 43,* 87–131.

Peabody, D., & Goldberg, L. R. (1989). Some determinants of factor structures from personality trait descriptors. *Journal of Personality and Social Psychology, 57,* 552–567.

Pearce, J. M., & Hall, G. (1980). A model for Pavlovian conditioning: Variations in the effectiveness of conditioned but not of unconditioned stimuli. *Psychological Review, 87,* 532–552.

Pearson, J. C., Turner, L. H., & Todd-Mancillas, W. (1991). *Gender and communication* (2nd ed.). Dubuque, IA: Brown.

Pederson, D. R., Morgan, G., Sitko, C., Campbell, K., Ghesquire, K., & Acton, H. (1990). Maternal sensitivity and the security of infant-mother attachment: A Q-sort study. *Child Development, 61,* 1974–1983.

Peele, S., Brodsky, A., & Arnold, M. (1991). *The truth about addition and recovery.* New York: Simon & Schuster.

Pelleymounter, M. A., Cullen, M. J., Baker, M. B., Hecht, R., Winters, D., Boone, T., & Collins, F. (1995). Effects of the *obese* gene product on body weight regulation in *ob/ob* mice. *Science, 269,* 540–543.

Penfield, W. (1975). *The mystery of the mind.* Princeton, NJ: Princeton University Press.

Penfield, W., & Rasmussen, T. (1950). *The cerebral cortex of man.* New York: Macmillan.

Perls, F. S. (1967). Group vs. individual psychotherapy. *ECT: A Review of General Semantics, 34,* 306–312.

Perls, F. S. (1971). *Gestalt therapy verbatim.* New York: Bantam Books.

Perls, F. S., Hefferline, R. F., & Goodman, P. (1951). *Gestalt therapy.* New York: Julien Press.

Peterson, A. C. (1988). Adolescent development. *Annual Review of Psychology, 39,* 583–607.

Peterson, A. C., & Ebata, A. T. (1987). Developmental transitions and adolescent problem behavior: Implications for prevention and intervention. In K. Hurrelmann (Ed.), *Social prevention and intervention.* New York: de Gruyter.

Peterson, L. R., & Peterson, M. J. (1959). Short-term retention of individual verbal items. *Journal of Experimental Psychology, 58,* 193–198.

Peto, R., Lopez, A. D., Boreham, J., Thun, M., & Heath, C., Jr. (1992). Mortality from tobacco in developing countries: Indirect estimation from national vital statistics. *Lancet, 339,* 1268–1278.

Petty, R. E., & Cacioppo, J. T. (1986). The elaboration likelihood model of persuasion. *Advances in Experimental Social Psychology, 19,* 123–205.

Petty, R. E., Harkins, S. G., Williams, K. D., & Latané, B. (1977). The effects of group size on cognitive effort and evaluation. *Personality and Social Psychology Bulletin, 3,* 579–582.

Petty, R. E., Ostrow, T. M., & Brock, T. C. (1981). *Cognitive responses in persuasive communications: A text in attitude change.* Hillsdale, NJ: Erlbaum.

Petty, R. E., Wells, G. L., & Brock, T. C. (1976). Distraction can enhance or reduce yielding to propaganda: Thought disruption versus effort justification. *Journal of Personality and Social Psychology, 34,* 874–884.

Phares, V., & Compas, B. E. (1993). Fathers and developmental psychopathology. *Current Directions in Psychological Science, 2,* 162–165.

Phillips, D., McCartney, K., & Scarr, S. (1987). Child-care quality and children's social development. *Developmental Psychology, 23,* 537–543.

Piaget, J. (1932/1948). *The moral judgment of the child.* New York: Free Press.

Piaget, J. (1954). *The construction of reality in the child.* New York: Basic Books.

Piaget, J. (1967). *Six psychological studies.* New York: Random House.

Pillemer, D. B., & White, S. H. (1989). Childhood events recalled by children and adults. In H. W. Reese (Ed.), *Advances in child development and behavior* (Vol. 21). New York: Academic Press.

Piner, K. E., & Kahle, L. R. (1984). Adapting to the stigmatizing label of mental illness: Foregone but not forgotten. *Journal of*

Personality and Social Psychology, 47, 805–811.

Pinker, S. (1995). *The language instinct.* New York: Harper Perennial.

Plawin, P., & Suied, M. (1988, December). Can't get no satisfaction. *Changing Times,* p. 106.

Plomin, R. (1988). The nature and nurture of cognitive abilities. In J. Sternberg (Ed.), *Advances in the psychology of human intelligence* (Vol. 4). Hillsdale, NJ: Erlbaum.

Plomin, R. (1989). Environment and genes: Determinants of behavior. *American Psychologist, 44,* 105–111.

Plomin, R., DeFries, J. C., & Fulker, D. W. (1988). *Nature and nurture during infancy and early childhood.* New York: Cambridge University Press.

Plutchik, R. (1980a). *Emotion: A psychoevolutionary synthesis.* New York: HarperCollins.

Plutchik, R. (1980b, February). A language for the emotions. *Psychology Today,* pp. 68–78.

Plutchik, R. (1994). *The psychology and biology of emotion.* New York: HarperCollins.

Pogue-Geile, M. F., & Zubin, J. (1988). Negative symptomatology and schizophrenia: A conceptual and empirical review. *International Journal of Mental Health, 16,* 3–45.

Pola, J., & Martin, L. (1977). Eye movements following autokinesis. *Bulletin of the Psychonomic Society, 10,* 397–398.

Pool, R. (1993). Evidence for homosexuality gene. *Science, 261,* 291–292.

Pope, H. G., & Hudson, J. I. (1986). Antidepressant therapy for bulimia: Current status. *Journal of Clinical Psychiatry, 47,* 339–345.

Pope, H. G., Hudson, J. I., Jonas, J. M., & Yurgelun-Todd, D. (1985). Antidepressant treatment of bulimia: A two-year follow-up study. *Journal of Clinical Psychopharmacology, 5,* 320–327.

Porter, L. W., & Steers, R. M. (1973). Organizational, work, and personal factors in employee turnover and absenteeism. *Psychological Bulletin, 80,* 151–176.

Posner, M. I. (1973). *Cognition: An introduction.* Glenview, IL: Scott, Foresman.

Posner, M. I., & Keele, S. W. (1968). On the genesis of abstract ideas. *Journal of Experimental Psychology, 77,* 353–363.

Posner, M. I., & Keele, S. W. (1970). Retention of abstract ideas. *Journal of Experimental Psychology, 83,* 304–308.

Post, R. B., & Leibowitz, H. W. (1985). A revised analysis of the role of efference in motion perception. *Perception, 14,* 631–643.

Powell, L. H., Shaker, L. A., Jones, B. A., Vaccarino, L. V., et al. (1993). Psychosocial predictors of mortality in 83 women with premature acute myocardial infarction. *Psychosomatic Medicine, 55,* 221–225.

Powell, R. A., & Boer, D. P. (1994). Did Freud mislead patients to confabulate memories of abuse? *Psychological Reports, 74,* 1283–1298.

Powers, S. I., Hauser, S. T., & Kilner, L. A. (1989). Adolescent mental health. *American Psychologist, 44,* 200–208.

Pressley, M., Levin, J. R., & Delaney, H. D. (1982). The mnemonic keyword method. *Review of Educational Research, 52,* 61–91.

Pribar, E. F., & Dinwiddie, S. H. (1992). Psychiatric correlates of incest in childhood. *American Journal of Psychiatry, 149,* 52–56.

Price-Williams, D. R., Gordon, W., & Ramirez, M. (1969). Skill and conservation. *Developmental Psychology, 1,* 769.

Prior, M., & Wherry, J. S. (1986). Autism, schizophrenia, and allied disorders. In H. C. Quay & J. S. Wherry (Eds.), *Psychopathological disorders of childhood* (3rd ed.). New York: Wiley.

Putnam, F. W., Guroff, J. J., Silberman, E. K., Barban, L., & Post, R. M. (1986). The clinical phenomenology of multiple personality disorder: Review of 100 recent cases. *Journal of Clinical Psychology, 47,* 285–293.

Pyle, R. L., Mitchell, J. E., & Eckert, E. D. (1981). Bulimia: Report of 34 cases. *Journal of Clinical Psychiatry, 42,* 60–64.

Pyle, R. L., Mitchell, J. E., Eckert, E. D., Hatsukami, D. K., Pomeroy, C., & Zimmerman, R. (1990). Maintenance treatment and 6-month outcome for bulimic patients who respond to initial treatment. *American Journal of Psychiatry, 147,* 871–875.

Pynes, J., & Bernardin, H. J. (1989). Predictive validity of an entry-level police officer assessment center. *Journal of Applied Psychology, 74,* 831–833.

Quadrel, M. J., Fishhoff, B., & Davis, W. (1993). Adolescent (in)vulnerability. *American Psychologist, 48,* 102–116.

Quay, H. C. (1965). Psychopathic personality as pathological sensation seeking. *American Journal of Psychiatry, 122,* 180–183.

Quina, K., Wingard, J. A., & Bates, H. G. (1987). Language style and gender stereotypes in person perception. *Psychology of Women Quarterly, 11,* 111–222.

Radford, A. (1990). *Syntactic theory and the acquisition of English syntax: The nature of early child grammars of English.* Oxford: Blackwell.

Rahe, R. H., & Arthur, R. J. (1978). Life changes and illness reports. In K. E. Gunderson & R. H. Rahe (Eds.), *Life stress and illness.* Springfield, IL: Thomas.

Raine, A., Venables, P. H., & Williams, M. (1990). Relationship between central and autonomic measures of arousal at age 15 years and criminality at age 24 years. *Archives of General Psychiatry, 46,* 1003–1007.

Randall, T. (1993). Morphine receptor clone-improved analgesics, addiction therapy expected. *The Journal of the American Medical Association, 270,* 1165–1166.

Ray, O. S., & Ksir, C. (1987). *Drugs, society, and human behavior.* St. Louis: Mosby.

Ree, M. J., & Earles, J. A. (1992). Intelligence is the best predictor of job performance. *Current Directions in Psychological Science, 1,* 86–89.

Ree, M. J., & Earles, J. A. (1993). g is to psychology what carbon is to chemistry: A reply to Sternberg and Wagner, McClelland, and Calfee. *Current Directions in Psychological Science, 2,* 11–12.

Reich, J. (1986). The epidemiology of anxiety. *The Journal of Nervous and Mental Disease, 174,* 129–136.

Reilly, R. R., & Chao, G. T. (1982). Validity and fairness of some alternative employee selection procedures. *Personnel Psychology, 35,* 1–62.

Reinisch, J. M., & Sanders, S. A. (1992). Effects of prenatal exposure to diethylstilbestrol (DES) on hemispheric laterality and spatial ability in human males. *Hormones and Behavior, 26,* 62–75.

Reinke, B. J., Ellicott, A. M., Harris, R. L., & Hancock, E. (1985). Timing of psychological changes in women's lives. *Human Development, 28,* 259–280.

Reis, H. T., Nezlek, J., & Wheeler, L. (1980). Physical attractiveness in social interaction. *Journal of Personality and Social Psychology, 38,* 604–617.

Reis, S. M. (1989). Reflections on policy affecting the education of gifted and talented students: Past and future perspec-

tives. *American Psychologist, 44,* 399–408.

Rescorla, R. A. (1968). Probability of shock in the presence and absence of CS in fear conditioning. *Journal of Comparative and Physiological Psychology, 66,* 1–5.

Rescorla, R. A. (1987). A Pavlovian analysis of goal-directed behavior. *American Psychologist, 42,* 119–129.

Rescorla, R. A. (1988). Pavlovian conditioning: It's not what you think it is. *American Psychologist, 43,* 151–160.

Rescorla, R. A., & Wagner, A. R. (1972). A theory of Pavlovian conditioning: Variations in the effectiveness of reinforcement and nonreinforcement. In A. H. Black & W. F. Prokasy (Eds.), *Classical conditioning II: Current research and theory.* Englewood Cliffs, NJ: Prentice-Hall.

Resnick, H. D., Kilpatrick, D. G., Dansky, B. S., Saunders, B. E., & Best, C. L. (1993). Prevalence of civilian trauma and post-traumatic stress disorder in a representative national sample of women. *Journal of Consulting and Clinical Psychology, 61,* 984–991.

Resnick, L. B. (1987). *Education and learning to think.* Washington, DC: National Academy Press.

Rest, J. R. (1983). Morality. In J. Flavell & E. Markman (Eds.), *Handbook of child development: Cognitive development.* New York: Wiley.

Reveley, M. A., Reveley, A. M., & Baldy, R. (1987). Left cerebral hemisphere hypodensity in discordant schizophrenic twins. *Archives of General Psychiatry, 44,* 624–632.

Revelle, W. (1987). Personality and motivation: Sources of inefficiency in cognitive performance. *Journal of Research in Personality, 21,* 436–452.

Revulsky, S. H. (1985). The general process approach to animal learning. In T. D. Johnston & A. T. Petrewicz (Eds.), *Issues in the ecological study of learning.* Hillsdale, NJ: Erlbaum.

Revulsky, S. H., & Garcia, J. (1970). Learned associations over long delays. In G. H. Bower & J. T. Spence (Eds.), *The psychology of learning and motivation* (Vol. 4). New York: Academic Press.

Reynolds, A. G., & Flagg, P. W. (1983). *Cognitive psychology.* Boston: Little, Brown.

Reynolds, B. A., & Weiss, S. (1992). Generation of neurons and astrocytes from isolated cells of the adult mammalian nervous system. *Science, 225,* 1707–1710.

Rhodes, S. R. (1983). Age-related differences in work attitudes and behaviors: A review and conceptual analysis. *Psychological Bulletin, 93,* 328–367.

Rhyne, D. (1981). Bases of marital satisfaction among men and women. *Journal of Marriage and the Family, 43,* 941–954.

Rice, M. L. (1989). Children's language acquisition. *American Psychologist, 44,* 149–156.

Richardson, J. D. (1991). Medical causes of male sexual dysfunction. *Medical Journal of Australia, 155,* 29–33.

Richardson-Klavehn, A., & Bjork, R. A. (1988). Measures of memory. *Annual Review of Psychology, 39,* 475–543.

Richmond, C. E., Bromley, L. M., & Woolf, C. J. (1993). Preoperative morphine pre-empts postoperative pain. *The Lancet, 342,* 73–75.

Rickels, K., Downing, R., Schweizer, E., & Hassman, H. (1993). Antidepressants for the treatment of generalized anxiety disorder. *Archives of General Psychiatry, 50,* 884–895.

Riggio, R. E. (1990). *Introduction to industrial/organizational psychology.* Glenview, IL: Scott, Foresman.

Robb-Nicholson, C. (1995). Posttraumatic stress. *Harvard Women's Health Watch, 11,* 2–3.

Robins, L. N., Helzer, J. E., Weissman, M. M., Orvaschel, H., Guenberg, E., Burke, J. D., & Regier, D. A. (1984). Lifetime prevalence of specific psychiatric disorders in three sites. *Archives of General Psychiatry, 41,* 949–958.

Roche, A. F., & Davila, G. H. (1972). Late adolescent growth in stature. *Pediatrics, 50,* 874–880.

Rock, I. (1986). The description and analysis of object and event perception. In K. R. Boff, L. Kaufman, & J. P. Thomas (Eds.), *Handbook of perception and human performance: Vol. 2. Cognitive processes and performance.* New York: Wiley.

Rodin, J. (1976). Crowding, perceived choice and response to controllable and uncontrollable outcomes. *Journal of Experimental Social Psychology, 12,* 564–578.

Rodin, J. (1981). Current status of the internal-external hypothesis of obesity: What went wrong? *American Psychologist, 36,* 361–372.

Rodin, J., & Salovey, P. (1989). Health psychology. *Annual Review of Psychology, 40, 533–579.*

Roediger, H. L. (1990). Implicit memory: Retention without remembering. *American Psychologist, 45,* 1043–1056.

Rolls, B. J., Federoff, I. C., & Guthrie, J. F. (1991). Gender differences in eating behavior and body weight regulation. *Health Psychology, 10,* 133–142.

Rook, K. S. (1987). Social support versus companionship: Effects of life stress, loneliness, and evaluation by others. *Journal of Personality and Social Psychology, 52,* 1132–1147.

Rorschach, H. (1921). *Psychodiagnostics.* Bern: Huber.

Rosch, E. (1973). Natural categories. *Cognitive Psychology, 4,* 328–350.

Rosch, E. (1975). Cognitive representations of semantic categories. *Journal of Experimental Psychology: General, 104,* 192–253.

Rosch, E. (1978). Principles of categorization. In E. Rosch & B. B. Lloyds (Eds.), *Cognition and categorization.* Hillsdale, NJ: Erlbaum.

Rose, A. S., & Blank, M. (1974). The potency of context in children's cognition: An illustration through conservation. *Child Development, 45,* 499–502.

Rosenbaum, M. E. (1986). The repulsion hypothesis: On the nondevelopment of relationships. *Journal of Personality and Social Psychology, 51,* 1156–1166.

Rosenman, R. H., Brand, R. J., Jenkins., C. D., Friedman, M., Straus,. R., & Wurm, M. (1975). Coronary heart disease in the Western Collaborative Group Study: Final follow-up experience of 8 1/2 years. *Journal of the American Medical Association, 233,* 872–877.

Rosenman, R. H., Friedman, M., Strauss, R., Wurm, M., Kositcheck, R., Hahn, W., & Werthessen, N. T. (1964). A predictive study of coronary heart disease. *Journal of the American Medical Association, 189,* 15–22.

Rosenthal, D. (1970). *Genetics of psychopathology.* New York: McGraw-Hill.

Rosenzweig, M. R. (1922). Psychological science around the world. *American Psychologist, 47,* 718–722.

Rosenzweig, M. R., Bennett, E. L., & Diamond, M. C. (1972). Brain changes in response to experiences. *Scientific American, 226,* 22–29.

Rosnow, R. L., Skleder, A. A., & Rind, B. (1995). Reading other people: A hidden cognitive structure? *The General Psychologist, 31,* 1–10.

Ross, C. A. (1989). *Multiple personality disorder: Diagnosis, clinical features, and treatment.* New York: Wiley.

Ross, D., Read, J. D., & Toglia, M. P. (Eds.). (1993). *Eyewitness testimony: Current trends and developments.* New York: Cambridge University Press.

Ross, G., Kagan, J., Zelazo, P., & Kotelchuck, M. (1975). Separation protest in infants in home and laboratory. *Developmental Psychology, 11,* 256–257.

Ross, L. D. (1977). The intuitive psychologist and his shortcomings: Distortions in the attributional process. In L. Berkowitz (Ed.), *Advances in experimental social psychology* (Vol. 10). New York: Academic Press.

Rossi, A. S. (1980). Aging and parenthood in the middle years. In P. B. Baltes & O. G. Brim, Jr. (Eds.), *Lifespan development and behavior* (Vol. III). New York: Academic Press.

Roth, E. M., & Shoben, E. J. (1983). The effect of context on the structure of categories. *Cognitive Psychology, 15,* 346–378.

Roth M., & Argyle, N. (1988). Anxiety, panic and phobic disorders: An overview. *Journal of Psychiatric Research, 22* (Suppl. 1), 33–54.

Rothbaum, B. O., Foa, E. B., Murdock, T., Riggs, D., & Walsh, W. (1992). A prospective examination of post-traumatic stress disorder in rape victims. *Journal of Traumatic Stress, 5,* 455–475.

Rothstein, H. R., Schmidt, F. L., Erwin, F. W., Owens, W. A., & Sparks, C. P. (1990). Biographical data in employment selection: Can validities be made generalizable? *Journal of Applied Psychology, 75,* 175–184.

Rotton, J., & Frey, J. (1985). Air pollution, weather, and violent crimes: Concomitant analysis of archival data. *Journal of Personality and Social Psychology, 49,* 1207–1220.

Rowe, D. C. (1981). Environmental and genetic influences on dimensions of perceived parenting: A twin study. *Developmental Psychology, 17,* 203–208.

Rowe, D. C. (1987). Resolving the person-situation debate. *American Psychologist, 42,* 218–227.

Rowe, J. W., & Kahn, R. L. (1987). Human aging: Usual and successful. *Science, 237,* 143–149.

Ruback, R. B., & Pandey, J. (1988). Crowding and perceived control in India. Unpublished manuscript, cited in J. Pandet (1990).

Rubin, D. C., & Kontis, T. C. (1983). A schema for common cents. *Memory and Cognition, 11,* 335–341.

Rubin, Z. (1973). *Liking and loving: An invitation to social psychology.* New York: Holt, Rinehart & Winston.

Rudd, M. D., Dahm, P. F., & Rajab, M. H. (1993). Diagnostic comorbidity in persons with suicidal ideation and behavior. *American Journal of Psychiatry, 150,* 928–934.

Rushton, J. P. (1988). Race differences in behavior: A review and evolutionary analysis. *Personality and Individual Differences, 9,* 1009–1024.

Rushton, J. P., Fulker, D. W., Neale, M. C., Nias, D. K. B., & Eysenck, H. J. (1986). Altruism and aggression: The heritability of individual differences. *Journal of Personality and Social Psychology, 50,* 1192–1198.

Rutter, M., Graham, P., Chadwick, O., & Yule, W. (1976). Adolescent turmoil: Fact or fiction? *Journal of Child Psychology and Psychiatry, 17,* 35–56.

Rutter, M., & Schopler, E. (1987). Autism and pervasive developmental disorders: Concepts and diagnostic uses. *Journal of Autism and Developmental Disorders, 17,* 159–186.

Ryan, E. D., & Kovacic, C. R. (1966). Pain tolerance and athletic participation. *Journal of Personality and Social Psychology, 22,* 383–390.

Saal, F. E., & Knight, P. A. (1988). *Industrial/organizational psychology.* Monterey, CA: Brooks/Cole.

Saari, L. M., Johnson, T. R., McLaughlin, S. D., & Zimerle, D. M. (1988). A survey of management training and education practices in U.S. companies. *Personnel Psychology, 41,* 731–743.

Sachdev, P., Hay, P., & Cummings, S. (1992). Psychosurgical treatment of obsessive-compulsive disorder. *Archives of General Psychiatry, 49,* 582–583.

Sackeim, H. A. (1985). The case for ECT. *Psychology Today, 19,* 36–40.

Sadalla, E. K., & Oxley, D. (1984). The perception of room size. The rectangularity illusion. *Environment and Behavior, 16,* 394–405.

Saegert, S., & Winkel, G. H. (1990). Environmental psychology. *Annual Review of Psychology, 41,* 441–477.

Safer, M. (1980). Attributing evil to the subject, not the situation: Student reactions to Milgram's film on obedience. *Personality and Social Psychology Bulletin, 6,* 205–209.

Sakai, K. (1985). Neurons responsible for paradoxical sleep. In A. Wauquier (Ed.), *Sleep: Neurotransmitters and neuromodulators.* New York: Raven Press.

Salthouse, T. A. (1989). Age-related changes in basic cognitive processes. In M. Storandt & G. R. VandenBos (Eds.), *The adult years: Continuity and change.* Washington, DC: American Psychological Association.

Sameroff, A. J., & Cavanaugh, P. J. (1979). Learning in infancy: A developmental perspective. In J. D. Osofsky (Ed.), *Handbook of infant development.* New York: Wiley.

Samuelson, F. J. B. (1980). Watson's Little Albert, Cyril Burt's twins, and the need for a critical science. *American Psychologist, 35,* 619–625.

Sandler, J., Dare, C., & Holder, A. (1992). *The patient and the analyst: The basis of the psychoanalytic process* (2nd ed.). Madison, CT: International University Press.

Sands, L. P., Terry, H., & Meredith, W. (1989). Change and stability in adult intellectual functioning assessed by Wechsler item responses. *Psychology and Aging, 4,* 79–87.

Sanua, V. D. (1987). Standing against an established ideology: Infantile autism, a case in point. *Clinical Psychology, 4,* 96–110.

Satir, V. (1967). *Conjoint family therapy.* Palo Alto, CA: Science and Behavior Books.

Saunders, N. A., & Sullivan, C. E. (Eds.). (1994). *Sleep and breathing* (2nd ed.). New York: Marcel Dekker.

Sauser, W. J., & York, C. M. (1978). Sex differences in job satisfaction: A reexamination. *Personnel Psychology, 31,* 537–547.

Scarborough, E., & Furumoto, L. (1987). *Untold lives: The first generation of American women psychologists.* New York: Columbia University Press.

Scarr, S., & Eisenberg, M. (1993). Child care research: Issues, perspectives, and results. *Annual Review of Psychology, 44,* 613–644.

Schacter, D. L. (1987). Implicit memory: History and current status. *Journal of Experimental Psychology: Learning, Memory, and Cognition, 13,* 501–518.

Schacter, D. L. (1992). Understanding implicit memory: A cognitive neuroscience approach. *American Psychologist, 47,* 559–569.

Schacter, S. (1971). Some extraordinary facts about obese humans and rats. *American Psychologist, 26,* 129–144.

Schacter, S., & Gross, L. P. (1968). Manipulated time and eating behavior. *Journal of Personality and Social Psychology, 1,* 98–106.

Schaie, K. W. (1974). Translations in gerontology–from lab to life: Intellectual functioning. *American Psychologist, 29,* 802–807.

Schaie, K. W. (1983). The Seattle Longitudinal Study: A 21-year exploration of psychometric intelligence in adulthood. In K. W. Schaie (Ed.), *Longitudinal studies of adult psychological development.* New York: Guilford.

Schaie, K. W. (1993). The Seattle Longitudinal Studies of Adult Intelligence. *Current Directions in Psychological Science, 2,* 171–175.

Schaie, K. W., & Strother, C. R. (1968). A cross-sequential study of age changes in cognitive behavior. *Psychological Bulletin, 70,* 671–680.

Schaie, K. W., & Willis, S. L. (1986). *Adult development and aging* (2nd ed.). Boston: Little, Brown.

Scharf, B. (1978). Loudness. In E. C. Carterette & M. P. Friedman (Eds.), *Handbook of perception.* New York: Academic Press.

Schau, C. G., Kahn, L., Diepold, J. H., & Cherry, F. (1980). The relationships of parental expectations and preschool children's verbal sex typing to their sex-typed toy play behavior. *Child Development, 51,* 266–270.

Scheerer, M. (1963). Problem solving. *Scientific American, 208,* 118–128.

Scheier, M. F., & Carver, C. S. (1992). Effects of optimism on psychological and physical well-being: Theoretical overview and empirical update. *Cognitive Therapy and Research, 16,* 206–228.

Scheier, M. F., & Carver, C. S. (1993). On the power of positive thinking: The benefits of being optimistic. *Current Directions in Psychological Science, 2,* 26–30.

Scheier, M. F., Matthews, K. A., Owens, J. F., Magovern, G. J., Lefebvre, R., Abbott, R. C., & Carver, C. S. (1989). Dispositional optimism and recovery from coronary artery bypass surgery: The beneficial effects of optimism on physical and psychological well-being. *Journal of Personality and Social Psychology, 57,* 1024–1040.

Schelling, T. C. (1992). Addictive drugs: The cigarette experience. *Science, 255,* 430–433.

Scher, S. J., & Cooper, J. (1989). Motivational basis of dissonance: The singular role of behavioral consequences. *Journal of Personality and Social Psychology, 56,* 899–906.

Scherer, K. R. (1986). Vocal affect expression: A review and model for future research. *Psychological Bulletin, 99,* 143–165.

Schiff, B. B., & Lamon, M. (1989). Inducing emotion by unilateral contraction of facial muscles: A new look at hemispheric specialization and the experience of emotion. *Neuropsychologia, 27,* 923–925.

Schmidt, F. L. (1992). What do data really mean? Research findings, meta-analysis, and cumulative knowledge in psychology. *American Psychologist, 47,* 1173–1181.

Schmidt, F. L., & Hunter, J. E. (1993). Tacit knowledge, practical intelligence, general mental ability, and job knowledge. *Current Directions in Psychological Science, 2,* 8–9.

Schmidt, F. L., Ones, D. S., & Hunter, J. E. (1992). Personnel selection. *Annual Review of Psychology, 43,* 627–670.

Schmitt, H. N., Schneider, J. R., & Cohen, S. A. (1990). Factors affecting validity of a regionally administered assessment center. *Personnel Psychology, 43,* 1–12.

Schmitt, N., & Robertson, I. (1990). Personnel selection. *Annual Review of Psychology, 41,* 289–319.

Schmitt, R. C. (1966). Density, health, and social disorganization. *American Institute of Planners Journal, 32,* 38–40.

Schooler, N. R., & Keith, S. J. (1993). The clinical research base for the treatment of schizophrenia. *Psychopharmacology Bulletin, 29,* 431–446.

Schroeder, S. R., Schroeder, C. S., & Landesman, S. (1987). Psychological services in educational settings to persons with mental retardation. *American Psychologist, 42,* 805–808.

Schuckit, M. A. (1989). *Drug and alcohol abuse: A clinical guide to diagnosis and treatment* (3rd ed.). New York: Plenum.

Schultz, D. P., & Schultz, S. E. (1990). *Psychology and industry today.* New York: Macmillan.

Schultz, R., & Alderman, D. (1974). Clinical research on the "stages of dying," *Omega, 5,* 137–144.

Schultz, R., & Decker, S. (1985). Long-term adjustment to physical disability: The role of social support, perceived control and self-blame. *Journal of Personality and Social Psychology, 48,* 1162–1172.

Schwartz, P. (1983). Length of day-care attendance and attachment behavior in eighteen-month-old infants. *Child Development, 54,* 1073–1078.

Scogin, F., & McElreath, L. (1994). Efficacy of psychosocial treatments for geriatric depression: A quantitative review. *Journal of Consulting and Clinical Psychology, 62,* 69–74.

Scott, K. G., & Carran, D. T. (1987). The epidemiology and prevention of mental retardation. *American Psychologist, 42,* 801–804.

Scott, M. D., & Pelliccioni, L., Jr. (1982). *Don't choke: How athletes become winners.* Englewood Cliffs, NJ: Prentice-Hall.

Sears, P. S., & Barbee, A. H. (1977). Career and life satisfaction among Terman's gifted women. In J. Stanley et al. (Eds.), *The gifted and the creative: Fifty year perspective.* Baltimore: Johns Hopkins University Press.

Segall, M., Dasen, P., Berry, J., & Poortinga, Y. (1990). *Human behavior in global perspective.* Elmsford, NY: Pergamon.

Segall, M. H., Campbell, D. T., & Herskovits, M. J. (1966). *The influence of culture on visual perception.* Indianapolis: Bobbs-Merrill.

Seligman, M. E. P. (1975). *Helplessness: On depression development and death.* San Francisco: Freeman.

Selkoe, D. J. (1990). Deciphering Alzheimer's disease: The amyloid precursor protein yields new clues. *Science, 248,* 1058.

Selye, H. (1974). *Stress without distress.* Philadelphia: Lippincott.

Selye, H. (1976). *The stress of life.* New York: McGraw-Hill.

Sennecker, P., & Hendrick, C. (1983). Androgyny and helping behavior. *Journal of Personality and Social Psychology, 45,* 916–925.

Serbin, L. A., Sprafkin, C., Elman, M., & Doyle, A. B. (1984). The early development of sex differentiated patterns of social influence. *Canadian Journal of Social Science, 14,* 350–363.

Serpell, R., & Deregowski, J. B. (1980). The skill of pictorial perception: An interpretation of cross-cultural evidence. *International Journal of Psychology, 15,* 145–180.

Shadish, W. R. (1984). Policy research: Lessons from the implementation of deinstitutionalization. *American Psychologist, 39,* 725–738.

Shadish, W. R., Montgomery, L. M., Wilson, P., Wilson, M. R., Bright, I., & Okwumabua, T. (1993). Effects of marital and family psychotherapies: A meta-analysis. *Journal of Consulting and Clinical Psychology, 61,* 992–1002.

Shaffer, G. S., Saunders, V., & Owens, W. A. (1986). Additional evidence for the accuracy of biographical data: Long-term retest and observer ratings. *Personnel Psychology, 39,* 791–809.

Shaffer, M. (1982). *Life after stress.* New York: Knopf.

Shapiro, D. H., Jr. (1985). Clinical use of meditation as a self-regulation strategy: Comment on Holmes's conclusions and implications. *American Psychologist, 40,* 719–722.

Shaver, P., Hazan, C., & Bradshaw, D. (1988). Love as attachment: The integration of three behavioral systems. In R. J. Sternberg & M. L. Barnes (Eds.), *The psychology of love.* New Haven, CT: Yale University Press.

Shaywitz, B. A., Shaywitz, S. E., Pugh, K. R., Constable, R. T., Skudlarski, P., Fulbright, R. K., et al. (1995). Sex differences in the functional organization of the brain for language. *Nature, 373,* 607–609.

Shedler, J., & Block, J. (1990). Adolescent drug use and psychological health: A longitudinal study. *American Psychologist, 45,* 612–630.

Sheer, D. E. (Ed.). (1961). *Electrical stimulation of the brain.* Austin: University of Texas Press.

Shekelle, B., Hulley, S. B., Neaton, J. D., Billings, J. H., Borhani, N. O., et al. (1985). The MRFIT behavior pattern study II: Type A behavior and the incidence of coronary heart disease. *American Journal of Epidemiology, 122,* 559–570.

Shekelle, R. B., Gale, M. E., & Norvis, M. (1985). Type A scores (Jenkins Activity Survey) and risk of recurrent coronary heart disease in the Aspirin Myocardial Infarction Study. *American Journal of Cardiology, 56,* 221–225.

Sheridan, C. L., & Perkins, A. (1992). Cross-validation of an inventory of stressors for teenagers. *Medical Psychotherapy, 5,* 103–108.

Sheridan, C. L., & Smith, L. K. (1987). Toward a comprehensive scale of stress assessment: Norms, reliability, and validity. *International Journal of Psychometrics, 34,* 48–54.

Sheridan, K., Humfleet, G., Phair, J., & Lyons, J. (1990). The effects of AIDS education on the knowledge and attitudes of community leaders. *Journal of Community Psychology, 18,* 354–360.

Sherman, S. J., Judd, C. M., & Park, B. (1989). Social cognition. *Annual Review of Psychology, 40,* 281–326.

Sherman, R. T., & Thompson, R. A. (1990). *Bulimia: A guide for family and friends.* Lexington, MA: Lexington Books.

Shertzer, B. (1985). *Career planning* (3rd ed.) Boston: Houghton Mifflin.

Shiffman, L. B., Fischer, L. B., Zettler-Segal, M., & Benowitz, N. L. (1990). Nicotine exposure among nondependent smokers. *Archives of General Psychiatry, 47,* 333–340.

Shiffman, S. (1992). Relapse process and relapse prevention in addictive behaviors. *The Behavior Therapist, 15,* 99–111.

Shimamura, A. P. (1986). Priming effects in amnesia: Evidence for a dissociable memory function. *Quarterly Journal of Experimental Psychology, 38A,* 619–644.

Shipley, T. (1961). *Classics in psychology.* New York: Philosophical Library.

Shippee, G., & Gregory, W. L. (1982). Public commitment and energy conservation. *American Journal of Community Psychology, 10,* 81–93.

Shirley, M. C., Matt, D. A., & Burish, T. G. (1992). Comparison of frontalis, multiple muscle site, and reactive muscle site feedback in reducing arousal under stressful and nonstressful conditions. *Medical Psychotherapy, 5,* 133–148.

Shotland, R. L. (1985). When bystanders just stand by. *Psychology Today, 19,* 50–55.

Shulman, H. G. (1971). Similarity effects in short-term memory. *Psychological Bulletin, 75,* 399–415.

Shulman, H. G. (1972). Semantic confusion errors in short-term memory. *Journal of Verbal Learning and Verbal Behavior, 11,* 221–227.

Shweder, R. A., & Sullivan, M. A. (1993). Cultural psychology: Who needs it? *Annual Review of Psychology, 44,* 497–523.

Sibai, B. M., Caritis, S. N., Thom, E., Klebanoff, M., McNellis, D., et al. (1993). Prevention of preeclampsia with low-dose aspirin in healthy, nulliparous pregnant women. *The New England Journal of Medicine, 329,* 1213–1218.

Siegler, R. S. (1983). Five generalizations about cognitive development. *American Psychologist, 38,* 263–277.

Siegler, R. S. (1989). Mechanisms of cognitive development. *Annual Review of Psychology, 40,* 353–379.

Silva, J. M., Hardy, C. J., & Crace, R. K. (1988). Analysis of momentum in intercollegiate tennis. *Journal of Sport and Exercise Psychology, 10,* 346–354.

Simkins-Bullock, J. A., & Wildman, B. G. (1991). An investigation into the relationships between gender and language. *Sex Roles, 24,* 149–160.

Simon, H. A. (1990). Invariants of human behavior. *Annual Review of Psychology, 41,* 1–19.

Sims, E. A. H. (1990). Destiny rides again as twins overeat. *New England Journal of Medicine, 322,* 1522–1523.

Skinner, B. F. (1938). *The behavior of organisms: A behavioral analysis.* Englewood Cliffs, NJ: Prentice-Hall.

Skinner, B. F. (1956). A case history in the scientific method. *American Psychologist, 11,* 221–233.

Skinner, B. F. (1957). *Verbal behavior.* Englewood Cliffs, NJ: Prentice-Hall.

Skinner, B. F. (1983). Intellectual self-management in old age. *American Psychologist, 38,* 239–244.

Skinner, B. F. (1984). *A matter of consequence.* New York: Knopf.

Skinner, B. F. (1987). What ever happened to psychology as the science of behavior? *American Psychologist, 42,* 780–786.

Skinner, B. F. (1989). The origins of cognitive thought. *American Psychologist, 44,* 13–18.

Skinner, B. F. (1990). Can psychology be a science of mind? *American Psychologist, 45,* 1206–1210.

Skolnick, A. (1979). *The intimate environment* (2nd ed.). Boston: Little, Brown.

Slobin, D. I. (1979). *Psycholinguistics.* Glenview, IL: Scott, Foresman.

Small, J. G., Klapper, M. H., Kellams, J. J., Miller, M. J., Milstein, V., Sharpley, P. H., & Small, I. F. (1988). Electroconvulsive treatment compared with lithium in the management of manic states. *Archives of General Psychiatry, 45,* 727–732.

Smalley, S. L. (1991). Genetic influences in autism. *Psychiatric Clinics of North America, 14,* 125–139.

Smeaton, G., Byrne, D., & Murnen, S. (1989). The repulsion hypothesis revisited: Similarity irrelevance or dissimilarity bias? *Journal of Personality and Social Psychology, 56,* 54–59.

Smith, A., & Stansfield, S. (1986). Aircraft noise exposure, noise sensitivity, and everyday errors. *Environment and Behavior, 18,* 214–226.

Smith, C. P. (Ed.). (1992). *Motivation and personality: Handbook of thematic content analysis.* Cambridge: Cambridge University Press.

Smith, D. (1987). Conditions that facilitate the development of sport imagery training. *The Sport Psychologist, 1,* 237–247.

Smith, G. B., Schwebel, A. I., Dunn, R. L., & McIver, S. D. (1993).

The role of psychologists in the treatment, management, and prevention of chronic mental illness. *American Psychologist, 48,* 966–971.

Smith, M. L., Glass, G. V., & Miller, T. I. (1980). *The benefits of psychotherapy.* Baltimore: Johns Hopkins University Press.

Smith, P. C. (1976). Behavior, results, and organizational effectiveness: The problem of criteria. In M. D. Dunnette (Ed.), *Handbook of industrial and organizational psychology.* Skokie, IL: Rand McNally.

Smith, S. (1979). Remembering in and out of context. *Journal of Experimental Psychology: Human Learning and Memory, 5,* 460–471.

Smith, T. W. (1992). Hostility and health: Current status of a psychosomatic hypothesis. *Health Psychology, 11,* 139–150.

Smither, R. D. (1994). *The psychology of work and human performance.* New York: HarperCollins.

Smyrnios, K. X., & Kirkby, R. J. (1993). Long-term comparison of brief versus unlimited psychodynamic treatments with children and their parents. *Journal of Consulting and Clinical Psychology, 61,* 1020–1027.

Snarey, J. (1987). A question of morality. *Psychology Today, 21,* 6–8.

Snarey, J. R., Reimer, J., & Kohlberg, L. (1985). Development of social-moral reasoning among kibbutz adolescents: A longitudinal cross-sectional study. *Developmental Psychology, 21,* 3–17.

Snow, M. E., Jacklin, C. N., & Maccoby, E. E. (1983). Sex-of-child differences in father-child interaction at one year of age. *Child Development, 54,* 227–232.

Snyder, S. H. (1984, November). Medicated minds. *Science 84,* pp. 141–142.

Snyderman, M., & Rothman, S. (1987). Survey of expert opinion on intelligence and aptitude testing. *American Psychologist, 42,* 137–144.

Sobal, J., & Stunkard, A. J. (1989). Socioeconomic status and obesity: A review of the literature. *Psychological Bulletin, 105,* 260–275.

Somers, V. K., Dyken, M. E., Mark, A. L., & Abboud, F. M. (1993). Sympathetic-nerve activity during sleep in normal subjects. *The New England Journal of Medicine, 328,* 303–307.

Sommer, R. (1969). *Personal space: The behavioral basis of designs.* Englewood Cliffs, NJ: Prentice-Hall.

Sorensen, J. L., Wermuth, L. A., Gibson, D. R., Choi, K., et al. (1991). *Preventing AIDS in drug users and their sexual partners.* New York: Guilford.

Soyka, L. F., & Joffee, J. M. (1980). Male mediated drug effects on offspring. In R. H. Schwarz & S. J. Yaffe (Eds.), *Drug and chemical risks to the fetus and newborn.* New York: Alan R. Liss.

Spanos, N. P., & Barber, T. F. S. (1974). Toward convergence in hypnosis research. *American Psychologist, 29,* 500–511.

Spanos, N. P., Menary, E., Gabora, N. J., DuBreuil, S. C., & Dewhirst, B. (1991). Secondary identity enactments during past-life regression: A sociocognitive perspective. *Journal of Personality and Social Psychology, 61,* 308–320.

Spear, N. E., Miller, J. S., & Jagielo, J. A. (1990). Animal learning and memory. *Annual Review of Psychology, 41,* 169–211.

Spearman, C. (1904). "General intelligence" objectively determined and measured. *American Journal of Psychology, 15,* 201–293.

Spence, J. T. (1985). Gender identity and its implications for concepts of masculinity and femininity. In T. Sondregger (Ed.),

Nebraska symposium on motivation. Lincoln: University of Nebraska Press.

Spencer, D. D., Robbins, R. J., Naftolin, F., et al. (1992). Unilateral transplantation of human fetal mesencephalic tissue into the caudate nucleus of patients with Parkinson's disease. *The New England Journal of Medicine, 327,* 1541–1548.

Sperling, G. (1960). The information available in brief visual presentation. *Psychological Monographs, 74* (Whole No. 498).

Sperling, G. (1963). A model for visual memory tasks. *Human Factors, 5,* 19–31.

Sperry, R. (1968). Hemispheric disconnection and unity in conscious awareness. *American Psychologist, 23,* 723–733.

Sperry, R. (1982). Some effects of disconnecting the cerebral hemispheres. *Science, 217,* 1223–1226.

Spitz, H. (1986). *The raising of intelligence: A selected history of attempts to raise retarded intelligence.* Hillsdale, NJ: Erlbaum.

Springer, J. P., & Deutsch, G. (1981). *Left brain, right brain.* San Francisco: Freeman.

Squire, L. R. (1986). Mechanisms of memory. *Science, 232,* 1612–1619.

Squire, L. R. (1987). *Memory and the brain.* New York: Oxford University Press.

Squire, L. R. (1992). Memory and the hippocampus: A synthesis from findings with rats, monkeys, and humans. *Psychological Review, 99,* 195–231.

Squire, L. R., Knowlton, B., & Mussen, G. (1993). The structure and organization of memory. *Annual Review of Psychology, 44,* 453–495.

Squire, L. R., & Slater, P. C. (1978). Bilateral and unilateral ECT: Effects on verbal and nonverbal memory. *American Journal of Psychiatry, 135,* 1316–1320.

Stall, R. D., Coates, T. J., & Huff, C. (1988). Behavioral risk reduction of HIV infection among gay and bisexual men: A review of results from the United States. *American Psychologist, 43,* 878–885.

Standing, L. (1973). Learning 10,000 pictures. *Quarterly Journal of Experimental Psychology, 25,* 207–222.

Standing, L., Canezio, J., & Haber, R. N. (1970). Perception and memory for pictures: Single-trial learning 2500 visual stimuli. *Psychonomic Science, 19,* 73–74.

Staw, B. M. (1984). Organized behavior: A review and reformation of the field's outcome variables. *Annual Review of Psychology, 35,* 627–666.

Stechler, G., & Halton, A. (1982). Prenatal influences on human development. In B. B. Woolman (Ed.), *Handbook of developmental psychology.* Englewood Cliffs, NJ: Prentice-Hall.

Steenbarger, B. N. (1994). Duration and outcome in psychotherapy: An integrative review. *Professional Psychology: Research and Practice, 25,* 111–119.

Stein, B. A. (1983). *Quality of work life in action: Managing for effectiveness.* New York: American Management Association.

Stein, J. A., Newcomb, M. D., & Bentler, P. M. (1990). The relative influence of vocational behavior and family involvement on self-esteem: Longitudinal analyses of young adult women and men. *Journal of Vocational Behavior, 36,* 320–328.

Steiner, M., Steinberg, S., Stewart, D., Carter, D., Berger, C., Reid, R., Grover, D., & Steiner, D. (1995). Floxetine in the treatment of premenstrual dysphoria. *The New England Journal of Medicine, 332,* 1529–1534.

Steinhausen, H. C., Göbel, D., Breinlinger, M., & Wolleben, B. (1986). A community survey of of infantile autism. *Journal of the American Academy of Child Psychiatry, 25,* 186–189.

Stenchever, M. A., Williamson, R. A., Leonard, J., Karp, L. E., Ley, B., Shy, K., & Smith, D. (1981). Possible relationship between in utero diethylstilbestrol exposure and male infertility. *American Journal of Obstetrics and Gynecology, 140,* 186–193.

Stephan, W. (1985). Intergroup relations. In G. Lindsey & E. Aronson (Eds.), *Handbook of social psychology* (3rd ed.). New York: Random House.

Stern, D. (1977). *The first relationship.* Cambridge, MA: Harvard University Press.

Stern, L. (1985). *The structures and strategies of human memory.* Homewood, IL: Dorsey Press.

Stern, P. C. (1992). Psychological dimensions of global environmental change. *Annual Review of Psychology, 43,* 269–302.

Sternberg, R. J. (1979). The nature of mental abilities. *American Psychologist, 34,* 214–230.

Sternberg, R. J. (1981). Testing and cognitive psychology. *American Psychologist, 36,* 1181–1189.

Sternberg, R. J. (1985). *Beyond IQ.* New York: Cambridge University Press.

Sternberg, R. J. (1988). *The triarchic mind.* New York: Viking Press.

Sternberg, R. J. (1990). *Metaphors of mind: Conceptions of the nature of intelligence.* New York: Cambridge University Press.

Sternberg, R. J., & Wagner, R. K. (1993). The g-centric view of intelligence and job performance is wrong. *Current Directions in Psychological Science, 2,* 1–5.

Stevenson, H. W., Lee, S. Y., & Stigler, J. W. (1986). Mathematics achievement of Chinese, Japanese, and American children. *Science, 231,* 693–696.

Stiles, W. B., Shapiro, D. A., & Elliot, R. (1986). "Are all psychotherapies equivalent?" *American Psychologist, 41,* 165–180.

Stinnett, N., Walters, J., & Kaye, E. (1984). *Relationships in marriage and family* (2nd ed.). New York: Macmillan.

Stokols, D. (1972). On the distinction between density and crowding: Some implications for future research. *Psychological Review, 79,* 275–277.

Stokols, D. (1990). Instrumental and spiritual views of people-environment relations. *American Psychologist, 45,* 641–646.

Stokols, D. (1992). Establishing and maintaining healthy environments. *American Psychologist 47,* 6–22.

Stoner, J. A. F. (1961). *A comparison of individual and group decisions involving risk.* Unpublished master's thesis, Massachusetts Institute of Technology, Cambridge.

Storandt, M. (1983). Psychology's response to the graying of America. *American Psychologist, 38,* 323–326.

Streissguth, A. P., Aase, J. M., Clarren, S. K., Randels, S. P., La Due, R. A., & Smith, D. F. (1991). Fetal alcohol syndrome in adolescents and adults. *Journal of the American Medical Association, 265,* 1961–1967.

Strickland, B. R. (1992). Women and depression. *Psychological Science, 1,* 132–135.

Strupp, H. H. (1986). Psychotherapy: Research, practice, and public policy (How to avoid dead ends). *American Psychologist, 41,* 120–130.

Strupp, H. H., & Binder, J. L. (1984). *Psychotherapy in a new key.* New York: Guilford.

Stumpf, H. (1993). The factor structure of the Personality Research Form: A cross-national evaluation. *Journal of Personality, 61,* 27–48.

Stunkard, A. J. (1988). Some perspectives on human obesity: Its causes. *Bulletin of the New York Academy of Medicine, 64,*

902–923.

Stunkard, A. J., Harris, J. R., Pederson, N. L., & McClearn, G. E. (1900). The body-mass index of twins who have been reared apart. *New England Journal of Medicine, 322,* 1483–1487.

Stunkard, A. J., Søtorensen, T. I. A., Hanis, C., et al. (1986). An adoption study of human obesity. *New England Journal of Medicine, 314,* 193–198.

Sue, D. W., & Sue, D. (1990). *Counseling the culturally different: Theory and practice* (2nd ed.). New York: Wiley.

Sue, S., & Okasaki, S. (1990). Asian-American educational achievements: A phenomenon in search of an explanation. *American Psychologist, 45,* 913–920.

Suinn, R. M. (1980). *Psychology in sports: Methods and applications,* Minneapolis: Burgess.

Suler, J. R. (1985). Meditation and somatic arousal: A comment on Holmes's review. *American Psychologist, 40,* 717.

Surgeon General. (1988). *The health consequences of smoking, Nicotine addiction.* Rockville, MD: U.S. Department of Health and Human Services.

Surtman, R. J. (1985). Alzheimer's disease. *Scientific American, 247,* 62–74.

Surwit, R. S., Feinglos, M. N., & Scovern, A. W. (1983). Diabetes and behavior. *American Psychologist, 38,* 255–262.

Swaim, R. C., Oetting, E. R., Thurman, P. J., Beauvais, F., & Edwards, R. W. (1993). American Indian adolescent drug use and socialization characteristics: A cross-cultural comparison. *Journal of Cross-Cultural Psychology, 24,* 53–70.

Swedo, S. E., Rapoport, J. L., Leonard, H., Lenane, M., & Cheslow, D. (1989a). Obsessive-compulsive disorder in children and adolescents. *Archives of General Psychiatry, 46,* 335–341.

Swedo, S. E., Schapiro, M. B., Grady, C. L., Cheslow, D. L., et al. (1989b). Cerebral glucose metabolism in childhood-onset obsessive-compulsive disorder. *Archives of General Psychiatry, 46,* 518–523.

Szasz, T. S. (1960). *The myth of mental illness.* New York: Harper-Collins.

Szasz, T. S. (1982). The psychiatric will: A new mechanism for protecting persons against "psychosis" *and* psychiatry. *American Psychologist 37,* 762–770.

Takanishi, R. (1993). The opportunities of adolescence—research, intervention, and policy. *American Psychologist, 48,* 85–87.

Tandon, R., & Greden, J. F. (1989). Cholinergic hyperactivity and negative schizophrenic symptoms. *Archives of General Psychiatry, 46,* 745–753.

Tannenbaum, S. I., & Yukl, G. (1992). Training and development in work organizations. *Annual Review of Psychology, 43,* 399–441.

Tanner, J. M. (1973). Growing up. *Scientific American, 179,* 34–43.

Tanner, J. M. (1981). Growth and maturation during adolescence. *Nutrition Review, 39,* 43–55.

Taylor, W., Pearson, J., Mair, A., & Burns, W. (1965). Study of noise and hearing in jute weaving. *Journal of the Acoustical Society of America, 4,* 144–152.

Tenopyr, M. L. (1981). The realities of employment testing. *American Psychologist, 36,* 1120–1127.

Teplin, L. A., Abram, K. M., & McClelland, G. M. (1994). Does psychiatric disorder predict violent crime among released jail detainees? A six-year longitudinal study. *American Psychologist, 49,* 335–342.

Terenius, L. (1982). Endorphins and modulation of pain. *Advances in Neurology, 33,* 59–64.

Termine, N., Hrynick, T., Kestenbaum, R., Gleitman, H., & Spelke, E. S. (1987). Perceptual completion of surfaces in infancy. *Journal of Experimental Psychology: Perception and Performance, 13,* 524–532.

Tesser, A., & Shaffer, D. R. (1990). Attitudes and attitude change. *Annual Review of Psychology, 41,* 479–523.

Thackwray-Emerson, D. (1989). The effect of self-motivation on headache reduction through biofeedback training. *Medical Psychotherapy, 2,* 125–130.

Thayer, W. P. (1983). Industrial/organizational psychology: Science and application. In C. J. Scheirer & A. M. Rogers (Eds.), *The G. Stanley Hall lecture series* (Vol. 3). Washington, DC: American Psychological Association.

Thibault, J. W., & Kelley, H. H. (1959). *The social psychology of groups.* New York: Wiley.

Thomas, A., & Chess, S. (1977). *Temperament and development.* New York: Brunner/Mazel.

Thomas, M. B. (1992). *An introduction to marital and family therapy.* New York: Macmillian.

Thompson, C. I. (1980). *Controls of eating.* Jamaica, NY: Spectrum.

Thompson, C. P. (1982). Memory for unique personal events: The roommate study. *Memory and Cognition, 10,* 324–332.

Thompson, J. W., & Blaine, J. D. (1987). Use of ECT in the United States in 1975 and 1980. *American Journal of Psychiatry, 144,* 557–562.

Thompson, R. (1969). Localization of the "visual memory system" in the white rat. *Journal of Comparative and Physiological Psychology, 2,* 1–17.

Thompson, R. (1981). Rapid forgetting of spatial habit in rats with hippocampal lesions. *Science, 212,* 941–947.

Thompson, R. (1986). The neurobiology of learning and memory. *Science, 233,* 941–947.

Thompson, R. (1990). Neural mechanisms of classical conditioning in mammals. *Philosophical Transactions of the Royal Society of London, 329,* 161–170.

Thorndike, A. L., Hagen, E. P., & Sattler, J. M. (1986). *The Stanford-Binet intelligence scale, Fourth edition: Technical manual.* Chicago: Riverside.

Thorndike, E. L. (1911). *Animal intelligence.* New York: Macmillan.

Thornton, G. C., III, & Cleveland, J. N. (1990). Developing managerial talent through simulation. *American Psychologist, 45,* 190–199.

Thurstone, L. L. (1938). Primary mental abilities. *Psychometric Monographs* (No. 1).

Tice, D. M., & Baumeister, R. F. (1985). Masculinity inhibits helping in emergencies: Personality does predict the bystander effect. *Journal of Personality and Social Psychology, 49,* 420–428.

Tilley, A. J., & Empson, J. A. C. (1978). REM sleep and memory consolidation. *Biological Psychology, 6,* 293–300.

Tobin-Richards, M., Boxer, A., & Peterson, A. C. (1984). The psychological impact of pubertal change: Sex differences in perceptions of self during early adolescence. In J. Brooks-Gunn & A. C. Peterson (Eds.), *Girls at puberty: Biological, psychological, and social perspectives.* New York: Plenum.

Tohen, M., Waternaux, C. M., & Tsuang, M. T. (1990). Outcome in mania. *Archives of General Psychiatry, 47,* 1106–1111.

Tolman, C. W. (1969). Social feeding in domestic chicks: Effects of food deprivation of non-feeding companions. *Psychonomic Science, 15,* 234.

Tolman, E. C. (1932). *Purposive behaviorism in animals and men.* Englewood Cliffs, NJ: Prentice-Hall.

Tolman, E. C., & Honzik, C. H. (1930). Introduction and removal of reward and maze performance in rats. *University of California Publication in Psychology, 4,* 257–275.

Tomkins, S. S. (1962). *Affect, imagery, consciousness: Vol. I. The positive affects.* New York: Springer.

Toro, P. A., Trickett, E. J., Wall, D. D., & Salem, D. A. (1991). Homelessness in the United States: An ecological perspective. *American Psychologist, 46,* 1208–1218.

Torrey, E. F. (1988). *Surviving schizophrenia: A family manual.* New York: HarperCollins.

Torrey, T. W., & Feduccia, A. (1979). *Morphogenesis of the vertebrates.* New York: Wiley.

Travis, C. B. (1988). *Women and health psychology: Mental health issues.* Hillsdale, NJ: Erlbaum.

Treffert, D. A. (1988). The idiot savant: A review of the syndrome. *American Journal of Psychiatry, 145,* 563–572.

Triandis, H. C. (1990). Theoretical concepts that are applicable to the analysis of ethnocentrism. In R. W. Brislin (Ed.), *Applied cross-cultural psychology.* Newbury Park, CA: Sage.

Triandis, H. C. (1993). Collectivism and individualism as cultural syndromes. *Cross-Cultural Research, 27,* 155–180.

Triandis, H. C., Brislin, R., & Hui, C. H. (1988). Cross-cultural training across the individualism-collectivism divide. *International Journal of Intercultural Relations, 12,* 269–289.

Triplett, N. (1898). The dynamogenic factors in pacemaking and competition. *American Journal of Psychology, 9,* 507–533.

True, W. R., Rice, J., Eisen, S. A., Heath, A. C., Goldberg, J., Lyons, M. J., & Nowak, J. (1993). A twin study of genetic and environmental contributions to liability for postraumatic stress symptoms. *Archives of General Psychiatry, 50,* 257–264.

Tucker, D. M. (1981). Lateral brain function, emotion, and conceptualization. *Psychological Bulletin, 89,* 19–46.

Tulving, E. (1962). Subjective organization in free recall of "unrelated" words. *Psychological Review, 69,* 344–354.

Tulving, E. (1972). Episodic and semantic memory. In E. Tulving & W. Donaldson (Eds.), *Organization of memory.* New York: Academic Press.

Tulving, E. (1983). *Elements of episodic memory.* New York: Oxford University Press.

Tulving, E. (1985). How many memory systems are there? *American Psychologist, 40,* 385–398.

Tulving, E. (1986). What kind of a hypothesis is the distinction between episodic and semantic memory? *Journal of Experimental Psychology: Learning, Memory, and Cognition, 12,* 307–311.

Tulving, E., & Schacter, D. L. (1990). Priming and human memory systems. *Science, 247,* 301–306.

Tulving, E., & Thompson, D. M. (1973). Encoding specificity and retrieval processes in episodic memory. *Journal of Experimental Psychology: Learning, Memory, and Cognition, 8,* 336–342.

Tung, R. (1988). *The new expatriates: Managing human resources abroad.* New York: HarperCollins.

Turk, D. C. (1994). Perspectives on chronic pain: The role of psychological factors. *Current Directions in Psychological Science, 3,* 45–48.

Turnbull, C. (1961). Some observations regarding the experiences and behaviors of the Bambuti pygmies. *American Journal of Psychology, 74,* 304–308.

Turner, J. A., Deyo, R. A., Loesser, J. D., Von Korff, M., & Fordyce, W. E. (1994). The importance of placebo effects in pain treatment and research. *The Journal of the American Medical Association, 271,* 1609–1615.

Turner, J. S., & Helms, D. B. (1987). *Contemporary adulthood.* New York: Holt, Rinehart & Winston.

Tuttle, T. C. (1983). Organizational productivity: A challenge for psychologists. *American Psychologist, 38,* 479–486.

Tversky, A., & Kahneman, D. (1974). Judgment under uncertainty: Heuristics and biases. *Science, 125,* 1124–1131.

Tyrer, P., & Shawcross, C. (1988). Monoamine oxidase inhibitors in anxiety disorders. *Journal of Psychiatric Research, 22* (Suppl. 1), 87–98.

U.S. Bureau of the Census. (1991). *Statistical Abstract of the United States* (111th ed.). Washington, DC: U.S. Government Printing Office.

U. S. Bureau of the Census. (1994). *Statistical Abstract of the United States* (114th ed.). Washington, DC: U. S. Government Printing Office.

U.S. General Accounting Office. (1992). *Elderly Americans: Health, housing, and nutritional gaps between the poor and the nonpoor.* Washington, DC: United States General Accounting Office.

Ulrich, R. E., Stachnick, T. J., & Stainton, N. R. (1963). Student acceptance of Generalized Personality Inventory. *Psychological Reports, 13,* 831–834.

Underwood, B. J. (1957). Interference and forgetting. *Psychological Review, 64,* 49–60.

Unger, R., & Crawford, M. (1992). *Women and gender: A feminist psychology.* New York: McGraw-Hill.

Valenstein, E. S. (1980). *The psychosurgery debate: Scientific, legal, and ethical perspectives.* San Francisco: Freeman.

Valenstein, E. S. (1986). *Great and desperate cures.* New York: Basic Books.

Vallerand, R. J., Colavecchio, P. G., & Pelletier, L. G. (1988). Psychological momentum and performance inferences: A lpreliminary test of the antecedents-consequences psychological momentum model. *Journal of Sport and Exercise Psychology, 10,* 92–108.

Valliant, G. E. (1983). *The natural history of alcoholism: Causes, patterns and paths to recovery.* Cambridge, MA: Harvard University Press.

Valliant, G. E., & Valliant, C. O. (1990). Natural history of male psychological health, XII: A 45-year study of predictors of successful aging at age 65. *American Journal of Psychiatry, 147,* 31–37.

Valtes, P. B., & Baltes, M. M. (1990). Selective optimization with compensation. In P. B. Baltes & M. M. Baltes (Eds.), *Successful aging: Perspectives from the behavioral sciences.* New York: Cambridge University Press.

Van Horn, J. D., & McManus, I. C. (1992). Ventricular enlargement in schizophrenia: A meta-analysis of studies of the ventricle/brain ratio (vbr). *British Journal of Psychiatry, 160,* 687–697.

van Ijzendoorn, M. H., & Kroonenberg, P. M. (1988). Cross-cultural patterns of attachment: A meta-analysis. *Child Development, 59,* 147–156.

VandenBos, G. R. (1986). Psychotherapy research: A special issue. *American Psychologist, 41,* 111–112.

Vander Wall, S. B. (1982). An experimental analysis of cache recovery in the Clark's nutcracker. *Animal Behavior, 30,* 84–94.

VanderPlate, C., Aral, S. O., & Magder, L. (1988). The relationship among genital herpes simplex virus, stress, and social support, *Health Psychology, 7,* 159–168.

Varca, P. E. (1980). An analysis of home and away game performance of male college basketball teams. *Journal of Sport Psychology, 2,* 245–257.

Vaughn, B. E., & Langlois, J. H. (1983). Physical attractiveness as a correlate of peer status and social competence in preschool children. *Developmental Psychology, 19,* 561–567.

Ventura, J., Nuechterlein, K. H., Lukoff, D., & Hardesty, J. P. (1989). A prospective study of stressful life events and schizophrenic relapse. *Journal of Abnormal Psychology, 98,* 407–411.

Verillo, R. T. (1975). Cutaneous sensation. In B. Scharf (Ed.), *Experimental sensory psychology.* Glenview, IL: Scott, Foresman.

Vernon, P. E. (1960). *The structure of human abilities* (rev. ed.). London: Methuen.

Vernon, P. E. (1979). *Intelligence: Heredity and environment.* San Francisco: Freeman.

Vertes, R. P. (1984). Brainstem control of the events of REM sleep. *Progress in Neurobiology, 22,* 241–288.

Vinacke, W. E. (1974). *The psychology of thinking* (2nd ed.). New York: McGraw-Hill.

Vitz, P. C. (1990). The use of stories in moral development. *American Psychologist, 45,* 709–720.

Voevodsky, J. (1974). Evaluations of a deceleration warning light for reducing rear-end automobile collisions. *Journal of Applied Psychology, 59,* 270–273.

Vokey, J. R., & Read, J. D. (1985). Subliminal messages: Between the devil and the media. *American Psychologist, 40,* 1231–1239.

Vorhees, C. F., & Mollnow, E. (1987). Behavioral tertatogenesis: Long-term influences on behavior from early exposure to environmental agents. In J. O. Osofsky (Ed.), *Handbook of infant development* (2nd ed.). New York: Wiley.

Vroom, V. (1964). *Work and motivation.* New York: Wiley.

Wagner, L. A., Kessler, R. C., Hughs, M., Anthony, J. C., & Nelson, C. B. (1995). Prevalence and correlates of drug use and dependence in the United States. *Archives of General Psychiatry, 52,* 219–229.

Wakefield, H., & Underwager, R. (1992). Recovered memories of alleged sexual abuse: Lawsuits against parents. *Behavioral Sciences and the Law, 10,* 483–507.

Walker, L. J. (1989). A longitudinal study of moral reasoning. *Child Development, 60,* 157–166.

Wallace, P. (1977). Individual discrimination of humans by odor. *Physiology and Behavior, 19,* 577–579.

Wallace, R. K., & Benson, H. (1972). The physiology of meditation. *Scientific American, 226,* 85–90.

Wallach, H. (1987). Perceiving a stable environment when one moves. *Annual Review of Psychology, 38,* 1–28.

Wallas, G. (1926). *The art of thought.* New York: Harcourt Brace Jovanovich.

Walsh, B. T., Hadigan, C. M., Devlin, M. J., Gladis, M., & Roose, S. P. (1991). Long-term outcome of antidepressant treatment for bulimia nervosa. *American Journal of Psychiatry, 148,* 1206–1212.

Walsh, B. T., Kissileff, H. R., Cassidy, S. M., & Dantzic, S. (1989). Eating behavior of women with bulimia. *Archives of General Psychiatry, 46,* 54–58.

Walster, E., Aronson, V., Abrahams, D., & Rottman, L. (1966). Importance of physical attractiveness in dating behavior. *Journal of Personality and Social Psychology, 4,* 508–516.

Walster, E., & Festinger, L. (1962). The effectiveness of "overheard" and persuasive communications. *Journal of Abnormal and Social Psychology, 65,* 395–402.

Walster, E., Walster, G. W., & Berschied, E. (1978). *Equity: Theory and research.* Boston: Allyn & Bacon.

Walters, G. C., & Grusec, J. E. (1977). *Punishment.* San Francisco: Freeman.

Walton, G. E., Bower, N. J. A., & Bower, T. G. R. (1992). Recognition of familiar faces by newborns. *Infant Behavior and Development, 15,* 265–269.

Walton, G. E., & Bower, T. G. R. (1993). Newborns form "prototypes" in less than 1 minute. *Psychological Science, 4,* 203–205.

Wamboldt, F. S., & Reiss, D. (1989). Defining a family heritage and a new relationship identity: Two central tasks in making of a marriage. *Family Process, 28,* 317–335.

Warner, L. A., Kessler, R. C., Hughes, M., Anthony, J. C., Nelson, C. B. (1995). Prevalence and correlates of drug use and dependence in the United States: Results from the National Comorbidity Survey. *Archives of General Psychiatry, 52,* 219–229.

Warrington, E. K., & Weiskrantz, L. (1968). New method of testing long-term retention with special reference to amnesic patients. *Nature, 217,* 972–974.

Warrington, E. K., & Weiskrantz, L. (1970). Amnesic syndrome: Consolidation or retrieval? *Nature, 228,* 629–630.

Watkins, L. R. & Mayer, D. J. (1982). Organization of endrogenous opiate and nonopiate pain control systems. *Science, 216,* 219–229.

Watkins, M. J. (1990). Mediationism and the obfuscation of memory. *American Psychologist, 45,* 328–335.

Watson, C. J. (1981). An evaluation of some aspects of the Steers and Rhodes model of employee attendance. *Journal of Applied Psychology, 66,* 385–389.

Watson, J. B. (1919). *Psychology from the standpoint of a behaviorist.* Philadelphia: Lippincott.

Watson, J. B. (1925). *Behaviorism.* New York: Norton.

Watson, J. B. (1926). What is behaviorism? *Harper's Monthly Magazine, 152,* 723–729.

Watson, M. W., & Amgott-Kwan, T. (1984). Development of family-role concepts in school-age children. *Developmental Psychology, 20,* 953–959.

Waugh, N. C., & Norman, D. A. (1965). Primary memory. *Psychological Review, 72,* 89–104.

Weaver, C. N. (1980). Job satisfaction in the United States in the 1970s. *Journal of Applied Psychology, 65,* 364–367.

Webb, W. B. (1975). *Sleep, the gentle tyrant.* Englewood Cliffs, NJ: Prentice-Hall.

Webb, W. B. (1981). The return of consciousness. In L. T. Benjamin (Ed.), *The G. Stanley Hall lecture series* (Vol. I). Washington, DC: American Psychological Association.

Webb, W. B., & Cartwright, R. D. (1978). Sleep and dreams. *Annual Review of Psychology, 29,* 223–252.

Wechsler, D. (1958). *The measurement and appraisal of adult intelligence* (4th ed.). Baltimore: Williams & Wilkins.

Wechsler, D. (1975). Intelligence defined and undefined: A relativistic reappraisal. *American Psychologist, 30,* 135–139.

Wechsler, D. (1981). Manual for the Wechsler Adult Intelligence Scale–Revised. New York: The Psychological Corporation.

Weekley, J. A., & Gier, J. A. (1987). Reliability and validity of the situational interview for a sales position. *Journal of Applied Psychology, 72,* 484–487.

Weil, A. T., Zinberg, N., & Nelson, J. M. (1968). Clinical and psychological effects of marijuana in man. *Science, 162,* 1234–1242.

Weisberg, R. W. (1986). *Creativity: Genus and other myths.* San Francisco: Freeman.

Weiskrantz, L., Warrington, E. K., Sanders, M. D., & Marshall, J. (1974). Visual capacity in the hemianopic field following a restricted occipital ablation. *Brain, 97,* 709–728.

Weisner, W. H., & Cronshaw, S. F. (1988). A meta-analytic investigation of the impact of interview format and degree of structure on the validity of the employment interview. *Journal of Occupational Psychology, 61,* 275–290.

Weiss, J. M. (1973). The natural history of antisocial attitudes: What happens to the psychopaths? *Journal of Geriatric Psychology, 6,* 236–242.

Weissman, M. M. (1988). The epidemiology of anxiety disorders: Rates, risks and familial patterns. *Journal of Psychiatric Research, 22* (Suppl. 1), 99–114.

Weissman, M. M., & Klerman, G. L. (1992). The changing rate of major depression. *Journal of the American Medical Association, 268,* 3098.

Weissman, M. M., Klerman, G. L., Markowitz, J. S., & Ouellette, R. (1989). Suicidal ideation and suicide attempts in panic disorders and attacks. *The New England Journal of Medicine, 321,* 1209–1214.

Welch, W. W., Anderson, R. E., & Harris, L. J. (1982). The effects of schooling on mathematics achievement. *American Educational Research Journal, 19,* 145–153.

Weldon, E., & Gargano, G. M. (1988). Cognitive loading: The effects of accountability and shared responsibility on cognitive effort. *Personality and Social Psychology Bulletin, 14,* 159–171.

Wellman, H. M., & Gellman, S. A. (1992). Cognitive development: Fundamental theories of core domains. *Annual Review of Psychology, 43,* 337–375.

Wells, G. L. (1993). What do we know about eyewitness identification? *American Psychologist, 48,* 553–571.

Wells, G. W., Luus, C.A.E., & Windschitl, P. D. (1994). Maximizing the utility of eyewitness identification evidence. *Current Directions in Psychological Science, 3,* 194–197.

Wertheimer, M. (1961). Psychomotor coordination of auditory and visual space at birth. *Science, 134,* 1692.

West, M. A. (1985). Meditation and somatic arousal reduction. *American Psychologist, 40,* 717–719.

Wheeler, R. J., & Frank, M. A. (1988). Identification of stress buffers. *Behavioral Medicine, 14,* 78–89.

Whitehurst, G. (1982). Language development. In B. Wolman (Ed.), *Handbook of developmental psychology.* Englewood Cliffs, NJ: Prentice-Hall.

Whiting, B., & Edwards, C. P. (1973). A cross-cultural analysis of sex differences in the behavior of children ages three through eleven. *Journal of Social Psychology, 91,* 177–188.

Whitman, F. L., Diamond, M., & Martin, J. (1993). Homosexual orientation in twins: A report on 61 pairs and three triplet sets. *Archives of Sexual Behavior, 22,* 187–206.

Whyte, L. L. (1960). *The unconscious before Freud.* New York: Basic Books.

Wickens, C. D. (1992). *Engineering psychology and human performance* (2nd ed.). New York: HarperCollins.

Wickens, D. D. (1973). Some characteristics of word encoding. *Memory and Cognition, 1,* 485–490.

Widner, H., Tetrud, J., Rehncrona, S., et al. (1992). Bilateral fetal mesencephalic grafting in two patients with Parkinsonism induced by 1-methyl-4-phenyl-1,2,3,6 tetrahydropridine (MPTP). *The New England Journal of Medicine, 327,* 1556–1563.

Wiggins, J. S., & Pincus, A. L. (1992). Personality: Structure and assessment. *Annual Review of Psychology, 43,* 473–504.

Wilcox, D., & Hager, R. (1980). Toward realistic expectations for orgasmic response in women. *Journal of Sex Research, 16,* 162–179.

Wilkes, J. (1986). Conversation with Ernest R. Hilgard: A study in hypnosis. *Psychology Today, 20(1),* 23–27.

Williams, J. E., & Best, D. L. (1990). *Measuring sex stereotypes: A multination study.* Newbury Park, CA: Sage.

Williams, K., Harkins, S., & Latané, B (1981). Identifiability as a deterrent to social loafing: Two cheering experiments. *Journal of Personality and Social Psychology, 40,* 303–311.

Williams, K., Nida, S. A., Baca, L. D., & Latané, B. (1989). Social loafing and swimming: Effects of identifiability of individual and relay performance of intercollegiate swimmers. *Basic and Applied Social Psychology, 10,* 73–82.

Williams, K. D., & Karau, S. J. (1991). Social loafing and social compensation: The effects of expectations of co-worker performance. *Journal of Personality and Social Psychology, 61,* 570–581.

Wilson, G. T. (1982). Adult disorders. In G. T. Wilson & C. M. Franks (Eds.), *Contemporary behavior therapy: Conceptual and empirical foundations.* New York: Guilford.

Wincze, J. P., & Carey, M. P. (1992). *Sexual dysfunctions: A guide for assessment and treatment.* New York: Guilford.

Winett, R. A. (1995). A framework for health promotion and disease prevention programs. *American Psychologist, 50,* 341–350.

Winett, R. A., Southard, D. R., & Walberg-Rankin, J. (1993). Nutrition promotion and dietary change: Framework to meet year 2000 goals. *Medicine, Exercise, Nutrition, and Health, 2,* 7–26.

Wing, L. (1989). *Diagnosis and treatment of autism.* New York: Plenum.

Wing, L., & Gould, J. (1979). Severe impairment of social interaction and associated abnormalities in children: Epidemiology and classification. *Journal of Autism and Developmental Disorders, 9,* 11–29.

Winter, D. G. (1987). Leader appeal, leader performance, and the motive profiles of leaders and followers: A study of American presidents and elections. *Journal of Personality and Social Psychology, 52,* 196–202.

Winter, D. G. (1988). The power motive in women—and men. *Journal of Personality and Social Psychology, 54,* 510–519.

Winter, D. G., & Stewart, A. J. (1978). The power motive. In H. London & J. E. Exner (Eds.), *Dimensions of personality.* New York: Wiley.

Winters, K. C., Weintraub, S., & Neale, J. M. (1981). Validity of MMPI code types in identifying DSM-III schizophrenics. *Journal of Consulting and Clinical Psychology, 49,* 486–487.

Winton, W. M. (1987). Do introductory textbooks present the Yerkes-Dodson Law correctly? *American Psychologist, 42,* 202–203.

Wisensale, S. K. (1992). Toward the 21st century: Family change and public policy. *Family Relations, 41,* 417–422.

Witenberg, S. H., Blanchard, E. B., McCoy, G., Suls, J., & McGoldrick, M. D. (1983). Evaluation of compliance in home and center hemodialysis patients. *Health Psychology, 2,*

227–238.

Witmer, J. F., & Geller, E. S. (1976). Facilitating paper recycling: Effects of prompts, raffles, and contests. *Journal of Applied Behavior Analysis, 9,* 315–322.

Wittchen, H., Shanyang, Z., Kessler, R. C., & Eaton, W. (1994). *DSM-III-R* generalized anxiety disorder in the National Comorbidity Survey. *Archives of General Psychiatry, 51,* 355–364.

Wollen, K. A., Weber, A., & Lowry, D. H. (1972). Bizarreness versus interaction of mental images as determinants of learning. *Cognitive Psychology, 3,* 518–523.

Wolpe, J. (1958). *Psychotherapy by reciprocal inhibition.* Stanford, CA: Stanford University Press.

Wolpe, J. (1969). Basic principles and practices of behavior therapy of neuroses. *American Journal of Psychiatry, 125,* 1242–1247.

Wolpe, J. (1981). Behavior therapy versus psychoanalysis. *American Psychologist, 36,* 159–164.

Wolpe, J. (1982). *The practice of behavior therapy* (3rd ed.). New York: Pergamon Press.

Wood, C. (1986). The hostile heart. *Psychology Today, 20,* 10–12.

Woodruff, V. (1994). Studies say the kids are all right. *Working Woman,* October, p. 12.

Worringham, C. J., & Messick, D. M. (1983). Social facilitation of running: An unobtrusive study. *Journal of Social Psychology, 121,* 23–29.

Wright, L. (1988). The Type A behavior pattern and coronary artery disease. *American Psychologist, 43,* 2–14.

Wysowski, D. K., & Baum, C. (1989). Antipsychotic drug use in the United States, 1976–1985. *Archives of General Psychiatry, 46,* 929–932.

Yalom, I. D. (1985). *The theory and practice of group psychotherapy.* New York: Basic Books.

Yaniv, I., & Meyer, D. E. (1987). Activation and metacognition of inaccessible stored information: Potential basis for incubation effects in problem solving. *Journal of Experimental Psychology: Learning, Memory, and Cognition, 13,* 187–205.

Yapko, M. (1993). The seduction of memory. *The Family Therapy Networker, 17,* 42–43.

Yates, A. (1989). Current perspectives on the eating disorders: I History, psychological and biological aspects. *Journal of the American Academy of Child and Adolescent Psychiatry, 28,* 813–828.

Yates, A. (1990). Current perspectives on eating disorders: II Treatment, outcome, and research directions. *Journal of the American Academy of Child and Adolescent Psychiatry, 29,* 1–9.

Yates, A. J. (1980). *Biofeedback and the modification of behavior.* New York: Plenum.

Yates, F. A. (1966). *The art of memory.* Chicago: University of Chicago Press.

Yerkes, R. M. & Dodson, J. D. (1908). The relation of strength of stimulus to rapidity of habit-formation. *Journal of Comparative Neurology and Psychology, 18,* 459–482.

Youngstrom, N. (1991, May). Serious mental illness issues need leadership. *APA Monitor,* p. 27.

Yuille, J. C. (1993). We must study forensic eyewitnesses to know about them. *American Psychologist, 48,* 572–573.

Zadeh, L. (1965). Fuzzy sets. *Information and Control 8,* 338–353.

Zajonc, R. B. (1968). Attitudinal effects of mere exposure. *Journal of Personality and Social Psychology* (Monograph Suppl.), *9,* 1–27.

Zajonc, R. B., & Markus, H. (1982). Affective and cognitive factors in preferences. *Journal of Consumer Research, 9,* 123–131.

Zanna, M. P., & Rempel, J. K. (1988). Attitudes: A new look at an old concept. In D. Bartal & A. W. Kruglanski (Eds.), *The social psychology of knowledge.* New York: Cambridge University Press.

Zedeck, S. (1987). *The science and practice of industrial and organizational psychology.* College Park, MD: Society for Industrial and Organizational Psychology.

Zedeck, S., & Cascio, W. F. (1984). Psychological issues in personnel decisions. *Annual Review of Psychology, 35,* 461–518.

Zedeck, S., Tziner, A., & Middlestadt, S. E. (1983). Interviewer validity and reliability: An individual analysis approach. *Personnel Psychology, 36,* 230–237.

Zelnik, M., & Kantner, J. F. (1980). Sexual activity, contraceptive use, and pregnancy among metropolitan-area teenagers; 1971–1979. *Family Planning Perspectives, 12,* 230–237.

Zigler, E., & Hodapp, R. M. (1991). Behavioral functioning in individuals with mental retardation. *Annual Review of Psychology, 42,* 29–50.

Zilbergeld, B., & Evans, M. (1980). The inadequacy of Masters and Johnson. *Psychology Today, 14,* 28–43.

Zimmerman, M., & Coryell, W. (1989). *DSM-III* personality disorder diagnoses in a nonpatient sample. *Archives of General Psychiatry, 46,* 682–689.

Zinbarg, R. E., Barlow, D. H., Brown, T. A., & Hertz, R. M. (1992). Cognitive-behavioral approaches to the nature and treatment of anxiety disorders. *Annual Review of Psychology, 43,* 235–267.

Zohar, D. (1980). Safety climate in industrial organizations: Theoretical and applied implications. *Journal of Applied Psychology, 65,* 96–102.

Zuckerman, B., & Bresnahan, K. (1991). Developmental and behavioral consequences of prenatal drug and alcohol exposure. The *Pediatric Clinics of North America, 38,* 1387–1406.

Zuckerman, M. (1978). Sensation seeking and psychopathology. In R. D. Hare & D. Shalling (Eds.), *Psychopathic behavior.* New York: Wiley.

Zuckerman, M., Buchsbaum, M. S., & Murphy, D. L. (1980). Sensation seeking and its biological correlates. *Psychological Bulletin, 88,* 187–214.

Zuckerman, M., Eysenck, S., & Eysenck, H. J. (1978). Sensation seeking in England and America: Cross-cultural, age, and sex comparisons. *Journal of Consulting and Clinical Psychology, 46,* 139–149.

Credits

Photo Credits

Unless otherwise acknowledged, all photographs are the property of Scott, Foresman and Company. Page abbreviations are as follow: (t) top, (c) center, (b) bottom, (l) left, (r) right, (bg) background.

3 Bob Thomas/Tony Stone Images   5 Michael Schwarz/Image Works   6 Rob Trimgali, Jr./Sports Chrome West, Inc.   9 Courtesy of Josh Gerow   10 By permission of the DARWIN MUSEUM, DOWN HOUSE, Courtesy of Mr. G. P. Darwin.   11 Archives of the History of American Psychology, University of Akron   14 Corbis-Bettmann   15 Corbis-Bettmann   17 Anthro-Photo File   18 Frank Pedrick/Image Works   21 Merlin D. Tuttle/National Aububon Society Collection/Photo Researchers   22 Bob Daemmrich/Image Works   24 John David Fleck/Gamma-Liaison   30 Jon Riley/Tony Stone Images   31 UPI/Corbis-Bettmann   37 Superstock, Inc.   39 Custom Medical Stock   48 Llewellyn/Uniphoto   54 Bruce Curtis/Peter Arnold   59 Photo Researchers   62(r) Guy Charneau/Gamma Liaison   62(l) Courtesy of Nancy Gerow   69 James Porto/FPG   71 Amy C. Etra/PhotoEdit   72 J.P. Ferrero/Explorer/Photo Researchers   81(both) Pat Field   81 C&D Bromhall/OSF/Animals   87 Joseph Sterling/Tony Stone Images   92 Tony Latham/Tony Stone Images   94 Tony Freeman/PhotoEdit   96 Tom Hanson/Gamma Liaison   100 Darryl Torckler/Tony Stone Images   107(t) Superstock, Inc.   108 Superstock, Inc.   109(b) Murray & Associates, Inc.   109(t) DeRichemond/Image Works   119 J.W. Burkey/Tony Stone Images   121(br) Superstock, Inc.   121(bl) James Schnepf/Gamma Liaison   121(tr) Superstock, Inc.   121(tl) Tom McCarthy/PhotoEdit   127 Will & Deni McIntyre/Photo Researchers   128 Giraudon/Art Resource   130 Lonnie Duka/ Tony Stone Images   133 L. Kolvoord/Image Works   136 Moscou/Gamma Liaison   139 Lawrence Midgale/Tony Stone Images   141(b) Bob Daemmrich/Tony Stone Images   141(tr) Robert Brenner/PhotoEdit   141(tl) Jeff Greenberg/PhotoEdit   143 Claudia Andujar/Photo Researchers   149 Tony Arruga/Tony Stone Images   151 Toss/Sovfoto   157 Tony Freeman/PhotoEdit   160 Scott Pauly/Black Star   162 Bob Daemmrich/Image Works   167 Alan Carey/Image Works   169 Superstock, Inc.   174 Jim Pickerell/Image Works   177 Hank Morgan/Discover Syndication/Walt Disney Company   180(all) From A. Bandura and R. Walters/Photo courtesy of Dr. Albert Bandura   187 Superstock, Inc.   190 Vince Streano/Tony Stone Images   193 Robert Brenner/PhotoEdit   194 D&I MacDonald/Picture Cube, Inc.   196 Photofest   198 Bob Daemmrich/Image Works   201(b) Doug Meneuz/Stock Boston   201(tr) Richard Hutchings/PhotoEdit   201(tl) Elizabeth Zuckerman/PhotoEdit   203 Tom McHugh/Photo Researchers   208 Robert C. Burke/Gamma Liaison   210 Superstock, Inc.   215 Eslami Rad/Gamma Liaison   221 Chris Speedle/Tony Stone Images   227 Charly Franklin/FPG   232(t) Cynthia Johnson/Gamma Liaison   232(bl) Bonnie Kamin/PhotoEdit   233(br) Ioannis Stergiou/Gamma Liaison   238 Tom Stewart/Stock Market   240 Roger Ball/Picturesque   241 Billy E. Barnes/PhotoEdit   245(t) Frank Steman/Picture Cube, Inc.   245(br) Porter Gifford/Gamma Liaison   245(bl) Keith Bernstein/Gamma Liaison   248 Richard Hutchings/PhotoEdit   251 Paul Chesley/Tony Stone Images   254 Kobal Collection   256 Superstock, Inc.   261 Bob Daemmrich/Image Works   262 Roger Ball/Picturesque   275 David Hanover/Tony Stone Images   277 Garry Watson/Photo Researchers   278 American Cancer Society   280 Myrleen Ferguson/PhotoEdit   282 Enrico Ferorelli   285 Anderson/Monkmeyer Press   287(all) George Zimball/Monkmeyer Press   288 Tony Freeman/PhotoEdit   292 Sylvain Grandadam/Photo Researchers   293 Bonnie Schiffman/Onyx   295 (both) The Huntington Library and Art Gallery, San Marino, CA.   296 Elizabeth Zuckerman/PhotoEdit   298 Margaret Miller/Photo Researchers   302 David Young-Wolff/PhotoEdit   304 Tony Freeman/PhotoEdit   305 Richard Hutching/Photo Researchers   306 Bob Daemmrich/Image Works   309(b) Jerry Cooke/Photo Researchers   309(tr) Woodfin Camp & Associates   309(tl) Michael Newman/PhotoEdit   313 Superstock, Inc.   314 A. Rousseau/Image Works   316 Michael L. Osborne   323 David Harry Stewart/Tony Stone Images   326 Spencer Grant/Gamma Liaison   327 Seth Resnick/Gamma Liaison   330 AP/Wide World   331 Corbis-Bettmann   332 Association for the Advancement of Psychoanalysis of the Karen Horney Psychoanalytic Institute and Center, New York   334 Tony Freeman/PhotoEdit   343(r) Lawrence Manning/Tony Stone Images   343(l) Donna Day/Tony Stone Images   346 David Young-Wolff/PhotoEdit   348 Peter Steiner/Stock Market   357 Bill Ross/Westlight   359(r) John Eastcott/Image Works   359(l) Ron Sanford/ Black Star   360 Francis de Richemond/Image Works   362 George Goodwin/Picture Cube, Inc.   364 Starr/Stock Boston   367(r) McLaughlin/Image Works   367(l) Bob Daemmrich/Image Works   371 Superstock, Inc.   372 Bodine/Custom Medical Stock   374 Gabe Palmer/Stock Market   379 C. Niklas Hill/Gamma Liaison   381 Sepp Seitz/Woodfin Camp & Associates   382(r) Sohm/Stock Market   382(l) Blair Seitz/Picturesque   384(r) Michael Newman/PhotoEdit   384(l) Dennis MacDonald/PhotoEdit   389(tl) Art Wolfe/Tony Stone Images   389(b) Kathy Bushue/Tony Stone Images   389(tr) Art Wolf/Tony Stone Images   390(all) 1975/Dr. Paul Ekman/Human Interaction Laboratory   391(all) 1973/Dr. Paul Ekman/Human Interaction Laboratory   397 Michael Simpson/FPG   399 Tony Freeman/PhotoEdit   400 Kenneth Gabrielsen/Gamma Liaison   402 Tom McCarthy/PhotoEdit   407 Mark Richards/PhotoEdit   408 Dan McCoy/Rainbow   411 R. Lord/Image Works   412 Nathan Benn/Woodfin Camp & Associates   414 Jonathan Kirn/Gamma Liaison   416 Bob Daemmrich/Image Works   418 American Cancer Society   421 Vanessa Vick/Photo Researchers   427 Frank Herhold/Tony Stone Images   429(r) Glen Allison/Tony Stone Images   433 Sygma   436(r) Michelle Bridwell/PhotoEdit   436(l) Andy Levin/Photo Researchers   439 Brad Markel/Gamma Liaison   443 Vanessa Vick/Photo Researchers   446 Jim Pickerell/Image Works   448 Mark Richards/PhotoEdit   450 Ogust/Image Works   454 Louise Williams/SPL/Photo Researchers   456 Brookhaven National Laboratory and NYU Medical Center   463 David McGlynn/FPG   465 Bridgeman/Art Resource   467 UPI/Corbis-Bettmann   468 James Wilson/Woodfin Camp & Associates   471 Michael Newman/PhotoEdit   473 Michael Newman/PhotoEdit   476 David Austin/Tony Stone Images   478 Michael Newman/PhotoEdit   480 Carl Rogers Memorial Library   481 Michael Alexander   482 Jeff Greenberg/PhotoEdit   483 Lawrence Migdale/Tony Stone Images   486 Myrleen Ferguson/PhotoEdit   487 Tony Stone Images   495 Joe Viesti/Viesti Associates, Inc.   497 Tony Shonnard/Tony Stone Images   499 John Team Russell/Gamma Liaison   500 Jacques M Chenet/Gamma Liaison   501 Mark Antman/Image Works   504 Image Works   507 Michael Newman/PhotoEdit   509 Mary Kate Denny/PhotoEdit   510 Ethan Hoffman/Archive Photos   511 Jon Riley/Tony Stone Images   517 THE FAR SIDE ©FARWORKS, INC./Dist. by UNIVERSAL PRESS SYNDICATE. Reprinted with permission. All rights reserved.   519 Terry McKay/Picture Cube, Inc.   521 Michel Gowerner/Gamma Liaison   523 Henley & Savage/Picturesque   526 Superstock, Inc.   531 Michael Newman/PhotoEdit   533 Jeff Isaac Greenberg/Photo Researchers   536 Tom Hollyman/Photo Researchers   538 Skojold/Image Works   541 David Young-Wolff/PhotoEdit   543(r) Walter Hodges/Tony Stone Images   543(l) Dick Durranof/Woodfin Camp & Associates   547(b) Arthur Grace/Stock Boston   547(c) John Coletti/Stock Boston   547(tr) Stephen Frisch/Stock Boston   547(tl) Bob Daemmrich/Stock Boston   549(b) Louis Goldman/Photo Researchers   549(tr) Stephen Frisch/Stock Boston   549(tl) Ken Graham/Allstock   550 Mark Segal/Tony Stone Images   554(r) David Woodfall/Tony Stone Images   554(l) Bob Daemmrich/Image Works   556 Alon Reininger/Contact Press Images

Text Credits

Ch. 2 From "Action Potentials Recorded from Inside a Nerve Fiber" by A.L. Hodgkin and A.F. Huxley. Reprinted by permission from *Nature,* Vol. 144, No. 3651, October 1939. Copyright 1939 by Macmillan Magazine Ltd.

Fig. 3.1 From "Contemporary Psychophysics" by Eugene Galanter from New Directions in Psychology. Copyright © 1962 by Holt, Rinehart and Winston, Inc. Reprinted by permission of the author.

Fig. 3.29 Adapted from "Pictorial Perception and Culture" by Jan Deregowski, Scientific American, November 1972. Copyright © 1972 by *Scientific American,* Inc. All rights reserved. Reprinted by permission.

Fig. 5.10 From "Introduction and Removal of Reward, and Maze Performance in Rats" by E.C. Tolman and C.H. Honzik from *University of California Publications in Psychology,* Volume IV, 1928-1931. Reprinted by permission.

Fig. 6.2 From "Short-term Retention of Individual Verbal Items" by Lloyd R. Peterson and Margaret J. Peterson from *Journal of Experimental Psychology* (September 1959), the American Psychological Association. Reprinted by permission of the authors.

Fig. 6.3 Fig.ure, "Statements About Eyewitness Testimony with Which the 'Experts' Agree" by S.M. Kassin, P.C. Ellsworth, and V.L. Smith from *American Psychologist,* Vol. 44, 1989. Copyright © 1989 by the American Psychological Association. Reprinted with permission.

Fig. 6.5 From "Long-Term Memory for a Common Object" by Raymond S. Nickerson and Marilyn Jager Adams in *Cognitive Psychology* 1979, 11. Copyright © 1979 Academic Press. Reprinted by permission.

Fig. 6.6 From "Narrative Stories as Mediators for Serial Learning" by Gordon H. Bower and Mical C. Clark from *Psychonomic Science,* Vol. 14 (4), 1969. Copyright © 1969 by Psychonomic Journals, Inc. Reprinted by permission.

Fig. 6.7 From "Mnemotechnics in Second-Language Learning" by Richard C. Atkinson from *American Psychologist,* Volume 30, August 1975, Number 8. Published by the American Psychological Association. Reprinted by permission of the author.

Fig. 6.8 From "Bizareness vs. Interaction of Mental Images as Determinants of Learning" by Keith A. Wollen, Andrea Weber and Douglas H. Lowry from *Cognitive Psychology,* 1972. Copyright © 1972 by Academic Press, Inc. Reprinted by permission.

Fig. 6.10 From "Properties of Learning Curves under Varied Distribution of Practice" by Mary J. Kientzle from *Journal of Experimental Psychology* 36 (June 1946). Published by the American Psychological Association, Inc. Reprinted by permission of the author.

Fig. 7.2 From *The Nature of Human Intelligence* by J. Guilford. Copyright © 1967 by The McGraw-Hill Companies. Reprinted by permission of The McGraw-Hill Companies.

Fig. 7.13 From "Problem Solving" by Martin Sheerer from *Scientific American,* Vol. 208, 1963.

Fig. 8.9 From "Human Mate Selection" by David M. Buss from *American Scientist* (January-February, 1985). Reprinted by permission of American Scientist.

Fig. 8.14 Adapted from "Growing Up" by J.M. Tanner as appeared in *Scientific American,* September 1973. Copyright © 1973 by Scientific American, Inc. All rights reserved. Reprinted by permission.

Fig. 10.7 From Lazarus, 1993. Reproduced, with permission from the *Annual Review of Psychology,* Volume 44, © 1993 by Annual Reviews, Inc. (Must appear on-page as in last edition)

Ch 10 Drawing by Frascino; © 1991. *The New Yorker Magazine, Inc.* (on-page credit)

Fig. 12.1 From *The American Psychiatric Association's Psychiatric Glossary.* Reprinted by permission of American Psychiatric Association.

Fig. 12.3 From *OCD: When a Habit Isn't Just a Habit.* Copyright © 1991 by CIBA-GEIGY Corporation.

Fig. 12.4 Adapted from *Is It Alzheimer's? Warning Signs You Should Know.* Reprinted by permission of Alzheimer's Association, 919 North Michigan Avenue, Suite 1000, Chicago, IL 60611-1676.

Fig. 13.1 From *Reason and Emotion in Psychotherapy* by Albert Ellis (New York: Citadel, 1962) and *A New Guide to Rational Living* by Albert Ellis and Robert A. Harper (North Hollywood, CA: Willshire Books, 1975) Copyright © by The Institute for Rational-Emotive Therapy.

Fig. 15.1 From *Training in Organizations: Needs Assessment, Development, and Evaluation,* Second Edition, by I.L. Goldstein. Copyright © 1986, 1974 by Wadsworth, Inc. Adapted by permission of Brooks/Cole Publishing Company, Pacific Grove, CA 93950.

Name Index

Subject Index